D0934110

Max Weber
and his Contemporaries

Max Weber and his Contemporaries

Edited by
WOLFGANG J. MOMMSEN and
JÜRGEN OSTERHAMMEL

THE GERMAN HISTORICAL INSTITUTE

London
UNWIN HYMAN
Boston   Sydney   Wellington

© German Historical Institute, 1987
This book is copyright under the Berne Convention.
No reproduction without permission. All rights reserved.

Allen & Unwin, the academic imprint of
Unwin Hyman Ltd
15/17 Broadwick Street, London W1V 1FP, UK

Unwin Hyman, Inc.
8 Winchester Place, Winchester, Mass. 01890, USA

Allen & Unwin (Australia) Ltd.,
8 Napier Street, North Sydney, NSW 2060, Australia

Allen & Unwin (New Zealand) Ltd in association with the
Port Nicholson Press Ltd,
60 Cambridge Terrace, Wellington, New Zealand

First published in 1987
Second impression 1988

British Library Cataloguing in Publication Data

Max Weber and his contemporaries.
  1. Weber, Max
  I. Mommsen, Wolfgang J. II. Osterhammel,
Jürgen III. German Historical Institute
301′.092′4   HM22.G3W4
ISBN 0–04–301262–0

Library of Congress Cataloging in Publication Data

  Max Weber and his contemporaries.
Includes index.
1. Weber, Max, 1864–1920. 2. Sociology—Germany—
History. I. Mommsen, Wolfgang J., 1930–
II. Osterhammel, Jürgen. III. German Historical
Institute in London.
HM22.G3A3 1986   301′.092′4   86–14198
ISBN 0–04–301262–0 (alk. paper)

Typeset in 10 on 11 point Times by
Mathematical Composition Setters, Ltd, Salisbury
and printed and bound in Great Britain by
Biddles Ltd, Guildford and King's Lynn

LIBRARY
ALMA COLLEGE
ALMA, MICHIGAN

Contents

Preface   *page* xi

Abbreviations   xiii

1 Introduction   1
   Wolfgang J. Mommsen

Part I Max Weber and the Social Sciences at the Turn of   **23**
         the Century

2 A Science of Man: Max Weber and the Political Economy of the   25
   German Historical School
   Wilhelm Hennis

3 Gustav Schmoller and Max Weber   59
   Manfred Schön

4 Max Weber and the 'Younger' Generation in the Verein für   71
   Sozialpolitik
   Dieter Krüger

5 Max and Alfred Weber in the Verein für Sozialpolitik   88
   Eberhard Demm

6 Personal Conflict and Ideological Options in Sombart and   99
   Weber
   Arthur Mitzman

7 Varieties of Social Economics: Joseph A. Schumpeter and   106
   Max Weber
   Jürgen Osterhammel

8 Robert Michels and Max Weber: Moral Conviction versus   121
   the Politics of Responsibility
   Wolfgang J. Mommsen

9 Mosca, Pareto and Weber: A Historical Comparison   139
   David Beetham

10 Georges Sorel and Max Weber   159
   J. G. Merquior

11 Mill and Weber on History, Freedom and Reason   170
   Alan Ryan

12 Weber and Durkheim: Coincidence and Divergence   182
   Anthony Giddens

Part II Max Weber's Relation to the Theologians   **191**
          and Historians

13 Max Weber and the Evangelical-Social Congress   193
   Rita Aldenhoff

14 Max Weber and the Lutherans   203
    W. R. Ward

15 Friendship between Experts: Notes on Weber and Troeltsch   215
    Friedrich Wilhelm Graf

16 Max Weber and Eduard Meyer   234
    Friedrich H. Tenbruck

17 Karl Lamprecht and Max Weber: Historical Sociology within   268
    the Confines of a Historians' Controversy
    Sam Whimster

18 Otto Hintze and Max Weber: Attempts at a Comparison   284
    Jürgen Kocka

Part III   The Realm of Politics   **297**

19 Friedrich Naumann and Max Weber: Aspects of a Political   299
    Partnership
    Peter Theiner

20 Max Weber and Walther Rathenau   311
    Ernst Schulin

21 Gustav Stresemann and Max Weber: Politics and Scholarship   323
    Gangolf Hübinger

22 Dietrich Schäfer and Max Weber   334
    Roger Chickering

23 Eduard Bernstein and Max Weber   345
    John Breuilly

24 Max Weber, Karl Kautsky and German Social Democracy   355
    Dick Geary

25 Max Weber's Relation to Anarchism and Anarchists: 367
    The Case of Ernst Toller
    Dittmar Dahlmann

26 Max Weber and Antonio Gramsci   382
    Carl Levy

Part IV   Max Weber and Philosophical Thought   **403**

27 Weber and Nietzsche: Questioning the Liberation   405
    of Social Science from Historicism
    Robert Eden

28 The Ambiguity of Modernity: Georg Simmel and Max Weber   422
    David Frisby

29 Weber and the Southwest German School: The Genesis   434
    of the Concept of the Historical Individual
    Guy Oakes

30 Max Weber and Benedetto Croce   447
    Pietro Rossi

31   Weber and Freud: Vocation and Self-Acknowledgement   468
     Tracy B. Strong

32   Passion as a Mode of Life: Max Weber, the Otto Gross   483
     Circle and Eroticism
     Wolfgang Schwentker

33   Ernst Bloch and Georg Lukács in Max Weber's Heidelberg   499
     Éva Karádi

34   Max Weber, Oswald Spengler and a Biographical Surmise   515
     Douglas Webster

35   Karl Jaspers: Thinking with Max Weber in Mind   528
     Dieter Henrich

Part V   Max Weber: the Enduring Contemporary   **545**

36   Max Weber and the World since 1920   547
     Edward Shils

37   Max Weber and Modern Social Science   574
     Ralf Dahrendorf

Contributors   581

Index   585

Preface

The collection of essays presented in this volume originated at an international conference on 'Max Weber and his Contemporaries', held from 20 to 23 September 1984 at the German Historical Institute, London.[1] As the Introduction describes in more detail, this conference attempted to ascertain Max Weber's intellectual position around the turn of the century vis-à-vis his contemporaries in the social sciences, in history and theology, in philosophy and in the contemporary political arena. Scholars from Great Britain, West Germany, the United States, Canada, Italy, France, Hungary, the Netherlands and Brazil, representing various academic disciplines ranging from history, political science and sociology to theology and economics participated in the conference. Even so, it was not possible to cover equally all aspects of Weber's work and its contemporary ramifications. We are grateful to Professor Dieter Henrich for allowing us to include in this collection a Memorial Lecture on Karl Jaspers, which made it possible to fill what otherwise might have been a glaring gap in this volume.

However incomplete this collection may still seem, it presents a fairly comprehensive account of Max Weber and his relationship to various scholarly disciplines in his own time. We hope it will be considered a useful contribution to our understanding of the intellectual history of the late nineteenth and early twentieth centuries, and of Max Weber's achievements in particular. Preparing the papers for publication, however, was not an easy task, if only because of the considerable problems involved in procuring adequate translations of the papers originally presented in German. Likewise, it was not easy to achieve a fair degree of consistency in rendering the extremely difficult terminology of Weber (and also, of course, of other thinkers) in English. Existing translations were used as far as possible. Sometimes they had to be corrected or amended. It is to be hoped that in due course a new English edition of Weber's writings, based on the *Max Weber–Gesamtausgabe* currently being prepared by a team of German scholars including the undersigned, will remedy the present unsatisfactory state of affairs regarding the texts by Weber available in English.

Without the efforts of Dr Angela Davies of the German Historical Institute, who assisted in editing the texts and prepared the index, this volume would probably not have come about. Special thanks go to Dr Sam Whimster, who acted as a collaborative editor on the papers which had to be translated into English. In particular, he checked the texts for terminological consistency and also for stylistic presentation. Thanks are also due to Dr Abraham Anderson of Columbia University, Dr Gangolf Hübinger and Mr Niall Bond of the University of Freiburg, and to Dr Wolfgang Schwentker of the University of Düsseldorf, who will be editing jointly with the undersigned a parallel German version of this volume (to be published by Vandenhoeck & Ruprecht, Göttingen, in the series Publications of the German Historical Institute). Last but not least, the staff of the German Historical Institute should be mentioned.

---

1 Cf, the report on this conference by Jürgen Osterhammel, in Bulletin of the German Historical Institute, London, no. 18 (1985), pp. 11–20.

Without the assistance of Jill Williams, Ingrid Materner, Georg-Peter Schröder, Jane Rafferty and John Lupton the conference would not have been a success, nor would it have been possible to master the problems of editing a collection of essays of this size in a satisfactory manner. Finally, thanks are due also to the Director of the German Historical Institute, Professor Adolf M. Birke, who, as my successor, was so kind as to lend his support to the publication of this volume. In addition, I should like to express my particular gratitude to Mrs Jane Harris-Matthews and Mr Gordon Smith of Allen & Unwin for their unceasing help and encouragement over the last years.

Düsseldorf, 1986   Wolfgang J. Mommsen

Abbreviations

AfSSP   *Archiv für Sozialwissenschaft und Sozialpolitik.*

Biography   Marianne Weber, *Max Weber: A Biography*, translated and edited by Harry Zohn (New York, 1975).

CoS   Max Weber, *Critique of Stammler*, translated, with an introductory essay, by Guy Oakes (New York and London, 1977).

ES   Max Weber, *Economy and Society: An Outline of Interpretive Sociology*, edited by Guenther Roth and Claus Wittich, 2 vols (Berkeley, Los Angeles and London, 1978).

GASS   Max Weber, *Gesammelte Aufsätze zur Soziologie und Sozialpolitik* [edited by Marianne Weber] (Tübingen, 1924).

GASWG   Max Weber, *Gesammelte Aufsätze zur Sozial- und Wirtschaftsgeschichte* [edited by Marianne Weber] (Tübingen, 1924).

GEH   Max Weber, *General Economic History*, translated by Frank H. Knight, new edn (New Brunswick and London, 1982).

GPS^1 Max Weber, *Gesammelte Politische Schriften* [edited by Marianne Weber] (Munich, 1921).

GPS^2 Max Weber, *Gesammelte Politische Schriften*, 2nd edn, edited by Johannes Winckelmann (Tübingen, 1958).

GPS^3 Max Weber, *Gesammelte Politische Schriften*, 3rd edn, edited by Johannes Winckelmann (Tübingen, 1971).

FMW   *From Max Weber: Essays in Sociology*, translated, edited and with an introduction by H. H. Gerth and C. Wright Mills (London, 1947).

Jugendbriefe   Max Weber, *Jugendbriefe* [edited by Marianne Weber] (Tübingen, n.d. [1936]).

Lebensbild   Marianne Weber, *Max Weber: Ein Lebensbild*, 3rd edn (Tübingen, 1984).

MSS   Max Weber, *The Methodology of the Social Sciences*, translated and edited by Edward A. Shils and Henry A. Finch (New York, 1949).

MWG   *Max Weber-Gesamtausgabe*, edited by Horst Baier, M. Rainer Lepsius, Wolfgang J. Mommsen, Wolfgang Schluchter and Johannes Winckelmann (Tübingen). Abteilung [series] I: *Schriften und Reden.* Vol. I/2: *Die römische Agrargeschichte in ihrer Bedeutung für das Staats- und Privatrecht*, edited by Jürgen Deininger (1986). Vol. I/3: (in two parts): *Die Lage der Landarbeiter im ostelbischen Deutschland*, edited by Martin Riesebrodt (1984). Vol. I/15: *Zur Politik im Weltkrieg: Schriften und Reden 1914–1918*, edited by Wolfgang J. Mommsen in collaboration with Gangolf Hübinger (1984).

PE   Max Weber, *Die protestantische Ethik*, 2 vols, edited by
             Johannes Winckelmann.
             Vol. 1: *Eine Aufsatzsammlung*, 6th edn (Gütersloh, 1981).
             Vol. 2: *Kritiken and Antikritiken*, 4th edn (Gütersloh,
             1982).

PESC   Max Weber, *The Protestant Ethic and the Spirit of
             Capitalism*, translated by Talcott Parsons, 2nd edn
             (London, 1976).

RaK   Max Weber, *Roscher and Knies: The Logical Problem of
             Historical Economics*, translated, with an introductory
             essay, by Guy Oakes (New York, 1975).

RS   Max Weber, *Gesammelte Aufsätze zur Religionssoziologie*,
             Vol. 1 (Tübingen, 1920), Vol. 2 (Tübingen, 1921), Vol. 3
             (Tübingen, 1921).

WG   Max Weber, *Wirtschaftsgeschichte. Abriß der universalen
             Sozial- und Wirtschaftsgeschichte*, edited by Sigmund
             Hellmann and Melchior Palyi, 3rd edn (edited by Johannes
             Winckelmann) (Berlin, 1958).

WL[1]   Max Weber, *Gesammelte Aufsätze zur Wissenschaftslehre*
             [edited by Marianne Weber] (Tübingen, 1922).

WL[2]   Max Weber, *Gesammelte Aufsätze zur Wissenschaftslehre*,
             2nd edn, edited by Johannes Winckelmann (Tübingen,
             1951).

WL[3]   Max Weber, *Gesammelte Aufsätze zur Wissenschaftslehre*,
             3rd edn, edited by Johannes Winckelmann (Tübingen,
             1968).

WL[4]   Max Weber, *Gesammelte Aufsätze zur Wissenschaftslehre*,
             4th edn, edited by Johannes Winckelmann (Tübingen,
             1973).

WuG[5]   Max Weber, *Wirtschaft und Gesellschaft. Grundriß der
             verstehenden Soziologie*, 5th edn, edited by Johannes
             Winckelmann (Tübingen, 1972).

1 Introduction

WOLFGANG J. MOMMSEN

In recent years there has been a considerable resurgence of interest in the work of Max Weber among scholars all over the world. More than ever before he is recognized as one of the great European thinkers of the turn of the century. After some delay, he has been granted a prominent place in European intellectual history, in company with Emile Durkheim and Vilfredo Pareto, as one of the founders of sociology as a scholarly discipline. Max Weber's unique contribution was to conduct his empirical sociological research from a universal-historical vantage point. He was a historian before he became a social scientist and, eventually, in the narrow sense, a sociologist. As a social scientist, he continued to be particularly interested in historiography. And although the ideal-typical theorems in which Weber tried to encapsulate the culturally significant problems of his time as precisely as possible were expressed in ever more abstract terms he intended thereby to create important conceptual tools for historiography as well as for sociology. In his late work, *Economy and Society*, Weber tried to grasp social reality in systems of 'pure types', all of which were constructed only with regard to systematic factors, allowing the contingencies of historical time to retreat into the background. None the less, Weber's conceptualization incorporated all that was known of the history of the Western world at his time. Also, in his classic studies on the sociology of world religion, a historical dimension is always evident. One reason for the present worldwide interest in Max Weber's work is that he succeeded in posing sociological questions against a historical horizon of unusual breadth, whose relevance for our present situation is obvious.

In his own lifetime, Max Weber had only limited influence on the development of the social sciences, especially on the establishment of sociology as an intellectual discipline, although his role as a founder of the Deutsche Soziologische Gesellschaft and as an organizer of scholarly enterprises, and even more as someone who encouraged concrete empirical research, should not be underestimated. He did not found a 'school' in a narrow sense. Much of his scholarly work was published only in the last years of his life. Most of it appeared posthumously, and then not always in a very satisfactory form, like *Economy and Society*, for example. Nevertheless, the impact of his person and his work was far-reaching and lasting.

Contrary to a long-established myth, Max Weber was the most cited and the most influential sociologist in Germany during the Weimar Republic.[1] In the late 1920s, his writings on methodology were already the subject of detailed scholarly analysis. The impact of his substantive sociological works was more diffuse, but equally strong. However, Weber's influence was not enough to lead German sociology out of the rut of an idealist, spiritual and sometimes organological approach.

Among historians, Weber's work attracted attention from the start, although few took a serious interest in his methodology. Otto Hintze applied ideal-typical methods in his work on European constitutional history. Other historians – Friedrich Meinecke, for example – expressed admiration for Weber as a great thinker, without adopting his methods in their own work. Max Weber's plea, before and during the First World War, for the 'parlamentarization' of the German constitution, and his energetic advocacy of a new democratic order between 1918 and 1920 were not forgotten. But, as German political culture drifted to the right, these factors no longer encouraged scholars to take a close interest in Weber, especially as the rigour of his thinking and the originality of his political ideas meant that he did not fit easily into any particular political camp. Historically, the strongest impact of Weber's ideas is found in the work of Carl Schmitt where, of course, they appear in a form that is surely not in line with Weber's original intentions.[2]

When the National Socialists came to power in Germany, interest in Weber's work did not cease immediately, but it soon faded. Christoph Steding, who had already described Max Weber in 1932 from a fascist point of view as the anachronistic representative of a bourgeoisie condemned to decline, came to represent National Socialist ideology,[3] while most social scientists working in the tradition of Max Weber had to leave Germany. The break was almost complete.

Thus the main interest in Weber shifted to Western Europe and the USA. In 1935, Raymond Aron published *La Sociologie allemande contemporaine*,[4] which contained a comprehensive appreciation of Weber. Talcott Parsons's major work, *The Structure of Social Action*,[5] was published in the USA in 1937. In Britain, interest in Weber concentrated mainly on his thesis about the relationship between Protestantism and 'the spirit of capitalism'. It was received critically, but with interest, above all in the works of R. H. Tawney.[6] In 1940, Carlo Antoni's *Dallo storicismo alla sociologia* appeared.[7] Although Antoni's assessment of Weber's political and sociological work was rather critical and reserved, Weber provided him with important evidence for his argument that German historical thinking was in the process of leaving behind the traditions of classical historicism (*Historismus*) and turning to sociological methods and approaches.

In the 1940s and 1950s, the tradition of Max Weber's work was continued by Anglo-Saxon scholars, especially in the USA, whose interest was then communicated back to Europe, and to the Federal Republic of Germany in particular, stimulating scholars there to take a fresh look at Weber's work. At that time, American scholars were interested primarily in Weber's sociological work. Weber's *Kategorienlehre* was the starting point for Talcott Parsons's theory of structural functionalism. Other scholars built on Weber's empirical research. Added to this was a newly awakened interest in political sociology and in Max Weber's involvement in day-to-day politics. H. C. Gerth and C. Wright Mills made Weber's writings widely available in their pioneering selection in English, *From Max Weber. Essays in Sociology*.[8] Contemporaries of Max Weber, in particular Paul Honigsheim and Karl Löwenstein,[9] also helped to interest English-speaking scholars in his work.

This upsurge of interest in Max Weber in Britain and the USA also had specific historical causes. Weber's sociology was fundamentally individualistic, and critical of all attempts at a substantive reconstruction of history. It was appropriate, therefore, at a time when 'holistic' philosophies of history, as described by Karl Popper in *The Poverty of Historicism*, were suspect as potentially leading to totalitarian forms of government.[10] In the era of neo-liberalism, when the principles of individualism and a free market, a liberal state and society, were held up against past and present totalitarian systems, Max Weber's liberal theory of society was received favourably, as was his highly effective critique of 'bureaucratic domination'. Further, his work offered, or at least so it seemed, a consistent and convincing alternative to socialism, which was seen as a political order that produced ever more govern-mental bureaucracies and human alienation. His analyses of the disadvantages of centrally directed socialist economies provided telling arguments against Marxism−Leninism with its inherent tendency to develop totalitarian forms of government.

Historiography was not affected to the same extent by contemporary issues such as these. Historians saw Weber as one of the thinkers who had intellec-tually prepared the break-through to a liberal society and a market-oriented industrial system in the West, and had pointed out its significance in scholarly analyses of a high standard. More than other German sociologists, Weber was receptive to social and political developments in the West. He incorporated Anglo-Saxon approaches into his sociological work, although in many ways his thinking remained indebted to the traditions of German idealism and historicism. This was also true of his political views.

Weber was among the thinkers who early distanced themselves from late nineteenth-century positivism and its naive belief in progress, without, however, succumbing to the opposite extreme of irrationalist theories of evolu-tion, or organological theories of society. He represented the grand tradition of European enlightenment at the moment of its partial disenchantment by modern science. This, above all else, made him a key figure in the development of European thought in the early twentieth century. In 1958, H. Stuart Hughes published his book *Consciousness and Society. The Reorientation of European Social Thought 1890−1930.*[11] He attributed an unusually high degree of intellectual productivity to the generation of thinkers who began writing and teaching in the 1890s. Hughes saw in their work a force that contributed substantially to shaping our present world. Their main achievement was to raze the bastions of a degenerate positivism and of a formalized idealism that had made the grand ideals of the Enlightenment one-sidedly concrete, and had compromised them by reducing them to a naive idea of predominantly materialist progress. This cleared a space for a new beginning in European intellectual history. Hughes saw Max Weber and Sigmund Freud as particularly important in this process, and placed Benedetto Croce, Emile Durkheim and Vilfredo Pareto in respected but subordinate positions.

In the following decades, almost no attempts were made to deal with Max Weber's work within large-scale syntheses of the history of European ideas. Scholars turned instead to the sociological and epistemological aspects of Weber's work, and only in this context was the question of Max Weber's place in the intellectual life of his era pursued any further. Richard Bendix's *Max Weber. An Intellectual Portrait*, published in 1960,[12] and numerous mono-graphs on Weber's methodological work, on his studies on the sociology of religion, and on his theory of bureaucracy, prepared the way for a new, more broadly based understanding of Max Weber, especially in the Anglo-Saxon world. Criticism was also heard, in particular of Max Weber's political views. (Much of this criticism was informed by Jakob Peter Mayer's book, *Max Weber in German Politics*, published in 1944.[13]) On the whole, however, a pragmatic attitude prevailed among scholars convinced of the direct applicability of Max Weber's sociological theories to further empirical research. The 1964 *Soziologentag* in Heidelberg was dedicated to the memory of Max Weber and represented the culmination of this feeling that a new era was beginning. Even here, however, distanced or overtly critical interpretations of Max Weber were heard. They included Raymond Aron's well-considered paper on 'Max Weber und die Machtpolitik', and Herbert Marcuse's paper 'Industrialization and Capitalism', in which he accused Weber of being an unreserved adherent of purely technocratic reason and thus an uncritical apologist of capitalism.[14]

During the following years there was a marked decrease of interest in Max Weber among social scientists. Empirical social research that was to lead to a new age marked by the 'end of ideology' (Daniel Bell) was in the ascendancy, making Weber's macro-sociological method, with its historical dimension and its commitment to a fundamental plurality of values, seem less relevant. Only his precept that 'science' must avoid *Werturteile* (value-judgements) found wide acceptance, but it was often interpreted in a purely positivistic sense that neglected the dimension of *Wertbeziehung* (value-reference). The converse was true of neo-Marxist positions influenced by the 'student revolution' of the 1960s. To adherents of these views, Weber represented an upper middle class that belonged to the past. Behind his rational and conceptual language, tending towards objective statements, they thought they detected quintessentially bourgeois values. In the Marxist–Leninist camp, Lukács's interpretation of Weber as a typical representative of the bourgeoisie's irrationalist thinking in the era of imperialism long maintained canonical status.[15]

Among historians, there has been continual interest in Max Weber, first because his methodology provided a link, acceptable to both sides, between the social sciences and historiography, and secondly because the ideal type proved to be a suitable tool for comparative social history. The same applies to political science. British political scientists had not often looked to Europe, but they now began to take a stronger interest in Max Weber. Particular mention must be made of David Beetham's book, *Max Weber and the Theory of Modern Politics*, which was the first full-scale assessment of Weber's political sociology in the Anglo-Saxon world.[16] John Rex and Anthony Giddens applied Weber's sociological theories to the problem of social action;[17] W. D. Runciman subjected Weber's methodological position to a thorough critique.[18] Moses I. Finley and Arnaldo Momigliano successfully applied Weber's work on ancient history to the problem of writing a social history of Antiquity.[19]

In West Germany, interest was initially directed towards Max Weber's theory of science. Dieter Henrich's pioneering, if controversial, study, *Die Einheit der Wissenschaftslehre Max Webers*, was published in 1952.[20] It was followed some years later by Friedrich H. Tenbruck's classic essay on the genesis of Weber's methodology.[21] From the mid 1960s, a rich stream of monographs appeared, nourished by Johannes Winckelmann's attempts to have Max Weber's main works republished in revised, corrected editions.

In 1956 he had already published a reorganized and expanded fourth edition of *Wirtschaft und Gesellschaft*, which, however, was not free of editorial flaws.[22] Wolfgang Schluchter, in *Aspekte bürokratischer Herrschaft* (1972), was one of those who alerted sociologists and historians to the significance of Max Weber's work in interpreting Western society of our day.[23] Schluchter subsequently published several studies in which he systematically investigated Weber's sociological work; his main theme was the rationalism of world domination (*Weltbeherrschung*).[24] Following the publication of my book, *Max Weber und die deutsche Politik 1890–1920*,[25] a controversy broke out, initially about Max Weber as a politician. Later it spread to the issue of Weber as a social theorist, placed between Marx and Nietzsche, and finally to that of Weber as a student of world history.[26]

In recent years, research on Max Weber has taken a wide range of directions. The literature on Weber has grown beyond measure. Rationalization and the related problem of bureaucratization have aroused particular interest. Weber's studies on the sociology of religion have also attracted renewed attention. For a time, his sociology of religion had been considered outdated and irrelevant; Kurt Samuelsson, for example, sharply criticized Weber's work on the Protestant ethic as empirically unsound.[27] Now a new and lively interest is being expressed in this aspect of Weber's sociology, especially as it relates to the sources of rationalization in the West.[28] It is not yet possible to identify any clear trend in recent research; all disciplines within the social and human sciences, from jurisprudence to theology, have turned to Weber's work with an overwhelming variety of approaches and methods.

For sociologists, the most recent upsurge of interest in Max Weber is related to the fact that the high-flown expectations harboured by empirical sociology in the 1950s and 1960s were disappointed. It had been hoped to achieve a new level of insight into society by means of an ahistorical, empirically based social science that strictly abstains from value-judgements and orients itself purely by instrumentally rational considerations. In response to this disappointment the need arose to proceed to new macro-sociological approaches; even though they could perhaps only be cast in hypothetical terms, such approaches could nevertheless provide guidelines for empirical research. At the same time a new interest has been awakened in the historical dimension of the social sciences. Weber's sociology provides an obvious starting point for ventures of this kind, because it poses its questions against a universal-historical background, and explicitly takes the historical dimension into account. This seems to us to explain part of the attraction of Max Weber for today's sociologists, although, as Ralf Dahrendorf shows in this volume, detailed research in sociology has long overtaken Weber. Weber's sociology offers a conceptual and theoretical orientation to historians also. Historiography has recently turned more strongly to intellectual history and the history of science, in an attempt to provide new intellectual guidelines in an age that, after the Enlightenment and the optimistic belief in progress characteristic of the nineteenth century, has lost its self-confidence.

In this situation, an attempt to redefine Max Weber's position within the intellectual and political constellation at the turn of this century seems appropriate. As the state of scholarship is constantly changing over a broad front, this would pose an impossible task for any individual. There is certainly no lack of specialized studies on individual aspects of the relationship of Max Weber's work to contemporary intellectual and political movements. Yet few studies deal comprehensively with larger sections of Weber's work while also taking account of the contemporary context. Those that exist are not always fully up to date with the latest research. Apart from this, Weber scholars are scattered widely over the English-speaking world and Europe, and may lack the necessary international connections. These considerations led us to hold an international conference in order to bring together the various strands and methodological approaches current in Weber scholarship, and to attempt a redefinition of Max Weber's position within the intellectual, sociological, political and philosophical environment of his time.

We deliberately chose not to structure the contributions around any particular theme, however important or central – such as, for example, Weber's model of the development of Western culture, the image of man that runs through his entire *oeuvre*, or his notion of societal change. Max Weber's work deals with a large variety of themes; any attempt to distinguish a dominant one, however it may be defined, would involve a considerable degree of arbitrariness and be attended by great interpretive difficulties – all the more so when the aim is to do justice to the development of Weber's thought through time and in his exchanges with contemporaries. The approach chosen here has been to examine Weber's work, with its wealth of perspectives and approaches, in the context of his own contemporary horizon, thus defining Weber's position within the spectrum of European thought in the first two decades of the twentieth century. This involves tracing the numerous parallels, or the mutual or unilateral influences, that existed between Max Weber and the many sociologists, historians, theologians and philosophers with whom he had a direct connection. It also requires an examination of the contrasts between Max Weber and contemporary thinkers with a commensurate *oeuvre*.

The contributions to this volume concentrate on the generation that began to be intellectually productive around 1890. Only in individual cases has this temporal limit been extended – for example, in those of Nietzsche and John Stuart Mill, who can truly be called Weber's 'enduring contemporaries'. The politicians and political thinkers of Weber's time also had to be considered. Political thought and politics were always important to Max Weber. Although he never became an active politician himself, he was, as Dolf Sternberger put it, a *politischer Bürger* in the true sense. It has been shown that Weber's strictly sociological work incorporates numerous observations and perceptions of a political kind, which Weber owed to the passionate interest he took in the political struggles of his time. Politics formed an important part of his scholarly work – although he always insisted that political value-judgements should play no part in it. Thus politics represents an autonomous dimension of Weber's work; it is not a mere biographical appendage that can be ignored with impunity.

The contributions to this volume express the most varied interpretations. From the start the project presupposed openness and a plurality of approaches to Weber's thinking and work. This means that no theoretical premises were imposed, and that extremely varied philosophical and political standpoints and methodological positions should be given equal representation. This procedure was intended to open up new vistas in an area that has become almost impenetrable, and thus allow new insights to be gained. Against the background of the intellectual and cultural movements of his day, Max Weber's achievements and his methodological originality emerge more clearly than has hitherto been the case. Conversely, we also see that Weber had important themes in common with his contemporaries, although he often gave them a particular twist.

The extremely diverse nature of Max Weber's relationships with his contemporaries, the subject of this volume, ruled out any standardization of individual contributions. Often, a personal or scholarly connection provides the starting point, as, for instance, in the discussion of the sociologists of the 'younger' generation in the Verein für Sozialpolitik, most of whom knew Max Weber personally. When discussing Robert Michels or Karl Jaspers, for example, it would be absurd not to give their personal relationship a central place in the analysis. Both were deeply influenced, personally and in their scholarly work, by their direct contact with Max Weber. In the majority of cases, however, a personal connection did not exist and, often, no traces of direct influence could be discovered in Weber's work either. At most, the influence operated only in one direction. Here, the aim has been to extract from the intellectual positions or argumentative models in each case the elements that were comparable, or, more often, to relate them to each other in the context of the time. It is important – in these cases – to show clearly the contrasts between the thought and work of Max Weber and that of his contemporaries. Ultimately, these essays are intended to document the changes that took place in European intellectual thought during the first two decades of this century.

Naturally, we cannot present anything even approaching a comprehensive assessment of Max Weber's intellectual environment. The personalities discussed in the volume were selected either because they maintained a scholarly or political relationship with Max Weber, or because a direct or indirect scholarly connection with him existed; however, those whose intellectual positions were diametrically opposed to Max Weber are also given due attention. The personalities under discussion here represent distinctive scholarly, philosophical or political positions of the age. They can be divided into four, in some respects extremely heterogeneous, groups. The first group consists of representatives of the social sciences in Weber's time; the second includes theologians and historians who were receptive to his work and who, in their turn, influenced him. Members of the third group belong to the realm of politics, and together make up an almost complete spectrum of the politics of the Kaiserreich as Max Weber saw it. The fourth group, transcending all these spheres of social reality, comprises philosophers and the exceptional figure of Sigmund Freud. Constraints of space meant that unfortunately the field of jurisprudence and constitutional law – including, for example, Georg Jellinek – could not be considered.

Part I, 'Max Weber and Social Science at the Turn of the Century', starts by dealing with those thinkers who made up Max Weber's immediate intellectual environment. Taking Karl Knies as an example, Wilhelm Hennis examines the long-neglected relationship between Max Weber and the political economy of the German Historical School. Manfred Schön looks at Max Weber's relationship with Gustav Schmoller, the father figure of the older school of

Kathedersozialismus (academic socialism), who made an enormous impact on contemporary social sciences in Germany. His political position, holding out the hope that a bureaucratically led, semi-authoritarian state would solve the major social problems of the day, was highly influential. Dieter Krüger discusses the 'younger' generation in the Verein für Sozialpolitik, who hoped that a liberalization of the state would lead to improved social conditions. Thus they came into conflict, sometimes sharply, with the majority of the *Kathedersozialisten* (academic socialists), led by Schmoller. Eberhard Demm introduces Alfred Weber, with whom Max Weber led intellectual attacks on the 'dominant opinion' within the Verein für Sozialpolitik until 1906. Thereafter the two brothers went their separate ways, and a common front in political matters did not develop between them again until after the First World War. Arthur Mitzman's topic is Werner Sombart, one of the most brilliant members of Max Weber's intellectual environment. Although Weber repeatedly fought fierce intellectual battles with Sombart, he regretted that Sombart was denied a 'normal' academic career commensurate with his abilities. Jürgen Osterhammel deals with Joseph Schumpeter, one of the few economists of the younger generation who can be considered true intellectual heirs to Max Weber. Finally, under the direct influence of Max Weber, Robert Michels developed from a committed anarchist and socialist into a sociologist. In many respects Michels occupies a mediating position between socialist social theory with a radical democratic slant and the Italian elite theories of the age. To Weber, he was also important as a link with Italian and Dutch anarchists, syndicalists and socialists.

These essays, which deal with Weber's immediate circle, as it were, are followed by studies of the great social theorists of the age, who made a lasting impact on European thought of the late nineteenth and early twentieth centuries: Gaetano Mosca, Vilfredo Pareto, Georges Sorel, John Stuart Mill and Emile Durkheim. The principle of contemporaneity in the sense of belonging to the same generation has been followed less strictly here, for reasons that are obvious in each case. In some respects, European thought and the far-reaching changes it underwent in the first two decades of the twentieth century can be diagrammatically represented as five interrelated poles. We have already alluded to parallels between Weber's political sociology and Mosca's and Pareto's theories of the circulation of elites. The contrast between Georges Sorel's gloomy picture of Western historical development and Max Weber's at least at first glance coolly rationalistic model of the development of the West could not be greater. But, if we consider Weber's theme of 'disenchantment', progrssive bureaucratization and the danger of ossification in Western culture, there is a surprising degree of agreement in their diagnoses of the crises of European culture, although not in the therapies each recommends. The relationship between John Stuart Mill and Max Weber, who acknowledged that he was strongly influenced by Mill, primarily concerns the empirical dimension of Weber's sociological work; it also raises the still unclarified issue of the connection between British and Continental thought in the nineteenth and early twentieth centuries. The relationship between Max Weber and Emile Durkheim, the two opposite poles of European sociology before the First World War, defies simple definition. Although their sociological questioning reveals clear parallels, their thoughts on politics and society show clearly developed differences. The success of Durkheim's sociology long prevented the reception of Max Weber's work in France, although the Durkeim school later appropriated certain elements of Weber's theory.

Part II, 'Max Weber's Relation to the Theologians and Historians', examines one dimension of the intellectual climate that was of the greatest importance for Max Weber's development. During the 1890s, Weber maintained contact with leading members of the progressive wing of German Protestantism that, in the Evangelical-Social Congress, had created for itself an influential public forum. These were Otto Baumgarten, Paul Göhre, Rudolf Sohm and Friedrich Naumann, who, in his later role as an active politician, is the subject of a separate essay. Rita Aldenhoff's contribution shows clearly how much the young Max Weber owed to German *Kulturprotestantismus* (cultural Protestantism). He shared the commitment of the young theologians who worked in the Evangelical-Social Congress, but not the naive idealism with which they believed they could solve the 'social question'. Max Weber's relationship to Lutheranism in the narrow sense was, by contrast, rather distanced. He believed Lutheranism to be largely responsible for the authoritarian mentality of the German middle classes, and held up against it the alternative model of Puritan religiosity. The remarkable inner-worldly achievements of Protestantism, especially in political respects, made him see Lutheranism in a thoroughly unfavourable light. He accused it of promoting a quietistic attitude to the big political issues. 'The fact that our nation has never, in *any* form, gone through the school of hard asceticism is ... the source of all that I find hateful in it (and myself)', Max Weber once wrote to Adolf von Harnack, in the context of an argument about the value – or lack of value – of Lutheranism.[29] W. R. Ward's essay allows the specific features of Weber's image of Lutheranism to stand out clearly against the background of the German Lutheranism of his time.

Weber's relationship to German Protestantism, and more specifically, to the Protestant theology of his age, was deeply influenced by Ernst Troeltsch, with whom he shared a house in Heidelberg for many years. Without the continuous dialogue he maintained with Troeltsch, Max Weber would probably never have written his studies of Protestant sects or of the 'spirit' of modern capitalism. In some respects Weber saw Troeltsch's book, *Die Soziallehren der christlichen Kirchen und Gruppen*, as a continuation of his own approach. While respecting it greatly, he also experienced feelings of rivalry. Partly because Troeltsch had given such a masterly account of this aspect of the inner-worldly activities of various Christian denominations,[30] Weber in 1915 turned to the economic ethic of the other world religions, with the intention of locating 'points of comparison with Occidental development that require further analysis'.[31] Weber's intellectual dialogue with Troeltsch, the leading representative of liberal theology in the early twentieth century, continued throughout his life, despite occasional personal tensions between them. If Weber had lived longer, it would have been revitalized because Weber intended, after completing his studies of the Asiatic world religions and ancient Judaism, to return to the development of the Christian doctrine and its significance for the creation of the modern, disenchanted, rationalistic culture of the West in his own day.

Max Weber's relationship with the historiography of his time has not yet been dealt with in an altogether satisfactory way. There is no question that in many respects Weber stood in the tradition of historicism (*Historismus*), although his own work can be interpreted as an ambitious attempt to free the humanities (*Kulturwissenschaften*) from the predominance of historicist methods and approaches, without doing away with those contributions by historicism that represented real epistemological progress. This includes, of course, the method of 'understanding' or 'empathy' that Weber wanted to transform into an epistemological method subjected to rational intellectual control throughout.

Taking a particularly impressive example, Friedrich H. Tenbruck shows that thematically, too, Max Weber owed a great deal to German historiography. Eduard Meyer's *Geschichte des Altertums*, which we know was valued highly by Max Weber, contains rudimentary forms of the ideal-typical model of charisma inevitably subjected to routinization in the course of time, which occupies a key position in Weber's historical sociology. There is undoubtedly a need for further studies of this type, that illuminate the historiographical findings of Max Weber's work. Only then will it be possible to determine more exactly the place of Weber's scheme of a 'societal history of the Occident' (Schluchter) – or, perhaps more correctly, of a plurality of 'societal histories' which together constitute the 'Occidental world'[32] – against the background of contemporary historiography. Unfortunately, we have not been able to take into consideration Max Weber's relationship with Theodor Mommsen, which seems to have been that of an uncommonly gifted pupil, with an independent mind, to a master. We can expect this issue to be clarified in Jürgen Deininger's introduction to the forthcoming second volume of the *Max Weber-Gesamtausgabe*, which will contain the early work, *Die römische Agrargeschichte in ihrer Bedeutung für das Staats- und Privatrecht* (1891). It appears that Weber was writing against Mommsen here, trying throughout to distance himself from Mommsen's findings. For the time being, however, it still deserves investigation whether or not Theodor Mommsen's historical typology of the Roman republic as presented in *Römisches Staatsrecht* influenced Max Weber's ideal-typical method.

Sam Whimster turns to a different aspect of Max Weber's place in the historiography of his time – his position in the historians' controversy that took place in Germany at the turn of the century, centring on the issue of cultural versus political history. It has gone down in history as the 'Lamprecht dispute'. Karl Lamprecht is generally seen as the pioneer of a new form of history writing, aspiring to a synthesis of social history, economic history, cultural anthropology and social psychology. 'Dominant opinion' among German historians rejected Lamprecht for allegedly using Marxist methods; this stance can also be read as a repudiation of all sociological methods. German historiography revolved around the concept of the modern, powerful nation-state, to which was attributed an ethical-moral quality in Hegel's sense. In this controversy, Weber sided with 'official' historiography rather than with Lamprecht. Lamprecht's organological and psychologizing method seemed even further from Weber's ideal of a historiography working with rational and precisely defined concepts than did contemporary German political historiography, with whose strengths and weaknesses Weber was fully familiar. And indeed, it must be said that, even if the Lamprecht dispute had ended in a different way, the Lamprecht school would not have produced the symbiosis of history and social science to which, in emulation of Max Weber, some branches of historiography aspire today.

In fact, the strongest connection, relatively speaking, between Max Weber's interpretive sociology and contemporary historiography could be found not in the field of social history, but in comparative institutional and constitutional history. A master in this field was Otto Hintze, one of the few historians whose breadth of perspective and universal-historical orientation did not fall short of Weber's. As Jürgen Kocka shows in his essay, it is not surprising that Hintze recognized the heuristic value of ideal-typical concepts for comparative constitutional and institutional history. These concepts made it possible to reconstruct the development of European states and their institutions during a period of 500 years. There were, however, clear differences between Hintze and Weber as far as their methods and heuristic interests were concerned. Nevertheless, Hintze's method of writing European constitutional history was closer to Weber's reconstruction of historical processes, whose cultural significance unfolds in the context of universal-historical development, than was the work of any other historian of his time.

At first sight, Part III, 'The Realm of Politics', takes us into a completely different field. Weber himself insisted that scholarly research and political conviction must be kept separate by all means. Scientific research is based on the principle of controlling its results in a strictly rational way and avoiding all value-judgements, political or other. Politics, by contrast, is a struggle: its specific means are force and violence, not rational deliberation and the adducing of empirical evidence. Politics can only be successful if it is governed by ultimate personal ideals which, regulated by an ethic of responsibility, are translated into determined political action. However, a rational awareness of the chances of effective personal action and of its consequences in the light of these ideals is a prerequisite for political conduct governed by the ethic of responsibility. Conversely, a rational understanding of the world in scientific terms is only possible in a meaningful way with reference to ultimate value-convictions, which serve as guidelines for research; these are, however, always conditioned by the political reality in which the individual lives. Max Weber made rigorous attempts to separate politics and science as different spheres of life, precisely because both, in equal degrees though in different ways, determine human existence and the intellectual horizons of man.

In the context of contemporary politics, Max Weber's own position can be described as that of a 'liberal in despair'. In order to preserve the central principles of liberal politics in an age of mass democracy and bureaucratic infiltration of the processes by which political objectives were being defined, Weber went beyond the postulates of classical liberalism.[33] An example of this is his ambivalent attitude towards Natural Law. Like Gaetano Mosca and Vilfredo Pareto in some respects, Weber tried to link democratic and elite or, more precisely, 'intellectually aristocratic' procedures of developing political objectives, and to combine them with the bureaucratic and demagogic instruments of mass democracy. Weber placed great stress on forward-looking political leadership, notwithstanding the institutional factors that condition political action, which he otherwise regarded as extremely important. At the end of his life, Weber believed that he had found a definite solution to the problem of leadership in modern democracy: he advocated a combination of plebiscitary leadership and bureaucratic control by means of party machines, with the role of parliaments being restricted primarily to providing a counterweight and a corrective to the leader's policies.

With ideas like these, Weber did not fit easily into the contemporary political scene. During the 1890s he was attracted more by the National Liberals than by progressive liberalism. After the turn of the century he approached first the Freisinnige Vereinigung (Liberal Union) and later the Fortschrittliche Volkspartei (Progressive People's Party), which was formed in 1911 as a federation of various radical liberal political groups. On social policy issues, Weber tended to be on the left of liberalism; on questions of national policy, however, he would have met with greater approval from the National Liberals. Throughout his life he remained a sharp critic of the Social Democrats, but repeatedly toyed with the idea of sacrificing his intellect and joining the party that belonged to the 'negatively privileged' political groups in Wilhelmine society. He always opposed the conservatives, especially the East Elbean variety; none the less, he respected conservative positions whenever they rose above narrow interest politics. Strictly speaking, Weber's political convictions did not match any of the established party positions; politically, he was a loner.

The 'realm of politics' in which Weber found himself is represented in this volume by prominent German politicians in the late Kaiserreich with whom he either maintained a more or less close connection or had an antagonistic relationship. This allows Weber's own place in the political spectrum of his time – a position in the centre, tending towards the left – to be established clearly.

Friedrich Naumann from the Christian Socialist camp was an intellectual precursor of the resolute liberalism of the period before and during the First World War; he was also, although this is not generally recognized, an extremely active politician both at parliamentary and at party level. In many respects, Naumann followed Weber's political line closely, though with a certain time-lag. In some ways, Naumann acted as a mediator between Max Weber and active politics. He repeatedly introduced Weber's political advice into parliamentary deliberations, notably on constitutional issues, often in co-operation with other leading liberal politicians such as Conrad Haußmann and Ernst Müller-Meiningen. Like Max Weber, Walther Rathenau stood outside the political arena, but nevertheless took an active interest in it. Ernst Schulin shows that there are many parallels in the political thought and work of these two men. They agreed in emphasizing the role of charismatic personalities, especially in democratic political systems. On the other hand, Weber never approved of Rathenau's state socialist ideas; he consistently advocated a market-oriented capitalism controlled by entrepreneurs in the grand style.

Contrasting Max Weber and Gustav Stresemann is of considerable interest. They came into direct confrontation only on the occasion of the debate about unrestricted submarine warfare in 1916; Stresemann wrote a memorandum in order to refute Weber's passionate plea against the unrestricted use of submarines even at the risk of bringing the USA into the war. In 1918–19 Weber, electioneering for the German Democratic Party (Deutsche Demokratische

Partei), rejected Stresemann's claim to a leading role in building up German democracy in Weimar because Stresemann was completely compromised by his expansionist stance during the war. Fundamentally, however, Weber and Stresemann agreed in their assessments of the nature of politics, and on the necessity for farsighted, responsible political action that did not look only to immediate success. But within the existing party political spectrum they occupied different positions, Stresemann arguing passionately against the doctrinaire professor who was ostensibly pursuing pure party politics, while Weber accused Stresemann of having irresponsibly acquiesced in the nationalist extravagance of the time, purely for tactical reasons and contrary to his better judgement. Subsequent developments proved that neither assessment was entirely correct.

There can be no doubt, however, about the diametrical opposition between Dietrich Schäfer and Max Weber. Schäfer can be regarded as the prototype of the sort of politician who bore no relation at all to Weber's 'ideal' politician, who acts with a sense of proportion and responsibility. Schäfer came from a humble social background, but he had made a successful academic career and held a distinguished post. As a 'social climber' he was naturally predestined to adopt pronounced nationalist views. During the First World War, these views led Schäfer to agitate actively in favour of unrestricted submarine warfare and extreme annexationist war aims. Schäfer was a 'professional politician' of the type that Weber abhorred most deeply: he had no scruples about mixing 'scholarship' and politics, and did not hesitate to use his professorial position to promote pan-German war aims. Lack of moderation, a total inability to consider political problems rationally, hollow demagogy based not on real issues but purely on emotion, conspiracy against the Reich leadership in collusion with the Reich Navy Office – in Weber's eyes, all this made Schäfer someone to be taken altogether less seriously than many other politicians. But, in ideal-typical terms, Schäfer represented the important and influential group of extreme nationalist politicians who corrupted German politics deeply during the First World War and continued to do so in the Weimar Republic.

Finally, Weber's attitude towards contemporary socialism deserves particular attention. His writings contain many scathing criticisms of German Social Democracy. He repeatedly made the accusation that, by adhering to an illusory strategy of 'revolutionizing the minds', German Social Democracy had from the start forfeited any chance of successfully pursuing strategies of practical reform. Weber criticized the Social Democrats' constant evocations of ultimate victory while they actually had almost no real influence, and their disparagement of the existing social system while pointing to a utopian vision of a future socialist society that would come about automatically. In Weber's opinion, this behaviour was bound merely to strengthen the existing order's immune system. There can be no doubt about Weber's personal preference: he opted for a policy of gradual reform in co-operation with the progressive sections of the liberal bourgeoisie.

This was also the line taken by the 'revisionists' within the German Social Democratic Party. Accordingly, Max Weber tried to establish a scholarly and personal connection with Eduard Bernstein, whom he also sought to recruit as an author for the *Archiv für Sozialwissenschaft und Sozialpolitik*, while he strongly opposed the ideologically centrist course taken by German Social Democracy and represented above all by Karl Kautsky. Dick Geary's essay shows that Weber's assessment of the ideological struggles within German Social Democracy was not necessarily as realistic as he himself suggested on several occasions. Conversely, Dittmar Dahlmann's essay on Weber's relationship to anarchism reveals that his preference for a 'realistic' (that is, revisionist) strategy by no means excluded considerable sympathy for anarchist and syndicalist positions. In any case, Weber never accused the anarchists of a lack of courage, determination and intellectual integrity.

On the whole, Weber's attitude towards contemporary socialism can be described as fundamentally critical, but nevertheless receptive and fair. This distinguishes him from the vast majority of his bourgeois contemporaries. Weber himself repeatedly emphasized that he was 'a member of the bourgeois classes', in contradistinction to a conceivable proletarian orientation. But Antonio Gramsci's analysis of Weber's political writings shows that Weber's work as a political theorist went beyond a purely bourgeois position. Despite Weber's support for free market capitalism – in which management and labour would be at liberty to fight out their class antagonisms – his theory of modern democracy was of considerable interest for democratic socialism.

'The Realm of Politics' should have been supplemented by a discussion of the historical relationship between Max Weber and Lenin; particular circumstances made this impossible. In any case, in his observations on political developments in Russia after 1917, Max Weber did not really recognize Lenin as a great leader. Nevertheless, a systematic comparison would be useful. It could be argued that, in some respects, Lenin's political success disproved Weber's thesis that, once a bureaucratic system of domination is firmly established, it cannot be destroyed – Lenin demolished the Tsarist bureaucracy within a few months. On the other hand, Weber's prognosis that centrally governed socialist systems will always ultimately lead to the subjection of the proletariat to the omnipotent rule of a class of bureaucratic functionaries, who will hold the rest of society under domination, has been strikingly fulfilled in the Communist states of Eastern Europe.

The synthesis attempted here of the intellectual climate created and experienced by Max Weber and his contemporaries culminates in Part IV: 'Max Weber and Philosophical Thought'. We have limited this section to a discussion of those philosophers who occupied important positions on Max Weber's scholarly horizon. It has long been recognized that Max Weber's intellectual roots lie in the philosophy of neo-Kantianism, although this is not universally accepted. Only recently, however, have Weber scholars taken greater notice of the formative impact of Nietzsche on Weber. As long as Weber scholars, under the influence of the empirical social sciences, looked mainly to Weber's empirical research and regarded the meta-scientific premises of his interpretive sociology as relatively unimportant, the Nietzschean elements in Weber's thought were largely overlooked, despite isolated studies of Nietzsche's significance for Weber – for example, Eugène Fleischmann's essay, 'De Weber à Nietzsche', published in 1964.[34] In his chapter in this volume, Robert Eden shows that Nietzsche had a lasting influence on Weber's work, although Weber tried all his life to distance himself from Nietzsche's disdain for the masses, his theory of resentment and his cultural pessimism. In strict chronological terms, of course, Nietzsche lies outside the scope of this study. But Max Weber was intensely interested in Nietzsche precisely during the period of Nietzsche's belated reception in Germany, that is, during what is generally, but not very felicitously, known as the 'Nietzsche Renaissance', beginning early in the 1890s. The few biographical references we have suggest that Max Weber's understanding of Nietzsche was strongly influenced by Ferdinand Tönnies's extremely successful book on Nietzsche,[35] and especially by two books by Georg Simmel: *Schopenhauer und Nietzsche* (1906), and *Philosophie des Geldes*.[36] Weber's own copy of the latter work is extant, and contains a number of highly instructive marginalia and comments on Simmel's interpretation of Nietzsche.

Simmel's significance as a pioneer of modern sociology is currently being recognized anew. For Max Weber, he was not merely a sociologist and philosopher who represented a link with Nietzscheanism and *Lebensphilosophie*; in this respect, Weber followed Simmel only to a limited extent. Simmel's *Die Probleme der Geschichtsphilosophie*,[37] and his *Philosophie des Geldes* referred to above, are models of the sort of discussion of social phenomena against the background of relatively broad theorems of a substantive philosophy of history that was widespread at the end of the nineteenth century. Of course, their empirical content and the level of their epistemological reflection distinguish them from evolutionist social theories as put forward by Roscher or Knies. David Frisby's essay takes us into largely unexplored territory, but it already seems clear that in many respects Max Weber built on Simmel – for example, in his theory of modern rational capitalism, or in his model of social action that, because it derives from value-rational or instrumentally rational motives, can be 'comprehended' in terms of its intentionality.

Methodologically, Max Weber regarded himself as a neo-Kantian or, at least, he had no difficulty in justifying his own methodological position with reference to the work of Heinrich Rickert. Rickert's *Grenzen der naturwissenschaftlichen Begriffsbildung* is probably the book Weber cites most often in his essays on the theory of knowledge. This may, however, be misleading, as self-interpretation is not always the best guide for establishing the philosophical position of a social thinker. In his essay on Max Weber and the Southwest German school of neo-Kantianism, Guy Oakes points out the limits of Max Weber's adoption of neo-Kantian positions. It is well known that Weber found Rickert's assumption of the existence of objective cultural values unacceptable, but the consequences of this are seldom fully realized. By introducing the term 'value-reference' not only as a means of 'individuating' historically given objects, but also in order to construct ideal-typical models to demonstrate the cultural significance of certain phenomena, Weber actually went far beyond neo-Kantian epistemology. Value-references are made possible only by a choice – in principle decisionist – between different value-hierarchies that are in eternal conflict with each other. Oakes demonstrates convincingly that Weber took from Rickert's philosophy those elements that he considered useful as theoretical pillars on which to support his own 'interpretive sociology'; he did not, however, adopt the central tenets of neo-Kantianism.

As far as we know, Max Weber clarified his own methodological position by means of a constant dialogue with Emil Lask, who himself occupied an intermediate position between neo-Kantianism and a *Lebensphilosophie* following Nietzsche and Simmel. Unfortunately, we could not devote a separate essay in this volume to Lask, who, until his early death, was very close to Max Weber and had been a frequent guest in Weber's house in Heidelberg.

Weber's relationship to contemporaneous *Lebensphilosophie* and to the aesthetic movements of that time is a particularly difficult topic and has not yet received adequate treatment. As far as we know, Weber was not aware of Henri Bergson. Bergson's theories pointed in a direction that ran totally counter to Weber's affirmation of a basically rational understanding of the world. To be sure, however, Weber's view that it was modern man's destiny to live in a disenchanted world shaped by instrumentally rational institutions, where the personality was pushed back into the non-committal sphere of private life, also contained a non-rational dimension. Weber himself admitted that, at the end of this secular process of rationalizing all areas of life, the ancient struggle of world images (*Weltanschauungen*) among themselves would break out again in a new form: 'Many old gods ascend from their graves; they are disenchanted and hence take the form of impersonal forces. They strive to gain power over our lives and again they resume their eternal struggle with one another.'[38] In one sense, Weber's attempt rigidly to rationalize his own life-conduct and constantly to subject his own ultimate value-ideals and the options they determined to a rigorous check led into an irrational world of values whose validity could no longer be established objectively, but only by a personal life-conduct that embodied them adequately.

Thus Weber's position is not quite so far removed from the *Lebensphilosophie* of his time as is generally thought. Further, the incipient substantive value ethic inherent in his concept of an ethic of responsibility has some things in common with the phenomenological philosophy of value, developed by Max Scheler during Weber's lifetime and taken further in Edmund Husserl's phenomenology. The work of Alfred Schütz, who saw himself as a successor to the phenomenological school, thus to a certain extent also stands in the tradition of Weber's work, although as far as we know, Weber tended to reject phenomenological ways of arguing. Philosophically, however, Weber was certainly closer to phenomenology than to the idealistic neo-Hegelianism of Benedetto Croce, despite the fact that they shared a central theme: the question of how freedom is possible in the modern world, and how it can be realized in concrete terms. But, in Weber's view, Croce's answers to these questions were much too optimistic, quite apart from the fact that intellectually Weber could not accept Croce's unilinear reconstruction of historical processes, even if it were only the history of the Occident, as a 'history of progress towards freedom'. The few points of contact between their work, as Pietro Rossi shows, relate primarily to methodological issues. The relationship between Croce and Weber can be summed up as a mutual demonstration of respect at a distance, combined with criticism in matters of detail. Weber never dealt systematically with Croce's philosophy; neither did Croce systematically examine Weber's work, even in the 1930s.

Weber has generally been seen as standing fully in the tradition of European rationalist thought since the Enlightenment. He is therefore considered to have fundamentally rejected all aestheticizing or irrational forms of thought. But the closer Weber pushed the postulates of a rational knowledge of the world to the limits of the conceivable, the more clearly did the principle of rationality split into two components that could not easily be reconciled with each other: 'formal' and 'substantive' rationality. Weber came to the conclusion that, in the light of certain ultimate value-ideals, a rational conduct of life was in principle possible from the most diverse positions, regardless of the fact that the modern capitalist and bureaucratic organization of Western societies favours purely instrumentally rational forms of life-conduct. This made the question of the value-ideals that alone confer meaning on the life of an individual ever more urgent.

For this reason, and especially towards the end of his life, Max Weber was extremely interested in philosophical positions that attempted to offer a counterweight to the instrumental rationality of the modern world. In this context, Sigmund Freud took on increasing significance for Weber. Freud pointed to deeper levels of human existence that, as it were, blocked the rigid, methodical life-conduct in the service of ultimate, non-everyday ideals, modelled on Puritanism, that Weber had so far favoured. Suddenly, Weber was made uncertain: perhaps the alternative of living out one's erotic feelings, regardless of the destructive impact on one's environment with its complex networks of social and moral obligations, was the more correct course after all. Immersing himself in the question raised by Freud regarding to what extent every individual's life conduct is determined by natural drives, Weber eventually decided against Freud. But on these issues Weber remained vulnerable, in both his intellectual and his private existence, for the rest of his life. In the *Zwischenbetrachtung* he addresses this problem with commendable clarity. The type of rationalization that follows from an ethical position of Puritan origin, affecting all spheres of life and not least one's personal life-conduct, he writes here, stands in indissoluble conflict with 'any unselfconscious abandonment to the most intense varieties of life experience: the artistic and the erotic'.[39]

Thus it is not surprising that Max Weber became increasingly receptive to philosophical and aesthetic positions that more or less radically rejected his own basic postulate of a rational understanding and mastering of the world. Their declared aim was to confront a social order that had become rigid in its emphasis on a purely instrumental rationality with new meanings and values, even if they were only of an emotional nature. However, emotional ways of arguing and a charismatic appeal, based on an extreme cultivation of the ideal of the individual personality, were in his view not enough to achieve this. They had to be joined by a readiness to adopt a personal life-conduct in which the various ideal postulates could be put to the test of reality.

This explains Max Weber's relationship − a mixture of rejection and fascination in equal parts − to Otto Gross and the community he founded in Ascona. Its members tried to put into practice the principles of free love and an 'alternative' life-conduct that withdrew from the pressures of a 'civilized society'. 'Passion as a mode of life' − as Wolfgang Schwentker sums it up − was incompatible with the principles of the Puritan ethic. Max Weber saw this as a salutary challenge to which, however, he did not find a definitive response.

Weber's relationship to Stefan George was similar, but it was located at a different level. Everything in Weber resisted the extreme personal stylization and aesthetic refinement of life-conduct practised by George, a *Dichterfürst* surrounded by a 'primarily artistic type of charismatic discipleship', who had a relatively secure financial basis.[40] All the same, Weber could not help respecting George. Friedrich Gundolf, incidentally, a follower of George's, regularly attended Weber's soirées at his home at 17 Ziegelhäuser Landstraße in Heidelberg. Unfortunately, it was not possible to devote an essay to Stefan George in this volume.

The aestheticizing trend of the day, represented by Stefan George, could be seen as a radical alternative to Weber's consistent and, in certain respects, heroic rationalism. In a way, Ernst Bloch and Georg Lukács were also a part of this movement. As Éva Karádi shows in her contribution to this volume, Ernst Bloch and especially Georg Lukács were regarded within the movement as 'figures of the opposite pole' – that is, opposite to the purely formal aestheticism represented by George. Ernst Bloch, in particular, presented himself to Max Weber as a philosophical apocalyptist, and did not hesitate to play the part of a prophet. Weber found it difficult to accept this; he was deeply suspicious of Bloch's attitude and thus withdrew, vis-à-vis Bloch, into the role of a critical scholar whose intellectual integrity did not allow him to pronounce on meta-scientific matters. Fundamentally, however, Weber was extremely interested in philosophical positions that attempted to find alternatives to the instrumental rationality of the modern world, provided they were translated into a corresponding personal life-conduct. In the case of Georg Lukács, Max Weber found total consistency between ultimate values and personal life. For this very reason, Lukács represented a constant challenge to Weber's own ultimate values. He was particularly interested in Lukács's attempts to find an independent philosophical basis for a theory of aesthetics. Weber could here perceive an independent sphere of intellectual reality, inaccessible by means of his own interpretive sociology, but apparently of the greatest 'scientific' value in as much as it raised highly significant cultural issues. Further, Lukács's position pointed to the existence of alternative forms of intellectual orientation in the world and of alternative ethical attitudes towards it. Weber recognized that this position was fundamentally in line with his own ethic of ultimate ends, but it pushed them radically further, seemingly leading to new shores.

Part IV is rounded off by Dieter Henrich's essay on Karl Jaspers and Max Weber. Originally written as a speech for the 100th anniversary of Karl Jaspers's birth, it documents the deep and lasting impression that Weber's work and personality made on everyone in his immediate vicinity. *Max Weber. Politiker, Forscher, Philosoph* (1932) by Karl Jaspers is arguably the most profound appreciation that a great thinker has ever received from someone who could call himself an intellectual 'pupil'. 'His existence', writes Jaspers, 'was an encouragement to all those who stride into the future without illusions, active as long as it is granted to them to be so, and full of hope as long as not everything is lost.'[41] By his own testimony, Jaspers was strongly encouraged by Max Weber to practise philosophy in his own way; it is not by chance that Jaspers became the spokesman for the circle around Marianne Weber dedicated to keeping alive the memory of Max Weber for future generations. In doing so, Jaspers did not always avoid the danger of idealizing Weber. Henrich shows that, in old age, Jaspers attempted to rectify this; he did not, however, alter his basic assessment that Weber had been 'the greatest German of our time'.[42]

Part V, the conclusion to this volume, consists of essays by Ralf Dahrendorf and Edward Shils. They provide a change of perspective in that they look back to Max Weber's work and personality from the vantage point of the present day. Edward Shils discusses the basic social changes that have taken place in the West since Max Weber's death and asks: what are the enduring elements of Weber's scholarly work and his philosophical position? Ralf Dahrendorf pays tribute to Weber as a sociologist in the light of present-day sociology, which in terms of both methods and substance has developed far beyond Weber's work. This is in line with Weber's own view that as the 'great cultural problems' change, 'science' too must 'constantly change its standpoint and its conceptual apparatus'.[43]

It was initially hoped that an assessment of Max Weber's work and personality in the context of Oriental and, in particular, Indian culture could also be included. Weber had an intense interest in this area, but under the given circumstances, he was unable fully to overcome a Eurocentric view. The critical assimilation and contemplation of Weber's work has only just begun in Asian cultures. To respond to this challenge would have been beyond the scope of this volume, but it should be recommended for future attention. This also applies to Weber scholarship in countries belonging to the Marxist–Leninist camp. Here, the ideological condemnation of Max Weber as a representative of the bourgeoisie that, during its phase of decline, subscribed to an irrational nationalism, has at long last given way to a more sober assessment of the analytical value of his sociology. Marian Orzechowski has recently pointed out, with some justification, that there are 'indeed striking analogies between Lenin and Weber, in their seizing on the same political questions during the era of imperialism, and in the nature of their observation despite all their ideological and methodological differences'.[44] The discussion of Max Weber as one of the great European thinkers of the early twentieth century will continue, and will certainly transcend the boundaries between scholarly, philosophical and political doctrines.

Notes: Chapter 1

This chapter was translated by Angela Davies.

1 Cf. H. Fogt, 'Max Weber und die deutsche Soziologie der Weimarer Republik. Außenseiter oder Gründervater?', in M. R. Lepsius (ed.), *Soziologie in Deutschland und Österreich 1918–1945*, Kölner Zeitschrift für Soziologie und Sozialpsychologie, Sonderheft 23 (Opladen, 1981), pp. 245–73; D. Käsler, *Die frühe deutsche Soziologie 1909–1934 und ihre Entstehungsmilieus* (Opladen, 1984).
2 Cf. W. J. Mommsen, *Max Weber and German Politics, 1890–1920* (Chicago, 1984), pp. 389ff.
3 C. Steding, 'Politik und Wissenschaft bei Max Weber', phil. diss., Breslau, 1932.
4 R. Aron, *La Sociologie allemande contemporaine* (Paris, 1935).
5 T. Parsons, *The Structure of Social Action* (New York, 1937).
6 R. H. Tawney, *Religion and the Rise of Capitalism: A Historical Study* (London, 1926).
7 C. Antoni, *Dallo storicismo alla sociologia* (Florence, 1940), transl. as *From History to Sociology* (Detroit, 1959).
8 H. C. Gerth and C. W. Mills, *From Max Weber: Essays in Sociology* (London, 1946).

20   Max Weber and his Contemporaries

9 Cf. among others, P. Honigsheim, *On Max Weber* (New York, 1968); K. Löwenstein, *Max Webers staatspolitische Auffassungen in der Sicht unserer Zeit* (Frankfurt, 1965).

10 K. R. Popper, *The Poverty of Historicism* (London, 1957).

11 H. S. Hughes, *Conscicusness and Society: The Reorientation of European Social Thought 1890–1930* (London, 1959).

12 R. Bendix, *Max Weber: An Intellectual Portrait* (London, 1960).

13 J. P. Mayer, *Max Weber in German Politics* (London, 1944), 2nd edn. London, 1956.

14 Cf. O. Stammer (ed.), *Max Weber und die Soziologie heute. Verhandlungen des 15. Deutschen Soziologentages* (Tübingen, 1965).

15 G. Lukács, *Die Zerstörung der Vernunft* (Berlin, 1954).

16 D. Beetham, *Max Weber and the Theory of Modern Politics* (London, 1974), 2nd edn, Cambridge, 1985.

17 A. Giddens, *Politics and Sociology in the Thought of Max Weber* (London, 1972); J. Rex, *Max Weber and Modern Sociology* (London, 1971).

18 W. G. Runciman, *A Critique of Max Weber's Philosophy of Social Science* (Cambridge, 1972).

19 Cf., among others, M. I. Finley, *The Ancient Economy* (London, 1973); idem, *Ancient Slavery and Modern Ideology* (London, 1980). A. Momigliano, *Contributo alla storia degli studi classici e del mondo antico*, 7 vols (Rome, 1956–75); idem, *Essays in Ancient and Modern Historiography* (Oxford, 1977).

20 D. Henrich, *Die Einheit der Wissenschaftslehre Max Webers* (Tübingen, 1952).

21 F. H. Tenbruck, 'Die Genesis der Methodologie Max Webers', *Kölner Zeitschrift für Soziologie und Sozialpsychologie*, vol. 11 (1959), pp. 573–630.

22 He undertook to compile the *Staatssoziologie*, which Max Weber never wrote, from his *Politische Schriften*, ostensibly excluding the 'value-judgements' they contained.

23 W. Schluchter, *Aspekte bürokratischer Herrschaft. Studien zur Interpretation der fortschreitenden Industriegesellschaft* (Munich, 1972), 2nd edn, Frankfurt, 1985.

24 idem, *Rationalismus der Weltbeherrschung. Studien zu Max Weber* (Frankfurt, 1980); idem, *Die Entwicklung des okzidentalen Rationalismus. Eine Analyse von Max Webers Gesellschaftsgeschichte* (Tübingen, 1979).

25 1st edn, Tübingen, 1959; 2nd edn, Tübingen, 1974, with an afterword and documentation of the controversy. For the English translation, see n. 2 above.

26 Cf. G. Abramowski, *Das Geschichtsbild Max Webers. Universalgeschichte am Leitfaden des okzidentalen Rationalisierungsprozesses* (Stuttgart, 1966); W. J. Mommsen, *Max Weber. Gesellschaft, Politik und Geschichte* (Frankfurt, 1974), pp. 442ff.

27 Cf. K. Samuelsson, *Ekonomi och Religion* (Stockholm, 1957). English edition: *Religion and Economic Action*, ed. by D. C. Coleman (Stockholm, 1961).

28 Cf. F. H. Tenbruck, 'Das Werk Max Webers', *Kölner Zeitschrift für Soziologie und Sozialpsychologie*, vol. 27 (1975), pp. 663–702; idem, 'Wie gut kennen wir Max Weber?', *Zeitschrift für die gesamte Staatswissenschaft*, vol. 131 (1975), pp. 719–42; further, W. Schluchter (ed.), *Max Webers Studie über das antike Judentum. Interpretation und Kritik* (Frankfurt, 1981); idem (ed.), *Max Webers Studie über Konfuzianismus und Taoismus* (Frankfurt, 1983); idem (ed.), *Max Webers Studie über Hinduismus und Buddhismus* (Frankfurt, 1984); idem (ed.), *Max Webers Sicht des antiken Christentums. Interpretation und Kritik* (Frankfurt, 1985).

29 Letter from Max Weber to Adolf von Harnack, 5 February 1906, Deutsche Staatsbibliothek, East Berlin, Harnack papers.

30 E. Troeltsch, *Die Soziallehren der christlichen Kirchen und Gruppen* (Tübingen, 1919).

31 RS, Vol. 1, p. 12.

32 Cf. W. J. Mommsen, 'Max Webers Begriff der Universalgeschichte', in J. Kocka (ed.), *Max Weber, der Historiker* (Göttingen, 1986), p. 64.

33 Cf. W. J. Mommsen, *The Age of Bureaucracy: Perspectives on the Political Sociology of Max Weber* (Oxford, 1974), especially the chapter 'A Liberal in Despair'.

34 E. Fleischmann, 'De Weber à Nietzsche', *Archives européennes de sociologie*, vol. 5 (1964), pp. 190–238.

35 F. Tönnies, *Der Nietzsche-Kultus. Eine Kritik* (Leipzig, 1897).

36 G. Simmel, *Schopenhauer und Nietzsche* (Leipzig, 1907); idem, *Philosophie des Geldes* (Leipzig, 1900).

37 idem, *Die Probleme der Geschichtsphilosophie* (Leipzig, 1907).

38 FMW, p. 149.

39 RS, Vol. 1, p. 563.
40 Cf. ES, Vol. 1, p. 245.
41 K. Jaspers, *Max Weber. Politiker, Forscher, Philosoph*; this quotation from 3rd edn (Munich, 1958), p. 8.
42 ibid., p. 7.
43 WL^4, p. 214.
44 M. Orzechowski, *Polityka Wladza panowanie. W. teorii Maxa Webera* (Warsaw, 1984), p. 416.

Part I

Max Weber and the Social Sciences at the Turn of the Century

2 A Science of Man: Max Weber and the Political Economy of the German Historical School

WILHELM HENNIS

In the first essay that he wrote on Max Weber's work, Friedrich H. Tenbruck referred to the 'historical isolation' surrounding the interpretation of Weber's writing, an isolation that has closed off important aspects of its historical and genetic context.[1] Little has changed since 1959; on the contrary, the progressive consolidation of modern sociology has ensured that this situation remains fixed and unchanging. There is, of course, a mountainous literature on the so-called 'reception' of Weber.[2] Equally evident is the fact that this literature contributes very little to the understanding of Weber's work. The various evolutions in the game of Chinese whispers can certainly be highly amusing, but here as in scientific 'receptions' we do not expect the original message to survive the process. Or might we – to take the most 'fruitful' example – draw conclusions about Weber's 'interpretive sociology' on the basis of Talcott Parsons's *Theory of Social Action*? Parsons certainly thought so,[3] and a whole generation of sociologists has learnt to read Weber through his eyes.

Even the rapid accumulation of studies on the relations, influences and possible parallels between Weber's work and that of his contemporaries (Rickert, Lask, Münsterberg, Troeltsch, Jellinek, Sombart) – who all without doubt prompted here and assisted there, stimulated, corrected and so forth, but nevertheless did not really *mould* the basic features of the work – has not led to any of these studies being able to contribute very much to a fundamental understanding of the work, for they assume without exception that Weber is to be understood as a founding father of modern sociology.[4] Consequently, interest from the very first has been directed to the process of development that sociology has undergone. Weber had nothing in common with the sociology of a Comte or a Spencer or a Durkheim (who, in fact, is never once mentioned), and Weber's *verstehende* sociology clearly distanced itself from the 'organic' variants of Schäffle and Gumplowicz. Here, we are obviously dealing with a 'founding father' of a sociology *sui generis*, *ex nihilo*, a pure intellectual invention. At the most, Tönnies and Simmel seem to belong to the same 'genetic' context, although wherever Weber greets them as kindred spirits he makes sure to keep a certain distance.

Max Weber maintained a distance wherever it was possible; his work is not free of an addiction to laboured originality.[5] However, if we disregard the mannerisms of *verstehende* sociology, then Weber's writings are seen to fall within the broad stream of later nineteenth-century German human and social sciences, a period in which these sciences truly blossomed. Such a point of view robs the work of none of its greatness! But let us reverse this perspective. Taking up Tenbruck's formulation, let us examine the connections which are historically and genetically *relevant* to the work, and which *lead up* to it. 'Reception history' is a diversion; the history of contemporary influences and contacts remains of importance, but cannot lead us to the origins of the work. Where do these origins lie – from which formative traditions does the work develop?

In two earlier essays I have sought to demonstrate that Weber's central problem – in his words, his *zentrale Fragestellung* – concerns the 'fate of humanity' under conditions of modernity. This can be regarded as a fundamentally 'anthropological' problem or, to use a term then current, a 'characterological' question; it is this question that generates the thematic thread running through the work: namely, the relation of 'personality and life orders' – another of Weber's formulations.[6]

Anyone familiar with the history of political philosophy will notice at once that Weber's problem and theme – when properly defined – share little with the specifically sociological traditions associated with the names of Comte, Spencer or Durkheim. On the other hand, there is a striking resemblance to the central themes of political philosophy from the Greeks up to Rousseau.[7] To use Comte's formulation, sociology developed as a *politique positive* from moral philosophy, and especially from politics – and in this process effected a decisive emancipation. The central point of 'practical', 'moral' and 'social' sciences is no longer the political community – in modern terms the state as *societas perfecta cum imperio*; in its place there appears *society* in its ideal form, *societas perfecta sine imperio*, constituted by those who are in principle free and equal. 'Society', with the market as an ideal type of sociability in which power and influence are freely competed for, delineates the extreme bounds for human action. The political order becomes subordinate, a sub-system of the social system. The result is a radical intellectual reorientation, which encountered (and not only in Germany)[8] particularly intense and stubborn resistance – Treitschke's post-doctoral thesis on the 'science of society' need only be recalled here.[9] The question to be posed in this essay aims at an understanding of the characteristic features of Weber's science between a waning tradition of 'politics' on the one hand and an up-and-coming sociology on the other, within the German academic context of the late nineteenth century. Is it possible, therefore, to understand Weber properly if he is viewed unquestioningly as the great sociologist, as the German founding father of sociology?

First, we must recall a few biographical details of significance in Weber's development, before moving on to examine the special character of that science into which Weber entered and with which he identified himself at the beginning of his academic career.

From Jurisprudence to Political Economy

In the first sentence of the first letter by Max Weber known to contemporary researchers, a letter from the twelve-year-old Max to his mother, we read: 'I have taken a look at Uncle Julian Schmidt's books and glanced at Herder's

Cid, and am at the moment reading Machiavelli's *Principe*, which Herr Dr Brendicke has lent me. Later I want to borrow *Anti-Machiavell* too.'[10] In April 1888, he writes to his uncle Hermann Baumgarten that he has to 'continually think about public affairs'.[11] And a year before his death, at the time when his chance of being elected to the National Assembly had finally come to nothing, he wrote to a friend: 'And then the political (I am now able "to speak of it more freely...") – that is my old "secret love".'[12] As we know, Max Weber never did find a path into practical politics. But what role should this 'secret love' be given in his scholarly work? Does this question help us in our search for its origins and for its basic working principles?

Weber studied law, that much is known, taking the broad approach that was usual at the time, but all the same not transgressing the usual boundaries. Thus, in addition to law, he read theology, philosophy, a great deal of history and also political economy. Law and political economy had always been closely associated in the German cameralist tradition. He gained a doctorate in law, completed his period as a junior barrister without any especial enjoyment and became an assistant judge (*Assessor*); he therefore became a qualified lawyer and was qualified as such in Berlin. Drawn into legal practice, he at first doubted his aptitude for scholarly work. The chance of working as a syndic in Bremen, i.e. practical work in the full sense of the term, fell through[13] and he did after all write a post-doctoral thesis and complete his 'Habilitation': in German and Roman law as well as in commercial law. Shortly after this, Friedrich Althoff, who had in mind great things for Weber, conferred on him an associate professorship in German and commercial law in Berlin.

If we wish to appreciate properly Weber's interests and his way of thinking, it is illuminating to look rather more closely at what Weber wrote on law in his lifetime. I hope that nothing has escaped my attention but my conclusion is that he devoted scarcely a single line to that which lawyers call *de lege lata*. The doctoral dissertation and the post-doctoral thesis deal with questions of legal *history*, questions that would never pall for him. But what he writes on law in the more restricted sense concerns legal policy – and this is written from the viewpoint of the legislator, *de lege ferenda*. The earlier themes concern social and commercial law: law of inheritance, law of residence, law of entailment and – reaching out even further – the law of the stock exchange and of bonds. In the final years, his interest turns to constitutional and public law. Weber now actually sees himself in the role of a *législateur*. The titles of his main articles express his intention with an almost provocative tone: in May 1918, 'Parliament and Government in a Reconstructed [i.e. to be reconstructed] Germany'; finally, in January 1919, summarizing the essays from the period November–December 1918: 'Germany's Future State Form'. During his entire life, legal questions were of interest to Weber only in relation to their potential political effect; questions of legal doctrine never caught his interest.[14]

And so, in 1894, the fully qualified lawyer, who in a letter of 1889 confessed to having in the meantime 'become one-third economist'[15] cagerly seizes the opportunity of exchanging his easily attained Berlin appointment in commercial law for the Freiburg chair in *Nationalökonomie*. His work for the Verein für Sozialpolitik on the condition of rural labourers in the eastern provinces had brought him recognition among contemporary economists. He felt equal to the tasks of the new discipline, even if he did claim, with some exaggeration, that he had for the first time attended principal economics lectures – given by himself.[16] For a time the Freiburg opening was not completely assured, and he wrote to his mother: 'I would be sorry if I remained harnessed to the relatively barren province of law.'[17] By assuming the Freiburg chair Weber by no means said goodbye to politics, as is sometimes assumed; he rather sought and found a way into a more practical politics[18] – into a science more 'political' than law could be, where anyone who wanted to make a career had to devote their efforts to work on positive law. One of the attractive aspects of the appointment to a small university like Freiburg was the possibility of participating in practical political work. Later, when Weber assumed chairs in Heidelberg and Munich, he was in each case quite aware that political activity (for example, appointment to the Reichstag) would scarcely be compatible with the more demanding commitments of teaching.[19]

The reasons for the shift from law to economics are primarily scholarly in nature, and relate to the differences existing between the two disciplines. Marianne Weber summarized them as follows:

> a change of discipline suited him. As a science, economics was still elastic and 'young' in comparison with law. Besides, it was on the borderline of a number of scholarly fields; it led directly to the history of culture and of ideas as well as to philosophical problems. Finally, it was more fruitful for a political and socio-political orientation than the more formal problems of legal thought.[20]

Before turning to a closer examination of the discipline that Weber joined, it might be of use to recall briefly the work that Weber left at his death. Can it, viewed from the perspective of 1920, be straightforwardly assigned to sociology? Weber had certainly been the driving force behind the foundation of the German Sociological Society. However, the society was hardly established before he left it.[21] He nearly always referred to sociology in a distancing fashion (for instance, in the opening passage of *Economy and Society*) and the tone is often distinctly ironic. Wherever he accepted the term for his own work he sought, by using specifying adjectives (*verstehend*, 'interpretive') not only to isolate it, but actually to singularize it. The 'later' Weber only admitted a sociology conducted in *his* fashion ('for sociology in our sense which is restricted to subjectively understandable phenomena – a usage which there is no intention of attempting to impose on anyone else')[22] – a Weber who, in the usual genetic reading, arrived at his 'mature' sociology in the first pages of *Economy and Society* via political economy and 'cultural science'.

Is such a view of Weber's development beyond doubt? Does an uncritical acceptance of the conventional wisdom contribute to a more precise acquaintance with the overall character of the work? For Weber the real task of science was precisely the casting of doubt on the 'taken-for-granted', at the very least to recognize the existence of a problem, to be on guard. On closer examination, then, the first 56 pages of *Economy and Society* with the essay on categories published in 1913 certainly are 'sociology'. But 'basic concepts', 'categories'? What are they for? For a contribution – *Economy and Society* – to an outline of social economics, *all* of whose remaining contributions (contents and authors all selected by Weber) were arranged according to a 'social economic' perspective and purpose. Weber chose for himself, and delivered, the section on 'Economy and the social orders and powers'.[23] Does *Economy and Society* represent a sociology? It cannot be disputed that the object was approached through an interpretive framework, constructed in Weber's own fashion, and that was what the unavoidable 'basic concepts' were for. But does the application of a sociological method to a given material make a 'sociology'? That is a scholastic question in whose ramifications we are not interested here. What is of interest to us is Weber's own conception of his academic standpoint and how his contemporaries regarded this position. For them, Weber was an economist: an economist with an uncommon breadth of interest and a subtlety of approach. But none of this was, in principle, alien to the discipline! The first contribution to the memorial volume for Max Weber provides an appreciation of his contribution to economics.[24] This is treated as perfectly natural — for what was he if not an economist? Had he occupied anything other than professorial posts in economics? In Munich, he changed the name of Lujo Brentano's chair into one concerned with social sciences, in an attempt to protect himself from the full range of duties connected with the post. Despite this, both Ministry and Faculty routinely continued to treat the chair as one in economics and Weber did lecture, for good or ill, on 'general economic history'. Until his death, Weber was officially bound to the disciplinary domain that he had entered in 1894 — whatever the label might be that the history of the sciences chose later to hang on his work.

As some have experienced for themselves, it is quite usual for academics to discuss among themselves the question of whether this person or that is a 'real' economist, lawyer, historian and so on. In spite of his admiration for Weber, Joseph Schumpeter was brave enough in his *History of Economic Analysis* to doubt whether Weber was a 'real' economist.[25] But to what did his doubts relate? Primarily, to Weber's 'almost complete ignorance' of economic theory as understood by that 'strong partisan of economic theory, in the Marshallian sense'. But Weber understood enough of this to state that, in Schumpeter's words, 'he saw no objection of principle to what economic theorists actually did, though he disagreed with them on what they thought they were doing'.[26]

In these amusing passages from Schumpeter's masterpiece it becomes clear that these attributions and delimitations are chiefly expressions of shifts within the discipline — in fashionable terms, expressions of a 'paradigm shift'. For Schumpeter, Weber belonged to a superseded epoch in economics, an epoch of which Schumpeter was no longer a part. And this is quite true. Weber declared himself repeatedly to be a student of the 'Historical School of German Political Economy' — and, if we are to understand the attraction that economics held for the young Weber, then it is to *this* school that we should direct our attention. In his Freiburg Inaugural Address, Weber reduced his critically distanced, partly polemical (but none the less irrevocable) relation with the Historical School to the formula: economic science is a 'political science'.[27] What did he mean by this statement? It is certainly rather provocative, but all he fundamentally does is to reduce the barely disputed contemporary character of political economy to the most concise formulation: a formulation that encapsulates, in our opinion, almost the entire 'secret' of Weber's work, and especially of *Economy and Society* and the 'Economic Ethic of World Religions'.

Economics as Political Science and as a Science of Man

It is not possible to arrive at a historical interpretation of the foundations and basic principles of Weber's work from the perspective of present-day sociology. As far as today's sociology is concerned, political economy is part of a pre-history existing at the same level as the work of Aristotle, Montesquieu, Machiavelli and many others: all those 'predecessors' who contributed to the eventual breakthrough. In no area of historical science is such a naive and simple faith in progress still to be found as in the history of science.[28] From the perspective of contemporary sociology, it is impossible to develop a genetic characterization of Weber's work that avoids prejudice and anachronism.

First of all, it is necessary to identify historically the academic location of Weber's *oeuvre*. However massive this *oeuvre* might be, however much it overflows the boundaries of defined academic disciplines, it must none the less have a place among disciplines established to be both taught and learnt. It must be related to the distinctions existing between faculties; it must be situated within the domains of competence of academic journals, monograph series, associations and so on. Once again: where does Weber's work belong? Or, as I would prefer to put it: out of which framework does it develop?

Weber *never* uttered a word about this, he never wrote anything resembling a 'history of doctrines'. The essay on Roscher and Knies expressly refuses any claim to such a history.[29] Despite this, Weber's work, in fact, is full of remarks that make it possible to summarize his own estimation of the position he occupied: within 'the science of human action' in the widest possible sense.[30] It is quite apparent from the work that he had a *perfect* command of the doctrinal history of the subject in which he assumed a chair in 1894. This was taken for granted by economists of his generation, because *all* theoretical controversy up to Walras and Marshall was almost exclusively a question of doctrinal positions and their disputes – Methodenstreitigteiten. Any doubt on this point is removed by referring to the comprehensive bibliography of Weber's unpublished 'Grundriß' of 1898 and to the notes in the *Nachlaß*.

In the Federal Republic of Germany today the history of economics has become the hobby of a few outsiders, and among professional economists we would not even need the fingers of one hand to name them. It would be quite incomprehensible to German readers that a book on the history of economics from Dugald Stewart to Alfred Marshall, a period in which political economy sought to break loose from its traditional integration with political science, should be entitled *That Noble Science of Politics*,[31] and no German publisher would accept such a title. Nevertheless, late nineteenth-century German economics had remained particularly close to the common point of departure for all national 'schools' of economics, namely and in particular moral philosophy and its most important sub-discipline, political science. It is *here* that the real difference is to be found that divides the Western 'classics' from German economic thought since Adam Müller and Friedrich List – a way of thought that culminated in the 'older' Historical School of Bruno Hildebrand, Wilhelm Roscher and Karl Knies, where it assumed an unmistakable profile when compared with 'Western', 'economistic' and 'cosmopolitan' economics.

Some basic facts: Adam Smith was a professor of moral philosophy, and his famous work was written within the framework of this academic domain. If politics was simply the science concerned with the public good in general, then *political economy* related to the economic good, in particular to 'popular welfare'. For Smith, this simply meant wealth, since his conception of 'welfare' was already a restricted one. As is stated in the opening passage of Book 4 of the *Wealth of Nations*: 'Political Economy, considered as a branch of the science of a statesman or legislator, proposes two distinct objects ... It proposes to enrich both the people and the sovereign.' This objective of political economy, deriving from natural law and emphasizing the centrality of wealth, or more precisely 'productivity', was one that Weber vehemently opposed, for along with the entire German economic tradition he did not believe that such a conception could be *scientifically* justified. However, this should not disguise the possibility that Weber's questioning of practical ends (which he shared with the older school) caused the German perspective of economics from the viewpoint of a 'statesman or legislator' to remain a much more radically 'political' one. If it is possible to summarize the development of English economics up to Marshall by saying that 'political economy' was finally struck out of academic nomenclature, being replaced by the laconic 'economics',[32] it can be seen that, by comparison, German economics remained up to the early 1950s a definite 'science of the state' (*Staatswissenschaft*): more precisely, the 'economic science of the state' as most of the chairs in economics were designated. During the nineteenth century, and in some cases even later, *Nationalökonomie*, while retaining this collective name, moved out of the Faculty of Philosophy into the Faculty of Law and Politics.[33] This could not occur in England, because there existed no such relationship between law and economics. In Germany, on the other hand, political economy remained a science with close links to the state and administration, continuing a line going from Cameralism and *Policeywissenschaft* via Friedrich List and Lorenz von Stein. To this day, we have a memorial to this tradition in Robert von Mohl's *Zeitschrift für die gesamte Staatswissenschaft*. In Weber's time, the leading economic journal, generally referred to as *Schmoller's Jahrbuch*, was properly called the *Journal for Legislation, Administration and Economy*, and Braun's *Archiv*, which Weber with Sombart and Jaffé took over in 1904 as the *Archiv für Sozialwissenschaft und Sozialpolitik*, had as a subtitle: *New Series of the Archive for Social Legislation and Statistics*. Brief consideration of this terminology provides a background to a reading of the Freiburg Inaugural Address, leading us to a closer understanding of Weber's *own* conception of his discipline, as well as the continuing effects of this conception after his illness.

The Freiburg Address is, to use a formulation of Wolfgang Mommsen, 'the most significant documentation that we have of Max Weber's political philosophy until the war years'.[34] In contrast to its political content, little attention has been paid to its programmatic scientific provenance, its documentary value for Weber the academic; for it is generally believed that the 'work proper' begins only in the years following his illness. In the discussion on value judgements in 1913, Weber certainly distanced himself from the 'in many respects immature form' of the address, finding that at many points he could no longer identify himself with it. This is, however, a mere rhetorical figure, for in the same sentence he proceeds to recall that at the time he had sought to make the point that 'social orders, however they might be organized, are ultimately to be assessed in terms of the chances offered to particular human types to assume a position of domination'.[35] The question (what social order produces what sort of human type? or, as we put it: what sort of man will come to predominate?) can scarcely be of more import within the framework of a human (inner-worldly) science – beyond that question lie other ways of attaining 'salvation'. I would argue that we have to locate the axis and fulcrum of the *oeuvre* in the above position, already outlined in the 1895 lecture, and it is obvious that this question is central to the whole of political science from Aristotle to Rousseau and Tocqueville: namely, what chances are there in the configuration of a political order for a particular human type to achieve prominence; not a statistical predominance but an ethical model, a representative and a setter of standards? Economics was not the least of the disciplines in nineteenth-century Germany that upheld this tradition and incorporated it into a science of man. In his Freiburg Address, Weber stands within an as yet unfractured tradition.

There are two central passages in which Weber expresses the older 'moral philosophical' tradition of political economy, and we have to consider both in some detail. The first thesis, repeated in altered form in 1913, states: '[. . .] a science of man, and that is what economics is, inquires above all into the quality of men who are brought up in those economic and social conditions of existence.'[36] And the second is the laconic statement: 'The science of economic policy is a *political* science.'[37] In coming to terms with this protestation, with which Weber confronted his listeners in 1895 – and it is no more than new wine served up in the old bottles of the German Historical School – let us begin with the second statement.

Economics as a 'Political Science'
What did it mean for a German economist in 1895 to state that his science was a 'political' one? An assurance, delivered in national-imperialistic tones, that it should not be 'unpolitical'? Not at all. In the terminology of Weber's time the opposite to 'political' is not 'unpolitical', but 'cosmopolitical'. This is true of an unbroken line from Adam Müller to Karl Knies. The fourth and fifth books of Adam Müller's *Elemente der Staatskunst* [Elements of Statecraft] (1809) are dominated by a critique of the 'cosmopolitanism' of the Smithian school. The case of Friedrich List is no different, the title of whose principal work, *The National System of Political Economy* (1841) contains in the word 'national' a definite critical connotation.[38] Chapter 1 of Book 2 (Theory) in List states the opposition perfectly clearly: 'Political and cosmopolitical economy'.[39] According to List, things had gone wrong from the time of the Physiocrats:

> Quesnay...was the first who extended his investigations to the whole human race, without taking into consideration the idea of the nation. [Quesnay demands] that we must imagine *that the merchants of all nations formed one commercial republic*. Quesnay undoubtedly speaks of *cosmopolitical* economy...in opposition to political economy...Adam Smith sees his task as consisting in the justification of the cosmopolitical idea of the absolute freedom of world commerce...Adam Smith concerned himself as little as Quesnay did with true political economy, i.e. that policy

which each separate nation had to obey in order to make progress in its economic conditions. He entitles his work 'The Nature and the Causes of the Wealth of Nations' (i.e. of all nations of the whole human race)...He seeks to prove that 'political' or *national* economy must be replaced by 'cosmopolitical or world-wide economy'.[40]

Wilhelm Roscher's *Grundriß zu Vorlesungen über die Staatswirtschaft. Nach geschichtlicher Methode* [Outline of Lectures on Political Economy, According to the Historical Method] (1843) is usually treated as the inaugural text of the Historical School of political economy. It begins with the classic line, aimed right at the heart of Smithian doctrine: 'For us, as for others, the question of how national wealth might be best promoted certainly is of prime importance; *but it does not in any respect constitute our actual purpose* [my emphasis, W. H.]. *Staatswirtschaft* is not a mere chrematistics, the art of becoming wealthy, but a political science in which the judgment and domination of men is at issue.' In the sentence that follows, we can see clearly how a Weberian 'sociology' develops out of the 'cognitive purpose' of the Historical School: 'Our objective is the representation of that which peoples have, in economic terms, thought, wanted and felt, what they have striven for and have achieved, why they have striven and why they have achieved. This approach is only made possible by the closest association with the other sciences of national life, in particular legal, state and cultural history.'[41]

'Cosmopolitanism' as a means of characterizing the specific 'one-sidedness' of the Smithian school likewise runs like a red thread through the text, which can be regarded as the true methodological foundation of the Historical School: Bruno Hildebrand's *Die Nationalökonomie der Gegenwart und Zukunft* [Political Economy of the Present Day and of the Future] (1848), a text marked by intellectual penetration, scholarly urbanity, a feeling for social justice and a masterly style.[42] A basic principle of the Historical School concerns the practical problems of economic policy, promoting human conscience, judgement and political responsibility as against a conception of economics (classically represented by Ricardo) as one of calculation and the application of cosmopolitan laws 'remote from time and space' − laws that are founded in the relationship of man to material goods.[43]

And finally, Karl Knies (1821−98) took up the argument against the 'cosmopolitanism' of Western theory in his most important book, *Die politische Oekonomie vom geschichtlichen Standpuncte* [Political Economy from the Historical Point of View],[44] the economic textbook that indicated to Weber, while still a student, the path that his research would later take. Knies took up the earlier theoretical objections to 'cosmopolitanism' (i.e. its disregard of geographical, political and temporal differences), transforming them into the concept of 'absolutism' or the 'abstractness' of theory − a terminology that Weber adopted in his 1898 'Grundriß'.[45]

A long passage from Part 3 in Knies's text can show us the appropriate context within which we have to understand the meaning of Weber's Freiburg dictum that economics is a political science. It follows a long passage on protective tariffs and free trade, which emphasizes the 'absolutism of the solution', and which precedes the chapter on 'The principle of relativity', which is itself a classic in the teaching of economic judgement. The degree to which this anticipates Weber's central problem is concisely summarized by the list of contents of the section from which the passage is drawn:

9. The uniform features of the endeavours and activities of individuals and peoples. Significance of non-economic factors and goods for the settlement of economic questions. Decisional norm relating to the principle of the conflict of obligations. Application to the controversial issues of modern trade policy.[46]

If I suggest that the Freiburg Address is a modernized paraphrase of pp. 401–40 of Knies's book, this is no belittlement of Weber. With a few good cigars, the whole thing could be finished off in a couple of mornings. So to the passage:

The economic life of a people is so closely interwoven with other areas of its life that any particular observation can only be made if one keeps in view its relation with the whole, existing as a truth in the complexity of empirical reality; just as a divination of the future development of the economy can only be made on the basis of the entire development of the life of a people. If political economy were to limit itself to the elaboration of laws in a world of material goods, or seek only to establish a technico-economic theory of enterprises, it would have to give up the title of economics and make way for a new independent discipline. If, however, political economy genuinely bases its observations and deductions on the real facts of people and state, if it seeks to solve the problems arising in the life of people and state, then it should not detach its domain and task from that of life in its entirety, but must rather treat both as a living member of a living body... Since political economy has to respect this context, and in its own concerns contributes to the solution of the moral–political problems of the whole, it is therefore enjoined to take its place with the *moral and political sciences*. Only then does it effect a proper connection to real life, for in fact the individual as well as entire peoples and states seek to realize the objectives of their whole life through economic endeavour and economic success. In this way economic concern for material goods attains the level of political and ethical activity.[47]

What makes economics a political science, therefore, is that which Weber rather obscurely and unnecessarily refers to as the 'heteronomy of ends' in all economic actions. Economic action, especially the economic policy of a *nation*, is never oriented to *merely* economic ends.[48]

In 1894, Weber entered a discipline whose German variant, marked by the influence of the cameralist tradition, distinguished between so-called general or 'theoretical' economics and economic policy. It had to make this distinction so that it might bring together both the accumulated practical knowledge of the cameralist disciplines and the theoretical advances of the 'classics'. Weber's doctrine of the ideal type and the postulate of value freedom develop out of this evolving disciplinary matrix, and he presents his solution in the essay on objectivity. Some further steps remained to be taken at the end of the Inaugural Address, but the basic lines of the solution are evident in the

Address and the 'Grundriß' of 1898. 'As a science of explanation and analysis economics is international',[49] referring here in the Freiburg Address to a 'cosmopolitan' classicism; '*theory* is ethically *indifferent*', we find on the second page of the Heidelberg 'Grundriß'. Since this is the case, it is possible to employ an ideal type, and this Weber does in the 'Grundriß' with a thoroughness and comprehensiveness to be found nowhere else in the whole of his published writings. The passage, therefore, has to be cited in its entirety:

To ascertain the most elementary life conditions of economically mature human subjects it [theory] proposes a *constructed* 'economic subject', in respect of which, by *contrast* with empirical man, it

(a) *ignores* and treats as *non-existent* all those motives influencing empirical man which are *not* specifically *economic*, i.e. not specifically concerned with the fulfilment of material needs;

(b) *assumes* as existent qualities that empirical man does not possess, or possesses only incompletely, i.e.

   (i) complete *insight* into a given *situation* – economic omniscience;

   (ii) unfailing choice of the *most appropriate means* for a given end – absolute economic rationality.

   (iii) complete dedication of one's powers to the purpose of acquiring economic goods – 'untiring acquisitional drive'.

It thus postulates an *unrealistic* person, analogous to a mathematical model.[50]

Here we have *homo oeconomicus*, the archetype of the ideal type; an ideal type that, in this form, was not Weber's invention, but had been declared by the 'classics' (pre-eminently by John Stuart Mill in his canonical *Principles of Political Economy* of 1848) to be quite plainly a fiction employed for theoretical ends.

The 1898 'Grundriß' demonstrates to us how thoroughly Weber was acquainted with the 'box of tools' (Schumpeter) of 'analytic science', that is, state of the art 'theory'. But it is not this that really is of interest to him. What he finds interesting are the questions concerning 'values', 'political' questions relating to the 'cultural tasks of the present time' (a term used by Knies as early as 1853) in so far as they are affected by the economy. And so we read in the Address: 'The economic policy of a German state, and the standard of value adopted by a German economic theorist, can therefore be nothing other than a German policy and a German standard.'[51]

Before we examine more closely Weber's admission – 'half unconscious but all the same dominating' – that economics (i.e. *including* its theoretical parts) is a science of man investigating 'above all else the *quality of. . .human be-ings*', and before we turn to the intention and 'polemical' meaning (in Carl Schmitt's sense) of the other programmatic statement contained in the Address, let us briefly return to the actual content of the Address.

Weber begins with a summary of his findings from the Verein für Sozialpolitik investigation into rural labour. As in later works, he takes pleasure in beginning with 'dry data'.[52] On the eastern borders of the German

Empire, there is an economic struggle taking place between the German and the Polish populations. At stake are 'protective tariffs' and 'free-trade policy', except that this time the product in question is human labour. Bismarck had closed the frontiers to eastern migrant workers in the interest of national exclusiveness; Caprivi gave way to pressure from the big agricultural employers and opened them up again. Adopting the point of view of a state that wished to be a national state, Weber demanded a return to Bismarck's policy. At this point, the properly scientific part of Weber's address begins; he poses the question of how one relates to this demand from the point of view of economic policy: 'Does it [economic policy] treat such nationalist value-judgements as prejudices, of which it must carefully rid itself in order to be able to apply its own specific standard of value to the economic facts, without being influenced by emotional reflexes? And *what* is this standard of value peculiar to economic policy?'[53] First of all, Weber destroys the picture of 'peaceful' economic competition:

> The German peasants and day-labourers of the East are not being pushed off the land in an open conflict by politically superior opponents. Instead they are getting the worst of it in the silent and dreary struggle of everyday economic existence, they are abandoning their homeland to a race which stands on a lower level, and moving towards a dark future in which they will sink without trace. There can be no truce even in the *economic* struggle for existence; only if one takes the semblance of peace for its reality can one believe that peace and prosperity will emerge for our successors at some time in the distant future. Certainly, the vulgar conception of political economy is that it consists in working out recipes for making the world happy; the improvement of the 'balance of pleasure' in human existence is the sole purpose of our work that the vulgar conception can comprehend.

This 'vulgar' conception is brusquely rejected. It is factually incorrect:

> the deadly seriousness of the population problem prohibits eudaemonism; it prevents us from imagining that peace and happiness lie hidden in the lap of the future, it prevents us from believing that elbow-room in this early existence can be won in any other way than through the hard struggle of human beings with each other.[54]

Weber has no time either for the normative aspects of 'vulgar' eudaemonism: 'The question which leads us beyond the grave of our own generation is not "how will human beings *feel* in the future" but "how will they be". *In fact this question underlies all work in political economy* (my emphasis, W. H.).'[55] Weber reveals the ultimate objectives of his scientific and political thought when he states: 'We do not want to train up feelings of well-being in people, but rather those characteristics we think constitute the greatness and nobility of our human nature.'[56]

The young man assuming a chair in economics begins his appointment by denying his discipline the capacity of providing itself with ultimate standards of judgement. Everywhere, the economic way of thought was on the advance. Even in pandectic textbooks (this is five years before the introduction of the

Civil Code) it was possible to detect here and there a quiet but insistent economic current. 'A method of analysis which is so confidently forging ahead is in danger of falling into certain illusions and exaggerating the significance of its own point of view.'[57] In much the same way that the diffusion of the material of philosophical reflection among a lay public had often led to the opinion that 'the old questions of the nature of human knowledge are no longer the ultimate and central questions of philosophy, so in the field of political economy the notion has grown in the minds of the coming generation that the work of economic science has not only immensely extended our *knowledge* of the nature of human communities, but also provided a completely new *standard* by which these phenomena can ultimately be *evaluated*, that political economy is in a position to extract from its material its own specific ideals.'[58] But wherever one sought to establish a specifically 'economic' principle of judgement, one relapsed into vague uncertainties. 'In truth, the ideals we introduce into the substance of our science are not peculiar to it, nor have we worked them out independently: they are *old-established human ideals of a general type.*'[59]

Weber does not yet express himself with the precision that he would achieve in the essay on objectivity. But already here it is a question of making the value-relation more precise, through which is to be gained the *specific* objectivity — at base a radicalized *subjectivity* — which alone appears to be solely realizable in the social sciences. This 'value relation', however, is and remains none other than that stated in the Inaugural Address: the 'quality of human beings', which is, 'bound up with the distinct imprint of humanity that *we* find in *our* own nature'.[60] We might hope 'that the future recognizes in our nature the nature of *its own ancestors*. We wish to make ourselves the forefathers of the race of the future with our labour and our mode of existence.'[61] Directly following this, we find the crucial sentence that is always read as a nationalistic statement: 'The economic policy of a German state, and the standard of value adopted by a German economic theorist, can *therefore* be nothing other than a German policy and a German standard.'[62] The ultimate standards of value are 'political'; for Weber they are only conceivable as individual and specific.

Weber follows this statement immediately with a discussion of the question of 'cosmopolitanism', and this is further proof that this passage should be read in a 'politico-anthropological' manner, and not nationalistically.

> Has the situation perhaps changed since economic development began to create an all-embracing economic community of nations, going beyond national boundaries? Is the 'nationalistic' standard of evaluation to be thrown on the scrapheap along with 'national egoism' in economic policy?...We know that this is *not* the case: the struggle has taken on *other forms*, forms about which one may well raise the question of whether they should be viewed as a mitigation or indeed rather an intensification and a sharpening of the struggle.[63]

The emergent world economy is merely another form of the struggle of nations one with another,

> and it *aggravates* rather than mitigates the struggle for the maintenance of one's own culture, because it calls forth in the very bosom of the nation

material interests *opposed* to the nation's future, and throws them into the ring in alliance with the nation's enemies. We do not have peace and human happiness to bequeath to our posterity, but rather the *eternal struggle* for the maintenance and improvement by careful cultivation of our national character.[64]

With this we come back to the second programmatic statement, Weber's recognition that economics is a science of man concerned above all with the *quality* of men, who are reared under the influence of economic and social conditions of existence.

Economics as a Science of Man

It is possible to associate Weber with Social Darwinism on the basis of such terminology only if his precise clarification is consistently ignored.[65] He has as little to do here with Social Darwinism as had Nietzsche, i.e. nothing, but it is patently Nietzsche's conception of *moral* 'breeding' that Weber here has in mind. He points out 'the irrelevance...of the disputes in natural science over the significance of the principles of selection, or over the general application *in natural science* of the concept of "breeding", and all the discussions which have taken this as their starting-point. This is in any case not my field'. He hopes (quite in vain, as the Weber literature shows) 'that a misunderstanding of their meaning is impossible for anyone who knows our literature.'[66] The idea of human 'breeding' was characteristic of even the Platonic state. When Weber characterizes economics as a science of man, we are placed not on the terrain of a (pseudo-) natural science, but on the most ancient ground of political science; the mutual relation of 'conditions of existence' (political in the older context, social in the modern) and the quality ('virtue') of man. This pair constituted the specific theme of political science for more than two thousand years, from Plato and Aristotle to Rousseau, and it remained one of the themes, if not the central one, of political economy even after Adam Smith.[67] Weber took it further, not in any particular original fashion theoretically – but the manner in which he worked through this theme in a perspective of 'universal history' reaching from distant China to the Mormons of Utah[68] secures him a permanent place in the history of political science.

How did Weber come to recognize that economics was a 'science of man'? In the same way as the idea that runs parallel with it: that economics is a 'political science'. What Weber states here is no more than a truism repeated remorselessly from textbook to textbook in the Historical School. And just as in the conceptual pair 'political–cosmopolitical', the formula 'Wissenschaft vom Menschen' has an unmistakably delimiting, 'polemical' sense.[69] It should be read as 'the science of the whole man', countering a science of 'ascribed', 'constructed' and 'unrealistic' beings, the 'mathematical ideal model' of 'abstract theory'. It was exactly on this point that the debate with 'Western' theory had turned, led in the older Historical School primarily by Roscher and Knies; this issue was also in the background of the dispute conducted between Schmoller and Menger – in which there was a considerable amount of misunderstanding and waywardness, as is usual in such disputes. But the bitterness with which this dispute was conducted was itself a consequence of the fundamental nature of the positions at issue.[70]

Here, I will confine myself to only the most necessary proof that 'science of man' should be polemically read in historical context as 'science of the whole man'. The proof consists of the most relevant statements from the inception and the twilight of the Historical School — formulae that provide disciplinary self-definition — and further, exact proof from the author who must be regarded as Weber's real economic teacher. In the beginning — as in the Old Testament — is the first sentence, set off from the rest, of Roscher's *System der Volkswirthschaft* [System of Political Economy], Vol. I, which concerns itself with the foundations of political economy: 'Point of departure and objective of our science is man.' The sentence opens paragraph 1 ('Goods') in Chapter 1 ('Basic Concepts'). Here is note 1, for it makes the delimiting and polemical sense quite plain:

> Well emphasised by Schäffle (*Deutsche Vierteljahresschrift*, 1861). Quite characteristically Smith's system (*Wealth of Nations*, 1776) begins with the concept of annual labour; that of J.–B. Say (*Traité d'économie politique*, 1802) with the concept of *richesses*; that of Ricardo (*Principles of Political Economy and Taxation*, 1817) with the concept of value.[71]

At the twilight of the Historical School we can cite a passage from an essay by Schmoller, the 'honoured master'. He wrote in 1897:

> Contemporary economics has arrived at a historical and ethical perception of state and society, in contrast to rationalism and materialism. From a mere theory of market and exchange, a kind of business economics which at one time threatened to become a class-weapon of the propertied, it has once again become a great moral and political science, which alongside the production of goods investigates their distribution, alongside value forms investigates economic institutions, which once more places man at the centre of the science instead of the world of goods and capital.[72]

We can cite as additional proof of the quite routine nature of this view, which is nevertheless the essence of the difference separating the Historical School from the 'economism' of the Classics, the circular sent by Schmoller to Treitschke (1874–5):

> The entire argument over the limits of economic freedom remains as a whole at a formal and superficial level. This formality has its own significance and its own history...But what is and remains important...is that we become more cultured, more hard-working, more intelligent and more just human beings. And the forms of life orders which lead us most directly along this path are the just ones.[73]

It might be recalled here that we are involved in a quasi-biographical approach to the 'character' and 'peculiarity' of Weber's work. What was the contemporary state of social science from which it grew, what position did Weber assume in contemporary debate? Since we cannot believe that after his recovery he created sociology virtually *ex nihilo*, we are trying to locate the point in the formative years from which everyone, even the greatest genius, must develop. The conception of economics as a science of man and as 'political' in the Inaugural Address restates the conventional positions of the Historical School, albeit with great precision. Can we see more exactly how Weber's work 'stands on the shoulders' of this tradition?

We can find out from Karl Knies. There is little point in looking at Weber's essay on Roscher and Knies (1903–6)[74] when seeking elements determining his 'formation'. This essay in fact deals, as Weber remarks in the section on Roscher, with 'long-superseded conceptions'. In our present context it is not at first clear why Weber feels compelled to expose the *remnants* of 'emanationism' and 'naturalism' in such a clumsy and persistent fashion. Was this really the most significant thing about Roscher's work? That the 'problem of irrationalism' went to the heart of Knies's work – Weber failed to make this clear to anyone who had not only flogged through to the end of Weber's essay, but had also taken the trouble, this time with decidedly greater profit, with Knies's main work.

Two decades *before* Weber wrote his critique of Knies he must have felt much the same. In the early letters we have the sole example of a development in Weber's capacity at judging the status of one of his teachers. On 2 May 1882 Weber reported to his mother on the lectures that he had attended: 'First Institutions with Bekker, a fine and extremely likeable old bachelor'. It is also a constant source of pleasure to listen to his lecturing, 'he makes things very easy for one, scatters here and there pretty and witty remarks, and never, and this should not be ignored, becomes boring like Professor Knies'. At the end of the following semester (23 February 1883) he writes to his father: 'In Knies's lectures political economy and finance are dealt with thoroughly; while not interesting (the content prevents this), I have at some time or other to attend these lectures.' In the summer of 1883 (letter to his father 5 May 1883) he finally realizes: 'Now that I have gained a few basic economic concepts through studying Adam Smith and others. Knies makes a quite different impression on me than he did a year ago, when in mid-semester I went once and found it dreadfully dreary. Only he speaks too fast, one has the greatest difficulty in taking notes from what he says, for his lecturing is even more fluent than that of Kuno Fischer. It is only his voice – it always seems troubled by the world, as if he regretted all the facts that he introduces – that weakens the impact of his extremely intelligent and creative disquisitions.'[75]

Weber's 1905 judgment on Knies's literary style ('so awkward as to be almost incomprehensible') was certainly influenced by his recollections of Knies's oral delivery. None the less, if Weber took note of the 'wealth of ideas streaming forth' it was pardonable if now and then a sentence 'went to pieces syntactically'. Weber's respect for Knies's 'scientific importance' is unmistakable. And what Weber says of Knies can just as well be applied to Weber himself: 'Anyone who proposes to undertake an exhaustive reconstruction of this book – a work eminently rich in ideas – has the following task. First, he must separate intertwined strands of ideas which, as it might be put, come from different balls of yarn. This accomplished, he must then systematize each of these collections of ideas independently.'[76] Let us try to establish the threads linking the Knies of 1883 with Weber's own 'skeins of thought'.

The two parts of 'Roscher and Knies' which, according to the headings, are devoted to Knies certainly give us precious little to go on. The product of a commission taken on for a university *Festschrift*, they betray markedly ignoble qualities in Weber. The task of honouring an important teacher, his predecessor, of delivering a balanced assessment – this seems to have gone sour for Weber.[77] Of the 188 pages apparently devoted to Knies, only around twenty can be said to be pertinent and these are written as if haunted by an obsession with Knies's 'fundamentally emanational ideas'. Weber must have sensed the awkwardness of his erratic, if not to say confused, article, for he admits that the picture he gives of Knies's scientific importance is 'clearly by no means adequate'; it could indeed seem that 'I am using Knies only as a "pretext" in order to discuss the problems raised here'.[78] This admission, however, cannot prevent us from taking note of the *overwhelming* importance of Knies in Weber's socioeconomic education.[79]

Karl Knies's action-oriented political economy

What has now to be demonstrated is Knies's precise contribution to a conception of economics as a 'science of man'. It must be remembered that the second edition of Knies's textbook was published in the very same semester as that in which Weber finally recognized the quality of his teacher. This new edition contained additions involving areas of work in which Weber, two or three decades later, would first make his great reputation.

For Knies, the idea that economics has to do with the complete human being is one that is so fundamental that there are only a few statements where it is not linked to other conceptions, but these also point forward in the direction that Weber was to take. As a consequence of the specifically German notion of 'humanity', conceived as 'the urge to establish moral foundations for everything that has force' in life and as a result of a 'real historical sense for the process of historical development, not simply the Englishman's sense of observation' (p. 329),[80] 'the philosophical trait of German intellect had turned to a revision, an examination and clarification of general basic concepts as the founding elements of the system'. By 'taking account of moral and political moments (and in contrast to the doctrine of the universal benefits of self-interest), the horizon of political economy has extended beyond the perspective of Adam Smith' (p. 330). The 'theoretical' (Weber will call it 'ideal-typical') character of 'abstract' economics is precisely outlined: 'Economics has as a point of departure a series of explicit or implicit assumptions which are employed as permanent means of support. These are treated as unconditional and constantly uniform and are derived from the general homogeneity of the material means of production as well as human beings (who for the purposes of *economic* analysis are regarded as acting from purely *selfish* motives) and also implicitly assumes as self-evident a specific state of social organization and a particular legal and constitutional order' (p. 497). Knies provides an exemplary introduction to the basic ideas and limitations of a 'pure economic analysis', leading from Ricardo to the mathematical models of Walras. Comte and Spencer are analysed, Marx's theory of value is critically discussed[81] and it is continually emphasized that 'this science, while dealing with questions arising from the world of material goods is always concerned with human beings, with persons possessing intellect and motivated by non-material forces' (p. 490). It appeared to Knies of prime importance 'to establish the *real* domain of investigation for economics as a science of nations (*Volkswirtschaftslehre*) and to emphasize the primary relation between economic phenomena and the remaining important spheres of human communal life' (p. iii). 'Was this so unimportant, since specialist studies had wasted no words on it?' he queried. It was not. All of Weber's 'special sociologies', led by the sociology of religion, are anticipated *in nuce* by Knies. Above all, Weber's theoretical orientation to *action* can be traced directly back to Knies.

Weber is *only comprehensible* on the basis of the polemical posture of *Nationalökonomie* with respect to Western theory, which constituted the object of its scientific endeavour in the so-called basic economic concepts (goods, value, property, wealth, economy, etc.) that had led economists into a 'domination of the word', as expressed in the title of Gottl's famous book, *Die Herrschaft des Wortes. Nationalökonomie* sought to free itself of this tyranny, and it did so by conceiving of 'the economy' as the outcome of man's 'economic activity' under real historical conditions and subject also to the 'heteronomy of ends'. The real aim of the Historical School was to place empirical man at the centre of economic reflection – while recognizing the methodological utility of 'constructed' man. None of the older school had expressed this with more sophistication than Knies, and, as a student, Weber had the greatest difficulty in keeping up with this stream of thoughts. His Heidelberg 'Grundriß', as well as the work done after the recovery, testify to the great impression made by his old teacher. The degree to which Weber's 'sociology' – 'as a science which seeks to understand social action interpretively and thereby explain the origins of its course and effects' – was conditioned by the Historical School, which for him culminated in the work of Knies, can now be demonstrated by way of a summarized 'reading guide' (Schumpeter) of Knies's principal text. The affinities with Weber will be detected without any difficulty.

A Reading Guide to Karl Knies's 'Die politische Oekonomie vom geschichtlichen Standpuncte'

A scientific approach to householding and economising activity is related at all times to '*human actions, human conditions* and *human tasks* oriented to the fulfilment of *human purposes*'; at issue is the 'investigation of one region out of the entire domain of human life and endeavour' (p. 2). Material *objects* (wood, grain, iron) which are worked up into economic goods, are only taken into consideration by economics to the degree that they are 'objects of human desire and action, employed as a means for the satisfaction of human needs'.

From this it follows that all questions of technique, like that of the hunter, fisher and miner, do not belong to political economy. At stake is not a mere *economics*, but a *political economy* (p. 2).[82] The object of investigation in the sciences of state and society consists of 'actions or works of man and of the resulting forms of socialized and legally ordered communal life' of many individuals and entire peoples. The object of reflection is not, as in the humanities (*Geisteswissenschaften*) 'the world of thoughts and ideas of the inner man, but processes and conditions to be found in the world of perceptible appearances'. This suggests parallels to the natural sciences; yet, in contrast to them, the 'investigation of the causes of these external phenomena leads back to the spiritual regions of the human interior' (p. 6). We also note that which the soul of man has lent to these external phenomena. 'In war and riot, market and fair, in the assemblies of popular representatives and of manual workers, we do not note the movements of an organized natural being, in the way that we observe the results of attraction and cohesion in natural bodies. If domination, subordination, happiness, misery, freedom, lack of freedom, order and disarray are expressed in the communal life of man, then the meaning of such perceived phenomena will only be grasped through immersion in the relationships between these phenomena and human spiritual life' (p. 6).

At stake here is thus 'neither an "inner" nor an "outer" human world. Instead, we are concerned with a perceptible "outer-world" of phenomena conditioned by "inner-worldly" causation and therefore not entirely accessible through the methods of natural-scientific research. From this "bifurcation" there follows a task which, although not necessarily more difficult, is certainly more complicated, and there will emerge many significant differences on basic methodological issues' (p. 7).

Knies clearly sees how the 'industrialism' of the modern period,[83] with its consequences for 'modern cultural life', has drawn the results of political economy into the struggle about current issues (p. 10). 'The conflict in the endeavours and demands of practical life is reflected in the antagonisms between scientific theories' (p. 11). Knies, following the 'relativism' of German historical orthodoxy (and here 'relativism' should be understood exclusively as a counter-concept to the 'absolutism' of abstract theory) emphasizes the significance of the 'differences' of given situations, possibilities and conditions of peoples for economic life, in which not only soil and climate but also the 'interest in and capacity for work' of humans has to be considered (pp. 44 ff.).

According to Knies, it is only possible to talk of economic activity and economic productivity in so far as they appear as the outcome 'of the combination of combined effects of forces and objects provided by external nature and *the activity of man*'. 'The second part of this generalized discussion, therefore, consists of the *investigation of human nature*, to the extent that this is relevant to the *economic* activity of man' (p. 67). But such investigation of the 'conditions given in the nature of man' is not only neglected by political economy, but also in many other disciplines which continually have to return, from the most abstract level of discussion, to 'concrete and historically-given men' (p. 67).

'Perhaps even more striking than the physical differences of people in individual countries are the differences of *inner capabilities and drives*, and of intellectual endowments.' Within the line separating the cultural level of the white race from the remainder it is possible to demonstrate 'manifold stages of intellectual ability and different modes in which this ability tends to be expressed' (pp. 75–6). General writing in history has shown many a time that 'some peoples are given to contemplativeness and passivity, while others display a strong drive to study, know and understand; that alongside a people slow to stir and holding stubbornly to traditional forms there exist peoples eager for renewal; that frontiers divide satisfied and equable people from pleasure-seekers and achievers, the indolent from the active and busy' (p. 76). All such features are not merely characteristic for the representation of the general history of nations, 'but they must also have great and lasting effects precisely in the field of economic affairs' (p. 76).

We find in Knies a comprehensive review of the factors that have an effect on the economic occupations of peoples, a review which becomes analytically ever more differentiated. Man itself must be regarded as an economic force. It is not sufficient to recognize the difference in which the negro replaces the Indian as a mineworker, to be then spared death in the cultivation of cane sugar, a death which easily carries off the 'Caucasian', or that 'the American redskin, in the midst of the white population, dies the *death of civilisation*' [my emphasis, W. H.].[84] 'The national nature of humans also renders the economic position of individual peoples differentiated, concrete, characteristic' (p. 78).

As an 'economic labour force' humanity is conditioned 'by the influence of general occurrences which in the course of historical time affect the life of peoples' (p. 91). Throughout all historical time the economically active person is subject to 'the changing effects of state and society which condition relations among a working population both quantitatively and qualitatively'. It is thus only a question of recognizing the significance of these circumstances for the general development of historical economies. However often 'purely economic causes' might in the course of time have had an impact on the change in material circumstances, they then have as a rule 'been overtaken by general historical relations or circumstances' (p. 100).

The first non-economic conditioning factor for economic life that Knies deals with is the 'influence of general state power on the form and development of the economy amongst historically-given nations' (pp. 106 f). Even those who assign 'to economics the task of composing a system of naturally given laws, immovable, complete and with identical effects whatever the circumstances, corroborate such a view when they see fit to complain of the intervention of the state in the economy having resulted in hundreds of years of misguidedness up to that day when the government renounces all such intervention; and in so doing they ascribe to state power a far greater influence in economic affairs than that which we have in mind with respect to historical experience' (p. 107). Not every era and not every people have in their economic activity wanted and striven for the same things that 'our wills are inclined towards' (p. 108).

Following on from the influence of 'general state power' – here we could say: of the character of domination in Weber's sense – Knies examines with especial care 'the actual influence of the second great force in life': that of the church and of religion. Curiously, remarks Knies, 'these have never been sufficiently appreciated or generally noted' (p. 110). It is here – already suggested in the terminology – that the central question of Weber's sociology of religion is prefigured.[85] The influence of religion is exerted 'upon inner man', and, because the psychological element in 'man as a factor contributing to the production of goods' is of such predominant importance, 'it is vital to pay attention to the influence of religious doctrine on economic relations'. The vocation of the church has always consisted in being 'the bearer and guardian of this influence on inner man'. For the 'external significance of the church, the impact of religion (in its canonical forms) on inner man has always been decisive' (p. 111). Knies complains that he 'can by no means exhaust the total mass of materials relevant to a consideration of this issue'. He has to settle, therefore, 'so that doubt might be dispelled', for a brief discussion of the influence of Christianity on the economy, contrasted with the religion of the ancient peoples, and he adds to this a sketch of the 'extent and form of influence exercised by the Catholic church during its formative period on the configuration of economic factors' (p. 111).

Pre-Christian religions are presented as national religions; 'they possess a relation with the body politic and with general state power that is so close one is hardly aware of an independent influence of the church on life unconnected with political forces' (p. 111). But 'not on the inner man, for the moral character of national religions coincides with the moral character of the national state'. 'The state identifies itself with religion and religion with the state; religious decrees are laws of the state and those laws are consecrated as such by religion.' The theocratic states of the ancient Orient are characterized by 'such a close relation of religious with political life, and of church with state power, that we often link together as one the ruling powers of the church and of the state, and treat the control of each power's domain as being combined personally in the same individual' (p. 112).

One cannot 'emphasize too strongly the manner in which Christianity contrasted decisively' with this state of affairs. Christ countered law and entitlement with duty and obligation, 'love of one's neighbour with selfishness' (p. 113). 'The moral character of the individual was placed on an entirely new footing by such ideas, ideas which the ancient world could not assimilate' (p. 113). Christianity dispelled the aura 'employed by the national religions to exalt the political egoism of a people' (p. 114), presenting itself as a world religion, 'a religion for all humankind, heathen and Jew alike; it outlawed national selfishness by announcing the equality of all beings and peoples before God'. No further elaboration is needed to see 'the changes that this implied specifically for economic relations, placing upon a new basis internal as well as external intercourse, the relationship of individuals as well as of peoples to each other. Everything which could be connected to duty, fairness and the equality of all peoples of humanity is here brought into direct association. It is perhaps no overestimation to see the consequences of these principles at their most effective in the area of economic life' (p. 114).

Christian doctrine regarding the profits of trade and its estimation of trade in general are dealt with in detail. Similarly, Christian maxims on the question of money lent at interest are outlined: 'The main principle was that loans should be negotiated for consumption and on the part of the poor on account of want, so that in such circumstances the Christian's love for his neighbour appeared to enjoin good works' (p. 118).[86]

One also has to 'emphasize the influence of the church on economic conditions, for its real and lasting calling is the cultivation of religious interests and the exhortation that they be realized in the practical activity of man'. Especial emphasis has to be laid on this today, since it has been 'historically authenticated' that 'in theory the morality of economic activity and the morality of Christian religion are two quite separate things' (p. 121). It is precisely consideration of the religious motives of human beings that brings to mind the truth that 'economic *forces* and *phenomena* of the present day are to be comprehended as a mere *historical fragment*, and are *neither* to be treated as *entire and universal for all economic phases and evolutions, nor as typifying such phases and evolutions*' (p. 122).

In an addition to the 1883 edition, Knies can then write – and once more it is to be remembered that, at the time that this edition appeared, Weber was attending Knies's lectures and had difficulty in keeping up with all the elaborations and deviations: 'The preceding three decades form one of those epochs in which the relation between the *religious* ideas of human beings and the economic phenomena of daily life becomes recognizable even to the most shortsighted observer. We have a constant and emphatic example in the economic results of a fatalistic oriental Islam, and East Asian Buddhism has also tried out its typically utilitarian doctrine among Chinese migrants in California. The great difference in the "economic morale" of the Jewish and Christian religions has also been felt more sharply in Germany since the political emancipation of the Jews. Of course, for all those Jews and Christians who do *not* practise their religions, this difference is not effective, for example, in the case of Christians who demand standards of behaviour from others very different to those which they themselves practise with respect to their "nearest".' We can also 'observe the far-reaching relationship of religion and economic life with respect to the fact that, among many individuals and in great sections of social strata, *all* religious belief has lapsed. This fact has results quite immeasurable in economic life – whether this draining away of religious belief is connected with the "advance of modern natural science" or with "philosophical proofs" as can be found in the "old and new belief" of David Strauss; with the savage scorn of a popular agitator or with the dire poverty of life and the "happiness of the unjust"' (p. 125).

Knies lays proud emphasis on the originality of his views with regard to the reciprocal effects of religion and economic life, and also outlines the 'significant relations between *economy and law* (legal norms and economic life)' (pp. 126–7). Regarding the large number of obvious connections existing between 'economic life and legal order' he thinks it to be striking that 'for so long even extremely perceptive theorists have neglected this aspect' (p. 128).

Reference is also made to the importance of political ideas to economic life; here, also, it is a question of the 'emotive endeavours and instinctive motives of inner man, whose strongest roots strike into an invisible foundation'. The peculiar character of individual historical periods rests in the main on the fact that 'specific ideas and intellectual currents become preponderant, achieving and sustaining a dominance over people's minds' (p. 123). Passionate affects take hold with single-minded energy 'seeking everywhere to transform the old and the traditional'. 'Despite the slow development of a reaction which assists in the setting of natural limits, a different epoch is inaugurated, and the effects of excess' cannot be totally undone (p. 123). It is by no means the case that one only finds particular ideas dominating 'where they are writ large and prominent on the tablets of history'. 'It is no different during periods of "calm" – even here particular underlying tones dominate, distinguishable above the total mass of phenomena'[87] (p. 123).

In conclusion, Knies outlines what could be called a cultural sociology applicable to economic life. Human beings, 'bodies with souls or sensual-*intellectual* beings' possess 'an inner world of self-consciousness and soulful existence; the presence and influence of the "psyche" in ideas, feelings, judgements, etc., whose nature we seek principally through self-observation, apprehending its specific character and its separate existence from the sensuous appearance of material things in their manifold expressions'. In particular, the relation of man to his outer world is determined by this psychic inner world, his 'action' seeking to satisfy material needs and also to shape the 'outer' world, which includes other persons. 'On the other hand, in the human spiritual inner world general recognition is given to the link of such external occurrences with conditions of the soul and spirit of the human being. On the basis of such connections we speak of "civilization" or "culture", phenomena peculiar to man. They include every legal order. And because the inner life of man is not simply open to variation, but is capable of development, it is not only possible to speak of a specific state of civilization for individuals, groups of individuals or even entire peoples, but also necessary to take account of the great differences and developmental stages existing in human civilization' (pp. 138–9).

Hence, all further discussion is superfluous 'for the provision of especial proof that scientific investigation of human "economic life" has of necessity to be linked with an inquiry into psychic processes by means of psychological and ethno-historical studies'. The concepts are precisely differentiated by Knies: 'the "soulful" and "spiritual" or "psychic" aspect of man which forms the basis of all manifestations of culture is not the same as the "moral" or "ethical" dimension in the German sense of the words' (p. 139).

'For the scientific study of the causal system operative in the domain of economic life'[!], 'manners constitute a considerable force in themselves, especially in addition to law, public administration and the free will of individuals and communities.' The actual efficacy of manners has considerably declined. 'One need only recall the contrast with a time in which guild organization has established in law that which had previously been customary in the workshop, the actual effectiveness of such guild regulation being guaranteed by a constancy in the customs of consumption.' (pp. 140–1).

The modernity and portentous nature of Knies's ideas is shown by the concise comments, more thoroughly dealt with in his monographs,[88] on the influence of modern means of communication such as the railway and the telegraph. In particular he points 'to the far-reaching influences of the most modern means of communication on the *psychic life of human beings*' [my emphasis, W. H.]. This is the precise problem, on the basis of which Weber, thirty years later, was to approach the investigation of associations and of the press.[89] Knies also elaborates the difference, so important for Weber, between the traditional motives of economic action and the forces that disrupt such traditions. 'While the peasant learns how to adapt himself to an uninvestigated rule of providence and is thus receptive to the authoritative power of worldly government, commercial activity will promote a "rationalistic" attitude and the urban dweller will be prompted to introduce the question of "accountability" everywhere. Hence the great cultural significance of any considerable alteration in the proportions between urban and rural populations' (p. 166). [90]

To close this brief guide, which cannot pretend to an exhaustive account of the links between Knies and Weber, we might recall once again the basic idea of Knies's book: to redefine the character of political economy as an 'ethical science', developing further the work of predecessors and contemporaries. He sees this as the 'cardinal point of economics' (p. 235). He does not seek to gain truth by means of a 'monologic abstraction of ideas' but rather through 'exact observation of historical life in its progressive development and the psychological study of man' (p. 235). Quite naturally, Knies argues within the framework of contemporary academic doctrine and controversy, conditioned as it was by the 'classical' assumption of self-interest as the sole relevant basic economic motive. But he goes beyond this question which, with the search for further 'basic motives', had occupied German economics so intensively between Hildebrand and Schmoller. What interests him, to express it in Weber's terms, is a 'science of reality', the influence of human beings on a historical material context which rebounds upon them. This can be seen above all in his efforts to establish a balanced and considered intermediate position between 'capitalism' and 'socialism': 'If on the one hand society is atomized in order to completely liberate the individual, so on the other the individual is robbed of a soul so that material need might be abolished among an undifferentiated mass. In the former the freedom of the individual is also the rough justice of the strong, while in the latter order means stagnation and death' (pp. 292–3). Knies's position between the two fronts can be characterized as sceptical, but the view of a thoroughly political man all the same. What are the logical bridges, and what bridges of living experience, lead from 'freedom' to 'distributional justice'? 'Here we are only faced with a *petitio principii*! Since every human being is not by nature thoroughly good and just, there is no guarantee of justice if persons acquire only that which they can win by their own efforts *in one way or another*. And how could one properly estimate the justness of the actual outcome for the respective parties' claims in the struggle among individuals, equipped with unequal powers and positions, for their share of the income that is to be distributed? Rewards for equal effort which are unequal over time and space permit of no evidence by analogy and render baseless even the first attempts at the constitution of a theodicy in this area. And the time is long past when people subscribed to that cloudy fascination, that unclear desire which supposed that goodness and justice would rule on earth if only unconditional freedom of desire and action could be secured for all' (pp. 307–8). Whoever fails to hear an echo of this 'mood' in Weber's Inaugural Address twelve years later – although in a decidedly harsher tone, the result of a generational change (and of Nietzsche!) – must be completely insensitive to intellectual relationships. *Economic science is a science of man.* 'However much one may refer to the effects and the effectiveness of eternally unchanging natural laws, there will always be found in the domain of economic affairs the presence of man – as an individual and as a fragment of state and nation – as the living bearer of all economic activity, and alongside material conditions and relationships personal elements must have their effect. The first will in all material questions become more predominant, while the latter will prevail everywhere that spiritual and ethical factors are to be observed.' National differences will become emphasized 'when the political and ethical questions concerning the optimal distribution of goods, the proper proportioning of economic activities in the complete context of the tasks of national life, and the purposiveness of economic creation gain significance' (p. 317). Only these last questions interested Weber. Just as 'law' was of interest to him solely from the viewpoint of the legislator, so the economy was considered as the 'most fundamental', most 'worldly' factor of man's life – in its vitality, its power or, to use the old word, its 'virtue'.

On Weber's New 'Methodological' Beginning

Having run through the important positions of Knies that are here of relevance and having established Weber's indisputable debt to them, when we return to the essay on Roscher and Knies we are left with a bad taste in the mouth. All representatives of the Historical School of economics had related 'whole' man to the specific features of human economic action. State, religion, law and ethics were constantly kept in mind, with all other natural and personal features. It is thus quite natural that what they understood by 'economy' was 'the complex of measures' (to borrow Weber's expression in the 1898 'Grundriß') 'brought about by the economic activity of an individual or of a human community.'[91] No one had expressed more clearly than Knies the view that political economy concerns human *actions* and 'human circumstances' for the fulfilment of 'human objectives', that here there existed '*one* section of the entire area of human life and endeavour' to be studied. Since Weber, in 1898 the immediate successor to Knies in Heidelberg, demonstrably relies on Knies's basic positions in his 'Grundriß' – and since he continues to propose, right up to *Economy and Society*, that 'social action' be the specific object of *verstehende* sociology – the paltry analysis that Weber devotes to Knies is curious, to put it mildly. There is no point in seeking to rectify the many misrepresentations of Knies's position that we find here. Weber graciously accepts 'for the present' the standpoint of Knies 'without any further discussion. In his [Knies's] view, the sciences in which human *action* – whether exclusively or only pre-eminently – constitutes the *subject matter* of the investigation are logically related in such a way that they belong together'.[92] One often has the impression that Weber here goes to enormous trouble to reproduce Knies's thoughts in such a way that the reformulation leaves no echo of the original. When one is aware of the importance of the concept of 'personality' for Weber, and the manner in which he defines it, then it is quite simply irritating to see the way in which he shakes off the dust of Knies's concerns. Weber works with insinuations[93] which have no basis at all in Knies, where we often read exactly the reverse of what Weber wishes to impute to Knies.

It is obviously *necessary* for Weber to attribute to Knies the 'atrophied remains of the great Hegelian ideas': 'emanatist ideas', 'panlogicism'[94] – although I find this completely incomprehensible, given the fact that Knies is silent on or even radically distances himself from such ideas.[95] In closing the essay he announces that 'in fact we shall see that the pre-eminence of this view is explicit in Knies's methodology',[96] that is, the theme of another article. We have *never* seen this – the announced article was never written. Perhaps Weber himself recognized the unedifying nature of this kind of analysis devoted to an important former teacher – truly a form of patricide – and let things be.

What is certain is that Marianne Weber is here also correct when she states in relation to the work following the recovery that 'Weber did not forget his scholarly past'.[97] If this is not given due recognition (as in the assumption of a 'completely fresh start') if a 'genetic' interpretation refuses to see in the early economic writings the foundation, the 'genetic code' as it were, of the work as a whole, then the work must remain unintelligible – a 'marvel' in the strongest sense, 'a work of pure inspiration'.[98] It is not possible here to deal in any greater detail with Weber's debt to German political economy. However, it can be generally stated that Weber simply radicalizes the positions of the Historical School, including those of Knies – whether it be as a consequence of his own inclination to favour the extreme over moderation, or whether it be a consequence of the much more radical disillusionment of his generation with the 'universalist' and 'harmonious' remnants of Enlightenment thought. Nietzsche cleared such remnants away, and that has here to be left at that. But an attempt should be made to establish in a few points what Weber carried with him from the Historical School.

From the above it should have become clear that Weber 'carried with him' not only the definition of *verstehende* sociology in terms of the action of the 'whole' man, but also his concern to 'uncover the causative relations between economic development and *all remaining social phenomena*'.[99] Apart from the sociology of music, I can detect no 'sociological' theme in Weber for which one of the older school, in particular Knies, had not laid the basis or at least provided an impulse.[100] How is it, then, with the new beginning in methodology?

The two most comprehensive treatments of Weber's *Wissenschaftslehre* which we have – from Alexander von Schelting and Dieter Henrich[101] – are free of any mention of political economy as a starting point for Weber's work. Since the publication of these two studies, it has been generally accepted as a canonical truth that Weber's methodological position developed out of a debate on neo-Kantianism. The sole text that deals in detail with the methodological writings as having developed from contemporary debates on *economic* methodology is Friedrich H. Tenbruck's article of 1959,[102] where it is suggested that 'the tendency and context of these works [on methodology] is apparent only to the reader aware of the historical co-ordinates in which they are placed'.[103] We refer to this important article, because there is another point that emerges from it. For Tenbruck in 1959, Weber's writing can be divided into three periods. The writings of the first period are within the bounds of German political economy. 'One can see the doctoral and post-doctoral student following more or less uncritically the customary paths of academic labour';[104] there is no word here from Weber the methodologist. The break with this initial period is registered with the Freiburg Address.[105] The second period begins with the article on Roscher, and culminates in the essay on objectivity. Finally, the third period begins with the *Protestant Ethic*, leading via the essay on categories and the 'Economic Ethic of World Religions' to *Economy and Society*. With respect to Weber's methodology,

Tenbruck claims, it is only the second phase that is relevant, and within this really only the essay on objectivity. Weber places the 'axis of the whole question'[106] in the opposition of the historical to the theoretical tendency of *Nationalökonomie*, especially in the dispute between Menger and Schmoller. Carl Menger appears as *the* quintessential exponent of the 'theoretical' tendency. But Tenbruck sees quite clearly that the background to the essay on objectivity is to be found in the entire recent history of economic science since the demise of Cameralism.[107] So much for Tenbruck.

In the objectivity essay, Weber, in line with the Historical School, uses the term 'abstract theory' when referring to the 'theoretical tendency'. Menger is not directly named once, although clear allusions to him exist ('the creator of the theory').[108] 'The question as to how far, for example, *contemporary* "abstract theory" should be further elaborated is ultimately also a question of the strategy of science, which must, however, concern itself with other problems as well. Even the "theory of marginal utility" can be subsumed under a "law of marginal utility".'[109]

If the objectivity essay is once more read against this great historical background, it becomes apparent that the problems of 'contemporary' 'abstract' theory reflect at base those of the entire history of German economics. After a few opening remarks, the essay states that 'our science...first arose in connection with practical considerations. Its most immediate and often sole purpose was the attainment of value-judgements concerning measures of state economic policy. It was a "technique"...' Weber is able to assume familiarity with the context in stating that 'it has now become known how this situation was gradually modified. This modification was not, however, accompanied by a formulation of the logical distinction between "existential knowledge", i.e. knowledge of what "is", and "normative knowledge", i.e. knowledge of what "should be"...With the awakening of the historical sense, a combination of ethical evolutionism and historical relativism became the predominant attitude in our science...None the less we can and must forgo a discussion of the principles at issue. We merely point out that even today the confused opinion that economics does and should derive value-judgements from a specifically "economic point of view" has not disappeared but is especially current, quite understandably, among men of practical affairs.'[110] We can see that Weber here directly takes up the central question of the Inaugural Address without the merest indication of a 'breakthrough': does economic policy generate its own standards of value? The answer is likewise the same: 'it can never be the task of an empirical science to provide binding norms and ideals from which directives for immediate practical activity can be derived.'[111] If we add to this 'binding everywhere and at all times' then we have the precise position of the Historical School, which had in another respect reached a position which it is generally assumed Weber gained only with the assistance of neo-Kantian philosophy: the fundamental distinction of 'what is' from 'what ought to be'. Here again, there was something which Weber could take with him.

With Weber this distinction would gain a philosophical, moral and 'existential' significance that cannot be compared with Roscher's straightforward methodological distinction of the two 'principal questions' to be applied to 'every science concerned with the life of a people': '*what is* (what has occurred, and how? etc.) and *what should be.*'[112] For Weber this division is not merely a methodological one (this cannot be discussed here), but rather a matter of fundamental principle, confronting the actor with his existential responsibility. It is only possible to understand properly and appreciate Weber's distinction in all its ethical rigour ('the profound seriousness of this situation') against the background of Nietzsche. It is a distinction which marks him off from the 'optimistic syncretism' of the older school.[113] Despite this, and however awkward the actual mode of expression might have been, it was the Historical School that first elaborated this distinction. It had to do so in order that it might bring together two unrelated streams of scientific thought: the German tradition of technical and practical Cameralism and English 'theory'. This disparate inheritance was, and still is, embodied in the two principal lecture courses in economics: 'General and theoretical economics' and 'Practical economics' or 'Economic policy'. Weber himself recognized in the essay on objectivity that, alongside the socialist critique, it was the 'work of the historians' (i.e. the older teachers of the Historical School), which had made a *beginning* with the transformation of 'the original evaluative standpoints'.[114] Weber becomes hazy and unclear, as in all the sections of the essay devoted to the historical background of its arguments, when he claims that 'the vigorous development of biological research on one hand and the influence of Hegelian panlogism on the other prevented economics from attaining a clear and *full* understanding of the relationship between concept and reality'.[115] The work of the German Historical School of political economy is expressly noted as one of the factors resisting the 'infiltration of naturalistic dogma'.[116] In order to give his own position an added stature, he needed to present the superseded position as one that had not really understood the problem *to its full extent*. Only in this way can the distortions of Knies's position be explained. The 'old teachers', primarily Knies, had made the distinction in a manner adequate to their own 'philosophical needs'. If this distinction is then existentially radicalized by Weber for quite different needs and related to quite distinct experiences, it must be remembered that even in *this* instance, in the ominous opposition of 'fact and value', Weber simply *continues* a long tradition initiated by the Historical School. Weber's position has to be seen against this background and that of Nietzsche. The oft-praised contemporary 'logicians' merely helped in lending the affair a 'scientific' gloss. Something had changed, however, in the real world, and Weber outlines this in striking terms at the close of the essay on objectivity: the practical cultural problems had been transmuted, old cultural problems had been replaced by new ones. Who wishes to doubt this? Weber's attempt to confront the new situation in a scientific manner none the less drew on positions already 'prepared' by the masters of the German Historical School.

Notes: Chapter 2

This chapter was translated by Keith Tribe.

1   F. H. Tenbruck, 'Die Genesis der Methodologie Max Webers', *Kölner Zeitschrift für Soziologie und Sozialpsychologie*, vol. 11 (1959), pp. 573–630. This is particularly true of the early economic writings, which are left to political historians on account of their lack

of sociological usefulness. A real change is marked by L. A. Scaff's 'Weber before Weberian sociology', *British Journal of Sociology*, vol. 15 (1984), pp. 190–215.

2 A useful attempt to provide an overview is to be found in A. Zingerle, *Max Webers historische Soziologie* (Darmstadt, 1981).

3 Virtually a final statement: T. Parsons, 'On the relation of the theory of action to Max Weber's "verstehende Soziologie"', in W. Schluchter (ed.), *Verhalten, Handeln und System* (Frankfurt, 1980), pp. 150 ff.

4 Most recently an interpretation of Weber on the basis of his 'founding' and 'legislative role' – S. S. Wolin, 'Max Weber: legitimation, method and the politics of theory', *Political Theory*, vol. 9 (1981), pp. 401–24.

5 Weber's anxiousness for originality is very well shown in a passage from a letter to Georg von Below (23 August 1905): 'Troeltsch's impressive work might in many points be traced back to promptings of our conversations and my essays (perhaps more than he knows) – but he is the theological expert.' (Zentrales Staatsarchiv Merseburg, Weber papers).

6 W. Hennis, 'Max Weber's "central question"', *Economy and Society*, vol. 12 (1983), pp. 135–80; idem, 'Max Webers Thema', *Zeitschrift für Politik*, vol. 31 (1984), pp. 11–52.

7 John Stuart Mill's pet project of 'ethology' (the science of character formation) is squarely in this political-philosophical context.

8 For the British debates concerning the priority of 'social sciences' or 'sociology' over 'political science', see P. Abrams, *The Origins of British Sociology 1834–1914* (Chicago, 1968). Above all, however, see S. Collini, D. Winch and J. Burrow, *That Noble Science of Politics: A Study in Nineteenth-Century Intellectual History* (Cambridge, 1983).

9 Treitschke's *Habilitationsschrift* on *Die Gesellschaftswissenschaft* (1859) sought primarily to defend the old unity of politics. See in relation to this the various writings of M. Riedel, in particular 'Der Staatsbegriff der deutschen Geschichtsschreibung des 19. Jahrhunderts in seinem Verhältnis zur klassisch-politischen Philosophie', *Der Staat*, vol. 2 (1963), pp. 41 ff.

10 *Jugendbriefe*, p. 3.

11 ibid., p. 293.

12 Cited in E. Baumgarten (ed.), *Max Weber: Werk und Person* (Tübingen, 1964), p. 671.

13 After the Bremen plan fell through, he wrote to Hermann Baumgarten regretfully that it would have been very useful for him to have learnt 'for a few years the practice of large-scale trading, particularly in this position, which would have involved a continuing engagement in publicistic activity of a scientific nature (Max Weber to Hermann Baumgarten, 3 January 1891, *Jugendbriefe*, p. 326).

14 Among the intellectual connections that are not yet closely investigated are those to the work of Rudolf von Ihering. To call Weber's conception of law 'positivist' is not adequate.

15 Max Weber to Hermann Baumgarten, 3 January 1891 (*Jugendbriefe*, p. 326). More modestly, he wrote to Adolph Wagner after the assumption of the Freiburg chair: 'I regard myself as a beginner on nine-tenths of the area that I have to cover' (Max Weber to Adolph Wagner, 14 March 1895, Zentrales Staatsarchiv Merseburg, Weber papers).

16 *Biography*, p. 202.

17 Max Weber to his mother, 26 July 1893, *Jugendbriefe*, p. 372.

18 Clearly argued in L. A. Scaff, 'From political economy to political sociology: Max Weber's early writings', in R. M. Glassman (ed.), *Max Weber's Political Sociology* (Westport, Conn., 1984), pp. 87–8.

19 Cf. here W. J. Mommsen, *Max Weber and German Politics, 1890–1920* (Chicago, 1984), pp. 35–6.

20 *Biography*, p. 200.

21 Max Weber to Robert Michels of 9 December 1912: 'I have left the "sociologists" committee. In the long run my nerves cannot stand struggling with such cloying insects as Herr G.' To Michels on 20 December 1913: 'Beware of giving a paper on the Sociological Society, since I *no longer belong to it*.' (Zentrales Staatsarchiv Merseburg, Weber papers).

22 ES, Vol. 1, pp. 12–13.

23 'Sozialökonomik' (first employed by H. Dietzel in *Zeitschrift für die gesamte Staatswissenschaft*, 1883) seemed to Weber the best and most modern expression for something that, at the time, possessed no unitary terminology – without its leading to particular misunderstandings. He suggested to the publisher that the third section of the *Grundriß* ('Wirtschaft und Gesellschaft', of which Weber had taken on the second part 'Die Wirtschaft und die gesellschaftlichen Ordnungen und Mächte') should bear the title 'Social conditions of the economy' ('Gesellschaftliche Bedingungen der Wirtschaft'). The publisher

ignored this and retained 'Wirtschaft und Gesellschaft'; but it makes clear how one should read the 'special sociologies' of *Economy and Society*. If J. Winckelmann added as a subtitle 'Grundriß der verstehenden Soziologie' to the later editions, then at any rate he was aware that this did not correspond to Weber's intentions. During the preliminary work on the Weber edition, Winckelmann examined the correspondence between Weber and the publisher Siebeck, and it became clear that Weber referred as a shorthand to 'my "sociology"' when what is today known as *Economy and Society* was being discussed, but emphasized that this could by no means be the actual title (Max Weber to Siebeck, 6 November 1913).

24   G. von Schulze-Gävernitz, 'Max Weber als Nationalökonom und Politiker', in M. Palyi (ed.), *Erinnerungsgabe für Max Weber*, vol. 1 (Munich, 1923), pp. x–xxii.

25   'Indeed, he was not really an economist at all. In an atmosphere not disturbed by professional cross-currents, it would be the obvious thing to label him a sociologist.' J. A. Schumpeter, *History of Economic Analysis* (London, 1954), p. 819.

26   ibid. In the Merseburg Archive are copies of two letters from Weber to Robert Liefmann, which give unambiguous clues to the innermost interests of Weber, even during the whole of his 'later' work. In reply to Liefmann's accusation that Weber had done so little for economic theory, Weber replied on 12 December 1919: 'I regret myself that I have been able to do so little, or virtually nothing, for theory, but one cannot do everything. I do not hold theory in any less esteem. The other things also need to be done.' What 'other things'? A letter dated 3 March 1920 makes more clear Weber's ultimate interest (cf. the 'Vorbemerkung' to RS, Vol. 1); here, there is a more concrete response to Liefmann's accusation that Weber was more interested in 'special' and not 'theoretical' relations: '*Yes* if one calls the question: *why only* in the West does rational (profitable) capitalism emerge, a 'special' relation. There have to be people to look into this question.' A similar line can be seen in Weber's letter of 10 April 1919 to Hans Ehrenberg, in which he writes that 'I yearn for the simplicity and massive grasp of realities – not like you for the penetration of the "idea" which for the moment must (unfortunately!) be regarded as a "luxury" of "low marginal utility"' (Zentrales Staatsarchiv Merseburg, Weber papers). All that is at stake here is to understand what Weber means by 'realities'. In any case: not desires ('Wünschbarkeiten') in the sense of Nietzsche's scornful expression.

27   Max Weber, 'The national state and economic policy' (transl. by B. Fowkes), *Economy and Society*, vol. 9 (1980), pp. 428–49.

28   On this whole problem see Collini *et al.*, *That Noble Science of Politics*, (Cambridge, 1983), pp. 3 ff. At root this was also the theme of W. Hennis, *Politik und praktische Philosophie* (Neuwied, 1963).

29   RaK, pp. 53, 210, 236. Weber called this essay his 'Seufteraufsatz' which means literally 'essay full of sighs' (*Biography*, p. 278).

30   Weber characterized the science that he practised as one concerning human action or 'Sich-Verhalten', in contrast to 'dogmatic' science.

31   Collini *et al.*, *That Noble Science of Politics*.

32   ibid., pp. 312, 332–3.

33   In Freiburg, this faculty coup was the work of the newly appointed Max Weber. See, for Weber's time in Freiburg, the detailed dissertation of F. Biesenbach, *Die Entwicklung der Nationalökonomie an der Universität Freiburg i. Br. 1768–1896* (Freiburg i. Br., 1969), pp. 200 ff.

34   Mommsen, *Max Weber and German Politics*, p. 36.

35   The 'Gutachten' is printed in Baumgarten (ed.), *Max Weber*, pp. 102–39; the relevant passage on p. 127.

36   Max Weber, 'The national state', p. 437.

37   ibid., p. 438.

38   'Smith's system should really be called "atavistic cosmopolitanism", for it is not only directed against all national bonds, but in addition it divides all individuals into two parts, into producers and consumers.' This pregnant formulation by List in 1843 is cited by Hans Gehrig in the foreword to his edition of F. List, *Das nationale System der politischen Ökonomie* (Jena, 1950), p. xxviii.

39   F. List, *The National System of Political Economy* (London, 1916), p. 97.

40   ibid., pp. 97–8 (transl. revised).

41   W. Roscher, *Grundriß zu Vorlesungen über die Staatswirtschaft. Nach geschichtlicher Methode* (Göttingen, 1843), p. iv.

42 Cited from H. Gehrig's edition (Jena, 1922).

43 ibid., p. 22 (against Smith) and p. 87 (against the socialists).

44 First edition, 1853; second revised and expanded edition, Brunswick, 1883. Citations here are from the second edition. Weber was nineteen when it appeared and was at this time attending Knies's lectures.

45 Cf. the references to the 'Grundriß' of the first book of the lecture course 'Allgemeine (theoretische) Nationalökonomie' (Summer Semester 1898) in W. Hennis, 'Max Weber's "central question"', pp. 176–7.

46 Knies, *Die politische Oekonomie*, p. xi.

47 ibid., pp. 436 ff.

48 The most impressive treatment of the 'heteronomy of aims' is to be found in Weber's 'Intermediate reflections' ('Zwischenbetrachtung') in the first volume of the *Religionssoziologie*. Two letters in the Merseburg Archive make clear much more plainly what Weber had in mind. He wrote to Sombart on 8 February 1897, expressing thanks: 'You have more or less arrived at the old liberal ideal of the "greatest welfare of the greatest number" and suffer from the optical illusion thereby to have steered clear of the heteronomy of ideals. It is not possible that this is your final word on the subject.' On 2 April 1913 he wrote from Ascona to Robert Wilbrandt: 'I believe that our views would diverge at the point of involving a *general theory* of "means". In the sphere of values I consider that *irreconcilable* conflict, i.e. the constant necessity to make compromises, is dominant; nobody, not even revealed religion, can seek to forcibly decide *how* such compromises are to be arrived at...What is for example "human economy"?...What human *qualities* are to be developed through this? Not only physical ones of course. But what qualities of the soul? Perhaps only those of an anti-economic nature and effect?'

49 Max Weber, 'The national state', p. 437.

50 'Grundriß', (as in n. 45 above), p. 2.

51 Max Weber, 'The national state', p. 437.

52 ibid., p. 428.

53 ibid., p. 435.

54 ibid., p. 436.

55 ibid., p. 437 (my emphasis, W. H.).

56 ibid.

57 ibid., p. 439.

58 ibid., p. 439–40.

59 ibid., p. 440.

60 ibid., p. 437 (my emphasis, W. H.).

61 Ibid.

62 ibid. (my emphasis, W. H.).

63 ibid., pp. 437–8.

64 ibid., p. 438.

65 For example Mommsen, *Max Weber and German Politics*, p. 41.

66 Max Weber, 'The national state', p. 448.

67 These questions were central to the project directed by Istvan Hont at King's College Research Centre from 1978–84. A first impressive result: I. Hont and M. Ignatieff (eds), *Wealth and Virtue* (Cambridge, 1983).

68 Cf. Weber's reference to the fate of the Indians in Utah: MSS, p. 26.

69 Whether in Carl Schmitt's sense, or Reinhart Koselleck's 'counterconcepts' – cf. the latter's *Futures Past* (Cambridge, Mass., 1985).

70 Cf. the reference to the 'bitter conflict about the apparently most elementary problems of our discipline' at the beginning of the essay on objectivity (MSS, p. 51). The English debate on the 'dismal science' became embittered over the very same 'anthropological' questions.

71 I cite here according to the second (1883) edition, the year in which Weber intensively studied economics; the passage cited here is from p. 1. It should be noted that this does not appear in the first edition of 1854.

72 G. Schmoller, *Über einige Grundfragen der Socialpolitik und der Volkswirtschaftslehre* (Leipzig, 1898), pp. 337–8.

73 ibid., p. 68.

74 RaK; on the background to the essay see *Biography*, pp. 259, 325 ff.

75 *Jugendbriefe*, pp. 41, 71, 74.

76 RaK, p. 95.

77   This is also shown by a letter to Marianne relating to Knies's death. Weber wrote on 9 August 1898 from a sanatorium in Konstanz: 'I first heard of Knies's death from the newspapers; I wrote to the family following your letter confirming his death. It would in any event be difficult to make a memorial speech for the 77-year-old man. I am really glad to be away'. And further: 'I am on the other hand sorry that I was not able to devote a few words to Bismarck in my lectures' (Zentrales Staatsarchiv Merseburg, Weber papers). A peculiarly cold tone, even if one remembers that Weber was ill.

78   RaK, p. 237.

79   I ask that the restriction be noted: Weber's socioeconomic education. It is *not* claimed here that Weber was a 'student' of Knies and only to be understood in terms of Knies! But Weber received from Knies, leading proponent of the 'Historical School' as he was, his first instruction in the material of *Nationalökonomie* and was provided with the perspective of the School, a perspective that Weber never renounced. Knies gave Weber the 'material' for the direction that he took; the 'spirit' came from a far more important event − later it will be necessary to discuss Nietzsche.

   [Addendum, December, 1985] In November of 1985 the author was able to examine the 'Wissenschaftliche Manuskripte Max Webers' (Rep. 92 − Nachlaß Max Weber Nr. 31, Bd. 1−6) in the Weber papers at the Zentrales Staatsarchiv Merseburg, which were not accessible on the author's first visit in March 1985. First of all, a look at these materials makes abundantly clear the basis of political economy/political science on which Weber's work was founded. With the exception of the special studies on the sociology of religion, it was during the period when he was lecturing at Freiburg and Heidelberg that he acquired mastery of the materials (at least in their basic aspects), which then flowed into *Economy and Society*. Also the 'methodological' issues are already present as questions − even if they are not worked through with such conceptual stringency as they were from 1902.

   The thesis of this chapter on the pre-eminent significance of Karl Knies in Weber's scholarly development is confirmed in the *Nachlaß* (Nr. 31, Bd. 6, 'notes'), where we find excerpts from Knies's main work, which Weber had taken with painstaking care. (Weber had these excerpts carefully transcribed (Blatt 76−111). In another envelope (Blatt 112) are more excerpts under the heading 'Knies I: Maxims and Ethics'.) On the back of the excerpts Weber has written down the key headings of the book: for example, for p. 303 of Knies 'conflict of obligations' (*Pflichtenkollision*); for p. 42, 'setting of main question'; for p. 209, 'no theodicy'. This places it beyond question that Weber had studied Knies most carefully. It also confirms the hypothesis (see note 86 below) of the particular significance of Knies's main work on finance, *Geld und Kredit*. This work was a fundamental text for Weber's extensively probing lectures on 'finance theory' (*Finanzwissenschaft*) (Nachlaß Nr. 31, Bd. 4) and the lecture on 'Money, Banking and the Stock Exchange' (Nr. 31, Bd 3). The lecture notes also confirm Weber's intensive preoccupation with Marx and Marxism, in particular the lecture course on the 'labour question' (Nr. 31, Bd. 5).

80   K. Knies, *Die politische Oekonomie vom geschichtlichen Standpuncte*, 2nd edn (Brunswick, 1883). Page references in brackets refer to this work.

81   Dealt with in more detail in K. Knies, *Geld und Kredit*, 2 vols (Berlin, 1873−9); see Vol. 1, pp. vii−viii; in more detail, pp. 117 ff. It is clear from the bibliography in the 1898 'Grundriß' that Weber was familiar with Marx's theory of value. In a note to paragraph 3.3 a special 'critique of the value theory of the Classical School and of Socialism' is announced; following a long list of texts relating to the most recent theory of value (Menger, Böhm-Bawerk and many others), there is: 'from the older theory, refer to: Karl Marx, *Das Kapital*, Vol. 1'.

82   Whereby the expression 'politische Oekonomie' must also mean for him 'sociale Oekonomie'.

83   Knies employed this parallel concept to 'capitalism', which was usual in English discussions up to the 1840s.

84   Cf. n. 68, above.

85   The biographical impulse for Weber's interest in the sociology of religion has already been intensively studied, in the greatest detail, by J. Weiss, *Max Webers Grundlegung der Soziologie* (Munich, 1975), pp. 105 ff. (the pious mother, the Roman monastery library, the course of Jellinek's 'human rights', etc.); most recently also by G. Poggi, *Calvinism and the Capitalist Spirit* (London, 1983), pp. 1 ff. Since the basic character of Weberian sociology as a sociology oriented to the historical conditions of human action and its consequences has not been sufficiently recognized, the origins of Weber's interest in religion (in which he

previously declared himself to be 'unmusical' or 'tone deaf') must also have remained obscure until now.

86 On the question of interest and money-lending, see the detailed account in Knies, *Geld und Kredit*, Vol. 1, part 2 (Berlin, 1876), pp. 328 ff., and Vol. 2, part 2 (1879). This second half bears the subtitle 'The Nature of Interest and the Conditional Causes of its Level'.

87 Only lack of space prevents the documentation of a filiation, almost sentence-for-sentence, in Weber's work.

88 K. Knies, *Die Eisenbahnen und ihre Wirkungen* (Brunswick, 1853); idem, *Der Telegraph als Verkehrsmittel* (Tübingen, 1857).

89 See Hennis, 'Max Weber's "central question"', pp. 167 ff.

90 Weber's central concern in the 'evaluation' of the East Elbean movement of rural workers; cf. Hennis, 'Max Webers Thema', pp. 30 ff.

91 'Grundriß', paragraph 2, 'Begriff der Wirtschaft'.

92 RaK, p. 98.

93 See, especially, ibid., pp. 202–5: 'this claim, as we can see, is very close to the knowledge...' (p. 202); for Knies 'homogeneity is the primary element' (p. 203); his substantive ideas are 'quite in the spirit of Romanticism' (pp. 204–5); the 'implicit foundation of Knies's book' (p. 205).

94 ibid., pp. 206–7.

95 Thus, in a crystal clear and ironically hostile reference to Hegel and all his 'direct descendants and distant relatives' (Knies, *Die politische Oekonomie*, pp. 368–9). Particularly annoying is the confusion of Weber's lifelong scorn for the proponents of 'ethical culture' such as Friedrich W. Foerster (whose triviality was as distasteful to Weber as was the 'vulgarity' of the 'pleasure principle') with the understanding Knies had for the idea of 'ethical science'. There is not the slightest connection between them. Moreover, nobody had so clearly analysed the nonsense of quasi-natural economic 'laws' as had Knies (ibid., pp. 24 ff., 351 ff). In his critique of the 'stages theory' being acceptable as an 'ideal type', Weber merely took further that which had already been carried a long way by Knies (ibid., pp. 358 ff).

96 RaK, p. 205.

97 *Biography*, pp. 326–7, supplemented in Baumgarten (ed.), *Max Weber*, p. 301, following reports from Marianne: 'The illness has not in any way shaken his fixed intellectual form... He has not as a result of the illness 'changed direction' – to 'deeper' thoughts, or ones previously hidden from him... He now has time to elaborate in all directions on his older perspectives: to China and India even. But the perspective of those analytical religious studies, which are now certainly pursued *universalistically*, are neither surprising to him nor to her. When she met him as a 26-year-old they were already there in place.' There is in my opinion not the slightest reason to cast doubt on the correctness of this view of the 'biography of the work'. Only a misplaced sociological 'patriotism' has to insist on the 'completely fresh start'.

98 A basis for an understanding of other aspects of Weber's debt to previous developments of German political economy can be found in H. Winkel, *Die deutsche Nationalökonomie im 19. Jahrhundert* (Darmstadt, 1977). This is true above all for Weber's emphatic affirmation of the educative task of political economy and directly related to this (and not at all opposed!) is the typical training in powers of judgement (these are learnt, and not simply given) resulting from involvement with the issues of economic policy.

99 From the 'Geleitwort' on taking over the *Archiv* in 1904: AfSSP, Vol. 19 (1904), p. ii (my emphasis, W. H.).

100 A closer exposition of the context in which the so-called 'Sociology of Music' relates to Weber's basic problematic ('Why only us?') is awaited from Christoph Braun.

101 A. von Schelting, *Max Webers Wissenschaftslehre* (Tübingen, 1934); D. Henrich, *Die Einheit der Wissenschaftslehre Max Webers* (Tübingen, 1952).

102 Tenbruck, 'Die Genesis der Methodologie Max Webers'.

103 ibid., p. 576.

104 ibid., pp. 580–1.

105 The primary intention of this essay is to point out the fundamentally traditional features of the Inaugural Address. There can be no question of a 'break' with the Historical School; the critical discussion remains within the bounds of the School. See for further details W. Hennis, 'Max Weber in Freiburg', *Freiburger Universitätsblätter*, no. 86 (December, 1984), pp. 33–45.

106   Tenbruck, 'Die Genesis der Methodologie Max Webers', p. 589.
107   It is to be hoped that Tenbruck's wish (Chapter 16 in this volume) to make the social scientist Weber a man of 'History' will not lead to any confusion. Certainly Eduard Meyer's *Anthropologie* was for Weber a stimulating book. A glance at Weber's own copy (in the private possession of Dr Max Weber-Schäfer, Konstanz) shows that Weber took from it only factual material relating to antiquity. The anthropological-characterological interest of Weber was developed in the context of the discipline within which the Tenbruck of 1959 still knew how to interpret Weber: *Nationalökonomie* – and in clear recognition of the debates over method current at the time. At stake here is the specifically 'economic' (and this does not simply mean acquisitive) conduct of the whole human being, in contrast with the calculations of *homo oeconomicus* in 'economistic' theory.
108   MSS, p. 87.
109   ibid., p. 89 (my emphasis, W. H.).
110   ibid., pp. 51–2.
111   ibid., p. 52.
112   W. Roscher, *System der Volkswirtschaft*, Vol. 1 (Stuttgart, 1854), p. 33, also Knies, *Die politische Oekonomie*, pp. 42 ff. The specific task of propagating the doctrine of *Nationalökonomie* is something that is assumed in all the textbooks. The *particular* emphasis on the value of statistics can also be explained by the cameralistic-political tradition. Both of Weber's principal teachers – Knies and Meitzen – were recognized masters of statistics.
113   MSS, p. 57.
114   ibid., p. 86.
115   ibid. (my emphasis, W. H.).
116   ibid.

3 Gustav Schmoller and Max Weber

MANFRED SCHÖN

A comparison of Schmoller and Weber involves contrasting the represent-atives of two generations of scholars in early twentieth-century economic and social science who, from the point of view of their attitudes, their conception of science and their political aspirations or temper, were so remote from each other that indeed, in some respects, they could be classified as intellectual antipodes.[1]

But, despite all their disagreements and differences of opinion, Weber did see and praise Schmoller as one of the outstanding figures in political economy and social policy in the German Reich of the late nineteenth century. These points are encapsulated in Weber's letter to Schmoller on the occasion of the latter's seventieth birthday:

(1) At a time most unfavourable to the influence of *universities* on public life in the sphere of your *interests* you have raised their influence to a level that has never been even nearly approached since the period between 1837 and 1848.

(2) Your prudence and moderation alone enabled the socio-political idealism of the academically *educated* classes to find an instrument, under the guise of the Verein für Sozialpolitik, which made itself felt not only in public opinion, but also with those who *had power*. This, in any case, would not have been possible without your leadership. And this despite the fact that – as you have often enough experienced it yourself – the 'contents' of the ideals which individuals served were frequently not only varied but also different from your own. No matter how frequent and stormy the battle against your *opinion* was on occasions, you made it morally impossible even for those who disagreed with you to fight against you as a *person*. So far as I can see, the conviction that *your* leadership was indispensable and the confidence placed in you by social policy-makers of the most heterogeneous character has never been shaken for one moment.

(3) At a time of the most barren economic rationalism you have created a home for *historical* thought in our science in a way that has not been found in any other nation to the same extent and with the same consequences even to this day. The scientific needs of the different generations in the sphere of our discipline oscillate between theoretical and historical knowledge – as you have often enough acknowledged. No matter that it is now perhaps high time to concentrate on the theoretical aspect: the fact *that* the time for theoretical work may be 'ripe' again, the fact *that* we have before us such

a powerful structure of knowledge at all – in historical penetration, psychological analysis and philosophical formation – which we, as the younger generation, may attempt to add to by means of *theoretical* construction of concepts – all this we ultimately owe primarily to your incomparably successful work of many decades.[2]

What cannot be overlooked in this 'birthday letter' (this does not mean to say that this letter was written purely and simply from the aspect of 'conventional reverence'), although understandably expressed in a subtle form and, as it were, 'dialectically' encoded, is that it is suggestive of the demand for increased theoretical research in the field of economics. When Weber talks about 'theory', for him this means research proceeding from the accomplishments of the 'Austrian School' or the representatives of the theory of marginal utility whose importance cannot be overestimated for Weber, the economic specialist. After all, Weber belongs to those German economists of his time who were the most unbiased in their acknowledgement and recognition of the theoretical efforts of the circle around Carl Menger. Thus the published 'Grundriß zu den Vorlesungen über Allgemeine ('theoretische') Nationalökonomie' [Outline of Lectures on General (Theoretical) Economics] of 1898 is largely oriented towards the theory of marginal utility.[3]

In 1903 it is Weber who recommends the nomination of von Böhm-Bawerk for an honorary doctorate at the University of Heidelberg:

> Equally outstanding in logical stringency, stylistic refinement and in the elegant objectivity of his polemics, he is undoubtedly the most important representative of the abstract and deductive work done by the school of Austrian political economists... He would make a particularly happy complement to the strictly historically inductive work by Professor *Schmoller*, whose promotion has been recommended by the other side.[4]

Thus it seems hardly accidental that, with Friedrich von Wieser, one of the main representatives of the Austrian School could be won over to the theoretically fundamental parts of the *Grundriß der Sozialökonomik*, initiated by Weber.

This in itself does not signify very much. The best approach towards an understanding of Weber's attitude to (pure) economic theory is without doubt that which can be inferred from his methodological writings, in which the infamous *Methodenstreit* (methodological dispute) between Schmoller and Menger forms the background. There Weber intervenes with his neo-Kantian conception of the social and cultural sciences.[5]

It is precisely the Menger of the *Methodenstreit* whom Weber credits to be the first (even before Rickert) to have discovered the fundamental methodological distinction or logical opposition between law-based science (*Gesetzeswissenschaft*) and the science of concrete reality (*Wirklichkeitswissenschaft*), between law-based knowledge and historical knowledge; this distinction did not spring from a difference in the object to be investigated (as in Wilhelm Wundt), but from the respective specific epistemological goals and interests, namely, the consideration of the particular or the general, or, alternatively, the individual or the universal.

Menger's objection to the Historical School of political-economy was that they confused economic history with economic theory or mistook its true character: the task of theory is the formulation of regular interconnections by means of general but one-sided concepts, that is to say, by means of the isolating-abstracting method. It searches for 'types' and their 'typical relations', i.e. the laws of appearances. In this, it proceeds from the most basic elements of all reality

> not considering whether these exist in reality as *independent* appearances, indeed even without considering whether they are in fact presentable independently in their full purity. By these means theoretical investigation arrives at the *qualitative* typical forms of appearances that cannot be tested against full empirical reality (because the forms we are talking about here, e.g. absolutely pure oxygen, an individual who pursues only economic ends, etc., exist in part only in our idea) yet none the less are the foundation and prerequisite for the attainment of *precise laws*.[6]

The 'precise laws' thus attained have, of course, equally to be abstracted from empirical reality. The approximation to what Weber was to classify as an 'ideal type' is evident, without thereby asserting that Menger was the only source stimulating Weber to formulate the 'ideal type'. Weber does, however, reproach the *disciples* of Menger for their 'naturalistic prejudice', their concept of the 'laws' of economics as equivalent to the way laws are constructed in the natural sciences.[7] This, according to Weber, is what they most definitely are not: the concepts and so-called 'laws' (or, better, tenets[8]) of theoretical economics are rational constructs; they are 'ideal types' of consistent rational action.[9] Weber is less interested in pure economic theory as such, since its elaboration is again governed by the principle of marginal utility,[10] but rather in its functional and pragmatic (its heuristic) significance in the context of causal empirical research.[11]

The relevance of the economic construction of concepts is illuminated particularly in Weber's discussion with one of the leading representatives of the Historical School, Lujo Brentano, in the review essay 'Marginal utility theory and the so-called fundamental law of psychophysics' ('Die Grenznutzenlehre und das "psycho-physische Grundgesetz"'). Apart from the fact that the theory of marginal utility manages to find mathematical formulae for the processes of economically relevant action,[12] its central significance resides in the understanding of the modern era ruled by capitalism:

> the historical distinctiveness of the capitalistic epoch, and thereby also the significance of marginal utility theory (as of every economic theory of value) for the understanding of this epoch, rests on the circumstance that... under today's conditions of existence the approximation of reality to the theoretical propositions of economics has been a *constantly increasing* one. It is an approximation to reality that has implicated the destiny of ever-wider layers of humanity. And it will hold more and more widely, as far as our horizons allow us to see.[13]

Perhaps it is Weber's sense of justice that makes him defend so vehemently the theory of marginal utility vis-à-vis a representative of the Historical School. This also finds expression in his simultaneous correspondence with Brentano, in which reference is made to Menger (and Schmoller):

> I am of the opinion: 1) that Menger expresses what he wants to say, to be sure in an awkward manner, but unpretentiously, simply and clearly; 2) that it is absolutely *un*justifiable to see him as a mere carbon copy of Gossen or *whomsoever* – to produce evidence for this would take too long here. It is true, he vastly overrates himself, but he has his *very* substantial merits and he was *right* on important points of the matter at *issue*, even in the dispute with Schmoller. [14]

The spirited exchange of letters with Brentano on the subject of the latter's treatment of the theory of marginal utility contains one (perhaps the real) reason for Weber's rejection of founding economic theory on a psychological base: 'The "doctrine of marginal utility" has in my opinion nothing more to do with "psychology" than with astronomy or Lord knows what else; it is objectionable to give the impression that it is in *need* of "psychological" support. In my opinion this opens the way to *Schmollerism*, which tends to work with "psychology".' [15]

What Weber ultimately rejects is the arrangement of the sciences in a hierarchy along Comtean lines or the attempt to see some disciplines as 'fundamental' to economics. The link with the other sciences results purely and simply from each individual line of inquiry. [16] Ironically, it is therefore Weber who, for pragmatic reasons, protects 'theory' against the psychological critique of the Historical School. [17] Theory works with ideal-typical rational constructs; it is not in need of psychological support as Schmoller had always propagated it: 'Psychology for us is the key to all the cultural sciences and therefore to political economy as well.' [18]

This takes us to Weber's disagreement with Schmoller's conception of science. Weber's critique does not challenge Schmoller's scholarly *practice*, the historical orientation of his studies and research with their valuable individual results, but rather his *goal*: a gigantic research project from the viewpoint of design, considering economic factors in their 'total context' and ultimately leading to a 'universal social science' to replace a specialist discipline. [19] An additional factor is that science along the lines of inductive-cumulative progress serves merely as preliminary grounding for a 'perfect' deductive science in the distant future. This has the fatal consequence of neglecting the construction of concepts and of leaving this to the envisaged 'perfect' science, an idea that is based on understanding concepts not as pragmatic constructs, but 'as reflections of "objective" reality'.

> If one perceives the implications of the fundamental ideas of modern epistemology, which ultimately derives from Kant, namely, that concepts are primarily analytical instruments for the intellectual mastery of empirical data and can be only that, the fact that precise genetic concepts are necessarily ideal types will not cause one to desist from constructing them. The relationship between concept and historical research is reversed for those who appreciate this; the goal [of the Historical School] then appears

as logically impossible, the concepts are not ends but are means to the end of understanding phenomena which are significant from concrete individual viewpoints.[20]

The importance of Weber's appeal to Rickert's methodology is to be judged in this context: the selection principles of cultural meaning and value relevance literally 'exonerate' him from Schmoller's epistemological or scientific position, which is oriented to Comte.

The institution in which the different political and scientific views and tempers of both Schmoller and Weber were accentuated and highlighted to a particular extent was the Verein für Sozialpolitik. It was Weber's essays on the agricultural workers east of the Elbe that made members of the Verein aware of him. Schmoller, as well as Knapp, applauded the scientific treatment of this topic. Because of this, Weber, the agricultural specialist, was considered as the potential successor of Max Sering at the Agricultural Institute (*Landwirtschaftliche Hochschule*) in Berlin. Schmoller thought that Weber was predestined to succeed him also because of his basic conservative attitude: 'He [Weber] combines his knowledge with a moderate political standpoint, a Prussian patriotism. He is free of all the Anglomania characteristic of Brentano's students, and [free] of any socialist tinge, although he earnestly and energetically advocates any sound social reform.'[21]

For a few years Weber's illness forced him to take a background position in the Verein, only then to emerge during the decade between 1905 and 1914 as one of the most outstanding but also most controversial figures of the Verein, as a speaker at general assemblies and most of the committee meetings, as a co-initiator of the inquiry into the selection and adaptation of industrial workers, as well as becoming the chief opponent in the debate on value-judgements.[22]

Three problem areas in particular show where Weber's and Schmoller's different scientific and political choices clash: (1) the distinctiveness and sociopolitical self-understanding of the Verein; (2) the function and importance of bureaucracy; (3) the question of freedom from value-judgement in the sciences.

Schmoller's conflict with Friedrich Naumann at the Mannheim general assembly of 1905 highlights Schmoller's ideas regarding the science policy orientation of the Verein für Sozialpolitik. The reason for the controversy was Naumann's discussion paper concerning Schmoller's lecture on 'the relationship between cartels and the state', in which Schmoller made a plea for moderate intervention by the state and, among other things, recommended a change in company law: the Reich government as well as the individual states should be able to send some delegates to the supervisory boards of joint stock companies owning more than 75 million marks equity capital, in order to 'safeguard the political and economic interests of the Reich and state together with those of the company'.[23] In contrast, Naumann in his contribution to the debate advocated the free and unimpeded development of large-scale industry. In his view, intervention by the state in large-scale industry would be 'nonsense, both from a technical and national-economic point of view', since the state was acting as the executive organ for chiefly agrarian interests, i.e. serving ultimately middle-class interests.[24]

In his closing speech, Schmoller, who felt personally attacked by this (although he was not named), called Naumann a 'demagogue' who without real knowledge of the actual subject-matter based his arguments on 'the old Marxist slogans and the, for me, dubious truth of the materialist conception of history supported by very scanty evidence'. Moreover, Schmoller emphasized that – to judge by the 'frenetic applause' Naumann's speech received – he [Schmoller] would be forced to resign his chairmanship of the Verein if he could not defend his standpoint.[25]

In the ensuing discussion, Weber intervened on behalf of Naumann (who was no longer present, and was particularly opposed to the fact that Schmoller in an authoritarian manner invoked his position as chairman of the Verein in order to prejudice the outcome of the proceedings).[26] The issue arose as to whether the Verein should serve as a 'free debating chamber' for all socio-political opinions or as a conservative-ruled debating circle.

The conflict escalated in the weeks that followed, although it was indeed Max and Alfred Weber as well as Eberhard Gothein who, in an open letter, repudiated the critique that had been expressed by the *Frankfurter Zeitung* after the Mannheim general assembly. This article spoke of the polemic against Naumann, which had allegedly been brought about by Schmoller's 'defeat'. The two Webers and Gothein felt they needed to defend Schmoller from this misrepresentation.[27] Despite leaving the door open for reconciliation the dispute escalated through a Naumann article in *Die Hilfe* as well as through Schmoller's 'Open Letter' in the *Tägliche Rundschau*, in which he radicalized his previous stance at the Mannheim general assembly in so far as he now made his retention of the chairmanship of the board dependent on a majority of moderate votes.[28] Weber vehemently resisted the attempt to transform the Verein into an 'association for well-behaved social policy'[29] in which the Left of the Verein acted as mere 'pieces of décor and token radicals'.[30] 'I refuse to collaborate on a stage which wants to offer the audience a little bit of radicalism, but only for appearance's sake and not too vociferously...'.[31]

Given the background of his own open letter to the *Frankfurter Zeitung* and the attitude taken by Schmoller, Weber was prepared to publish a reply. This, however, was not done because Lujo Brentano advised him strongly against it, so as not to endanger the unity of the Verein, and also because, in the meantime, Schmoller and Naumann had privately settled their quarrel.[32] Moreover, Brentano feared Schmoller's immediate resignation of the chairmanship if the letter were published. Schmoller later confirmed this and stated that, in his opinion, Weber's public attack would 'probably have led to a split' in the Verein für Sozialpolitik.[33] Thereupon, Weber offered Schmoller his voluntary (but, in the end, unsuccessful) resignation from the Verein's committee, since he did not doubt Schmoller's leading position and did not want to see it challenged.[34] The question of censoring members of the Verein remained. Weber proposed cancelling the general assembly entirely, while Brentano put forward the motion to abolish the respective chairmen's summary of the individual debates. The latter motion was later adopted by a committee meeting in January 1907.[35]

The main motive for Schmoller's conduct was undoubtedly his fear that right-wing members, particularly Conrad, Neumann, Sering and Wagner, threatened to leave the Verein on account of Naumann's speech, something which Schmoller was trying to prevent at all costs: 'Just as much as the left wing of the Verein is necessary as the progressive element, the right wing is equally necessary, because it corrects exaggerations and gives the Verein influence over the broad bourgeois classes whose social education is our main task.'[36] The central function of the Verein could only be achieved by appearing as a 'united social reform party' to the outside world. But, in truth, its unity of course was bought only at the price of a continuing gradual change in its function: the 'spearhead of social reform' was transformed into a mere academic debating circle. Even Schmoller harboured no illusions about this.[37] He placed emphasis on the safeguarding of the unity of the Verein again in 1909, when he received irritated letters about the conduct of the Weber brothers and Sombart after the debates on value-judgement in Vienna:

> Among all of those on the Right the indignation about the Webers is great. I for one cannot share it. They are after all neurotics, but they are the leaven and they animate our general assemblies; they are honest people and enormously talented. To be sure they act as explosives in our Verein, which for my part has to be held together for as long as possible. If we split up, the left wing will become a body of radical officers without an army, while the right will turn into a troop of corporals; both without power and influence, something we still have by virtue of our togetherness.[38]

Schmoller wanted to present a moderate image of the Verein to the outside world, mainly because the actual addressee of its socio-political activities was the Prussian bureaucracy. The appraisal of Prussian officialdom in particular constitutes one of the great points of difference from Weber. Schmoller's exceedingly positive image of the bureaucracy does not stem from sociological analysis, but rather from his historical studies and particularly his personal experience. Schmoller, like Delbrück and more particularly Harnack, belongs to those representatives of the 'governmental intelligentsia'[39] who were in close contact with the important decision-makers of the Prusso-German regime of officials. For Schmoller, bureaucracy, the regime of officials, is a neutral authority beyond the particular interests of party and class, an authority that becomes the most important vehicle for the enforcement of socio-political measures: 'The monarchy ultimately has always a greater liking for any major social reform than do ruling millionaires and industrialists.'[40] Moreover, he appreciated the civil service as a reservoir or as 'sphere for selection' for political elites:

> Our local government is better today than that of the English, because our municipal councils, our local and staff committees, contain so many elements which have undergone civil service training. Indeed, one can say even of our parliaments that their prominent members and party leaders originate from officialdom. One could say that our great statesman, the founder of the German Empire, has accomplished unrivalled achievements only because he was able to rise above *Junker*dom to officialdom.[41]

This view of an officialdom above class and the legitimacy of its rule corresponds with the rejection of the parliamentary system of government: 'for this we lack the aristocracy, the leaders, the large parties.'[42]

This is the absolute antithesis to Max Weber's ideas on the relationship of politicians to officials. If the official administers impartially, *sine ira et studio*, carries out instructions given to him in a manner appropriate to the case even if they contradict his own convictions, then the medium of the politician is that of conflict and in his action he is duty-bound only by his own sense of responsibility.[43]

Schmoller's proposals, even though moderate, on the issue of cartels in 1905 led Weber to a fundamental critique of Schmoller's concept of the state. Here, for the first time, the critique of the ruling bureaucracy and pseudo-constitutionalism is formulated, a theme which pervades a large part of Weber's writings and general commentary from that time onward. 'The great works of Professor Schmoller on the history of Prussian officialdom belong ... among the classics of our science; they have influenced us and will influence us as long as we think scientifically. But here too Goethe's maxim is applicable: "We all live by the past and perish by the past."'[44] Weber questions the empirical character of the contemporary Prussian state, or rather the competence of its bureaucratic elites to intervene in the issue of cartels. He arrives at an entirely negative conclusion:

> What kind of people are those who occupy the ministerial posts today? Absolutely excellent in their way, but this way means: matter-of-fact men, businessmen... None of these gentlemen who occupy their ministerial posts today will claim to be statesmen... They are matter-of-fact men, who know how to adapt, have to adapt, themselves to the given situations, due to dynastic wishes and other pressures.[45]

This is the reason why Weber can only emphatically warn about the community of interests shared by state and industry. It would lead to an undue influence on the state exercised by capitalist interests and interested parties. This fact stirred him four years later, at the Verein's general assembly in Vienna, to draw the humorous comparison that the state would play 'not the role of Siegfried, but that of King Gunther with Brunhilde'.[46] It is precisely the 1909 debate on the 'economic enterprises in the municipalities', in which Weber presents the negative consequences of bureaucracy and the results of increasing bureaucratization in their socio-political, power-political and universal historical dimensions. Not to consider this and to ignore the outcomes of these processes arises − and Weber addresses himself here explicitly to Schmoller − from a prejudice: 'the faith in the omnipotence of the high moral standards, doubted by no one, of our German officialdom'.[47] This indeed, although exaggeratedly, touches the core of Schmoller's relationship with officialdom. Friedrich Meinecke, in his retrospective considerations of Schmoller and his generation, arrives at roughly the same conclusion: 'He trusted... the rational forces of history too much, which in our conditions he found embodied in the monarchy and officialdom of Prusso-Germany.'[48]

Just as antithetically as Weber construes the relationship between official and politician, he apprehends a similar antithesis between empirical knowledge and value-judgement. *Tertium non datur*. The principle of freedom from value-judgement, formulated for the first time in the 1904 essay on objectivity, was aimed at the historical-ethical school of political economy. From about 1909, Weber found himself operating on two fronts in so far as a group of economists now used the postulate of the freedom from value-judgement as a vehicle in their struggle against the Verein für Sozialpolitik, in particular, and against all social policy, in general. Given this background, it becomes comprehensible that Weber was one of the main proponents, indeed was an initiator, of a social policy demonstration on the fortieth anniversary of the foundation of the Verein für Sozialpolitik. It would be a demonstration that was to document – once again apparent to all – the ties of younger economists to the still surviving founding members, particularly Schmoller: '*Nothing more embarrassing* could happen to Harms, Pohle, Adolf Weber, but also the gentlemen *Elster* and consorts, than a co-operation under the auspices of Schmoller, Cohn, *Lexis* and yourself [i.e. Brentano], which encompasses all of *you*.'[49] And in a letter to Werner Sombart he explained his active participation by the fact that he had in recent times always been 'played off against the Verein and Schmoller'.[50] At Schmoller's own request this demonstration never took place. He obviously doubted the sense and wisdom of such an event and, indeed, he expected renewed problems for the unity of the Verein rather than a contribution to its stability.[51]

The debate on value-judgement in the Verein für Sozialpolitik, which had been started in 1909 in Vienna by Weber's polemic against the economic concept of productivity, reached its peak in 1914 during an extended committee meeting, which was specially called on this theme. Schmoller insisted on no minutes being taken, in order to prevent the differences from being shown publicly and outsiders interpreting these to the detriment of the Verein.[52]

At this point, it is appropriate to give a brief sketch of Weber's position in the debate on value-judgement. The radical distinction between 'what is' and 'what ought to be' corresponds with the rejection of the transcendental basis of cultural values and that of any objectively valid value-system. This rejection is the consequence of the radical destruction of Christian religion and philosophical metaphysics, which Nietzsche had accomplished before him. Values are no longer objective entities but mere points of orientation, which are 'valid' only in so far as one believes in them and submits them to the test of everyday life. They are subjective categories for guiding one's own conduct; they can change historically and therefore have to be denied an absolute meta-historical character.[53] It is the fate of Western man, deprived of meaning in a disenchanted world, to create from his 'own heart' the values from which his life should develop and orient itself.[54]

It is only with this background in mind that we can understand the intensity with which Weber came to speak of Schmoller, and especially of the new version of Schmoller's article 'Volkswirtschaft, Volkswirtschaftslehre- und -methode' ['The national economy and the doctrine and method of economics'] in the *Handwörterbuch der Staatswissenschaften* [Concise Dictionary of Political and Social Sciences] in his report made available for the debate.[55] Schmoller, in the completely reworked concluding part of his article, had chiefly criticized Weber and his postulate of the freedom from value-judgement and had arrived at a diametrically opposed position, a position that elucidates the epistemological absurdities and perplexities of 'ethical' economics in an almost ideal-typical way. As Schmoller puts it, just as there are objective value-judgements resulting from the increasing assimilation of value-judgements by individuals, classes and societies, so there is an ethic which increasingly becomes the subject of an empirical science.[56]

> Ethics, of course, is as much a realistic science to me as economics. I consider the transcendental and purely formal ethic, which Max Weber ... makes out to be the only justifiable one, to be misguided, ...[57]

> M. Weber does not want the highest ethical ideals that move the human soul to penetrate into the 'technical-economic' sphere. This is an ethical purism which I cannot support... Our science lies at least on the borderline between the technical-economic and ethical spheres. M. Weber would not have been able to write his beautiful essays on the Protestant Ethic if he did not himself deeply sense the closest interrelationship between the economic and ethical spheres.[58]

This is not the place to recapitulate all the individual points made by Weber, but only to emphasize two. First, Weber rejects a 'realistic' ethic, i.e. the idea of arriving for example, at a normative ethic by empirically demonstrating the socio-economic determinateness of particular evaluative standpoints.[59] Secondly, he criticizes the identification of ethical principles with particular, in each case only temporally valid, cultural values, an identification that ultimately ignores or underestimates the heterogeneity and possible antagonism of individual value-spheres to each other or vis-à-vis ethics.[60] Perhaps this is the point where Weber and Schmoller most strongly differ from each other. The antagonism between values or value-spheres was totally alien to the representative of the Historical School, who argues with *juste milieu* value-judgements. Hence it may be warranted to conclude by citing Weber's characterization of Roscher, one which in essence may also apply to Schmoller – at least to the later Schmoller:

> So we see that the numerous claims Roscher makes concerning economic policy are a consequence of his liberal, sober and temperate personality. But they are in no sense the expression of a clear ideal which has been thought through to its logical conclusions. Genuinely serious and enduring inconsistencies between the march of historical destiny and the tasks which God sets for individuals as well as for peoples are quite impossible. The autonomous selection of his ultimate goals is not a possibility for the individual.[61]

Notes: Chapter 3

This chapter was translated by Elizabeth King.

1   Cf. also F. Meinecke, 'Drei Generationen deutscher Gelehrtenpolitik. Friedrich Theodor Vischer, Gustav Schmoller, Max Weber', *Historische Zeitschrift*, vol. 125 (1922), pp. 248–83.
2   Max Weber to Gustav Schmoller, 23 June 1908, in: *Reden und Ansprachen gehalten am 24.*

Juni 1908 bei der Feier von Gustav Schmollers 70. Geburtstag. Nach stenographischer Aufnahme. Als Handschrift gedruckt (Altenburg, 1908), pp. 67–8. Corrected on the basis of the original letter, Tübingen University Library, Schmoller papers (Md 1076), no. 48, fasc. 2.

3 The 'Grundriß' is also interesting because, although the term does not appear, the *substance* of the 'ideal type' of action does. See the citation in Chapter 2 above (p. 35).

4 Max Weber to the Philosophische Fakultät of\the University of Heidelberg, 26 May 1903, University Archives, Heidelberg, H-IV-102/135. 'The other side' refers to the historian, Erich Marcks, who had been the chief advocate of an honorary doctorate to be given to Schmoller.

5 For the relationship between Max Weber and Carl Menger, cf. F. H. Tenbruck, 'Zur Genese der Methodologie Max Webers', *Kölner Zeitschrift für Soziologie und Sozialpsychologie*, vol. 11 (1959), pp. 573–630. Weber's annotated personal copy of Menger's *Untersuchungen über die Methode der Socialwissenschaften und der Politischen Ökonomie überhaupt* (Leipzig, 1883) survives at the Alfred-Weber-Institut at Heidelberg. See also C. Brinkmann, *Gustav Schmoller und die Volkswirtschaftslehre* (Stuttgart, 1937), p. 135, n. 126.

6 Menger, *Untersuchungen*, p. 41.

7 WL³, p. 188; MSS, pp. 87–8.

8 Cf. also H. Dietzel, *Theoretische Socialökonomik*, Vol. 1 (Leipzig, 1895), p. 76.

9 WL³, pp. 189 ff.; MSS, pp. 88 ff.

10 WL³, p. 190; MSS, p. 89.

11 WL³, p. 193; MSS, p. 92.

12 Max Weber, 'Marginal utility theory and the so-called fundamental law of psychophysics' (transl. by L. Schneider), *Social Science Quarterly*, vol. 56 (1975), p. 30; WL³, p. 392.

13 Max Weber, 'Marginal utility theory', p. 33; WL³, p. 395.

14 Max Weber to Lujo Brentano, 30 October 1908, Bundesarchiv Koblenz, Brentano papers, no. 67.

15 Max Weber to Lujo Brentano, 29 May 1908, ibid.

16 Max Weber, 'Marginal utility theory', p. 31; WL³, p. 393.

17 Cf. MSS, p. 88; 'Abstract theory purported to be based on psychological *axioms* and as a result historians have called for an *empirical* psychology in order to show the invalidity of those axioms and to derive the course of economic events from psychological principles.' (WL³, pp. 188–9).

18 G. Schmoller, *Grundriß der allgemeinen Volkswirtschaftslehre*, Vol. 1, 2nd edn (Munich and Leipzig, 1919), p. 108.

19 ibid., p. 124.

20 MSS, p. 106.

21 Gustav Schmoller to Friedrich Althoff, 3 March 1893, Zentrales Staatsarchiv Merseburg, Althoff papers (A I, no. 62, vol. 133).

22 'For the next session we need new rules of procedure whose first article should limit the Weber brothers' speaking time to 55 minutes in one hour.' Schmoller, quoted in O. von Zwiedineck-Suedenhorst, 'Vom Wirken von Max und Alfred Weber im Verein für Sozialpolitik', in E. Salin (ed.), *Synopsis. Alfred Weber, 30.7.1868 – 30.7.1948* (Heidelberg, 1948), p. 785.

23 'Verhandlungen der Generalversammlung in Mannheim', in *Schriften des Vereins für Sozialpolitik*, Vol. 116 (Leipzig, 1906), p. 271.

24 ibid., p. 367.

25 ibid., p. 420.

26 ibid., pp. 432–5.

27 *Frankfurter Zeitung*, no. 274 (3 October 1905), evening edn, p. 2.

28 *Die Hilfe*, no. 40 (8 October 1905); *Tägliche Rundschau*, no. 489 (18 October 1905).

29 Max Weber to Gustav Schmoller, 23 October 1905, Zentrales Staatsarchiv Merseburg, Schmoller papers, no. 158.

30 Max Weber to Alfred Weber, n.d. [October 1905], Zentrales Staatsarchiv Merseburg, Weber papers, no. 4.

31 Max Weber to Carl J. Fuchs, 24 October 1905, Tübingen University Library, Fuchs papers (Md 875).

32 Max Weber to Gustav Schmoller, 23 October 1905, Schmoller papers (as in n. 29 above), no. 158.

33 Gustav Schmoller to Lujo Brentano, 29 October 1905, quoted in F. Boese, *Geschichte des Vereins für Sozialpolitik* (Berlin, 1939), p. 120.

34 Max Weber to Gustav Schmoller, 16 November 1905, Schmoller papers (as in n. 29 above), no. 158.

35   Boese, *Geschichte*, p. 121.
36   Gustav Schmoller to Lujo Brentano, 29 October 1905, quoted in Boese, *Geschichte*, p. 119.
37   Gustav Schmoller to Lujo Brentano, 10 October 1912, Brentano papers (as in n. 14 above), no. 58.
38   Gustav Schmoller to Arthur Spiethoff, 15 October 1909, Basle University Library, Spiethoff papers. Partly printed in E. Salin, 'Alfred Weber', in idem, *Lynkeus. Gestalten und Probleme aus Wirtschaft und Politik* (Tübingen, 1963), p. 62.
39   Cf. R. vom Bruch, *Wissenschaft, Politik und öffentliche Meinung. Gelehrtenpolitik im Wilhelminischen Deutschland (1890 – 1914)* (Husum, 1980), p. 16.
40   G. Schmoller, 'Die englische Gewerkvereinsentwickelung im Lichte der Webbschen Darstellung', *Schmollers Jahrbuch*, vol. 25 (1901), p. 313.
41   G. Schmoller, 'Der deutsche Beamtenstaat vom 16. – 18. Jahrhundert. Rede gehalten auf dem deutschen Historikertag zu Leipzig am 29. März 1894', *Schmollers Jahrbuch*, vol. 18 (1894), p. 714.
42   Gustav Schmoller to Georg Friedrich Knapp, 26 April 1906, Schmoller papers (as in n. 29 above), no. 131b.
43   MWG, Vol. I 15, pp. 450 ff. Cf. also W. J. Mommsen, *Max Weber and German Politics, 1890–1920* (Chicago, 1984), pp. 163 ff.
44   GASS, p. 402.
45   ibid.
46   ibid., p. 415.
47   ibid., pp. 415–16.
48   Meinecke, 'Drei Generationen', p. 269.
49   Max Weber to Lujo Brentano, 3 July 1912, Brentano papers (as in n. 14 above), no. 67. Cf. also MSS, pp. 6 ff.
50   Max Weber to Werner Sombart, 7 July 1912, Weber papers (as in n. 30 above), no. 30, Vol. 6.
51   Max Weber to Gustav Schmoller, 15 July 1912, Schmoller papers (as in n. 29 above), no. 204a.
52   Cf. Boese, *Geschichte*, pp. 145 ff.
53   WL[3], p. 152; MSS, p. 55.
54   WL[3], p. 40; RaK, p. 89.
55   G. Schmoller, 'Volkswirtschaft, Volkswirtschaftslehre und ihre Methode', in *Handwörterbuch der Staatswissenschaften*, 3rd edn, Vol. 8 (Jena, 1911), pp. 426–501.
56   ibid., pp. 493, 495.
57   ibid., p. 497.
58   ibid., p. 497.
59   Max Weber, 'Äußerungen zur Werturteilsdiskussion im Ausschuß des Vereins für Sozialpolitik' [1913], quoted from E. Baumgarten (ed.), *Max Weber: Werk und Person* (Tübingen, 1964), pp. 115–16.
60   ibid., p. 117.
61   WL[3], p. 40; RaK, p. 89.

4 Max Weber and the Younger Generation in the Verein für Sozialpolitik

DIETER KRÜGER

If one views the development of Weber's works in the context of problems and controversies in modern social science one's interest becomes focused on one organization which, unlike many others, stamped the development of social science in Imperial Germany. Together with the Evangelical-Social Congress (Evangelisch-Sozialer Kongress) — though not founded before 1890 — the Verein für Sozialpolitik (Social Policy Association) holds a special position in the enormous number of cultured bourgeois institutions and associations which characterized this epoch.[1] The Verein was the manifest link between the dominant socio-scientific paradigm and socio-political conviction. Since the 1870s, the Historical School had emerged as the leading tendency in German political economy. The search for the laws of economic behaviour was replaced by the explanation of prevailing economic and social structures, as well as the interpretation of their perspectives in relation to their historical development. This concept came to dominate the academic discipline of *Nationalökonomie*. It was accompanied by the prevailing opinion among scholars and the cultured bourgeoisie that the outmoded institutional system should be amended in favour of an improvement in the situation of the working classes. Academic knowledge and socio-political convictions thereby legitimated and stimulated each other. Both were cultivated under the roof of the Verein: it was, on the one hand, an academic association with important research and publication programmes. Almost all younger scholars were academically 'socialized' by it. On the other hand, the Verein was a 'combat patrol of social reforms', that is, a platform for cultured bourgeois commitment to social reforms. In this capacity it appealed mainly to state and public opinion, backing its demands with academic authority. Since the turn of the century, however, the Verein had increasingly lost influence, after being highly noted before as a critical accompaniment to the government's social policy.[2]

The emergence of lobbies was largely responsible for this loss of influence. The public relations activities of pressure groups (based on propaganda departments which benefited from a sophisticated organization) were taking the place of the cultured bourgeois and the scholar as the dominant source of social interpretation. After 1890, the rapid expansion of university education also indicated a slow disintegration of the cultured bourgeoisie itself. A salaried class with university degrees replaced the traditional propertied amateurs. In combination with these external factors, four basic contradictions within the academic discipline of political economy became continually more opposed after the turn of the century. They led the Verein für Sozialpolitik into paralysis by the beginning of the First World War.

First, it was a question of the difference between a more social-liberal and a more social-conservative concept of social policy. This difference already marked the older generation, with Lujo Brentano and Karl Bücher in the former camp and Gustav Schmoller and Adolph Wagner in the other. Secondly, a generational conflict emerged between three groups: (1) the founders of the Verein, born between 1835 and 1850; (2) the second generation, born between 1855 and 1870 (Max Weber, Werner Sombart, Heinrich Herkner, Ferdinand Tönnies, Gerhart v. Schulze-Gävernitz, Walther Lotz, Carl J. Fuchs and others); (3) the third generation born after 1870 (Joseph Schumpeter, Arthur Spiethoff, Robert Wilbrandt, Leopold v. Wiese, Johann Plenge and others). Corresponding to a changing economic and political context, the respective younger generations tried to find new academic and socio-political paradigms. Because of this, the concepts of the previous generations were inevitably put in question. Eventually, around the turn of the century, a group of economists formed itself (Julius Wolf, Richard Ehrenberg, Ludwig Pohle, Andreas Voigt, Ludwig Bernhard and others) which radically called into question the socio-political accord existing between more liberal and more conservative social scientists. In addition, the increasing sterility of the historical method, which had difficulty in formulating theoretical tools, began to show. At the same time there was an increase in the specialization and heterogeneity of research interests, above all within the third generation.

Conceptions of Social Policy among the Second Generation

The discussion in the Verein, in 1890, in which the younger scholars of the second generation had to explain their position, seemed characteristic of the basic dissent mentioned above. Brentano criticized Bismarck's patriarchal social policy. Pointing to positive experience in England, he recommended reforms that were to support the organization of workers into trade unions. In his opinion, only in this way was it possible to realize the value of the commodity 'labour' in line with the market within a principally free-enterprise economic system. The quintessence of Brentano's conclusions was the free organization of inevitably antagonistic interests, with the aim of their peaceful settlement through wage agreements, instead of state repression. It was based on the British experience of trade unions. Britain's social order was the model according to which German conditions had to be shaped. Brentano was supported here especially by his students Herkner and Schulze-Gävernitz.

Not only did the representative of the Central Association of German Manufacturers (Centralverband deutscher Industrieller) criticize the (in his opinion) incorrect image of Britain and the demand for transfer of British institutions to Germany, but also Schmoller criticized this in the discussion in the Verein. He feared the emergence of 'terrorist' trade unions, on the one hand, and, on the other, of capitalist 'giant monopolies' combined with a total crushing of small- and medium-scale industry. In opposition to this, he supported co-operation between employers and workers controlled by the state. The workers' organizations should be formed according to the conditions in their respective trades. This corresponded to the conviction shared by the majority of senior economists that capitalist expansion should be curbed by state bureaucracy oriented to public welfare. Here, a gloomy picture was painted of a future, purely industrial nation in which a broad working class, possibly set on 'revolutionary action', was opposed to a small group of capitalist magnates. In contrast to that, the bureaucracy of the authoritarian state should seek to maintain a broad and politically loyal middle class, based on small businesses and agriculture.[3] In short, the liberal social reformers aimed at equal participation of workers in the 'free play of forces'. Their conservative colleagues, on the other hand, strived for restriction of the 'free play of forces' itself.

Besides Weber, virtually all representatives of the second generation – who took up senior university appointments in the 1890s – started their academic work under the influence of the Historical School, and they remained all their life in part committed to it in certain aspects of their work. The majority and the most important leaders, however, followed for the time being not Wagner's or Schmoller's conception of social policy but that of Brentano and Bücher. Bücher's commitment to social policy was indeed less spectacular than Brentano's. But, in his theory of economic stages, Bücher had already made an attempt to outline a theoretical concept of capitalist development.[4] In this, he anticipated the concern of the younger scholars to transcend the antagonism between Schmoller and Menger in their dispute about method.[5] In this sense, Bücher may have influenced Sombart, Max Weber, Spiethoff and Plenge. Bücher's political background was based as much on free-trade liberalism as was Brentano's. Max Weber recognized in him the 'head' of the younger economists.[6]

Initially, Brentano's students were totally influenced by him. In an early study on the cotton industry of Alsace, Herkner supported, to Schmoller's displeasure, the introduction of the right of association into the Imperial territory (*Reichslande*), whose patriarchal social order became the target of his criticism.[7] He considered the raising of the purchasing power of the masses by wage increases to be a solution to the problem of stagnating productivity combined with stagnating consumption. Higher wages he regarded as a possible means for stimulating technical progress and the transition to large-scale enterprise as well as to joint-stock companies. Referring to Britain, Herkner demanded free rights of association. Owing to the so-called *Arbeitswilligenschutz* (protection of non-strikers) and to legally non-binding associations (paragraphs 152, and 153 of the Imperial Trades Regulations), right of association was in fact subject to substantial restrictions in Germany. At the Verein, Herkner stressed that organizational parity of workers with employers would be the best method of reducing the revolutionary activities of the working class.[8] With his support of the dockworkers' strike in Hamburg in 1897, Herkner (and also Tönnies) drew practical conclusions from these convictions – at the expense of his career.

Backward small-scale industry, poor wages, oppression of the workers, low level of organization and prevalence of revolutionary convictions within the working class were features of backward capitalism in the opinion of Schulze-Gävernitz. While he considered this stage already overcome in Britain, he saw it still prevailing in Germany. The solution to the problem was seen by him in the combination of technological advance, transition to mass production and the development of trade unions. After all, organization of workers was the precondition for their collective agreement with employers, in the context of their shared interest in the prosperity of the various trades.[9]

Schulze-Gävernitz emphasized the element of mediation between capital and workers more than Schmoller's student, Sombart, who regarded competitive economic struggle as the nature of capitalist expansion. The right of association was for him the precondition for the successful struggle of workers with employers about the price of the labour commodity. Nevertheless, as he underlined before the Verein für Sozialpolitik in 1897, he always saw agreement to be the aim of wage conflicts. Basically he thought that social policy always meant class politics. Any society was characterized by the irreconcilable antagonism between emerging and decaying classes. Thus Schmoller's and Wagner's conception of social policy, aiming at redistribution of income, class reconciliation and control of capitalist development, was fundamentally wrong. Social policy should rather be oriented to the 'development of productive forces' and to the 'class representing economic advance'.[10] Concretely this meant to promote capitalist expansion to the maximum instead of curbing it. The struggle for social policy was class struggle led by workers against employers. In a speech to the Verein in 1899, Sombart made it perfectly clear that there was no place in this scenario for backward groups within the middle class.[11] Sombart's expectation that capitalism would evolve into a socialist order contrasted sharply with the convictions of the older social-liberal economists. A similar stance was taken also by Tönnies and later by Wilbrandt and Plenge.

According to Tönnies, capitalism had replaced former 'communal' relationships in predominantly rural societies by the principle of 'society'. With Max Weber, one might speak of the preponderance of instrumentally rational social relationships. Tönnies considered the working class to be the promoter of a new ideal of solidarity. He thought that a new co-operative organization on the basis of joint property would take the place of economic competition and class struggle. Thus, in Tönnies's opinion, social policy was tantamount to the support of trade unionism and, especially, of the co-operative movement. However, he also considered an advancing capitalism as the most effective trend towards socialism. In his view, this trend inevitably would lead to the nationalization of large-scale industry. On this point Tönnies agreed with Wagner, a state socialist, although unlike Wagner he assumed until 1914 a critical attitude to the Prussian state. Tönnies can be regarded as an early representative of a corporatism that oscillated between conservatism and socialism. During the First World War, such a point of view was to find a number of followers, among them Edgar Jaffé, Wichard v. Moellendorff, Paul Lensch (at that time a right-wing Social Democrat), Konrad Hänisch and others.[12]

In contrast to Sombart and Tönnies, Bücher's and Brentano's commitment aimed at realizing and stabilizing a liberal bourgeois social order by the integration of the working class. Though Brentano's students Herkner and Schulze-Gävernitz shared this aim, they soon took other paths to that of their teacher. In the early writings of Schulze-Gävernitz, it was already apparent that he did not consider as sufficient the institutionalization of the class struggle by collective bargaining and arbitration bodies. Conflicting social interests should rather reach agreement within an overarching ethical canon. In a way similar to the ethics of conservative *Kathedersozialisten* (academic socialists), Schulze-Gävernitz objected to classical liberalism and materialism in the last analysis as being both equally utilitarian. In contrast to that, Brentano's clear aims were always 'the greatest happiness of the greatest number' and the refinement of classical liberalism.[13] This liberalism, at once simple and practical, did not meet with much approval from economists of the second generation. Schulze-Gävernitz derived his ideas of social reconciliation from the classics of modern philosophy – Kant especially. However, he interpreted the teachings of German idealism in favour of social engineering and in an increasingly nationalist and imperialist spirit.[14]

As early as 1891, arguments for social reform, based on power politics, became noticeable in Herkner's ideas: 'The future belongs to the nation that has the best social relations among its citizens.'[15] With his first speech before the Verein on the problems of rural workers, Max Weber underlined this point of view. In his Freiburg Inaugural Address he called the struggle for power a normal relationship between nations. In order to make certain that Germany could stand up to this struggle, he demanded unrestricted promotion of capitalist development of industry combined with colonial expansion. Both required the integration of the working class, which could only be achieved by political and social reforms.[16] According to both the opinion of younger scholars and also of Brentano, there existed good prospects for eventually achieving this integration. Of course, the politically influential Junker class and the upper bourgeosie fought determinedly against any attempt at reform that could limit their considerable privileges. The Verein and individual academic advocates of social reform had to face constant attacks by persons representing large-scale industrial interests. Consequently, Max Weber sharply criticized the conservative elites.[17] Tönnies and Schulze-Gävernitz, in particular, followed him in this. With Max Weber, Schulze-Gävernitz became an advocate of liberal-social policy in connection with imperialist aggrandizement.

After the turn of the century, Schulze-Gävernitz tried to demonstrate that British free-trade capitalism was being replaced by a 'modern British' imperialism, motivated above all by ethics and no longer by pure economics as was the declining 'Manchesterism'. Schulze-Gävernitz predicted the transition of Britain to tariff protection and to the economic isolation of the Empire. For Germany, the practical consequences were as follows: promotion of large-scale capitalist development (especially of banks and joint-stock companies) as weapons in the peaceful economic struggle of nations; *Weltpolitik*, colonial expansion and naval rearmament as military and political complements; social and political reforms, aimed at winning over the working class by granting equal rights; reduction of the political influence of the Junker class, which was detrimental to both capitalist development and institutional reforms.[18]

Notable in this context is the changing use of 'model Britain'. If the reference to that economically successful and socially advanced nation served Brentano and the early Schulze-Gävernitz as a justification for liberal demands for reform, so did the recourse to Britain now justify imperialist modifications of the liberal concept. After Brentano had criticized his student's work, Schulze-Gävernitz consequently stated that they now followed divergent paths.[19] Actually the differences in opinion about the acclaim, which Schulze-Gävernitz orchestrated for Chancellor von Bülow's *Weltpolitik*, seemed also characteristic of the second basic difference – the generational conflict – in the liberal camp. In accordance with W. J. Mommsen's ideal-typical definitions, one could define the differences between Schulze-Gävernitz and Max Weber, on the one hand, and Brentano and Bücher, on the other, as the difference between 'liberal imperialism' and 'pragmatic anti-imperialism' of free traders.[20] Max Weber only found open to criticism in the imperialism of Schulze-Gävernitz the 'exaggeration of ideas which I also share'.[21] Between the two, who for a certain period taught at the same university in Freiburg, there existed, however, a rather reserved personal relationship. While in the opinion of Schulze-Gävernitz Weber believed too often in the 'power of the conference table', Weber for his part regarded Schulze-Gävernitz as 'clever' although he recounted 'the greatest trivialities with a voice shrouded in mystery'.[22] Schulze-Gävernitz appears, indeed, in many respects as the great simplifier of Weber's ideas. On the other hand, his inclination to passionate emotion and to rhetorical effect as well as his personal charisma during public appearances strengthened his influence on public opinion and on his students.

Certainly Max Weber did not share Sombart's or Tönnies's socialist visions – or, if so, then only in the form of the gloomy fiction of a bureaucratically paralysed society. Neither did Weber endorse Schulze-Gävernitz's philosophical views. Despite all differences, he nevertheless clearly formulated the basic aims of social policy shared by the majority of the younger economists: (1) modernization of the political and social system in favour of equal rights and integration of the working class; (2) unconditional acceptance of large-scale capitalist development in Germany. The second point expressed a differing position from a group within their own generation (Gustav Ruhland, Karl Oldenberg, Max Sering and Ludwig Pohle), which complied more with the political interests of large-scale landowners. This group, together with Adolph Wagner, proposed an artificial halt to Germany's development as an industrial state.[23]

Conflicts in the Verein für Sozialpolitik

These objectives of the younger generation were only approved with reservations by the majority of older economists, who regarded a monarchical and bureaucratic state, with the broadest possible agrarian basis, as guarantor against the paralysis of the Reich by class struggle. Their commitment to social reforms (often very courageous) had its limits in these objectives. This became visible in the cultured bourgeois campaign against the Subversion Bill (*Umsturzvorlage*) of 1895. On the initiative of Max Weber, Schulze-Gävernitz and Lotz, a statement was made that differed from the position of the older *Kathedersozialisten*. Its first version stressed 'retributive justice' and the necessity of 'sacrifices' by the ruling classes. In contrast to that, the second version underlined the fact that 'freedom of opinion and association combined with basic social reforms' worked 'for the interest of peaceful social development as well as economic advance'.[24]

The naval policy set up in those years met with the support of both tendencies (with few exceptions such as Tönnies!). With the expiry of the trade agreements signed under Caprivi and with Bülow's impending new customs tariffs, the following question was raised, however: would the navy become a military complement to a free-trade policy oriented to exports (as intended by Max Weber, Brentano, Schulze-Gävernitz and others) or a social-imperialist instrument in the hands of protectionist industrial and agrarian interests? This was the background of a dispute within the Verein für Sozialpolitik in 1901. In his speech, Lotz took Brentano's view entirely. In opposition to that, Pohle declared himself in favour of the joint protection of agriculture and industry. He wanted to 'maintain the right mixture of an agrarian and industrial state'; development towards an industrial nation depending on exports was to be retarded. Cautiously, Schmoller and Sering supported Pohle. Sering underlined the combination of customs tariffs with a compensatory social policy for the working class. In company with Heinrich Dietzel, Heinrich Sieveking and Eberhard Gothein, Schulze-Gävernitz also argued against protective tariffs. Industry oriented to exports alone could procure the means for naval rearmament. In a sharp polemic against Pohle, Alfred Weber expressed the common conviction of most of the younger economists that 'the future of our industry can only be in the production of finished goods'. In view of the strength of agrarian pressure groups in conjunction with heavy industry supporting protective tariffs, Friedrich Naumann expressed doubts concerning the hope of Sering (and in the end also of Schmoller) that it would be possible to balance the consequences of the tariffs by means of social policy.[25]

Naumann, with a political background in the Christian-Social movement, was supported especially by Max Weber, Brentano and Schulze-Gävernitz. The co-operation with Naumann was partly a reaction to the difficulties of working together on questions of social policy with the more conservative majority in the Verein. When, in 1896, Naumann founded the National Social Association (Nationalsozialer Verein), Max Weber and Schulze-Gävernitz especially pressed for a liberal-imperialist platform. The naval propaganda of the Association indeed found certain favour with the working class, whereas its social policy demands met with hardly any interest on the part of the bourgeoisie. The Association, with its old cultured bourgeois ideals, did not have any electoral success. Eventually Brentano and Schulze-Gävernitz supported its integration into the left-liberal Liberal Union (Freisinnige Vereinigung). Naumann became more and more a political spokesman for liberal social scientists and popularized their ideas through his writings.[26]

In 1905, because of his strong rhetoric, Naumann unexpectedly became the centre of a severe clash between the younger and older scholars in the Verein für Sozialpolitik. Already, in the debate about working conditions in large-scale industry, the younger generation (Naumann, Max Weber, Sombart) had radicalized their position, with Brentano leading the way. In particular, Max Weber attacked the authoritarian stance of German large-scale industrialists. Brentano's proposition to strengthen the relatively weak organization of workers in the face of the increasing power of large-scale industry by legal compulsory organization with obligatory negotiations, however, did not meet with Weber's approval. Schmoller regarded the capacity of the state to effectively force through public interest against individual interest as endangered by the increasing organization of industry into cartels. In addition to an office for the control and supervision of cartels, he proposed that in large joint-stock companies the state should occupy one-quarter of all mandates on the board of directors and the supervisory board. Beside Robert Liefmann and Theodor Vogelstein (who belonged to the youngest generation) and Lotz, the Weber brothers criticized Schmoller's 'strange ideas' (Alfred Weber). Both were afraid of the paralysing effect of the politicization of economic decisions. In their opinion, international competition was a major argument against limiting capital concentration. Max Weber blamed Schmoller for ignoring the reality of the present Prussian state. In fact, the civil servant oriented to public welfare who (according to Schmoller) should be a member of the managing board, hardly existed any more. On the contrary, Weber feared the sinecurism of political parties and lobbies. So did Naumann: in view of the government's *Sammlungspolitik*[27] he foresaw the defensive influence of agrarians and *Mittelstand*. Schmoller's suggestions seemed to him similar to plans by an 'association of small shopkeepers wanting to kill the department store'. Schmoller retorted by accusing the 'demagogue' Naumann of 'empty Marxist talk', without naming him personally. Finally, he threatened to resign the chairmanship of the Verein für Sozialpolitik, should the majority share Naumann's view. In response, Weber protested sharply.[28]

This meeting was followed by a fierce dispute fought out partly in public. Eventually, it could be settled, although the reason for the crisis, which was the different conception of social policy supported by the younger generation, had not been removed.[29] After all, however, in the liberal camp they shared the conviction that Schmoller was 'for the time being the only possible chairman'.[30] Should they really 'shift modestly to the left', as Georg F. Knapp, a rather conservative member and personal friend of Schmoller,[31] suggested, the danger could emerge that the Verein would break up. Schmoller stated that 'any change in the leadership can lead easily to a division into a left and a right wing. Some time ago, Pohle, Andr. Voigt had resigned their membership. I have prevented others from doing likewise ... Even Sering appears unbearably conservative to the Webers. But many other colleagues have a similar colouring. Conrad has been irritated for a long time. Even among Brentano's students rebellion prevails. Herkner is almost more conservative, more distant from Brentano than I am... If there remained only the left wing, Brentano, the Webers, Gothein, Sombart, the Verein would lose a considerable part of its political influence. Moreover, these are not the persons capable of producing good publications in which things are considered from every viewpoint.'[32]

In fact, even representatives of the younger generation had taken a conservative turn. This was true of Fuchs (who approved of Schmoller's propositions of 1905) and, above all, of Herkner. In the fifth edition of his standard work on social policy, *Die Arbeiterfrage*, he came to an assessment of the role of state bureaucracy that was practically identical to Schmoller's views. Even in the sixth edition, published during the First World War, he expressed himself cautiously in favour of the so-called protection for non-strikers, although its abolition was finally on the agenda.[33] At this point, Herkner also shared with Schmoller certain 'anti-industrialist and anti-capitalist feelings'.[34] After the clash of interests in 1905, he suggested the progressive shift of the Verein's concerns towards an academic perspective. Interest in social policy should recede into the background in favour of an erudite professional association. This victory over the formerly successful dual nature of the Verein was to take place under the auspices of Herkner after the First World War. Sombart's conservative development, too, started after the turn of the century. If, as recently as 1902, he did declare the profit impulse of capital to be the driving force of capitalist development, so now he increasingly broke with his Marxist attitudes. His commitment to social policy was rapidly replaced by elitist aestheticism. In his second edition of *Moderner Kapitalismus*, Sombart returned to a more historical method.[35] The conservative Berlin faculty supported this development by offering him the succession to Wagner's chair in 1916. On the whole, many younger scholars did not share any longer the more critical position of the Weber brothers in relation to social policy.

Thus the appearance of the brothers before the Verein in 1909 not only provoked later protests by Fuchs and Eugen v. Philippovich (in a letter to Schmoller)[36], but also Schulze-Gävernitz intervened during the meeting against the Weber brothers. In fact, he was now closer to the conservative scholars than before the turn of the century – in line with his great sympathy for Bülow and his conservative ethics. The dispute was stirred up again in connection with the question of how much the state should intervene in the economy. In view of the alleged favourable attitude, shared by the majority of the Verein, towards an extension of state- or community-owned enterprises, Alfred Weber made clear that he would expect a decline in personal initiative and political commitment in connection with an expansion of a state bureaucracy such as was much admired by the older generation. Contrary to Wagner's and Schmoller's ideal of the socially compensatory bureaucracy he defined the Prussian bureaucracy as 'a dependency of the ruling classes'. Like his brother, Max Weber declared that bureaucratization of the world was inevitable, due to the increasingly extensive organization of society. Unlike the majority of the Verein, he did not wish to speed up this development. Wagner, on the other hand, had stressed again the historical achievements of bureaucracy and had emphasized the reactionary attitude of employers.

Considering the development of German power, the Weber brothers demanded strict separation of economic and political spheres. The economic sphere should be freely subject to the laws of capitalist accumulation. In opposition to that, Schulze-Gävernitz was prepared to support nationalization, above all in order to finance the expensive naval policy. In consideration of the low ethical and cultural maturity of employers compared with civil servants, he did not share Weber's resentment against bureaucracy. He thought the reform of the Prussian electoral system to be more important.[37]

Indeed, supporters were won among the younger generation in favour of the demand for introducing the Imperial Electoral Law in *Länder* and municipalities, and partly even for a government responsible to a parliament. In contrast to this, conservative economists did not even accept the Imperial Electoral Law without reservations.[38] In the opinion of the younger generation, political reforms were necessary to ensure stronger control of a bureaucracy open to various influences by interest groups by-passing parliament. Moreover, as Max Weber, opposing Wagner, explained before the Verein in 1907, they expected from the political emancipation of the Social

Democrats the strengthening of the reform-oriented party bureaucracy that would later enter the municipal authorities of the big cities.[39] They expected that a practical establishment of the right of association as well as political emancipation would bring the labour movement from 'negative integration' to positive co-operation with the system.[40]

Blocking political commitment of scholars for these aims was not only a new reactionary campaign against social policy, which started by 1912, but also the unclear situation in the Verein. In 1911, Schmoller stated before the Verein that its previous dual nature had changed more and more in favour of a professional association.[41] Genuine agitation for social policy was now carried out by the Gesellschaft für soziale Reform [Society for Social Reform], founded in 1901. Brentano and other liberal social scientists did not play any important role here.[42] Although, as mentioned above, external developments endangered the once successful conception of the Verein, the Weber brothers brought the crisis to a head by their criticism of ideas associated with the authoritarian state, expressed by Schmoller, Wagner and others. Max Weber's criticism, repeated at several meetings of the Verein and also in his writings on methodology, of the combination of (socio-)political value-judgements with what should be scientific statements struck a nerve in the self-image of the *Kathedersozialisten*. In the last analysis, ethical and political convictions and academic positions formed here a scarcely separable unity, whose elements fed each other and indicated the road ahead. During the Verein's time of glory it was just this combination of social scientific interests with social policy that brought about its influence on public opinion. Max Weber's criticism of the Historical School, however, did not signify any radical break, because many of his ideas were rooted in questions raised by the Historical School itself.[43] Weber's demand for scientific statements and conceptions free from value-judgement was probably led by the intention (strictly speaking, in itself *also* political) to strip the aura of scientific objectivity from the demand for the preservation and support of the bureaucratic authoritarian state (if necessary at the expense of economic efficiency). To this extent, the conflicting situation in the Verein may have pushed Weber to formulate clearly his ideas on bureaucracy and on the methodology of the social sciences. But he did not meet with unanimous approval among the younger generation.

Divergencies among the Younger Generation

Although the younger social scientists succeeded in creating their own influential periodical with their *Archiv für Sozialwissenschaft und Sozialpolitik* (whose title shows that they wanted to stick to the successful combination), no joint activity was forthcoming. Like Schmoller, Max Weber was basically convinced that 'nine out of ten colleagues would shift to the right should the Verein be split up'.[44] Moreover, the generational conflict had its effects within this group, too.

In 1908, a break occurred between Brentano and Naumann. Characteristically enough, on this occasion Max Weber and Schulze-Gävernitz backed Naumann, who had not dissociated himself from Carl Peters, a colonial pioneer, in the way expected by Brentano. Brentano took this to be an affirmation of 'Pan-Germanism', of which Naumann had been suspected for some time.[45] Nor did Brentano agree to the anti-Polish policy of settlement in eastern Europe, which was supported by Naumann and Schulze-Gävernitz. When Naumann, in line with the Bülow bloc, voted for an Imperial Law of Association which proposed a new restriction in the liberty of association (language clause), Brentano, loyal to his own principles, could no longer co-operate with Naumann.

Faced with the new campaign against social policy and the isolation of Brentano after his break with Naumann, the idea of holding an important meeting on social policy emerged in circles around Brentano. Its organizational basis was planned to be among the 'leftists' of the Verein, who hoped to find a new enduring basis for an academic social policy along social-liberal lines. But the project failed because of three contradictions. As the supporters of protective tariffs and the opponents of social reforms were largely identical, Brentano intended to act against both groups. Yet it was precisely the problem of free trade on which a majority could not be established in the Verein. Max Weber rejected the combination of a commitment to the maintenance and extension of the right of association with trade issues. He believed that it was barely possible to find supporters for Brentano's position. Furthermore, the Weber brothers and Naumann had already cast doubt on Brentano's proposal to establish compulsory trade unions. Naumann stated that there was a 'strange degree of accord in Brentano's ideas with the advocates of state interventionism'.[46] As Brentano now even suggested legislation on wage regulation the conflict also loomed there. But, in the last analysis, what was decisive was the dispute concerning the invitation of Social Democrats to the planned meeting. Brentano, Tönnies and Wilbrandt had insisted on that, but Max Weber firmly rejected it. He regarded the meeting as political and, in order to ensure a broader public response, he wanted to refrain from inviting Social Democrats. Furthermore, he obviously still trusted in the capability of the bourgeoisie to deal with reactionaries within its own ranks. This again must have appeared to Brentano to be a repetition of the unclear situation in the Verein.[47]

Not only the dissent between Brentano and Weber but also the change of interests and opinions of the younger generation were to blame for the failure of the project. Thus Wilbrandt withdrew, as a majority against the co-operation with Social Democrats was to be expected, even though he was one of the representatives of that generation with the greatest interest in social policy. However, he also believed that any social policy in a capitalist society should primarily be guided by the profit interests of capital. With the early Sombart and with Tönnies, he shared the opinion that the organizational trend of modern capitalism would lead to socialism; one would have to choose 'between a socialism without competition or a capitalism without competition'. Like Tönnies, he envisaged a communal economy (*Gemeinwirtschaft*) organized on co-operative lines. The 'really powerful force capable of bringing about such an economy can only be the movement of the unpropertied classes themselves'.[48] Like Rudolf Goldscheid, who was little appreciated by Weber and Sombart, Wilbrandt regarded himself as a socialist and was closely associated with the Social Democrats.

Leopold v. Wiese, also interested in social policy, did not believe in any future for the co-operatives. The acquisitive drive was still the main economic impulse for him. But, at the same time, he wondered himself 'whether the old paths of social reform . . . continued to be the right ones'. As a result of the continuation of state social policy, he feared an 'increase of administrative power'. In his opinion the danger of 'splitting up into groups of trades and classes' loomed, if the working class took matters into their own hands by using the right of association. Unlike Wilbrandt, and agreeing on that point with the Webers, he considered 'the increasing of security rather than the growth of freedom' to be the 'tenet of social policy'.[49] Both positions show that agreement on maxims of social policy continued to wane in the third generation.

Johann Plenge's lack of interest in the meeting planned by Max Weber is also characteristic. Bücher's student, supported strongly by Max Weber himself, no longer had any special interest in social policy. On the contrary, he suggested to Max Weber a reorganization of the Verein into a pure body of experts (which came close to Herkner's ideas). This body was supposed to reflect primarily on a basic conception of the present and future world. Social policy would then be only one line of social sciences among many others.[50] If the second generation turned increasingly towards the search for theoretical conceptions of development, this was all the more true for the youngest generation. Issues of social policy and economic history were increasingly replaced by interest in economic and social theories. This was particularly true for Joseph Schumpeter, who nevertheless did not totally lose track of economic history with his *Theory of Economic Development*.[51] This work developed in the climate of a renewed interest in the theory of economic cycles and crises. Franz Eulenberg, Pohle, Schmoller's student Arthur Spiethoff and, to a lesser degree, Plenge gave important stimuli in this field. As early as 1903 the Verein discussed the problem of economic crises. The meeting became unusually theoretical, not least because of Spiethoff's paper.[52] This newly raised interest was reflected by the debates of the Verein in 1909, when many representatives of the youngest generation intervened (Othmar Spann, Otto Neurath, Otto v. Zwiedineck-Südenhorst). On this occasion, however, the discussion concerning value-judgements was already a strong factor in the debate.[53]

In 1913 the Verein called a committee session on the problem of value-judgement. Max Weber again demanded strict separation of scientific from political judgements. Problems concerning social policy, in particular, could not in his opinion be decided by scientific methods. Only the means for the realization of an aim, the probable consequences resulting from the application of these means and the existence of competing aims can be explained by science. Decisions concerning aims are made in the sphere of politics, not in that of science. Eulenburg followed Weber's ideas practically without modification. In his opinion, science could not formulate any instructions concerning action. In contrast to that, Oldenberg, mistrusting methodological considerations altogether, took the more traditional historical position. He regarded ethical value-judgement to be both the starting point for and driving force behind research in social science. Albert Hesse and Goldscheid believed such values to be inherent in the classification of empirical material according to cause and effect. Goldscheid was convinced that it was possible to work out scientifically cognitive interests that also would include ethical value-judgements. Wilbrandt and Wiese took an intermediate line. They held that, except in theoretical economics, value-judgements were necessary when assessing social and economic policy. One should nevertheless use them sparingly. Spann distinguished between nomothetic elements of cognition and elements related to values. The latter could either be oriented towards an organic conception, i.e. concerning the whole society, or towards an individualist conception aimed at maximal benefit for individuals.

On the whole, Weber's critical position met with a rather sceptical response among the younger generation. Weber made clear, however, that he was at least as much interested in the purity of science as he was in protecting politics against those academics who tried to lend scientific authority to their personal political convictions. Therefore, he demanded the elimination of value-judgements from academic teaching. The university teacher should not teach *Weltanschauung* but, as a specialist, should limit himself to professional lectures. Consequently, in his opinion *Menschenbildung*, the education of human beings in a broad and emphatic sense, had ceased to be the task of universities. By that he argued in favour of increasing professionalism, which was indeed developed strongly. No less shocking for many senior colleagues must have been his view that even the most profound expert knowledge of a professor did not give him any superiority in practical judgements. Both opinions diametrically contradicted the self-image of the *Kathedersozialisten*, who deduced from their academic qualifications and their ethic of conviction their claim to be those first heard by public opinion.

Weber was basically correct in maintaining that even if the Verein had propagated the validity of other standards of value than those of business profitability alone, it had never been capable of agreeing on one of the conflicting values. He was also right in insisting that, on principle, one should admit a plurality of views if one wanted to give a judgement as a university teacher. Actually Schmoller, influential in decisions concerning the appointments to economic chairs, had always rejected Marxists and followers of 'Manchesterism' as unqualified for such positions. Paradoxically, these statements reveal the implications for practical politics inherent in Weber's demand for the freedom from value-judgement. This political interest was only of second-rate importance to many younger members. Schumpeter's reaction in that context seems typical. He believed that the conflicting positions were far too exaggerated. He also fundamentally mistrusted the interest in 'practical ideas'. 'Judgement and interests' had to take second place when compared with the 'ideal of knowledge for knowledge's sake'.[54]

On the whole, interest in social policy decreased noticeably. It was often replaced by the commitment to new forms of teaching and research. The foundation of many commercial colleges (*Handelshochschulen*) with private funding, after the turn of the century, should be emphasized in this context. Many younger scholars were offered their first positions in such institutions.[55] At that time, specialized institutes such as the Institut für ostdeutsche Wirtschaft [Institute for East German Economy] and the Institut für Weltwirtschaft [Institute for International Economy] in Kiel were also founded. Plenge's plan to open, with the support of Westphalian heavy industry, an institute for the training of political economists oriented to practical problems failed mainly because of the outbreak of the First World War.[56] These developments indicated an increasing specialization and professionalism in the social sciences. With that, social policy gradually lost its leading role in the concern for an improvement of the situation of the working class, a concern that had been inspired by ethics, propagated by the bourgeoisie and legitimated by science. Social policy became a mere chapter within a comprehensive concept of social science as social theory. Now social policy was considered (for example, by Wiese or Zwiedineck-Südenhorst) as a subject and instrument of the struggle for power between social groups.[57]

The Opponents of Social Reform

In 1905, Bernhard Harms, also a member of the youngest generation, had supported Brentano's plans for compulsory membership of trade unions. During the prewar years he pleaded for a halt to social policy. This benefited his successful foundation of the Institut für Weltwirtschaft, since he resorted to private funds. Industry had been seeking for some time to exert influence on the appointment of professors to chairs in economics. In this, their practical interest was, on the one hand, to provide a more practically oriented training for future executives and, on the other, to diminish an unwelcome orientation towards social policy. A scientific criticism of the stance on social policy held by the older political economists could enhance one's chances of making a career in the context of campaigns against social policy and *Kathedersozialismus*: for example, as a 'punitive professor' who was appointed next to a professor committed to social policy. The camp of anti-*Kathedersozialisten* was increasing in size continually.

Julius Wolf, in 1897 appointed next to Sombart, was the first to represent this line of 'punitive professor'. He supported again the traditional position – which the Verein für Sozialpolitik had almost eliminated from universities – that high productivity combined with free competition would resolve the social problem automatically. He regarded social policy as a danger to economic productivity. Despite methodological differences, Ehrenberg followed him in his struggle against social policy. Ehrenberg looked for support (not least financially) from industrial circles to provide a planned academic institute; this met with determined resistance from the majority of economists. Industry, in turn, referred to him as a chief witness against academics in favour of social policy. In 1907, Pohle and Voigt resigned from the Verein. They had developed 'doubts', as Pohle wrote to Schmoller, 'about the way of dealing with economics, which led to the formulation of all kinds of demands concerning social policy'.[58]

Later, both sided with the camp of anti-*Kathedersozialisten*. They took charge of the *Zeitschrift für Sozialwissenschaft*, which had been successfully established by Wolf, and developed it into a renowned organ dedicated to theoretical interests and in which political ideas were avoided as much as possible. With this journal the dominance of those periodicals edited by *Kathedersozialisten* was put in question. The arguments 'of those pseudo value-free and tendentious elements backed by the determined partisanship of influential lobbies' (Max Weber)[59] became especially explosive, as these were in certain aspects identical with Weber's and Sombart's criticism of 'ethical economics'. Pohle blamed the majority of economists for having left 'the course of the unconditional discipline which pursues pure knowledge' and having descended 'to the level of political discussion'. The Verein, especially, pursued politics and not, as it pretended, science. Pohle defined the methods of investigation in economic policy in a similar way to Weber: description of the development of special problems, investigation of the consequences of political measures, explanation of the underlying principles of the measures, analysis of the standards of political judgement itself. Proceeding from the postulate that scientific research is free of value-judgements, Pohle described virtually all demands concerning social policy by *Kathedersozialisten* as being unscientific and motivated by politics alone, thus turning upside down the latters' claim that their position was one 'beyond politics' and related directly to the aim of public welfare. Finally, Pohle could also refer to the doubts concerning state social policy expressed by younger scholars (e.g. Wiese and Alfred Weber).[60] This criticism served as an academic accompaniment to the campaign of industrial and *Mittelstand* pressure groups in favour of a halt to social policy, which had started by 1912. The older *Kathedersozialisten* increasingly showed disconcertion when faced with the criticism of their younger colleagues, as this was similar to that of their sworn enemies. The foundation of a special organization did not seem to be advisable to most of the younger scholars, for the same reason. Max Weber was not at all interested in putting an end to academic social policy; on the contrary he wanted to give it new forms and meanings.

On the whole, Max Weber carried on the tradition of liberal academic social policy, while giving it an imperialistic emphasis. In this, he supported a position prevailing among the second generation of the Verein. His sharp criticism of the mainly conservative, older *Kathedersozialisten* was supported only with reservations by the youngest generation. He directed its members towards problems of economic theory. But this was connected with an increasing lack of interest among the third generation in traditional problems concerning social policy. Max Weber's criticism of the mixing-up of politics and science, which, by and large, was accepted by the majority of the youngest generation, was both a symptom of the crisis of traditional scholarly politics and an important contribution to this crisis. His criticism was adopted also by those social scientists who, as spokesmen of the emerging lobbies, worked against social policy. There remained less and less space for the traditional political commitment of scholars – with its claim for scientific objectivity, impartiality and orientation towards the public welfare. In so far as Max Weber experienced political isolation during the First World War, he also became a victim of this development.

Notes: Chapter 4

This chapter was translated by Leena Tanner.

1 On the relationship of scholars and public opinion see R. vom Bruch, *Wissenschaft, Politik und öffentliche Meinung. Gelehrtenpolitik im Wilhelminischen Deutschland (1890–1914)*

(Husum, 1980), with many further references. For the 'Evangelisch-Sozialer Kongress', see Chapter 13 by R. Aldenhoff in this volume.

2   On the history of the Verein für Sozialpolitik see M.–L. Plessen, *Die Wirksamkeit des Vereins für Sozialpolitik von 1872–1890* (Berlin, 1975); A. Müssiggang, *Die soziale Frage in der historischen Schule der Nationalökonomie* (Tübingen, 1968); D. Krüger, *Nationalökonomen im wilhelminischen Deutschland* (Göttingen, 1980). The most important work for the period discussed here still is: D. Lindenlaub, *Richtungskämpfe im Verein für Sozialpolitik* (Wiesbaden, 1967).

3   See 'Verhandlungen der Generalversammlung 1890 in Frankfurt/M.', in *Schriften des Vereins für Sozialpolitik*, Vol. 47 (Leipzig, 1890).

4   See K. Bücher, *Die Entstehung der Volkswirtschaft* (Tübingen, 1920).

5   See also H. Winkel, *Die deutsche Nationalökonomie im 19. Jahrhundert* (Darmstadt, 1977), pp. 138 ff.

6   Max Weber to Karl Bücher, 16 May 1910, Leipzig University Library, Bücher papers.

7   See H. Herkner, *Die oberelsässische Baumwollindustrie und ihre Arbeiter* (Strasburg, 1887).

8   See especially, H. Herkner, *Die Sociale Reform als Gebot des wirtschaftlichen Fortschritts* (Leipzig, 1891).

9   See G. v. Schulze-Gävernitz, 'Der wirtschaftliche Fortschritt, die Voraussetzung der sozialen Reform', *Archiv für soziale Gesetzgebung und Statistik*, vol. 5 (1892), pp. 1 ff.

10   W. Sombart, 'Ideal der Sozialpolitik', *Archiv für soziale Gesetzgebung und Statistik*, vol. 10 (1897), pp. 1 ff., especially p. 44.

11   See 'Verhandlungen der Generalversammlung 1899 in Breslau', in *Schriften des Vereins für Sozialpolitik*, Vol. 88 (Leipzig, 1900).

12   See F. Tönnies, *Gemeinschaft und Gesellschaft* (Leipzig, 1887, and 2nd edn 1912). See also A. Mitzman, 'Tönnies and German Society 1887–1914', *Journal of the History of Ideas*, vol. 32 (1971), pp. 507 ff.

13   L. Brentano, *Mein Leben im Kampf um die soziale Entwicklung Deutschlands* (Jena, 1931), p. 98, pp. 101–2.

14   See Krüger, *Nationalökonomen*, pp. 50 ff.

15   Herkner, *Sociale Reform*, p. 111.

16   See 'Verhandlungen der Generalversammlung 1893 in Berlin', in *Schriften des Vereins für Sozialpolitik*, Vol. 58 (Leipzig, 1893), pp. 62 ff; GPS[3], pp. 1–25.

17   See especially, W. J. Mommsen, *Max Weber and German Politics, 1890–1920* (Chicago, 1984), pp. 68 ff.

18   See G. v. Schulze-Gävernitz, *Britischer Imperialismus und englischer Freihandel* (Leipzig, 1906).

19   See Gerhart v. Schulze-Gävernitz to Lujo Brentano, 21 September 1906, Bundesarchiv Koblenz, Brentano papers.

20   See W. J. Mommsen, 'Wandlungen der liberalen Idee im Zeitalter des Imperialismus', in K. Holl und G. List (eds), *Liberalismus und das Problem liberaler Parteien in Deutschland 1890–1914* (Göttingen, 1975), pp. 109 ff., especially pp. 122–3.

21   Max Weber to Alfred Weber, 30 January 1907, Zentrales Staatsarchiv Merseburg, Max Weber papers.

22   Max Weber to Alfred Weber, 2 January 1895 (ibid.); Gerhart v. Schulze-Gävernitz to Lujo Brentano, 16 August 1895, Brentano papers (as in n. 19 above).

23   See K. D. Barkin, *The Controversy over German Industrialization 1890–1902* (Chicago, 1970).

24   See *Die Grenzboten*, vol. 54 (1895), nos. 6 and 11.

25   See 'Verhandlungen der Generalversammlung 1901 in München', in *Schriften des Vereins für Sozialpolitik*, Vol. 98 (Leipzig, 1902).

26   See Chapter 19 by Peter Theiner, in this volume.

27   'Refers to a defensive alliance of capitalists and landowners, convergent protectionist forces united by fear of foreign competition and democratic reform'. G. Eley, *Reshaping the German Right* (New Haven, Conn., 1980), p. 4 (editor's note).

28   See 'Verhandlungen der Generalversammlung 1905 in Mannheim', in *Schriften des Vereins für Sozialpolitik*, Vol. 116 (Leipzig, 1906).

29   See also Chapter 3 by Manfred Schön in this volume.

30   Lujo Brentano to Gustav Schmoller, 26 October 1905, Zentrales Staatsarchiv Merseburg, Schmoller papers.

31   Georg Friedrich Knapp to Gustav Schmoller, 1 February 1906 (ibid.).

32 Gustav Schmoller to Georg Friedrich Knapp, 30 January 1906 (ibid.).
33 See H. Herkner, *Die Arbeiterfrage*, 5th edn (Berlin, 1908), pp. 51 ff., and 6th edn (Berlin, 1916), Vol. 1, pp. 184 ff.
34 Heinrich Herkner to Gustav Schmoller, 21 October 1905, Schmoller papers (as in n. 30 above).
35 See W. Sombart, *Der moderne Kapitalismus*, 2nd edn, 4 vols (Leipzig, 1916–17).
36 See F. Böse, *Geschichte des Vereins für Socialpolitik 1872—1932* (Berlin, 1939), pp. 136–7.
37 See 'Verhandlungen der Generalversammlung 1909 in Wien', in *Schriften des Vereins für Sozialpolitik*, Vol. 132 (Leipzig, 1910). For the differences in Max and Alfred Weber's positions, see especially Chapter 5 by Eberhard Demm in this volume.
38 See Lindenlaub, *Richtungskämpfe*, pp. 393 ff.
39 See 'Verhandlungen der Generalversammlung 1907 in Magdeburg', in *Schriften des Vereins für Sozialpolitik*, Vol. 125 (Leipzig, 1908), pp. 294 ff.
40 See D. Groh, *Negative Integration und revolutionärer Attentismus. Die deutsche Sozialdemokratie am Vorabend des Ersten Weltkriegs* (Frankfurt, 1973).
41 See 'Verhandlungen der Generalversammlung 1911 in Nürnberg', in *Schriften des Vereins für Sozialpolitik*, Vol. 138 (Leipzig, 1912), pp. 1 ff.
42 See U. Ratz, *Sozialreform und Arbeiterschaft* (Berlin, 1980).
43 See also Chapter 2 by Wilhelm Hennis in this volume.
44 Max Weber to Lujo Brentano, 3 July 1912, Max Weber papers (as in n. 21 above).
45 Brentano, *Mein Leben*, p. 276.
46 F. Naumann, *Die Hilfe*, vol. 11 (1905), n. 41, p. 5.
47 See B. Schäfers, 'Ein Rundschreiben Max Webers zur Sozialpolitik', *Soziale Welt*, vol. 18 (1967), pp. 261 ff; Mommsen, *Max Weber and German Politics*, pp. 118 ff.; Krüger, *Nationalökonomen*, pp. 111 ff.
48 *Schriften des Vereins für Sozialpolitik*, Vol. 116 (as in n. 28 above), p. 334.
49 L. v. Wiese, *Einführung in die Sozialpolitik* (Leipzig, 1910), pp. 147, 201.
50 See Krüger, *Nationalökonomen*, pp. 116–17.
51 J. A. Schumpeter, *Theorie der wirtschaftlichen Entwicklung* (Leipzig, 1911).
52 See 'Verhandlungen der Generalversammlung 1903 in Hamburg', in *Schriften des Vereins für Sozialpolitik*, Vol. 113 (Leipzig, 1903).
53 See *Schriften des Vereins für Sozialpolitik*, Vol. 132 (as in n. 37 above).
54 See 'Äusserungen zur Werturteilsdiskussion im Ausschuss des Vereins für Socialpolitik', printed in manuscript (n.p., 1913).
55 See H. Kellenbenz, 'Handelshochschulen, Betriebswirtschaft, Wirtschaftsarchive', *Tradition*, vol. 10 (1965), pp. 301 ff.
56 See Krüger, *Nationalökonomen*, pp. 102 ff.
57 See O. v. Zwiedineck-Südenhorst, *Sozialpolitik* (Leipzig and Berlin, 1911).
58 See Böse, *Geschichte*, p. 125.
59 Max Weber, in Äusserungen zur Werturteilsdiskussion' (as in n. 54 above), p. 89.
60 See L. Pohle, *Die gegenwärtige Krisis in der deutschen Volkswirtschaftslehre* (Leipzig, 1911). On Ehrenberg, see also D. Lindenlaub, 'Firmengeschichte und Sozialpolitik', in K. H. Manegold (ed.), *Wissenschaft, Wirtschaft und Technik. Festschrift für Wilhelm Treue* (Munich, 1969), pp. 273 ff.

5 Max and Alfred Weber and the Verein für Sozialpolitik

EBERHARD DEMM

From childhood onwards Max and Alfred Weber had a very close, although often tense relationship, and frequently collaborated on many political and intellectual questions.[1] This collaboration occurred particularly within the Verein für Sozialpolitik. I would like first of all to describe the standing of the two brothers in the Verein and then, using a convenient authentic example, to discuss in detail their method of collaboration.

The Verein für Sozialpolitik (Social Policy Association), founded in 1872, disapproved of both revolutionary socialism and the *laissez-faire* liberalism of classical political economy. It endorsed legislative interventions by the state into the economy, which would benefit the common good rather than selfish class interests and, above all, take the edge off the social question through economic and social emancipation of the working class. The Verein organized and financed extensive investigations into the most important economic and social issues of its time and tried, through discussion of the existing deplorable state of affairs, to influence public opinion and give the necessary impetus to legislation.[2]

Within the Verein there were three main trends, represented by the long-serving President, Gustav Schmoller, and Professors Adolph Wagner and Lujo Brentano. Wagner, although he was comparatively isolated and even resigned from the Verein from time to time, styled himself a 'state socialist' and demanded nationalization of the most important branches of industry, banks and transport companies.[3] Schmoller advocated above all a comprehensive state social policy, which would win workers over to the state and bourgeois society. Brentano, who considered Germany's social policy both authoritarian and undemocratic, was in favour of separating the state and social reform. Abolition of laws and regulations against trade unions would mean that workers gained the opportunity of shaping their futures freely and independently.[4]

Since the turn of the century a younger generation of political economists had begun to participate in these debates. Among them were not only Gerhart von Schulze-Gävernitz, Werner Sombart, Ferdinand Tönnies and Robert Wilbrandt, but also Max and Alfred Weber. The Weber brothers stood out as the socio-political avant-garde of the Verein, and were once described by Schmoller as the 'stimulus and catalysts of our meetings'.[5] Alfred Weber later said repeatedly that his brother and Werner Sombart were 'indisputably both in personality and practical ability the leaders of the younger members, superior to all the others',[6] and there is no reason to doubt this verdict. This is not to say that Alfred was overshadowed by his brother in the Verein; indeed, a look at the minutes shows that he was actually more prominent in the talks and discussions at general meetings than was Max.[7] Alfred Weber had also taken on numerous organizational and editorial duties in the Verein.[8] To a certain extent, the disputes over the direction of the movement were aggravated by this younger group of scholars. The Webers and their friends criticized in particular the political conservatism, the naive mixing of scientific understanding with ethical value-judgements, and the more subjective rejection of Marxist socialism that was characteristic of some of their older colleagues. These disagreements soon came very close to splitting up the Verein.[9] We should not speak over-hastily of a generational conflict here, however, since the contradictions cross-cut the generations; nor should we allow these conflicts to make us lose sight of the common interests fundamental to the Verein. Both Webers, like most other members of the Verein, were convinced that social reform was necessary. They thus presented a united front against other young economists, such as Richard Ehrenberg or Julius Wolf, who were very much in favour of business enterprise and against reform.

The brothers had both studied under leading representatives of the Historical School of political economy — Max Weber with Karl Knies, Alfred with Gustav von Schönberg and Schmoller. This school was not only committed to historical method, as its name suggests, but also devoted explicit attention to social problems — a fact that is often forgotten. Wilhelm Hennis has provided evidence of similarities between Knies and Max Weber in this respect.[10] Schmoller, once referred to by his pupil Heinrich Herkner as 'one of the greatest sociologists there are',[11] was also interested from an early stage in social trends and the psychological basis of economic phenomena. In 1893 he was already predicting that 'political economy ... will have to transform itself into a social science'[12] and, in his *Grundriß der Volkswirtschaftslehre* [Outline of Political Economy], he treated sociological themes such as, for example, the class structure of society.[13] Schmoller was in no doubt that his pupils would adhere to the lines of the historical school. In a fundamental article on political economy in the *Handwörterbuch der Staatswissenschaften* [Concise Dictionary of Political and Social Science], he wrote in 1911: 'the vast majority of contemporary German political economists, now gathered together in the Verein für Sozialpolitik, founded in 1872, are making progress towards establishing their aims, position and method with reference to the above-mentioned general texts'.[14] (In addition to other texts, he had just reviewed his own *Grundriß*.) The Weber brothers are also among the individually named representatives of this school.[15] In fact, when he was a young lecturer in Berlin, Alfred Weber had emphasized his own intellectual independence from Schmoller, his doctoral supervisor, by openly adopting the opposing position of marginal utility theory as represented by Menger and Böhm-Bawerk.[16] In his work, *Theory of the Location of Industries*[17] however, he attempted to find a synthesis between the two schools, and in his essays on cultural sociology he reverted once more to a historical orientation.

In their basic social and political orientation, the Weber brothers were closer to Brentano than to Schmoller. In a letter on the occasion of Brentano's sixtieth birthday, Alfred Weber described him as 'the inspiration of my youth ... even from afar ... the patron of my adulthood... Among the whole great generation that went before me, I have actually only ever felt close to you.'[18] Numerous agreements in the work of the two scholars are indeed to be found, both in their scientific concerns and political tendencies. The same holds true for Max Weber. The Weber brothers did not merely adopt Brentano's theory of workers' organizations as the bearers of social reform, but also fought for the same goals as he did: for free trade against protectionism, for spontaneity in social progress, against excessive cartelization, against increasing bureaucracy in political life, against 'yellow unions', the so-called 'protection of non-strikers', and against the political and economic power of the Prussian Junkers.[19] Alfred and Max Weber also held the same fundamental political beliefs as Brentano: they were members of Friedrich Naumann's National Social Association (Nationalsozialer Verein) and favourably disposed to Social Democracy. The Weber brothers and Brentano were also involved in the same campaigns within the Verein für Sozialpolitik. Brentano's suggestions and influence, openly recognized by Alfred Weber, were certainly important to Max Weber as well.

One of the most important issues to concern Max and Alfred Weber before the First World War was the increasing encroachment of personal freedom by the large and expanding industrial concerns in Germany. Schmoller remarked on this as early as 1890 at a meeting of the Verein für Sozialpolitik, when he said: 'huge monopolies on the one hand, and, on the other, a self-contained working class that will probably become hereditary in time ... a large proportion of today's competition and a large proportion of today's industrial freedom will simply vanish.'[20] With these words, he formulated the whole question concerning the position of workers and salaried employees in modern large-scale industry. From 1908–11 there was a wide-ranging investigation by the Verein für Sozialpolitik, in which the Weber brothers played a prominent part. This inquiry may be used here to demonstrate in detail how Max and Alfred Weber worked together and where their intellectual positions concurred or differed.

In the course of his researches into home-based industry, Alfred Weber had already been confronted with the effects of work on the working population's mental and physical health. He criticized in harsh terms that 'the health of the German working class in today's forms of production within home-based industries is being destroyed by overwork, undernourishment and filth'.[21] This problem continued to interest him. In a lecture in Vienna in 1902 he demanded 'protection for the capacity for work', i.e. measures to increase the workers' efficiency by improving working conditions, and called for higher wages, a shorter working day and cheap food and accommodation, as well as adequate education.[22] While teaching in Prague, he was interested in the handing on of acquired characteristics, public health and 'degeneration'.[23] Poor working conditions, which damaged the workers' health, were a problem belonging to this complex of issues, for they affected the next generation also and, for example, impaired the ability to do military service. In 1905, after previous consultation with Brentano, Alfred Weber proposed to the Verein für Sozialpolitik an investigation into the problems of degeneration, but his motion appears to have been rejected. When he was invited to take up a chair at Heidelberg in 1907, he decided the time had at last come to begin a research project on this subject. He talked first to his brother about it. Max had obviously already had similar ideas, for in a letter written on 3 September 1907, he puts forward various recommendations for an investigation of 'mental work in modern large-scale industry', in which he wanted to include for consideration the type of skilled labour chosen, job opportunities and job changes.[24] He refers to corresponding suggestions made by Alfred and promises to support Alfred's interest in the degeneration question in the Verein, and to involve himself in it personally. A few weeks later, Max Weber did recommend the project to the Verein's president, Schmoller, and gained his consent. The decisive meeting of the managing committee took place in Magdeburg on 29 September. First of all, an application by the absent Brentano to conduct a systematic investigation of 'degeneration' was dismissed, as this appeared to the members of the committee to be too difficult. Following this, Herkner and Alfred Weber formulated the title 'industry and workers', and Schmoller suggested this should include an analysis of the life histories of workers employed in industry.[25] It was Alfred Weber, however, who finally determined the main subject areas of the investigation: (i) the mental, physical and psychological demands made on the worker by large-scale industry and (ii) the changes in personality undergone as a result.[26] Finally a sub-committee was set up, led by Karl Bücher and including the Weber brothers, Schmoller, Herkner and seven other economists. The Weber brothers took over most of the work involved in preparing the investigation. Alfred drew up a research plan and constructed a questionnaire, guided by a conviction, held since his Prague days, that the concepts and methods of natural science should be adopted by economics, and he demonstrated this by using Darwin's terms 'adaptation' and 'selection'.[27] He had been a convinced Social Darwinist since his student days, but advocated a democratic variant of this theory.[28] Naturally, he often discussed the planned project with his brother, but Max was much more sceptical about the methodological possibilities.[29] On the other hand, he paid far more attention to this aspect than did Alfred: he contacted the psychologist Emil Kräpelin, one of Wilhelm Wundt's pupils, who had already done some research into the symptoms of exhaustion among workers, and examined the possibility of using Kräpelin's experimental method in the Verein's inquiry. With direct reference to Alfred Weber's research outline and his terminology, Max wrote a detailed methodological study, entitled 'Data concerning selection and adaptation (choice of job and its prospect) among the workforce in large, self-contained industrial enterprises'.[30] Here, and in a further article on the psycho-physics of industrial work, he drew upon the statistical documents of Carl David Weber's, his late uncle's, textile factory in Oerlinghausen. He further attempted, albeit in vain, to collaborate with Adolf Levenstein, who was setting up a similar investigation at the same time.

The sub-committee of the Verein für Sozialpolitik met in Eisenach on 13 June, where the Weber brothers were conspicuous for the great number of suggestions they put forward. They dominated the debate to such an extent that Schmoller facetiously suggested that their talking time be limited to fifty-five minutes per hour at the next meeting. From the memoirs of another member of the committee, Otto von Zwiedineck-Südenhorst, the surviving questionnaires and Max Weber's methodological study, we can see that, in spite of their close collaboration, the two brothers had very different objectives. Alfred Weber was interested above all else in the personal fate of the worker, his motives in choosing a particular job, or changing it, and the difficulties he experienced during his working life.[31] Max, on the other hand, was primarily concerned with worker productivity in the capitalist production process. This is why he mainly discussed issues concerning the psycho-physics of work, e.g. symptoms of exhaustion, statistics relating to the intensity of work and its correlation with working conditions, consumption of alcohol, dietary habits – so thoroughly in fact that he was recently accused of putting the Verein's inquiry directly at the service of the capitalist state.[32] However, since his report is explicitly based on Alfred's drafts and he also quotes him verbatim, we find passages in the final section of his work that are far more typical of Alfred's orientation: the psychological adaption of the worker to conditions in industrial production, his leisure interests and the pattern of his working career.[33]

Until now, these pages have been held to reflect Max Weber's beliefs only, but the fact that such ideas occupy a rather isolated position in his *oeuvre* is in itself suspicious. Nowhere is the human being the focal point of his discussion – neither in his research into psycho-physics, nor in his comments at the congress of the Verein für Sozialpolitik in Nuremberg in 1911, which refer only to methodology, during discussion of the results of the inquiry; nor in his later investigations of bureaucracy. Rather, he concentrates solely on bureaucratic and economic constraints and structures. So we must conclude that it was Alfred Weber who inspired the relevant passages in the report. Originally, it seems, evidence of the brothers' collaboration was to be provided by the signatures of both at the end, for, in a letter written on 19 September 1908, Max Weber informs his brother that finally he alone has now signed.[34] In recognition of Alfred's contributions, Max stresses in his introduction that his work is based on a circular sent out by his brother and frequently draws on the results of discussions with him.[35] But since this introduction was omitted from the reprint of the report in Max Weber's *Gesammelte Aufsätze zur Sozialpolitik*, Alfred Weber's assistance has been forgotten. Some obscurities do remain, however, since Max Weber does not explain which points in the report originate from his brother. We will consider this in further detail later on.

At the second meeting of the sub-committee on 11 October 1908 (on Bücher's resignation, Alfred Weber, Herkner and Schmoller had jointly taken over the chairmanship), final decisions about the practical work were made. The researchers engaged to undertake the investigation were to receive the following to assist them: Max Weber's description of the method; a schedule drawn up in earlier discussions of the sub-committee; various points listed by Alfred Weber and Herkner; the questionnaire that Alfred Weber had conceived and revised a number of times.[36] The interviewing of the workers took place from 1908 to 1911, and the results were published between 1910 and 1912 in six volumes of the series published by the Verein für Sozialpolitik.[37] A good example of the method they used is an investigation by Marie Bernays into 'selection and adaption among the workers in large, self-contained industrial enterprises, based on conditions in the Gladbach spinning and weaving company in Mönchen-Gladbach'. Her work is especially valuable to us because it offers detailed information about the Weber brothers' differing areas of interest. For, as she explains in her introduction, Marie Bernays was guided in the first part of her work by Alfred Weber, at a time when the completed questionnaires had not yet been printed; for the second part of her investigation, she received suggestions and advice from Max Weber.[38] In the first section, inspired by Alfred Weber and entitled 'Choice of occupation and conditions of employment of the working class', Marie Bernays examined the workers' social and geographical origins, their employment in relation to age, the course of their working lives, and the significance of marriage and family. The second part, supervised by Max Weber and entitled 'On the psycho-physics of work in the textile industry', shows how profitable its workers were for the company, above all when correlated with the findings of the first section. The influence of age, origin, family status, living conditions and even the seasons on the industrial workers' performance were all analysed.[39]

This, then, is clear evidence of the Weber brothers' differing concerns. Max Weber is interested in the psycho-physics of work, Alfred in the workers themselves and their problems. Our assumption that the last pages of Max's report are based on suggestions made by Alfred and do not represent the interests of the older brother himself is borne out by Marie Bernays' investigation.

Why is the Verein's inquiry so significant? Not necessarily because it deals with those particular questions, for similar issues had already been examined in other investigations – the workers' biographies written on Paul Göhre's initiative, for example, or in Ernst Abbé's studies of the effects of shorter factory working hours. Rather it is the use of a strict empirical method, based on Kräpelin's experimental psychology, that breaks new ground and makes the Verein's inquiry stand out from similar contemporary projects, including the simultaneous investigation by Adolf Levenstein.[40] Since Levenstein's work has been overestimated and directly pitted against the Verein's inquiry,[41] a brief comparison of Levenstein's and Bernays's work would seem appropriate at this point.

Levenstein sent to eight thousand workers a questionnaire with a total of twenty-six questions relating to their psychological attitude to work, their social expectations, and their leisure interests. This covers fewer areas than the Verein's questionnaire with its twenty-five questions, but Levenstein deals in greater detail with the workers' enthusiasm for their jobs, and their mentality. As Bernays pointed out in her review of Levenstein's book, the responses, each one clearly written up, provide a 'treasure trove for the psychology of work'.[42] The methodology applied and the scientific evaluation of the material have several failings, however. Marie Bernays spent a number of weeks working in the factory she had chosen, to gain the workers' trust, and then asked them questions in person. Levenstein contented himself with sending out question-naires, sometimes via a third person, and letting the workers complete them themselves. Various percentages are incorrectly calculated in Levenstein's report[43] and, except for age and wage brackets, he does not generally note any of the correlations so frequent in Bernays's report. The subjective descriptions given by the workers of symptoms of exhaustion, for example, were not checked by exact measurements, which Bernays did.[44] Although Levenstein quotes the workers' responses word for word, which makes his work fascinating to the modern historian, the analytical assessment, so admirably executed in Bernays's work, is of a more descriptive nature, the results are hardly related to each other, and the whole thing is very short. From a total of 406 pages, 340 pages are devoted to reproducing the responses and 66 pages to an analysis that is endearingly unscientific in approach, compared with Frau Bernays's report. The promised 'general overview' entitled 'technology and emotional life' never appeared.

This brief comparison demonstrates the methodological advances that the Verein's inquiry had made in empirical social research, thanks to the Weber brothers' combined talents. At the general meeting of the Verein in 1911, Ludwig Sinzheimer recognized the inquiry as 'a major scientific advance' — a description that is indeed justified. [45]

When the findings of the inquiry were discussed by the Verein at its general meeting in Nuremberg on 10 October 1911, the differing interests of the two brothers were demonstrated yet again. While Max Weber commented particularly on methodology, referring to Kräpelin's method among others, Alfred Weber drew special attention to career problems experienced by industrial workers. In contrast to professional careers, where the best positions are often reached after the age of forty, a manual worker is so exhausted and worn out by the time he reaches this age that he either retires altogether from the working process, or sinks into badly paid jobs. [46] In order to make working in industry emotionally healthier, Alfred Weber called for an additional pension for older workers, but this proposition met with opposition from his colleagues. In later lectures and publications, Alfred Weber repeatedly focused on the worker's alienation in the modern production process and on his passive, totally ruined existence as a 'Promethean slave, chained in place by the capitalist machine'. [47] He suggested several ways of humanizing the working environment and by so doing, encouraging the development of the individual. This does not mean that Max Weber would have dismissed possible reforms in this area, for he certainly favoured a liberal social policy but, as Jürgen Kocka has shown, not for reasons of charity or sympathy. For him, it was a necessary domestic complement to a successful *Weltpolitik*. [48]

It is noticeable that several speakers at the Nuremberg general meeting mentioned Max Weber's contribution to the conception and execution of the inquiry, whereas Alfred Weber found no such recognition. The reason for this is that, although Alfred Weber provided the decisive intellectual impetus and made suggestions about the method to be adopted, it was Max Weber who, unlike his brother, was free from teaching commitments and, therefore, could play a more prominent part in following the inquiry through.

A similar situation is found in another of the brothers' research projects, on bureaucracy, which is closely related to the industrial worker inquiry. Unfortunately, however, in this case the stages of their collaboration cannot be traced in such detail. Suffice it to say that discussions on that theme did take place — with Friedrich Naumann among others. From 1904 onwards, Naumann had raised the question of how each individual's independence could be preserved in large-scale factories. [49] Max Weber had already worked on the historical dimension of bureaucracy, whereas Alfred probably became more interested in it as a result of the industrial worker inquiry. We may assume this because, in a memorandum to the Verein's sub-committee, he stressed the fateful significance of the 'machine' (*Apparat*) in the organization of large-scale industrial production. Later, he applied the same term to state bureaucracy. [50] At a meeting of the Verein für Sozialpolitik in Vienna in 1909, Alfred Weber made a widely noted speech, in which he sharply attacked colleagues who exalted state and bureaucracy in emotive terms and ascribed to them a position of authority over human beings. He conceded the outstanding mechanical efficiency of bureaucracy, which makes it totally indispensable for running the state and large business concerns, but warned of the psychological consequences — 'our entire society is being rendered narrow-minded and philistine', 'threatens to stifle any independent intellectual stirrings' and creates a new type of human being who is 'German, loyal and pensionable'.[51] Here, of course, he is criticizing the 'state metaphysics' of colleagues such as Schmoller and Wagner, and it is not surprising that almost all members of the Verein strongly opposed him. The only speaker who supported him without any reservations and agreed emphatically with his views was Max Weber.[52] Upon closer examination, however, a difference in the real object of their criticism is apparent. Alfred Weber thought that bureaucracy threatened the development of strength (both physically and mentally) by the population, whereas Max Weber criticized bureaucracy above all for endangering the growing political power of the German Reich.[53] Here, as in the industrial worker inquiry, the differing interests of the two brothers are clearly visible. Max is interested first and foremost in the theory of bureaucratic domination and the political and economic assertion of state power. Alfred's most pressing concern is the individual and his or her relief from social, economic and political pressures.

The common denominator that most readily enables us to summarize the discussion about bureaucratization and the situation of workers in large-scale industry, and by which we can place it in intellectual context, is the concept of alienation. It can be defined in its broadest sense as the problem that occurs when forms of organization created by man become an independent 'machine', controlling and de-humanizing life itself.[54] With this, the Weber brothers are following a long tradition of European thought, which began with Rousseau and German idealism; the individual, who in the natural state is free to develop his or her personality autonomously, loses this freedom as a result of the development of political institutions and the division of labour, with which alienation and inequality begin.[55] Marx saw class antagonism and capitalist property relations as the primary sources of alienation and hoped, by removing private ownership of the means of production, to reinstate the freedom and humanity that had been lost. The Weber brothers, by contrast, saw the omnipotence of bureaucratic power structures as the decisive factor and, for this reason, they did not expect socialization to bring any redress.[56] Even so, there are considerable divergences in their assessment of this phenomenon, which stem from their fundamentally different outlooks on life.

Alfred Weber in his own synthesizing and eclectic manner merged idealist and liberal traditions with elements of *Lebensphilosophie*. In agreement with idealist thinking, he held the highest goal of man to be an all-round self-realization achieved through creativity. As a liberal, he wanted to maintain the freedom of the individual against the state and, like Friedrich Naumann and others, he also turned this demand against bureaucratic organization of industry. In accordance with *Lebensphilosophie*, he demanded that ultimate priority should be given to experience, the *élan vital*, and to developing the ability to create. These would counter the objectivizing process of civilization (rationalization in Max Weber's terminology) in areas of state and economy.[57]

According to his principles of cultural sociology, individuals should be able to develop spontaneity and creativity freely in the cultural movement, against the constraints imposed by the civilizing process. In order that this might become possible for the broader masses, rather than the selected few, ways must be found of reinstating individual autonomy in the modern production process, and changing work from being a factor for capitalist exploitation into a factor for developing the individual personality.[58]

Max Weber's outlook on life is far harder to define. The neo-Kantianism with which he is commonly identified is scarcely sufficient as an explanation. He clearly does not share his brother's ultimately optimistic view that the personality of what Alfred later came to term 'Man Mark III' (*Der dritte Mensch*), oriented towards freedom and autonomy, could still be maintained in modern society. Max Weber is resigned — indeed, fatalistic — and sees no way out of the cage of modern bureaucratic serfdom. To us, he seems to embody a modern point of view that might perhaps be called functionalism, which accepts the absolute inevitability of constraints determined by organization and profitability. Compared with him, Alfred Weber held an idealistic liberal position, which valued person above institution, an attitude that is still part of the liberal credo today, although in many cases it appears inadequate when actually enforced and indeed is only developed consistently in fringe groups with an alternative lifestyle. The discrepancy between the two attitudes, one of them, in Karl Mannheim's terminology, a conservative position that clung to what existed already and was averse to anything 'possible' or 'speculative', and the other a progressive stance, consciously aware of the possible and perhaps even of Utopia,[59] today still influences discussions about the status of human beings in modern industrial society.

Notes: Chapter 5

This chapter was translated by Caroline Dyer.

1   E. Demm, 'Alfred Weber und sein Bruder Max', *Kölner Zeitschrift für Soziologie und Sozialpsychologie*, vol. 35 (1983), pp. 1–28.

2   H. Winkel, *Die deutsche Nationalökonomie im 19. Jahrhundert* (Darmstadt, 1977). pp. 159 ff.; D. Lindenlaub, *Richtungskämpfe im Verein für Sozialpolitik* (Wiesbaden, 1967).

3   ibid., p. 95; Winkel, *Die deutsche Nationalökonomie*, pp. 130 ff.; F. K. Ringer, *The Decline of the German Mandarins: The German Academic Community, 1890–1933* (Cambridge, Mass., 1969), p. 148.

4   Lindenlaub, *Richtungskämpfe*, p. 204; W. Krause and G. Rudolph, *Grundlinien des ökonomischen Denkens in Deutschland 1848 bis 1945* (Berlin, 1980), p. 103; J. J. Sheehan, *The Career of Lujo Brentano: A Study of Liberalism and Social Reform in Imperial Germany* (Chicago and London, 1966), pp. 40, 54.

5   E. Salin, 'Alfred Weber', in idem, *Lynkeus. Gestalten und Probleme aus Wirtschaft und Politik* (Tübingen, 1963), p. 62.

6   A. Weber, 'Werner Sombart zum 70. Geburtstag', *Frankfurter Zeitung*, no. 49/50, 19 January 1933.

7   Max Weber's contributions at the general meetings of the Verein add up to about 52 printed pages, while those of Alfred Weber reach a total of 57 pages. Calculated from the relevant bibliographies: for Max Weber the one compiled by M. Riesebrodt in H. Baier *et al.*, *Prospekt der Max-Weber-Gesamtausgabe* (Tübingen, 1981); for Alfred Weber J. Kepeszczuk

(comp.) *Alfred Weber: Schriften und Aufsätze 1897–1955. Bibliographie* (Munich, 1956). A supplementary bibliography is to be found in E. Demm (ed.), *Alfred Weber. Politiker und Gelehrter* (Stuttgart, 1986).

8 For example, organizer and editor of the inquiry into domestic industries, organizer of the debates on the question of cartelization (1905), co-organizer of the inquiry into the selection and adaptation of the work force in large-scale industry.

9 Cf. D. Krüger, *Nationalökonomen im wilhelminischen Deutschland* (Göttingen, 1983), pp. 76 ff.; Lindenlaub, *Richtungskämpfe*, pp. 272 ff.; W. J. Mommsen, *Max Weber and German Politics, 1890–1920* (Chicago, 1984), pp. 118 ff.

10 See Chapter 2 by Wihelm Hennis in this volume. Biographical data on Alfred Weber's education and professional training can be found in the Alfred Weber papers, deposited at the Bundesarchiv Koblenz.

11 H. Herkner, 'Gustav Schmoller als Soziologe', *Jahrbücher für Nationalökonomie und Statistik*, vol. 118 (1922), p. 3.

12 G. Schmoller, 'Die Volkswirtschaft, die Volkswirtschaftslehre und ihre Methode' [1893], in idem, *Über einige Grundfragen der Socialpolitik und der Volkswirtschaftslehre* (Leipzig, 1898), p. 283

13 idem, *Grundriß der allgemeinen Volkswirtschaftslehre*, 4th edn (Leipzig, 1901), Vol. 1, pp. 391 ff.

14 idem, 'Volkswirtschaft, Volkswirtschaftslehre und ihre Methode', in *Handwörterbuch der Staatswissenschaften*, 3rd edn, Vol. 8 (Jena, 1911), p. 448.

15 ibid.

16 A. Weber, 'Die Jugend und das deutsche Schicksal. Persönliche Rückblicke und Ausblicke', in E. Kern (ed.), *Wegweiser in der Zeitwende* (Basel and Munich, 1955), p. 60. See also his letter to Georg Jellinek of 24 December 1907, where he deplores 'the dreadful platitudes to which the historical school . . . has ultimately led us'. Bundesarchiv Koblenz, Jellinek papers.

17 A. Weber, *Über den Standort der Industrien. Teil I. Reine Theorie des Standorts* (Tübingen, 1909). An English translation was published in Chicago in 1929.

18 Alfred Weber to Lujo Brentano, 16 August 1928, Bundesarchiv Koblenz, Brentano papers, no. 66.

19 See, for wide-ranging surveys of these issues, Sheehan, *The Career of Lujo Brentano*, pp. 122, 127 ff., 134 ff., 139, 159, 171; and Mommsen, *Max Weber and German Politics*, pp. 91 ff. Alfred Weber's relevant texts are: 'Forderungen zur Kartellpolitik', *Die Hilfe*, vol. 8, no. 39 (28 September 1902), p. 3; idem, 'Die Kartellfrage', in *Protokoll über die Verhandlungen des Nationalsozialen Vereins (7. Vertretertag) zu Hannover vom 2. – 5. Oktober 1902* (Berlin, 1903), pp. 54–71, 86; idem, *Arbeitswilligenschutz* (Munich, 1914); idem, 'Agrarier und Reichsfinanzreform', *Vossische Zeitung*, no. 262, 11 June 1909.

20 G. Schmoller, 'Diskussionsbeitrag', in *Schriften des Vereins für Sozialpolitik*, Vol. 47 (Leipzig 1890), p. 205.

21 A. Weber, 'Die Hausindustrie und ihre gesetzliche Regelung', in *Schriften des Vereins für Sozialpolitik*, Vol. 88 (Leipzig, 1900), p. 12.

22 idem, 'Die gemeinsamen wirtschaftlichen Interessen Deutschlands und Österreichs', *Deutsche Worte*, vol. 5 (1902), p. 149.

23 M. Brod, *Streitbares Leben. Autobiographie 1884–1968*, new edn (Frankfurt, 1979), pp. 207–8; Alfred Weber to Lujo Brentano, 22 December 1903, Brentano papers (as in n. 18 above), no. 66.

24 Max Weber to Alfred Weber, 3 September 1907. I am grateful to Wolfgang J. Mommsen and M. Rainer Lepsius for allowing me to read this letter and others; they are hereafter cited without giving their location.

25 F. Boese, *Geschichte des Vereins für Socialpolitik* (Berlin, 1939), pp. 129–30. See also A. Oberschall, *Empirical Social Research in Germany, 1848–1914* (Paris and The Hague, 1965), pp. 113 ff.; P. Hinrichs, *Um die Seele des Arbeiters. Arbeitspsychologie, Industrie- und Betriebssoziologie in Deutschland 1871–1945* (Cologne, 1981), pp. 85 ff.; and a general overview: I. Gorges, *Sozialforschung in Deutschland 1872–1914. Gesellschaftliche Einflüsse auf Themen und Methodenwahl des Vereins für Sozialpolitik* (Königstein, 1980).

26 H. Herkner, G. Schmoller and A. Weber, 'Vorwort' in M. Bernays, *Auslese und Anpassung der Arbeiterschaft der geschlossenen Großindustrie* (Leipzig, 1910) = Schriften des Vereins für Sozialpolitik, Vol. 133, p. vii.

27 *Biography*, p. 330.

28 On democratic forms of Social Darwinism cf. A. Kelly, *The Descent of Darwin: The*

Popularization of Darwinism in Germany, 1860–1914 (Chapel Hill, NC, 1981), pp. 7, 22 ff., 101, 119 ff.

29 *Biography*, p. 331; Max Weber, 'Diskussionsbeitrag in der Debatte über Probleme der Arbeiterpsychologie', in *Schriften des Vereins für Sozialpolitik*, Vol. 138 (Leipzig, 1912), p. 190.

30 Max Weber, *Erhebungen über Auslese und Anpassung (Berufswahl und Berufsschicksal) der Arbeiterschaft der geschlossenen Großindustrie*, printed in manuscript (Altenburg, 1908).

31 O. von Zwiedineck-Südenhorst, 'Vom Wirken von Max und Alfred Weber im Verein für Sozialpolitik', in E. Salin (ed.), *Synopsis. Alfred Weber, 30. 7. 1868 – 30. 7. 1948* (Heidelberg, 1948), pp. 784–5.

32 Hinrichs, *Um die Seele des Arbeiters*, p. 98.

33 Cf. Max Weber, *Erhebungen*, pp. 34, 54–5

34 Max Weber to Alfred Weber, 19 September 1908.

35 Max Weber, *Erhebungen*, p. 3.

36 Herkner, Schmoller and Weber, 'Vorwort', pp. viii–xiv.

37 *Schriften des Vereins für Sozialpolitik*, Vols 133–138 (Leipzig, 1910–12). For a summary of the conclusions, see M. Bernays, 'Berufswahl und Berufsschicksal des modernen Industriearbeiters', AfSSP, vol. 35 (1912), pp. 123–76, vol. 36 (1913), pp. 884–915.

38 Bernays, *Auslese und Anpassung*, pp. xvi–xvii.

39 ibid., passim. Cf. also Max Weber, 'Zur Psychophysik der industriellen Arbeit', GASS, pp. 61–255.

40 A. Levenstein, *Die Arbeiterfrage. Mit besonderer Berücksichtigung der sozial-psychologischen Seite des modernen Großbetriebs und der psycho-physischen Einwirkungen auf die Arbeiter* (Munich, 1912).

41 Cf. Oberschall, *Empirical Social Research*, p. 95; Hinrichs, *Um die Seele des Arbeiters*, p. 90.

42 M. Bernays, Review of Levenstein, *Die Arbeiterfrage*, AfSSP, vol. 35 (1912), p. 833.

43 For example, Levenstein, *Die Arbeiterfrage*, p. 13 (table).

44 Bernays, 'Berufswahl und Berufsschicksal', p. 170.

45 L. Sinzheimer, 'Diskussionsbeitrag', in *Schriften des Vereins für Sozialpolitik*, Vol. 138 (Leipzig, 1912), p. 179. Cf., for similar assessments, R. Dahrendorf, *Industrie- und Betriebssoziologie* (Berlin, 1967), p. 33; E. K. Scheuch, 'Methoden', in R. König (ed.), *Fischer-Lexikon Soziologie* 19th edn (Frankfurt, 1978), p. 187.

46 A. Weber, 'Diskussionsbeitrag', in *Schriften des Vereins für Sozialpolitik*, Vol. 138, p. 150. See also idem, 'Das Berufsschicksal der Industriearbeiter', AfSSP, vol. 34 (1912), p. 388.

47 ibid., p. 393.

48 Cf. J. Kocka, 'Otto Hintze, Max Weber und das Problem der Bürokratie', *Historische Zeitschrift*, vol. 233 (1981), p. 100.

49 Cf. T. Schieder, 'Einleitung', in F. Naumann, *Werke*, Vol. 2 (Cologne and Opladen, 1964), p. xxxvi. See also F. Naumann, 'Die politischen Aufgaben im Industriezeitalter', in idem, *Werke*, Vol. 3 (Cologne and Opladen, 1964), pp. 6, 9; idem, *Die Erziehung zur Persönlichkeit im Zeitalter des Großbetriebs* (Berlin, 1907), pp. 35 ff.

50 A. Weber, 'Der Beamte' [1910], in idem, *Ideen zur Staats- und Kultursoziologie* (Karlsruhe, 1927), p. 82.

51 idem, 'Diskussionsbeitrag in der Debatte über die wirtschaftlichen Unternehmungen der Gemeinden', in *Schriften des Vereins für Sozialpolitik*, Vol. 132 (Leipzig, 1910), pp. 239–40, 244.

52 Max Weber, 'Diskussionsbeitrag', ibid., p. 282; reprinted in GASS, p. 413.

53 This difference has already been spotted by Lindenlaub, *Richtungskämpfe*, p. 396.

54 This definition is based on A. Gehlen, 'Über die Geburt der Freiheit aus der Entfremdung', in idem, *Studien zur Anthropologie und Soziologie* (Neuwied and Berlin, 1963), p. 232.

55 Cf. J. Israel, *L'aliénation de Marx à la sociologie contemporaine. Une étude macrosociologique* (Paris, 1972), pp. 38 ff.; W. Weisskopf, *Aliénation, idéologie et répression* (Paris, 1976), pp. 53 ff.

56 Cf. W. J. Mommsen, 'Kapitalismus und Sozialismus. Die Auseinandersetzung mit Karl Marx', in idem, *Max Weber. Gesellschaft, Politik und Geschichte* (Frankfurt, 1974), p. 157; Demm 'Alfred Weber', p. 9.

57 Cf. A. Weber, 'Der soziologische Kulturbegriff' [1913], in idem, *Ideen*, pp. 45–6.

58 idem, 'Das Berufsschicksal', p. 401.

59 Cf. K. Mannheim, 'Das konservative Denken', AfSSP, vol. 57 (1927), pp. 84–5.

6 Personal Conflict and Ideological Options in Sombart and Weber

ARTHUR MITZMAN

Werner Sombart, economist, sociologist and German ideologist, is perhaps best known for his work on modern capitalism, the two editions and several parts of which were published between 1900 and 1930.[1] In the context of this work on the evolution and sources of the capitalist system, his ideas are eminently comparable with those of his contemporary Max Weber. Both born in the mid-1860s, they earned their ideological spurs in the 'Richtungskampf' of the Verein für Sozialpolitik, taking the modernist position against the upholders of a patriarchal social policy. From 1902 onwards they were joint editors (with Edgar Jaffé) of the *Archiv für Sozialwissenschaft und Sozialpolitik*. They also devoted considerable attention to the sources and evolution of the 'spirit' of modern capitalism, and were given to disputing freely with one another.[2]

At the level of personal origins and development there are other similarities between Sombart and Weber, which make their divergences during the years 1900 to 1920 so much the more interesting and worthy of investigation. Both men came from well-to-do families of the Berlin upper middle class, with a partly Calvinist background. The personal history of both men in their twenties seems to have been based on an oedipal struggle to oppose and distinguish themselves from the ideological positions and values of their fathers in particular and of the older generation of social reformers in general. Around 1900, both men went through a crisis, bound up with the relation to the father — more serious in Weber's case, but no less evident in Sombart's.

Yet the differences between the two are at least as important as the similarities. Apart from their different points of academic origin (Weber studied law, Sombart economics), Sombart was far more representative of the intellectuals of his generation than was Weber. Although Weber engaged in fierce polemics on political and social subjects during and before the First World War, they usually had the character of one-man guerilla actions against the puerile enthusiasms of his contemporaries: what he once called 'the power of stupidity'. Sombart was much closer to the mainstream of German social thought. After his 'modernizing' polemics of the 1890s against the patriarchal social policy of the older generation of *Kathedersozialisten* [academic socialists] — polemics which he shared with Weber and others — Sombart rapidly retreated from the modernist position to a nostalgic embrace of pre-capitalist *Gemeinschaft* [community].[3] The main intellectual influence in this phase was that of Tönnies, but Sombart's ideological framework for implementing the ideas of Tönnies, himself a reluctant and unofficial social democrat, brought him close to the values and social perspectives of the conservative and fashionable *völkisch* movement of the prewar period. Although he always retained some of the central ideas of Marx and Tönnies, he turned in the following decade (1910–20) more and more to kitsch-Nietzschean models of entrepreneurial and national heroism, also popular among his compatriots.

Weber, by way of contrast, pursued a lonelier path. Always at odds with the ideological self-deception of his contemporaries, he retained and refined a sort of liberal self-consciousness. He investigated in his own Calvinist background the sources of his personal dilemmas and of the iron cage of bureaucratic capitalism. He never betrayed his liberal, modernist standpoint as Sombart did, by falling into the trap of *völkisch* sentimentalism. And his acceptance of Nietzsche, when it occurred around 1910, remained in a framework of bourgeois individualism – his aristocratic values, his recognition of the role of charisma in politics, signaled the Nietzschean influence, but he never engaged in the modish identification of a Nietzschean *Herrenmoral* with the German nation, as Sombart did.

On the whole, we can say that both men underwent an existential crisis around 1900, which was reflected in their ideological values and scholarly directions, that both men participated in the movement of the times away from liberal rationalism towards an appreciation of the irrational forces motivating social life – forces embodied both in the culture of the elite, such as the George-Kreis and German expressionism and in the mass phenomena of *völkisch* nationalism. In Sombart, however, the temptation to abandon the liberal bourgeois position for the *völkisch* enthusiasms of the *Mittelstand* and their intellectual apologists appeared irresistible, while Weber was immune to such enthusiasms.

This leads us to a double question, the answers to which must at this time remain both speculative and brief:

(1)   What is the difference in personal evolution discernible behind the different ideological options of the two editors of the *Archiv für Sozialwissenschaft und Sozialpolitik*?
(2)   What are the larger social implications of these personal evolutions and ideological options?

At a personal level, we can see in Sombart and Weber two different ways of coping with oedipal conflict, and it is probably this difference in personal development that led the two men to such fundamentally different ideological options. Though each went through a short phase in his student period of identification with his father, preceding the outspoken rejection of him in the 1890s, this phase was in Sombart's case probably stronger and undoubtedly of greater importance in the later ideological choices. Weber's identification with his father was discernible only in the career and life-style choices of his first year of study.[4] Afterwards, through most of the 1890s, his political and social options as well as his innermost values betrayed the profound influence of his mother's personality and Calvinist heritage. With Sombart, the father's patriarchal values were visible in his first scholarly studies of 1888 on family economic life in Italy. Soon after, and throughout the 1890s, the patriarchal values were replaced by a clearly 'modernist' support for capitalist efficiency and for a moderate 'revisionist' socialism.

In comparing the personal evolution and ideological options of Sombart and Weber, a gap in the published – and perhaps unpublished – sources poses a problem. In Weber's case, it is clear both from his *Jugendbriefe* and from his wife's biography of him that the values that guided his scholarship in the 1890s were basically those of his mother. In the case of Sombart, lack of ego-documents and an adequate biography make it impossible to say anything at all about the mother. None the less, the Institute for Social History in Amsterdam does have the invaluable letters between Sombart and the close friend of his youth, the Swiss socialist Otto Lang, written in the 1880s and 1890s, and from these we can see that the 'red' phase in Sombart's life, his adoption of a number of revisionist Marxist ideas, was in large measure mediated through the friendship with Lang.

In fact this relationship with Lang was the first – perhaps the most profound – of a series of such friendships: with adherents of the left-leaning Berlin naturalist circle in the 1890s, with Carl Hauptmann and the Schreiberhau intellectuals after 1900. On the whole, such horizontal emotional ties seem to have been more important in the life of Sombart than in that of Weber, who was more dominated by the vertical relations with father and mother. Nevertheless, in Sombart's case too the vertical oedipal relationship was important. It is impossible to establish if Sombart's relationship with his mother was involved in his embrace of *Gemeinschaft*-like values in the period after 1900. About his personal life in this period, we know only that he left his wife and family around 1900, and had an important extra-marital affair, which greatly influenced his writing of *Die deutsche Volkswirtschaft im 19. Jahrhundert* [The German Economy in the 19th Century] (1903), the book in which he comes closest to a *völkisch* outlook based on Tönnies's communitarian ideal. It is also remarkable that he explicitly stigmatized the entrepreneurial style of his father in this book as a 'Sklavensinn'.[5] By 1910, at which time the integration of Nietzschean *Herrenmoral* was evident in his new view of the capitalist entrepreneur, Sombart had returned to his wife and was favourably mentioning his father's economic role for the first time.

Thus, on the one hand, the trajectory of Sombart's psycho-sexual development led him personally, after rejecting his father and dropping out of his marriage, to a rediscovery of the father and a new and more ruthless endorsement of his entrepreneurial role. The ideological aspect also signifies a return, twenty years after turning his back on his father's patriarchal values, to the current mask for those values, the aggressive nationalism of the First World War period. In Weber, on the other hand, the rejection of the father in the 1890s, unambiguously founded on the mother's social values, was capped by a total collapse following his father's death in 1897, and the way out of this collapse lay not in an acceptance of the father but in a rigorous analysis of the values he had received from his puritanical mother and which he had used to defy his father shortly before the latter's death. His later evolution continued, as Wolfgang J. Mommsen and others have shown, in the direction of a truly Nietzschean transvaluation of values, keyed into the aesthetic and mystical currents of European thought in the early twentieth century, but utterly remote from the *völkisch* enthusiasm and the kitsch-Nietzscheanism that for a time captivated Sombart. If Mommsen is correct in stressing the nationalism of the later as well as that of the earlier Weber it is also true that Weber's hard-earned sobriety about the course of modern history kept him at a critical distance from the febrile xenophobia of most of his intellectual compatriots during the First World War.

The ideological options and psychological life-courses of Sombart and Weber may possibly have a much broader historical and cultural significance. I am thinking of two contexts. One is the relative significance for character formation and for social history of the two frameworks for socialization that I have noted in Weber and Sombart – the vertical oedipal relation and the horizontal peer relation. The other is the connection between the voluntarist values of post-heroic liberalism and the anti-modern movements of the pre-industrial strata.

The oedipal relationship, which became the keystone of a Freudian notion of personality, was a highly appropriate framework for viewing the son–parent relationship in the nineteenth and twentieth century bourgeois family. The tense dialectic of emulation and rejection of the father and of a complex love for the mother undoubtedly characterized the growth to maturity of Weber, Freud and a good many others in European bourgeois culture. The case of Sombart, however, reminds us that other agents of socialization – alongside and sometimes instead of the parental model – could and did significantly influence the growth of personality in childhood and adolescence. Sombart's student relationship with Lang signifies in this respect a world of influence on personality development that stands outside the narrow child–parent nexus of the isolated nuclear family.

Anthropologically, this isolated nuclear family was something of an anomaly, because it was far more common historically to see nuclear family ties attenuated by three other agencies of socialization: the kin-network of cousins, aunts, uncles and grandparents, supplemented among the well-to-do by household servants; the intertwined socialization networks of neighbourhood, religious and professional organizations which characterized city and town life before the nineteenth century; above all, the adolescent peer group.

This last seems to be the most stubborn of all the agencies of character formation outside the nuclear family. Time and again, during the roughly two hundred years that the bourgeois family structure has been liberated from larger kin-networks and from the older corporate agents of socialization, the adolescent peer group – earlier institutionalized in the traditional popular culture – has re-emerged as a powerful seed-bed of creativity in European elite culture, usually with markedly anti-bourgeois values. Sombart himself compared his student days with Lang to the 'storm and stress' of the eighteenth century.[6] Closer to his own time were the *Burschenschaften* [student fraternities] of early nineteenth century German nationalism; ten years away was the beginning of the German Youth Movement, the *Wandervogel*, recruited from the bourgeois youth of Berlin. In France, the high tide of romanticism around 1830 revealed a variety of aesthetically oriented bourgeois youth circles, most of which condemned the bourgeois utilitarianism and opportunism of the time ('Jeune France' and the 'bousingots' were the most visible). At a less organized level, Flaubert's intimate adolescent bond with Alfred Le Poittevin can stand for a considerable number of such peer-relationships, indifferent or hostile to the world of the parents, among the budding intellectuals and artists of early and mid-nineteenth century France.[7] Indeed, Jesse Pitts has analysed the more or less permanent influence in French social life of what he calls 'the delinquent peer group'.[8] Such phenomena among the English elites stem from the intimate male ties of the public school and university days: Oscar Wilde, E. M. Forster and a good part of the Bloomsbury circle are obvious examples of this, with comparable anti-bourgeois values to those we have found in France and Germany. Post-Second World War successors to these peer-group bonds made the decade of the 1960s the most turbulent in recent European and American history.

Although bourgeois society has generally tolerated such youth friendships and associations, their political and social implications have more often than not been hostile to bourgeois society itself, sometimes to the point of revolutionary terrorism; they in fact are echoes of popular youth associations and rituals of the pre-industrial society, which both the bourgeoisie and its predecessor in matters of public morals, the church, condemned as immoral and suppressed as disruptive of civilized social existence.[9]

The repeated anarchic and explosive reappearance of such youth groups in the modern world constitutes for bourgeois society a return of the repressed, whose implications both for character formation and for social structure have been insufficiently studied. To return to Sombart and Lang, for example, it would be worth knowing in how many other situations the late adolescent peer relation helped to radicalize bourgeois social consciousness in Imperial Germany. Was it important for the Berlin naturalists as a whole? For the *Jungen*[10] to whom Sombart was sympathetic in the 1890s? For the poets of the George-Kreis? For the German expressionists? For the right-wing *völkisch* movements?

This last — the *völkisch* movement of the backward-looking *Mittelstand* — leads to a final question raised by the comparison of Weber and Sombart. In both men, a post-heroic liberal value-system hinged around the polarity of determinism and voluntarism. In Sombart's evolution, this polarity was decisively modified by the fascination he came to feel for *völkisch* 'communitarian' values, then largely the property of conservative ideologists of the *Mittelstand*. These values were also tied in with an emerging militant nationalism, which two decades later found its way into Nazism. Sombart never fully embraced the Nazi cause, but his ultra-nationalist celebration of heroism and community brought him close. We can certainly speak of a partial collapse of his earlier liberalism into *völkisch*, *Mittelstand* nationalism, a collapse that did not occur in Weber's case, whose nationalism retained its liberal bourgeois character.

The collapse of Sombart's liberal principles, his attraction to the revolutionary nationalist energies located primarily in the *völkisch* beliefs of the *Mittelstand*, was anything but a unique case in Germany. What is most interesting is that the same phenomenon is discernible in mid-nineteenth-century France, notably in the person of the historian Jules Michelet. Michelet's early work shows a post-heroic liberal ideology similar to Sombart's and Weber's: the celebration of political free will against the determinants of race, geography and social structure. This ideology dominated his perspective from 1830 to 1840. Then, after the death of his first wife, he underwent a psychic crisis bound up with his love for a woman who was dying of cancer. Under

the influence of this woman, in whom he saw an ideal mother, his entire social
and historical philosophy became matriarchally tinted – he came to view both
God and *la patrie* as nurturant mothers. Concomitantly his voluntarist principles became blurred, just as Sombart's later did, and were partly replaced by
a popular ideology of community,[11] derived from the backward-looking strata
of the lower middle class. Like Sombart, his social ideal became that of the
artisan-artist, with which he identified himself. The ideological development
of the French historian appears then as strikingly similar to that of the German
political economist.

And yet, the differences between Michelet and Sombart, in terms of the
political and social meaning of their communitarian pro-artisan phases, are
enormous. Michelet was viewed in the 1840s as a left-radical, ardently supported by the same elements of students and radical craftsmen who, in 1848,
were to topple Louis Philippe (just as in 1830, they had brought down Charles
X). His social role in the 1840s was to lead the anti-clerical battle against the
returning Jesuit influence on education during the last phase of the July
Monarchy. Sombart's role was quite simply reactionary, back-pedalling as
swiftly as he could from his earlier support for the socialists.

The difference lay in the social and political meaning in France and
Germany of the pre-industrial popular strata that had as their base the communitarian ethos. In France, these strata were bound up throughout the nineteenth century with the radical traditions of the French Revolution and became
the seed-bed, at the end of the century, of the modern socialist movement.
Because these strata had been in alliance with the liberal elite in the revolutionary movements of 1789–92 and 1830, their folk culture and social ideals
were largely adopted by the social romanticism of the July Monarchy, which
was the larger framework for Michelet's turn from pure liberalism in the
1840s.

For reasons that we have no time to discuss here, the same pre-industrial
social and economic stratum of artisans, peasants and shopkeepers had an
exclusively reactionary significance in Imperial and Weimar Germany. Since
the tragically split revolutionary movements of 1848, German liberals viewed
the revolutionary nationalism of the *Mittelstand* only as a threat, and both the
artisan and the new proletariat, however deep their mutual hostility, knew they
could never rely on the liberals in moments of political crisis.[12] All three
worlds were separate and hostile, which explains perhaps why Sombart's
ideological course after the 1890s took the drastic turn that ultimately led him
to be a fellow-traveller of the violently anti-liberal ideology of Nazism.

That these worlds of the artisan, the bourgeois and the proletarian were in
France less shut off from one another than in Germany, helps us to understand
Michelet's ability to retain many of his liberal nationalist values after his
conversion to the communitarian 'fraternal' creeds of the artisan radicals; it
also clarifies for us why Sombart's course was rather a one-way street, and
how Weber managed to avoid such a course only by never entering that street.
That differences in personal character may also have been significant in the different trajectories of Weber and Sombart goes without saying. But we should
never forget that character is formed in the dark and ultimately unfathomable
crucible that merges social and parental influences with hereditary
dispositions.

Notes: Chapter 6

1 W. Sombart, *Der Moderne Kapitalismus. Historisch-systematische Darstellung des gesamteuropäischen Wirtschaftslebens von seinen Anfängen bis zur Gegenwart*, 2 vols (Munich and Leipzig, 1902); 2nd edn, 4 vols (Munich and Leipzig, 1916/17); 7th edn, 6 vols (Munich and Leipzig, 1928). The second, expanded edition was, according to Sombart's introduction to it, 90 per cent re-written. The seventh edition contains the four volumes of the second plus two new ones on *Das Wirtschaftsleben im Zeitalter des Hochkapitalismus*. Apart from these volumes, *Der Bourgeois. Zur Geistesgeschichte des modernen Kapitalismus*, (Munich and Leipzig, 1913) might well be viewed as part of Sombart's work on modern capitalism, as could *Luxus und Kapitalismus*, Vol. 1 of *Studien zur Entwicklungsgeschichte des modernen Kapitalismus* (Munich and Leipzig, 1913). For a discussion of Sombart's life and work before 1918, see A. Mitzman, *Sociology and Estrangement: Three Sociologists of Imperial Germany* (New York, 1973), pp. 135–264.

2 For a recent analysis of the polemic with Weber about the relative importance of Calvinism and Judaism in the origins of a 'spirit' of modern capitalism, see S. Z. Klausner's introduction to the reissue of the English translation of *Die Juden und das Wirtschaftsleben*: W. Sombart, *The Jews and Modern Capitalism* (New Brunswick, NJ, 1982), pp. lxxiv–lxxxv.

3 Traces of this nostalgia for 'Gemeinschaft' appear in *Dennoch* (1901) and are fully developed in *Die deutsche Volkswirtschaft im 19. Jahrhundert* (Berlin, 1903). Sombart's contributions to the journal, *Der Morgen*, which he founded with Hugo von Hofmannsthal, Richard Strauss and Georg Brandes, show his anti-modernist values in their purest form. See A. Mitzman, *Sociology and Estrangement*, pp. 194–233.

4 See A. Mitzman, *The Iron Cage: An Historical Interpretation of Max Weber* (New York, 1970), p. 73 (2nd edn with new introduction, 1984).

5 Sombart, *Die deutsche Volkswirtschaft*, p. 119.

6 'Who among us did not revel in the raptures of Werther; who did not enthuse with Rousseau for pure nature; who did not feel infinite development in Byronic romanticism; who was not a devotee of Schopenhauer, a republican and a Social Democrat'. Letter from Sombart to Lang, June 1889 (original in the International Institute for Social History, Amsterdam) cited in Mitzman, *Sociology and Estrangement*, p. 215.

7 Zola with Cézanne, Maxime Du Camp with Louis de Cormenin, the brothers Hugo with each other, likewise the brothers Goncourt, Jules Michelet with Paul Poinsot, Alfred Dumesnil (Michelet's son-in-law) with Eugène Noël, de Musset with Tattet.

8 See J. R. Pitts, 'Continuity and change in bourgeois France: the traditional French value system', in S. Hoffmann (ed.), *In Search of France* (New York, 1963), pp. 235–62.

9 Cf. N. Z. Davis, 'The reasons of misrule: youth groups and charivaris in sixteenth-century France', *Past and Present* no. 50 (1971), pp. 41–75; A. Burguiere, 'The charivari and religious repression in France during the ancient régime', in R. Wheaton and T. K. Hareven (eds), *Family and Sexuality in French History* (Philadelphia, Pa, 1980), pp. 84–110; Y.-M. Bercé, *Fête et révolte. Des mentalités populaires du XVIe au XVIIIe siècles* (Paris, 1976); R. Muchembled, *Culture populaire et culture des élites dans la France moderne* (Paris, 1978); A. Esler, 'After the youth revolution – what?', in idem (ed.), *The Youth Revolution: The Conflict of Generations in Modern History* (Lexington, Mass., 1974); M. Crubellier, *L'Enfance et la jeunesse dans la société française 1800–1950* (Paris, 1979), pp. 57–122, 143–86, 309–36; R. J. Bezucha, 'Masks of revolution: a study of popular culture during the Second French Republic', in R. Price (ed.), *Revolution and Reaction: 1848 and the Second French Republic* (London and New York, 1975), pp. 236–53.

10 See Chapter 4 by Dieter Krüger in this volume.

11 This retreat is clearly evident in Jules Michelet's *Le Peuple* (Paris, 1846). The complex issue of the feminization of Michelet's social and historical outlook in the 1840s is briefly sketched in A. Mitzman, 'Sociability, creativity and estrangement: a psychohistorical approach to Michelet and Flaubert, or history as epos and anti-epos', in *Geschiedenis, Psychologie, Mentaliteit. Negen Discussiebijdragen* (Amsterdam, 1982), pp. 102–16, 180–2.

12 I deal with this problem in the introduction to the Transaction edition of my *Sociology and Estrangement* (New Brunswick, NJ, 1986).

7 Varieties of Social Economics: Joseph A. Schumpeter and Max Weber

JÜRGEN OSTERHAMMEL

I

Like Georg Lukács, the other Eastern prodigy among Max Weber's friends and collaborators, Joseph Alois Schumpeter, born in Moravia in 1883 and educated in Vienna, was a member of the generation that was formed intellectually in the closing years of the nineteenth and the opening decade of the twentieth century. Its first literary attempts were published at the same time as the masterpieces of the older generation were coming off the press. The publication of Schumpeter's earliest article coincided with that of Max Weber's first essay on the protestant ethic. Schumpeter's first book, *Das Wesen und der Hauptinhalt der theoretischen Nationalökonomie* [The Nature and the Principal Doctrines of Theoretical Economics], was published in 1908.[1] It was favourably received in Britain and France, but had only a limited impact on economics in Austria and Germany.[2] His second book, *The Theory of Economic Development* (1911),[3] which he never surpassed as a creative achievement, established Schumpeter's international fame. It was widely discussed and studied, also by Max Weber, whose annotated personal copy has survived.[4] After the death of Eugen von Böhm-Bawerk in 1915, Schumpeter enjoyed the reputation of being the foremost economic theorist writing in the German language. He retained this stature after he left Vienna in 1925 to take up a chair in Bonn, later moving to Harvard University in 1932.

Schumpeter and Weber were contemporaries in a literary sense, aware of each other's writings and interests, for a little less than a decade between Schumpeter's emergence as a major economist and Weber's death. Yet, it is important to note that most of Schumpeter's seminal ideas germinated during this particular period – the second decade of the twentieth century. Almost his entire American *oeuvre* can be traced back to the period before 1920. In *Business Cycles* (1939) he restated his theory of economic development in a refined and vastly expanded form, more subtly argued and historically fleshed out, but still based on the fundamental insights of 1911. *Capitalism, Socialism and Democracy* in 1942 revived arguments first suggested in the 1920 article 'Sozialistische Möglichkeiten von heute' ['Socialist opportunities of the present day']. And the posthumous *History of Economic Analysis* (1954) was a massive and immeasurably learned elaboration of the chapter on 'Epochen der Dogmen- und Methodengeschichte' ['History of economic doctrines and methods'] which had been published in 1914 under Max Weber's editorship in the first volume of the *Grundriß der Sozialökonomik* [Outline of Social

Economics]. By 1920, then, the basic outlines of Schumpeter's thinking had become visible. The contours of his specific variety of social economics had been boldly sketched in; they were worked out, and shading and colour were added, in subsequent decades.

Max Weber rarely mentions Schumpeter in his published works and never discusses his ideas at any length. Without referring to manuscript material, it is difficult, therefore, to demonstrate that such ideas in Weber's later writings as have a Schumpeterian ring reflect any kind of direct influence. Somewhat more evidence exists that Schumpeter was influenced by Weber. Of Schumpeter's numerous biographical essays, his obituary of Max Weber[5] is the only one entirely free of critical objections. Weber is hailed as an 'intellectual leader', a 'prince of science', a 'knight in shining moral armour', a polymath of unparalleled erudition. His main achievement, in Schumpeter's view, was to have transcended the limits of the German Historical School, inaugurating a 'scientific' approach to history along lines first laid down by Karl Marx. Yet in spite of the fulsome praise heaped upon Weber the man, Schumpeter is strangely reticent about Weber the thinker, writer and social scientist, and he never discusses his work in any detail. Many years later, in the *History of Economic Analysis*, Weber appears as a marginal figure in a crowd of German exponents of 'historism'.[6] Schumpeter in no way belittles or denies Weber's importance. But he draws a clear distinction between an evaluation of Weber as an intellectual figure and an assessment of his contribution to what lies at the heart of Schumpeter's own concerns – 'economic analysis'. 'Indeed, he was not really an economist at all. In an atmosphere not disturbed by professional cross-currents, it would be the obvious thing to label him a sociologist. His work and teaching had much to do with the emergence of Economic Sociology in the sense of an analysis of economic institutions, the recognition of which as a distinct field clarifies so many "methodological" issues'.[7] Schumpeter's reading of Weber is governed by his own systematic interests, which are those of a theoretical economist.

Although he saw himself primarily as a contributor to the mainstream of neo-classical (post-Ricardian and pre-Keynesian) economic theory, Schumpeter nevertheless retained a broad vision of social economics in the pre-1914 Continental sense. This remained for him the wider matrix in which rigorous theory had to be embedded. His own *oeuvre* spans a whole range of academic disciplines: economics, sociology, economic history, political science and methodology. Though his writings do not obviously fall into an overall systematic pattern, he was fundamentally a systematic thinker, committed as François Perroux has correctly pointed out, to 'un esprit unificateur et non éclectique'.[8] Schumpeter's hidden system therefore deserves a closer look.

Schumpeter saw himself as the heir to the particular kind of economic reasoning that had found its mature expression in the works of David Ricardo. This 'classical' tradition, as Schumpeter explained in his early chapter on the history of economic doctrines, had since fallen into decline, especially after John Stuart Mill's *Principles of Political Economy* (1848), the swansong of grand theory. Especially in Germany, economic theory had been sliding into disarray and disrepute. 'Theoretical economics had never become firmly entrenched in Germany, nor had it entered deeply into the consciousness of most people; it was an alien plant which, moreover, had been transplanted by hands which were by no means especially skilful. Its representatives could not prove attractive and its doctrines could not possibly provide intellectual satisfaction'.[9] At the time when Schumpeter embarked on his own career, he was only able to identify two economists who had preserved the theoretical sophistication of the 'classical' tradition: Karl Marx and Léon Walras. Marx, purified of Hegelian metaphysics and unwelcome political partisanship, remained relevant to Schumpeter as a master of subtle theoretical thinking, as the leading interpreter of the dynamics of capitalism and as the man who had envisaged an integrated system of the social sciences that would incorporate economics, sociology and history.[10] Even if most of his answers had been refuted, Marx had asked questions that were clearly still of central importance. Walras, on the other hand, provided at least some of the answers, if only within the limited sphere of a theory of economic statics. Walras, of course, was only one of several economists who had sparked off the marginalist revolution and laid the foundations for neo-classical theory. But, as Schumpeter saw it, he was superior to William Stanley Jevons, Carl Menger or Alfred Marshall, on three counts. First, his mathematical language was more advanced, especially in comparison with the Austrian school. Secondly, he had extended the analysis of individual acts of exchange on particular markets to an exact description of exchange relations within the national economy as a whole. Thirdly, he had given a definitive statement of general equilibrium theory that was unlikely to be improved upon. In short, neo-classicism in general and its Walrasian variety in particular had laid a firm theoretical basis on which to build the vast edifice of social economics according to the Marxian blueprint.

Schumpeter had studied under Eugen von Böhm-Bawerk and Friedrich von Wieser at the University of Vienna and had thus been exposed to a thoroughly 'marginalist' atmosphere. Far from being recruited for Austrian orthodoxy, however, from his early writings onwards he displayed an independence of mind that enabled him to rise above the protracted academic quarrels of his time. In addition to the fact that his preference for Walras to Menger was less then loyally 'Austrian', Schumpeter's sympathy for Marx (if not for Marxism) contrasted sharply with the anti-Marxist critique of Böhm-Bawerk and of Walras's successor at the University of Lausanne, Vilfredo Pareto. Schumpeter's esteem for Marx had been stimulated by his fellow-student Otto Bauer and by his contacts with other Austro-Marxists, rather than by the partial rediscovery of original Marxism among the 'younger' generation within the Verein für Sozialpolitik. Finally, the young scholar was confronted with the alternative of 'theory *or* history' that lingered on, even though the methodological dispute between Menger and Schmoller had cooled down by the turn of the century. From the start, Schumpeter refused to take sides. His later verdict that the whole battle had been 'substantially a history of wasted energies which could have been put to better use'[11] was already expressed in his earliest writings. Although in a sense he was the purest of the Austro-German pure economists, adamant in his insistence on the methodological autonomy of economic reasoning, he never endorsed Menger's onslaught against the very possibility of historical economics. Few have appraised Schmoller's work as sympathetically as Schumpeter did in his great essay of 1926.[12] Even so, he left no doubt that historical economics, properly constituted as economic history, should not be allowed to challenge the position of neo-classical theory at the heart of a system of social economics.

Schumpeter never came close to achieving the ambitious synthesis himself, although *Business Cycles* went a considerable way towards exemplifying what he had in mind. In his last work he outlined a comprehensive 'economic analysis' which was to consist of four sub-disciplines: theory, statistics, economic history and economic sociology.[13] From the point of view of this system, Max Weber became relevant only in so far as his research fitted into the slot of economic sociology. Theory, at the centre of the system, meant neo-classical theory and, in this sense, Weber 'was not really an economist at all'. This accounts for Schumpeter's lack of *systematic* interest in Weber's work.

At a different level — that of unacknowledged influence as opposed to explicit discussion — Weberian themes reverberate through Schumpeter's texts. It is tempting to suggest that Weber was a constant presence, hovering over Schumpeter's desk, too important to be explicitly invoked. Such influence is hard to substantiate with reasonable accuracy. Instead of measuring Schumpeter's distance from Weber on individual issues, I shall attempt to compare their views on three topics: the methodology of the social sciences, classical capitalism and the transformation of the capitalist system in the twentieth century.

II

Schumpeter unconditionally endorsed Weber's stance, as he understood it, on the issue of value-judgements. He reminded his readers that the principle of avoiding value-judgements had never been disputed by the classical economists.[14] By sweeping away obscurantist German notions of science as an arbiter in matters of practical life, Weber had simply restored an almost trivial classical convention. Schumpeter showed little interest in the Neo-Kantian intricacies of Weber's position on value-orientation, and he chose to disregard the epistemological and ethical implications involved. To him, refraining from value-judgements merely meant objectivity of reasoning and political neutrality of action. He rejected the notion that the scholar had *any* public responsibility or political role. When he joined the cabinet of Chancellor Karl Renner as a non-party minister of finance in 1919, he apparently regarded himself as a mere expert and mouthpiece of undiluted economic logic. This self-conception contrasted sharply with the highly controversial policies that he introduced or recommended. In the end, he was forced to resign, having antagonized almost all the relevant political forces in Austria.[15] Schumpeter's self-image of being a neutral financial technician in the midst of party politics and social antagonisms was sometimes regarded as the cause of an unprincipled opportunism. Professor Schumpeter, as the great satirist Karl Kraus remarked, was a man 'with more different views than were necessary for his advancement'.[16] Putting aside both the ethic of responsibility and the ethic of conviction and ignoring the tension-ridden nature of politics, Schumpeter predicated his practice of *Werturteilsfreiheit* on threadbare Weberian credentials.

Schumpeter is much more impressive as an economic methodologist. His first book was an introduction to Walrasian theory, but at the same time also a methodological treatise. Schumpeter suggested 'a kind of Monroe doctrine for economics': economic theory was to be constituted as self-contained and autonomous, protected against interference from neighbouring disciplines, above all from sociology, psychology and ethnology. It was to be conceived as *pure* theory, independent of all kinds of extra-economic knowledge.[17] The main contemporary challenge to the autonomy of theory came from psychological approaches. Schumpeter had in mind especially Friedrich von Wieser's idea that the laws of economics could be discovered through the economist's 'introspection'.[18] Schumpeter did not claim that this was impossible. He believed that it was unnecessary. He argued against epistemological over-determination: if economics could do without psychology – why should it not choose to be as self-reliant as possible?

In 1908, the same year as Schumpeter's book was published, Max Weber launched his own defence of economics against psychology. In his essay 'Marginal utility theory and the so-called fundamental law of psychophysics',[19] he took issue with Lujo Brentano, who had asserted that the laws postulated by marginalist theory were based on the findings of experimental psychology and would be invalidated if the latter were to be empirically disproved. Like Schumpeter, Weber not only defended the independence of pure economics, but also went on to attempt to redefine the epistemological status of neo-classical theory. Whether or not Weber believed marginalism to be relevant to his own concerns as a *Nationalökonom* was immaterial to the purpose of his critique of Brentano. His intention was to explain the 'logic-in-use' of the 'Austrians', and to compare it not only with Brentano's distortions but also with their own 'reconstructed logic',[20] especially Menger's methodology. Weber thought that the Austrians were not doing precisely what they believed they were doing. Marginalism had to be defended not only against its detractors (such as Brentano) but also against its creators and leading representatives.

Against the critics, Weber points out that the theorems of marginalism are not based on psychology but on 'pragmatic' assumptions, i.e. the categories 'end' and 'means' which govern the 'commercial calculus' in every-day life.[21] Against Menger and his followers, he reverts to his earlier critique (put forward in his 1904 essay on objectivity) of Menger's claim that knowledge in economic theory was derived from grasping the evident nature of pre-existing 'laws'.[22] In 1908, Weber demonstrates that the tenets of marginalism are not statements about reality, but mental constructs, useful in representing the complexity of the empirical world and in heuristically paving the way for further analysis. He thus goes much further than Schumpeter in elucidating what economic theorists are actually doing, and provides a masterly example of 'saving criticism' in Lessing's sense: marginalist theory is defended against its own advocates. Although Weber is more successful in this than Schumpeter, their basic thrust is almost identical: both try to develop a set of *minimal* epistemological requirements, which marginalist theory has to fulfil in order to pass as scientific knowledge. Both are opposed to Carl Menger's 'realist' or 'Aristotelian' views, according to which the 'laws' of economics, analogous to those of the natural sciences, possess an objective existence.[23] Whether – as in other varieties of 'Austrian' thinking – they can be derived from 'introspection' (Friedrich von Wieser) or from insight into *a priori* given modes of rational conduct (Ludwig von Mises) is of secondary importance.

Weber and Schumpeter both favour a 'nominalist' position, but for different reasons. Weber is indebted to Neo-Kantian epistemology, whereas Schumpeter is influenced by Henri Poincaré's 'conventionalism'.[24] According to Poincaré, scientific theories are conventions, agreed upon by the community of scholars. Poincaré's methodology is unsatisfactory on two counts: it gives no criteria by which to determine the adequacy of theories, and it fails to explain progress in science; it was later superseded by Karl Popper's 'revolutionary falsificationism.'[25] In 1908, however, conventionalism was a fairly radical position to take up, especially so within the context of Austrian economics.

To claim that the 'laws' of economic theory were nothing but 'hypotheses made up by us', 'just as arbitrary as definitions' and only to be judged in terms of their 'utility',[26] was to fly in the face of Vienna orthodoxy. It was much nearer to Weber's position than to that of Menger, but a difference still remained. Weber, captivated by the concept of value-orientation, was not a conventionalist. Scientific thinking was not, as Schumpeter believed, totally unrelated to a choice between conflicting values. To Weber, the intersubjective consensus among scholars did not provide the kind of validation of theoretical reasoning that it offered to the conventionalists. Weber also refused to detach concept formation from the question of cultural meanings, something that fell victim to Schumpeter's sharp 'razor'. Yet Weber was a methodological constructivist,[27] and Schumpeter, as one of very few economists, joined him in this at an early stage.

Das Wesen und der Hauptinhalt der theoretischen Nationalökonomie remained Schumpeter's principal contribution to economic methodology. Thereafter, he seldom returned to reflections on method and, if he did, it was in a critical rather than in an affirmative vein. He did not elaborate a prescriptive methodology, and has therefore not entered the ranks of the great law-givers of economics. Yet, especially in *Business Cycles*, he showed himself keenly aware of methodological issues. *Business Cycles* demonstrates the use of models – in this case of a dynamic model of capitalist development – with a degree of circumspection rarely paralleled since.[28] Schumpeter carefully discusses each step of model-building, its preconditions and limits. He starts from the proposition that capitalism never actually existed in the pure form that economic theorists commonly believed it to have assumed. The theorist, of necessity, has to design a model or 'schema' that is an ideal abstraction rather than a mirror-image of real life. Such a model is nothing but a useful fiction, a 'set of analytical tools', convenient for structuring the endless variety of empirical phenomena. A model can neither be derived by logical induction from the observation of reality, nor can it be deduced from general theoretical statements. On the other hand (and here Schumpeter moderates his earlier conventionalism), a model is not assembled arbitrarily. The model-builder is equipped with the given state of theory and a body of pre-scientific practical knowledge, which he shares with the businessman. A model cannot be refuted by confronting it with reality; the criteria of falsificationism do not apply to it. It can, however, be replaced by a better model, which combines an equal descriptive capacity with a higher degree of structural clarity. Schumpeter does not invoke Weber's authority when commenting on his model-building procedures. Yet they closely approach Weber's ideas about using ideal types. There have been few practitioners of an ideal-typical method, but innumerable interpreters of it. In *Business Cycles*, Schumpeter shows himself to be one of those who work with rather than within Weber's spirit.

Schumpeter, as far as he has been appreciated as a methodologist at all, has been credited with elaborating the doctrine of methodological individualism, first explicitly introduced into economics by Carl Menger.[29] Perhaps more remarkable than the doctrine itself is Schumpeter's insistence on separating methodological from political individualism. Taking the individual, equipped with exchangeable commodities and a set of preferences, as the basic unit of analysis does not necessarily imply commitment to a system of libertarian capitalism. Classical and neo-classical economic theory does not lead directly to 'Manchesterism' in economic and social policy, as many of its critics, mainly in Germany, believed. Here, Max Weber wholeheartedly concurred. He firmly objected to 'the tremendous misunderstanding to think that an "individualistic" *method* should involve what is in any conceivable sense an individualistic system of *values*',[30] and in his own work by and large upheld the principle of methodological individualism.

Schumpeter never saw himself as a champion and follower of Weberian methodology. He even doubted its relevance to economic theory. Yet, when viewed within the context of contemporary methodological positions, Schumpeter comes close to Weber in a number of important points: in his defence of autonomous economic reasoning, in a basically nominalist and constructive stance, in a certain preference for the ideal-typical method and in the defence of methodological individualism.

III

Schumpeter's theory of economic development is an explanation not of the historical genesis of capitalism, but of its dynamic functioning. It is a theory of the capitalist process. In the original version of 1911, its time-scale is limited to the individual developmental cycle; only later, in Volume 2 of *Business Cycles*, is it extended into a long-term historical analysis of the Western economies. Schumpeter's theory of 1911 is inconceivable without the theoretical background of nineteenth-century thinking on the sources of social and economic change. Yet it does not directly compete either with Marx's examination of 'primitive accumulation' and its consequences, or with Weber's ideas on the role of beliefs in the rise of capitalism, let alone with the eclectic approach of Sombart, whose shoddy scholarship and lack of theoretical sophistication Schumpeter severely criticized. Schumpeter's characteristic theme had different roots. It was shaped by historical experience and by the state of the art. The historical experience was that of contemporary Austria, marked by relative economic stagnation and the failure of *laissez-faire* capitalism to surmount the social and political obstacles impeding its development.[31] The state of the art was indicated by a gaping hole left in the Walrasian system: how were the dynamic features of capitalism (so obvious, for example, in Germany and the United States) to be accounted for in terms of the neo-classical theory of general equilibrium? The founding fathers of neo-classicism had by no means disregarded the problem; Walras's system was stationary, not static. It did not exclude the possibility of quantitative growth and qualitative change, and it provided, for example, for the adaptation of the economy to exogenous processes such as population growth. But the dynamics of the economic system were of a purely reactive kind, set in motion by external stimuli alone. Schumpeter's problem was whether an endogenous source of development could be identified and whether it could be reconciled with the basic principles of neo-classical theory. A Marxian problem was to be dealt with in Walrasian terms.

Schumpeter, therefore, took as his starting point not a historically concrete form of pre-capitalist society, but a theoretically defined state of equilibrium, which could not be located in historical time and space. This equilibrium is upset by individuals who take on the function of an entrepreneur: they 'innovate' by bringing given economic resources together into new 'combinations' (technologies, marketing strategies, forms of business organization, etc.) and by actually translating these combinations into reality. Since the entrepreneur, by definition, is not an owner of capital, new combinations can only be realized – and development can therefore only take place – if the entrepreneur is given access to credit. This is the function of the capitalist, i.e. the owner of capital, or more specifically, under modern conditions, the banker. Capitalism is defined as 'that form of private-property economy in which innovations are carried out by means of borrowed money, which in general though not by logical necessity, implies creation of credit'.[32] This is a functional, not a substantive definition. Rather than a 'social formation' or a specific 'social system', capitalism is merely the linking of the function of the innovating entrepreneur with that of the financier under conditions in which the means of production are privately owned. Schumpeter's entrepreneur is the bearer of one specific economic function. He does not occupy a position within a given social structure. It would be absurd, in Schumpeterian terms, to speak of a *class* of entrepreneurs. That entrepreneurial success is likely to help an individual to join the capitalist class (in turn providing funds for a new generation of entrepreneurs) is quite a different matter and does not affect the basic argument. Schumpeter's theory of economic development is thus constructed around a hard core of 'pure' economic logic. He offers a model of equilibrium being disturbed and re-established at a higher level. No non-economic assumptions have to be introduced in order to explain the basic mechanisms of growth. Individual motivation, social conditions of action, class structures, belief systems, anthropological presuppositions and historical contexts do not enter into the model itself. Schumpeter's theory of economic development remains firmly in the neo-classical orbit, an illustration of his own 'Monroe doctrine', maintaining a clear distance to all kinds of psychology, sociology or political economy of the Historical School.

However, by supplementing his economic theory with sociological interpretations, Schumpeter himself moves on from economics to *social* economics, that is, into Max Weber's territory. Schumpeter's notion of human or social 'types' which correspond to economic functions and embody particular kinds of conduct, provide a bridge from economic theory in a technical and narrow sense to a wider concept of social *and* economic interpretation of reality.[33] The hallmark of the entrepreneur's conduct is his disruption of that daily routine which characterizes the way in which non-innovative 'mere managers' go about their business. The entrepreneur, a force of unconditioned dynamism, bursts into the ever-revolving system from outside, throws it off course and imbues it with a kind of economic quantum impulse. He acts as a creative destroyer, personifying the force of extraordinariness in economic life. Normality, marked by equilibrium and circular flows, by the 'individual's routine work as determined by material circumstances',[34] will eventually be restored, but only at a new level of systemic performance and in modified form. This is not the result of social evolution or of the workings of anonymous forces and masses. The cycle of eternal recurrence of the same can only be cracked open by the initiative of the enterprising few, those who are both willing and able to provide leadership.[35]

From a sociological perspective, therefore, the entrepreneur's conduct is discernible as a particular manifestation of the basic type of social action that Schumpeter calls 'leadership'. 'Social leadership', he explains in his essay on social classes (1927), 'means to decide, to command, to prevail, to advance.'[36] It is universal and constitutes a fundamental moving force at all levels of human communal life from the family to the nation state. Leadership shapes history; it, in turn, is shaped by the transpersonal conditions of life. The prevalent type of leadership in classic capitalism is *economic* leadership; the prevalent type of leader is the daring industrialist − the risk-taking founder rather than the well-established industrial dynast of the second or third generation. During the short time that his genuine leadership lasts, he is something of a classless individual, too dynamic to fit into any kind of social structure as yet, still on the move and impinging on his environment in the process. It may not be a coincidence that the social outsider Benjamin Disraeli appeared to Schumpeter as the classic representative of *political* leadership.[37]

As Schumpeter points out in his essay on social classes, this sociological concept of leadership should not be confused with 'individual leadership of the great mind or of the genius'.[38] The industrial leader, for example, is only significant as the incarnation of a social type; he does not possess a recognizably individualistic ethic or personal charisma of the sort that characterizes Nietzsche's or Weber's great individuals. In the final analysis, the entrepreneur − whatever his personal motives may be − serves as the unwitting instrument by which the universal process of rationalization is put into practice. He is 'the pioneer of modern man and of level-headed thinking, utilitarian philosophy and forms of life that are essentially individualistic'.[39] The creativity and boldness of the entrepreneur, his disruption of routine and matter-of-fact business, is not only a necessary condition for economic growth but also, in the wider perspective of social economics, a crucial force contributing to a 're-organization of economic life along the lines of private economic rationality'.[40] Rationalization is the sum total of individual initiatives rather than the result of relentlessly advancing trans-individual bureaucratization. Even so, the individual cannot escape.

Schumpeter regarded the long-term prospects of social and economic development with the equanimity of the tough-minded economic theorist. He did not disguise his contempt for the 'forms of life' brought about by modern capitalism with 'its utilitarianism and the wholesale destruction of

Meanings',[41] and he deplored the loss of aura surrounding central manifestations of culture: 'The stock exchange is a poor substitute for the Holy Grail.'[42] The entrepreneur is a strangely ambivalent 'type' , because he is affected by this process of disenchantment. Economically speaking, he is the vehicle of the pure logic of capitalism. Culturally, however, he still partakes of the magic spell of the hero, who is propelled by decidedly non-rational motives, which conform neither to the anthropology of classical political economy nor to that of the theorists of marginal utility. The entrepreneur's behaviour 'does not seem to verify the picture of the economic man, balancing probable results against disutility of effort and reaching in due course a point of equilibrium beyond which he is not willing to go'.[43] Much more to the point, he is driven by 'the dream and the will to found a private kingdom, usually, though not necessarily, also a dynasty. The modern world really does not know any such positions, but what may be attained by industrial or commercial success is still the nearest approach to medieval lordship possible to modern man'.[44] Yet if the entrepreneur is the last hero, he is a hero only in a limited sense – a leader and a revolutionary only as far as economic matters are concerned, but no longer the exponent of a homogenous and unfragmented style of life. At times, Schumpeter appears to look back to an age when a pre-modern wholeness and unity of life still seemed possible. His comments on modern capitalism are tinged with a faint melancholy which, however, is nowhere allowed to interfere seriously with the sobriety of scientific analysis. Schumpeter the critic of modern culture never takes over from Schumpeter the social economist.

IV

Schumpeter's social-economic analysis of capitalism is marked by three distinctive features. First, it is a functional rather than a genetic analysis, not primarily concerned with the origins of modern capitalism. Secondly, it is built around a theory of economic development that is devised in essentially neo-classical terms and is only supplemented by sociological interpretation at a later analytical stage. This order of priority differs sharply from Max Weber's political social economics as exemplified in the early studies on rural labour.[45] A political dimension is largely absent from Schumpeter's writings on capitalism before 1920. Thirdly, Schumpeter subscribes to the cosmopolitanism of the classics. He does not accept the national state as a unit of analysis or as the repository of political values. Few of Weber's utterances are further removed from Schumpeter's concerns than the Freiburg Inaugural Address. Schumpeter's science of economics is by no means oblivious of the problems raised by the German Historical School of political economy, but in no sense is it a '*National*-Ökonomie'.

As far as the analysis of contemporary capitalism was concerned, Max Weber and Schumpeter disagreed most conspicuously in their assessment of the role of bureaucracy. This is clearly apparent in their respective theories of democracy. For Weber and Schumpeter alike, democracy cannot be isolated from the issue of leadership. Both men share a distrust of substantive theories of democracy, especially those deriving from Rousseau or from concepts of Natural Law;[46] both agree that educating and selecting political leaders according to formalized procedures is the foremost task of parliaments. These similarities in outlook have often been noticed and commented upon. On the other hand, there are two important differences, which have received less attention. Firstly, Schumpeter's leaders act above all on considerations of political feasibility, while Weber's leaders are mainly guided by ultimate convictions. In other words, Schumpeter goes much further than Weber towards a purely pragmatic, formal and ethically neutral theory of politics. Secondly, for Weber the central antagonism at the heart of the theory is that of political leadership and bureaucracy, whereas for Schumpeter the crucial relationship is that between the leader and his followers, extending to the masses on which the art of plebiscitary mobilization is exercised. When Schumpeter speaks of bureaucracy (at least as far as the theory of democracy is concerned) he refers to the political 'machines' at the disposal of the leader rather than to the executive power of the state in the Continental European sense. To Schumpeter, bureaucracy does not figure as a contrasting principle to plebiscitary leadership democracy. It is an integral part of it.

Both Schumpeter and Weber keenly observed the effects of bureaucratization on the development of capitalism, but arrived at quite different conclusions. Schumpeter paid particular attention to the evolution of the bureaucratic giant company and the 'trust'. As his essay 'Sozialistische Möglichkeiten von heute' (1920) makes clear, he regarded the transformation of competitive capitalism into organized capitalism as an irreversible process. Although he personally deplored this process, he did not see it as leading to disastrous economic consequences. While Max Weber believed in a close connection between economic dynamism and the existence of a stratum of entrepreneurs operating in comparatively free markets,[47] Schumpeter did not exclude the possibility that the function of the entrepreneur would be transferred to the bureaucratic management of the giant company. As he wrote in 1920: technological progress had already become 'the result of systematically conducted scientific research'; it occurred almost 'automatically' and was no longer dependent on the bold action of imaginative individuals.[48] This was equally true of other types of innovative achievement that had been the domain of the classic entrepreneur. What was rapidly becoming obsolete was not the function of the entrepreneur in general, but only the *individualistic* manifestations of this function.[49] Schumpeter therefore did not expect capitalism to stagnate, as did Max Weber;[50] much less did he foretell its collapse on account of an economic crisis. Capitalism, by definition, was incapable of stagnating.[51] Finally, writing in the aftermath of the Great Depression, Schumpeter went so far as to welcome the bureaucratic corporation, operating in monopolistically or oligopolistically structured markets, as 'the most powerful engine' in the process of creative destruction that defined capitalism.[52] Hence, there were no viable economic arguments in favour of individualistic entrepreneurship. The regime of the managers differed from the regime of the heroic industrial pioneers only in respect of culture and the dominant life-forms but not in economic efficiency. To put it very simply, Schumpeter was an economic optimist.

On the other hand, he was a cultural pessimist. Nowhere in his work is the contradiction between these two attitudes satisfactorily resolved. It must be emphasized, however, that Schumpeter's prognosis of the inevitable self-destruction of capitalism – the very part of his work where the two different standards of interpretation clash most sharply – is by no means the centre-piece of his *oeuvre*, even if much writing on Schumpeter tends to give this impression. *Capitalism, Socialism and Democracy* is an attempt at *haute vulgarisation* rather than the sum of its author's scientific insight.[53] The famous self-destruction thesis is offered in a spirit of playful reflection on tendencies and prospects for the future: it must not be taken as the apogee of Schumpeter's thinking; Schumpeter never claimed scientific validity for it in the way he did for his theory of economic development. He himself was keenly aware that the thesis could not easily be derived from his own *economic* theory of capitalism. It is based exclusively on ad hoc assumptions about cultural change in capitalist societies. The self-destruction thesis is based on socio-cultural, not on economic, arguments.

Any attempt to link the two strands of reasoning more closely than Schumpeter himself does must go back to the concept of rationalization that lies behind so many of Schumpeter's more general statements. A connection may then be construed as follows: capitalism of the classic type developed its specific mode of functioning and its characteristic economic rationality within a sociocultural environment that was only partly affected by the process of rationalization. Rationalization proceeds at different speeds in different spheres of human communal life. Non-rational orientations were retained much longer in the cultural sphere, where the predominant human 'types' and the characteristic 'forms of life' consequently continued to be hybrid and ambivalent. Modern economic life remained permeated by traces of pre-modern mentality; the entrepreneur himself was cast in the decidedly pre-modern role of the heroic leader and his life-style was prone to subsequent gentrification, turning erstwhile industrial pioneers into *bourgeois gentilhommes*.

But rationalization advances relentlessly. The same process that raises capitalism from the level of individualistic entrepreneurship to the (formally and materially) more rational one of the bureaucratic giant company, also erodes the sociocultural buffers that had protected classic capitalism: private property becomes ever more abstract and is ultimately transmogrified into the ownership of shares; 'extra-rational loyalties' to the central institutions of society disappear, as do the remaining pre-capitalist or semi-capitalist 'protect-ive strata'; intellectuals are free to sabotage the basic consensus of values on which capitalism rests.[54] Thus, capitalism is by no means brought down by the impact of the 'superstructure', as Schumpeter calls it, deliberately using the Marxist term.[55] There is no such simplistic reversal of Marx in Schumpeter's work. As far as Schumpeter is concerned with determination 'in the ultimate instance' – and he is not concerned with this in his major writings, with the single exception of *Capitalism, Socialism and Democracy* – he does in fact look to the economic sphere for the most profound sources of historical dynamics. Rationalization originates from the economic sphere, but it bursts through its boundaries and extends its sway over the much more resistant sociocultural environment. Eventually, the protective atmosphere withers away as the world is immersed in the blinding light of unshaded rationality.

Socialism is the final phase in this process. When Schumpeter talks about socialism, he excludes all humanistic and Utopian connotations and narrows down the concept to a purely economic definition.[56] Socialism is the type of economic system in which a 'central body controls all means of production, devises and implements economic planning to the extent of taking charge of the distribution of consumer goods to the individual citizens'.[57] Whether the means of production are privately or publicly owned is of little importance as long as they are effectively under centralized control. Thus, socialism is little more than a prolongation of tendencies already present in organized capitalism, marking a further step in the universal process of rationalization.

Joseph Schumpeter was not a socialist. He saw his prophecies of the impending victory of socialism as resulting from his sober contemplation of the ways of the world. To argue for or against the desirability of socialism seemed to him to be beside the point. However, he gave his opinions on the more limited question of the feasibility of socialism. In contrast to Max Weber, and especially the younger Austrian school (F.A. v. Hayek, L. v. Mises), he regarded a socialist economy as perfectly capable of functioning as smoothly as, and perhaps more rationally than, a capitalist market economy. In the 'planning versus free market' debate that was conducted around 1920 and to which Max Weber contributed a few incisive pages in *Economy and Society*,[58] Schumpeter sided with those who did *not* accept economic arguments against the practicability of socialism (it should be pointed out, however, that Schumpeter's notion of socialism bore little resemblance to that of some of his comrades-in-arms). Moreover, he was not particularly worried about the prospect of a bureaucratized socialism. Provided that certain technical arrangements were made – especially for the continued operation of a system linking reward with performance – 'human material of supernormal quality' would soon occupy the key positions as it had done under capitalism.[59] Elitist socialism would not mean a dramatic break with the past. Schumpeter did not share the visions of horror held by liberal anti-socialists: economic irrationality, political serfdom and social levelling. To him, the highest price to be paid for socialism would be the obliteration of Meaning by the operation of totally unrestrained rationality. Schumpeter faced this prospect in a mood of ironic pessimism.

Notes: Chapter 7

1   J. A. Schumpeter, *Das Wesen und der Hauptinhalt der theoretischen Nationalökonomie* (Leipzig, 1908).
2   Cf. E. Schneider, *Joseph A. Schumpeter. Leben und Werk eines großen Sozialökonomen* (Tübingen, 1970), p. 19.
3   J. A. Schumpeter, *Theorie der wirtschaftlichen Entwicklung* (Leipzig, 1911), hereafter quoted from the English translation by R. Opie, new edn (New Brunswick, NJ, and London, 1983).
4   At the Max-Weber-Arbeitsstelle of the Bayerische Akademie der Wissenschaften, Munich. The most recent contribution to Weber and Schumpeter is R. Collins, *Weberian Sociological Theory* (Cambridge, 1986), pp. 117–42. This important book was published after the present chapter had been finalized.
5   J. A. Schumpeter, 'Max Webers Work' [1920], in idem, *Dogmengeschichtliche und biographische Aufsätze* (Tübingen, 1954), pp. 108–17.
6   J. A. Schumpeter, *History of Economic Analysis*, ed. from manuscript by E. B. Schumpeter (London, 1954), p. 818–19.
7   ibid., p. 819.

8 F. Perroux, *La Pensée économique de Joseph Schumpeter: les dynamiques du capitalisme* (Geneva, 1965), p. 179.

9 J. A. Schumpeter, *Economic Doctrine and Method: An Historical Sketch*, transl. by R. Aris (London, 1957), pp. 161–2.

10 Cf. ibid., pp. 182 ff.; idem, 'Marie Esprit Léon Walras', in idem, *Ten Great Economists: From Marx to Keynes* (London, 1952), pp. 74–9.

11 idem, *History of Economic Analysis*, p. 814. See idem, *Das Wesen*, pp. vii, ix.

12 idem, 'Gustav v. Schmoller und die Probleme von heute', in idem, *Dogmengeschichtliche und biographische Aufsätze*, pp. 148–99. This masterly essay was not translated in *Ten Great Economists*.

13 idem, *History of Economic Analysis*, pp. 12 ff.

14 Cf. idem, *Das Wesen*, pp. 78–9. See also Schumpeter's 1915 lecture to students in Czernowitz, 'Wie studiert man Sozialwissenschaft?', in idem, *Aufsätze zur ökonomischen Theorie* (Tübingen, 1952), pp. 555, 559.

15 For this episode, see E. März, *Österreichische Bankpolitik in der Zeit der großen Wende 1913–1923. Am Beispiel der Creditanstalt für Handel und Gewerbe* (Vienna, 1981), pp. 318–44; W. F. Stolper and C. Seidl, 'Einleitung', in J. A. Schumpeter, *Aufsätze zur Wirtschaftspolitik* (Tübingen, 1985), pp. 15–32

16 K. Kraus, 'Die allerletzten Tage der Menschheit', *Die Fackel*, no. 513–530 (February 1920), p. 158.

17 Schumpeter, *Das Wesen*, pp. 536, 539 ff.

18 F. v. Wieser, *Der gesellschaftliche Werth* (Vienna, 1889), p. 4; idem, *Theorie der gesellschaftlichen Wirtschaft*, 2nd edn (Tübingen, 1924), pp. 8–10.

19 WL⁴, pp. 384–99. An English translation of this essay (by L. Schneider) can be found in *Social Science Quarterly*, vol. 56 (1975), pp. 21–36. See also Chapter 3 by Manfred Schön in this volume.

20 For these terms, see A. Kaplan, *The Conduct of Inquiry: Methodology for Behavioral Science* (San Francisco, Calif., 1964), pp. 3–11.

21 WL⁴, pp. 396, 394. This discussion has to disregard Weber's general attitude towards contemporary psychology. See, for example, T. E. Huff, *Max Weber and the Methodology of the Social Sciences* (New Brunswick, NJ, 1984), pp. 29 ff).

22 WL⁴, p. 187; MSS, p. 87.

23 Cf. T. W. Hutchison, *The Politics and Philosophy of Economics: Marxians, Keynesians and Austrians* (Oxford, 1981), pp. 178 ff.; idem, 'Some themes from "Investigations into Method"', in J. R. Hicks and W. Weber (eds), *Carl Menger and the Austrian School of Economics* (Oxford, 1973), pp. 15 ff).

24 Cf. H. Poincaré, *La Science et l'hypothèse* (Paris, 1902).

25 I. Lakatos, *The Methodology of Scientific Research Programmes* (Cambridge, 1978), p. 21.

26 Schumpeter, *Das Wesen*, p. 46.

27 Cf. W. J. Mommsen, *Max Weber. Gesellschaft, Politik und Geschichte* (Frankfurt, 1974), p. 226.

28 J. A. Schumpeter, *Business Cycles: A Theoretical, Historical and Statistical Analysis of the Capitalist Process*, 2 vols (New York and London, 1939), especially Vol. 1, chs 1–5. See also his presidential address to the American Economic Association, 'Science and ideology', *American Economic Review*, vol. 39 (1949), pp. 350–1.

29 F. Machlup, *Methodology of Economics and Other Social Sciences* (New York, 1978), p. 545; M. Blaug, *The Methodology of Economics or How Economists Explain* (Cambridge, 1978), pp. 309 ff.; W. Heine, *Methodologischer Individualismus* (Würzburg, 1983), pp. 116–22.

30 ES, Vol. 1, p. 18.

31 Cf. E. Streissler, 'Schumpeter's Vienna and the role of credit in innovation', in H. Frisch (ed.), *Schumpeterian Economics* (Eastbourne and New York, 1982), pp. 60–83; E. März, *Joseph Alois Schumpeter: Forscher, Lehrer und Politiker* (Munich, 1983), pp. 92–8; F. Meissner, 'The Schumpeters and the industrialization of Třešť', *Zeitschrift für die gesamte Staatswissenschaft*, vol. 135 (1978), pp. 256–62. The thesis of Austrian stagnation has recently been called into question by D. F. Good, *The Economic Rise of the Habsburg Empire, 1750–1914* (Berkeley, Calif., 1984), pp. 125 ff.

32 Schumpeter, *Business Cycles*, Vol. 1, p. 223.

33 idem, *Theory of Economic Development*, pp. 82–3.

34 ibid., p. 88 (translation amended following *Theorie der wirtschaftlichen Entwicklung*, p. 128). On Schumpeter's entrepreneur, see also K. W. Rothschild, 'Capitalists and en-

trepreneurs: prototypes and roles', in H.-J. Wagener and J. W. Drukker (eds), *The Economic Law of Motion of Modern Society* (Cambridge, 1986), pp. 186–96.

35   ibid., pp. 84 ff.
36   J. A. Schumpeter, 'Social classes in an ethnically homogeneous environment', in idem, *Imperialism and Social Classes*, transl. by H. Norden (New York, 1951), p. 217.
37   idem, 'The sociology of imperialisms', in ibid., pp. 9 ff.
38   idem, 'Social classes', p. 216.
39   idem, *Theorie der wirtschaftlichen Entwicklung*, p. 134 (the existing English translation of this passage is inaccurate).
40   ibid.
41   J. A. Schumpeter, *Capitalism, Socialism and Democracy*, 3rd edn (London, 1950), p. 129.
42   ibid., p. 137.
43   idem, *Theory of Economic Development*, p. 92.
44   ibid., p. 93.
45   Cf. L. A. Scaff, 'Weber before Weberian sociology', *British Journal of Sociology*, vol. 35 (1984), pp. 190–215, here pp. 200 ff.
46   See, for example, Schumpeter, *Capitalism, Socialism and Democracy*, pp. 250–68. For Weber, see W. J. Mommsen, *Max Weber and German Politics, 1890–1920* (Chicago, 1984), pp. 392–3.
47   Cf. D. Beetham, *Max Weber and the Theory of Modern Politics* (London, 1974), pp. 82–3.
48   J. A. Schumpeter, 'Sozialistische Möglichkeiten von heute', in idem, *Aufsätze zur ökonomischen Theorie*, p. 467.
49   This important point was made by C. Napoleoni, *Grundzüge der modernen ökonomischen Theorie* (Frankfurt, 1968), p. 84.
50   Cf. Mommsen, *Max Weber and German Politics*, p. 82.
51   Schumpeter, *Capitalism, Socialism and Democracy*, p. 82.
52   ibid., p. 106.
53   See also H. Kirsch, 'Joseph Alois Schumpeter', *Journal of Economic Issues*, vol. 13 (1979), p. 151.
54   Schumpeter, *Capitalism, Socialism and Democracy*, pp. 144 ff.
55   ibid, p. 121.
56   For a good critique of Schumpeter's concept of socialism, see T. Bottomore's introduction to the 5th edn (London, 1976) of *Capitalism, Socialism and Democracy* (especially p. xi).
57   Schumpeter, 'Sozialistische Möglichkeiten', p. 458.
58   WuG⁵, pp. 53–62. See also K. Novy, *Strategien der Sozialisierung. Die Diskussion der Wirtschaftsreform in der Weimarer Republik* (Frankfurt and New York, 1978), pp. 82 ff.
59   Schumpeter, *Capitalism, Socialism and Democracy*, p. 204.

8 Robert Michels and Max Weber: Moral Conviction versus the Politics of Responsibility

WOLFGANG J. MOMMSEN

Robert Michels (or Roberto, as he renamed himself on emigrating to Italy) occupies a special position among the contemporaries of Max Weber in the social sciences. It is impossible to classify him unequivocally under any single heading among the tendencies within the social sciences of his day. As David Beetham rightly emphasizes, his significance as a scholar must be sought primarily in his remarkable capacity to co-ordinate and combine divergent theoretical positions.[1] Throughout his life, he also played the role of a mediator between the German and Italian social sciences and, in a sense, between Germany and Italy in general. Born into an upper bourgeois Cologne family in 1876, he formed a special relationship with France and Italy at an early stage in his development. Having obtained a doctorate in history under Johann Gustav Droysen at the University of Halle, he went on to pursue extensive studies in history and the social sciences in France and Italy, where he came into close contact with syndicalist circles and became personally acquainted with Georges Sorel and Arturo Labriola.[2]

At the age of 24, Michels joined first the Italian and then the German Socialist Party, becoming actively involved in Marburg with a group of socialist intellectuals of markedly anarcho-syndicalist coloration. As someone who had become a socialist on grounds of ethical and moral conviction, he found himself more or less on the margins of German Social Democracy. Almost from the beginning of his involvement in Social Democratic politics, he criticized it from the perspective of a political strategy with syndicalist leanings, which owed a great deal to his concrete knowledge of conditions within the Italian Socialist Party. His membership of the Social Democratic Party proved an obstacle to his Habilitation (qualification for university teaching) in Marburg. When, a little later, in 1906, he made a renewed attempt to obtain his Habilitation, in Jena, he was debarred on the same grounds during preliminary negotiations. As a result, Michels emigrated in 1907 to Turin, where he finally got his Habilitation with Achille Loria. Though he considered Italy his second home and felt 'at heart' an Italian, in his scholarly interests he remained primarily oriented towards the German scientific community. In Turin, he did, however, become acquainted with Gaetano Mosca and later also with Vilfredo Pareto. The writings of both men were to have considerable influence on his own work.

We do not know when Max Weber and Robert Michels first met. The first letter we have from Weber to Michels dates from 1 January 1906 and in it Weber responds very positively to a 'projected piece of work' by Michels. This is probably a reference to an article on 'German Social Democracy' which was published in the *Archiv für Sozialwissenschaft und Sozialpolitik* in the same year.[3] That article, however, had been preceded by an essay on 'The Proletariat and the bourgeoisie in the socialist movement in Italy', for which Weber's support had certainly not been lacking; indeed it seems possible to attribute its publication essentially to his initiative.[4] One way or another, from the spring of 1906 onwards an extremely close relationship developed between Michels and Weber, which has no equal for intimacy and intensity in the rest of Weber's life. Michels confirms this retrospectively in an obituary for Weber, written in 1920:

> The writer had the good fortune of enjoying a close friendship with Max Weber for many years of his life, which, however, at the beginning of the First World War suffered a shock from which it did not completely recover after the war had ended.[5]

Between Weber and Michels there arose what I have described elsewhere as an 'asymmetrical partnership', the effects of which on the development of the work of Michels – and indeed of Weber – in the social sciences were considerable.[6] As Wilfried Röhrich has so appositely remarked, where Michels was concerned, Max Weber took on the role of a critically questioning mentor, lending support to him in his scientific work with constant advice and critical appraisal.[7] But the full scope of his interest in Michels went far beyond this, extending, indeed, into an existential dimension. In a certain sense, Max Weber saw in Michels the personification of a conduct according to the ethic of conviction and in this respect his *alter ego* – some one who, from premises which were in many respects identical to his own, tended to draw moralist consequences which he, by his rigorous, rationalistic self-criticism (corresponding to the postulate of the ethic of responsibility) denied himself. It is not by chance that Weber's letters to Michels contain the most spontaneous and direct expressions of his views about political, scientific and personal problems that we possess.

From the material at our disposal – despite the occasional obliqueness of its reference – we may conclude that Weber was principally interested in Michels the socialist, or more precisely in Michels as a conviction socialist and, particularly, as a syndicalist who possessed close contacts to both German and Italian social democrats. We know from other contexts of the trouble taken by Weber throughout his life to encourage socialists to participate in the *Archiv*, in his attempt to find possible ways of breaking the monopoly of bourgeois social science. The young Michels was optimally qualified to present the problems of socialism and Social Democracy in the *Archiv* as an insider, that is to say, from the standpoint of a committed partisan. The fact that Michels's socialism denied him access to an academic career in Germany may have provided an additional motivation for Weber's overtures to him and the interest Weber took in his work. Whether or not this was the case, Weber argued vigorously in Michels's favour in the ensuing years and sought, wherever possible, to smooth a path for him. The refusal of a professorial title

to Michels gave Weber occasion publicly to charge the *Kaiserreich* with allowing 'freedom of scholarship' only within boundaries defined by the limits of
courtly tolerance; this, he said, represented 'disgrace and ignominy for a
cultured nation [*Kulturnation*]'.[8] It was Weber who recommended Michels to
Achille Loria, also a former student of August Meitzen, for a Habilitation in
Turin. More importantly, however, he did his best to open the doors of the
Archiv to Michels; almost all the more significant of Michels's writings in
subsequent years first appeared in the *Archiv für Sozialwissenschaft*, particularly those articles that were later to be presented in a unified form in his
famous *Political Parties*, published in 1911. In addition, Weber made efforts
to persuade Michels to participate in the work of the Verein für Sozialpolitik
(Social Policy Association). He enlisted him as an author in the *Grundriß
der Sozialökonomik* (Outline of Social Economics), of which he had been
editor since 1909. As early as 1908, he also began to press for Michels to
become a joint editor, with Jaffé, Sombart and himself, of the *Archiv für
Sozialwissenschaft*, despite the fact that this might have necessitated his own
withdrawal from the editorial board. Only in 1913 was this ambition realized;
however, Michels's editorship then came to an abrupt end after the entry of
Italy into the First World War, essentially on account of political differences.
Despite a subsequent bitter quarrel over an article Michels had published in a
Basle newspaper arguing that Italy's entry into the war on the side of the Allies
was justified, Weber continued to defend Michels against criticism from third
parties.[9]

Throughout these years, Weber continued to nurture the greatest expectations of Michels as a scholar. Yet he was never blind to Michels's weaknesses,
the most serious of which, in his view, was a tendency to publish prematurely
work that was more of a publicistic than a scholarly character, in which his
arguments had not yet been sufficiently thought through. Weber's greatest
hope of Michels was that he might produce a 'cultural history of the modern
proletarian movement' in its ideological, or, in Weber's own terms, its 'world-
view' aspects. He urged him repeatedly to concentrate his efforts on a great
undertaking of this kind rather than dissipate his talents in the production of
essays and articles on current political questions. He considered such an undertaking to be 'an immense task, for which, to my knowledge, *only you* in the
whole wide world, are fitted'.[10] Later still, he extracted from Michels the
promise of an article for the *Grundriß der Sozialökonomik* on the socialist
movement. Michels promised to tailor the contents to guidelines laid down by
Weber, but the article did not see the light of day until after Weber's death.
For his part, Michels provided Weber with numerous contacts in socialist
circles; this was how the Dutch anarchist Nieuwenhuis, for example, came to
write in the *Archiv*.

Robert Michels's early works are concerned predominantly with the German
and Italian socialist movements and, at the same time, with the role of the
socialist trade unions. It was his perspective as an observer steeped in the ideas
of Western-European-style syndicalism that inclined Michels to view German
Social Democracy critically. An attendant factor in the judgements he passed
on it was, however, his own ethic of conviction, which led him to identify with
the proletarian movement and to regard it as a fruit on the tree of capitalism,
destined in the end to receive its inevitable inheritance. His essay on party

membership and social composition in German Social Democracy, which was published in the *Archiv* in 1906, already makes unequivocal reference to the points on which he diverged from the predominant political current within Social Democracy, one particular instance of which was his view on the relative distance between party and unions, which he saw as a major cause of the weakness of Social Democracy in the German Reich. He concluded, however, on the optimistic note that 'the German proletariat, the German wage labourers' represented the 'well-spring' of German Social Democracy, 'a well-spring that was far from exhausted as yet'.[11] However, Michels grew increasingly disillusioned with the quietistic course steered by the leadership of the Social Democratic Party, which was revolutionary only in its language – something incompatible with his ethics of conviction. Furthermore, his frustration mounted at the impotent and isolated position of intellectuals within the party, where they were treated with distrust and a general lack of appreciation. This led him rapidly towards an increasingly critical assessment of German Social Democracy.

For Michels, the quietism and merely verbal radicalism of the party were to be ascribed primarily to its leaders; thus he became a sharp critic both of the Kautskyan strategy of 'revolutionizing the minds' and of the pragmatism of the trade union leaders, who wanted no truck with a politics of revolutionary struggle involving the active participation of the unions, and were particularly opposed to the strategy of the political 'mass strike'. It was in this context that the problem of the gradual alienation of the Social Democratic leaders from the mass of the workers first posed itself for Michels; their step-by-step transition from a proletarian to a petty-bourgeois existence, and the shifts of position in politics and world-view which this engendered, seemed to Michels to have played a major part in producing an ossification of the leadership and a quietist political strategy, which paid lip-service to the classic revolutionary goals of the party, but did not pursue them in practice. Michels concluded that petty-bourgeois modes of thought had got the upper hand in the party.

On this point, Michels's views were very close to those of Max Weber, who, from premises that were to some degree opposed, had arrived at essentially the same conclusion, namely that a petty-bourgeois mentality predominated within German Social Democracy. It may be presumed that Weber and Michels discussed their differences on this question at great length, both in conversation and; from the evidence which we have to hand, also in writing. Certainly, Weber made plans to visit Michels in Rome in 1906 for the Italian Socialist Party Congress, where he hoped to attend the sessions as an observer. In the end, nothing came of the plan, which had arisen out of Weber's lively interest in the political situation in Italy. He did, however, attend the Social Democratic Party Congress in Mannheim in 1906, where he witnessed the famous Strategy Debate on the political role of the unions. The debate ended, in effect, in a fundamental renunciation of the concept of the political strike and a rejection of the idea of a politically aggressive role for the trade unions. He gave Michels a relatively extensive account of the proceedings:

> Mannheim was rather miserable. Bebel and Legien referred at least ten times to 'our *weakness*'. Furthermore, all this extremely petty-bourgeois de-meanour, these numerous complacent publican-faces, the lack of dynamism,

the inability to draw the necessary conclusions from the fact that the path
to the left is blocked, or at least appears to be so, and embark upon a rightist
policy — these gentlemen don't frighten anyone any more. [12]

Michels's immediate reaction to this letter is not known, though there can be
little doubt that he too held the party's petty-bourgeois demeanour essentially
responsible for its belief that the 'path to the left was blocked'. In Michels's
view, access could be gained to what he saw as a desirable leftward path for
the party, if necessary by employing the weapon of the political mass-strike.
Weber, by contrast, took quite the opposite view, bemoaning the failure of
Social Democracy to respond to prevailing social conditions by openly adopting a coherent revisionist line in alliance with the Left Liberals. Instead the
Social Democrats seemed to prefer to act as a force of 'inoculation', whose
function was to protect and sustain the existing, semi-constitutional political
order. [13] In his essay 'The German Social Democratic movement in its international context', which was published a year later in the *Archiv*, Michels took
the German socialists to task in no uncertain terms for their political strategy,
which he found wanting above all by comparison with the other European
socialist parties of the Second International. [14] He referred with obvious disapproval to the 'universal acclaim' accorded to 'the relegation of the weapon of
the general strike' at the most recent party congress in Mannhiem, 'to the
farthest corner of the party lumber-room' and pointed out that, 'perhaps with
the exception of the Danish party, the German Social Democratic Party is the
only one remaining within international socialism whose policy excludes the
tactic of the general strike, as indeed it excludes any form of direct action, even
including peaceful street demonstrations. And yet this is precisely the party
with the poorest prospects of even the remotest degree of success, as far as
alternative strategies are concerned'. [15]

In a similar vein, he registered with some bitterness the absolute irresolution
and quietism of German Social Democracy in relation to the measures that
might possibly be taken in the struggle to prevent a European war. In this context, he quoted extensively from the statements of numerous socialist leaders
from other parties. The conclusions he then drew on the state of Social
Democracy in many respects foreshadow the critique which today goes by the
name of 'secondary integration'. For Michels, the condition of total impotence in which German Social Democracy found itself had arisen not simply
in spite of, but indeed precisely because of its remarkably high level of
organization. Although purportedly anticipating revolution, it could no longer
claim to be a revolutionary party. Its 'purely verbal revolutionism, which lives
in constant anticipation of the automatic catastrophe' was not matched by any
will to revolutionary action. 'It is a characteristic feature of German Social
Democracy that it assembles under its single umbrella the most flagrant of contradictions: revolutionary intransigence at election-time is ranged against the
anti-revolutionary quietism of its general posture; high-sounding phraseology
in its theory sits alongside a resigned compliance in its practice; its language
is that of inflamed prophecy, yet in its actions it is almost totally paralysed.' [16]

As far as their diagnosis of the condition of German Social Democracy was
concerned, Michels and Weber appear at this stage to have belonged more or
less in the same camp. Both deplored the quietism of Social Democracy's

political strategy, bound up as it was with a purely verbal radicalism, whose ultimate goal was a mental disciplining of the masses and in which there was no place for the will to concrete political action. And Weber saw just as clearly as Michels (who was possibly the first to bring the subject to his attention) that qualitative changes in the party's political strategy – among other things, a weakening of its revolutionary élan – had been brought about by its advancing bureaucratization. At the same time, he did point out to Michels that this was a universal phenomenon, valid even for bourgeois parties; he referred him in this context to studies by James Bryce and Maurice Ostrogorski on American political parties.

Max Weber and Robert Michels did, however, draw very different conclusions from their common diagnosis of the situation. Weber considered the process of bureaucratization in modern mass parties to be irreversible; what is more, in the specific case of Social Democracy, he did not particularly disapprove of its effects. Quite the contrary, in fact, for he saw the increasing bureaucratization of the Social Democratic Party as a guarantee against any serious danger of revolutionary activity from that quarter. In the contemporary context, he judged the bourgeois fear of the much-evoked 'Red Peril' to be completely without foundation. It was during the debates of the Verein für Sozialpolitik at Magdeburg in the autumn of 1907 that Weber expounded these views, putting renewed emphasis on the disappearance from the party of any will for revolutionary action – indeed, even for constructive reformist politics. His statements were entirely in line with Michels's position; indeed Weber borrowed a number of Michels's own formulations. German Social Democracy, said Weber, 'is today clearly in the process of transforming itself into an enormous bureaucratic machine'. The long-term price of that transformation would, he maintained, inevitably be paid by those elements within Social Democracy who were the bearers of 'revolutionary ideologies'. At the same time, he denounced the 'petty-bourgeois physiognomy' of Social Democracy, which had, as he saw it, put 'lame, bombastically griping and grumbling debate in the place of the Catilinarian energies of faith to which we have hitherto been accustomed'.[17] This caustic use of public polemic was, however, too much for Michels. Evidence of his vigorous letter of protest to Weber may be gleaned from Weber's reply of 6 November 1907, which is all that remains of the exchange. Weber's deliberations on the subject in this context are presented in a mode that was very characteristically his own. He sets out the arguments both from his own value-perspective and from the value-perspective which he assumes would be adopted by the 'syndicalist' and partisan of the proletariat, Michels:

> The crazy idea that a class party with alleged class ideals coula ever become anything other than a 'machine', in the American sense of the term, is the key issue. Therefore I preach to my peers: 'you fools, the Social Democratic Party, whether parliamentary or syndicalist, is not, and never will be, anything worse (from *your* point of view) than a quite ordinary party machine'. As far as you are concerned, the conclusion would have to be: *political* democratization is the only thing that is perhaps attainable in the foreseeable future, but this is by no means a negligible achievement. I cannot prevent you from believing that more is possible, neither can I force myself to do so.[18]

Disregarding the shared premiss that both started out from, namely, a common perception of the absence of any propensity for revolutionary action in a German Social Democratic movement, whose radicalism was purely verbal, Weber here confronts central points of dissension between Michels and himself. Michels was convinced in principle that a syndicalist strike strategy could gradually undermine the existing system, and that it could ultimately bring about the victory of the socialist movement. For his part, Weber respected Michels's view, but demanded that it be regarded as a position to be justified on grounds of ethical conviction, rather than as a realistic strategy that might expect to meet with concrete success in empirical reality. And when Michels declared his sympathy for the spontaneous revolutionary mass-strike, a strategy that was being propagated at the time by Karl Liebknecht and Rosa Luxemburg and which he regarded both as a weapon of attrition to be employed against the existing social order and as a means of developing the revolutionary consciousness of the workers, Weber opposed him with some vigour:

It cannot possibly have escaped you that a *very* considerable proportion of all strikes (such as the defeated Hamburg dockers' strike) achieve the opposite of their desired effect, not only in the unions (this you would not mind) but on every kind of progress within the working-class movement, which they set back by years if not by decades. Their effect is exactly the opposite of what must be desired by anybody who measures the value of a strike by its contribution to the advance of 'socialization' or to the unification of the proletariat as a class or to whatever (provisional) socialist 'goals' you like. It is the most bizarre assertion that can ever be made to say, in the light of these experiences, that every strike works in the direction postulated by socialism, *ergo*, *every* strike is justified. And then there is this measuring of 'morality' by 'success'. Have you totally forgotten your Cohen? Surely he must have succeeded in curing you of *this* at least. Most particularly in curing Michels the *syndicalist*. The syndicalist M[ichels] ought to (is indeed compelled to) view the *conviction* which motivates a strike as 'proper' *in every case*; it is *patriotic* (patriotic to the class) – *ergo*, and so on. Yet what weakness is displayed in this obsequious courting of success! And in this violation of the facts before you![19]

Michels, for his part, was in no way inclined at this stage simply to abjure his fundamentalist conception of democratic rule, which, though it owed much to Rousseau's idea of direct democracy, was also strongly influenced by anarchistic ideas of a society free from domination; neither was he prepared, as an alternative, to embrace the pragmatic concept of democracy advocated by Weber. On the contrary, he continued to attribute Social Democracy's unwillingness to engage in revolutionary action under the conditions of the Wilhelmine semi-constitutional system chiefly to a corruption of the revolutionary impulses that were proper to the proletariat as a class. Their leaders, he claimed, had led them into quietism and a thoroughgoing accommodation to the existing political system; that corruption stemmed from a progressive bureaucratization, and indeed from an oligarchization of the party's leading cadres. In the forefront of this process, as Michels saw it, was the steadily increasing distance of the leaders from what we would today call 'the grass-roots'. What was more, he claimed, the leaders had sought to preserve their own positions through a gradual usurpation of power. The developing bureaucratic apparatuses had revealed themselves as wholly appropriate instruments for the attainment of this goal; at the same time, they themselves produced a further distancing of the leadership from the masses and from the proletarian milieu in general. Conversely, Michels also identified a need among the masses to subject themselves willingly to the leaders once these had been elected. All these factors together had, as he saw it, caused the internal party process, whereby opinions and conceptions were formed only to degenerate into a struggle for supremacy among a small leadership elite, who used demagogic techniques to form and influence opinion among the mass of the membership.

The source of Michels's ideas in this context was Gaetano Mosca's theory of the 'political class', that class which holds political power once and for all in its hands. He also drew upon Vilfredo Pareto's theory of the 'cyclical succession of political elites', although he did not allow it to undermine his own radical-democratic position. The first cogent formulation of such theses by Michels occurs in an essay on 'The oligarchic tendencies in society', which was published in the *Archiv* in the spring of 1908.[20] Most of the key terms, which make up the core of the book that he was to publish some three.years later, *Political Parties* (Zur Soziologie des Parteiwesens in der modernen Demokratie), are to be found in this essay. Since, however, Mosca and Pareto were still expressly characterized as anti-democratic thinkers, Michels avoided any possibility of the direct identification of his ideas with theirs.

Michels's and Weber's perceptions of the empirical facts of Social Democracy overlap considerably; their interpretations, however, are diametrically opposed. To illustrate the asymmetrical relationship between their positions, in what follows two themes will be extracted somewhat arbitrarily from Michels's work which also play a central role in the work of Max Weber, although they do so in a characteristically modified form. These are, first, the role of bureaucracy as a means of 'self-defence', in other words, as an instrument for the stabilization of the rule of the 'political class' and, secondly, the interpretation of the relationship between the leaders and the led as a relationship of domination.[21] There can have been no doubt as to how these two phenomena would be evaluated within Michels's political value-system; in his view, both tendencies were to be thoroughly deplored. It was his hope that to simply demonstrate the ways of their functioning might bring about an improvement in the situation they produced. In no sense was he yet prepared to call into question the criteria by which he sought to assess modern society, and the Socialist parties in particular, which latter he considered to be the true standard-bearers of the idea of the egalitarian principle and democracy. He particularly did not wish to question the ideal of a democracy, which should be a direct democracy to the highest possible degree and immune from corruption either by power-seeking strata of representatives or oligarchies of leaders, an ideal that was very much alive in the anarchist tradition in particular. He did, however, indicate that such an ideal was valid only as a yardstick against which reality could be measured; it was not to be regarded as a realizable postulate.

Max Weber's reaction to this line of argument was at once positive and extremely critical. He was convinced that Michels's radical-democratic perspective, which remained oriented towards the ideal of a more or less egalitarian democratic society of a socialist type organized along syndicalist lines, would inevitably come to grief when confronted with reality. He did not, however, in any sense deny the validity of Michels's perspective from the viewpoint of an ethic of conviction. Indeed he showed great interest in it, though more as a thought-experiment than anything else. In his response to Michels, he reiterates his belief that it is possible to sustain two antithetical perspectives – the one pragmatic and realist, the other moralistic – on the postulate of the realizability of a perfect socialist democracy even though the ultimate consequences of each display differences of a far-reaching nature:

> Your last piece of work in the *Archiv* is, however, considered *very* important by the people here; it has been mentioned to me in a number of different contexts. I found it thoroughly correct and commendable in its critical sections. But how much resignation will you still have to put up with? Such notions as 'will of the people' and 'genuine will of the people' have long since ceased to exist for me; they are fictitious notions. The same difficulties would present themselves if you tried to talk about a 'will of the boot consumers' which was to set the terms for the way the cobbler was to order his technique. There are two possibilities here.

> They are, set out (f)ormally:

> (1)   'My kingdom is not of this world' (Tolstoy) *or* a syndicalism *thought through to its logical conclusions*, which is *nothing other than* a translation of the proposition 'the goal is nothing to me, the movement everything' into revolutionary ethics, the sphere of the personal – a syndicalism which (of course) *you yourself* have not thought through to its conclusion! – or:

> (2)   An affirmation of culture (i.e. culture that expresses itself objectively, in technical – or other – achievements) which goes hand in hand with an accommodation to the sociological conditions underlying *all* 'techniques', be they economic, political, or whatever (all of which would find their *most highly developed expression* precisely in collectivist societies).

> In case number 2, all talk of revolution is quite farcical. Any idea of abolishing the domination of man over man by any socialist system whatsoever or by any sophisticated form of democracy whatsoever is Utopian. Your own critique in this matter does not by any means go far enough. The moment anyone who wishes to live as a 'modern individual', in the sense of having a newspaper every day and railways, electrical goods, etc., vacates the terrain of revolutionism *for its own sake*, that is, revolutionism without any goal, indeed revolutionism for which no goal is even *conceivable*, he necessarily *renounces* all those ideals which float before *your* eyes. You are a thoroughly honest chap and will yourself – as the [sober] sections of your article show – carry through the process of critical reflection which long ago brought me round to this way of thinking and stamped me, by virtue of that reflection, as a 'bourgeois' politician, at least for as long as the little that one *can* desire does not recede beyond the horizon.[22]

In the course of the following two years, Michels further elaborated the conceptions that he had begun to develop in his articles on Social Democracy, and had first presented systematically in his essay, 'The oligarchical tendencies in society'. The piecemeal arguments developed there were now set down in coherent fashion in his *Political Parties*, the first edition of which was published in 1911.[23] Although we have only limited concrete evidence of his continuing discussions with Max Weber, they cannot have been without consequence for his work in this period. Michels himself expressly acknowledged Weber's influence in the Preface to the second edition and, indeed, dedicated the first edition to him.[24] Michels complied only to a very limited extent with Weber's insistence that he should extend the basis of his analyses of modern parties by incorporating the available research on bourgeois parties; he did, however, in the more general sections of the book, take Ostrogorski's works on the subject into account. And he was clearly prepared to acknowledge, to a much greater extent than in 1908, the Utopian status of that total direct democracy, which had originally served as his normative guideline and which he had also judged to be a desirable form for the process of the formation of ideas within the party. He no longer regarded classical anarchism, which rejected on principle any form of centralization of power – including, of course, the formation of parties – as a logically imperative theoretical position.[25] In essence, however, his ultimate conclusion remained that of 1908. The conclusion to be drawn from his work, he claimed, was a practical maxim of continued struggle against the party system's structurally conditioned tendency towards the formation of oligarchies and, more generally, against all forms of domination.[26] The critical analysis of the 'ailments of democracy' presented by Michels aimed, by providing 'a clear and unembroidered insight into the oligarchic dangers of democracy, not to be in a position to prevent these altogether, but at least to be able to reduce them'.[27] For Michels, democracy still remained the 'lesser evil' by comparison with other forms of rule in general, and with pure aristocracy (as the classical form of oligarchic power) in particular.[28] Michels's critique of the democratic party-system was not yet a product of right-wing thinking but of a radical democratic position, which had its principal intellectual roots in the anarcho-syndicalist doctrine of a society completely free from domination. But contrary tendencies have a habit of coinciding in history, and indeed this is how things were to turn out in Michels's case.

When Robert Michels dedicated his *Political Parties* to Max Weber, he did so in part in recognition of the many years of support he had received; in part, too, he was expressing his gratitude for the numerous suggestions and clarifications provided by Weber, largely during the period in which he wrote the numerous articles that formed the basis of the book. Weber's reaction to the work was by no means uncritical. He criticized it on a series of crucial points of detail, one of which was the concept of power (*Herrschaft*) employed by Michels. For one thing, he argued, the use of the concept was ambiguous; further, Michels had failed to recognize that all forms of social relations – even the most personal – were, in a sense, power relations (*Herrschaftsbeziehungen*).[29] The core of his interpretation may be viewed as diametrically opposed to Michels's roots in anarcho-syndicalism, in so far as Weber declared the idea of a social order free from domination – whatever form this may take – to be inconceivable. His criticism here runs along much the same lines as his earlier critique of Michels's position, which had condemned it as resting on idealist postulates that must necessarily come to grief when confronted with empirical reality.

Michels's arguments did, however, converge with Weber's own views on a number of central points: for example, in his emphasis upon advancing bureaucratization and its consequences for political parties and, by extension, for the formation of political objectives in general. The two authors were at their closest in their views on the function of political leaders, whose demagogic capabilities which directly corresponded to the masses' need for leadership (which Weber termed their 'submissiveness' [Fügsamkeit]) effect the submission of the masses to the system of domination. Weber's emphatic insistence that, in any political system, political decisions always rest in the hands of a few leading personalities is well known. The 'principle of the small number, that is, the superior political power of manoeuvre of *small* leading groups, always governs political action'.[30] His entire sociology of domination revolves around the question of the circumstances and the constitutional conditions that guarantee an optimum of capable political leadership. Weber's main argument for the parliamentarization of the constitution of the German Reich was that, in the prevailing circumstances, the parliamentary system represented the best possible way of selecting political leaders of proven ability. And, in the early stages of the Weimar Republic, his political demands climaxed in a call for a 'leadership democracy with a "machine"', as an alternative to the 'leaderless democracy' whose restoration in the course of 1919 seemed apparent despite all revolutionary changes.[31]

It would seem reasonable to raise the question of whether Max Weber does not at this point, display an affinity – if not in form then at least in content – both with Gaetano Mosca's theory of a 'political class' that has definitively taken over the role of political leadership and, more particularly, with Pareto's theory of the circulation of political elites. One might even take the view that Schumpeter's well-known theory of democracy, which he views as a competitive struggle between political leaders for the allegiance of the masses, and therefore for power, represents a logical extension of Max Weber's democracy theory as it might be developed from the standpoint of Pareto's circulation theory. There can be no doubt that Michels drew Weber's attention both directly and indirectly to the works of Mosca and Pareto. Already in his early article, 'Oligarchic tendencies in modern society', both authors are quoted extensively and it is difficult to imagine that their theories played no part in the numerous conversations between Michels and Weber, whether in Heidelberg or Turin, even though, as far as I can ascertain, Mosca and Pareto are nowhere mentioned in the parts of the correspondence we possess. (Guilhelmo Ferrero, whom Weber considered insignificant and second-rate by comparison with Theodor Mommsen, is the only name occasionally mentioned.)[32] One looks in vain, however, for any explicit reference to the theories of Mosca or Pareto in Weber's work.

What does, however, emerge quite clearly from the comparison between Michels and Weber, is the more or less absolute opposition between their interpretations of the empirical material that formed the basis of Michels's *Political*

Parties. Michels evaluated his material from a democratic fundamentalist standpoint, which regarded the principles of equality and popular sovereignty at the very least as binding value-standards for scientific judgement, though not always as maxims for political action. Weber, by contrast, increasingly came to judge the issues at stake primarily in terms of the question of how effective political action (and, for him, this in practice meant effective political leadership) might be possible. He continued to hold all types of conviction politics (*Gesinnungspolitik*) in the highest regard, including the syndicalist variety so prominently expounded by Michels (he did himself constantly feel tempted to let himself be swayed by 'a conviction ethic' rather than to maintain the sober rein on his own passions that his 'ethic of responsibility' demanded). For Weber, however, such moralist politics remained unrealistic – even Utopian – in the circumstances of the time.

It is not possible, within the limited scope of this chapter, to give a full exposition of this question here. We shall therefore restrict ourselves to two examples. In Robert Michels's view, it was, firstly, demonstrably the case that the bureaucratization of parties and of the political system in general had, as a necessary consequence, resulted in a diminution in the quality of political leaders. In the first instance, he saw this simply as an effect of an increasing distance between the leaders and their own party membership, though it also resulted from an inevitable tendency among leaders to make the preservation of their own status their dominant political goal. Hence the vehemence of his declaration that 'the beginning of the formation of professional leadership' was to be seen as 'the beginning of the end of democracy'.[33] Max Weber, as we know, drew very different conclusions from the evidence of an increasing bureaucratization within modern parties. Not only did he consider the trend towards 'plebiscitarian democracy', which inevitably involved a substantial enhancement of the role of political leaders at the expense of the 'led', to be irreversible; he saw it also as a positive development, in that it served as a counterweight to the bureaucratization of the apparatuses of power.

Similarly, Weber viewed as fundamentally positive both the replacement of the older parties of notables by modern, bureaucratically organized mass parties and, with them, the rise of the professional politician who, of course, lives from politics, but also lives for politics. Particularly in the German political context of his day, he welcomed the demise of the older type of *Weltanschauungspartei* and its replacement by professionally led political parties, since only these latter appeared to have 'a chance of ever acquiring effective political power within the Wilhelmine political system'. From this point of view, the progressive discarding of a revolutionary programme within the Social Democratic Party and its replacement by a realistic pragmatic politics involving a commitment to reforms bearing on specific current problems, seemed to him a further positive development. Weber tended, to an extent, to judge the process of oligarchization identified by Michels within the Social Democratic Party – and within political parties in general – as part of a universal process of rationalization that extended to all spheres of life; in the medium term, he was inclined to emphasize the positive effects of this process, rather than the ultimate consequences it entailed for the liberal societies of the West.

In Weber's sociology of political parties (first formulated, at this stage in largely unsystematic form, in the years 1912–13) there is, however, evidence that he was by no means deaf to the objections raised by Michels over the question of the bureaucratization of parties.[34] To the extent that bureaucratization and the attendant trend towards plebiscitarian democracy afforded the leaders in the upper echelons of modern parties far greater practical chances of success in transforming political reality, Weber certainly welcomed both developments; on the other hand, he was equally aware of the danger that progressive bureaucratization might stifle political leadership altogether. Yet, rather than merely bemoaning the creeping growth of bureaucracy in the organization of power, Weber aspired towards a combination of the two opposing principles of 'charismatic leadership' and bureaucratic organization, which he hoped would optimize the power of the party leadership to shape and form society. The power base of the Great Politicians, whose personal charisma made leadership their 'calling', was, he argued, independent and personal-plebiscitarian in nature; equipped with a bureaucratic organization, they would be able to realize their goals all the more effectively. This view finds paradigmatic expression in Weber's famous statement in 'Politics as a vocation':

> There is only the choice between leadership democracy with a 'machine' and leaderless democracy, that is to say, the rule of professional politicians without a calling, i.e. without the inner charismatic qualities that make a leader.[35]

Weber's argument here displays parallels with the theory that he first developed systematically in his outline of the basic categories of social organization, in which modern plebiscitarian democracy is regarded as an anti-authoritarian variant of charismatic domination.[36] This later work marks a shift away from his own earlier interpretation of democratic rule as a value-rational variant of legal domination and towards a more strictly elitist or – if we may call it such – an 'aristocratic' conception of democratic rule. On the basis of observations on the party system and the transformations of the democratic system in the prevailing conditions of the twentieth century – observations which, to a great extent, he shared with Michels — Weber thus ultimately finds himself consigning the principle of popular sovereignty once and for all to the realm of mere fiction.

It appears perhaps only superficially paradoxical that Robert Michels's subsequent development should not only have led him along the same road as Weber, but that it in fact took him a good deal further. It may indeed be impermissible to reduce an issue of such extraordinary complexity to a simplifying formula of this kind. The issue to which we are referring is, of course, Michels's conversion to Italian fascism, which involved an almost complete reversal of his political value-system. In chronological terms, Michels's conversion took place after the beginning of the First World War and thus lies outside the period in which it is possible to talk of the relationship between Weber and Michels as an 'asymmetrical partnership'. Michels's conversion would possibly, indeed almost certainly, have made irreversible the break between the two men, which had begun to heal somewhat after the end of the war. Yet there is a connection to be made with Weber, if only an indirect one, in so far as Michels justified his decision to support Mussolini and the Italian Fascist *Führerstaat* by express reference to Max Weber.[37] Among other things, Michels was able to invoke Weber's explicit claim that the emotional attachment of the broad masses to the leader constitutes the specific characteristic of charismatic authority, and that the leader determines the content of policy on his own ultimate authority alone, while the assent of his following resides purely in their trust in the leader's charismatic leadership qualities as such, rather than in their concurrence with the particular objectives he lays down. For Weber, 'plebiscitarian democracy', which he views as the most significant among the forms of leadership democracy, 'is, in its genuine sense, a type of charismatic domination which conceals itself beneath the *form* of a legitimacy deriving from the will of the ruled and only persists as a result of that will. The leader (demagogue) rules, in fact, by virtue of an allegiance to and a faith in his *person* as such'.[38] As I have demonstrated elsewhere, such a conception of democratic rule, according to which the 'recognition' of the leader's qualities by his following takes on to a large extent a formal quality, yet is at the same time expressly claimed to be essential in principle, was certainly by no means immune from possible reinterpretation along anti-democratic lines.[39]

The perpetuation of an element of 'recognition by the ruled' in the form of democratic elections, already formalized to an excessive degree in Weber, was declared by Michels, as it was by Carl Schmitt, to be dispensable. That recognition could, Michels argued, find equally adequate expression in forms other than democratic elections within a constitutional parliamentary system. More precisely, it could, he said, be much more directly articulated in the form of popular acclamation than could ever be possible within a system of parliamentary representation. Indeed, Michels went so far as to characterize the former type of 'recognition' of the leader as imperfect and impure:

> under charismatic leadership, the masses delegate their will in conscious admiration and veneration of the leader, in a form which appears almost as an unquestioned and voluntary sacrifice. In democracy, by contrast, the maintenance of the act of delegation of the will sustains the appearance of a will which remains potentially in the hands of those who delegate it to their elected leaders.[40]

Pushing to its radical ends a reasoning which Weber had already elaborated in rudimentary form, in so far as he held that the charismatic leader does not simply consider himself 'the electors' mandatary', but rather creates his following by virtue of his own specific demagogic qualities, Michels came to the conclusion that true political consensus could only be achieved through the elimination of the election of parliamentary representatives, since such an election constituted an act of falsification of the popular will. Weber's theory of the charismatic leader who attracts a following outside the sphere of parliament and parties by virtue of his personal demagogic capacities could be adapted with relative ease to suit Michels's ends:

> Charismatic leaders... make themselves masters of the body politic independently of, or even contrary to, the traditional methods of conferring the

authority of the state upon individuals... Their power rests on the worship which their personality inspires and is circumscribed by it.[41]

This was the line of argument that led Michels finally to defend the rule of Mussolini expressly by reference to the 'tipologia politica di Max Weber, il saggio di Eidelberga'.[42] Analogously, he at the same time cast doubt on the possibility of considering the principle of the 'selection of leaders' – a principle much vaunted by Weber – to be a 'specific characteristic' of democracy alone. It should rather be interpreted, he maintained, in the light of Pareto's theory of the circulation of elites. The principle according to which the leaders 'never gave way to the masses, but only ever to other new leaders' seemed to him fundamentally valid for all political systems; there was nothing exceptional in this regard about parliamentary democracy.[43]

It would, of course, clearly be inappropriate to attribute Michels's shift towards fascism even indirectly to Max Weber's influence. At the very most, Michels might be seen to have taken Weber's advice on the necessity for him to take stock of reality and revise the conviction postulates of his fundamentalist conception of democracy just a shade too literally! Yet indications of an inclination towards protofascist ideas are to be found at a relatively early date in Michels's work, for example in his 1908 article 'Homo Oeconomicus and co-operation', where Michels declares that 'the age of individualism in the economic sphere' is today to be regarded as 'definitively at an end'.[44] In his view, forms of co-operative organization of economic activity were advancing to replace individualism on all fronts. Taking co-operative organization as the lowest common denominator, he was able to produce that hypothesis through a sweeping amalgamation of the socialist movement of worker co-operatives in both production and distribution with the co-operative societies of the lower middle classes and the prevailing tendencies towards the formation of trusts and cartels, within which he saw private capital as being transformed into 'social or impersonal capital'.[45] The signs of the time pointed, he maintained, towards a continuing transformation of the existing system of market-oriented competitive capitalism, and towards a growth in the 'co-operative organization of social production to the exclusion of free competition'.[46] In other words, in predicting the rise of a 'corporatively organized capitalism', Michels's work may be seen in a certain sense to foreshadow the idea of a corporative state, which was later to be propagated by Italian fascism. The advance of what he called 'co-operative' forms of social organization (we might equally term them 'corporative' forms) seemed to Michels to have deprived the Marxist theory of classes of much of its interpretive power; above all, since 'the tendency to form oligarchies reveals itself in that class with exactly the same vigour as in all the other classes of society', the mass movement of socialism seemed to him necessarily doomed to founder.[47]

Michels's work on co-operative organization certainly offers numerous points of departure for his later defection into the camp of fascism, with its promise of a future society where producers would live together in relative harmony under the aegis of the openly oligarchic rule of charismatic leaders, a society in which the historical contradiction between labour and capital would increasingly lose all meaning. In this sense, his relationship with Max Weber can in no way be seen as the sole cause of that defection. We may note also that Max Weber, not surprisingly, found this very essay on 'Co-operation' superficial and vague and did not hesitate, even though he was perfectly well aware of Michels's sensitivity to criticism of too direct a nature, to write to Michels in all frankness that, 'as a scholarly essay', it had been decidedly below his 'usual standards', since 'it was vague, side-stepped a variety of issues and failed to clarify any problem'.[48]

Although Michels had already left both the Italian Socialist Party and Social Democracy by 1907, we should none the less avoid dating his renunciation of socialism and of his radical-democratic standpoint too early (as Röhrich in particular is inclined to do). In Michels's article on August Bebel, which was published in the *Archiv für Sozialwissenschaft* in 1913, he still shows a substantial degree of sympathy with the socialist workers' movement.[49] Although his enthusiasm for Bebel had clearly waned by comparison with earlier years, he still saw in him the genuine representative of the wishes of the proletarian working class of Germany.[50] In this context, he referred, among other things, to the opinion expressed by Bebel that those elements 'who attacked him as an opportunist, and rallied to the standard of radicalism, or even of anarchism, within the party', most usually, 'tended suddenly to re-emerge a short while later on the most extreme right wing of Social Democracy, if not indeed within the bourgeois camp'.[51] In a certain sense, Michels himself fell victim to the same fate. The ultimate reasons for Michels's political transformation lie outside the field of the present study, since we are concerned here only with an interpretation of his work in its relation to Max Weber. However, a twofold observation may appear in place here. On the one hand, Michels's biography serves as an example of the political dangers inherent in an adoption of positions on ground of conviction alone. We may also conclude, on the other hand, that to a certain extent the same danger emerged from Max Weber's all too radical formalization of the substance of democratic rule, as it appears, for example, in his sociology of domination; it was for this reason that Michels could, after all, continue to consider himself a disciple of Max Weber even after he had become an apologist for Italian fascism.

Notes: Chapter 8

This chapter was translated by Erica Carter and Chris Turner.

1   'Michels and his critics', *Archives européennes de sociologie*, vol. 22 (1981), pp. 81–99.
2   The ideas developed here bear closely upon the argument of my earlier article, 'Max Weber and Roberto Michels: an asymmetrical partnership', *Archives européennes de sociologie*, vol. 22 (1981), pp. 100–16. See also W. Röhrich, *Robert Michels. Vom sozialistisch-syndikalistischen zum faschistischen Credo* (Berlin, 1972) and his concise essay on Robert Michels in D. Käsler (ed.), *Klassiker des soziologischen Denkens*, Vol. 2 (Munich, 1978), pp. 226–53; A. Mitzman, *Sociology and Estrangement: Three Sociologists of Imperial Germany* (New York, 1973), pp. 267–344. For a trenchant critique of the interpretations of both Röhrich and Mitzman, see D. Beetham, 'From socialism to fascism: the relation between theory and practice in the work of Robert Michels', *Political Studies*, vol. 25 (1977), pp. 3–24, 161–81; see also F. Pfetsch, 'Robert Michels als Elitentheoretiker', *Politische Vierteljahresschrift*, vol. 7 (1966), pp. 208–27, and, on the relationship between Weber and Michels, W. J. Mommsen, *Max Weber and German Politics, 1890–1920* (Chicago, 1984),

especially pp. 107 ff., and the article by L. A. Scaff, 'Max Weber and Robert Michels', *American Journal of Sociology*, vol. 86 (1981), p. 1269 ff.

3 Max Weber to Robert Michels, 1 January 1906, Fondazione Luigi Einaudi, Turin. The article is R. Michels, 'Die deutsche Sozialdemokratie', AfSSP, vol. 23 (1906), pp. 471–556.

4 R. Michels, 'Proletariat und Bourgeosie in der sozialistischen Bewegung Italien', AfSSP, vol. 21 (1905), pp. 347–416, and vol. 22 (1906), pp. 80–125, 424–66, 664–720.

5 R. Michels, 'Max Weber', *Nuova Antologia*, 16 December 1920, p. 7.

6 Mommsen, 'Max Weber and Roberto Michels', pp. 100–1.

7 Röhrich, *Robert Michels*, p. 14.

8 Max Weber, 'Die sogenannte "Lehrfreiheit" an den deutschen Universitäten', *Frankfurter Zeitung*, 20 September 1908, 3rd morning edn. Cf. Mommsen, *Max Weber and German Politics*, pp. 112–13.

9 Max Weber to Robert Michels, 21 October 1915, Zentrales Staatsarchiv Potsdam, Weber papers. See also Mommsen, 'Max Weber and Roberto Michels', p. 102.

10 Max Weber to Robert Michels, 19 August 1909, Fondazione Luigi Einaudi, Turin.

11 Michels, 'Die deutsche Sozialdemokratie', p. 555.

12 Max Weber to Robert Michels, 8 October 1906, Fondazione Luigi Einaudi, Turin. See Mommsen, *Max Weber and German Politics*, p. 107.

13 See Max Weber, 'Zur Lage der bürgerlichen Demokratie in Rußland', AfSSP, vol. 22 (1906), pp. 120–1.

14 R. Michels, 'Die deutsche Sozialdemokratie im internationalen Verbande', AfSSP, vol. 25 (1907), pp. 148–231.

15 ibid., p. 179.

16 ibid., pp. 219–20.

17 GASS, p. 410.

18 Max Weber to Robert Michels, 6 November 1907, Fondazione Luigi Einaudi, Turin. Michels was in fact later to describe the party in similar terms. See his *Zur Soziologie des Parteiwesens in der modernen Demokratie. Untersuchungen über die oligarchischen Tendenzen des Gruppenlebens* (Leipzig, 1911), p. 293, n. 2. An English translation of this work (from the Italian) was published under the title *Political Parties: A Sociological Study of the Oligarchical Tendencies of Modern Democracy* (London, 1915).

19 Max Weber to Robert Michels, 19 August 1908, Fondazione Luigi Einaudi, Turin. See Mommsen, *Max Weber and German Politics*, p. 108.

20 R. Michels, 'Die oligarchischen Tendenzen der Gesellschaft. Ein Beitrag zum Problem der Demokratie', AfSSP, vol. 27 (1908), pp. 73–135.

21 ibid., pp. 77–8, 118 ff.

22 Max Weber to Robert Michels, 4 August 1908, Fondazione Luigi Einaudi, Turin. See Mommsen, *Max Weber and German Politics*, pp. 104–5.

23 Michels, *Zur Soziologie* (as in n. 18 above).

24 The 2nd edn was published by Kröner in Leipzig in 1925 and reissued in Stutgart in 1957, with an introduction by Werner Conze.

25 Michels, *Zur Soziologie*, 1st edn, p. 349. In the more emphatic formulation in the 2nd edn (p. 340), anarchy is said not to have 'succeeded in realizing its theory in any practically applicable form'.

26 ibid. (1st edn), pp. 387 ff.

27 ibid., p. 391; see also 2nd edn, p. 377.

28 ibid.

29 See the undated letter from Weber, written sometime in 1911, in which he thanks Michels for the dedication and lists a whole series of points of criticism, Fondazione Luigi Einaudi, Turin. It is worth noting that the same letter is explicitly mentioned in Michels's Preface to the second edition. 'For the first time the opportunity now presents itself to give this detailed letter, containing a critique which is both positive and negative, the attention it deserves', ibid., p. xxviii.

30 MWG, Vol. I/15, p. 483.

31 Cf. Mommsen, *Max Weber and German Politics*, pp. 339 ff., and idem, *The Age of Bureaucracy: Perspectives on the Political Sociology of Max Weber* (Oxford, 1974), pp. 89–94.

32 See n. 19 above.

33 This formulation does not, however, appear until the 2nd edn of Michels, *Zur Soziologie* (p. 130).

34   WuG^5, pp. 531–40. In Weber's 'Parlament und Regierung im neugeordneten Deutschland' (MWG, Vol. I/15, especially pp. 454–64) of 1917, his position on the sociology of parties appears in fully developed form; it stands in direct contrast to the hypotheses developed by Michels, despite the fact that the contents of their analyses are, to a large extent, the same. It was not until 1919–20 that Weber set his study of political parties within the framework of a 'typology of forms of domination' (WuG^5, pp. 167 ff.).

35   GPS^3, p. 532.

36   See WuG^5, pp. 155–7, and the comments in Mommsen, *Max Weber and German Politics*, pp. 401 ff.; also idem, *The Age of Bureaucracy*, pp. 90–4.

37   See Röhrich, *Robert Michels*, pp. 143 ff., and Beetham, 'From socialism to fascism', pp. 175–7.

38   WuG^5, p. 156.

39   See Mommsen, *Max Weber and German Politics*, pp. 381 ff.

40   R. Michels, 'Grundsätzliches zum Problem der Demokratie', *Zeitschrift für Politik*, vol. 17 (1927), pp. 291–2.

41   idem, 'Authority', in *Encyclopaedia of the Social Sciences*, Vol. 2 (New York, 1939), p. 319, quoted from Röhrich, *Robert Michels*, p. 164.

42   ibid., p. 160.

43   Michels, 'Grundsätzliches zum Problem der Demokratie', p. 295.

44   R. Michels, 'Der Homo Oeconomicus und die Kooperation', AfSSP, vol. 29 (1909), pp. 59–83 (quote from p. 79).

45   ibid., p. 66.

46   ibid., p. 68.

47   ibid., p. 65.

48   Max Weber to Robert Michels, 19 August 1909, Fondazione Luigi Einaudi, Turin.

49   R. Michels, 'August Bebel', AfSSP, vol. 37 (1913), pp. 671–700.

50   See Röhrich, *Robert Michels*, pp. 55 ff.

51   Michels, 'August Bebel', p. 697.

9 Mosca, Pareto and Weber: A Historical Comparison

DAVID BEETHAM

What kind of understanding are we after when we relate a writer to his or her contemporaries? There are clearly different kinds. The most basic is interpretive: a writer's work can only be made intelligible, not by treating it as an isolated enterprise, but by situating it in the context of the intellectual tendencies and debates which help define its meaning and elucidate its purpose. A second form of understanding is causal: we seek to identify the influences to which a writer is subject, and their contribution both to the creation of specific works and to the process of his or her development as a whole. A third understanding is evaluative: it is only by comparison with others that it is possible to define the distinctive character of a writer's work, and assess the quality of its 'achievement'. These interconnected forms of understanding, easy to specify in principle, are of course more difficult to attain in practice, and are the subject of considerable methodological dispute. The characterization of 'Weber and his contemporaries' as a study of the relationships between particular individuals, for example, is itself only one, by no means uncontroversial, way of defining such a project.

Whatever the possible divergences of practice, however, it would be agreed that the modes of understanding indicated above presuppose at least that we can identify an actual historical connection between a writer and given contemporaries. But what kind of 'relationship' can we speak of between people who never met, and who may never have read each other's work, even if only to dismiss it? Such seems to be the case with some of the figures considered in our programme, among whom Mosca, Pareto and Weber can be included. A sharp-eyed reader would be hard put to find any references in Weber's work to Mosca and Pareto, or of the last two to Weber. (The well-known references of Mosca and Pareto to one another, uniformly disparaging, need not concern us here.) We have the evidence of Michels that Weber, 'who spoke Italian with a certain elegance and verve', had a high regard for Mosca's work, though he knew Pareto 'only from hearsay', while Pareto knew Weber 'only by name'.[1] In the absence of any internal evidence, however, it is difficult to know what weight to put even on Michels's suggestion of a connection between Mosca and Weber; it is certainly insufficient to amount to 'influence', or even intellectual 'engagement'. The most obvious historical connection between the three writers is through those of the next generation whom they jointly influenced, in particular Schumpeter and Michels himself. But to read back from this a connection between their elders would be a mere anachronism.

What stands out, in short, is precisely the lack of any direct connection between Weber, on the one hand, and Mosca and Pareto, on the other. This negative fact is not only striking in itself; it raises the question of how we should proceed in seeking to relate them to one another. If the tracing of a direct historical affiliation is excluded, we are left with the very different enterprise of systematic comparison, of elucidating the major similarities and differences in the content and methods of their respective works. Such a comparison, however, if it is not to be merely arbitrary or contrived, has to engage with the broadest social and intellectual currents of the period in question: on the one hand, to identify those general features of the time that give their works a certain recognizably common 'stamp'; on the other, to distinguish those elements of national culture and politics, as well as of individual history and circumstance, that explain the differences in their response to problems whose outline can be characterized more generally. Such an enterprise is necessarily both more ambitious and more speculative than the tracing of historical connections between thinkers who are known to have engaged with each other's work directly.

My starting point will be to assume that there were indeed common elements in the intellectual and political experience of the different European countries in the two decades 1895–1914, which gave to the social science of the period, and to our three writers in particular, a certain distinctive character. Among these elements the following seem to me the most significant:

(1) Changes in the structure of capitalism, combining the developing monopolization or cartelization internally with intensified competition externally, and the increasing importance of the skilled functionary within the individual enterprise. The period also witnessed the emerging prominence and confidence of labour movements and socialist parties, using the expansion of the suffrage to put a new range of issues on to the political agenda (the so-called 'social question'). Both developments posed new tasks for, and a new challenge to, the state.

(2) A crisis of political ideologies, both of Marxism and liberalism, engendered directly by the above changes: in the case of the former, because they did not accord sufficiently with the prognostications of the Communist Manifesto; in the case of the latter, because they put in jeopardy the tenets of classical liberalism. Of the two, it is the crisis of liberalism that will be more the concern of this chapter, given the political complexion of its subjects. Basic themes of this crisis were the decline of individual liberty in the face of the changing structures of capitalism and increased state intervention, and the threat to parliamentarism posed by the development of mass parties and labour movements; with both went a profound loss of confidence in the capacity of the bourgeoisie to defend the liberal tradition and values.

(3) The establishment of sociology as a recognized academic discipline within the universities. In the first instance, this can be seen as the product of an internal development within the social sciences, and in particular within political economy. On the one hand, the increased security of the 'scientific' status of political economy provoked a challenge to the other social sciences; on the other hand, this security was obtained at the cost of a degree of specialization and a narrowing of focus which rendered political economy no longer capable of comprehending the broader social changes of the period or of expressing its arguments in a manner accessible to the intelligent lay person. The two decades 1895–1914 were the period in which sociology took over

from political economy (as the latter had from political philosophy) the role of the most general form of social consciousness of the bourgeois intelligentsia. And with this sociology took over political economy's ideological function also. The definitive rebuttal of Marxism, and the reformulation of liberal ideology, now became the province of sociology, and were expressed in typically sociological categories.

The above features serve to define the common milieu in relation to which the work of Mosca, Pareto and Weber will be considered. To take first the establishment of sociology as an academic subject: all three moved to sociology from longer established disciplines, Pareto and Weber from political economy, Mosca and Weber from constitutional law, all three from various forms of historical study. Chief attention will be given here to the shift from political economy to sociology, both because it was the decisive academic change in the period within the social sciences, and because the character of sociology was itself distinctively shaped by the scope and method of the political economy from which it grew, and against which it sought to define itself. This fact is also important for the understanding of Mosca's work as well as that of Pareto and Weber. It was not altogether fortuitous, however, that Mosca and Weber also came to sociology from the study of constitutional law. A characteristic feature of the sociology of this period was the study of *Herrschaft* or *dominio*, of the structure and organization of social and political hierarchies. It was in the categories of an essentially *political* sociology that the significant changes of the period were analysed in the work of the three writers, and in terms of these that both their critique of socialism and their reformulation of liberalism was advanced.

If we can thus identify certain common key elements, a common 'agenda' even, in the work of Mosca, Pareto and Weber, their work also differed markedly in the manner and effectiveness with which this agenda was prosecuted. It is conventional to relegate Mosca and Pareto to a 'second league' of sociological thinkers in this period. However, the awarding of marks on some Paretian elite scale suggests that the differences between them were a matter simply of individual genius and temperament. One concern of this chapter will be with some of those broader differences of intellectual tradition and historical experience that made certain perceptions more readily accessible within one culture than another. The experience of parliamentary intrigue and *trasformismo* in Italy, of the mass manipulations of Bonapartism and Boulangism in France, of the bureaucratization of political institutions and movements in Germany, gave a characteristic difference of emphasis to the political sociology of Mosca, Pareto and Weber respectively. Such differences of experience, however, and in the subjects of study to which they gave rise (clientelist politics, crowd psychology, organization theory), could be readily assimilated across national boundaries by those interested in comparative analysis, as the three writers all were. More decisive in my view were those deeper differences of cultural tradition, between the German historical tradition of *Kulturwissenschaft* and the more positivist tradition of French and Italian social science, which influenced the methodology first of political economy and then of the sociology that subsequently developed from it. It is this difference that explains a different quality and level of coherence in Weber's work when compared with the other two. It also goes some way to

explaining those absences of communication, those 'silences', which are otherwise such a surprising feature of the historical record.

From Political Economy to Sociology

The development of sociology from political economy in this period is well
illustrated by a comparison of Pareto and Weber. With regard to Pareto,
the development can be charted through his major theoretical publications:
in the *Cours d'économie politique* (1895) sociology occupies an appendix; in
the *Manuale di economia politica* (1906) it forms a substantial introduction;
in the *Trattato di sociologia generale* (1916) political economy is reduced to a
mere rump. The most important period in the development of his thought was
from 1895 to 1905. It was in those years that he began to give a course of
lectures on sociology at Lausanne, that he published a number of articles on
the scope and method of sociology, and that he wrote *Les Systèmes socialistes*
(1902–3) in which his critique of socialist ideas moved from the plane of
economic analysis (as in his 1893 Introduction to extracts from *Das Kapital*)
to that of social structure and psychology.

What were the reasons for Pareto's shift from political economy to
sociology? By his own admission, it was his increasing awareness of the
importance of non-economic factors to an explanation even of the economy
itself, and his dissatisfaction with the inability of political economy to account
for them. The success of political economy in developing a body of scientifically valid laws was gained precisely because of the self-limitation of its range
and assumptions and the separation of its subject matter from that of the other
social sciences. Political economy was like an overgrown branch on the tree
of social science, in which the other branches remained stunted:

> Having reached a certain point in my researches in political economy I
> found myself in a blind alley. I saw empirical reality but could not com-
> prehend it, because of certain obstacles in my way: among others the mutual
> dependence of social phenomena, whereby one cannot completely isolate
> the study of the different classes of these phenomena from one another, and
> it is impossible for one of them to progress indefinitely if it is deprived of
> help from the others.[2]

Marxism offered one model for studying the effect of different social factors
upon each other, but, following a conventional critique of historical materialism, Pareto argued that it fell into the error of economic reductionism, of
reducing a process of mutual interaction to a unilinear chain of cause and
effect. The full understanding of this interaction was the task of sociology:
'The special sciences, which study the different categories of social phenomena, are, so to say, united by another science, which considers these same
phenomena in their totality and in so far as they influence one another. It is
to this science that we give the name of sociology.'[3]

Pareto's account of sociology as the most general social science was broadly
similar to those of Comte and Spencer, but had to be purged, he argued, of

their evolutionary schemata and of the influences of 'sentiment and prejudice' with which their work, like that of most other sociologists, was contaminated. The elimination of prejudice could most effectively be achieved by making the study of ideology itself a central part of the sociological project. Here Pareto offered a more precise demarcation between the terrains of political economy and sociology: where the basic assumption of the former was the rational or logical character of human actions, the latter in contrast should concern itself with the non-logical, with the sentiments, beliefs, customs, etc., which were not grounded in 'experimental fact' but which none the less exerted a decisive influence on social behaviour. Once again this definition took its starting point in the demonstrable limitations of political economy. Economists, Pareto contended, were capable of offering a definitive refutation of false social theories; but their assumption of the rationality of human behaviour was quite incapable of explaining why such theories continued to win adherents despite all their refutations: 'Economists have made the mistake of ascribing too much importance to reason as the determining motive of human action. They have believed that by simply exposing the emptiness and falsity of their adversaries' theories they have reduced them to impotence.'[4]

This inadequacy of political economy had been conclusively demonstrated in Pareto's own political experience during the 1890s. On the one side were liberal politicians, supposedly convinced of the general advantage of free trade and a limited state, yet readily resorting to protectionism for the benefit of particular industries and to the use of state welfare to buy off working-class opposition. On the other side were socialist leaders, continuing to pursue the Utopian projects of revolutionary overthrow and the classless society long after the labour theory of value and the economics of distribution according to need had been finally refuted by political economy. Both political tendencies, Pareto argued, had a common social basis in the process of elite circulation. Above stood a decadent elite, lacking the self-confidence either to compete in the market place or openly to confront its working-class opposition; below was a rising and vigorous counter-elite, using the support of the masses to mount a determined challenge to the existing order. Both groups in their turn were obeying a common psychological law in clothing their actions, which expressed their own sentiments and interests, in the garb of reasoned principle. Humanitarian and socialist doctrines, both based on false empirical assumptions and socially harmful, nevertheless prevailed because they accorded with the psychological needs of the times and the particular stage of elite rise and decay.

Thus, for Pareto, it was sociology, combining the analysis of social structures with psychological laws, that could make intelligible those contemporary social phenomena which political economy was unable to comprehend: the condition of bourgeois rule and the socialist opposition; the persistence of erroneous ideas and doctrines; the nature of the 'social question' and the extension of state activity in response to it. Sociology could do so only because it broke with political economy's assumption of the rationality of human behaviour, and transcended its narrowly economic subject-matter. However – and this is the crucial point – Paretian sociology remained fundamentally conditioned in both substance and method by the political economy that it sought to transcend. Its subject-matter offered a kind of mirror-image of

Pareto's political economy. In contrast to the market, with its assumption of the individual rational pursuit of interests in conditions of free exchange, was counterposed a concept of political society as the arena of collective action, the exercise of power and the struggle to win it, the prevalence of sentiment and ideology. A non-sociological conception of the economy produced by antithesis a sociological caricature of political society. Thus, for example, policies of state interventionism, by definition an 'aberration' from the free market, could only be explained as the product of non-rational collective forces, not of the changing *structure* of capitalism. Pareto's social theory produced a fundamental divide between economy and society, between the subject-matter of political economy and sociology, a divide which, despite the existence of certain common categories (wealth, population, 'selection'), frustrated the integrated understanding that his own project for the social sciences required.

At the methodological level, Pareto's sociology was also moulded by its origins in political economy, in that he transferred the assumptions of scientific method directly from one to the other. These assumptions can be characterized as 'positivist', not in the strict Comtean sense, but in the more general sense that they blurred important distinctions between the natural and social sciences. Pareto held that the differences between sciences were differences of complexity only, and that the success of political economy resulted from its faithful replication of the methods of the natural sciences, in two particular respects. One was the abandonment of everyday language and the assumptions of common sense. In his sociology this produced a sharp divergence between what he called the 'subjective' and the 'objective' viewpoint, between a person's own version of their motivations and their real ones. The result was a largely behavioural account of social action, in which individuals formed simply a point of intersection between psychological forces on one side and social structures on the other, and their conscious intentions were discounted.

A second assumption was that the goal of social science was to attain a knowledge of general empirical laws by inductive method. 'Science looks for the constant elements in phenomena in order to get at uniformities', Pareto wrote; '. . . my sole interest is the quest for social uniformities, social laws.'[5] Where the programme of Paretian political economy was the study of behavioural regularities and those constants of economic life revealed by statistics (e.g. the law of the distribution of wealth), his sociology followed in its train. The point of studying history was to provide the data for generalization; indeed, the past served better than the present because the researcher was less likely to be influenced by sentiment and prejudice. Pareto's determined expulsion of all values from the activity of the social scientist meant that they also lost any role in providing a criterion for the significance of what was studied. What gave the present its significance for science was its exemplification of some social uniformity. The general was more significant than the particular, the constant than the variable. It is questionable whether, in practice, Pareto remained consistently true to this somewhat arid methodological postulate, but such at least was its explicit formulation.

Before turning to Weber, it is worth remarking that Mosca's account of sociological method was very similar to Pareto's. Mosca, of course, was never a political economist; he began his career as a student of constitutional law. Like Pareto, he left his first subject because it proved incapable of providing an adequate account of his own political experience, in particular the gap between constitutional formulae and political actuality. The starting point of his political sociology was thus also the critique of ideology. As with Pareto, however, he derived his methodological postulates for the new subject – a detachment from subjective experience and the search for 'those great constant laws that manifest themselves in all human societies' – from the 'most advanced' social science. A positivist conception of method in political economy thus replicated itself in his sociology also.

With Weber we see a process of transition from political economy to sociology parallel to that of Pareto, but with markedly divergent results, appropriate to a different tradition of political economy. The interpretation of this process is also more controversial. At one level, the development is clear enough. In the period 1895–1905 Weber saw his work exclusively as that of a political economist or *Nationalökonom*, and his references to sociology are almost always disparaging. He criticized sociology for the teleological implications of its evolutionary perspective, and for its treatment of social institutions, using the analogy of natural organisms, as transcendent entities whose intrinsic character was independent of the individuals who comprised them. From 1909 onwards, however, when he took part in the founding of the German Sociological Association, Weber increasingly described his work as that of a sociologist, and it was as such that *Economy and Society* was conceived and executed, and as sociology that his collected writings on religion were published at the end of his life.

Two different interpretations of this development can be given. One is that it was largely contextual or institutional, and did not correspond to any substantive change in the character or method of his work. The German tradition of *Sozialökonomik*, it could be argued, allowed precisely for that study of the interrelationship between the economy and other social factors that was absent from other traditions of political economy, such as Pareto's. It was itself a form of sociology. The fact that *The Protestant Ethic*, a work of *Nationalökonomie*, could subsequently be reclassified as sociology suggests the interchangeable character of the two activities. On this view, Weber's shift from political economy to sociology was largely a matter of intellectual climate and context – his dissatisfaction with the social policy emphasis of the Verein für Sozialpolitik and the developing impetus of German sociology through the work of Simmel, Tönnies and others, in a manner freed from those faults that Weber had previously associated with the subject.

Such would be the interpretation of those who wish to stress the essential unity of Weber's work. It seems to me, however, that Weber's shift from political economy to sociology was not merely one of adjustment to a changing academic climate, but corresponded to certain substantive shifts of emphasis in his work, in two respects which I think are familiar:

(1) Although the German tradition of political economy was broadly based, it naturally treated economic phenomena as central to its concern, and it was within such a perspective that Weber's earlier work was written. In particular, despite his criticisms of Marxism for its historical method and account of capitalist origins, with other members of the younger generation of the

Historical School Weber regarded the concept of capitalism as a focal concept for understanding the contemporary world. A distinctive feature of his later work, however, is that capitalism comes to be treated as simply one aspect of that wider process of rationalization which he saw as characteristic of all aspects of modern society. Thus, in the foreword to the *Grundriß der Sozialökonomik*, he writes: 'Our starting point was the idea that the development of the economy should be primarily conceived as a particular manifestation of the general rationalization of life.'[6] What is involved here is not just a change of categories, from an economic to a broader social one; the concept of rationalization now provides the framework in terms of which capitalism itself comes to be reinterpreted. This broadening of focus can be traced in miniature in the development of the *Protestant Ethic* argument: in the first version of 1904, it is the origins of capitalism that is central; in his anti-critique of 1910, Weber insists that it is the effect of the *Berufsethik* on the character of modern man that is most important; in the revised edition of 1919, the argument is set firmly within the broader rationalization theme. This change from the concept of capitalism to that of rationalization, and the subsumption of the economic category into the broader social one, corresponds to a change in Weber's self-designation, from political economist to sociologist. It marks the attempt to develop a conceptual framework that will grasp the different aspects of modern society in their interconnectedness, to comprehend it as a totality, albeit in a very different fashion from the Marxist alternative that Weber at the same time sought to transcend.

(2) The shift from political economy to sociology represented a broadening of perspective in Weber's work in a further sense: from the descriptive historical approach of the Historical School of political economy to the more generalizing focus of a theoretical sociology. At most, the distinction between history and sociology is a relative rather than an absolute one. In particular, in characterizing sociology as a generalizing science, Weber did not mean thereby a search for universal laws of the kind that he had specifically rejected as the goal of social science in his methodological writings of 1903–6. The purpose of comparative historical study was rather to develop those theoretical concepts that would help define and elucidate the historical *specificity* of particular social formations. Referring to *Economy and Society* in a letter to Georg von Below in 1913, Weber wrote: 'What is *specific* to the medieval city ... can only be elucidated by establishing what other cities lack, and so on. It is then the task of history to explain this specificity ... but the very modest preliminary work of elucidation is one that sociology, as I understand it, can perform.'[7] It can be said that, in the course of its composition, *Economy and Society* came to outgrow this modest 'underlabourer' conception of sociology, to become a work of historical and theoretical synthesis in its own right. Yet Weber's concern with historical specificity persisted throughout.

Sociology for Weber, in sum, provided the means to understand modern society both in its totality and in its historical distinctiveness. Such an understanding could only be attained by moving beyond the more limited concerns of political economy, in its concentration on economic phenomena and a more descriptive historical approach. As with Pareto, however, the character of Weberian sociology was moulded by the political economy from which it developed. This is not the place for a discourse on Weber's methodology or on the many problems of interpretation to which it has given rise. It seems to me, nonetheless, that one of the keys to that methodology is the attempt of Weber's generation to resolve the *Methodenstreit* between the historical and theoretical schools of German political economy, as Sombart sought to do via an extension of Marxist method in *Der moderne Kapitalismus* and Weber, in a different and more theoretical manner, attempted in his methodological writings of 1903–6. The ideal-type method, as expounded there and employed self-consciously for the first time in *The Protestant Ethic*, combined the hypothetico-deductive method of the Menger school (with its constructions of how rational agents might be expected to behave in given circumstances) and a historical insistence that what was rational depended upon belief systems that were culturally specific. (Thus, in turn, the calculating, goal-maximizing assumptions of theoretical political economy were shown to be historically conditioned.) This combination of a hypothetico-constructive and a historical method also lay at the heart of the more complex theoretical ideal types of Weber's sociology.

More particularly, its origins in German political economy gave Weberian sociology a very different character from that of Pareto. At the substantive level, the tradition of *Sozialökonomik*, with its less abstracted and narrow conception of the economy, allowed for a more integrated treatment of economy and society in Weber's sociology than was possible for Pareto. This contrast was heightened by a crucial methodological difference. As we have seen, Pareto's social theory comprised a gulf between his assumption of the unconstrained rationality of economic action, and his psycho-structural explanations of social behaviour, from which intentionality was squeezed out. The starting point of Weber's understanding of both economy and society, in contrast, was a common one in the intentions and purposes of agents, albeit as these were defined by culturally given patterns of belief and situated within historically delimited structures. Other methodological differences between the two writers are equally striking. Where the aim of comparative history for Pareto was to discover historical uniformities, the universal laws of psychology and social processes, this aim was specifically rejected by Weber in his methodological writings; the goal of the comparative method, in contrast, was to develop those theoretical concepts that would help make intelligible the historical distinctiveness of a given social formation or epoch. Finally, with their differing accounts of the nature of sociological theory went a different account of what gave the activity its significance. Pareto's explicit elimination of all value standpoints from the activity of social science deprived social phenomena of any significance other than as manifestations of some general law. Weber's methodological concept of 'value relevance', in contrast, enabled him to make explicit what at most was only intermittent and implicit in Pareto's work: that the significance of particular social formations lay in the possibilities they offered or foreclosed for the realization of distinctive human values.

A comparison of the work of Pareto and Weber thus reveals a common pattern of development from political economy to sociology, a development which reflects a basic transition point in the social science of the period. In each case their sociology was moulded by the character of the political economy from which it developed, but with markedly differing results according to the different character of that tradition. There is perhaps nothing remarkable, therefore, in the absence of any contact between the two, especially when Weber had explicitly rejected the main methodological assumptions on which Pareto's sociology was founded. For all their *methodological* differences, however, their work also showed a significant convergence of *substantive* themes, as the next section will explore.

Political Sociology as the Critique of Ideology

A common focus of the sociology of Mosca, Pareto and Weber, as it distinguished itself from political economy, is to be found in the central place it gave to the analysis of structures of authority or domination (*Herrschaft*), and to the study of ideology in relation to such structures. Their sociology was in essence a political sociology, not just in the narrow sense of a sociology of the state, but in its preoccupation with societies and social institutions as hierarchically organized, divided between those exercising authority and those subordinate to it. If the assumption that all societies and social institutions are structured in this way constituted the central tenet of political sociology, then its chief field of investigation consisted of a systematic analysis of the most general variations between such structures, in the following respects:

(1) The basis of authority, and the manner of its exercise and organization. Authority was held to be based not on mere force, but on the performance of some specific social function, which in turn determined the form of the authority and its administration.

(2) The character and quality of leadership, and its typical pattern of recruitment. The character of a society or social institution was held to be chiefly determined by the quality of its elite, and this in turn by the pattern of its recruitment and training, among other factors.

(3) The nature of the political formula, myth, or legitimizing principle underpinning both the above. Ideologies served to sustain a belief in the legitimacy of authority on the part both of those exercising it and of those subordinate to it; they also played a crucial part in the organization of a following to challenge an existing authority structure.

These characteristic propositions of so-called elite theory were common to the political sociology of all three writers. They provided both a broad programme for comparative historical analysis, and a framework within which the changes in contemporary society could be made intelligible. Within this common scheme there were, of course, considerable differences of emphasis between the three writers. True to their generalizing methodological programme, with its cyclical conception of history, Mosca and Pareto devoted considerable effort to proving the universality of elite domination, and to demonstrating the recurrence of its main historical variants. Of the two, Mosca was responsible for giving definitive formulation to the law of oligarchy, which he derived initially from his experience of Italian parliamentarism, while Pareto offered the more dynamic conception of elite circulation, which he drew from his analysis of the contemporary class struggle. In contrast to both, Weber tended to take the general assumption about the inevitability of oligarchy for granted, and in accordance with the more unilinear emphasis of his historical method, to concentrate on those differences in the basis and organization of rule that distinguished the major historical epochs from one another and, in particular, modern society from its past. This difference of emphasis, combined with a greater concentration on the phenomenon of *individual* leadership, has given the impression that Weber should not properly be included in the category of 'elite theorist'. The question of labelling is a relatively unimportant one, however. More decisive is that the propositions itemized above can be shown to have informed Weberian sociology every bit as much as those of Mosca or Pareto.

The common framework of assumptions about the hierarchical structure of society and the legitimizing function of ideology are nowhere more clearly demonstrated than in the self-conscious 'realism' with which political sociology confronted and exposed the prevalent contemporary 'illusions' of radical democracy and socialism, particularly in their Marxist form. As has often been remarked, the development of political sociology took place not only by a process of differentiation from political economy, but in conscious opposition to Marxism also. Where political economy, however, could only offer a critique, and hence a simple rejection, of Marxism, political sociology sought also both to comprehend it sociologically, and to assimilate its valid insights by transposing them into the categories of its own theory.

The attack on Marxism was directed at two central points in its theory. First was the overall scheme of historical materialism: on the one side, its assertion of the causal primacy of the economy and its identification of private property as the source of political domination; on the other, its confidence in a future society without any such domination. Against the latter, political sociology insisted on the universality of the striving for power and advantage as irreducible features of human nature, and a hierarchical structure of authority as necessary to the organization of complex tasks in any society. The universal laws characteristic of Moscan and Paretian methodology gave their rebuttal a particularly definitive formulation: the category of 'scientific impossibility'. In attempting the impossible, so it was argued, socialists would only succeed in creating a more powerful oligarchy than any known to past history, through the concentration of economic and political power in the same hands. 'Everyone will have to kowtow to the men in government', wrote Mosca. 'They alone can dispense favour, bread, the joy or sorrow of life. One single crushing, all-embracing tyranny will weigh upon all.'[8]

We can recognize in these arguments the classical tenets of liberal political philosophy, concerning the essential competitiveness of the human condition, and the necessary limitation of power, re-presented in sociological form. They were reinforced by a broader critique of historical materialism. Its confidence in a future without structures of domination, so it was argued, derived from a misreading of the past. The private ownership of property was only one possible basis for the exercise of political power; a monopoly of military, priestly or intellectual functions could serve as well, and historically had done so. Marxism made the mistake of building a general theory from the particular instance of capitalism, with the erroneous conclusion that, once private property had been abolished, the domination of a minority over the majority would end with it. In fact, the future power-holders of a socialist society – this characteristically Weberian thesis was merely adumbrated by Mosca and Pareto — were already evident in that stratum already proving its indispensability in the most advanced sectors of capitalism: the skilled functionaries. Their monopoly of expertise in both economy and state would provide the basis for a new power structure of the future. In contrast to Marxism, therefore, it was political hierarchy that could be shown to be the universal phenomenon, and the possession of property as only one possible basis for its exercise.

The second Marxist tenet challenged by political sociology was the conception of the labour movement and the socialist party as the instrument for the self-emancipation of the working class. In contrast, political sociology identified the workers' movement as the agency for the rise of a new elite, whose members would either be assimilated into the established order, with a consequent dilution in their socialist commitment, or seek to overthrow it, only to impose on their followers a new dictatorship. In this sociology of popular movements and parties, the self-activating class of Marxist theory was replaced by the notion of 'the mass' as its central concept. In its anthropological version, this category postulated the innate passivity and incapacity of the popular masses (described characteristically by Pareto as 'the incompetent, those lacking energy, character and intelligence: in short, that section of society which remains when the elites are subtracted').[9] In its social-psychological form, it indicated how the masses could be manipulated in the hands of a demagogic leadership and, if aroused, their capacity only for irrational, destructive action. Pareto made the most work of this category, though it was present also in Mosca and Weber. However, Weber combined it with the argument based on the superior strength and manoeuvrability conferred on the leadership of the socialist movement by its organizational function, in comparison with the dispersed and fluid character of its following (the 'law of the small number'). Together these arguments pointed to the inexorable subordination of the workers' movement to the will and policies of its leaders, and ruled out the idea of its self-emancipation as Utopian.

It is not my purpose here to analyse how far the understanding of Marxism on which these criticisms were based was accurate, nor how far the criticisms were justified. It is common for a theory's opponents to take the more simplified versions of it to attack, and such were the ones in fact most readily available in this period. What was characteristic of the critique of Marxism by Mosca, Pareto and Weber, however, was that in criticizing it they also sought to assimilate it, by incorporating it as a special case of their own theories. Thus the possession of private property became *one* of the possible bases for political domination; the concept of class, one of a threefold typology of class, status and political power; the class struggle, one of the historical forms of elite circulation. By thus assimilating Marxism they neutered it, and at the same time gave it a sociological explanation: as the Utopian ideology that confirmed the self-confidence of a rising elite, and provided a secular religion for the masses mobilized in its support.

It should be said that, in their account of Marxism's social function, our authors did not see it as wholly negative. The radical democratic and communist beliefs that it comprised had a certain social value, not so much in their explicit aims, but in what followed as 'by-products' from them. Thus,

Rousseauesque notions of equality had contributed to securing a wider representation of social forces in government and careers open to talent. In their socialist form they had given the working class a confidence in defence of their basic interests and a sense of collective solidarity and even moral elevation. The danger was that such ideas would be taken literally, and driven to their logical extreme. Thus the belief in democratic equality could result in 'hyper-democracy' and threaten to slide into anarchy (Mosca). The socialist 'religion' tended to degenerate into intolerant fanaticism (Pareto). Revolutionary 'romanticism' would consolidate the divisions in the polity, and pre-empt the gains that could be won from an openly reformist practice (Weber).

Political sociology thus counterposed to the Utopianism of ideology the 'realism' of its own theoretical analysis. It provided both a critique of ideology and an explanation for its persistence, despite, or indeed perhaps because of, its falsity. We might ask, however, what purpose such an exposé could serve. At times the 'destruction of illusions' was advanced with almost missionary zeal. Yet, if socialist and Marxist doctrines persisted because they served important social needs and interests, if their degree of validity bore no relation to the enthusiasm with which they were received, then it would seem that little purpose would be served by exposing them as false. The straightforward answer is that it was not the popular masses who constituted the main 'audience' for political sociology, but members of the bourgeoisie itself, including those whom Marx and Engels had characterized in the *Communist Manifesto* as of loftier understanding, who had 'gone over to the camp of the proletariat'. It was in undermining the self-confidence of the bourgeoisie that Marxism was politically most dangerous. 'What makes socialism so dangerous', wrote Pareto, quoting Le Bon, 'is not the very modest changes which it has so far induced in the popular consciousness, but the profound shifts it has brought about in the consciousness of the ruling classes.'[10] The critique of ideology could thus make an important contribution to bourgeois defence. This combination of academic and political purpose that a properly scientific political sociology could serve was given classic expression by Mosca in the closing pages of the first edition of the *Elementi*:

> Socialism will be arrested only if a realistic political science succeeds in demolishing the metaphysical and optimistic methods that prevail at present in social studies − in other words, only if the discovery and demonstration of the great constant laws that manifest themselves in all human societies succeed in making visible to the eye the impossibility of realising the democratic ideal. On this condition, and on this condition only, will the intellectual classes escape the influence of social democracy and form an invincible barrier to its triumph.[11]

It can be argued that, for Weber, this political purpose was more muted, and the academic purposes of his sociology more diverse, than was the case for either Mosca or Pareto. If so, this does not alter the fact that Weber's political sociology constituted a 'massive rejoinder' to Marxism, or that his work equally gave expression to a crisis of the liberal consciousness, all the more effective, perhaps, because it was less overt and more deeply ingested into the terms of his sociology. A consideration of this crisis, and of the reformulation of liberal ideology, will form the subject of the concluding section.

The Reformulation of Liberalism

Mosca, Pareto and Weber all gave expression in their work to a sense of crisis in liberal values, which put in question the preservation of individual freedom in face of the changes in contemporary society. All three in turn perceived this 'crisis' as the product of liberalism's own success, although in different ways. According to Pareto, the increase in wealth generated by the operation of the free market led to a humanitarian degeneration of the bourgeoisie, and to demands for increased state intervention from the working class, both of which restricted the free operation of the market. For Weber, the energies unleashed in the age of competitive individualist capitalism transformed capitalism in a bureaucratized direction, and so undermined that same individualism. For Mosca, more exclusively political in his concerns, the doctrine of the rights of man, which had provided the impetus for an expansion of individual liberties, now served as the justification for a radical democracy, which threatened to destroy them. Such conceptions expressed the pathos of a generation that attributed to the success of its forbears its own dilemmas.

One dimension of the problems was a loss of confidence in the bourgeoisie as defenders of liberty. A theoretical perspective, which regarded the quality of a society's elite as essential to its well-being, was bound to be particularly sensitive to evidence of its decline. The fear of bourgeois decadence was a recurrent one in all three writers. On the economic plane, evidence was found in the desire of the entrepreneurial classes to escape the harsh winds of economic competition for the safe haven of a rentier existence (Weber) or the easy winnings of a protectionist or 'politically oriented' form of capitalism (Pareto, Weber). In the sphere of relations with the working classes, bourgeois weakness was displayed either by the resort to a crass authoritarianism (Weber) or in a craven surrender to the workers' demands (which Pareto termed 'humanitarianism'). At the political level, all three bemoaned the decline of political leadership and the prevalence of demagogues and placemen at the expense of the intellectually cultured (Mosca), the men of determination and independent will (Pareto) or the politicians who combined passion with a sense of proportion (Weber).

Such judgements betrayed a significant difference of emphasis in the precise qualities necessary for an elite, and in the explanation for its supposed decline. For Pareto, it represented one of those secular shifts in the process of elite circulation, whereby a self-enclosed leading group corroded from within, and new vigorous forces emerged from below to challenge it. Evidence of this shift lay abundantly to hand in the toughness and readiness for sacrifice on the part of the socialist leadership when compared with the softness of its opponents. Pareto's exhortations to the bourgeoisie to abandon its humanitarianism alternated with predictions that, in the coming struggle, the socialists would win because they were more ready to use force and to shed blood. However, Pareto did not discount the possibility of the survival of the bourgeois order if it could harness new forces in its defence from the popular classes, 'where are preserved intact the virile energies of the race'.[12] He could thus hail both the Bolshevik revolution and the Fascist march on Rome as 'decisive proof' of his sociological theories.

Pareto's conception of elite qualities betrays a fairly crude form of Social Darwinism. According to his theory the social struggle, like that of the natural order, was a struggle for survival: the 'unfit' were more likely to be eliminated in the course of life from the lower orders, which thereby came to possess a toughness which the children of the elite must lack. In addition, the qualities necessary for survival were assumed without question to be those also necessary to political leadership. For Mosca, in contrast, the fate that awaited the 'unfit' was merely their subordination, not their outright elimination, and the qualities needed for 'fitness' to rule were not all the same as those for brute survival. On the contrary, to Mosca it was precisely the social acquisition of an intellectual culture, characteristic of the middle strata of the bourgeoisie, that was decisive for the capacity to govern. It was this that he saw under threat from the advance of representative democracy and the extension of the suffrage. By a process of 'negative selection', the middle strata were losing ground in the electoral struggle to plutocrats who could purchase votes with their money, or demagogues who could win them by flattery. Squeezed between the forces of large capital and the advancing proletariat, the men of intellectual culture and independent judgement, capable of transcending the narrow interests of class, were being lost to public life, a loss that was only accelerated by the economic ruin of this stratum in the postwar period.

Mosca's oft repeated eulogy on the civic virtues of the bourgeois intelligentsia reflected his own close identification with a stratum from which Pareto's experience had personally alienated him and whose political value he specifically rejected. From their different perspectives, however, both saw the decline of the bourgeois political elite as a European-wide phenomenon. Weber's concerns were initially more local, with the specific problems of a German bourgeoisie that had never attained a position of leadership in the state, and whose chief political characteristics were a subservience to the Prussian Junkers on one side and a fear of Social Democracy on the other. Weber realized, however, that legislative measures to abolish the privilege of the former and hasten the political incorporation of the latter would not themselves guarantee the quality of political leadership, as his late wartime writings make clear. At this point, his analysis of the problem appears much closer to that of Mosca than to Pareto. It is how to secure a place in the polity for those of independent means and judgement, who are capable of living 'for' rather than 'off' politics, in the sense that they neither depend on it as a source of livelihood nor use it to advance narrow sectional interests.

Weber's definition of the ideal political elite is very similar to Mosca's. The means he advocated to achieve it, however, are very different, and reveal a fundamental difference in their respective conceptions of electoral politics. Mosca's understanding of this was wholly traditional, according to which the parliamentary representative was an independent figure, accountable to his constituents alone. Only by a limitation of the suffrage, he believed, could a sufficient number of cultivated persons be elected to make an impact on public life. Weber rejected any such limitation out of hand. His conception of electoral politics as organized on strict party lines, with parties themselves as disciplined hierarchical structures, allowed room for a leavening of the independent-minded to make an impact in positions of party leadership. Such a possibility was further enhanced by his conception of the individual plebiscitary leader, able to appeal directly to the electorate over the head of his party and across class boundaries.

A comparison of the three writers together thus reveals a measure of disagreement about what were precisely the requisite qualities for political leadership. The sociological form of the argument could not hide the fact that the definition of such qualities was largely a matter of subjective judgement, as was also any definition of bourgeois 'decline'. There was more agreement between them, however, on the nature of the threat to liberty itself. This was seen as coming from two main sources. First was the expansion of the state's activity, with the increasing regulation of social and economic life, and the growth of the state administration. How could individual rights and freedom of movement be guaranteed against this increasingly intrusive power?

Here, as just previously, there was a clearer division in the answers given between Pareto and the other two. Pareto stood in the tradition that saw the guarantee for all individual liberties as residing in economic property rights, and the condition of *laissez-faire* as maximizing personal freedom on all fronts. The extent of freedom was to be measured by the absence of regulation of economic activity, and by the proportion of its product that was left for individual (as opposed to state) consumption. In accordance with these basic principles of his political economy, Pareto's 'solution' to the problems of freedom in contemporary society could only be to advocate a return to *laissez-faire*. As suggested earlier, such a response overlooked the existence of power relations within actual markets, and the fact that it was partly economic developments themselves that had made the growth of state activity unavoidable. Pareto's conception of liberty allowed no way of reconciling individual freedom with an expanded state, or of distinguishing between different forms of state activity in their varying implications for personal freedom.

Mosca and Weber, although of course committed to private property, developed their reformulation of liberalism from a more pluralist and sociological tradition, whereby the chief guarantee of individual liberties was seen to lie in the existence of a plurality of power centres in state and society. According to Mosca's theory, this pluralism should, ideally, have a number of different dimensions. One was a separation between polity and economy, not as an absence of state intervention, but such that the groups of elites exercising power in each should not overlap. Associated with this was a balance of forces within civil society, so that there was no one preponderant social or class power; indeed, it was one of the functions of the state to regulate conditions (e.g. the relations between capital and labour) to ensure this. A further dimension of pluralism was to be found within the state itself, between the bureaucratic and the representative elements. Mosca recognized the development of bureaucracy into an independent element within the state, and gave a correspondingly strong emphasis to the role of representative institutions and assemblies in guaranteeing individual rights and liberties, or 'juridical defence' as he called it.

All these were also typically Weberian themes. Indeed here more than anywhere it might be possible to speculate on some tangible consequence of Weber's 'high regard for Mosca's work'. As elsewhere, however, Weber gave to the themes an emphasis entirely his own. In his view, the threat to individual liberty came not only from the state but from the advance of bureaucratic structures throughout society, and from the threatened monopolization of specialist expertise this represented. Social and political pluralism required a process of competition between bureaucratic hierarchies, both within and between the different sectors of social life. Another, typically Weberian touch was the transfer of individualism − formerly attainable in principle by all, but now no longer − to the summit of bureaucratic structures, where it was realized in the person of the industrial chief or party leader, in the exercise of which others below might enjoy a kind of vicarious satisfaction, a 'freedom of movement' by proxy.

The other major threat to individual liberty was seen to derive from the extension of democracy. One characteristic objection to democratic politics advanced by all three writers was its encouragement of sectional demands on the state and the tendency for policy to be subordinated to a succession of particular social interests. In his postwar *Trasformazione della democrazia*, Pareto portrayed an acute form of this process as typifying the state of contemporary politics. The placation of one set of social forces after another had encouraged the growth in the power of sectional elites at the expense of the political centre, to the extent that they now constituted a 'new feudalism', oppressive of individual liberty. The weakening of state institutions was exacerbated by a second feature, also typical of democratic politics: the encouragement by demagogic leaders of popular illusions and antipathies, of exaggerated expectations, which could not be fulfilled. The most likely end of this centrifugal process, this decomposition of sovereignty, would be the inauguration of a new form of dictatorship.

This scenario embodied the familiar theme of the conflict between freedom and democracy. How could liberty, then, be preserved in face of the democratic tendencies towards political disintegration? The question resolved itself into the search for a form of parliamentary democracy that would meet two essential criteria: on the one hand, it should represent the main social forces or interests of society; on the other, it should also keep a certain distance from them, so that it was not exposed to direct popular pressures or insupportable demands, and could maintain its decisional integrity. Such has been the recurrent agenda for liberal political theory in the democratic era, at least since J. S. Mill's *Representative Government*. Its contradictory requirements have not always been easy to fulfil, particularly the second of them, which was dealt with very differently by the three writers with whom we are concerned. Pareto's solution was, in effect, what would today be termed neo-liberal or Hayekian: the integrity of the market, and with it individual freedom, could only be secured by protecting its operation from the realm of the *political* market-place and the pressures of electoral auctioneering, if necessary by authoritarian means. Of the three, Pareto's theory led in the most explicitly anti-democratic direction, as his support for Mussolini's coup was to show, though he would have been dismayed if he had lived to see the latter's economic policies in practice.

If Pareto's solution to the problem was authoritarian, Mosca's can best be described as old-fashioned. In his theory the bureaucracy constituted the authoritative principle in the state, and representation the democratic one. The degenerative potential of the latter was, however, to be checked by a limitation of the suffrage, sufficient to secure representation for the popular classes, without their overwhelming the representation of that 'moral and intellectual aristocracy' on whose presence in the state the protection of individual liberties depended. In this, Mosca did not advance beyond the 'fancy franchises' of J. S. Mill. There was, however, an important terminological innovation in his account of democracy, which was taken up by later writers. In his view, the democratization process had an inherent tendency to overreach itself, to become 'hyper-democracy', because this was implicit in its basic ideas of equality, popular sovereignty, etc. Since such ideas were of their nature incapable of realization, it made more sense to redefine 'democracy' in a way that did not arouse such expectations. In effect, this is what Mosca proceeded to do. For him democracy meant juridical defence, the career open to talents, the representation of a plurality of social forces, all of which were eminently compatible with liberty. Indeed, the two terms were almost interchangeable, as they have since in fact tended to become.

The really substantial innovation in liberal democratic theory, however, was that made by Weber. In contrast to Mosca, Weber was quick to appreciate the implications of the new electoral politics, based upon party discipline, and the demise of the independent representative whom it replaced. He was also aware, from his reading on American and British politics, of the extent to which the context of mass campaigning allowed for the emergence of a strongly personalized element in electoral politics, in which the personality of the party leader came to count for more than the details of a party's policy. Elections were becoming a vote of confidence (or loss of it) in the capacities of the individual leader, a confidence that gave him both considerable prestige within his party and wide scope for the determination of policy. Weber called this the 'plebiscitary' or 'Caesarist' element in electoral politics. The conceptual originality of the latter term in this context has not always been appreciated. By convention, Caesarism designated the authoritarian, if also popular, military dictatorship that typically followed the disintegration of a representative democracy. Weber incorporated the concept into his account of democratic politics itself, where it expressed just that combination of democratic and decisionist elements that liberal theory required. According to this conception, the role of elections was reinterpreted as providing a general legitimation for the party leader, who was then left to get on with the business of government in a manner independent of popular constraints.

The extent to which Weber's theory of competitive leadership democracy, popularized by Schumpeter and others, has become a commonplace of present-day political sociology, indicates the subtlety of his grasp of contemporary political developments, some of which had not even then fully matured. Like Pareto and Mosca, Weber was concerned to offer a reformulation of liberalism in elitist terms, but his reformulation alone was strictly compatible with the formal requirements of a parliamentary democracy. The vigorous authoritarian elite that Pareto espoused, quite opposite in character to Italy's established political class and the associated intellectual stratum from which he had himself been personally alienated since the 1890s, could in practice only assert itself by undermining parliament and the democratic electoral process. Mosca's defence of the political virtues of precisely this same intellectual stratum, to which he of course belonged, required in its turn an explicit restriction of universal suffrage. Both of them, fixated respectively on the vices and virtues of Italy's political class, proved unable to transcend in their theorizing the local conditions of Italy's political system. Their historical method also, concentrating as it did on the recurrent and cyclical aspects of the historical process, suggested to them the possibility of a return to the past – to the age of *laissez-faire* or limited suffrage – which was in fact an illusion. At this point, Weber's comparative sociological method, at once more universal in scope and more genuinely historical, offered a more thorough understanding of the significance of contemporary develop-ments in mass democracy, and one that was more sensitive to its irreversible aspects.

If we are to identify Weberian theory as offering the most distinctive, and also the most cogent, reformulation of liberalism in this period, what can be said, finally, about its adequacy? Any assessment of it depends ultimately upon our judgement concerning the original definition of its problem, and the categories of the political sociology in which this is formulated. It depends, that is, upon whether the problem of limiting democracy, of keeping the masses 'at arms' length' from the political process, represents a *universal* dilemma of the democratic age, a categorical conflict between the principles of democracy and individual freedom, or whether it constitutes instead a more localized and specific agenda, necessitated by the political requirements of a late capitalist society. On this latter view, the requisite limitations of democratic principle, of the values of equality and participation, are not the product of some intrinsic deficiency of the popular masses or the represent-ative process, but are necessitated by the requirements of a system of private property ownership, which demands the isolation of economic and industrial activity from the operation of democratic norms, the preservation of the state's independence from the disruptive consequences of class inequality and the lack of agreed principles on the distribution of the social product, and a largely passive political role for a population that offers the state a generalized legitimacy and guarantees to it, in return, a wide sphere of autonomy both in action and in defining the terms of political debate.

It seems to me that the latter, more localized, interpretation is the more accurate one. The separation of political sociology from political economy, and its transposition of Marxism into more general political categories, necessarily obscured from it the origins of its own theorizing in a specifically capitalist location, and allowed it to present its solution to the problems of democratic politics as definitive. Yet the compromise between representative and decisionist elements, the redefinition of democracy in liberal terms, so that it does not 'go beyond' the level of citizen participation that is tolerable within the existing order, is at best an unstable one, which the revolutionizing tenden-cies of capitalism itself repeatedly threaten to upset. And it is when the shocks imparted by the latter generate new popular demands and mobilizations – the rational expression of unmet needs rather than the pathological manifestation of mass psychology and demagogic excitation – that the authoritarian and manipulative aspects of the liberal-democratic state come to the fore, and that the illiberal potentialities implicit in the reformulation of liberal theory considered here become manifest.

Notes: Chapter 9

1　R. Michels, *Bedeutende Männer* (Leipzig, 1927), pp. 113–14.
2　Quoted in C. Mongardini, *Vilfredo Pareto, dall 'economia alla sociologia* (Rome, 1973), p. 21. Mongardini's book provides a useful collection of Pareto's early sociological writings.
3　V. Pareto, 'Il compito della sociologia fra le scienze sociali', *Rivista italiana di sociologia*, July 1897; reprinted in Mongardini, *Vilfredo Pareto*, p. 94.
4　Mongardini, *Vilfredo Pareto*, p. 24.
5　V. Pareto, *A Treatise on General Sociology*, Vol. 1 (New York, 1935), pp. 144–5, cf. p. 45.
6　*Grundriß der Sozialökonomik*, 1. Abteilung, 1. Teil (Tübingen, 1914), p. vii.
7　Quoted in G. v. Below, *Der deutsche Staat des Mittelalters*, 2nd edn (Leipzig, 1925), p. xxiv.
8　G. Mosca, *The Ruling Class* (New York, 1939), p. 285. Mosca's attitude towards socialism is set out most systematically in his reply to a survey in 1902, reprinted in *Ciò che la storia potrebbe insegnare* (Milan, 1958), pp. 649–56.
9　V. Pareto, *Sociological Writings*, ed. S. E. Finer (London, 1966), p. 134.
10　V. Pareto, *Les Systèmes socialistes*, Vol. 2 (Paris, 1902), p. 397.
11　Mosca, *The Ruling Class*, p. 327.
12　V. Pareto, *Oeuvres complètes*, Vol. 18 (Geneva, 1974), p. 456. See the two articles 'La borghesia può risorgere?' and 'Il crepuscolo della libertà' collected in the same volume, pp. 396–413.

10 Georges Sorel and Max Weber

J. G. MERQUIOR

Our conventional wisdom about 'Sorel and Weber' normally consists, I suspect, in presenting them as two thinkers with altogether different social, professional and intellectual backgrounds who, although largely contemporary, wrote in ignorance of one another but were both outstanding figures in that general revolt against positivism[1] so typical of Belle Epoque social theory. Sorel and Weber were, of course, worlds apart in their main concerns and most of their approaches to social and political phenomena; yet the quasi-Nietzschean sociology of Weber and the Bergsonian radicalism of the elder man do evince in many regards a certain family resemblance. Then there is a modicum of biographical *connection par personne interposée* in the Michels bridge between them, Robert Michels being the man who theorized on the iron cage of bureaucracy within the very object of Sorel's sharpest strictures: the socialist political party.

I would like to suggest a few points of convergence and divergence between Sorel and Weber in four broad areas: their idea of social science, their moral stance, their political views and their historical outlook, with special reference to their image of man in modern society.

I

The agreement seems to be most patent in their epistemological positions. Like Weber, Sorel starkly rejected historicism, i.e. logic-of-history narratives in both evolutionist (Comte, Spencer) or dialectical (Hegel, Marx) fashion. To him, also, 'historical laws' and historical determinism were just tall orders never actually demonstrated. The arguments employed by Sorel to rebut the coarse deterministic historical materialism of Plekhanov are not in essence different from the criticisms Weber addressed to 'organic' and morphological theories of history as respectively defended, for instance, by a Stammler or a Lamprecht. Whether rosy and idealist as in Stammler or gloomy and anti-progressivist as in Spengler, historicisms, as entelechic views of history, were never countenanced by Weber; but neither were they for a moment accepted by Sorel, who once formed with Labriola and Croce a fiercely anti-determinist Holy Trinity of Latin Marxism. If anything, it was Sorel, rather than Weber, who probed deeper into the general philosophy of anti-determinism, thanks to his timely reading of Cournot. From his earliest writings, Sorel held on to Cournot's belief that the whole universe – not just the social world – is an unstable mix of strict determinism, probability and chance.[2]

An empirical corollary of the antihistoricism shared by Weber and Sorel may be found in what I am tempted to dub the Bernstein convergence: for both of them concurred with the great revisionist in dismissing the three main predictions of Marx: the immiseration thesis, the forecast of further class polarization and the breakdown prophecy. More often than not, left critics of Second International Marxism, such as Rosa Luxemburg, were firm believers in *Zusammenbruchstheorie*. Sorel was not – and the reason lies in his Weber-like antihistoricism. Not even his beloved Vico was exempt from his critique of unproven finalism in history.[3]

So much for historicism. But what about historism – the brainchild, not of Hegel, but of Herder and Ranke, which substituted a search for historical uniqueness for the assertion of doubtful 'historical laws'? It is a commonplace to think of Weber as a conspicuous heir to *Historismus*. However, he definitely departed from mainstream historism on a key aspect. Historists – whether historians or philosophers – were, almost to a man, holists: they set out to grasp social wholes. In so doing, they were surely akin to classical sociological theory; but the classic they resembled, or foreshadowed, was not Weber but Durkheim. As for Weber, he so distrusted holism that he put under strong suspicion even the concept of development, cherished by his friend Troeltsch. In his view, all 'organic' holistic notions were just romantic fakes.

To Sorel, they were no better. In 1895, in the pages of *Le Devenir social*, he criticized Durkheim precisely for his misty holist conceptual weaponry. Sounding like a Weberian, he resisted the Durkheimian 'collective consciousness', insisting that social processes ought to be described by means of sensible empirical-minded psychological categories. Durkheim was right to discard asocial individualism as a standard of sociological analysis, but one should beware not to throw the baby out with the bathwater: asocial individualism was to go, individual psychology continued to be required. Indeed, some have held Sorel to be pretty close to Tarde when it comes to matters epistemological.[4] At any rate, social theory could never reasonably hope to grasp the whole of social processes, let alone of society: rather, it was forced to look into just parts of it. Sorel called this *disremption* – something to a certain extent analogous to, though certainly not identical with, the stylization of social reality implied in Weber's 'ideal types'.

One last epistemological point reveals a kind of halfway convergence. Weber, in his critique of Eduard Meyer, claimed that the idea of historical effectiveness was not enough as a driving force in historical research, because the meaning of the past is not, so to speak, 'out there' – rather, it is largely a projection of our own presentist concerns. Now, in the introduction to his little known study, *Le Système historique de Renan* (1905), a work almost contemporary with his three key texts published in 1908 (*Reflections on Violence*, *The Illusions of Progress* and the lecture *The Decomposition of Marxism*), Sorel also states that causal effectiveness – typified by the famous 'battle of Marathon' problem in Meyer – was just one of two possible, indeed necessary, perspectives on history, the other being the recovery of the psychological experience of historical actors in order to understand their intentions as the source of events and social processes. Focus on outcomes had to be complemented by a *verstehende* analysis. Their convergence on this point stemmed from different motivations. The ever-pious Sorel was just trying to salvage the spiritual meaning of human behaviour in the history of religion, a level of meaning greatly shaken by the elegant scepticism of Renan. On the other hand, Weber, who was to stress so much the need for an interpretive level in social science, was not, at this juncture, interested in historical meaning *as the actors' intentions* but rather in the subjective perspectives *of historians*. He had embarked on a Nietzschean supersession of classical historist (i.e. Rankean) objectivism. Yet in either case the upshot went well beyond the methodological canon of positivist historiography.

However, neither Weber nor Sorel meant to overlook historical causality. For all its historist concern with the character of a historical individual – the modern West at birth – *The Protestant Ethic and the Spirit of Capitalism* is above all a superb inquiry into the causal power of religious ethics. Moreover, it is also a sociological treatise on the irony of human action. With perfervid belief, the Puritans built an institutional shell – modern capitalism – where today most of us live and even work in an increasingly un-Puritan way. No doubt Weber had mixed feelings about it, but that does not detract from his perceptiveness as a master of sociological irony – a point that was not lost on one of his ablest disciples, Joseph Schumpeter.

As far as I can remember, Sorel did not tell any ironical tale worth comparing with the 'hollow shell' of ex-ascetic capitalism in Weber, or with capitalism's undoing of its own 'protective strata' in Schumpeter – nor, for that matter, with the capitalists' sensible and yet suicidal behaviour, strangling the rate of profit, depicted in Book 3 of *Das Kapital*. But he devoted a good deal of Chapter 5 in his *Saggi di Critica del Marxismo* (1902) to stress that, because (as Aristotle remarked in one of his shrewdest jibes at Plato's Utopianism) society can scarcely act as an individual (and therefore the social body can hardly be a 'tool' pliable to one's wishes), the social plural is bound to be entwined into action at cross-purposes, likely to lead to many outcomes at a far remove from many an original intention. Translation: Sorel, also, knew that Clio is an ironical muse. Like Vico, he was alive to the need for correcting the *jus naturale* dictum: 'homo *non* intelligendo fit omnia'.[5]

II

Sorel is renowned for his championship of ethical socialism. But his brand of moral socialism differed from similar trends, such as social Christianity or Tolstoyan sects, in that it had a strong heroic temper. As he puts it in *Reflections on Violence*, he wanted 'rendre plus héroique la notion socialiste'. He tried to instil into syndicalism a Roman, even Spartan ethos, where morality was to be a blend of virtue and morale. Moreover, he set great store by personal dignity and professed an ethics definitely closer to the Kantian ideal of rigorism and autonomy than to the utilitarian creed. In David Beetham's felicitous words, Sorel upheld two basic moralities: the already mentioned heroic one, best described as a morals of morale, and an ascetic one, boiling down to a work ethic.[6]

If we put these few traits together, we get an overall picture that is not identical to, but greatly resembles Weber's own ethic beliefs and moral subject-matter. Naturally, the 'Roman' side, with its accent on morale, is less prominent in the portrait of intramundane asceticism classically drawn by Weber, though it is not altogether absent from charisma – a blend, in Arthur Mitzman's view, of mysticism and Nietzschean heroics. Weber's own morals, in any event, had little room for collective sentiment, leaning as it famously did towards an 'existential' stress on *personal* heroism. But the value attached to individual autonomy, the anti-utilitarian ethos and the sympathy towards the work ethic are obvious areas of agreement between Weber and Sorel. Indeed, it is hard to think of two theorists more adverse not just to utilitarianism in its more hedonic forms, but to eudaemonism *tout court*. To Sorel, the 'socialist superstition' (in the title wording of his 1885 essay) was Utopianism, and Utopia was but a deceitful figment of the eudaemonist imagination. He pitted Marx's *Critique of the Gotha Programme*, with its stern antidistributivist stand, against the mirage of bliss in which the young Marx still indulged.

One of Sorel's best recent interpreters, Richard Vernon, has suggested a telling kinship between Weber's celebrated two ethics, of conviction and of responsibility, and Sorel's 'The ethics of socialism'.[7] This text of 1899 prefigures the already mentioned distinction between looking at social phenomena from the outside, as causal sequences of events, and seeing them from the inside, as springing from the actors' intentions. In his book on Renan, Sorel puts this distinction to a primarily epistemological use; in 'The ethics of socialism' the focus is, of course, on the moral side. The point is: Sorel's socialist intentions are moral absolutes, just like Weber's 'ultimate ends' in 'Politics as a vocation'.

Modern scholarship on the evolution of the moral thought of each of our two thinkers yields a curious kind of chiasmus effect. On the one hand, Weberology tends of late to reduce the gap between Weber's two ethics. The trend is especially visible in the work of Wolfgang Schluchter. Dissatisfied with Weber's own hint (towards the very end of 'Politics as a vocation') at a synthesis between *Gesinnungsethik* and *Verantwortungsethik*, seen as complementary rather than as contrasting, Schluchter makes a twofold move: first, his reading of Weber reasserts the primacy of the ethic of responsibility as the only morals germane to our age; secondly, and more important, he claims that such an ethic, far from being ruled by adaptive success, contains an intrinsic *Gesinnung* element, a component of inner obligation not a bit less strict than the moral duties imposed by 'ultimate ends'. In 1972, Hans Henrik Bruun had forcefully defended the thesis that Weber ultimately preached a 'responsible ethic of conviction'; Schluchter, I am tempted to say, has argued a powerful case for extracting from Weber a conviction-like ethic of responsibility.[8] In spite of the wide gulf between his and Schluchter's bold respective ways of eliciting a thematic unity from Weber's fragmentary *oeuvre*, one can, I think, discern much of the same trend at work in Friedrich Tenbruck's pathbreaking re-examination of Weber's theory of history. According to Professor Tenbruck, the key question in Weber is not so much a probing into the nature of the West (later universalized as the 'modernization' problematic) as a general inquiry into the role of rationality in world history, undertaken in the *Collected Essays on the Sociology of Religion*. The driving force of rationality as a world-historical process was in turn religious rationalization built on the problem of theodicy – a creative cultural response to the often tragic human experience of misery, distress and frustration.[9] If so, Weber emerges as still closer to the ingrained *pietas* of Sorel's cast of mind, both as a minor historical sociologist and as a great radical moralist.

To a certain extent, therefore, both Tübingen and Heidelberg (Tenbruck and Schluchter) have since the 1970s burnished the slightly tarnished effigy of Weber the moralist and cryptomystic – the Baumgarten streak in his thought, if we are to believe his biographers. Weber the prophet of widespread instrumental action, still so dear to the Frankfurt school indictment of the Enlightenment as a culture, seems to be fading away; pride of place is now given to the theorist of *Wertrationalität*. Stephen Kalberg's lucid explication of the several meanings of rationality in Weber appears to partake of the anti-instrumental new look in Weber studies. Kalberg draws attention to the fact that, for Weber, the only type of rationality capable of introducing and sustaining methodical ways of life is *substantive* rationality operating as value-rational action, since (a) *theoretical* rationality bears no direct relation to conduct, (b) *practical* rationality, based on subjective interest, reacts to situations rather than ordering behaviour and (c) *formal* rationality stamps no comprehensive imprint on life. [10] During the Heidelberg congress held in commemoration of Weber's centennial, Talcott Parsons protested against making *Zweckrationalität* into the keystone of Weber's historical sociology. Today, he would scarcely have to worry about it: *Wertrationalität* is carrying the day.

While Weberologists were busy restoring the saliency of the non-consequentialist side in Weber's view of man and history, Sorel scholarship took, as it were, the opposite path. More and more, from Georges Goriely to Vernon and to John Stanley's *The Sociology of Virtue*, [11] it chooses to stress that Sorel's moral absolutes went hand in hand with a strict weighing up of the duties and obligations of socialism towards civilization and mankind. Weber saw that Simmel, in his pithy book on Nietzsche (and Schopenhauer) was right in inferring from the doctrine of eternal recurrence an increase in human responsibility. In similar vein, Sorel realized that Bernstein had every reason to believe that if socialism was not the product of blind historical necessity, then the moral burden of socialists became all the more heavy – and Sorel kept such a belief well after the end of his flirtation with the parliamentary politics of Bernsteinian revisionism. In sum: while Weber scholars are carefully revising our traditional belief in the alleged superiority of an ethic of responsibility in Weber, Sorel experts now tend to refrain from presenting him as an uncompromising partisan of moral dogmas. Weber readings shifted from responsibility to conviction; Sorel interpretations, from conviction to responsibility. Therefore, halfway, Weber and Sorel once again meet.

III

Sorel's programme of a history of morals and his lifelong concern with 'living ethics', historically effective ideals, do in fact irresistibly remind us of much that is central in Weber's work. Nevertheless, this significant degree of convergence in moral outlook is offset by the wide discrepancy in the political views of the two men. At its root there lies the undeniable fact that, while Weber has always been reckoned the foremost name in the rescuing of politics from the reductionist claws of sociologism or economism, Sorel, like his master Proudhon, was a stubbornly antipolitical radical who not only scorned representative democracy but had no use for the polity, as opposed to the economy and the societal sphere. Of Lenin it has been said that he tacitly transformed Marxism from a theory of class society into a praxis of party politics. But to Sorel, one of the greatest merits of Marx was to have led socialist theory from party (that is, from Blanquiist insurrectional sects) into class (that is, into the study of labour and capital). [12] (This, incidentally, may help explain his glaring misconstruction of the October revolution as a syndicalist affair.)

Even so, there are striking points of contact between some of the aspects of Sorel's political views and those of Weber – provided that we take 'contact' to mean just a conceptual overlapping, not a shared political belief. For instance, it has been noticed that Sorel's workers constitute less a class than a status group (*Stand*). Classes, to Sorel, are pre-eminently 'cultures', that is, strata, defined by their life styles. In so far as the distinction between the bare 'economicness' of a class, defined, in quasi-Marxian fashion, by its sole market situation, and a status group, marked by a specific set of cultural traits, is one of the best-known loci of *Economy and Society*, one could say that Sorel's concept of the working class (as well as of its bourgeois opponent) is a brilliant if unwitting illustration of Weber's theory of stratification in its more original part.

Again, Weber reckoned that political participation of the masses could defuse class struggle. In his view, the fact that, in Wilhelmine Germany, the workers refused capitalism as such instead of fighting to improve their lot within the system was largely due to the circumstance that their class organizations were kept apart from an adequate participation in political decision-making processes. This was hardly a popular opinion among liberal-conservatives, yet Weber had stuck to it since his plea for 'social unification' at his Freiburg inaugural lecture. Now Sorel also earnestly believed that political integration went against class war. The only difference is that, whereas Weber would welcome such an upshot, he held such a prospect in utter abomination.

The purist, schismatic flavour of Sorel's unpolitics makes his radicalism vulnerable less to criticisms from moderate politics than to some strictly sociological queries. One of these, voiced by John Stanley, [13] is impeccably Weberian: Sorel laboured on the assumption that the revolutionary voltage of a lower class is compatible with its organizational stability. In fact, however, it should be rather difficult to relate the charismatic energy of revolutionism to an institutional basis. Routinization of charisma is a moot practical issue.

Both Sorel and Weber fully acknowledged – in contrast to Marx or Durkheim – that society is bound to be always an arena; in itself, social conflict is the norm, not a historical disease. But Sorel thought that politics was an unhealthy form of this. Engineer Sorel wanted to preserve the advanced technology as well as the dynamic economy of capitalism (and poured contempt on any kind of regressive communism) – but he would have no truck with modern democracy, with the politics of popular sovereignty and representation. In *The Decomposition of Marxism* he chided Bernstein for not seeing that the root evil of Blanquiism – revolutionism perverted into the despotism of the literati – was not as much conspiracy and 'putschism' as the fateful idea of a revolutionary party and a popular state. As a foretaste of modern critiques of Leninist ideocracy, this sounds remarkably prescient. Yet

Sorelian social theory was to remain politically crippled, for it contemplated no positive alternative to the nastiness of 'political socialism'. Sorel's 'left antidemocratism' (as the Belle Epoque label had it) was doomed to political barrenness.

On the other hand, Weber's attitude towards politics did not lack a fair amount of disturbing shadows either. To begin with, Weber was highly ambivalent as regards professional politics. It was not only bureaucracy that he viewed as a dangerous foil to charisma: career politicians, too, with their Ostrogroskian and Michelsian parties, were quite a nuisance and a hurdle. Nobody ever managed to produce a convincing picture of Weber as a genuine democrat. No wonder his typology of legitimate domination is wholly presented from the viewpoint of the rulers, a crucial point I tried to pin down as the main blindspot in his political sociology and which Frank Parkin has been, I think, the latest to stress.[14] There was a time when we used to deem Weber an elitist liberal. I am afraid we have to change the order of the words: at bottom, he was rather a liberal elitist.

We simply can no longer afford to ignore the depth of Weber's allegiance to the peculiar notion of open-yet-authoritarian elite in the political culture of the post-Bismarckian Kaiserreich. And as Walter Struve has conclusively shown a decade ago, such German liberal elitism meant democratic personnel selection but definitely not democratic decision-making or popular control of rule.[15] It is true that, unlike most German liberals of that time, Weber favoured universal suffrage and demanded 'Western' institutions – but also a caesarist 'leadership democracy' that would put power in the hands of a consitutional dictator. He was consistently anti-'feudal' (that is, anti-Junker), but, as a young man, he mocked at social-democrats as 'petty-bourgeois philistines' and for several years before defeat was suspicious of prospects of a liberal alliance with them. He strongly opposed rule by a caste of officials, but was not a bit less hostile to popular pressures on government. And if he saw the need for parties and party competition, he apparently failed to understand the logic of mass politics and in any case so bluntly identified party following with blind obedience to a *Führerprinzip* that he came to speak (in 'Politics as a vocation') of 'intellectual proletarianization' as a desirable condition for the led masses. All this is quite well known, especially since Wolfgang J. Mommsen's decisive research into the relation between Weber and German politics – a work that as a whole has stood the test of time much better than most. We are also more than aware of the shaky Social Darwinian–Nietzschean assumptions on which (as the late Raymond Aron indicated at Heidelberg in 1964) Weber erected the pessimist metaphysics underpinning his anachronistic power politics. Nor do we need feel any embarrassment at Weber's authoritarian politics, the shortcomings of his theoretical (as distinct from his historical) political sociology or the apocalyptic overtones in his world-view in order to go on acknowledging, as we should, his towering greatness as a historian-sociologist.

IV

Like Weber, Sorel was a Faustian thinker: he extolled the creative energy of a dynamic economy (except Hobson, no one from the left was to my mind more spirited in the defence of markets and free trade) and hailed a conquering technology. On reflection, he and Weber − alongside Veblen − were perhaps the prime examples of Faustian thought turned pessimistic, since both before and after Spengler Western *Kulturpessismismus* was not, as a rule, Faustian: neither Schopenhauer nor Burckhardt nor, much closer to us, the Frankfurt school were exactly appreciators of capitalist restlessness and scientific-technological prowess. What irked Sorel was the *ideology* of progress − certainly not progress as such, in its Promethean temper.

However, while, to the ex-Catholic Sorel, capitalist dynamism (something that, faithful to Marx, he did not even dream of jeopardizing in revolution) was associated with a Proudhonian fondness for crafts, Weber uttered famous fears about the reign of the expert in bureaucratic-technological society. Sorel was a guild-Faustian. His 'savoir à fond sa partie' reads as an echo of Goethe's *Wilhelm Meisters Wanderjahre* and a whole bourgeois tradition of calling and conscientious professionalism. But by the same token, it seems part and parcel of the world we have lost. No wonder most of French industry, in his time, was still a paradise of skilled work on a 'small-is-beautiful' scale. Weber's professionals, on the other hand, were career people, not craftsmen. And it took a disgruntled humanist such as Erich von Kahler, a product of the George-Kreis, to scold him for espousing without qualms the specialist's ideal. On the contrary: he was only too aware that they might turn out to be 'specialists without spirit'.

Sorel was no individualist (here lies one of his few but decisive departures from Proudhon); Weber remained one to the very last. Understandably, Sorel wrote (against Bergson) in praise of team-work as routine. Weber, as we know, preferred to play charisma against the humdrum drudgeries of *Alltäglichkeit*. Again, whereas Sorelian unions were 'natural' guilds, Weber showed an almost Tocquevillian concern for voluntary associations; he once went as far as to describe modern man as a *Vereinsmensch*. While Weber, the legal scholar, liked to think of charisma as a rule-breaking force, Sorel, ever so keen on roots and tradition, was a strikingly juridical conscience amid radical thinkers − and so on and so forth.

Which one, in his image of man and history, says more to our post-modern sensibility? Not long ago, Sir Isaiah Berlin construed Sorel as a Belle Epoque Marcuse minus Marcuse's libidinal Utopia − a counterculture rebel *avant la lettre*.[16] The real trouble with this kind of interpretation is not just its obvious, conscious clash with some key aspects of Sorel's thought, such as his Puritanism. At a deeper level, it is the neglect of a whole conceptual structure, where some central tenets of counterculture ideology simply do not make sense. I will give just one − but clinching − instance of this. There is no room, in Sorel, for the idea of alienation − the crucial Gnostic dogma in counter-culture thought. A Pascalian thinker, he was thoroughly unable to conceive of (social) man as a fallen angel promised salvation through history. The Jansenist among Marxists (in Kolakowski's apt phrase), he never assumed a good, fine human essence denied by exploitation and retrievable by revolution.

Ironically, it is the liberal-conservative Weber, not, as might be expected, the radical Sorel, who, in some key regards, seems closer to the reservoir of romantic ideology tapped by revolutionism and the counterculture. Although Sorel was decadence-obsessed, and to that extent shared one of the most widespread among the many neoromantic *Leitmotive* of Belle Epoque culture, he never put forward anything so darkly romantic as Weber's sombre views on the ebbing of charismatic energy. For all the anachronism of his uncompromising dismissal of utilitarian attitudes, his stern exorcism of 'the materialism of interests', the truth is that Sorel kept the radical flag a far cry from the worst delusions of the lay *ersatz* religions foisted upon us by intellectuals at war with the cultural core of modern society. This is more than one can say for Western Marxism – that brainchild of Lukács (who thought of himself as a Sorelian in his communist beginnings). Did not Western Marxism end up, in its Frankfurt idiom, by perpetrating a spectacular neoromantic appropriation of Weber's uneasy diagnosis of modernity?

No matter. In the end, what remains truly living, rather than their visions, are the analytical tools they forged. To be sure, unlike Weber, Sorel did not bequeath us a sharp analytic geared to the apprehension of modernity. And Weber supplies, in particular, concepts that are extremely fruitful when it comes to understanding revolution and the counterculture – provided that we use his work with a modicum of imagination.

We can, for instance, as I have suggested elsewhere,[17] regard the Leninist revolutionary party – the backbone of most social revolutions in our century – as a Weberian hybrid: a robust blend of charisma and bureaucracy. The crux of the matter is that (a) in Leninist parties, charismatic virtues, like fervent devotion to the Cause, its gospel and its leaders, work as a key factor of meritocratic career advancement – one of the defining criteria of bureaucracy in Weber; (b) such parties usually display a remarkable aptitude to overlap with state apparatuses, reinforcing in the process their bureaucratic elements while, at the same time (c) catering for the legitimacy demands of modernizing societies, thanks to a deft administration of democratic and national symbols endowed with charismatic aura.

Weber himself, as Guenther Roth reminded us,[18] did allow for an impersonal, ideological charisma of reason,[19] active in Jacobin-like revolutionism. So much, then – within our confines – for social revolution. What about the counterculture? François Bourricaud has construed the ideological rough weather that prevailed after the 'end-of-ideology' days as a shift in the complexion of the two main democratic passions, liberty and equality. What has happened since 1968 is that, whereas much of the ideology of liberty has ceased to be liberal and become libertarian, most of the ideology of equality has dropped the theme of equality of opportunities resulting in a meritocracy in order to embrace egalitarianism pure and simple.[20]

Likewise, Roth tends to see the libertarian egalitarianism of the counterculture communes of the late 1960s and early 1970s as a revival of the charisma of reason in the above sense.[21] Although substantially agreeing with both analyses, I would like to add a farewell qualification. The counterculture seems to me to feed rather on the charisma of *unreason* – by which I mean the prestige of irrational and romantic motives in the mainstream humanist culture of advanced industrial society. The humanist ideology in our midst is keen on enacting an antinomian posture vis-à-vis the rationalized basis of modern social culture. The state clerisy of academic bureaucrats and the youth of the affluent bourgeoisie tend to form a vast counterculture reserve army, where 'existential' communes and leftist militant 'groupuscules' are just a conspicuous if intermittent avantgarde. As Gellner points out,[22] Weber's fears about a polar night of overrationalization in the iron shell of bureaucracy did not reckon with this phenomenon — yet it seems that it has come to stay, in our most un-Sorelian age of automation, widespread narcissism and permissive morals.

The mistake Sorel made was to trust work-ethic people with a cultural revolution. Modern revolution is not — except in modernizing countries — the business of ascetics, but of an 'official marginality' made up of well-fed professional romantics (and then, it is not a real revolution — rather it is just a language and a ritual). Weber's mistake was to think that rationalization and disenchantment would not entail chronic, near-institutionalized backlashes of re-enchantment creeds and trends, and to believe that the 'last form' of large-scale ideological charisma died under the guillotine of Thermidor. In fact, it had just been born.

Notes: Chapter 10

1   If I may borrow H. S. Hughes's phrase from his *Consciousness and Society: The Reorientation of European Social Thought, 1890–1930* (London, 1959), Chapter 2.
2   See Sorel's 1894 series of articles 'L'ancienne et la nouvelle métaphysique', posthumously published in book form as *D'Aristote à Marx* (Paris, 1935).
3   Cf. G. Sorel, 'Etude sur Vico', *Le Devenir social*, vol. 2 (1896), pp. 787–817, 906–41, 1013–46.
4   T. Clark, introduction to his edition of G. Tarde, *On Communication and Social Influence* (Chicago, Ill., 1969), p. 11. Nowadays the position of Tarde in the holism/individualism debate begins to be reassessed. What mattered to Tarde was not so much the individual as such as the differential element produced either between two persons or within the same person — the 'infinitesimal' idea of imitation or opposition emerging from the phenomenon of contiguity in countless (chance) meetings. See I. Joseph, 'Gabriel Tarde: le monde comme féerie', *Critique*, no. 445–46 (1984), p. 551.
5   On this point, see J. G. Merquior 'Defence of Vico against some of his admirers', in G. Tagliacozzo (ed.), *Vico and Marx: Affinities and Contrasts* (London, 1983), pp. 407–13.
6   D. Beetham, 'Sorel and the left', *Government and Opposition*, vol. 6 (1969), p. 309.
7   R. Vernon, *Commitment and Change: George Sorel and the Idea of Revolution* (Toronto, 1978), p. 43.
8   Cf. H. H. Bruun, *Science, Values and Politics in Max Weber's Methodology* (Copenhagen, 1972), p. 284; W. Schluchter, 'Die Paradoxie der Rationalisierung', *Zeitschrift für Soziologie*, vol. 5 (1976), pp. 280–1, translated as Chapter 1 of G. Roth and W. Schluchter, *Max Weber's Vision of History* (Berkeley, Calif., 1979), pp. 53–9. See also, ibid, pp. 76–92 (translation of Schluchter's essay 'Wertfreiheit und Verantwortungsethik', first published in 1971).
9   F. H. Tenbruck, 'Das Werk Max Webers', *Kölner Zeitschrift für Soziologie und Sozialpsychologie*, vol. 27 (1975), pp. 663–702, quoted here from the slightly abridged English translation, 'The problem of thematic unity in the works of Max Weber', *British Journal of Sociology*, vol. 31 (1980), pp. 316–51, especially pp. 329–40.
10   S. Kalberg, 'Max Weber's types of rationality', *American Journal of Sociology*, vol. 85 (1980), pp. 1164–71.
11   Cf. G. Goriely, *Le Pluralisme dramatique de Georges Sorel* (Paris, 1962); Vernon, *Commitment and Change*; J. Stanley, *The Sociology of Virtue: The Political and Social Theories of Georges Sorel* (Berkeley, Calif., 1981).
12   G. Sorel, 'The decomposition of Marxism', translated by I. L. Horowitz as an appendix to his book, *Radicalism and the Revolt against Reason: The Sociological Theories of Georges Sorel* (London, 1961), pp. 242–3.
13   Stanley, *The Sociology of Virtue*, p. 326.

14 Cf. J. G. Merquior, *Rousseau and Weber: Two Studies in the Theory of Legitimacy* (London, 1980), pp. 130–6; F. Parkin, *Max Weber* (London, 1982), pp. 74–80.

15 W. Struve, *Elites against Democracy: Leadership Ideals in Bourgeois Political Thought in Germany, 1890–1933* (Princeton, NJ, 1973), pp. 3–11. Struve's fourth chapter is entirely devoted to Max Weber.

16 I. Berlin, 'Georges Sorel', in idem, *Against the Current: Essays in the History of Ideas* (London, 1979), pp. 327–32.

17 Cf. Merquior, *Rousseau and Weber*, pp. 122–30.

18 G. Roth, 'Charisma and the counterculture', in Roth and Schluchter, *Max Weber's Vision of History*, p. 134.

19 ES, Vol. 2, p. 1209.

20 F. Bourricaud, *Le Bricolage idéologique* (Paris, 1980).

21 Roth, 'Charisma and the counterculture', pp. 137–42.

22 E. Gellner, *Legitimation of Belief* (Cambridge, 1974), pp. 191–2.

11 Mill and Weber on History, Freedom and Reason

ALAN RYAN

To write about Mill in the intellectual context of Weber's sociological and political writings is a task of some intellectual awkwardness. At the risk of sounding complaining, I might even say that it is intellectually quite awkward to display just what that awkwardness consists of. Mill was an empiricist, a liberal, an individualist – both methodologically and morally; he was obsessed by the ambiguous nature of progress, by the relationship between masses and individuals: he was concerned about the dislocating effects of the secularization of Europe and anxious about the prospects of re-establishing some sort of transcendental justification for our social and political allegiances in an increasingly 'rationalized' society; he was equally anxious to square the demands of democracy and participation with the demands of efficient, bureaucratic administration.

Almost all of this might equally well be said of Weber; yet it would be utterly misleading to suggest that they had much in common, either intellectually or methodologically or politically. Space prevents me from even attempting a task which ignorance would prevent my accomplishing; I shall not try to offer a blow-by-blow comparison of their views on every topic that they both touched on. I shall say something quite general about history, rationality, individuality and liberalism in Mill, leaving it to others better equipped than myself to bring out the extent of the contrast with Weber.

In particular, I shall not try to say anything about the area in which, at first sight, one might think they had most in common – the area of methodology, or the philosophical discussion of what sort of results the social sciences might hope to discover, the kind of causation that social affairs displayed, and so on. There is certainly much that might be said about this. Weber was conscious that the explanatory tasks of the social sciences were not accomplished when we had achieved a merely plausible interpretation of the phenomena we were concerned with. We might 'see how it was', and yet be quite wrong about the actual causation of events: adequate interpretive understanding had to be bolted to the phenomena by causal adequacy. Plainly, Weber understood causal adequacy much as Mill had done before him – to claim that one event was the cause of another was at least to say that without the first event the second would not have happened, and that (in those conditions) the occurrence of the first was a sufficient condition of the occurrence of the second. Equally plainly, Mill stood as a sort of methodological conscience not only to Weber but to most social theorists of the later nineteenth century. I do not mean that they never turned and rejected his views – I think that almost every thinker who took him seriously did so – but Mill's account of what made social science a respectable empirical discipline was inescapable as a starting point.

But the interest of Weber's views – especially to a student of Mill – is greatest just where Mill is at his thinnest. Weber was not a philosophically sure-footed analyst of the *concept* of causation, as Mill was, but Weber saw into corners that Mill's empiricism could not illuminate. The analysis of rational action, for instance, is a matter on which Mill is very thin. Given his causal theory of action, Mill could not readily distinguish between, say, rational and traditional conduct, other than by alluding to the different goals that served as the causal prompting of action. He never followed up the insights which seem in retrospect to be implicit in his own account of the methods of economics – that is, he described the method of political economy as 'geometrical', but instead of going on from there to consider what difference it made that in economics a course of action could be shown to be a priori the 'best possible' or a unique solution to a maximizing problem, he fell back on the thought that economics was geometrical in the sense that, like geometry, it involved an abstraction from the facts. If Weber's views about the peculiarity of rational jurisprudence and economics are neither wholly persuasive nor wholly intelligible, they are altogether richer than Mill's.

Why, if there is so much that separates Mill and Weber, is it worth mentioning them in the same breath at all? The answer is that Mill was almost unique among British writers of the earlier nineteenth century in his willingness to learn from European thinkers and in his impact on them. Mill's 'Works' were collected in a German edition a century before they were collected in an English (actually Canadian) one. The German term for the human sciences which so many writers think *peculiarly* German and un-Anglo-Saxon – *Geisteswissenschaften* – was given to the Germans by Mill. When his *System of Logic* was translated by Gomperz, Mill's term for the human sciences – the 'moral sciences' – produced this new and much used term in German. Of course, no sooner was the expression successfully Germanized than Dilthey denied that Mill's empiricist – perhaps more importantly 'inductivist' – account of the human sciences would do; but, by the time Weber came to discuss the connections between 'interpretive' and 'causal' explanations of social action, Mill's influence on the context of the discussion was firmly established. Nor is this all. If Mill's liberalism was partly derivative from de Tocqueville – and it certainly was – it was also partly derivative from Goethe – whose motto 'many-sidedness' Mill took as his own after his 'mental crisis' of 1826, and Mill's borrowings from Carlyle and Coleridge also amount to borrowings from German thinkers of the early nineteenth century.

But Mill was inevitably an Anglo-Saxon thinker first and foremost. His liberalism was distinctively English – British, perhaps; he was an unrepentant disciple of Bentham and his father who saw himself as responding to the needs of the age by infusing his teachers' narrow and businesslike rationalism with the emotional insights of Romantic poets such as Wordsworth and Coleridge, and with the historical perspectives of French sociologists, German philosophers and their English interpreters. It was also distinctively English in ways that separated it from Continental liberalism – there was no place for anti-clericalism in Mill's liberalism; he did not see the English middle-class as a social group that somehow lacked the political self-confidence to take political power for itself; he did not live in a country whose national identity was so insecure that liberalism had to ally itself with nationalism. So Mill was both part of and separated from Continental strains of liberalism.

But what made Mill a fully paid-up member of the European intellectual community — besides the simple intellectual distinction that gained the grudging admiration of Marx and Taine — was his sense that social and political thought had to be essentially historical. Whether Mill was the first English writer to think this, I don't know; it is plain that after him the rise of the 'comparative method' made the belief a platitude. But what Mill thought was that his predecessors — especially his father and Bentham, but eighteenth-century radicals generally — had written 'timelessly' about almost every subject, but about politics especially, as if the only question to be asked was what was the best form of government, its installation then being a matter of will-power and technique. This, he thought, would no longer do; questions of political reform were essentially historical. Unless we know what stage of their historical development a people has reached, we cannot know what political reforms will enable it to progress.

Mill's commitment to this view started early in life, and was frequently reaffirmed. His revolt against Bentham and his father in the 1830s involved an appeal to the insights of Coleridge: in his famous comparative essays on Bentham and Coleridge, Mill insisted that, whereas Bentham could see in the past nothing but a storehouse of error and superstition, Coleridge had tried to look for the 'spirit' of an age; such intuitive spiritual commitments were generally dismissed by Bentham as 'unexamined generalities', but Coleridge saw in them a source of wisdom, which certainly needed to be drawn out of the verbal formulae in which it was enshrined, but which could not be understood at all save by sympathetic attempts to retrieve its meaning for those who had believed it. This did not mean, said Mill, that we should uncritically accept whatever our forbears believed — Mill was eager to recruit Coleridge's insights in the cause of reform, not conservatism; it did mean that we should be conscious of what it was we were reforming; it also meant that we should — in a rather Hegelian fashion — become aware of the sources of our ideals in our existing lives, not think of them as deliverances of pure reason.

This concern to 'recapture' the meaning of the past did not exhaust Mill's interest in history. For Mill also borrowed from Comte a view of the determinants of the broad sweep of history. No more than Weber did Mill wish to accept a 'one-sided idealism', and no more than Marx did he think of history as the progress of the Idea. But, it was certainly to changes in ideas that Mill looked for the basic movements in history. If we ask '*what* ideas?', Mill's answer is not systematic. But, it is evident that he includes in these 'ideas' both the growth of scientific knowledge and changes in our moral commitments. The French Revolution, he says, is rightly explained by Carlyle as the result of the *ancien régime* being detected in a 'giant imposture'; all the glories of the *ancien régime* were built upon a lie. When people ceased to believe in the lie, the regime lost its hold on them, and vanished with hardly a blow struck. As to what the 'lie' was a lie about, Mill (like Carlyle) is not explicit, but we can locate at least a couple of dimensions of the answer. Thus, it is a more or less literal untruth that the French aristocracy were entitled to their privileges in virtue of the protection and other services they rendered to their inferiors. But, they might have survived their uselessness if people had thought that tradition itself entitled them to their social position and their privileges, or that God had appointed them to that position. This, however, was what people had ceased to believe; for practical purposes, they were becoming wholly secular in their habits of thought.

Although Mill never offered an *histoire raisonnée* of morality, it is not too difficult to see that he supposed that morality bore the marks of mankind's intellectual development in general. Theistic beliefs about the natural order would support a positive ethic in which morality was thought to be a series of divine commandments; belief in 'natural powers', which Comte identified as the metaphysical, pre-positive stage of science, would support an ethics of natural law and natural rights; contemporary science, with its analysis of causation as a matter of pure, physical regularity, can only sustain something like a utilitarian ethics − for morality is now revealed as essentially a human invention, the 'art' as Mill describes it, that corresponds to the science of social psychology.

This picture of history is a 'rationalist' one, then, inasmuch as it makes the historical process hinge on the progress of human reason, and makes that progress a matter of increasingly rational understanding of the natural world and an increasingly rational ethics. This sustains not only *Liberty* but Mill's *Considerations on Representative Government* as well; for there also, Mill argues, as he had in his youth, that which constitutes the best form of government for a country depends on the stage of its history that the country has achieved. Unlike Weber, Mill is happy to say that representative government is the absolutely best form of government; its only competitor is that form of aristocracy − such as the Venetian − which, in practice, approximates to bureaucracy. One can see in this an argument for the East India Company's government of the Indian sub-continent, which in Mill's eyes was admittedly despotic, and in that sense non-responsible, but was precisely what India needed in order to be able to progress towards genuine self-government. Good habits of administration, the defeat of corruption, economic and political self-reliance, which were the preconditions of self-government, would be inculcated by the East India Company, which would thus put itself out of business and leave India to govern itself.

This is the moment to notice that Mill's account of the workings of representative government is light-years away from Weber's discussion of democracy, with its obsession with parties and leadership. It is not quite true that Mill did not discuss leadership, or that he had no conception of leadership, but it is true that Mill had no time for *Führerdemokratie*. It is true twice over, in fact. As an empirical phenomenon, it corresponded to the government of Napoleon III, whom Mill detested. In principle, there was no room for it in Mill's conception of politics, just as there was no room for political parties in it. (Paradoxically, Mill was a very good party MP when he was a member of the House of Commons, by no means averse to behaving as lobby-fodder and by no means averse to slanging the Tory opposition.) The reason why there is next to no room for leadership is that Mill's moral rationalism, like that of his radical predecessors, represented the political battle as a conflict between the 'people' or the 'public good' and 'sinister interests'. There would not be political conflicts, or at any rate not party conflicts, if there were no sinister interests. Although Mill was eager to preserve 'antagonism of opinions'

(Tocqueville's great influence on Mill secured that), he thought of parties as, at best, only bodies of people united around a common view about what was best for the community. The only sort of leadership this allows is something like intellectual and moral leadership: voters ought to defer to the wisest and the noblest among us – how they are to be recognized Mill does not say, or what pleasure they are likely to get out of a life in politics – but the notion of leadership as such is quite unexplored.

I stress this as much as I do because it allows me to end these few remarks about Mill's view of history by observing that, however much he learnt from Carlyle, Mill was never an enthusiast for the 'great man' theory of history. He certainly thought that some great men had made a great deal of difference: what he never thought was that some great men had so to speak taken events by the scruff of the neck and made history by main force. Nor did he look to any to do so now. It also allows me to open my few remarks about rationality by pointing out that Mill never shared Weber's interest in the non-rational imposition of values on a culture or a political system.

Mill's rationalism is not easy to characterize. Although he seemed at that well known point in *Utilitarianism* to fall into the fatal trap of offering to 'prove' that utility was the only possible principle from which to derive a moral system, Mill's usual position, in *Utilitarianism* and elsewhere, was that matters of value are not susceptible of proof, strictly speaking. There are two reasons. The first, which is no doubt one he shares with Weber, is that the only way one can show something to be desirable is to show that it leads to something independently agreed to be desirable; but this, though it may work for subordinate goals, cannot work for ultimate goals – since they, *ex hypothesi*, are what determine the value of means to them, but are not themselves determined as valuable by anything else. The second, less well known, is that Mill distinguished between what he called 'art' and 'science': 'art' was the realm of practice, instructions, imperatives; 'science' was the realm of the 'is'. No matter what we learn about what is, it teaches us nothing about what we 'ought' to do. It follows, therefore, that reason has a limited role in matters of value. Mill does say, in *The System of Logic*, that there is a 'philosophia prima' of the Art of Life or Teleology, but there is nothing comparable to his elaborate discussion of the philosophy of the inductive sciences to explain what he thought that 'philosophia prima' involved. On the face of it, however, teleology must be parasitic on the science of psychology, since teleology's ranking of the goals of life in terms of their contribution to human happiness must owe almost everything to the psychologist's discovery of what gives us how much happiness.

The whole subject, however, is plunged into confusion by Mill's best known distinction – between quantity and quality of happiness. Once this comes into play, rationality must cease to be a matter of the calculation of effective means to happiness, because we have to decide between different 'qualities' of happiness as well. It is this that makes Mill's politics – and his liberalism generally – so hard to pin down. For, there is a strong impression that rationality in the sense of the rational calculation of means to ends may well be inimical to rationality in the sense of the exploration of the ultimate goals of life. Mill's version of Weber's iron cage is that the society in which he lived would settle for a conception of what was worth while in life that would cramp mankind's moral development. It was (as in Weber) a subject that bore on the role of bureaucratic administration. Mill feared that his friends, such as Chadwick, would tidy up social arrangements so enthusiastically that all that would be left for people to do would be to settle gratefully into the niche organized for them.

Of course, it was essential to improve such things as the supply of drinking water and the disposal of sewage in order to stop the ravages of typhoid fever: but, it was also essential to leave room for the exploration of alternative ends in life. How far could this exploration be rational? The answer is hard to give. Perhaps the best answer is that Mill thought that whatever we discovered about the ends of life was a discovery about the sources of human happiness; since he held that appeals to utility 'rationalized' the Art of Life, these discoveries would be fitted into something that had in aspiration some (how many is a question I simply duck on this occasion) of the properties of a rational calculus.

Equally important is the fact that these discoveries would be empirical ones: a rational ethics is one that is not dependent on authority or 'intuition', and this ethics would not be so dependent. It would, of course, be vulnerable to just the sort of disagreements that Weber identified as putting ethical values beyond the scope of rational determination – members of different cultures would simply not recognize each others' purported 'discoveries'. Mill's reply can only be what it was in *Utilitarianism*, that those who had tried out both in practice could pronounce authoritatively. Weber, I imagine, would have denied that we could make much sense of the thought experiment – could the Samurai who thought it quite all right to try out his new sword on a passing peasant really share the experience of a Wilberforce wrecking his health in an attempt to emancipate the slaves of British West Indian planters? None the less, whatever the difficulties of Mill's case, it is clear that Mill did not want to drive *such* a wedge between rational calculation and moral imagination that his widened utilitarianism would have to be accounted 'non-rational'.

But Mill and Weber would have found much to agree about on the subject of the rationalization of the social world. Mill's essay on 'Civilisation' argues that there is a near-inevitable process of change whereby industry becomes more productive, the units of government and economic organization generally become larger or at least more functionally effective, the role of force diminishes, the role of inherited and traditional authority diminishes. Moreover, this change is associated with what Mill terms 'the predominance of masses over individuals', a thought he *might* have got from Tocqueville a little later, but seems to have picked up from the Saint-Simonians or even to have worked out for himself. To some extent, this is a restatement of the point noted above, that organizational factors become salient in economic growth, governmental efficiency and the like. It also implies what of course obsesses Mill, that the impact of the individual on public opinion, on the moral climate, on politics must diminish. For a movement to be effective, it has to grip a mass audience. This is a complicated issue. I have said already that Mill does not discuss leadership as such in the same way as Weber; to some extent, this is because Weber's anti-rationalism was so acute and Mill's not. What Mill felt most acutely was that the imaginative moralist was likely to feel lonely and isolated; it wasn't a matter of how he could lead a mass movement that interested Mill, but of how the masses (by which he means the middle-class mass audience, not 'the masses' in the sense of the lower classes) can be persuaded to listen to a message that is meant for each of them individually, not for potential members of a movement.

There are innumerable reasons why Mill and Weber should have come together partially, but only partially. Aside from anything else, the fact that they lived at opposite ends of the nineteenth century is quite enough to explain why their concerns are so different – Mill hardly lived into the age of really large-scale economic and political organization; the rise of the mass political party began in Britain in the years immediately after his death. Equally crucially, the philosophical background from which they started was strikingly different. Mill's picture of 'legal-rational' authority has next to nothing in common with Weber's, although it is hard to explain quite why. But, it is clear that Mill thinks of legal arrangements as simply imposed by legislation rather than as springing from an attempt to rationalize relationships by ensuring that there is always a rule to cover a case. It is true that Mill thinks of the application of rules to cases as the deductive inference of a decision from a rule and appropriate facts: but he has none of that curiosity about how rules 'grow' to meet cases, which common lawyers in Britain have (and Savigny shared), or the curiosity about how rules become rational expressions of social purpose, which Hegel had. And, lastly, it is obvious enough that the impact of British politics on Mill must inevitably have been very different from the impact of German politics on Weber.

One feature of Mill's work that this touches on is his half-hearted belief in the need for a 'religion of humanity' to provide some sort of transcendental justification for people's everyday existences. Weber is the great theorist of disenchantment and its ambiguous benefits – science being the obvious benefit, a loss of 'meaning' in life being the most obvious drawback. Mill never reached the plangent note that Weber struck so easily; none the less, he asked himself the awkward question whether people would be sufficiently motivated by simply working out what would be the right way to behave in the various social and political exigencies they confronted, and he found it hard to believe that the answer was yes. Yet, as I have said, he was convinced that in France secularization had already gone too far to be stopped, and that in England it was proceeding apace. The answer had to be what he, following Comte and the Saint-Simonians, termed 'the religion of humanity'. Unlike Comte, he was entirely uninterested in mimicking the apparatus of Catholic ritual (not for Mill the worship of the earth itself as *le grand être*), but he did want some way of associating the members of the present generation in the projects of their descendants and in the hopes and fears of their predecessors. We are not exactly to *worship* humanity, but some sort of cult of spiritual leaders like Socrates and great men like Washington seems to be envisaged. Immortality in the usual sense of the term is not something that can be demonstrated philosophically, although it may be hoped for; a partial equivalent for it lies in the imaginative association of each of us with the projects of mankind at large – for when we die, not everything we value will die with us. It is part of Mill's intellectual charm that he is so willing to admit that the loss of religious faith involves genuine losses, although he himself was unusual in never having had a faith to lose and therefore unusual in suffering none of the familiar Victorian pangs when it vanished. It is also part of Mill's intellectual charm that he drops his usual austere manner when discussing Comte's philosophy – nobody who had ever laughed could have drafted Comte's proposals for a humanist liturgy, says Mill, and goes on to mock them thoroughly.

I shall not try to compare Mill's attitude to the role of religion with Weber's. It is perhaps worth pointing out that Weber's notion of the 'meaning' that religion gives to life is not exactly paralleled in Mill. Mill's concerns are with motivation rather than 'meaning'; it is possible to translate much of what is gestured at by the notion of the 'meaning of life' into considerations of the ontological truth of religion and the motivational consequences of its truth, but I at least feel that something is left over when such a translation is made. Weber, writing against the background of the hermeneutic tradition, would have found it entirely natural to write about the meaning that a religious culture possesses for its members; Mill, writing against the empiricist background that permeates the *System of Logic*, would not.

This, perhaps, bears also on Mill's individualism. Mill was in many ways the heir of the Puritan tradition: his entire conception of the individual's aspirations for self-perfection is unintelligible outside the Puritan tradition. But he never defended Puritanism: *On Liberty*, for example, strongly attacks the Puritan obsession with individual moral virtue; harmless enjoyments are always to be allowed. Mill's conception of individual development is much more closely tied to Greece than to Jerusalem; it is Athenian expansiveness rather than Puritan self-restraint that he defends. The place of individuality in Mill's ethical and political theory is not entirely simple to describe, but it may be summarized something like this.

Since the age is one in which masses predominate over individuals, our age needs, more than other ages, to protect individuals from the pressures of public opinion. Public opinion is a more important threat to individuals than political tyranny – at any rate in Britain; Mill always thought that the Continent was superior to Britain in matters of what one might call social freedom, although Britain was vastly superior in matters of straightforward political freedom. It is clear that Mill always found the social manners of the French and Italians much easier and more agreeable than those of the English: we have a vision of him travelling through Naples, deploring the tyranny of the Bourbons and applauding the colour and gaiety of the inhabitants, while working out the finishing touches to *On Liberty*. But the argument involves a great deal more than that. Mill's intellectualist account of history made ideas central, and therefore made intellectual conformism the great threat to progress. Public opinion is more of a menace than straightforward tyranny in some ways because opinion, so to speak, permeates the minds of the individuals subject to its pressure, whereas threats of physical injury, imprisonment and the like certainly inhibit the transmission of ideas but commonly arouse intellectual resistance rather than acquiescence. So, it is the nineteenth century that has to watch against intellectual stagnation as no other century has, because it is the nineteenth century that is dominated by the democratic notion that public opinion is entitled to get its own way.

To argue as passionately as Mill did on this score, we need to hold another of his views – that one man with an idea can have more effect than ninety-nine with an interest. He always held that the doctrine that men's behaviour is determined by their interests is either drearily tautological or importantly false. The interesting question – if we allow the principle to be tautological – is what makes people entertain one conception of their interests rather than another. It must be some idea or other, and therefore the interesting and important causal factor is that idea. So Mill's concern for the individual turns on his concern for the individual as the source of all the ideas on which historical change depends. Unless we hold society back, and leave individuals room to breathe intellectually and emotionally, we shall end in that famous condition of 'Chinese immobility'. This, of course, is the point at which those who disbelieve in Mill's views often make objections – Puritanism was exceedingly good for intellectual progress, but there was absolutely no question of individuals being left to think what they liked. But Mill has rather more resources to cope with that observation than seems likely at first sight. He does not attain to the subtlety of Popper, who produces a much more elaborate account of the sociology of intellectual invention and criticism, but it seems likely that Mill would have shared many of Popper's views on this. It *looks* as if he thinks of intellectual endeavour as a matter of individuals somehow accumulating truer and truer views about the world, but in *On Liberty* he insists that no opinion is more reliable than it shows itself in the face of criticism, and that suggests something much nearer 'criticalism' than 'inductivism'. My own view, which is admittedly contentious, is that Mill's inductivism is a form of criticalism; what it is not is a sociologically very sophisticated form of criticism. That is, there is nothing in Mill to match Popper's account of how we need the right social setting to encourage inventiveness in putting forward hypotheses and to provide a critical environment in which to scrutinize them against the evidence.

None the less, what Mill more or less takes for granted is the possibility of creating an intellectual community of the desired sort. There is little in Mill to suggest that intellectual life is essentially *lonely*. It is true that people need self-discipline and a certain toughness in order to keep going under criticism, but once again the heroic note struck by Nietzsche and the plangent note struck by Weber are absent from Mill's work. He simply doesn't think in what you might call thoroughgoing sociological terms – but then he was primarily a philosopher. The other aspect of individuality, which Mill was eager to defend, was what he discussed in *On Liberty* as one of the great goods of life. In spite of the extended discussion in the third chapter of his most famous essay, it is not *quite* clear what the nature of individuality is. Basically, individuality is a matter of each person being able to say of his or her own life, ideas and the rest that they really were his or her own. Independence, autonomy, self-government in thought and action – these seem the obvious terms to apply. And these define both Mill's individualism and Mill's liberalism. One important feature of Mill's account is that it separates individualism as a moral and political value from any sort of economic individualism and *laissez-faire*.

Mill's ability to effect this separation is part of his legal positivism. There is no natural right to property, so there is no argument from the natural right to liberty to the right to do as you choose with your abilities and property. All property is conventionally created and its treatment is a proper matter for government decision; that decision must be utilitarian in the widest sense. That widest sense is the sense offered in *On Liberty*, where Mill appeals to the interests of man considered as a progressive being, and makes it clear that libertarian considerations are fundamental to this widened utilitarianism. As I have argued elsewhere, and shall therefore not argue now, Mill contemplates as a possibility, though one for the future, an economy of self-governing worker co-operatives as the successor to the regime of the individual capitalist or the capitalist joint-stock company. That there is no chance to become a capitalist in the current sense is not for Mill an infringement of liberty in the sense in which *On Liberty* attacks such infringements. Since property rights are something close to social privileges, individuals can only claim such property rights as will achieve the goals set out by enlarged utilitarian reflection. This, though, leaves all the other rights Mill is eager to defend perfectly intact.

Thus, there could be no question of making it illegal or difficult for people to campaign against co-operativism once it was installed – though, just as we now forbid incitement, it would have to be done in the proper fashion, not by inciting people to wreck their firms. There could be no question of governments taking a moral stand on what co-operatives ought to produce; so far as I can see, if there were a co-operative that wished to sell cannabis cigarettes, Mill would think that it ought to be allowed to do so, though drivers, soldiers, and so forth would rightly be forbidden to smoke dope on duty. In other words, it would be very much like the situation with drink, where Mill takes a fierce view of prohibitionists, though he allows that where taxation occurs for the sake of revenue rather than as a form of prohibition, it is reasonable to tax drink rather than more necessary items of consumption.

And, although *laissez-faire* is, for Mill, once again a matter of policy rather than a matter of rights, Mill's liberalism does pull him in the direction of demanding a large measure of *laissez-faire* all the same. By this stage in this essay, the reasons ought to be obvious enough. Individual effort and individual responsibility are both the driving force of progress and part of the goal of progress. The defect of constant governmental intervention is not so much that it is inefficient – Mill thinks it often is, for all the familiar reasons – as that it replaces diverse individual projects with uniform collective ones. There is plenty of work for governments to do that does not breach this commitment – for example, governments can set up schools more or less in competition with those set up by everyone else, and they can do this to keep up standards and to increase diversity rather than to reduce it; again, governments can set up some sort of national examination system, so that everyone can see how well different schools do in meeting various tests – but they ought not to impose any particular method of teaching, ought to set examinations only in strictly examinable subjects, and must resist the temptation to interfere where they do not know best.

This, then, means that freedom for Mill is consistent with a socialist (of sorts) organization of the economy, but that it is likely to be threatened by the same forces, under socialism, as it is threatened by under a capitalist regime. The pressures to uniformity and centralization, many of them humanitarian in origin, many of them entirely defensible in terms of efficiency, which frighten Mill in the present order, will be exactly as strong in the new order. Indeed, there will be an added problem, whose nature shows clearly just how far Mill was a child of the early nineteenth century. Mill's discussions of the varieties of socialism in his *Principles* and in the *Chapters on Socialism* are mostly couched in terms which a twentieth-century reader follows without difficulty. One exception is his anxiety about population. Mill thought at first that any system which ensured that workers would be kept at a tolerable standard of living, no matter what, would collapse under the weight of unchecked expansion of population. He, like most of his orthodox contemporaries, had been terrorized by Malthus's discussion of population into believing that it was only the natural check of misery that kept population down; if the workers were able to escape the consequences of imprudent over-breeding, they would infallibly bring on the eventual destruction of the system. Early on, he saw that birth-control would effect a cure – he spent a night in jail at the age of sixteen when caught distributing birth-control leaflets in a working-class area. But it would need social pressure and education to make sure that whatever birth-control techniques were available were used. So Mill's anxiety took the form of thinking that enough social pressure to keep population in check would itself threaten to become a form of tyranny; the existing order kept population in check by brutal and random means, but they were at any rate not under anyone's control. Put the power to control population in the hands of a bureaucracy such as the Saint-Simonians envisaged in command of their society, and the road to serfdom was wide open before them. The general form of the dilemma is familiar – to make a socialist economy work is either impossible, because neither the information nor the techniques of management are to be had, or else it is possible but intolerable, because those with the authority and the techniques of control will inevitably be corrupted and become tyrannical. What is to us archaic (though doubtless not to the Chinese and the Indonesian readers of Mill, if there are any) is the subject that attracts the anxiety.

The conception of freedom on which all this hangs is, then, the familiar liberal conception. The great enemy of individual freedom is the state, although in the modern world, social pressure is if anything more dangerous still. The remedy is a clear and rational sense of where the proper boundaries ought to be drawn between individual choice and social requirements. It is essentially a moralist and a philosopher addressing society that we hear. What there is not is the sense of freedom as an accomplishment or as something collective, or as something essentially tied up with boldness and innovation in politics. In contrast with Weber, for instance, there is no suggestion in Mill that the act of political decision-making in itself, the actual exercise of power, is a risky business, and that in seizing the chance of action in spite of its risks there is a special sort of freedom to be had. The same thing applies to Mill's unconcern with either national independence or group self-confidence. It is not that Mill had nothing to say about nationality – but what he had to say was merely that groups which wished to be one nation ought to be so; the complications attendant on that simple thought were dismissed with the solution of federalism. The idea that anyone could think that their nation's national project was what freedom was all about is not one that occurs to Mill. The explanation of Mill's indifference is not obvious, nor is it clear what sort of explanation we ought to look for. Is it to be found in the tradition of English utilitarianism, with its assumption that all real problems have rational optimizing solutions? Or in the social position of the utilitarians, who generally occupied professional positions of a safe kind, where politics was indeed a matter of rational problem-solving? Or in the ascendancy of the English middle class, which had no cause to fight for its own view of the world in the desperate fashion envisaged by Weber? What is clear, though, is the extent to which Mill's views hang together – that his rationalism, individualism and liberalism form a coherent ideological perspective, one that legitimates and is legitimated by the historical perspective that attends it, and what is then equally clear is how different this perspective was, and inevitably was, from Weber's.

12 Weber and Durkheim: Coincidence and Divergence

ANTHONY GIDDENS

Let me start from a puzzle, one that must interest everybody concerned with these two major figures in the history of social thought. Weber and Durkheim are regarded as among the principal founders of modern sociology – together with Marx, probably the three dominant figures who have established the major parameters of modern social science. Yet, on the face of things, it seems distinctly odd that Weber and Durkheim should be so frequently discussed in the same breath. Not only did they work in different national traditions, their writings at first sight seem to have very little similarity indeed to one another.

Durkheim tirelessly promoted the cause of sociology throughout his lifetime. By 'sociology', he understood a discipline established largely along the lines set out by Comte in the middle of the nineteenth century. Durkheim's idea of sociology was of a science of social institutions, employing wherever possible analogous methods to those used in the natural sciences. For him, the problem of establishing sociology upon a firm basis was that of catching up, in the realm of social activity, with the achievements of natural science in understanding a world of material reality. Although Durkheim may have changed certain of his views rather substantially during the course of his career, he never relinquished this overall ambition. Weber, by contrast, was chary of the notion of 'sociology', and would have little to do with that version of social analysis that most strongly influenced Durkheim. Comte's writings were for the most part not highly esteemed in Germany, and certainly Weber had little sympathy with the idea of establishing a science of social institutions along the sort of lines proposed by Durkheim. In his lifetime, Weber was not regarded either by himself or by others as primarily 'a sociologist', but saw himself, and was seen, as a historian, economist and theorist of jurisprudence. No reference to the work of Durkheim appears in Weber's writings. Contrary to the views of certain scholars, this should not be regarded as particularly surprising. Weber certainly knew of the work of Durkheim and of Durkheim's collaborators in the *Année sociologique* school but there can be little doubt that he was barely influenced at all by this body of writers. The same applies in a reciprocal vein: Durkheim knew of Weber's work, and there is a minor reference to aspects of it in one passage in Durkheim's writings[1] but he claimed no particular kinship with those of Weber's ideas with which he was familiar.[2]

Whose view, therefore, is correct? Should we accept the opinion, commonly held today, that Durkheim and Weber were groping their way towards something of a common standpoint in social science?[3] Or should we rather take the view that they held of themselves: that is, that neither the orientation of their work nor the main suppositions underlying it have much in common with one another? There are two ways in which we can seek to answer these questions. First, we can investigate how far apart their views were in reality. Perhaps their writings, in spite of the inclinations of their authors, reveal some underlying similarities. Secondly, given that they started from different perspectives, we can seek to elucidate how far there was an increasing convergence between their views during the course of their respective careers.

The first of these problems can be divided into three: (1) We can enquire into the sources they drew upon, looking at how far these overlapped. (2) We can look at their methodological ideas, asking how far there were similarities between the modes of enquiry they respectively sought to foster in social science. (3) We can look into the content of their substantive writings, to see whether there are resemblances between the content of their investigations.

If we enquire about the respective backgrounds of Weber and Durkheim, we discover some interesting similarities. Durkheim studied in Germany, as a young man, in 1885–6, and throughout his life he kept up with the German literature in social science. *L'Année sociologique* gave a good deal of attention to German publications – in the shadow of the imminent First World War, Durkheim was strongly attacked, in fact, for giving too much weight to German social thought in his own concerns. Durkheim's early publications include some lengthy review articles based on the research he carried out in Germany.[4] He was especially impressed by Wundt and Schäffle and devoted a good deal of attention to their writings. At a later phase, he produced discussions of the writings of Simmel and Tönnies. However, it must be pointed out that those forms of social thought to which Durkheim was most attracted were the very same about which Weber was most strongly critical. Durkheim admired Schäffle, for example, because of that writer's demonstration that the qualities of social wholes could not be derived from those of their individual members.[5] Weber, of course, had little time for this sort of viewpoint.

If there is a main connection between the traditions of thought which Weber and Durkheim drew upon, it is one mediated by their respective critical relationships to neo-Kantianism. It is well known that neo-Kantianism strongly influenced certain aspects of Weber's thought. It is much less common to indicate that something similar was true of Durkheim. Durkheim was in a certain sense much more preoccupied with Kantian themes than was Weber. In *The Division of Labour*, Durkheim's concern with the social conditions promoting the autonomy of the individual, or what he calls 'moral individualism', represents a sociological concern with a distinctly Kantian theme.[6] Unlike Kant, Durkheim did not regard the dignity and moral value of the individual as simply a philosophical given. Rather, he sought to 'sociologize' Kant by demonstrating how the issue had come to the fore in a particular set of social and historical circumstances. Durkheim's interest, later on in his writings, in the framing and classification of knowledge also has a distinctly Kantian thrust. In *The Elementary Forms of the Religious Life* we find essentially a sociological investigation of the Kantian categories. Durkheim concludes that the categories of knowledge are not an inherent part of the human mind, but are created in and through social association.[7]

The elements which Weber and Durkheim respectively drew from Kantianism were quite different. These differences are plainly reflected in the divergent methodological ideas that each of the two thinkers held. Durkheim was indebted methodologically to Comte and to Boutroux. His sociological programme can be understood in substantial part as an attempt to separate the basic methodological framework found in Comte from the substantive content of Comte's ideas, most of which Durkheim rejected. Durkheim was not a Kantian in respect of method. Kantian thought was important to Durkheim not as a philosophical resource in and of itself, but as indicating a set of themes which needed sociological investigation. Weber, on the other hand, was indebted to neo-Kantianism methodologically and drew extensively upon it in formulating more philosophical aspects of his standpoint. Their respective relationship to neo-Kantianism, therefore, drove their positions apart rather than brought them together. In most respects, their methodological views are plainly opposed.

I see no reason to doubt that Weber meant what he said when he advocated a version of what today would be called 'methodological individualism'. There is an obvious association of a logical kind between Weber's insistence upon the significance of studying subjective meaning, and his emphasis upon the individual and the individual action as the concrete realities with which social science deals. The logical qualifications he entered about the use of so-called 'collective' concepts were also entirely in line with these emphases. Whether Weber had actually read Durkheim's *Rules of Sociological Method* we do not know, but it is certain that he would have found in it a prime example of doctrines of which he himself had the greatest suspicion.[8] Durkheim, for his part, had almost certainly not read Weber's methodological writings. During Weber's lifetime, these were never collected together in an accessible form corresponding to Durkheim's own book, and always remained in large part reflections upon established practices of social and historical research, rather than constituting a methodological manifesto in their own right. Such a manifesto is certainly what Durkheim intended to produce in *The Rules of Sociological Method*. One would be hard put to it to claim that Durkheim derived his precepts of sociological method from the more concrete investigations that he undertook. On the contrary, it makes more sense to say that these investigations were designed by Durkheim to exemplify principles of method he had already elaborated.

It would be out of the question in a relatively short discussion like this to compare the whole range of substantive themes in the writings of Durkheim and Weber. There are manifestly major differences in the two styles of work. Durkheim was an evolutionary thinker, and from *The Division of Labour in Society* through to *The Elementary Forms* he adopted a conception of evolutionism. He was basically uninterested in detailed historical research, and fond of constructing generalized interpretations of social development. Neither the detailed studies of economic history and the development of law, which Weber undertook at the beginning of his career, nor the open-ended comparative research, which culminated in the volumes of *Economy and Society*, have much of an echo in Durkheim's work. Durkheim was certainly alive to the importance of comparative sociology, and was one of the first to see the significance of modern fieldwork in anthropology for sociological issues. As Gouldner has pointed out, Weber and Durkheim belonged to the first generation that broke in a fairly systematic way with a Europe-centred outlook in social science. But there is not much resemblance between them in the manner in which this was accomplished.

Let us consider one main aspect of their writings in order to demonstrate this. Rather than picking what has seemed to many commentators to be the main line of connection between them – their work on the sociology of religion – I shall take their writings on the state and politics. A continuing concern with the nature of politics, with forms of modern government, and with the origins of state power, are found in both writers. Weber, of course was actively involved in the sphere of practical politics for fairly lengthy periods of his life. Durkheim, on the other hand, played little active part in politics, save for being marginally involved in some of the events relating to the Dreyfus affair.[9] Although he did not in his lifetime publish a book specifically concerned with politics and government, Durkheim gave several major lecture-courses, which after his death were published in book form. These provide us with a clear idea of the systematic position which he elaborated on these issues.[10]

Durkheim saw himself as a critic of Marxist interpretations of the state and politics on the one hand and of conservative theories on the other. Marxist thought he attacked, not only because of its misleading emphasis upon class dynamics, but because it failed to develop an account of the origins of political power. That is to say, Marxist theory, in Durkheim's view at any rate, sees the state as primarily an economic form of organization. The state exists as a mechanism of class domination, and hence can be transcended in a society in which classes no longer exist. In such a society, economic regulation is all that will be required to allow individuals to live free and fulfilling lives. Durkheim tried to show that this theme, deriving in substantial part from Saint-Simon, cannot provide an account of the nature of modern government. The state is not just the perpetuator of class domination, but fulfils a range of more positive functions. It cannot be transcended in a socialist society of the future, but is likely to expand the range of its activities with the progression of social development. On the other hand, Durkheim had little time for those theories of government that associate the state with the highest values of human social life. That is to say, he accepted that the state has its origins in civil society and remains inherently tied to it. It is just as wrong to over-value the significance of the state as it is to claim that the state is an epiphenomenon of class domination.

Durkheim therefore tried to work out an account of the character of the modern state that differed from each of these perspectives at both an analytical and a normative level. The progressive development of the state, in his view, is a result of the expanding differentiation of human society. The more complex society becomes, the more there is a need for a greater range of governmental functions. Each of the two perspectives he set out to criticize have mistaken assumptions about the desirable form of the state. For Marxism, the problem is to re-absorb the state into society and so transcend it. To the degree to which this is a realizable proposition, however, the result would be, if achieved, a political system without stability of orientation or policy. A modern society without central direction is one in which the whims of the populace control the direction of political activity. There would be nothing to inhibit the erratic influences of collective emotions and sentiments. Those who over-value the state, by contrast, fail to see the unfortunate consequences that can stem from overwhelming state power. If a state achieves too much power in a modern society, the result is despotic government, which is not at all responsive to the needs or the interests of the mass of the population.

In steering a way between these two positions, Durkheim developed a challenging and important conception of democratic government.[11] A democracy is a political order in which the state is in touch with the views and ideas of the population that it governs. In other words, there must be consistent and developed channels of communication from the majority of the population to those in the governing circles. However, democratic government presumes avoiding each of the situations that are in fact actively sought for by the two perspectives Durkheim discards. Communication from populace to government should not be confused with the subordination of state power to the immediate wishes and demands of that population. The government must be strong enough to be capable of overriding at least some sectors of public opinion in order to help initiate progressive programmes of social reform, which correspond to the longer-term interests of the majority. Democracy is equally impossible, however, where a state is able effectively to ignore the wishes of those who are governed. A democratic state, therefore, presumes the existence of secondary associations intervening between the individual and the state. Such secondary associations protect the individual from state power and, at the same time, help to buffer the state from the petty day-to-day concerns of the mass. Durkheim saw revitalized occupation associations, or *corporations*, as the main form of secondary association likely to emerge in the modern world.

There was therefore a direct tie between Durkheim's theory of the division of labour and his account of the nature of democratic government. The division of labour, as it increases in complexity, creates the need for an expanding role for occupational associations; at the same time, these occupational groupings provide the political means of intervening at levels between the individual on the one side and the state on the other.

Both Weber's definition of the state in general, and his account of the nature of modern democratic politics in particular, differ very markedly from those offered by Durkheim. For Weber, the two prime characteristics of states are their territoriality and their association with legitimate monopoly of the means of violence. Territoriality and control of violence play no role in Durkheim's conceptualization of the state. In fact, Durkheim specifically rejects them as defining characteristics of state power. States have not always been territorial, he says, giving the example of nomad empires. Moreover, there have been non-political forms of association linked with territorial boundaries. Therefore, we cannot regard territoriality as a defining characteristic of the state. Much the same applies to control of the means of violence. Durkheim hardly ever discusses military power or its role in history. It seems fairly evident that his views are closely related to those of many earlier nineteenth-century social thinkers, who saw a major division between the tradition of societies of the past and the emerging industrial order of the future. For such thinkers, while militarism and militaristic adventurism may have characterized many societies in the past, the newly emerging industrial order was to be one based upon economic exchange rather than upon violence. Industrial society is portrayed as fundamentally a peaceful order, in which the expanding division of labour brings individuals into greater and greater interdependence, both nationally and on an international scale.

Durkheim's sociology, unlike the political views developed by Weber, simply had no place to accommodate the First World War. Durkheim was shattered intellectually and personally by the advent of war, since all his writings lead to the idea that what will come about in the modern world is an increasingly co-operative industrial commonwealth of nations. During the course of the war, Durkheim wrote two pamphlets concerned with German militarism. What impresses the reader about these documents is not their insight, but the highly forced and unconvincing arguments that Durkheim deploys in order to analyse the German war aims. German culture is regarded as a 'pathological' deviation from the normal course of development associated with progressive social differentiation. It is a society in which – for reasons which Durkheim is unable to specify at all adequately – imperialistic impulses towards cultural domination come to the fore. [12] Those elements that figure most prominently in Weber's discussion of the war, the specific geopolitical situation of Germany and its interests in relation to encircling European powers, barely make an appearance in Durkheim's interpretation. As with other aspects of their writings, the differences between their respective views are surely more impressive than the similarities.

Where does all this leave us? I would characterize the relation between Weber and Durkheim as one of 'contextual association and dissociation'. That is to say, they were contemporaries working in two European countries, whose fate was tied together historically and by the conjunctions of war. The 1870–1 Franco-Prussian War both connects and separates them, as a backdrop to their early work, just as the First World War does towards the end of their respective careers. So far as Weber was concerned, the outcome of the 1870–1 War was the need to deal with the consequences of the unification of Germany under Bismarck. Germany had become a unified nation, but one that needed to promote a rapid phase of industrialization, with the divisive consequences which this was likely to produce internally, and with the need to consolidate its position in Europe externally. Weber's preoccupation with problems of leadership – something that finds no echo in Durkheim – was evidently strongly influenced by his appraisal of the impact on Germany of Bismarck's domination. Although his investigation of the nature of bureaucracy and of bureaucratic power was undertaken with characteristically developed scholarship over a broad front, it is difficult to resist the supposition that Weber's preoccupation with bureaucratic administration was itself strongly influenced by the circumstances existing in Germany. The relation between charismatic leadership, on the one hand, and dull bureaucratic routine, on the other, undoubtedly connects to the twin roles of Bismarck and the Prussian bureaucracy in influencing the fate of Germany. Durkheim neither admired great leaders in the way that Weber did, nor did he see bureaucratic routine as the menace to individual freedom that it was for Weber. The term 'bureaucracy', even when referring to state power, hardly appears in Durkheim's writings, and there certainly is no systematic discussion of the development of bureaucratic administration.

Durkheim was strongly influenced in his thinking by the legacy of the

1870–1 War. But, in France, the consequences of the war, and the implications of it perceived by political thinkers, were quite different from those in Germany. For liberal republicans such as Durkheim, the French defeat in the war signalled the need for considerable internal reconstruction. *The Division of Labour in Society* can be regarded as an attempt to provide a general backdrop to the necessary social reforms as Durkheim saw them. The book demonstrated that the development of liberal individualism is not some sort of distortion of traditional values, but signals a generic set of processes of social transformation – from mechanical to organic solidarity. The problem of social progression is one of propelling forward the social trends that will stabilize a complex industrial order, involving a ramified division of labour. In political terms, this meant, for Durkheim, realizing the long-term implications of the 1789 Revolution. That is to say, the Revolution had promised a series of structural changes in French society, but the achievement of these changes could not be an affair of the revolutionary transition itself. They demanded long-term social reorganization. Durkheim's concern with the achievement of moral 'solidarity', in relation to the furthering of individualism and the consolidation of a democratic state, have to be understood in these terms.

It makes some sense to see both Weber and Durkheim as attempting to reconstruct liberalism in the context of a critique of Marxism, on the one side, and of conservative thought, on the other.[13] Both thinkers rejected the idea that nineteenth-century liberalism (that is to say, economic liberalism tied to utilitarian philosophy and the reign of free markets) offered a solution to the problems faced by the European societies at the turn of the twentieth century. Even if Weber was much more directly influenced by Marxism, and schooled in Marxist thought, than was Durkheim, they both perceived its importance and saw the need to combat it in its own terms. They were each attracted similarly by certain aspects of conservative thought, but also decisively rejected the main orientations of such thought. Each appropriated elements from socialism and conservatism to provide a defence of a restructured liberalism. Weber's defence – typical of the man, when compared with Durkheim – was much more qualified and fractured. Although interpreters of Weber have quarrelled about this, I think there can be little doubt that, for him, democracy was never more than a means to other ends. Weber's philosophical stance did not provide a mechanism for validating democratic values in and of themselves.[14] Durkheim, on the other hand, was committed throughout his life to liberal republicanism, and in his sociological thought attempted to provide reasoned justification of the values associated with liberal individualism. The depth of the differences between their views in this respect is symptomatic of what I have called disassociation through contextual association. If Weber and Durkheim are considered, as no doubt they should be, to be among the leading founders of modern sociology, we have to acknowledge the depth of the differences between their respective legacies. Durkheim's programme for the development of sociology was unequivocal and clear. For him, sociology was to inherit some of the tasks previously assumed by philosophy, but should use empirical methods to accomplish them. By adopting a framework of positive method, the social sciences could recapitulate a similar order of established findings to those achieved within the natural sciences. Weber's scepticism of this view, and his distaste for too programmatic a methodological position, distanced him quite irrevocably from any such aspirations. If, in the end, he produced a defence of sociology, it was one much more hedged about with reservations than anything to which Durkheim could have assented.

Notes: Chapter 12

1 In a report, 'Le premier congrès allemand de sociologie', *L'Année sociologique*, vol. 12 (1913).
2 Georges Davy has emphasized that Durkheim 'connaissait très mal les oeuvres de Weber'. Personal communication to Steven Lukes, reported in Lukes, *Emile Durkheim: His Life and Work* (London, 1973), p. 397.
3 T. Parsons, *The Structure of Social Action* (New York, 1937).
4 'La science positive de la morale en Allemagne', *Revue philosophique*, vol. 24 (1887), pp. 33–58, 113–42, 275–84.
5 'Le programme économique de M. Schaeffle', *Revue d'économie politique*, vol. 2 (1888), pp. 3–7.
6 E. Durkheim, *The Division of Labour in Society* (London, 1984), new translation.
7 idem, *The Elementary Forms of the Religious Life* (New York, 1965).
8 idem, *The Rules of Sociological Method* (London, 1982), new translation.
9 idem, 'L'individualisme et les intellectuels', *Revue bleue*, 4th series, vol. 10 (1898), pp. 7–13.
10 idem, *Socialism* (London, 1959); idem, *Professional Ethics and Civic Morals* (London, 1957).
11 idem, *Professional Ethics and Civic Morals*.
12 idem, *'L 'Allemagne au-dessus de tout': La mentalité et la guerre* (Paris, 1915).
13 Cf. A. Giddens, *Capitalism and Modern Social Theory* (Cambridge, 1971).
14 idem, *Politics and Sociology in the Thought of Max Weber* (London, 1972).

Part II

Max Weber's Relation to the Theologians and Historians

13 Max Weber and the Evangelical-Social Congress

RITA ALDENHOFF

The early writings of Max Weber have been receiving increasing attention in recent scholarship. Interest has mainly been directed towards the possibility of demonstrating lines of continuity, even at this early stage, between the general body of his theoretical work and his political concerns.[1] Attention focuses primarily on Weber's theoretical and political assessment of the advance of agrarian capitalism in the German East, where the dismantling of existing patriarchal structures had, he argued, increasingly undermined the national interests of the German Reich.[2] In this context, Weber's hitherto largely unresearched participation in the Evangelical-Social movement during the Wilhelmine period assumes a particular significance. What were the motives for his involvement in the Evangelical-Social Congress (ESC)? Did he seriously envisage the possibility of exerting a moral or religious influence upon existing relations of social organization or authority,[3] or were the reasons underlying his action of a different order? In what follows, we shall attempt to draw out Weber's central concerns as they emerge from his exchanges with various groups and individuals within the Evangelical-Social Congress.

The founding of the Evangelical-Social Congress in 1890 was entirely in the spirit of the general reorientation of social policy that occurred at the beginning of the 1890s. In place of the repression of the Social Democratic movement, increased efforts were now to be made to find solutions to social problems, particularly those of the industrial workforce, through changes in social policy. The signal for these changes was given in the Kaiser's February proclamations on social policy, which contained promises of stronger national measures for the protection of workers, as well as announcing an international conference on workers' welfare.[4]

In April 1890, there followed a pronouncement from the Protestant High Consistory, which, as a body directly answerable to the head of state,[5] effected a parallel change of course in social policy. On the one hand, the clergy were exhorted to continue the fight against Social Democracy; they were, however, also to recognize and take account of the legitimate social needs of the workers. The improvement of material welfare was declared one of the preconditions for raising religious and moral standards. It was further recommended that the clergy participate in the formation of Protestant workers' associations, and in workers' meetings.[6]

One month later, the first meeting of the Evangelical-Social Congress took place in Berlin.[7] The initiative for the founding of the Congress had come from the conservative court preacher, Adolf Stoecker, who saw it as creating a potential forum for debates on social problems among representatives of diverse theological and political tendencies within the Church. It was as a result of a decision by Stoecker that Adolf Harnack, the leader of the liberal theological tendency was also invited, in spite of the considerable political and theological differences that existed between them. In this way, the theological current inspired by the Göttingen theologian Albrecht Ritschl was also drawn in.[8] In addition to numerous clergymen, candidates for ordination, theological students and a string of university theologians, senior civil servants and university teachers from other faculties also participated in the Congress, among them the military historian Hans Delbrück and the economist Adolph Wagner, both long-standing members of the so-called Action Committee.[9] It was, above all, the relatively high level of participation by university teachers and senior civil servants that gave the ESC a high public profile, which was also true in this same period of the Verein für Sozialpolitik.[10]

Although, as we shall demonstrate in greater detail below, Stoecker's original plans had been somewhat different, the Congress did not see its objective as residing in intensified agitation against Social Democracy, but rather in 'the unprejudiced investigation of social conditions among our people, the evaluation of those conditions against the touchstone of the moral and religious commandments of the Gospels, and the attempt to implement these commandments in contemporary economic life in ways which make them more fruitful and effective than they have hitherto been'.[11] Not only were social and socio-ethical questions dealt with in extensive reports at annual conferences,[12] but in addition to these — and this is characteristic of the Congress's work in the years that followed — in meetings conducted along the lines of academic courses, the clergy were familiarized with the principles of political economy. It was the resultant collaboration between the clergy and political economists that laid the foundations for Max Weber's long and energetic participation in the Evangelical-Social Congress.

Weber was a regular participant in the annual conferences, up to and including that of 1897; from 1892 on, he was a member of the Council that directed the movement.[13] After his move to Baden in 1894, he also became a member of the Council of the local Evangelical-Social Union, one of the provincial unions affiliated to the ESC.[14] He made contributions to a series of courses in political economy for the clergy, of which his October 1893 lectures in Berlin are perhaps the best known. Weber spoke there in company with such widely reputed economists as Adolph Wagner, Karl Oldenberg and Wilhelm Stieda on a number of basic economic problems, in particular on agriculture and agrarian politics.[15] Further courses, in which Weber lectured on questions pertaining to the Stock Exchange and, again, on agrarian politics, followed in 1896 and 1897.[16] To these must be added — with four individual papers delivered to the Evangelical-Social learned societies and the Upper Hessian society for Home Missions[17] — his collaboration on Martin Rade's *Die christliche Welt* [The Christian World] and the *Mitteilungen des Evangelisch-sozialen Kongresses* [Communications of the Evangelical-Social Congress]. Lastly, his work as director of the Inquiry into Rural Workers, which the ESC carried out in 1892–3 in the manner of the earlier survey undertaken by the Verein für Sozialpolitik, is of fundamental significance.

Now that the considerable extent of Weber's participation in the Evangelical-Social movement has become clear, we are all the more urgently impelled to ask what motives lay behind that participation. It will be our concern in what follows to cast light on those motives and to demonstrate that, by the beginning of the 1890s, Weber was already developing lines of inquiry that were to mark out the directions of his later work, both with regard to practical politics and to theory. The present study will proceed through the presentation of two individuals (Otto Baumgarten and Paul Göhre) and one group (the liberal theological tendency gathered around Adolf Harnack, Martin Rade and Hermann von Soden), with whom Weber had a particular affinity within the ESC.[18] An analysis of the arguments they put forward for the work of the Evangelical-Social movement will allow Weber's own motives to emerge more clearly.

Weber's interest in the Evangelical-Social Congress was aroused, in the first instance, by his cousin, Otto Baumgarten. Baumgarten, a fellow-student of Weber's in Heidelberg, came to Berlin in 1888, where he served as chaplain in an orphanage. In 1890, he became a university lecturer in Berlin and, in the same year, he was appointed Assistant Professor at the University of Jena. In 1894, he became Professor of Practical Theology at Kiel. Baumgarten was the editor of *Evangelisch-soziale Zeitfragen* [Evangelical-Social Contemporary Issues], a series of pamphlets close in spirit to the ESC. The series had set itself the goal of 'reinstating the Protestant Church as the conscience which moves the Protestant people in their dealings with economically weaker members of the nation'.[19] According to Baumgarten, Weber lent his assistance in the elaboration of the programme for the 'Contemporary Issues' series.[20] There is no evidence for this in Weber's own writings, though it has been established that he took on occasional editorial work for Baumgarten and canvassed for the project in Berlin.[21] He did, for example, visit the Berlin political economist Adolph Wagner in an attempt to win his support for the series.[22] He had also originally planned to contribute a pamphlet on the rural workers' question.[23]

For Otto Baumgarten, in contrast to Max Weber, religious motives doubtless played the decisive role in his commitment to the Evangelical-Social movement. Yet the two men did have one objective in common. Both were striving to come to terms with the National Liberal heritage of their fathers. Baumgarten felt his vocation lay in 'bolstering the social conscience of the National Liberal Party'.[24] Although Weber felt by no means so closely associated with national liberalism as Baumgarten, who had been deputy chairman of the Thuringia National Liberal Party during his time as a teacher in Jena,[25] he too entertained hopes that the traditional reticence of liberalism in matters of state social policy might be overcome. For Weber, a failure to move with the contemporary tide in social policy was one of the most far-reaching errors that liberalism could commit. In his view, such an error could appreciably impair liberalism's future chances of success.[26] Yet for all that, there was one specific point on which Baumgarten and Weber broke faith with the liberal heritage. The social reforms they fought for were not to be informed by patriarchal conceptions. Rejecting the line in social policy advocated by Stoecker, who, in his desire to prevent the workers from coming of age politically, ultimately treated them (in Baumgarten's words) 'as the object of the Church's mission',[27] they wished to see social policy grounded in a recognition of the rights of working people to independent organization and self-determination. This was to include a recognition of their right to political and social representation.

Thus, on specific socio-political issues, as for example when pressing the case for the development of workers' housing in Kiel, Baumgarten worked with Social Democrats.[28] He was also one of the signatories of the appeal for a settlement by arbitration in the Hamburg dockers' strike of 1897.[29] Weber does not in fact figure among the signatories of that appeal, but, in an address in Saarbrücken in January 1897, he came down unequivocally on the side of the dockers.[30] Both Baumgarten and Weber signed a declaration against the Subversion Bill (*Umsturzvorlage*) with which the government sought to revive repressive measures against the Social Democrats.[31] At the Evangelical-Social Congress of 1894, Weber called for the extension of freedom of association to agricultural workers.[32] By so doing, he contributed decisively to the exacerbation of the conflict between the so-called Old and New Guards within the ESC and thus ultimately to the secession of the Stoecker tendency in 1896.[33]

In sum, we may conclude that Weber's collaboration in the ESC – like Baumgarten's – arose out of a desire to gain acceptance for certain principles of social policy. What this entailed for Weber was, on the one hand, a critical engagement with the patriarchal Stoecker tendency and, on the other, educational work on the preconditions of social policy in general. This work of education was performed through the courses and lectures on basic questions of political economy mentioned above. Weber maintained a sharp distinction between the lectures he gave under the aegis of the Evangelical-Social movement and the educational seminars conducted by the Volksverein für das katholische Deutschland [The People's Association for Catholic Germany] and by the Protestant Workers' Associations. In the latter, he contended, religious, ethical and political issues had been conflated with economic problems. Naumann, for one, used such seminars to win the Protestant Workers' Associations over to a single common programme.[34] By contrast, Weber endeavoured to use his lectures and courses to put forward only theoretical arguments, and thus to maintain a strict separation between these various spheres.

On this issue, Weber found himself in agreement with the so-called 'Cultural Protestant' (*kulturprotestantisch*) tendency, which played a major role in the ESC. This liberal theological tendency, inspired by the work of Albrecht Ritschl, was represented in the ESC most prominently by Adolf Harnack, Martin Rade and Hermann von Soden. Harnack, an ecclesiastical historian, whose appointment to Berlin in 1888 had been the subject of violent controversy, achieved particular notoriety in 1892 in the course of the *Apostolikumsstreit* [the dispute about the Creed] when he advocated a new, modernized version of the Apostles' Creed.[35] Martin Rade, who served during the 1890s as chaplain at the Paulskirche in Frankfurt-am-Main and from 1904 onwards was Assistant Professor of Systematic Theology at Marburg, was the founder and editor of *Die christliche Welt*, the review which formed a focus for the Ritschl school.[36] The New Testament scholar, Hermann von Soden, who worked in Berlin from the end of the 1880s as a preacher and a university teacher and later, from 1893, as Assistant Professor, was, with Adolf Harnack, a leading light in the movement against the protestant High Consistory's new draft liturgy, through which it was proposed to institutionalize the traditional order of service.[37]

Weber's closest personal contact in this group was Martin Rade, the brother-in-law of Friedrich Naumann. Weber produced a series of articles for

Rade's review, *Die christliche Welt*. In none of these, however, did he take up any position on theological questions. Indeed, he described himself as a 'layman' where theological matters were concerned.[38] On the other hand, he did show deep concern over controversies in church politics. He took up the defence of Paul Göhre, the General Secretary of the ESC, against the attacks of the influential theologian, August Hermann Cremer, who was regarded as the head of the orthodox 'Greifswald School'.[39] Furthermore, he participated in the movement against the proposed new liturgy. He signed a petition to the Protestant High Consistory drafted by Harnack and others at von Soden's instigation.[40] This called for a greater freedom of operation on the order of service for individual parishes, particularly in respect of the status and use of the Apostles' Creed.[41]

Beyond all this, there is, however, an affinity of principle, which accounts more generally for Weber's initial involvement in the work of the ESC. Stoecker had originally conceived of the Congress as a 'Social-monarchist Union', the principle objective of which would be to agitate against Social Democracy.[42] His conception was rejected by the liberal theological tendency. Harnack made his participation dependent upon the Congress's not becoming 'a party political gathering'.[43] In his opinion, it should rather prepare 'information of an expert nature',[44] as a precondition for meaningful social assistance, and carry on debates on the desired extent of the Church's involvement in attempts to resolve social problems.[45] Harnack was successful in gaining acceptance for this idea of the Congress as a forum for the discussion of social ethics, social policy and social-scientific questions.[46] It was, in turn, only this new understanding of the Congress's functions that enabled Weber to present himself to some extent as a specialist in law and political economy, willing to serve Protestant aspirations by carrying out his work of theoretical 'enlightenment'.

During the period of his work in the ESC, Weber's most important relationship was with the theologian Paul Göhre. The bond that kept him closer to Göhre than to Baumgarten or the 'Cultural Protestant' tendency was their common research interest. It was thanks to Göhre that, in the early 1890s, Weber lighted upon the basic elements of certain sociological questions and methods that were to set the directions of his later work.

In the late 1880s, Paul Göhre worked as an assistant editor on *Die christliche Welt*; from 1891 to 1894, he was General Secretary of the ESC; in 1896, with Friedrich Naumann, he founded the Nationalsozialer Verein [National-Social Association] and became the second chairman of that body. In 1899, he left the Association and joined the Social Democratic Party. After giving up the cloth and leaving the Church, he became a deputy in the *Reichstag* (1910–1918), Under-Secretary of State in the Prussian War Ministry (1918–19) and Secretary of State in the Prussian Ministry of the Interior (1919–23).[47]

During the period of his participation in the ESC, Göhre drew attention to himself by a series of projects and initiatives. His particular interest lay in research into the economic and social conditions of specific population groups or, in the terminology of the theologian, specific groups of parishioners. In order to gain a clear picture of the 'actual situation of those for whose sake we have a social or workers' question', Göhre had himself spent three months working incognito as a factory-hand in the heavily industrialized province of Saxony and had published the account of his experiences in a widely aclaimed study.[48] Even today, this is considered a remarkable piece of field-work.[49] For Otto Baumgarten's 'Evangelical-Social Contemporary Issues' series, Göhre planned comparable, if somewhat briefer, studies by members of the clergy on the economic and social situation of their parishioners.[50] This plan of Göhre's was based not only on his own investigations but also on work by a clergyman from Saxony, who had produced a detailed study of the material situation of those of his parishioners living on low incomes.[51] Weber showed great interest in these plans. Although he had only begun the evaluation of the copious material of the Verein für Sozialpolitik's Inquiry into the condition of rural workers a few months before,[52] he could already clearly see the shortcomings of that survey. For one thing, the Verein had used the agricultural employers as its sole source of information; secondly, the material collected by the Verein only shed light on the economic factors that had led to the visible decline in the East of the time-honoured patriarchal form of labour relations. No indication was given as to the psychological causes of that decline.[53] Yet, if insight was to be gained into the process of fragmentation of traditional rural labour relations, then in Weber's view the psychological factors seemed at least as important as the economic. Not only were these factors, for him, an essential component of the process of that collapse, 'partly as contributory causes, partly as symptoms or as consequences', they were also of decisive importance in the subsequent 'developmental trends'.[54] The clergy seemed to Weber ideally placed to investigate these psychological factors, given the position of trust they held within the parish community. Using a questionnaire, which Weber and Göhre had developed together,[55] clergymen were not only to be required to serve in the illumination of the complex interplay between economic, social and psychological factors but, in the process, they were themselves to come to 'understand the psychological consequences of modern economic development and class formation, the necessary and contingent effects of these on the traditional foundations of family life and on the relation between human beings and their work, and to understand fully how these elements were interrelated'.[56]

The problematic, which Weber had already formulated in the context of the ESC's Inquiry into the rural workers, also set the terms of his later investigations into the industrial workforce, albeit in a modified form. Here too, his central concern was with the interrelation of economic and social variables, such as, on the one hand, the conditions of labour in 'integrated large-scale industry' and, on the other, the psychological consequences to which they gave rise. These psychological consequences, with the particular 'qualities produced by the ethnic, social and cultural background, traditions and living conditions of the workforce', could then, in turn, be seen to react upon the 'development potential' of large-scale industry and 'the direction of that development'.[57]

To recapitulate then, three motives may be adduced to explain why Weber participated in the ESC. In the first instance, he wished to win support for certain socio-political positions. By contrast with liberalism, with its traditional reticence where state social policy was concerned, and by contrast also with conservative parties, who either approached social problems from a patriarchal perspective or from a perspective determined by their own political interests, the ESC seemed to offer Weber serious and commendable points of departure for the implementation of a state social policy based on a recognition that the economic and political interests of working people should find representation. In his attempt, in numerous lectures, to disseminate the rudiments of political economy (to the Protestant clergy and to lay people), Weber hoped simultaneously to demonstrate the possibilities and limitations of the changes that could be brought about by social policy. Finally, in directing with Paul Göhre the ESC's Inquiry into rural workers, Weber was pursuing a specific scholarly interest, which also laid the foundations for his later research on the industrial workforce. All three motivations, the socio-political, the 'educative' and the scholarly, lasted beyond the early 1890s and were of significance in Weber's later work. There is, however, no evidence that, at the beginning of the 1890s, Weber believed in the possibility that effective political action could be conducted on a Christian basis. Rather, his analysis of the rural workers' question had made him aware, at an early date, that modern development tended to replace personal power with impersonal domination by a class of property owners. Thus it also follows that 1894, the year in which Weber reproached Friedrich Naumann for his failure to recognize that it was impossible – given the increasing depersonalization of social authority – to influence prevailing conditions by religious or moral means,[58] does not mark a break with preceding years. This is all the more clearly shown to be the case because Weber's involvement in the ESC did not end in 1894.[59] As has been demonstrated above, there is evidence to show that he participated further in the endeavours of the Evangelical-Social movement, at least until 1897.

Notes: Chapter 13

This chapter was translated by Erica Carter and Chris Turner.

1 On this point, see W. Hennis, 'Max Webers Thema', *Zeitschrift fur Politik*, vol 31 (1984), especially pp. 21–32, and L. A. Scaff, 'Weber before Weberian sociology', *British Journal of Sociology*, vol. 35 (1984), pp. 190–215.

2 On this early work on agrarian topics, see the recent article by K. Tribe, 'Prussian agriculture – German politics: Max Weber 1892–7', *Economy and Society*, vol. 12 (1983), pp. 181–226, and M. Riesebrodt, 'Vom Patriarchalismus zum Kapitalismus', *Kölner Zeitschrift für Soziologie und Sozialpsychologie*, vol. 37 (1985), pp. 546–67. On the origins and organization of the Inquiry into the situation of the East Elbean rural workers, conducted by Weber in 1892 under the aegis of the Verein für Sozialpolitik, see the very important introduction and editorial commentary contributed by Martin Riesebrodt to the re-edition of the Inquiry in MWG, Vol. I/3, pp. 1–33. Vernon K. Dibble has already pointed out the particular significance of this survey in 'Social science and political commitments in the young Max Weber', *Archives européennes de sociologie*, vol. 9 (1968), pp. 92–110. In his 1980 essay, 'Der autoritär verfasste Kapitalismus. Max Webers Kritik am Kaiserreich', Wolfgang Schluchter compares Weber's writings on Roman agrarian history and Prussian agrarian labour conditions in a systematic manner. See Schluchter, *Rationalismus der Weltbeherrschung. Studien zu Max Weber* (Frankfurt, 1980), pp. 134–69.

3 This is the argument of Johannes Weiß. Weiß starts out from the assumption that Weber's involvement in the Christian-Social movement up to 1894, that is, until his thoroughgoing critique of Friedrich Naumann in the article 'Was heisst Christlich-Sozial?' ['What does "Christian-social" mean?'] 'was accompanied by a reflection on and evaluation of the possibility of... combining Christianity with practical politics', *Max Webers Grundlegung der Soziologie* (Munich, 1975), p. 120. Weber's article was published in *Die christliche Welt*.

Evangelisch-Lutherisches Gemeindeblatt für Gebildete aller Stände, no. 20 (17 May 1894), cols 472–7.

4   K. E. Born, *Staat und Sozialpolitik seit Bismarcks Sturz* (Wiesbaden, 1957), pp. 7–10.

5   K. E. Pollmann, *Landesherrliches Kirchenregiment und soziale Frage* (Berlin, 1973), pp. 11 ff.

6   ibid., pp. 81–4.

7   On the history of the ESC, see P. Göhre, *Die evangelisch-soziale Bewegung, ihre Geschichte und ihre Ziele* (Leipzig, 1896); H. Eger, *Der evangelisch-soziale Kongress* (Leipzig, 1931); K. Apel, *Die soziale Frage im Lichte der Verhandlungen des Evangelisch-sozialen Kongresses* (Kirchhain, n.d. [1940?]); J. Herz (ed.), *Evangelisches Ringen um soziale Gemeinschaft. Fünfzig Jahre Evangelisch-Sozialer Kongress, 1890–1940* (Leipzig, 1940); G. Kretschmar, *Der Evangelisch-Soziale Kongress* (Stuttgart, 1972); H. Liebersohn, 'Personality and Society: the Protestant Social Congress, 1890–1914' (PhD thesis, Princeton, 1979); Pollmann, *Kirchenregiment*, pp. 107–23; W. R. Ward, *Theology, Sociology and Politics* (Bern, 1979), especially pp. 55–88; E. I. Kouri, *Der deutsche Protestantismus und die soziale Frage 1870–1919* (Berlin, 1984), especially pp. 99–154.

8   Pollmann, *Kirchenregiment*, p. 109.

9   R. vom Bruch, *Wissenschaft, Politik und öffentliche Meinung. Gelehrtenpolitik im Wilhelminischen Deutschland, 1890–1914* (Husum, 1980), pp. 267 ff.; Pollmann, *Kirchenregiment*, p. 118.

10   M. Schick, *Kulturprotestantismus und soziale Frage* (Tübingen, 1970), p. 80.

11   So runs the 1891 programme of the Congress, published in *Bericht über die Verhandlungen des Zweiten Evangelisch-sozialen Kongresses abgehalten zu Berlin am 28. und 29. Mai 1891* (Berlin, 1891), p. 126.

12   See the review of themes discussed in Kretschmar, *Der Evangelisch-sozialer Kongreß*, pp. 118–125. At the first congress, discussion centred on socio-political questions and on the relationship with Social Democracy. The reports and debates were published annually under the title, *Bericht über die Verhandlungen des Evangelisch-sozialen Kongresses*.

13   This information comes from an item in the minutes of the ESC (Archiv der Versöhnungskirche Leipzig-Gohlis A II 1: Evangelisch-sozialer Kongress. Akten und Schriftwechsel 1890–1910).

14   *Mitteilungen des Evangelisch-sozialen Kongresses*, no. 7 (September 1897).

15   *Grundriss zu den Vorlesungen im Evangelisch-sozialen Kursus zu Berlin, October 1893*, (Berlin, no date).

16   *Mitteilungen des Evangelisch-sozialen Kongresses*, no. 6 (September 1896), no. 7 (September 1897).

17   See the accounts of Weber's papers in *Frankfurter Zeitung*, no. 72, 13 March 1895, evening edn, and no. 68, 8 March 1896, 3rd morning edn; also in *Frankfurter Volksbote*, no. 47, 24 November 1895; *Straßburger Neueste Nachrichten*, no. 288, 9 December 1897, 3rd edn.

18   On Weber's relationship with Friedrich Naumann, see Chapter 19 by Peter Theiner in this volume.

19   O. Baumgarten, *Meine Lebensgeschichte* (Tübingen, 1929), p. 215.

20   ibid.

21   Max Weber to Hermann Baumgarten, 3 January 1891, *Jugendbriefe*, pp. 324–5.

22   H. Rubner (ed.), *Adolph Wagner. Briefe, Dokumente, Augenzeugenberichte, 1851–1917* (Berlin, 1978), p. 260.

23   Max Weber to Hermann Baumgarten, 18 April 1892, *Jugendbriefe*, p. 344.

24   Baumgarten, *Meine Lebensgeschichte*, p. 217.

25   ibid., p. 216.

26   Max Weber to Hermann Baumgarten, 3 January 1891: 'For that reason we do not feel Liberalism's future looks too black, provided that it does not commit errors in national politics. One such error would be not to go along in a principled manner with the present tide of socio-political development, which, as far as it presents certain difficulties, has anyway more or less reached its high water mark.' (*Jugendbriefe*, p. 329); also the letter of 1888 quoted in *Biography*, pp. 124–5.

27   Baumgarten, *Meine Lebensgeschichte*, p. 217.

28   ibid., p. 219.

29   Published in *Die Hilfe*, no. 5 (31 January 1897), pp. 8–9.

30   Cf. the report in the *St. Johanner Zeitung*, no. 10 (13 January 1897): 'There it is said, as in the present Hamburg strike: "We do not negotiate with such people." This is to play the lord and master, a position which, in this context, the speaker roundly condemns.'

31 Published in *Die Hilfe*, no. 9 (3 March 1895), pp. 3–4.
32 *Bericht über die Verhandlungen des 5. Evangelisch-sozialen Kongresses, abgehalten zu Frankfurt-am-Main am 16. und 17. Mai*, (Berlin, 1894), pp. 74–5.
33 In July 1896, Stoecker founded the *Freie kirchlich-soziale Konferenz*. See Pollmann, *Kirchenregiment*, pp. 269 ff.
34 Max Weber, 'Die Evangelisch-sozialen Kurse in Berlin im Herbst diesses Jahres', *Die christliche Welt. Evangelisch-Lutherisches Gemeindeblatt für Gebildete aller Stände*, no. 32, (3 August 1893), col. 766.
35 On this, see E. R. Huber and W. Huber, *Staat und Kirche im 19. und 20. Jahrhundert. Dokumente zur Geschichte des deutschen Staatskirchenrechts*, Vol. 3 (Berlin, 1983), pp. 645 ff.; A. von Zahn-Harnack, *Adolf von Harnack*, 2nd edn. (Berlin, 1951), pp. 144 ff.
36 *Die christliche Welt. Evangelisch-Lutherisches Gemeindeblatt für Gebildete aller Stände* was edited by Martin Rade from 1887 to 1931. On Rade, see J. Rathje, *Die Welt des freien Protestantismus* (Stuttgart, 1952); C. Schwöbel, *Martin Rade* (Gütersloh 1980).
37 Adolf Harnack to Martin Rade, 29 October 1893, Marburg University Library, Ms 684/53.
38 'Zur Rechtfertigung Göhres', *Die christliche Welt*, no. 48 (24 November 1892), cols. 1104–5, 1107.
39 ibid., cols. 1104–9.
40 Adolf Harnack to Martin Rade, 29 October 1893 (see note 37).
41 The petition, with more than 800 signatures, was printed in *Chronik der christlichen Welt*, no. 11 (15 March 1894), cols. 82–3 and no. 12 (22 March 1894), cols. 89–92.
42 Pollmann, *Kirchenregiment*, pp. 109–10. On Stoecker, see also the recent work by G. Brakelmann *et al.*, *Protestantismus und Politik, Werk und Wirkung Adolf Stoeckers* (Hamburg, 1982).
43 A. Harnack, 'Der Evangelisch-soziale Congreß zu Berlin', *Preussische Jahrbücher*, vol. 65 (1890), p. 566.
44 ibid., p. 567.
45 ibid., pp. 567 ff.
46 Pollmann, *Kirchenregiment*, p. 110. The reservations of the cultural-Protestant tendency with regard to political economy should not, of course, be left out of account here. Martin Rade, in particular, warned against the overestimation of this relatively young science. Besides concerning himself with political economy, the clergyman must also without fail study 'the people itself', Martin Rade, 'Vom Evangelisch-sozialen Kongress zu Berlin', *Die christliche Welt*, no. 25 (22 June 1890), col. 581.
47 J. Brenning, *Christentum und Sozialdemokratie. Paul Göhre: Fabrikarbeiter – Pfarrer – Sozialdemokrat. Eine sozialethisch-historische Untersuchung*, Theology thesis (Marburg, 1980), pp. v–vii.
48 P. Göhre, *Drei Monate Fabrikarbeiter und Handwerksbursche*, (Leipzig, 1891), p. 1.
49 See, for example, A. Oberschall, *Empirical Social Research in Germany, 1848–1914* (Paris, 1965), p. 28.
50 P. Göhre, 'Die Evangelisch-sozialen Zeitfragen', *Mitteilungen des Evangelisch-sozialen Kongresses*, no. 1 (24 November 1891), p. 4.
51 ibid. The article in question is by the Saxon pastor Borchardt, 'Zur sozialen Frage auf dem Lande', *Der Arbeiterfreund*, vol. 28 (1890), pp. 213–24.
52 Weber had begun the evaluation of the questionnaires by mid-February 1892 at the earliest. See the editor's commentary in the re-issue of Weber's survey of rural workers of 1892, MWG, Vol. I/3, p. 24.
53 Max Weber, 'Privatenquêten über die Lage der Landarbeiter, 2', *Mitteilungen des Evangelisch-sozialen Kongresses*, no. 5 (1 June 1892), p. 6.
54 Weber defined the aim of the survey as follows: 'The material and economic causes of this development [the dissolution of traditional labour relations, R.A.] are, for the most part, known to us; it will, however, have to be the task of unofficial local studies to discover the psychological factors which appear partly as contributory causes, partly as symptoms or as consequences of the transformation. Only local surveys are able to achieve this and their task is all the more important in that it is pre-eminently this subjective state of affairs which will determine the subsequent trend of development.' (ibid.).
55 The questionnaire is reproduced in the Preface contributed by Weber to the first pamphlet published by him in the series, 'Die Landarbeiter in den evangelischen Gebieten Nordwestdeutschlands': S. Goldschmidt, *Die Landarbeiter in der Provinz Sachsen, sowie den älteren Herzogtümern Braunschweig und Anhalt* (Tübingen, 1899), pp. 1–8.

56   ibid., p. 10 (Preface).

57   Max Weber, 'Methodologische Einleitung für die Erhebungen des Vereins für Sozialpolitik über Auslese und Anpassung (Berufswahlen und Berufsschicksal) der Arbeiterschaft der geschlossenen Großindustrie' (1908), GASS, p. 1. On the continued presence of this problematic in Weber's work, cf. Tribe, 'Prussian agriculture', p. 202.

58   Max Weber, 'Was heisst Christlich-Sozial?' (see n. 3 above), especially col. 475; 'Die deutschen Landarbeiter', *Bericht über die Verhandlungen des 5. Evangelisch-sozialen Kongresses* (see n. 32 above), pp. 72–3.

59   In view of this, Liebersohn's description of Weber's activities ('Personality and Society', pp. 39–40) as a sort of 'flirtation with Christian socialism' is also wide of the mark.

14 Max Weber and the Lutherans

W. R. WARD

Max Weber, the unbelieving scion of a family descended on the one side from those protestant refugees from the Habsburg lands who had so often generated religious revival, and in another branch from that ancient Huguenot community in Frankfurt, whose congregation outside the walls was a permanent memorial to the pugnacious determination of the Frankfurt town council to maintain the Lutheran character of a place full of Calvinists and Jews, derived from his pedigree a degree of detachment, even alienation, from his milieu, which is doubtless one of the qualifications of a sociologist. Family circumstances, political events and intellectual interests were, however, to bring him into close contact with a group of Lutheran theologians, all of whom had strong reasons for wishing to remain within their *Landeskirchen*, and so made the intellectual running in these establishments, that they are now almost the only theologians in the period of intellectual interest. To this group, the neo-Ritschlians, Weber came to be important, partly because of his analysis of German society and partly because he was powerfully engaged with intellectual issues cognate with those that they had inherited from Ritschl. The intellectual significance of this group in no way disguises the fact that they were a minority, even a persecuted minority, in the great *Landeskirchen* of their day, and heavily dependent on state protection in academic appointments, protection that did not extend to providing a career for one distinguished Old Testament scholar among them, Hermann Gunkel.[1] One of the unspoken reasons for Troeltsch's transfer from theology to philosophy when he moved from Heidelberg to Berlin in 1915 may very well have been that no one wanted another row with the Evangelisch Oberkirchenrat like that which had been staged when Harnack had been brought in from Marburg in 1890.[2] Confessional Lutheranism remained as strong as ever in the Saxon church; to the fury of Ritschl, it came to provide a shelter for all the tendencies of anti-Prussian separatism in Hanover and the middle states;[3] the power of the Positive Union, meticulously consolidated at the court of Wilhelm I, remained unbroken in the Old Prussian Union at the time of his grandson's abdication.[4]

Political antipathy was not the only barrier between Weber and the conservatives who were in possession in the German churches. All of these groups still resisted in the name of dogma the historical outlook for which Weber stood and, even on the level of social understanding, moved in another world. Rudolf Todt had tried to derive social policy from the Bible; Stoecker was not merely an anti-semite, but thought that political agitation provided a way to sublimate the divisions in the national life by focusing on enthusiasm for God, Church and Emperor; while the whole protestant-social enterprise was an affront to the demand for a value-free social science for which Weber had come to stand. Indeed, the third edition of Martin von Nathusius's book, *Die Mitarbeit der Kirche an der Lösung der sozialen Frage* [The Contribution of the Church to a Solution of the Social Question] (1st edn, Leipzig, 1893–4; 3rd edn, 1904), which gave Troeltsch a push towards the studies that led to his *Social Teaching of the Christian Churches*, sought to derive from Christianity the principles of a natural social order, of a Christian sociology with the virtual status of revelation. And, if Weber made no contact with the various styles of conservatism dominant in the *Landeskirchen*, the interest he aroused among theologians was equally clearly terminated by the demise of the Ritschlian party. It was Karl Barth, a pupil of Wilhelm Herrmann, and one of the successors of that friend of Weber's youth, Paul Göhre, as assistant to Martin Rade on *Die christliche Welt*, who most notably turned from his neo-Ritschlian origins to new ways; although Barth vituperated wildly against Naumann, Troeltsch and Harnack, he left hardly a reference to Weber in the whole of his gigantic corpus. The deaths of Naumann, Weber and Troeltsch in rapid succession concluded a chapter, and that conclusion was underlined by the rise of the dialectical theology.

Weber would probably have been drawn to the Ritschlians in any case. His mother was devoted to the Protestant-social cause on religious grounds,[5] and his Baumgarten cousins were also involved in it. Otto Baumgarten was a friend of the pastor and professor, Baron von Soden, who was active in the Evangelisch-sozialer Kongress [Evangelical-Social Congress; ESC], and was commissioned to produce a semi-official sheet, the *Evangelisch-soziale Zeitfragen*. In this enterprise he made use of Weber and of the political economists who gathered at the Weber household.[6] Of more importance for our present study is that Otto Baumgarten's childhood friends had included Friedrich Loofs and Albert Eichhorn, later to be two leading members of the Ritschlian group, and Otto Ritschl, the son and later the distinguished biographer of the great Albrecht himself.[7] Thus, although Weber was confirmed in the profession of sociologist by an invitation, in 1893, from Paul Göhre, secretary of the ESC, to continue on behalf of that body the inquiry into the conditions of rural labour in the provinces east of the Elbe, which he had begun for the Verein für Sozialpolitik, he already stood not far from the Ritschlian group, into whose hands the ESC fell after the secession of Stoecker and the conservatives in the great political crisis of 1895.[8] And although the Baumgartens were Carlylean[9] and analytically not very rigorous, the main intellectual preoccupations of the Ritschlian group had a significance for Weber, as his secularized mind had for them.

Albrecht Ritschl had begun his intellectual life as a disciple of Baur and the Tübingen school, and as a young man viewed the intellectual and political problems of his day much in Young Hegelian terms. Some bridge had to be found between the factual truth, arising from the positive sciences, and the subjectivism, which seemed the last refuge of a faith in God that had lost its grip on history and the world; some alternative to the bleak choice between the scientific destruction of revelation in the manner of Strauss, and the doctrinaire confessionalism of Hengstenberg; some version of what Schleiermacher had called 'the contract' between Christian faith and scientific research.[10] At first, Ritschl thought that Hegelianism might provide the organizing concept, but, like Marx and Feuerbach, Ritschl accepted the Left

Hegelian pursuit of the concrete, of the real world and of practical ends; by the 1850s, he had got rid of Hegelianism altogether and reintroduced Kant as the Protestant philosopher *par excellence*. According to Kant, there was no theoretical way of transcending the limits of finiteness; the only possibility of a break-through to the divine lay in the sphere of practical reason, in the experience of the moral imperative. From this point of view, Ritschl contributed to the heavy emphasis on personality and the cultivation of ethics in German Protestant theology in the late nineteenth century, and exemplified one of the ways in which theology, like so many other branches of scholarship, was feeling the impact of historical studies. He also provided a systematic backing for his view that the survival of Protestantism in the Rhineland depended on the Prussian Union Church, and that the recovery of national unity in Germany depended not on confessionalism but on the Prussian state.

The organizing concept of the system that Ritschl had constructed by the time of the founding of the Second Empire, which held together his philosophy of religion and history, his exegesis, dogmatics and ethics, was that of the kingdom of God. The kingdom of God was God's purpose for the world; there was thus a sense in which the social and cultural development of mankind was rooted in the nature of God himself. The hierarchy of natural communities – family, profession, national state – was, both statistically and morally, a precondition of the kingdom of God. In one system Ritschl had despatched the world-denying attitudes of monasticism and pietism, the particularism of Hanover and also of the Centre party, the narrowness of the sects, and the grandiose presumption of the Hegelian idealism in which he had been raised. His recourse to history rather than metaphysics, his ethical impulse, his return to Luther, were particularly attractive to young men raised upon confessional or mediation theology. [11]

If Ritschl sought to assign a religious value to history and culture, he was also a practitioner of historical inquiry on a greater scale than is commonly allowed. In December 1885, Harnack sent Ritschl the first copy of the first volume of his *History of Dogma*, with the inscription: 'It is necessary for me, in putting this volume in your hands, to thank you again heartily for all I have received from you. Seventeen years ago my own theological labours began with the study of your *Rise of the Old Catholic Church*, [12] and since then scarcely a quarter has passed without my learning something new from you. The present book is a sort of conclusion of long years of study; without the foundations you laid, it would never have been written, imperfect as it is.' [13] It appears, indeed, that Harnack derived the framework of his famous book from Ritschl, though he built upon it in his own way. [14] Ritschl also produced a massive three-volume *Geschichte des Pietismus* [History of Pietism] (Bonn, 1880–6; reprinted, Berlin, 1966). This work has suffered in esteem because of its polemical object. Ritschl believed intensely that the failure of the Protestant establishments to hold the masses was the fault of the alliance between the Pietists and the confessional party in his own lifetime. These groups had severed the links with culture that every healthy religious appeal needed, and had sought to convert individuals to deny worldly affections instead of strengthening them ethically to pursue temporal vocations. The *Geschichte des Pietismus* was designed to make this implausible charge stick. It was, nevertheless, a very considerable work in its own right. The Pietist literature was, in Ritschl's time, much more difficult to trace than it is now, and almost the only reputable work on which he could build were the studies of the religious life of the Rhineland by that remarkable historian Max Goebel. And, at the end, with whatever defects of scholarship and partisanship, Ritschl had produced a massive general survey of the field on an international and inter-denominational basis, which no subsequent scholar has had the courage to rival or even revise.

Much more important from the standpoint of our present study is that Ritschl had adumbrated at intervals in his treatise a typology of the Christian life, of the sort that had already concerned Max Goebel in his discussion of Rhineland sects and, later, was to concern Weber and Troeltsch. Ritschl held that mysticism was a Hellenistic phenomenon alien to Christianity; Christianity was world-affirming and active in the world. It followed that since Pietism and its precursors among the Anabaptists embodied mysticism and asceticism, they could not have been derived from primitive Christianity but only from Catholicism. The age of Bernard of Clairvaux and the monastic reform movement had shown that medieval Catholicism was a collection of incompatible concepts. The Church as a legally organized institution sought world domination, while prescribing to individuals world renunciation and mystic union with Jesus beyond the world. Power was the object of the institution: monasticism, mysticism and asceticism the aims imposed on individuals. The incompatibility was bearable, at least for a time, because the distance between the world and mankind, on the one hand, and God on the other, was understood in very abstract terms, but it was an inherently unstable arrangement. Ascetic mysticism was a force always ready to appeal to its ideals of other-wordly perfection against the institutions of the church and also against the content of its faith. It was prepared to burst the bonds of universal social unity for which the church stood in monasticism, sectarianism, mysticism and individualism.

Luther's achievement was to rediscover the Christian faith as a spiritual power in the world. The church now gave up the legal and political functions that had inhibited its religious development, and the state, taking responsibility for legal protection and the discipline of the Christian life, cleared the way for the church to purify social life by universal love. The individual, free to appropriate God's promise of love, could realize his own value in quiet trust in God in the pursuit of his temporal calling. The church, which alone had the gospel of justification and the certainty of salvation, had the job of keeping individuals up to scratch in a world necessarily imperfect. If there were difficulties in this, there was no solution at all in defending the idea of a holy congregation. Perfection could not be the character of the church in the world; the mark of the church's presence was the preaching of the gospel. What imperilled the Lutheran church was the misapplication of the idea of 'freedom in the law'. Political circumstances and the struggle with Catholicism had brought into Lutheranism many of the features of the old church system to which it was opposed, had separated it from the ethical and religious aspirations of the people and had given much too great a weight to doctrine. Nor was the balance preserved on the Reformed side. Here, doctrine effaced the Lutheran distinction between law and religion, discipline and grace, state and church, and attempted to create a new theocracy. A hard biblicism attempted to give universal sanction to the transitory institutions of the New Testament church. Ascetic strictness approximated to monastic flight from the world. The Reformed church was well equipped to contend with the universalist as well as the separatist tendencies in Catholicism, but the logic of its own position was to dissolve into independency. Illogicality, refusal to accept the consequences of its assumptions, was a strength in the Reformed tradition, as it was a weakness in the Lutheran.

These tendencies, which had contributed to the break-up of the Catholic church system, continued to ferment in the Reformed world. Having established apostolic doctrine, the Lutheran churches did not attempt to recover an apostolic church-form; having recovered an apostolic church-form, the Reformed churches tended to subject all moral choices to canons of apostolic sanctity, and to abolish the category of things indifferent. This moral ideal was bound to be ruinous to the idea of a *Volkskirche*, and to encourage the formation of separate religious societies. Pietism was the offspring not only of Anabaptism, but also of Calvinism. There was a further typology of Anabaptism to be established, in which Franciscan features were to be observed again, the spiritualist and the biblicist. Again men became indifferent to natural human conditions, became 'world-deniers', and took up the cudgels not against sin but against men's creaturely condition. This might issue in Quietism (a phenomenon which, as Ritschl had learnt from Heinrich Heppe, had arrived from France) or in eschatological enthusiasm, which aimed a revolutionary blow at the course of history and the development of society. But both roads led to separatism and to a rejection of the church's mission to reshape society. In Reformed territories, this frame of mind led to the formation of free churches, which sustained the utmost hostility towards the confessional churches from which they had sprung; in Lutheran territories, it tended to turn against the whole congregational idea, and to aspire to a sort of philadelphia without word or sacrament in the Lutheran sense, or local roots and constitution. Some barrier against this had been created by Spener, who revived the domestic order in the Lutheran system and strengthened professional life. In addition to his basic typology, Ritschl offered various explanations, drawn from national character and social history, about the variety of ways in which the story had worked out in the various confessional territories; but all ended in separation, all were strong among the lower social orders (sometimes they needed the patronage of wealthy women, but only the nobility and the civil service remained true to the *Landeskirchen*), and all were unwilling to admit the degree to which forms of church life were necessarily deeply influenced by particular historical circumstances. [15]

Thus, very remarkably, Anabaptism, Calvinism, Pietism and enlightenment turned out to be derived from the bad features of medieval Catholicism, and it was Lutheranism that offered a model for an age of liberalism and science. It was now a question whether Ritschl's successors could continue to derive the same organizing advantage from the concept of the kingdom of God, whether his typology and historical periodization would be found satisfactory (Troeltsch, for example, started from Ritschl's point and ended with something very different), and whether, when the encouragement of the Kaiser in 1890 induced in academics of all kinds an obsession with the 'social question', Ritschl's hints towards social policy would be thought enough. For although his concept of the kingdom of God ascribed a positive significance to the world process, and hence implied the possibility of a social dogmatic and a social ethic, Ritschl himself drew almost no social inferences. His view of the long slow way by which Protestantism drew its adherents to the law of Christ was limited to religious education in which the congregation, the family, and the state took part.

Two interconnected groups of younger Ritschlians began to form, each finding problems with the master, and it was with these younger men, and especially with one group of them that Weber was to be connected. In 1876, Martin Rade, a theological student in his fourth semester at Leipzig, made the acquaintance of the young Harnack, then a *Privatdozent*, and formed a durable circle of friends who made a considerable mark on theological studies in Germany and Switzerland, men such as Wilhelm Bornemann, Friedrich Loofs, Paul Drews and Wilhelm Wrede. In 1886, Rade's circle launched the journal which the following year became *Die christliche Welt*, and developed into one of the most famous of all liberal-Protestant journals.[16] At first it took up the anti-Catholic element in Ritschl's heritage and backed the Evangelische Bund, but in championing Harnack's claims to appointment in Berlin, and supporting him in the doctrinal battles in which he became engaged, the journal took a decisive turn to the left, its editor, Martin Rade, the only one of the younger Ritschlians to enjoy any longevity, continuing to move leftwards till his death in 1940 at the age of 83. Like Friedrich Naumann, whose sister Dora he met in 1887 and married in 1889, Rade was attracted to social questions by interest in the career of Stoecker. Moreover the journal could not but be deeply affected by the history of the ESC, for with Naumann its correspondent on Inner Mission affairs, Paul Drews on social questions, and Paul Göhre coming in as Rade's parish assistant and the paper's expert on socialist affairs, *Die christliche Welt* was almost an organ of the 'young' group at the ESC. By this time, Rade was well aware of intellectual difficulties in the heritage of Ritschl. Like Harnack, Rade was overwhelmed by the importance of a historical approach to Christian doctrine, and was indeed optimistic enough to think that historical studies offered a way to peace and an end to dogmatic feuding.[17] Not surprisingly therefore, while sharing Ritschl's hostility to natural theology. Rade was not in the least interested in the teleological devices by which Ritschl had ascribed theological significance to society and culture in his doctrine of the kingdom of God. Ritschl indeed began to look like another theologian who had sacrificed truth to system. For, if theology had its basis in a historical revelation, then that basis could be established by the same methods of historical enquiry as obtained in profane history. This in turn implied that the problem of the relation of religious knowledge and knowledge of the world, which Ritschl thought he had solved by his system, returned in an acute form. Moreover, history figured greatly in the Rade group's sense of mission – their calling to redeem the church as well as the world. This very fact, however, raised acutely the question of the relation of present and past in historical inquiry. Could historical inquiry be determined by present concerns, and what relation might there be between a present sense of mission and the Christian past? More generally, if theology could be considered a historical science, what was its relation to Christian practice, not merely to ethics but to preaching? Rade and his friends managed to convince themselves that Ritschl's unsuccessful textbook, *Unterricht in der Christlichen Religion* [Instruction in the Christian Religion] (1875) could all be preached. It became apparent, however, that one's view of the relation of theory and practice would be influenced by one's understanding of the relation of theology to historical scholarship, of Christianity to culture. Abstract as these questions were, they underlay the individual's judgement of what social groups the congregation could co-operate with and what special task it could set itself. To Martin Rade, whose first choice was for a pastoral rather than an academic career, these questions were, and remained, paramount.[18]

The academic young Ritschlians, nevertheless, came by their own route to much the same point at the same time. A group jovially known as the *kleine Fakultät* had begun to form under Ritschl's wing at Göttingen in the 1880s; it included Eichhorn, Gunkel, Wrede (from Rade's original circle), Bousset, Weiss and Troeltsch, all of them, except Troeltsch, North Germans, and all, except Eichhorn and Troeltsch, Bible scholars. They began to claim that the historical-critical school gave too much heed to philology and too little to the general historical background of the religious origins of the past; they disregarded the 'historical constitution' of all literary documents; still worse they sacrificed the variety of the New Testament to the necessities of system.[19] Even Harnack, the farthest left of the older group, now became unco-operative; having made himself unpopular in his youth by emphasizing Hellenistic influences upon the history of Christian dogma, he was now attacked for not going nearly far enough. The young were impressed by the great works of secular history of Ranke and Mommsen,[20] and were concerned to insist that the religious development of Israel and the church could not be separated from general history, conceived very broadly indeed. The pressure of current social questions opened their eyes to the influence of such issues in the religious history of the past. More than this, historical research was held to have obliterated the frontiers between Christianity and non Christian religions, between natural and supernatural areas of study. To the younger party, the older Ritschlians seemed to be pushing aside the questions thrown up by history, while they themselves were seeking to subject the whole religious life of men to the same methods of research. Rade called for the foundation of new chairs in *Religionsgeschichte*, the history of religion in this general sense, while older Ritschlians stood firm against any further reduction of the absoluteness of Christianity. The issue here raised was not unlike the issue raised at the ESC: that is, whether a specifically Christian politics was possible; the break-up of the Ritschlian party, which began with an attack by Troeltsch on Julius Kaftan in 1893, coincided fairly closely with the break-up of Congress.

By the early 1890s the circle was complete. Weber was the centre of a professorial discussion-group at Heidelberg, which included Troeltsch among its members; he was lecturing for the ESC and assessing its work in Rade's journal, *Die christliche Welt*;[21] and if the ESC confirmed Weber in his vocation as a sociologist, he contributed to the break-up of that body by his reports. Weber's exposure of the hollow basis of the public pretensions of the Eastern aristocracy was absolutely intolerable to the Right in their great counter-attack of the mid-1890s, and helped to make Stoecker's position in the ESC impossible; by contrast, his analysis gave some standing-ground in policy to Naumann and the left wing of that body. Weber could not have failed to draw some stimulus from the discussions in the Ritschlian circle, as well as from the investigations into which they pushed him. In return, he exercized a disturbing intellectual influence on the group. This has always been recognized in the case of that other outsider whom the Ritschlians drew to them, Friedrich Naumann. [22] Naumann used Ritschl's language and concepts, but seems never to have bothered with Ritschl himself, and his views were shaped by his own pastoral experience and by a wide reading of socialist literature uncommon among the clergy of the establishment. Like Ritschl, Naumann came to employ the kingdom of God as an intellectually unifying concept, but the content of the concept was derived from his own social experience. The kingdom of God was the process of establishing social justice, a process that might find room for both the charitable activity of the Inner Mission and the social engineering contemplated by the socialists. The methodological clash between the younger and the older Ritschlians, signalled by the attack by Troeltsch on Julius Kaftan in 1893, had its counterpart in a clash between Kaftan and Naumann at the ESC in the same year. Kaftan, in the Ritschlian way, addressed himself to the question of 'Christianity and the economic order', in principle two quite different things, from the standpoint of the concept of personality. He concluded that, since there was no eternal life in God without moral education and activity, it was a Christian obligation so to shape the economic order that it offered scope for the Christian ideal. [23] In opening the discussion, Naumann showed how his encounter with Marx had moved him in the direction of vocabulary which became characteristic of Weber. The question was whether Christianity had an inner-worldly ideal (a term earlier employed by Max Goebel). Social-democracy was the first great protestant heresy, because it had exaggerated the inner-worldly ideal of the church to the point of chiliasm, making the impossible demand that perfect conditions be introduced on earth; it was, in fact, an inner-worldly chiliasm. In resisting the heresy, the church had in fact forgotten the principle that the heresy perverted, had forgotten that Jesus was one who brought help to the suffering, and that some means must be found for doing this in a machine age. The two great guides were Jesus and Marx. Marx showed how the world worked and what its needs were; Jesus, 'the man of the people', offered inner dynamism, hope, faith, and liberation from the tyranny of concepts imposed by Marx's professed disciples. [24]

Though the language might be Weberian, Weber set himself to destroy the substance of Naumann's doctrine. In 1894, Rade invited Weber to review a collection of Naumann's essays in *Die christliche Welt*. In this review Weber paid tribute to Naumann personally, but derided both his claim to have created a theological politics, and his optimism about the future. This jolt to Naumann, [25] however, was as nothing to that occasioned by Weber's Freiburg Inaugural address. This ferocious blast, with its implicit demand for a value-free political sociology, was in every way a challenge to the political theology that Naumann had been struggling to develop, and some of its thrusts – the refusal to substitute 'state-help' for 'self-help', even while establishing the power interests of the nation, and the attack on those who substituted 'social policy in place of politics ... cultural and economic history in place of political history' – seemed aimed directly at him. The pitiless perspective of the Freiburg Inaugural upon international politics thoroughly upset Naumann's balance. Reporting the lecture for his own journal *Die Hilfe*, he asked in a famous phrase 'is he not right? Of what use to us is the best social policy, if the Cossacks come? The man who wishes to pursue domestic policy must first secure the nation, fatherland and frontiers; he must look after the national power. This is the weakest point of Social Democracy. We need a socialism that is fit to govern ... Such a socialism must be German-national'. Convinced by Weber that the world was not what he and Marx had supposed it to be, pressed by Rudolf Sohm to separate religion and politics in the interests of confessional purity, driven by the recognition that in the conditions of the mid-1890s the church was not a useful vehicle for social policy, Naumann founded his Nationalsozialer Verein[26] and entered on a process of minimizing the scope of religion. This left him little to talk about beyond the concept of personality that had so preoccupied the elder Ritschlians, and finally silenced him as a religious writer for almost the whole of the last fifteen years of his life.[27] On the other hand, in *Demokratie und Kaisertum* [Democracy and Empire] in 1900, Naumann skilfully used Weber's methods of social inquiry to answer his criticisms of the Nationalsozialer Verein. Weber had held that it was hopeless to attempt to combine working-class and middle-class elements in a single party, when modern political parties were based on the concrete and distinct separate interests round which the classes themselves had formed. Naumann now argued that if political realism were induced all round, it ought to be possible to produce a grand left-bloc 'from Bassermann to Bebel', which could force the imperial government to negotiate; the price of co-operation would be electoral reform and the consequence of electoral reform would be the destruction of the parliamentary strength of the conservatives and their privileged relation to the Kaiser. There was room in the modern Germany for capitalism, socialism and *Weltpolitik*; no room for the alliance of Emperor and a basically particularist coalition of the right. If the ESC had made a sociologist of Weber, he had in turn made a sociologist of Naumann, and in so doing had acquired a life-long friend and ally.

Weber's influence was equally marked upon the more theoretically minded members of the Ritschlian group. If their preoccupation with questions of religious typology and the concern with problems of large-scale historical periodization, which flowed from their belief that Protestantism had taken its opportunities at the beginning of the modern era but seemed to be losing them now, had propelled Weber in the direction of the studies on the Protestant ethic and the spirit of capitalism, his agrarian studies gave a sharp actuality to the economic influence upon religious outlook to men who were very inclined to see religious groupings and institutions as the expression of religious ideas, and reinforced the assumptions of the *religionsgeschichtliche* school. Troeltsch repeatedly looked back to Weber's dominant influence upon him[28] as he turned to sociology at this point: 'All the previous solutions gave rise to new problems. At the same time I came under the spell of the powerful personality of Max Weber, for whom the marvels dawning upon me had long been foregone conclusions. And from that point I was powerfully gripped by the Marxist theory of infrastructure and superstructure: not that I swallowed it without more ado.'[29] It is, however, also true that Troeltsch gave Weber the benefit of his vast reading, when the latter gave his mind to the social consequences of religious belief.

There were, moreover, further complexities in the interchange between the two. Of the older group of Ritschlians, the only one to keep in any kind of touch with the younger men was Harnack, and although Harnack publicly resisted Rade's pressure for the foundation of chairs in the field of *Religionsgeschichte*, Rade felt that he must use Harnack's *Essence of Christianity*, the most famous of all expositions of Christianity for the plain man, given as inter-faculty lectures at Berlin in the winter semester of 1899–1900, as a banner to rally the party.[30] Two difficulties lay in the way. Harnack summed up Christianity in a very individualist way – 'God and the soul – the soul and its God';[31] although he accepted that the preaching of the kingdom of God had social implications, and (under a political hat) was prepared to talk about the priority of the state over the individual,[32] it was now unlikely that this would satisfy either Lutheran high-churchmen beating the drum about the church, or the younger Ritschlians' preoccupation with the community-forming power of Christian groups of various kinds. More fundamental was the very notion of an 'essence' of Christianity. It is true that this notion had had a long history,[33] and that Troeltsch himself had used language of this kind in the mid-1890s. The difference now was that the younger Ritschlians had been exposed to Max Weber, who had been refining the ideas they had all played with on the subject of religious typology, into his concept of 'ideal types'. On the surface the 'essence of Christianity' appeared to be an 'ideal type' of that complex phenomenon, and Troeltsch said as much in his essay on 'Modern philosophy of history' (1904).[34] Immediately, however, Max Weber made it clear that this was not the case.[35] He distinguished between value-related judgements, which historians must make in their choice of source materials, and value-judgements proper. The historian must not turn his technical operations into value judgements. Harnack's 'essence' might convey the notion of a force operating in history, and it might be a normative concept designed to recall Christianity to its true self; in neither case was it a Weberian ideal type. An ideal type for Weber was simply a generalization, whose adequacy, greater or less, made it more or less useful for comparing or measuring reality.

This confusion was to be important for Troeltsch's future work. Troeltsch's reception of Harnack's book in a serial review he wrote for *Die christliche Welt* was decidedly cautious, and he quietly made more than seventy alterations of substance in the review when it was included in his *Gesammelte Schriften* [Collected Works].[36] What Troeltsch wanted in the *religionsgeschichtliche* manner was to proceed 'from general history and its methods to Christianity in its whole breadth, and to the question of the validity of Christianity,'[37] but he found that this programme did not get him out of the toils. Apart from the difficulty of explaining a religion that claimed to be a final revelation in terms of its context, there was the problem of the contradictions within the Christian tradition. Troeltsch believed (and said) that Catholicism was 'a deviation from the essence of Christianity';[38] he knew that this was a value judgement, and obscured its effect when the essay came to be included in his collected works. In his subsequent rumination upon this problem, Troeltsch could not find a way of insisting on the pursuit of modern historical inquiry wherever it led, and yet stopping short of scepticism and relativism; or, to put the matter in another way, of combining a historical treatment of Christianity with actual dogmatic construction. From this dilemma, Weber's emphasis on the value-free nature of his ideal types seemed to offer some way out. And when Troeltsch had got to the end of his *Social Teaching of the Christian Churches*, he maintained that 'perceptions of eternal ethical values are not scientific perceptions and cannot be proved along scientific lines'. [39] He went on, nevertheless, to suggest four social and ethical 'ideas and energies', which had certain status as revelation. In short, the logical acumen of Weber enabled Troeltsch to clarify his scholarship, but in the end did not save him from dogmatizing from a personal standpoint. Troeltsch was in the same position as the orthodox conservatives he had represented as primeval ignoramuses.

There were rumours that Troeltsch, who was better at getting into print than Weber, irked Weber by anticipating some of his ideas in the *Social Teaching of the Christian Churches*. Whatever the truth of this, the two of them with Harnack and other Ritschlians continued to co-operate in trying to seek constitutional reform during the war, an early peace, the erection of constitutional government with generous provision for the churches, and the launching of the German Democratic Party (DDP). It was death that left them with unfinished work in both politics and scholarship.

Notes: Chapter 14

1 W. Klatt, *Hermann Gunkel* (Göttingen, 1969), pp. 17, 41–3.
2 O. Baumgarten, *Meine Lebensgeschichte* (Tübingen, 1929), p. 187.
3 O. Ritschl, *Albrecht Ritschls Leben* (Freiburg, 1892–6), Vol. 2, pp. 162–3.
4 G. Kögel, *Rudolf Kögel. Sein Werden und Wirken* (Berlin, 1899–1904).
5 W. J. Mommsen, *Max Weber and German Politics, 1890–1920* (Chicago, 1984), p. 19.
6 Baumgarten, *Meine Lebensgeschichte*, pp. 215–6.
7 ibid., pp. 82–4, 89.
8 All these topics are briefly treated in W. R. Ward, *Theology, Sociology and Politics: The German Protestant Social Conscience, 1890–1933* (Bern, 1979), pp. 63–73.
9 Carlyle could be taken seriously as late in Germany as in England. A three-volume collection of his *Sozial-politische Schriften* was published at Göttingen as late as 1899.
10 In Schleiermacher's second letter to Friedrich Lücke. K. Nowak (ed.), *F. D. E. Schleiermacher, Theologische Schriften* (Berlin [GDR] 1983), p. 442.
11 On Ritschl, see Ritschl, *Albrecht Ritschls Leben*; G. Koke, *Die theologische Schule Albrecht Ritschls und die evangelische Kirche der Gegenwart* (Berlin, 1904), Vol. 2, pp. 4–25; H. Timm, *Theorie und Praxis in der Theologie Albrecht Ritschls und Wilhelm Hermanns* (Gütersloh, 1967), especially pp. 29–36, 62–73, 81–5; A. Harnack, *Reden und Aufsätze* (Giessen, 1904–30), Vol. 4, pp. 341–4; Klatt, *Hermann Gunkel*, p. 19.
12 2nd edn, Bonn, 1857.
13 A. von Zahn-Harnack, *Adolf von Harnack* (Berlin, 1936), p. 135.
14 E. P. Meijering, *Theologische Urteile über die Dogmengeschichte. Ritschls Einfluss auf von Harnack* (Leiden, 1978), p. 11.
15 M. Wichelhaus, *Kirchengeschichtsschreibung und Soziologie im neunzehnten Jahrhundert und bei Ernst Troeltsch* (Heidelberg, 1965), pp. 44–50.
16 The history of this journal forms much of the substance of J. Rathje, *Die Welt des freien Protestantismus* (Stuttgart, 1952).
17 C. Schwöbel, *Martin Rade. Das Verhältnis von Geschichte, Religion und Moral als Grundproblem seiner Theologie* (Gütersloh, 1980), p. 39.
18 ibid., pp. 31–3.
19 Klatt, *Hermann Gunkel*, pp. 18–21, 26–7. The history of the 'kleine Fakultät' has recently been taken much further by F. W. Graf, 'Der "Systematiker" der "Kleinen Göttinger

Fakultät". Ernst Troeltsch's Promotionsthesen und ihr Göttinger Kontext', in H. Renz and F. W. Graf (eds), *Troeltsch-Studien*, Vol. 1 (Gütersloh, 1982), pp. 235–90.

20   When Harnack found himself in the company of historians of Rankean derivation in 1906, he became unpopular again, preaching toleration towards Catholics despite the government's politically inspired anti-Catholicism. R. vom Bruch, *Wissenschaft, Politik und öffentliche Meinung. Gelehrtenpolitik im Wilhelminischen Deutschland, 1890–1914* (Husum, 1980), p. 390.

21   ibid., pp. 254, 265 n. 208.

22   On Naumann, see T. Heuss, *Friedrich Naumann. Der Mann, das Werk, die Zeit* (Stuttgart, 1937; 3rd edn, Munich and Hamburg, 1968); H. Timm, *Friedrich Naumann. Theologischer Widerruf* (Munich, 1967); I. Engel, *Gottesverständnis und sozialpolitisches Handeln. Eine Untersuchung zu Friedrich Naumann* (Göttingen, 1972); A. Lindt, *Friedrich Naumann und Max Weber* (Munich, 1973); Ward, *Theology, Sociology and Politics*, pp. 89–118; F. Naumann, *Werke* (Cologne and Opladen, 1964–7). P. Theiner, *Sozialer Liberalismus und deutsche Weltpolitik. Friedrich Naumann im wilhelminischen Deutschland* (Baden-Baden, 1983) and Chapter 19 by Peter Theiner in this volume.

23   *Berichte des Evangelisch-sozialen Kongresses*, vol. 4 (1893), p. 12.

24   It is another sign of the toils into which the Ritschlian school was getting, that Naumann's contribution was attacked by Harnack on historical grounds. ibid., pp. 41–3.

25   F. Naumann, *Werke*, Vol. 1, pp. 402–24; Timm, *Friedrich Naumann*, pp. 38–40.

26   On the fate of this political association, see D. Düding, *Der Nationalsoziale Verein, 1896–1903. Der gescheiterte Versuch einer parteipolitischen Synthese von Nationalismus, Sozialismus und Liberalismus* (Munich, 1972).

27   Naumann, *Werke*, Vol. 1, p. 632.

28   'Max Weber, one of the mightiest of Germans and one of the most comprehensive, and also methodologically one of the strictest scholars of the age'. E. Troeltsch, *Gesammelte Schriften*, Vol. 3 (Tübingen, 1922), p. 565.

29   ibid., Vol. 2 (Tübingen, 1922), p. 11.

30   Schwöbel, *Martin Rade*, p. 122.

31   A. Harnack, *What is Christianity?* (London, 1901), p. 34.

32   idem, *Reden und Aufsätze*, Vol. 4, pp. 280–1.

33   H. Wagenhammer, *Das Wesen des Christentums. Eine begriffsgeschichtliche Untersuchung* (Mainz, 1973).

34   Troeltsch, *Gesammelte Schriften*, Vol. 2, p. 723.

35   M. Brodbeck, *Readings in the Philosophy of Social Science* (New York, 1968), pp. 503–4.

36   For this, see S. W. Sykes, 'Troeltsch and Christianity's essence', in J. P. Clayton (ed.), *Ernst Troeltsch and the Future of Theology* (Cambridge, 1976), p. 143. The paper as a whole is a valuable discussion of the relations of Weber and Troeltsch at this point.

37   Troeltsch, *Gesammelte Schriften*, Vol. 2, p. 400.

38   ibid., p. 404.

39   E. Troeltsch, *The Social Teaching of the Christian Churches* (London, 1931), p. 1004.

15 Friendship Between Experts: Notes on Weber and Troeltsch

FRIEDRICH WILHELM GRAF

Ernst Troeltsch was one of the few men to whom Weber referred publicly on more than one occasion as a 'friend'.[1] Conversely, Troeltsch acknowledged a 'friendship' with Weber.[2] There was no Heidelberg colleague, apart from this theologian who was only a few months his junior, with whom Weber had such close and lasting ties. It is all the more remarkable, then, that at present we know of no letters exchanged between them and no printed evidence that might throw further light on the nature of their long-standing association. We have a few secondary accounts – from Marianne Weber's *Lebensbild* and especially from various recollections by Paul Honigsheim[3] – as well as the two obituaries published by Troeltsch a few days after his friend's death,[4] but these give only an indistinct picture of their personal relations. This paucity of evidence has proved, however, to be an ideal starting point for attempts to make up for our lack of factual knowledge by means of psychologistic intuition and the construction of value-judgements that exceed the evidence. Thus Eduard Baumgarten, for example, discovered in Troeltsch a 'need to avoid having *too* much to do with Weber' and surmised that 'Weber's attacks on Rachfahl were *perhaps* due to "object-transference"'.[5] And, in the current controversy among Weber experts, the advocate of 'humanity' (*Menschentum*) is linked with the representatives of universal evolution at least by the ability, where Troeltsch is concerned, to transcend the limits of historical reason. Wilhelm Hennis is convinced that the appearance of *The Social Teaching of the Christian Churches* 'must have rankled with Weber',[6] and in the school of Friedrich Tenbruck it is known 'for certain' that Weber read the first parts of 'The Economic Ethics of World Religions' to his friend in 1913.[7] Since there is no evidence for such surmises, I should like – while claiming no expertise as regards Weber, although I have gleaned some knowledge from Troeltsch's critique of historical reason – to devote Part I of what follows to defining the limits of our *present* knowledge[8] of the biographical facts. Part II will attempt an *exemplary* account of the complex relations between the work of Troeltsch and that of Weber. Part III will then briefly propose a systematic approach to their interpretation: the potent presence of each man's work in that of the other is an indication and a consequence of their interdisciplinary co-operation in analysing the historical 'vital force' (*Lebensmacht*) of religion. Their mutual recognition of shared interests, however, encompasses at the same time profound contrasts at an interpretive level, which surface especially in their differing assessments of the present social relevance of religion under the conditions imposed by modern Western rationalism.

I

Up to now, we know nothing about when Troeltsch and Weber first met. There is no evidence of any personal contact between them until Weber's move from Freiburg to Heidelberg. Before this time, however, they may have been aware of each other's writings as contributors to Martin Rade's *Die christliche Welt*, or at least heard of each other, for some close friends of Weber's cousin Otto Baumgarten were also close friends of Troeltsch.

- It was through Baumgarten that Weber met the theologians Eduard Grafe, Eduard Simons and Hans von Schubert while he was a student.[9] In April 1887 Baumgarten joined his friend Grafe in Halle to prepare for his licence to teach theology. Here he took lodgings with the ecclesiastical historian Albert Eichhorn, who had a significant influence on Troeltsch's theological development.[10] Weber continued to maintain various contacts with Baumgarten's 'wide circle of acquaintance' through letters and personal visits.[11] Troeltsch also belonged to this circle. There were close intellectual and personal links between a group of Göttingen doctoral and post-doctoral students of theology who were substantially influenced by Troeltsch – and later came to be known as the 'School of Religious History' – and the Halle theologians just mentioned. They all saw themselves as an avant-garde whose purpose was to establish a new historically critical concept of theology, the systematic structure of which was determined by precisely the same empirical interest in the effect of religion on the way people conduct their lives that also shaped Weber's concept of the sociology of religion. Theology was not speculation about dogma or the guardianship of a body of beliefs professed by a particular church, but a science of 'living' or 'lived' religion, which was prosecuted as part of 'cultural history'; it described real religious practice and interpreted the practical relevance of religion to culture, its role as a *Lebensmacht*.[12] The tensions between religion and culture, the attempts to achieve a productive release of such tensions, the practical significance of 'piety' for the individual and the social effects of communal religious activity (worship, etc.) – these were the most important subjects discussed by the theologians with whom Weber associated from the mid-1880s. It is not possible at present to prove directly that he met Troeltsch in this circle of so-called *Jungritschlianer* (pupils of the Göttingen systematician, Albrecht Ritschl, who were turning away from their teacher's dogmatic theology and enthusiastically embracing the novel study of religion as it actually existed), but it seems likely: it can be shown that both frequented Grafe's 'open house' before 1890,[13] and, when Troeltsch went to Bonn as professor in 1892, he had such close links with Weber's circle that the two men were probably introduced to each other by mutual friends. Whether or not this *assumption* is correct, we can say that even before their time in Heidelberg, both men had a common background of experience that could in essence be defined as an interest in the social relevance of religion, which was to be studied theoretically (theology as the history of religion) and also given a practical direction.

Being isolated within the Heidelberg faculty of theology, Troeltsch preferred the company of younger colleagues from other disciplines. 'Most of my contacts are with people outside the Faculty. Max Weber, Hensel, Carl Neumann ... are very dear friends of mine.'[14] At present, we can say only vaguely what is meant by Marianne Weber's statement that 'new and distinguished friends joined their [the Webers'] circle: Georg Jellinek, Paul Hensel, Carl Neumann, and *above all* the theologian Ernst Troeltsch'.[15] Since Weber and Troeltsch remained in close contact for a good seventeen years – with lengthy interruptions due to Weber's many journeys – the lack of recorded information must in the main reflect the stability of their relations with each other. In the spring of 1910, at the invitation of the Webers, Martha and Ernst Troeltsch moved in with them in the old Hausrath house on the Neckar; Troeltsch's later statement, in the *Frankfurter Zeitung* obituary, that '*for years*' he had experienced the 'infinitely stimulating force' of Weber's intellect in their '*daily* contacts' probably refers primarily to this period when they shared the same house. Letters that Troeltsch wrote to third parties testify to his sympathetic concern about Weber's illness and his considerable familiarity with his friend's plans for future publications.[16] Just as in 1905 Weber referred to one of Troeltsch's forthcoming publications when it was not yet complete in manuscript,[17] Troeltsch too was in the habit of quoting texts by Weber that had not yet appeared in print. As early as 1919 he referred to the findings of Weber's work on the sociology of music, which was not published until after Weber's death. And Troeltsch was well informed about plans for the posthumous publication of Weber's unpublished works.[18] Troeltsch regularly attended the Sunday meetings of Weber's circle and developed personal and enduring contacts with some of its younger members, contacts which he maintained after his move to Berlin.[19] Unlike Weber, who saw himself deprived, from 1903 onwards, of all institutional means of exerting his influence in the University, Troeltsch had a substantial pull in university politics – becoming pro-rector in March 1906, and representing the University in the lower house of the Baden parliament from 1909 to 1914. On at least one occasion he used his influence – admittedly without success – in a cause that Weber supported, by campaigning strenuously for the appointment of their mutual friend Georg Simmel to a chair.

It is only when they are in distant parts that the written records become informative. We know substantially more about the five weeks or so[20] that they spent together in the United States in the summer of 1904 than we do about the whole seventeen years of their everyday life in Heidelberg. The accounts of the journey given by Marianne Weber and Troeltsch agree even in details of formulation – in particular, in their expression of horrified fascination at the socio-cultural consequences of capitalist modernization. Although Weber, we are told, was 'constantly informative in the most interesting manner', Troeltsch was more in sympathy with Marianne's religiously inspired criticism of the United States (she began to have doubts about freedom and immortality when faced with the 'millions living under the scourge of gold') than he was with her husband's enthusiasm. As a result they had 'some theoretical disagreements'.[21] We have a similar report from Hans Haupt, an American pastor of German descent to whom the travellers had written before leaving Heidelberg with a request for scholarly assistance:

'They asked him to collect as much material as possible about American denominations and their moral teachings and attitudes, especially in relation to economic practices ... When his distinguished visitors arrived, they spent several days with him. In between an inspection of the town of Towanda and visits to nearby Niagara Falls, they talked and argued all the time. But they hardly asked for Haupt's opinion and failed to inspect the material he had gathered, but they took it with them. Haupt had the impression that the professors knew all that could be known without having to weigh empirical evidence.'[22] The fact that the visitors took possession of his material admittedly seems to indicate the contrary.[23]

Although Troeltsch was on terms of close friendship with prominent supporters of Friedrich Naumann and was at least well acquainted with Naumann himself, he was not a member of the National Social Association (Nationalsozialer Verein), but opted in his first years in Heidelberg for the National Liberals.[24] It is thought that by 20 January 1905 at the latest, at an 'American evening' organized by the Association, he was seen in the company of Naumann's supporters and from then on, with Adolf Deissmann, came out publicly in support of Naumann on several occasions. Weber is said to have urged Troeltsch even before 1903 to 'take an active part in politics', but Troeltsch is said to have refused, 'despite considerable sympathy with liberalism' because his Christianity prevented him from becoming exclusively involved with any *doctrinal* liberalism.[25] In 1906 this pious sceptic ascribed his 'disagreements with Weber' specifically to his friend's 'optimistic belief in progress'.[26] Conversely, Weber, in the extended version of his essay on sects, drew attention to 'a few points' on which he disagreed with views expressed by Troeltsch in his Evangelical-Social Congress lecture on 'Politische Ethik und Christentum', delivered in Breslau in 1904. Troeltsch, who was a democrat not out of conviction or principle but out of a sense of historical responsibility,[27] had maintained in his lecture that there was no religious legitimation for a doctrine of democracy founded on natural law, arguing that the Christian ethic, which insisted on the autonomy of the individual personality, always included a 'conservative' element that involved raising the individual above the mass and was hence essentially 'aristocratic'. Weber, by insisting on a constitutive difference between 'conservative' and 'aristocratic', was first and foremost calling upon his friend to adopt a more critical attitude towards the Wilhelmine system of government. The fact that, before the war, Troeltsch became increasingly radical in his demands for the democratization of the Reich and in his strictures against the exclusion of the Social Democrats from government was probably due to Weber's influence. On the other hand, Weber publicly lent his support to the church policy of the liberal minority among German Protestants, a policy which was drawn up largely by Troeltsch.[28] However, too little research has been done on Troeltsch's political life before the war for us to be able to determine the precise nature of the lasting 'differences of politics and principle' to which he attributed the momentous row he had with Weber in the autumn of 1915.[29]

Even Marianne Weber mentioned in 1926 that Weber, who during the war served as a disciplinary officer at the military hospital administration at Heidelberg, had been very touchy in his relations with his colleagues.[30] Troeltsch too sought to explain the conflict to himself as a result of Weber's nervous state. Although, on 31 August 1914, he had reported to Paul Siebeck that Weber was putting up with 'the intense work' of a twelve-to-thirteen hour day 'better than expected', his first letter from Berlin stated that Weber was 'at the moment so irritable that our relations have suffered a severe blow' and that this had to a large extent 'marred the end of his stay' in Heidelberg.[31]

According to Marianne Weber's account, 'not until five years later were the stubborn men brought together again by their wives.'[32] This must have been sometime in 1919. We have no further details. It is true that as early as March 1916 Weber attended a speech given by Troeltsch to the Deutsche Gesellschaft von 1914, and it is likely that there were at least some indirect contacts through the dense communications network of the anti-annexionist academic politicians. Despite profound disagreements over the theoretical justification of the war and over the kind of democracy that would be appropriate in the new political order in postwar Germany, they were clearly in agreement on important matters of practical politics: they both signed the Delbrück-Dernburg Petition; Weber supported the Volksbund für Freiheit und Vaterland, which Troeltsch had a large hand in shaping, while Troeltsch was a champion of the Heidelberger Vereinigung. All this may have been conducive to a personal reconciliation.[33] We may *surmise* that it was effected in the March or April of 1919. There may have been pressing practical reasons for patching up the quarrel. Both were now involved in politics. Troeltsch had a prominent role as a member of the Prussian National Assembly and, from March 1919 to July 1920, was Under-Secretary of State in the Ministry of Science, Art and Education. He was intensely active in public in support of the German Democratic Party and, as the party's main Berlin candidate in the elections to the Prussian National Assembly, he had to attend numerous party meetings. Of course there was no question, for purely practical reasons, of going back to the close daily contact they had enjoyed in the Ziegelhäuser Landstraße. Yet it is noteworthy that it was Troeltsch whom Marianne Weber asked to speak at the memorial service held for Weber in Munich. For practical reasons Troeltsch was unable to give the 'funeral oration',[34] but it was later printed. In it, we find Troeltsch's only reference so far known to the nature of his friendship with Weber: 'The only emotional friendship he had to my knowledge was with Paul Göhre ... *All* his other associations arose primarily from shared interests'.[35]

II

It is far from easy to determine the 'shared interests' which brought Troeltsch and Weber together. We not only have to surmount the considerable hurdles we encounter in studying the history of their reception (which is equally problematic in both their cases): we also have to dismantle the prejudices that exist within their respective disciplines, that prevent representatives of either discipline from appreciating the inner complexity of *both* men's work. Even more serious is a methodological difficulty. In the whole history of modern scholarship, we know of few authors of comparable stature whose work *may have been* shaped by such intense mutual communication resulting in fruitful scholarly interaction[36] during 'years of daily association'. Each of them is a hero within his own discipline, and those who see themselves called upon to guard the reputations of their heroes will have to be prepared to cross the inter-disciplinary divide; for it is not possible for sociology to say the last word about the scholarly activity that went on at Ziegelhäuser Landstraße, nor can the theologians stage a revelation of the mystery – for there is still an element of mystery attaching to those 'important scholarly discussions',[37] which went on between the genius and his friends amid dense clouds of tobacco smoke.

As long as no further sources come to light about the life the two men led together – in particular, about the transactions of the Eranos Circle – we can reconstruct the content of their scholarly exchanges only from *references to each other in their writings*. Well-founded judgements regarding possible mutual influences cannot be based on the numerous more or less vague thematic parallels that undoubtedly exist in the sphere of the sociology of religion, but only on *explicit references* – quotations, acknowledgements and other such sound evidence – to each other's publications. This approach is, of course, somewhat pedantic – but it serves to 'avoid the confusions', of which there is no lack in the literature on religious typology.[38] Because of the 'enormous tangle ... of reciprocal influences'[39] existing between the works of Weber and Troeltsch (especially in the field of the sociology of religion), we can deal here with only one aspect of the complex 'causal relations', and even this can be treated with reference to only one single *example*: Weber's recep-tion of writings of Troeltsch in the *Protestant Ethic* of 1904/05.

The complex history of their reciprocal references begins with a short men-tion by Troeltsch of the first article in Weber's 'Roscher and Knies' essay published in 1903.[40] Conversely, Weber first refers to one of Troeltsch's publications in the first part of the *Protestant Ethic*; the work in question is a review, written by Troeltsch in the early summer of 1900, of the second volume of a history of dogma by the nationalistically oriented Lutheran theologian, Reinhold Seeberg.[41] Weber accuses most 'theological writers' of providing a 'still insufficiently clear analysis of the concept of "lex naturae"'[42] and expressly refers to Troeltsch's demand for a more differentiated investi-gation of the notion of natural law. Troeltsch had argued that this notion was the systematic distillation of the general interest in a reconciliation of religious ideas with the harsh realities of the world, in terms of practical culture. In justifying his demand for an integrated treatment of the many heterogeneous links between religious ideas and other cultural factors (a treatment which would 'bring together theological, legal, economic and philosophical knowledge'), Troeltsch was already sketching certain central elements of his view of the history of Christianity, which he later elaborated, especially in the *Social Teaching of the Christian Churches* and various subsequent additions to that work.[43] These central elements were: the eschatological remoteness of the culture of early Christianity; the dualistic concept of asceticism peculiar to the unified culture of the Middle Ages; his critique of the quietistic indifference of Lutheranism to the 'shaping of social culture'. This was the reason why Troeltsch subsequently referred on a number of occasions to his review of Seeberg's work as containing the nucleus of the programme he set out in full in the *Social Teaching* – usually in the context of attempts to establish his own independence *vis-à-vis* Weber.[44]

In the *Protestant Ethic*, which Weber wrote after his journey to the United

States, Troeltsch is referred to specifically as an *'expert'* in theology in the course of a fairly long footnote. In this footnote Weber acknowledges the reliance of his 'sketch' (!) on the 'intensive and liberal-minded theological work of many centuries' and makes the first of those curiously earnest protestations of scholarly modesty with regard to theology that recur in his writings on the sociology of religion right up to the 'Economic Ethics of World Religions'. The *non-expert*, he says, works at 'second hand' and can 'lay no claim whatever to originality'. Despite having studied the sources for himself (admittedly with the handicap of the non-expert), it is 'quite inevitable' that he should 'seek guidance' from secondary literature in the field of theology in order to understand them. Hence no one 'familiar with the most important theological literature', and in particular no expert, will find anything 'new ' in his (Weber's) account, except 'in so far as everything is related to those points of view which *we* find important, some of which, though of crucial significance for us ... are naturally of less concern to theological writers'.[45] Weber could not have stated more clearly his *productive* dependence on a mass of theological literature, which he regrets being unable to quote in full 'for reasons of space'. He claimed originality only with regard to the questions he himself raised or to the new systematic structuring of familiar theological material arising from these questions. Yet in all this Troeltsch played at least an indirect part: 'Some other points of view ... receive only summary treatment here, because I hope that E. Troeltsch, in his contribution to the Hinneberg volume, will deal with these matters (*lex naturae*, etc.) in detail, having studied these questions for years, as witness his work on *Gerhard and Melanchthon* and especially his numerous reviews in the *Göttingische Gelehrte Anzeigen*. He is naturally better equipped to clear them up, being an expert, than I could ever be with the best will in the world'.[46] The 'contribution' Weber was referring to was an extensive account of modern Protestantism, running to a good 200 pages of print, which appeared in January 1906.

At the same time Troeltsch published, in Hinneberg's *Kultur der Gegenwart*, a short sketch of the fundamental problems involved in a systematic 'science of religion'.[47] On 24 October 1904 he completed the German version of the lecture he had given in St. Louis; after this, he worked on his two contributions to the Hinneberg volume, interrupting this work only to write a few reviews on subjects germane to it and a contribution to the controversy over fundamental theology which had been sparked off by his work, *The Absoluteness of Christianity and the History of Religions*. The *terminus ad quem* for the completion of his big work on Protestantism, which contains a number of references in the footnotes to Weber's two essays on the Protestant Ethic in the *Archiv* (the second one appeared in June 1905), was 22 October 1905. Troeltsch thus had a few months to fulfil his friend's publicly expressed hopes. That there was simultaneous influence in the opposite direction is clear from the fact that, while Weber was prepared, in his account of ascetic Protestantism, to expatiate on his *own* 'points of view' (those which make his particular perspective different from that found in the older theological literature), he wished only to indicate certain other 'points of view' which also needed to be treated, though by Troeltsch rather than by himself. And, in fact, those writings by Troeltsch that Weber specifically mentions – *Vernunft und Offenbarung bei Johann Gerhard und Melanchthon. Untersuchung zur*

Geschichte der altprotestantischen Theologie (Göttingen 1891), numerous reviews, and a substantial lexicon article of 1903 on 'English moralists'[48] – do indeed prove that Troeltsch had 'studied these questions for years'.

A comparison between the *Protestant Ethic* and these works by Troeltsch reveals at least *one* instance of Weber's reliance on his friend: he was indebted to him for his knowledge of most of the theological literature he drew upon in his historical account of ascetic Protestantism. This debt is evident from the number of quotations alone: much of the specialist theological literature he used consists of works that Troeltsch also drew upon (in the same editions!) for his studies on the history of ethics and which he in some cases subjected to a detailed critique. Both men often quote the same crucial passages. Moreover, the critical commentaries with which Weber introduces certain theological works (despite his self-imposed reserve as a non-expert) offer judgements that are remarkably close to those that the same works elicited from Troeltsch. A particularly significant instance is Weber's treatment of Albrecht Ritschl's writings on the history of dogma.

This 'philological' finding – that Troeltsch was Weber's adviser on the theological literature – may at first appear trivial, but it is of relevance to the content of the two men's work in that, without exception, those works by Troeltsch that Weber cites are remarkably close to the *Protestant Ethic* both in the subjects they treat and the arguments they advance. *With regard to his assessment of the history of Lutheran theology Weber is directly dependent on Troeltsch, and to a greater extent than would appear from the brief references in the footnotes.* It was from Troeltsch's dissertation, a study of Lutheran theology in the sixteenth and seventeenth centuries oriented towards 'cultural history', that Weber adopted the *critical* view of historical Lutheranism which constitutes *one* of the *decisive* conditions for his account of the specific significance of Calvinist Protestantism in the development of culture. Among the topics Weber discusses are: the central position occupied by the concept of Law in all 'old Protestant' doctrinal systems, the attribution of ethical differences between the Protestant confessions to competing interpretations of God's Law, the impotence of Lutheranism as a practical cultural force resulting from a specific version of the doctrine of grace, the adoption by late Lutheran orthodoxy, largely inspired by Melanchthon, of traditions regarding natural law that were at variance with Luther's teaching on the Law, the rejection of Ritschl's critique (based on his own religious politics) of Lutheran mysticism and pietism. These were not, as Weber's method of quoting might now and then suggest, generally accepted historical judgements going back to the older literature on the history of dogma, but extremely provocative individual assessments with decidedly political implications (Lutheranism being the predominant variety of Protestantism in Prussian Germany). Such assessments had first been voiced – to a considerable chorus of criticism from fellow theologians – in Troeltsch's dissertation. This dissertation, moreover, influenced Weber's linguistic usage: this is seen particularly clearly in his adoption of the term 'old Protestant',[49] which Troeltsch admittedly did not invent, but was the first to use as a designation for a historical period. Contemporary theological critics of Weber were right to see this coinage – which they admittedly felt to be problematical – as due to the influence of Troeltsch.

With regard to other writings by Troeltsch that are cited by Weber, it is not maintained that the latter was dependent on the former, as this would be inadmissible on methodological grounds. True, all these writings evince a fascinating conceptual and thematic affinity to Weber's account of ascetic Protestantism. In some of the footnotes to the first 'Roscher and Knies' article, published in October 1903, we find what was probably Weber's first public reference to the connection between the 'genesis of the capitalist spirit' and 'Puritan ideas'.[50] In the same year (we cannot be more precise about the date), Troeltsch published his article, 'English Moralists'. In it, Troeltsch described the 'Calvinist ethic' in terms that were without exception fundamental to Weber's account of Calvinism and referred specifically to the theological literature on which this account was based. This applies not only to the *theological features* of Calvinism, such as 'bibliocracy', the central position of the 'idea of predestination', the inner connection between 'predestined grace' and 'conformity with the Law' (because 'moral attainment ... is overt proof of election, the dogma of predestination is the source of extreme energy in action'), 'the church as the sanctifier of the predestined', etc., but also for the *description* of the 'reformed ethic' in terms of the *'history of culture'* as the 'great point of intersection in modern intellectual development':

> [in the] Calvinist countries ... there prevails ... a freer attitude to economic activity and the capital which promotes it. By contrast with the patriarchal conservatism of the Lutherans, with their attachment to the closed household economy, the Calvinists believe in political and economic utilitarianism ...; and this utilitarianism is supported by the Christian requirements of moderation, probity and diligence, in which the Gospel proves to be conducive to material as well as to spiritual wellbeing. In this way those countries which have adopted the reformed faith become supporters of the capitalist economy, of trade and industry, and of a kind of utilitarianism which is tempered by Christianity and has significantly influenced both their cultural theory and their actual strength. It has given a powerful boost not only to modern political development but also to economic development. Anyone who is so absolutely sure – through predestination – of his earthly goal and his salvation hereafter can apply his natural powers all the more freely to the acquisition of wealth as a natural principle of life and need not fear an excessive attachment to earthly goods. It was thus possible for the reformed ethic to become linked with the purely secular theories which had evolved in the fields of politics and economics, and for some of its cultural components to become autonomous agents in purely worldly concerns ...[51]

Even though Weber referred to this text in 1905, we are *not* justified in concluding that his description of ascetic Protestantism is *dependent* on Troeltsch. For, on the one hand, both Troeltsch and Weber later stated that they had been made aware of the subject by Jellinek's work on human rights.[52] We know that, in an indirect critique of Troeltsch's assertion (made in 1906) that Weber's 'capitalist spirit' was partly influenced by that of Sombart, Weber stated that he had lectured on the subject of the *Protestant Ethic* as early as 1898. There are at present no legitimate grounds for doubting this. Certainly, the *affinity* between the *Protestant Ethic* and writings by Troeltsch published before 1904 may equally be explained as the result of Weber's influence on Troeltsch through verbal communication. Yet we can no more show that Troeltsch was *dependent* on Weber than we can show the converse.

True, there was a lively exchange of ideas between the two men at least by the time when Weber was working on the *Protestant Ethic* — and this was not necessarily confined to the Eranos Circle, founded in 1904. This exchange of ideas has to be understood as a kind of co-operation, which cannot be adequately described in terms of direct one-way influence. For Troeltsch did not simply give Weber 'technical' advice on the theological literature relevant to the religious profile of ascetic Protestantism; one should rather say that Weber adjusted the thematic scope and the layout of his work to the work Troeltsch was doing on a closely related subject at the same time (or at least with an overlap of a few months). The hope that Troeltsch would treat those matters 'which for this reason are only indicated here'[53] soon becomes a *presumption*: 'The great importance, for the *social* character of reformed Christianity, which attaches to the Calvinist idea that in order to gain salvation it is necessary to be received into a *community* which conforms to divine precepts will, I presume, be treated at length in the essay mentioned before. As regards *our* particular points of view, however, the central issue is somewhat different.'[54]

III

For both Troeltsch and Weber the most important condition for their co-operation was their mutual recognition of the independence which each of them claimed. They both interpreted this independence as primarily a formal matter, relating to specific differences between the disciplines of their respective fields. They saw their co-operation as interdisciplinary collaboration between autonomous sciences, each of which defined the object of its knowledge independently but was obliged, in order to arrive at a concrete understanding of this object, to adopt and assimilate the findings of the other discipline or to engage in a scholarly exchange of ideas. This kind of interdisciplinary collaboration was, so to speak, a practical necessity: in view of the cultural complexity of the give-and-take between religion and society, it was impossible for a sociologist who was resistant to theology, or for a theologian who was resistant to sociology, to do justice to his claims to knowledge. Both men were vehemently critical of representatives of their respective disciplines who refused to participate in such interdisciplinary activity. At the same time they clearly defined the limits of their own subjects. In 1906, for instance, Troeltsch stood in for his friend and gave a lecture on 'The importance of Protestantism for the emergence of the modern world'; in it, he regretted that 'those parts of the theme relating to politics, economics and sociology ... could not receive expert treatment'.[55] Similarly, Weber stressed more than once that parts of the work programme on the sociology of religion, which hc had sketched out in the concluding parts of the *Protestant Ethic*, had in the meantime been dealt with by Troeltsch 'in a manner of which I, as a non-theologian, should not have been capable'.[56]

The fact that Troeltsch and Weber defined their working relations formally in terms of interdisciplinary collaboration rather than in terms of subjects of common interest does not mean that there were not numerous thematic parallels between the two *oeuvres*. One particularly important parallel is the recognition of the fact that social reality is significantly influenced by religion. Yet their shared interest in the analytical investigation of religion as a *Lebensmacht* did not constitute a sufficiently solid basis for a definition of the relation between their theoretical programmes, inasmuch as these differed considerably in their constructive aims. In their formal interpretation of the relations between their work, Weber and Troeltsch were able not only to take advantage of these differences but to narrow them down in a productive manner. However abstract the interpretation of their working relations as interdisciplinary collaboration may appear, it was precisely this formality of approach which allowed both men to co-operate pragmatically on the one hand, without on the other hand having to conceal from each other serious differences of content. These too relate primarily to religion as a *Lebensmacht*: despite the genetic relevance of ascetic Protestantism to the establishment of modern industrial capitalism, Weber was unable to accord any continuing social function to religious values; Troeltsch, by contrast, sought to adapt the ethical content of Christianity to modern social problems: faced with the destructive consequences of capitalist modernization, the social potentialities of religion were in this way to be rendered effective (once again) in favour of a humane shaping of society.

The extent to which Weber's research into the sociology of religion was influenced by the work of Troeltsch through their common interest in religion as a *Lebensmacht* can be demonstrated *within the context of Weber's writings* above all by reference to the substantial modifications he made to his original programme of work. The fact that, in 1910, Weber rejected Felix Rachfahl's attempt to treat Troeltsch and himself as a team and stated 'emphatically that there had been no team-work, even of a latent kind',[57] does not imply that there was no relevant inner connection between his writings on the sociology of religion and Troeltsch's publications. Between 1909 and 1919/20, Weber stressed on several occasions that certain central problems, which he had only touched upon in the *Protestant Ethic*, had meanwhile been 'taken up in the most felicitous manner' by Troeltsch, who had approached them from the perspective of his own ideas and dealt with them with 'far greater expertise'.[58] The revision of the *Protestant Ethic* and the essay on sects, as well as the extension of the scope of his inquiry to include the general historical links between religion and society, are to be interpreted largely as a response to the reception of Troeltsch's publications[59] – in particular of his *Social Teaching*, to whose composition Weber had contributed with advice on problems of economic history, references to the relevant literature, and critical comments.[60] In assessing the extent to which the *Social Teaching* and other works of Troeltsch relating to the history of religion influenced the categories and material content of Weber's later work on the sociology of religion, we must admittedly take into account the fragmentary nature of the 'Economic Ethics of World Religions'; since Weber was not able to complete the final volume on the 'Christianity of the West', we can do no more than attempt an indirect reconstruction of *his* view of how its content differed from that of Troeltsch's 'Universalgeschichte der Ethik des okzidentalen Christentums'.[61] We may surmise that in this fourth volume of the 'Economic Ethics' Weber would have thought it necessary, in view of the close parallels between the two in both subject matter and method, to complement Troeltsch's references to him in the *Social Teaching* by indications of where they diverged. In December 1913, Weber announced the 'Sociology of Religion' of *Economy and Society* to Paul Siebeck with an express reference to Troeltsch: 'sociology of salvation doctrines and different religious ethics – what Troeltsch has provided, with reference now to all religions ...'.[62] Troeltsch's view of their contrasting positions is relatively well documented in numerous sociologically inspired texts on the history of Christianity, and especially in various fragments of his late work on the philosophy of history.[63]

These contrasts find their fullest expression in competing systematic definitions of the current historical relations between Western rationality, ethics and Christianity. Both men were in broad agreement over the alarming consequences of capitalist modernization and the threat it posed to freedom. They saw how the individual's scope for independent action was being increasingly restricted by widespread bureaucratization and the growing rigidity of social institutions, so that the normative conceptions of modern culture formulated during the Enlightenment of the late seventeenth and eighteenth centuries had by now proved illusory. Yet Troeltsch differed from Weber on the practical cultural or ethical consequences to be drawn from the recognition of the potential for crisis inherent in the universal process of rationalization, brought about primarily by economic factors. Differences between their theoretical programmes do not relate to their respective analyses of the age: Troeltsch agreed with Weber's diagnosis of the threat to individual freedom posed by 'high capitalism'[64] and was, if anything, more radical than Weber, imagining apocalyptic scenarios, so to speak, for the 'decline of the individual'. For this reason, he inevitably concerned himself with the question that arose from this diagnosis: was there any way out of the iron cage? Yet Troeltsch's answer was in a certain sense more complex than Weber's.

All the evolutionary theories current among philosophers of history arrived, by way of a merely one-dimensional dogmatic abstraction, at the supposition that the modern age would see the definitive end of religion in the West. Troeltsch, by contrast, expressly included religion in his analyses as a factor which might *possibly* have present relevance in the shaping of society; in doing so, he concentrated his theoretical attention above all on the question of whether, even under conditions of capitalism, religion could be turned into a force that would have the counter-effect of strengthening individual freedom. Not that his answer to the question of how it 'might *still be possible*, in view of the overwhelming tendency towards bureaucratization, to rescue *some* remnants of freedom of movement which might in *some* sense be called "individual"'[65] was any more clear or more optimistic than Weber's. He considered the religion which then existed in Germany to be little more than an instrument of class rule, and he called Prussian Lutheranism, with its patriarchal and illiberal values, the 'religion of the ruling class'. His analysis of the 'religious situation' was altogether too critical for him to be able to set simple piety against Weber's *'heroic scepticism'*.[66] Yet he was profoundly convinced that there was no such thing as a society without religion. Secularization was seen by him not as a progressive loss of religion but as a transformation of religion's cultural and social function. Therefore, when it came to the question of finding possible ways to relativize the bureaucratic levelling of the 'soul', it was necessary to include the resources of religion among the subjects to be discussed: *if* one were going to save a 'residue of humanity' from the 'parcelling off of the soul',[67] then it would be absurd to ignore that form of consciousness which by definition aims at *transcendence* and to this extent not only gives scope to individuality, but promotes *free involvement in society*. For Troeltsch was not only unable to envisage a society without religion: from the perspective of his sociologically informed theory of religion he was equally unable to believe in subjective religion, i.e. forms of piety that did not find objective expression in institutions or remained socially irrelevant.

Religion had in particular *two* functions that might *possibly* make it an evolutionary factor in modern societies. Troeltsch wrote a number of programmatic sketches and preliminary studies for what was to have been, with a treatment of material ethics, his 'principal work' – a comprehensive 'Systematic Science of Religion' or 'Philosophy of Religion'.[68] In the programmatic writings he discussed, on the one hand one specific function of religious consciousness, namely, the *promotion of individuality*. Like F. D. E. Schleiermacher,[69] the 'classical' representative of the theory that saw religiosity as being capable of assuming a modern form, Troeltsch regarded religious consciousness as the sphere in which true individuality could assert itself. For religion is the communion of the soul with God, the relating of the finite consciousness to the ultimate generality, which transcends and relativizes all supra-individual generalities (state, society, etc.), or the self-realization of individual subjectivity in a transcendent sphere of freedom. The metaphysical content of religion furnishes the individual with the potential for distinguishing himself from the generality of the world around him. To this extent religion can give stability to personal identity – what Troeltsch, in the parlance of the age, called 'personality' – or strengthen the individual's consciousness of his autonomy. Religion thus provides a view of man which is in permanent contrast with the socially produced experiences that seem to confirm the insignificance of the individual: whereas in society the particular is at the disposal of the general and the individual is reduced to a function, in religion we have a symbolic assurance of the 'infinite value of the human soul'. This symbolic function of religion, however, has its own social relevance. For Troeltsch, as for Weber and other contemporary thinkers, all social relations were relations between the rulers and the ruled: thus, in describing the antagonism between the individual and society, he never ceases to be aware of the real potential for conflict within society, and even reinforces the individual's capacity or readiness to engage in conflicts.[70]

On the other hand, religion also has a social function. Objective religion in particular – that is, the cultural institutions of religion (religious activity within the community, worship, etc.) – furnishes a potential for social integration. It is true that Troeltsch found it far more difficult to define the precise nature of this integrative function of religion than to explain its individualizing function. This is partly due to the concrete political content of his theory of religion, which was formulated with specific reference to the political and social conditions obtaining in the Wilhelmine Reich and the early Weimar Republic – a society, in other words, which was characterized not only by class antagonisms but also by deep religious divisions (denominational fragmentation or the competition between the churches and new religious movements based on eclectic concepts, which were in the main decidedly critical of Christianity), which were a serious impediment to the integrative effects of religion. Troeltsch was aware of the basic dilemma facing all theories of integration. For the sake of integration a certain amount of rational content must be shown to command general consent. Yet to lay down certain principles of rationality with regard to the content of religious faith – certain values for which general validity is claimed – represents in itself a threat to individual freedom. Because of the highly rational cast of his thinking, Troeltsch shared Weber's critical sensitivity to the dangers inherent in any postulation of general principles. However, he did not endorse Weber's solution of the 'problem of values', which was an exclusively formal understanding of rationality, calling into question the possibility of universalizing principles of rationality, hence a plea for a permanent political war between subjective sets of values. For, according to Troeltsch, even Weber could not escape, through recourse to the concept of 'polytheism', the dangers to freedom which would arise if mere particular beliefs were given absolute status. The theologian therefore adopted the opposite course: being politically much more able than Weber by reason of his theoretically established readiness to compromise, and realizing that politics has to be understood not just as conflict, but as an endeavour to shape a common will, Troeltsch attempted to harness the potential of religion for communication in the cause of *open* integration. To do this, he embarked upon a ridge-walk through the philosophy of history, knowing of course that the risk of losing his balance was much greater than the prospect of reaching his destination. The aim was to discover, through a religiously inspired reconstruction of Western history, a set of material, politically practical and relevant principles that would command a consensus and be recognized as valid throughout European–American culture. In the interests of freedom, however, it was imperative not to lose one's awareness of the factual relativity of any consensus – of the possibility that it might at any time be superseded. Whether Troeltsch was able to do justice to both these insights is open to dispute, given the fragmentary nature of his work. This very open-endedness was seen by him as an inevitable consequence of the historical limits to which any definition of general principles is subject. He ascribed a theological quality, as it were, to the antinomies of his philosophy of history: they gave expression to our awareness that, within the framework of history, the absolute values of religion cannot be stated positively and definitively. It is impossible to institutionalize social orders that will be permanently valid, and there are no such things as eternal norms and ultimate values. Great though the contrasts may be between Weber's critical philosophy and Troeltsch's religious metaphysics, the differing basic structure of their theoretical programmes clearly reflects a common interest in preventing a positive delimitation of freedom.

Notes: Chapter 15

This chapter was translated by D. R. McLintock.

1   Max Weber, '"Kirchen" und "Sekten" in Nordamerika. Eine kirchen- und sozialpolitische

Skizze', *Die christliche Welt. Evangelisches Gemeindeblatt für Gebildete aller Stände*, vol. 20, (1906), cols 558–62, 577–83, here col. 580; idem, 'Antikritisches zum "Geist" des Kapitalismus', PE, Vol. 2, p. 149. This article is a contribution to the discussion of E. Troeltsch, 'Das stoisch-christliche Naturrecht und das moderne profane Naturrecht', in *Verhandlungen des Ersten Deutschen Soziologentages vom 19. – 22. Oktober 1910 in Frankfurt a. M.* (Tübingen, 1911), p. 196.

2 E. Troeltsch, 'Max Weber', *Frankfurter Zeitung*, no. 447 (20 June 1920), p. 2 (hereafter quoted as 'FZ obituary').

3 *Lebensbild*; P. Honigsheim, 'Der Max-Weber-Kreis in Heidelberg', *Kölner Vierteljahreshefte für Soziologie*, vol. 5 (1926), pp. 270–87; idem, 'Wie man in Heidelberg für Simmels Berufung gekämpft hat', in K. Gassen and M. Landmann (eds), *Buch des Dankes an Georg Simmel. Briefe, Erinnerungen, Bibliographie* (Berlin, 1958), pp. 262–8; idem, 'Max Weber in Heidelberg', in R. König and J. Winckelmann (eds), *Max Weber zum Gedächtnis. Materialien und Dokumente zur Bewertung von Werk und Persönlichkeit* (Cologne and Opladen, 1963), pp. 161–269; idem, 'Zur Hegelrenaissance im Vorkriegs-Heidelberg. Erkenntnissoziologische Beobachtungen', *Hegel-Studien*, vol. 2 (1963), pp. 291–301.

4 Apart from the obituary mentioned in n. 2 above, which is reprinted in a slightly abridged form in König and Winckelmann (eds), *Max Weber zum Gedächtnis*, Troeltsch published a second, 'Max Weber als Gelehrter', *Deutsche Allgemeine Zeitung*, no. 290 (19 June 1920, evening edn), p. 1 (hereafter quoted as '*DAZ* obituary').

5 E. Baumgarten (ed.), *Max Weber. Werk und Person* (Tübingen, 1964), p. 624.

6 W. Hennis, 'Max Webers Fragestellung', *Zeitschrift für Politik*, vol. 29 (1982), pp. 241–81, here p. 263.

7 G. Küenzlen, *Die Religionssoziologie Max Webers. Eine Darstellung ihrer Entwicklung* (Berlin, 1980), p. 61. All that is *attested* is that Georg Lukács was one of the 'friends' to whom Weber read the first parts of the 'Economic Ethics of World Religions'. Cf. G. Lukács, *Briefwechsel 1902–1917*, ed. É. Karaádi and É. Fekete (Stuttgart, 1982), p. 362. Altogether Küenzlen's book represents a considerable advance in the attempt to place Weber's sociology of religion within the context of the history of ideas. Cf. the detailed review by V. Drehsen, *Zeitschrift für evangelische Ethik*, vol. 28 (1984), pp. 233–7.

8 It is to be hoped that the publication of Weber's correspondence will enable us to define his relations with Troeltsch more precisely than we can at present.

9 *Jugendbriefe*, pp. 57, 65, 117, 171, 223–4; P. Honigsheim, 'Max Weber: His Religious and Ethical Background and Development', *Church History*, vol. 19 (1950), pp. 219–39; V. Drehsen, 'Religion und die Rationalisierung der modernen Welt: Max Weber' in K. W. Dahm et al., *Das Jenseits der Gesellschaft. Religion im Prozess sozialwissenschaftlicher Kritik* (Munich, 1975), pp. 89–154; J. Weiss, *Max Webers Grundlegung der Soziologie. Eine Einführung* (Munich, 1975), pp. 105–33. For Baumgarten, see especially F. W. Graf, 'Lex Christi und Eigengesetzlichkeit. Das Grundproblem der ethischen Theologie Otto Baumgartens', in W. Steck (ed.), *Otto Baumgarten* (Kiel, 1986).

10 H. Gressmann, *Albert Eichhorn und die Religionsgeschichtliche Schule* (Göttingen, 1914), pp. 7–11; O. Baumgarten, *Meine Lebensgeschichte* (Tübingen, 1929), pp. 81–92. Baumgarten's autobiography received a detailed evaluation from a remarkably competent authoress: Marianne Weber, 'Otto Baumgarten als Theologe und Politiker', *Die christliche Welt*, vol. 44 (1931), cols 161–5.

11 *Jugendbriefe*, p. 268.

12 An account of the understanding of religion current among the 'Jungritschlianer' or 'Religionsgeschichtler' is given by F. W. Graf, 'Der "Systematiker" der "Kleinen Göttinger Fakultät"', in H. Renz and F. W. Graf (eds), *Troeltsch-Studien*, Vol. 1 (Gütersloh, 1982), pp. 235–90.

13 Gressman, *Albert Eichhorn*, p. 12; *Jugendbriefe*, pp. 223–4; frequent references in Renz and Graf (eds), *Troeltsch-Studien*, Vol. 1.

14 Troeltsch to Wilhelm Bousset (5 August 1898) in E. Troeltsch, 'Briefe aus der Heidelberger Zeit an Wilhelm Bousset 1894–1914, herausgegeben von E. Dinkler – von Schubert', *Heidelberger Jahrbücher*, vol. 20 (1976), pp. 19–52, here p. 32. This comment on Weber by Troeltsch, the earliest so far known, suggests that Weber was known to Bousset too. Contacts possibly came through the Evangelical-Social Congress or through mutual friendship with Friedrich Naumann.

15 *Biography*, p. 227.

16 Troeltsch to Heinrich Rickert, 10 March 1899; idem to Carl Neumann, 2 January 1906; idem

to Karl Vossler, 19 May 1913. In the last of these we read: 'Max Weber ... does more work than five healthy men, but he is not healthy. At the moment he is revising and organizing Schönberg's old *Handbuch der Nationalökonomie* and turning it into a completely new work...' Copies of these and other unpublished Troeltsch letters are kept in the Troeltsch Archive at the University of Augsburg. I am very grateful to Horst Renz for his help in working through the unpublished material.

17   Max Weber, 'Die protestantische Ethik und der "Geist" des Kapitalismus. II. Die Berufsidee des asketischen Protestantismus', AfSSP, vol. 21 (1905), pp. 1–110, here pp. 3–4, n. 3, p. 14, n. 20.

18   We can presume at least some contact with Marianne Weber on these matters from the fact that in Troeltsch's *Historismus* (whose first part-volume was issued by Mohr-Siebeck simultaneously with Weber's *Gesammelte Aufsätze zur Wissenschaftslehre*) he announced this collection with precise details of those essays by Weber that were to be included and – no doubt with *Economy and Society* in mind - predicted that Weber's scholarly achievements would only be demonstrated after the appearance of his posthumous works. At all events, he did not learn of the plans for their publication from their joint publisher, P. Siebeck. Troeltsch had a copy of his *Historismus* volume sent to Marianne Weber by the publisher. See archive of the publishers J. C. B. Mohr (Paul Siebeck), Tübingen.

19   So far as we know that, in particular, Emil Lask and Paul Honigsheim kept up close contacts with Troeltsch. In 1919 Troeltsch got Honigsheim a post as Max Scheler's assistant.

20   Troeltsch had to cut short his visit to the USA because of a bereavement.

21   Copy of two letters from Troeltsch to Martha Troeltsch of 3 September 1904 and 14 September 1904 (Troeltsch Archive, Augsburg).

22   W. Pauck, *Harnack and Troeltsch: Two Historical Theologians* (New York, 1968), p. 72.

23   It is worth noting that Haupt himself published on the subject: H. Haupt, *Die Eigenart der amerikanischen Predigt* (Giessen, 1907); idem, *Staat und Kirche in den Vereinigten Staaten von Nordamerika* (Giessen, 1909).

24   Cf. M. Dibelius, 'Ernst Troeltsch und die Heidelberger Theologie', *Kölnische Zeitung*, edition C, no. 321, 27 June 1936 (supplement to the morning edn). The statement that 'social and democratic ideals' were 'alien to Troeltsch's strongly bourgeois instincts' (*Biography*, p. 228) is questionable in view of his extremely intensive socio-political activity within various 'liberal' contexts in the Baden parliament. Marianne Weber's psychological assessment of Troeltsch (ibid.) is open to doubt in so far as numerous obituaries offer a distinctly different picture of his personality. Cf. the obituary written by the well-known Heidelberg Islamic scholar, C. H. Becker, who knew both Troeltsch and Weber: 'Ernst Troeltsch. Ein Gedenkwort', *Berliner Hochschul-Nachrichten*, ed. by P. Kersten and E. R. Marschall, 9th semester, no. 1 (May 1923), pp. 4–5.

25   Quoted from W. Köhler, *Ernst Troeltsch* (Tübingen, 1941), p. 292. Köhler's quotation (presumably from a letter) has not yet been verified.

26   Troeltsch to Carl Neumann of 2 January 1906 (Troeltsch Archive, Augsburg).

27   Max Weber, 'Kirchen', cols. 580–1, f.n. For Troeltsch's view of democracy, cf. the precise definition given by H. Ruddies: 'Democracy is a factual imperative, but not a "product of doctrine"; for this reason it must be made transparent by way of a historical reflection *as* a practical necessity, but not justified on the basis of a theory or doctrine of democracy *by arguments as to* necessity'. H. Ruddies, 'Soziale Demokratie und freier Protestantismus. Ernst Troeltsch in den Anfängen der Weimarer Republik', in H. Renz and F. W. Graf (eds), *Troeltsch-Studien*, Vol. 3 (Gütersloh, 1984), pp. 141–74, here p. 161.

28   Cf. for instance the criticism (largely inspired by Otto Baumgarten and Troeltsch) by liberal Protestant professors of the repressive policy of the Prussian church authorities towards Pfarrer C. Jatho. See the declaration of the 40 trustees of *Die christliche Welt* on the Jatho Case in *An die Freunde. Vertrauliche d.i. nicht für die Öffentlichkeit bestimmte Mitteilungen*, no. 37 (Marburg, 20 September 1911), pp. 411–12; and the declaration of 73 university professors against the tribunal in the Jatho case in *Christliche Freiheit. Evangelisches Gemeindeblatt für Rheinland und Westfalen* (ed. by G. Traub), vol. 27, no. 15 (Bonn, 9 April 1911), p. 229. Both declarations were publicly supported by Weber.

29   Cf. the letter from Troeltsch to Paul Honigsheim of 12 June 1917 quoted in Baumgarten (ed.), *Max Weber*, p. 489. For the notorious 'military hospital conflict', see *Biography*, p. 524.

30   ibid, p. 522.

31 Troeltsch to Paul Siebeck, 17 April 1915, Archive of the publishers J. C. B. Mohr (Paul Siebeck), Tübingen.
32 *Biography*, p. 524.
33 For Troeltsch's political life, cf. now the detailed evidence for numerous 'new' texts, political speeches and appeals in *Ernst Troeltsch Bibliographie*, edited with introduction and commentary by F. W. Graf and H. Ruddies (Tübingen, 1982). Also Ruddies, 'Soziale Demokratie', and the essays by B. Sösemann, ('Das "neue Deutschland". Ernst Troeltschs politisches Engagement im Ersten Weltkrieg') and by J. R. C. Wright ('Ernst Troeltsch als parlamentarischer Unterstaatssekretär im preussischen Ministerium für Wissenschaft, Kunst und Volksbildung') in Renz and Graf (eds), *Troeltsch-Studien*, Vol. 3, pp. 120–44 and 175–203.
34 'His widow asked me to speak at the graveside. Being overburdened with urgent business and being myself close to the limit of my nervous energy as I now am, I was unable to accede to her wish. And so I should like to say here roughly what I should have been able to say at the graveside...' (*FZ* obituary). There is no doubt about the honesty of this statement, since Troeltsch, as Under-Secretary of State, had been involved since mid-June in non-stop conferences on the revision of the Prussian Church.
35 *FZ* obituary.
36 Cf. *Biography*, p. 228.
37 ibid., p. 369.
38 Comprehensive references to the extensive literature on the subject are given by S. D. Berger, 'Die Sekten und der Durchbruch in die moderne Welt. Zur zentralen Bedeutung der Sekten in Webers Protestantismus-These', in C. Seyfarth and W. M. Sprondel (eds), *Seminar: Religion und gesellschaftliche Entwicklung. Studien zur Protestantismus-Kapitalismus-These Max Webers* (Frankfurt-on-Main, 1973), pp. 241–63; M. T. Steemann, 'Church, sect, mysticism, denomination: periodical aspects of Troeltsch's types', *Sociological Analysis*, vol. 36 (1975), pp. 188–204; W. H. Swatos jun., 'Weber or Troeltsch? Methodology, syndrome and the development of Church–Sect Theory', *Journal for the Scientific Study of Religion*, vol. 15 (1976), pp. 129–44; H. Ralston, 'The typologies of Weber and Troeltsch: a case study of a Catholic religious group in Atlantic Canada', *Archives des sciences sociales des religions*, vol. 50/1 (1980), pp. 111–27.
39 PE, Vol. 1, p. 77.
40 Cf. E. Troeltsch, *Das Historische in Kants Religionsphilosophie. Zugleich ein Beitrag zu den Untersuchungen über Kants Philosophie* (Berlin, 1904), pp. 109–10.
41 Review by Troeltsch of R. Seeberg, *Lehrbuch der Dogmengeschichte. Zweite Hälfte: Die Dogmengeschichte des Mittelalters und der Neuzeit* (Erlangen, 1899), in *Göttingische Gelehrte Anzeigen*, vol. 163 (1901), pp. 15–30. A slightly abridged version is printed in E. Troeltsch, *Gesammelte Schriften* (Tübingen, 1922–25, reprint Aalen, 1962–77), Vol. 4, pp. 739–52.
42 Max Weber, 'Die protestantische Ethik...I', AfSSP, vol. 20 (1904/05), p. 41, n. 1.
43 Relatively soon after the appearance of the *Social Teaching*, Troeltsch began work on a second enlarged edition; in addition, he published several pieces, which he expressly called supplements or extensions. Cf. especially *Augustin, die christliche Antike und das Mittelalter. Im Anschluss an die Schrift 'De Civitate Dei'* (Munich and Berlin, 1915).
44 Cf. especially, Troeltsch, *Gesammelte Schriften*, Vol. 1, pp. 950–1, n. 510.
45 Max Weber, 'Die protestantische Ethik...II', AfSSP, vol. 21 (1905), pp. 3–4, n. 3.
46 ibid.
47 E. Troeltsch, 'Wesen der Religionen und der Religionswissenschaft', in *Die christliche Religion mit Einschluss der israelitisch-jüdischen. (= Die Kultur der Gegenwart. Ihre Entwicklung und ihre Ziele. Herausgegeben von Paul Hinneberg. Teil I, Abteilung IV, II. Hälfte: Systematische christliche Theologie)* (Berlin and Leipzig, 1906), pp. 461–91.
48 Cf. Max Weber, 'Die protestantische Ethik...II', AfSSP, vol. 21 (1905), pp. 3–4, n. 3, pp. 5, 14, 31, 37–8.
49 Cf. Max Weber, 'Die protestantische Ethik...I', AfSSP, vol. 20 (1904/05), p. 52.
50 WL³, pp. 32–3.
51 E. Troeltsch, 'Moralisten, englische', in *Realencyklopädie für protestantische Theologie und Kirche*, Vol. 13, 3rd edn (Leipzig, 1903), pp. 436–61. Here quoted from the slightly modified reprint in Troeltsch, *Gesammelte Schriften*, Vol. 4, pp. 374–429 (here pp. 391–3).
52 Cf. Weber's speech on Jellinek; also Troeltsch's review, written at Camilla Jellinek's request, of the posthumous collection of his writings: 'Ausgewählte Schriften und Reden. Von Georg

Jellinek, Berlin 1911', *Zeitschrift für das Privat- und öffentliche Recht der Gegenwart*, vol. 39 (1912), pp. 273–8.

53   Max Weber, 'Die protestantische Ethik...II', AfSSP, vol. 21 (1905), p. 4, n. 3.
54   ibid., p. 14, n. 21.
55   E. Troeltsch, *Die Bedeutung des Protestantismus für die Entstehung der modernen Welt* (Munich, 1906), p. 1, n. 1.
56   RS, Vol. 1, p. 206, n. 1.
57   PE, Vol. 2, pp. 149–50. Although he objected to being treated by Rachfahl only as a part-owner of a 'joint scholarly firm', Troeltsch attached more importance than Weber to the 'team' (the word he used was 'Arbeitsgemeinschaft') of 'Heidelberg scholars who complement one another so successfully'. '... the personal exchange of ideas and the chance circumstance of personal propinquity has a certain importance which can be recognized in their writings themselves' (ibid., pp. 188–9).
58   ibid., p. 54. Cf. also pp. 151 and 345, and RS, Vol. 1, pp. 18, 206, n. 1.
59   Weber incorporated into his text in 1920 quotations adduced by Troeltsch in the Hinneberg chapter and the *Soziallehren*, which could be taken as confirmation of the first version of the *Protestant Ethic*. As to the changes in the content (the extent and importance of which is disputed by Weber scholars), it is important to understand in particular the new profile given to the difference between asceticism and mysticism as the result of a more precise formulation (*not* a correction) of Weber's original position; the new formulation was due to Troeltsch's influence. (A critical comparison between the two early versions and the late version of the essay on sects has still to be made.) For the role played by Troeltsch in the modifications that Weber made to his research programme on the sociology of religion, cf. the indications given in W. Schluchter, *Die Entwicklung des okzidentalen Rationalismus. Eine Analyse von Max Webers Gesellschaftsgeschichte* (Tübingen, 1979), pp. 216 ff., 232, 243–4, 249. The 'work programme of Troeltsch' (ibid., p. 216, n. 47), which has to be taken into account in reconstructing the history of Weber's work on the sociology of religion, was, however, much more comprehensive than Schluchter assumes.
60   From the copious footnotes in the *Soziallehren* we have testimony to Weber's continual involvement in the complicated development of the work over several years. Even while he was writing those parts of his text that first appeared in the *AfSSP*, Troeltsch was taking advice from Weber. After the *Archiv* publication, Weber informed Troeltsch of corrections and additions, which Troeltsch then used in the revision and enlargement of the first version.
61   This is how Weber described the *Soziallehren* in 1919/20. Cf. RS, Vol. 1, pp. 17–18, n. 1.
62   Quoted from Schluchter, *Die Entwicklung*, p. 123.
63   The Troeltsch bibliography, cited in n. 33 above, contains references to many texts often published in obscure places during the last years of Troeltsch's life. For Troeltsch's systematic criticism of Weber, we must not only consult his obituary in the *Deutsche Allgemeine Zeitung* (see n. 4 above), but also various texts assembled in Vol. 3 of the *Gesammelte Schriften*. In addition to the references to Weber given in the index to Vol. 3, see also ibid., pp. 43, 59, 123–4, 307, 313, 432, 706, 758–9.
64   Max Weber, 'Zur Lage der bürgerlichen Demokratie in Russland', GPS[3], pp. 63–4. This article met with Troeltsch's approval. Cf. his *Die Bedeutung des Protestantismus für die Entstehung der modernen Welt* (Munich, 1906), pp. 65–6, and the greatly expanded second edition (Munich and Berlin, 1911), pp. 102–3.
65   GPS[3], p. 333. Cf. also Mommsen, *Max Weber and German Politics*, pp. 16, 88, 162 ff.
66   FZ obituary; Troeltsch, *Gesammelte Schriften*, Vol. 3, p. 568. Cf. also W. J. Mommsen, 'The antinomian structure of Max Weber's political thought', in S. G. McNall (ed.), *Current Perspectives in Social Theory*, Vol. 4 (Greenwich, Conn., 1983), pp. 289–311.
67   GASS, p. 413.
68   In the recent debate about Troeltsch (which has produced over thirty monographs in the last decade!), proper attention has at last been paid to the central importance of his programmes on the philosophy of religion. Cf. G. W. Reitsema, *Ernst Troeltsch als godsdienstwigsgeer* (Assen, 1974); R. Morgan and M. Pye (eds), *Troeltsch and the Science of Religion: Writings on Theology and Religion* (London, 1977), pp. 234–52; K.-E. Apfelbacher, *Frömmigkeit und Wissenschaft. Ernst Troeltsch und sein theologisches Programm* (Munich, Paderborn and Vienna, 1978), especially pp. 129–60; G. Becker, *Neuzeitliche Subjektivität und Religiosität. Die religionsphilosophische Bedeutung von Herkunft und Wesen im Denken von Ernst Troeltsch* (Regensburg, 1982), esp. pp. 298–344.

69 Cf. W. E. Wyman jun., *The Concept of Glaubenslehre: Ernst Troeltsch and the Theological Heritage of Schleiermacher* (Chico, Calif., 1983).
70 Cf. F. W. Graf, 'Religion und Individualität. Bemerkungen zu einem Grundproblem der Religionstheorie Ernst Troeltschs', in Renz and Graf (eds) *Troeltsch-Studien*, Vol. 3, pp. 207–30.

16 Max Weber and Eduard Meyer

FRIEDRICH H. TENBRUCK

Eduard Meyer and Max Weber, younger by nine years, belonged to a generation that took their orientation from history and expected to find it within the historical sciences (*Geschichtswissenschaft*). Meyer gave expression to this need, one that was shared with Weber, when he acknowledged that the striving for a unified and historically anchored view of the world had been his innermost driving force in taking up his profession.[1] Having grown up in the same educational world, they both entered the academic profession of historian. However, while Eduard Meyer, carefully prepared by schooling as well as disposition, immediately turned to universal history,[2] causing a sensation at the age of twenty-nine with his *Geschichte des Altertums*, Max Weber began his studies with legal, economic and social history, and the universal historical direction of his work only revealed itself at the end of his life.

Real differences did exist between the two men in their personal qualities and, even more important, in their intellectual character, which informed the style and expression of their presentation. Where Weber, from logical disposition and legal training, was at ease with endless conceptual distinctions, then produced a staccato of impenetrable massed facts and then moved easily from deep insight to forceful depiction, Meyer's presentation is always an even flow that moves unhurriedly from question to answer and is content with the style and expression of educated prose. On matters of fact, Meyer's presentation is clear and pertinent, but his general statements rely upon the context rather than conceptual explanation, while at the same time maintaining a small number of basic ideas. It is worth noting that, when both men wish to say the same thing, their style and ways of thinking are so different that the contrast in expression is very apparent.

If the significance of Eduard Meyer for Max Weber is to be considered, this presupposes that Weber himself started as a historian. Certainly he did not opt for the narrower subject of history, but rather for political economy (*Nationalökonomie*) and the Historical School, to which he remained faithful despite later reservations.[3] He stood not only within the tradition and concerns of German political economy but also in the midst of all those sciences whose joint concern was to know the historical reality of man. These were the disciplines of 'history' against which Windelband in his famous Rector's Address of 1894 had counterposed 'natural sciences'.[4] Correspondingly, his *Wissenschaftslehre* (Methodology) gathers together the historical disciplines, which represent a specific type of science — namely, the science of concrete reality (*Wirklichkeitswissenschaften*) — under the generic name of 'history'. This 'History' (*Historie*) — as we shall call it from now on — considers reality in its individual and therefore historical quality in terms of the causal relation between actual causes and effects.[5]

Weber's sociology develops from the historical work carried on in the ensemble of the historical sciences. It was this that made sociology feasible; it owed its advance to the positions and concerns of history, in all its breadth, as well as to the historians of the time. Eduard Meyer is only one of many historians who had a significant part in Weber's development.

This assertion, of course, runs counter to current views. In the literature on Max Weber, Eduard Meyer, if he appears at all, does so only as a scholar who is dismissed with polemical sharpness in the *Wissenschaftslehre*. The reasons for this we shall come to later. In general, however, we are told nothing of the essential influence of the historians on Weber's development; for various reasons, this is completely ruled out and the reasons for this have to be considered next.

Max Weber as a Historian

Anyone who seriously approaches the work of Max Weber is presented with the question of how Weber, who started out as a historian, could become a sociologist, as he tentatively called himself at a later stage of his career. This is no mere antiquarian interest, for the answer gives us the solution to the puzzle regarding what Weber intended by his sociology, and this obviously is not to be obtained directly from *Economy and Society*.

It is regrettable that the meaning of Weber's sociology has been defined by an immanent interpretation of his later work. This procedure was a reflection of the notion that, because the work of his own time was incommensurable with Weber's own achievement, the sociology had therefore to be understood in its own terms. Thus, the genesis of the sociology appeared as uninteresting. Even when those who were knowledgeable traced its origins back to the early writings, their conclusions were barely noted by the discipline.[6] Attempts to uncover the substantive origins of sociology in the sciences of the day have been totally absent – at least in respect to History, if by History we mean following the *Wissenschaftslehre*, a type of science that can comprise the most varied disciplines. Reference is frequently made to the position of the scientific disciplines within which Weber was placed, but it is the methodological controversies that attract attention and not the existing substantive questions. In the former, Weber seems to distance himself from the historical sciences with his critique of 'intuitionism'.

However, quiet reflection would have indicated that Max Weber's work could have originated only on the basis of highly developed historical scholarship. An empirically based sociology with universal historical perspectives obviously presupposes that historical research has reached out beyond the collection and description of particular processes and has been able to order the mass of material according to comprehensive viewpoints. Even Max Weber could not have imagined the goal of his sociology – much less reached it – had not History given him the necessary foundations. Historical research already had to have reached a level where abstraction and comparison would yield firm concepts and theories, capable of assessing in universal historical terms the basic configurations of the orders and powers of society. The basic level of *Economy and Society* consists of themes that had already been posed by History. Max Weber did not need – and indeed could not collect – one by one the facts with which *Economy and Society* overwhelms us; he found them already available, admittedly subject to debate, structured by concepts and theories. So, at the basic level, we continually encounter the themes and theories that are already prepared by History. In relation to the themes *Economy and Society* is concerned with, these debates had for the most part already become focal points of historical research. At this basic level, the work is an attempt to decide between the competing theories of the historians by means of the examination of facts and the critique of concepts.

As long as we remain unaware of the themes, theses and theories of the historical disciplines of the time that are arrayed in *Economy and Society*, it is not possible to grasp Weber's particular achievement. Only when we know which traditions, facts, concepts and theories have gone into *Economy and Society* are we able to gauge Weber's contribution and intention. If today, in spite of the significant progress that research has made, especially in the last decades, in regard to extensive sections we still stand 'prior to the systematic reconstruction of Weberian sociology',[7] this relates above all to the fact that we lack a 'historical' reconstruction of the work and that we do not know where Weber's original systematization begins. Given the condition of the *oeuvre* and the increasing lack of knowledge of History as it existed at that time, it may well be the case that this 'historical' reconstruction has already become practically unattainable. Even if this is the case, it still remains our duty to try, and it is to our credit to at least point out that a systematic reconstruction can no longer be validly achieved.

This now allows us to define with greater precision the point at which Weber's work stemmed from History. It occurred at the point where historical research, because of its continuous progress, was confronted with new sorts of problems, which it was not able to surmount with its own traditional means. Descriptive history-writing was faced with the problem of absorbing increasing amounts of historical data in a way that would lead to history being broken up into fragmented images. This problem became plain with the entrance of the 'modern' disciplines alongside the traditional history, the latter being oriented mostly towards political events and figures. The modern disciplines of economic, legal, constitutional, administrative, social, cultural and religious history began to establish themselves in a way that, even without intending to, undermined in practice the claims of the older history-writing to be the valid description of history ('as it really was'). Indeed, in the end, they fed the doubt as to whether it was at all possible to understand historical reality in all its fullness in a scientific way. Weber grew up in these new, neighbouring disciplines and hence could not avoid the problematization of historical knowledge and the specialization of research that had become clearly evident.

This was the case, above all, in social and economic history, i.e. in Weber's own disciplines. Here the formless mass of data did not permit an ordering by the traditional methods because what was at issue was a concern with overall conditions (*Zustände*) as opposed to actions.[8] Procedures were therefore developed that worked with 'evolutionary stages' or even 'evolutionary laws', to bring order to the disparate plurality of individual facts. It is sufficient to recall Friedrich List, Karl Rodbertus, Wilhelm Roscher or Karl Bücher, not to mention Karl Marx, who thought they could construct very different sequences from the same facts; this finally led to the controversy about what justification, if any, there was for constructing such ideas as 'evolutionary stages' and 'evolutionary laws'.

So Max Weber found himself personally tied into the problem of concept construction. Also the Historical School of political economy, from which by his own testimony he originated, had worked with 'economic stages'; indeed the Historical School hoped as the culmination of its work to uncover the 'laws' of economic action and of economic evolution. Max Weber had himself gone in this direction in his *Römische Agrargeschichte*, which he later counted as one of the 'sins of his youth'.[9] And it was above all professional historians, namely Eduard Meyer and Georg von Below, who with their decisive critique of Karl Bücher's '*oikos*-theory' of the ancient economy revealed the questionability of all stage theories and thereby woke Weber (one might say) 'from his dogmatic slumbers'. Weber, as an economist, was then confronted with the practical questions of concept construction, the relation of theory to history and the 'objectivity of social scientific knowledge'.[10]

Similar questions concerning the construction of concepts surfaced in the remaining 'neighbouring disciplines', indeed even in the mother discipline, which with the increasing penetration of its burgeoning data moved beyond the depiction of historical series of events. This allowed the orders and powers that stood behind the historical figures and events to come into view. The diversity of the findings now demanded concepts, in order to make possible a material definition and historical identification of constructs such as 'city', 'feudalism', 'patrimonialism', 'church', 'state', '*polis*', '*Genossenschaft*', 'estate', 'class', and so on. Consequently, the writing of history reached a new level, where by means of analogy and comparison, and by means of abstraction and generalization, it pressed forward to definite concepts; it also considered regularities and started to deploy theories. Thus traditional history-writing was not only challenged by the increasing independence of the neighbouring disciplines, but found itself confronted with its own problems.

The essays that were later collected in the *Wissenschaftslehre* are evidence of the successive efforts by Weber to cope with this situation. Although they benefit from his talent and penchant for 'logical' disquisition, they grew from the demands of the questions with which he was faced in his own work. When he speaks of the 'uncertainty' that 'unambiguously is the case at present as regards history',[11] this also applied to Weber himself, as the 'sins of his youth' testify. His methodological works grew from within the practical problems of research and were not externally imposed upon research. It was not the great methodological controversies of his time, or even the demand inspired by positivism to raise history to the level of a science, that led Weber to inquire into the logical basis of his work; it was rather the open question of constructing concepts for practical purposes that lay behind Weber's interest in methodological debates: 'methodology can only bring us reflective understanding of the means which have demonstrated their value in practice'[12] – here Weber is in agreement with Eduard Meyer.[13] Therefore, the essays of the *Wissenschaftslehre* were attempts to solve problems that had arisen within and between the historical disciplines. All the interpretations of Weber that latch on to the general methodological problems instead of proceeding from the real requirements of historical research, to which Weber's work is everywhere oriented, are therefore insufficient.

In his essays on methodology, Max Weber appears first of all as a historian among historians. When he refers to 'historians', he has the image of a 'logical type of science'[14] in which he includes not only historians in the narrow sense of the word, the professional historians, but also the historians of the neighbouring specialist disciplines,[15] and so naturally also the 'historians of our subject', those of *Nationalökonomie*.[16] The description varies according to the context: the 'descriptive', the 'political'[17] or even the 'modern' historian[18] are referred to, and these divisions cannot be completely subsumed under the established disciplines. The changing usage reflects the complicated situation within historical scholarship. However, we must first establish: 'when "history and its related sciences" are referred to it remains wholly unsettled what those sciences are. Where the word "history" by itself is used, it is always meant in its widest sense [including political, cultural, and social history]'.[19]

The *Wissenschaftslehre* begins with the defence of the historical disciplines, which face 'common problems'[20] because the change in cultural interests ('the light of the great cultural problems moves on')[21] presents them with new concerns: 'Since the "viewpoints" that are oriented towards "values", from which they become "objects" of historical research, change, and because and in so far as this is so, new "facts" and in a new way will always become historically "essential"'.[22] Under the impact of social and economic changes, History came face to face with the new problems of economic and social history for which it had to find solutions through the further refinement of its conceptual apparatus. Its own progress, in widening its field of research, threatened to burst through the existing conceptual apparatus that was no longer able to organize the diversity of facts.

Weber interpreted this problem not as a crisis or as a failure but rather as normal for the progress of the historical sciences: 'The intellectual apparatus which the past has developed through the analysis, or more truthfully, the analytical rearrangement of the immediately given reality, and through the latter's integration by concepts which correspond to the state of its knowledge and the focus of its interest, is in constant tension with the new knowledge which we can and desire to wrest from reality. The progress of cultural science occurs through this conflict. Its result is the perpetual reconstruction of those concepts through which we seek to comprehend reality. The history of the sciences of social life is and remains, therefore, a continual interaction between the attempt to order reality analytically through the construction of concepts – the dissolution of these analytical constructs through the expansion and shift of the scientific horizon – and the reformulation anew of concepts on the foundations thus transformed.'[23]

It was in such a process of transformation of its conceptual apparatus that Weber found History and even himself placed. He never doubted the ability of history to meet this challenge through substantive work. When the light of cultural problems has moved on, then science equips itself to follow it. His problem is rather that 'as a result of considerable shifts in the "viewpoint"... the idea emerges that the new "viewpoint" also requires a revision of the logical forms in which the "enterprise" has heretofore operated and when, accordingly, uncertainty about the "nature" of one's own work arises'.[24] He feared that the practical concerns of history would be weighed down by the methodological quarrels over its nature. Therefore, Weber inspected the demands for revision, first of all in the essays on Roscher and Knies; he found that the leading figures of the Historical School were incapable of mounting a coherent defence of History, which he himself now took in hand. On the one hand, invoking our need to understand concrete reality, he refutes the positivistic transformation of history into a science of laws (*Gesetzeswissenschaft*). On the other hand, he opposed 'subjectivizing theories'[25] arguing that assertions were unprovable without causal explanation.

The task of history, according to Weber, has always been causal explanation, and so it should always remain. Although it must sometimes further develop its concepts in the light of new problems in its subject matter, this does not necessitate a revision of its logical form. Because it is already a causal method, it does not need to raise itself to a higher level. It is only at first sight that history appears to be an unstructured collection and description that does not provide any valid knowledge. In fact, its explanation uses concepts and knowledge about the regularities of social life, and without these no causal attribution would be possible. As is well known, Weber specified the particular character of historical concepts and knowledge of regularities — namely as ideal-typical. Equally he worked out the role of *Verstehen* and, what is usually overlooked, the role of the 'analysis of values' (*Deutung*) as a guide for this other 'historical', i.e. causal, form of interpretation, which cannot be entered into here.[26] It is clear that the *Wissenschaftslehre* represents a defence and legitimation of History.

This concern of the *Wissenschaftslehre* has time and again been interpreted as a general indictment of the historian, against which Weber's indebtedness to history must appear as absurd. This interpretation only picked up Weber's occasional complaint about the historians' aversion to concepts and misunderstood its sense and application. It overlooked that Weber carefully limited his disapproval: 'The major error into which several, but not all, historians fall is that the complexity and fluidity of historical phenomena do not permit the use of definite and precise concepts.'[27] Weber's critique of the apparent 'concept-less' *praxis* of the historian is also misunderstood. Weber had clearly protested against the opinion 'that history is a discipline which devotes itself exclusively to the collection of material, or if not that, is a purely descriptive discipline'. He promised to show 'how little truth lay in the naive but widespread opinion that history is the "mere" description of a pre-existent reality or the simple reproduction of "facts" '.[28] He directed his objections not at the work of the historian but at the naive presentation of the logical nature of his work: 'It is indeed unfortunate, especially in the *manner* in which the professional historians have sought to justify history in the "disciplinary" sense of the word, that they have contributed not a little to the strengthening of the prejudice that historical work is something substantively other than "scientific" work, that "concepts" and "rules" "don't have anything to do with" history.'[29] Only a wholly un-Weberian understanding of science could interpret this as a critique of historical work and as a general desire to methodologically enlighten the historians. Rather, Weber advised the historians to put methodological questions 'simply to one side and to be satisfied with the gaining of "valuable" knowledge through practical work',[30] to which, as Eduard Meyer knew, methodological enlightenment could contribute almost nothing.[31]

Finally, it is an erroneous view that Weber was aiming at political history and professional history itself, and it is therefore mistaken to attack political history in Weber's name. For this fails to recognize that Weber dealt with the entirety of the historical sciences, within which he distinguished between the 'typical' problems, achievements and possibilities of the various disciplines, with particular regard to the relation of his own special subjects to the mother discipline. Corresponding to the change in problem, there occurs a change in the kind of nomological knowledge required. Political history, in particular, is scarcely in need of explicit formulation, because it deals with the action of individuals and groups; when we know the circumstances, those actions are for the most part comprehensible in terms of the rules of everyday experience.[32] If one wanted 'to decorate the historical (or economic) description with references to laws wherever possible', this would be a 'sort of naturalistic vanity'.[33] In order to grasp the significance of events, the historian unavoidably works with ideal types, such as individualism, feudalism or capitalism, but he can be excused for not formulating them explicitly. 'In a great many cases, particularly in the field of descriptive political history, their ambiguity has not been prejudicial to the clarity of the presentation. It is sufficient that in each case the reader should feel what the historian had in mind.'[34]

So the professional historian is given considerable leeway, indeed is expected, to speak 'the language of life'.[35] Yet, in modern History, new problems emerge that demand clear concepts and rules. Weber demonstrates this in the modern disciplines. Here, he thinks first of all of his own subject: 'In general we are not in the favourable position of the political historian, for whom the cultural contents to which his description relates are normally unambiguous – or appear to be.'[36] Yet it is the same for the other modern historical disciplines. Therefore the 'Critique' of Eduard Meyer in the *Wissenschaftslehre* exceeds its primary purpose. It starts as a technical explanation of the general uniqueness of history (as well as of political economy)[37] as distinct from natural science, and then separates from History 'the disciplines that seek the "rules" and "laws" of social life'.[38] But History as a whole is dependent upon 'concepts' and 'rules' in so far as it takes on modern questions; so, in practical application, this cuts across all its disciplines. Therefore, Weber disassociated himself from that wing of the Historical School in his own subject area which – exactly as did the 'theoretical' school – misunderstood the ideal-typical character of rules; this led to a false presumption about the final nature of laws and, therefore, the too hasty rejection of the need for concepts and rules. Weber directed his charge of aversion to concepts not only against the less extensive history (i.e. standard history) but more so against the Historical School of political economy. It was not primarily from the modern historical disciplines but from the older tradition that he obtained support: for instance, from Eduard Meyer and Georg von Below, who posed the modern questions about the economy, society and the state, and in doing so demanded clear concepts. Georg von

Below, in particular, unceasingly criticized the Historical School's aversion to concepts and thereby contributed to Max Weber's position in the *Wissenschaftslehre*, which he welcomed immediately and unreservedly.[39]

This must suffice to establish that it was not only the late sociological work but also the *Wissenschaftslehre* which grew out of the difficulties that History was undergoing at the time. Max Weber represented political economy and was stamped by the tradition of its Historical School, and this in no way should be belittled or misunderstood; the proof of its 'anthropological' position has been furnished by Wilhelm Hennis. However, we have to reckon with the further fact that political economy, and Max Weber with it, belonged to the larger and living context of History (or equally the cultural sciences) and especially shared its interest in the 'anthropological'. This context determined the traditions, facts and questions of all the historical disciplines. Weber's work, both with regard to the facts as well as in defining the problems, takes its bearings from the whole field of History. His work grew out of the concerns that History was facing at the time.

If interpretation of Weber's work has scarcely taken account of this fact, it is because (leaving aside the blind-spots of immanent interpretation) we have lost sight of the state of knowledge from which Weber's sociology developed. At best, there are now specialists who deal only with the individual parts of the overall picture of the time. Furthermore, the interpretation is undertaken by philosophers, methodologists and sociologists, who hardly know anything of the real position and problems of History any more.[40] This is even more the case abroad: in England, the state of knowledge in Weber's time is scarcely known; in America, where the history of science (and, in particular, sociology) is written, it is completely unknown.[41] In Germany, the history of these sciences is totally forgotten, so that already an erroneous picture of History at that time has entered circulation, one that excludes the influence of the historians on Weber's evolution as a sociologist.

In this way, the myth originated that the historical sciences in Germany were politically reactionary and intellectually had lagged far behind, on account of the fact that they had produced the cult of the unique and concept-less 'intuitionism', which only allowed space for the deeds of great men, ignored the role of institutions, completely left out the masses and mass phenomena, and took no interest at all in 'regularities', 'the law-like', and 'theory'. This myth is usually completed with the observation that the historians – with the exception of Otto Hintze – had impeded and had meant to impede scientific progress, especially that of sociology.

The propagation of this caricature, while being amended slightly, is still the one currently circulating. It derives from the indictment of the political beliefs of the historians, who have to put up with the examination of their democratic credentials. Where these appear to be acceptable, this involves the individual theses, theories and subjects being torn out of the context of overall History and being held to stand for some particular direction within political history, while the extensive field of 'modern' (to use Weber's term) historians does not appear to exist at all. Against this, it has to be decisively established that the German historians were most emphatically in the vanguard of the progress of knowledge, both in relation to social and economic phenomena and in the field of theoretical reflection. A knowledge of the scientific situation at that time shows the current accusations to be a nonsensical myth. Instead, it is correct to say that History, especially in Germany, was marching forward on a broad front – by moving into new areas and perspectives, through the development of new disciplines with new concepts and theories and by the employment of new methods.

Certainly, Weber was convinced of this. It was not the *Wissenschaftslehre* alone that evinced an unshakeable belief in the progress of historical knowledge through substantive work. In spite of the insight that all sciences (as also today) work with the conceptual apparatus of their time and therefore (as today) consider the preparation of their subject matter as an 'end in itself',[42] Weber was strongly influenced by the turbulent progress of History. As often as he emphasized the serious challenge posed by new questions[43] and, therefore, did not restrain criticisms, so he did not for a moment doubt the new course of History. It is because the light of great cultural problems moves on that science equips itself 'to change its standpoint and analytic apparatus'.[44] And when science pursues those stars 'which alone can impart significance and direction to its labour',[45] it is therefore obvious that it is not Max Weber alone who has opened up new channels.

Max Weber's work has evolved from the position outlined above; it develops from the concerns of History, and as a solution to these concerns. So the foundation of the *Wissenschaftslehre* originated from the problems of historical research, and the basic level of *Economy and Society* from its findings. In this respect, Weber's sociology has been the consistent continuation of developments that were already in train within History. And, therefore, we have to look to the historians in order to find the models, the forerunners and the colleagues, without whom Weber's sociology could not have emerged. When we proceed from the more normal methods – immanent interpretation and the popular 'theory comparison' – very many things will appear differently. However, we can only learn what Weber really intended by his sociology if we follow the procedure outlined above.

The Critique of Eduard Meyer

Of all the essays in the *Wissenschaftslehre*, the 'Critique of Eduard Meyer' has rated the least. The meaning of this text is mistaken if we adjudge it to be an *opusculum* in which Weber gave free rein to his polemic. From this, the erroneous view has sprung up – and this is all that will be considered here – that Eduard Meyer was merely an object of criticism for Max Weber.

Max Weber not only followed in detail the path-breaking *Geschichte des Altertums*, above all for the richness of its knowledge, but also, despite individual criticisms, admired it. The 'Critique' is written against the backdrop of an extraordinarily high estimation of Meyer's work. Weber regarded Meyer as 'one of our most eminent historians', an outstanding scholar, terming him a historian of the first rank, and counted himself an 'admirer of this great work'.[46] In his personal reminiscences, Paul Honigsheim confirms these estimations – as 'brilliant', 'convincing' and 'commendable'. He states: 'the methodology book seemed to him to be important enough to be the focus of a separate article. . . Also Weber said, at least in my presence, nothing at all about Eduard Meyer's methodology. Whereas he had unreserved admiration for Meyer's scholarship of ancient and, not least, oriental history, even if he did criticize him in particulars.'[47]

The admiration corresponded to the extraordinary significance that Meyer's writings occupied in Weber's own work. We have already mentioned the contribution that Meyer's critique of K. Bücher had played in the formation of Weber's fundamental methodological self-definition. Weber later expressly confirmed that Meyer's historical work had already been the impulse for the ideal-typical construction of concepts: 'It is as well to acknowledge that the progress of the historians (Ed. Meyer and his students), which has been correct, *especially* in regard to the dispute with K. Bücher and others, and has been achieved (fortunately) by taking up the tools of the economic theorists whom they once despised, and so have obtained clear concepts.'[48] In no way did History descend into concept-less intuitionism; Eduard Meyer had already clearly practised the methods, which Weber first made explicit in the *Wissenschaftslehre*.

Another factor is surely much more important. There are in Weber's own works – above all in the *Agrarverhältnisse im Altertum* (The Agrarian System in Antiquity), 'The Economic Ethic of World Religions', and also in *Economy and Society* – not only countless historical and ethnological 'facts' that derived from Meyer, but also the 'theories' by which Meyer (and other historians) had focused their view of history by means of ideal-typical application. These 'theories' of the 'modern' historians form the foundation for the themes, and often the theses, that Max Weber employed, used for comparison, criticized and advanced in *Economy and Society*.

Finally, and this can only be dealt with summarily here, Eduard Meyer's work on the early peoples and cultures of the Orient, his studies on Judaism and Christianity, also on the Mormons and Islam, as well as his comments on the 'civilizational arena (*Kulturkreis*) of the Indo-Chinese' helped to continuously expand the universal historical interests of Max Weber, which were initially concentrated on Europe. Meyer should be seen as providing the model for Weber's implementation of world historical comparison on the firm grounds of historical facts in combination with the setting of actual problems in ideal-typical terms for the purpose of gaining knowledge of universal significance and validity. It was through his acquaintanceship with Meyer's work that Weber came to maturity.

Nowhere does the 'Critique' diminish the rank and significance of Eduard Meyer the historian; only his methodological statements are criticized. Although Weber does not seem to be uninhibited in his comments – 'surprising', 'questionable', 'unclear', 'insufficient', and 'contradictory', everywhere these expressions are immediately qualified: one gets the 'impression', one is led 'to surmise' or so it 'appears' as though Meyer is caught up in contradictions or allows himself to be drawn into inconsistencies. Consequently, it must always be borne in mind that Meyer 'in the main things is correct',[49] 'has come quite close many times to the logically correct formulation', and in general 'the usual kernel of truth is contained in the views which are here criticized', which 'is indeed is to be expected of a historian of such distinction who discusses his own procedure'.[50] So the methodological critique deals predominantly with questions of formulation, which in the end led Weber to an embarrassed admission that the effort was in no way proportional to the outcome.[51]

Yet Weber's criticism is explained not solely by his impatience with the insufficiency of Meyer's formulations. As still remains to be shown, there is much at issue in the 'Critique'. The footnote at the end makes clear that the 'Critique' should defend history against the generalization that every science should search after laws. In addition, Max Weber wishes to make especially clear what connects 'the disciplines that search out the "rules" and "laws" of social life' with the disciplines of History (in the less extensive sense), and also what might separate them both.[52] It should now be clear that the particular significance of the 'Critique' merely confirms the importance of Eduard Meyer for Max Weber.[53]

Eduard Meyer's 'Anthropology'

We must now turn to Eduard Meyer's *Geschichte des Altertums*, published in 1884 (Vol. 1), which was immediately recognized as a scientific, indeed cultural achievement of the first rank. It expanded the intellectual horizon of history by being the first to provide a unitary context to perceive classical civilization alongside oriental civilizations. If the work already attracted interest because of its universal historical outlook, it also adopted a 'more open and comprehensive standpoint'. Consequently, its conclusions stood in opposition to the basic assumptions that predominated not only in historical but also in ethnological research. This research took tribe and people (often termed society) to be valid 'as the primary unit, as the pre-given original elements and as something unchangeable with which it could operate and which further development has to follow'.[54] Eduard Meyer was forced to break with this model, because he placed tribes, peoples and cultures in their historical contexts and realized that 'All peoples and certainly all nationalities of our cultural world are the products of a complicated process of development that is influenced by the most various historical individual events'.[55] By doing this, he opened up new avenues for sociological and historical study, because he took the process of socialization into groups as his starting point, and inquired into the creation and demise of these different orders. Thus he discovered that the political and cultural influences of associations on one another originated from the civilizational arena, within which the real 'flow of historical life' occurred.[56] In this the 'universal religions' with 'their claim to be world religions'[57] have played a decisive part, so that Eduard Meyer could write: 'However,... these civilizational arenas – the Oriental and the Hellenic in Antiquity (that then becomes the Graeco-Roman) and the Christian and Islamic in the Middle and Modern Ages – are so intertwined in their development...that only an overall consideration that holds each in equal regard allows the full understanding of their history. The third great civilizational arena, the east-Asian (Indo-Chinese)...'[58]

It is clear that with his *Geschichte des Altertums* Eduard Meyer developed new tendencies which, although occurring in History, took on a new emphasis and form in his work. It is difficult to grasp how his 'more open and comprehensive standpoint' influenced historical thinking in Germany and how its concerns opened up new directions and problems. In any case, parts of the late works of Max Weber read as though they only could have been written on the canvas of universal history that Eduard Meyer had prepared.

How single-mindedly Eduard Meyer broke with tradition in his *Geschichte des Altertums* is particularly indicated by the 'Introduction', which he had provided in advance for the first edition of the work.[59] There, in the first ten paragraphs covering only fifteen pages, he set out the 'Elements of Anthropology', by which he meant 'that science of the evolution of man', which at that time pulled together the anthropological theory of evolution, the comparative specialisms, the developmental constructions of ethnology and the other theories of progress. In spite of its widespread popularity, in political history (at least) it stood accused of inadmissible generalization, as the Introduction makes clear: 'whereas beforehand the interests of the historians were completely opposed to these questions, and in some opinions they had caused astonishment and censure'.[60] And then, in the second edition in 1907, Eduard Meyer continues, 'at present where these questions are the order of the day, a justification will no longer be necessary',[61] which makes it clear how historical interests had changed so totally in the meantime.

Meyer's 'Introduction' had also changed fundamentally and, excluding the statements on methods, had swollen in size from 15 to 183 pages; it appeared as a volume in its own right. In place of the barely considered outline, there now appeared, after the main work had been completed, a view of the total findings;[62] Eduard Meyer was not afraid to dismiss his earlier remarks[63] and to rescue them from the shadows of evolutionary laws. The anthropology had now moved from being a 'science of the evolution of man' to a 'theory of general forms of human life and human development'.[64]

In fact, in 1884 Eduard Meyer had already deliberated on whether he should call his introduction 'sociology'; while accepting that it had similar concerns,[65] he regretted that anthropology often appeared 'under the label of sociology'.[66] He rejected this appellation for himself, since sociology would make the 'state' (which was, for Meyer, all those associations with the power to establish right) into a mere appurtenance of society. So we ought to define the 'Introduction' as the sort of sociology that Eduard Meyer had gained from the study of the history of the Oriental–Hellenic–Roman civilizational arena, which included such comparative references to other ethnographic and historical material as was necessary for a unified presentation. 'The Introduction in no ways owes its existence to its interest in these problems alone', acknowledged Eduard Meyer, 'but rather to the indispensable need for a scientific and intellectually unified history of Antiquity. This question faces every historian in all specialist fields; the historian should at all times describe the origins of individual peoples and cultures and to do this he is totally incapacitated if he does not consider these problems as a whole and does not confront them with a logically thought out position.'[67]

Weber could have described his position in a similar manner, had he gone further in his consideration of the economy of peoples and eras and sought out the 'principal questions'. Still more noticeable is the basic agreement between the even closer statements by Weber and Meyer on the meaning and purpose of this 'Anthropology'. Obviously the starting point is the same: History concerns itself with the interpretation of the actions of man or, more precisely, with the description of the external course and internal relation between events and developments in their concrete uniqueness. It can never reproduce reality, but must select viewpoints in terms of significance,[68] which it defines according to historical effectiveness as well as intrinsic value – here Meyer had taken on board Weber's criticism[69] – and according to points of view that are significant in the present. While anthropology derived its facts from history, ethnology and other comparative sciences in order to obtain general statements and to illustrate these,[70] History conversely required a nomological knowledge, taken from the sciences, in order to explain historical events in their particularity.[71] For History, all law-like statements are only presuppositions and givens, which are used as means for the comprehension and description of individual occurrences.[72] History requires 'the aid of abstract constructions' as a means of knowledge, which do not in themselves possess any reality;[73] even if it must proceed empirically throughout, 'it can thereby as little do without hypotheses and final conclusions as any other science' and works, therefore, with analogies and parallels.[74] And, in regard to the construction of 'stages of economic development' and its relation to 'determinate political frameworks', we read, 'Historical knowledge contains none of these statements; *historically* they are nothing other than empty concepts. Historical knowledge always obtains its concepts from the fullness and diversity that attaches to the individual historical occurrence. Concepts may indeed serve as guiding threads in the getting and organization of facts, and very often provides a high degree of probability for the surmise that something is, or has been, or will come about: there is always a need for conjecture in order for the rules of experience within the historical facts to be sufficiently recognized.'[75]

In practical terms, the standpoint represented here is unmistakably the same as Max Weber's in the *Wissenschaftslehre*. Undoubtedly Max Weber would have expressed himself differently, and would have objected to the more irregular and inconsistent of Eduard Meyer's formulations. Moreover, Eduard Meyer had held firm to a few conceptions: those in the first edition of the Introduction of 1884 as well as in the *Theorie und Methodik der Geschichte* of 1902 had already been criticized by Max Weber in his 'Critique of Eduard Meyer'. However, the criticisms concerned matters of formulation, which were often insufficient for the sense and meaning of Meyer's own purpose – as Max Weber himself recognized and which Meyer extensively clarified in the second edition of the above-named work. We also have to reckon that the second edition of the 'Anthropology' of 1907 could and had been influenced by Weber's 'Objectivity' essay of 1904 as well as by his 'Critique of Eduard Meyer' of 1906. Even so, we have to acknowledge that Eduard Meyer in 1884 – however unaided and however ill-defined – had aimed at a fundamental understanding of historical knowledge, which Weber was to present fully developed in the 'Objectivity' essay twenty years later. Only in this way is Meyer's statement of 1902 explicable, and here we have to bear in mind it occurs a year before Max Weber's wish to try out the utility of Rickert's ideas.[76] Eduard Meyer, looking back at his old Introduction, whose youthful sins in relation to historical laws he now corrected, wrote, 'Anyway it is a great pleasure for me that recently H. Rickert has presented the thoroughly re-

searched point of view whose conclusion, while vigorously contesting the existence of historical laws, agrees nearly completely with the remainder of the
substance of my statements at that time'.[77] It is not meant by this that Eduard
Meyer's 'Introduction' had lit the way for the methodical clarification of the
particularity of history, whose solution could now be realized in the
Wissenschaftslehre. However, we should emphasize that Meyer had taken a
methodological position in the same sense as the *Wissenschaftslehre* – for this
is the important point – and in this way had prepared the ground. This is as
far as we can go with the question of methods that so aroused Weber's interest
in the 1902 text.

The real revolutionary importance of the 'Introduction' lay elsewhere. It actually had been revolutionary that, in 1884, a historian should demand that an
'anthropology' or 'sociology' be an indispensable complement and aid for
history and that he had developed the first outline. The full significance of this
can only be seen when, twenty-three years later, Eduard Meyer began to draw
up the 'anthropological' summary of his work.

The complaint is always heard that the door to sociology was kept closed,
casting Simmel, Tönnies and Weber as exceptions, and that the historians in
particular, excepting Otto Hintze, were blind to sociological questions and had
nothing to contribute. This indestructible myth could only have originated by
placing greater value on the theoretical positions, academic niceties and
general outlooks than on the substantive research. There can be no doubt that
substantive sociological questions were handled thoroughly and broadly in
German political economy, social science and also History. Max Weber's
sociology could not have developed from History if the corresponding work
had not been undertaken. As important as all this may have been for *Economy
and Society*, there was no work, even projected let alone started, that was
universal historical, empirically anchored in historical research, and operating
with a sociology that sought out the comparison of peoples and civilizations
according to ideal-typical rules of historical events that have a universal
significance and validity. If the project that Max Weber undertook with
Economy and Society had already been conceived of anywhere else, then this
was done by Eduard Meyer. If anything could have inspired Weber's project,
it was the completion of the later edition of the 'Anthropology'.

It is not my intention here to go through the contents of that book. It must
suffice to note that Eduard Meyer divided the contents analytically according
'to the two main headings of political and cultural history',[78] without thinking
of this as a real divide. Then follow the societal orders and powers, and the
interactive and conflicting process of formation and change of social,
economic and political evolution, on the one hand, and religious, intellectual
and cultural evolution, on the other.

The publication of the *Geschichte des Altertums* was closely followed by
Weber: 'each successive volume providing more interest for social history'.[79]
He had acquainted himself with the short 'Introduction' of 1884, referring to
it at significant points in his 'Critique of Eduard Meyer' in 1906,[80] though
admittedly only by way of 'logical' sallies. From Weber's side, we do not know
how he received the 'anthropological' (or 'sociological') presentations of
Meyer and whether he absorbed the factually so sparse and conceptually so
simple expressions that were so often disguised by contemporary jargon. In his

'Critique', Weber only noted that Meyer had in the meantime moved away from 'historical laws', owing to the influence of Rickert, but that the 'dubious formulation of the relations between the "general" and the "particular" '[81] as well the acceptance of the opposition between necessity and freedom had been retained. The second edition of the 'Introduction' added practically nothing new to these analytic, basic questions (that is, in relation to the position attained in the 1902 edition), so that Weber's reservations in the *Wissenschaftslehre* certainly remained. In the intervening period stood only an enlarged single-volume 'anthropological' (or 'sociological') exposition, which caused Weber to comment on his first impressions: 'it contains much that is very valuable, but also a number of general reflections which seem disputable'.[82] What was valuable lay in the 'concrete', in the orders and powers arrived at through a universal historical treatment, in the sociological types and rules of events, and in the systematic requirements of description.

So, better prepared, we come closer to the question whether the 'Anthropology' was significant for *Economy and Society* and we are now able to narrow down the possibilities. First, we need to note that the 'Introduction' to the second edition only appeared after the completion of the printing of *Agrarverhältnisse im Altertum*,[83] and thus was only able to have an influence on the 1913 essay, 'Some Categories of Interpretive Sociology', on the 'Economic Ethics of World Religions' and on *Economy and Society*. Since Weber's sociology had only found a definite form in *Economy and Society*, we will stay with this work. For several reasons, it is meaningless to compare the two works item by item; this is something that has to be given over to further research. Such a comparison, whatever it might turn up, will not lead to definitive results about the significance of Eduard Meyer's 'Anthropology' for Weber's sociology. In order to arrive at a provisional answer, we need a sure criterion for additional deliberations on the simple circumstances, thus enabling us to find out provisionally what distinguishes *Economy and Society* from all earlier works, including *Agrarverhältnisse im Altertum*. What, then, was specifically and characteristically new and was it perhaps already present in the essay on the 'Categories of Interpretive Sociology' or in the 'Economic Ethics of World Religions'? Or, conversely: what was completely absent from the earlier works? By means of this comparison we come to the question of how Max Weber, the historian, became the sociologist, and what was intended by this 'sociology'.

We should establish at this point that, in spite of the continuities in method and substance in parts of the three named works, which are explicitly called 'sociology' by Weber, there is nevertheless a jump that cannot simply be explained in terms of mere development. However much *Economy and Society* relates to the works that had led up to *Agrarverhältnisse im Altertum*, there is, nevertheless, little reason to extrapolate *Economy and Society* from this line of development. Weber must have got hold of something new. Whatever the reason, we cannot reliably know it, particularly because the interval from 1906 to 1914, which relates to his scientific development, remains very much in the dark — especially the move to 'sociology', of which we scarcely know more than the external circumstances (the foundation of the German Sociological Society).[84] At any rate, Marianne Weber's testimony could have made clear that *Economy and Society* was more than the strict continuation of preceding studies, that it was not simply a decision determined by Weber's personal situation to 'supplement the old *Verein* in the field of purely scholarly discussion' through the agency of the 'Sociological Society' (which corresponded to the interests of the younger generation of academics). The Society would exchange ideas not only with political economists but also 'with philosophers, theologians, jurists, theoretical ethnologists and so on' and would 'cope with the enormous cluster of problems purely scientifically and without an ethical–political emphasis'.[85] When he was active in the new Society, Weber obviously put forward the most varied proposals for collective work,[86] yet throughout this period he had no intention of creating his own 'sociology'. For the reasons why Weber made his decision and how he alighted upon his programme, we are dependent upon the riddle Marianne Weber presents us with in her important remark (probably referring to 1911 or 1912):

> For one of his birthdays, therefore, his life's companion wished him concentration on his own work to create enduring things: "Actually, all my wishes boil down to this blasphemous one: The devil take the Sociological Society for which you fritter yourself away on penny-ante stuff, for besides the nice conventions it will remain a machine that runs idle." To this Weber replied: "All right, then, you shall have your will to the extent that this is in my power, even though I don't know what great things this will produce. As it is, I now have to start all sorts of essays which are intended for the *Grundriß*. They will open up problems which may then lead to further things. But everything will go quite *slowly*, for the gestation period should really have been even longer. I am far from having absorbed all the new things and have not yet made them my own.[87]

All attempts to explain the origin of *Economy and Society* will have to be measured against this yardstick, even if this cannot be carried out exactly. Accordingly, what is it that appears as unexpectedly new in Max Weber's intellectual horizon, enabling him to develop the programme of *Economy and Society*? For the first time, he reached a level of knowledge that superseded his previous work and makes this work so distinctive. Leaving aside the indeterminate areas, there are three new, basic characteristics of the late 'sociological' work and they are certainly integral to *Economy and Society*, namely: the systematic programme, the universal historical realization and, finally, the theory of charisma, to which we turn next.

Charisma

Unlike other concepts, the theory of charisma suddenly appears without any recognizable forerunners in the 'Economic Ethics of World Religions'. The only references in the literature are those of Rudolf Sohm and Karl Holl, which Weber himself had cited. We assume from this that Weber came across the concept and phenomenon of charisma in Sohm and Holl, and that his own theory was so pre-arranged that he only had to place the concept within it.

However, even if Weber discovered the concept in its general significance and, on the basis of his own knowledge, knew how to deploy it in other historical cases, this would hardly have led him to the supposition of the universal historical and revolutionizing force of charisma; to have done so, he would have been faced with the insoluble problem of going through and reinterpreting an infinite amount of unrelated and unprepared material on world history, in order to be able to announce his radical assertion. The other categories of Weberian sociology were only able to grow from the highly advanced historical scholarship, which for some length of time had gone beyond the collection of simple facts and the description of particular events and had taken up general problems and concepts. So, likewise, the theory of charisma presupposes that the historical and ethnological state of knowledge had prepared the ground for the appropriate viewpoint in its world historical aspect to such an extent that the uncovering of the revolutionary power of charisma (however else this was later added, clarified and systematized), if not spelt out by historical scholarship, certainly allowed its confirmation.

We have to exclude the possibility that Sohm and Holl had completed the necessary preparation, because their work is limited to a specific subject – early canon law and monasticism. According to Max Weber's own description, neither man had any inkling of the historical significance of charisma. No significance should be attached to the fact that Sohm in his description had foregone the term charisma, which Holl had made the central concept in his presentation in relation to the theological literature on the 'gift of grace'.[88] Hence they had got hold of a wholly limited phenomenon and had not realized its universal significance. This is the sense when Weber writes:

> The concept of 'charisma' ('gift of grace') is taken from the vocabulary of early Christianity. Rudolf Sohm, in his *Kirchenrecht*, was the first to clarify the substance of the concept for the Christian hierocracy, even though he did not use the same terminology. Others (for instance, Holl in *Enthusiasmus und Bußgewalt* [1898]) have clarified certain important consequences of it. It is thus nothing new.[89]

And, even more clearly, he says:

> It is to Rudolf Sohm's credit that he worked out the sociological character of this kind of power structure; however, since he developed this category with regard to one historically important case – the rise of the ecclesiastic authority of the early Christian church – his treatment was bound to be one-sided from the viewpoint of historical diversity. In principle these phenomena are universal, even though they are often most evident in the religious realm.[90]

Although the concept of charisma was sufficiently prepared and linked with specific phenomena, the failure to realize its universal historical significance was so complete that not once had it been inquired into.[91]

Accordingly, we need to ask – indeed *must* ask – how Max Weber came to the realization of the revolutionary power of charisma, when in his early writings there is not even a trace that charismatic phenomena exist at all, despite the fact there had been occasion to note them in the *Protestant Ethic*, within the 'Protestant Sects' and in the studies on the decline of the ancient world. The absence of charisma is not accidental; types of concerns and forms of presentation, which occupy all the early works, meant that this whole area is excluded.[92] Therefore, Weber had to create new fields of inquiry for the discovery of charisma as a world historical force, and these fields of inquiry ought to have been 'all the new things' which he was 'still far from having absorbed'. He had suddenly realized the significance of what had previously been an inaccessible field of inquiry and which he had not yet been able to integrate into his thinking. This is the significance of 'I have not yet made them my own'.

References in the studies on religion at this time do not give any further obvious help; yet it still remains uncertain whether Weber had undertaken these studies as a result of his awakened interest in charisma. Although these studies helped him to conceptualize and define charisma more precisely, by the same token they contributed little to the perception of charisma as a world historical force beyond religion. And the references to the obligation towards *Economy and Society* remain wholly inappropriate, yet at that time there still existed a general commitment for many contributions to the *Grundriß der Sozialökonomik*, but still no defined plan existed and this is fully confirmed by Marianne Weber. It is simply erroneous to suppose that *Economy and Society* could have developed as a consequence, and without break from, the early works, so that it only needed the request of the publishers for a new edition of Schönberg's *Handbuch der politischen Ökonomie* for *Economy and Society* to take its place as part of a series planned for the *Grundriß der Sozialökonomik*. And, conversely, the torso which we know by the name of *Economy and Society* could not have emerged in its fragmented form as a result of the decision to summarize and extend Weber's previous work. Rather, it came about because a new and unforeseen field of inquiry had come into being, the treatment of which led to the project of *Economy and Society*.

We should accept that Eduard Meyer's 'Anthropology' has played an important role here, because for many reasons Weber was actively engaged with the work – indeed, it must have become a challenge for him. Here, Max Weber came across a universal historical theory of general forms of human life and of human development that was empirically worked out and, therefore, a 'sociology' devised by a historian. In spite of the profound differences of expression and substance, we cannot read the work without noticing its kinship to *Economy and Society*; indeed, over extensive sections we can find themes and solutions jointly worked out, which anticipate what is characteristically new in *Economy and Society*. At any rate this is true for the second part of the 'Anthropology' which presents the 'spiritual evolution'. For there we find almost all the important concerns of Max Weber's sociology of religion in their characteristic interconnections prefigured in Meyer's statements on mythical thought, magic, belief in gods, ritual priesthood, the stages of religious evolution, the origin of ethical salvation religions, the distinction between priest and founder of religions, the separation of ethical and exemplary prophecy, the break up of the tribal community by the construction of the individual community on account of universal prophecies of salvation, and thus the determination of the origin and development of the various arenas of civilization. Obviously, some of these insights were already to be found elsewhere in scholarship; however, it was Eduard Meyer who first placed the fragmented state of discoveries on the basis of a universal historical intent and knowledge in its totality, which is known to us through Weber's sociology of religion.

The above relates to the central theory of the second part of the 'Anthropology': a revolutionary power which always breaks up the traditionalism into which life has become embedded and which, in its turn, finally hardens into tradition. This power, which can appear everywhere, only gains its world historical significance in connection with universal emissaries (*Botschafter*); by virtue of their attempts to bring about a unity of the psychic and ethical world, the progress of civilization results. In order to exemplify this, I have linked together various passages from Eduard Meyer that pursue the idea that, in the course of religious evolution, there originates the ethical postulate, which demands that the gods be ethical powers:

But all major and revolutionary movements do not come from the circles of the priesthood as such... They come rather from the individual personalities, who are seized by religious ideas... In all periods such inspired personalities appear..., who are so completely dominated by the seriousness and force of religious ideas that they embody in themselves those ideas and govern all their actions and words according to those ideas; they [become] path-breakers of a new religious idea and as such effect an internal transformation of traditional culture and its views... It is the singular conviction, the inner compulsion of certainty, that the individual personality carries and which has such a consequential effect. In such figures the subordination to an external authority is unthinkable; what they preach has the stamp of their own personality whose name and individuality adheres to their doctrine and is inseparable from their prophecy, since its truth is based on their own inner experience alone... Therefore its appearance is always revolutionary and its results create transformation, precipitous upheaval and [extend] far beyond the specifically religious sphere into all areas of human life, even while it might vehemently reject rather than pursue such a transformation... At no time can it establish itself without hard struggle with its opponents..., and the people, swayed by the opposing interests and persuasions, oscillate between the everyday and the traditional, on the one side and, on the other, the new idea to which the people can for a period commit themselves with enthusiasm...; this means that religious movements, which are individual and transformative in nature, still appear in the form of mass movements... Next to the indigenous cultic communities of the tribal followers appears, by virtue of voluntary association, the creation of an independent cult association that seeks to become not a community of people (*Volksgenossen*) but of human beings... The universality of religious forms comes to predominate, both in its striving to bring about the unity of the physical and ethical world as well as in its claim to be world religions. As always, when this idea is realized, it turns into its opposite... In place of free movement and the spontaneous religious perception, comes tradition, which is systematized anew and subjects all action and thought to a fixed rule... Out of this appears the power of custom, the very first idea from which man could not free himself... [93]

Evidently, then, the 'Anthropology' provided the rehearsal of the concerns for Weber's own sociology of religion, and the former prefigures the important themes, even making the same interconnections. Given that Weber's earlier work is marked by the absence of a serious attempt at universal historical comparison as well as a systematic sociology of religion, we have to consider whether the 'Anthropology' provided the impetus.[94] In any case, Meyer had established the basic ideas of Weber's sociology of religion: that religious evolution of a civilization is to be understood as a process of rationalization of the spirit. This is advanced by charismatically inspired intellectuals according to the requirements of a meaningful and unified explanation of the world, and is successful by means of the formation of community, and through dissemination and mass-following becomes significant even in world-historical terms; but it always takes the form of revolutionary missions prizing apart the normality of hardened traditions and customs, only for itself to become unavoidably frozen within the patterns of the normal everyday.

Certainly, Meyer had set down his thinking in terms of descriptive sketches rather than systematic conceptualization. He always concentrated on presenting the particular and left other parts out of the picture. Everything is successively mentioned, but not in fixed concepts that are maintained throughout. Moreover, the findings are always overlaid by retrospective observations on the 'basic forces of historical life', interpreted according to the formula that Weber found so offensive: the opposition of 'individual and general factors'.[95] Obviously, the expression, charisma, was absent (as in Sohm), also the precision that Weber brought to the term. We are always coming across formulations that, taken in themselves, appear to differ completely from Weber's definition of charisma, necessitating the search for additions and qualifications. Leaving aside the conceptual precision and the fructification of material that accrued in Weber's usage, we still have to establish that Eduard Meyer provided the model for the basic ideas of Weber's sociology of religion; the essential statements were advanced by Weber in his own ways and developed as an interrelated problem, especially in regards to the basis of his own researches into charisma, which presented charisma as the revolutionary force 'from within' in history. So there appeared a new field of inquiry on Weber's horizon, which he has first 'to make his own'. Obviously, this is the field of inquiry that first determined and made possible the particular sociological work of Weber.

But the story does not end here. In 1912, Eduard Meyer published a work that he had started in America, *Ursprung und Geschichte der Mormonen. Mit Exkursen über die Anfänge des Islams und Christentums*. He was fascinated by the possibility that the origin and history of a new religion of revelation, Mormonism, could be traced down to the last detail 'from the extraordinarily rich supply of countless documents, all precisely dated, of its adherents and opponents',[96] thus enabling a comparison with the origin and emergence of Islam. These two cases of 'prophetic revelation' were then to be further compared with Christianity. The study proceeds from the founders of the religion, who did not originate from the priesthood but rather felt themselves to be personally called, in the way Weber outlined, as the basic characteristic of the 'prophet'.[97] While Meyer distinguishes between the true prophets of revelation and the religious teacher, Weber lumps both together as 'prophets', only to separate them immediately into the instrument of revelation and the bearer of religious doctrine – here, he uses the same examples as Eduard Meyer;[98] Weber ignores Meyer's gradations, and then sharpens up the distinction into the pure typology of 'ethical' and 'exemplary' prophecy.[99]

What is of interest here is that, for Meyer, charisma grows out of the psychic capacities of its bearers, while, for Weber, it appears to derive from the belief of the followers in the charisma of the bearer. The 'fundamental problem'[100] for Meyer stems from the fact that the prophets actually experience revelations and visions and, in their turn, the followers themselves believe those visions to be of supernatural origin. 'Rationalism exposes these prophets as common swindlers',[101] and Meyer takes their conscious deceit as self-evident in his explanation:

Therefore it is as impossible to understand Joseph Smith as it is to understand Amos or Isaiah, Mohammed or Joan of Arc. One has solely to mention the fact that he was a young, completely uneducated country lad, who concerned himself with visions and clairvoyance, with treasure divining and miracle cures, in order to see the falsity of an interpretation that holds that every word of his book and his revelations bore the imprint of his spiritual nature; similarly, this interpretation is just as little able to explain the fact that the prophet, the alleged instrument, stands in the same relation of superiority at the start to his followers – including here the much better educated Rigdon, the supposed string puller – as did Mohammed to Abu Bekr and Omar; and that they at no time expressed any doubt in his inspiration, never mind exposing the alleged deceit, although they all fell out with him later and were banished from the Church.[102]

Mormonism therefore showed that, in all cases, we have to proceed from the following facts:

Inspired personalities of the same sort as Joseph Smith have always existed in their thousands – in the distant past as well as in the present. In all societies and religions there are people who, while retaining a practical understanding of many things and quite often great cunning, possess an inner life that at important moments deviates from the normal and comes close to the area of mental illness – so, for example, enthusiastic mystics, visionaries and dreamers, seers and miracle workers. There are countless gradations of individual peculiarities and spiritual worth: from the predominantly theistically understood spirituality of prophets, like Amos or Isaiah, to the ecstatic fanatics (*Schwärmer*) whom the spirit drives to raptures and frenzied behaviour like the bands of prophets under whom Saul fell and to whom belonged Elijah, and finally to the really lunatic whom the Orient even now still reveres as holy. What they all hold in common is a mental outlook in which the actual material world unfolds before a super-sensory world of the spirit and both worlds are merged together into an indissoluble unity; hence there is a complete failure to perceive the frontiers between both worlds, and consequently truth and reality are completely absent in the way they exist for normal people.[103]

Meyer is clear, therefore, that extraordinary psychic capability does not ensure a significant, or even world-historical effect; rather, the bulk of these gifts disappear without trace, and those remaining, reaching a limited success according to circumstances, range from 'saints and properly recognized seers and prophets, or instruments of the devil, to heretics and charlatans'.[104] Meyer also gives an account of how the qualification in question is possessed not only by eminent personalities: 'Neither Joseph Smith nor Mohammed were outstanding personalities; one would not place them in the same rank with the great figures of the Old Testament prophets, with Zoroaster, with countless similar Christian or the most eminent of the Buddhist saints'.[105] However, he is unwavering in his assertion that an extraordinary *habitus* of the bearer is the most secure basis for the genuine phenomena of charisma, whereas Weber locates this solely in the beliefs of the followers – or so, at least, interpretation has insisted.

Finally, there is the question whether Max Weber's theory of charisma actually possesses the particular features of Meyer's 'Anthropology' whatever other stimulus the latter may have had upon Weber. If we turn to those passages in the older part of *Economy and Society* where Weber sets forth the nature and impact of charisma, it is surprising to note that even Weber himself adds that, in the case of the extraordinary strengths which the holders of valid charisma must themselves possess, 'Not everyone has the capability to achieve ecstasy and thus to produce those effects. . ., which are only attained through experience'.[106] The capacity for ecstasy, as in Eduard Meyer, is tied to 'manic seizure', 'constitutional epilepsy', etc.[107]

> For us, both forms of ecstasy are not edifying; neither is the kind of revelation found in the Holy Book of the Mormons; if we were to evaluate this revelation, we would perhaps be forced to call it a rank swindle. However, sociology is not concerned with such value-judgements: rather, the head of the Mormons and those 'heroes' and 'magicians' proved themselves as charismatically gifted in the eyes of their adherents. Because of this gift. . .they practised their art and authority.[108]

So, when Weber discusses charisma, he makes a direct link to Meyer's book on the Mormons and confirms once again that he discovered the basic idea of charisma – the revolutionary power of world history and its inevitable routinization – in Eduard Meyer; likewise, the question of 'religious rationalization' that also defines Weber's sociology of religion. It has already been noted that Weber came across charisma as a revolutionary power in the field of social and cultural phenomena,[109] which he later worked up into a separate type of domination that was only implicitly associated with Meyer. And as Weber continues, in the previously quoted passage:

> It is to Rudolf Sohm's credit that he worked out the sociological character of this kind of power structure; however, since he developed this category with regard to one historically important case, his treatment was bound to be one-sided from the viewpoint of historical diversity. In principle these phenomena are universal, even if they are most evident in the religious realm.[110]

So Weber himself confirms for us that he was indebted to Eduard Meyer for the insight into the universality of charisma and its routinization.

Max Weber's Transition to Sociology

The significance of Eduard Meyer is visible in Weber's sociology of religion and that influence extends over the theory of charisma, to the areas of the sociology of domination and, finally, to *Economy and Society* in general. However, it should be accepted that Eduard Meyer had helped Max Weber on his way — this at least should now be clear.

At any rate, Meyer was the single historian who was motivated to take up universal history in his own research and to consider this from the aspect of pre-history and ethnology (*Völkerkunde*), an area that had worked with flimsy constructions about the early stages of civilization. Weber grew up in the subject area whose interest derived from European civilization — its nations and its classical legacy. For a long time, his writings maintain not only an accidental disinterest in primitive peoples (*Naturvölker*) but a declared disinterest;[111] Honigsheim also reported that it was only later that Weber discovered ethnological material.[112]

This late, fundamental change cannot be explained by external circumstances — such as the foundation of the German Sociological Society or the planning of the *Grundriß der Sozialökonomik*. Weber's sociological work becomes unrecognizable when seen through the study of foreign civilizations and the interest in ethnological data. This change did not happen by itself, but was occasioned by Eduard Meyer's demonstration, in his 'Anthropology', of how it was possible to obtain highly valuable knowledge of general validity by means of comparison and the extension of research to the non-European civilizations.

Finally, we need to take note of a simple fact, which is usually overlooked. What was new about *Economy and Society* was not actually the ideal-type method of *Verstehen*, where Weber conceptualized an already established *praxis*.[113] What was new about the comparative method was not the method itself but its extension to universal history. On the other hand, what was new was the systematic character of the work. From the start, the *Wissenschaftslehre* had adopted the standpoint that History at the minimum required an analytic intelligibility of nomological knowledge, but at no time did this necessitate its systematization.[114] History, therefore, requires the help of other subjects when its own experience does not suffice; these subjects make available to History 'adequate rules of occurrences' for the explanation of concrete events.[115] History works with ad hoc types chosen for their usefulness; this also excludes a systematization of the social sciences.[116]

Naturally, *Economy and Society* does not provide a closed and final system: Max Weber untiringly warned sociology against taking this road.[117] Nevertheless, in *Economy and Society* he broke with his earlier position that ideal types could only be developed in an ad hoc way. This at least is new about his 'sociology'. Therefore the question arises: what had caused him to change his tune in *Economy and Society*?[118] The answer is that a historian had resolved simply   and   uniquely   to   move   to   a   'systematic   presentation   of anthropology',[119] which by means of universal historical comparison would provide a 'theory of the general forms of human life and of human evolution'.[120] In many respects, Meyer's findings could not suffice for Max Weber; Part 1 is challenged and refuted in *Economy and Society*, where Weber puts forward an entirely different interpretation of the state. Yet Meyer's attempt to create a sociology of the orders of society and its powers must have been a challenge for Weber. If we ask for a model that would give such a coincidentally effective sketch with which the table of contents of *Economy and Society* surprises us, then it is to be found neither in Schmoller's *Allgemeine Volkswirtschaftslehre* or anywhere else in the camp of the Historical School, nor obviously in Dilthey's sequence on 'natural' orders and 'systems of culture', but rather it is to be found in the 'Anthropology', which provides the guide to the succeeding volumes. Weber considered the societal orders and powers according to their relation to the economy, while for Meyer these remained general; he concerned himself with 'modern' developments about which Meyer showed no interest or regard. Therefore, a completely independent work had come into being, yet without Meyer's 'Anthropology' it would have come into existence only with difficulty.

Conclusion and Prospect

The historical sciences in the nineteenth century were concerned in the main with a set of problems that rapidly unfolded and diversified, while at the same time historical work underwent a deep-seated change in its cultural interests. Max Weber's work was an attempt to clarify these problems in order to secure the progress of historical knowledge. It is in this sense that History develops from, and as a solution to, these concerns.

Max Weber's sociology arose on the basis of the knowledge of the historical disciplines. At the basic level, it was situated on the known 'theories' of History as it existed at that time, which consequently established sociology along an identifiable direction that was already independently developed in the subject area of history; therefore, the historians were the models, forerunners and colleagues, and among them Eduard Meyer played a special role, although he was by no means the only one.

Therefore, we shall only learn to understand Max Weber's sociology to the extent that we know the complex concerns of the historical disciplines in Weber's day. The specific character of Weber's sociology is only clearly revealed when we know what scholarship, aims and directions it had taken over from the historical disciplines.[121] Only in this way do we have some hope of finally understanding what Weber intended by his sociology.

Appendix: On the Relationship of Max Weber to Georg von Below

In the picture of German sociology, Georg von Below appears, as is well known, as the model of the narrow-minded historian who, on the basis of pure ideology, opposed the progress of knowledge and was, therefore, a sworn enemy of sociology. It is time to correct this myth, less for Below's sake than for the history of German sociology and history. This overdue rectification can only be preparatory, beginning with some remarks about the relationship between Max Weber and Below.

In 1904, Below published a series of articles in the *Zeitschrift für Socialwissenschaften* under the title 'Towards an appreciation of the Historical School of political economy', in which he expanded on his earlier critique of this school, in particular the younger wing of this school led by Schmoller. His critique, in its essential points, was the same as Max Weber's position in the 'Objectivity' essay, whose profound discussion he underlined with the sentence: 'No historian should neglect to consider it' (G. v. Below, 'Zur Würdigung der historischen Schule der Nationalökonomie', *Zeitschrift für Socialwissenschaften*, vol. 7 [1904], p. 370). Below's reference to the 'Objectivity' essay (apparently published at the same time) is most simply explained by supposing that Max Weber made the proofs available to him. We may further conjecture that there was a closer scholarly relationship between the two, which other factors suggest. A certain parallelism of themes and problems should not be overlooked, as in the critique of the Historical School, in the preoccupation with the city, with feudalism and with patrimonialism. Also to be noted is Below's 'The origin of modern capitalism', which was published in the *Historische Zeitschrift*, vol. 55 (1903). This connection would also be supported by the well-known letter (the only evidence we currently have) of 21 June 1914 from Max Weber to Below, concerning the 'forthcoming' publication of *Economy and Society* (ES, Vol. 1, pp. lviii ff.). If we bear in mind Weber's character and the facts of the situation, this letter clearly documents the scientific esteem with which Weber acknowledged the 'modern historian', Georg von Below, as well as probably indicating a closer scholarly connection.

Even if we suppose that there is not a relation between the two, it is certainly the case that there is a considerable substantive and, in parts, almost simultaneous parallelism of themes and problems, which by concentrating on the same questions affirms the unity of History. In spite of some major differences (in important methodological questions and, in part, questions of content), Below adopted a fundamentally similar position to Max Weber; moreover, he did so rather earlier than Weber, even though the overlap was relatively undefined. This shows how little separated the two disciplines were. Still more clearly, perhaps, than Eduard Meyer in his 'Anthropology' and books on the Mormons and ancient history, Below, putting the normal descriptive history-writing behind him, grappled with questions concerned more with 'overall conditions' (*Zustände*) than 'events'. Therefore he felt himself as much responsible for the concerns of the specialist historical disciplines as, conversely, for the questions of History in so far as it pursued particular overall conditions. In this way, we can understand Below's interest in legal, political and social orders and, in particular, in economic relationships; thus we are able to comprehend his continuous debate on the historical aspect of political economy. The converse also holds: for him, the specialist historian has to occupy himself with works of general history in so far as it takes account of more than mere 'events'. We should not forget that political economy saw itself as a 'Historical School' with reference to the entirety of cultural phenomena, when it was not concerned solely with economic, or economically determined facts (MSS, p. 166). Even *Economy and Society* is still founded on such a perspective, and, as the *Wissenschaftslehre* puts it, it most certainly is not 'forerunner of a general social science' (WL², p. 166). Instead it recognizes:

> that the analysis of social and cultural phenomena with special reference to their economic conditioning and ramifications was a scientific principle of creative fruitfulness and with careful application and freedom from dogmatic restrictions will remain such for a very long time to come. (MSS, p. 68.)

As this text shows, although the origin of the specialist historical disciplines created new concerns in history, it would be wholly erroneous to split these specialisms up into separate compartments, or to play them against each other. It was not the case that the representatives of general history-writing took no interest in the legal, political, social or economic questions that the specialist disciplines had taken on. In so far as a line of separation existed, it crosscuts the separate columns along the lines of the question: is History exhausted by the mere description of intelligible action, or should it not also interpret the overall conditions, or orders and powers, which lie behind these actions and which can only be grasped by means of the deliberate construction of explicit concepts?

This was in any case how Max Weber saw the situation, in which he decided in favour of the 'new' or 'modern' direction (he uses the two terms interchangeably); this did not mean, of course, the abandonment of a descriptive and factual history, but its complementing. He represents, therefore, the progress of historical knowledge and not solely the endeavours of his own speciality, which was still to become a 'general social science'. Far from standing alone, he had many colleagues in all the specialist branches of History (and elsewhere), who wished to improve the historical verification of cause and effect. Eduard Meyer impressed him in this way, and bearing in mind the 'theoretical' implications that attend all historical statements, it was Meyer who pressed beyond historical description to 'clear concepts' (GASWG, p. 279). By the same token, he must have esteemed Below, who went much further than Meyer in relation to clear concepts and theories. Therefore, Below is referred to in *Economy and Society* and already distinguished in the *Wissenschaftslehre* as a 'modern historian' (RaK, p. 223, n. 54); Max Weber freely acquainted Below with his plans for *Economy and Society*, as, conversely, Below often valued Max Weber's work. Accordingly, Below is another fraternal colleague, along with Meyer, who stands for progress in historical knowledge along the lines put forward by Weber. Below's work is part of the antecedents of Weber's work, and traces of it remain in the *Wissenschaftslehre* and the basic stage of *Economy and Society*. It is more surprising, as well as disturbing, to find that the history of sociology allots a wholly different role to Below than that which he should rightfully occupy. A few remarks about the interrelation of the historical disciplines will be squeezed in here.

The interconnection and interplay of the human sciences (*Geisteswissenschaften*) strikes anyone who has taken the trouble to open the books and journals of the time. As his education shows, Max Weber was placed within this framework, and his work is part of it. This was obvious to the older generation of commentators, who grew up in this tradition and recognized its unities and differences. Today, however, sociology in the professionalization of its subject is cut off from this knowledge, and it reads *Economy and Society* as a 'necessary forerunner to a general social science'. A blind faith prevails that we shall understand Max Weber if we compare him with Marx, Durkheim or Parsons. At long last, we have found a history of sociology that spares us the trouble of going into the real history of sociology and of taking stock of the writings to which Max Weber was oriented.

Here, we come to the role Below is portrayed as playing in the history of German sociology. Only by a distortion can one show that Below was the reactionary opponent of sociology and Max Weber, and that he was the epitome of concept-less history-writing. We have the letter, already mentioned, that reports on the forthcoming publication of *Economy and Society*. This is interpreted as the younger Max Weber petitioning the threatening high priest of conservative historians and thereby merely trying to play down the sociological character of his book. The facts gain weight if we remember that Below was seen in the 1920s and again in the last decade as the most important representative of 'bigoted' and 'reactionary' history-writing and as the leader of a bitter struggle against sociology – an 'obligatory myth' which saves further study of the facts. Whatever we may think of Below the historian, it is nevertheless correct that he waged a relentless struggle from all sides for a scholarly (*wissenschaftliche*) history in its substantive and theoretical work. His political beliefs actually did not stop him from pitilessly attacking colleagues (e.g. G. Schmoller) who were of the same conviction as himself, if he considered their work dropped below his standard of scholarly research.

It is a measure of sociology's understanding of these matters that it makes Below (and so History) into a bogyman. For the substantive issues are not entered into. Rather Below is 'strung up' because he came out openly against Tönnies's student, H. L. Stoltenberg, who with the Minister of Culture, C. H. Becker, was responsible (with Tönnies's backing) for the establishment of sociology as a permanent subject. In his 'Sociology as a subject. A critical contribution to the reform of higher education' (which was published in *Schmollers Jahrbuch*, vol. 43[1919], pp. 1271–1322), he held the same position as Max Weber had taken, who likewise did not wish to see the establishment of sociology as a regular subject. Karl Jaspers informs us that Max Weber, when in post as an economist, was 'against the establishment of chairs in sociology' (K. Jaspers. *Max Weber, Politiker, Forscher, Philosoph.* [Bremen, 1946] p. 39):

He did not hide from himself that, since it was a subject that stood on other people's territory for an important part of its own research, it demanded an unusual amount of critical self-reflection. 'Most of what goes under the name of sociology is a fraud', he said in his Heidelberg farewell lecture.

Below took exactly the same position; although he had nothing against sociological methods, he opposed the establishment of sociology as a regular academic subject; this was no different from Max Weber, who therefore took occasion to specify the nature of the teaching duties included in sociology upon taking up his chair in Munich (cf. H. H. Bruun, *Science, Value and Politics in Max Weber*, Copenhagen, 1972, p. 38, as well as G. Roth and W. Schluchter, *Max Weber's Vision of History*, Berkeley, 1979, p. 120). This fits in with the many statements of Max Weber, who saw sociology as playing the role of a preparatory work for the investigation of the 'historical', and in performing this function it has to be resigned to realizing that it merely provides 'in all events usable questions for the specialist' (WL^2, p. 572).

This suffices to show that the description of the history of sociology and, in consequence, sociology's own self-understanding, is oriented for the main part to academic positioning and the recognition of the subject, without taking account of the virtually contiguous substantive questions. In order to present Max Weber as the key witness of today's sociology, it has diligently ignored Max Weber's rejection of sociology as an academically taught subject. Conversely, Below, who took the same standpoint as the *Wissenschaftslehre*, is caricatured as representing the reactionary sentiment of History in Germany in its opposition to sociology, allegedly because History was so blinkered and narrow-minded. The dissemination of this myth shows the indifference to substantive questions, which from the viewpoint of History were so important for both Below and Weber, and this myth complacently congratulates itself that it has adequately grasped the issues of scholarly debate as they existed at that time.

This involves not merely being fair to Georg von Below. His case is a good illustration in that it shows how far sociology has become distanced from the substantive questions from which Weber's work arose. Accordingly, his case deserves a detailed and comprehensive treatment, for which this chapter serves only as an indication.

Notes: Chapter 16

This chapter was translated by Sam Whimster. An Italian version of this chapter was published in *Communità*, vol. 39, no. 187 (1985).

1 E. Meyer, *Geschichte des Altertums*, Vol. 1, Part 1, 'Einleitung. Elemente der Anthropologie', 8th edn (Darmstadt, 1978), p. ix.
2 *Geschichte des Altertums*, *Ursprung und Geschichte der Mormonen*, *Urgeschichte des Christentums*, and *Caesar's Monarchie und das Principat des Pompeius* are now available in facsimile. For an appreciation of Eduard Meyer, see the contributions by his students, written at the time of his death: W. Otto, 'Eduard Meyer und sein Werk', *Zeitschrift der deutschen morgenländischen Gessellschaft*, vol. 85 (1931), pp. 1–24; W. Otto, 'Nekrolog', *Jahrbuch der Bayerischen Akademie der Wissenschaften*, vol. 18 (1930/31), pp. 43–7; U. Wilcken and W. Jaeger, *Eduard Meyer zum Gedächtnis* (Stuttgart, 1931).
3 WL^2, pp. 163–4, 208.
4 WL^2, p. 3, n. 2.
5 WL^2, pp. 174, 237.
6 Previous work remains under the shadow of the very valuable but also very general contribution of E. Francis, 'Kultur und Gesellschaft in der Soziologie Max Webers', in K. Engisch *et al.* (eds), *Max Weber. Gedächtnisschrift* (Berlin, 1966). Since then, G. Roth in his Introduction to *Economy and Society* (New York, 1968), and later in R. Bendix and G. Roth *Scholarship and Partisanship* (Berkeley, Calif., 1971), as well as W. J. Mommsen in several contributions, have traced important categories of *Economy and Society* back to the earlier works; to date, sociology does not appear to have seriously absorbed this knowledge. Nevertheless, D. Käsler has attempted to draw out the continuities in Max Weber's work in his *Einführung in das Studium Max Webers* (Munich, 1979). Particular mention should

be given to the outstanding MA thesis of Elisabeth Kraus, 'Feudalismus im Werk Max Webers. Zur Genese eines Typenbegriffs' (Tübingen, 1982), which with a rare penetration investigates the origin of the concept of feudalism in the work of Max Weber.

7 Thus, completely correctly M. R. Lepsius, 'Max Weber in München', *Zeitschrift für Soziologie*, vol. 6 (1977), pp. 103–18.

8 Cf. A. Heuß, 'Vom geschichtlichen Wissen', *Historische Zeitschrift*, vol. 239 (1984), pp. 11–21.

9 GASWG, p. 287.

10 Cf. E. Meyer, 'Die wirtschaftliche Entwicklung des Altertums', appearing first in *Jahrbücher für Nationalökonomie und Statistik*, vol. 84 (1895) pp. 696–750, then in *Kleine Schriften*, Vol. 1 (Halle, 1910). Of G. v. Below's numerous important works see, among others, 'Über Theorien der wirtschaftlichen Entwicklung der Völker', *Historische Zeitschrift*, vol. 50, (1901), pp. 1–77, and the later *Probleme der Wirtschaftsgeschichte* (Tübingen, 1920).

11 WL^2, p. 218; MSS, p. 116.

12 WL^2, p. 217; MSS, p. 115.

13 Meyer, *Geschichte des Altertums*, Vol. 1, p. 187.

14 WL^2, p. 268.

15 ibid., pp. 215–6.

16 ibid., pp. 184 and 209.

17 ibid., pp. 199 and 209.

18 ibid., p. 23, n. 2.

19 ibid., p. 47; RaK, p. 98 [transl. altered].

20 WL^2, p. 216.

21 ibid., p. 214; MSS, p. 112.

22 WL^2, pp. 261–2; MSS, p. 159. Cf. WL^2, pp. 167, 182, 206–7, 218.

23 WL^2, pp. 206–7; MSS, p. 105. Cf. WL^2, pp. 182, 218, 262.

24 WL^2, p. 214; MSS, p. 116.

25 WL^2, pp. 70 ff.

26 ibid., pp. 251; MSS, p. 114. Cf. WL^2, p. 262.

27 GASWG, p. 280.

28 WL^2, pp. 216 and 237; MSS, pp. 114 and 135.

29 ibid., pp. 216–7; MSS, p. 115 [transl. altered].

30 WL^2, p. 265, n. 1.

31 ibid., pp. 217–8.

32 ibid., pp. 111–2 and 235.

33 ibid., pp. 112–3.

34 ibid., p. 193; MSS, p. 93.

35 WL^2, pp. 113, 209 and 278.

36 ibid., p. 209; MSS, p. 107 [transl. altered].

37 WL^2, p. 162.

38 ibid., p. 216.

39 For this, see my more detailed Appendix, pp. 257–61 in this volume.

40 If we follow the secondary literature in chronological order, it is noticeable how the understanding of Weber has changed over time according to the disciplinary background and education of the interpreter. Between the wars, German interpretation was still marked by its familiarity with the historical sciences. To be sure the specialist historians remained rather reserved, as seen in the great exponents such as Friedrich Meinecke; yet there was no lack of interest on the part of the remaining human sciences for which the scientific field was accessible. Because of their background in the Historical School, the economists of this period (one thinks of names like Carl Brinkmann or Bernhard Pfister) were drawn to the work of Max Weber given their interest in the social sciences.

Whereas interpretation since 1945 has increasingly become cut off from the field of problems from which Weber's work derives (in so far as *Nationalökonomie* has become restricted to Anglo-Saxon 'economics') sociology has professionalized itself into a separate subject, and the cultural sciences – or at least the social sciences – have taken on a positivistic theoretical stance. These disciplines have lost their connection with the historical cultural sciences, whose concerns have now vanished in the face of demands for a systematic theory of society. It was Parsons's attempt to take Weber down this road that signalled the change. There has grown up a new Weber literature, which takes scarcely any notice of the older works and regards itself as exempted from inquiring into the ways in which Weber was tied into the scientific situation of his day. Works, which because of their real knowledge of the history of scholarship or because of their philosophical interests no longer fit the picture, have scarcely any prospect in the social sciences today. The original position of Weberian sociology has completely sunk into oblivion as American sociology has moved into its predominating position and is able to write the history of the subject according to its own lights.

The Weber renaissance has been little able to change this. In America, the lack of knowledge of foreign languages debars access to the original as well as to the German Weber literature, just as the lack of familiarity with the history of German scholarship blocks the way to its origins. It is only with regret that one states that the in some ways so vital Weber literature in America for the most part still only takes account of English-language publications. However, the German Weber literature, in spite of important individual contributions, is evidently no longer informed by a real understanding of the history of the German social sciences. Thus the exegesis of Max Weber is entrusted to disciplines that possess no connection with the historical cultural sciences from which Weber's sociology developed.

41 I have attempted to show in my book, *Die unbewältigten Sozialwissenschaften und die Abschaffung des Menschen* (Graz, 1984), that the powerful development of an independent American sociology has had some very profound consequences.

42 WL^2, pp. 182, 207 and 214.

43 ibid., pp. 154 or 588.

44 ibid., p. 214; MSS, p. 112.

45 ibid.

46 WL^2, pp. 215, 232, and 265; MSS, pp. 113, 130, 163.

47 P. Honigsheim, 'Erinnerungen an Max Weber', in R. König and J. Winckelmann (eds), *Max Weber zum Gedächtnis*, Kölner Zeitschrift für Soziologie und Sozialpsychologie, Sonderheft 7 (Cologne, 1963), pp. 206–7.

48 GASWG, p. 279; *The Agrarian Sociology of Ancient Civilization*, trans. by R. I. Frank (London, 1976), p. 370 [transl. altered].

49 WL^2, p. 219; MSS, p. 117.

50 WL^2, pp. 232–3; MSS, pp. 130–1.

51 WL^2, p. 265, n. 1; MSS, p. 163, n. 30.

52 WL^2, p. 216; MSS, p. 114.

53 The 'Critique of Eduard Meyer' derives its sharpness not from the severity of its factual errors, which Weber reckoned to have uncovered – as is the case in the critique of Stammler or Ostwald and, to a lesser extent, Brentano – but rather from the high expectations that Weber must have placed on Meyer's statements on methodology. He counted Meyer (as well as G. v. Below) as a 'modern' historian who was calling for 'clear concepts' (GASWG, p. 279). The opening of the 'Critique' already makes it very clear what significance would inevitably attach to any contribution from Eduard Meyer to the intense debate about the nature of History. In particular, the 'Critique' has to be read with the actual situation in mind; so perhaps we can infer from it Max Weber's position on the role of the classical world in *Gymnasium* education, which occupied such an important place in contemporary debate. Thus, Weber's criticism replaces Meyer's contention that History is only concerned with historical 'effectiveness' in its causal connection to the present with the view that the study of antiquity (and other historical phenomena) is valued 'for its own sake' (WL^2, p. 257; MSS, p. 155). The conclusion of the 'Critique' makes it abundantly clear that Weber wished to protect Eduard Meyer from those who would devalue the educational value of the ancient world: 'And all the admirers of his great work rejoice that he cannot at all proceed with any fidelity to these ideas, and they hope that he will not even attempt to do so for the sake of an erroneously formulated theory.' (WL^2, p. 265; MSS, p. 163).

As Weber continuously repeated, the 'Critique' predominantly concerned matters of formulation. This is confirmed if we refer to the 2nd edition – in Vol. 1 of his *Kleine Schriften* (Halle, 1910) – where Eduard Meyer willingly accedes to Weber's criticisms. He immediately corrects his earlier statement that the effective is the object of historical study, and he himself now stresses that History must also be oriented to the significance of phenomena in their own right. More of Weber's points are scattered among the footnotes by Meyer, while the intended sense of his formulations are corrected in the light of Weber's logically analytical reading. On the whole, we need to say that the situationally defined questions that are prominent in the 'Critique' did not form its real contents; these are to be sought elsewhere and are still scarcely explored. In any case, W. J. Mommsen has already shown that, in the 'Critique', the *Wissenschaftslehre* seeks for the earlier differentiation between the historical sciences (in the narrower sense) and the actual social sciences, without, however, having pursued this in the meantime (WL^2, p. 216). Research has completely passed over the long passages on value-interpretation, the validity of values and value-analysis (WL^2, pp. 241 ff), even though it might have played an important role in the genesis of the interpretive sociology.

54   Meyer, *Geschichte des Altertums*, Vol. 1, p. 77.
55   ibid., p. 80.
56   ibid., p. 81.
57   ibid., p. 155.
58   ibid., p. 199.
59   See the table of contents, *Geschichte des Altertums*, Vol. 1.
60   ibid., p. ix.
61   ibid.; cf. also E. Meyer, *Zur Theorie und Methodik der Geschichte* (Halle, 1902), p. 6.
62   Meyer, *Geschichte des Altertums*, Vol. 1, p. vii.
63   Meyer, *Theorie und Methodik*, p. 59.
64   Meyer, *Geschichte des Altertums*, Vol. 1, p. 3.
65   Meyer, *Theorie und Methodik*, p. 6.
66   Meyer, *Geschichte des Altertums*, Vol. 1, p. 16.
67   ibid., p. ix; idem, *Theorie und Methodik*, pp. 5–6.
68   Meyer, *Geschichte des Altertums*, Vol. 1, pp. 188 ff.
69   WL^2, p. 257.
70   Meyer, *Geschichte des Altertums*, Vol. 1, p. 184.
71   ibid., p. 186.
72   ibid., pp. 185 ff.
73   ibid., p. 4.
74   ibid., pp. 15 and 202; idem, *Theorie und Methodik*, p. 32.
75   Meyer, *Theorie und Methodik*, p. 33.
76   WL^2, p. 7, n. 1.
77   Meyer, *Theorie und Methodik*, p. 31.
78   Meyer, *Geschichte des Altertums*, Vol. 1, p. 194.
79   GASWG, p. 279; *Agrarian Sociology*, p. 369.
80   WL^2, pp. 228 and 230.
81   WL^2, p. 231.
82   GASWG, p. 279; *Agrarian Sociology*, p. 369.
83   ibid.
84   Still instructive about this 'change', despite some exaggerations, is E. Francis, 'Kultur', p. 89 ff (see n. 6). The continuities with Max Weber, the historian, have in the meantime been better worked out by G. Roth and W. J. Mommsen. The development of Max Weber's sociology from the point of view of the sociology of religions has been considered by G. Küenzlen, *Die Religionssoziologie Max Webers* (Berlin, 1980) pp. 46–55.
85   *Biography*, p. 420.
86   ibid., pp. 420–1.
87   ibid., pp. 421–2. We hope that at some point the *Max Weber-Gesamtausgabe* will throw some light on these points, which are so important for the genesis of Max Weber's sociology.
88   Cremer, 'Geistesgaben', 'Charismata', in *Realencyclopädie für protestantische Theologie und Kirche*, (Leipzig, 1899).
89   WuG^5, p. 124; ES, Vol. 1, p. 216.
90   WuG^5, pp. 654–5; ES, Vol. 2, p. 1112.
91   This concerns the fundamental difference that always exists between the properly conceived ideal type and the illustrative clarification of the 'essence' of any behaviour, on the one side, and, on the other, its actual historical appearance and significance. Weber had made this fundamental distinction in the example of 'exchange' in a money economy; overall, this has the same general characteristics but only gains its cultural significance for the first time when it appears as a 'mass phenomenon'. See MSS, pp. 77–8.
92   To be sure, the *Protestant Ethic* corresponds to the 'process of revolution which puts an end to all traditionalism' (RS, Vol. 1, p. 50), but this can only signify the strength of the 'idea' of the 'rational' conduct of life in search of the assurance of salvation. The leaders of these sects were *not* charismatic but instead evidenced the power of their new doctrines. Similarly,

Weber later refers explicitly to the 'charismatic glorification of reason' as the 'final form that charisma has adopted in its fateful historical course' (WL^2, p. 734; ES, Vol. 2, p. 1209). This late concept of a charisma of ideas (cf., among others, E. Shils, 'Charisma, order and status', *American Sociological Review*, vol. 30 [1965], pp. 199–213, and G. Roth, 'Socio-historical model and developmental theory', *American Sociological Review*, vol. 40 (1975), pp. 148–57) obviously presupposes that charisma had already been discovered. Even in this presentation of charisma, there is no predecessor in the earlier works.

93 Meyer, *Geschichte des Altertums*, Vol. 1, pp. 149 ff. This also indicates that Eduard Meyer could have found almost similar passages to those quoted here scattered in the contemporary literature, above all in theology and the history of religion; so, at the very least, this literature provided a stimulus, and indeed was used directly. In the general comprehension this theme was, so to speak, in the air. Actually Meyer's formulation bears the stamp of authenticity, because it has unmistakably developed from the comprehensive research of the whole of the European Middle-Eastern area of civilization in antiquity; it has been tested against those facts and also been realized in the history of antiquity. Weber could not have been convinced without the idea of a revolutionary power in world history that derived from the charismatic qualifications of certain persons. Decisive for Weber's persuasion was Eduard Meyer's well-versed knowledge and the broad historical realization of the thesis. It is not possible to go further into how Weber used and moulded these ideas to his own purposes.

94 While universal history was an initial interest for Eduard Meyer, for Max Weber it was the product of a later development. His writings and interests (and so, essentially, his knowledge) for a long time were confined to the field of European history. The *Protestant Ethic* did not extend beyond the insight into the 'fateful power' of capitalism and whatever it bore within it. When, in 1908, he answered the demands of his critics for a 'counter-example' he did so methodologically but did not consider a civilizational comparison; cf. PE, Vol. 2, pp. 48 and 54. Even in the 'Economic Ethics of the World Religions' the breakthrough to universal historical thinking of a 'typology and sociology of rationalism' only really occurs in the 'Intermediate Reflections' (RS, Vol. 1, p. 237). It is the case that, even in the pioneering 3rd edition of *Agrarverhältnisse im Altertum*, which displays an expertise of the classical world when measured against existing concerns and, not least, Eduard Meyer's extension of the historical horizon, Weber only thought about the contrasting of civilizations as the comprehension of the orders and powers, seen from a universal historical point of view and in civilizational comparison; this was only first given form in the 'Economic Ethics of World Religions' and in *Economy and Society*. And the same goes for the 'systematic' sociology of religion, which, while it could accommodate within itself the *Protestant Ethic*, was not however prepared in that work.

What we have indicated in broad outline is that Max Weber's otherwise continuous development of new questions was determined by the surprise discovery of new fields. Weber himself was well aware of this turning point. As has already been noted above, Marianne Weber registered the opening up of new fields, as likewise did Max Weber in his acknowledgement of a measure of success in his letter of 1914 to G. v. Below, which announced the impending publication of *Economy and Society* (See Appendix, especially p. 258). In this, Weber himself recognized universal historical comparison when he wrote that it was only possible to explain the medieval city historically if one grasped its particularity, and this could only be known through its difference from the Ancient, the Chinese and the Islamic city. He thereby made it clear that he had reached a new position that had not been attained in the *Agrargeschichte des Altertums* – however useful this work remained. Weber informed his colleague, G. v. Below, who stood for clear concepts, of his new positions in the hope that he, the 'modern' historian, would be in agreement with it.

95 Meyer, *Geschichte des Altertums*, Vol. 1, p. 173.
96 E. Meyer, *Ursprünge und Geschichte der Mormonen* (Halle, 1912), p. 1.
97 WuG^5, p. 268.
98 Meyer, *Mormonen*, pp. 8–13.
99 WuG^5, pp. 268 ff.
100 Meyer, *Mormonen*, p. 8.
101 ibid., p. 10.
102 ibid., p. 11.
103 ibid., pp. 2–3.
104 ibid., p. 3.

105   ibid., p. 4.
106   WuG[5], p. 245.
107   WuG[5], p. 654; ES, Vol. 2, p. 1112.
108   ibid.
109   Talcott Parsons had already remarked that Weber first discovered charisma as a revolutionary force in history and only later recognized it as a source of legitimacy. See T. Parsons, *The Structure of Social Action*, Vol. 2 (New York, 1968), pp. 662 ff.
110   WuG[5], p. 654; ES, Vol. 2, p. 1112.
111   WL[2], p. 274.
112   P. Honigsheim, 'Erinnerungen', pp. 216–17. In relation to this, Honigsheim relates that Weber for a long period limited himself to the orbit of European history in which antiquity played an important role (see pp. 204–10 passim).
113   Basically, E.Francis has correctly emphasized that Weber did not discover ideal types and their construction, which had been practised for a long time, but only analysed and articulated the logical structure of this method even though he did not follow through the implications and consequences of his clarification; see Francis, 'Kultur', p. 107.
114   WL[2], p. 113.
115   ibid., pp. 175, 179 ff and 208.
116   ibid., p. 184.
117   The position of sociology today can almost be described as one of a split consciousness. Sociologists work untiringly for a definitive and final theory of society and, just as untiringly, claim Max Weber as their founding father. From his side, Max Weber untiringly worked against such an enterprise, which sought a definitive theory of society. The *Wissenschaftslehre* is, not least of all, a thoroughgoing warning against what Weber regarded as the substantively meaningless and practically dangerous intent to develop sociology as a definitive system, and he maintained this position in *Economy and Society*. In the later work there is indeed something new, for 'Weber restructures and systematically arranges such "ideal types"', as Marianne Weber puts it (*Biography*, p. 678). She continues with the warning: 'it is well to bear in mind that he could have no use for their arrangement into a system for the sake of an integrated conception of the world. For these types were not intended to be definitive fixations but only temporary stopping places in the flow of a constantly changing process of historical cognition.' In the *Wissenschaftslehre*, Weber had presented the ideal type as the specific method of the cultural sciences; in the *Agrargeschichte* and in the 'Economic Ethics of World Religions' he pushed ahead with the development of several ideal types. Yet *Economy and Society* only resolves 'to systematically arrange such "ideal types"' as a 'stopping point' to inquire into the 'orders and powers of society' in respect of their relation to the economy, but not, however, as a 'forerunner of a general social science'. This attempt to systematize the 'temporary stopping places' is what is unmistakably new about *Economy and Society*.
118   I will not pursue here another side of the origin of *Economy and Society*, which so far as I can see has not been investigated elsewhere. As stated in the text above, Weber understood the history of the cultural and social sciences, in general – History, as a succession of ever new syntheses that light the way for new cognitive interests and possibilities; this continues until science lays them aside when they are 'mature', and as the light of the cultural problems moves on it demands progress in the conceptual apparatus; where this is achieved in a grand manner, this for Weber is always the act of genius – to be able to define an epoch (WL[2], pp. 182 and 208). In this respect the possibility of a new conceptual apparatus, of a new synthesis, was seen in *Economy and Society* as early as the 'Objectivity' essay; it is not fortuitous that the Stammler essay in the *Wissenschaftslehre* is part of an attempt to develop basic categories. Nevertheless, the decision to write *Economy and Society* as a unified work with a thorough conceptual apparatus stemmed from a much later period and is not the product of an earlier intent. We can expect clarification of this only through further research and from the *Max Weber-Gesamtausgabe*.
119   Meyer, *Geschichte des Altertums*, Vol. 1, p. ix.
120   ibid., p. 13.
121   In conclusion, it is necessary to emphasize the difficulty of this problem. On the one side, there is the long neglect of an appropriate history of the discipline subject and, overall, a distancing from the state of German scholarship at that time. On the other side, there is the still-living unity of the 'historical' or, overall, the disciplines of the human sciences of that time; because of the ramifications of influences and commonalities (as indicated in the in-

dividual case in n. 93), the identification of sources is uncertain. Both can only be furthered through the tenacious pursuit of Weber research. It has been a major purpose of this chapter on Max Weber and Eduard Meyer to provide a stimulus for such research.

17 Karl Lamprecht and Max Weber: Historical Sociology within the Confines of a Historians' Controversy

SAM WHIMSTER

Is there an accepted nomenclature for 'methodological disputes', or is the term generic to all such disputes? It is probably a pointless exercise trying to answer this question. Like the bubonic plague, its outbreaks are intermittent yet part of a series, often localized but still part of a general occurrence and with effects sometimes more, sometimes less, severe. I tend to regard the historians' *Methodenstreit*, which is the phenomenon that concerns this chapter, as subsidiary to the first major *Methodenstreit* – which was the long-drawn-out dispute between the claims of the new marginalist economics and the Historical School of political economy – and more distantly connected to the second dispute – which was the science/political value-distinction argued out, again over a lengthy period of time, pre-eminently in the Verein für Sozialpolitik (Social Policy Association).

In contrast, the historians' dispute was relatively well contained. Its outbreak was sudden, although not unexpected, and within a decade the major arguments were played out and exhausted. However, within the quite well-defined cockpit of the historians the dispute was conducted with considerable savagery and centred upon the works and views of one man, Karl Lamprecht. Single-handedly and without any significant predecessors, he challenged the dominant conception of history writing, and in less than ten years of the appearance of the first four volumes of his massive *Deutsche Geschichte* (History of Germany) was effectively ostracized from the centres of influence within the historians' profession.

My interest in this dispute is not to re-write this episode in the history of the historians' discipline, or to rehabilitate Lamprecht's contribution to social or cultural history; this has been done elsewhere. [1] What the Lamprecht dispute does provide, because of its well-defined and 'in-house' character, is an opportunity to study that complex interaction between debates internal to a discipline and their relation to a more general crisis 'out there' which, for me, is nothing less than the dissolution of the educated middle class (*Bildungsbürgertum*). In this sense, the historians' *Methodenstreit* is a sub-set of the wider argument. Furthermore, the way we look back at the dispute is itself problematic, for in opposing internalist accounts of 'disciplines' against some external background, it is easy to overlook that, in the course of this interaction, the specifically modern, twentieth-century concepts of disciplines and academic knowledge were worked out.

The Lamprecht dispute raises in a particular form one of the central questions of social theory: the relation between individual action and a notion of collective entity. Yet when we follow the course of the dispute, there is a continuous feeling that something else is being addressed and that the stakes are immensely high. Nominally, it is an academic debate, and one – as we are now aware – that is not easy to resolve. But the conduct of the debate was anything but academic: there was little studied and measured deliberation of the issues involved; intead the answers came quickly, delivered often as not with considerable personal malice and high-minded appeals to 'obvious simplicities', and the whole dispute was managed with an immoderate haste. The solution reached firmly repudiated the positivistic direction within history writing, so that not only was the status of individual action in history decided but also a whole range of accompanying issues: the nature of proper scholarship, the correct mode of discourse in history-writing, demarcations within the discipline and between neighbouring disciplines, and the less clearly defined role of the historians' own political values. Despite the fact that the solutions reached did hold, and for a surprising length of time, we cannot fail to note that those solutions were also particularly unreceptive to the newly developing social sciences and their philosophies.

However, when one approaches the dispute with a different set of questions and asks what insecurities and loss of direction were experienced by the historians, a more comprehensible picture emerges. For instance, the issues of the respective claims of individual vs collective action and the role of rational and irrational action in history are far more indicative of the apprehensions of a key section of the educated middle class in the face of the 'materialism' of industrialization than of what they provide in methodological utility. Hence this paper will attempt to explore some avenues into this 'other side' of the historians' dispute.

Such an exploration is also pertinent, I believe, to Max Weber's appearance in the debate. His appearance in the Lamprecht dispute is peripheral, and he participates as an outrider in the main battle against positivism in the human sciences. His intervention is partially predictable in terms of the place of individual action, and he provides a crucial advance concerning the significance of the rational and irrational and how the cultural sciences can handle these categories of behaviour. But his intervention in respect to an assessment of the relation of cultural/economic to political history adds little when the really big questions are confronted. Specifically, if we take Max Weber's three-way comparison of the developmental tendencies in the pre-modern West, Antiquity, and the Orient that figures so prominently in *The City*, the *Sociology of Law* and *The Agrarian Sociology of Ancient Civilization*, the reader is hardly prepared for how such a comparative history should be handled. Indeed, we are tempted to opine that the direction within Weber's methodological writings leads to and culminates in 'Science as a vocation', which is a different and in some ways a separate preoccupation from one that would serve as a practical historiographical guide in approaching the large historical questions: such as the interplay between, on the one side, man's self-determination and the structures of representation and, on the other, the embeddedness of cultural and material life.

However, this is to overreach the subject of this chapter. First, Lamprecht must be given a serious reading; then, we must ask why his proposals were considered such a threat and how they were consequently handled by his fellow historians; finally, we must consider Max Weber's contribution to the dispute.

Karl Lamprecht's *Deutsche Geschichte*

The *Deutsche Geschichte* is a strange work by any standard. It does not sit easily within any compartmentalization of history-writing or social science, and it is partly this maverick quality, cross-cutting as it does all the accepted criteria, that makes it so interesting. Its critics, so far as I can judge, never did manage to pin the work down exactly and, as a result, many critical attacks failed to deliver the final mortal thrust. The interest in these critiques is Lamprecht's ability to goad his antagonists into revealing some of their own fundamental presuppositions, not to say prejudices, about the proper nature of history-writing. By today's standards, especially for an outsider, the work falls into the category of the bizarre. It is hard to understand how it could be castigated for its Marxist and materialist conception of history, yet at the same time offer a 'scientific' account of the evolution of the German people and its superior national consciousness.[2] A final preliminary consideration is the fact of its popularity; although pushed to the outer regions of the historian's profession, Lamprecht could and did claim some justification because of its success. Why it was popular, and who it was popular with, are relevant to a consideration of its reception.

The *Deutsche Geschichte* is evolutionist in conception and utilizes Herbert Spencer's idea: 'from simple homogeneity to complex heterogeneity'. Unlike Spencer, though, the history advances a rather excessive seven cultural epochs through which the social psyche (*Sozialpsyche*) develops. These seven epochs are subsumed, however, into a more conventional tripartite periodization of pre-history and middle ages; secondly, modern history; finally, the most recent era. In pre-history, culture is named animism, symbolism in the early middle ages, and successively typical and conventional in the middle ages. The modern period is a culture of individualism (1600–1750) and subjectivism (1750–1820). The most recent period (1830 to the present) is a culture of stimulus (*Reizsamkeit*).

Unlike many contemporary evolutionists in the Historical School of political economy, Lamprecht is not content to operate his theory as an analogy to biological evolutionism. The social psyche does actually evolve, and the stages are not regarded as manifestations of some presumed core as in Roscher's work. Moreover, this core, the entity of the social psyche, is scientifically knowable. Whereas, for an organicist such as Otto von Gierke, the entity at the core of collective life was an unknowable mystery. The *Deutsche Geschichte* sought to establish the course of this entity as an agency in history and to research how the entity grew in intensity, differentiation, extent and energizing force. Having assumed the existence of this social psyche in history, Lamprecht set himself the task of empirically verifying the effects that he hypothesized would result from the development of this agency.

In short, Lamprecht had a well worked out monist position, and, if it makes any sense, we could describe his system as a positivized Hegelianism. Lamprecht held that it was possible to develop an independent science of the psychic life of the people that would explain (i) the behaviour of individuals within any one cultural epoch, (ii) the movement from one epoch to another. In a summarization of his history, presented in a book of lectures (*Moderne Geschichtswissenschaft*, 1905), he secures his own epistemological position. How is he, as a historian, able to discern the laws and movements of something that sets the limits of individual consciousness? His answer is that the most modern era is the first period in history to have produced individuals capable of understanding its laws of movement.[3]

His explanation of movement from one era to another does not make the assumption of an automatic linear progress. The movement out of an era is the result of psychic disequilibrium that prompts a return to the dominant values of an epoch which, no longer suited to the overall conditions of society, triggers the dissolution of those values and the creation of a new social psyche. As in all advanced monist positions, the use of dialectics is well developed in order to handle the various interchanges between scientists and the world, individuals and the cultural soul of society, and epoch in relation to epoch. Lamprecht does not exactly come clean on this feature of his theory and method, for he wants to insist on the 'scientificity' of his methods according to positivist criteria. So he presents his method as a deductive one, which then seeks to confirm empirically the hypotheses suggested by the theory. This, as may be imagined, caused considerable confusion.

Lamprecht's handling of the relation between individuals and the dominant psychic force of an epoch shows some genuine insights, and it is interesting to note that his treatment leans in a Durkheimian direction. In the first chapter of his *Moderne Geschichtswissenschaft*, he simplifies evolution into two contrasting periods, which are, as it were, the two poles of the development of the social psyche. In the first period, the psychic existence of the individual is inseparable from that of the collective psyche. It was impossible for the individual to act independently from the rest of the tribe or clan, for he did not have a separate form of imagination. The age of symbolism expressed a primitive unity of imagination. For the warrior

> the world was not yet something conceivable, capable of portrayal, but only such as he saw it before him. The world was reproduced allegorically, and its meaning repeated in mental relationships which expressed it externally by means of symbols. Thus intuition and thought coincided and mental culture, the psychic existence of the time, took a symbolic form.[4]

In this period, thought, law and religion were mediated through symbols. Philosophy merged into mythology, which in its turn transformed the most important phenomena of nature and human life into a world of gods who lived behind those phenomena, creating and guiding them.

> In this world of symbolic life the individual vanishes; he becomes at once the actor in a psychic life, becomes part of a whole, a co-equal member of a community side by side with others of the same standing.[5]

Leaving aside the primitive egalitarianism, there are clear affinities with Durkheim's collective representations in elementary religion.

At the other end of the polarity is the modern cultural epoch. The collective soul has evolved to such an extent that the individual owes his independent existence to the differentiation within the overall culture. The mental life of the individual is pre-given and, as a result, is subordinate to the mental life of the whole. Individuality is never a taken-for-granted ontological assumption, but is made possible through the differentiation of culture. 'The collective mental life, marked by the deviation of the individual within it, is a thing in itself.' This borderline Durkheimianism is also evidenced in Lamprecht's comments on the problems of excessive individualism in modern life. The era of *Reizsamkeit* leads to the over-suggestibility of the individual to outside influences, an excitation that leads to the pathos of the modern individual. This may result in two pathologies: individuality can turn inwards to introspection, which way lies suicide, or else there occurs a complete effacement of individuality with outside stimuli, a case being excessive nationalism.[6]

The Move to Naturalism

It is clearly fanciful to suggest that Lamprecht was some overlooked and underestimated Durkheimian in the fraternity of German historians. Yet it is possible to discern parallels: the same difficulty in grappling with the interrelation between a social collective entity – treated evolutionistically – and the individual, and in endeavouring at the same time to frame the investigation as a scientific enterprise. Lamprecht asserted that the social psyche was no different from any other subject in the natural world and should, therefore, be studied according to the methods of the natural sciences, just as a plant or human body might be studied. This was a bold innovation, but was subsequently undermined by an uncritical emphasis on the philosophical claims of naturalism. Unlike Durkheim, whose enterprise was a science of collective representations, Lamprecht did not stay to construct a science particular to the social psyche. Instead, he called to his aid a positivistic form of psychology.

Within the human sciences (*Geisteswissenschaften*) it was psychology, according to Lamprecht, that had gone furthest in adopting a properly scientific approach. His Leipzig colleague, Wilhelm Wundt, had developed a psychology that treated the mind as being determined by causal laws. Lamprecht saw the collective psyche as no less susceptible to causal analysis, where cause was defined as a law-like regularity from which particular effects could be deduced. Exactly why Wundt's psychology (and that of his followers: Ebbinghaus, Münsterberg and Lipps)[7] was selected as appropriate for the study of the social psyche is justified by a particularly bogus piece of sociological reasoning. Because the individual is a product of the collective psyche, the individual's mind is a stamp from the pattern of the collective mind. Psychology provides laws of the individual mind and so these laws give one an entrée to the original stamping mechanism, the collective mind. 'History in itself is nothing but applied psychology, hence we must look to theoretical psychology for interpretation.'[8] With this move to a naturalistic psychologism of the social psyche, the role of individual behaviour is wholly subsumed under the laws of the collective mind. In a calculated insult to his historical colleagues, Lamprecht held that the great personality is unable to effect the development of the social psyche, which sets the limits to all individual behaviour. The earlier usage of regularities of the social psyche become resolved in favour of the law-like behaviour (*Gesetzmäßigkeit*) of mass phenomena. Separate individual behaviour, when aggregated, achieves a unity called the collective will. The individual's ideas and perceptions are structured by this higher unity. This determinism consigns free will to a residue; it becomes a realm of the accidental and spontaneous, which has no efficacy upon the movement of the collective psyche.

Lamprecht equates free will with the irrational. To act freely is to act not as a consequence of the social psyche but according to an undeterminable (and irrelevant) caprice. This is precisely counter to Durkheim's thinking on the subject. For Durkheim, the free expression of the personality meant the exercise of rational faculties, and this attribute was not particular to the person 'but belongs to human reason in general'. Further: 'The senses, the body and, in a word, all that individualizes, is, on the contrary, considered as the antagonist of the personality by Kant.'[9]

In a characteristic piece of Wilhelmine bravura, Lamprecht suggests a way out of the determinism of modern contemporary life. Here, the problem is to protect the individual's personality and maintain its inner harmony against the multiple impressionism of the external world. The great artist, notes Lamprecht, has the force of personality to be not only creative but to impose his style upon the world. The artist is the exemplar who shows how a mastery over the world sets the individual psyche free and creates a total personality. But free will operates in the realm of the irrational and is not susceptible to scientific study. Fittingly, it is the study of art that provides insights into the irrational.[10]

Lamprecht tells us in the supplementary volume of his *Deutsche Geschichte* that he did not introduce psychology as the underpinning science of his concept of history until the seventh volume, which is on the modern period of subjectivity. Obviously he regarded the move to naturalism as the best reply to his critics, so much so that he boasted that he was able to replace the preface to the third edition of the first volume of the history, which carried a complete bibliography of the critiques of the work and his replies, with one that could claim complete scientific certainty.[11] Whatever the reasons for this move, it closed down the dialectical possibilities in the treatment of the social psyche and replaced the heuristic potential of his notion of an agency in history with a far more (and intentionally so) mechanistic conceptualization of the law-like nature of the social psyche, both in relation to individuals in any one period and to the forward development of the social psyche itself. This was a regrettable move, because it cut him off from the romanticist and idealist sources of his inspiration, notably Herder (*Volksseele*) and Burckhardt, without at the same time attaining a scientific penetration of the agency in history, the social psyche, which was ultimately, despite the recourse to *Naturphilosophie*, unknowable.

The Reception of Lamprecht's *Deutsche Geschichte*

The list of antagonistic critics of Lamprecht's work embraced some of the leading historians of the day — Eduard Meyer, Friedrich Meinecke, Max Lenz, Hans Delbrück, Heinrich Finke, Felix Rachfahl, Hermann Oncken and Georg

v. Below. [12] Before looking at two of the leading spokesmen of the historians' profession, Meinecke and Below, we need to try and estimate just how popular Lamprecht's *History* was.

It had gone through five editions by 1920. Given its massive size — it was brought out in 18 separate books, divided into twelve volumes plus concluding volume, covering over 7,500 pages — this was no mean achievement. Heinrich v. Srbik notes, *Deutsche Geschichte* 'was meant for a large intellectually interested reading public and it also reached this public'. [13] Lamprecht declared that the work was not written for the specialist, who was only interested in pointing out particular mistakes, but for his contemporaries

> who feel the need to be instructed on the inner connectedness of the more important historical occurrences of our time, and to make available the informing extent of German history in relation to all its events for those who do not have access to what can only be produced by and large by the expert. [14]

What was the extent of this reading public? Did it extend beyond the boundaries of the *Bildungsbürgertum*, that hard-to-define Protestant intellectual elite of high officials, higher education and senior secondary school teachers, writers, journalists and the intellectually inclined of the officer class and the industrial and financial bourgeoisie? Alfred Kelly, in a most interesting study, makes the point that in an age of mass literacy, before the advent of radio and television, the market for popularization was immense. The popularizers

> were the writers (a few of them important thinkers in their own right) who sought to break down the growing barriers between the increasingly complex world of scholarship and an ever expanding reading public. Such efforts are traceable back to the seventeenth century; but it was only in the late nineteenth century, with the advent of mass literacy and the first impact of science upon daily life, that the popularizer emerged as a cultural type, above all in Germany. [15]

Lamprecht can be seen as a popularizer straddling the world of historical scholarship and the reading public. He stood in a tradition of the popularization of Darwinism. Kelly presents the Darwinists as those who offered a Weltanschauung that explained everything from man's relation to nature, the position of the German nation and state in a league table of the evolution of different cultures, to providing a position on politics and religion.

Lamprecht collaborated with his Leipzig colleague and friend, Wilhelm Ostwald, who was a chemist and an early Nobel prizewinner in that field. Ostwald was a popularizer. As president of the Monist League and successor to Ernst Haeckel — the man who introduced Darwin's theories (or a version of them) to the German public — Ostwald peddled his own particular contribution, which sought to reveal the unity of man and nature and the commonality of their laws. Ostwald held that basic laws of energy, of increase and exploitation, underlie both matter and culture. To propagate his form of *Naturphilosophie* he founded a journal, the *Annalen der Naturphilosophie* (1902–1911), that would bring together the leading experts in their respective disciplines and would try to show the interconnections between the natural and human worlds. Among its contributors, in addition to Ostwald himself, were Mach, Wundt, and – of course – Lamprecht. The *Annalen* were decidedly serious and meant to be so.[16] Ostwald also wrote popular works, such as *Monism as the Goal of Civilization*, that outlined the practical, political and religious advantages of monism. In this, Ostwald managed to combine sun worship with energy conservation.[17]

I do not know whether Lamprecht was a member and an activist in the Monist League, but he did work alongside Ostwald in a presentation of German history that aimed to educate the separate groups and classes of the Wilhelmine Empire regarding their respective historical places in the present society. It is probably fair to say that there must have been a considerable market for his brand of philosophy of history and one that stretched beyond the educated stratum. This stratum itself, as Fritz Ringer's study[18] suggests, was becoming larger, originating from a wider social background and, increasingly, through the expansion of the *Technische Hochschulen*, open to the influence of science and technology.

The major point I want to make here is that, even within the educated stratum, and putting aside the issue of the wider reading public, Lamprecht was offering a decisively new conception of history. I would argue that the increasing heterodoxy of this educated audience opened the way to the popularity of the *Deutsche Geschichte*. Lamprecht, with his philosophy of history, had caught the temper of the times, and offered an entirely new version of the history of the German state and nation. His version gave scientific certainty, and a cast-iron assurance that the emergence of the economic and political strength of the German state was confirmed by the laws of evolution. The particular force and strength of the German people had been identified as a social psyche and its progress scientifically demonstrated. The social entity within which the historical laws of evolution were acted out was the nation, and the state its organizational form.

The successful transmission of this new conception of German history was, I believe, the major reason for the sense of outrage felt by the professional historians. It has to be remembered that history-writing occupied a very special niche in the training (*Erziehung*) of the educated elite. Even at its most confident (for instance, Treitschke's *History of Germany in the Nineteenth Century*), history was still meant to be instructive, to show why Prussia emerged as the leading power because of the demonstrable superiority of its laws, its political thinkers and its rulers compared with the backward and feudalistic petty principalities with their bombastic princes and reactionary advisers. Above all, Treitschke's narrative concerns the voluntarism of power – with the wrong policies and the wrong decisions, the outcome would not have been triumphant. Its tone was celebratory, but also instructive.

Meinecke's *Cosmopolitanism and the National State* (1908) was a representative work showing the orthodox outlook of the historian and his function as educator. The becoming of the nation is a moral tale. In the Rankean tradition, the state was a repository of ethical values and customs and, for Meinecke, the progress of the modern state and the creation of a national community involved the perspicacity, the wisdom and the moral sense of the ruler and his advisers. What was crucial for Meinecke was the ability of certain key thinkers to endorse the correct ideas, so that the proper line of development of the national state would be perceived. There was nothing ordained about the becoming of the national state; the reactionary and romantic feudalism of Ludwig v. Gerlach misidentified the personality of the state as the property of the ruler, and the universalistic philosophy that European nations could form one cultural community to maintain peace led to the gross errors of Friedrich Wilhelm IV. Meinecke's acuity in his presentation of ideas, the wrong-headed and the right, revealed the essential precariousness of the development of the national state. The major figures of Hegel, who gave the national state a personality and identity, Ranke, whose idealism unearthed the mysteries of the cultural nation and whose empiricism anchored the history of the nation, and Bismarck, whose realistic thinking gave national state power its first effective expression, are the salutary personages in Meinecke's history. [19]

Meinecke's opposition to Lamprecht was inevitable. The duality of nature and intellect, power and ethics, the general and the unique that are so prized in Meinecke's conception are completely subverted in Lamprecht's system. The role of the moral, autonomous intellect is reduced to irrelevancy, an object of artistic consideration. The state is no longer a precious receptacle of the moral forces of the nation; it is not even an organism – which might have been a half-acceptable naturalization – but a mechanism. And the exercise of power loses the frightening lability that demands a mature realism on the part of the statesman.

An even more acute cognitive dissonance resounded because, in their entirely different ways, Meinecke and Lamprecht were talking about the same thing. The cultural soul for Meinecke was something that the major figures and intellects could divine, although ultimately the cultural ideas of a nation were unknowable and mysterious. Lamprecht rudely asserted that Ranke's notions about the being of the nation were not empirical truths but were an ascribed mystery. His science of history would replace such etherealism with a scientific, non-metaphysical scrutiny of this once sacred object. Presumably the transmutation of the central object of the idealistic historiographical tradition into the object of deterministic science must have filled Meinecke, at the very least, with repugnance.

Beyond Tolerance

The above list of antinomies does not in itself explain the ostracism Lamprecht suffered – in part because of the policy of Meinecke, who was the young editor of the historians' periodical, the *Historische Zeitschrift*. In an ideal academic world those antinomies should have made for debate. I am not persuaded by the prejudice that Lamprecht was substandard, owing to his inaccuracies, his flights of fanciful argument and deficiencies of presentation, and that therefore he was beneath consideration. He clearly represented an intellectually valid approach to the study of society and history that, had it been received in a more open atmosphere, might have led to more constructive debate. For instance, had he been a professor of *Nationalökonomie*, he could perhaps have expected a different intellectual engagement. [20]

History was the sensitive faculty within higher and, indeed, secondary education. It instructed the 'civics' of national becoming and, in this sense, occupied a niche equivalent to philosophy in the French university and lycée system. In a past-minded nation the historians were the soothsayers of national destiny. In his essay, 'Drei Generationen deutscher Gelehrtenpolitik', Meinecke writes: 'Max Weber recognized perfectly rationally that: "The fatherland is not for us the land of the fathers but of their descendants." The complete idea of the national state demands, however, that it is the country of both.'[21] It seems that even Weber was not to escape the ethic of history.

However, to return to the matter in hand, Lamprecht with his *Deutsche Geschichte* had interposed not only an entirely different approach to history-writing but also how the reader should interpret history. In the period of high industrialization of the German Empire, the demands of the young Rankeans within the historical profession were out of tune with the awakening interest in economic and social history. The hegemony of political history asserted by Dietrich Schäfer, although ascribed to within the profession, was less suited to the new expectations of its audience in the educated middle class.[22] Lamprecht's *Deutsche Geschichte* offered an entirely new ideology of past-mindedness, one, as has been noted, that offered a comprehensive assurance to a more complacent and self-satisfied audience. For Meinecke, that it might be erroneous was nothing compared with the dangerous and facile conclusions drawn by its large readership. It was because Lamprecht had usurped and defiled the Rankean heritage, one of intellectual and moral authority over its audience, that the leading organ of the historians' profession expressed first strong disapproval and then refusal to recognize his academic existence.[23]

The methodological debate was conducted in terms of the role of the singular to the general and the appropriate methods of history; however, what was really at stake was not only a conflict of Weltanschauung but the right to disseminate the correct philosophy of history. A series of philological critiques were entered by Heinrich Finke, Felix Rachfahl and Georg v. Below. These corrected the errors of detail and fact in the *Deutsche Geschichte* and demanded a return to the scholarly use of primary sources. They argued that it was inadmissible to trust to secondary sources and by implication, given the present impossibility of mastering all primary sources, urged the abandonment of wide-ranging (in both time and space) history. Lamprecht dismissed these critics as *Detaillisten*, and in part this was justified.[24] But more interesting is part of the fall-out from this debate. History-writing became empiricized, and this was a new disciplinary standard that had not existed in the same way before. Ranke had called for new historical standards of accuracy against the metaphysical-speculative vein of history-writing epitomized by Hegel. However, as Iggers has shown, this did not exclude an idealistic theory of 'immanent becoming' in Ranke's own writing.[25] The new philological standards, as an exclusive criterion of proper history writing, was the response of withdrawal, of inward-looking disciplinary norms, in the face of the challenge to its authority.

The line of attack, led by Georg v. Below, was to deny the right to generalize in historical writing. Nominally a dispute between a generalizing and a particularizing science, it was in fact one of ontological and moral claims. Lamprecht's method was a materialist philosophy of history that, by subsuming the actions of the individual within the orbit of laws, denied any autonomy to the individual. In making this critique, Georg v. Below unfolded his own, countering, ontology. Because the individual was free, he could always have acted differently, hence free will always confounds the imposition of laws of history. Moreover, following his revered mentor, Treitschke, he asserted that the individual, the personality, must always remain a riddle and, therefore, closed to the gaze of human sciences. The attempt to extract laws of history by ranging over a long time-span and the use of comparative history is, like the new subject of sociology, merely a form of dilettantism.[26]

Enter Weber

I would presume that Weber's stance in this dispute was a little different from Meinecke's. Weber, perhaps more than any other academic, wanted to remove the baleful influence of a positivistic conception of history writing, and for the same underlying reason: its denial of a moral realm to knowledge and to the bearer of that knowledge, the scholar. Unlike Meinecke, though, he was much more aware of the crisis in the role and function of the academic and his knowledge. Meinecke continued in the old tradition, with a highly refined sensibility of the moral role of the historian. Weber realized the more prosaic and 'materialistic' nature of Wilhelmine society. The receptiveness of the educated middle class to the moral sensibility of the scholar could no longer be taken for granted. Moreover, within the business of producing knowledge itself, new professional standards internal to the disciplines and the academy were increasingly distancing knowledge from the old moral community of the educated middle class.[27]

We know Weber's solution: a moral egalitarianism within the educated middle class – so that professors no longer, by virtue of their position, had the right to act as moral authorities for their audience – and a differentiation of moral judgements from knowledge statements. Henceforth, the production of knowledge was to be an occupation just like any other in the modern world, and its practitioners were no more privileged and no less absolved from moral responsibility.[28]

Whatever we think, and however we interpret Weber's position, it was novel and a breakthrough in recognizing the changing realities of the production of knowledge and the relation of knowledge to society. For the purposes of this essay, I want to mention two aspects. First, the intense competition and hostility that Weber was faced with when propounding his viewpoint and, secondly, the detrimental effect this struggle had on 'technical' questions of methodology.

These aspects can be seen in Weber's engagement in the Lamprecht dispute. The most damaging part of Lamprecht's theory was his scientific conception of knowledge, for this essentially denied meaningful autonomy to the individual and relegated free will to the realm of the irrational. If the old-style scholar were out of touch with new realities, this was nothing compared to the new positivism. With the old school, the place of morality had only(!) to be re-positioned, whereas the new scientization of knowledge presumed to subsume morality under the working of laws. Positivism was public enemy number one and all other issues were secondary. Although today we see a line of continuity back to Heidelberg neo- Kantianism, Weber himself sometimes must have wondered whether that position was not surrounded and over-whelmed by the claims of a positivistically conceived science. In philosophy, psychology, law, economics and sociology, the idea of a determinative science and related organicist concepts were gaining the upper hand.

It is perhaps surprising that Lamprecht did not become the victim of one of Weber's obsessional and annihilating reviews in the *Archiv für Sozialwissenschaft und Sozialpolitik*. Instead, the more peripheral figure of Wilhelm Ostwald drew his ire, so conferring on Ostwald an ironic posterity – in the social sciences at least. Lamprecht suffered a more lingering death, im-paled on a series of dismissive footnotes and asides. He figures as a barely acknowledged worst point. Roscher's organicism, for instance, at least had the virtue of not seeking the essence of the progress of the *Volk*, whereas Lamprecht's does. Wundt's so-called laws of history misguidedly suggest that there can be a scientific foundation to meta-historical values, but this is as nothing with the 'appalling' Lamprecht who seeks to deploy these into cultural history. Roscher saw cultural values as essential because of their place in the continuity to the present, but it takes the 'amateurish' Lamprecht to commit this mistake in respect to art history.[29] As editor of the *Archiv*, Weber opined to the psychologist Willy Hellpach: 'It seems to me that for us [at the *Archiv*] no possible good can come from an essay that takes him as scientifically serious.'[30] Despite Weber's belief that Lamprecht was a fraud and a charlatan, the *Archiv* did carry a review of Lamprecht.

For Weber, it was the general battle that counted: truly one for the hearts and minds. But, in securing this major front, Weber gave himself very little room to manoeuvre when clarifying the relationship between history and sociology. The historians' debate was located on the terrain of the respective claims of cultural vs. political history. But the way through to a cultural history had been totally discredited by Lamprecht. In so far as Weber entered the historians' dispute, he had to back the orthodox historians. Major methodological essays on the possibilities of a developmental historical sociology have as their starting point an endorsement of the historians – Eduard Meyer and Georg v. Below – against Lamprecht.

It is often suggested that Weber is placed *mid*-way between anti-positivism and empiricism, and from that point he proceeded to build his own position by virtue of the epistemological and procedural novelty of the ideal type. However, I would argue that the *Wissenschaftslehre* is predominantly caught up in a resistance to positivism and the remainder leaves little scope for the more substantive issues of a comparative history. Weber's hostility to positivism meant that he was a methodological hostage to the historians. Even though he sought to redefine the empiricist position of the historians, he agreed on the fundamentals: pre-eminently, the assertion of the particularity of history and the ontological assumption that somehow the particular is more meaningful and less de-natured than any more general statement.[31]

An excellent illustration of this is a comparison of Otto Hintze's review of Lamprecht. Meinecke himself was later to admit that Hintze's review was one of the most balanced and fructifying in the dispute.[32] Hintze declared:

I agree with Lamprecht in the view that historical scholarship must be placed on the broad basis of thorough and profound research in social psychology...This is an enlargement of previous scholarly endeavours, not the overthrow of historical scholarship. As it appears to me, it will not result in the regularly recurring pattern of events but in the comprehension of an altogether singular development. In what we call universal history – i.e. the connected cultural development of ancient and modern peoples – the single nations represent distinct stages in the development of the wider whole, rather than a recurring pattern of a recurring national development.[33]

While Hintze rejects the idea of a regular re-occurrence, he does give himself room to formulate a developmental concept of 'the distinct stages of the development of the wider whole'. In a later essay on sociology, he says that sociologists compare 'in order to discover the general that lies at the basis of what is compared, while the historian compares in order to understand more clearly the uniqueness of each part of that which is compared...'[34] Hintze's position does not preclude the possibility that the study of comparative history can produce concepts that reflect the imputation of the real existence of stages or patterns of history. Exactly what we should term these concepts – pragmatically conceived 'real types'[35] – or precisely how we locate them in a philosophy of science[36] cannot be entered into here. The point to note is that Weber forecloses any such possibility, when it seems to me his own comparative sociology would have benefited from this recognition. (Notwithstanding the fact, as has been noted elsewhere, that he does actually 'slip' and uses 'real types'.)[37]

In contrast to Hintze, Weber denies that a general concept could reflect a real situation. Weber reveals *in nuce* his position in the oft-quoted letter to Georg v. Below. He *apologizes* for starting out with the comparative and systematic *Economy and Society* and assures Below that the purpose of comparison is to determine what is specific to, say, the medieval town. Comparison leads to the grasp and isolation of the *particular*, and 'the task of history is to find a causal explanation for these specific traits'.[38] This is not a precautionary gesture, lest he suffer the dreaded Below's scorn for sociology, but a genuine statement of Weber's ambition for a comparative historical sociology.

Obviously this point needs to be argued systematically in relation to Weber's whole work. Here, the approach is from the vantage point of the contemporaneous historians' dispute. This suggests that Weber shared not only their detestation of Lamprecht, his methods and *Weltanschauung*, but more crucially the threat posed by a positivist conception of knowledge that would totally redefine the old moral stance of the cultured individual. Weber recommends new ways out of the impasse precipitated by the break-up of the old knowledge community, in terms of both his own epistemology and his redefinition of the relationship between science and morality. Looking back at his proposals today, we cannot help but notice that his involvement in the fundamental questions was a limiting condition – at least for *him* – in the foundation of an independent historical sociology: one that had the freedom to explore the complex questions of the study of enduring regularities, the nature of their development over the long *durée*, and the form of their interaction with the forces that intervene, redirect and reform those regularities.

Perhaps we should agree with the veteran of an earlier historians' dispute, Eberhard Gothein, that what was needed was not a dispute between an individualizing and a collective concept of history, but an analysis of the differing value and significance to be placed on the raw, brutal material powers, on the one side, and the mental and cultural forces in history, on the other.[39]

Notes: Chapter 17

1 G. Oestreich, 'Die Fachhistorie und die Anfänge der sozialgeschichtlichen Forschung in Deutschland', *Historische Zeitschrift*, vol. 208 (1969), pp. 320–63; also E. Engelberg, 'Zum Methodenstreit um Karl Lamprecht', in J. Streisand (ed.), *Studien über die deutsche Geschichtswissenschaft*, Vol. 2 (Berlin [GDR], 1965); K. Weintraub, *Visions of Culture* (London, 1966); finally, the most informative study by L. Schorn-Schütte, *Karl Lamprecht. Kulturgeschichtsschreibung zwischen Wissenschaft und Politik* (Göttingen, 1984). Unfortunately, due to its recent publication, I was not able to utilize this study as much as I would have wished.

2 Franz Mehring had to disavow Lamprecht's alleged reputation as a *historical* materialist. He has also been criticized for his national cultural-imperialism. See Oestreich, 'Die Fachhistorie', nn. 7 and 122.

3 *Moderne Geschichtswissenschaft* (Leipzig, 1905); I have used the English translation, *What is History?* (London, 1905), p. 8.

4 Lamprecht, *What is History?*, p. 42.

5 ibid., p. 45.

6 ibid., p. 124.

7 ibid., p. 32.

8 ibid., p. 26.

9 E. Durkheim, *Elementary Forms of the Religious Life* (London, 1915), p. 8. Weber makes the same point against the empiricizing historians (and against G. v. Below specifically), who asserted the irrational and therefore unpredictable force of personality in history. Weber, however, does not appeal to a foundationalist belief in the universality of reason. Instead, Weber held that we act rationally when we act in terms of the understanding we have of the normal rules, norms and expectations that govern social life. See RaK, p. 271, n. 54.

10 Lamprecht, *What is History?*, p. 132.

11 *Deutsche Geschichte. Zur jüngsten deutschen Vergangenheit*, 3rd edn (Berlin, 1912), pp. v–vii. See also Preface to *Zweiter Ergänzungsband* (Berlin, 1903), p. 5: 'if we are to present the German social and economic development not from the specifically national and social-economic approach but rather from a general evolutionary and social psychological approach, then the explanation has to be far-reaching and broad-based: in particular the up till now valid theories of economic stages have to be replaced by a new psychological theory of stages...'

12 See Oestreich, 'Die Fachhistorie', p. 352.

13 H. v. Srbik, *Geist und Geschichte des deutschen Humanismus bis zur Gegenwart* (Salzburg, 1951), p. 229.

14 Lamprecht, 'Preface' to *Deutsche Geschichte*, Erster Ergänzungsband (Berlin, 1901), p. ix.

15 A. Kelly, *The Descent of Darwin: The Popularization of Darwinism in Germany, 1800–1914* (Durham, NC, 1981), p. 4.

16 W. Ostwald, 'Einführung' to *Annalen der Naturphilosophie*, Vol. 1 (Leipzig, 1902).

17 See D. Gasman, *Scientific Origins of National Socialism* (London, 1971), p. 69.

18 F. Ringer, *Education and Society in Western Europe* (Bloomington, Ind., and London, 1979), Chapter 2. There appears to be an absence of a study that links both the changing composition of the *Bildungsbürgertum* and the full range of ideas it was increasingly susceptible to. This need is alluded to by K. Vondung (ed.), *Das wilhelmische Bildungsbürgertum. Zur Sozialgeschichte seiner Ideen* (Göttingen, 1976).

19 F. Meinecke, *Cosmopolitanism and the National State* (Princeton, NJ, 1970), pp. 192 ff.

20 Is it a coincidence that both Eberhard Gothein and Max Weber gravitated to this department?

Gothein had earlier offended the profession with some mild criticisms of Dietrich Schäfer's assertion of the primacy of the political in history writing. Within the Rankean conception there was space to cultivate a cultural history without detriment to the political, Gothein argued. See P. Alter, 'Eberhard Gothein', in H-U. Wehler (ed.), *Deutsche Historiker*, Vol. 8 (Göttingen, 1982).

21   F. Meinecke, 'Drei Generationen deutscher Gelehrtenpolitik', *Historische Zeitschrift*, vol. 125 (1922), p. 283.

22   See Oestreich, 'Die Fachhistorie', pp. 351 ff.

23   Meinecke, as editor of the *Historische Zeitschrift*, unleashed a third and exceedingly hostile review by Georg v. Below. Given the history of abuse between Below and Lamprecht that led to a libel case in 1893, Meinecke's attitude can only be described as unfriendly. After Below's eighty-page tirade against Lamprecht's 'new historical method', Meinecke in a letter to Below, counsels a tactic of ignoring rather than engaging the combative and prolific Lamprecht. 'Indeed it's impossible to keep the man quiet, he will always produce confusion in weak minds – he's a hydra. I think a better tactic than one of continuing polemic – provisionally at least – is to let him scribble and to see him off in short reviews now and then that are quickly done. Then if he is still bearing fruit, we can perhaps give him a much stronger swipe with the blade.' F. Meinecke, *Ausgewählter Briefwechsel* (Stuttgart, 1962), pp. 15–17. To an extent, this tactic was successful and Lamprecht was forced out from the main stream. However, he was not silenced and at Leipzig he founded the grandiose *Königlich Sächsisches Institut für Kultur- und Universalgeschichte bei der Universität Leipzig*. On the attitude of the *Historische Zeitschrift*, see T. Schieder, 'Die deutsche Geschichtswissenschaft im Spiegel der Historischen Zeitschrift', *Historische Zeitschrift*, vol. 185 (1959), pp. 48–51.

24   See Srbik, *Geist und Geschichte*, p. 230.

25   G. G. Iggers, *The German Conception of History* (Middletown, 1968).

26   G. v. Below, 'Die neue historische Methode', *Historische Zeitschrift*, vol. 81 (1898), pp. 193 ff. Below was more than just a foot soldier in this dispute. His position within history writing was very complex and he obviously had a formidable and feared reputation. Below's opposition to Lamprecht was multi-layered. Against Lamprecht's conception of cultural history, Below asserted the primacy of political history. This, in its turn, demanded the appropriate methodology: one that venerated the every act and intention of the historical individual. There was a further, bottom-layer debate about the nature and origin of public authority in the medieval period. Lamprecht's first work, *Deutsches Wirtschaftsleben im Mittelalter* (Leipzig, 1886), had emphasized the role of local landlordship in the feudal period, while Below vigorously propounded the continuity of public authority. The salience of these arguments was their linkage to the status and origin of the medieval town councils: were they founded by private landlordship, were they conferred by some public authority, or were they autonomously created by the medieval burghers? This debate was abstruse, was constitutionalist in character, yet nevertheless carried clear resonances to and from the academics' stance to contemporary politics. To name only a few of the contributors, and it should be recognized that the debate predates the generations writing in the 1890s, Gierke formulated a dialectic between *Herrschaft* and *Genossenschaft* in the development of German state and society, Below championed the growth and persistence of a state public authority, Lamprecht stressed the role of the medieval town corporations and their integrative character in pre-class society and Max Weber drew attention to the autonomous role of the medieval burghers in the *coniuratio* movement. There is a case for opining that these debates were the substantive bedrock of argumentation in the historical sciences.

27   Max Weber: 'Universities do not have it as their task to teach any outlook or standpoint which is either "hostile to the state" or "friendly to the state". They are not institutions for the inculcation of absolute or moral values. They analyse facts, their conditions, laws and interrelations; they analyse concepts, their logical presuppositions and content. They do not and they cannot teach what should happen – since this is a matter of ultimate personal beliefs and values, of fundamental outlook, which cannot be "demonstrated" like a scientific proposition.' *Max Weber on Universities*, transl. and ed. by E. Shils (Chicago, 1973), p. 21.

28   FMW, pp. 129–56.

29   RaK, p. 244, n. 60; p. 111; p. 214, n. 10.

30   Max Weber to Willy Hellpach: 'Could you decide to leave Lamprecht out of the picture...It seems to me that no possible good will come from an essay that takes him scientifically seriously, for it will be necessary – and probably I'll have to be the executioner – to say that from our side we take him for a swindler and charlatan of the worst sort in so far as he passes

himself off as a *Culturkritiker* and cultural historian.' And 'His [Lamprecht's] theory of cultural stages appropriates facts according to the following motto: "skip to our tune or else", is long since anticipated by Comte and Roscher, takes over since Burckhardt the conceptual method into the field of history, the concept of social psychology correctly formulated by Eulenburg is continually mixed up with metaphysical questions by him, in short: not even the errors of detail are original. However, this is only to advertise...' Quoted in Schorn-Schütte, *Karl Lamprecht*, p. 93.

31 See also W. G. Runciman, *A Critique of Max Weber's Philosophy of Science* (Cambridge, 1972), pp. 78 ff.

32 F. Meinecke, *Erlebtes, 1862–1901* (Leipzig, 1941), p. 204.

33 *The Historical Essays of Otto Hintze*, ed. by F. Gilbert (New York, 1975), p. 366.

34 O. Hintze, *Gesammelte Abhandlungen*, Vol. 2 (Göttingen, 1964), p. 358.

35 See W. J. Mommsen, 'Max Weber und die historiographische Methode in seiner Zeit', *Storia della storiografia*, vol. 3 (1983), p. 38.

36 W. G. Runciman, *A Critique*; see also R. Keat, *The Politics of Social Theory* (Oxford, 1981).

37 As noted by F. H. Tenbruck, 'The problem of thematic unity in the works of Max Weber', *British Journal of Sociology*, vol. 31 (1980), p. 333.

38 Max Weber to Georg v. Below, 21 June 1914, transl. in G. Roth, 'Introduction', in ES, Vol. I, p. lxiv. This point is developed in S. Whimster, 'The profession of history in the work of Max Weber', *British Journal of Sociology*, vol. 31 (1980), pp. 352 ff.

39 See Oestreich, 'Die Fachhistorie', p. 355.

18 Otto Hintze and Max Weber: Attempts at a Comparison

JÜRGEN KOCKA

To investigate the influence of the Berlin historian Otto Hintze (1861–1940) on Max Weber is to pursue a rather fruitless line of inquiry. To my knowledge, Weber did not make a serious study of Hintze; it is not clear how familiar he was with Hintze's work; doubtless Hintze was not one of the writers who made any special impression on Weber. Conversely, Hintze had sceptically taken note of Weber's critique of bureaucracy even before 1914. Weber's articles on constitutional politics in the *Frankfurter Zeitung* in 1917 might have influenced Hintze, because in the same year he began to draw closer to parliamentary ideas, also owing to the influence of the war and the domestic political situation. After the First World War, Hintze's concept of the state grew closer to Weber's – the state as 'enterprise' (*Betrieb*) and 'institution' (*Anstalt*). Certainly Weber's works may have played a part here, but probably the experiences of the war, the German defeat and the collapse of the Wilhelmine Empire were of greater importance. In 1927, Hintze wrote briefly but admiringly about Max Weber, in the form of a review of Marianne Weber's biography. Around 1930 he refined his views on historical type formation – emphasizing the 'real type' (*Realtypus*) – by moving away from Max Weber, whose ideal type seemed too nominalistic to him. Weber thus influenced Hintze, but we shall not inquire into that any further in this chapter.

Our intention is, rather, to sketch some attempts at a comparison between Hintze and Weber (concentrating on the period up to 1920), in order to contribute to a distinction between what in Weber's thought and work was typical of his age, and what was specifically his, and to reach a clearer appreciation of Weber's and Hintze's achievements and limitations. For all their differences (which are so great as to make comparisons between the two difficult), they resembled each other in that the civil service and bureaucracy were the central objects of their scientific and political interests. From their scientific and journalistic concern with this theme, essential similarities and differences in their works emerge. The following section compares their research and views on bureaucracy and politics. From there I go on to develop some central theoretical and methodological differences between Weber and Hintze. Finally some conclusions are suggested.

Bureaucracy and Politics

At the centre of Hintze's work up to 1914 is his meticulously researched treatment of Prussian administrative and constitutional history, particularly in the seventeenth and eighteenth centuries. From here, he branched out in three directions. In the first place he did comparative work on other European states, pursuing the objective of a general administrative and constitutional history of the modern world of states, although the Prussian case retained paradigmatic importance for him, at any rate until the First World War. Secondly, he penetrated far into economic, social and cultural history, particularly that of Prussia, by investigating some of the many aspects of early modern administration: the conditions for it and resistance to it, its consequences and concomitant circumstances. To the extent that monarch and bureaucracy under the *ancien régime* were the initiators and driving forces of social modernization, administrative and constitutional history, as Hintze conceived it, could open out into a general social history – albeit from the point of view of the administration. Finally, Hintze extended his longitudinal studies in constitutional and administrative history more and more frequently into the nineteenth century and linked them with political science analyses.

Within this framework, Hintze's concept of bureaucracy and his assessment of the relationship between bureaucracy and politics under the Empire took shape. Starting from the Prussian-German example, he analysed the modern civil service both as an institution and as a social group. Several years before Max Weber summarized, sharpened and universalized the ideal type of 'bureaucracy', Hintze had marked out many of its characteristics: the public service/loyalty relationship between civil servant and state as opposed to the simple contract of employment; the principle of the 'whole person'; the element of delegated exercise of authority; the lifelong duration, the security, the honour, the salary and other socioeconomic aspects of the civil servant's status, particularly the principle of official duty in contrast to business interests. Hintze neglected three important aspects of the later Weberian type: the strictly hierarchical structure, the developed specialization and, lastly, vocational training and examinations as conditions of entry to most civil service posts. Accordingly, Hintze praised 'honesty, sense of duty and simple loyalty' as civil servants' virtues, but not so much the bureaucratic efficiency and purposive rationality in the execution of orders so central to Weber's analysis.

In principle Hintze, like Weber, stressed bureaucracy's nature as a means and viewed public (or indeed private) officialdom as the ruler's (or entrepreneur's) instrument of authority and administration, as an intermediate stratum, as the 'link from the rulers to the ruled, from the entrepreneurs to the workers'. To this extent, for Hintze as well, the bureaucracy referred upward to an extra-bureaucratic top, which in Prussian Germany meant primarily the monarch. On the other hand, he knew from his studies of traditional European absolutism, particularly in Prussia, that 'administration is much more closely linked with government and thus with aspirations of power than is commonly assumed'. Against this background, it seemed to him neither surprising nor particularly reprehensible that even in the administrative reality of his day 'at the summits of the civil service state' 'the concept of service' actually blended with that of 'authority'. More implicitly than explicitly, Hintze thus distanced himself from a way of thinking which – like Weber's – maintained (or even required) that there was a division and a qualitative difference between the extra-bureaucratic top and the bureaucratic apparatus. He was approaching, albeit unwittingly, a less dualistic conception of the relationship between leadership and administration, such as was more often found in the less bureaucratic Anglo-American sphere and is implied in the concept of 'management'. For this concept denies the deep split between the top and the apparatus that is so central to Weber's conception of bureaucracy. In this way Hintze succeeded in making a realistic analysis of government and administration in the monarchical, civil servant state (*Beamtenstaat*). He captured the reality of a structure of authority that was characterized in its upper ranks by gradually increasing power, but not by a split between leader and apparatus.

Hintze mainly saw advantages in this monarchical, bureaucratic form of rule. He argues that, for historical reasons which persisted, civil service posts in Prussian Germany had been taken up by the best personnel; hence, the selection of leading ministers from the ranks of the civil service was much more promising than any other selection mechanism. Therefore, the civil service, this 'invaluable product of the political-military education of our people since the days of the Great Elector', could not be surpassed in Germany for talent, independence of judgement, esprit de corps and 'impartial objectivity'; these merits would only suffer from parliamentarization. Moreover, the monarchical bureaucratic government was above the party and class interests, and was thus particularly suited to providing a 'firm course towards definite political goals in the long term', the smoother running of politics and a disciplined leadership of state and society.

In accordance with his basic principle of regarding state constitutions and social structure as partly, if not primarily, shaped by the influence of 'external state formation' and constellations in international politics, Hintze considered it impossible for continental Germany to afford parliamentariza- tion – threatened as it was on many sides and forced to rely on its army, striking power and disciplined leadership. The untested implication of this argument, which Weber would have disputed at the time and which most historians would dispute today, consisted in assuming that the monarchical constitutional system possessed greater powers to act than did the parliament- ary system. Secondly, he referred to significant obstacles to parliamentariza- tion in Germany, namely the federalist structure, the fragmentation of German society according to class and religion, but above all to the irrespons- ible behaviour of inept, fragmented, polarized and ideologized parties. He conceded that a social integration and transformation of the party system in the long run might perhaps be more likely to result from parliamentarization. In contrast to Weber, however, he refused to accept the risk in the increasingly tense foreign political situation – so hostile to parliamentarization.

Thus far Hintze (unlike Weber) was firmly in the prevailing tradition of German political thought of his day, which approved a special path for Germany's constitutional history (constitutional monarchy instead of parlia- mentarization). But, even before 1914, Hintze qualified that by saying that this rigid authoritarian system impeded 'the natural urge of the people towards the activation of a co-operative spirit in public life', helping to arouse social democracy's 'venemous enmity towards the state' and preventing politics from becoming the internal and social 'politics of peace'. But only when the First World War had conspicuously demonstrated how greatly a state's possibilities of exercizing power depended on its internal cohesion, its citizens' readiness to participate and hence the democratic opportunities to participate; when the weaknesses in co-ordination and leadership of the pre-parliamentary German system had become all too clear in the final phase of the war; when the 'elemental force' of the democratic movements had manifested itself more powerfully than ever before, and defeat was already looming ahead – only then did Hintze draw the necessary conclusions in terms of criticism of the constitution. In autumn 1917, he proposed a limited extension of suffrage in Prussia and practical steps in the direction of parliamentarization, which would, however, be kept within bounds by corporatist elements in the composition of the Upper Chamber and by new plebiscitary elements. Admittedly, Hintze was very reserved as far as comments on constitutional politics were concerned after the end of the war. He did not come out against the new state, but neither did he defend it: he maintained a retiring 'contemplative stance', full of scepticism towards the new democracy and its impotence in foreign affairs. But the Prussian military and civil service state ceased to be the paradigm, model and centre of his historical comparisons, which were now even more far-reaching than before. Rather than Germany, it was the constitutional history of the West European states with their gradual adoption of parliamentarization that came to represent the paradigm case, endowed with superior historical justification.

Weber approached the problem of bureaucracy quite differently from Hintze – not via the historical study of the early modern military and civil service state, in which the rising modern civil service had actually played a progressive part in the process of modernizing the state, society and the economy, at least in Prussia. Rather, it was, first, his historical studies of the economic history of antiquity and, secondly, his empirical sociological research into the situation of the East Elbean farm labourers that alerted him to the role of bureaucracies. The former work dealt with the question of the conditions governing the emergence and decline of a capitalist economic system in the Roman Empire; the latter intensified his critical interest in the socioeconomic and sociopolitical problems of the German Empire, whose increasingly modern capitalist economy he saw as being in sharp contrast to the social and political constitution that was shaped by remaining structures of the feudal and authoritarian state. In both these problem areas Weber pursued two questions that were central to the rest of his work. What were the conditions that made possible the emergence of capitalist economic systems? What are the conditions and factors that determine its continued existence or its destruction? It should be remembered that, for Weber, modern capitalism meant – and this became increasingly evident in the course of his later work – not only a methodical and rational economic system; it also signified the socioeconomic dimension of a complex cultural tradition, occurring originally only in the Occident and which aimed at anti-traditionalist mastery of the world. This was described by Weber as 'rationalization' – and, as such, was desired by him. In his studies of the economic history of antiquity and in the sociological investigation of his time, bureaucracy enters Weber's analysis chiefly as a threat to that socioeconomic dimension of rationalization. The dynastic bureaucracy of the Roman monarchy established a 'liturgical' state on the Graeco-Egyptian pattern that had helped, in Weber's opinion, to strangle capitalism in the ancient world. Similarly, the pre-bourgeois political system of the Kaiserreich, with its late feudal as well as bureaucratic characteristics, threatened, as he saw it, to impede the development of an emergent capitalism, of an autonomously self-regulating bourgeois society and a strong national state. On the basis of extensive universal historical and comparative sociological studies, he soon came to perceive that modern capitalism itself became the driving force of further bureaucratization, and that modern bureaucracy – alongside the rational economy, positive law and empirical science – itself represented a dimension of modern 'rationalization'.

This is the background, of which only an outline is given here, to Weber's concept of bureaucracy and his assessment of the relationship between bureaucracy and politics under the Kaiserreich. It was chiefly from his actual observations of the Prussian-German civil servant that he abstracted the ideal type of 'bureaucracy'. This has influenced sociological research ever since, in a manner unequalled by any other conceptual system. By comparison with pre-bureaucratic forms of administration, especially the traditional patrimonial administration and the administration by notables in the nineteenth century, he demonstrated in a way that was more convincing and conceptually more incisive than Hintze's, the superior efficiency of bureaucracy as the means of carrying out legal authority as well as an instrument for effecting organizational aims of any kind.

Thus it is scarcely surprising that Weber had an equally high opinion of the Prussian-German professional civil service as had Hintze. Even during the 1918–19 revolution, he defended it vehemently. He praised its moral virtues and its technical efficiency. Yet at the same time – in total contrast to Hintze and most of his contemporaries – he was one of the most scathing critics of the German civil service of his day; this was so in three respects.

First, in a way that was more consistent than Hintze's, he regarded the civil service as one social group among many and as part of a society that was characterized by conflict and a heterogeneity of interests. He viewed the civil service as a social group which, like any other social group, represented particular interests; he critically analysed the language of *raison d'état* and the institution of the official secret, regarding them as instruments of the preservation and extension of bureaucratic power. In strong contrast to Hintze, he questioned the civil servants' claim to be non-partisan trustees of the common weal. The same critical intent lay behind his repeated charges against the Prussian bureaucracy: that behind the veil of *raison d'état* it was under too much of an obligation to agrarian interests and that it bore the stamp of conservative, neo-feudal traditions.

Secondly, Weber, quite unlike Hintze, emphasized the categorical difference between bureaucratic administration on the one hand, and political leadership on the other. It is well-known that he denied the civil servants' right and competence to engage in political action. On the basis of delegated powers of authority and specialized knowledge, with responsibility for the office and in the service of given objectives, good administration proceeded in a steady, calculable and efficient manner. Precisely because good civil servants met this requirement, with their professional ethos, their mode of conduct and their value-orientations, they were, he claimed, unsuitable as politicians. For, in politics, one had to make decisions on the basis of one's own responsibility with reference to the public realm of value-conflict. He passionately reproached the bureaucracy in Germany for having usurped politics. The weaknesses of German politics – a lack of unity, a lack of energy, particularly in pursuing national political objectives, as well as a lack of dynamism at home – he ascribed to the fact that there was basically rule by civil servants, and not the rule of one or another social class. Much as Weber defended and welcomed bureaucracy as a means of rule and goal-attainment in institutions of every kind, he emphatically rejected bureaucracy as the rule of civil servants and as the source of goal-formulation. In order to eliminate the rule of civil servants or at any rate to restrict it, he developed his well-known ideas of parliamentarization and democratization. He did this at a much earlier stage than Hintze and in a much more radical way.

Ultimately Weber's critique of the Prussian-German civil service state and his proposals for constitutional reform were part of a fundamental scepticism about the long-term consequences of bureaucratization. However much bureaucracy was a consequence and a means, a force and expression of the specifically occidental tradition of rational and methodical world mastery, and was, moreover, a process that could only be halted or turned back, if at all, at the price of technical-economic and sociopolitical regression, Weber was none the less convinced that, in the long term, bureaucratization would become a danger to individuals' realization of their own freely chosen values and their readiness to transcend given conditions, a danger also to the development of a dynamic capitalist economy, and finally a danger to open social relations and to politics in general ('the future cage of bondage'). Such ideas were foreign to Hintze.

Basic Concepts

The difference in the way they assessed bureaucracy and politics points to fundamental dissimilarities between Hintze and Weber, which we shall now summarize in four points.

(1) If Weber saw the Prussian-German civil service as one social group among others and critically analysed the ideological component of its particular interests, demonstrating its affinity with agrarian interests and feudal traditions, he did this on the basis of an analysis of both the class structure and the economic and cultural situation in the German Empire. As Weber put it, this was 'characterized on the one hand by the disintegration of the economic preconditions of the Prussian landowners' national position, on the other hand by the appropriation of the feudal values by the industrial, capitalist bourgeoisie, while the proletariat remains negatively integrated into the Empire'. The class-conscious bourgeois Max Weber regarded the landowners and not the proletariat as the principal class adversary of the bourgeoisie, and criticized the latter harshly for its tendency towards politico-social adjustment, 'state piousness' and the 'feudalization' of its values and mode of life. He saw German society as split by diverging interests and ridden with conflicts, and strove to bring these conflicts out into the open. From this point of view, that of society, he looked at bureaucracy.

Hintze, whose origins, temperament and perspective brought him much closer to the character of the Prussian civil servant, lacked two things: the bourgeois anti-Junker commitment as a spur to action, and – at least until the end of the war – the ability to regard the bureaucracy (and the state) from the vantage point of society, 'from below', so to speak. He had never systematically analysed the Prussian-German civil service and its relative dependence on individual social groups and classes, although his essays undoubtedly contain historical instances and illustrations of such a dependence. Nor had he deemed it impossible to use the concept of *raison d'état* in the sense of a state objective governing action, instead of relativizing it in terms of an ideological critique as Weber did.

Here a central difference between the two writers becomes evident. At first glance, Weber and Hintze (the former more drastically than the latter) frequently based their conceptions of political goals on the primacy of state and power politics. Economic developments, social reforms and constitutional changes were evaluated, advocated or resisted by both (though by no means exclusively) according to their effects on the power and greatness of the national state. But Hintze, at least until 1918, adopted this outlook as an analytical perspective; that is to say, his choice of scientific approach, his points of view, methods and explicatory models were primarily influenced by the state, by the political aspect, frequently by foreign affairs, and, almost like a civil servant, he tended to consider economic and social phenomena only as far as they could be seen as conditions or results of state action. Whereas Weber, despite his political identification with power-state interests, adopted a sociological approach, in so far as he attempted to view state organs and decisions primarily (if not exclusively) in their dependence on and their function in a heterogeneous, conflict-ridden society.

Accordingly, the relations between state and society were interpreted differently by Hintze and Weber. Around 1900, Hintze saw 'society' as the sphere of mutual needs, of 'material culture', of economic life, of 'external culture', of exchange, of collective forces that were only partly becoming conscious. Economy and society seemed to him to be the 'organic' foundation, developing slowly and relatively regularly, on which the state rested. The sphere of the state, on the other hand, was dominated by conscious will, the individual. Hintze viewed the state as a 'personality', the general individuality which inspired the 'striving to guide, to lead, to dominate'. The 'state personality' and its organs, namely the monarch and the civil service, appeared to him to be the major progressive factors in historical change. And, for this reason, despite the consideration he gave to economic and socio-historical factors, a sociological conception of the state remained just as foreign to him as a genuinely socio-historical interpretation of universal history – at any rate until the end of the First World War.

To Weber, on the other hand, the state was an 'enterprise' (*Betrieb*), that is, an instrument defined by functional characteristics for the realization of the most various, changeable, not necessarily self-imposed goals. For Weber, the state ceased to be any kind of embodiment of the universal; it became a means, albeit an excellent one, and thus had to be analysed in relation to those changing, diverging forces whose realization and implementation it served. Weber identified these forces as material and ideal interests, as groups and classes, and as the value-related decisions and aspirations of individuals. He thereby opened the door to a sociological or socio-historical consideration of state and bureaucracy.

This is documented not only in his analysis of the civil service under the Empire, but also in his fundamental assessment of bureaucratization in a long-term universal-historical perspective. He saw the rise of modern bureaucracy, and bureaucratization in general, as conditioned by preceding socioeconomic and sociocultural processes (the market and money economy, the anti-traditional 'disenchantment' of the world, the increasing division of labour, social differentiation and specialization, which demanded co-ordination). Conversely, he showed the strength of bureaucracy – once it had formed – to influence, to promote and to endanger those socioeconomic and sociocultural processes. In other words, at this universal-historic level, also, his analysis of bureaucracy is firmly rooted in a socio-historical outlook. There is nothing in Hintze's work that corresponds to this. Hintze attempts no fundamental socio-historical explanation of the processes of internal and external state formation, which are at the centre of his interest and whose principal element he considers to be the rise, structure and achievements of the civil service.

(2) It was Weber's profound disappointment with what he saw as the inadequate leadership of German foreign policy that prompted his sharpest attacks on the monarchical civil service state. With some justification, he linked the lack of clear co-ordination and leadership in foreign policy, and the absence of personal responsibility in cases of glaring failure, with the weakness of a pre-parliamentary system of government that had no strong majority support. He reproached the civil servants with being bureaucratically incompetent in matters of power politics. For reasons that were primarily to do with foreign policy, he became a critic of domestic politics.

Hintze, who was also a firm believer in the goal of the expansion of national power, still gave muted praise and sober assent to the imperial government's successes in foreign policy in 1913–14, which indicates that the two men assessed the same events by different yardsticks. Much as he supported the German world power and naval policies, Hintze did not believe in the inevitability of war or the exclusiveness of struggle in the relations between nations. Indeed, he trusted in a solidarity within a system of power that was based on international law and a common culture, quite in the tradition of Leopold v. Ranke. Admittedly these powers were in rivalry and the system itself was constantly endangered, but nevertheless it ultimately tended towards a balance. World power politics, as he understood it, was a continuation of earlier power politics of states, albeit with new methods and on an ever more global scale; it was in no way a 'bid for world power'. This view tended to render him politically moderate; analytically, it obstructed his insight into the specifically new aspect of contemporary imperialism: that is, its specific explosive force connected with its mass-mobilizing function and its link with the expansionist requirements of an industrial capitalism that, in global terms, was extremely unevenly developed.

For Weber, international politics was more clearly and exclusively a struggle for power, elbow-room and survival than it was for the moderate, cautious Hintze. His passionate commitment made him hypercritical of the political errors and inconsistencies of German power politics. To a certain extent he was the more modern of the two: politically in his nationalism, analytically in his sense of the role of mass phenomena in contemporary politics, which he sought to capture in the category of charismatic rulership and the analysis of the modern mass party.

(3) The two writers' diverging analyses of bureaucracy demonstrate their understanding of politics and historical reality in general. In his methodological essays, Weber always emphasized that the norms and goals of political action cannot be deduced from an analysis (no matter how precise) of the observable historico-social reality, because historical reality – and here he differed fundamentally from any Hegelianizing approach – does not carry its goal and its meaning within it. History cannot specify the criteria for its own future development from within itself. But, at the same time, he vigorously denied any predetermined, unhistorical fixed order of binding values in the Christian natural-law sense, or in the Rickertian sense. He saw politics primarily as decision, as a struggle in which one was responsible to one's own chosen values, and as an open clash between diverging interests, but not as the expression of some kind of predetermined common weal. From this partly pluralist, partly antagonistic concept of politics, it is evident that he denied the exclusive right of any social group – no matter how intelligent and well-educated – to lay down and implement whatever was considered politically correct at any one time. He principally required of a politician aggressive qualities that could only be but feebly developed in the civil service; in his opinion, expertise and conscientiousness alone would not make a good politician. Impartiality as the attribute of a politician was either an indication of failure, or, more frequently, a smoke-screen. For him, bureaucracy could not and should not be a medium of politics, because it did not enable the inevitable conflict to take place, or it disguised such conflict.

But it is also perfectly valid to reverse this causal relationship, and it is hard to say which aspect was more strongly conditioning, and which more strongly conditioned, in the genesis of Weber's thought. Precisely because Weber was profoundly dissatisfied with the achievements of Prussian-German politics, not least because of his extreme and aggressive nationalist expectations that remained unfulfilled by imperial politics, and because of his anti-feudal stance, precisely for these reasons he attempted to demarcate the limits of bureaucratic action in politics both analytically and normatively, and to formulate as sharply as possible the qualitative difference between politics as decision, struggle and commitment to values, on the one hand, and civil service administration as the implementation of decisions in terms of a rational orientation to specific ends, on the other. Weber's concept of political action was developed with a polemical intent under the conditions of a pre-parliamentary civil service state. He regarded this state with the utmost scepticism, and this helps to explain his sharpness, rough edges and exaggerations.

In all this, Weber differed fundamentally from Hintze. At least until the end of the Wilhelmine Empire, Hintze did not reveal the foundations of his thought – and thus his concept of politics – to the same extent as Weber. From brief references, however, we may deduce that he based himself vaguely and implicitly on the existence of a common weal (albeit discernible with difficulty) beyond the struggle and compromises of divergent and unsecured value-choices, and above particular interests and parties. By this common weal, the *raison d'état* as he termed it, he meant at least the realization of power and prosperity, of law and security, of internal and external peace. He obviously never contemplated the possibility that sensible people might have different opinions on these principles; at any rate, such a notion did not enter into his theoretical arguments. How were these not easily reconcilable objectives of the state to be realized at any given time? Characteristically, this depended to a certain extent on what he called 'historical necessities'. Among these he included, for example, historical tradition, the geopolitical conditions and above all the external threat to a state.

In a certain respect, historical reality obviously prescribed several basic rules for good politics in Hintze's view. For him history was not, as it was for Weber, meaningless happenings, a chaotic torrent of events, even though it certainly did not appear to him as a clearly structured, purposeful movement. It would be going too far to impute to him a way of thinking in categories of historical determinism; but, much more strongly than Weber, he viewed the action of the politician as the consequence of historical conditions and the historically developed, given situation; its analysis as expertly and objectively as possible became the crucial precondition of good politics. Hintze did not deny the conflicts between interests, classes, confessions, and so on, but neither did he stress them; this was in contrast to the conflicts (which he emphasized but did not explain more fully) between the states, in whose 'banging and barging' he claimed to find much of the explanation for the internal developments within states. Privately, he seems to have been convinced that the fundamentals of good politics might consist of the insight and the deliberations of intelligent, unemotional, well-meaning, honest, talented and educated people (and for Hintze where were they to be found if not in the civil service?), and it was neither permissible nor necessary to leave politics to the unpredictable result of conflict and compromise.

From all this it is understandable that, unlike Weber, Hintze theoretically had little reason to plead for a rigorous separation of politics and administration: according to his view of history, it was right and proper for them to exist in the closest conjunction. Moreover, because Hintze was largely in agreement with the results of German politics under the Empire, he also lacked the topical impetus which prompted Weber's conceptual dichotomization of politics and bureaucracy.

(4) Weber's demand for a clean conceptual as well as practical separation of politics and bureaucracy has its methodological counterpart in his insistence on a sharp distinction between normative and analytical statements, and in his position in the dispute on value-freedom. True, Weber clearly saw and demonstrated that the values and viewpoints of the scientist are bound to influence his choice of themes, his conceptualization and reasoning, just as he also conceded, conversely, that analytical scientific findings are not irrelevant to the decision about objectives and values. But, nevertheless, a dominant feature in his methodological essays is a commitment to the sharp division between analysis and evaluation, between statements about what is and what ought to be. The fact that Weber insisted so fiercely on this division is closely linked with his criticism of bureaucracy's encroachment into the field of politics, a domain that was not its proper concern. For if, in Weber's view, bureaucrats usurped politics, they did so ultimately with reference to their expertise: that is, to science in the broadest sense, the capabilities of which

were thereby fatally overstretched. The lack of a clear division between expertise (science) and politics was a central element in the bureaucratization of politics, as criticized by Weber. Weber's polemics in the dispute on value-freedom draws its strength and its incisiveness from this background.

Without Weber's polemics against the mingling of politics and administration in the Kaiserreich, Hintze characteristically failed to arrive at a sharp epistemological division between norm and analysis. His position in the dispute on value-freedom remains unclear; his works teem with implicit and explicit value-judgements. Whereas Weber's postulate of value-freedom was partly devised in his minority struggle against the Schmoller-led majority of the Verein für Sozialpolitik, it seems likely that Hintze, had he been present, would have come down on Schmoller's side rather than Weber's.

A Comparative Summing-Up

This discussion of the contrasting aspects of the work of Weber and Hintze from different points of view might now be employed to arrive at a comparative assessment of the stature and limitations of the differing approaches of the two scholars. For all the brilliance and perspicacity of Hintze's analysis of the civil service, a comparison with Weber the critic of bureaucracy makes clear how much this analysis was shaped and limited by a traditionalist view of the bureaucratic, authoritarian state. Hintze's fundamentally *étatiste*, pre-pluralist and undoubtedly pre-democratic stance emerges most clearly from a comparison with Weber's more liberal and more democratic approach. This was connected with the methodological limitations of Hintze's otherwise impressive work, which we are not able to appreciate to the full here. A comparison also underlines these limitations: his distance from genuine social-historical approaches; a lack of clarity in his analysis of modern phenomena – partly due to the over-hasty transfer into contemporary history of categories that had been proved by research into the Europe of the *ancien régime*; his readiness to introduce the power struggle between the states as an explanatory factor, but scarcely or not at all as something itself in need of explanation. Without devoting too much attention to the distinction between descriptive-analytical and normative statements, and thus reflecting the related problems of the objectivity and contextual nature of scientific statements, the otherwise methodologically well-versed Hintze seems almost a little pre-critical in the mirror of the Weberian critique. All this applies with greater force to the Hintze of the Kaiserreich period. In many respects, he later came closer to Weber, though this later position remained incomplete and not properly connected with the earlier period.

Conversely it is true that the comparison with the much more old-fashioned, liberal conservative Hintze, whose outlook bore the stamp of the authoritarian state, demonstrates the uncommon incisiveness of Weber's vision, the strength of his analysis and – in connection with this – the radical nature of his liberal, democratic and nationalist commitment. But the comparison would also reveal weaknesses and difficulties in Weber's approach, which Hintze avoided. This could be demonstrated in their attitudes to social policy, to the demand for social security for the lower strata and to the emergent welfare state, which

Hintze welcomed but Weber, in a hopelessly anachronistic manner, deprecated.

The fact that, in reality, there is a gradual, graded difference rather than a qualitative, dichotomous one between political leadership and high bureaucracy, that bureaucracies change internally in the transition from authoritarian to functional administration and that they themselves can become sources of dynamism – these facts were more clearly and realistically recognized by Hintze, schooled in the example of pre-modern Europe, than by the modern, liberal Weber. The latter's prognosis of the ossification of bureaucracy, which has not been fulfilled to this day, was not shared by the reflective Hintze. Finally, much of Hintze's concept of politics is impressive, in contrast to Weber's. Despite its *étatiste*, pre-pluralist and pre-democratic features, it was more receptive to the fact that politics does not consist only of struggle and that the development of an informed opinion is also always connected with expertise, analysis and some common objectives, such as 'welfare', 'justice' and 'peace'.

Note: Chapter 18

This chapter was translated by Barrie Selman.

For detailed references to sources and literature see J. Kocka, 'Otto Hintze, Max Weber und das Problem der Bürokratie', *Historische Zeitschrift*, vol. 233 (1981), pp. 65–105. See also idem, 'Otto Hintze', in H.-U. Wehler (ed.), *Deutsche Historiker* (Göttingen, 1973), pp. 275–98, and O. Büsch and M. Erbe (eds), *Otto Hintze und die moderne Geschichtswissenschaft* (Berlin, 1983). An important general study is R. vom Bruch, *Wissenschaft, Politik und öffentliche Meinung. Gelehrtenpolitik im Wilhelminischen Deutschland (1890–1914)* (Husum, 1980). A selection of Hintze's writings is easily accessible in F. Gilbert (ed.), *The Historical Essays of Otto Hintze* (New York, 1975), which contains an excellent introduction by the editor. The full German edition of the essays is O. Hintze, *Gesammelte Abhandlungen*, ed. by G. Oestreich, 3 vols., 2nd edn (Göttingen, 1962–7).

Part III

The Realm of Politics

19 Friedrich Naumann and Max Weber: Aspects of a Political Partnership

PETER THEINER

If we are looking for lasting traces of Max Weber's influence on the politics of the late-Wilhelmine Reich, we shall encounter his political and personal friendship with Friedrich Naumann – a relationship maintained until Naumann's early death. 'Many years of my own life and hopes die with him', wrote Weber in August 1919;[1] a comment which conveyed not only his deep personal sorrow, but also his fundamental sympathy with Naumann's political aims. Such concord is rare in the history of Max Weber's relations with his political environment. He had, after all, a general reputation as an extremely strong-willed personality, not easily integrated into political categories or organizations.

This chapter attempts to outline the various phases and high points of this political relationship. It may be possible to arrive at a more precise estimation of Weber's direct and indirect influence on the political events of his time by tracing the course of the relationship between him and Naumann. But at the very least we shall be able to put the political scenario of the late-Wilhelmine Reich into sharper perspective by establishing correspondences, or at least similarities, in their political aims, and by considering the conflicts between their aims, and the causes of these conflicts. We shall also be able to determine more precisely how much room for manoeuvre the forces of reform found at their disposal. Max Weber and Friedrich Naumann, we must remember, were the exponents of a variety of Wilhelmine liberalism that aimed to make fundamental changes in the sociopolitical system of the late Kaiserreich.

At first sight there was very little to suggest political affinity or political co-operation between them. Friedrich Naumann, four years older than Max Weber, was the son of a clergyman and followed in his father's vocational footsteps. He studied theology, trained for his pastoral vocation and, in the course of his theological training, opted for practical activity in Protestant social work. For three years he exchanged his academic milieu for one that would give him more immediate insights into the living conditions of the lower echelons of society, and became an assistant in the so-called 'Rough House' founded near Hamburg by Johann Hinrich Wichern. The experience gained there proved useful in his first pastoral appointment, in Langenberg. He attracted the attention of his superiors in the ecclesiastical hierarchy of Saxony by his unusually strong and intensively pursued interest in the living conditions of his congregation; he began to publish his observations and reflections on social ethics, extremely tentative though they were at this period. His 'Working Man's Catechism',[2] of 1889, is typical of this phase of his development.

It was written entirely in reaction to the increasing share of votes won by the Social Democrats in the Reichstag elections, and was an attempt to re-establish the status of the church, and of values upheld by the church, among a proletariat that was on the point of turning its back entirely on church and religion.

The young clergyman advocated cautious reform, rejecting radical concepts of social change. He was appalled by the increase in the employment of women and by the disintegration of the family, which this in his view entailed, and he polemicized against the programmes and propaganda of the Social Democrats. Nevertheless – and here we have some indications of his role as dissident in the ecclesiastical and social politics of Protestantism in his time – there were significant differences of detail between Naumann's early publications and the forms of social apologetics usually produced by the church at that time. He claimed to be 'a Socialist on the basis of the state as presently constituted',[3] and thereby distanced himself clearly from a purely pastoral conception of his vocation as clergyman. His claim was viewed by his ecclesiastical superiors with considerable scepticism, but this concept of his identity did place him in the tradition of a Christian socialism of Protestant persuasion.

The gap between church and society had become all too evident by the time of the 1848 Revolution; Naumann continued efforts made by others to bridge this gap and if possible to close it, by working in the field of social ethics. A typical pioneer of this epoch was Johann Hinrich Wichern, with his scheme for a large-scale re-Christianization of society, in a spirit of counter-reformation.[4]

But if Wichern was concerned to mitigate the destructive consequences of pauperization and early industrialization by means of charitable organizations and by a common front of church and state against 'revolution', the second phase of development (as seen from a typological standpoint) had already encountered a changing situation. The movement, led by the Berlin Court preacher, Adolf Stoecker, was a typical product of the 1870s. Stoecker's attempt to regain a proper place in society for religion culminated in the foundation of a political party. Impelled by the increasing electoral successes of the Social Democrats and by the increasing secularization of broad strata of society, he adopted methods for demagogic mobilization of the masses, in order to ward off the decline of the bastions of ecclesiastical power. Like many Protestant clergy, Stoecker legitimized his own role in society by an excess of nationalistic zeal and, for good measure, enhanced his militant anti-socialism with anti-Semitic images of the enemy. The movement that he inaugurated hastened the demise of traditional conservatism and created an ideological platform for the right-wing radical dissident parties of the late Kaiserreich, but did not actually advance the original aim of re-Christianizing society.[5]

It is against this background that we must appreciate the young Naumann's attempts to recover the ground lost by the church's remoteness from the social changes of his time, from his position as parish priest and later as clergyman of the Home Mission. Naumann specifically placed himself in the tradition of Protestant social reformers begun by Wichern, but made efforts to go beyond what he saw as the all too patriarchal limitations of the Home Mission.

Within the broad context of the Christian Social movement influenced by Stoecker, Naumann swiftly made himself a name as the unifying figurehead of a group of young clergy that emerged in the early 1890s. The most significant area of activity of this group included the Protestant workers' organizations (Evangelische Arbeitervereine) and the Evangelical-Social Congress (Evangelisch-sozialer Kongreß); in this latter forum, Friedrich Naumann had an opportunity to define the differences between the 'younger' Christian Socialists and the middle-class, socially conservative character of Stoecker's movement. The 'younger' Christian Socialists saw themselves as the shock-troops of Protestant reform of society, and sought to free themselves from the embrace of conservatism, in which Stoecker's movement had become ever more firmly enfolded. They had visions of a 'Protestantism open to the workers' claims for emancipation.[6] For Naumann, it was no longer vital to fight Social Democracy on the side of an authoritarian social conservatism. On the contrary, in his speech to the Evangelical-Social Congress, he described Social Democracy as a 'heresy', whose core of truth should be accepted and developed by the church with the long-term aim of eventually inheriting the legacy of Social Democracy by pursuing a thoroughgoing self-renewal of Protestantism.[7] This constituted a turning-point in the development of the Christian Social movement, since it was predictable that theses of this kind would soon cease to base themselves on the platform of traditional socially conscious Protestantism.

However, it emerged on closer inspection that the policy programme of the 'younger' Christian Socialists under Friedrich Naumann's leadership was anything but clear and coherent. It oscillated curiously between a frenzy of reforming zeal and the patriarchal concepts of order to which it still partly clung. Naumann attacked the quietism of church institutions and appealed to the social conscience of property and culture – but failed to explain how socialism with a Christian bias could be incorporated in institutional form, or be conveyed through the realities of an industrial society. The slogan 'Organize the people, fight capitalism'[8] revealed that this variant of Christian Socialism was as much at sea in social politics as any other; it was precisely this irritating mixture of reforming zeal and traditionalism that provoked Max Weber's opposition. The scepticism that distanced Weber from Paul Göhre's conclusions on agrarian policy, as a result of the inquiry that they had jointly conducted for the Evangelical-Social Congress, was also evident in his reaction to Naumann's efforts in the Christian Social movement, which Weber followed with critical sympathy in the early 1890s.[9]

He approved of Naumann's detachment from Stoecker's Christian Socialism, but could make very little of Naumann's distinction, in this form at least, between 'concentration of industry', which was to be encouraged, and 'concentration of capital', which was to be opposed. Behind Naumann's attempts to accept technical progress without facing up squarely to its consequences (especially to the depersonalization of social relations), Max Weber detected theologically inspired wishful thinking and deep-seated mistrust of industrial development in general. He countered Naumann by arguing that the 'crucial characteristic of modern development' was the 'disappearance of personalized relations in government' and their increasing replacement by the 'impersonal rule of the *property-owning* class'. This undermined the central premiss of Christian Social policy—that is, the assumption that social conflicts could largely be resolved by appealing to the consciences of those involved. On the contrary, he argued, the gathering momentum of modern class-formation and the increasing erosion of patriarchally biased social organizations would eventually force Naumann to declare where he stood in political terms.[10]

This intervention by Max Weber had a far-reaching effect on the young Naumann's development. The absence of intellectual restraint, with which Naumann had hitherto advocated Christian Social initiatives, gave way to a sceptical view of the chances that such initiatives would be realized at all. In addition, the canonical lawyer Rudolf Sohm extended the critical examination of Naumann's policies, and demanded that Naumann should make a clear distinction between religion and politics. Sohm was concerned on theological grounds to avoid any conflation of religious articles of faith with political aims, whatever their colour. Christianity was to be established as it were above the sphere of political and social conflicts, which in his view could not be solved by theologically based prescriptions.[11]

Weber and Sohm were not the only ones with whom Friedrich Naumann found himself on the defensive. Max Weber had intended to provoke him into a rigorously precise definition of his position, and thus to initiate the demythologization, as it were, of his concepts of the political and social order. But it was the behaviour of the Protestant church authorities that precipitated a more sober reaction among Christian Socialists. The initial goodwill of the church's ruling authorities towards internal impulses for reform had been replaced, after the Evangelical-Social Congress in 1894, at which Weber and Göhre had presented the findings of their inquiry, by a strategy of calculated intimidation of the dissidents on the left wing of the Christian Social movement. Furthermore, not only the major Prussian landowners east of the Elbe, organized in the Conservative Party, but also the owners of heavy industry saw the activities of the rebellious clergymen as a political provocation, and exerted all their strength to denounce the sociopolitical involvement of the Naumann circle as a conscious preliminary to 'revolution'.

The 'younger' Christian Socialists grouped around Naumann could no longer avoid the choice between retreating to their clerical posts or attempting to form an independent group outside Protestantism. In view of the futility of further attempts to reform church organizations from within, Naumann opted for the foundation of a political organization.[12]

When Naumann finally turned his back on Christian Socialism and began to carve out a political image for the National Social Association (National-sozialer Verein), which was then in the process of formation, it was again Max Weber who provided what must have been the decisive political conceptual impetus. It is not simply that Weber's inaugural lecture at Freiburg in 1895 was given an enthusiastic reception in Naumann's weekly, *Die Hilfe*;[13] it is also clear that Naumann's political thought developed in a different direction in response to Weber's sensational address. What had been discernible merely in the background of his publications now became a constant factor in his political attitudes and critiques: a nationalistic imperialism, sometimes extremely crass in tone, henceforward characterized Naumann's speeches and writings, and also the political image presented by the National Social movement under Naumann's leadership.

Friedrich Naumann's account of his renunciation of Christian Socialism –

partly forced on him by outside circumstances and partly precipitated by intellectual influences – is given in a form that illuminates the changes in his political orientation and demonstrates that these changes were an experience characteristic of his whole group. After a visit to Palestine in 1898, he felt that what had been the 'younger' Christian Socialists' typical habit of annexing the Gospel for their own sociopolitical ends could not continue to carry much conviction, in view of the manifest discrepancy between the Holy Land and the reality of the industrial society currently in the making.[14] Naumann's *Letters on Religion* (*Briefe über Religion*) marked a staging post in this process of theological disillusionment, in so far as they rejected Christian belief as a guide for social change, and confined it to the private sphere of personally held values. 'Religion', he concluded in the summary of this self-appraisal, 'lies not merely in speaking, but often equally in keeping silence'.[15]

None the less, Max Weber was disappointed in the hope that the National Social Association, founded by Naumann in 1896, might be a congenial political entity within the spectrum of Wilhelmine political parties, in which his own political will might be effectively embodied. Even during the preliminaries to the foundation of the National Social party, it was pertinently said of his relation with Naumann that everything turned on 'extracting Naumann from his socialists haverings'.[16] Weber was forced to admit that he had not made much real headway with Naumann in this regard. His strong criticism of the foundation manifesto for the organization planned by Naumann highlighted the weak spots in Naumann's early concept of a political party and, even before these plans were put into effect, diagnosed that the enterprise would fail in political reality. For Weber, Naumann's plan had two fundamental defects. Firstly, he saw no reason, as a class-conscious member of the bourgeoisie, to involve himself with a party with vaguely socialist undertones, especially since the position of Naumann's group on the matter of class politics seemed to him highly dubious. In his view, Naumann's National Social Association might indeed become an ineffectual 'party of those who labour and are heavy laden', but it would never be a genuine proletarian party. And, secondly, Weber detected a lack of genuinely '*political* thinking'[17] – he was prepared to interest himself in a 'national party of civil liberty',[18] but not in a group that had by now abandoned its original main initiative as a 'movement against the major landowners',[19] because the founding members had such vastly divergent notions of what their aims should be. Moreover, Weber perceived a considerable apolitical element in Naumann's concept of the constitution, which did after all envisage a considerable reduction of the Reichstag's budgetary powers. Such a notion is a vivid instance of the excessively 'nationalistic thinking', which continued to be in evidence among the members of the National Social Association; it also demonstrates how little common ground there actually was between Naumann's concepts of policy and Weber's fundamental convictions, especially in the area of constitutional policy.

And, indeed, the National Social Association did remain a party of middle-class outsiders, which failed to make headway in the tangled undergrowth of the Wilhelmine party system. Sociopolitical quarrels – particularly the commitment of the left wing to the interests of the industrial proletariat, and the devious tactics pursued by Naumann's group on the issue of a second ballot – brought the Association on several occasions to the verge of schism, and

prevented it from evolving a well-defined programme. Two discouraging electoral defeats proved that Naumann could not command an adequate number
of votes either in the bourgeois camp or among the industrial proletariat.[20]

Of all the political ideas that Naumann absorbed during the period of his
rejection of a Christian socialism, he retained his adherence to imperialist
Weltpolitik, despite the fact that Max Weber had wished to see this imple-
mented in an entirely different party political context, and did not share the
Anglophobia popular in National Social party circles. The common factor in
Weber's support for naval armament and the National Social agitation for the
construction of a battle fleet was that neither Naumann nor Weber could raise
any enthusiasm for an armaments policy of the kind represented by Miquel's
Sammlungspolitik. Both politicians regarded the catchword notion of
Sammlung as a distortion of *Weltpolitik*, which failed to take account of the
crucial alternative between agrarian and industrial development of the Reich.
At the same time, they rejected the 'exploitation of the military question as a
weapon against unwelcome opposition parties'.[21] This expression of Weber's
and the phrase coined in the Naumann circle about the unwanted 'prison navy'
(*Zuchthausflotte*),[22] voiced their shared conviction that the linking of
Weltpolitik to a repressive home policy, especially towards the organized
proletarian movement, was tantamount to turning *Weltpolitik* into something
akin to its opposite. Both for Max Weber and for Naumann, the integration
of the proletariat into the political system of the Reich was one of the crucial
preconditions for the prospective success of any imperialism of a progressive
kind. Their relatively unprejudiced appraisal of Social Democracy, and their
contempt for the widespread fear of the 'red peril', elevated Weber and
Naumann far above the average level of understanding of their bourgeois contemporaries. As liberal imperialists, Naumann and Weber had no differences
of opinion about the course of action to be taken on this matter – for them,
neither modernization of the political system nor the prospect of successful
expansion abroad could be entertained unless the basic dogmas of Miquel's
Sammlungspolitik were repudiated.

None the less, significant differences remained between them in the short
term on the subject of the constitutional policy options open to liberal
imperialism. The frequently emotional rhetoric of Naumann's attitudes to
Great Britain was in Weber's eyes misguided, since he hoped for a German
Weltpolitik co-ordinated with that of England. Nor could he approve of the
corollary to this in home policy – Naumann's equally emotionally coloured
image of Wilhelm II. One can, of course, always point to the basic fact that
the structural model of the Wilhelmine party system, which Naumann outlined
in his political essay *Democracy and Empire* (*Demokratie und Kaisertum*), and
his conclusion that German political culture was being extensively obstructed[23]
tallied to a great extent with Max Weber's assessment of the situation. But
Naumann's suggested solution of a democratic autocracy, embodied in
Wilhelm II of all people, was inevitably seen by Weber as a dangerous political
illusion. He had advised against the founding of a political party based on
personal belief in a reconciliation between bourgeoisie and proletariat, and he
was equally unable to bring his concepts of constitutional political order into
any kind of association with the charisma of Wilhelm II – which for him was
non-existent in any case. On this point, the sociologist was worlds apart from

the erstwhile clergyman, who could never quite detach himself from his vocational past, even in the full flow of political argument. In this regard, the political partnership between Naumann and Weber could in many of its phases be described as a lifelong process of learning. Weber never tired of reminding Naumann of the objection, which he had already voiced in his early critique of Naumann's Christian Social policy programme – that it was not sufficient to appeal to the charitable feelings of property owners or to the progressiveness of a monarch. The essential aim was to change socioeconomic and political structures.

The political collapse of the National Social Association after the Reichstag elections of 1903 had justified in ample measure Max Weber's scepticism about Naumann's political false start. The question that he had persistently asked at the meeting held to found the party ('What exactly was Naumann trying to *do*?') now presented itself to Naumann with renewed urgency. The party political amalgamation between the remnants of the National Socials and Theodor Barth's Liberal Union (Freisinnige Vereinigung), a left-wing liberal splinter party, opened up a new field of political action for Naumann.[24] If we examine Naumann's political activities in the context of this group, we gain the impression that he was in many ways belatedly following Max Weber's advice. For instance, he abandoned his attempts to unite proletariat and bourgeoisie in one single party. The 'Pan-Liberalism',[25] which Naumann had already outlined in 1901, was now directed in party political terms towards an internal consolidation of the liberal camp, especially of its left wing.

After his move to the liberal camp, Naumann became one of the most vociferous advocates of an amalgamation of the three separate groups into which the left wing of the liberals had divided. Until 1910, his prime aim in domestic politics remained the creation of a unified left-wing liberal party, willing as far as possible to co-operate closely with the National Liberals. To achieve this end, a change was necessary in the traditional methods of mobilizing the electorate – the use of notable personalities would be abandoned and a stable party organization would be set up, with professional 'party officials'.[26] In terms of content, Naumann's political identity was very similar to the aims of Theodor Barth. Barth also shared the basic assumptions of the liberal imperialists, and he regarded as obsolete reservations towards imperialist *Weltpolitik*, especially those traditionally held in the left-wing liberal circles led by Eugen Richter. Like Naumann and Weber, he too had come to reject Bismarck's foreign policy. After the early 1890s, he had rallied like Naumann to the task of harnessing the momentum of imperialist *Weltpolitik* as far as possible for the benefit of the liberal movement, and avoiding relegation to the backwaters of foreign policy. In the eyes of Naumann and Barth, it was only thus that liberalism could be built up into a potential alternative government to the parties of reaction.[27] In addition to this change in the orientation of foreign policy, the interest of the liberal revisionists, to use a term of Theodor Barth's,[28] was equally engaged by a change in their estimation of the Social Democrats. After the publication of Bernstein's sensational policy statement, *Evolutionary Socialism*, Naumann made intensive efforts to develop contacts with the Social Democratic Revisionists, and never flagged in keeping his readers abreast of the changes and conflicts of policy among Social Democrats. For Naumann, Revisionists and

Reformists alike were symptomatic of a structural change gradually taking place in the proletarian movement; he wished to encourage this change as far as possible, in order to break out of the paralysing round of Social Democratic agitation and shrill anti-revolutionary panic scares among the bourgeoisie. On the tactical level, this culminated in attempts to bring together Social Democrats and liberals in agreements on a second ballot.[29]

At least from 1903 onwards, Naumann seems to have responded positively to Weber's admonitions to define his political aims with more precision, in that he had by then become the most eminent representative of a concept of politics that sought to make fundamental changes in the Wilhelmine system. The principal aim, according to this concept, was to bring to an end the continuing domination of the pre-industrial elites, and to lead the liberals, in alliance with the right wing of the Social Democrats, into reform-oriented policies. Just how ardently Max Weber's political hopes were concentrated on Naumann is shown in a letter to Lujo Brentano, which includes the comment: 'Sole ray of hope – Naumann'.[30]

It was not only on the level of practical party work that Naumann's political career underwent a change of direction – his range of sociopolitical options changed at the same time. Werner Sombart's writings on the genesis of modern capitalism particularly influenced the decision that Naumann, heavily involved in publishing contributions to the turn-of-century debate on the industrial state,[31] now took to relinquish definitively any attempt at a Christian Socialist social policy. Naumann attempted to reflect in his apologetics the theme that preoccupied both Sombart and Weber: the growth of modern industrial capitalism and its effects upon the field of action open to individuals and to groups in society. Naumann was by now convinced that no religiously based ethos was alone sufficient to control the impersonality of social relations in industrial society. At the same time, he thought it utterly unlikely that the capitalist order could be unhinged by any strategy of the socialists. His observation of the processes of industrial concentration and rationalization led him rather to evolve the theory that capitalism, both as an economic system and as a way of life, had achieved such a degree of momentum and stability that the only feasible approach was to seek opportunities for individual liberty within it. Naumann's publicity campaigns against 'industrial feudalism' frequently give the impression of being the pragmatic political offshoot of Max Weber's dictum that an 'iron cage of the new serfdom'[32] was even now ready and waiting. Naumann's political tracts functioned in this connection rather like a reflector to a wider public of Weber's diagnosis of the age: 'There are men of earnest purpose who see centuries of renewed feudal bondage descending upon us like the hosts of a hostile army'.[33]

For Naumann, it was not only the generally reserved attitude of the left-wing liberals towards *Weltpolitik* that was behind the times; the complement to this was his conviction that a change of direction by the liberals on social politics was also vital. Faced with the challenge of the modern rise of large-scale industrial enterprises, Eugen Richter's left-wing liberalism, with its dogmatically rigid stance on issues of social policy, seemed to Naumann to have no adequate solution to offer, because Richter had shown himself largely uninterested in the question of 'the fate of liberty in the large-scale industrial organizations'.[34] Once the liberal postulates on law and order were carried,

Naumann perceived 'a new unfreedom arising in the midst of the free interplay of forces',[35] and accordingly sought remedies, as parliamentarian and as publicist, for the deficiency in the liberal party programme. For example, at parliamentary level he made efforts to overcome the reservations on the part of the leadership of the Reich towards the participation of trade union secretaries in the much mooted Chambers of Labour (*Arbeitskammern*) which in the end were never actually set up.[36] This is one example of his deep concern that equality of opportunity should exist as far as possible between all parties to industrial negotiations in the labour market. Naumann also regarded as anachronistic traditional left-wing liberal reservations towards any degree of state intervention, however small; he ascribed the liberals' loss of electoral potential in no small degree to the sociopolitical abstentionism of the left-wing liberal groups. In conjunction with this, he canvassed within his own political camp for a more down-to-earth approach to the as yet rudimentary schemes for a system of social insurance, and for the urgent expansion of this system as 'a necessary corollary to the free contract of labour'.[37]

None the less, he did not consider adequate a social policy which was merely oriented towards the principles of provision at minimum subsistence level. He pleaded in addition for a progressive industrial order: in the factories, employee participation should be institutionalized by the introduction of a 'factory parliamentarianism'. Contrary to current practice, this should not be a matter of patriarchal mollification of the workers by in-house arrangements for welfare, but of guaranteed participation in internal decision-making.[38] The premisses from which Naumann conducted these arguments were in many respects heavily dependent on Max Weber. Weber's notion of the 'iron cage' had its parallel in Naumann's expression of the fear that the achievements of liberalism might prove no more than an 'interlude', given the modern rise of large-scale industry.[39]

Naumann's contributions to sociopolitical debates, especially those made before the Verein für Sozialpolitik, advocated (like Weber's) more scope for the activities of the proletarian movement as organized in trade unions, and attacked the biased intervention of government institutions in support of the interests of industrial manufacturers. Naumann did this in a form not often found among parliamentarians of the non-socialist camp; no doubt it was therefore in the area of social policy that Ernst Troeltsch's judgement was particularly apt that, 'as refracted and focused through Naumann', Weber's political ideas 'had exercised a historic influence upon the German people'.[40]

However, this judgement only holds good with the important proviso that we constantly bear in mind the delayed reactions that characterized Naumann's political career. This applies particularly to Naumann's thinking on constitutional policy. Not until long after the failure of his National Social experiment was he constrained to admit that the hope associated with this ex- periment – the hope of a democratic Caesarism, often expressed in messianic terms – was unrealistic and destined to remain so. Even during the preliminaries to the formation of the Bülow Bloc, Max Weber had counselled that all such illusions should be firmly repudiated, and that at all costs a situa- tion should be avoided in which the election slogan for the imminent Reichstag elections became a 'vote of confidence in the Kaiser'.[41] By contrast, Naumann at first welcomed the political constellation of the Bülow Bloc, since it did after all appear to present an opportunity of bringing the left-wing liberal splinter groups closer together at parliamentary level. Furthermore, he anticipated that support of the 'Conservative–Liberal mating' in the Reichstag would produce considerable progress on the question of Prussian franchise.

Not until the 'Daily Telegraph affair' was Naumann finally and belatedly brought to admit that he had misjudged the monarch for many years, and only then was his thinking on constitutional policy propelled much more firmly in the direction indicated earlier by Weber.[42] But this did finally open the way for a thorough revision of his ideas on the constitution. After the collapse of the Bülow Bloc policy, Naumann strove to achieve a broadly based reform coalition of the centre left, with the motto 'from Bassermann to Bebel'; as one of the very few representatives of politically organized liberalism, he began to canvas for a re-modelling of the constitutional monarchy along the lines of a system of parliamentary government.[43] In a series of parliamentary and publicity campaigns, during the period immediately preceding the First World War, he attempted to gain popular support for the notion that the 'full establishment of the Reich' would not come about for the time being, in view of the dogged and still unbroken persistence of leading conservative elites.[44] It must be said, of course, that a political survey of the liberal revisionists under the late-Wilhelmine Reich shows little more than isolated successes, confined to certain areas and certain periods. In 1910, the Progressive People's Party (Fortschriftliche Volkspartei) was formed in spite of considerable opposition from the left-wing liberal splinter groups; this was an important organizational preliminary to the second-ballot vote from the left-wing liberals in support of the Social Democrats in the Reichstag elections of 1912.[45] Furthermore, the foundation of the Hanseatic Federation (Hansabund), to which Naumann gave enthusiastic public support, marked a decisive advance in the field of political alliances against the supremacy of agrarian and heavy industry group interests.[46]

In the field of constitutional policy, however, Naumann was forced to resign himself to the fact that the solution of the question of Prussian franchise ultimately remained blocked because of Bethmann Hollweg's half-hearted attempts at reform. None the less, at parliamentary level the left-wing liberals did succeed in liberalizing the government's original scheme for the reform of the constitution of Alsace-Lorraine, and in forcing the Conservatives into isolation – a procedure repeated with spectacular success in 1913 during the altercations about the cover-up of the large military reserve.[47]

As far as his ideas on social policy were concerned, Naumann remained in a minority in the Progressive People's Party, as he had done in the Liberal Union. Modest ventures, such as a public appearance of famous sociologists planned in 1912 in support of a new start in social policy, gained no support from within the party, and finally foundered on the irreconcilable differences between Lujo Brentano and Weber. Naumann and Weber were forced to accept that the foundation of a new sociopolitical alliance failed because of the difference of direction within the Verein für Sozialpolitik. This defeat became all the more serious for the sociopolitical ideals of the two scholar-politicians as conflicts about social policy sharpened noticeably on the eve of the First World War.[48]

None the less, we may emphasize the fact that the policy programme devised by Naumann in constant intellectual exchange with Max Weber, and especially his conception of a political alliance of the centre left, increasingly took on the character of a latent alternative to the existing system, even for the political leadership of the Reich. Bethmann Hollweg's illuminating remark that in financial politics he was unable 'to pursue any large-scale bloc policy' – although that is precisely what happened with the introduction of the Imperial Income Supplement Tax in 1913[49] – is startling evidence that Naumann's political goals cannot simply be written off as Utopianism.

Of course, the outbreak of the First World War put an end for the time being to any thoughts of reform in constitutional policy. But the successful formation of an all-party committee (*Interfraktioneller Ausschuß*), to which Naumann made a decisive contribution, revealed afresh in the summer of 1917 the problem of the ungovernability of the late Kaiserreich, and thus also pointed the long and difficult way to the Weimar coalition.

To this extent, the liberal imperialists Naumann and Weber were to remain a minority with much experience of defeat. The significance of their impulse for reform was something which the ruling elites of the Kaiserreich were unable to assimilate in time.

Notes: Chapter 19

This chapter was translated by J. M. Tudor.

1 Cit. T. Heuss, *Friedrich Naumann. Der Mann, das Werk, die Zeit*, 3rd edn (Munich and Hamburg, 1968), p. 534. Friedrich Naumann's writings are listed in A. Milatz, *Friedrich-Naumann-Bibliographie* (Bonn, 1957). Many aspects of the relationship between Naumann and Weber (from Max Weber's point of view) are described in W. J. Mommsen, *Max Weber and German Politics, 1890–1920* (Chicago, 1984); cf. also the study by P. Theiner, *Sozialer Liberalismus und deutsche Weltpolitik. Friedrich Naumann im wilhelminischen Deutschland* (Baden-Baden, 1983).
2 F. Naumann, *Werke*, ed. by T. Schieder, Vol. 5 (Cologne and Opladen, 1964), pp. 1 ff.
3 ibid., p. 45.
4 G. Brakelmann, *Kirche und Sozialismus im 19. Jahrhundert. Die Analyse des Sozialismus und Kommunismus bei Johann Hinrich Wichern und bei Rudolf Todt* (Witten, 1966).
5 G. Brakelmann et al., *Protestantismus und Politik. Werk und Wirkung Adolf Stoeckers* (Hamburg, 1982).
6 K. E. Pollmann, *Landesherrliches Kirchenregiment und soziale Frage. Der evangelische Oberkirchenrat der altpreußischen Landeskirche und die sozialpolitische Bewegung der Geistlichen nach 1890* (Berlin, 1973).
7 *Werke*, Vol. 1 (Cologne and Opladen, 1964), p. 336.
8 ibid., p. 363.
9 Mommsen, *Max Weber and German Politics*, pp. 21 ff.
10 Weber's review of Naumann's collected essays (they appeared under the title *Was heißt Christlich-Sozial?*) was published in *Die christliche Welt*, 17 May 1894, cols 472–77.
11 R. Sohm, *Der Christ im öffentlichen Leben. Verhandlungen des 28. Kongresses für Innere Mission in Posen vom 23.–26. September 1895* (Posen, 1895), pp. 31 ff.
12 Pollmann, *Landesherrliches Kirchenregiment*, pp. 276 ff. D. Düding, *Der Nationalsoziale Verein. Der gescheiterte Versuch einer parteipolitischen Synthese von Nationalismus, Sozialismus und Liberalismus* (Munich and Vienna, 1972).
13 *Die Hilfe*, vol. 1, no. 28 (14 July 1895), p. 1.
14 F. Naumann, *Asia* (Berlin-Schöneberg, 1899).
15 *Werke*, Vol. 1, pp. 566 ff., especially p. 631.
16 Cit. Mommsen, *Max Weber and German Politics*, p. 127 (Letter of 15 October 1896).
17 GPS[1], p. 27.

18   ibid., p. 28.
19   ibid., p. 27
20   Düding, *Der Nationalsoziale Verein*, pp. 124 ff., pp. 175 ff.; Theiner, *Sozialer Liberalismus*, pp. 86 ff., pp. 122 ff.
21   GPS[1], p. 31.
22   *Die Hilfe*, vol. 5, no. 49, 26 November 1899, p. 4.
23   See especially *Werke*, Vol. 3, pp. 255 ff.
24   K. Wegner, *Theodor Barth und die Freisinnige Vereinigung. Studien zur Geschichte des Linksliberalismus im wilhelminischen Deutschland (1893–1910)* (Tübingen, 1968).
25   *Werke*, Vol. 4, pp. 215 ff.
26   Theiner, *Sozialer Liberalismus*, pp. 140 ff.
27   Wegner, *Theodor Barth*, pp. 68 ff.
28   T. Barth, *Neue Aufgaben des Liberalismus* (Berlin-Schöneberg, 1904).
29   Theiner, *Sozialer Liberalismus*, pp. 129 ff.
30   Max Weber to Lujo Brentano, 6 February 1907; quoted in Mommsen, *Max Weber and German Politics*, p. 133.
31   K. Barkin, *The Controversy over German Industrialization 1890–1902* (Chicago, 1970).
32   GPS[1], p. 63.
33   *Werke*, Vol. 5, p. 363.
34   ibid., p. 362.
35   ibid., p. 363.
36   See Naumann's speech in the *Reichstag*, 11 March 1908, *Stenographische Berichte über die Verhandlungen des deutschen Reichstages*, Vol. 231, pp. 3731D–3735D.
37   *Werke*, Vol. 3, p. 502.
38   ibid., pp. 418 ff.
39   *Werke*, Vol. 5, p. 365.
40   E. Troeltsch, *Deutscher Geist und Westeuropa* (Berlin, 1925), quoted in Mommsen, *Max Weber and German Politics*, p. 136.
41   Max Weber to Friedrich Naumann, 14 December 1906, GPS[1], p. 452.
42   Naumann to Weber, 30 October 1908, Zentrales Staatsarchiv Potsdam, Naumann papers, no. 106, fol. 86.
43   *Werke*, Vol. 2, pp. 362 ff.
44   *Die Hilfe*, Vol. 16, no. 28, p. 443,
45   Theiner, *Sozialer Liberalismus*, pp. 212 ff.; J. Bertram, *Die Wahlen zum Deutschen Reichstag vom Jahre 1912. Parteien und Verbände in der Innenpolitik des Wilhelminischen Reichs* (Düsseldorf, 1964), pp. 224 ff.
46   S. Mielke, *Der Hansa-Bund für Gewerbe, Handel und Industrie 1909–1914. Der gescheiterte Versuch einer antifeudalen Sammlungspolitik*, Göttingen 1976. Theiner, *Sozialer Liberalismus*, pp. 195 ff.
47   ibid., pp. 208 ff., pp. 214 ff.
48   Mommsen, *Max Weber and German Politics*, pp. 118–19; K. Saul, *Staat, Industrie und Arbeiterbewegung im Kaiserreich. Zur Innen- und Außenpolitik des Wilhelminischen Deutschland 1903–1914* (Düsseldorf, 1973).
49   Theobald v. Bethmann Hollweg to Karl v. Eisendecher, 23 March 1913, quoted in P. C. Witt, *Die Finanzpolitik des Deutschen Reiches von 1903 bis 1913. Eine Studie zur Innenpolitik des Wilhelminischen Deutschland* (Lübeck, 1970), p. 365.

20 Max Weber and Walther Rathenau

ERNST SCHULIN

Personal Knowledge

Max Weber and Walther Rathenau (1867–1922) were virtually of the same age. Both grew up in Berlin. Both took as their starting-point modern socioeconomic facts and problems: Weber was mainly interested in political economy and agrarian questions, and Rathenau in technology and industrial organization. Both sought to have an influence on politics that was similar in its nationalist stance and its liberal critique of Wilhelminism. Their supporters, who by and large came from the same social background and shared similar attitudes, revered them as models of great stature; this was particularly so for those young people seeking new political and ideological goals. Whether as political thinkers relevant to the time or as charismatic leaders, they were seen as persons denied position – to the detriment of Germany. The equal of this esteem (one might say, over-esteem) was not shown to any other contemporary in this way, and it was enhanced by the unexpectedly early death of Weber and the murder of Rathenau in the critical initial stages of the Weimar Republic.

Considering that the two men had so much in common, it is surprising that there is no record of an acquaintanceship between the two or of the influence of one upon the other. As well as possessing many friends, Rathenau also had an extraordinarily wide circle of acquaintances; he associated with the leading figures in economics, politics and culture, and was proud of knowing 'all the important men of Europe and America now living'.[1] He must have been aware of the esteemed sociologist of religion from Heidelberg, and even more so of the critic of constitutional politics writing in the *Frankfurter Zeitung*. Apart from the university and close political friends, Weber was much less concerned with making acquaintances. He was not curious to meet 'celebrities'; for all his interest in modern economic development and for all his views about the (as he saw it) dubious influence of the large companies, he hardly seems to have associated with leading practitioners of finance and industry. This fact is more remarkable than his similar reserve with regard to government circles.

When searching for mutual friends of Weber and Rathenau, we might think of Friedrich Naumann; his relations with Rathenau seem, however, to have been very distant. Hence it is Werner Sombart and Ernst Troeltsch who are of greatest interest in this connection. Weber and Rathenau were probably kept informed about each other by these two. Sombart had been in Berlin since 1906 and must have got to know Rathenau shortly afterwards, by 1911 at the latest.[2] Troeltsch only arrived in Berlin from Heidelberg in 1915, but soon came into contact with Rathenau through the 'Deutsche Gesellschaft 1914', and discovered in him a political *confrère*.[3] Weber and Rathenau might well have met each other in this club. Both were members, though, as a

Heidelberger, Weber was not often present; it is probable that he gave a lecture only once, on 3 April 1916, and obviously did not feel at ease in the interesting and diverse circle of politicians, soldiers, journalists, scientists and artists.[4] His comment, in a letter from Berlin on 17 January 1918, that Rathenau was still betting on three years of war[5] might derive from a personal conversation, for in Rathenau's newly published pamphlet *Die neue Wirtschaft* [The New Economy] this view is not, of course, so clearly stated. The two men might have formed a closer acquaintanceship if Weber had seen fit to join the Second Socialization Commission in April 1920; instead, he proposed his brother Alfred, who subsequently did take part.[6] Here we can already observe some characteristic differences: while Rathenau had declared in 1919 that he was deeply offended at not being invited to take part in the First Socialization Commission, in 1920 Weber actually declined the invitation.

Even more striking than the lack of reports of personal meetings or correspondence is the fact that they virtually never commented on each other. We must certainly make allowances here for a characteristic typical of both men: they wished to appear even more original than they were, and so they were reluctant to record explicitly their sources of inspiration. There is only one recorded comment on Weber by Rathenau. This was noted down by Wolfgang Schumann, a writer and publisher from Dresden, who knew Weber from the Lauenstein Cultural Meetings in 1917. Rathenau had 'great respect' for Weber, but is reported to have said about his sociology of religion, 'The man squanders a lifetime's energy proving things that anyone with eyes can see are true at a glance. More notes than text.'[7] This is probably a reference to the version of *The Protestant Ethic* that was published in 1920 in the first volume of the *Gesammelte Aufsätze zur Religionssoziologie* and whose 'malignant tumour of footnotes' Weber himself considered in need of justification.[8] Behind Rathenau's remark, we glimpse his oft-expressed aversion to science and professorial wisdom, to the laborious argumentation, fact-grubbing and evidence-hunting of scholarly erudition. To this he opposed the intuitive 'truth' of his short, apodictic statements, although he was forced to register the fact, with injured pride, that he was generally not taken seriously by academics.

Weber's silence with regard to Rathenau as a theoretician might also be connected with this. Except for the passage from the letter mentioned above – and perhaps in others, hitherto unpublished – Weber mentioned Rathenau only in the pamphlet *Wahlrecht und Demokratie in Deutschland* [Suffrage and Democracy in Germany] (1917), placing him in the list of the leaders of the economy, and therefore as a practitioner.[9] Similarly, Sombart had quoted scattered passages from Rathenau's works simply as interesting statements by a practitioner; in doing so he had passed over the *Kritik der Zeit* [Critique of the Age] (1912), merely alluding to the symptomatic success of the concept of 'mechanization' used there , and ignoring the fact that Rathenau had intended this work to be a corrective elaboration of the interpretations of the modern capitalist world attempted by political economists and sociologists such as Tönnies, Sombart and Weber.[10] Experts such as Gerhart von Schulze-Gävernitz, Franz Oppenheimer and Richard Ehrenberg, for all their criticisms, had clearly acknowledged this theoretical achievement of Rathenau's.[11] We may thus presume that the reserve of Sombart and Weber implied a certain degree of dissent, which did not need to be voiced in view of the well-known 'unscholarliness' of the industrialist. Weber's silence about Rathenau's conspicuous and contradictory activities during the First World War cannot, however, be explained in this way. Rathenau's impressive organization of the supply of raw materials and his much read book *In Days to Come* (Von kommenden Dingen) (1917) on the economic and political demands for change should have made an impression on Weber, and even have provoked him. It is astonishing that, in the violent public arguments about Rathenau, Weber never said anything, even in private, in defence of the patriotic Jew, or anything critical about the anti-capitalistically speaking capitalist.

Common Features

Let us now examine more closely the features that Weber and Rathenau had in common. Despite their respect for the historical achievements of Prussia, its landed nobility and its army, they were both in favour of the modern development of Germany into an 'industrial state' with a corresponding political strengthening of the bourgeoisie, in particular the industrially active stratum. The pamphlet by the agrarian-conservative political economist, Karl Oldenberg, on *Deutschland als Industriestaat* [Germany as an Industrial State] (1897) was the starting-point for Weber's rejection of the Conservatives and likewise for Rathenau's successful conversion of the editor of *Die Zukunft*, Maximilian Harden, to industrialism.[12] Related stances on imperialism, liberalism, parliamentarism, the critical comments on the position of the Kaiser and on the selection of responsible figures in politics and diplomacy are also similar. This was political criticism of the prevailing social and political conditions from the modern, national point of view. According to this, the strong German national state depended on the promotion of modern economic power, and hence on the leadership of a new bourgeois elite, which should by all means learn political responsibility from the previous ruling strata but should not allow itself to become feudalized. These opinions were held by Weber and Rathenau in the prewar Wilhelmine period independently and probably without the knowledge of the other.

Weber's political views found hardly any published expression until 1917. To begin with, a more tangible parallel may be drawn with Weber's brother, Alfred. In 1907 Rathenau, influenced by Bülow's 'bloc' policy and the growth of liberalism in other European states, had first publicly come out in favour of a stronger constitutional influence and an increase in self-government; in the same year, Alfred Weber had asserted the suitability of parliamentarism for Germany in an argument with Schmoller.[13] In the discussion of these issues, which in Germany generally was very sporadic, during the following years, Rathenau's clear statement in a newspaper article entitled 'Parliamentarism' on 12 April 1914 is noteworthy for the way in which he stressed the 'automatic selection' of leading political figures in the parliamentary state in which parties bore a political responsibility; there was nothing comparable to this in Germany.[14] This and other newspaper articles by Rathenau between 1911 and 1914 can only have had, at most, the effect of further confirming Max Weber's views. Rathenau's comments on Judaism and anti-Semitism

(1911) were more sensational, but Weber hardly concerned himself with this problem.

At the outbreak of war in 1914 they both reacted with equal patriotism and pessimism. Too old for the front, they both sought to do war service at home, Rathenau as a civilian working for the Raw Materials Organization of the Prussian War Ministry, Weber even in uniform at the Heidelberg hospital administration. Neither of them took part in the widespread patriotic surge of publications, the 'tribal cry' of the literati and professors, as G. F. Knapp called it. For all their criticism of the political leadership, they wanted to do their duty, to dispel all defeatism, and they sought at first to influence the government privately through memoranda. Their specialist areas in foreign affairs differed in accordance with their prior knowledge and interests, as did, in part, their assessment of the principal dangers. Weber's model, as far as domestic German changes were concerned, was certainly England and America; but in foreign affairs he spoke chiefly as an expert on Polish and Russian conditions. This was due to his familiarity with East Elbean affairs and to the interest that he took as early as 1905 in the changes in the Russian constitution. Now, in wartime, he regarded England simply as 'the bitterest enemy at present' and Russia as the 'gravest future danger', considering the 'destruction of tsarism' to be the only (though very positive) result that Germany had achieved.[15] In his memoranda, Rathenau depicted England almost throughout as the most long-term and most dangerous adversary, as did most industrialists and experts on world economics. For this reason he considered it necessary to safeguard raw materials and to form a central European, if not continental, economic union. But in their warnings against unlimited submarine warfare they were both in complete agreement; also to a large extent in rejecting the public discussion of the German war aims.[16]

Even more clear and publicly visible was their common interest in the question of domestic political transformation. In March 1917, Rathenau's book *In Days to Come* was published; it immediately aroused widespread attention and was respectfully received by important reviewers such as Ernst Troeltsch, Gustav von Schmoller and Ferdinand Tönnies. It contained his criticism of German conservatism and the *rentier* mentality of the bourgeoisie, as well as his renewed and now even more emphatic demand for a 'thoroughgoing reform of German parliamentarism'.[17] Under the 'domestic truce', questions relating to constitutional reform had been set aside since the outbreak of war. They were raised almost exclusively in private memoranda, and even then were generally restricted to the reform of the Prussian three-class electoral system. The adoption of Western parliamentarism, with parties responsible for the work of government, was seen as unsuitable or even dangerous for the Prussian-German state. These are the views of writers such as Schulze-Gävernitz, Harnack, Delbrück and Troeltsch, expressed in 1915–16, and are particularly clearly stated in Friedrich Meinecke's essay 'Die Reform des preussischen Wahlrechts' [The reform of Prussian electoral law] in December 1916.[18] Only Hugo Preuss in his booklet *Das deutsche Volk und die Politik* [The German People and Politics] in 1915 criticized the 'unmitigated antagonism of government and parliament' and pleaded for the development of a 'people's state' (*Volksstaat*), admittedly more by means of political education than by constitutional reform. In the same year, Alfred

Weber in his *Gedanken zur deutschen Sendung* [Thoughts on the German Mission] deplored 'the lack of an apparatus for parliamentary selection which would attract the talented'.[19] Thus the thoughts on parliamentarism that Rathenau wrote down in the autumn of 1916 are not isolated; however, they were developed very early and were not only contrary to the views currently held by his own social class, but also more far-reaching than those of the majority of liberal political thinkers. In elaborating his essay of 1914, he stressed the necessary development of political parties, parliamentary groups and committees for the democratization of the executive and legislature. Ideas of a distinctively German form of the state counterposed to the West, he treated simply as prejudices to be overcome. 'The strange and not always agreeable parliamentary apparatus is, however, indispensable because it is a selection and a school of the statesmen and politician – or ought to be.'[20]

These thoughts appeared in *In Days to Come* in March 1917, at exactly the right time in the public discussion that had been triggered off more than anything else by Bethmann Hollweg's announcement of the domestic political 're-orientation' at the end of February 1917. This discussion was dominated, as we know, by Max Weber's penetrating and incisive statement of his views, which he published from the end of April to the end of June 1917 in five articles in the *Frankfurter Zeitung*, and then in May 1918 as a pamphlet entitled *Parlament und Regierung im neugeordneten Deutschland* [Parliament and Government in a Reconstructed Germany]. We may assume that he had been prompted to this by, among other things, Rathenau's statement of opinion on the topic, which was similar in tendency but remained vague and sketchy. He did not wish to trump him with the authority of the scholar, for, like Rathenau, he believed that the 'choice among ultimate commitments cannot be made with the tools of science' and also, in stressing the merely relative significance of 'state *form*', they were in agreement.[21] He criticized far more aggressively, however, the constitutional and social development originated by Bismarck and followed since, ruthlessly attacking the advocates of a special path for Germany. He also took up the issue of parliament as the arena for the selection of political leaders. Rathenau also considered this a matter of urgent necessity, but he was much less emphatic than Weber in underlining the contrast between political leadership and the specialist mentality of the ruling bureaucracy. It is easy to see why the ideas of the less well-informed Rathenau paled in comparison and were forgotten.[22]

If we look for further features in common during the war, they may also be found in their similarly ambivalent attitude to the problematic leader, Ludendorff. Both put some of their hopes in him, tried to influence him and were in a similar state of excitement after personal meetings with him.[23] Rathenau's despairing plea for national defence at the beginning of October 1918, after Ludendorff's request for a cease-fire, was surely also in Weber's spirit in its extremely nationalistic underlying attitude, though the latter does not mention it directly.[24] In terms of party politics, they both declared their support for the left-liberal German Democratic Party from the beginning of the building of a new Germany after the war. But they both occupied a rather precarious special position within it, as they came to terms with parliamentarism and party politics more theoretically than practically.

It may be seen that the features common to Weber and Rathenau, some of which have been discussed in more detail, some merely indicated, are largely characteristic of the widespread but not particularly numerous group of left-liberal critics of Wilhelmine Germany. Both are distinguished from this group by their much more pronounced nationalism, which was not so much ideological as strongly emotional in character. That this did not lead to visible co-operation may be attributed to the differences between them, which we shall now examine.

Differences

In 1912, as set out in his work *Zur Kritik der Zeit*, Rathenau had seen the principal characteristic of the modern world not in capitalism or in the advance of technology but in 'mechanization', that is, mass production imposed by the density of population and made possible by machinery and industry, and in the related loss of individuality and 'dehumanization' (*Entseelung*) of life as a whole. On the basis of these irreversible facts, he wished to create a future worth living through rational organization and by finding new meaning, that is a re-evaluation that would prevail over materialism. The term 'mechanization' rapidly spread, appearing to be an apt designation of a cultural problem; it became a slogan, as Sombart, for instance, ascertained with some misgivings.[25] As such it also played a part in the Cultural Meetings at Lauenstein, which were initiated in May and October 1917, by the publisher Eugen Diederichs, with the Social Democrat and theologian turned neo-conservative, Max Maurenbrecher. Characteristically, the political economist Plenge poked fun at this gathering 'with Maurenbrecher...as the bearer of a new truth and Rathenau as the subject of discussion'.[26] Maurenbrecher did, in fact, speak about overcoming 'capitalist mechanization' by an idealistic state which would be set up by a 'party of intellectuals'.[27] Weber retorted, as recorded in a minute, that we were 'doomed for the foreseeable future to mechanization, manifesting itself in the extremely strong bureaucracy on the one hand, and proliferating, overpowering capitalism on the other. There is no remedy for that in our classics; Maurenbrecher's state party of intellectuals would, if it came to power, be forced to acquire a bureaucracy and to peter out, just like social democracy or the trade unions. The struggle against materialism had rather to draw its strength from the sober facts of the day; the wild dogs of the material interest groups would have to be set loose on one another...'[28]

The difference in positions is clearly seen here. The material clash of interests was for Weber preferable to their being overcome by the state, intellectuals or anything else, which would only lead to bureaucratic ossification. He saw bureaucratization as a principal characteristic and problem of the modern world. Ever since he had championed this view with his brother at the Vienna meeting of the Verein für Sozialpolitik in 1909 against other political economists more favourable to the state and civil service – who referred to it as the 'over-excited family view of the Webers'[29] – it had been one of his most important criteria of evaluation. He saw this tendency not only in the state, but also in advanced capitalism and in socialism – all the more so if the spheres were mixed.

By contrast, Rathenau based himself on his experiences of mixed economic practices in the large-scale enterprise of AEG (Allgemeine Electricitäts-Gesellschaft). He saw in these organizations managed along lines of public administration a beneficial attenuation of the competitive struggle and an objectification of an entrepreneurial greed. He also believed that he could thereby render the state and the international power struggle more civilized and efficient. Unlike Weber, he considered military conflicts to be obsolete in view of the modern forms of economic competition.

This difference becomes all the more clear after Rathenau's wartime experience of raw materials organization and his corresponding reflections on the future. As the organizer of raw materials supply in the War Ministry, he had demonstrated in a practical way the possibility of non-bureaucratic work of reconstruction through government agencies and private firms, and he sought to develop these forms of organization to create better conditions for the future peacetime economy. He was not alone in this. There was a general discussion of state socialism and the planned economy, in which he gained great importance as a practitioner and theoretician. Since the outbreak of war several political economists had talked about the end of the hitherto individualistic order of economy and society – not without stressing the English (hence un-German) origins of this order. Prominent in this was Johann Plenge, whose 'ideas of 1914' were also affirmed by Ernst Troeltsch. Social Democrats such as Paul Lensch, Ernst Heilmann and the journalist Georg Bernhard advocated the 'transfer of the private monopolies into the administration and ownership of the state'.[30] In Austria in 1917, Karl Renner coined the phrase about 'the progressive encroachment of the state into the economy which in wartime had increased precipitately', and in the same year Rudolf Goldscheid published a draft programme for a 'reappropriation of the state' and a systematic, organized extension of the communal economy based on it.[31] Political economists who were close to Max Weber also expounded similar views: Edgar Jaffé, Werner Sombart, Gerhart von Schulze-Gävernitz and even his brother Alfred Weber.[32] The AEG engineer, Wichard von Moellendorff, who had decisively influenced Rathenau in 1914 in the planning of the raw materials department, came to be a particularly impassioned advocate of an anti-liberal, centrally controlled economy. He regarded the state-controlled but self-governing war corporations (co-ordinating distribution of raw materials) as prototypes of future corporatively oriented organizations, as he explained in his book *Deutsche Gemeinwirtschaft* [German Corporate Economy], published in the summer of 1916. Even Harnack took up the idea of a national communal economy in a speech in August 1916, thereby eliciting protests from many industrialists.[33]

Because discussion mainly centred on mixed forms and not on an absolute state socialism, in the first three years of the war we find that the objections were hardly fundamental ones. In addition to Leopold von Wiese, mention should be made of Franz Oppenheimer, who gave exaggerated warnings of the Utopia of a 'marketless economy', in which 'the proletarian socialist Scheidemann' would come together with 'the Christian socialist Plenge, the Platonist Moellendorff and the Saint-Simonist Rathenau'.[34] Max Weber, however, was vehemently opposed to this tendency, particularly at the end of 1917 in his work *Wahlrecht und Demokratie in Deutschland*. He defended the preservation of private economic principles, contrasting the great creative individual entrepreneur with state-socialist bureaucratization. Communal or co-operative economy or progressive 'state control' (*Durchstaatlichung*) were for him claptrap, no less than corporatist conceptions of social order. As usual in his polemics, he mentions no names but speaks of 'ideologues intoxicated with writing', 'inkwell romantics' or, most often, naive 'literati'.[35] This epithet, which he clearly prefers to that of 'journalists' or 'intellectuals', is used by him in an idiosyncratic manner. Whereas it was previously applied by the government and its supporters to writers who expressed critical or 'irresponsible' ideas about the state, Weber uses it to denote those who write in the interest of the state or of an obsolete order. He especially applied it to the opponents of parliamentarism. In the present case, the most curious thing is that with his use of the epithet he obviously did not intend to snipe at experienced practitioners such as Moellendorff and Rathenau, although they quite clearly advocated the ideas he was attacking. By emphasizing the importance and vital independence of the great 'leaders of the economic system' and mentioning Rathenau in company with Stinnes, Thyssen and others,[36] he was actually playing off the practitioner against the theoretician: Rathenau the industrial organizer against Rathenau the man of letters.

If Weber was here obscuring a difference with Rathenau, this may be partly explained by the fact that the 'literati', particularly the political economists among them, were closer to him and affected him all the more deeply. The ideological 'profundities' at, say, the Lauenstein meetings must have got on his nerves. Rathenau's similar views were well-known from his lecture 'German raw materials provision' and his book *In Days to Come*, but they did not achieve prominence until after the publication of his pamphlet *Die neue Wirtschaft* in January 1918. This pamphlet unleashed a storm of indignation because, a few months after the Russian Revolution, it dared to prophesy that the old economic order would burn down and that the old foundations of the social order would also catch fire.[37] Moreover, it was possible to link the work with the state-controlled economic projects of the War Ministry and similar plans of the Imperial Commissariat for a transitional economy.

In 1918 the general trend of the debate moved against the advocates of a communal economy. 'In the first year of the war it was good form to enthuse about "German organization" ', wrote the economic journalist Arthur Feiler in July 1918. 'Today the enthusiasts of yesterday are complaining at the top of their voices about "state control", the "economy of ruination".'[38] When it came to personalities, the philosophizing economic organizer Rathenau made an appropriate target for the main attack. It is striking that the wartime economy that had been so successful in Germany was more popular abroad than at home as a model for thinking about the planned economy, and hence as a main inspiration of modern planning for the future. As British Minister of Munitions, Lloyd George recognized its importance and ruthlessly incorporated those industries that were vital to the war effort into a purely state-controlled and planned economy. Bukharin and Lenin had Germany in mind when they developed their idea of state capitalism, of the state as the sole entrepreneur and of the possibility of a long-term planned economy.[39] In Germany itself, the wartime economy did not lead to any lasting augmentation of state influence on the economy; rather the reverse, as may be seen from the attempts at socialization of the postwar period.

In the final year of the war, after the publication of Rathenau's *Die neue Wirtschaft*, Max Weber no longer took any part in this discussion. Undoubtedly, alongside the differences about the relationship between state and economy mentioned above, there were many points on which he agreed with Rathenau with regard to the 'transitional economy' that had to be organized. This applied, for example, to the necessary 'rational economy of production' and the 'rational formation of goal-oriented organizations (*Zweckverbandsbildungen*) on the largest scale', which would have to succeed the wartime economy.[40] But it is probably less important to refer to this than to emphasize another, unspoken difference which always existed between the two men. Rathenau considered a change in consciousness more vital to the solution of contemporary problems than governmental and economic reforms. Weber, too, wished to see changed human beings and 'modes of conduct', but he set no store by didactic sermons, appeals and ideological professions of faith. Nor could he have much sympathy with Rathenau's harmonizing and syncretic world-view, given his conception of eternally antagonistic values. It was more important for him to investigate what religious, political and economic preconditions would make possible the development of individually and socially desirable types of human beings. For this reason, he sought to collaborate on the constitutional reorganization of Germany.

Conclusion

It might seem far-fetched to reflect on a non-relationship, a dialogue that did not take place. But it should now be plain that some kind of problematic connection must have existed from Weber's point of view, if not from Rathenau's. It was not simply because of his activities as Foreign Minister of the Weimar Republic and because of his assassination that Rathenau became a well-known public figure; he had already achieved this status during the First World War. Everyone discussed and argued about his publications, which seemed so out of keeping with his work as president of AEG. To this extent we are justified in asking why Weber did not take part in these arguments and why (to date) we do not even know of any relevant private comments.

Weber and Rathenau not only have a good deal in common in their political orientation, but also as men. Both were versatile, charismatic and ambitious personalities who, however, repeatedly sought to curb their drive to achieve power and influence by forearming themselves with an impartial objectivity or a scholarliness free of value-judgements. Weber alternated between science and politics, theory and practice. Rathenau lived a dual existence as a practical businessman and a philosophizing writer, and also sought to enter politics. During the war, from 1915 onwards, both were distressed by the fact that they were denied any politically responsible task in this critical period. As a substitute they wrote memoranda, newspaper articles and other works, and made speeches. In their despair at the plainly visible, yet unchecked domestic political shortcomings, which were affecting the country's ability to cope with the war, they both compared themselves indirectly with the prophets of the old Israelites and lamented the present-day hostility to prophets.[41]

Weber probably viewed the relationship differently. As he himself was virtually excluded from practical activity all his life and suffered from this, he was bound to see Rathenau as the prototype of the successful practitioner, the 'born leader', who, characteristically for Germany, entered industry and not the government or a political party.[42] During the course of 1916, Rathenau's vital organization of raw materials management became public knowledge. In comparison Weber must have felt the insignificance of his own work at that time in the Heidelberg hospital administration. It may have been for this reason that he refrained from making critical comments on Rathenau the writer. By the standards that he otherwise applied to his contemporaries he must have found Rathenau not merely unscientific but also vain and full of empty phrases in matters of which he understood nothing.

Many other contrasts and comparisons could be made. It is doubtful whether personal contacts would have developed if Weber had lived to see Rathenau's involvement in foreign affairs in 1921–22. He could have supported Rathenau's attempt to de-emotionalize international relations, but he would probably have had misgivings about a Jew assuming this extremely difficult and vulnerable task, as did many independent observers – even those free from anti-Semitism.[43] For us, despite all their differences, they are both like-minded representatives and critics of Wilhelmine Germany, alarmingly receptive and perceptive, like few of their contemporaries, personally unhappy and beset by worries, suffering from the problems of their age. Both worked hard not merely to arrive at an understanding of the world, but also to do whatever was in their power to help it.

Notes: Chapter 20

This chapter was translated by Barrie Selman.

1   W. Rathenau, *Hauptwerke und Gespräche*, ed. E. Schulin: *Walther-Rathenau-Gesamtausgabe*, Vol. 2 (Munich and Heidelberg, 1977), p. 794.
2   *Walther Rathenau. Industrialist, Banker, Intellectual and Politician: Notes and Diaries 1907–1922*, ed. H. Pogge v. Strandmann (Oxford, 1985), p. 123. Reference is made here to meetings on 11 and 14 May 1911. See also *Walther-Rathenau-Gesamtausgabe*, Vol. 2, p. 704. They may well have met earlier through Maximilian Harden or Felix Deutsch. Cf. W. Rathenau and M. Harden, *Briefwechsel*, ed. H. D. Hellige: *Walther-Rathenau-Gesamtausgabe*, Vol. 6 (Munich and Heidelberg, 1983), p. 563, n. 2, and p. 735, n. 15.
3   In 1917 he wrote a detailed review of *Von kommenden Dingen* in the *Vossische Zeitung*, cf. *Walther-Rathenau-Gesamtausgabe*, Vol. 2, p. 563 ff. There is also a reference in F. Meinecke, *Autobiographische Schriften*, ed. E. Kessel (Stuttgart, 1969), p. 236 ff. In the *Neue Rundschau*, no. 33 (1922), Troeltsch wrote an obituary entitled 'Dem ermordeten Freunde', reprinted in E. Troeltsch, *Deutscher Geist und Westeuropa*, ed. H. Baron (Tübingen, 1925), pp. 258–64.
4   MWG, Vol. I/15, pp. 777 ff.
5   *Biography*, p. 620.
6   W. J. Mommsen, *Max Weber and German Politics, 1890–1920* (Chicago, 1984), p. 309.
7   *Walther-Rathenau-Gesamtausgabe* , Vol. 2, p. 749.
8   RS, Vol. 1, p. 89.
9   MWG, Vol. I/15, p. 358.

10 W. Sombart, *Der Bourgeois* (Munich and Leipzig, 1913), pp. 217, 238 and 247, quotations from Rathenau's *Reflexionen*, cf. *Walther-Rathenau-Gesamtausgabe*, Vol. 2, p. 528. Rathenau's allusions to other interpretations of capitalism in the *Kritik der Zeit*: ibid., pp. 27 and 71. There is a direct reference on p. 71 to Sombart's book *Die Juden und das Wirtschaftsleben* (Munich, 1911).

11 Cf. the reviews quoted in *Walther-Rathenau-Gesamtausgabe*, Vol. 2, pp. 513–18.

12 Mommsen, *Max Weber and German Politics*, p. 97; *Walther-Rathenau-Gesamtausgabe*, Vol. 6, pp. 304 ff.

13 W. Rathenau, *Die neue Ära*, newspaper article of 12 February 1907, reprinted in idem, *Nachgelassene Schriften* (Berlin, 1928), Vol. 1, pp. 15–22. On the argument between Alfred Weber and Schmoller in the Vienna *Neue Freie Presse*, which was commented on by Friedrich Naumann in his periodical *Die Hilfe*, see T. Eschenburg, *Die improvisierte Demokratie* (Munich, 1963), p. 22.

14 W. Rathenau, *Parlamentarismus*, reprinted in idem, *Gesammelte Schriften* (Berlin, 1925), Vol. 1, pp. 233–49. According to Rathenau, written in 1913. In July 1912 he had advised Bethmann Hollweg in conversation to make parliamentary reforms, but had declined to commit his ideas to writing owing to his lack of expertise: Rathenau, *Notes and Diaries*, pp. 163 ff.; L. Albertin, *Liberalismus und Demokratie am Anfang der Weimarer Republik* (Düsseldorf, 1972), p. 233. For Rathenau's political writings at this time, see E. Schulin, *Walther Rathenau* (Göttingen, 1979), pp. 51–5.

15 MWG, Vol. I/15, pp. 159 and 751.

16 See G. Hecker, *Walther Rathenau und sein Verhältnis zu Militär und Krieg* (Boppard, 1983), pp. 333 ff. and 391 ff.

17 *Walther-Rathenau-Gesamtausgabe*, Vol. 2, pp. 471–91.

18 On this discussion see Albertin, *Liberalismus und Demokratie*; R. Patemann, *Der Kampf um die preussische Wahlreform im Ersten Weltkrieg* (Düsseldorf, 1964); R. Opitz, *Der deutsche Sozialliberalismus 1917–23* (Cologne, 1973); G. Schmidt, *Deutscher Historismus und der Übergang zur parlamentarischen Demokratie* (Lübeck and Hamburg, 1964); B. Sösemann, 'Ernst Troeltschs politisches Engagement im Ersten Weltkrieg', in H. Renz and F. W. Graf (eds), *Troeltsch-Studien*, Vol. 3 (Gutersloh, 1984); and particularly K. Schwabe, *Wissenschaft und Kriegsmoral* (Göttingen, 1969), pp. 130–145, and D. Krüger, *Nationalökonomen im wilhelminischen Deutschland* (Göttingen, 1983), pp. 199–231.

19 H. Preuss, *Das deutsche Volk und die Politik* (Jena, 1915), pp. 9, 56, 186; A. Weber, *Gedanken zur deutschen Sendung* (Berlin, 1915), p. 20, also p. 25 and in the final section p. 105. The diaries of the journalist Theodor Wolff show how strongly he, too, advocated the 'parliamentary regime' or the 'parliamentary system' in place of the Prussian electoral reform – after the outbreak of war more clearly in conversation than was possible in newspaper articles. See T. Wolff, *Tagebücher 1914 1919*, ed. B. Sösemann (Boppard, 1984), especially p. 161 (conversation with Bethmann Hollweg, 9 February 1915), p. 442 (with Bülow, 9 October 1916) and p. 480 (with Riezler, 12 February 1917).

20 *Walther-Rathenau-Gesamtausgabe*, Vol. 2, p. 474.

21 MWG, Vol. I/15, p. 432.

22 The Heidelberg agrarian scientist Adolf Mayer stresses Rathenau's poorer grasp of the subject compared with Weber in a review of *Von kommenden Dingen*, quoted in *Walther-Rathenau-Gesamtausgabe*, Vol. 2, p. 584. Albertin, *Liberalismus und Demokratie*, p. 233, points out the striking similarities.

23 Rathenau, *Notes and Diaries*, pp. 215–18; *Biography*, pp. 686–9.

24 Mommsen, *Max Weber and German Politics*, p. 309.

25 On this point see my comment in *Walther-Rathenau-Gesamtausgabe*, Vol. 2, p. 528.

26 Quoted in Krüger, *Nationalökonomen*, p. 235.

27 MWG, Vol. I/15, p. 702.

28 ibid., p. 706.

29 E. Baumgarten (ed.), *Max Weber. Werk und Person* (Tübingen, 1964), p. 17.

30 Lensch's phrase, quoted in Krüger, *Nationalökonomen*, p. 159.

31 K. Renner, *Marxismus, Krieg und Internationale. Kritische Studien über offene Probleme des wissenschaftlichen und praktischen Sozialismus in und nach dem Weltkrieg* (Stuttgart, 1917); see K. Novy, *Strategien der Sozialisierung. Die Diskussion der Wirtschaftsreform in der Weimarer Republik* (Frankfurt-on-Main and New York, 1978), pp. 98 ff; R. Goldscheid, *Staatssozialismus oder Staatskapitalismus* (Vienna, 1917), reprinted in idem and J. A. Schumpeter, *Die Finanzkrise des Steuerstaates*, ed. R. Hickel (Frankfurt-on-Main, 1976).

32   See especially Krüger, *Nationalökonomen*, chapters 7 and 8; F. Zunkel, *Industrie und Staatssozialismus* (Düsseldorf, 1974), pp. 51–9.

33   K. Braun, *Konservatismus und Gemeinwirtschaft. Eine Studie über Wichard von Moellendorff* (Duisburg, 1978).

34   From the lecture probably given in 1917 entitled 'Gemeinwirtschaft', printed in F. Oppenheimer, *Wege zur Gemeinschaft* (Munich, 1924), quotation p. 295. See Krüger, *Nationalökonomen*, p. 133; L. v. Wiese, *Staatssozialismus* (Berlin, 1916), and idem, *Freie Wirtschaft* (Leipzig, 1918).

35   MWG, Vol. I/15, pp. 355 ff.

36   ibid., p. 358.

37   W. Rathenau, 'Die neue Wirtschaft', in idem, *Gesammelte Schriften*, Vol. 5, p. 258.

38   In an article in the *Frankfurter Zeitung* under the heading 'Kriegssozialismus und Wirtschaftsfreiheit', reprinted in A. Feiler, *Vor der Übergangswirtschaft* (Frankfurt-on-Main, 1918), p. 33.

39   P. Scheibert, 'Revolution und Utopie', in *Epirrhosis. Festgabe für Carl Schmitt*, Vol. 2 (Berlin, 1968), p. 634. Within a larger framework, the problem of the development of the controlled economy through the First World War is now treated in W. H. McNeill, *The Pursuit of Power* (Oxford, 1983), pp. 317 ff.

40   MWG, Vol. I/15, pp. 353 and 357. Cf. also the reference of D. Stegmann, *Die Erben Bismarcks* (Cologne and Berlin, 1970), p. 514.

41   *Biography*, p. 627. For Rathenau's part see, in particular, his pamphlet *An Deutschlands Jugend* (1918).

42   MWG, Vol. I/15, p. 481.

43   For a comparable statement of opinion by Weber, see Baumgarten (ed.), *Max Weber*, pp. 610–12. On Weber and modern Judaism, see H. Liebeschütz, *Das Judentum im deutschen Geschichtsbild von Hegel bis Max Weber* (Tübingen, 1967), especially pp. 322–8. On Rathenau, see my essay 'Walther Rathenau und sein Integrationsversuch als "Deutscher jüdischen Stammes" ', in W. Grab (ed.), *Jüdische Integration und Identität in Deutschland und Österreich 1848–1918. Jahrbuch des Instituts für Deutsche Geschichte*, Beiheft 6 (Tel Aviv, 1984), pp. 13–38.

21 Gustav Stresemann and Max Weber: Politics and Scholarship

GANGOLF HÜBINGER

If we measure the career of Gustav Stresemann against the ideal-typical virtues of the political leader, as Max Weber defined them, then the result is extremely ambivalent. On the one hand, Weber believed politicians such as Stresemann to be indispensable for the establishment of a capitalist society organized along liberal-bourgeois lines. For, in such a society, the interpenetration of politics and economics is constantly growing: 'Politics is penetrating into the economic order at the same time that economic interests are entering into politics.'[1] On the other hand, it is precisely in Stresemann that Weber diagnosed characteristics of political behaviour that he vehemently rejected on ethical grounds, such as tactical manoeuvring, a readiness to compromise, opportunism, sinecurism and an advocacy of limited and particular interests. All this contrasts sharply with Weber's ideal of a life guided by an ethic of responsibility and oriented towards the political welfare of the whole nation.

The relationship between Weber and Stresemann is shaped by the tensions between Weber's ideal types of the career politician, on the one hand, and the actual career patterns of professional politicians in late-Wilhelmine Germany, on the other. There was no personal relationship between the two men, but rather the mutual attention paid to each other by two personalities prominent in public life. Weber was esteemed as one of the most perceptive and far-sighted analysts of political and social conditions in the Kaiserreich;[2] Stresemann, under precisely these conditions, developed to become a political leader of European stature.[3] At the same time both were prominent representatives of the conflicting camps within the liberal Wilhelmine bourgeoisie. Stresemann, who made his career as a legal adviser (*Syndikus*) to business associations, represented the values and interest of industry.[4] Weber represented and upheld the values and norms of an academic middle class (*Bildungsbürgertum*) that was undergoing metamorphosis under the impact of advanced industrialization; as an academic and politician (*Gelehrtenpolitiker*) he fought to get these values accepted.[5]

It is understandable that the numerous frictions between the industrial bourgeoisie and the academic middle class influenced the ways in which Stresemann and Weber perceived each other. The representative of industry saw in the professor an arrogant 'know-all', while the professor noticed in the other, above all, the selfishness of the lobbyist. Nevertheless, a comparison of their two positions has to recognize their extensive agreement in principle on political ideas and values. As is well known, the corner-stones of Weber's political thought were the struggle for world power status of the national state, the parliamentarization of the constitution and the replacement of patriarchal patterns in social policy. Against the background of his investigations into the bureaucratization of all spheres of society, there was also his assessment of the indispensability of modern interest groups to a rational economic life and of the professionalization of party leaders, were the latter to prevail in the parliamentary struggle. Those who initiated and promoted such a policy of modernization, as advocated by Weber, can – formally at least – be described as ideal-typical political reformers, thus coming close to Weber's own political values. The career politician Gustav Stresemann fitted well into this category.

Stresemann, born in 1878, and fourteen years younger than Weber, stood for a new political generation that no longer embarked on a career with the epigonal civil service mentality inherited from Bismarck, but with a self-confidence derived from the business milieu. Stresemann took his doctorate in Leipzig in 1900 with Karl Bücher, who was, like Weber, a representative of the 'left' in social policy among the liberal political economists. After having briefly been with the Association of German Chocolate Manufacturers, Stresemann became secretary of the Dresden-Bautzen district of the League of Industrialists (Bund der Industriellen) in 1902. He achieved his professional and political advance by his own merits without recourse to the normal student corporation connections. In the same year, he became a legal adviser to the Association of Saxon Industrialists, and he represented the interests of the manufactured goods industries in Saxony against the big landowners and heavy industry, with great organizational talent. His political breakthrough in the National Liberal Party came with an important speech at the party conference in Goslar, in October 1906. In 1907 he was elected to the Reichstag and in the subsequent legislative period became recognized as the 'crown prince' to the party leader, Ernst Bassermann. During this time he con-solidated his leadership positions in the business associations. In 1911 he became chief executive of the Federation of Industrialists, and in 1912 adviser to the management committee of the Hanseatic Federation (Hansabund). Stresemann, therefore, became an important co-ordinating figure for in-dustrial interests and National Liberal politicians who wanted a change of course in the right-wing liberal *Sammlungspolitik* at the turn of the century. This led, in 1912, to Stresemann not only losing his Reichstag seat after serious election attacks by the Conservatives and the Agrarian League (Bund der Landwirte), but also to the heavy industry wing of the National Liberals voting him off the party's management committee. In December 1914 he was re-elected to the Reichstag at a by-election in Aurich, but with policies that were not in line with the extensive war-aims of heavy industry. After Bassermann's death, he became parliamentary leader; in this role he was the chief spokesman of the party majority in its demands for large-scale annexations abroad by a victorious Germany. After the war he founded the German People's Party (Deutsche Volkspartei, DVP) and became its leader. In June 1920, at the time of Max Weber's death, Stresemann's DVP was one of the victors in the Reichstag election, which had been called following the Kapp putsch. With his renewed self-confidence, he imagined himself becoming chancellor or foreign minister.[6] In fact, he was chancellor from August to November 1923; he took over the foreign ministry at the same time and retained it through subsequent cabinets until his death in October 1929.

However much Weber, in his political theory, acknowledged business politi-

cians of Stresemann's type to be necessary pathbreakers for a liberally constituted capitalism,[7] his rigorous ethical position gave him a very low opinion
of the character and everyday behaviour of such politicians. This can be
demonstrated by his judgement of the adroit and often unscrupulous
Stresemann. At the same time, Weber's reservations about a parliamentary
system dominated by professional politicians living *from* and not *for* politics
can be clearly seen. In biographical terms, these reservations are an example
of the 'antinomic structure of Max Weber's political thinking';[8] in
sociocultural terms, the high social and moral demands Wilhelmine scholars
made of politics continued to determine Weber's assessment of the political
leaders of the period. Consequently, the tension between principles of political
theory and everyday political judgements must be borne in mind when interpreting the direct and indirect points of contact between Weber and
Stresemann.

Weber, like Stresemann, acquired early practical political experience in
Friedrich Naumann's National Social Association (Nationalsozialer Verein).
Weber commented on the party's foundation in 1896 with his typical 'mixture
of sympathy and strong rejection'.[9] He charged the delegates not to undertake, like 'political puppets', a politics of the social integration of 'those that
toil and are heavy laden', which had no chance of success, but to take part
in the struggle of interest 'between today's leading classes' on behalf of
'bourgeois capitalist development'.[10] As a student, Stresemann had also joined
the National Social Association and was deputy chairman of the Dresden
district association until the dissolution of the whole party after the debacle
in the 1903 Reichstag elections. While Weber withdrew after this first and for
the time being 'only connection with active political involvement',[11]
Stresemann joined the National Liberal Party.

Here Stresemann made his mark on the left wing, emphasizing the 'distinctively liberal element' in addition to the national one.[12] He advocated a policy
of forced industrialization, in sharp opposition both to conservative anti-
capitalist policies, and – significantly in constructive debate with Naumann –
the Social Democrats' ideology of class struggle.[13] He always began his
speeches with the rhetorical opposition between an 'agrarian state' and an 'industrial state',[14] developing the guiding principles of his politics from this
point. 'Industrialism', he said, was the irreversible tendency of the age, and
the parties were, above all, the bearers of economic policies. Consequently, the
National Liberals as the 'party of industry' had to ensure the competitiveness
of manufacturing industry against the cartel policies of heavy industry and
against the big landowners and their interest groups.[15] An indispensable
precondition was, according to Stresemann, an active social policy, based on
the assumption that business and workers both had an interest in an expanding
economy. Stresemann was a sharp opponent of Social Democracy, which he
saw as undermining this common interest. But, like Weber and in contrast to
Naumann's harmonious ideal of the 'industrial citizen', he accepted the basic
pattern of the economic struggle of interest. He conceded the trade unions'
political legitimacy within this framework and accepted freedom of
association.[16] But he also saw an active social policy as the most effective
instrument for recruiting the 'new middle class' of white-collar workers as the
mass base for his planned liberal industrial party.[17] Stresemann, like Weber,

was not pursuing social policies for their own sake; both regarded the 'welfare of each class in the country'[18] as the necessary precondition of Germany's future role as a world power. Stresemann and Weber both shared the hierarchy of liberal-imperialist values, in which the foundation of the Reich not only demanded the maintenance of national autonomy but also worldwide economic expansion and political self-confidence, and consequently also an aggressive colonial policy with all the appropriate military and financial measures.

Weber was a close observer of the National Liberals' break-out from the conservative *Sammlung*, in which Stresemann was one of the initiators. He himself, in a speech given in Saarbrücken in 1897 on 'The bourgeois development of Germany and its significance for population movements', had already argued that big business had to be in a position to compete on the world market, and that the 'broad mass of workers had to be integrated into Germany's bourgeois development'. As a result, a National Liberal group offered him the opportunity of standing against the industrialist, Karl Freiherr von Stumm, in the 1898 Reichstag elections.[19] The letters that Weber wrote to Naumann between 1906 and 1908 confirm that, in principle, he felt his basic political viewpoint to be closer to the course of reform proposed by Stresemann and the Young Liberals within the National Liberal Party than to the Liberal Union (Freisinnige Vereinigung), which Naumann had joined.[20] For Weber's central political theme, repeatedly signalled by the catch-phrase *Weltpolitik*, was the transition from an authoritarian society, embodied in 'personal rule' and the 'subordination of the barrack-room', to a liberal form of bourgeois capitalism, with parliamentary supports and accompanied by social reforms.[21]

The question may be asked why Weber and Stresemann, who shared the same basic point of reference, never found a common political forum, which Theodor Heuss, with reference to Naumann's slogan 'from Bassermann to Bebel', believed to be quite possible.[22] But if we take into account how firmly each followed the particular standards of his own milieu – universally binding social morality on the one side, interest group efficacy on the other – then that is where the principal explanation is likely to be found.

Stresemann's aims and his new style of business politics in conjunction with party politics have been clearly described by Hans-Peter Ullmann in his study of the League of Industrialists.[23] Stresemann carefully and determinedly built up his interest group politics around four elements, combining them with his activities in party politics. He held that the imbalance between the economic importance of industry and its limited political influence had to be corrected; representatives of industry must have greater influence on legislation; in the age of 'industrialism', parties and members of parliament could no longer be judged by their legal and political qualifications but by their economic qualifications; finally, the support of a broad section of public opinion was essential to the success of industrial interests. Stresemann attempted to attract the desired mass-base by trying to convince the working class of its common interest with business by means of limited social concessions, by winning white-collar workers with pension insurance schemes and by using the German Farmers' League (Deutscher Bauernbund) to detach the peasantry from the Agrarian League (Bund der Landwirte).

Weber accepted 'mass organizations' and 'modern interest group organizations' as new forms of economic and political power struggle.[24] He also recognized the political competence their leaders acquired in the 'struggle with political opinion'.[25] As parliamentary forms develop, it is from the ranks of such interest-representatives, of modern party officials and professional journalists that the political elite is recruited.[26] But it is Stresemann who also provides Weber with material for his categorical distinction between living *from* politics and living *for* politics. According to Weber, not only do party journalists and officials, and employees of the trade unions and chambers of commerce, agriculture and trades live from politics, but also, of course, do employees of employers' organizations such as Stresemann. Like civil servants, they have enormous expert knowledge, but their dependency on their material interests prevents the development of a charismatic personality. Their eligibility as political leaders is small by comparison with the career politician who is economically independent, responsible only to himself, fights 'for his own power'[27] and therefore lives for politics.

There is no question that his orientation towards the ideal type of the politician as an independent advocate led Weber to underestimate the possibilities offered by creative interest group politics – and hardly anyone knew how to use these as skilfully as did Stresemann. He was able to increase the influence of industry representatives on legislation, to replace political notables by politicians trained in economics and to win the support of a broad section of public opinion for 'industrialism'. In particular, he attempted to draw the 'new middle class' to his programme by an attractive social policy. Stresemann achieved political prominence in the 'everyday struggles of private economic interest',[28] which Weber described as the decisive feature of the age. However, while Stresemann regarded the development by which the parties were drawn into the economic process as irreversible, and consciously promoted it, Weber insisted on his ideal of the independent leader, living *for* politics, free of 'plutocratic' interests and acting on behalf of the whole in an awareness of power relationships.

The antithetical viewpoints of the politician, Stresemann, and the scholar, Weber, built up barriers which disturbed any possibility of communication so strongly that the only direct points of contact were brief and conflict-laden. One such point of contact was the 'Ehrenberg Affair' in 1908–9. Ernst Budde, business politician and director of Siemens and Halske AG, had, as chairman of the Institut für exakte Wirtschaftsforschung (a research institute friendly to business), suggested setting up an additional chair of political economy at Leipzig University and promised 30,000 RM to fund it. Richard Ehrenberg, who had ensured the support of industry by his research in applied economics as well as his attacks on the 'academic socialism' of the Verein für Sozialpolitik, was proposed for the chair. Such a pro-industry professorship suited Stresemann's interest group politics, so he played the role of intermediary to the Saxon minister of culture. This aroused massive protest from university teachers against the 'attempt to buy the appointment of a political professorship (*Tendenzprofessur*) with money'. Professorial resentment at interference in their administrative autonomy was given public expression above all by Max Weber at the University Teacher's Conference at Leipzig in October 1909.[29] Stresemann countered by asking whether it was 'an example of scientific judgement when ... Herr Professor Weber presents his democratic-socialist ideas at the great conferences of the university teachers'.[30] In a further response to Weber's attack, he justified his support of Ehrenberg, but claimed to have acted as a private individual and not as official representative of the Association of Saxon Industrialists.[31] Although he never actually named Stresemann, Weber's conference speech publicly dismissed him as a 'lobbyist'.[32] Weber himself was less interested in Stresemann as an individual. After his experiences with the representatives of industry at the Mannheim conference of the Verein für Sozialpolitik, he now drew a straight line from the General Secretary of the Central Association of German Manufacturers (Centralverband deutscher Industrieller), Henry Axel Bueck, to the initiators of the Ehrenberg professorship.[33]

Two years later, Stresemann, having already lost his constituency, was outmanoeuvred by the heavy industry wing in the elections to his party's management committee. This was followed in 1913 by the setting up of the Cartel of Productive Estates (Kartell der schaffenden Stände), and Stresemann could only make his political comeback at a Reichstag by-election in December 1914 by largely swinging behind the annexationist course of heavy industry and the Agrarian League. As a result, Stresemann and Weber were once more opponents. On one side stood Stresemann, an advocate of a 'victorious peace', a Pan-German and an extreme annexationist, supporter of unlimited submarine warfare and 'chancellor toppler'; on the other side was Weber, a spokesman for a negotiated peace and 'real guarantees', an opponent of unlimited submarine warfare and a supporter of Bethmann Hollweg. These prominent spokesmen, one for national-liberal big business, the other for the radical-liberal academics, demonstrate the polarization in the liberal middle class, which largely determined the new foundation and the limitations of liberalism after the 1918 collapse. Discussion circles such as the German Society 1914 (Deutsche Gesellschaft 1914), which brought together business and academic middle classes under the mediating direction of Ernst Jäckh, and in which Stresemann and Weber both participated, failed to moderate these antagonisms,[34] although Friedrich Naumann did all he could to draw not only Weber but Stresemann as well into his plans for a 'central Europe'.[35]

A significant sign of the increasing hardening of positions is Stresemann's reply to Weber's well-founded warning that intensified or unlimited submarine warfare would inevitably provoke the entry of America into the war and seal the German defeat. This was the tenor of his memorandum, 'The intensification of submarine warfare', which he sent to the government and to party leaders in mid-March 1916.[36] Stresemann, who only returned from a Balkans trip at the height of the crisis, reacted promptly, mocking Weber's 'calculations' from the 'standpoint of a practical man'. In his admiration for Ludendorff, he allowed all his considerations of geopolitical changes to rest on the victory guarantees given by the military leadership. He saw only the promised opportunities, particularly of a decisive defeat of England, and, unlike Weber, did not reckon the dangers.[37]

In the autumn of 1916, Weber expanded a lecture given in Munich on 'Deutschlands weltpolitische Lage' ['Germany's international situation'], into an essay for the journal *Die Hilfe*. In it he flailed the 'conqueror's vanity', as expressed, for example, in the memorandum of the six economic interest groups of 20 May 1915. Stresemann had shared responsibility for the memorandum and felt himself directly addressed. Weber had spoken of the irresponsible and self-interested politics of those 'who stayed at home in their offices' , and denounced the Pan-Germanism of their influence on government policy. Stresemann reacted sharply: 'If the gentleman in question continues to presume to insult the leaders of German economic life in the manner of a fish-wife...then we would like to give Herr Professor Weber the good advice that he first of all accomplish in his academic activity what the leaders of the League of Industrialists and of the Central Association of German Manufac-turers have achieved in this war for the adaptation and efficiency of German industry so that war production could be established.'[38]

Weber, of course, was not concerned with reprimanding industry as such, whose achievements he acknowledged without reservation.[39] His concern was the absence of rational calculation in achieving the highest war-aim, one that he also supported, of securing for the German Reich its historically rightful place among the European world powers. However, extreme annexationist demands, and 'plutocratic' internal and social policies were, as Weber saw it, the most unsuitable means imaginable of achieving this.[40]

At the same time as he was involved in these war-aims controversies with Weber, Stresemann had recognized the necessity of opposing the Conserv-atives and of contributing to a new course in internal politics. With a radicalism that startled many left-wing liberals, he demanded parliamentariz-ation, and in particular, a parliamentary foreign affairs committee.[41] Stresemann, like Weber, wanted the fundamental re-organization of the Imperial Constitution to lead to a parliamentary monarchy. In his articles at this time, Weber's only direct mention of Stresemann refers to his agreement with the proposal that the parliamentarization of the Prussian departmental ministries should not be a matter of principle, in order not to exclude from politics civil servants with a capacity for political leadership.[42]

Likewise, Stresemann used arguments similar to Weber's to oppose economic theories that aimed to replace the capitalist economic order with a state-organized 'co-operative economy'.[43] However, for Weber, this funda-mental political agreement counted less than concrete political mistakes. In his eyes, Stresemann was discredited once and for all, at the latest after his approval of the Zimmermann telegram, and for the role, which as confidant of the Military High Command he had played in the fall of Bethmann Hollweg.[44]

As a result, Weber fully shared the political inflexibility displayed by his brother Alfred and by Theodor Wolff. In November 1918, at the conference on the unification of the liberal tendencies, they, as spokesmen of the newly founded German Democratic Party (Deutsche Demokratische Partei, DDP), excluded members of the 'old compromised parties', Stresemann in particular.[45] In his series of articles on 'Deutschlands künftige Staatsform' ('Germany's future state'), as later in his election speeches for the DDP, Weber formulated his demand for a replacement of party leaders by direct reference to Stresemann. 'If, for example, the National Liberal Party were to continue to exist, as a part of it wishes to do, then it is impossible for a democratic new order that it appears before the electors with leaders who joined in the denigration of "Western" democracy, or that it appears before the League of Nations with leaders who wanted to annexe Flanders or Briey, supported the insane Baltic policy, praised the unbelievable note to Mexico and, above all, who by their demagogy helped to enforce the submarine warfare. Otherwise, the election campaign will not be a struggle for the future, but an angry settling of past accounts.'[46]

The Kapp putsch, as an early test of republican commitment, did indeed show that Weber's thesis, that Wilhelmine politicians were untrustworthy occupants of the republic's leading positions, was not so far from the truth. Whereas Weber completely condemned the putsch, Stresemann's behaviour was altogether equivocal.[47] On the other hand, it was not surprising that on the paramount question of national autonomy, both Weber and Stresemann were deeply convinced of the necessity of rejecting the Versailles Treaty, although the consequences were perfectly clear to them.[48] Nevertheless, Stresemann as foreign minister, operating in 'power politics', and with a 'realistic assessment of the European balance of power', succeeded, with the conclusion of the Locarno Treaties of 1925, in returning Germany to the circle of 'European world powers'.[49]

It has been shown how Weber and Stresemann fought for the establishment of an adequate political framework for industrial-bourgeois-capitalist society. For them, the boundaries between academic left-liberal politics and right-wing liberal business politics were not clearly defined. Nevertheless, in the choice of means and on many individual questions, the scholar's scheme of values on the one hand and interest group politics on the other were decisive in producing antagonisms. 'Realistic politics' meant something different to Weber than did *Realpolitik* to Stresemann. Weber himself summed up this tension in a much-quoted formula: 'A politician *must* make compromises; a scholar *must not* cover them.'[50] It was in this revolutionary mood with respect to political ends and means that, in November 1918, the resignation of the old political elite, Stresemann in particular, was demanded, not least by Weber. It was in the same atmosphere that the proposal was made to Weber to exchange the role of political analyst for that of political actor, as party leader or minister. The question whether Weber could have fulfilled the expectations placed in him is hypothetical, and must ultimately be answered in the negative.[51] His real contacts with politics did not go beyond his professional advice to friends such as Friedrich Naumann, Conrad Haußmann, Hugo Preuss and Ludo Moritz Hartmann. The brilliance of political analysis was bought at the cost of a (partly desired) renunciation of anything but a sporadic involvement in the everyday sphere of 'politics as a vocation'. By contrast, Stresemann's sovereign command of this sphere assured him of a swift political comeback. In Weber's words in another context, he was the 'weathercock of a general trend'. Despite Weber's analyses, it was precisely under parliamentary conditions that Stresemann established himself and really began his career as a 'political leader' and statesman.

Notes: Chapter 21

This chapter was translated by Erica Carter and Chris Turner.

1   ES, Vol. 1, p. 299.

2 Cf. D. Beetham, *Max Weber and the Theory of Modern Politics* (London, 1974); W. Schluchter, 'Der autoritär verfaßte Kapitalismus. Max Webers Kritik am Kaiserreich', in idem, *Rationalismus der Weltbeherrschung* (Frankfurt-on-Main, 1980), pp. 134–69; W. J. Mommsen, *Max Weber and German Politics, 1890–1920* (Chicago, 1984).

3 Cf. E. Kolb, 'Probleme einer modernen Stresemann-Biographie', in O. Franz (ed.), *Am Wendepunkt der europäischen Geschichte* (Göttingen, 1981), pp. 107–34. For a survey of research on Stresemann, see idem, *Die Weimarer Republik* (Munich and Vienna, 1984), pp. 194 ff. A recent biography is F. Hirsch, *Stresemann. Ein Lebensbild* (Göttingen, 1978), and a comprehensive bibliography is M. Walsdorff, *Bibliographie Gustav Stresemann* (Düsseldorf, 1972).

4 Cf. H.-P. Ullmann, *Der Bund der Industriellen* (Göttingen, 1976), pp. 138 ff.; D. Warren, *The Red Kingdom of Saxony: Lobbying Grounds for Gustav Stresemann, 1901–1909* (The Hague, 1964).

5 For the different types of involvement of German scholars in politics, see R. vom Bruch, *Wissenschaft, Politik und öffentliche Meinung. Gelehrtenpolitik im Wilhelminischen Deutschland (1890–1914)* (Husum, 1980), and idem, 'Forschungen und Arbeiten zur politischen Sozialgeschichte des deutschen Bildungsbürgertums im 19. und frühen 20. Jahrhundert mit besonderer Berücksichtigung der Hochschullehrerschaft', in *Jahrbuch der historischen Forschung 1982* (Munich, 1983), pp. 36–41.

6 Hirsch, *Stresemann*, p. 126.

7 MWG, Vol. I/15, especially pp. 456–7.

8 Cf. W. J. Mommsen, 'The antinomian structure of Max Weber's political thought', in S. G. McNall (ed.), *Current Perspectives in Social Theory*, Vol. 4 (Greenwich, Conn., 1983), pp. 289–311.) Gustav Radbruch, for example, noticed a sharp distinction between Weber's value-free observation as 'a principle of theoretical and scientific thinking' and Weber's practical conduct: 'In his practical conduct, Weber was an ethical absolutist and rigorist.' G. Radbruch, *Der innere Weg. Aufriß meines Lebens* (Stuttgart, 1951), p. 88.

9 Mommsen, *Max Weber and German Politics*, p. 127. See also P. Theiner, *Sozialer Liberalismus und deutsche Weltpolitik. Friedrich Naumann im Wilhelminischen Deutschland (1860–1919)* (Baden-Baden, 1983), pp. 53 ff.

10 GPS³, pp. 27, 28.

11 Mommsen, *Max Weber and German Politics*, p. 123.

12 *Neunter allgemeiner Vertretertag der nationalliberalen Partei am 6. und 7. Oktober 1906 in Goslar. Protokoll auf Grund stenographischer Aufzeichnungen* (Berlin, n.d.), p. 54.

13 Speech in the Reichstag, 12 April 1907, *Stenographische Berichte über die Verhandlungen des Deutschen Reichstags*, Vol. 227, pp. 709–15.

14 See the collection of his speeches: G. Stresemann, *Wirtschaftspolitische Zeitfragen* (Dresden, n.d. [1910]) especially p. 72.

15 ibid., p. 145.

16 Speech in the Reichstag, 12 April 1907 (as in n. 13 above).

17 Stresemann, *Wirtschaftspolitische Zeitfragen*, pp. 49, 74–5.

18 ibid., p. 101. See also J. J. Sheehan, *German Liberalism in the Nineteenth Century* (Chicago, 1978), p. 261.

19 Cf. the report on Weber's speech in *Saarbrücker Zeitung*, 13 January 1897. See also *Biography*, p. 223.

20 Cf. Weber's letters to Naumann written between 14 December 1906 and 18 November 1908, in GPS¹, pp. 451–8. For Weber's views on the Young Liberals, cf. 'Ein Rundschreiben Max Webers vom 15. Dez. 1912, ed. and introd. by B. Schäfers', *Soziale Welt*, vol. 18 (1967), pp. 261–71 (here p. 270).

21 Here I am following Schluchter's conclusions, 'Der autoritär verfaßte Kapitalismus', pp. 168–9.

22 T. Heuss, *Erinnerungen 1905–1933* (Tübingen, 1933), p. 80: 'Gustav Stresemann had moved into the ranks of the Young Liberals after having spent his political youth with Naumann. We watched his development with interest, but also with certain misgivings.'

23 Ullmann, *Der Bund der Industriellen*, pp. 138 ff.

24 Cf. MWG, Vol. I/15, pp. 460, 534.

25 ibid., p. 534.

26 GPS³, p. 545.

27 MWG, Vol. I/15, p. 468; also p. 502.

28 ibid., p. 378.

29 The quotation is taken from Weber's letter to the *Frankfurter Zeitung*, no. 290, 19 October 1909, 1st morning edn. See also Warren, *The Red Kingdom of Saxony*, pp. 80–1; Vom Bruch, *Wissenschaft, Politik und öffentliche Meinung*, pp. 296 ff., 438–9. In his review of Adolf Weber, *Die Aufgaben der Volkswirtschaftslehre als Wissenschaft* (AfSSP, vol. 29, 1909, pp. 615–20), Max Weber included a critical comment on Ehrenberg's 'punitive professorship' against the 'Kathedersozialisten' that had been inspired by the big industrial interests. For his speech at the Leipzig meeting, cf. *Verhandlungen des III. Deutschen Hochschullehrertages zu Leipzig am 12. und 13. Oktober 1909* (Leipzig, 1910), p. 16.

30 G. Stresemann, 'Eine "Tendenzprofessur" an der Universität Leipzig', *Sächsische Industrie*, vol. 6, no. 3 (1909–10), pp. 35–8 (here, p. 36).

31 'Die Leipziger "Tendenzprofessur"', *Leipziger Tageblatt*, no. 286, 15 October 1909. That Stresemann was the author of this anonymous article is proved by a letter from Karl Bücher to Hans Delbrück, dated 19 October 1909 (Bundesarchiv Koblenz, Delbrück papers, no. 30). See also Stresemann's later explanation of his behaviour in *Frankfurter Zeitung*, no. 54, 28 October 1909, 2nd morning edn. I am grateful to Rüdiger vom Bruch for providing these references.

32 Cf. Warren, *The Red Kingdom of Saxony*, p. 81.

33 *Verhandlungen des III. Deutschen Hochschullehrertages* (as in n. 29 above), p. 16. For Stresemann's practical opposition to Bueck in central issues of the policy of the Central-verband, see F. Blaich, *Staat und Verbände in Deutschland 1871–1945* (Wiesbaden, 1979), especially pp. 43 ff.

34 Cf. E. Jäckh, *Der goldene Pflug* (Stuttgart, 1954), pp. 187 ff.; Hirsch, *Stresemann*, p. 86.

35 After the inaugural meeting of the 'Arbeitsausschuß für Mitteleuropa', Arndt v. Holtzendorff told Albert Ballin that as late as August 1915 Naumann had invited Stresemann to co-operate. But: 'The *Vereine* pursue interest group politics; the group around Stresemann is totally opposed to the group around [Theodor] Wolff; it is therefore impossible to combine the two.' Bundesarchiv Koblenz, Ballin papers, R1, v. Holtzendorff's report no. 358, 23 February 1916, p. 4.

36 MWG, Vol. I/15, pp. 115 ff. and the editorial report, pp. 99 ff.

37 Stresemann's reply is cited in W. J. Mommsen, *Max Weber und die deutsche Politik 1890–1920*, 2nd edn (Tübingen, 1974), pp. 515 ff. This passage was omitted in the English translation of Mommsen's book (as cited in n. 2 above).

38 [G. Stresemann], 'Die Schimpfrede eines deutschen Professors', *Deutscher Kurier*, no. 312, 12 November 1916. Stresemann refers to the first version of Weber's article in *Die Hilfe*, 9 November 1916, now in MWG, Vol. I/15, pp. 161 ff. (especially pp. 167–8). The *Deutscher Kurier*, edited by Stresemann, returned to the issue on 6 January 1917 ('Professor Max Weber und die deutsche Industrie').

39 Cf. Weber's speech 'An der Schwelle des dritten Kriegsjahres' (1 August 1916), MWG, Vol. I/15, especially p. 666.

40 As far as this supreme principle of a liberal imperialism was concerned, there was indeed an affinity between Weber's and Stresemann's positions, as has been pointed out by M.-O. Maxelon, *Stresemann und Frankreich* (Düsseldorf, 1972), pp. 28, 276. A wide-ranging analysis of Stresemann's politics during the First World War is M. L. Edwards, *Stresemann and the Greater Germany, 1914–1918* (New York, 1963).

41 See, in particular, Stresemann's speech in the Reichstag on 26 October 1916, *Stenographische Berichte*, Vol. 308, pp. 1019 ff. Cf. Theiner, *Sozialer Liberalismus*, pp. 229–30.

42 MWG, Vol. I/15, p. 575. Stresemann had thus commented on the formation of a government by Graf Hertling: 'With these new appointments there is no question of a parliamentary system as it is known abroad. German sentiment would never tolerate a ministry being held by a parliamentarian who would lack the necessary expertise.'

43 G. Stresemann, 'Die isolierte Industrie', *Vossische Zeitung*, no. 503, 1 October 1916. Cf. also Weber's lecture on socialism: MWG, Vol. I/15, especially pp. 611–13.

44 Thus Weber in his Heidelberg electioneering address on behalf of the German Democratic Party (17 January 1919). Cf. MWG, Vol. I/16 (forthcoming).

45 Cf. T. Wolff, *Tagebücher 1914–1919. Zweiter Teil*, ed. B. Sösemann (Boppard, 1984), pp. 658–9. The entry for 19 November 1918 includes the following remarks: 'This morning I telephoned Fischbeck, he hopes to achieve an agreement, and I will make sure that Weber does not behave in a personally offensive manner again. I told him that we had been annoyed because they had sent us Wiemer and Stresemann.' It is curious, and will probably never be definitively explained, that Wolff and Stresemann erroneously believed Max and not Alfred

Weber to have been the moving spirit at the November 1918 conference. Wolff, in a diary entry of 18 November (*Tagebücher. Zweiter Teil*, p. 658) mentions 'Max Weber'. In his diary entry of 24 February 1919, Harry Graf Kessler records a conversation with Stresemann, which took place on the same day: 'He told me about the negotiations with Professor Weber concerning the founding of the Democratic Party, during which Weber had thrown him out in the most insulting manner...He found out later, however, that Weber had already been in a mental hospital twice.' Kessler, *Tagebücher 1918–1937*, ed. W. Pfeiffer-Belli (Frankfurt-on-Main, 1982), p. 140. The most likely source of this confusion was not ignorance of their Christian names, but a syncretization of the political rigorousness of both brothers, producing an ideal figure 'Weber'. Max Weber was in Heidelberg at the time and intended to go to Frankfurt to work in the editorial office of the *Frankfurter Zeitung* 'for a few weeks'. See his letter to Helene Weber, 18 November 1918, from Heidelberg, in GPS[1], p. 481.

46 GPS[3], p. 455. Further documentation will be published in MWG, Vol. I/16 (forthcoming).
47 Cf. Mommsen, *Max Weber and German Politics*, pp. 328–9; H. A. Turner, *Stresemann – Republikaner aus Vernunft* (Berlin, 1968), pp. 57 ff.
48 Cf. ibid., pp. 47 ff., and Mommsen, *Max Weber and German Politics*, p. 320.
49 Cf. Kolb, *Die Weimarer Republik*, pp. 62 ff.
50 Letter to Klara Mommsen, quoted from *Biography*, p. 689. See also Weber's letter to Carl Petersen, 14 April 1920: 'The politician ought to and *has to* reach compromises. My profession, however, is that of a *scholar*.' MWG, Vol. I/15, p. 1.
51 Cf. Mommsen, *Max Weber and German Politics*, pp. 329–30. Mommsen here emphasizes Weber's self-conscious loyalty to the ideals of the Kaiserreich era – in contrast to Stresemann's facile opportunism. Yet, here again, Stresemann and Weber ultimately move close to each other. Stresemann's veering between constitutionalist revisionism and republicanism was deeply influenced by his experience in the Wilhelmine period.

22   Dietrich Schäfer and Max Weber

ROGER CHICKERING

Dietrich Schäfer and Max Weber arrived in the faculty at the university in Heidelberg within a year of one another and were colleagues for six years, until 1903, when Schäfer was called to Berlin. The relationship between the two in Heidelberg was cordial, if not particularly close, restricted in any event by the emotional turmoil that plagued Weber during these years.[1] Both men were noted for their nationalist convictions, particularly for their opposition to the growing influence of Poles in eastern Germany, and they displayed their convictions together as members of the Eastern Marches Society (Deutscher Ostmarkenverein) and the Pan-German League (Alldeutscher Verband).[2] After Schäfer's departure for Berlin, however, the relationship between the two scholars deteriorated. Like most historians in Imperial Germany, Schäfer took a dim view of the emergent discipline of sociology, and he clashed with Weber over the candidacy of Georg Simmel for a chair in Heidelberg, an appointment that Weber favoured.[3] The antagonism then culminated in a bitter debate during the First World War. Schäfer emerged as the foremost public advocate of an ambitious programme of German annexations in Europe and abroad, as well as the champion of unrestricted submarine warfare. Weber moved more reluctantly into the debate, but, as the war dragged on, he became a leading opponent of both the kind of naval warfare that Schäfer advocated and the grandiose war-aims with which his former colleague had become associated.[4]

The growing conflict between the two men is of more than casual interest. It raises questions of political temperament and style, a disciplinary conflict, and divergent conceptions of German history and politics. At the root of the antagonism, however, stood conflicting ideas about the proper relationship between scholarship and political action.

The values and orientations that underlay Dietrich Schäfer's politics were largely those of his academic guild. It must remain a matter of speculation, though, whether the passion and rigidity with which he held them and the energy with which he broke with his colleagues' traditional disdain for political activism were not psychological by-products of a remarkable career.[5] During his astounding social ascent from the shipyards of Bremen to a chair at the country's leading university, the most enduring influence on Schäfer was that of his teacher, Heinrich von Treitschke. Schäfer was in fact known variously as Treitschke's foremost disciple or his epigone — and both claims were accurate.[6] The premises of the primacy of the nation-state and the inevitability of international conflict informed the scholarship of teacher and student alike, but Schäfer's writings lacked the power of Treitschke's and were marked instead, to borrow Charles McClelland's apt description, by 'the sober, humorless, pedantic spirit of the petty-bourgeois schoolmaster'.[7]

Nor was Schäfer's in any sense an original or penetrating mind, and many of the critical issues that occupied Max Weber and other thinkers at the turn of the century did not interest him. That the historian was to strive for objectivity in scholarship and that this objectivity could to a substantial degree be realized were to him self-evident principles. In his inaugural lecture in Tübingen, which he republished with but slight modifications on the eve of the war, Schäfer spoke of the 'ever higher demands on [historical] criticism' and of the importance of 'determining the fundamental facts, uninfluenced by any *Tendenz* or preconceived opinions'.[8] On another occasion he denounced as one of the 'worst errors a historian can commit' the practice of 'gauging the past by standards of the present'.[9] It would be unfair to accuse Schäfer of intellectual dishonesty; his problem was rather a lack of detachment, of a capacity for self-criticism, which made it impossible for him to recognize how patently he himself was guilty of just the errors he criticized. In the same passage in which he cited present-mindedness as a cardinal sin, he announced that he was not going to commit it, but that his own account would 'remain constantly conscious of the state of affairs which is portrayed in our perceptions as the product of historical development – the state of affairs,' and here Schäfer left little doubt about the extent of his debt to Treitschke, 'that is characterized by the competition of nations, above all the leading nations for world power'. His own work, he concluded, would see in just this state of affairs a 'lodestar, particularly with respect to the selection of the [historical] material'.[10]

It might be possible to claim that in these and other similar passages in his work, the historian was, in good Weberian fashion, merely making manifest the values he intended to impose upon his subject-matter and cautioning the gullible reader not to attach claims of scientific validity to these values. Schäfer insisted, however, that values that related to the nation-state were of an entirely different order than those of a confessional or partisan character, which did indeed, in his opinion, impair historical objectivity. The historian did not, Schäfer believed, impose national values on the historical process; historical scholarship instead 'flows along chiefly in a national bed'; it is 'chiefly guided by the national principle which rules the present'.[11] Or, as he put it shortly afterwards in a similar image, historical scholarship 'floats in the wake of the nation [*im nationalen Fahrwasser*]'.[12] The national moment, the impulse to national consciousness, amalgamation, political unification, and self-assertion, thus not only informed the historical drama; it was an immanent imperative which operated upon the historian no less than on those whose acts the historian chronicled. Historical scholarship divorced from the realities and values generated by the nation-state was not only senseless, it was inconceivable.[13]

The concept of the nation, therefore, had both epistemological and moral significance, and it guided the historian in both facets of the preceptorial role that Schäfer thought was properly his. The historian was to mediate between the past and present, not only by the employment of national categories to draw out of the past the lessons it contained for the present. 'It will also henceforward be the task of the historian,' he announced in an early lecture, 'to bring the state to understand its origin, its development, the conditions of its existence, its responsibilities.'[14] For Germans specifically, the function of the historian was to 'furnish the historical record, to influence their judgement...by providing a closer understanding of the nature of things that have developed and the preconditions of [the country's] continued existence'.[15] Schäfer openly endorsed the label of 'historical writing with a political *Tendenz*' to describe the kind of history he had in mind.[16] He did not, however, in any sense thereby demean the significance of the results of historical inquiry. The knowledge that the historian was to disseminate, as it related both to the meaning of the historical record and to the imperatives that this record prescribed, would be objective and scientifically valid, if only the historian undertook the project in the proper spirit.

Schäfer practised these principles in his own historical scholarship. He trained with Georg Waitz as a medievalist, and his professional reputation rested largely on the work he did on the Hanseatic League.[17] But the lessons that the history of the League offered for the German Empire in the twentieth century were never far from the historian's mind. He argued that the decline of the League was due in the main to the fact that its members could not rely on the kind of consolidated political and military power that its newly emergent rivals enjoyed. The disappearance of German maritime supremacy in the north was then an aspect of the general deterioration which beset the nation's economy, politics and culture for the next four hundred years.

By the turn of the century Schäfer's interest had turned from the history of the *Hanse* to broader topics, and he began to promote naval history as a genre. He also produced two broad historical surveys designed for a more popular audience.[18] In these, he presented a more extended statement of the historical panorama implied in his earlier work. The historical record now revealed the centrality of national consciousness, that this consciousness required the foundation of the state for its full expression, and that the power of the state went hand-in-hand with maritime prosperity and naval might.

Schäfer's work was, of course, not only an analysis of the historical record: it was a secular theology, a broad vision of fall and redemption. In this vision, the era inaugurated in the reign of Otto the Great (936–73) represented the pinnacle of German power, prosperity, and culture, the 'most brilliant [period] of our nation', the era in which 'the best of our nation gathered around the imperial monarchy, and upon every last man in it there fell a part of the brilliance that spread out over the nation'.[19] The fall was ushered in by the diversion and contamination of the monarchy in Roman affairs, which in turn led to political fragmentation and the loss of commercial hegemony in the north. Roman influence sealed the tragedy in the cultural fragmentation and political prostration of the nation, which resulted from the era of religious warfare. Even at the nadir of its fortunes, however, national consciousness glowed on in the legacy of Luther, until its cultural political resurgence in the eighteenth and nineteenth centuries.

Schäfer's vision of the historical drama was, to employ Hayden White's schema, a romance – a story of self-fulfilment, vindication, and triumph over a multitude of adversities.[20] The drama was, however, by no means at its end at the point when Schäfer recounted it, for in the historian's cycs, past and present were a continuum along which a single set of forces and challenges operated. To the generation of Germans who inherited the great legacy of national unification fell now the obligation to extend the achievement in an age of industrial growth and worldwide struggle among the great powers.

A vision which so systematized the past, present and future in the play of moral forces might well be described as an ideology, a *Weltanschauung*. It would, in any case, be no misrepresentation to describe Dietrich Schäfer as an ideologue and moralist. And these traits made him at home in the Pan-German League, where he found the company of other upwardly mobile men with academic training, who shared his vision of history and the nation's destiny and who articulated an aggressive set of policies designed to fulfil that destiny. [21] Schäfer was, however, although the label is almost a contradiction in terms, a moderate among the Pan-Germans. He never subscribed to the racism with which the ideologists in the League sought after the turn of the century to impose a more rigid scientific order on the past. [22] Nor did he, at least prior to the war, endorse some of the more extravagant schemes, such as the settlement of eastern France with Germans, which some of the League's leadership advocated. [23]

Moderate as Schäfer might have been in the company of the Pan-Germans, his activism made him a more extreme case among his professional colleagues. Although his assumptions about historical scholarship, about the indispensability of evaluative criteria offered by the nation-state, were generally shared by German academic historians in the Wilhelmine epoch, Schäfer differed from his colleagues in the enthusiasm with which he attempted to translate the lessons of scholarship into political action. [24] In this respect, he stood closer to his mentor, Treitschke, than he did to most of his fellow-historians, whose ethos emphasized the detachment of an academic vocation and who, at least until the outbreak of the war, tended to confine their commentary on issues of contemporary politics to the lecture room. [25] Schäfer, by contrast, plunged into the political arena, as a regular contributor to political journals and as a featured speaker not only for the Pan-German League but also for practically every other patriotic society in the country. The reason why he was such an asset to these organizations was not only the prestige that attached to his profession, but also his interpretation of his professional role. He appeared draped in the mantle of scholarship and publicly invoked the authority of his profession in support of the causes and policies that these societies advocated.

Two causes were of particular significance to him. The first was the Germanization of the Prussian eastern provinces (the cause in which he and Weber joined forces in the 1890s). Schäfer claimed expertise on this subject on the basis of research he had done on German colonialization of the north-east in the fourteenth century. The legacy of this historical phenomenon was, he argued, not only the right, but the obligation of Germans to impose their hegemony over the Poles who inhabited the Prussian east – an obligation which, on Schäfer's authority, was also incompatible with the idea of democratic reform of the Prussian suffrage. [26] The other cause was the navy. Schäfer was the very model of the *Flottenprofessor*, who lent his services to the campaign being orchestrated out of Tirpitz's Imperial Naval Office for purposes of generating popular support for the construction of a battle fleet. Schäfer was in his element. His lectures on the subject emphasized the lessons of the history of the *Hanse* and drove home the moral that, as the abstract of one of his lectures explained, 'the prosperity of all nations rose as long as they had a great fleet at their disposal' and that 'the ruin of commerce and the decline of great nations always followed immediately on the ruin of the navy.'[27]

For Schäfer, the outbreak of war in 1914 marked no real hiatus, and none of his assumptions changed. His public engagement merely intensified. He mobilized most of his academic colleagues in uncompromising defence of the German war effort.[28] As leader of the so-called Independent Committee for a German Peace and as a leading figure in the mammoth Fatherland Party, Schäfer lobbied for a wide-reaching programme of war-aims, including not only renewed German colonization of the east but also German control of Belgium and northern France. More fatefully, he led the campaign that ultimately succeeded in committing the German government to unrestricted submarine warfare. For Schäfer, pursuit of these goals – particularly the eastern colonization and the relentless assertion of German naval power – was mandated by the same ideological vision that governed his perception of history. To this vision he clung tenaciously until the final days of the war, long after the very policies he had advocated had guaranteed the military defeat of his country.[29] In fact, not even defeat in war could challenge the integrity of this vision, and until his death in 1929 Schäfer's politics, in particular his loud opposition to the new republican government in Germany, were geared to it.

In the circles in which Schäfer moved during the war, Max Weber was regarded as a defeatist (*Flaumacher*) for his opposition to the policies these men promoted.[30] To fault Weber for want of patriotism would have been inconceivable to anyone who had followed his activities in the 1890s. At this time, most spectacularly in his inaugural address in Freiburg in 1895, Weber professed a faith in the German nation that was no less militant than Schäfer's, no less informed by a Darwinian vision of international conflict, and no less committed to a programme of overseas expansion and naval power.[31] Weber might have had reservations about the influence of Treitschke, whose student he too had been, but these were nowhere in evidence in his public exaltation of German power before the turn of the century, when the spirit of Treitschke animated his views just as much as they did Schäfer's.[32]

Even at this time, however, there was a critical difference between Weber's patriotic creed and Schäfer's. The difference lay beneath the surface, in the epistemological foundations of Weber's political beliefs, where it remained initially obscured amid the more obvious similarities. A discussion of this topic is difficult to confine, for it raises issues that have been central in the exegesis of Weber's work, especially of his methodology, for more than a half century – the relationship between the realms of politics and scholarship, particularly the place of value-judgements or normative standards in each, and Weber's success in observing the precepts of his methodology in his own work as scholar, political theorist and political actor.

To reduce the difference between the views of Schäfer and Weber to the most critical point, Weber denied the existence of a continuum between past and present along which a uniform set of evaluative criteria and moral imperatives operated. He was far more alive than Schäfer to what has been called the 'crisis of German historicism', and he reflected far more profoundly on the problems of historical objectivity, the ontological status of the historical record, and the admissibility of evaluative or normative statements of any kind in the cultural, social or historical sciences.[33] For Schäfer, all these problems evaporated once he admitted nationality as an indispensable category in the evaluation of the past. Weber's insistence upon the scientific inadmissibility of all evaluative categories was thus a repudiation of the epistemological assumptions on which Schäfer's whole vision of history rested.

Weber's position was not, of course, that the historical scholar could not be a nationalist. The scholar had only to remain intellectually honest and to recognize the fact that, like all political convictions, the belief in the heritage, quality and mission of a national group was a product of choice on the part of the observer. Because this belief embraced normative standards, it could in no way be documented or demonstrated in the empirical record of history. Weber struggled all his life with the implications of this radical separation of fact and value, of historical scholarship and political conviction. Nor did he always succeed in observing it (it is difficult to see how any human being could): occasional imprecision of language, a tendency, for example, to use loaded phrases such as the Germans' 'obligations to history' attested to the difficulties he faced.[34] Yet, to use the words of Günter Abramowski, the 'most fascinating thing about this scholarly personality' was the degree to which he did succeed in keeping separate the realm of his own values and judgements, on the one hand, and, on the other, a commitment to empirical research.[35]

Weber's devotion to German power lacked nothing in passion, but, unlike Schäfer's, it did not derive from a unified, all-embracing vision of history and politics. It was based instead upon a set of patriotic feelings for which Weber claimed to find no empirical support in historical scholarship. Weber's involvement with the Pan-German League was thus of a different character from Schäfer's. It reflected less an ideological affinity (for Weber was no ideologue in the sense that Schäfer was) than Weber's interest in a single issue, the Germanizing of the eastern provinces, a programme mandated in Weber's mind not by history but by calculations of German power. Significantly, Weber left the Pan-German League in 1899, once he recognized that the Pan-Germans' concern about the Polish threat was but part of a much broader ideological anxiety which featured all kinds of threats to the German nation.[36]

The practical consequence of Weber's methodology was that he approached questions of politics less ideologically encumbered than Schäfer did. His analysis, if not more tentative, was thus more flexible and open-minded, his calculations based upon a 'power-pragma', a given configuration of power, rather than upon some putative historical obligation.[37] History, Weber insisted, could not prescribe policies for the political actor or analyst; it could only suggest, by analogy, the possible consequences or repercussions of a given policy. Of course, the history of any configuration of power – the evolution of power-relationships over time – had to be given weight in the political calculation, but in this respect, also, the debt of Weber, the political observer, to history was of a different order to Schäfer's, for Weber believed that the principal contours of the power-configuration faced by his country dated back only to 1871.[38]

Weber's analysis of politics was thus more open to modification than was

Schäfer's. Although his political *desideratum* remained the maximization of German power, he was able, in a way that Schäfer was not, to adapt his strategies in the pursuit of this goal to political realities empirically perceived − to the point of advocating parliamentary democracy, which, for an outspoken nationalist in Imperial Germany, was unusual indeed. Weber's thinking on the subject of German foreign policy changed.[39] By the time he had emerged from his emotional crisis, his commentary on national issues had lost much of its earlier ferocity. His analysis of the revolutionary events in Russia in 1905 led him to break with Schäfer on the Polish problem and to argue that the interests of German power would be best served by a policy of accommodating the country's Polish minority.[40] In succeeding years, Weber's alarm grew about the consequences of the patriotic bombast that attended the build-up of the German navy and flavoured the public utterances of the country's leaders, most painfully of the Kaiser himself. It was a measure of Weber's concern, as well as of his flexibility, that he flirted momentarily with the peace movement, in the calculation that German interests demanded a more conciliatory foreign policy.[41]

A final consequence of Weber's ideas about the relationship between history and politics, between scholarship and value-judgement, was that he took pains to keep his political and scholarly roles distinct. In his political commentary he explicitly foreswore the authority of his academic profession and proffered his views as a layman. 'As a university professor,' he once told an audience in Munich, 'I can no more claim a special authority in questions of politics than can be presupposed of anyone else.'[42] And, although the structure of his commentaries occasionally left some confusion over where Weber the scholar yielded to Weber the political observer, his conception of his role was much more modest than Schäfer's.[43]

In part because of this modesty, Weber was initially more reticent than Schäfer in his political commentary. Once the war began, however, Weber took to the political arena in the attempt to counteract what he held to be the disastrous consequences of the agitation of Schäfer and his political allies. Weber's observations on the strategic and diplomatic constraints that Germany faced during the war were, with remarkably few aberrations, monuments of sober calculation and good sense. He branded as 'foolish' the proposition, advanced by Schäfer's camp, that the country should annexe Belgium and northern France; the consequence, he noted, could only be to benefit Russia, by guaranteeing that country in advance that a powerful Anglo-French coalition could be arrayed against Germany in any future conflict.[44] Weber's brief against the unrestricted use of submarines read like an accounting statement, which assessed the staggering ramifications of a strategic decision advocated and eventually adopted on the basis of the most dubious calculations of Allied shipping losses. The result could only be, as he wrote to his wife early in 1916, the enlargement of the Allied merchant fleet with the confiscation of interned German vessels, a half-million fresh American troops in the field, forty billions in cold cash for the country's enemies, three more years of war, and certain ruin. 'No one has ever thought,' he concluded, 'of anything more stupid.'[45]

Weber's own programme of war-aims was, as Wolfgang J. Mommsen has noted, not exactly modest.[46] In the West he advocated a peace of conciliation, but to the East he envisaged a network of small nation-states, whose cultural and political autonomy would be safe in the orbit of German commercial and military hegemony. This network would provide, Weber anticipated, the most secure bulwark against the enduring threat of Russia – one of the few political subjects on which Weber's views reflected the alarmism of Schäfer's.[47] But the accuracy of Weber's calculations of the consequences of U-boat warfare was not fortuitous. It grew out of a balanced appreciation of the realities of a critical situation and of the constraints that this situation imposed upon the pursuit of German power.

During the war, Weber had ample opportunity to ponder the significance of the radical nationalism that inspired those who gathered in the annexationist camp behind Dietrich Schäfer and the Pan-Germans. Weber's engagement with this phenomenon took place almost entirely within the categories of political analysis, his condemnation of the Pan-German extravagances being based upon considerations of their likely impact upon the exercise of German power. The language Weber employed in this condemnation was highly instructive. The Pan-Germans' policies were 'fantasies', 'raving demagogy', 'planless politics of emotion (*Gefühlspolitik*)', 'irresponsible amateur politics'; the men who concocted these politics were 'dilettantish *literati*', 'irresponsible beer-hall politicians'.[48] Theirs was a programme of 'vanity': it lacked every sense of proportion (*Augenmaß*), of realism and objectivity (*Sachlichkeit*), and it symptomized the political immaturity of the German nation.[49]

Weber's language betrays the extent to which his famous lecture, 'Politics as a vocation', not only had the wartime polemic with the Pan-Germans as one of its sources, but also represented Weber's most extended analysis of the Pan-Germans' significance.[50] Dietrich Schäfer, who in Weber's eyes was a symbol of the Pan-German phenomenon, thus represented the antithesis of the kind of political figure whom Weber hoped to see guide the country's destiny.[51] Weber's description of the characteristics that this politician was to possess was a catalogue of traits that he had found wanting in the Pan-Germans. The passion that was to animate this political figure was not the 'sterile excitability' of the Pan-Germans; it was rather a passion harnessed responsibly and always with a sense of proportion in the service of a clearly defined cause. And, as the two kinds of 'deadly sins in politics', Weber invoked irresponsibility and a lack of objectivity, epithets he had repeatedly hurled at the Pan-Germans during the war.[52] In the final analysis, Schäfer and his friends belonged to the proponents of an ethic of conviction (*Gesinnungsethik*), for they, no less than the anarchists, pacifists and radical socialists who, in Weber's mind, also populated this category, acted without regard for the political consequences of their actions.

Weber did not appreciate the full danger of what Schäfer represented.[53] He was, of course, not alone in his failure, and his early death makes it easier to understand. But it does reflect a limitation in his analysis of radical nationalism, which is significant enough to merit brief mention. Weber addressed the phenomenon of radical nationalism only in the categories and language of politics, in his capacity as political observer, not as a scholar. In his decision not to employ categories from his scholarship, Weber was perhaps influenced by his disdain for Schäfer, whose confusion of the bounds between academic scholarship and political commentary represented for Weber a betrayal of the profession as well as bad politics (and bad scholarship).[54] However, Weber's categories of political analysis could not comprehend the dynamism and attraction of radical nationalism. They lumped together anarchists and pacifists, whose emotional appeal was destined to remain limited because they could never credibly lay claim to the national symbolism, with Pan-Germans whose potential support was infinitely greater because they could. We can only speculate about the nature of Weber's conclusions had he approached the radical nationalists with the tools of his scholarship, as a sociologist of religion.

To make these kinds of demands of Max Weber is, of course, unfair. It also overlooks one final feature of his understanding of the phenomenon of radical nationalism. Weber's appreciation of the dangers posed by Schäfer and the Pan-Germans was limited, because politically he shared most of their goals and values. His conflict with them had less to do with their passionate engagement on behalf of German power than with the immediate political consequences of their inability to discipline this passion. Weber disagreed with them, in other words, more about questions of style and means than about goals, for he was convinced that their political passion must in the end defeat the very goals they themselves professed to serve. We are today in a better position than Weber to recognize that the passion of the radical nationalists was indicative of problems more far-reaching and profound than political irresponsibility, vanity, and a want of perspective.

Notes: Chapter 22

1 D. Schäfer, *Mein Leben* (Berlin and Leipzig, 1926), p. 129; *Biography*, p. 257.
2 Schäfer, *Mein Leben*, p. 153; W. J. Mommsen, *Max Weber and German Politics, 1890–1920* (Chicago, 1984), pp. 54–5; R. vom Bruch, *Wissenschaft, Politik und öffentliche Meinung. Gelehrtenpolitik im Wilhelminischen Deutschland (1890–1914)* (Husum, 1980), p. 431; GPS[2], pp. 152, 169–70; *Biography*, pp. 224–5. For these patriotic societies and for the full literature, see R. Chickering, *We Men Who Feel Most German: A Cultural Study of the Pan-German League, 1886–1914* (London, 1984).
3 See P. Honigsheim, 'Erinnerungen an Max Weber', in R. König and J. Winckelmann (eds), *Max Weber zum Gedächtnis. Materialien und Dokumente zur Bewertung von Werk und Persönlichkeit* (Cologne and Opladen, 1963), pp. 210–11.
4 For the roles of Schäfer and Weber in the war-aims debate, see K. Schwabe, *Wissenschaft und Kriegsmoral. Die deutschen Hochschullehrer und die politischen Grundfragen des Ersten Weltkrieges* (Göttingen, 1969).
5 See H.-T. Krause, 'Dietrich Schäfer: Vom Schüler Treitschkes zum ideologischen Wegbereiter des ersten Weltkriegs' (Diss. phil., Halle/Wittenberg, 1968); K. Jagow (ed.), *Dietrich Schäfer und sein Werk* (Berlin, 1925). See also H. Krause, 'Die alldeutsche Geschichtsschreibung vor dem ersten Weltkrieg', in J. Streisand (ed.), *Studien über die deutsche Geschichtswissenschaft* (Berlin, 1965), Vol. 2, pp. 207–19.
6 ibid., p. 208; cf. W. Goetz, *Historiker meiner Zeit. Gesammelte Aufsätze* (Cologne and Graz, 1957), p. 326.
7 C. E. McClelland, 'Berlin Historians and German Politics', in W. Laqueur and G. L. Mosse (eds), *Historians in Politics* (London and Beverly Hills, Calif., 1974), p. 199.
8 D. Schäfer, 'Das eigentliche Arbeitsgebiet der Geschichte' in idem, *Aufsätze, Vorträge und Reden* (Jena, 1913), Vol. 1, p. 269. On the modifications see vom Bruch, Wissenschaft, *Politik und öffentliche Meinung*, p. 383.
9 D. Schäfer, *Weltgeschichte der Neuzeit*, 2nd edn, (Berlin, 1907), Vol. 1, p. 5.
10 ibid.; cf. A. O. Meyer, 'Der Geschichtsschreiber', in Jagow (ed.), *Dietrich Schäfer*, pp. 75–84.

11 D. Schäfer, *Deutsches Nationalbewußtsein im Lichte der Geschichte* (Jena, 1884), p. 5.
12 ibid., p. 31.
13 See Schäfer, 'Arbeitsgebiet', pp. 270–9.
14 ibid., p. 279.
15 D. Schäfer, *Deutsche Geschichte* (Jena, 1910), Vol. 1, p. 12.
16 ibid.
17 H.-T. Krause, 'Dietrich Schäfer und die Umorientierung der bürgerlichen Hanseforschung zu Beginn des 20. Jahrhunderts', *Forschungen zur mittelalterlichen Geschichte*, vol. 17 (1970), pp. 93–117.
18 Schäfer, *Weltgeschichte der Neuzeit*; idem, *Deutsche Geschichte*.
19 Schäfer, *Nationalbewußtsein*, p. 11.
20 See H. White, *Metahistory: The Historical Imagination in Nineteenth-Century Europe* (Baltimore, Md, and London, 1973).
21 Chickering, *We Men*, pp. 74–121; cf. G. Pretsch, 'Dietrich Schäfer – der Alldeutsche', *Wissenschaftliche Zeitschrift der Karl-Marx-Universität Leipzig Gesellschafts- und sprachwissenschaftliche Reihe*, vol. 9 (1959/60), pp. 729–35.
22 Zentrales Staatsarchiv Potsdam, Bestand Alldeutscher Verband Nr. 455, Schäfer to Heinrich Class, 9 April 1912.
23 Schäfer, *Deutsche Geschichte*, Vol. 2, p. 470.
24 See G. Iggers, *The German Conception of History: The National Tradition of Historical Thought from Herder to the Present*, 2nd edn (Middletown, Conn., 1983); H.-H. Krill, *Die Rankerenaissance: Max Lenz und Erich Marcks. Ein Beitrag zum historisch-politischen Denken in Deutschland 1880–1935* (Berlin, 1962).
25 The fullest treatment of this whole problem is Vom Bruch, *Wissenschaft, Politik und öffentliche Meinung*.
26 Schäfer, 'Unser Recht auf die Ostmarken', in idem, *Aufsätze*, Vol. 2, pp. 305–20.
27 ibid., pp. 340–62 ('Englands Weltstellung und Deutschlands Lage'); idem, *Was lehrt uns die Geschichte über die Bedeutung der Seemacht für Deutschlands Gegenwart?* (Munich, 1900).
28 See F. Klein, 'Die deutschen Historiker im Ersten Weltkrieg', in Streisand (ed.), *Studien*, Vol. 2, pp. 227–50. For Schäfer's activities during the war, see Schwabe, *Wissenschaft und Kriegsmoral*, especially pp. 77–8, 98–101, 156–7, 161–2, 182–3; F. Fischer, *Griff nach der Weltmacht: Die Kriegszielpolitik des kaiserlichen Deutschland 1914/18* (Düsseldorf, 1961), especially pp. 199–200, 559–61.
29 Schwabe, *Wissenschaft und Kriegsmoral*, p. 174.
30 *Biography*, p. 559. Of course, in the circles in which Schäfer moved during the war, even he could on occasion be accused of abetting the *Flaumacher*: see E. Hartwig, 'Deutscher Wehrverein 1912–1935', in D. Fricke *et al.* (eds), *Lexikon zur Parteiengeschichte*, (Leipzig, 1983 ff), Vol. 2, p. 337.
31 'Der Nationalstaat und die Volkswirtschaftspolitik: Akademische Antrittsrede', GPS[2], pp. 1–25; cf. A. Bergsträsser, 'Max Webers Antrittsvorlesung in zeitgeschichtlicher Perspektive', *Vierteljahreshefte für Zeitgeschichte*, vol. 5 (1957), pp. 209–19. For Weber's concept of the nation, see D. Beetham, *Max Weber and the Theory of Modern Politics* (London, 1974), pp. 119–50; Mommsen, *Max Weber and German Politics*, pp. 35–8.
32 ibid., pp. 3–8.
33 See Iggers, *German Conception*, pp. 124–73. For a much fuller statement of Weber's approach, see H. H. Bruun, *Science, Values, and Politics in Max Weber's Methodology* (Copenhagen, 1972).
34 See R. Aron *et al.*, 'Max Weber and Power Politics', in O. Stammer (ed.), *Max Weber and Sociology Today* (Oxford, 1971), pp. 83–132; GPS[2], pp. 24, 171; C. Antoni, *From History to Sociology: The Transition in German Historical Thinking* (Detroit, Mich., 1959), especially pp. 138–42. In his *Antrittsrede*, Weber also came close to Schäfer's view that the national moment was immanent in history. 'In great moments, in time of war', he noted in speaking of the 'broad masses', 'the significance of national power impresses even them [*tritt auch ihnen vor die Seele*] – then it is clear that the nation-state rests on primeval [*urwüchsig*] psychological foundations even in the case of the broad, economically dominated strata of the nation and that it is by no means merely a "superstructure", the organization of the ruling classes' (GPS[2], p. 18). This riposte to Marx does little to parry the charge that Weber was in the final analysis an idealist; see G. Lukács, *Die Zerstörung der Vernunft*, (Darmstadt and Neuwied, 1974), Vol. 3, p. 57.
35 G. Abramowski, *Das Geschichtsbild Max Webers. Universalgeschichte am Leitfaden des*

okzidentalen Rationalisierungsprozesses (Stuttgart, 1966), p. 180; cf. H. Hughes, *Consciousness and Society: The Reorientation of European Social Thought, 1890–1930* (New York, 1958), pp. 278–335.

36   *Biography*, pp. 224–5.
37   K. Löwith, *Max Weber and Karl Marx* (London, 1982), p. 36; Aron, 'Max Weber and Power Politics', pp. 89–90.
38   GPS², p. 157; cf. Bruun, *Science*, pp. 254–5; Mommsen, *Max Weber and German Politics*, pp. 69, 137.
39   G. Schulz, 'Geschichtliche Theorie und politisches Denken bei Max Weber', *Vierteljahrshefte für Zeitgeschichte*, vol. 12 (1964), p. 337.
40   Mommsen, *Max Weber and German Politics*, pp. 56–60.
41   R. Chickering, *Imperial Germany and a World Without War: The Peace Movement and German Society, 1892–1914* (Princeton, NJ, 1975), pp. 151, 161; Mommsen, *Max Weber and German Politics*, pp. 140, 155.
42   W. J. Mommsen, *Max Weber und die deutsche Politik*, 2nd edn (Tübingen, 1974), 521. (This appendix was omitted from the English translation of Mommsen's book – editor's note.) Cf. Antoni, *From History to Sociology*, p. 121.
43   The Freiburg *Antrittsrede* invited, despite the author's disavowals, just such confusion, for its first part was a dry rehearsal of the results of his research: GPS², pp. 2–10. The structure of 'Politik als Beruf' was similar.
44   'Deutschland unter den Weltmächten', GPS², pp. 152–72; cf. Mommsen, *Max Weber and German Politics*, pp. 192–8.
45   *Biography*, p. 561; cf. Schwabe, *Wissenschaft und Kriegsmoral*, pp. 98–101.
46   Mommsen, *Max Weber and German Politics*, p. 206.
47   GPS², p. 164.
48   ibid., pp. 130–31, 136, 154, 211, 292, 360.
49   ibid., pp. 154–55, 290; Schwabe, *Wissenschaft und Kriegsmoral*, p. 255, n. 99.
50   GPS², pp. 493–548; cf. G. Schmidt, *Deutscher Historismus und der Übergang zur parlamentarischen Demokratie. Untersuchungen zu den politischen Gedanken von Meinecke, Troeltsch, Max Weber* (Lübeck and Hamburg, 1964), p. 231.
51   See GPS², p. 292; *Biography*, p. 575.
52   GPS², p. 535.
53   See E. Nolte, 'Max Weber vor dem Faschismus', *Der Staat*, vol. 2 (1963), pp. 1–24; Mommsen, *Max Weber and German Politics*, pp. 390–414.
54   Weber did not regard Schäfer's later historical surveys as serious scholarship: Honigsheim, 'Erinnerungen an Max Weber', pp. 210–11; cf. GPS², p. 292.

23 Eduard Bernstein and Max Weber

JOHN BREUILLY

There were contacts between Bernstein and Weber, although they were very limited. In 1904, Weber wrote to Bernstein asking for advice on nineteenth century Quaker thinking on usury. Weber was working on *The Protestant Ethic and the Spirit of Capitalism*. Bernstein had published his book on socialist thought during the English revolution. At one level this was, therefore, a simple communication between one scholar and another, who were working on related subjects. Weber also asked Bernstein to visit him while Bernstein was in Heidelberg and to contribute to the *Archiv für Sozialwissenschaft und Sozialpolitik*. [1] We do not know whether Bernstein did meet Weber and he did not contribute to the *Archiv*. I do not know whether Bernstein did have any advice or information to give Weber on the matter of Quaker views on usury and, if so, whether it had any influence on Weber's published treatment of that problem. At this level, therefore, the contact appears brief and insignificant.

However, this brief contact could be considered in another way. The initiative comes from Weber, a man of no practical political importance in bourgeois liberal politics, towards Bernstein, a man of apparently great significance within the German Social Democratic Party (SPD). Bernstein had recently returned from England. A year earlier his revisionist ideas had been overwhelmingly rejected by the Dresden congress of the SPD. Weber was concerned about how to strengthen the pressures for liberal reform within Germany. He saw in revisionist and reformist figures within the SPD and the Free Trade Unions possible allies for the bourgeois liberals, as well as seeing in the isolationism and revolutionary Marxist rhetoric of the SPD leadership a bogus politics which helped to strengthen anti-liberal politics within the German bourgeoisie. In a number of ways, Weber was concerned to open up the channels of communication between bourgeoisie and working class, liberals and socialists. One level was a purely personal one in the academic sphere: the ending of non-academic discrimination against scholars who were Social Democrats. Weber spoke out openly against the practice of refusing the *Habilitation* award to Social Democrats, irrespective of their scholarly achievements, and in particular was affected by the treatment of his protegé, Robert Michels. At one level, therefore, we can relate his invitation to Bernstein to this concern to open up the world of academe to socialist scholars. And we could see this, in turn, as part of a broader desire to encourage and strengthen the forces represented by Bernstein within the labour movement.

It is more difficult to relate Bernstein's broader intellectual and political concerns to this particular episode, precisely because he did nothing. We could take this as symbolic of the inability, for whatever reason, for revisionists within the labour movement actually to put into practice their ideas of constructing alliances with the bourgeoisie. But that would be very speculative. We could equally well argue that Bernstein was a busy man, who did not have time to waste on the interests of a political dilettante whose best-known political views called for anti-Polish colonization in eastern Germany and the energetic pursuit of *Weltpolitik*. The episode could become, in short, a non-event, symbolic not merely of the failure but even of the impossibility of some sort of Lib–Lab political alliance in Germany. Bernstein remained tied too closely, whether politically or intellectually, to illiberal Marxism, and Weber to illiberal nationalism, for there to be any prospect of co-operation.

That may be a reasonable conclusion, but it would be premature to jump from the non-event of their personal contact to such a broad conclusion without some intervening argument. I shall conduct this at three levels. First, I shall ask what intellectual convergence can be detected between Bernstein and Weber. Did they think about society in the same ways? Secondly, I shall ask what political convergence there might be between them. Did they think about what was politically possible and desirable in the same ways? Thirdly, I shall ask what bearing these broader intellectual and political affinities (or lack of them) had upon the prospects for collaboration between liberals and socialists. Is affinity of social and political thought an important element in the construction of political alliances? To anticipate my major conclusion, I shall argue that actually there were, in many ways, fewer affinities between Bernstein and Weber than might be thought – above all because Bernstein stood so much more closely than Weber to the classical liberal political tradition. But in turn, I shall argue that this had little to do with practical political relationships, which are concerned with short-term balances of costs and benefits for political interest groups and not with broader questions.

Intellectual Convergence?

The obvious place to begin is with the common critical response of Bernstein and Weber to orthodox Marxism as represented in the SPD.[2] Both rejected materialist determinism. Both insisted on the autonomy of values. Certain social groups might tend towards certain values, but one could not reduce these values to the material characteristics and interests of those groups. Both questioned some of the claims of orthodox Marxism about social and economic trends. The growth of cartels, the survival of intermediate classes, the increase in working-class prosperity, the dampening down of economic crises: all called into question the vision of polarization, immiseration and deeper crisis on which SPD politics was based. Both questioned the 'scientific' nature of Marxism. For Bernstein, the labour theory of value and the notion of surplus value represented an abstract truth for the whole of society but not a theory that could be used to analyse the detailed workings of an economy. For Weber, the alternative theory of value based on marginal utility offered a much more fruitful method of economic analysis. Both rejected the notion of the state as an instrument of the capitalist class; instead, they tended to see the state as having more universal functions and as being, in principle, capable of serving working-class interests without being turned into a dictatorship of the proletariat. Both, in short, saw the orthodox SPD position as a sterile one, which resulted in political passivity and a freezing of the status quo, and they based this judgement on intellectual criticisms of a similar kind.

But this similarity appears strongest when seen in relation to the common opponent, orthodox Marxism. When we look at the positive side of those criticisms several important differences emerge. For example, their actual treatment of values is very different. Bernstein is concerned with the autonomy of 'moral' values, which tend to be seen as feelings or instincts. He sees socialism as an ethical imperative that any decent human being would recognize. I do not think that Bernstein would recognize the glorification of war, of conquest, of social and national inequality and exploitation as just other moral values from those of socialism, but rather as immoral values. There is really none of Weber's tough-mindedness about the autonomy and incompatibility of ultimate values. Bernstein's whole evolutionary schema looks to an increasing extent to make compatible what he regards as the true moral values: international peace, prosperity, equality and individual liberty. In a way it is the tough-mindedness of orthodox Marxists about evolutionary progressivism against which Bernstein is reacting.

In connection with this, I do not think Bernstein understood the relationship between objects of investigation and the methods and concepts used in an investigation to anything like the same degree as Weber did. To take the issue of understanding society 'as a whole': Bernstein's critique of orthodox Marxism seems to be basically that too much precision is claimed of certain abstract concepts, such as the labour theory of value and the concept of surplus value. But there *is* such an entity as 'society as a whole', which can be broadly comprehended (thus it makes sense to talk of 'social surplus value'). But, Bernstein is then arguing that, at the 'abstract' level of 'pure science', we should recognize that this broadness leaves room for varying approaches (thus the abstractions of marginal utility theories of value can be admitted along with the abstractions of the labour theory of value), and, at the 'applied' level, we can leave room to modify, or even overturn, specific conclusions (e.g. about the polarization of society into a small capitalist class and a large proletariat) and their replacement with other conclusions (e.g. about the continued viability of small enterprises and the growth of a white-collar class in both public and private sectors). Weber does not take this naturalist-cum-eclectic position. 'Society as a whole' should be regarded as a 'thing-in-itself', i.e. unknowable. Concepts are not derived from the 'thing-in-itself' (what Guy Oakes in Chapter 29 calls a form of 'emanationist logic') but rather from the intellectual values of the investigator. It is this dimension of intellectual values – not to be derived from the object of investigation and not to be identified with ultimate moral values – which is missing in Bernstein and which is of central importance for Weber. For Weber, Bernstein's talk of 'society as a whole', the 'abstract truth' of the labour theory of value, the idea of society evolving (and being properly apprehended as evolving) in a progressive direction, and of an increasing capacity to reconcile ultimate 'good' moral values – all this is empty. Weber would agree with Bernstein about the falsity of specific Marxist predictions (and also on the emptiness of the intellectual attempts to save those predictions in some way), about the autonomy of values. But he could hardly go along with Bernstein's evolutionary, naturalist, progressivist alternative. Clearly Weber did have visions of the future (the iron cage of bureaucracy in both private and public sectors, with the nightmare of their merging in a socialist society) but they were not 'progressive', they were not explicitly based upon any claim to knowledge of 'society as a whole', and they were not based on extrapolations from short-term trends but rather from inferences about the potential of certain forms of social organization (e.g. the potential of bureaucracy) and a recognition of the incompatibility of ultimate ends (e.g. economic efficiency achieved by means of a market system and non-economic goals such as welfare provision or ethnic assertion).

Apart from the general difference in intellectual approach, there were also differences in their evaluations of specific trends. For example, Bernstein was positive in his evaluation of cartelization and the spread of ownership, which were seen in the perspective of the progressive socialization of the economy. Weber saw instead the impairment of economic efficiency as cartels managed to avoid the full rigours of competition and as direction shifted from a class of dynamic entrepreneurs to a class of bureaucratic officials. Weber was also much clearer than Bernstein in his recognition of the disadvantages of cartels as well as the largest economic enterprises, the great factories, for workers. If anything, Weber was both more consistent and closer to orthodox Marxists, in that his denial of polarization was based on the growth of a white-collar sector rather than the survival of small enterprises. At the same time, he saw that these large factories were arenas in which workers were at their weakest. He called for state intervention to bolster worker organization in these spheres. Weber, therefore, saw these developments negatively so far as the current and future interests of workers were concerned, just as did the orthodox and radical Marxists. Of course, his responses to this shared perception were very different. Marxists would reject with scorn the idea that the state might intervene to build up workers' organizations within these factories or to enforce competition upon cartels (with the possible exception of one capitalist sector, which suffered at the hands of another cartelized or protected capitalist sector, being able to get the state to act on its behalf), and could hardly agree that the form of 'control by officialdom' found in these larger enterprises and cartels was an anticipation of what socialism would really be like. Neither, of course, could Bernstein. But Bernstein never really reconciled this aspect of his theory with his equal stress upon the survival of old intermediate classes. Equally, he never really worked out a way of reconciling his later recognition of the disadvantages to which large-scale organization of capitalist enterprises put workers with his claim, at the time of the revisionist controversy, that this form of development fitted into his perspective of evolutionary socialism.

Weber seemed to have had less hope of continued economic heterogeneity than did Bernstein. His own work on East Elbean agriculture stressed, like orthodox Marxists, the economic irrationality of small-scale agriculture, and he quite consciously argued for its support on non-economic grounds (to combat Polish immigration and take-over of land and to replace the economically, but above all politically, disastrous form of Junker agriculture). In the industrial sphere, he seemed to identify the future with the large-scale integrated unit of production. Only independent state action could be looked for to deal with some of the negative political and economic consequences that could arise from such a development. At the same time, Weber could continue to think in terms of political pluralism because of the growth of a white-collar sector, the hope for the positive participation of blue-collar workers in the political process, and because of his pluralist conception of classes as such. This is another point that distinguishes him from Bernstein, who had a generally 'naturalist' view of class that was no more than an eclectic loosening up of the orthodox Marxist position.

To put it very crudely, both rejected the 'catastrophe' perspective of orthodox and radical Marxism. But Bernstein did this from the value-position of socialism seen as a 'natural' ethic and within the perspective of optimistic evolutionary progressivism, whereas Weber did this from the value-position of dynamic capitalism and nationalism seen as one set of values chosen from among many and within the perspective of pessimism concerning bureaucratic powers' potential, in the organized private and public sectors, to undermine the realization of these values.

Political Convergence?

Clearly, to have different views on how moral values relate to one another and to material questions, when undertaking an investigation of society, is no bar to political co-operation. Weber and Bernstein shared a negative view of the revolutionary posturing of the SPD. They wished to see how the labour movement could pursue common political objectives with middle-class groupings. Both wished to see anti-labour legislation halted and reversed. This is self-evident for Bernstein. But we should remember that Weber openly called for the repeal of the very restrictive clause in the Industrial Code on the conduct of strikes; he called for state intervention in helping to form independent worker organization in large enterprises. Weber, like Bernstein, called for a democratic reform of the Prussian franchise, which both saw as the key political obstacle to the advancement of an anti-conservative politics. Bernstein, for his part, called for changes in SPD policy on matters such as the agrarian question, which could attract support from non-working-class groups. Both men believed that in the wake of reforms of this sort the revolutionary rhetoric and isolationism of the SPD would break down and the labour movement would come to be led by reformist politicians and trade union officials. Clearly, the broader political expectations of the two were different. Weber would expect this to produce a healthy and limited form of class conflict within the stable framework of a democratic state and capitalist economy. For him, its great value would be in removing or weakening backward conservative and bureaucratic, corporatist forces within Germany. The elites of labour would always occupy a subordinate, even if a positive position within the economic and political order. For Bernstein, on the contrary, this development would be a step on the road towards the peaceful assertion of democratic socialist values (expressed mainly, though not exclusively, through the working class). But, we might argue, this longer-term difference in perspective need not prevent constructive co-operation in the short term against the common enemies, the 'revolutionary' wing of the SPD and the military and bureaucratic elites that dominated the Prusso-German political system.

But a number of problems stood in the way of such a short-term and medium-term political strategy. First, both men pursued their politics within their own political camps. Thus, even when pressing hard for a policy within the Verein für Sozialpolitik that would strengthen the trade union movement, Weber actually refused to work with trade union leaders and reformist Social Democrats. When heading the industrial sociology project of the Verein für Sozialpolitik between 1909 and 1911, Weber seems to have made no attempt to obtain support and co-operation from SPD and trade union people. It was in part trade union hostility which prevented the questionnaire survey getting a good response from workers. Weber was always counselling a bourgeois politics, initiated and controlled by bourgeois political forces, which might produce a positive response from the labour movement but which was not formulated in co-operation with that labour movement. Equally, as Dick Geary points out in Chapter 24, Bernstein argued his position wholly within the SPD and saw it in terms of a pure labour movement policy. In this context, it is important that Bernstein returned to Berlin when he came back to Germany and his politics was always pursued within the Prussian context. Thus, whereas south German reformist Social Democrats were actively exploring forms of co-operation with other political forces, in Bernstein's case this remained largely theoretical.

Secondly, we must remember that both still saw politics from a clear class perspective. There is nothing more anachronistic than the perspective that identifies Bernstein with post-1945 Social Democracy. Here was a man who supported political strikes, with all the potential bloodshed, illegality and repression they might entail (as well as the negative impact they would have on middle-class political opinion) in order to achieve reform of the Prussian franchise. And, since Mommsen's work, we can harbour no doubts about the hard-line taken by Weber, who opposed state-enforced collective agreements to help poorer, less organized and less skilled workers, because this was paternalist and undermined the development of a 'healthy' elite within the working class, and who saw everything within the perspective of national struggle and the assertion of a bourgeois German nation-state in world politics.

Thirdly, both men were hardly typical of broad political forces within Germany. This is most obviously true of Weber, who on foreign-policy issues stood near to the Pan-Germans (differing from them more often on pragmatic rather than principled grounds) and in domestic policy was nearer to the social liberals such as Lujo Brentano. We know now that one cannot (as Bernstein did and Weber most emphatically did not) identify the pursuit of *Weltpolitik* with the interests of Prussian conservatism. We know that there is no incompatibility in principle between a reformist modernizing domestic politics and an aggressive imperialism. But, by and large, the leading advocates of the one set of policies were not on the same political wavelength as the advocates of the other set. Weber, in this sense, was a political rogue figure. He was even more so by virtue of the intellectually ruthless but politically quite unsuitable way in which he analysed political problems and advocated policy.

This atypicalness is also true of Bernstein. Nothing is more misleading than the tendency to equate Bernstein with revisionism, revisionism with reformism, and reformism with all the major tendencies in the party which opposed radicals. First, there were different interest groups and types of reformism within the SPD and the Free Trade Unions. Secondly, Bernstein's views on foreign and domestic policy cut across what might be seen as the ideal-typical combinations of policy within the SPD. On the one hand, there were the revisionists who wished to alter the foreign-policy perspective of the SPD and who saw in a positive line on imperialism one means of bringing the labour movement into co-operation with non-working-class groups. The social imperialists who clustered around Joseph Bloch and the *Sozialistische Monatshefte* represented this position. Although Bernstein contributed to this journal, he did not share the views of these social imperialists, and when this became clear, after August 1914, collaboration between Bloch and Bernstein ceased. Bernstein remained true to an older form of internationalism, one with a radical as much as a socialist tradition, and which could not easily support an imperialist war against the democracies of western Europe.[3] Yet, at the same time, Bernstein had broken with those traditional elements within the SPD on matters of domestic policy. When his concerns on domestic policy were subordinated to those on foreign policy after 1914, he was forced into political collaboration with the radicals and some of the representatives of orthodoxy within the SPD. His membership of the Independent German Social Democratic Party (USPD) cut him off from those with whom, in the field of peacetime domestic politics, he had the most in common.

Their atypicalness in part helps to explain the political unimportance of both Bernstein and Weber, though I think there are other reasons connected with the nature of their personalities that also contribute to this political isolation.

Conclusion

But even if they had not been so atypical, if Bernstein had been more pro-*Weltpolitik*, if Weber could have descended from his high-minded view of politics as the ruthless and rigorous execution of the 'ethic of responsibility' to take into account the fudging and vagueness, the necessary hypocrisy and the mastery of the political machinery (rather than seeing these as conditions for the activity of politics) it is doubtful whether a much more fruitful co-operation would have been possible. Ultimately, everything in the way of an alternative political strategy was undermined by the short-term interests of political groupings within pre-1914 Wilhelmine Germany. I shall try to illustrate this with a couple of examples showing the fate of policies that Bernstein and Weber recommended.

Bernstein, for example, counselled a policy of support for small and medium-sized farms. We should bear in mind that this policy was rejected by the SPD before either an elaborate 'orthodox' or 'revisionist' position had been worked out. We should also bear in mind that the strategy of 'rural agitation' was pursued before a pro-agrarian position was formally rejected by the party, and that in appropriate areas (for example, in south Germany) the local Social Democrats continued to take a pro-agrarian line, irrespective of national party policy. On the basis of these observations, we can make a number of points. The rejection of the pro-agrarian policy had nothing to do with views about orthodox or revisionist Marxism. It was based upon two related considerations. One was that agrarian areas supported the enemies of the SPD (the Centre Party, the Farmers' League, etc.), independently of the line the SPD took. The other was that a pro-agrarian line could only mean in practice either higher food prices or higher taxes, and this would lose working-class support. The revisionist case was not lost because the party preferred the rhetoric of orthodoxy, and the revisionist case was not pursued silently in opposition to the rhetoric of orthodoxy. The revisionist case was lost, both in theory and in practice, because it clearly went against the immediate interests of the party. Now, we can examine how far earlier party policy was responsible for present party interest taking the form that it did, and we can argue that it would have been better to reduce the weight of immediate interest in party strategy. But neither point persuades me that the party leadership had much choice in this matter.[4]

So far as Weber is concerned, we can see that his foreign-policy views might command a good deal of middle-class support but had little chance of gaining much working-class support as long as domestic political arrangements so blatantly disadvantaged them. But what was the short-term bourgeois interest in Weber's domestic policy suggestions? Weber argued, for example, that liberals should support the strengthening of trade unions by positive state intervention in large factories and by throwing out many of the legal restrictions on strike action. In the long-term, Weber could plausibly argue, this would keep capitalism dynamic and weaken anti-modern conservative forces entrenched at the top of German politics. It is difficult to imagine a set of policy suggestions better designed to arouse hostility among the most powerful industrialists and those military and bureaucratic elites. When we accept that Weber's rejection of paternalist forms of social welfare also offended some of those among the circle of academic and professional social reformers, we can understand why he was unable to recruit much support for the policies he advocated.

The inability of Bernstein and Weber to be politically effective must also be related to their inadequate understanding of the politics of the class they opposed. I can only mention this briefly, because it goes beyond the specific concern of this chapter.

It is a truism that Bernstein's ideas are derived from his English experience. I think this also means that his understanding of liberalism is very English. Faced with a political system that seemed to represent a unified bourgeois political interest through parliamentary channels and that seemed to be in harmony with the socioeconomic system, Bernstein imagined that the German bourgeoisie could or should engage in a similar type of politics. The creation of the right institutions (above all, parliamentarization and democratization) would lead to the right state–society balance. If we question this 'English' understanding of German politics, we also automatically put into doubt the political strategy to which it gives rise.[5]

At the same time, Bernstein had a very 'English' perception of foreign policy. His internationalism and desire for peace based upon free trade and open diplomacy apparently put him close to the anti-war elements in the SPD. But really he was closer to the bourgeois peace movement and to people such as Philip Snowden and Ramsay MacDonald in the Independent Labour Party in Britain rather than to any important element within the German labour movement. And such a peace movement was very unimportant in the bourgeois politics of Wilhelmine Germany. Once again, Bernstein's advocacy of 'bourgeois' politics was not appropriate to German conditions.

Weber's inadequacies in an understanding of the German labour movement are of a rather different kind. His tough-mindedness about class relationships in capitalist society put him closer to Kautsky than to Bernstein. But although later writers have praised the insight of Weber's criticisms of the SPD, what they have really done (and with far less justification, given the benefit of hindsight) has been to recapitulate some of Weber's own errors. The central deficiencies are in the treatment of political ideology and the relationship between economic functions and political allegiances of the German working class.

Roger Chickering notes the limites of Weber's understanding of radical nationalism, that is, of a political ideology influential within middle-class circles.[6] The point applies even more to Weber's understanding of ideology in the labour movement. Weber treats Marxism as the dishonest language of a petty-bourgeois class of politicians, which is sustained by the lack of participation allowed to working-class elites and which serves as a pseudo-religion. But what Weber never tries to do is to construct some notion of a political culture of the labour movement, in which Marxism has a range of other functions. He fails to understand that Marxism made perfect sense even to many reformist elements within the labour movement, by investing the drive for reform with a wider significance, and by interpreting to activists the meaning of obdurate resistance to such 'reform' demands. If employers would not grant collective agreements or the Prussian government permit reform, this must mean that these were more than 'mere' reforms. To understand what that 'more' was, and at the same time to motivate people to fight hard for such 'mere' reforms, was an important function of Marxism within the labour movement. Historians, who later separate and oppose 'reform' to 'revolution' and assume that greater accommodation of reform demands would have undermined the remnants of a revolutionary attitude or rhetoric, are repeating the mistake.

The other defect is less understandable. Weber was a pioneer of political sociology, and we would have expected him to have sought to connect working-class experience to politics. Yet his major empirical study of contemporary workers, the industrial observations carried through under the auspices of the Verein für Sozialpolitik, almost completely lack a sociological perspective.[7] Instead, we have a series of close observations of workers as objective psycho-physical units, which were more concerned with improving the capacity of management to raise productivity than with understanding the subjective experience of the worker or with seeing the role played by group identities and relations at the workplace. It is not surprising that the trade union movement did not co-operate with this project. It is noticeable that Weber had less success than the 'worker sociologist', Adolf Levenstein. Even then, when Levenstein put open-ended questions about workers' aspirations on his questionnaire, Weber advised him to leave out such vague questions. Fortunately, Levenstein ignored Weber's advice, and the answers to those questions provide us with some of the best clues we have about how worker experience and support for the Marxist message of the SPD were connected.

Both deficiencies are perhaps grounded in Weber's tendency to treat class as an economic interest, rather than as a social experience or as a source of political loyalty. There are strands in his own thinking which could allow a fruitful combination of these elements. It would be better to take this aspect of Weber and apply it to an understanding of German workers and the SPD, rather than to repeat his own inadequate analysis. That inadequacy might help to explain why Weber was unable to construct a politics that could attract working-class support away from the SPD or tempt the SPD to abandon its Marxist language and rejection of the politics of class collaboration.

Some of Weber's and Bernstein's ideas were put into practice after 1914, though in a context that neither had anticipated or welcomed. Thus, the state did bolster worker organization in factories with the Auxiliary Service Law of December 1916, although by and large this law represented a form of state intervention that Weber opposed as strengthening the rule of officials. The SPD did collaborate with other parties and the state, but in order to support a war that Bernstein opposed. The war had changed the political context, and thereby the nature of the balance sheet of short-term costs and benefits for political interest groups, in such a radical way that some of the things Bernstein and Weber had advocated now occurred, though possessed of a quite different meaning. Thus, Weber came to accept a far more democratic form of state and a more pacific foreign policy for Germany after 1918. Arguably, this brought him closer to Bernstein's position, but it was based on Weber's own brand of realism and was never really accepted, even less understood, by the SPD or bourgeois parties. Generally, both Bernstein and Weber remained fairly isolated and powerless figures within their respective political camps. The fact that, in later periods, some of what they argued for was realized may say much for their prescience about long-term political trends and possibilities. But it also tells us a lot about their inability to pursue a practical and realistic politics in the very different circumstances of their own time. That, of course, tells us as much about what was practical and realistic politics as it does about the values and character of Bernstein and Weber. Each was a prophet, albeit a very different kind of prophet from the other; each was enclosed and isolated within his separate and class-based political milieu. It was that political context rather than political ideas which prevented them, or more broadly what they stood for, from coming together.

Notes: Chapter 23

These are just a few bare references to some important points in the article. This article is not based upon any special research and it would be misleading to provide any extensive references.

1   For the personal contacts between Bernstein and Weber, see W. J. Mommsen, *Max Weber and German Politics, 1890–1920* (Chicago, 1984), p. 112.
2   See Chapter 24 by Dick Geary in this volume.
3   For revisionists and foreign policy, see R. Fletcher, *Revisionism and Empire: Socialist Imperialism in Germany, 1897–1914* (London, 1984).
4   I owe much in this treatment of the agrarian question to the arguments of Athar Hussain in A. Hussain and K. Tribe, *Marxism and the Agrarian Question*, 2nd edn (London, 1983).
5   For a critique of this way of approaching Wilhelmine Germany, see G. Eley and D. Blackbourn, *The Peculiarities of German History* (Oxford, 1984).
6   See Chapter 22 by Roger Chickering in this volume.
7   For these aspects of Weber's work, see A. Oberschall, *Empirical Social Research in Germany, 1848–1914* (Paris and The Hague, 1965).

24 Max Weber, Karl Kautsky and German Social Democracy

DICK GEARY

Weber's intellectual development clearly owed a great deal to a dialogue with the ideas of Marx – or, to be more accurate, a dialogue with the theories of those 'vulgar' Marxists who found a home in German Social Democracy before the First World War and whose representative spokesman was Karl Kautsky. Weber also revealed considerable interest in the development of the German Social Democratic Party (SPD), regretted its isolation and persecution in Wilhelmine society, and yet was thoroughly critical of the party's immobilism and dogmatic faith in an inevitable triumph of socialism.[1] Yet it is fair to say that this interest was not *directly* reciprocated by Kautsky and his colleagues. Significantly, the great theoretical debates of German Social Democracy took place *within* the socialist camp, further testifying to its isolation and introspection. It was to Bernstein, rather than to 'bourgeois' critics, that Kautsky and Rosa Luxemburg responded. However, the fact that Weber constructed a critique of 'orthodox' Marxism, and that this critique was in many respects similar to that of the high-priest of 'revisionism', enables us to construct a kind of dialogue between him and the theorists of the SPD. The Weberian critique centred on the claims of 'scientific' socialism, on a refutation of the theories of immiseration, class polarization and inevitable crisis, and a rejection of the strategic consequences of such a prognosis, namely the strategy of proletarian isolation and self-reliance.

'Scientific Socialism'

Weber's neo-Kantian training made him highly critical of those who based their socialism on some claim to understanding the supposedly 'objective laws' of capitalist society or historical development. He did not believe that it was possible to know or comprehend the whole of social reality; the most one could do, and the only honest thing to do, was to construct 'ideal types' which explained as *hypotheses* a part of that reality. In fact, he argued that claims to know the laws of history were not only intellectually unsound but politically fatal for the SPD, causing an impotent immobilism. (Precisely the same charge was levied by Friedrich Naumann.)[2] Furthermore, according to Weber, historical materialism neglected the role of 'ideal interests' in the historical process. Socialism's foundation could not lie in the realm of 'science', a point made equally forcefully by the neo-Kantian revisionists and by Bernstein himself.

Kautsky's defence of what he repeatedly termed 'the materialist conception of history' faced this 'ethical' socialism with difficulty. For Kautsky, socialism was a science, an outcome of a correct analysis of capitalist society, and Bernstein's neo-Kantianism was anathema.[3] An ethical socialism relegated struggle to an individual/personal matter and could not meet the needs of a mass political movement.[4] In attacking the 'moralists', however, Kautsky was not saying that moral judgements were irrelevant for a Marxist, and he did speak of the struggle against inequality as part of man's 'moral nature'.[5] On at least two occasions he even claimed that the categorical imperative could serve as a formulation of the socialist aim to end all exploitation.[6] It was just that it was insufficient *alone* to underpin socialist theory.[7] This reveals – and Kautsky explicitly stated as much in a letter to Plekhanov[8] – how little philosophical understanding the SPD's leading theoretician possessed. For him, what mattered were the consequences of Bernstein's ethical formulation: for, if socialism were primarily a matter of individual conscience and not the outcome of the objective interests of a particular class in capitalist society, then there was no reason to believe in either the inevitability of its triumph or in that policy of proletarian isolation that was the cornerstone of Kautsky's political thinking.[9]

Kautsky was well aware of the connection between an ethical formulation of socialism and the advocacy of reconciliation with the bourgeoisie; and this was precisely why he insisted that revisionism implied a change in the SPD's established practice.[10] In capitalist society each class possessed its own ethic,[11] and only the working class could be truly socialist.[12]

Kautsky's rejection of neo-Kantian arguments was a corollary of his firm belief that his own theory rested on a correct analysis of the laws of capitalism. (So, for that matter, was Rosa Luxemburg's critique of Bernstein: she saw her major task as the defence of the materialist conception of history and the re-affirmation of the objective necessity of socialism. What was important was what revisionism had to say about the objective development of capitalist society.)[13] This confidence in man's ability to comprehend 'laws' of historical necessity was primarily a consequence of Kautsky's intellectual formation through Darwin and through that highly positivistic rendering of Marxism, Engel's *Anti-Dühring*. In ignorance of Hegel, Kautsky came to Marx via *The Origin of Species*. Darwin's work came to him as nothing less than a 'revelation' and, even after encountering Marx, Kautsky claimed that his Darwinism had been merely *modified*.[14] That great journal of international socialism *Die Neue Zeit*, which Kautsky edited from its foundation until 1917, was founded not only to propagate Marxism but also to spread knowledge of Darwin.[15]

For Kautsky Darwin's discovery was as significant for the study of society as for that of nature. Indeed, social science was simply a 'particular area' of the 'natural sciences', and Marx's great achievement was to unite the two. Although men were not the blind agents of historical destiny, Kautsky did believe that human behaviour was *governed* by inexorable laws.[16]

Some time ago Hans-Josef Steinberg pointed out that the influence of Darwin on Kautsky diminished after 1885, and that Kautsky's political thinking was far less fatalistic than Bebel's, on the one hand, and many revisionists, on the other, who used evolutionary biology as an argument against revolutionary politics.[17] More recently, Gary Steenson has made the same point, emphasizing the existence of non-deterministic elements in Kautsky's thought.[18] There is much to be said for this reinterpretation at a general/abstract level. Kautsky attacked 'darwinistelnde(n) Soziologen' for arguing from analogies with nature, insisted that social development had its own particular laws, and at times claimed that Marxism was a method, not an infallible list of laws governing the universe. He even came close to describing laws of social development as mere explanatory hypotheses.[19] He insisted that Marxism was not a fatalistic doctrine, that determinism and fatalism were not identical, and admitted that single individuals and fortuitous factors played a role in historical development. In short, men did make their own history, while the concept of 'economic necessity' did not mean that economic processes operated purely mechanically.[20] Time and again he stressed that Marx had not anticipated the automatic collapse of capitalism through purely economic causes.[21]

Kautsky's deviance from a simple model of economic reductionism is nowhere clearer than in his stress on the necessity of *political* organization and action. It was the conquest of political power, not the collapse of capitalism, that would bring socialism.[22] Revolutionary consciousness did not result from the sectional and economistic struggle of the unions but had to be instilled into the masses from *without*, by the party and revolutionary intellectuals.[23] (When Lenin lifted this theory wholesale from Kautsky in *What is to be done?*, he quoted Kautsky and *not* the revolutionary traditions of the Russian intelligentsia.[24]) Thus we can make a fair case from Kautsky's *general* remarks that he was no mere regurgitator of a positivistic, scientistic fatalism.

However, the charge is in no way utterly without foundation, even in relation to Kautsky's later works. Even if Kautsky claimed that society's laws of development were different from those of nature, he still believed there were such laws. What is more, the terminology employed by Kautsky is riddled with references to '*Naturnotwendigkeit*', '*Naturgesetze*', when talking about societal development. 'Economic necessity' was 'the decisive factor in history'. The small concern would decline as a 'natural necessity'. Revolution and socialism were always 'inevitable'. Economic 'laws' could not be overcome by human artifice.[25] If we look at Kautsky's approach to specific problems, namely the general strike debate, the Russian Revolution and the Nazi regime, then we are left with little room for a voluntarist interpretation.

As early as 1893 Kautsky had contemplated the possibility that the enemies of the proletariat might proceed against it by suspending the few democratic privileges it enjoyed. And Kautsky always asserted that violence should be met by violence, that in such circumstances the organizations of labour might have to call a general strike. But, even in 1893, and even more so during his altercation with Luxemburg in 1910–11, Kautsky drew up an enormous list of preconditions before such action could be contemplated. Virtually all the proletariat had to be organized, the state must already have been weakened, which he quite rightly pointed out – and with the concurrence of radicals such as Lenin and Parvus[26] – wasn't true in Germany, even if it was in Russia.[27] Similarly, even if the proletariat were to meet force with force, 'force' did not necessarily mean violence. It could be 'pressure by the majority', organizational superiority, or economic 'indispensability'. If the enemy none the less resorted to such a policy of repression, it was bound to fail against a class with 'economic necessity' on its side.[28] In short, however much Kautsky might talk about possible forms of action, in practice an economic determinism intruded to excuse inaction. Hence, the SPD was a 'revolutionary' but not a 'revolution-making' party. Therefore, the task was not to fight or not, but to *organize* for the fight or not; and time and time again Kautsky insisted that caution, an avoidance of provoking the bourgeoisie or the state into repressive counter-measures was preferable to what he saw as the adventurism of a mass-strike. [29] It was the combination of a radical social analysis – the need for a revolution to bring about a qualitative change in working-class existence, the prediction of increasingly bitter class conflict – with an almost total silence on tactical questions that led Pannekoek to describe Kautsky's Marxism as 'passive radicalism', that led to demands from the right (Bernstein) for 'action' in the shape of practical reformist politics in alliance with liberals, and from the left for a 'mass strike'.

Rosa Luxemburg's position on the mass strike clearly differed from that of her elder colleague. In the first place, her analysis of the contemporary situation was, from a revolutionary perspective, far more optimistic, in the sense that she believed that the age of revolution had now arrived, [30] and that the SPD had to decide either to place itself at the head of the revolutionary masses or be pushed aside by them. [31] However, she was far more sanguine about possible defeats than Kautsky, who counselled caution and believed that the labour movement could be set back years by *premature* conflict. [32] For Luxemburg, the essence of revolutionary politics consisted in pushing the objective contradictions of capitalism to their very limit. [33] The mass strike was not merely a means of winning specific concessions from the authorities; it was only really significant as part of a long-term process that generated revolutionary consciousness. Organization and class-consciousness were not necessary prerequisites of action, as Kautsky maintained, but often a consequence of such action. The masses, often unorganized, needed confidence in their *own* ability to resist exploitation, and such confidence came not through blind adherence to bureaucratic party organization. [34]

Luxemburg's hostility to 'organizational fetishism' was directed as much at Lenin's theory of a tightly disciplined vanguard party as it was at the SPD and trade union bureaucracies in Germany. Opportunism was not to be fought by erecting a highly centralized organization, but rather by allowing the working classes to develop their own abilities in action. [35] Organization, education and action were not distinct and sequential moments of the revolutionary process but complementary and different aspects of that process. [36] This critique of bureaucratic strangulation Luxemburg shared with Robert Michels and with Weber, who saw ossification as part of advanced capitalism and deplored the 'spiritual goose-step' engendered by party discipline in the SPD. But it is only fair to point out that Kautsky too was aware of the problems that bureaucratization could bring and regretted loss of initiative on the part of the rank and file. [37] However, his own perpetual advocacy of caution and organization was scarcely inclined to alleviate the problem. Although Luxemburg's theory of the mass strike seems to rediscover the dialectic of proletarian self-liberation in Marx, it has to be said that the differences between her and Kautsky are easily exaggerated. She never believed that the mass strike should replace parliamentary action, did not associate it with violence necessarily; above all, she insisted that a mass strike could not be called into being on party instructions. Arguably, her faith in the spontaneity of the masses, like her theory of imperialism as adumbrated in *The Accumulation of Capital* (1913), owed not a little to a deterministic model of social change.[38]

To return to Kautsky, the refusal to contemplate action characterized not only his position in the mass-strike debate of 1910/11 but also his attitude to the Bolshevik revolution. Socialism could only be built on the basis of a fully capitalist order, violence could not overcome economic laws, phases of development could not be bypassed. The collapse of the Bolshevik regime was inevitable;[39] so, claimed Kautsky in 1934, was that of German National Socialism, doomed by its economic contradictions.[40]

Thus, whatever Kautsky may have said at an abstract level about human intervention in the historical process, in practice the need for action disintegrated in the face of economic laws. And those laws Kautsky thought he knew with sufficient accuracy to predict the future.[41] In the end, we are confronted with a 'scientific socialism', which both Bernstein and Weber believed to rest on a quite inadequate understanding of the nature of the social, as distinct from the natural, sciences.

The Analysis of Capitalism

It was not only the claim to detect laws of capitalist development that Weber found objectionable. As far as he was concerned the substantive claims of the vulgar Marxists were empirically false, at least as far as the supposed immiseration of the proletariat, the polarization of the classes, the inevitability of crisis were concerned. Similar points were made by Bernstein and thus were dealt with by the Marxists in their response to revisionism.[42]

Kautsky did not attempt to deny Bernstein's or Weber's contention that working-class living standards had improved since the early days of capitalism. He pointed out – correctly in view of Marx's position in the last two volumes of *Das Kapital* – that the concept of immiseration was not a statement to the effect that workers would become worse off in *absolute terms*. (Indeed, Marx had explicitly criticised the Lassallean theory of the iron law of wages.) What the theory of impoverishment stated was that workers did not receive the full value of their labour, i.e. a quite different proposition from a claim about living standards declining in absolute terms. Kautsky recognized that trade-union struggle or state intervention could bring about improvements in wages or working conditions, but those improvements had to be seen in the context of higher productivity, engendered by the intensification of labour and technological modernization. This process meant that the worker was receiving a smaller percentage of the value of his labour than hitherto, i.e. that exploitation was increasing even at the same time as an absolute improvement in wages. Immiseration was thus a *relative* concept, denoting that profits rose faster than wages and that labour's *share* of the national cake was declining. In fact, Kautsky used – correctly – official income tax statistics to demonstrate that higher incomes rose by a greater percentage than lower incomes in the Second Empire.[43]

Kautsky was also concerned to defend the theory of inevitable economic crisis, rejected by Bernstein and Weber in the wake of Germany's recovery after the so-called 'Great Depression' of 1873–96. Weber and Bernstein believed that trusts, cartels, the development of new credit institutions and simply ever greater experience enabled firms to iron out some of the discrepancies between supply and demand, created mechanisms to control production, limit competition and thus reduced the risk of crisis. To the Marxists, as for Weber, the emergence of an increasingly organized capitalism was not to be denied. But the success of the system, in the long term, continued to be impossible. Initially working with an under-consumptionist model of capitalist production, linked to a structural explanation of imperialism as early as 1884, Kautsky insisted that as long as competition and production for exchange (i.e. capitalism) remained, so did economic crisis.[44] Even though he later rejected under-consumptionist models and stressed the disproportion between producer and consumer goods sectors,[45] he remained convinced that cyclical depression was inevitable, and he rejected Bernstein's argument that cartels and trusts could obviate the 'anarchy of production'.[46] They might lessen the impact of a depression on the industrialist, but they also brought new problems for the worker by increasing inflexibility and hence unemployment during depressions and by controlling wages when business was booming. Cartels were designed to maximize profits and keep prices high; they were not benevolent societies to protect the working class from insecurity.[47] In short, organized capital meant an intensification of exploitation and class conflict, in which unions found it increasingly difficult to defend their members against powerful industrial organizations – a point which Weber also recognized, which was made forcefully by Bebel in justifying the primacy of the party over the unions, and which was reflected in Rosa Luxemburg's infamous description of trade union work as a 'labour of Sisyphus'.[48] Only socialism could put an end to the anarchy of production.[49] One additional reason for this was the growth of imperialism. Although Kautsky's last theory of imperial expansion, the theory of ultra-imperialism, envisaged the possibility of a peaceful form of imperialism in the shape of international cartelization, the position he held earlier (before 1911) was also that of Bebel[50] and Luxemburg:[51] namely, that wars were inevitable under a capitalism that translated the anarchy of production from the domestic to the international plane.[52] In short, the theory of imperialism was part of an answer to those who believed that capitalism could regulate itself.

An important aspect of Weber's critique of Marxism was concerned not only to argue that *class* conflict was not as important as the Marxists imagined, but also that the concept of class was multi-faceted. There were several different class structures. Above all, and here again Weber found himself in agreement with Bernstein, the class structure was not becoming increasingly polarized. The proletariat was becoming more and more internally differentiated, as was the middle class. Above all, a numerous class of white-collar workers was emerging. Hence, to imagine that class conflict would increase as a result of a polarization of society was to share an illusion. (It is interesting to note that this argument entails a certain form of economic reductionism: structural changes will militate against class conflict. In some ways, Kautsky was less of a reductionist, as his concept of class entailed political/organizational and not merely structural characteristics.) Kautsky was fully aware that the theory of capital concentration was absolutely central to Marxism and to the revisionist controversy.[53] It was of crucial importance because, if untrue, a policy of working-class self-reliance was unrealistic and the chances of successful revolution slim. Kautsky argued in general that the industrial proletariat was growing in size, that the old small producers were disappearing in the face of competition from industrial giants using the most up-to-date machinery.[54] The thesis was far more problematical, however, when applied to agriculture. Originally, Kautsky had based his arguments on the technical superiority of the large agricultural concern, which he believed to be more productive and infinitely more adaptable than the peasant smallholding. Thus the peasant appeared doomed to extinction.[55] As Eduard David pointed out, there were not a few problems with this argument. Indeed, the actual increase in the number of smallholdings suggested that they were possibly superior to the large concern.[56]

Kautsky's response was firstly to demonstrate that the survival and multiplication of peasant farms did not indicate their economic health. Some peasants had only survived by becoming outworkers in domestic industry, some by working in rural factories. Thus the number of wage labourers was increasing without the expropriation of the peasantry.[57] According to Kautsky, some of the new smallholdings were in fact the property of relatively well-off miners; thus, the proliferation of small 'agricultural concerns' grew *together* with the proletariat.[58] Secondly, however, Kautsky conceded that developments in the agricultural sector were not identical with those in industry. There was a size of concern above which the advantages of scale disappeared, ground rent prevented investment in new technology, and large-scale agriculture was only viable where such technology, trained managers and skilled hands were available.[59] Thirdly, claimed Kautsky, the peasant had survived at the expense of agricultural progress and society at large. The smallholding could not provide the agricultural surplus essential for the creation of socialism.[60] Hence, albeit for different reasons, Kautsky always opposed those who advocated that the SPD adopt a policy of peasant protection to win the votes of rural society. (Kautsky's triumph over the opposition on this issue, at the party conference of 1895, was less a triumph of theory than of the simple fact that the SPD was overwhelmingly a party of the urban working class, who realized that peasant protection entailed higher food prices.) Kautsky's refusal to embrace the peasantry was not simply a consequence of an analysis of the structure of agriculture. It also rested on arguments about the *politics* of both the peasantry and the old *Mittelstand*. The continued existence of these strata could not diminish the severity of the crucial struggle between capital and labour, because these strata did not constitute classes in the fullest sense. And this was because they were incapable of pursuing *independent* politics. They were both hostile to advancing capitalism and yet clung to the ideal of private property. They were not bearers of a qualitatively different social order. Consequently, the peasantry and lower middle class veered wildly from course to course in their political allegiances.[61]

This was Kautsky's position on a number of occasions. On others, he saw more structured divisions *within* the *Mittelstand*, with one section supporting capital, the other labour in the class struggle.[62] But Kautsky's most usual argument was that the peasantry and petty bourgeoisie essentially defended existing property relations, were becoming increasingly reactionary and had sold themselves to the existing state for protection. They had rallied round the banner of imperialism and also formed the backbone of rabid anti-semitism. [63] Similar arguments were deployed against the contention of Bernstein and Weber that the emergence of a large class of white-collar workers both refuted the model of class polarization and implied a lessening of class conflict. Kautsky was perfectly well aware of the emergence of the white-collar *salariat*. [64] However, he denied that it constituted a separate class, for it was far too heterogeneous and its class loyalties were divided. The beneficiaries of surplus value – bank managers, company directors, opera singers (!) – identified with capital, while the clerks, faced with increasing competition and automation, came increasingly close to the industrial proletariat in both their objective situation and their attitudes. [65] Hence, the SPD did not have to abandon its class identity and become a *Volkspartei*, as Bernstein, David and fellow revisionists advocated. Not only that: the bourgeoisie was becoming more, not less reactionary, and hence Bernstein's dreams of class alliance were increasingly remote from reality. [66] In future, the SPD would face greater repression and isolation, and the bourgeoisie was already forsaking whatever liberal values it had once possessed. [67] This theme was shared by Bebel and Luxemburg, [68] and it was closely related to the Marxist theories of imperialism.

For Kautsky, imperialism was not simply an issue of international politics. With Luxemburg, he believed that imperial expansion was also related to new class alliances and a brutalization of domestic politics, in which the bourgeoisie would increasingly resort to violence. [69] Thus imperialism brought about alliances between landowners and industrialists, between the military and the bourgeoisie, which then pursued a common anti-labour strategy. [70] And thus the theory of imperialism was seen, at least in part, as an answer to those who wished Social Democracy to abandon its character as a *Klassenpartei*. Kautsky's insistence on a strategy of proletarian self-reliance was not without its ambiguities. In the early 1890s, he spoke of the need for compromise with progressive elements of the bourgeoisie and against the Lassallean concept of a reactionary mass. In the revisionist controversy his position hardened in defence of isolation. However, in 1911 he advocated a *temporary* electoral alliance with the Progressive Party (seeing the revival of liberalism as a consequence of the emergence of the 'new middle class'); while the theory of ultra-imperialism maintained that progressive elements of the bourgeoisie could be mobilized against violent colonialism and the threat of war. [71] Ironically, liberals such as Weber, who wanted the SPD to abandon its isolation, were unavailable for precisely this alliance. For, whatever else Weber was, he was also a nationalist who identified with Germany's *Weltpolitik*. For him, the arms race was unfortunate but inevitable. [72] On German foreign policy there could be no meeting of minds between Weber and the Marxists. [73]

The division between Weber and other 'liberals', on the one hand, and Marxists *and* the rank and file of the SPD, on the other, went deeper than this, however. National Liberal support for the politics of Empire increased the tax burden, especially via indirect taxation on the less affluent sections of the community. National Liberal support for economic protection also ran counter to the Social Democrats' attacks on the system and the high food prices it entailed. In the electoral propaganda of the SPD it was precisely such consumerist issues that dominated. [74] The isolation of the Wilhelmine working class and its political representatives was further enforced by the intransigent posture of German employers towards trade unions, reflected in the absence of collective wage agreements in the heavy industrial system, [75] while the retreat of the National Liberals on the issue of suffrage reform in Prussia further rendered hopes of co-operation illusory. Isolation was not imposed on the SPD by a dogmatic Marxism. Rather Kautsky's Marxism reflected the isolation of a party that was roughly 90 per cent manual working class in its social composition.

Against this, it may be objected that points of contact did exist across class lines. In the Reichstag elections of 1912, for example, it was the case that the SPD concluded a temporary electoral pact with the Progressives in the run-off. What is instructive, however, is the subsequent behaviour of the followers of the two parties. Whereas the Social Democratic electorate followed the party line and voted for the Progressive candidate where the SPD candidate had stood down, Progressive supporters did not display the same loyalty but usually voted against social-democratic candidates. In several cases, Progressive candidates even refused to stand down in accordance with the electoral pact. Similar reservations have to be made in connection with the much-vaunted collaboration of the SPD and Liberals in Baden. Founded on common hostility towards the Catholic Centre Party, this alliance had brought the workers of Baden little by 1913, and some even within the Baden SPD were disillusioned with the strategy of collaboration. More importantly, Baden was not the Reich, in which Prussia dominated two-thirds of the territory and three-quarters of the population. Within the SPD in the 1890s there were more Social Democrats in Berlin than in all of South Germany put together, as Bebel pointed out [76] and as those who stress the reformist nature of the SPD would do well to remember. Karl Liebknecht could claim with some justification in 1910 that 'the political and economic future of Germany is – unfortunately – certainly not Baden. South Germany's future is rather North Germany'. [77] In Hamburg and Saxony, the suffrage actually became more discriminatory after the turn of the century, while the state also moved with increasing harshness against those involved in industrial disputes, especially in 1912. [78] It is against this background that the possibility of integrating German labour into the Second Reich, the dream of the Verein für Sozialpolitik (Social Policy Association) must be assessed. SPD electoral success in 1912 coincided with the formation of the *Kartell der schaffenden Stände*, an anti-socialist alliance of agrarians, some sections of industry and parts of the *Mittelstand*. Such political polarization along class lines, even reflected in the sports and leisure organizations of Wilhelmine Germany, made at least some sense of Kautskyite theory.

A further aspect of Weber's attitudes towards the SPD reflects the distance between himself and the world of labour. Weber adopted Michels's contempt for the supposedly petty-bourgeois and bureaucratic mentality of the SPD's leadership, and regarded the party's rank and file as slavish, sheepish followers. But this picture is far removed from the vitality of local party organizations and grossly underestimates the role of dynamic local and shop-floor initiatives, which played a part both in the formation of the SPD's ancillary organizations and in most major strike waves. Weber's elitist concern with formal leadership thus placed him in no position to understand the dynamics of a movement that could only be won over by fundamental political reform and qualitative social change.[79]

Notes: Chapter 24

1   For Weber's position in general, see W. J. Mommsen, *Max Weber and German Politics, 1890–1920* (Chicago, 1984). For his relationship with the Social Democrats especially, ibid., pp. 108 ff.

2   F. Naumann, *Demokratie und Kaisertum* (Berlin, 1900), p. 3.

3   K. Kautsky, *Grundsätze und Forderungen der Sozialdemokratie*, 2nd edn (Berlin, 1899), p. 6; idem, *Bernstein und das sozialdemokratische Programm* (Stuttgart, 1899), p. 157.

4   ibid., pp. 3, 157.

5   K. Kautsky, *The Labour Revolution* (London, 1925), p. 108.

6   K. Kautsky, 'Kant und Sozialismus' (1922), manuscript in International Institute for Social History (Amsterdam), Kautsky papers, KA A 105, p. 3.

7   ibid.

8   Kautsky to Plekhanov, 22 May 1898, published in *Der Kampf*, no. 18 (1925), p. 1.

9   See R. Geary, 'Karl Kaustky and the development of Marxism', PhD thesis, Cambridge University, 1971, ch. 4.

10 Kautsky, *Bernstein*, p. 18.

11 This was the central argument of Kautsky's *Ethik und materialistische Geschichtsauffassung* (Berlin, 1922).

12 K. Kautsky, *Das Erfurter Programm*, 4th edn (Stuttgart, 1902), p. 229; idem, *On the Morrow of the Social Revolution* (London, 1909), p. 24.

13 R. Luxemburg, *Politische Schriften* (Leipzig, 1969), pp. 13, 16.

14 K. Kautsky, *Die materialistische Geschichtsauffassung* (Berlin, 1927), Vol. 1, p. 17; idem, *Erinnerungen und Erörterungen* (Amsterdam, 1960), p. 214; idem, *Das Werden eines Marxisten* (Leipzig, 1930), p. 4; idem, *Vermehrung und Entwicklung in Natur und Gesellschaft* (Stuttgart, 1910), pp. v, vii.

15 H.-J. Steinberg, *Sozialismus und Sozialdemokratie*, 2nd edn (Hanover, 1969), p. 51.

16 *Die Neue Zeit*, vol. 1 (1883), p. 73; Kautsky, *Erinnerungen*, p.365; idem, *Vermehrung*, p. 12; idem, *Die materialistische Geschichtsauffassung*, Vol. 1, p. vii; idem, *Die historische Leistung von Karl Marx* (Berlin, 1908), p. 8.

17 Steinberg, *Sozialismus und Sozialdemokratie*, passim and especially pp. 54–63. Bebel saw no difficulty in reconciling Darwinism and Marxism and firmly believed in the inevitable collapse of capitalism (ibid., p. 56). See especially his comments at the 1891 SPD party conference: *Protokoll über die Verhandlungen des Parteitages der Sozialdemokratischen Partei Deutschlands. Abgehalten zu Erfurt v. 14. – 21. 10. 1891* (Berlin, 1891), p. 172.

18 G. Steenson, *Karl Kautsky* (Pittsburgh, Pa, 1978).

19 *Die Neue Zeit*, vol. 3 (1885), p. 108. See also his attacks on Ferri and Brentano: *Die Neue Zeit*, vol. 13 (1895), part 1, pp. 710 ff., and vol. 19 (1901), part 2, p. 22; vol. 15 (1897), part 1, p. 228; Kautsky, *Vermehrung*, p. 11; idem, *Die materialistische Geschichtsauffassung*, Vol. 1, pp. 787 and i.

20 K. Kautsky, *Die proletarische Revolution* (Berlin, 1922), p. 5; idem, *The Social Revolution* (London, 1909), p. 41; idem, *Der Weg zur Macht* (Hamburg, 1909), p. 36; idem, *Nationalstaat, Imperialistischer Staat und Staatenbund* (Nuremberg, 1915), p. 7; idem, *Bernstein*, pp. 14–15; idem, *Das Erfurter Programm*, pp. 140–1; *Die Gesellschaft*, vol. 2 (1929), p. 493.

21 Kautsky, *Bernstein*, p. 45; idem, *Das Erfurter Programm*, p. 105; idem, *Die materialistische Geschichtsauffassung*, Vol. 2, p. 547; idem, *Sozialdemokratische Bemerkungen zur Übergangswirtschaft* (Leipzig, 1918), p. 163. In this respect Kautsky was closer to Rudolf Hilferding's *Das Finanzkapital* (Vienna, 1910) than to Rosa Luxemburg's *Die Akkumulation des Kapitals* (Berlin, 1913), which placed a limit on the possibility of capitalist reproduction.

22 *Die Neue Zeit*, vol. 12 (1894), part 1, p. 366; vol. 17 (1899), part 1, p. 688.

23 *Die Neue Zeit*, vol. 19 (1901), part 2, pp. 80–90.

24 V. I. Lenin, *Collected Works*, Vol. 5 (Moscow, 1961), pp. 383–4.

25 Kautsky, *Die materialistische Geschichtsauffassung*, Vol. 1, p. xiv; idem, *Das Erfurter Programm*, pp. 136, 141; idem, *The Labour Revolution*, p. 142; idem, *Grundsätze und*

Forderungen, p. 5; idem, *Der Weg zur Macht*, p. 24; idem, *Die Agrarfrage* (Stuttgart, 1899), p. 128; *Der Kampf*, vol. 15 (1922), p. 31.

26 Trotsky, reporting Lenin's opinion to Kautsky, 21 July 1910, Kautsky papers KA DXII 168; Parvus to Kautsky, 14 June 1910, Kautsky papers KA DXVIII 462.

27 For a fuller discussion of Kautsky's position on the general strike, see Geary, 'Karl Kautsky', ch. 6.

28 *Der Kampf*, vol. 24 (1931), p. 295; K. Kautsky, *Wehrfrage und Sozialdemokratie* (Berlin, 1928); *Die Neue Zeit*, vol. 21 (1903), part 2, p. 390; vol. 22 (1904), part 1, p. 657; vol. 25 (1907), part 1, p. 461.

29 *Der Sozialdemokrat*, vol. 8 (1881), p. 1; *Die Neue Zeit*, vol. 13 (1895), p. 712–13; vol. 17 (1889), part 1, p. 299; vol. 22 (1904), part 1, p. 1, and part 2, p. 581; vol. 30 (1912), part 2, p. 691; K. Kautsky, *Der politische Massenstreik* (Berlin, 1914), pp. 87, 99.

30 *Protokoll . . . Jena (1905)*, p. 320.

31 *Die Neue Zeit*, vol. 23 (1905), part 1, p. 573.

32 See note 29 above.

33 Luxemburg, *Politische Schriften*, p. 48.

34 R. Luxemburg, *Gewerkschaftskampf und Massenstreik* (Berlin, 1928), p. 568–9; idem, *Massenstreik, Partei und Gewerkschaften* (Leipzig, 1919), p. 31; *Protokoll . . . Magdeburg (1910)*, pp. 427 ff.

35 *Die Neue Zeit*, vol. 22 (1904), part 2, p. 532.

36 ibid., p. 488; *Protokoll . . . Jena (1905)*, p. 321; Luxemburg, *Massenstreik*, p. 46.

37 *Protokoll . . . Mannheim (1906)*, pp. 143, 257.

38 Luxemburg, *Gewerkschaftskampf*, p. 541; *Protokoll . . . Magdeburg (1910)*, p. 428.

39 Kautsky, *The Labour Revolution*, pp. 39, 144; idem, *The Dictatorship of the Proletariat* (London, 1918), pp. 124–5.

40 K. Kautsky, *Grenzen der Gewalt* (Prague, 1934), p. 44; *Der Kampf*, vol. 1 (1934), p. 9.

41 *Die Neue Zeit*, vol. 27 (1909) part 1, p. 188.

42 E. Bernstein, *Wie ist wissenschaftlicher Sozialismus möglich?* (Berlin, 1901).

43 Kautsky, *Bernstein*, pp, 123 ff.; idem, *Der Weg zur Macht*, p. 88; idem, *Das Erfurter Programm*, p. 36; idem, *The Social Revolution*, pp. 18 ff.; *Die Neue Zeit*, vol. 27 (1909), part 2, p. 522.

44 For an account of Kautsky's several – and often contradictory – theories of imperialism, see Geary, 'Karl Kautsky', ch. 5.

45 Kautsky, *Die materialistische Geschichtsauffassung*, Vol. 2, pp. 544–50.

46 *Die Neue Zeit*, vol. 12 (1894), part 1, p. 460; vol. 19 (1901), part 1, p. 176; vol. 20 (1902), part 2, p. 111.

47 *Die Neue Zeit*, vol. 20 (1902), part 2, p. 135; vol. 29 (1911), part 1, p. 882.

48 For Weber, see W. J. Mommsen, 'The antinomian structure of Max Weber's political thought', in S. G. McNall (ed.), *Current Perspectives in Social Theory*, Vol. 4 (Greenwich, Conn., 1983), pp. 301–2. For Bebel, see *Protokoll . . . Köln (1893)*, p. 201.

49 Kautsky, *Die proletarische Revolution*, pp. 59–60.

50 *VIIe Congrès Socialiste Internationale, Stuttgart 1907* (Paris, 1907), p. 114.

51 Luxemburg, *Akkumulation*.

52 *Texte zu den Programmen der deutschen Sozialdemokratie* (Cologne, 1968), pp. 176–7; K. Kautsky, *Sozialismus und Kolonialpolitik* (Berlin, 1907), p. 38.

53 *Die Neue Zeit*, vol. 20 (1902), part 1, p. 773; Kautsky, *Bernstein*, p. 8.

54 ibid., pp. 49, 81; idem, *Das Erfurter Programm*, pp. 21, 23, 48, 78; idem, *Die proletarische Revolution*, p. 15; *Die Neue Zeit*, vol. 12 (1894), part 1, p. 459; vol. 34 (1916), part 1, p. 569.

55 *Die Neue Zeit*, vol. 21 (1903), part 1, p. 750; vol. 29 (1911), part 2, p. 409; Kautsky, *Die Agrarfrage*, p. 265.

56 E. David, *Sozialismus und Landwirtschaft* (Berlin, 1903), p. 54.

57 Kautsky, *Die Agrarfrage*, pp. 174, 187.

58 *Die Neue Zeit*, vol. 13 (1895), part 2, p. 485.

59 *Die Neue Zeit*, vol. 29 (1911), part 2, p. 349; K. Kautsky, *Bolshevism at a Deadlock* (London, 1931), pp. 39–40; idem, *Die Agrarfrage*, pp. 145, 195.

60 ibid., p. 230; idem, *Georgien* (Vienna, 1921), p. 34; *Die Neue Zeit*, vol. 26 (1908), part 1, p. 253.

61 *Die Neue Zeit*, vol. 9 (1891), part 2, p. 752; vol. 16 (1898), part 1, p. 810; vol. 29 (1911), part 2, pp. 798–9.

62 Kautsky, *Die Agrarfrage*, p. 139; idem, *Social Revolution*, p. 24.

63 *Die Neue Zeit*, vol. 8 (1890), p. 398; vol. 17 (1899), part 1, pp. 293 ff.; vol. 18 (1900), part 1, p. 749; vol. 25 (1907), part 1, p. 329; vol. 26 (1908), part 2, p. 547; vol. 28 (1910), part 2, p. 368; K. Kautsky, *Are the Jews a Race?* (London, 1926), p. 159; idem, *Der Weg zur Macht*, p. 97.

64 *Die Neue Zeit*, vol. 25 (1907), part 1, p. 590; vol. 28 (1910), part 2, p. 620; vol. 35 (1917), part 2, p. 103.

65 *Die Neue Zeit*, vol. 34 (1916), part 1, pp. 363, 525; vol. 35 (1917), part 2, p. 103; Kautsky, *Bernstein*, p. 135; idem, *Georgien*, p. 19; idem, *Die materialistische Geschichtsauffassung*, Vol. 2, p. 16; idem, *Die proletarische Revolution*, pp. 34–7; idem, *Der politische Massenstreik*, p. 255,.

66 *Die Neue Zeit*, vol. 16 (1898), part 1, p. 811; vol. 17 (1899), part 1, p. 293; vol. 18 (1900), part 1, p. 597; vol. 19 (1901), part 1, p. 10.

67 *Die Neue Zeit*, vol. 27 (1909), part 1, p. 45; vol. 29 (1911), part 2, p. 97.

68 *Protokoll ... Jena (1905)*, pp. 291–2; R. Luxemburg, *Sozialreform oder Revolution?* (Leipzig, 1908), p. 19.

69 *Die Neue Zeit*, Vol. 18 (1900), part 1, pp. 200, 587; Kautsky, *Der Weg zur Macht*, pp. 81–2.

70 ibid.

71 Kautsky to Adler, 5 May 1894. Cf. F. Adler (ed.), *Viktor Adler. Briefwechsel mit August Bebel und Karl Kautsky* (Vienna, 1954), pp. 152 ff.; *Die Neue Zeit*, vol. 30 (1912), part 2, p. 103.

72 Mommsen, 'The antinomian structure', p. 295.

73 For Marxist criticisms of German foreign policy, see Geary, 'Karl Kautsky', ch. 5.

74 W. Maehl, *August Bebel* (Philadelphia, Pa, 1980), pp. 360 ff.; P. Domann, *Sozialdemokratie und Kaisertum* (Wiesbaden, 1974), p. 101; J. Roberts, 'Drink and the labour movement', in R. J. Evans (ed.), *The German Working Class* (London, 1982), p. 86.

75 A comparison of figures for collective wage agreements in Britain and Germany makes this abundantly clear:

	Britain (1910)	Germany (1913)
mining	900,000	82 (!)
metalwork	230,000	1,376
textiles	460,000	16,000

Source: P. Stearns, *Lives of Labour* (London, 1975), pp. 180–1.

76 Bebel, in *Vorwärts*, 30 November 1894.

77 *Protokoll ... Magdeburg (1910)*, p. 335.

78 For criticism of the argument that the Wilhelmine state became more liberal with the progress of time, see D. Geary, 'The SPD and the authoritarian state in Imperial Germany', in J. C. Fout (ed.) *The State and Political Parties in Imperial Germany* (New York, forthcoming).

79 For a critique of Michels, see C. E. Schorske, *German Social Democracy* (Cambridge, Mass., 1955), pp. 111–18, and especially K. Schönhoven, *Konzentration und Organisation* (Stuttgart, 1980). For a general critique of the idea of *embourgeoisement*, see R. J. Evans, 'Introduction' to R. J. Evans (ed.), *The German Working Class*, pp. 15–53, and D. Geary, *European Labour Protest* (London, 1981), pp. 107–26. For local SPD politics, see especially M. Nolan, *Social Democracy and Society* (Cambridge, 1981), and F. Boll, *Massenbewegungen in Niedersachsen* (Bonn, 1981). For the significance of informal networks and shop-floor militancy, see F. Brüggemeier, *Leben vor Ort* (Munich, 1983) and M. Grüttner, *Arbeitswelt an der Wasserkante* (Göttingen, 1984).

25 Max Weber's Relation to Anarchism and Anarchists: The Case of Ernst Toller

DITTMAR DAHLMANN

During Weber's life the points of contact between him and the anarchist trends of his time were rather marginal, whether considered from a political, scientific or personal point of view. They did in fact, though, frequently influence his way of thinking to no small degree; thus, his opposition of an ethic of ultimate ends (*Gesinnungsethik*) to an ethic of responsibility (*Verantwortungsethik*) seems to me hardly imaginable without reference to anarchist and pacifist ideas of the time; these appear on the fringe, only becoming explicit in a few passages. In his academic work, Weber discussed anarchism only to a limited extent,[1] above all the religious anarchism or pacifism as embodied by Lev Tolstoy[2] and the revolutionary syndicalism as it flourished as a political and social movement pre-eminently in France.[3]

In particular, Weber had personal contacts with the 'Bohemia' that in Wilhelmine Germany had mainly established itself in pre-war Munich[4] and in those 'strange, fabulous realms',[5] as Weber called Ascona, where the anarchists had founded a life-reforming commune on Monte Verità. It was here that he met Raphael Friedeberg,[6] a doctor and anarchist, who like himself delivered an opinion and gave advice in the Otto Gross case[7]: Weber a legal opinion and Friedeberg a medical one. Unfortunately though, there is practically no information about the relationship between Weber and Friedeberg. In the Gross case, Weber also gave a written judgement on the anarchist, Ernst Frick,[8] intimate friend of Frieda Gross, who had been sentenced to imprisonment for participating in an anarchist attack in Switzerland in 1913. Since 1905, Frick had edited *Der Weckruf*, which was the equivalent German publication to the journals *Réveil* and *Risveglio anarchico* (published by the Tessin anarchist, Luigi Bertoni). At the same time, Frick was a member of the Socialist Federation (Sozialistischer Bund), which was influenced by the ideas of Gustav Landauer.[9] Weber expressed a positive opinion about Frick in his letters, even though he had little sympathy for Frick's political views.[10]

Next to the personal contacts with the anarchists of Monte Verità, which are hard to document, foremost is the exchange of letters, with Robert Michels as intermediary, with the Dutch anarchist, F. Domela-Nieuwenhuis,[11] and Max Nettlau, a collector of anarchist literature and chronicler of the anarchist movement in Europe and overseas.[12] Impressed by their refusal to compromise, Weber undoubtedly had a certain sympathy for the anarchists at a personal level, but scarcely any at the level of realistic politics. In April 1914, he wrote to his wife from Ascona: 'The life of these people is without background, but not without pride and form...but I could not breathe for long in this atmosphere'.[13]

In terms of his own personal standards, he sharply rejected aspects of these people's behaviour. Thus, in a letter to Emil Lask, he called the anarchists of Munich who were ideologically close to Erich Mühsam 'imbeciles' and 'fainthearts who besmirch the honest word "revolution" with their bragging on paper' – 'rabble' who 'scrawl articles'.[14] As Mommsen writes with good reason, 'Weber could easily understand the kind of radical, emotional politics [*radikale Gesinnungspolitik*] that did not shrink from hopeless battles. He took the anarchists who were committed to social revolutionary action far more seriously than he did the Marxists, who took comfort from the belief that their eventual victory was a historical necessity.'[15]

But already, in Weber's lifetime, the success of the Bolsheviks in Russia indicated that the Marxists were definitely prepared to fight for their victory, whereas the fundamentalists in the anarchist camp failed in the 'bloody carnival', as the Munich Soviet Republic (*Räterepublik*) was called by its opponents. Also, Weber's judgement of the *Attentat* (the idea of assassination) missed the crux of the matter; for him it had no concrete purpose other than demonstrating the belief in the correctness of the anarchist doctrine.[16] According to the anarchists' convictions and their theory – in so far as we can talk of a theory – the propaganda of the deed, the *Attentat*, served a definite end and had a clear purpose. Only in a few cases were the assassination attempts made out of despair; mostly they were planned actions intended to contribute to the de-stabilization of the social and political order and to demonstrate a capacity to act. Moreover, they were a proof of the voluntaristic understanding of revolution by anarchism, which considered revolutionary action as being possible at all times and not just at propitious moments.[17]

As may be evident, Weber's interest in anarchist theory as well as his relationships with anarchists were not in general especially developed. They remained episodes, however much he appreciated individuals such as Ernst Frick and Raphael Friedeberg. Weber's lack of prejudice, his willingness to tolerate the ideas of political opponents, is shown with regard to anarchism in his published opinion in the debate on value-judgements. In opposition to almost all other German university teachers, he was of the opinion that an anarchist should be allowed to hold a professorship – he even chose the example of a professor of law. 'The anarchist can surely be a very good lawyer. And if he is, then this is the Archimedean point, which stands outside the conventions and assumptions that we take for granted, on which are placed his convictions (if genuine and actually practised), enabling him to see the basic conceptions of conventional legal doctrine as problematic – problems which escape those for whom such conceptions are all too self-evident.'[18]

It was only during the First World War, at the Meetings on Culture arranged by Eugen Diederichs (an editor from Cologne) in the spring and autumn of 1917 and held at Burg Lauenstein in the Thüringian forest, that Weber became more closely acquainted with a representative of the religious- and pacifist-oriented anarchism, namely the student, Ernst Toller. Terming Toller an anarchist is not without its difficulties; the term is scarcely appropriate in the Weimar period, yet his thinking was strongly influenced by the ideas of the anarchist Gustav Landauer and, in this sense, it is permissible to call Toller an anarchist. In addition to Landauer, the writings of the pacifist Friedrich W. Foerster made a strong impression on Toller. Toller was born in Samotschin near Bromberg in 1893. Despite being exempt from military service on account of his physical and psychological constitution, he announced that he was willing to do active service and at his own request he fought at the Front. He suffered a nervous breakdown in May 1916 and, after a prolonged stay at a military hospital and sanatorium, he was discharged as unfit for further service. In the winter of 1916–17 he started to study economics at the University of Munich and at the same time worked on his play, *Die Wandlung* [The Transfiguration], and wrote poems. [19]

Although strong differences existed between the two in every respect – most of all in political beliefs – there did emerge from their meeting at Burg Lauenstein a wholly personal relationship, which made a considerable impression on Toller's own work. Next to Gustav Landauer and Kurt Eisner, Max Weber was the third person who decisively influenced his thinking. This 'ancestry' may seem surprising, but it is to be explained by the personal impact that Weber had upon Toller, and Toller's virtually life-long preoccupation with the problematic of an ethic of ultimate ends and an ethic of responsibility, which Weber had raised.

In 1921, Toller, for the first time, wrote about his meeting with Max Weber. [20] 'In the winter of 1917 he [Toller] studies in Heidelberg and is frequently permitted to be a guest of Max Weber, the only university teacher in Germany who is a politician of significant import. And a personality. In Germany this counts for more.' [21] In his autobiography, *Eine Jugend in Deutschland*, Toller specifically refers to his meeting with Weber at the second Lauenstein Meeting in October 1917. 'Max Weber has arrived... The youth fasten on to Max Weber, drawn by his personality and his intellectual integrity. He hates all romanticism concerning the state, he attacks Maurenbrecher and all those university professors who cannot see reality for their own fancies.' [22] He regarded his meeting with Weber as a 'treasured friendship'. 'During conversation in the evening the pugnacious character of this scholar reveals itself. Using words which put his freedom and life in danger, he reveals the deficiencies of the Reich.' [23]

These lines, written more than ten years after the meeting, reveal the extraordinary impression that Weber had upon the twenty-four year old Toller. In opposition to Weber, who stood for substantive reforms and rationality in politics, Toller went in another direction. In a partnership with the 'youth' of Germany, he wanted to build a new foundation for Germany. He 'believes that a change in the external order also changes the man.' [24] When it comes to matters of the soul, politics according to Weber's conviction were not sufficient. [25] The questions of politics are only resolved by power; all politics are founded upon force. Although a radical pacifist ever since his experiences in the war, in April 1919 Toller was confronted with this problem of power and force, which he detested but now proved necessary to defend the Soviet Republic, of which he was a protagonist. He called this a 'tragic necessity'. [26]

Following the encounter with Weber at the first Lauenstein Meeting at Whitsun 1917, Toller left Munich for Heidelberg in order to continue his studies closer to Weber. In the summer he participated in the famous Sunday afternoons at the Webers, and he occasionally read aloud passages of his play,

Die Wandlung, on which he was working, or recited his poems. 'As a result of the Meeting at Lauenstein, in the winter of 1917/18 some socialist and pacifist students attend Weber's Sunday afternoons. They are profoundly shaken by the experiences of the war. Ernst Toller is one of them. He feels at home and brings some of his poems which he reads. The listeners are moved by the delicacy of a pure soul which believes in the original goodness and solidarity of human beings, and believes it possible to get the people, who are murdering one another at the behest of their governments, to throw away their arms.'[27] Although rejecting its aims, Weber felt quite sympathetic about the group of pacifists that formed around Toller in Heidelberg.

During the summer and autumn of 1917 the 'Cultural and Political Federation of German Youth' was formed in Heidelberg under Toller's leadership. Although mainly influenced by Landauer's theories, it also took up the pacifistic ideas of Friedrich W. Foerster. The guiding principles run: 'The League is a community of the like-minded. We want to lead by example. The whole is set alight by our ideas... Everyone works from their soul and their spirit, as person to person.' The aims of the Federation were, among others: '2. The Federation fights for the abolition of poverty. It supports an economic structure that will give rise to meaningful production and a just distribution of material goods ... 7. It strives for the harmony of body, soul and spirit. In the place of militarism it wants harmonious movement, invigoration of the soul and the enlivenment of the spirit, that is, a creative enthusiasm and beauty.'[28] The call to establish and support the Federation was sent to numerous people in public life,[29] and, because of an indiscretion, it was made public prematurely and published in the *Deutsche Tageszeitung*. Following its vigorous rejection by the German Fatherland Party, Toller had to provide an explanation in the Heidelberg press.[30]

Beside the persons referred to above, Gustav Landauer also received the declaration of the Federation. (His 'Call to Socialism' strongly influenced Toller.)[31] A letter written from Toller to Landauer in December 1917, the day before Toller was suspended from the university (probably at the direction of the Baden military command), clearly shows Toller's anarchist disposition and its already expressionistic coloration. He wants 'to fight against poverty and the state, the latter only knowing force and not justice (as a right); to replace the state by the community that is committed economically to the peaceful exchange of equivalent products of labour and exists as a spiritual community of free people.'[32]

The group of pacifist students, numbering hardly more than ten,[33] hoped to win over Max Weber as one of their leaders. But he firmly rejected any involvement in the group. He could not agree with the mixture of religious fervour, radical pacifism and socialist demands that was laid out in its declaration. In Weber's estimation, the group exhibited great idealism but lacked any rational judgement of the politically possible, and so there could be no agreement. Weber from his side evidently offered to discuss the theses of the Federation, but was turned down by Toller and the other members of the group.[34]

Weber indicated his relationship to the Federation and his assessment of its ideas in a letter to Professor Goldstein:

When the highly immature young people, some of whom were serious-minded, submitted their 'proclamation' to me, I offered to discuss the matter with them in some detail. That offer was declined ... Thereupon I wrote to the leader, Herr Toller, and declined to take responsibility for that sort of thing ... Either resist evil with force *nowhere* and then live like Saint Francis or Saint Clare or an Indian monk or a Russian narodnik. Anything else is fraud or self-deception. For this *absolute* demand there is only an *absolute* way, the way of the saint.[35]

He explained further that it was simply incomprehensible to him why a revolution or a civil war as a 'means to an end' had a different value basis than war or a 'just war of self-defence'.[36] Weber's thinking in extremes, his radical polarization of two possibilities reveals itself clearly here. The realm of the fundamentalist is 'not of this world' and whoever acts politically must accept violence as a means to an end.

After his suspension from the University of Heidelberg, Toller went to Berlin in December 1917.[37] There, he became acquainted with Kurt Eisner, whose political views were much closer to his own. A short while later they both travelled together to Munich, where Toller took part in the agitation during the January strikes of 1918.[38] At meetings and at factory gates, he recited from his play, *Die Wandlung*, and from his poems, just as he had done at the Sunday afternoons in Heidelberg. Toller – like Weber – was generally regarded to be a good and captivating speaker, who was able to hold the attention of his audience and influence the masses.[39] Because of his participation in the January strikes he was arrested in early February and put into military prison. Having learnt of his imprisonment, Weber applied to be heard in the case[40] and gave evidence on his behalf at the Baden military command in Karlsruhe.

After his release from prison, Toller returned for a short time to his mother's house in Landsberg/Warthe and then went on to Berlin. He renewed his political activities and spoke at a meeting at the end of October 1918 that had been organized by the Majority Social Democrat, Wolfgang Heine. He declared himself against national defence as formulated, for example, in Rathenau's demand for a *levée en masse*.[41] At the outbreak of the revolution, Toller was ill at Landsberg/Warthe, but already on 10 November he was travelling to Berlin and from there, a few days later, to Munich where, on 7–8 November, Kurt Eisner had proclaimed the Republic and formed a provisional government.[42]

Only a few days before, on 4 November, Weber had spoken in Munich. In his audience were Erich Mühsam and Max Levien,[43] both of whom later played leading roles in the Munich Soviet Republic. During Weber's speech, a vehement dispute took place between Weber on the one side and Mühsam and Levien and their followers on the other.[44]

After Toller's arrival in Munich there followed the few months of his life in which he played a leading political role and became an exponent of what its opponents labelled the pseudo-Soviet Republic or *Kaffeehausräterepublik*, which was led by 'literati' and writers. The circle of literary people, or 'literary dilettantes', as Weber already called the actors in the drama of November 1918, comprised, apart from Toller, Gustav Landauer, Erich Mühsam, Ernst

Niekisch and Ret Marut (later known as B. Traven but actually Hermann Albert Otto Max Feige) who was editor of the magazine, *Der Ziegelbrenner*. The writers Georg Kaiser, Friedrich Burschell, Oskar Maria Graf and Heinrich Mann played minor roles.[45] However, not only literary people in the narrow sense of the word took part in the revolution. In addition there were some academics: Edgar Jaffé, minister of finance up to the first Soviet Republic, Otto Neurath, chairman of the Socialization Commission, and Lujo Brentano, Weber's predecessor as professor of political economy at Munich – all three were not so distant from Max Weber. Brentano collaborated in the formation of the Council of Intellectual Workers, which to begin with was granted thirty and later six seats in the Workers' and Soldiers' Council, and he was also active in the Socialization Commission.[46]

Kurt Eisner, Bavarian prime minister from 7–8 November 1918 until his assassination on 21 February 1919, was also more writer than politician and preached unity of thought and deed. As Eisner wrote, the Bavarian revolution resulted from the inspiration of 'the most important idea which mankind knows: that no contradiction and interval of time should exist between thought and deed.'[47] He proposed the '*Realpolitik* of idealism'[48] and believed in the 'power of the idea'.[49] Influenced by the humanism of German classicism,[50] he considered that life and politics were a total work of art (*Gesamtkunstwerk*): 'Art is no longer a flight from life, but life itself. In the hugely powerful class struggle of the proletariat there glows the divine spark of pleasure, which lights the way out of a society of misery and chance to the work of art of the new society.'[51]

Even more so than Eisner, Landauer was more a literary person than a politician. Its leader and founder of the Socialist Federation, he campaigned for the re-creation of the political order through 'leagues of spontaneity' that would be organized on a federal basis (a constitutive part of anarchism); this would then lead to a 'union of mankind'.[52] There was no separation for him between thought and action. 'The socialism which is actualized immediately makes all creative powers vital. It is a work of warmth and recovery, of culture and re-birth.'[53] He wanted 'to create with fellow men the good life as a work of art.'[54]

Toller, who as Weber said was a 'disciple by nature',[55] was obviously completely seized by the ideas of Eisner and Landauer. In his evidence before the court-martial in the case against Toller, Weber reported on his impression of the relationship between Toller and Eisner: 'In Munich he came under Eisner's influence, who also was of an honest and pure nature but was nothing other than a *Literat* who let himself be intoxicated by words ...'[56] For Weber as an advocate of power politics, rationality in political action and an ethic of responsibility, nothing could be more alien than Eisner's and Landauer's conception of politics as a total work of art.

Toller's demands for a world ruled by Eros, 'the spiritual community of free people',[57] and the 'liberation of the people from professional politicians and politics'[58] were closely tied to those of Eisner and Landauer. Here, we can see clearly the contrast between Toller's and Weber's ideas; despite this, there still existed a sympathy between the two men, especially on Weber's part for the person of pure conviction. Toller's preoccupation with Weber's intellectual integrity and his devotion to the man who provided such a 'treasured friendship' continued to exert an influence during the periods of Weimar and his exile.

It is almost certain that Weber and Toller met each other in Berlin in December 1918, for the first time after the Heidelberg period. Toller spoke at a party meeting in Berlin. When some of the participants tried to silence him on account of his radical statements, Weber is said to have stepped on to the speaker's rostrum, to have put his hand protectively on to the shoulder of the slight Toller and declared: 'Let him speak. He is a man to be taken seriously. He has something to say.'[59] Only a short while after his arrival in Munich in the middle of November 1918, and despite his political experience being limited to the foundation of the Federation and his participation in the January strikes of 1918, Toller was elected at the end of November/beginning of December as the third chairman of the Executive Committee.[60] He stood as a candidate for the Independent Social Democratic Party (USPD) in the elections for the Bavarian Diet, in which the USPD received 1.6 per cent of the vote and three seats.[61] Eisner retained the post of prime minister, despite this devastating setback.

About two weeks after these elections Weber gave his lecture 'Politics as a vocation' in Munich, at the invitation of the 'Freideutsche Jugend'. According to Weber, Toller attended this lecture. 'In January 1919 Toller was a discussant opposed to the witness at a public meeting; here Weber already believed he was able to establish the strong influence of Eisner on the accused.'[62] The demand for the pursuit of responsible action in politics did not at this point receive a favourable response from Toller.

The most appropriate characterization of Toller as a politician was given by Ernst Niekisch, who at that time had close ties with him: 'In the revolutionary excitement of those days Toller had stepped on to the slippery ground of politics, for which he was in no way gifted. He was a man of feelings, not of cool calculation; of imagination, not of a dispassionate sense of reality. He was more overwhelmed by the situation than able to control it through impassive deliberation. Toller's political actions were impulsive, emotional gestures, improvisations, spectacular ideas and not those of the sure touch of strategic and tactical measures.'[63]

This is not the place to go into the events that finally led to the proclamation of the Soviet Republic in Munich on 6/7 April 1919. The actions and proclamations of the Soviet Republic were at turns both tragic and comic. Scarcely any of those in leading positions were politicians. Toller's demand for the abolition of the professional politician was translated into reality. For a few days the principle of an absolute ethic of pure conviction ruled instead of *Realpolitik* — to the extent that one can talk about power at all; the Communist Party kept itself aloof from this. On 8 April, Toller took over as chairman of the Revolutionary Central Committee from Ernst Niekisch, who resigned. In a flood of decrees the Central Committee determined to socialize the press and the monetary system, to disarm the police, to establish revolutionary tribunals, to ration accommodation and to disarm the bourgeoisie.

The pseudo-Soviet Republic as the communists called it ended after only seven days in a putsch by troops loyal to the government;[64] those arrested included Erich Mühsam. After the putsch had been suppressed by Red Guards, the Communist Party took over the leadership of the Soviet Republic.

However, the Communist leaders, too – Eugen Leviné and Max Levien among others – lacked the political experience necessary to keep the Soviet Republic afloat. Leviné was like Toller – he had studied at Heidelberg and was more of an artist than a determined revolutionary. Fedor Stepun, like Leviné of Russian descent and a student at Heidelberg, described him as 'an unusually tenderhearted young man, who versified the drumming of the autumn rain on the roofs of the workers' houses, and wrote a play about the life of pure and noble prostitutes. His socialism lacked any experience and was not of a dogmatic or fanatic nature; rather it was obviously stamped by ethical and pedagogic convictions.'[65]

Toller and Landauer offered to work together with the communist government of the Soviet. Toller, the radical pacifist, became a commander of troops and repulsed the attacking White Army at Dachau and Rosenheim.[66] He could not prevent the chaos of the final days of the second Soviet Republic, nor the shooting in the Luitpold Gymnasium of hostages who were members of the radical right, *völkisch* Thule Society, nor the break-up of the front due to the leadership's refusal to deviate from the principle of absolute voluntariness of the Red Army. After the breakdown of the Soviet Republic, Toller hid himself for a month in various places in Munich[67] until he was arrested on 4 June. In the middle of July (14–16), the case against Toller was heard in the court-martial. A few days before, Eugen Leviné had been sentenced for his part in the Soviet Republic and, under the jurisdiction of the military court, had been shot. A member of the Independent Social Democrats and one-time member of the Council of People's Representatives, Hugo Haase, acted as defending counsel in the case with two Munich lawyers, Gänßler and Kaufmann. Besides Max Weber, the writers Björn Björnson, Max Halbe and Max Martersteig among others gave evidence. Written statements were submitted by Carl Hauptmann and Thomas Mann.[68] They all testified to the fundamentally ethical disposition of Toller's writings. Weber, who felt himself constrained to give evidence on 'what I know in favour of the young man',[69] was called on the second day of the proceedings.

In his evidence Weber expressed his 'deep human sympathy for the defendant', a man 'of an entirely upright character', who had acted, however, without any sense of the consequences of action but did so from 'an ethic of ultimate ends'. Toller was 'an extremely unstable young man, who still holds the most confused views on the ideas and problems of our time. Without being aware of it he appealed to the hysterical instincts of the masses, allowing himself to be emotionally carried away beyond his original intention. He was innocent of all political realities. Regarding the time in Heidelberg, Weber stated that the group of young people knew absolutely nothing about economic and political matters, or about socialism. He repeatedly suggested to Toller that he distance himself from these movements.' Weber coined the expression that 'God in his wrath chose Toller to be a politician'.[70]

Neither Toller nor his defending counsel, Hugo Haase, accepted this characterization. In his plea, Haase argued 'The testimony of Professor Max Weber, which is based on observations made in 1917, cannot be decisive for a judgement of Toller as a politician, because Toller has in the meantime pursued extensive economic and sociological studies. It is entirely wrong to hold him responsible under criminal law for the fact that he is allegedly not up to the standard required of a political leader.'[71] As in the trial against Leviné, who was refused mitigating circumstances because of his 'dishonourable beliefs', the prosecutor in the Toller case sought to charge Toller with 'unprincipled actions'. Obviously Weber decisively rejected this. Kaufmann, the Munich lawyer, said in his plea: 'Professor Max Weber, cited by the prosecutor, also indignantly rejected the view that Toller has ever burdened himself with ethical guilt. Also if you believe that Toller has made political mistakes, this does not give you the right to judge him legally or ethically.'[72]

Toller definitely refused to accept his fundamentalist ethic as a mitigating circumstance. In his final words before the court he said: 'It is clearly shown that my case does not involve a psychopathic or a hysterical condition, which would justify mitigating circumstances. I carried out all my actions on rationally considered grounds, and I demand that you hold me fully responsible for these deeds.'[73] He wanted to take responsibility for his actions and was prepared to answer for his ideals with all their conceivable consequences, and moreover at the risk of being sentenced to death; a mode of conduct that always commanded Weber's respect.[74]

The contradiction between the ethics of conviction and responsibility, between idea and deed, between thought and action as Weber presented it in 'Politics as a vocation' occupied Toller in the further course of his life when he had finally left the political stage and was solely a writer. He still could not and did not wish to relinquish responsibility as a politically thinking and acting person. The role and function of the political leader, which he himself had become for a short period and which Weber had described in his political theory of parliamentary leadership democracy, even then frequently appeared at the centre of his political thought.

Toller discussed Weber's characterization of him as a fundamentalist in his autobiography, *Eine Jugend in Deutschland*. This was only published by the Amsterdam publishing house, Querido, after his emigration from Germany in 1933. In this, he obviously referred to Marianne Weber's biography; for example, the letter to Professor Goldstein of November 1918 already mentioned.[75] Toller dealt at length with Weber's demand that the person of pure conviction should radically renounce the world, as did Saint Francis, 'or else desire to resist evil by force, because otherwise *you share responsibility* for it.'[76] In *Eine Jugend in Deutschland* he wrote,

I ask myself what lies ahead for the man who wants to intervene in the fortunes of the world and so become a politically acting person, when he wants to actualize his perception of the just ethical idea in the struggle of the masses? Was Max Weber right in saying that, if we do not wish to resist evil by force anywhere, we must live like St Francis, that for this absolute demand there is only the absolute way, the way of the saint? Has the acting person to become guilty, again and again? Or if he does not wish to become guilty does he perish . . . ? Is not man individual and mass at the same time? Isn't the struggle between individual and mass played out in the interior of the man as well as in society? As an individual he acts according to the moral ideal which is seen as just. He will serve this ideal even though the world might collapse. As part of the masses he is driven by social impulses; he will achieve the objective even though he is forced to give up the moral ideal.

To me this contradiction seems to be insoluble, because I experienced it in my own actions, and I seek to give it form. Thus originates my play *Masses and Man*.[77]

The conflict described above was the stimulus for Toller's play *Masses and Man*, which dealt with the occurrences of April 1919 and was written in October 1919 during his imprisonment in the Niederschönenfeld fortress.[78] For Toller it seems that it was not so much the action that was important but rather the inner debate that preceded the action, the decision to act 'in spite of all', the will that fought for things and ideas that were just and good.[79] This problem of the consequences of action, the connection between the idea that is recognized as right and the effects that therefore follow, engaged Toller again and again. Only a few years after the collapse of the Soviet Republic he realized that the question of power so often referred to by Max Weber, which had been almost entirely ignored in April 1919, was central to thought and action. In a speech on the November revolution, which makes an indirect reference to 'Politics as a vocation', he said, 'Deed effects power. The means for the deed are not chosen by us alone. Today he who fights on the grounds of politics in interaction with economic and human interests must be clear that law and the effects of his struggle are determined by powers other than his own good intentions, that often the manner of defence and resistance are forced upon him, which he must regard as tragic and because of which he can literally bleed to death.'[80]

In almost all his speeches in the years of the Weimar Republic,[81] Toller called for the observance of political realities, the clear recognition of questions of power, and the exercise of patience in the realization of political aims. Even when the person who acts politically can be 'guiltlessly guilty', as Toller portrayed it in *Masses and Man*, in Toller's view he must exhibit, on the one hand, following Kurt Eisner, the 'courage for truth' or (from Toller's description of Max Weber) 'intellectual integrity' and, on the other hand, in order to act at all in the world, he must not lose track of political realities. The rigorous pacifism of the young Toller had not stood the test of reality during the period of the Munich Soviet Republic. It was gradually replaced, in particular during his years of exile, by the knowledge that it is also necessary to resist evil with force. A manuscript of a speech from the 1930s states, 'The state which fires the first shot is not the breaker of peace. The peace breaker is the state which prepares its people to glorify war... The only way to prevent it [the state] is if it knows that it would have the united world against it which is willing to punish the attacker... There is no democracy of ideas. Democracy of ideas leads to the despotism of the robber and the man of violence.'[82]

Over the years Toller, the person of pure conviction, came very close to a position of an ethic of responsibility – although obviously only through a supreme effort. He was not actually able to resolve the conflict between such extreme polarities. On the question of 'ethical action', on whether 'the end justifies the means', the political thinker gave a different answer from that of the writer.

In conclusion, the question of the basis of the relationship between Weber and Toller remains to be clarified; in particular, what brought about Weber's open concern for Toller? Weber, who often stressed 'his absolute scepticism towards the Credo',[83] who rejected the evaluation of ethical action in terms of its effects',[84] encountered in Toller the person of pure conviction who, in the short time of their acquaintanceship, dismissed any 'scientific rationalization of the processes of his decision-making'[85] and was prepared to put into practice his ethical ideals in a radical way. In his own political actions, Weber also tended towards an ethic of conviction although remaining perfectly aware that politics was unthinkable without compromise; therefore, he shrank back from the ultimate consequences of action, just as Toller accepted them, and acknowledged in Toller the 'ideal type' of a consistent fundamentalist who, without regard for the possible outcome, not only proposed action (*Aktion*) but also took a leading part in revolutionary actions.

Notes: Chapter 25

This chapter was translated by Leena Tanner and Sam Whimster.

1   There is no space here for a discussion of what might be understood by 'anarchism'. Instead, reference can be made to P. Lösche, *Anarchismus* (Darmstadt, 1977). On the anarchist movement in Germany, see U. Linse, *Organisierter Anarchismus im Deutschen Kaiserreich von 1871* (Berlin, 1969).
2   For Weber's interest in Tolstoy, which increased in 1905 as a result of Weber's writings on Russia, see his outline in 'Zwischen zwei Gesetzen', MWG, Vol. I/15, pp. 95 ff. On religious or pacifistic anarchism, see ES, Vol. 1, p. 595, and RS, Vol. 1, p. 547.
3   MWG, Vol. I/15, pp. 504, 550–1, 628, 633; and in the letters to Robert Michels, cited in W. J. Mommsen, 'Max Weber and Roberto Michels: An asymetrical partnership', *Archives européennes de sociologie*, vol. 22 (1981), pp. 108–9.
4   M. R. Lepsius, 'Max Weber in München', *Zeitschrift für Soziologie*, vol. 6 (1977), pp. 107–8. On Bohemia, cf. H. Kreuzer, *Die Boheme. Beiträge zu ihrer Beschreibung* (Stuttgart, 1968); W. Frühwald, 'Kunst als Tat and Leben. Über den Anteil deutscher Schriftsteller an der Revolution in München 1918/19', in *Sprache und Bekenntnis. Hermann Kunisch zum 70. Geburtstag* (Berlin, 1971), pp. 361–89.
5   *Biography*, p. 491.
6   For Friedeberg, cf. H. M. Bock and F. Tennstedt, 'Raphael Friedeberg. Arzt und Anarchist', in H. Szeemann (ed.), *Monte Verità. Berg der Wahrheit. Katalog zur Ausstellung in der Villa Stuck* (Munich, 1980), pp. 38–58.
7   For Otto Gross, cf. E. Hurwitz, 'Otto Gross. Von der Psychoanalyse zum Paradies', in Szeemann (ed.), *Monte Verità*, pp. 107–16. For Weber's judgement of Gross, see the letter to Else Jaffé, printed in E. Baumgarten (ed.), *Max Weber. Werk und Person* (Tübingen, 1964), pp. 644–8, and Chapter 32 by Wolfgang Schwentker in this volume. The theories of Otto Gross on libertarian sexuality, anti-authoritarian education free of repression, and his demand for emancipation of the self from traditional family and professional bonds had great influence on the anarchist movement, above all in Munich, and especially on Erich Mühsam. Gross's theories served to legitimate a liberated anarchistic practice. Cf. R. Kauffeldt, *Erich Mühsam. Literatur und Anarchie* (Munich, 1983), p. 190, as well as E. Mühsam, *Namen und Menschen. Unpolitische Erinnerungen* (Berlin, 1977), pp. 235–6 (first edition 1931).
8   *Biography*, p. 490.
9   Bock and Tennstedt, 'Friedeberg', p. 44; G. Landauer, *Sein Lebensgang in Briefen*, ed. by M. Buber (Frankfurt-on-Main, 1929), Vol. 1, p. 220.
10 *Biography*, pp. 491 ff.
11 Letters from Max Weber to Robert Michels, 7 February, 18 February and 7 August 1907: Roberto Michels papers, Fondazione Luigi Einaudi, Turin.
12 Letter from Max Weber to Max Nettlau, 27 October 1910, International Institute of Social History (IISH) Amsterdam, Nettlau papers. M.
13 *Biography*, p. 491.

14   Letter from Max Weber to Emil Lask, 25 December 1913, Zentrales Staatsarchiv Merseburg, Max Weber papers.
15   W. J. Mommsen, *Max Weber and German Politics, 1890–1920* (Chicago, 1984), p. 107.
16   WL[4], p. 514.
17   U. Linse, '"Propaganda der Tat" und "Direkte Aktion". Zwei Formen anarchistischer Gewaltanwendung', in W. J. Mommsen and G. Hirschfeld (eds), *Sozialprotest, Gewalt, Terror. Gewaltanwendung durch politische und gesellschaftliche Randgruppen im 19. und 20. Jahrhundert* (Stuttgart, 1982), pp. 237–69; C. J. Friedrich, 'The anarchist controversy over violence', *Zeitschrift für Politik*, vol. 19 (1972), pp. 167–77.
18   Baumgarten (ed.), *Max Weber*, p. 110.
19   For Toller, see T. Bütow, *Der Konflikt zwischen Revolution und Pazifismus im Werk Ernst Tollers* (Hamburg, 1974); C. ter Haar, *Ernst Toller. Appell oder Resignation?* (Munich, 1977); W. Frühwald and J. Spalek (eds), *Der Fall Toller. Kommentar und Materialien* (Munich, 1979).
20   E. Toller, 'Lebenslauf'. This test was written for a planned anthology, but was not published at the time. It appeared first in 1967 in H. Daiber (ed.), *Vor Deutschland wird gewarnt. 17 exemplarische Lebensläufe* (Gütersloh, 1967), pp. 90–1. Here cited as in H. Viesel (ed.), *Literaten an der Wand. Die Münchner Räterepublik und die Schriftsteller* (Frankfurt-on-Main, 1980), pp. 331–5.
21   Toller, 'Lebenslauf', p. 332. Gustav Radbruch, at that time Reichstag deputy for the SPD and Professor at Kiel, visited his former schoolfriend, Mühsam, and Toller in the fortress during September 1921. A police report records that 'Radbruch and Toller enthused over Weber as the focus of Heidelberg university'. From Toller's police record, 11 September 1921, printed in Frühwald and Spalek (eds), *Der Fall Toller*, p. 124.
22   E. Toller, *Eine Jugend in Deutschland* (Reinbek, 1979), p. 57. This book was first published in 1933 and was translated as *I was a German* (London, 1934). Since this translation is deficient for our purposes, we refer to the German version. For Weber at the Lauenstein meeting, cf. MWG, Vol. I/15, pp. 701–7.
23   Toller, *Jugend*, p. 58.
24   ibid.
25   FMW, p. 115.
26   Toller, 'Lebenslauf', p. 334.
27   *Biography*, p. 601.
28   'Leitsätze für einen kulturpolitischen Bund der Jugend in Deutschland', printed in E. Toller, *Gesammelte Werke*, (Munich, 1978), Vol. 1, pp. 31–4.
29   Among others, F. W. Foerster, Walter Hasenclever, Carl Hauptmann, Karl Henckell, Heinrich Mann and Walter von Molo associated themselves with the proclamation; see Frühwald and Spalek (eds), *Der Fall Toller*, p. 33.
30   *Heidelberger Zeitung*, no. 298, 20 December 1917: 'Erklärung des stud. jur. Ernst Toller'.
31   G. Landauer, *Aufruf zum Sozialismus* (Berlin, 1911; new edn, Cologne, 1967).
32   Toller, *Gesammelte Werke*, Vol. 1, p. 36. The original letter and a copy of the proclamation can be found in Landauer papers IISH Amsterdam, Toller correspondence.
33   Communication of Prorektor of Heidelberg University to Rektorat of Munich University, 30 January 1918, Staatsarchiv Munich, Staatsanwaltschaft 2242/II, p. 139. Some documents from the Toller case in the Munich Staatsarchiv are printed in F. Hitzer, *Der Mord im Hofbräuhaus. Unbekanntes und Vergessenes aus der Bayerischen Räterepublik* (Frankfurt-on-Main, 1981), pp. 149–95; M. Turnowsky-Pinner, 'A Student's Friendship with Ernst Toller', *Leo Baeck Institute Year Book*, vol. 15 (1970), pp. 216–17. It is certain that the Bund was principally the creation of Toller, as W. Rothe, *Ernst Toller* (Reinbek, 1983), p. 37, writes, and that all proclamations, etc., were written by him.
34   *Biography*, p. 601.
35   Letter from Max Weber to Goldstein, 13 November 1918; *Biography*, pp. 602–3. Emphasis in original. Cf. also the letter to the *Göttinger Tageblatt*, 24 December 1917, Zentrales Staatsarchiv Merseburg, Max Weber papers.
36   *Biography*, p. 603.
37   According to his own statement, he was there for treatment in a clinic. Statement of Toller to Munich Staatsanwaltschaft, 4 June 1919, Staatsarchiv Munich, Staatsanwaltschaft 2242/I, p. 130.
38   On 2 February 1918, Toller addressed a meeting on the Theresienwiese in Munich. Wochenbericht des Regierungspräsidenten, 4 February 1918, Bayerisches Hauptstaatsarchiv,

MINN 66283. For the January strikes in Munich, cf. W. Boldt, 'Der Januarstreik in Bayern mit besonderer Berücksichtigung Nürnbergs', *Jahrbuch für fränkische Landesforschung*, vol. 25 (1965), pp. 14 ff., and W. Albrecht, *Landtag und Regierung in Bayern am Vorabend der Revolution von 1918* (Berlin, 1968), pp. 295 ff.

39 For this, see the reports in Rothe, *Toller*, pp. 17–18; 'Protokolle der Baierischen Räterepublik', *Kürbiskern*, vol. 2 (1966), pp. 49–50; Bütow, *Konflikt*, Appendix, pp. 72 ff.; E. Niekisch, *Gewagtes Leben. Begegnungen und Erlebnisse* (Cologne, 1958), p. 98.

40 *Biography*, pp. 601 ff. Weber's testimony is not recorded, nor is it known what influence it had on Toller's release, which occurred in September 1918 after he had been psychiatrically examined.

41 Staatsarchiv Munich, Staatsanwaltschaft 2242/I, p. 131; Frühwald and Spalek (eds), *Der Fall Toller*, p. 13; for Weber's attitude to a *levée en masse*, see Mommsen, *Max Weber and German Politics*, p. 287; *Biography*, pp. 625–6.

42 For the course that the Bavarian Revolution followed, cf. A. Mitchell, *Revolution in Bayern 1918/19. Die Eisner-Regierung und die Räterepublik* (Munich, 1967); K. Bosl (ed.), *Bayern im Umbruch. Die Revolution von 1918, ihre Voraussetzungen, ihr Verlauf und ihre Folgen* (Munich, 1969). For Eisner, cf. F. Wiesemann, 'Kurt Eisner. Studie zu einer politischen Biographie', in Bosl (ed.), *Bayern*, pp. 387–426. For the actions and conceptions of the anarchists, see U. Linse, 'Die Anarchisten und die Münchner Novemberrevolution', in ibid., pp. 37–73.

43 R. M. Rilke, *Briefe aus den Jahren 1914–1921*, ed. by R. Sieber-Rilke and C. Sieber (Leipzig, 1927), p. 207; *Biography*, p. 627.

44 ibid.

45 P. Pörtner, 'The writers' revolution: Munich 1918–19', *Journal of Contemporary History*, vol. 3 (1968), pp. 137–51; Frühwald, 'Kunst als Tat und Leben', p. 369.

46 L. Brentano, *Mein Leben im Kampf um die soziale Entwicklung Deutschlands* (Jena, 1931), pp. 353 ff. The number of seats was reduced because of the 'eloquence of the intellectual workers', since these would otherwise have had too great a preponderance during meetings.

47 K. Eisner, *Die halbe Macht den Räten. Ausgewählte Aufsätze und Reden*, ed. by R. and G. Schmolze (Cologne, 1969), p. 289.

48 Frühwald, 'Kunst als Tat und Leben', p. 379.

49 K. Eisner, *Sozialismus als Aktion* (Frankfurt, 1975), p. 76.

50 ibid., p. 95.

51 K. Eisner, 'Die Heimat der Neunten', in idem, *Gesammelte Schriften*, Vol. 1 (Berlin, 1919), p. 154.

52 G. Landauer, 'Die 12 Artikel des Sozialistischen Bundes', in his *Aufruf zum Sozialismus*, 2nd edn (Cologne, 1967), pp. 187–8.

53 Letter from Gustav Landauer to the Action Committee, 16 April 1919, in Landauer, *Lebensgang*, Vol. 2, pp. 420–1.

54 Letter from Gustav Landauer to Louise Dumont-Lindemann, 8 January 1919, in ibid., p. 351. Eisner's and Landauer's view of themselves as 'dead men on parole' is clear in their statements: Eisner, *Gesammelte Schriften*, Vol. 1, pp. 5–6; Landauer, *Lebensgang*, Vol. 2, p. 341. This was a characterization also used by E. Leviné in his closing statement before the Standgericht, in T. Dorst (ed.), *Die Münchner Räterepublik. Zeugnisse und Kommentar* (Frankfurt, 1966), p. 167.

55 S. Großmann, 'Prozeß Toller', *Vossische Zeitung*, no. 363, 19 July 1919, evening edn, p. 2.

56 *Vorwärts*, no. 358, 16 July 1919, morning edn.

57 Toller, *Gesammelte Werke*, Vol. 1, p. 36 (letter to Gustav Landauer, December 1917).

58 ibid., p. 44: 'Die Friedenskonferenz zu Versailles', first published on 1 April 1919 in *Neue Zeitung*.

59 Mommsen, *Max Weber and German Politics*, p. 47, n. 50. Mommsen relies here on an oral report of the meeting given by Professor Hans Rothfels. After his release from the Military Prison in September 1918, Toller first spoke in public again at W. Heine's meeting in October 1918. In October 1918, Weber was not in Berlin but, in December 1918, he delivered two speeches there on 17 and 20 December. At this time Toller was in Berlin as a delegate of the Munich Independent Social Democratic Party (USPD) to the General Congress of the Workers' and Soldiers' Councils, which met from 16 to 21 December. *Allgemeiner Kongreß der Arbeiter- und Soldatenräte Deutschlands vom 16.–21. Dezember in Berlin. Stenographische Berichte* (Berlin, 1919), list of participants, p. 213.

60 In the literature, Toller is nearly always mentioned as the second chairman of the executive

committee, e.g. Frühwald and Spalek (eds), *Der Fall Toller*, pp. 13–14. In the list of participants mentioned in note 59, he is named as the third chairman. This must be regarded as the correct version.

61 Mitchell, *Revolution in Bayern*, p. 189. In March 1919, shortly after the murder of Eisner, Toller was elected chairman of the Munich USPD.

62 Since this was the sole lecture Weber gave in Munich in January 1919, and since the political activities of Toller meant that only important matters could take him away from Munich, it can be supposed that Toller was present at Weber's lecture. But his presence is not certain. In a letter to his publisher Kurt Wolff, Munich 24 January 1919, he writes: 'Tomorrow I am going as a delegate of the Executive Committee of the Bavarian W. C. to a conference in Bern'. *Kurt Wolff. Briefwechsel eines Verlegers 1911–1963*, ed. B. Zeller and E. Otten (Frankfurt-on-Main, 1966), p. 321. It is none the less probable that the dating involves a reading error on the part of the editor, since the International Socialist Congress only began in Bern on 2 February 1919 and it is improbable that Toller travelled to Bern more than a week before this date. The likely date of the letter is 29 January 1919. If the dating of the letter in the Toller papers (Yale University Library) is correct, then Weber is referring to the meeting with Toller during December 1918 in Berlin, which was mentioned above.

63 Niekisch, *Gewagtes Leben*, p. 99.

64 Mitchell, *Revolution in Bayern*, pp. 271 ff.; K. L. Ay, *Appelle einer Revolution* (Munich, 1968), pp. 27 ff.

65 F. Stepun, *Vergangenes und Unvergängliches. Aus meinem Leben. Erster Teil: 1884–1914* (Munich, 1947), p. 145. Cf. also G. Radbruch, *Briefe*, ed. by E. Wolf (Göttingen, 1968), p. 72; letter from Gustav Radbruch to Eugen Abel, 7 June 1919. The Action Committee of Revolutionary Artists continued during the second Soviet Republic.

66 On 26 April 1919 Toller resigned as commander of his army group since he regarded 'the present government as harmful to the working people of Bavaria'. He wished, however, to continue his duties until a new commander was appointed. Staatsarchiv Munich, Staatsanwaltschaft 2242/I, p. 160.

67 Bütow, *Konflikt*, Appendix, pp. 72 ff. For a few days, Toller hid with Fürst Karl zu Löwenstein.

68 Mann had already delivered a written statement in favour of Toller by the beginning of June 1919. T. Mann, *Tagebücher 1918–1921*, ed. by P. de Mendelssohn (Frankfurt-on-Main, 1981), p. 257: entry of 3 June 1919.

69 Letter from Max Weber to Marianne Weber of 19 June 1919, Collection Max Weber-Schäfer, in private hands.

70 Reports from *Münchener Neueste Nachrichten*, no. 277, 16 July 1919, evening edition, p. 2; *Frankfurter Zeitung*, no. 518, 16 July 1919, second morning edition, p. 3, as well as Staatsarchiv Munich, Staatsanwaltschaft 2241/I. As was obviously customary in the procedure of the court-martial, no record was made of testimony. The condensed report in the Munich archives records only the sequence in which witnesses were heard. Weber's statement will appear in MWG I/16. S. Großmann, 'Prozeß Toller', *Vossische Zeitung*, no. 363, 19 July 1919, evening edition, p. 3. It should not go unmentioned that a few months later, following a performance of Toller's 'Die Wandlung', the *Rote Fahne* wrote of Toller: 'a wonderful person, but a darling of the bourgeoisie who is politically completely ignorant'. *Rote Fahne*, no. 74, 19 December 1919, cited in ter Haar, *Toller*, p. 108.

71 S. Großmann, *Der Hochverräter Ernst Toller. Die Geschichte eines Prozesses* (Berlin 1919), p. 36.

72 *Der Kampf. Südbairische Tageszeitung der Unabhängigen Sozialdemokratie Deutschlands*, Munich, no. 16, 18 July 1919, p. 3.

73 Toller, *Gesammelte Werke*, Vol. 1, p. 49: closing statement before the court-martial, according to the *Münchener Post*, 17 July 1919.

74 Cf. Mommsen, *Max Weber and German Politics*, pp. 442–3. Toller was sentenced to five years' imprisonment. He served his whole sentence.

75 See above, p. 371.

76 *Biography*, pp. 603 ff. Emphasis in original.

77 Toller, *Eine Jugend*, pp. 158–9. In a manuscript for a speech in English dating from 1936 or 1937 Toller took up this line of thought once again. Toller, *Gesammelte Werke*, Vol. 1, p. 78.

78 Cf. Bütow, *Konflikt*, pp. 91–136.

79 ter Haar, *Toller*, pp. 52–3. The concept 'in spite of all' (*dennoch*) was of great significance

for the bourgeois left during the Weimar period, especially for the Weltbühne circle to which Toller also belonged. Cf. K. R. Grossmann, *Ossietzkiy. Ein deutscher Patriot* (Frankfurt-on-Main, 1973). Weber also used equally emphatically but in a different sense this *dennoch* in 'Politics as a vocation': FMW, p. 128.

80 Toller, *Gesammelte Werke*, Vol. 1, p. 162; speech on the occasion of the anniversary of the Revolution in 1925.

81 For Toller during the Weimar Republic, cf. S. Lamb, 'Ernst Toller and the Weimar Republic', in K. Bullivant (ed.), *Culture and Society in the Weimar Republic* (Manchester, 1977), pp. 71–93.

82 ibid., pp. 78 ff.

83 Letter from Max Weber to Robert Michels of 4 August 1908, Roberto Michels papers, Fondazione Luigi Einaudi, Turin.

84 *Biography*, p. 490.

85 Mommsen, *Max Weber and German Politics*, p. 442.

26 Max Weber and Antonio Gramsci

CARL LEVY

for James Joll

Introduction

In early 1898, a young German scholar suffered nervous collapse: 'an evil something out of the subterranean unconsciousness ... grasped him by its claws.'[1] Thirteen years later, an even younger Sardinian scholarship student at the University of Turin tottered on the brink of mental disintegration. Later he recalled that winter of 1911 when he had been seriously ill 'as a result of cold and exhaustion.' 'I used to be obsessed by the vision of a colossal spider which would come down from its web every night while I was asleep, and suck out my brains.'[2]

Incessant agonizing battles for mental stability were shared by Antonio Gramsci and Max Weber.[3] Both men were strongly puritanical, impatient with shoddy workmanship and did not suffer fools or windbags. They were outstanding polymaths and not a little difficult. Both belonged to a breed of irregulars who foresaw how specialization and rationalization were destroying the sociological conditions for the generation of further cohorts of generalist humanists.[4] They had in common a classical education, a firm grounding in political theory and philosophy, and a thorough immersion in Italo-German historicism. If Weber in his early maturity was an economist, historian, philosopher and self-educated theologian, Gramsci was qualified to teach linguistics, philosophy, history of literature and history. Weber came from the *Bildungsbürgertum* and Gramsci from its 'democratic' confrère, the *classe dei colti* (educated middle classes). Weber, like Gramsci's obsession, Benedetto Croce, lived as a rentier-scholar; the Sardinian came from the lower echelons of the intelligentsia. Gramsci was born into a rural Southern bureaucratic family, which to the unfamiliar eye might appear to share the same misery as its peasant neighbours. But the ability to read and even to send one's son to *liceo* and possibly to university and to a legal career, made them the object of envy and resentment. 'He is the greatest of Western Marxists', Tom Nairn writes of Gramsci, 'but it cannot be without some significance that he was also a product of the West's most remote periphery, and of conditions which, half a century later it became fashionable to call "Third World". No comparable Western intellectual came from such a background. He was a barbed gift of the backwoods to the metropolis, and some aspects of his originality always reflected this distance.'[5] During their lives Gramsci and Weber never achieved consistent success. Gramsci, the *maestro manqué*, sought to turn the Italian Communist Party into a pedagogic institution, and his final testament, the

Prison Notebooks, were written as *private* theoretical reflections on how Marxism might be taught and then 'spontaneously' incorporated into the everyday philosophies of working-class people. His greatest position of power, however, had been achieved not through moral suasion, but through the very mechanical process of Comintern co-option. Weber, who like Gramsci dreamt of advising the Modern Prince, could not hold his own among the caucus politicians. Furthermore, their intellectual genius was never fully appreciated before their deaths, owing in part to the unusual quality of their texts.

Weber's work was fragmentary and disconnected, 'found in journals or left unedited'. Marianne Weber's persistence and devotion played no little part in its collection and publication.[6] *Economy and Society* was in large part written 'without benefit of footnotes and other customary scholarly paraphernalia.'[7] As for Gramsci, besides his prolific and theoretically rich journalism (a profession that Weber, unlike many of his class, felt was important and honourable), he wrote his main text quite literally in an iron cage. For obvious reasons, Gramsci's testament was an extended series of notebooks (*note, noterelle, appunti*), not finished texts. He was never quite certain if his work would be confiscated and destroyed by his captors and, during his first two years in prison, he was allowed only to write personal letters. Indeed there is 'continuity and overlapping between *Letters from Prison* and *Prison Notebooks*'.[8] It took the timely interventions of Piero Sraffa, Tatiana Schult (his sister-in-law) and Palmiro Togliatti to preserve the notebooks from destruction. After the war, they were published in politically inspired spasms. We have only possessed a scientifically correct version since 1975, and we are currently witnessing a similar operation on the volumes of pre-1926 newspaper articles. There is certainly something ironic about the exegesis of these two polymaths' unfinished work, by younger generations of rationalized specialists. Indeed, we might argue that it is a last example of doctrinal texts disseminated through networks of scholars/scholastics. And, since the texts are incomplete, we can also, perhaps fancifully, imagine this as a form of intellectual's folklore; at least, I believe, both Gramsci and Weber would have found that deliciously ironic.

At the 1977 Florence Gramsci conference, it was claimed that a good deal of the political reflections found in the *Prison Notebooks* were characterized by explicit or implicit, specific or generic references to Max Weber.[9] This assertion is greatly exaggerated, but on the other hand there is scope for a comparison – necessarily synoptic – of the main themes found in Gramsci's and Weber's political and scientific writings – placing them in the broader sociocultural force-field which characterizes the still largely unexplored encounter of socialism and modern sociology. I think the most important are their attitudes towards and conceptions of leadership formation in mass societies (elites and democracy); legitimate domination and hegemony; intellectuals, bureaucracy and state formation; charisma and caesarism; religion and research methodologies; science. The following should be considered merely my own *noterelle*. However, after a preliminary survey of the field, I feel confident that a larger study of Weber and Gramsci, such as Löwith's beautiful essay on the affinities between Marx and Weber,[10] would not only add something to the histories of socialism and sociology but also serve as a mutually beneficial heuristic device. First, I turn to a short examination of the force-field which bound Gramsci's and Weber's project together; glancing at the fortunes of Weber in Italy in the 1920s and 1930s, and the extent of Gramsci's knowledge of Weber before incarceration and during his captivity.

The Educated Middle Classes in Germany and Italy: 1830–1914

Germany and Italy were both young nation states composed of a bewildering number of local subcultures, both were societies rent by regional, social, religious and class cleavages. The educated middle class dominated the pre-unification German liberal nationalist movement, as James Sheehan argues, 'precisely because in a society without an extensive communications system, without national markets, a national press, or unified political institutions, professional relationships, and above all, the nexus of the state's bureaucratic institutions [were] of great political significance, for the development of supralocal personal and political ties'.[11] In Italy, the *Risorgimento's* shock troops were largely young university graduates from the *ceto medio*.[12] In a country where less than 10 per cent of the population spoke the national language in 1861, an educated middle class was bound to play a role that far exceeded its numerical strength. However, while the *Bildungsbürgertum*, especially the vast majority of university professors and state functionaries, were easily integrated into Bismarck's expansive version of the Prussian civil service state, the Italian state remained weak; it never created an effective bureaucracy or educational system, nor did industrialization affect Italy as rapidly as it did Germany. Long-lasting alienation from the tarnished results of the *Risorgimento* affected sections of the *classe dei colti* and pushed some towards socialism as a form of populist salvation at first, and later, more importantly, as a strategy of modernization and national integration. Besides, the Italian Catholic landed elites, unlike the Junkers, opposed the new state: what we witness is a bifurcation of the *classe dei colti* into rulers and *sovversivi*; usually, after a few years or decades of 'crowd management', many of the latter would join and reinforce the former. Mosca and Pareto did not have far to search for living examples of a circulation of elites.[13]

Social/Political Apprenticeships

Gramsci became a socialist during the first post-positivist generation, when a majority of his intellectual contemporaries were embracing anti-socialist nationalism and philosophical idealism. His Marxism was refracted through the unorthodox lenses of *La Voce* and individuals such as Salvemini, Croce and Gentile.[14] With Weber, Gramsci shared an appreciation for Nietzsche.[15] Gramsci's superman, however (like Jaurès's), was the collective socialist party. Revolution was a revaluation of bourgeois values, and the modern proletariat served as the human dynamite to clear away the ruins of pre-capitalist humanist culture. Gramsci always retained a deep fascination for Russian and Italian Futurism.

If Weber had been born an Italian he certainly would have been able, if he had desired, to achieve a working relationship with the socialists. It was the generation reaching maturity in the 1890s that dominated Italian socialism before 1914. And Weber, like Robert Michels, would have been happily accepted by its university professor leadership. Michels had been active in the German and Italian socialist movements. He had had his German career abruptly terminated when he openly declared for the German Social Democratic Party (SPD). For Michels, the strain was too much and he sought succour at the University of Turin, rapidly becoming a relatively important socialist intellectual. In Italy, before the First World War, the university professor could retain and even increase his standing in certain sections of polite society by his membership of the Italian Socialist Party (PSI), while simultaneously mixing with the *braccianti* (landless labourers) of the Po Valley. It was a phenomenon which fascinated the chastened Michels when he wrote his useful if uneven study of the Italian educated classes' relationship to the labour and socialist movements.[16] Weber possessed greater political affinities with free-trade radical liberals cast in the Einaudi or, slightly more socialist in inclination, Salvemini mould. The SPD, however, could never form a lasting relationship with liberalism. The National Liberals were firmly attached to the anti-socialist coalition and attempts at creating electoral pacts with the Progressives merely drove left-liberal voters towards the anti-socialists. So Weber's position in Germany was a good deal more beleaguered and isolated than that of comparable Italian intellectuals. He liked to think of himself as a class-conscious bourgeois 'who opposed the entrenched Junkers and the rightwing romantics no less than the petty-bourgeois labour movement and the Utopian leftwing intellectuals'.[17]

Equally, Gramsci's mentors were neither far removed from Weber's basic outlook nor from his major political concerns. The sober free-trade liberalism of Einaudi, Giretti and Salvemini railed against the 'monarcho-bureaucratic Giolittian state'. Croce and Gentile, like Weber, lampooned the self-satisfied positivist evolutionism of the Italian Socialist Party. Gramsci's political coming-of-age occurred just when the first election under universal manhood suffrage (1913) signalled the decline and fall of the Post-*Risorgimento* elitist liberal compromise. It was the combination of his cultural apprenticeship, his direct experience of the Italian bureaucratic state in Sardinia and the heady modernizing atmosphere of Turin, joined with the universal European radicalization during the First World War, that laid the foundations for his 'pre-figurative', ethical and libertarian Marxism of the *Biennio Rosso* (1919–1920). Weber would have appreciated the voluntarism and ethical libertarianism of the young Gramsci (so similar to his Russian social revolutionary friends in Heidelberg), even if, on deeper reflection, he would have probably placed him in the category of 'romantic literati'.

Elective Affinities

Nevertheless, important themes join Weber to 'young'/'old' Gramsci. They shared a deep interest in identifying efficient mechanisms of capital accumulation and leadership generation. The inevitability of productivist criteria in industrial societies and an underlying and contradictory critique of bureaucratic growth can be found in both. For Weber and Gramsci, pre-capitalist institutions prevented the full flowing of modern 'healthy' capitalism. In turn, both respected vibrant Anglo-Saxon civil society and envied its rich selection of voluntary organizations. Both men were fascinated by 'Americanism' and impatient with the 'literati' radicalism that condemned Americans' lack of traditions or good breeding. It was a fortunate aspect of America that it lacked a large population of non-productive pre-capitalist classes, whom Gramsci called 'the pensioners of history'. In the Anglo-Saxon examples, they identified capitalist societies which compared favourably to the bureaucratic timidity found at their door-steps. There is also a certain symmetry in both thinkers' estimation of how bureaucracy affected capitalism's future. Gramsci thought that Agnelli the dynamic entrepreneur had, under the effects of imperialist monopoly capitalism, been transformed into *cavaliere* Agnelli: the plutocratic figurehead emperor of an empire ready to be self-managed by heroic Sorelian producers. Weber, 'the liberal in despair', predicted how capitalism reaching its maturity would generate spiritually noxious bureaucracies, threatening to strangle spontaneity and creativity and undermining free enterprise itself.[18] Both men exaggerated trends. Gramsci's strategy was severely weakened by his underestimation of the autonomy of the new technical middle classes and the ingenuity and flexibility of the capitalists.[19] Similarly, Weber's prophecies seem more coloured by the currents of cultural pessimism he swam in: real bureaucracies (state, capitalist or otherwise) were far more complex entities, cantankerously individualistic and certainly less rational than Weber's dark broodings would allow.[20]

Weber in Italy

Although one of Weber's chief legacies to social science is the notion of a separation of scientific inquiry from partisan preference, his reception in Italy was filtered through the cut-and-thrust of politics. Weber's work was known to a limited reading public during the *Biennio Rosso*, chiefly through the translation of *Parliament and Government in a Reconstructed Germany* (Bari, 1919), published under the guidance of Benedetto Croce.[21] Croce was one of the few Italian intellectuals who knew Weber's work, particularly his theory of rationalization, but he opposed its underlying assumptions. In his review, which served as an introduction to the English translation of Carlo Antoni's famous study, the Italian monograph that joined Weber's already existing reputation as a historian of religion, law and agriculture to his specific scientific methodology, Croce notes impatiently that Weber's disenchantment with reality flattened history; his 'attempts to explain causally and psychologically acts of spirit which are essentially free, original and creative', were dismissed.[22] Instead, Weber was used by two different groups of liberals. For an older or more moderate group, Weber was marshalled to show the continual necessity for technical and bureaucratic hierarchies in all modern societies. Italian variations of sovietism and homegrown syndicalism were discredited by using the arguments found in *Parliament and Government*.[23] On the other hand Weber's biting criticisms of uncontrollable and irresponsible bureaucracy found deep resonance in Italy. It was hoped that the war-swollen bureaucracy might be tamed and controlled by a vigorous parliamentary process, which decades of transformism had enervated. In this regard, Weber's *Parliament and Government* echoed Einaudi's postwar writing.

Younger liberals gathered around Piero Gobetti's series of pre-1926 Turin journals, especially *La Rivoluzione Liberale* and its associated Northern supporters' circles, used Weber in more radical fashion. The young liberals wanted to modernize and deprovincialize liberalism. Weber's notion of a Calvinist work-ethic found a ready audience here. Gobetti sought a new elite to replace the discredited and rapidly fading pre-fascist political ruling class. He identified in the skilled Turin working class the carriers of the bourgeois work-ethic, and envisaged a new industrial system similar to German co-determination after the Second World War. Capitalism, he argued, would be transfused with fresh blood from the shopfloor. Gobetti's heterodox political philosophy linked him with Gramsci's Sorelian producers' communism, on the one hand, and Walther Rathenau's version of organized capitalism, on the other. Gobetti's knowledge of Weber's *Protestant Ethic* came chiefly from a small group of neo-Protestants centred around the journal *Conscientia*. He rapidly assimilated the Calvinist work-ethic to American Taylorism or Fordism. In his review of Ford's autobiography, he anticipated and influenced Gramsci's reflections in the *Notebooks*, although it must be said that Gobetti's metaphorical equation Calvinism = Fordism was more heavily influenced by Weberian texts, whereas Gramsci's original interest in Taylorism and socialist machine culture came via Sorel, the Futurists and a group of Turin worker/technician anarchists. [24] Croce's critical interest and Gobetti's journals became chief sources of Weber's thesis. Giovanni Ansaldo, the editor of Genoa's reformist socialist *Il Lavoro*, compared the vigorous political culture of Anglo-Saxon capitalist nations with the lethargy and authoritarianism prevalent in Italy, using Sombart, Weber and Troeltsch as examples, while Mario Manilio Rossi and Filippo Burzio became their translators and specialists on their writings. Rossi's book, *L'ascesi capitalista* (1928), was the first organic exposition of Weber's thought in the Italian language. [25]

However, it should be recalled that a linkage between modern capitalist mentalities and Protestantism had been circulating in Italian intellectual circles for at least a generation. During the post-war crisis it became part and parcel of a larger controversy about the failure of the post-*Risorgimento* state and the *rivoluzione mancata*. [26] It was through this channel that part of Gramsci's knowledge and interest in Max Weber arises. Gramsci's *Southern Question* (1926) was just one text in a wide-ranging selection of critical analyses of the *Risorgimento* and its aftermath. Part of Gramsci's inspiration derived from the *Rivoluzione Liberale* group, particularly Guido Dorso's *La rivoluzione meridonale* (1925) and Gobetti's *Risorgimento senza eroi* (1924). Gobetti was a collaborator in the first two series of *L'Ordine Nuovo* and Gramsci occasionally contributed to his journals. Nevertheless, there were differences with certain collaborators in Gobetti's literary enterprises. Gramsci bitterly criticized the neo-Protestants in 1925 and 1926 for attempting to create a Marxist Protestant group within the maximalist rump of the PSI. Chiefly he objected to the tendency which emphasized the spiritual effects of the Protestant Revolution and disregarded the fine interplay of cultural and material interests. But his critical attitudes had been gestating for eight years, and can be traced back to his interest in the failure of the Reformation in Russia.[27]

There is a curious circulation of ideas going on here. Gramsci equates his biting and satirical criticism of the neo-Protestants with an earlier attack on Thomas Masaryk's study of Russia's failure to produce a religious reformation and how this had long-lasting and disastrous effects on its 'gelatinous' civil society. In 1918, Gramsci translated and published Trotsky's critique of Masaryk.[28] Trotsky argued that Russia's missing Reformation could be explained by a non-existent independent urban culture and its related economy. Gramsci assimilated this point into the later debate. The links between religious practice and urban culture bear a remarkable similarity to Weber's own sociology of religion. But there was another striking parallel. By 1916, Gramsci had argued that every revolution was preceded by an intense operation of cultural criticism; thus the Enlightenment preceded the French Revolution. However, without a necessary linkage with an emergent 'corporate' class, the *philosophes* would have remained irrelevant. Religion and ideologies prospered in so far as a social group seized upon their tenets to justify and codify its conduct. The serious weakness of the neo-Protestants, Gramsci recalled in the *Notebooks*, was their failure to link spirit with grubby quotidian reality. In the context of the middle twenties debate, this meant that Gramsci could show sympathy with left-wing liberals such as Dorso and Gobetti, who drew the correct historical analogies and envisaged an alliance of southern peasantry and northern producers (with the latter supplying the ideology), as the only solution to the crisis of elitist liberalism.[29]

Before prison, Gramsci was fully acquainted with *Parliament and Government* and had a firmer grasp of Weber's ex-student, Michels, than Gobetti had. Both were used in a synthetic fashion. In 1922, Gramsci commenced to construct a Marxist theory of fascism, which went beyond primitive varieties of the preventive counter-revolution thesis; at the same time, according to Leonardo Paggi, he translated Weber's example of Junker domination and distortion of the prewar German state into its Italian equivalent. The Italian bureaucracy, and the class that supplied its functionaries, had developed into a caste of its own, prepared to support Mussolini once he scored his initial victories in the countryside. The decline of the PSI was explained by its precocious bureaucratization due to the 'negative democracy' of the Italian parliament. The PSI, he explained in 1922, had substituted *travet* (pen-pushers') consciousness for the proletarian's. This usage of the sociology of elites was not restricted to Gramsci: many early Communists saw its utility. Zinoviev, for instance, had written a study of the deradicalization of the SPD, which leaned heavily on Michels, while Bukharin, during the war, displayed a keen interest (much to Lenin's annoyance) in Weber, Pareto, Mosca and Michels.[30]

Weber in the *Notebooks:* Overview

Even if Weber is cited sparingly in the *Notebooks*, this does not disallow his influence. An acquaintance with Gramsci's style shows how his usage of Weber indicates an interesting case of influence, one step beyond a series of elective affinities arising from a shared historical-cultural experience and similar intellectual problematics. His usage was not merely incidental. It evinced an attempt, spurred on by his precocious intellectual imagination, to bridge the gap between affinity and intimate knowledge. In this respect, the example of the Masaryk debate is an instructive example of how Gramsci digested and utilized the limited resources at hand in his prison cell. And in his footnotes to the passage and in others that recapitulate the argument, Gramsci assimilates the Czech's examination of Russian civil society with Gobetti's usage of Weber's *Protestant Ethic*. We are led to believe that Gramsci's trajectory would have given him a greater and more fruitful appreciation of Weber if he had known more of Weber's central works. There are certainly limits to Gramsci's knowledge of Weber and it is worth while underlining that Italian Eurocommunist theorists have overestimated it. We do not know what Gramsci would have done if he had survived. If he had returned to Sardinia to devote himself to study and writing, then Weber's work would have aided his project immensely. As a heuristic tool, Weber's historical sociology, and even his sociological methodology, would have sparked an interchange, although a full acceptance by Gramsci of Weber's methodology would have necessitated a complete break with Marxism. That is why this chapter does not seek to place Weberian sociology in a direct comparison with Gramsci's Marxism. Rather, the approach used here is to segment each thinker's grander system of thought into a series of converging underlying thematic components, highlighting the extent to which Gramscian Marxism approaches Weber's sociology and also pinpointing the inescapable differences in each.

Gramsci used three Weberian texts: *Parliament and Government* (1919), not available in prison but quoted from memory on several occasions; passages from *Economy and Society*, transmitted via an article by Robert Michels ('Les partis politiques et la contrainte sociale' *Mercure de France*, 1 May 1928), and *The Protestant Ethic*, available via an Italian serialization in 1931–1932 (in *Nuovi Studi di diritto, economia e politica*).[31] Michels was another source: Gramsci had several of his volumes in prison and was, as mentioned, fully conversant with his political sociology. (Both Michels and Mosca taught at the University of Turin when Gramsci was a student.) Gramsci had a copy of Michels's *Corso di sociologia politica* (1927), which introduced a number of Weberian concepts into Italy, although Gramsci did not possess Michels's partial translation of *Wirtschaft und Gesellschaft* (1934). More importantly, Gramsci had read Michels's *Bedeutende Männer* (1927), with its incisive biographical portrait of Weber. (It should be borne in mind that Gramsci was fairly fluent in German and, in fact, criticized the Italian translation of *Parliament and Government*.) Gramsci also had copies of Werner Sombart's *Il capitalismo moderno* (1925) and *Le socialisme et le mouvement social au XIX siècle. Chronique du mouvement social 1860–1897* (1898), as well as Georg Simmel's *Il conflitto della civiltà moderna* (1925). Finally, the Webers were fairly well known within Communist Party leadership, and Alfred's works were being used by Giuseppe Berti, Scoccimarro and Bordiga at the makeshift Party School for political prisoners on Lipari in 1927.[32]

Weber is mentioned in five passages of the *Notebooks:* in *Quaderno 2*

(1929–33, pp. 230–1), where his notion of charisma is placed alongside Michels's; in *Quaderno 3* (1930, pp. 386–8), where the weakness of prewar Italo-German liberal capitalism is compared, employing Weber's *Parliament and Government* as a central text; in *Quaderno 8* (1931–9, pp. 1086–7), where the *Protestant Ethic* and the equation modern Marxism = Calvinism makes its appearance; in *Quaderno 11* (1932–3, pp. 1389–92), where it reappears in a passage on how new conceptions of the world (hegemony) are disseminated and vulgarized; finally, in Gramsci's fascinating notes for a cross-national study of intellectuals (*Quaderno 12*, 1932, pp. 1526–7). Most of Gramsci's central concerns are repeated in each of these passages, and merge with others where Weberian concepts may have been adopted without direct reference. So, for instance, when Gramsci employs the analogy of Piedmont to Prussia as an example of passive revolution in the nineteenth century, he apparently refers, directly or indirectly, to *Parliament and Government* and certainly to other non-Weberian texts. Or, when Gramsci refers to Bonapartism/Caesarism and its routinization within bureaucratized parliamentary or presidential systems of government (MacDonaldism *et al.*), Weber's variety of 'caesars' and the routinization of charisma may not have been far from Gramsci's mind.[33]

Sociology and Science[34]

By now it is a commonplace that Gramsci criticized severely not only racially based Italian positivist sociology but also Third Internationalist variants of dialectical materialism (notably Bukharin's) for flattening the Marxist concept of praxis.[35] In short, when Gramsci thought of sociology, he imagined pseudo-laws and tautologies that petrified human action. This becomes particularly clear in his extended critique of Michels's political sociology, with its striking parallels to Weber's own well-known objections. However, Gramsci reached his position mainly by employing his education in philosophical idealism, and particularly its twentieth-century offspring Croceanism, to demolish Michels. He knew little, if anything, about post-positivist sociology. Like other Italians, Gramsci thought of Weber as a cultural historian and historian of religion; he knew nothing of his sociological methodology except the misleading interpretation of it by Michels. In addition, Gramsci's knowledge of German historiography was decidedly limited.[36]

Generally speaking, the gaps in Gramsci's sociological knowledge are quite astounding. He knew nothing of Durkheim (even if his culture was largely derived from French sources), Marcel Mauss, Lévy-Bruhl, Cooley, Znaniecki, Tönnies or Mannheim. Spencer is mentioned in passing, Veblen quickly liquidated and Schumpeter missing. Nor, for that matter, are many Marxist political economists mentioned, except Luxemburg, Graziadei (who gets a rough ride) and an intriguing reference to Grossmann.[37] For a man who considered Piero Sraffa as a close comrade, this is extraordinary. Notwithstanding recent Eurocommunist attempts to present Gramsci as a third in a triad of Weber, Keynes and Gramsci, his notes on the growth of state interventionism East and West are brilliant intuitions, crying out for that comparative reading of the moderns that Gramsci never had the chance to accomplish. He was very much one of the greatest graduates of prewar Italian humanist culture.

Nevertheless, an anti-functionalist interpretation of Gramsci does allow one to construct a provisional outline of a new 'sociology' (if I may employ that term without offending his shade), which attempts to go beyond the determinist/positivist model, and in this sense is certainly an interesting if underdeveloped challenger to Weber's methodological revolution. It attempts to understand society on three levels of abstraction, incorporating and transcending the automatic iron laws of elitist political science. First, there are habitual and intellectual behaviours that run in a continuum from *senso comune* or folkloric beliefs to hegemonic ideologies. Secondly, there are the primordial facts of any society: the 'technical' division of labour between rulers and ruled, specialist and layman. Finally, there are the dull constraints of the social infrastructure. These three levels can be equated respectively to civil society (voluntary organizations), political society (the state and its coercive apparatus) and economic society (the modes of production).[38] Gramsci's 'sociology' was an original synthesis of Marxist and Hegelian concepts, weighing heavily in the direction of analysis of the ensemble of superstructures (civil and political societies).[39] It was not that he simply forgot about the economic infrastructure. Rather, like Weber, he envisaged historical change arising from a struggle between social classes and contending world-views created by intellectuals (individual human beings), which are incorporated by classes. Ideologies are not mere reflections of differing modes of production; rather, they have a certain logic and independence of their own.

How Gramsci would have reacted to Weber's definition of science is an open question, yet it can be surmised that Gramsci's definition was rather closer than Weber's ex-student Lukács's. All of Gramsci's instincts would have attracted him to a Weberian notion of science. Certainly Gramsci's view stood closer to Weber's than to Croce's. Although he employed the arsenal of Italian philosophical idealism in his battle against positivism in all its varieties, he was careful to criticize Gentile and Croce for undermining the cultural prestige of the Italian scientific community.[40] Nor did Gramsci have any sympathy for Lukács's conception of science as an ideological superstructure of the bourgeoisie. Instead, he conceived of the scientific revolution and its effects on post-Galilean societies in much the same fashion as Weber. Joseph Femia has noted the affinities.

> Gramsci's concept of science, as a matter of historical fact, is not all that different from that of Weber, who – as is known – resolutely upheld the cognitive supremacy of the scientific method. Weber, too, thought that descriptions of natural phenomena had to be filtered through *a priori* assumptions, but also recognised that when these assumptions blatantly conflict with the data of the external world, they must be discarded. While scientists do not, to his mind, discover an external reality, totally independent of the human mind, neither do they 'produce' scientific theories in the same way that ideologists produce theories of man and society. There is no reason to believe that Gramsci disagreed with this characterisation of the scientific method.[41]

One could write an interesting essay contrasting the differences, and sorting out the affinities, between Weber's, Gramsci's, Croce's and Sorel's notions of science, and how they affected the creation of a critical and anti-positivist sociology. One line of argument would have to investigate how far Gramsci adopted the notion, or the approximate Sorelian notion, of the ideal-type (his *diremptions*).[42] Another avenue of exploration would contrast Weber's and Croce's notions of science with Gramsci's. Gramsci accepts Croce's criticism of the importation of the physical scientific method into historical investigation. On the other hand, he does not deny the need for some types of scientific criteria. A Marxist theory of historical reality, in the same fashion as Weber's, could only set out possibilities, not iron-clad laws. Even Gramsci's division of society between superstructures and infrastructure is recognized as a methodological convenience.[43]

To sum up, if we understand 'Gramscianism' to be a canon of historical research, and not a political system, then his idea of social science, incorporating structural constraints and voluntary action in any explanatory framework, comes quite close to Weber's. However, if we accept his system as a holistic philosophy, then his attempts to bridge the gap between science (fact) and ideology (value) arrive at entirely non-Weberian conclusions. At a rather sophisticated level, even Gramsci's Marxism must be classified as a scientific socialism, and he would have objected to the famous Weberian separation of ethical socialism, on one hand, from Marxism as a heuristic device, on the other. This, of course, is one of his central disagreements with Croce. In turn, Gramsci's image of his 'future city', the marriage of the cold expert with the passionate layman, would have been considered dangerously Utopian by Weber.[44]

Charisma and Caesarism

Gramsci and Weber shared Machiavelli's and the elitist sociologists' method of isolating ethical intentions from an empirical and technical science of politics.[45] Both thinkers, however, had their disagreements with elitists, especially Michels. Naturally the concept of charisma attracted Gramsci, especially as his political proclivities developed in an authoritarian direction.

Giorgio Galli has differentiated four phases of Gramsci's relationship with theories of elites.[46] First, there is an early Mussolinianism, when the party is considered a rejuvenating elite (1914–16). This is followed by Gramsci's council communist interlude (1916–20), when the entire Northern working class becomes a species of collective elite. A third phase is ushered in with the rise of Fascism and the bolshevization of the Communist Party: the worker elite is guided, as it were, by a remote-control Leninist vanguard. Finally, we arrive at the *Notebooks*, where he assimilates the elitists' imagery while criticizing their methodology. The pre-1926 Leninist vanguard is converted into a pedagogic elite. What we have is a Leninism that recent Eurocommunist interpreters have quite rightly compared with the Lenin of the last desperate struggles to tame the Soviet bureaucracy by administering cultural therapy.[47] Gramsci travelled a long way. In 1917, he renounced any comparison of the socialist movement with an army; socialist were not officers leading a proletarian infantry and, even as the proletariat's consciousness, he attached no sense of duality, no separation between scientific socialism and everyday experience, as did Kautsky and Lenin.[48] One year later 'the Russian Utopia' was preserved and defended through hierarchical and charismatic leadership. So that freedom could be 'organized', post-revolutionary Russia had installed a necessary dictatorship. It was, however, one that allowed a variety of institutions (Soviets, workers, councils, etc.) and socialist and anarchist parties and groups to exist at its base; at its apex was a freely accepted dynamic individual, Lenin, whose power was 'largely spiritual'.[49] Gramsci's obituary of Lenin six years later was simply entitled '*Capo*'. Lenin was a unique historical individual, the necessary dictator of the proletariat, since his dictatorship was progressive and laid the foundations for greater freedom. Gramsci still stresses the need for circulation of elites within the hierarchy and identifies most of Lenin's power as being in his charismatic power, not in the Cheka and the Red Army; however, the plurality of institutions and parties has disappeared:[50] there is only one party that incarnates the proletarian dictatorship.[51] In the *Notebooks*, historical studies and political values are so closely intertwined that it is difficult to fathom what position he really took.

We do know that Michels's versions of charisma and caesarism are roundly criticized by Gramsci. Both Weber and Gramsci take Michels to task for his shoddy scholarship and his famous iron law of oligarchy. Weber thought it an optical illusion. Michels had reified a series of interesting observations about modern political parties into an untenable universalizing conclusion.[52] Each historical case must be examined separately. 'Democracy as such', Weber explains, 'is opposed to the "rule" of bureaucracy, in spite and perhaps because of its unavoidable yet unintentional promotion of bureaucratization. Under certain conditions, democracy creates breaks in the bureaucratic pattern and impediments to bureaucratic organization.'[53]

Similarly, Gramsci is sceptical of Michels's discussion of socialist charismatic leadership. Lassalle's (and Stalin's?) leaderships were historically specific. 'So-called charisma', he explains, 'in the modern world will always coincide with a primitive phase of mass politics, when doctrine presents itself to the masses as something nebulous and incoherent and there is a need of an infallible pope to act as interpreter.'[54] Furthermore, Weber would wearily have nodded in agreement at Gramsci's characterization of Michels as the Linnaeus of political sociology, who classified political phenomena in a purely descriptive and ahistorical manner.[55] Weber had previously noted that Michels's iron law of oligarchy remained flawed precisely because he had drawn upon anecdotal material from France, Italy, and Germany, without noting the specific and highly original complexions of these nations' political and cultural histories.[56]

Democracy and Leadership[57]

The major theme of Weber's and Gramsci's works is the birth and death of liberal societies and the bureaucratization of economic and political life. Both men considered the need for skilled professional leadership in modern societies to be absolutely essential. Generals, Gramsci remarks in the *Notebooks*, can always reconstruct their armies. For Weber, regimes may come and go, but if the bureaucratic hierarchy remains in office, the state will continue to function.

The difference between Weber and Gramsci was essentially how many generals, or political leaders, were required to run the machine. Weber envisaged his charismatic leader as Lloyd George, the product of elite, liberal capitalist democracy, not Lenin, the product of democratic centralism.[58] In the *Notebooks*, Gramsci was extremely candid about methods of choosing leadership. Democratic centralism was contrasted to bureaucratic centralism, which he described as a form of political organization choked by a stultified caste of fanatics. If his Leninism was expansive it certainly was not pluralistic, not even in the 1918 sense of the word.[59] Weber, too, did not really believe in democratic culture as a universal.[60] 'The *demos* itself', Weber notes, 'in the shape of a shapeless mass, never "governs" larger associations, but rather is governed. What changes is only the way in which the executive leaders are selected and the measure of influence that the *demos* or, better, that social circles from its midst are able to exert upon the content and direction of administrative activities by means of "public opinion".'[61] Gramsci put it similarly: under democratic centralism the eternal question of leader and followers becomes a technical one. The orchestra, he was fond to opine, never believes the conductor to be an oligarch. Gramscian organic intellectuals linked *capo* with *gregari* and performed similar roles to Weber's parliamentary deputies, or the Webbs's middle-level ('NCO') trade unionists.[62] They all assured a ceaseless circulation of elites and information, restraining megalomania at the top and fighting apathy at the bottom.

It is quite easy to imagine this solution as functionalist, without the necessity of a shred of democratic culture around, which is David Beetham's main contention concerning Weber's politics: elite-guided democratization created a more efficient and therefore more powerful German nation to compete in the ceaseless world struggle.[63] A careful reading of the latest treatments of Gramsci's politics by a sceptic such as Femia[64] and a true believer such as Showstack Sassoon,[65] shows that democratic centralism ultimately rested on the goodwill of the leadership; they or he held all the cards in their hands. Nowhere do we find mechanisms that allow for the creation of independent pressure groups and alternative political parties. If Gramsci, at times, seems to be harking back to his quasi-syndicalist factory-council days, he never says if councils or unions could have a leadership that did not chime with the party state. What, indeed, would he have thought of the Polish August? Besides, it was precisely the 'cultural Lenin's' attempt to increase the power of the middle-level leadership and establish a control commission to supervise the operations of the entire Soviet bureaucracy, which served as Stalin's first power base.[66] Weber would not have been surprised.

Hegemony and Legitimate Domination

The striking similarities between Weber's, Durkheim's and Gramsci's treatment of the classical political problem of consent and coercion has not gone unnoticed by Gramsci scholars, even if this has occasioned embarrassed noises.[67] And an alternative reading of Gramsci can easily conflate his 'sociology' with functionalist interpretations by Weber and Durkheim. It is certainly true that Durkheimian themes lurk beneath Gramsci's rich ethical language. Gallino explains this as an unconscious transfer via Sorel, and a shared reading of Renan.[68] But others deny such a 'functionalist' Gramsci. Buci-Glucksmann likens Gramsci's notion of hegemony to Weber's legitimate domination, but quickly adds a disclaimer that the Italian 'avoids the stumbling block of a Weberian institutionalism (primacy of institutions over parties), for the hegemonic apparatus is intersected by the primacy of the class struggle'. Gramscian hegemony, she continues, cannot be reduced to 'a Weberian problematic of legitimacy that combines violence with the ends of social integration'.[69] But it really depends on which Gramsci we are talking about. The 'cultural Leninist' allows for a degree of voluntary movement. The emphasis is on how different conceptions of the world (hegemonic ideologies) rise and fall, and on the connection between masses, middle strata and great intellectuals/statesmen. This 'Gramsci' is heavily superstructural and drenched in ethical language and imagery. Cultural criticism precedes every major revolution, and the intellectual-cum-pedagogic politician raises the spontaneous activity of the lower orders to effective politics. This 'Gramsci' reflects on the importance of the factory-council movement from his prison cell:

> The Turin movement was accused simultaneously of being 'spontaneist' and 'voluntarist', of Bergsonianism ... The leadership was not 'abstract', it neither consisted in mechanically repeating scientific or theoretical formulae, nor did it confuse politics, real action, with theoretical disquisition. It applied itself to real men, found in specific historical relations, with specific feelings, outlooks, fragmentary conceptions of the world, etc. This element of 'spontaneity' was not neglected, even less despised. It was educated, directed, purged of extraneous contaminations; the aim was to bring it into line with modern theory. It gave the masses a 'theoretical' consciousness of being creators of *historical* and *universal values*, of being founders of a State.[70]

Through Antonio Labriola, Gramsci had assimilated the legacy of Neapolitan liberal Hegelianism to socialist politics. From an emphasis on the pedagogical nature of the modern state, stimulating active participation of citizens in its affairs, Gramsci and Labriola envisaged Marxism as a benevolent but critical teacher of the labour movement.[71] How to reconcile the all-encompassing universalism of Hegelian Marxism with the stubborn particularisms of popular movements was never resolved. Gramsci certainly had the tendency to assume that the masses and the leadership vibrated on the same wavelength. In this sense, a succession of regimes founded on legitimate domination or Gramscian hegemony allow little room for deviance. For Weber, there is no such thing as illegitimate domination, and, for Gramsci, belief systems not connected to scientific ideologies (*senso buono*) tend to be relegated to folklore. This tendency of Gramsci's to vacillate between an appreciation of spontaneous movements outside or with difficulty subsumed under a functionalist system and a 'functionalist' Gramsci is revealed in a passage in the *Notebooks* where Weber is directly quoted and central to the argument.

Gramsci is discussing one of his pet themes: how a new conception of the world supersedes older competitors. There is a direct comparison between the Calvinist notion of salvation and predestination and Marxist determinism.

Both systems, he argues, rely on activist psychologies, arrived at through Vichian historical cunning, but not merely because ideas become transcendental shattering forces in themselves. Rather, Marxist and Calvinist world-views had been grounded in specific economic and political organizations.[72] It is a curious and characteristic passage where a coldly Machiavellian political description of how any 'church' generalizes and maintains its world-view, is rapidly transformed into a pragmatic discussion of what the modern Marxist Prince must do. From descriptive historical sociology, the reader is confronted with a political programme. There are three main points: the masses must be educated in a catechistic fashion; the cadres/clergy must be elevated intellectually; there must be room and resources at the top for the production of charismatic statesmen-cum-intellectuals. Gramsci concludes by explaining that the ideological 'panorama of an epoch' is changed when a functional apparatus modelled on these three points works efficiently; especially if it allows for the constant production of cadres/clergy and high intellectuals.[73]

A 'functionalist Gramsci' is also evident in his conception of class formation, which parallels Weber's own stratification model. For Gramsci, classes only exist when they are conscious of their cultural and economic distinctiveness. Classes without such attributes are termed corporate groups or entities in the *Notebooks*. Without intellectuals, classes can never achieve self-realization. There is certainly more than a striking similarity to Weber's idea of status groups possessing higher degrees of cohesion than social classes, which tend to be subdivided into innumerable parts, owing to conflicting corporate interests in the marketplace.[74] There is a difference in their two systems, however. In Weber's, the universal class tends to be the bureaucracy, at least in his theoretical writings. Gramsci is more optimistic, as long as a lucid policy of political pedagogy is followed. Both Weber and Gramsci define political parties as voluntary organizations. But whereas Weber is utterly cynical about the long-term survival of *Weltanschauung* parties, and sees the political process merely as a method to spin off dynamic leadership, Gramsci's system is dependent on parties as carriers of contrasting 'state spirits'. Changes in universal world-views are thereby effected by the triumph of one 'state spirit' carrying party over its rivals. Weber was less optimistic; he never believed that politics meant active mass participation; Gramsci's system implied the permanent and *disciplined* mobilization of the population. For Weber, modern industrial systems pre-empted revolutions; he only allowed for a series of *coup d'états* where an organized party seized control of a nationally defined coercive bureaucratic machine.

Comparative Studies of Bureaucracies, State Formation and Intellectuals

If Gramsci's Marxism as a political project was quite different from Weber's, 'Gramscianism' as a canon of historical research (to paraphrase Croce's famous formulation) brings forth interesting comparisons. Mommsen explains that Weber wanted to present 'a genuinely *universal* interpretation of western civilisation and of the uniqueness of its value system as well as the patterns of human behaviour. This was to be done by means of a comparative analysis which sufficiently explained societies throughout the history of mankind.'[75] Gramsci's interests ranged over a rich selection of national examples and, even if he had not the time to enrich upon his notes, the scope of his intended study would have approached Weber's. He planned to study the national formation of intellectuals, the formation of nation-states and the effect of pre-modern bureaucracies and religions upon them and, finally but perhaps more speculatively, a comparison of modern statist interventionism (Fordism, Fascism and Stalinism). The concept of passive revolution served as a key methodological tool. By this, Gramsci meant the political action of traditional status groups and/or pre-modern or independent bureaucratic forms within capitalist and post-capitalist societies. Thus, the Restoration's bureaucracy merely codified and institutionalized the advances of the French Revolution. Or the intervention of Fascist Italian or New Deal American governments in the Depression economy, by socializing the private costs of capitalists prepared the way for a revolutionary scenario more or less equivalent to a Habermasian legitimation crisis.

It was through such cunning of historical reason that Gramsci could imagine how a series of molecular movements and changes led up to an organic crisis, a revolution or, as he put it, a war of movement. Passive revolution was his canon of historical research, but not, he explicitly added, a political programme.[76] In several ways, Weberian ideas are strikingly similar. To begin with, there is the Gramscian concept of the traditional intellectual, which is almost identical to Weber's cultivated man. The carrier of humanist culture, the enemy of specialists: the English gentleman, the French humanist or the Chinese mandarin are trans-epochal (in the Marxist sense of epochs equalling historical stages in the evolution of modes of production), appearing to be capable of passing from one mode of production to another without losing a distinctly ancient form of status-consciousness. Traditional intellectuals, Gramsci explains, 'feel the continuity of their category and their history, the only category which has an uninterrupted history'.[77] Each nation-state, Gramsci argued, had its own type of traditional intellectual (except the United States, which lacked any). They possessed great political and cultural power, even if their economic fortunes had declined relatively. And so Weber is cited in Gramsci's comparison of Junkers, with their great caste consciousness founded on military power which approximated a class of 'warrior-priests', with the compromises effected by the English gentry, who retained a 'quasi-monopoly' power over the upper reaches of the state, but had to share power further down with a large group of organic modern intellectuals.[78]

Another important question for Gramsci was the nationally specific mechanism for the production of functionaries. In certain cases Gramsci allows state bureaucrats to possess quasi-class-consciousness. Thus the examples of Italy and Germany are used once again. But he also notes how, in the Soviet Union, the Bolshevik reliance on 'statolatry' to inculcate the state spirit into a 'gelatinous' civil society was in danger of spawning a virtually independent bureaucratic class.[79] To what extent he would have reached Trotsky's last pessimistic conclusions cannot be known. But his endorsement of forced industrialization, plus a not-too-secret admiration for industrial productivism, might have led him to Bruno Rizzi's belief that bureaucratic totalitarian industrialism was a progressive step, merely because it was more productive, even if all else might be sacrificed.[80]

To sum up: as a historian Gramsci shared Weber's interest in the spread of bureaucratization, the rise of credentialization and the construction of a legal-rational order.[81] Like Weber, he appreciated the large degree of independence intellectuals and bureaucrats might have.

On the other hand, the method of Weber's historical sociology, at times, came quite close to Marxist monistic materialism, except that Weber merely extended the Marxist interest in the separation of the means of production from the producers to the fields of education, religion and politics. To a great extent Weber's underlying telos, even if he denied such a thing, was the worldwide growth of officialdom. It would not be difficult to identify Gramsci's telos as the universalization of the intellectuals and the intelligentsia's style of life. However, differences also remain. Weber became increasingly abstract, and his last cross-national comparative typologies do not retain historical evolutionary dynamics. Ideal-typical forms of domination clash with Marxist historical epochs. Weber quite deliberately placed the bureaucratic model of domination at the dawn of history, and to rub his point in, he compared the bureaucracy of ancient Egypt with the possible future fate of Soviet Russia.

Gramsci outlined a possible methodology that he would have used in his cross-national comparison of intellectuals. He wanted explicitly to avoid sociological models, but admitted a certain amount of schematic model-building would be needed, although he quickly added that it would have to be expressed in good literary style, not 'sociologese'. His methodology would have derived from a synthesis of *Kulturgeschichte* and political science. The result might have been fascinating, and we can see how his project approached Weber in parallel fashion, but it is hard to see how Gramsci's historical sociology would have avoided some type of evolutionary message. Indeed, as far as can be ascertained, Gramsci was more Eurocentric than Weber. One passage in the *Notebooks* is revealingly entitled 'The hegemony of Western culture over the whole world's culture.'[82] At least Weber's relativism could prevent him from creating historyless peoples. On the other hand, Weber's evolutionary legal-rational mentality does tend to undermine the conception of ahistorical ideal-typical forms of domination.

Comparative Studies of Religion

Many Weber scholars have stressed how close his sociology of religion comes to a Marxist approach.[83] Weber recognized the irreducibility of religious belief founded on irrational and incommunicable mystical experiences, but religions acquired their institutional permanence to the degree to which they were harnessed by sets of rational ideas. Religion codifies and justifies the worldview of a social class. Gramsci would have expressed this in terms of a historical bloc, where ethico-political ideas generated by intellectuals in a determinant social structure create ideologies employed by corporate-economic classes, allowing them to become leading partners in an alliance with other groups. The first historical bloc was the church, and this image, we have had cause to notice, was transferred to modern politics. Gramsci's comparative studies of religion parallel Weber's interests. We need only remember that both men drew attention to the central importance of clergy as traditional intellectuals/cultivated men; the rupture between Renaissance humanism and the Reformation; the gap between Catholic masses and clergy; the abyss that lay between Asian urban clergy and the rural laity; the intimate relationship of clergy and faithful in sectarian Protestant Europe and America and the direct effect on sustaining a rich voluntary organizational tradition, or the widespread practice of magic in all peasant cultures explained by the peasantry's reliance upon natural phenomena for daily survival. There are, finally, the underlying personal affinities of two religiously 'unmusical' intellectuals being deeply affected by religious institutions and imagery.

Conclusion: Regulated Society versus New Egypt

During the past decade or so, attempts to compare Gramsci and Weber have tended to be subsumed under the politics of Italian Eurocommunism. Italian theorists and their followers abroad identified Gramsci as a rigorously Marxist critic of both reformist welfare interventionism and sinister varieties of state-directed social revolutions. But what thinker predicted the social structures and the mechanisms of social control in modern Western Europe with greater accuracy? Weber's decisionist democracy is simplistic and dangerously authoritarian in that it generally dismisses social movements that refuse to abide by the logic of a rationalized bureaucratic game. In this regard, as David Beetham shows in his comparison of Mosca, Pareto and Weber, the elite sociologists, and liberal democratic theorists informed by their assumptions, usually play with loaded dice.[84] However, at the end of the day, taking into account all of his prejudices, Weber has a better grasp of the modern world than Gramsci. Certainly, it must be said that Gramsci's conception of the political process, at least in Western 'late' capitalist democracies, is downright archaic. To what extent are political parties ethico-political entities harbouring 'state spirits'? Has not the very nature of ideology and its articulation changed dramatically since Gramsci's death? Here, I am not arguing for the end of ideology, just for its transubstantiation. Gramsci's version of ideology, no matter how much he tried to connect it to the infrastructure, still smacks of a nineteenth-century battle of ideas between two sets of well educated elites. Gramsci still breathed the air of Spaventa and Croce. In the contemporary world styles of life, the very consumption and production of commodities have replaced traditional legitimating ideologies. As the Italian historian Galli della Loggia puts it, for the Hegelian tradition, that refrigerators and television sets can replace world-views is a monstrosity beyond the limits of the imaginable.[85]

Max Weber was firmly convinced that nothing in the long run would prevent the bureaucratization of the world. At best he imagined a plurality of bureaucratic organizations played off, one against the other, by charismatic politicians. To the extent that Gramsci described his future city as a regulated society, he shared a strangely analogous prophecy. For Gramsci, the state would evaporate as each citizen became a functionary.[86] Does this mean that civil society will break up the state; that Gramsci advocated creeping anarchism? Or did he imagine that the standardization of human behaviour made coercion redundant? If we all vibrate to the song of Taylorized machines, our synchronization with the master wavelength is that much easier. The Eurocommunist theorists thought, at least in the late 1970s, that Gramsci meant the first proposition. Thus, Badaloni writes that Gramsci advocated a 'new individualism' grounded in a socialized and self-managed economy.[87] Cerroni describes Gramsci's final aim in terms of communitarianism.[88] Vacca is positively lyrical and breaks a lance against Weber's iron cage. Gramsci's heirs were not interested in replacing one intellectual strata by another, communist entrepreneurs for capitalist, the hegemonic apparatus of the workers' party for that of the bourgeois state. Rather, they sought to create conditions for a 'social intelligence', which originates from the 'class of producers'.[89]

It is not surprising that the terms alienation and reification are non-existent in the Gramscian vocabulary, and ideology has positive connotations whereas in Marx they are entirely negative.[90] Taylorsim, Gramsci explained in the *Notebooks*, did not 'murder the human spirit'. In fact, with the standardization of human movements and their sublimation in the mind of the factory worker, the freedom to think – even subversively – might threaten the new industrial order. Taylorism could never create human gorillas.[91] It is just Gramsci's rather eager digestion of 'Fordism' and 'statolatry' which makes us pause and brings to mind one of Weber's more thoughtful passages in *Parliament and Government*:

> The future belongs to bureaucratization, and it is evident that in this regard the literati pursue their calling – to provide a salvo of applause to the up-and-coming powers – just as they did in the age of laissez-faire, both times with the same naïveté.[92]

Notes: Chapter 26

1   H. S. Hughes, *Consciousness and Society* (London, 1959), p. 296.
2   G. Fiori, *Antonio Gramsci* (London, 1970), p. 71.
3   For Weber, see A. Mitzman, *The Iron Cage* (New York, 1970).
4   FMW, p. 23.
5   T. Nairn, 'Antonu Su Gobbu', in A. S. Sassoon (ed.), *Approaches to Gramsci* (London, 1982), p. 161; P. Anderson, *Considerations on Western Marxism* (London, 1976), p. 54.
6   C. Antoni, *From History to Sociology* (Detroit, Mich., 1959), p. 10.
7   Hughes, *Consciousness and Society*, p. 324.
8   A. Pipa, 'Gramsci as a (Non) Literary Critic', *Telos*, vol. 57 (1983), p. 186.
9   L. Mangoni, 'Il problema del fascismo nei "Quaderni del Carcere"', in F. Ferri (ed.), *Politica e storia in Gramsci*, Vol. 1 (Rome, 1977), p. 409.
10 K. Löwith, *Karl Marx and Max Weber* (London, 1982). For more recent attempts to compare Marx and Weber, see A. Giddens, *The Class Structure of the Advanced Societies* (London, 1981), pp. 50–2, 78–81; B. Turner, *For Weber* (London, 1983), pp. 25–7.
11 J. Sheehan, *German Liberalism in the Nineteenth Century* (London, 1978), p. 21.
12 C. Lovett, *The Democratic Movement in Italy, 1830–1876* (Cambridge, Mass., 1982).
13 A. A. Rosa, 'La Cultura', in C. Vivante (ed.), *Storia d'Italia*, Vol. 4, Pt. 2 (Turin, 1975), p. 1055.
14 Fiori, *Antonio Gramsci*, pp. 89–114. A. Davidson, *Antonio Gramsci: Towards an Intellectual Biography* (London, 1977), pp. 48–112.
15 W. J. Mommsen, 'Universalgeschichtliches und politisches Denken bei Max Weber',

Historische Zeitschrift, vol. 201 (1965), pp. 557–612; O. Bucci, 'Nietzsche e il primo Gramsci', in F. Ferri (ed.), *Politica e storia in Gramsci*, Vol. 2 (Rome, 1977), pp. 326–35.

16 R. Michels, *Proletariato e borghesia nel movimento socialista italiano* (Turin, 1908); W. J. Mommsen, 'Max Weber and Robert Michels: An Asymmetrical Relationship', *Archives européennes de Sociologie*, vol. 22 (1981), pp. 100–16, and Chapter 8 by W. J. Mommsen in this volume.

17 See Introduction by Guenther Roth, in ES, Vol. 1, p. xcix.

18 F. Adler, 'Factory Councils, Gramsci and the Industrialists', *Telos*, vol. 31 (1977), pp. 67–90.

19 M. N. Clark, *Antonio Gramsci and the Revolution that Failed* (New Haven, Conn., and London, 1977).

20 P. M. Blau, *Bureaucracy in Modern Society* (New York, 1956); A. W. Gouldner, *Patterns of Industrial Bureaucracy* (Glencoe, Ill., 1954); A. Etzioni, *A Comparative Analysis of Complex Organizations* (New York, 1961).

21 N. De Feo, *Max Weber* (Florence, 1975); B. Mastrogiuseppe, 'Max Weber in Italia (1907–1980). Una bibliografia', *Rassegna Italiana di Sociologia*, vol. 12 (1981), pp. 227–53.

22 See Foreword by Benedetto Croce, in Antoni, *From History to Sociology*, p. iii.

23 De Ruggiero used such an approach when he summarized Weber's arguments for readers of *Il Tempo* (19 October 1919); see G. De Ruggiero, *Scritti Politici*, ed. R. De Felice (Turin, 1963), pp. 290–4.

24 C. Levy, 'The Italian Anarchists in 1919: A Preliminary Survey', *Risorgimento*, vol. 4 (1984).

25 S. Festa, *Gobetti* (Assisi, 1976), pp. 76, 83–7, 215–17, 252–69, 275–6, 319–29, 417–83.

26 C. Pogliano, *Piero Gobetti* (Bari, 1976), pp. 87–127; De Feo, *Max Weber*, pp. 96–8; De Ruggiero, *Scritti Politici*, pp. 73, 290–4; P. P. Portinaro, 'Robert Michels e Vilfredo Pareto: La formazione e la crisi della sociologia politica', *Annali della Fondazione Luigi Einaudi*, vol. 11 (1977), pp. 99–141; N. Bobbio, *Saggi sulle scienze politica in Italia* (Bari, 1969), pp. 219–24; E. Garin, *Cronache di Filosofia Italiana, 1900/1943* (Bari, 1975), Vol. 1, p. 27; Vol. 2, p. 403; P. Rossi, 'Max Weber and Benedetto Croce', Chapter 30 in this volume.

27 A. Gramsci, *Quaderni del Carcere*, ed. V. Gerratana (Turin, 1975), pp. 317–18, 893, 1155, 1178, 1684–5, 1986–7, 2764.

28 Originally published in *Der Kampf* (Vienna) 11 December 1914, see Gramsci, *Quaderni*, Vol. 2, pp. 893, Vol. 3, p. 1683.

29 A. Gramsci, *Cronache torinesi, 1913–1917*, ed. S. Caprioglio (Turin, 1980), pp. 99–103.

30 L. Paggi, *Gramsci e il principe moderno* (Rome, 1970), pp. 121, 377–83, 404; S. Cohen, *Bukharin and the Bolshevik Revolution* (New York, 1975), p. 21.

31 See Gramsci, *Quarderni*, Vol. 1, pp. 230, 231, 389; Vol. 2, pp. 1086–7, 1389; Vol. 3, p. 1527; Vol. 4, pp. 2407, 2559, 2614, 2761, 2825.

32 A. Gramsci, *Lettere dal carcere*, ed. S. Caprioglio and E. Fubini (Turin, 1965), p. 103.

33 Mangoni, 'Il problema del fascismo', p. 409.

34 For a recent overview of the connections between Gramsci's thought and sociology, see C. Grasso, 'Alcuni contributi ricenti sui rapporti tra il pensiero di Gramsci e la sociologia', *Quaderni di Sociologia*, vol. 29 (1980–1), pp. 349–59.

35 J. Joll, *Gramsci* (London, 1977), p. 77–8; L. Salamini, *The Sociology of Political Praxis* (London, 1981).

36 A. Baldan, *Gramsci come storico* (Bari, 1982), pp. 7, 55, 80, 82, 84.

37 L. Gallino, 'Gramsci e le scienze sociali' in P. Rossi (ed.), *Gramsci e la cultura contemporanea*, Vol. 2 (Rome, 1969), pp. 81–108.

38 ibid.; A. Pizzorno, 'Sul metodo di Gramsci: dalla storiografia alla scienza politica', in Rossi (ed.), *Gramsci e la cultura contemporanea*, Vol. 2, pp. 109–26.

39 N. Bobbio, 'Gramsci e la concezione della società civile', in ibid., Vol. 1 (Rome, 1969), pp. 75–100.

40 P. Rossi, 'Antonio Gramsci sulla scienza moderna', *Critica Marxista*, vol. 14 (1976), pp. 41–60.

41 J. Femia, *Gramsci's Political Thought* (Oxford, 1981), p. 111.

42 Hughes, *Consciousness and Society*, pp. 92, 173.

43 L. Paggi, 'Gramsci's general theory of Marxism', in C. Mouffe (ed.), *Gramsci and Marxist Theory* (London, 1979), p. 148.

44 U. Cerroni, 'Universalità + politica', in Ferri (ed.), *Politica e storia in Gramsci*, Vol. 1, pp. 127–60; B. De Giovanni, 'Libertà individuale e uomo collettivo in Antonio Gramsci', in ibid., p. 224.

45 Bobbio, 'Gramsci e la concezione'; Antoni, *From History to Sociology*, p. 137.
46 G. Galli, 'Gramsci e le teorie delle "elites"', in Rossi (ed.), *Gramsci e la cultura contemporanea*, Vol. 2, pp. 201–2.
47 See, for example, De Giovanni, 'Libertà individuale'.
48 A. Gramsci, *La città futura*, ed. S. Caprioglio (Turin, 1982), pp. 331–3.
49 A. Gramsci, *Scritti giovanili, 1914–1918* (Turin, 1958), pp. 280–7.
50 Gramsci, *Cronache torinesi*, pp. 12–16.
51 P. Bonetti, *Gramsci e la società liberaldemocratica* (Bari, 1980), p. 109.
52 Roth, 'Introduction', p. lxv.
53 ES, Vol. 2, p. 991.
54 Gramsci, *Quaderni*, p. 233.
55 ibid., p. 238.
56 Roth, 'Introduction', p. lxiv.
57 For Weber and Lenin, see J. G. Merquior, *Rousseau and Weber* (London, 1981), pp. 122–32; E. O. Wright, *Class, Crisis and the State* (London, 1978), pp. 181–215.
58 D. Beetham, *Max Weber and the Theory of Modern Politics* (London, 1974), p. 58.
59 M. Salvadori, 'Gramsci e il PCI: due concezioni dell' egemonia', in F. Coen (ed.), *Egemonia e Democrazia* (Rome, 1977), pp. 33–54.
60 Beetham, *Max Weber*, passim.
61 ES, Vol. 2, p. 985.
62 C. Levy, 'Fabianism, the nursery of organised socialism', Ms, The Open University, 1983.
63 Beetham, *Max Weber*, p. 112; see also Chapter 9 by David Beetham in this volume.
64 Femia, *Gramsci's Political Thought*, pp. 165–89.
65 A. S. Sassoon, *Gramsci's Politics* (London, 1980).
66 M. Krygier, 'Weber, Lenin and the reality of socialism', in E. Kamenka and M. Krygier (eds), *Bureaucracy* (London, 1978), pp. 84–6.
67 F. Lo Piparo, *Lingua intellettuali egemonia in Gramsci* (Bari, 1979), p. 121.
68 Gallino, 'Gramsci e le scienze sociali', p. 104.
69 C. Buci-Glucksmann, *Gramsci and the State* (London, 1980), pp. 48, 56.
70 Gramsci, *Quaderni*, p. 330.
71 P. Piccone, 'From Spaventa to Gramsci', *Telos*, vol. 31 (1971), pp. 35–66; H. Entwistle, *Antonio Gramsci: Conservative Schooling for Radical Politics* (London, 1979); Rosa, 'La Cultura', p. 1040.
72 Gramsci, *Quaderni*, Vol. 2, pp. 1389–92.
73 ibid., pp. 1390–2.
74 Gallino, 'Gramsci e le scienze sociali', p. 102.
75 Mommsen, *The Age of Bureaucracy*, p. 2.
76 Gramsci, *Quaderni*, Vol. 3, p. 1827.
77 ibid., Vol. 2, p. 769.
78 ibid., Vol. 3, p. 1526.
79 ibid., Vol. 2, pp. 1020–1.
80 B. Rizzi, *The Bureaucratization of the World*, ed. A. Westoby (London, 1985).
81 C. Boggs, *Gramsci's Marxism* (London 1976), p. 46.
82 A. Cirese, 'Gramsci's Observations on Folklore', in Sassoon (ed.), *Approaches to Gramsci*, pp. 212–47.
83 For one of the more recent examples, see F. Parkin, *Max Weber* (London, 1982), pp. 40–71.
84 See Chapter 9 in this volume by David Beetham.
85 E. Galli della Loggia, 'Le ceneri di Gramsci', in Coen (ed.), *Egemonia e Democrazia*, p. 81.
86 Gramsci, *Quaderni*, Vol. 1, p. 340.
87 N. Badaloni, 'Libertà, individuale uomo collettivo in Gramsci', in Feri (ed.), *Politia e storia in Gramsci*, Vol. 1, pp. 37–8.
88 Cerroni, 'Universalità e politica'.
89 G. Vacca, 'La "quistione politica degli intellettuali" a la teoria marxista dello stato nel pensiero di Gramsci', in Ferri (ed.), *Politia e storia in Gramsci*, Vol. 1, p. 478.
90 F. Fergnani, 'La "questione Gramsci": una proposta di riconsiderazione', *Aut-Aut*, no. 114 (1974), pp. 4–18.
91 Gramsci, *Quaderni*, Vol. 3, p. 2170–1.
92 ES, Vol. 2, p. 1401.

Part IV

Max Weber and Philosophical Thought

27 Weber and Nietzsche: Questioning the Liberation of Social Science from Historicism

ROBERT EDEN

Weber's relation to Nietzsche has recently come under closer scrutiny than social scientists had heretofore thought necessary.[1] This closer inspection has reopened questions that were widely believed (or wishfully thought) to be closed for good. Although Weber's teaching is inherently controversial, fundamental controversy, going to the roots of his thought, had almost disappeared from the social sciences.[2] My purpose in this chapter is to bring one topic from the renascent controversy about Weber's fundamental principles into clearer focus.[3]

Social scientists and historians have been taught for several generations that Weber liberated their disciplines from historicism.[4] Secure in this knowledge, they may hastily dismiss — will probably misconstrue — the thesis that Weber followed Nietzsche on the path to his own distinctive historicism.[5] The diacritic point in this contention is that we must distinguish with greater care between fundamentally different forms of historicism. If many scholars have been inclined to ignore such distinctions, it is primarily because a major transformation within historicist thought was not adequately mapped by our received historiographies and philosophies of social science.[6] In particular, the most influential accounts of the origins of social science failed to chart the traverse initiated by Nietzsche, away from *theoretical* historicism towards a *practical* (or existentialist) historicism.[7] This failure was of some consequence. It blinded many scholars to a possibility now under scrutiny: that in liberating the disciplines of history and social science from Hegel (and from the residues of Hegel in Marx), Weber had adopted Nietzsche's critique of theoretical historicism, thereby introducing the Nietzschean traverse (with some modification) into contemporary social science and historiography.[8]

To indicate where this Nietzschean traverse leads, and to illuminate Weber's response to Nietzsche's argument on historicism, I propose to discuss Part 7 in Nietzsche's *Beyond Good and Evil*, 'Our Virtues'.[9] Since my intention is not to advance a definitive account of Weber's distinctive practical historicism, but merely to clarify a few controversial questions raised by recent studies of Weber's relation to Nietzsche, I shall concentrate upon the initial steps of Nietzsche's argument, and keep close to the terms of discussion set by two prominent interpreters of Weber, Wolfgang Schluchter and Guenther Roth.[10]

Verstehen versus *Redlichkeit*

'Our Virtues,' follows a discussion of 'We Scholars' and makes a transition from science in general to history and the *Geisteswissenschaften* in particular.[11] In it, Nietzsche is concerned with what Tocqueville called the influence of democracy upon the movement of the intellect, or with the interplay between science, public opinion and the republic of letters. That interplay is presently dominated by the rise of the historical sciences and historicism, according to Nietzsche.[12] In the twenty-seven aphorisms in Part 7, Nietzsche plays on the bad conscience of his age, by vivisecting two virtues that characterize our epoch as an age of historicism.[13]

These contemporary virtues, 'the historical sense' and 'intellectual probity', stand high among the virtues Weber exemplified and stressed in his writings on method and ethics.[14] Curiously, Nietzsche argues that they are antithetical. *Verstehende Soziologie* or *Historie* forgives too much, because it understands indiscriminately.[15] It cannot comprehend what is remorseless and unforgiving in a closed and perfectionist culture; what it cannot understand is *measure*.[16] Devaluing the self-discipline that high art and human accomplishment demand, we who prize the historical sense shrink from each severe ranking of men and things. By contrast, intellectual honesty (*Redlichkeit*) is a ferocious virtue that *must* marshal a ranking of values and impose exacting self-discipline.[17] Thus, 'our virtues' contradict and misinterpret each other. From the standpoint of rigorous intellectual probity, the historical sense appears comically anti-historical: by mortifying our capacity to understand strict and noble standards of praise or blame, the historical sense *compels* us to misunderstand the peaks of past human accomplishment.[18] Paradoxically, a virtue prized by scientific historiography works against historical understanding.[19] Conversely, according to Nietzsche, steadfast intellectual honesty inevitably appears to votaries of the historical sense as immoralism and cruelty.[20] If Nietzsche is correct, these two virtues are antithetical and should cancel one another.[21]

The pride of our contemporaries is accordingly volatile and prone to fluctuate into self-contempt: either virtue, taken seriously, puts the other to shame.[22] We cannot do justice to the most consequential differences between cultures without transcending *Verstehen* or the historical sense: intellectual probity ultimately requires that we treat *Verstehen* as a vice.[23] Nor can we overcome the moral relativism that accompanies our indiscriminately sympathetic understanding of many cultures, unless we become 'immoralists'.[24] Thus the tension between our virtues cannot be stabilized. It must set us in motion, toward downfall or ascent.

Nietzsche was not one to repeat the Biblical warning that pride precedeth the fall.[25] Instead, he advocated a choice of *Redlichkeit* against the historical sense. Projected into practice by this choice, historicist pride in 'our virtue' could presage an ascent — toward active nihilism.[26] Thus Nietzsche's traverse, from theoretical historicism towards a practical, revaluing, destructive and creative historicism, is an ascent towards mastery over our virtue.[27] One thing needful is to subordinate the passively contemplative theoretical virtue of *Verstehen* to the remorseless and actively disenchanting virtue of *Redlichkeit*: Intellectual probity is the practical or active virtue par excellence.[28]

Nietzsche presents his argument with great elegance and subtlety, but even my crude rendition should make one ask if it is *possible* to combine *Redlichkeit* with *Verstehen*, or intellectual honesty with the historical sense, as Weber claimed to have done.[29] In Nietzsche's revaluation of theoretical historicism, the virtue of intellectual probity conquers the historian's virtue of *Verstehen*. *Redlichkeit* impels us toward a practical historicism that Nietzsche identified with nihilism.[30] Intellectual honesty becomes nihilistic when life as a whole is made an experiment of the knowers.[31] Thus, one topic of controversy that attention to Nietzsche may raise to high visibility is Weber's moralization or domestication of intellectual honesty. For, in Weber's social science, *Redlichkeit* appears to stand in the service of moral forces.[32] The question is whether Weber's refusal to embrace Nietzschean nihilism can be grounded in an intelligible argument. Why wasn't Weber a nihilist?[33]

A second topic of controversy concerns Weber's rejection of moral relativism and his denigration of moral philosophy. In Nietzsche's argument in Part 7, these themes are closely joined.[34] Nietzsche's critique of theoretical historicism entails a qualified rejection of moral relativism in one form; but the qualification is stringent enough to ensure that the critique leaves no path open back towards moral philosophy. The critique precludes any attempt to ground morality in transcendant ethical absolutes (as in the Socratic 'error' of the Good) or in human desires and aversions (as in utilitarianism).[35] Nietzsche heralds a nihilism that 'sails right over morality'; in Part 7, he claims that the notions of 'the general welfare', notions moral philosophers had tried to put in place of the absolute standards of Biblical morality, were 'not intelligible concepts'.[36] Problems of pleasure and pain are lower problems; a philosophy that does not ascend beyond them is a naivety.[37]

If Nietzsche's analysis is sound, Weber's denial that he was a moral relativist must be reconsidered: not because Weber failed to distance himself from moral relativism, but rather because he did so in the name of intellectual probity.[38] Can one consistently combat moral relativism under the aegis of intellectual honesty without embracing Nietzschean nihilism? What did this 'untimely' virtue, intellectual probity, mean to Weber? What kept him then – what keeps social science now – from ascending to (or from falling into) nihilism?

Max Weber and Our Contemporaries

Until recently, most of our contemporaries in sociology and political science held that the social science initiated by Max Weber provided the only reliable or rational knowledge of the bureaucratized world in which we are fated to live.[39] Such social science was not to 'partake of the contemplation of sages and philosophers about the meaning of the universe'.[40] Weber was widely celebrated as the founder of a sociology for disciplined empiricists, *Fachmenschen* who refused to 'tarry' either for transcendental speculation, for new prophets like Zarathustra, for the philosophy of the past, or for Nietzsche's 'philosophy of the future'.[41]

Such a radical break with philosophy was a necessary consequence of Weber's insight into the nature of the objects of social scientific knowledge, according to the most acute version of this contemporary view.[42] Weber understood the social sciences as historical disciplines governed by historical questions, which always concern individuals: individual groups, individual human beings, individual achievements, individual 'civilizations', distinctively individuated 'processes' of 'rationalization', and so on.[43] Philosophy might provide heuristic instruments for the pursuit of such knowledge of individuals; in particular, 'social philosophy' could aid in the formulation of theoretical ideal-types.[44] But the quest for knowledge of the actual required a strict subordination of philosophy to empirical research. Sociology had to be fortified to prevent philosophy from becoming an end in itself; philosophy was to be the handmaiden rather than the queen of the social sciences.

When it looked back to its origins, therefore, social science took pride in Weber's resoluteness in turning away from philosophy, his determination to work patiently amid its ruins to build an edifice emphatically *in* and *for* our world: the world of concern to us, a world disenchanted in the specific sense that it had broken the spell *of philosophy*. Weber's assertion of this resolutely anti-philosophical social science was, of course, assumed to be inseparable from the stance he took towards Nietzsche in his scholarly works, just as his rejection of Nietzsche's politics was integral to his political writings.

In this view of Weber's legacy, however, there was a double standard, if not an outright contradiction. The Weberian *Aufklärung* or enlightenment meant an end to the tutelage of social science by philosophy; it meant freedom for empirical or historical inquiry, freedom for the direct exercise of untrammelled reason. The social scientist or historian was said to be free at last to confront actuality without metaphysical blinkers.

On the other hand, Weber's claim that the objects of historical knowledge were ultimately individual and, even more critically, his assertion that the 'historical individual' of paramount concern for the social and historical sciences was 'the inescapable given of our historical situation', were assertions not warranted by historical fact.[45] They had rather to be affirmed by an 'ultimate commitment', a leap of faith. At best, they constituted a philosophical view; at worst, another ideology. So, instead of liberating social science entirely from philosophy, Weber required perpetual tutelage to a definite philosophical position: the imperative to be authentically contemporary, or to be true to our unique historical circumstances, became an indispensable tenet that was affirmed every day (as Weber put it) 'by my very work'.[46]

Thus one could cast out philosophy with Weber's pitchfork, yet unwittingly bring it back as part of the pitchfork itself. For well-informed observers, this reflexivity was subtle but stubborn evidence of Weber's debt to historicist philosophy of a specific kind: Nietzsche's attempt to supersede the theoretical historicism of Hegel by means of a novel, more radically practical historicism. If you cast out Hegel with Nietzsche's pitchfork, it should be no surprise that your historical, social scientific 'empiricism' brings back Nietzsche, ready-to-hand, among the tools of your trade.[47]

Nevertheless, it remains a surprise for our contemporaries, especially for scholars solicitous to transmit Weber's legacy as a living tradition. Consider the doctrine advanced recently by Wolfgang Schluchter and Guenther Roth. They contend that the great practical issue of our time is the rationality of modern society, or more precisely, 'the legacies and dynamics of Western rationalism, which have brought about ... the inescapable interdependence of all parts of the world and its irreversible dependence on scientific and technological world-mastery', the tremendous costs and dangers of which 'are clear to most of us'.[48] The contemporary political crisis of legitimacy is ultimately due to 'a profound crisis of faith in science' or to the collapse of critical rationalism within the 'dominant [liberal] tradition', which cannot provide 'a theoretically consistent and institutionally effective alternative to a directionless decisionism as well as a meaningless perfection of "the iron cage"'.[49] Because liberals do not understand 'the rationality of modern society', they cannot offer an alternative to 'a technocratic consciousness which functions as a background ideology for the progress of an industrial society'.[50] Liberalism cannot articulate the proper relations between religion, science, and politics, or secure a place for science as 'a politically relevant power', especially not in the face of a 'revolution in entitlements' appealing to 'natural rights legacies'.[51] Weber's vision is choiceworthy because it 'shows us the reasons for our discontent with modernity, but also makes clear why we will do well not to give in to this discontent'.[52] We are urged to adopt both Weber's diagnosis of modernity and 'his own position toward it, his philosophy of life, so to speak, insofar as it has relevance beyond his own person'.[53] Weber helps Schluchter 'to show that the notion of self-restraint can be an essential element of a political philosophy appropriate to the times'.[54] Under Weber's aegis, a new public philosophy for the defence of liberal democratic institutions can be advanced by scholars. 'The sciences can instill a social consciousness which counters decisionist as well as technocratic interpretations of politics; the sciences should 'participate in spreading an ethic of responsibility', for unless 'the citizens and especially the politicians accept it, the sciences cannot fulfil their tasks for politics'.[55] Weber has a programme: 'determining the function of science and politics is the dominant issue of the present'.[56] The choice is between a technocracy, which masters the world but is unconscious of ultimate questions, and the regime of critical rationalism, for which 'What is needed is conscious world mastery, the subjective correlate of which is self-control vis-à-vis one's own and alien "gods"'.[57]

Weber points the way to 'the ethical life style adequate for a disenchanted world', only, however, if 'we are ready to argue in his own terms against him'.[58] Weber's explicit doctrine of ethics and method rules out public philosophy or the instilling of social consciousness as an endeavour for science. To save liberal democracy we must turn from Weber to Schluchter, or move with him from the surface toward 'the foundations of Weber's position'.[59] Because Weber closed the route they wished to reopen through 'social philosophy' toward a renewal of our public philosophy, Roth and Schluchter necessarily treat many completed inquiries as 'matters left unfinished or insufficiently elucidated by Max Weber'.[60]

By thus modifying Weber, Roth and Schluchter hoped to distance themselves from the relativist and decisionist implications of Weber's doctrine of science. Although they did not fully admit that vulgar Weberianism, rampant in social science, had largely discredited Weber's doctrines of value-relevance and his version of the fact/value dichotomy, their remarks about a mindless 'decisionism' indicate that the critiques of Habermas, Strauss, Voegelin and others had hit home to them.[61] Their remedy was to jettison the baggage of vulgar Weberianism, in part by finessing the question of where Weber's doctrines of value-relevance and objectivity fit in with his work as a whole. By treating Weber's corpus as incomplete, Roth and Schluchter believed they could circumvent those doctrines and reconstitute a social philosophy from Weber's ethical dicta and example. In particular, they sought to rescue an 'ethic of responsibility' that was neither relativistic nor decisionistic. Weber's argument was insufficient for Roth and Schluchter, because it failed to leave open the path toward 'social philosophy' that would make the social sciences effective in resolving the most urgent question of our time, the question of the rationality of modern society.[62] Weber's argument seemed to leave modern society defenceless or unable to provide a rational grounding for the ethic of responsibility that Weber exemplified; consequently, Roth and Schluchter attempted to move beyond Weber's argument, and through Weber's personal example, towards a union of ethics and method, moral philosophy and historical inquiry.

The combination of vision and history, or of philosophy and history, that Roth and Schluchter advance under Weber's aegis is highly problematic. Schluchter's formulation raises the problem to high visibility, although unwittingly. For what the actualization of an ethic of responsibility requires, according to Schluchter, is nothing less than 'conscious world mastery, the subjective correlate of which is self-control vis-à-vis one's own and alien "gods"'.[63] Schluchter urges us to choose 'the world view that has an elective affinity to modern society ... a world view of immanence', and the core of this choice turns out to be Nietzschean world-affirmation, 'because the cosmos of ethical causality – the central values controlling and directing man – must be created and justified by man himself'.[64] The 'public philosophy' for which Schluchter calls goes beyond Weber to assert Nietzsche's doctrine of value-creation and value-justification, or a Nietzschean revaluation of values, albeit in a form so congenial to contemporary opinion that Schluchter evidently does not notice the Nietzsche in it. If he knows, he does not let on that Nietzsche advocated it as fully conscious nihilism.[65] What kept Weber then, what keeps social science now, from ascending to (or from falling into) nihilism? Schluchter dramatizes our question with exemplary panache – by falling in.

Weber's 'founding' of social science is not the defence of liberal democratic institutions and science that Schluchter and Roth desired. The received view of Weber is in this respect closer to Weber than their proposed revision. As Shils put it, 'For [Weber] ... a system of general concepts and a general theory was simply an instrument'.[66] In so far as Roth and Schluchter disregard Weber's strictures in order to restore social or public philosophy, their re-interpretation is a retreat toward theoretical historicism. Nevertheless, by introducing Nietzschean formulations, Schluchter comes close to uncovering the basis of Weber's hostility to theory. The difficulty with the received view was that it made Weber look like a positivist, and failed to explain the pathos of his attempt to combine anti-positivist *Verstehen* with a passion for intellectual probity unparalleled among the positivists.[67] Weber's studies of method and ethics are more intelligible if we take our cue from Schluchter, and consider them as a methodological revaluation of values akin to Nietzsche's critique of 'the prejudices of philosophers', or their 'normative' concerns.[68] When Schluchter asserts that 'the central values controlling and directing man must be created and justified by man himself', or that 'the cosmos of ethical causality' is a world that man must create, he comes close to contending that the logical completion of Weber's thought would be consistent Nietzschean nihilism.[69] As recent studies have shown, one can entertain this thesis without denigrating Weber's herculean effort to turn Nietzsche against Nietzsche, or to defend science against Nietzsche's philosophic leadership.[70]

So far, I have suggested that a clearer picture of Nietzsche's traverse away from theoretical historicism would help us to pinpoint precisely where Weber turned back from Nietzsche's radical path, and I have claimed that Nietzsche provides such a picture in Part 7 of *Beyond Good and Evil*. This is not the occasion for a full study of Part 7, or of its bearing on Weber. But a closer look at the preliminary stages of Nietzsche's argument on historicism may advance us a step further along his traverse, and help us understand a difficulty that has perplexed and bedevilled Weber's friends in social science: how could Weber so confidently deny that he was a moral relativist, despite his far-reaching attack upon normative moral philosophy and his exclusion from social science of any attempt to 'reconstruct public philosophy' along the lines Roth and Schluchter advocate?

Nietzschean Revaluation and Weber's Stance Toward Moral Relativism

Weber's posture is intelligible to the extent that 'public philosophy' and traditional political philosophy either promote moral relativism or blind us to the ultimate meaning of our own conduct. This is the charge that gives Weber's animus against normative political philosophy its pathos of 'serving moral forces', and distinguishes Weber's critique from (say) Karl Popper's. But it was Nietzsche who articulated the link between moral relativism and moral philosophizing most persuasively, and who first advanced the task of 'revaluing values' as *the* practical alternative to traditional political philosophy. A glance at Nietzsche's compressed history of political philosophy will help, therefore, before we turn to the considerations that gave Weber's critique its practical urgency and pathos.

In aphorism 212, which serves as a proem to 'Our Virtues', Nietzsche introduces the vivisecting of virtue as a problem that was formerly undertaken by philosophers, Socrates and Montaigne: that is, by political philosophers.[71] But evidently their influence and success recreated the fundamental problem or posed it in a new form. Montaigne and other early modern political philosophers combated the influence of Socrates; while Nietzsche thought himself compelled to provide an unprecedented alternative to both ancient and modern moral philosophy.[72]

In Nietzsche's view, contemporary moral relativism ultimately derives from Montaigne and the modern humanitarian project he set in motion.[73] Were we to combat the vicious consequences of Montaigne's bourgeois project by returning to Socrates, however, we would sacrifice the great 'legacy of all the strength, that the struggle against [Socratic] errors has bred' in us.[74]

Nietzsche regards this legacy as a heritage of habits and passions embodied in us, as a consequence of centuries of sustained willing. [75] Our virtues and vices are constituted by our history and constitute our historical individuality. [76] For Montaigne, moral relativism was a means of combating the Socratic errors of the pure *Geist* and the Good as such. He exhibited the fallibility and weakness of his own human, all-too-human *Geist*, teaching men to turn away from Socratic asceticism toward the things of this world, things good in relation to our human, all-too-human desires and aversions. Initially, then, modern moral relativism was inseparable from Montaigne's subtly subversive struggle against Plato and 'the Christian-ecclesiastical pressure of millenia'. [77]

Nietzsche argues that a radicalization of moral relativism is presently required to prevent the diminution of man and, for this purpose, Nietzsche relies upon the virtue of *Redlichkeit* or intellectual probity. [78] Relativism can be disenchanted or stripped naked by a resolute attack on modern moral philosophy. [79] Furthermore, moral relativism can be invigorated and radicalized by forcing it to contend against a spirited revaluation or reassertion of cruelty. Montaigne had argued against Socratic virtue by vivisecting it, that is, by removing its disguises and exhibiting it as human, all-too-human cruelty. [80] Nietzsche presents our contemporary disciples of Montaigne's humanitarianism with a new antagonist, by forthrightly celebrating cruelty. Cruelty is inseparable from every higher accomplishment of humanity: whether masked or open, cruelty is of the essence of *Geist*: not to be cruel is not to have a human mind. [81] To be consistently indulgent toward human frailty, Montaigne would have to believe in the inhuman, pure *Geist*, and thus return to Socratic asceticism. Cruelty is integral to the mind precisely because the mind (as Montaigne and his early modern followers thought), is impure and fully integral with the body and the passions. [82] Intellectual probity, by requiring consistency, can (as it were) put Montaigne on the defensive, or bring modern moral relativism back to its original spiritedness in defence of the body and the passions. [83]

Thus a new historiography of philosophy, displacing Hegel's, provides the comprehensive framework of Nietzsche's traverse away from theoretical historicism. The remarks on Montaigne and Socrates with which Nietzsche begins his traverse (aphorism 212) follow a critique of Hegel's history of philosophy (aphorism 211). Because no trace of such a historiography of philosophy remains in Weberian social science, one problem deserves to be mentioned in passing. [84] The academic disciplines with which Weber replaced Nietzsche's subtle histories of philosophy – the sociology of knowledge, and 'intellectual history' – are highly vulnerable to Nietzsche's contemptuous criticism: that they are '*impossible* literature' because they contain 'no realistic history of what was formerly thought (...*nichts von feinerer Wendung und Faltung eines alten Gedankens, nicht einmal eine wirkliche Historie des früher Gedachten*)'. [85] However this may be, Nietzsche's demolition of Hegel's theoretical historicism clears the ground for Weber's attempt to place the legislation of values or of practical ethics at the centre of attention in the social sciences and historical studies. [86] Were there space here, I would go on to suggest that Nietzsche's reinterpretation of *Geist* as a sublime refinement of human cruelty also had profound consequences for the social sciences and history as *Geisteswissenschaften*, and for Weber's 'methodological' writings.

The present inquiry must be restricted, however, to the initial stages of Nietzsche's argument for displacing traditional moral/political philosophy in order to overcome moral relativism. For these first steps in Nietzsche's traverse dramatically bring forward the considerations that gave Weber's stance toward moral relativism its practical urgency and pathos.

Hastening the Collapse of Moral Relativism

In the first fifteen aphorisms of Part 7 of *Beyond Good and Evil*, Nietzsche attempts to undermine esteem for the historical sense, as well as the complacency of modern psychology, by arguing that the climate of mutual toleration, promoted during the nineteenth century in Western Europe by modern doctrines of moral relativism, will not endure. He claims that contemporary historicism, the moderate and relatively tolerant residue of Hegelian cosmopolitanism, is unstable: moral relativism is only weakly supported by 'our virtues'; it is a transient and untenable position.[87] Nietzsche predicted that a politics of ultimate commitment, of extreme partisanship, would soon emerge from behind the façade of *fin de siècle* tolerance and moderation.[88] Nietzsche tried to quicken this collapse of moral relativism; Weber subsequently followed his lead in doing so.[89] Nietzsche acknowledged, as did Weber, that the abandonment of moral relativism would hasten the collapse of an ostensibly humanitarian politics, including the politics of compassionate social policy within the framework of the dynastic *Rechtsstaat* in Wilhelmine Germany.[90] Like Weber, Nietzsche found this politics to be predicated on a chimerical assumption, that compassion is unambiguously and necessarily humanitarian.[91] According to Nietzsche and Weber, social or moral philosophy, leading to a 'public philosophy' articulating 'the general welfare', cannot possibly provide any such unambiguous humanitarian foundation: 'the general welfare' is neither an ideal, nor a goal, nor a graspable concept of any kind, but solely a battering ram to use against selected bastions of privilege and prerogative.[92]

Thus, Nietzsche begins his traverse by discrediting both the history produced by theoretical historicism and the theory provided by moral philosophy; he emphasizes their inability to cope with what Paul Valéry later called 'the immediate political problem, which consists after all in determining the relations of one man with the mass of men he does not know'.[93] To accomplish this, Nietzsche presents a sketch of the immediate practical problem. It is difficult to evaluate our actions because they characteristically reflect several different standards of moral conduct.[94] This multiplicity of standards, according to Nietzsche, is not incidental. It reflects the realities of modernization or democratization. The modern state establishes a new relation between public and private life by excluding government from the politics of moulding the soul or character.[95] Hence our age is not one in which the virtues are public, stable, visible: 'our virtues' are hard to vivisect, because we first have to develop an adequate optics for bringing the living virtues up to the operating table.[96] It is not even settled that we will *have* virtues and vices; if we do have them, Nietzsche thinks these virtues will be very different and far less public in their manifestation. Our virtues are hard to revaluate, because they do not present themselves straightforwardly or foursquare, like the virtues of our forebears. [97]

The rise of the modern state is thus linked, on Nietzsche's analysis, to a masking or interiorizing of standards of virtue. If we moderns do have virtues, according to Nietzsche, they will not be public but will rather be linked to the hottest passions in the hidden recesses of our souls. [98] The rise of the modern state and its democratization promote the intermingling of peoples, classes and races. In Nietzsche's view, this intermingling necessitates both moral relativism and a politics of disguise. [99] Democratization within the impersonal modern state requires formerly segregated or isolated groups to take account of alien moral standards and adapt to the requirements of mutual toleration, but it does not require them to give up their traditions: inwardly, these diverse nations, *ethnoi*, classes and races, may adhere to the moral standards of their forebears. The surface we see is, therefore, respect for a multiplicity of standards, or moral relativism, but this respect is without deep roots and has nothing to do with 'the hottest passions in the hidden recesses of our souls'. [100]

Nietzsche thus intimates that the high value currently placed on the historical sense is a result of political need. The need finds expression in a quest for costumes and public masks. Nietzsche implies that this contemporary craving is comic, reflecting plebeian insecurities and the desire of parvenus for a public persona. [101] A less caustic and more Weberian formulation would be that the high contemporary evaluation of historicism is integral to the quest for dignity by groups who either cannot assert their old pride or are ambiguous about new forms. What they share in common is that they are all outsiders: they share hostility to any imposition of a ruling way of life: no one wants to be matter to be made over in someone else's image. The quest for disguises is for a haven from which one could emerge with full dignity. But even this more sympathetic view would not essentially alter Nietzsche's contention: that historicism is attractive because we crave masks, not because we take it seriously as a doctrine. Historicism and a relativist climate of opinion permit us to keep the surface of public life agreeably frivolous; they help to prevent anyone from moulding our will. It is possible that Weber's scepticism about natural right appeals is based on this Nietzschean insight that much of the modern rhetoric of rights is intended to provide public masks: not so much to disguise private interests (that does not concern Nietzsche), but rather to decrease the psychological and social tensions caused by the commingling of once clearly delineated, once clearly opposed ways of life. [102]

To recapitulate the initial stage of Nietzsche's argument: our 'immediate political problem' makes a certain intellectual sensibility dominant. Theoretical historicism seems to provide a grounding for the politics of mutual toleration and disguise. The next step in Nietzsche's traverse toward practical historicism is to show that this grounding is untenable. Nietzsche mischievously demonstrates how easygoing moral relativism can be radicalized. Serious or thorough going relativism is untimely or uncongenial to the age, because it can become a seminary of intolerance. That is why contemporary psychologists hold back from looking too closely at morality, and why 'moral philosophy' is so dangerous that it ought to be made as boring as possible. [103]

Compassion

Tolerant moral relativism is bound to break down, according to Nietzsche and Weber, because 'our contemporaries' are forcefully drawn to compassion as a basis for public policy. The need for a clear concept or a credible common ground for policy will become ever more urgent, because the passions aroused by the politics of compassion are suggestible and intensely divisive. Neither theoretical historicism nor ahistorical moral philosophy can provide such a clear concept: they therefore leave us prey to 'undisciplined instincts, sympathies and antipathies'.[104]

We have seen that, early in Part 7, Nietzsche stressed the comic side of contemporary public life, the parade of political fashions that makes democratic politics a series of costume-parties. This politics of disguise is highly congenial to the leadership of historicist opinion. But there is a moralistic politics that deracinated classes and races do take with almost religious seriousness, and that is the politics of compassion. When Nietzsche takes up pity later in his argument, he tries to exploit the following difficulty: a social policy that makes claims on the strong to help the weak in the name of compassion prompts the strong to compassionate their own kind.[105] The bull who is gored by the politics of compassion will make his suffering a counter-claim and bellow for help. When it becomes a case of compassion versus compassion, *as it must*, according to Nietzsche, the politics of toleration, secured by the *Rechtsstaat*, will give way to a politics of indignation and moralistic self-assertion, or of ultimate commitment.[106]

The immoralism for which Nietzsche is famous thus rests on a rediscovery of the hard lesson that morality is dangerous, potentially cruel – and for Nietzsche's purposes, therefore good.[107] The politics of compassion to which our contemporaries are drawn underestimates or overlooks this danger, and the 'historical sense' does nothing to sharpen our perception of the danger. It rather leads us to misperceive what taking rights seriously would actually mean for our politics and our way of life.[108] Hence, Nietzsche must rely upon our only remaining experience of a virtue that imposes a ranking of values. Amazingly, he relies on 'our virtue' of intellectual probity – the very virtue that makes us question and undermine morality – to teach us that every truly serious morality imposes a Yes and a No.[109] Morality requires what Weber later spoke of as 'ultimate commitment'. It requires not only that we affirm one way of life, but that we negate another. And willing destruction, actually living the No in a morality, is threateningly close to nihilism.[110]

This harsh side of morality would not have to be faced if we could rest moral conduct (or social policy) upon a principle such as compassion, a humanitarian principle. But upon Nietzsche's inspection, the principle of compassion proves to be unstable and fraught with potential conflict, for reasons that go beyond the elementary problems of group conflict sketched above.

Compassion has to be triggered by the sight of a suffering subject; for this reason, even compassion for 'humanity' can take diametrically opposed forms. Since all human beings are at once both creatures and creators, we can pity in them either the creature or the creator.[111] These options yield opposed standards for compassionate policy: for, if we compassionate the creature in man who is acted upon from without, we prove to be harsh and unyielding toward the creator in man who shapes the creature. If the struggle is one of compassion against compassion, therefore, it is also cruelty against cruelty. [112] The argument for compassion necessarily has a tougher side. We cannot defend a policy of compassion without embracing a harshly political code of conduct against those whose compassion goes out to the wrong beneficiaries. It is, therefore, not puzzling that proponents of compassionate morality are seldom hesitant to practise cruelty, or more broadly, the politics of force and fraud. [113]

With the emergence of a plurality of moral claims to compassion, the 'public philosophy' of modern moral relativism will become a seminary of intolerance. This predictable declension justified Nietzsche's anticipation that 'equality of rights' could all too easily change into an assertion of equality in wrongs (*Unrecht*), 'a vulgar warfare against everything rare, strange, exceptional ...' [114] Nietzsche and Weber shared this analysis, and both attempted to dispel the chimerical hope for a unifying politics of compassion. Weber's hostility to traditional political philosophy, and particularly to the doctrines Nietzsche attacks in aphorism 228 – hedonism, pessimism, utilitarianism, eudaemonism – was largely directed against this illusory hope. [115] Weber undoubtedly thought that by compelling men to render themselves an account of the 'ultimate meaning of their own conduct', he was defending a 'higher duty, higher responsibility' against vulgar *Rechthaberei* or self-righteousness. [116] To conclude: Weber's denial that he was propounding a defence of moral relativism is most intelligible in the context of the extended Nietzschean argument articulated above.

Why Wasn't Weber a Nihilist?

We may nevertheless question the stability of Weber's attempt to distinguish himself from the moral relativists and, at the same time, from Nietzschean nihilism. Nietzsche tried to accelerate the collapse of moral relativism in order to clear the ground for a comprehensive legislating of new values. [117] By contrast, Weber radicalized moral relativism, while denying that a new ranking of values was possible. [118] He made it a matter of principle to affirm a politics of ultimate commitment, of devotion to a cause, precisely in the absence of any ranking of values. And while he spoke – as did Nietzsche – of a politics of 'responsibility', Weber's defence of responsible pluralism was intended as a defence of just those liberal democratic institutions that normally shelter moral relativists. [119] Weber urged political men to eschew any alternative as *Weltablehnung*, a turning away from the world, and he branded Nietzsche's philosophic politics as an escape from the stern realities of our fateful times. [120] Instead of embracing nihilism, as Nietzsche did, in order to destroy the very foundations of contemporary moral relativism, Weber continued to speak of 'serving moral forces' where this could only mean 'serving moral pluralism' (and, *pari passu*, moral relativism). [121] Weber's work thus has the form of a Nietzschean revaluation of values only up to a point. Thereafter, Weber turns the rhetoric of revaluation against Nietzsche, and against philosophy in the grand style, rather than risk an ascent or fall into nihilism.

Did Weber provide a reasonable justification of this eclecticism? Did he ever adequately ground this selective approach to Nietzsche's thought? Weber warned that Marxian historical materialism was not a cab to be taken at will.[122] We must therefore determine whether he had discovered a fissure in Nietzsche's argument, a flaw that enabled him, without illogicality or *sacrifizio dell' intelleto*, to turn Nietzsche's revaluation of values against Nietzsche, rather than following it relentlessly to its destination – that is (if Nietzsche is right), to the conclusion to which intellectual honesty compels us.[123] Until such a fissure is convincingly shown, the result of sustained inquiry into Weber's relation with Nietzsche can only be to exhibit fundamental questions that are neither adequately posed nor answered within the circle of Weber's thought. Does the liberation of social science from theoretical historicism, like so many other liberation movements of our time, merely enthral us to another historicism, of a more resolute and remorseless kind?

... it is quite possible that the modern philosopher is in much greater need of reflection on his situation because, having abandoned the resolve to look at things *sub specie aeternitatis*, he is much more exposed to, and enthralled by, the convictions and 'trends' dominating his age. Reflection on one's historical situation may very well be no more than a remedy for a deficiency that has been caused by historicism, or rather by the deeper motives which express themselves in historicism and which did not hamper the philosophic efforts of former ages.[124]

Notes: Chapter 27

Translations in the text are my own and are based upon *Nietzsche Werke: Kritische Gesamtausgabe*, ed. by G. Colli and M. Montinari (Berlin, 1968 ff.), apart from quotations taken from F. Nietzsche, *Beyond Good and Evil: A Prelude to the Philosophy of the Future*, transl. by W. Kaufmann (New York, 1966). This volume will be quoted as BGE, numbers referring to the aphorisms as numbered by Nietzsche.

1 See R. Eden, *Political Leadership and Nihilism: A Study of Weber and Nietzsche* (Gainesville, Fla, 1984); idem. 'Bad conscience for a Nietzschean age: Weber's calling for science', *Review of Politics*, vol. 45 (1983), pp. 366–92; W. Hennis, 'Max Webers Fragestellung', *Zeitschrift für Politik*, vol. 29 (1982), pp. 241–81; W. Shapiro, 'Nietzsche, Weber and the foundations of political science' (paper presented at the Annual Meeting of the American Political Science Association, Washington DC, August 1980); idem, 'Nietzsche, Weber, human nature and sociology' (paper presented at the annual meeting of the Southern Sociological Society, Knoxville, Tenn., March 1980); idem 'The Nietzschean roots of Max Weber's social science' (PhD thesis, Cornell University, 1978); H. Baier, 'Die Gesellschaft – ein langer Schatten des toten Gottes. Friedrich Nietzsche und die Entstehung der Soziologie aus dem Geist der decadence', *Nietzsche-Studien*, vol. 10/11 (1982), pp. 1–22; K. Lichtblau, 'Friedrich Nietzsche und die klassische deutsche Soziologie – Aspekte einer nietzscheanischen Soziologie' (manuscript, Fakultät für Geschichtsissenschaft und Philosophie, Universität Bielefeld).

2 The best work on the controversies surrounding Weber is by S. P. Turner and R. A. Factor, *Max Weber and the Dispute over Reason and Values: A Study in Philosophy, Ethics and Politics* (London, 1984). See also J. Kocka, 'Kontroversen über Max Weber', *Neue politische Literatur*, vol. 21 (1976), pp. 281–301; H. Fogt, 'Max Weber und die deutsche Soziologie der Weimarer Republik: Aussenseiter oder Gründervater?' in M. R. Lepsius (ed.), *Soziologie in Deutschland und Österreich, 1918–1945. Materialien zur Entwicklung, Emigration und Wirkungsgeschichte* (Opladen, 1981), pp. 245–61. For the bitter controversy over Wolfgang J. Mommsen's study of Weber's politics, see his Afterword to the

second edition, translated into English as *Max Weber and German Politics, 1890–1920* (Chicago, 1984), especially pp. 415 ff.

3 Turner and Factor, *Max Weber*, pp. 209–33. The critique advanced by L. Strauss in *Natural Right and History* (Chicago, Ill., 1953), has been ignored rather than rebutted by social scientists; on the complexity of the issues posed by Strauss's chapter on Weber, see R. Eden, 'Why wasn't Weber a nihilist?' (paper presented to the Annual Meeting of the American Political Science Association, Chicago, Ill., 1983).

4 C. Antoni, *From History to Sociology: The Transition in German Historical Thinking* (London, 1962); H. S. Hughes, *Consciousness and Society: The Reorientation of European Social Thought, 1890–1930* (New York, 1958); G. G. Iggers, 'The dissolution of German historicism', in R. Herr and H. Parker (eds), *Ideas in History* (Durham, NC, 1965); K. R. Popper, *The Poverty of Historicism*, 2nd edn (London, 1960). As Georg Simmel put the liberationist creed, 'It is necessary to emancipate the self from historicism in the same way that Kant freed it from naturalism ... The definitive purpose of the ensuing investigations may, therefore, be described as follows: they attempt to emancipate the mind – its formative power – from historicism in the same way that Kant freed it from naturalism.' G. Simmel, *The Problems of the Philosophy of History: An Epistemological Essay*, transl. and ed. by G. Oakes (New York, 1977), pp. viii–ix.

5 This thesis is advanced with particular attention to Weber's Inaugural Lecture of 1895, in Eden, *Political Leadership and Nihilism*, pp. 15—71.

6 A classic work blissfully oblivious to the importance of historicism in Weber's thought is W. G. Runciman, *A Critique of Max Weber's Philosophy of Social Science* (Cambridge, 1972). Runciman argues that Weber's doctrine of value-relevance is an irrelevance: pp. 33, 37–41, 47–8, 92–3. It is, however, the *point d'appui* of Weber's relation to Nietzsche in the methodological writings. See further, E. F. Miller, 'Positivism, historicism, and political inquiry', *American Political Science Review*, vol. 66 (1972), pp. 796–817.

7 Strauss articulates the distinction between theoretical and practical historicism most clearly just prior to his critique of Weber: 'The radical historicist ... recognizes the absurdity of unqualified historicism as a theoretical thesis. He denies, therefore, the possibility of a theoretical or objective analysis, which as such would be trans-historical, of the various comprehensive views or "historical worlds" or "cultures". This denial was decisively prepared by Nietzsche's attack on nineteenth-century historicism, which claimed to be a theoretical view. According to Nietzsche, the theoretical analysis of human life that realizes the relativity of all comprehensive views and thus depreciates them would make human life itself impossible, for it would destroy the protecting atmosphere within which life or culture or action is alone possible. Moreover, since the theoretical analysis has its basis outside of life, it will never be able to understand life. The theoretical analysis of life is noncommittal and fatal to commitment, but life means commitment.' L. Strauss, *Natural Right and History*, p. 26.

8 See H. Caton, 'World in decay: Critiques of the historiography of progress', *Canadian Journal of Political and Social Theory* (in press).

9 For a supporting interpretation of the Preface, and Parts 6 and 9 of *Beyond Good and Evil*, see Eden, *Political Leadership and Nihilism*, pp. 53–63, 72–133.

10 For Weber's relation to the German Historical School of political economy, see Chapter 2 by Wilhelm Hennis in this volume. For a more extensive treatment of Roth's and Schluchter's account of Weber, see R. Eden, 'Weber's historical perspective', *Review of Politics*, vol. 46 (1984), pp. 142–5.

11 BGE 223, 224; and see Nietzsche's reinterpretation of *Geist* in BGE 229–30. I would question Alan Ryan's thesis, in Chapter 11 in this volume, ascribing primary importance to John Stuart Mill in the origin of the term *Geisteswissenschaften* in German scholarship.

12 BGE 214, 223–4. See the title to Vol. 2, Book 1, of Alexis de Tocqueville's *Democracy in America*.

13 Cf. BGE 212 with BGE 214, 218, 224 and 227. The term 'vivisection', introduced in BGE 212, occurs only once in Part 7, at the end of BGE 218.

14 T. Burger, 'Droysen and the Idea of *Verstehen*', *Journal of the History of the Behavioral Sciences*, vol. 14 (1978), pp. 6–19. The most sustained interpretation of the centrality of intellectual probity in Weber's thought is G. Hufnagel, *Kritik als Beruf. Der kritische Gehalt im Werk Max Webers* (Frankfurt, 1971).

15 I am aware that some readers may be jarred by the identification of 'the historical sense' with *Verstehen*. See the introduction by Guy Oakes to Simmel, *The Problems of the*

Philosophy of History; also Burger, 'Droysen'; and compare Nietzsche's description of the historical sense in BGE 224.

16 BGE 224 end: 'Measure is foreign to us, let us admit it to ourselves.'

17 BGE 227. I choose the term 'ferocity' advisedly, to highlight the link between Nietzsche and Machiavelli. That Nietzsche understands virtue in an extramoral sense as Machiavellian *virtù* may be suggested by his emphasis on discipline in BGE 226: among the 'free spirits' to whom Nietzsche speaks of 'we immoralists', Machiavelli leaps to mind even if one has not read BGE 28. Compare *The Prince*, ch. 26, with *On the Genealogy of Morals*, essay 2, aphorism 24 end; *The Prince*, ch. 25 end with *Genealogy*, essay 3, epigramme before aphorism 1.

18 BGE 224 end; BGE 223. See the discussion of 'monumental history' in *On the Use and Abuse of History for Life*, sections 2, 7.

19 Cf. *Genealogy*, essay 3, aphorism 26.

20 Consider the connection between BGE 226 and 227; and recall the juxtaposition of a pessimism of weakness (which we may safely identify with the historicism Nietzsche had criticized in *Abuse of History*) in BGE 208 with a pessimism of strength in BGE 209, a pessimism that Nietzsche identifies with Frederick the Great (and, pari passu, with Machiavelli?). See Eden, *Political Leadership and Nihilism*, pp. 84–7.

21 Consider BGE 212. The historical sense reinforces 'the taste of the time and the virtue of the time', which Nietzsche identifies with 'weakness of will' and professional specialization; probity, by contrast, can be a virtue of greatness and solitude.

22 On self-contempt, see BGE 222, and compare Nietzsche, *The Gay Science*, aphorisms 273–5.

23 As Simmel treats it in his critique of 'historical realism', *The Problems of the Philosophy of History*, p. 76. Compare BGE 224 end.

24 See BGE 226, 229–30.

25 Compare Nietzsche, *The Gay Science*, aphorisms 273–5, with L. Strauss, 'Machiavelli', in L. Strauss and J. Cropsey (eds), *History of Political Philosophy*, 2nd edn (Chicago, 1972), p. 271.

26 Compare BGE 230 end with BGE 208 and BGE 1 end.

27 In BGE 284, see the vow 'to remain master of one's ... virtues'.

28 BGE 227, 229–30, 208–9; compare the first paragraph of Martin Heidegger's *Letter on Humanism*. The importance of the first-person pronoun is clear from the title of Part 7. Variants of 'we' and 'our' occur 169 times in this Part. The first person plural possessive pronoun or adjective, 'our', occurs once in the title and 83 times in the text: the central occurrence identifies the historical sense as '*our* great virtue', BGE 224 (*Nietzsche Werke: Kritische Gesamtausgabe*, ed. by G. Colli and M. Montinari, Berlin, 1968 ff., Vol. 6, part 2, p. 165, lines 30–1). 'We' occurs 86 times; the central occurrences are both in BGE 226, in the opening phrase, 'we immoralists'. Of all 169, the central occurrence is in the command, 'Let us admit it to ourselves, measure is alien to us' (Das Maß ist uns fremd, gestehn wir es uns). The virtue of the historical sense is mastered when intellectual probity compels us to admit this as the vital shortcoming of our historical sense.

29 Cf. Hughes, *Consciousness and Society*. On intellectual honesty, see especially MSS, pp. 1–9. (That Weber was well aware of the tension between probity and *Verstehen* stressed by Nietzsche is indicated by Weber's remarks on p. 98.) See also 'Über einige Kategorien der verstehenden Soziologie', in WL³, pp. 427–41.

30 BGE 230 end; Eden, *Political Leadership and Nihilism*, pp. 98–133; M. Heidegger, *Nietzsche* (Pfullingen, 1961), Vol. 1, epigramme, and pp. 473–658.

31 Nietzsche, *The Gay Science*, aphorism 324; *Genealogy*, essay 3, aphorism 28.

32 Cf. Eden, *Political Leadership and Nihilism*, pp. 134–73.

33 See note 3 above.

34 BGE 214–17; 219; 228. Compare BGE 204.

35 Compare BGE Preface; 225, 228, 230 end.

36 BGE 23, 228.

37 BGE 225 end.

38 See Shapiro, 'The Nietzschean roots of Max Weber's social science', pp. 15, 31–2, 65, 163–8.

39 R. Bendix and G. Roth, 'Max Webers Einfluß auf die amerikanische Soziologie', *Kölner Zeitschrift für Soziologie und Sozialpsychologie*, vol. 11 (1959), pp. 38–53; O. Stammer (ed.), *Max Weber and Sociology Today* (New York, 1971).

40 FMW, p. 152.

41   ibid., pp. 153, 155. See Turner and Factor, *Max Weber*, pp. 180–201.
42   Cf. the remarks of Edward Shils in his introduction to MSS, p. vii.
43   Cf. Strauss, *Natural Right and History*, p. 37.
44   MSS, pp. 59, 72–4, 78–81, 89–92, 150–1.
45   FMW, p. 152; MSS, p. 67.
46   FMW, p. 152.
47   Cf. Miller, 'Positivism, historicism and political inquiry'.
48   G. Roth and W. Schluchter, *Max Weber's Vision of History: Ethics and Methods* (Berkeley, Calif., 1979), p. 11; W. Schluchter, *The Rise of Western Rationalism: Max Weber's Developmental History* (Berkeley, Calif., 1981), p. xv.
49   Roth and Schluchter, *Max Weber's Vision of History*, pp. 76, 112, 132, 136, 142, 147, 204.
50   ibid., pp. 11, 83.
51   ibid., pp. 42, 103, 142.
52   ibid., p. 59.
53   ibid.
54   ibid.
55   ibid., p. 107.
56   ibid., p. 71.
57   ibid., p. 58.
58   ibid., p. 53
59   ibid., p. 80.
60   ibid., pp. 1–2, 108–9.
61   See Schluchter's remarks on Habermas in ibid., pp. 74–6, 92–3, 111–12.
62   ibid., p. 107.
63   ibid., p. 58.
64   ibid., p. 52.
65   Schluchter mentions Nietzsche but offers no judgement on whether Weber was, or was not, a nihilist in Nietzsche's meaning of the term: ibid., pp. 58–9.
66   MSS, p. vii.
67   See Burger, 'Droysen', and Turner and Factor, *Max Weber*, pp. 180–233.
68   BGE 1–23, and especially BGE 6.
69   Roth and Schluchter, *Max Weber's Vision of History*, pp. 52, 58–9.
70   See Eden, *Political Leadership and Nihilism*, pp. 72–97, 134–73.
71   For the demonstration and deduction that the sixteenth-century philosopher discussed, but not named, in BGE 212 must be Montaigne, see Eden, *Political Leadership and Nihilism*, pp. 59–61.
72   BGE Preface; BGE 212; Eden, *Political Leadership and Nihilism*, pp. 54–9.
73   Cf. BGE 208 and 212.
74   BGE Preface.
75   Nietzsche, *The Gay Science*, aphorisms 110–111.
76   *Genealogy*, passim.
77   BGE Preface, 208.
78   BGE 222–30, 232, 238; BGE Preface, 203, 256; *Genealogy*, essay 1, aphorisms 11–12; essay 3, aphorisms 26–8.
79   BGE 228–30.
80   Montaigne, Essays, II.11, III.12. See L. Schaefer, 'The Good, the Beautiful and the Useful: Montaigne's transvaluation of values', *American Political Science Review*, vol. 73 (1979), pp. 139–53.
81   BGE 229–30.
82   BGE 230 end.
83   BGE 230.
84   See R. Eden, 'Bad conscience for a Nietzschean age', pp. 360–92.
85   BGE 228.
86   See Eden, *Political Leadership and Nihilism*, pp. 38–42.
87   Note the final sentence of BGE 214; compare FMW, p. 394.
88   BGE 208–9; see also BGE 242, 251; FMW, p. 125.
89   Cf. MSS, p. 98; GPS^2, pp. 13–14.
90   Compare BGE 222, 225, with Weber's critique of Bismarck's social welfare policy in 'Parliament and Government in a Reconstructed Germany', in ES, Vol. 2, pp. 1390–1. As Mommsen observed, 'He certainly did not favor social policy out of a sense of social respon-

sibility. His views were close to those of Nietzsche in this area; he held no brief for "pity".'
Mommsen, *Max Weber and German Politics*, p. 101. See also ibid., pp. 102–23.

91 BGE 225; see Weber's critique of the 'chief mistake' of the commission of inquiry on the Bourse, its 'moral approach'; Mommsen, *Max Weber and German Politics*, p. 74, citing Weber's denial that there could be for any nation 'a "fundamental" solution of economic questions based upon economic or social "justice" or, more generally, upon any ethical point of view ...'.
92 BGE 228; GPS², pp. 15–16, 24. Mommsen, *Max Weber and German Politics*, pp. 101–23.
93 P. Valéry, *History and Politics* (New York, 1962), p. 12.
94 BGE 216; see BGE 200.
95 See Eden, *Political Leadership and Nihilism*, pp. 43, 49–52.
96 BGE 214; compare BGE 230 end; BGE 262.
97 BGE 214, 216.
98 BGE 214; compare BGE 212.
99 BGE 223; compare BGE 242, 262 and especially 200.
100 BGE 214.
101 Combine BGE 222 and 223 and compare BGE 201–2.
102 BGE 223, 200, 262. Cf. Roth and Schluchter, *Max Weber's Vision of History*, pp. 142, 147.
103 BGE 218, 228.
104 GPS², p. 16. Compare Eden, *Political Leadership and Nihilism*, pp. 24 ff.
105 BGE 221, 225.
106 Is this the point of Nietzsche's enigmatic foreboding or hope at the end of BGE 214? Compare 'Why I am a Destiny', aphorisms 1–7, in F. Nietzsche, *On the Genealogy of Morals and Ecce Homo*, transl. by W. Kaufmann and R. J. Hollingdale (New York, 1967), pp. 326–35.
107 Compare BGE 226 and 229.
108 BGE 216, 217, 221, 224; BGE 262, 265.
109 BGE 224, 227, 229.
110 BGE 208; see *Ecce Homo*.
111 BGE 225.
112 BGE 225, 229–30.
113 Compare BGE 217, 212 end; FMW, p. 125.
114 BGE 212, near the end: *Nietzsche Werke: Kritische Gesamtausgabe*, Vol. 6, part 2, p. 151, lines 3–8.
115 BGE 225, 228; GPS², pp. 15–16, 24, 59–62.
116 FMW, pp. 152, 118, 125.
117 *Ecce Homo*.
118 FMW, pp. 148–9, 125–8. See Eden, *Political Leadership and Nihilism*, pp. 73, 136, 139, 148, 154–8, 183, 186, 188, 203–4, 218–20, 226–7.
119 See ibid., pp. 174–94.
120 FMW, pp. 127, 149, 153, 155–6.
121 FMW, p. 152; Eden, *Political Leadership and Nihilism*, pp. 134–73.
122 FMW, p. 125.
123 See note 28 above.
124 L. Strauss, 'Political philosophy and history', in idem, *What is Political Philosophy? and Other Studies* (New York, 1959), p. 71. See also M. Blitz, 'Radical historicism and the meaning of natural right', *Modern Age*, vol. 28 (1984), pp. 243–6.

3 The Ambiguity of Modernity: Georg Simmel and Max Weber

DAVID FRISBY

I

Despite the existence of a whole range of 'elective affinities' between aspects of the work of Georg Simmel and Max Weber – at the methodological, substantive and philosophical-historical levels – and despite the frequent personal contact between their two households after the turn of the century, there still exists no systematic examination of the relationship between the two figures either at the personal or intellectual level.[1] And, if we take a broader perspective at the personal level and include common acquaintances and students, then we are confronted with a remarkable 'intersection of social circles' around the two figures. Some of the materials for outlining the networks of personal contact are already to hand in memoirs, correspondence and substantive writings. To take some of the perhaps less obvious examples, it would be fruitful to examine the different and changing responses of Weber and Simmel to Stefan George and his circle.[2] Since both Weber and Simmel are often seen to be located within the neo-Kantian philosophical tradition of the Southwest German School, it is surely time to re-examine that relationship and question whether Simmel, for instance, despite his extensive correspondence with Heinrich Rickert, was not influenced by a much earlier neo-Kantian tradition.[3] In turn, the influence of Weber and Simmel upon their students could hardly overlook their respective response to the two maverick figures of Ernst Bloch and Georg Lukács.[4]

But, at the same time, an investigation of the interweaving of their social and academic networks could not ignore the very different nature of the two individuals and their responses to the options that lay open to them. Even though, in both instances, at various points in their lives, Weber and Simmel not merely wrote for a variety of audiences but also were faced with a range of seemingly contradictory options as far as their life-interests were concerned, they both contrived to resolve this diversity. In Weber's case, especially though by no means exclusively in his later years, the academy and the political sphere, including political journalism, were spheres into which he was drawn, producing a tension that can hardly be said to have been satisfactorily resolved. In Simmel's case, his full admission into the academy was achieved, if at all, only with the greatest difficulty, while the political option – as society's stranger – was never compelling aside from his brief foray into some socialist circles in the early 1890s.[5] And, to complete the comparison, it was seldom political journalism but rather an often aesthetic feuilletonism which either appealed to Simmel or into which he was drawn. In contrast to Weber, Simmel was seldom, if at all, drawn into the politically loaded methodological disputes that so preoccupied Weber. Indeed, Weber's political confidence with regard to the politics of the academy as well as society as a whole can perhaps be contrasted with Simmel's diffidence and even indifference. Thus, if there is little doubt that there existed a fascinating intersection of their social circles, the weight which Weber and Simmel placed upon each one was most often very different.

In terms of intellectual development, the relationship between Simmel and Weber appears to be largely a one-sided one. Since Simmel was so averse to referencing any of his major works, they present us with an enormous hermeneutic task of reconstructing their contexts in the light of his contemporaries and predecessors. In this respect, they still retain that virtuoso quality that was commented upon by so many of Simmel's contemporaries. At any event, they provide little or no illumination about Simmel's regard for Weber's works. In Weber's case, the explicit, published references to Simmel's work are largely confined to footnotes in his own writings from *The Protestant Ethic* onwards. Even the important unfinished assessment of Simmel as 'sociologist and theorist of the money economy' (probably 1908)[6] breaks off at precisely the point at which Weber is about to expound his criticisms of Simmel's sociology. Neither man reviewed or commented extensively upon the other's works. In this respect, the absent relationship between Durkheim and Weber – so often remarked upon – is paralleled by the incomplete relationship between Simmel and Weber as it is manifested in their published works. Simmel's work was reviewed by notable contemporaries such as Tönnies (*Über sociale Differenzierung* [On Social Differentiation][7] *Einleitung in die Moralphilosophie*[8] [Introduction to Moral Philosophy]) and Durkheim (*Philosophy of Money*[9] among other writings), but not by Weber. Conversely, the only work by a contemporary German sociologist that Simmel reviewed was a now neglected monograph by Tönnies (*Der Nietzsche-Kultus*).[10] In the social sciences in Germany as a whole, Simmel did review works by the economist Knapp (1888),[11] Stammler (1896)[12] – a decade before Weber's critical response – and Schmoller (1900).[13] Like Weber, Simmel remained largely silent on the works of Durkheim – despite his correspondence with Celestin Bouglé – though he did review the works of important contemporary French contributors to the social sciences such as Gabriel Tarde (1891)[14] and Gustav le Bon (1895).[15]

But perhaps the absence of any judgement by Simmel upon Weber's writings is not surprising if we examine more closely the period within which they were both making a contribution to sociology. Before 1900, Weber's research was concentrated in the areas of economics, politics, law and economic and cultural history understood in their broadest sense. Before 1900, probably the first to teach courses exclusively on sociology as an independent discipline in Germany (other figures who might come into question are Ernst Grosse in Freiburg, Paul Barth in Leipzig and Ferdinand Tönnies in Kiel) was, even as early as 1894, Georg Simmel. Even in 1899, Simmel himself declared to Bouglé that 'sociology is a very specialized discipline for which there is no representative in Germany apart from myself'.[16] Within a single decade between 1890 and 1900, that is, between the publication of Simmel's *Über sociale Differenzierung* (1890) and *The Philosophy of Money* (1900), Simmel had not only also published a range of articles on sociology – including the crucial 'The problem of sociology' (1894), described by its author as 'the most fruitful one that I have written', and by 1900 translated into English, French and Italian – but to his own satisfaction had established sociology as an independent discipline. Furthermore, Simmel's works were already reaching an international sociological public. The very first issue of *L'Année Sociologique* (1896) contained as its second contribution an essay by Simmel. Between 1896 and 1910, largely as a result of the initiative of Albion Small, nine of Simmel's sociological essays appeared in the newly established *American Journal of Sociology*. We need only contrast this state of affairs with the much later reception of Weber's 'sociological' works.

There exists, therefore, some justification for Tenbruck's claim that 'Simmel's sociological work is thus confined to a single decade. Hence he is specifically and in the strict sense not a contemporary of Max Weber. As the latter commenced sociological work, the former had already taken his leave of it.'[17] It is certainly true that within this decade Simmel had established the basic framework for his sociology and that, after 1898, he ceased to preface his substantive articles on sociology with a justification for the grounds of such a discipline. But this is to restrict too greatly Simmel's interest in sociology. Between 1894 – when Simmel first taught a course simply entitled 'Sociology' (for which 152 students enrolled) – and 1908, he taught a course on sociology annually. Thereafter, that is, after the publication of his major *Soziologie* (1908), he taught sociology courses only in the winter semesters of 1909/10, 1911/12 and 1917/18 (1917 saw the publication of his *Grundfragen der Soziologie* [Basic Issues in Sociology]). On the other hand, it is true that Simmel's *Soziologie* is largely composed of articles already published between 1888 and 1908. One important exception is the excursus: 'How is Society Possible?' This should not be taken to imply that Simmel's intellectual productivity was in decline, but merely that it increasingly changed direction or at least broadened its base into a central concern with a philosophy of culture. Although suggested for the presidency of the new German Sociological Association, and even though he gave the opening address to its first congress in Frankfurt in 1910, Simmel's interests seemed increasingly to lie elsewhere.

Nevertheless, if it is the case that Simmel had already produced a formidable array of contributions to the new field of sociology before Weber turned his attention towards it, what was it that Weber felt compelled to respond to? It is well known that Weber studied *The Philosophy of Money* (1900) intensively after his nervous breakdown at the turn of the century and prior to the first version of his *The Protestant Ethic and the Spirit of Capitalism*. There, Weber praised Simmel's 'brilliant analysis' of the spirit of capitalism, although at the same time he suggested that 'the money economy and capitalism are too closely identified to the detriment of his concrete analysis'. Indeed, in *The Philosophy of Money*, Simmel 'tends to move from a discussion of the money economy to the effects of capitalism without realising that there is a distinction between the two'.[18] None the less, in all probability, Weber felt compelled to confront Simmel's characterization of capitalist rationality for this very reason, especially since Simmel offered a very different account of the origins of the capitalist spirit, while taking up many of the central features that Weber subsequently delineated. In this respect, Weber's arguments on the capitalist spirit may not merely be seen as a reply to Sombart and others but also, to some extent, to Simmel too. It does seem likely that Weber was impressed by Simmel's analysis of the nature of economic rationality and, in particular, by his detailed discussion of the teleology of means and ends, even to the extent that it may have found its way subsequently into Weber's own conception of purposive social action. The rationalization and functionalization of social relationships that Simmel illuminates in the context of a money economy may also have reinforced Weber's already implicit pessimistic philosophy of history. In other words, as Levine suggests, Weber found 'a provocative interpretation of the all-pervasive effects of rationalization in modern society and culture' [19] – a theme already announced, however, in Tönnies's *Community and Association* (1887) and especially his 'Historismus und Rationalismus' (1895). [20] Not merely Weber but Tönnies and Simmel before him had all, in their different ways, come to view any possible socialist society that might succeed capitalism as the highest or most extreme form of rationalization. This Simmel made clear in his *Philosophy of Money*.

It has also been argued that Simmel's *Philosophy of Money* was important at the methodological level. Schnabel, for instance, has suggested that in this work 'Weber found those methods outlined and in part carried out which he made use of in his later analysis of capitalism, *The Protestant Ethic and the Spirit of Capitalism*. He found a mode of procedure described there ... which did not remain content with the derivation and application of mere ideal types but rather extended them into embodiments of whole complexes of meaning which grasped the distinctiveness of levels of historical development.' [21] Yet it was precisely the demarcation of levels of historical development that Weber found to be unclear in Simmel's account of the money economy.

Of greater methodological significance for Weber was the second edition of Simmel's *The Problems of the Philosophy of History* [22] (1905), which he confronted extensively in his early development of the concept of *Verstehen*. Indeed, in his essay on Roscher and Knies (1903–6), Weber declared that 'the logically most fully developed attempts at a theory of *Verstehen* are to be found in the second edition of Simmel's *Probleme der Geschichtsphilosophie*'. In outlining his own theory of historical understanding, Weber confronts Simmel's theory of historical interpretation. But it is clear that Weber wishes to move in a different direction to Simmel. On one occasion, Weber points to Simmel's examples 'of expressions occasioned by "prejudice, anger, sarcasm", etc. However, the really decisive question is the following. Was there, for whatever reason, *cognitive reflection* concerning this *motive* for the expression – even if the purposes of this reflection were practical? What we call "interpretation" *in this paper* becomes applicable *only if* this condition is satisfied.' [23] Weber was already outlining a theory of the rational interpretation of human motivation (later in terms of interests) that could not be reduced to psychological states of the individual consciousness. Simmel, from his earliest writings onwards, was interested in the constellation of social psychological motivations for human interaction.

The Roscher–Knies essay also contains an indication that Weber intended a full-scale critique of Simmel's work, as when he remarks that 'my purpose is not to offer a systematic critique of Simmel's views. His theses are invariably artfully developed and technically refined. Shortly I shall return to the examination of some of these theses, probably in the *Archiv für Sozialwissenschaft und Sozialpolitik*.'[24] Though this commitment was never realized, this is perhaps the origin of the unpublished and unfinished outline of a critique of Simmel 'as a sociologist and theorist of the money economy' (1908). Such a possibility is reinforced by Weber's succeeding statement in this note, that the reader should consult the criticisms already advanced by Othmar Spann. These same criticisms, with which Weber largely concurred, recur again in Weber's own unfinished critique of Simmel.

It has been suggested that one reason why this critique remained unpublished was that its preparation coincided with Weber's (and Gothein's) recommendation of Simmel for the second chair of philosophy at Heidelberg University in 1908, should Rickert not accept it. Its publication could have damaged Simmel's chances of success. As it was, and although Rickert declined the chair, Simmel was not successful in Heidelberg and did not obtain a chair (of philosophy) until 1914 at Strasbourg University. Be that as it may, the then unpublished and incomplete critique remains the most sustained attempt by Weber to confront Simmel's sociology. There, Weber expressed his own ambiguous attitude towards Simmel's two major works: *Philosophy of Money* and *Soziologie*. Each of Simmel's works 'abounds in important theoretical ideas and the most subtle observations' and, 'even when he is on the wrong path', Simmel 'fully deserves his reputation as one of the foremost of thinkers, a first-rate stimulator of academic youth and academic colleagues'.[25]

Weber recognizes that the orthodox specialist is likely to be exasperated by Simmel's works because, 'where the specialist is dealing with questions of "facticity", empirical questions, Simmel has turned to look at the "meaning" which we can obtain from the phenomenon'.[26] And often this meaning is accessed via an 'analogical procedure' which Weber wished to criticize for 'the dubiousness of its basic principles (particularly pronounced in Simmel's treatment of sociological problems)'. Equally annoying for the specialist is the fact that, even where he is dealing with 'technical, substantive questions', Simmel's 'ultimate *interests* are directed to metaphysical problems, to the "*meaning*" of life'.[27] In passing it is worth noting both that this is indeed an explicit intention in his *Philosophy of Money*, and that the whole problematic of the meaning of life was given a greater urgency in part by both Simmel's and Weber's confrontation with the writings of Nietzsche (and Weber studied Simmel's *Schopenhauer und Nietzsche* [1907] with great interest).[28]

Had Weber completed his critique, he would have no doubt gone on to concur largely with the criticisms made earlier by Spann[29] of Simmel's concepts of 'society' and 'sociology', even though, Weber maintained, Simmel's 'recently published *Soziologie* shows some notable, but not fundamental, modifications'. Spann had argued that Simmel adhered to a 'psychologistic concept of society' that rested upon 'the definition of *societal* interaction as the interaction of *psychic* entities'. Simmel was unable to establish the basic premises for sociology, since its basic problematic – society – was defined 'more in the sense of a collective name' for diverse forms of interaction. Spann concluded that 'Simmel is ... the sole and first epistemologist of psychologistic sociology'. Weber could hardly have fully concurred with

Spann's criticism, since his own sociology does not take its central problematic to be a holistic conception of society.

Perhaps more seriously, Weber objected to Simmel's grounding of sociology in '"interactions" amongst individuals', largely because 'this concept of "interaction" extended so far that only with the greatest artificiality will one be able to conceptualize a pure "one-way" influence, i.e., an instance of one man being influenced by another where there is *not* some element of "interaction"'.[30] Clearly, Weber was already committed to a starting point in social action with an emphasis upon the intentionality of individual actors. In this context, however, and in the light of Simmel's emphasis upon typification and idealization in his role theory (especially in 'How is society possible?'), it has been suggested by Uta Gerhardt that 'it hardly requires additional evidence in order to make explicit the parallels between this determination of the *intentionality* of social action by Simmel and the conception of *rational* action by Weber', even though the latter 'sees in typification more a scientific method than a basic process of social interaction'.[31] It was, of course, the basic processes of social interaction and forms of sociation that constituted the focal point of Simmel's sociology.

It is perhaps significant that Weber's criticisms of Simmel are largely concerned with those 'crucial aspects of his methodology which are unacceptable'. In the first two decades of this century, Weber was seeking to refine his own epistemological foundation of sociology on the way to the development of sociology as a *Wirklichkeitswissenschaft*, a science of concrete reality. The nature of the reality that sociology was to deal with was not necessarily identical in the case of Simmel and Weber. Yet crucially they did share a conception of sociology that shifted the focus of its problematic away from an overarching notion of society. Indeed, if Simmel's occasional definitions of society are deliberately elusive and point toward society as, at most, a 'regulative idea', for Weber's sociology society is an absent concept.[32] Simmel shifts his focus to the study of forms of social interaction or 'sociation', though he does at least pose the quasi transcendental question of how society is at all possible. Weber, rejecting Simmel's concept of *interaction*, takes social *action*, its intentionality and the meanings individuals attach to such action, as his central focus.

II

Thematically, there exists a whole range of parallels that could be drawn between the works of Simmel and Weber. We think here of their discussions of bureaucracy, domination, conflict, religion and, of course, the analysis of the whole process of rationalization. In order to illuminate the parallels and differences between the two, it may be useful to examine briefly one theme that has returned to the forefront of sociological debate in Germany and elsewhere: the sociology of modernity. This has itself been understood as part of a wider ongoing discussion of the theory of rationality and rationalization in the work of Weber.

There is little doubt that Weber provides us with one of the most impressive, if incomplete, theories of modernization, which centres around his account of the development of modern Western rationalism and its consequences, among which is modern Western capitalism.[33] Several writers have pointed to the difficulties of clarifying the notion of rationality in its variants of instrumental, substantive, formal and conceptual rationality (Levine, Kalberg).[34] In addition, Levine has argued that we can detect in Weber's work a 'distinction between subjective and objective manifestations of rationality' that not merely echoes Simmel's subjective and objective culture distinction but which might form the basis for a central thesis in the dialectics of modernity. Indeed, it has been argued recently by Berman that Simmel 'intimates, but never really develops, what is probably the closest thing to a twentieth-century dialectical theory of modernity',[35] though what he has in mind is largely the outcome of Simmel's theory of the inevitable clash between subjective and objective culture.

The most recent attempt to develop a social theory of modernity – which retains its links with the discussion of the process of rationalization – is provided by Habermas in his essay on modernity and, more recently in his *Theory of Communicative Action* (1981).[36] In both these works Habermas focuses crucially, though not exclusively, upon Weber.

But when we turn to this recent attempt to outline Weber's theory of modernity, we find that Habermas acknowleges a number of difficulties. On the one hand, Weber's theory of rationalization offers 'the most promising beginning for the explanation of social pathologies, which appear as a result of capitalist modernization', while, on the other hand, 'the pathologies of modernity', arising out of the rationalization process, are considered by Weber solely from the standpoint of a theory of the rationalization of the systems of action that is itself confined to the standpoint of purposive rationality. As such, it is incapable of analysing the 'moral–practical and aesthetic –expressive aspects' of modernity. Weber's diagnosis of the present instead focuses upon the related processes of bureaucratization as 'a key phenomenon for the understanding of modern societies' and upon rationalization as the key to the emergence of capitalist society.

The new type of purposive-rational oganizational form is grounded in the rational calculation of production within capitalist enterprises and in public administration by legally trained officials. In both cases, the objectification of social relations in organizations produces depersonalized 'rationally functioning machines' in such a way that the dead machine in manufacture and the living machine in bureaucratic organization combine as 'the iron cage'. The formally organized spheres of action are distanced dramatically from the life-world: 'organizations gain autonomy via a *neutralizing demarcation over against the symbolic structures of the life-world*; confronted with culture, society and the personality, they thereby become fundamentally *indifferent*.'[37] What are the consequences of these processes for individuals?

Habermas sums up Weber's diagnosis of the present somewhat schematically under the headings of loss of freedom and loss of meaning for individuals. In the former case, rather than seeing the individual's loss of freedom as arising out of the rationalization process *per se*, Habermas argues that it actually arises out of an 'uncoupling of system and life-world' in such a way that orientations to action in the latter are conditioned by the former. With the lack of private orientation consequent upon the decline of inner-motivation from a generalized work-ethic, the private sphere increasingly lacks any focus for orientation. Weber speaks in this context of 'specialists without spirit' and 'hedonists without heart'. In the public sphere, legitimation of political authority demands increasingly the exclusion of the ethical sphere from the political. What originally gave meaning to the life-world is either fragmented or removed entirely.

In short, Habermas implicitly indicates a theory of modernity in Weber's work which, as a disjunction of social system and life-world and in its contemporary diagnosis, comes to resemble Simmel's separation of objective and subjective culture. The problem of individual orientation, in a similar way, is also acute. Weber saw the disenchantment of the world, arising out of the domination of a restricted form of rationality, as combining with the loss of meaning in the world (with no rationality of ends) to produce a threatening absence of value orientations for individuals:

> As intellectualism suppresses belief in magic, the world's processes become disenchanted, lose their magical significance, and henceforth simply 'are' and 'happen' but no longer signify anything. As a consequence, there is a growing demand that the world and the total pattern of life be subject to an order that is significant and meaningful. [38]

Simmel, concerned with 'the preponderance of objective over subjective culture', seems to reach similar conclusions while starting out from a different problematic. The 'measuring, weighing and calculating exactness of modern times', 'the growing transformation of all elements of life into means', and 'the peculiar levelling of emotional life that is ascribed to contemporary times' are all conditioned if not determined by the mature money economy. [39] The result is not merely the impoverishment of subjective culture, of the chances for individual creativity, but the elimination of human purposes and meanings that go beyond those provided by an objective culture. In other words,

> the conceivable elements of action become objectively and subjectively calculable rational relationships and in so doing progressively eliminate the emotional reactions and decisions which only attach themselves to the turning points of life, to the final purposes. [40]

Simmel's analysis of the domination of means over ends and the attendant self-estrangement of the individual seems, then, to have been echoed later in Weber's own assessment of modernity.

But there is an important difference between Weber's and Simmel's accounts of modernity. If it is the case that Weber's analysis is incapable, as Habermas argues, of dealing with the 'moral–practical and aesthetic–expressive aspects' of modernity or, more broadly, the modes of experiencing the life-world of modernity, then the same cannot be said of Simmel's account of modernity. In other words, Weber's account of the process of modernization as rationalization may be more firmly grounded than that of Simmel, but the latter's attempt to capture the *experience* of modernity was surely more successful.

Indeed, Simmel may be the first sociologist to have provided a social theory of modernity that accords with the sense given to modernity by Baudelaire nearly half a century earlier as the experience of the world as 'transitory, fleeting and contingent'.[41] Simmel, like his contemporaries. Tönnies, Durkheim and Weber, sought to grasp that which is 'new' or 'modern' in contemporary society. Yet the 'new' must be recognized in its transitoriness and thus presupposes crucial changes in our consciousness of time. Furthermore, if modernity as a distinctive mode of experiencing (social) reality involves seeing society and the social relations within it as (temporally) transitory and (spatially) fleeting, then this implies, conversely, that traditional, permanent structures are now absent from human experience. The earlier, less threatening notion of the steady accretion of progress gives way to a situation in which, as Tönnies put it, 'l'évolution sociale prend la form d'une *désagrégation spontanée*'.[42]

The equivalent conception in Simmel's account of modernity is that reality is experienced in flux. In other words, the shock of 'movement' in production, society and history first experienced with the French Revolution and subsequently in the revolutions of the nineteenth century, though at first bounded by actual 'social movements', could be experienced at the turn of the century as movement as such, as permanent flux. As Simmel puts it: 'In reality itself things do not last for any length of time; through the restlessness with which they offer themselves at any moment ... every form immediately dissolves in the very moment when it emerges; it lives, as it were, only by being destroyed; every consolidation of form into lasting objects ... is an incomplete interpretation that is unable to follow the motion of reality at its own pace.'[43]

This makes more difficult the search for the 'laws of motion' of social reality. Instead, the modernist is tempted to search out 'the ideal system of eternally valid lawfulness', to distil the eternal from what is transitory, to try to capture the dialectic of the permanent and the transitory. This might explain the intention behind Simmel's 'snapshots *sub specie aeternitatis*'. Of course, for Simmel, the social phenomenon par excellence, which embodies both the labyrinth of movement and the dialectic of flux and permanence, is money, since 'there is no more striking symbol of the completely dynamic character of the world ... It is, as it were, an *actus purus*'.[44] Symbolizing the transitory and the fleeting it is 'the most ephemeral thing in the external-practical world'.

If everything is in flux and transitory, then social reality itself no longer exists as a pre-ordered totality. Further, experience of the world as transitory, fleeting and fortuitous suggests the disintegration of fixed ways of experiencing the world and, instead, experience of the discontinuity of time, space and causality, even the dislocation of the present from the past and the future. This, of course, presents the social theorist with formidable problems. And, in this connection, Simmel could perhaps turn to advantage that for which Weber later criticized him. Simmel's analysis of modernity emphasizes the cultural dimensions of modernity rather than the structural features of modernization. It does not purport to be a systematic theory, but rather the illumination of fragments of modernity. In this respect, it did not require the elaboration of concept formations into a systematic whole. In important respects, Simmel looks for an aesthetic totality that is to be found in the work of art – a direct contrast to Weber's delineation of the progress of science in 'Science as a vocation'. What also stands out is the attention that Simmel devotes to the psychological dimensions of the experience of modernity. Again, Weber probably concurred with Spann's criticism of the psychologistic foundations of Simmel's conception of society. But, in terms of an analysis of modes of experiencing modernity, Simmel was compelled to turn to the 'inner' life of human beings, to the *psychology* of modernity. This is an important emphasis, given sociology's attempts at the end of the nineteenth century to demarcate itself as an independent discipline, not merely from history, from philosophy, but also from psychology. Simmel, who started out in the *Völkerpsychologie* of Lazarus and Steinthal,[45] retained a sensitivity to psychological processes that proved essential to his analysis of the modes of *experiencing* modernity. Simmel was not merely a master in the sociology of fleeting encounters and interactions; he was also a key figure in the development of a sociology of emotions and intimate interaction, as Birgitta Nedelmann has persuasively argued,[46] and, one must add, of a psychology of emotional life. This was an urgent task for the social theorist of modernity who viewed 'the essence of modernity' as 'psychologism, the experiencing and interpretation of the world in terms of the reactions of our inner life and indeed as an inner world, the dissolution of fixed contents in the fluid element of the soul, from which all that is substantive is filtered and whose forms are merely forms of motion'.[47] All the central features of modernity, which Simmel analyses in the 'outer world', as it were, are expressed and manifest themselves in the 'inner' life of individuals. Simmel sought to gain access to this inner world in his 'psychological microscopy' rather than in the analysis of the major institutions of society. It is possible to see in Simmel's major works, especially his *Philosophy of Money* but also his shorter essays on the metropolis, the adventure, the senses, etc., the outlines of a theory of modernity that tries to do justice to the 'life-world' of modernity, to examine the ways in which modernity is experienced. Like Baudelaire's poetic examination half a century earlier, these experiences are those of the neurasthenic, the metropolitan dweller and the consumer of commodities. Some of these very features of his methodology that Weber criticized enabled Simmel to examine more closely the fragmentary life-world of modernity. Simmel remained convinced that the 'fortuitous fragment of reality' could produce 'a deeper and more accurate' understanding of society than 'the mere treatment of major, completely supra-individual total structures'. Even the most systematic of Simmel's works – *The Philosophy of Money* – is held together by 'the possibility ... of finding in each of life's details the totality of its meaning'. The ideal of progress in science (via more refined concept formation), to which the early Simmel also subscribed, is supplemented by an aesthetic ideal (already announced in Simmel's essay 'Soziologische Aesthetik' of 1896), in which 'the typical is to be found in what is unique, the law-like in what is fortuitous, the essence and significance of things in the superficial and transitory'.[48]

Simmel's exploration of the life-world of modernity through that which seems insignificant, through the 'fortuitous fragments of reality' and fleeting social relations, despite often its lack of conceptual refinement, can be seen to serve as a complement to his theory of the widening gap between subjective and objective culture as well as to Weber's own theory of modernity. The consequences of living in a world that generates indifference to values, though recognized by Weber, were more fully developed at the level of individuals' experience of it by Simmel.

Notes: Chapter 28

1   For two recent comparisons, see Y. Atoji, *Sociology at the Turn of the Century* (Tokyo, 1984), ch. 2, and J. Faught, 'Neglected Affinities: Max Weber and Georg Simmel', *British Journal of Sociology*, vol. 36 (1985), pp. 155–74.

2   On Simmel and Stefan George, see M. Landmann, 'Georg Simmel und Stefan George', in H.-J. Dähme and O. Rammstedt (eds), *Georg Simmel und die Moderne* (Frankfurt, 1984), pp. 147–73.

3   For Weber and the neo-Kantian tradition, see Chapter 29 by Guy Oakes in this volume. On the early development of neo-Kantianism, see, most recently, K. C. Köhnke, *Entstehung und Aufstieg des Neukantianismus* (Frankfurt, 1986).

4   On Weber's relation to Bloch and Lukács, see Chapter 33 by Eva Karádi in this volume.

5   See D. Frisby, *Georg Simmel* (Chichester, London and New York, 1984), pp. 73–6.

6   Max Weber, 'Georg Simmel as sociologist', *Social Research*, vol. 39 (1972), pp. 155–63.

7   F. Tönnies, Review of G. Simmel, *Über sociale Differenzierung*, in *Jahrbücher für Nationalökonomie und Statistik*, vol. 56 (1891), pp. 269–77.

8   F. Tönnies, Review of G. Simmel, *Einleitung in die Moralphilosophie*, in *Zeitschrift für Psychologie und Physiologie der Sinnesorgane*, vol. 4 (1893), pp. 393–400, and vol. 10 (1896), pp. 473–80.

9   E. Durkheim, 'Philosophie des Geldes', *L'Année Sociologique*, vol. 5 (1900–1), pp. 140–5.

10   G. Simmel, 'Ferdinand Tönnies. Der Nietzsche-Kultus', *Deutsche Literaturzeitung*, vol. 17, no. 42 (1897), cols 1645–51.

11   idem, 'Die Bauernbefreiung in Preussen', *Baltische Monatsschrift*, vol. 35 (1888), pp. 257–81.

12   idem, 'Zur Methodik der Sozialwissenschaft', *Jahrbuch für Gesetzgebung, Verwaltung und Volkswirtschaft*, vol. 20 (1896), pp. 575–85.

13   idem, 'Einige Bemerkungen zu Schmollers "Grundriß der allgemeinen Volkswirtschaftslehre"', *Allgemeine Zeitung* (Munich), 28 October 1900, p. 222.

14   idem, Review of G. Tarde, *Les Lois de l'imitation*, in *Zeitschrift für Psychologie und Physiologie der Sinnesorgane*, vol. 2 (1891), pp. 141–2.

15   G. Simmel, 'Massenpsychologie', *Die Zeit* (Vienna), no. 5, 23 December 1895.

16   See Frisby, *Georg Simmel*, p. 14.

17   F. H. Tenbruck, 'Georg Simmel (1858–1918)', *Kölner Zeitschrift für Soziologie und Sozialpsychologie*, vol. 10 (1958), p. 593.

18   PESC, p. 193.

19   D. N. Levine, Introduction in *Georg Simmel. On Individuality and Social Forms* (Chicago, 1971), p. xiv.

20   F. Tönnies, 'Historismus und Rationalismus', *Archiv für systematische Philosophie*, vol. 1 (1895), pp. 227–52.

21   P. E. Schnabel, 'Georg Simmel', in D. Käsler (ed.), *Klassiker des soziologischen Denkens*, Vol. 1 (Munich, 1976), pp. 288–9.

22   G. Simmel, *The Problems of the Philosophy of History*, transl. and ed. by G. Oakes (New York, 1977).

23   RaK, p. 254.

24   ibid., p. 258, n. 54.

25   Max Weber, 'Georg Simmel as sociologist', p. 158.

26   ibid., p. 161.

27   ibid.

28   See chapter 27 by Robert Eden in this volume

29   O. Spann, *Wirtschaft und Gesellschaft* (Dresden, 1907); reprinted in O. Spann, *Frühe Schriften in Auswahl* (Graz, 1974), especially pp. 223–60.

30   Max Weber, 'Georg Simmel as sociologist', p. 163.

31   U. Gerhardt, *Rollenanalyse als kritische Theorie* (Neuwied and Berlin, 1971), p. 39, n. 30.

32   K. Schrader-Klebert, 'Der Begriff der Gesellschaft als regulative Idee', *Soziale Welt*, vol. 19 (1968), pp. 97–118.

33   For Weber's developmental history, see W. Schluchter, *The Rise of Western Rationalism* (Berkeley, Calif., and London, 1981).
34   See D. Levine, 'Subjective and Objective Rationality in Simmel's "Philosophy of Money", Weber's Account of Rationalisation and Parsons' "Theory of Action"', Paper presented to the 10th World Congress of Sociology, Session on Simmel's "Philosophy of Money", Mexico City, 1982, and S. Kalberg, 'Max Weber's types of rationality', *American Journal of Sociology*, vol. 85 (1980), pp. 1145–79.
35   M. Berman, *All That is Solid Melts into Air* (New York and London, 1983), p. 28.
36   J. Habermas, *Theorie des kommunikativen Handelns* (Frankfurt, 1981). (An English translation was published in 1984.)
37   Habermas, *Theorie*, p. 455.
38   ES, Vol. 1, p. 506.
39   G. Simmel, *The Philosophy of Money*, transl. by T. Bottomore and D. Frisby (London and Boston, 1978), ch. 6.
40   ibid., p. 431.
41   D. Frisby, *Fragments of Modernity* (forthcoming), ch. 2.
42   F. Tönnies, 'Considerations sur l'histoire moderne', *Annales de l'Institut Internationale de Sociologie*, vol. 1 (1895), pp. 245–52, especially p. 246.
43   Simmel, *The Philosophy of Money*, p. 510.
44   ibid., p. 511.
45   See Frisby, *Georg Simmel*, pp. 69–71.
46   B. Nedelmann, 'Georg Simmel – Emotion und Wechselwirkung in intimen Gruppen', *Kölner Zeitschrift für Soziologie und Sozialpsychologie*, Sonderheft 25 (1983), pp. 174–209.
47   G. Simmel, *Philosophische Kultur*, 3rd edn (Potsdam, 1923), p. 196.
48   G. Simmel, 'Soziologische Aesthetik', *Die Zukunft*, vol. 17 (1896), pp. 204–16, especially p. 206. An English translation (by K. P. Etzkorn) is in G. Simmel, *The Conflict in Modern Culture and other Essays* (New York, 1968), pp. 68–80.

29 Weber and the Southwest German School: The Genesis of the Concept of the Historical Individual

GUY OAKES

The Problem

'I have finished Rickert', Weber wrote to his wife from Florence in the spring of 1902. 'He is *very* good.'[1] This was, of course, the philosopher Heinrich Rickert, Weber's friend from his Freiburg period,[2] and the book Weber had just finished turns out to have become the major work of Rickert's career: *Die Grenzen der naturwissenschaftlichen Begriffsbildung* [The Limits of Concept Formation in Natural Science], an attempt to develop a philosophy of history independent of both positivism and neo-Hegelian idealism along lines already sketched by his teacher, Wilhelm Windelband, in the 1890s. In a note of uncharacteristic modesty, Rickert admits that the main thesis of *Die Grenzen* had already been clearly articulated by Windelband in *Geschichte und Naturwissenschaft* [History and Natural Science] his famous inaugural lecture as rector of Strasbourg University in 1894. Rickert even suggests that the reader who has thought his way through the consequences of Windelband's lecture may find parts of his own treatise superfluous.[3] During the twenty years of his Strasbourg period, Windelband became the leader of the Baden or Southwest German School of neo-Kantianism, thus named because its leading figures held appointments at southwest German universities: Windelband at Strasbourg and later at Heidelberg, Rickert at Freiburg and then at Heidelberg, and Emil Lask – Rickert's student at Freiburg and subsequently Windelband's postdoctoral student at Heidelberg – at Heidelberg as well.

The impact of the Southwest German School on Weber's methodological work in the period 1903–7 is, of course, well documented. In addition to the testimony of Rickert, Weber's wife Marianne, and the frequent citations and remarks in Weber's own writings, there is the fact that Weber regularly uses the ideas and arguments of these philosophers. Rickert's concepts of the historical individual and value-relevance and his distinction between values and value-judgements, and Lask's analysis of theories of concept formation and his account of his *hiatus irrationalis* between concept and reality, name only a few of the most obvious borrowings. To these considerations, we should add Weber's close personal relations with Rickert and Lask – in the case of Rickert, well known; in the case of Lask, not so widely appreciated, but still well documented – and the fact that Weber was uncommonly receptive to the work of acquaintances with whom he enjoyed a close personal relationship, especially those to whom he was sympathetically inclined. Therefore, the fact that the Southwest German School – Rickert and Lask directly, and through them, Windelband – played some part in the genesis of Max Weber's early methodological ideas may be taken as established. In light of this fact, the purpose of the ensuing discussion is to determine what is responsible for it and how it can be explained. Is it a contingent fact of Weber's intellectual biography, a datum in the history of ideas that can be accounted for by tracing the network of Weber's acquaintances, the books he read, and the order in which he read them? Or are there more systematic considerations that explain Weber's relationship to this philosophical tradition, reasons that are essential to Weber's thought and which in some sense necessitated the acceptance of certain ideas that he found in the Southwest German School? In sum, does the impact of the Baden neo-Kantians call for a historical or a philosophical explanation?

Culture, Cultural Science, and the Historical Individual

As Weber repeatedly stresses, the social sciences as he conceives them are sciences of reality, defined by reference to their interest in the individual significance of concrete reality and its qualitatively distinctive properties. According to Weber, we ascribe meaning, significance and value only to phenomena that we regard as essential or distinctive because of their individual qualities.

> The transcendental presupposition of every *cultural science* is not that we find a certain 'culture' (or indeed any 'culture' at all) *valuable*, but rather that we *are* cultural beings, endowed with the capacity and the will to take a deliberate *position* towards the world and to ascribe a *meaning* to it. Regardless of what this meaning may be, it will lead to the fact that in life we will *judge* certain phenomena of human collective existence on its basis and take a position on them as being (positively or negatively) *significant*. Regardless of the content of this position, these phenomena have a cultural *significance* for us. Their scientific interest rests on this significance alone.[4]

The connection between culture, the cultural being and cultural science as a science of cultural phenomena or historical individuals may be explained as follows. Weber defines culture by reference to the concrete value commitments of the individual person. It is the sphere of persons, actions, and their artefacts that are identifiable as such by reference to the meaning that a certain type of human being – the cultural being – ascribes to specific concrete phenomena. The character or personality of cultural beings is formed by the choices they make in the face of radical value conflicts. As a result of these choices, they ascribe meaning to certain phenomena and value them in the light of this meaning. In the language of Weber's early methodological writings, the life of cultural beings, their actions and their artefacts, and the phenomena that acquire meaning as a result of the value choices they make, constitute the domain of cultural phenomena or historical individuals.[5]

This means that Weber's conception of cultural science presupposes an account of the conditions under which knowledge of historical individuals is possible. Put another way, it depends upon a philosophy of history that provides a theory of historical or cultural knowledge. It is the problem of knowledge of historical individuals that marks the essential point of contact between Weber's early methodological work and the Southwest German School. The decisive influence of the Baden neo-Kantians on Weber's thought can be articulated in the following way: In the philosophy of history developed by Windelband, Rickert and Lask, Weber found an epistemology of the cultural sciences which, in his view, established the conditions under which knowledge of the historical individual is possible.

The Philosophy of History of the Southwest German School and the Theory of Individual Concept Formation

As regards its bearing on the problem of knowledge of the historical individual, the basic outlines of this philosophy of history can be sketched as follows. First, Windelband formulated the ideal of a historical science, the distinctive interest of which lies in knowledge of individual or concrete reality. This is the methodological ideal of idiographic knowledge, which Rickert later analyses more precisely as knowledge of the historical individual. Secondly, in Lask's account of the analytical and emanationist theories of concept formation and in his discussion of the *hiatus irrationalis*, Weber found an analysis of the conditions under which knowledge of the historical individual is possible. Thirdly, in Rickert's theory of historical knowledge, Weber found an account of the conceptualization of individual entities, which undertakes to show how the problem of the *hiatus irrationalis* between concept and concrete reality can be solved; not by surmounting the gap between concept and reality, however, but rather by employing it as an essential premiss for the development of a theory of historical concept formation. Rickert's account, therefore, can be conceived as an attempt to show that the conditions for the possibility of knowledge of the historical individual are satisfied.[6]

   This is the main thrust of the neo-Kantian impact on Weber's early methodological thought: a methodological ideal for historical knowledge that identifies a theoretical interest in the historical individual; an analysis of concept formation and the relation between concept and reality that specifies what the requirements for knowledge of the historical individual are; a theory of individual or historical concept formation that attempts to show that these requirements are met. These three doctrines – each of which is incorporated into Weber's methodological essays of the period 1903–7 – together constitute an argument which entails that the basic epistemological condition of his conception of cultural science (the possibility of knowledge of historical individuals) is satisfied.

Windelband: the Methodological Ideal of Idiographic Knowledge

In one of his last critical appreciations of Kant's importance in modern philosophy, Windelband introduces some observations on Kant's conception of historical knowledge, and thereby reaffirms one of the main doctrines of his own philosophical programme: to understand Kant is to go beyond him. Kant conceived the scope of science as limited to the enterprise of Newtonian natural philosophy: the attempt to discover the necessary and universally valid laws that account for the properties of the phenomenal world. Historical claims to knowledge, on the other hand, are particular and contingent. In the final analysis, history has an inferior cognitive status, because it fails to qualify as a science according to the criteria for scientific knowledge that Kant elaborates in his *Critique of Pure Reason:* historical propositions lack the necessity and general validity that would qualify them as possible objects of scientific knowledge. Windelband argues that this is the point on which the Kantian theory of knowledge is most in need of revision.[7] Arguing against Kant thirteen years earlier in *Geschichte und Naturwissenschaft*, Windelband holds that the possibility of history as a science rests on three premises: an individualistic conception of value; a nomological or nomothetic conception of the limits of natural science; an individualistic or idiographic conception of historical science.

Windelband claims that values can be ascribed only to phenomena that are unique and incomparable in their individuality. This thesis is ultimately grounded in the individualistic conception of value introduced by Christian theology in its polemic against the axiological universalism of Greek philosophy. The Christian idea that values can be ascribed only to individual phenomena has its origins in the conception of the Creation, the Fall, and the events of the life of Christ as unique occurrences endowed with unprecedented significance. Windelband claims that this idea represents the first powerful insight into what he calls 'the inalienable metaphysical right of history':[8] its interest in reality as unique and unrepeatable. According to this conception of value, we lose interest in an object if we discover that it is nothing more than a representative case of a general phenomenon. This consideration entails the individuality of values: The attribution of values must always have a concrete and singular referent. The source of our interest in knowledge of individual phenomena lies in this basic fact of philosophical anthropology: that we ascribe values exclusively to individuals.

This theoretical interest cannot be satisfied by natural science, which abstracts from the unique and qualitatively distinctive properties of real phenomena in order to disclose the laws on which they depend. This is the sense in which natural science is nomothetic. It has no intrinsic interest in the individual events of concrete reality. On the contrary, the individual datum is relevant to natural science only to the extent that it can be represented as a type, an instance of a generic concept, or a case that can be subsumed under a general law. This is a consequence of the ultimate theoretical purpose of natural science, which is to produce a system of maximally abstract and general laws, nomological regularities that govern all events. Nomothetic knowledge, therefore, represents the triumph of abstract thought over our perception of concrete reality. The interest of historical science, on the other hand, is idiographic. Here the purpose of knowledge is to comprehend the distinctive properties of the unique event itself. History is not interested in a phenomenon because of what it shares with other phenomena, but rather because of its own definitive qualities. Unlike the natural scientist, the historian attempts to establish knowledge of the concrete and singular features of reality. Therefore, it is historical science that will realize the theoretical ideal generated by our interest in knowledge of individual phenomena.

The main theses of *Geschichte und Naturwissenschaft* – the individualistic conception of value, the nomothetic conception of the limits of natural science, and the methodological ideal of idiographic knowledge – are also major doctrines in Rickert's philosophy of history. In addition, the basic problem generated by the arguments of *Geschichte und Naturwissenschaft* also becomes the fundamental question that Rickert attempts to solve in *Die Grenzen*.

Windelband alludes to this problem in the final paragraphs of the lecture. The occurrence of individual events cannot be explained by general laws. Put another way, there is no set of nomological statements, regardless of how exhaustive and precise, from which any description of an individual event can be deduced. This is why our theoretical interest in individual phenomena cannot be satisfied by natural science. As Windelband claims, nomothetic and idiographic cognitive interests are independent and juxtaposed to one another: The law and the event remain as the ultimate and incommensurable entities of our world-view.[9] But if natural science cannot establish knowledge of individual phenomena, how is such knowledge possible? In response to this problem, Windelband offers nothing more than a few obscure and metaphorical suggestions. At the end of the lecture, we are left with the conclusion that the individual historical datum represents 'a residuum of incomprehensible brute fact'. It is 'an inexpressible and indefinable phenomenon'.[10]

Lask: The Problem of the Irrationality of Concrete Reality

Although the purpose of historical science is knowledge of individual phenomena, such phenomena are incomprehensible. Under what conditions is this sort of knowledge possible? Weber found what he regarded as an exemplary answer to this question in Lask's precociously brilliant doctoral dissertation on Fichte's philosophy of history.[11]

For the Southwest German School, epistemological questions are concerned with the formation of concepts. The conditions for the possibility of knowledge of an object are conditions for the possibility of forming concepts of that object. An item becomes an object of knowledge when it is brought under concepts, or when concepts are formed that represent the item. Valid concept formation, therefore, constitutes knowledge. It follows that the problem of historical knowledge is the problem of individual concept formation: the question of the conditions under which concrete reality can be conceptualized or represented by means of concepts. This relationship between knowledge and concept formation in the epistemology of the Southwest German School explains why Lask attacks the problem of historical knowledge by analysing theories of concept formation.

Lask claims that all theories of the concept fall into either of two main groups. One theory, which is typified by the work of Kant, he calls an analytical logic of concepts. The other, which was consummated by Hegel, he calls an emanationist logic.

The analytical theory holds that the concrete object of immediate experience is the sole reality, the basis from which all concept formation begins. Reality itself, however, cannot be conceptualized. Individual existence, which is unique and unfathomable, marks the limit of concept formation. The concept itself is an artificially abstracted part or aspect of reality, produced by analysing elements that actually exist together in a diffuse or inchoate fashion. Because of its abstract character, the concept is general, articulating what is common to a plurality of phenomena. This is the sense in which concept formation qualifies as an analysis of what is immediately given. The concept recasts the reality it represents in such a way that this reality is conceived as an instance of the application of the concept itself. As a result, the relationship between the concept and its object is not one of real dependence. It is a purely logical relationship established by thought and without any ontological foundation. Because the concept is an artificial intellectual construct, reality is ontologically richer than the concept. Indeed, the more abstract and general the concept, the more remote from reality it becomes. Thus, even though concrete reality is subsumed under concepts, it cannot be derived from them. This is because concepts – as ontologically empty products of intellectual abstraction – cannot contain reality itself. Because concrete reality cannot be conceptualized, it is 'irrational': that is, it is not a possible object of knowledge.

The definitive theses of the analytical theory of concept formation, therefore, may be summarized as follows. (1) Concept formation represents an analytical abstraction from reality. (2) This is responsible for the substantive poverty or the ontological emptiness of the concept. (3) As a result, there is a dualism of concept and reality. The concept is what can be comprehended or known, even though it has no ontological status. Individual existence, on the other hand, is not a possible object of conceptualization, even though it is the sole reality. (4) Thus, reality is irrational in the sense that it is inaccessible to conceptualization.[12]

The emanationist theory rejects each of these theses. The concept is not an abstracted aspect or part of reality. On the contrary, individual existence realizes or embodies the content of the concept, from which it emanates. It follows that concrete events can be deduced from concepts, which are ontologically richer than these events and in this sense represent a higher reality. As a result, individual existence is not only subsumed under concepts; the content of individual existence is also included in the content of concepts. Thus, the purely logical relation between concept and reality maintained by the analytical theory becomes an ontological relationship in the emanationist theory. The dialectical or logical process of thought becomes a *Weltprozess*, a universal or cosmic process of real events. This means that logic is also a metaphysics and an ontology.[13] Because the concept is fully real and because individuality, which emanates from the concept, is fully rational, the dualism of concept and reality collapses. Thus, the irrationality of reality is nullified as well. Because the content of individual reality can be exhaustively derived from concepts, what is real is rational, and what is rational is real.

Although Lask admits that the logic of the emanationist theory is sound, he cannot accept the main premiss that generates the theory: Hegel's account of the concept and the Hegelian thesis that concepts are more real than individual existence.[14] As a student of Rickert and Windelband, Lask also regards concepts as artificial intellectual constructs that abstract from reality. This means that, in returning to Kant in order to confront the problem of historical knowledge, the Southwest German School is committed to the analytical theory. And yet this theory entails a consequence that seems to preclude conceptualization of the individual: the dualism of concept and reality and the irrationality of individual existence.

Borrowing an expression from Fichte, Lask claims that the contingent, arbitrary and anomic character of individual existence represents a '*hiatus irrationalis*' between thought and reality. This is a result of the absolute dualism of concept and reality.[15] There is a hiatus because reality cannot be derived from concepts. And it is irrational because reality can be rationalized only by conceptualizing it, which according to the analytical theory is impossible. Thus, as Windelband notes in the conclusion of his lecture, concrete reality simply must be accepted as an incomprehensible brute fact. Even though individual existence is subsumed under laws, it cannot be deduced from them, and even though it follows laws, it does not follow from them. Therefore, the law and reality, or concepts and reality, are incommensurable quantities.[16] In summary, Lask's analysis of theories of concept formation entails that historical knowledge is possible only if the problem of the *hiatus irrationalis* can be solved.

Rickert's Theory of Individual Concept Formation

In the light of the *hiatus irrationalis*, is there any strategy by means of which knowledge of the historical individual is possible? Weber found an answer to this question in Rickert's theory of individual concept formation, which begins with the following question: Given that the concrete perceptual manifold of reality is not a possible object of knowledge, and given our interest in the historical individual, is it possible to distinguish the concrete perceptual manifold of reality from its individuality in such a way that the latter can be identified as an object of knowledge? In demarcating historical science or cultural science from natural science, Rickert argues that the object of cultural science is the individuality of reality, or reality in so far as individuality can be ascribed to it. Since he also argues that reality as *anschaulich* – the immediate experience, actuality, or perceptual manifold of reality – cannot be conceptualized by any science, this distinction is indispensable to Rickert's theory of historical knowledge.[17] In other words, because cultural science, like natural science, cannot reproduce the concrete perceptual manifold of reality, it also requires what Rickert calls a principle of selection on the basis of which the essential aspects of reality – those that matter to us in such a way that knowledge of these aspects satisfies our theoretical interests – can be distinguished from the inessential aspects.[18] Unlike natural science, the theoretical interest of cultural science is anchored in the value we ascribe to the individual. It follows that this principle of selection must identify some sense in which the individuality of reality can become a possible object of knowledge. It must discriminate or select certain individually defined aspects of reality that qualify as important in relation to our values. The search for this principle is the primary objective of Rickert's philosophy of history and the main issue of *Die Grenzen*. He calls it 'the problem of historical concept formation'.

The reasoning that leads Rickert to a solution begins with the attempt to establish the sort of distinction he needs. The concrete perceptual manifold of reality can be distinguished from its individuality by differentiating two kinds of individuality. The premisses crucial to Rickert's reasoning may be outlined as follows.

(1) Individuals in the most general sense – discrete, independently identifiable phenomena – are all unique. (2) However, we do not regard all such phenomena as irreplaceable. On the contrary, if their uniqueness is of no interest to us, they become objects of knowledge only because they fall under some general concept. This is the sense of individuality in which the perceptual quality of reality is equivalent to individuality, and all reality qualifies as individual. (3) There is another kind of individuality that cannot be ascribed to a phenomenon simply because it is unique in this most general sense. Rickert calls it in-dividuality, and the objects to which it is ascribed are called in-dividuals. A phenomenon qualifies as an in-dividual when it is constituted by a coherence and an indivisibility that it possesses in virtue of its uniqueness. (4) However, this individuality is not defined by reference to all the properties of the phenomenon. It obtains only by virtue of specific properties that we regard as indispensable because we see them as responsible for the coherence and indivisibility of the phenomenon. (5) Precisely for this reason – because we regard phenomena constituted in this way as irreplaceable – their uniqueness is of interest to us.

How is the distinction between individuality and in-dividuality made? How does the in-dividuality of a diamond differ from the individuality of a lump of coal? It is clearly because the coherence or indivisibility characteristic of the uniqueness of the former has a significance for us that the latter lacks, a meaning that is determined by the values we attach to it. In other words, the in-dividuality of a phenomenon is due to the value we ascribe to the singular coherence and indivisibility that are responsible for its uniqueness.

The ultimate basis of Rickert's individuality/in-dividuality dichotomy is neither metaphysical nor epistemological. On the contrary, it is grounded in a very general fact about human experience that lies within what might be called the universal pragmatics of human life. Human beings set certain values, they act on them, and they attempt to realize them. However, it is impossible for everything in the domain of human experience to have the status of an in-dividual. This is because action is possible only on the basis of an orientation to generalizations or general rules of experience[19]. The possibility of ascribing values to certain objects presupposes other objects for which this is not possible. Or, to employ Rickert's language, the possibility of in-dividuals presupposes individuals, entities that fall within the domain of our experience and interest us only as instances of general concepts. Thus, the praxeology of human life entails that experience cannot be comprised exclusively of in-dividuals. On the other hand, the fact that we ascribe values to individuals by virtue of their distinctive properties shows that there must be some in-dividuals. If all individuals were nothing more than representative cases of general concepts, then we would have no basis for differentiating one such case from any other, and thus no basis for an interest in any given individual. Therefore, it is because human beings ascribe values to certain things that some individuals become in-dividuals.

The in-dividual is constituted as a historical individual, and thus as a possible object of historical science, by reference to what Rickert calls the purely theoretical value-relation (*Wertbeziehung*). Put another way, an in-dividual can be conceptualized as a historical individual only if it falls under some value-relation. Because of the connection between value-relations and the constitution of historical individuals, Rickert claims that the elimination of value-relations from historical science would also eliminate the object of cognitive interest in history, and thus the possibility of historical knowledge as well. The doctrine of value-relations or value-relevance is Rickert's solution to the problem of individual or historical concept formation.

This doctrine is constituted by four theses, each of which places constraints on the values that define historical individuals. In other words, each thesis states certain conditions that must be satisfied by the values to which historical individuals are related. The first thesis holds that a commitment on these values must be made by the historical actors whose conduct is the ultimate datum of a historical investigation, and thus the ultimate object of historical concept formation. In Rickert's language, the 'historical centres' of a historical investigation must take a position on these values. The second thesis holds that these values cannot be purely personal or private. They must express the general concerns of a culture. In Rickert's language, they must be cultural values. The third thesis holds that these values must be objective in the sense that an unconditionally general validity can be ascribed to them. They are not merely empirically general values to which all the members of a society are in fact committed. Nor are they merely normatively valid values, commitment to which is required by a social norm that all the members of a society in fact acknowledge. On the contrary, they are unconditionally general values: their validity or binding force represents a categorical commitment that is independent of both empirical maxims and hypothetical imperatives. The fourth thesis holds that the historical investigation itself cannot take a position on these values. It must rather relate them to the historical individual in a purely theoretical fashion.

The first thesis rests on the distinction between the investigator's values and the values of the historical actor, or between the values of the historian and those of the historical centre. In Rickert's terminology, this is also the distinction between the values of the historical subject and those of the historical object. The second thesis rests on the distinction between personal or private values and general cultural values. The third thesis rests on the distinction between subjective and objective values.

The fourth thesis rests on the distinction between a valuation or value-judgement and a purely theoretical value-relation. Rickert claims that 'in so far as the value-perspective is decisive for history, this concept of the "value-relation" – in opposition to "valuation" – is actually *the* essential criterion for history as a pure science'.[20] In his attempt to clarify the importance of this distinction, Rickert considers the methodological status of a history of religion that is based on confessional assumptions. Such a history, he claims, is not grounded in a purely theoretical value-relation. This is why it cannot possess scientific objectivity. Why is this the case?

Consider two different confessional biographies of Martin Luther, a Roman Catholic account and a Protestant account. Because they are committed to rival subjective valuations, Rickert claims that it is impossible to resolve the conflicts between them. Historical accounts of this sort can never be regarded as purely scientific, because their valuations will never be valid for all scientists. According to Rickert, this is one sense in which the domain of values is irrational: There is no principle by means of which conflicts between such rival valuations can be resolved. It follows that if the domain of values were exhausted by valuations historical science would be impossible. The purpose of the value/valuation dichotomy is to avoid this consequence by showing that there is a sphere of purely theoretical value-relations that is independent of valuations.

Suppose that the two biographies of Luther were not grounded in the confessional commitments of Protestantism and Roman Catholicism. Suppose that the historian simply defines Luther's individuality by reference to religious values in general and does not take any stand on their validity. In that case, the issue of value-irrationality – the question of whether there is a principle on the basis of which conflicts between value-judgements can be resolved – simply does not arise. If the conceptualization of Luther's individuality is based exclusively on such value-relations, then the problem of historical knowledge of Luther can be solved, or so Rickert claims. Because the purely theoretical value-relation that defines religious values will be valid for both Roman Catholics and Protestants, the same aspects of the individual that we identify as 'Luther' will also prove to be essential for historians of both persuasions. Thus these aspects will be synthesized to form the same historical concept. In other words, they will constitute the historical individual 'Luther' as an object of historical knowledge in the same way. As a result, the value/valuation dichotomy preserves the objectivity of historical knowledge from the consequences of the irrationality of subjective valuations.

In summary, the doctrine of value-relations may be formulated in the following terms. Consider an entity *I* that is an in-dividual and a value *V* that satisfies the following conditions: *V* is a general cultural value on which the historical actors of a given society take a position, and it is also unconditionally valid. If *V* is linked to *I* in a purely theoretical fashion, then *I* qualifies as a historical individual, and thus as an object of historical concept formation. To link *I* to *V* in this fashion is to conceptualize it historically, as a result of which it becomes an object of historical knowledge. In *Die Grenzen*, therefore, Rickert attempts to show that the conditions for the possibility of cultural science are satisfied by elaborating a theory of individual concept formation based on the doctrine of value-relevance. It should be noted that the doctrine of value-relevance does not attempt to solve the problem of conceptualizing the individual by surmounting the *hiatus irrationalis* or closing the gap between concept and reality. On the contrary, the dualism of concept and reality is presupposed by this solution. If reality could be exhaustively derived from concepts, there would be no grounds for the claim that any one individual aspect of reality is more significant than another. In that case, the ultimate basis for the doctrine of value-relevance – the distinction between individuals and in-dividuals – would collapse.

Concluding Remarks

If this analysis is sound, then the explanation of the neo-Kantian influence on Weber's early methodology lies in the immanent requirements of his thought. The Southwest German School provided what Weber needed: a solution to the problem of knowledge of the historical individual that he could accept. Because of the intimate connection between the problem of knowledge, the problem of concept formation, and the theory of value in the Southwest German School, this means that its distinctive contribution to Weber's early methodology lies in two areas: a theory of concept formation and a theory of values.[21]

However, Weber's commitment to the theory of values of the Southwest German School remained compromised and somewhat muddled. Rickert, for example, bases the possibility of knowledge of the historical individual on a theory of objective cultural values. If we examine his theory of culture, we find that culture is defined by reference to unconditionally valid values: general normative imperatives, commitment to which is unconditionally obligatory. In Rickert's work therefore, the distinction between hypothetically binding cultural norms and categorically binding ethical imperatives is blurred, if not erased altogether. However, Weber repeatedly insists on the indispensability of the distinction between cultural and ethical values, and he rejects the Southwest German doctrine of objective values. Rickert's objective value hierarchies collapse into an irreconcilable plurality of conflicting value commitments, the implacable struggle between the antagonistic gods or demons of modern culture. This consideration poses an interesting problem. When Weber finished Rickert's book, how well did he understand what he had read? In his critique of Stammler, Weber informs the reader that he is employing Rickert's concept of culture.[22] Since Rickert's theory of culture rests on a doctrine of objective values that Weber rejects, that cannot be the case. This suggests that, although Weber may have regarded *Die Grenzen* as an impressive piece of work to the extent that it either seemed to confirm conclusions he had already reached independently or seemed to offer what he regarded as satisfactory solutions to some of his own methodological difficulties, he failed to grasp some of Rickert's most important arguments, even though they were directly relevant to the central questions of his own thought. Thus it can be said that Weber adopted the Southwest German School's theory of values only within certain limits and with reservations that he did not fully understand.

In embracing the neo-Kantian theory of concepts and, with reservations, its theory of value, Weber created certain difficulties for his own methodological thought. By way of a summary of the foregoing remarks, two of the most important difficulties may be sketched: the implications of the neo-Kantian theory of concepts for Weber's theory of the ideal type and the problematic status of Rickert's value/valuation dichotomy.

The distinctive conceptual tool that Weber develops in order to identify, characterize and explain historical individuals is the ideal type. Weber repeatedly refers to the respects in which ideal-typical concepts approximate or depart from reality, and he claims that the use of ideal types depends upon comparing them with reality. He also speaks of measuring reality against the ideal type.[23] Given Weber's commitment to the neo-Kantian theory of concepts and its absolute duality of concept and reality, however, such operations appear to be impossible in principle. Reality as such, independent of its conceptualization, is unintelligible. Therefore, it is not possible to compare ideal types with reality. It is possible only to compare reality as constituted by some ideal type with reality as constituted by another ideal type. Weber, however, claims that the role of ideal types in providing explanations depends upon their verification by comparing them with reality. In that case, Weber's commitment to the neo-Kantian theory of concepts seems to entail that Weberian cultural science – which rests on explanations by means of ideal types – is impossible.

As a solution to the problem of how knowledge of the historical individual is possible, Weber accepts Rickert's doctrine of value-relevance and the absolute distinction between values and valuations on which it rests. The validity of this dichotomy depends upon the thesis that value-relations are independent of valuations. Should this thesis prove to be mistaken, then Rickert's dichotomy and his solution to the problem of knowledge of the historical individual collapses.

In his defence of this thesis, Rickert claims that a conflict over value-judgements is possible only if the conflicting valuations presuppose a common value, which must obtain independently of the value-judgements that depend upon them. For example, a conflict about political value-judgements presupposes that the partisans to the conflict acknowledge a common domain of political values. Otherwise, Rickert argues, political values could not be distinguished from the universe of the non-political. The main idea of this defence – that a controversy over value-judgements necessarily presupposes a common valuation-free value-relation – seems to be mistaken. Consider a case in which two partisans find themselves in a controversy over the valuation of a given value because one of them refuses to acknowledge its status as a value. In this case, the presupposition of a common value-relation on which both value-judgements are based does not obtain. That presupposition is precisely the point of the controversy. Because of his value-judgements, one partisan refuses to acknowledge the value that the other accepts. If such a case is possible, then it is clear that there are instances in which value-relations necessarily presuppose valuations. This is because – in an ironic reversal and refutation of Rickert's position – valuations prove to be conditions for the possibility of value-relations. So it is not the case that conflicting value-judgements necessarily presuppose a common value-relation. On the contrary, a common value-relation may presuppose an agreement in value-judgements. If this reasoning is sound, if value-judgements are indispensable to value-relations, then Rickert's value/valuation dichotomy collapses, and with it falls his solution to the problem of knowledge of historical individuals, the solution on which Weber's own methodology rests.

Notes: Chapter 29

1 *Biography*, p. 260.
2 Rickert and Weber had been colleagues since the time of Weber's professorship at Freiburg (1894–7), where Rickert was a Privatdozent in philosophy. Rickert completed his doctoral

studies under Wilhelm Windelband in 1888 with a monograph on the logic of definition (*Zur Lehre der Definition*). He then moved to Freiburg for his *Habilitation*. Completed in 1891, this was a general introduction to the problems of the theory of knowledge (*Der Gegenstand der Erkenntnis*). When a professorship in philosophy at Freiburg fell vacant upon Alois Riehl's departure for Kiel, Weber successfully supported Rickert's candidacy. In the year that followed this letter to his wife, Weber characterized his first and most ambitious methodological study as, in part, an attempt to test the value of Rickert's ideas for his own methodological purposes. See WL[3], p. 7. For the influence of Rickert's epistemology on Weber's theory of concept formation, see T. Burger, *Max Weber's Theory of Concept Formation* (Durham, NC, 1976).

3   H. Rickert, *Die Grenzen der naturwissenschaftlichen Begriffsbildung* (Tübingen, 1902), p. 302. Windelband (1848–1915) received his doctorate in philosophy at Berlin in 1870 and completed his *Habilitation* at Leipzig in 1873. Studies with Kuno Fischer at Jena and Rudolf Hermann Lotze at Göttingen were the principal influences on his conception of the aims and limits of philosophy. For an account of the genesis of the neo-Kantian movement that focuses on the development from Kant through Fichte and Lotze to the immediate pre-history of neo-Kantianism in the 1850s and 1860s, see G. Lehmann, 'Kant im Spätidealismus und die Anfänge der neukantischen Bewegung', *Zeitschrift für philosophische Forschung*, vol. 10 (1963), pp. 438–56. Hans-Ludwig Ollig provides a good general account of the two main tendencies of the neo-Kantian movement, the Marburg School and the Southwest German School. See H.-L. Ollig (ed.), *Neukantianismus* (Stuttgart, 1982). One of the best recent accounts of neo-Kantianism is contained in the introductory materials with which Werner Flach and Helmut Holzhey preface their anthology of neo-Kantian logic and epistemology. See W. Flach and H. Holzhey (eds), *Erkenntnistheorie und Logik im Neukantianismus* (Hildesheim, 1980). For a general account of the neo-Kantian movement in English, see T. E. Willey, *Back to Kant* (Detroit, Mich., 1978).

4   MSS, p. 81; WL[3], pp. 180–1.

5   ibid., p. 178.

6   This is obviously not a genetic account of how the thinking of the Southwest German School in fact developed, but rather a reconstruction of the manner in which Weber appropriated its theory of historical knowledge.

7   W. Windelband, *Präludien. Aufsätze und Reden zur Philosophie und ihrer Geschichte*, 2 Vols., 9th edn (Tübingen, 1924), Vol. 2, pp. 13–14.

8   ibid., p. 156.

9   ibid., p. 160.

10   ibid., p. 159.

11   E. Lask, 'Fichtes Idealismus und die Geschichte', in idem, *Gesammelte Schriften*, Vol. 1 (Tübingen, 1923). Lask (1875–1915) studied with Rickert in Freiburg (1894–6, 1898–1901) and with Windelband in Strasbourg (1896–8). 'Fichtes Idealismus' was completed under Rickert's supervision in 1901.

12   ibid., pp. 30–1, 43–4.

13   ibid., p. 67. See also ibid., pp. 30, 66, 72, 88.

14   ibid., p. 72.

15   ibid., pp. 63, 117–18, 144–5.

16   ibid., pp. 173–4.

17   H. Rickert, *Die Grenzen der naturwissenschaftlichen Begriffsbildung*, 5th edn (Tübingen, 1929), p. 303.

18   ibid., pp. 293–5, 297.

19   ibid., p. 319.

20   ibid., p. 329.

21   An investigation of the influence of Windelband, Rickert and Lask on Weber's early methodology does not, of course, qualify as a complete account of the relationship between Weber's work and the Southwest German School. Such an account would have to explore several questions that are not considered here. For example: the relationship between Rickert's schematism of values in 'Vom System der Werte', *Logos*, vol. 4 (1913), and Weber's sociology of value spheres, especially as this is articulated in Weber's sociology of religion; the relationship between Weber's various fragmentary discussions of the theory of value and Rickert's value theory, especially as systematized in Rickert's *System der Philosophie* (Tübingen, 1921).

22   WL[3], p. 343.

23   ibid., pp. 190 ff.

30 Max Weber and Benedetto Croce

PIETRO ROSSI

I

Direct contacts between Weber and Croce are few. Reviewing the Italian translations of 'Science as a vocation' and 'Politics as a vocation' in 1948, Croce's thoughts went back forty years. 'I had met Weber at the 1908 International Philosophy Congress in Heidelberg, he was friendly with friends of mine and they thought highly of him; I had no further contact with him, nor did I follow his scholarly work – from which I had only read his early book *Roman Agrarian History*.'[1] It was mainly Karl Vossler who was responsible for these few contacts; at that time a lecturer in Heidelberg, he had been asked by Windelband to convey to Croce the offer of delivering one of the principal addresses at the Congress (Croce chose as his theme 'Pure intuition and the lyric character of art').[2] Croce sent Weber – again with Vossler as intermediary – the first edition of his *Logica*, which had appeared during 1905 in the series *Atti dell' Accademia Pontaniana*;[3] the following year Weber responded by sending Croce offprints of the third part of 'Roscher and Knies', and 'Critical studies in the logic of the cultural sciences'.[4] On this latter occasion Croce had asked his friend Vossler whether the author of both pieces 'were the same Weber who has written on Roman agrarian history', and announced his intention of sending the reprinted edition of his essays, *Historical Materialism and the Economics of Karl Marx*.[5] Contact between Weber and Croce was interrupted at this point, the interruption lasting until Croce suggested the Italian translation of *Parliament and Government in a Reconstructed Germany*. This mutual esteem never became a dialogue. News of the death of Weber did, however, move Croce to write to Vossler, who had the previous year informed Croce of Weber's appointment at Munich, that 'I have heard of Weber's death with genuine pain, one of the finest minds of our time and a serene spirit'.[6]

There is, nevertheless, no lack of reference in the work of both writers to each other's thoughts.[7] Weber, two years the elder, was the first to take up an important point and discuss Croce's doctrine of intuition as presented in Karl Federn's 1905 translation of *Aesthetics as Science of Expression and General Linguistics* (1902).[8] The discussion appears in the first few pages of the third part of the article on Roscher and Knies published (in vol. 30 of *Schmollers Jahrbuch*) in 1906. In the second part of this essay, Weber had expanded his criticism of the Historical School of political economy into a critique of the methodological remnants from romantic thought, which were widespread in late nineteenth-century German philosophy; here, he also rejected the attempts at founding the specificity of historical knowledge on the method of *Verstehen*, which excluded resort to causal explanation. His initial target was principally the contrast of '"free" and therefore irrational individual action of persons on the one hand, law-governed determination of the naturally given conditions of action on the other'[9] – a contrast which resulted in the denial of the possibility of a rational explanation of human action in principle. Weber's polemic was concerned with the methodology of the human sciences propounded by Wilhelm Wundt, in particular his concept of 'creative synthesis'; it led further to a rejection of the Kantian conception of causality through freedom. Consequently the concept of interpretation assumed a leading role in Weber's analysis, and he emphasized the inability of this concept to distinguish between the procedures of historical and natural scientific knowledge. His criticism was expressly directed against Hugo Münsterberg's *Grundzüge der Psychologie* [Outline of Psychology] (1900), the second edition of Georg Simmel's *The Problems of the Philosophy of History* (1905) and Friedrich von Gottl-Ottlilienfeld's *Herrschaft des Wortes* (1904). In the background, however, there also emerged references to Dilthey and Rickert, marked in different ways. In the case of Dilthey, it was not only the distinction of natural from human sciences that was rejected on the grounds that its objective foundation was methodologically misleading, but also the conception of *Verstehen*, together with the relation between experience (*Erleben*) and *Verstehen*; in the case of Rickert, Weber accepted not only the distinction of natural from cultural sciences on the basis of their different cognitive purposes, but also the general methodological approach that was laid out in his *Grenzen der naturwissenschaftlichen Begriffsbildung* [The Limits of Concept Formation in Natural Science] (1902). And, finally, the polemic against the reduction of epistemology to psychology (and against the confusion of an epistemological with a psychological approach) found support in Edmund Husserl's *Logical Investigations*, which had been published in 1900–1.

It is this rejection of psychologism that forms the point of departure in the third part of the essay on Roscher and Knies, discussing the theory of empathy formulated by Theodor Lipps in his *Grundlegung der Aesthetik* [Fundamentals of Aesthetics] (1903) and Croce's theory of intuition. At first glance, this association of Lipps and Croce might seem surprising, for Lipps's theory is concerned with a psychological foundation for aesthetics, even assuming a conception of aesthetics as a 'psychological discipline' or a 'discipline of applied psychology'.[10] Croce, on the other hand, employs the concept of intuition to define art as a form of knowledge distinct from intellectual knowledge; more precisely, as a 'stage' of the mind's theoretical activity, which pre-exists and is independent of 'knowledge through concepts', i.e. philosophy. The association seems even more surprising when it is recalled that, in the historical part of his *Aesthetics*, Croce expressly rejects Lipps's position as a representative of a 'pure psychological and associationist orientation' of aesthetics,[11] while Weber regards Croce as 'the ingenious Italian counterpart of the views of Lipps and those committed to psychologism within philology and aesthetics in general'.[12] There is, nevertheless, justification for the association. With regard to Lipps, Weber criticizes the claim of deriving intellectual understanding from empathy, conceived as a purely internal act, a kind of 'inner imitation'; in Croce, he criticizes the thesis (central to Croce's

Aesthetics as well as his later *Lineamenti di une logica come scienza del concetto puro* [Outline of Logic as the Science of the Pure Concept] (1905) that individual 'objects' can be only known 'artistically' without resort to relational concepts.[13] With respect to Lipps, Weber objects that 'the claim that empathy includes "more" than mere "intellectual understanding" cannot imply that empathy has more "theoretical value" or a better claim to "validity"... It is only a way of saying that empathy is not a matter of objectified "knowledge", but rather a matter of pure "experience"'.[14] Similarly, Weber identifies in Croce the 'naturalistic errors' supporting the conclusion that 'history cannot be the object of a "logical" evaluation, for logic concerns only (general) concepts and their definitions.'[15]

According to Weber, essentially three errors are made. The first is that 'only relational concepts and ... only relational concepts of absolute precision, i.e. those which can be expressed in terms of causal equivalents, are genuine "concepts"'.[16] Weber remarks with respect to this standpoint that 'even physics employs concepts which fail to satisfy this condition'; the implication of this criticism is that Croce's view is dependent on an artificial (and, one should therefore add, historically backward) model of empirical science. The second error is the statement that '"concepts of objects" are not "concepts", but rather "institutions"' − a statement which is 'the consequence of the reciprocal commixture of different meanings of the category of "intuitivity"', namely, of the 'intuitive self-evidence' of a mathematical proposition with the intuitive character of experience. With regard to Croce's denial of the possibility of 'concepts of objects', Weber argues that 'when empirical evidence treats a given manifold as a "thing", and therefore as an "entity" − e.g. the "personality" of a concrete historical person − then it is invariably the case that this object is only "relatively determined". That is, it is a conceptual construct which always includes aspects that are empirically "intuited". But, at the same time, it is a thoroughly synthetic construct. Its "unity" is constituted by the selection of those aspects which are "essential" from the point of view of specific theoretical goals. It is, therefore, a product of thought, which bears only a "functional" relation to the "given". In consequence, it is a "concept"...' In this manner, Weber emphasizes the *constructional character*, and this means the cognitive character, of every object (whether natural or historical) as the product of a process of unification of the empirically given, and thereby reveals the arbitrariness of the correspondence that Croce postulates between the concept of the 'object' and intuition (and also the similar correspondence between relational concepts and conceptual knowledge). The third and final error is the 'widespread popular view of history accepted by Croce ... the view according to which history is a "reproduction of (empirical) intuitions", or a copy of prior "direct experience" (either a first-person or a third-person experience)'. Here, Weber recapitulates the criticism that he had formulated against historical intuitionism in general, emphasizing that 'as soon as it becomes the object of a *thought*, not even a first-person experience can be "reflected" or "reproduced" in inner experience. That would not constitute thought *about* the experience, but rather another "experience" of the earlier experience. Or rather, since this is impossible, a *new* "experience", "accompanied" by the "feeling" − which, from an analytical point of view, invariably proves to be only relatively grounded – that one has already "experienced" "this".' He concludes by emphasizing that 'even the most simple "existential proposition" ... presupposes logical operations as soon as it constitutes a "proposition" the "validity" of which – for *this* is the only relevant question – is to be established. Although these logical operations do not include the "justification" of general concepts, they certainly do include their constant *use*. Therefore, they include abstraction and comparison.'

As with Lipps, Weber's critique of Croce is not directed against his aesthetics but rather against the implications of such an aesthetics for the notion of *Verstehen* or, more generally, for historical knowledge. The target of Weber's polemic is with Lipps the possibility of founding knowledge of the individuality of others upon empathy, and therefore upon *Erleben*. In the case of Croce, it is rather the possibility of reducing history to intuition and hence 'art', opposing this to intellectual knowing. The aspect of Crocean thought that Weber criticizes is that 'subsumption of history under the general concept of art', which had been theorized in an early academic paper by Croce[17] and to which he returned in *Aesthetics* in terms of the distinction between the two kinds of theoretical activity. Croce claims that outside intuition (or expression) and concepts, that is outside the forms of art and of science (conceived in the sense of philosophy and not of natural science, which is regarded as 'non-authentic science'), 'the knowing spirit has no other'; consequently, historicity was denied by Croce of the possibility of being a 'third, theoretical form', as it is 'not form, but content'.[18] From this, there follows the conclusion that 'history neither seeks laws nor mints concepts; its procedures are neither inductive nor deductive; It is organized *ad narrandum*, *non ad demonstrandum*; it creates no general concepts and abstractions, but rather gives rise to intuitions.'[19] Certainly, Weber could not accept this position, for although it approached, on the one hand, Rickert's thesis on individuality of the historical object, on the other it shifted this idea of individuality into the domain of intuition, i.e. the domain of non-conceptual knowledge. Weber certainly shared the idea that history neither sought laws nor minted concepts, but saw the employment of empirical rules and general concepts as indispensable; for Weber, too, history has a narrative rather than demonstrative character, but its logical structure consists of causal explanation, not of narration. In his essay on 'Objectivity in social science and social policy', Weber argued that 'if the causal knowledge of the historians consists of the imputation of concrete effects to concrete causes, a valid imputation of any individual effect without the application of "nomological" knowledge – i.e. the knowledge of recurrent causal sequences – would in general be impossible'.[20] For Weber the problem was not, as it was for Croce, one concerning the presence or absence of concepts of historical knowledge, but instead their function and logical specificity. It was here that his deep and insuperable difference with Croce, as author of *Aesthetics* and *Lineamenti*, lay.

In his subsequent writings Weber was not to direct himself to Crocean ideas. The intention, announced in the essay on Roscher and Knies, of returning elsewhere to the *Lineamenti*,[21] was never realized; neither was Weber's intention to write a 'critical comment' on the new edition of *Historical Materialism and the Economics of Karl Marx*, an intention alluded to in a letter from Vossler to Croce in October 1907.[22] The sole further reference to Croce that is to be found in Weber's work appears as a footnote to the first part of 'Critical studies in the logic of cultural sciences', i.e. in the essay 'A Critique of Eduard Meyer's methodological views', where he accuses Croce and Vossler of confusing '"valuation" and (causal) "explanation"' and hence denying the autonomy of the latter.[23] In fact, neither the process of constructing a philosophy of spirit on a Hegelian basis which had been undertaken by Croce after the 1906 essay 'What is living and what is dead of the philosophy of Hegel?', in *Philosophy of the Practical. Economic and Ethic* (1909) and in the revisions to *Logic as the Science of the Pure Concept* (1909) nor the identification of history and philosophy and the consequent definition of philosophy as the 'methodology of historiography' (this appeared in *Theory and History of Historiography*, in German in 1915 and Italian in 1917) was of interest to Weber. The doctrine of art as 'lyric intuition' or the studies on the literature of the new Italy would have interested him even less.[24] The link with Croce was a marginal episode in the context of critical exchanges, on the basis of which Weber developed the methodology of the socio-historical sciences.

II

But it was the same for Croce. During the years in question his knowledge of Weber's work was quite limited and remained so in the years following. Croce had read the *Roman Agrarian History* in his youth; according to his correspondence with Vossler in July 1906, he later read both of the offprints sent to him by Weber, or at least he read the pages that referred to him. However, he did not reply to Weber's criticism, not even indirectly: the reference to Hegel, underlying his shift of thinking in that period, led to a growing distance in relation to contemporary German philosophy, in particular that which provided the most significant philosophical 'source' for Weber – value-theory. The influence of Giovanni Gentile directed the 'system' of the philosophy of 'spirit' (in *Philosophy of the Practical* and the revised *Logic*) in an idealistic direction, and this was to be typical right up to the final years.[25] The different tendencies of neo-Kantianism became the object of an at times fierce polemic. Croce published his essay 'Intorno ai così detti giudizi di valore'[26] in *La Critica* during 1910, denying value-judgements all logical character and treating them as simple 'expressions of feeling'. The sole legitimate employment of the concept of value was that which identified it with forms of spirit, i.e. with the 'categories' of spiritual life, and this to the extent that 'without categories judgement and therefore history is impossible; without knowledge of the Good, i.e. of ethical life, of the beautiful, i.e. the aesthetic life, of the useful, i.e. the economical life, of the true, i.e. the life of thought – without all these one is unable to recount history, relating to specific objects or to others, if they exist'.[27] To the degree that Croce allowed a legitimacy to value-theory, it was placed alongside the theory of forms of spirit as the foundation of historical judgement – a judgement that no longer occurred on the level of intuition, but which was ascribed a genuine intellectual, i.e. philosophic, character.

World war and the crisis of Germany reawakened Croce's interest in Weber;

but this was now Weber the politician, the author of *Parliament and Government in a Reconstructed Germany* (1918). Having quickly obtained a copy via Switzerland, Croce pressed the translation on the publisher Laterza, 'so that this painful and critical confession made by Weber of the bureaucratic conception of politics, cultivated and exalted as it is by the Germans in contrast to the free people of Western Europe, should bear fruit in Italy'.[28] The translation, entrusted to Enrico Ruta, was published in the summer of 1919 with an extremely positive foreword by the translator, who underlined the validity of Weber's interpretation. The Italian publication of this book, shortly followed by the translation of Rathenau's *Die neue Wirtschaft* [The New Economy] and Naumann's *Mitteleuropa* [Central Europe], which Croce had also proposed, testifies to Croce's intense interest in the dramatic collapse of the German Empire and also to his hopes for a German democratic renewal. It is not accidental that Croce, in a letter to Vossler on 17 June 1920, connects his sorrow at Weber's death with 'sorrow for that which you say about the German situation', in which he saw suffering that 'concerns not only Germany, but us all'.[29] Much later, in 1948, he underlined again the relation between Weber's personal fate and the political fate of Germany. Weber seemed to him to be 'a victim of these circumstances, being both intolerant and inflexible'.[30]

Nevertheless, the historico-sociological work of Weber's last decade remained alien to Croce. He did contribute the essay 'Die Grenzen der Sprachsoziologie'[31] to the memorial volume for Weber, but he took no notice of either *Economy and Society* or the various collections of Weber's writings published during the first half of the 1920s – he did not even read them. Irrefutable proof of this is provided not least by the lack of precise reference to Weber's writings in Croce's work in the subsequent period but also the absence of these writings in his library – with the exception of *Wirtschaft und Gesellschaft* and *Politische Schriften*.[32] There are occasional references to Weber, for example in the extremely negative review of Troeltsch's *Der Historismus und seine Überwindung*, printed during 1927 in *La Critica*, and in the review published in the same journal during 1933 of Karl Heussi's *Die Krisis des Historismus*, but nothing more. One has to wait until a further review in 1940, of Antoni's *From History to Sociology* – which subjected German historicism and Weber's thought to criticism inspired by Croce – to find an explicit judgement on Weber. The sole essay by Weber that prompted some interest on the part of Croce during the inter-war period was the *Protestant Ethic*. While he did not agree with the general thesis of the essay, he did recognize its importance,[33] and he made attempts to get Piero Burresi's translation published by Laterza.[34] The commercial failure of *Parliament and Government* meant, however, that Croce's intervention was unsuccessful; the translation had to wait a few years until publication of *Nuovi studi di diritto, economia e politica* [New Studies of Law, Economics and Politics] in 1931–2.

The boundaries of Croce's interest in Weber's work, as well as his actual knowledge of it, did not pertain to Croce alone: they reflected the contemporary state of Italian culture. Translations were at first few in number, not without error and not without unhappy terminological renderings. Before the appearance of *Parliament and Government*, the only Italian translation of

Weber's writing was the *Roman Agrarian History*, published during 1907 in Pareto's *Biblioteca di storia economica*. Apart from those translations published during the two subsequent decades that have already been noted, all that was published was a selection from *Economy and Society* under the title 'Carismatica e i tipi del potere'; this was arranged by Robert Michels in 1934 for the *Nuova collana di economisti stranieri e italiani* [New Collection of Foreign and Italian Economists] in the volume entitled *Politica ed economia* where it was published alongside the Communist Manifesto, and texts by Labriola, Loria, Pareto and Simmel. Quite apart from these translations, however, the interest in Weber was restricted to a few groups, and concentrated on the thesis concerning the Calvinist-Puritanical origin of the capitalist spirit. During the first half of the 1920s, this interest established itself in the environment of Gobetti's journal *Rivoluzione liberale*, and among Protestant circles, in particular the journal *Conscientia* and the publisher Doxa – both areas of Italian culture remote from Croce's predominance. Weber's thesis was mostly put to ideological use, seeking to demonstrate the far-off roots of the 'failed revolution' in Italy or the superior modernity of Protestantism in comparison with Catholic ethics, which were held to be permeated by anti-capitalist motives. The reception of the thesis among economic historians was also quite limited and patchy, thanks to the work of historians such as Gino Luzzatto, Mario M. Rossi, Amintore Fanfani, Armando Sapori and others. Rossi tried to develop a spiritualistic interpretation of Weber in his *L'ascesi capitalistica* (1928), representing Weber as a kind of 'Anti-Marx'; while in the early 1930s Fanfani sought to demonstrate, with the aid of Weber, that a Catholic social ethics was incompatible with capitalism and that capitalism must be overcome by a form of corporatism of both Catholic and Fascist inspiration. Discussion on the origins of capitalism and on the presence of capitalist economic forms in the later Middle Ages did tend, in general, more towards Sombart's *Modern Capitalism* (partially translated in 1925 by Luzzatto) than towards Weber. The only reliable presentation of Weber's scientific stature is to be found in Ernesto Sestan's essay in the 1933–4 volume of *Nuovi studi di diretto, economia e politica*. Other aspects of Weber's historico-sociological work were unknown territory to all but Michels. The first general outline, if one-sided and marked by strong prejudice, is to be found in Carlo Antoni's 1938 essay in *Studi germanici*, later reprinted in his book *From History to Sociology*.

The publication of this book, and the succeeding translation in 1948 of 'Science as a vocation' and 'Politics as a vocation' in the Einaudi volume *Il lavoro intellettuale come professione* – with an important introduction by Delio Cantimori – gave Croce renewed opportunity to consider Weber's work. Supported by his secure confidence in the superiority of his own historicism to that of the Germans, his judgement assumed a tone quite distinct from that of his correspondence with Vossler in the first decades of the century, where he had adopted the position of admiring respect. The admiration is certainly there, but it relates only to the 'honesty and courageousness of the man, and the vivacity of his mind in the comprehension of aspects of reality'; but not the historico-sociological work, and even less its methodological presuppositions.[35] Such writing was for Croce – as it was for Antoni – an expression of the involutionary tendency of German culture, a process which had led from historicism to the human sciences (*Geisteswissenschaften*) and ultimately to sociology. Even Weber 'suffered from the decadence or interruption of the great German speculative tradition'; for Croce, it was here that the limit of his work was to be found. Thus 'the faults of the famed derivation of modern liberty from the spirit of Calvinism, and from the concept of vocation and divine election' arose from the fact that 'it was a psychological derivation and not a historico-philosophical explanation which is quite necessary for the treatment of an intellectual category'. Weber's criticism of historical materialism, in Croce's view, similarly failed to account for the fact that 'this doctrine was philosophical ... and could not be criticized without the re-insertion and rediscovery of proper speculative concepts'. But the greatest of Weber's mistakes seemed to him to be the attempt at 'the logical construction of a sociology' without taking into consideration that it was 'a pseudo-science, seeking to resolve philosophical problems in a non-philosophical manner'. This contrast of philosophy with the empirical sciences and the claim that the latter were pseudo-conceptual in nature served the older Croce for a summary judgement upon Weber, accusing him of an incapability of 'recognizing that philosophy is exactly the supersession of its boundaries, limiting it, justifying it and illuminating historically that which is the *concretum* of philosophy'.

III

There was, nevertheless, a common area of research and discussion between Weber and Croce: criticism of historical materialism and the dicussion of Marx. Here, Croce was practically a decade ahead of Weber. His essays, later collected in *Historical Materialism and the Economics of Karl Marx* (1899), were written in the last decade of the nineteenth century, between 1896 and 1899. Subsequently, Croce was to return to Marx and Marxism from time to time – after the Second World War in a markedly obsessive fashion – but the period which he himself dubbed the 'Marxist parenthesis' of his life[36] can be regarded as one that had closed by the turn of the century. The impulse for Croce arose from two essays by Labriola, 'In memoria del Manifesto dei Communisti' (1895) and 'Del materialismo storico, dilucidazioni preliminari' [Historical materialism: preliminary explanations] (1896), which proposed a humanistic, anti-metaphysical and anti-positivistic interpretation of Marxism. The young Croce, barely thirty years old, wished to agree substantially with Labriola, and in the essay 'Sulla forma scientifica del materialismo storico' (1896) sought to demonstrate that historical materialism was not a philosophy of history, denying or countering the idealist conception of history, in that it 'involves an entire abandonment of all attempts to establish a law of history, to discover a general concept under which all the complex facts of history can be included'.[37] For Croce, historical materialism was no 'new philosophy of history or a new method; but it is properly this: a mass of new data, of new experiences, of which the historian becomes conscious';[38] that is to say, using a formula that was to become emblematic, a canon of historical interpretation. The recognition of the importance and fertility of Marxist doctrine is balanced by a refusal to ascribe a precise theoretical or methodological status to it.

The argument that Croce developed in an essay appearing two years later ('Per la interpretazione e la critica di alcuni concetti del marxismo') is more elaborate. His analysis no longer referred just to Labriola; Croce took a stand in the European debate on Marxism and dealt not only with Sombart's essay 'Zur Kritik des ökonomischen Systems von Karl Marx' (which reviewed Vol. III of *Das Kapital* in the 1894 volume of *Schmollers Jahrbuch*) but also with texts of the late Engels, and of Lange, Kautsky, Bernstein and, above all, Georges Sorel. His intention was to define the specific character of the form of investigation followed by Marx, and to distinguish it from, on the one hand, the historical analysis of modern capitalist society and, on the other, from economic science. Primarily, Marx's work was for Croce an 'abstract investigation' whose object was not the 'historically existing' capitalist society of a particular country or of a specific period; it was rather 'an ideal and formal society, deduced from certain hypotheses, which could indeed never have occurred as actual facts in the course of history. It is true that these hypotheses correspond to a great extent to the historical conditions of the modern civilized world; but this ... does not alter its nature.'[39] Marx's investigation is thus not descriptive but instead seeks an 'understanding' relating to 'one special economic system, that which occurs in a society with private property in capital, or, as Marx says, in the phrase peculiar to him, *capitalist*.'[40] In this attempt Marx follows a comparative method based on the law of equivalence of value and labour. Referring to Sombart, Croce notes that 'Marx's labour-value is not only a logical generalization, it is also a fact conceived and postulated as typical,' which has the function 'of a term of comparison, of a standard, of a type'. The purpose of this is 'to show with what divergencies from this standard the prices of commodities are fixed in capitalist society, and how labour-power itself acquires a price and becomes a commodity.'[41] The equivalence between value and labour appeared to him to be the formulation of a model of 'economic society in so far as it is a working society', which disregards the existence of class relations and which must serve to present a comparison 'between capitalist society and economic society as such.'[42] In anticipation of Weber, and without knowing Jellinek, Croce attributed in this fashion an ideal-typical character to Marx's theory, which was to serve as the foundation for the analysis of historical forms of capitalist society. This makes it possible for him to distinguish Marx's investigation from a genuine historical investigation and also to attribute to the principle of class struggle the 'limited value as a standard of interpretation',[43] i.e. the value of a criterion on the basis of which it can from time to time be ascertained whether and when social classes exist, what their contrasting interests might be and how far they are conscious of this contrast. By using an ideal-typical approach, it was also possible for him to differentiate between Marx's economic theory and economic science, ascribing to the first the character of an economic sociology or that of a comparative 'sociological economics'.[44] While 'pure' economics − here Croce has in mind doctrine from Smith and Ricardo to Jevons and Marshall, the Austrian school, Pareto and Pantaleoni − is the 'general science of economic facts', Marx offers a study of a model of society conceived as an 'abstract working society',[45] and hence quite compatible with the principles of economic science.

Croce was soon to move away from this position, probably influenced by the quite distinct manner of reading Marx suggested by Gentile in his *La filosofia di Marx* of 1899. Having repeatedly defended the legitimacy of historical materialism as a canon of historical interpretation – against Loria, Labriola and also Rudolf Stammler – Croce claimed in 1899 that 'historical materialism was erroneous as a general scientific thesis'.[46] He adopted that interpretation of Marx and Marxism that in the preceding years he had systematically criticized: now he argued that it was on the one hand materialistic, and on the other represented a 'conception of historical process which unfolded along predetermined lines, a variant of the Hegelian philosophy of history'.[47] In his eyes, historical materialism assumed a metaphysical character and, in this regard, was countered with a 'living' as distinct from a 'dead' Hegel – Croce seeking in this way to oppose the dialectical apprehension of reality to the Hegelian system as such. What remained of the encounter with Marx and Marxism was reduced to a recognition of the autonomy of that which was of 'utility' as a form of practical activity – this idea is central to *Philosophy of the Practical* – a form which could not be reduced to ethics and which includes not simply the relations of production and labour, but also political and legal relations, the life of states and the relationships between classes. Croce was to explain several years later: 'From the point of view of theory I did not take up anything from Marxism, for its value was pragmatic rather than scientific in nature; and as a science all it offered was a pseudo-economics, a pseudo-philosophy and a pseudo-history.'[48] Thus the encounter with historical materialism concluded with its drastic liquidation.

During the same period Weber also was studying Marx's work, under the joint impulse of his own investigations into ancient history and his participation in the activities of the Verein für Sozialpolitik; he too, in all probability, followed the debate about Marxism that was particularly lively at the turn of the century. His thought was especially influenced by the revision of Marxist doctrine represented by Bernstein's *Evolutionary Socialism* in 1899; he did not hesitate to side with Bernstein in his polemic with Kautsky, even if he did not intervene directly.[49] His critique of historical materialism, however, is to be found in the years following, at a time when Croce's 'Marxist period' was already closed: from 1904 to 1907, coinciding with the formulation of Weber's methodology. The interpretation of Marxist theory that Weber adopts is also distinct from that of Croce. Historical materialism is, or seeks to be, a general historical interpretation that has to be refuted as such. As Weber put it in a well-known passage in the essay '"Objectivity" in social science and social policy': 'The so-called "materialist conception of history" as a *Weltanschauung* or as a formula for the causal explanation of historical reality is to be rejected most emphatically ... this conception ... with the crude elements of genius of the early form which appeared, for instance, in the Communist Manifesto still prevails only in the minds of laymen and dilettantes.'[50] At the methodological level, his critique of historical materialism is dealt with in terms of the problem of historical explanation. Weber rejects historical materialism's claim to be a '"universal" canon which explained all cultural phenomena ... as, in the last analysis, economically conditioned.'[51] His criticism was directed against both the distinction of base and superstructure and an explanatory model founded upon a presumption of reduceability − even if 'in the last instance' − of superstructural phenomena to a structural, i.e. 'economic' base. He also rejected in principle the thesis of the 'primacy of the economic' and the consequent consideration of the various aspects of the historical process as functioning 'for the benefit of certain economic class interests'.[52] This critique of historical materialism was, however, only a special case in the critique of an explanatory model, in which one 'factor' or series of factors was privileged as the *ultimate* foundation of cultural phenomena − whether this be 'material interests' or relations of production and labour, or racial qualities, or religion. It was no accident that this is counterpointed by Weber's criticism of the 'thesis of the conditionality of all cultural phenomena "in the last instance" *only* by religious motives' in the essay on Stammler.[53] Historical materialism, race theory and a spiritualistic conception of history are all united by the same error: accepting one aspect of the historical process as dominant, as an explanatory base to which the remaining aspects must, directly or indirectly, be related.

It was, nevertheless, precisely this view that made it possible for Weber to approach the materialist conception of history in a positive manner and to underline its heuristic value. As he wrote in the 'Objectivity' essay: 'we believe nevertheless that the analysis of social and cultural phenomena with special reference to their economic conditioning and ramifications was a scientific principle of creative fruitfulness and, with careful application and freedom from dogmatic restrictions, will remain such for a very long time to come.'[54] From this standpoint, Weber defended the legitimacy of an economic interpretation of the historical process as one possible mode of analysing (and explaining) cultural phenomena. Even if he rejected 'the explanation of everything by economic causes alone' as 'never exhaustive', he was prepared to allow that 'the justification of the one-sided analysis of cultural reality from specific "points of view" − in our case with respect to its economic conditioning ... is in general only a special case of a principle which is generally valid for the scientific knowledge of cultural reality'.[55] Later, in the 'Economic ethic of world religions' and in *Economy and Society*, or in the posthumous lectures on economic history, Weber's critique of historical materialism did not take the form of an attempted 'supersession', but rather of a 'positive' critique, which had to be conducted in terms of the analysis of mutual relations between economic forms and forms of social organization in specific historical circumstances. Hence, they led to a different conclusion from that of Croce: not a philosophical 'refutation' of Marx and Marxism, not an alternative general conception of history, but a recognition of the scientific validity of historical materialism as a method, even if limited by the unavoidable onesidedness that was the property of this, as of all other, points of view.

IV

These years at the turn of the century were the time when, in their critique of historical materialism and in the debate with Marx, Croce and Weber came closest. But no dialogue developed between them. Weber was first to learn of Croce's essays when they were sent to him by the author in 1906 − that is, just at the point when Weber had formulated his position; and it can be doubted whether Weber then read the book, since his critique of Stammler does not once refer to the analysis of the same text that had been made earlier by Croce.[56] After this point, their paths were to diverge, and any comparison of Croce's system of the philosophy of mind – from *Aesthetics* to *Theory and History of Historiography* – with Weber's methodology can only be indirect.

Croce's views with respect to historical knowledge underwent a radical change in the first decade of the twentieth century. In the *Lineamenti di Logica*, he had already dispensed with the thesis according to which history was to be reduced to art, recognizing the joint presence in historical judgement – or, better, the synthesis – of a representative element (of an artistic nature) and a conceptual element; in this way he characterized historical principles as a 'third series of theoretical products' with art and philosophy.[57] Some years later, in *Logic as the Science of the Pure Concept*, Croce reintroduced a rigorous dichotomy between art and philosophy; but, owing to the theory of identity between the determining judgement of philosophy and the individual judgement of history, historiography no longer coincided with art, but with philosophy. On the one hand, philosophy was reduced to the role of defining and elaborating categories, founding historical judgement and constituting the logical foundation of the four forms of spirit; on the other hand, this judgement presented itself as the characterization of an individual 'fact' founded by a category – characterized then as either artistic, logical, economic or ethical fact. In this fashion, historical knowledge became for Croce the sole possible cognitive form beyond artistic intuition, while philosophy – as in the since well-known formulation – assumed the role of a 'methodology of historiography'. This became possible thanks to the denial of the cognitive value of the sciences – empirical as well as abstract sciences, i.e. mathematics and 'pure' economics – which Croce developed in *Logic*, invoking the empirio-criticism of Mach and Avenarius and more generally the irrationalistic tendencies of the late-nineteenth-century critique of the sciences. The sciences are constructs made up of pseudo-concepts, i.e. of 'conceptual fictions'; they are constructions for the purpose of classification in the case of the empirical sciences and for the purpose of measurement in the case of the abstract sciences. Both draw their contents from history and work them up with regard to a practical objective. Only philosophy concerns itself with the pure concept and its categorical forms; only philosophy can found historical judgement, which in turn ultimately dissolves philosophy. Croce's epistemology allows to philosophy and historiography a monopoly of conceptual cognition and drives the sciences back into the sphere of economic form, that of the non-theoretical but practical spirit. In relation to the social sciences, Croce's position becomes increasingly deprecatory; from 1905, there is a continual polemic against positivistic sociology, which results in the denial of legitimacy to sociology as such.[58]

By contrast, Weber developed neo-Kantian historicism further. This historicism distinguished the human or cultural sciences from the natural sciences through the method they employed, the objects they dealt with, or both; and in so doing, he fully recognized the cognitive value of each. For Dilthey and Simmel, for Windelband and Rickert, and also for Weber, they are of different types but possess a similar level of objectivity in comparison with the scientific apprehension of the natural world: it is in relation to them that philosophy has to undertake a critical (in the Kantian sense) analysis, without, however, being either reduced or assimilated to them. Dilthey had distinguished the human and the natural sciences on the basis of the contrast between understanding and explanation, and he sought the foundation of the human sciences in a procedure that connected experience, expression and understanding. Rickert, on the other hand, wished to define the sphere of cultural sciences on the basis of their historical orientation, that is, their orientation to the individual. In both cases, however, the argument for the autonomy of a group of disciplines with respect to the natural sciences was accompanied by the attempt to clarify the distinct standards of their scientificity. It was in this way that Weber regained nomological knowledge for historical cognition (employing a methodological perspective taken over from Rickert's *Die Grenzen*) and distinguished the role it played here from that which it performed in the natural sciences. For Weber there is a distinction, but no dichotomy, between historical knowledge and the scientific apprehension of the natural world; the requirements that have to be met in order to be considered objective knowledge – the exclusion of value-judgements and resort to causal explanation – are common to both. Historical knowledge is founded upon a value-relation as a principle of selection within the variety of the empirically given, and at the same time as a criterion for the construction of its object; causal explanation becomes the explication of a process in its individuality; causality does not exclude understanding, but rather is united with it; all these properties are the differentiating aspects of a specific form of scientific knowledge, and nothing more. It is the same with the instrumental function attributed to general concepts and empirical rules. The doctrine of the ideal type enabled Weber to combine individualizing historical research and the systematic cultural sciences, as later – in the 1913 essay 'Über einige Kategorien der verstehenden Soziologie' and in the first chapter of *Economy and Society* – it did enable him to recognize the relative independence of sociology from history and at the same time their reciprocal relation.

Croce counterposed historiography to the social sciences – whether it be the economy theory or the 'empirical science of politics'; for the first, he reserved a cognitive value while assigning the second, like the natural sciences, to the domain of economic intellectual forms. For Croce, historical judgement – the sole form of judgement to which cognitive validity was ascribed – ruled out any kind of resort to general concepts, apart from categorical determinations of mind, that is, of its 'forms'. More radically, he ruled out the invocation of laws or procedural regularities that might be empirically apparent, since he believed that the spirit always operated through individual works that were – as products of spiritual activity – constantly different and hence only to be drawn together for the purpose of classification. For Weber, on the contrary, ideal types (and thus the social sciences, which consist of ideal types organized in a systematic fashion) are indispensable means of historical knowledge; that which is individual can only be recognized with the assistance of general concepts and the rules of experience. Here, the postulate of the explanatory character of historical knowledge once more emerges, the postulate that had led Weber in the essay on Roscher and Knies to take up a critical position in relation to Croce. Historiography had initially meant for Croce the 'description' or 'narration' of facts in an artistic manner, and then was subsequently developed as the historico-philosophical reconstruction of the individual course of events, or more precisely as 'recalling' established by the spirit under the stimulus of an 'interest in contemporary life'.[59] The subject of historical knowledge coincided with the subject of history, and this coincidence secures not only its possibility, but its 'truth'. For Weber, on the other hand, every form of knowledge, and hence also historical knowledge, must be causal explanation. The specificity of historical knowledge, therefore, had to be sought in the particular type of explanation that it offered, as well as in the varying function of nomological knowledge.

The distance separating Weber from Croce appears to be greater when the ontological presuppositions in which Croce anchored his epistemology are considered. In his attempt at extracting the 'living' heart of Hegelian philosophy from its systematic structure, Croce arrived at the dissolution of the idea in consciousness and he denied the independent existence of nature; instead of being the precondition and the antecedent of intellect (as in *Aesthetics*), nature became an abstract construction, which created spirit for practical ends. Reality thus identified itself with spirit, and spirit with history; in this way, every 'fact' became a historical fact, an individual moment in the unfolding of spirit conceived as the infinite 'subject' of history. The thesis itself, according to which 'each judgement is a historical judgement or is itself history' was supported, as it was formulated in *History as the Story of Liberty* (La storia come pensiero e come azione) by the assumption that 'the judged fact ... is always a historical fact, a process of becoming, a historical process'.[60] It is on this that the well-known conclusion is based, that 'reality is history and can only be recognized historically'.[61] The philosophy of spirit thus became 'absolute' historicism, a historicism that, by dissolving reality in the spirit, treated the spirit as identical with history, in that 'the spirit is never in itself and for itself, but is always historical'.[62] Within this Hegelian conception of history the human individual lost all solidity and became a manifestation of spirit, became a complex of 'works' produced by spirit itself, and hence a simple 'institution', if not a 'symbol', of spiritual activity.[63] It would be hard to think of anything further from Weber's thoughts, writing as he did in *Economy and Society* of sociology having as its object social action, '"social" insofar as its subjective meaning takes account of the behaviour of others and is thereby oriented in its course',[64] and where 'social relationship' is defined as denoting 'the behaviour of a plurality of actors insofar as, in its meaningful content, the action of each takes account of that of the others and is oriented in these terms'.[65] Weber would certainly have seen in absolute historicism a kind of emanationism of a Hegelian form far more rigid than that which he had rejected in the work of Roscher. The mature Croce would have seemed far more remote than the Croce of *Aesthetics*, against whom he had once directed his criticism.

V

Neither is the distance separating Weber and Croce at the level of the substantive interpretation of history any less. In the period between the wars, Croce reworked the theory of spiritual forms and laid less emphasis on their distinction (and the consequent autonomy of political life in relation to morals) and more on their mutual relation and − within this relation − underlined the central role of the ethical form whose fundamental value he saw as in freedom. The polemic against Fascism led him to identify the core of historical process in 'the history of *moral or ethical life* . . . of a people or of mankind in general' − or in 'history in general, history par excellence',[66] to which particular histories of other spiritual forms had to be traced back. On this basis, Croce had confirmed the priority of ethico-political history, a synthesis of the history of culture and of states, whose object was 'the constitution of moral institutes in the broadest sense' and the work of their 'creators', those 'political geniuses and aristocrats or political classes from which they arise and which they also create and maintain'.[67] This conception of history as ethico-political history is more apparent in relation to the conception of freedom, in which Croce saw the 'eternal creator of history, the subject of all history',[68] the forming principle and at once the 'practical idea' of moral conscience.[69] Because spirit is by definition freedom (and simultaneously necessity), history becomes the history of freedom, its progressive realization and its progressive self-consciousness. In this fashion, Croce invoked the Hegelian conception of history as the development of spirit towards ever greater freedom; at the same time, he allowed the liberal conception of life to coincide with absolute historicism. He saw in the intellectual and moral history of the nineteenth century the time of the conclusive assertion of a philosophy founded upon the principle of immanence, as well as the historical epoch of the victorious confrontation of liberalism with the 'opposing forms of religious belief'.[70]

This viewpoint is at the basis of that historical work by Croce that corresponds most closely with the theoretical assumptions of his philosophy: *History of Europe in the Nineteenth Century*, published in 1932.[71] For Croce, what distinguishes this period from the preceding one is the emergence of the liberal conception of life − set free from the 'abstract rationalism' of the Enlightenment − in the form of a religion, more precisely in the form of a 'religion of freedom'. During the course of the nineteenth century, liberalism proved its superiority both as a general conception of reality and as an ethical idea corresponding to this, over the other 'religious forms of belief', whether these be inherited from the past like Catholicism and monarchial absolutism, or a creation of the Enlightenment, such as the democratic ideal, or even the new ethico-political ideal of communism. There are two aspects of this superiority. First, this is a theoretical or intellectual superiority, the superiority of an immanent and thus dialectical conception of life over a conception based on the idea of transcendence. In fact, the nineteenth century had given a profound impulse to the 'process of secularization' in institutions and society, and demonstrated the superiority of 'worldly thought and knowledge' over traditional religious perspectives.[72] Secondly, however, it is also an ethico-political superiority, that is, the superiority of liberalism as the principle of social progress, as a principle that 'does not coincide with the so-called free trade' even if it 'emerges at the same time . . . but always in a provisional and accidental manner'[73] irreducible to a specific economic policy, but which from time to time realizes itself in particular directions and measures. This superiority has, as a consequence, that this freedom can undergo periods of eclipse and of crisis, can endure long 'parentheses' (and, for Croce, Fascism is such a parenthesis in the continuity of historical development); but it is doomed to decline, for the liberal ideal 'is the only one which withstands criticism and represents for human society the point around which, in constant fluctuation and frequent disharmony, balance is eternally restored'.[74] On the basis of this view Croce is able to respond, in the epilogue to the work, to the question, 'whether freedom will belong to what is called the future', by stating that freedom has 'something better: eternity'.[75]

Ethics played an important role in the historical process for Weber too; he saw it as the element that oriented human action in relation to the realization of particular values. Among the various behavioural forms that affect the structure of a society is quite certainly that which he called 'religious or magically motivated action', action that is aimed at influencing natural events by magic means or (whether in this world or the next) securing the salvation of the individual or the community.[76] At the centre of Weber's interest from the analysis of the 'spirit' of capitalism onwards stood the problem of the relations between social structures and religious life; as is known, this constituted the theme of his investigations into the sociology of religion. It was precisely in the economic ethic of world religions that he saw the link between economy and religion: the means by which a religion assumed an attitude with respect to economic action, adapting to its conditions, rejecting them or seeking to subordinate them to its purposes. The point of departure for this can be found in the *Protestant Ethic* of 1904, in which a specific economic ethic founded upon ascetic Protestantism is linked to the 'spirit' of capitalism; from here, the investigation led Weber to the question of the peculiar nature of the modern Occident. But here the analogy with Croce's position ends. However important ethics might be, they do not for Weber provide the ultimate motive for human action; on the contrary, Weber is of the view that 'interests (material and ideal) and not ideas directly control human action'.[77] Ethics, be it of ultimate ends or of responsibility, is the outcome of a process of rationalization and to a certain extent of a process of sublimation, restricting interests and subordinating them to the realization of values. Weber does criticize historical materialism, but does not because of this, as we have seen, accept Stammler's thesis on the dependence of human action on religious causes. Not only are 'the most elementary forms of behaviour motivated by religious or magical factors ... oriented to *this* world',[78] while religious actions possess for the most part a practical objective, but the development of religious life (even redemptive religions) depends on the relation with social structures, political institutions and the forms of economic activity. The economic ethic may express the 'religious determination of life-conduct', but this is 'only *one*' of the factors determining life-conduct, among many others.[79] Two determining tendencies meet within the economic ethic: the determinacy of religious life in relation to specific social strata, and the determinacy of economic life by religious motives. Neither the one nor the other can in principle be given a privileged role.

Weber's conception of the historical process was very different from that of Croce, who gave a central place to the development and dialectics of ideas; it is these ideas which are, for Croce, the sole factor capable of lending meaning to the course of events, and thus also to political, economic and social circumstances. For Weber, the history of mankind is characterized by a process of rationalization, which he sees at work in all societies and at all times; a process leading, on the one hand, to the dissolution of the 'natural' bonds of kinship and magic and, on the other, to the progressive substitution of new forms (particularly rational forms) of action in place of more traditional forms. This process is not, however, unambiguous: it varies according to the possibility that it be oriented towards a particular value postulated as an unconditional objective or towards an objective adapted to the means and conditions of its realization, and according to the values and concrete ends to which it relates. This founds the possibility in turn of there being two major tendencies in the process of rationalization, inspired by the principles of either formal or material rationality; within these tendencies, there exists the possibility of variously oriented types of rationalization. The process of rationalization is indeed universal, but it develops variously in different societies and historical epochs. The formally constituted rationalization process typical of the modern West represents only one *particular* tendency in this process.

For Croce, at the pinnacle of the historical process there stands the liberal conception of life, founded upon the principle of immanence and upon the recognition of spirit as the subject of history. This pinnacle had for him been attained in nineteenth-century Europe, in the period that he called the liberal era. For Weber, the culture of the modern West and its characteristic features – from capitalism as 'economic rationalism' to the bureaucratic state and formal-rational law, and from rational science to the 'disenchantment' of life – must always be accounted for as the product of a particular process, its realization made possible by specific conditions, which in turn lend it its individuality. There is no criterion – neither historical, nor even metahistorical – that might make possible an evaluative comparison between these features and corresponding ones in other societies. The Crocean conception of history is a dialectical one, in which past elements of the historical process are maintained and 'overcome' within later periods. Croce's Eurocentrism thus possesses an axiological character. His postulate of the unity (and unilineal character) of history prevents him from recognizing the existence of cultures other than those that participated in the process leading from the ancient to the modern European world, finding their objective in the 'religion of freedom'. For Weber, on the other hand, world religions – and the cultures of which they are an expression – possess their own individuality and represent diverse, axiologically equivalent positions in relation to the 'world' (as is apparent in the analysis carried out in the 'Intermediate reflections'). The specificity of an inner-wordly orientation cannot imply its superiority. At most, we can allow a technical superiority in some areas to the rationalistic culture that emerges from the secession from the religious conditions of Protestant reform. The concept of 'progress' possesses no further legitimacy apart from its technical significance.[80]

The formally oriented process of rationalization in the modern world is indifferent to the freedom and liberal conception of life to which Croce gave a central place. In the political domain, as in others, this process primarily took the form of bureaucratization, as the development of an impersonal administrative apparatus open to use by the state and also by internal or external power-groupings (mainly parties). Bureaucracy is, however, a form of administration that is universally applicable. It can place its technical competence at the service of the state founded, as the modern 'bourgeois' state is, on the principles of legitimacy; or at the service of a state pursuing the objectives of material justice, such as the aim of socioeconomic equality. It corresponds rather more closely to the requirements of a mass democracy, arising as it does from the victory of the modern state over the particularism of the *Stände* and from the increasing levelling of social differences. The process of rationalization does not require in a formal sense the conditions of greater freedom; it does not necessarily have as its objective a society based on liberal or liberal–democratic principles. It can also lead to a quite different outcome, symbolized by the 'iron cage' that appears in the closing pages of the *Protestant Ethic*. If Croce's last word consists in the consoling claim that freedom possesses not future, but 'eternity', Weber's last word is rather the prospect of a world in which bureaucratization and mass democracy tend to limit and restrict the freedom of the individual. But Croce's freedom was the freedom of spirit, and as such imperishable; the freedom in Weber's thought was a restricted and precarious freedom of people living in a world possessing no 'meaning' in itself, a world to which they had to lend meaning through their actions – a value, that must be conquered and maintained and which could thus also be lost.

Notes: Chapter 30

This chapter was translated by Keith Tribe.

1   *Quaderni della Critica*, no. 12 (November, 1948), later reprinted in B. Croce, *Terze pagine sparse*, Vol. 1 (Bari, 1955), pp. 130–3, here p. 130.
2   *Carteggio Croce–Vossler (1899–1949)* (Bari, 1961), pp. 106–7. Karl Vossler to Benedetto Croce, 13 October 1907.
3   ibid., p. 58, Karl Vossler to Benedetto Croce, 11 July 1905.
4   ibid., pp. 94–5, Croce to Vossler, 12 July 1906. Daniela Coli claims that 'it is not possible on the basis of the correspondence to understand which of Weber's pieces Croce had read'; *Croce, Laterza e la cultura europea* (Bologna, 1983), p. 83 fn. This is true, but it is possible to make such an identification by considering the writings of Weber that Croce had in his library.
5   ibid.
6   *Carteggio*, p. 243, Benedetto Croce to Karl Vossler, 17 June 1920.
7   The one attempted investigation of the relation of Croce and Weber is the piece by F. Tessitore, 'Su Croce e Weber', in *Comprensione storica e cultura* (Naples, 1979), pp. 285–95. Less useful is the article by S. Cirrone, 'Sul rapporto Croce–Weber: una ipotesi', in A. Bruno (ed.), *Benedetto Croce trent' anni dopo* (Bari, 1983), pp. 179–88. There is no reference to this relationship in the important book by G. Sasso, *Benedetto Croce. La ricerca della dialettica* (Naples, 1975). Eugenio Garin gives a general assessment of Croce's thought within the framework of European culture at the turn of the century in 'Appunti sulla formazione e su alcuni caratteri del pensiero crociano' in idem, *Intellettuali italiani del XX secolo* (Rome, 1974), pp. 3–31, as well as in his important book, *Cronache di filosofia italiana (1900–1943)* (Bari, 1955).
8   *Estetica come scienza dell' espressione e linguistica generale*. An English translation was published in 1909. The German translation referred to here appeared in 1905 under the title *Aesthetik als Wissenschaft des Ausdrucks und allgemeine Linguistik. Theorie und Geschichte*.
9   RaK, p. 96 [transl. revised].
10 T. Lipps, *Aesthetik, Psychologie des Schönen und der Kunst.* Bd. 1: *Grundlegung der Aesthetik* (Leipzig, 1901), p. 1.
11 *Estetica come scienza dell' espressione e linguistica generale* (Bari, [1902]), 12th edn (Bari, 1973), p. 455.

12 RaK, p. 167 [transl. revised].
13 ibid.
14 ibid., p. 166.
15 ibid., p. 167.
16 The citations here are from pp. 167–9.
17 'La storia ridotta sotto il concetto generale dell' arte', paper read in Accademia Pontaniana, Naples, 5 March 1983. Later printed in *Primi saggi* [1918], 3rd edn (Bari, 1951), pp. 1–41.
18 *Estetica*, p. 31.
19 ibid.
20 MSS, p. 49.
21 RaK, p. 263, fn. 66: 'I hope to return to this work on another occasion'.
22 *Carteggio*, p. 107, Karl Vossler to Benedetto Croce, 13 October 1907: 'Weber has not yet read your economic book, for he is at present engaged with other things; he did however tell me that he will write a critical comment on it.'
23 MSS, p. 149. The reference is to Karl Vossler's *Die Sprache als Schöpfung und Entwicklung* (1905); and we should bear in mind the many pages of Croce–Vossler correspondence devoted to discussion of this (see especially pp. 58–90).
24 For the doctrine of art as 'lyric intuition', see, apart from Croce's 1908 Heidelberg address, *Breviario di estetica* (Bari, 1913), reprinted in *Nuovi saggi di estetica* (Bari, 1920), pp. 1–91. The essays on the literature of the new Italy were published in *La Critica* from its first volume, and in 1914–15 were collected into four volumes.
25 The literature on Croce's thought and its development is extensive, but is often of quite limited usefulness. For the construction and transition to the 'system', we should not forget (apart from Garin's important studies) A. Mautino, *La formazione della filosofia politica di Benedetto Croce*, 3rd edn, ed. G. Solari and N. Bobbio (Bari, 1953). See also M. Corsi, *Le origini del pensiero di Benedetto Croce* (Florence, 1951). The works by M. Abbate, *La filosofia di Benedetto Croce e la crisi della società italiana* (Turin, 1955) and E. Agazzi, *Il giovane Croce e il marxismo* (Turin, 1962), are questionable and restricted ideologically, developing Gramsci's interpretation. See also, A. Bausola, *Filosofia e storia nel pensiero crociano* (Milan, 1955) and idem, *Etica e politica nel pensiero crociano* (Milan, 1966), which offer a 'reading' of Croce from a Catholic position. Even Sasso's path-breaking reconstruction (*Benedetto Croce*) is not free of some subtle apologetics, and its findings are not always acceptable.
26 *La Critica*, vol. 8 (1910), pp. 382–90. On this, see G. De Ruggiero, 'La filosofia dei valori in Germania', *La Critica*, vol. 9 (1911), pp. 369–84, 441–84 and vol. 10 (1912), pp. 41–61, 126–32, 211–19, written with the encouragement of Croce. Further reference to value-theory and, in particular, to Rickert can be found in the correspondence with Vossler, and afterwards in the review of the system of philosophy in *La Critica* vol. 22 (1924), pp. 108–12.
27 B. Croce, *Ultimi saggi* (Bari, 1935), p. 400.
28 *Terze pagine sparse*, Vol. 2, p. 130. For the translation of *Parliament and Government*, see Coli, *Croce*, pp. 149–50.
29 *Carteggio*, p. 249.
30 *Terze pagine sparse*, Vol. 2, p. 133.
31 In M. Palyi (ed.), *Hauptprobleme der Soziologie. Erinnerungsausgabe für Max Weber* (Munich, 1923), pp. 361–89.
32 The following works of Weber are to be found in Croce's library: the original editions of *Römische Agrargeschichte*, *Wirtschaft und Gesellschaft*, *Politische Schriften*, the offprints of Pt 3 of 'Roscher and Knies' ('Critical studies in the logic of the cultural sciences'), the essay on Stammler, and the 1918 pamphlet *Wahlrecht und Demokratie in Deutschland. Parlament und Regierung* is missing, this was most probably kept by the translator. Translations that can be found are *Parlamento e governo nel nuovo ordinamento della Germania* and *Il lavoro intellettuale come professione*.
33 See 'Calvinismo e operosita economica', *La Critica*, vol. 36 (1938), pp. 399–400. Neither from this piece nor from other allusions made by Croce is it possible to conclude that he read the famous 1904 essay very closely, where the thesis was first formulated; it is, by contrast, possible to claim without reservation that Croce never read the later essays on the sociology of religion.
34 Cf. Coli, *Croce*, pp. 83–6.
35 This and following citations come from *Terze pagine sparse*, Vol. 2, pp. 130–2.
36 In the essay 'Marx's problem and pure economics'; see also, 'Come nacque e come morì il

marxismo teorico in Italia (1895–1900)', *La Critica*, vol. 36 (1938), pp. 35–52, 109–24, reprinted as an appendix to *Materialismo storico ed economia marxistica*, 6th edn (Bari, 1941), pp. 279–322.

37   *Historical Materialism and the Economics of Karl Marx* (London, 1914), p. 10.
38   ibid., p. 12.
39   ibid., p. 50.
40   ibid., pp. 50–1.
41   ibid., p. 56.
42   ibid., p. 64.
43   ibid., p. 86.
44   ibid., p. 67.
45   ibid., pp. 75, 66.
46   ibid., p. 115.
47   'Come nacque . . .', reprinted in B. Croce, *Materialismo storico ed economia marxistica* (6th edn), p. 302.
48   ibid., pp. 319–20; cf. Mautino, *La formazione*, ch. 3.
49   Particularly relevant here is the allusion made in PESC, p. 258, fn. 188. Still of relevance today when considering the relation of Weber and Marx are the essays of A. Salomon, 'Max Weber', *Die Gesellschaft*, vol. 3 (1926), pp. 131–53; and K. Löwith, *Max Weber and Karl Marx* [1932] (London, 1982). More recently, attention might be drawn to M. L. Salvadori, 'Le critica del materialismo storico e la valutazione de socialismo' in P. Rossi (ed.), *Max Weber e l' analisi del mondo moderno* (Turin, 1981), pp. 247–88.
50   MSS, p. 68.
51   ibid., p. 70.
52   ibid., p. 71.
53   CoS, p. 65.
54   MSS, p. 68.
55   ibid., p. 71.
56   Karl Vossler to Benedetto Croce, 13 October 1907: 'Weber has not yet read your economic book' (*Carteggio*, p. 107). By this time, Weber's essay on Stammler had been published in AfSSP.
57   'Lineamenti di una logica come scienza del concetto puro', read in Accademia Pontaniana, Naples, 10 April 1904, 1 May 1904 and 2 April 1905. Reprinted in A. Attisani (ed.), *La prima forma della Estetica e della Logica* (Messina and Rome, 1925), p. 185.
58   See 'A proposito di une discussione sulla sociologia', *La Critica*, vol. 3 (1905), pp. 533–5.
59   B. Croce, *Teoria e storiạ della storiografia* [1916] 11th edn (Bari, 1976), pp. 15–16.
60   idem, *La storia come pensiero e come azione* [1938] 7th edn (Bari, 1965), p. 19.
61   ibid., p. 316.
62   B. Croce, *Il carattere della filosofia moderna* [1940] 3rd edn (Bari, 1963), p. 23.
63   For Croce's conception of history and its relation to his historiographical work, see F. Chabod, 'Croce storico', *Rivista storica italiana*, vol. 64 (1952), pp. 473–530; N. Abbagnano, 'L'ultimo Croce e il soggetto della storia', *Rivista di filosofia*, vol. 44 (1953), pp. 300–13; P. Rossi, 'Croce e lo storicismo assoluto' in idem, *Storia e storicismo nella filosofia contemporanea* (Milan, 1960), pp. 285–330.
64   ES, Vol. 1, p. 4.
65   ibid., p. 26.
66   For the predominance of ethico-political history, see *Etica e politica* (Bari, 1931), pp. 273, 277–9. See Chabod's important essay ('Croce storico') for this, and G. Galasso, 'Croce storico', in idem, *Croce, Gramsci e altri storici*, 2nd edn (Milan, 1978), pp. 1–85.
67   Croce, *Etica e politica*, p. 279.
68   idem, *La storia*, p. 46.
69   See the essay 'Principio, ideale, teoria: a proposito della teoria filosofica della liberta', in *Il carattere della filosofia moderna*, pp. 104–24. For the Crocean conception of freedom, see N. Bobbio, 'Benedetto Croce e il liberalismo', in idem, *Politica e cultura* (Turin, 1956), pp. 211–68.
70   This is the title of the second chapter of *Storia d'Europa nel secolo decimonono* [1932] 11th edn (Bari, 1964). The opposing religious forms are Catholicism, monarchial absolutism, democracy and communism.
71   See the critical comments of A. Gramsci, *Il materialismo storico e la filosofia di Benedetto Croce* (Turin, 1952), pp. 192–7, but, above all, Chabod, 'Croce storico', pp. 220–33.

72 Croce, *Storia*, pp. 288–9.
73 ibid., pp. 41–2.
74 ibid., p. 358.
75 ibid.
76 ES, Vol. 1, p. 400.
77 RS, Vol. 1, p. 252.
78 ES, Vol. 1, p. 399 ff.
79 RS, Vol. 1, p. 238.
80 See the essay, 'The meaning of "ethical neutrality" in sociology and economics', in MSS, pp. 34 ff.

31 Weber and Freud: Vocation and Self-acknowledgement

TRACY B. STRONG

> It is true that the path of human
> destiny cannot but appal him who
> surveys a section of it. But he
> will do well to keep his small
> personal commentaries to himself, as
> one does at the sight of the sea or
> of majestic mountains, unless he
> knows himself to be called and
> gifted to give them expression in
> artistic or prophetic form.
>> Max Weber, *The Protestant Ethic and
>> the Spirit of Capitalism*,
>> (Author's Introduction)

Max Weber once noted that any honest modern scholar must admit 'that he could not have accomplished crucial parts of his own work without the contributions [of Marx and Nietzsche]'. He concluded that 'our intellectual universe has been largely formed by Marx and Nietzsche'.[1] From the perspective of another sixty years, we can surely add Weber and Freud to that list. Yet it is not clear what relation all of these men bear to each other, let alone to us. I propose here to suggest some relations between Weber and Freud, leaving aside the broader question.

A starting point does come from the fact that both Weber and Freud share a complicated relationship with Nietzsche. Each took Nietzsche seriously as an analyst of practical ethics and of modernity. It might be said, however, of both Weber and Freud that they also took some pains to distance themselves, at least publicly, from Nietzsche.[2] There is thus a genealogical reason for attempting a comparison of Weber and Freud. Yet the mere fact of a common genealogy does not tell us much about on what terms they could (let alone should) be brought together. The Frankfurt school, for instance, were heavily influenced by Weber and also found resources in Freud's thought for an analysis of the sources and dynamics of prejudice; they sought there an analogy from the personal dimension to the Marxian social and economic analysis of repression; lastly, they thought to find in the speech acts of the successful therapeutic situation a model of emancipation and freedom.[3] The resultant analysis, which we might see as a kind of socially informed Kantianism, is interesting in itself and has certain apparent affinities with some of Weber's thought. But Freud appears almost as an antidote to Weber (and Marx): the topics that the Frankfurt school sought to address in Freud are not at the forefront of Weber's concerns. The reasons this is so are themselves interesting (I shall address them below) but this still does not seem an arena in which Freud and Weber might shed some light on each other.

We might seek other themes, even more general, by posing Freud and Weber as pessimistic diagnosticians of the bourgeoisie. Both do see contemporary humans as caught in prisons of their own making, made powerless to escape by their own forces, with even every move towards liberation a forced repetition of the terms of their imprisonment. A comparison of the end of *Civilization and its Discontents* and the beginning of 'Politics as a vocation' reveals striking similarities, with both writers at least appearing to eschew the temptation to rise up before their fellows as prophets. Here, however, we have to note that, if the bourgeoisie was in crisis, it was in crisis for a lot of thinkers. Carl Schorske has recently detailed a vast range of artists, musicians, architects and politicians who responded to a crisis in the European middle classes;[4] it is not hard to add Weber to this group (Schorske already includes Freud), but it is not clear what is gained by it except the (perhaps) important recognition that Weber shared much with his time.

Still other, perhaps even more fruitful, grounds for comparison offer themselves as well. The structure of explanation in each thinker is strikingly similar. The categories used by Freud to explain analytical experience bear, as Paul Ricoeur has noted, 'a much greater resemblance to historical understanding than to natural explanation.'[5] In fact, we might argue, again with Ricoeur, that from an epistemological point of view there is a strong resemblance between Freudian categories and Weber's ideal types, in that both are designed to impart to historical understanding the character of intelligibility that is required for history to be an object of knowledge.[6]

Yet in all these areas the comparison is not so much strained as too loose. Weber and Freud were working out similar problems in the afterglow of neo-Kantian and post-Nietzschean critical thought. The separation of the natural from historical sciences, which seemed required by the intellectual dynamics of the early part of this century, set certain limits within which both Weber and Freud operate. But this field they share with a great number of other thinkers: Dilthey, Bultmann, the Lukács of *History and Class-Consciousness*, Vaihinger, perhaps even Sorel or Wittgenstein. And thus, while it is possible to give a reading of the parallels between Weber's and Freud's approaches to knowledge, it only makes sense to do so in terms of a cultural history, not in terms of them as individuals.

Finally, we might also venture, as has been done with some success, a 'Freudian'-based interpretation of Max Weber, bringing together the man and his work in such a manner that each casts light on the other. This was already implicit in Meinecke's perceptive review of Marianne Weber's *Lebensbild* in 1927, as well as explicit in Mitzman's important biographical reading and Jameson's extension of it in a literary direction.[7] Although some of what I say below constitutes the reverse of this operation (a Weberian reading of Freud), I shall not have much more to say directly here about these enterprises, since they do not really consist in bringing the two men together.

A more interesting question would rather seem to me to be: What keeps them apart? As far as I can determine, Freud never spoke publicly of Max Weber. It is highly probable that he had not read Weber, at least none of

Weber's sociological (as opposed to journalistic) writings. Weber, however, did know of Freud relatively early on and, by 1908, had read his 'major works'. (This probably includes *The Interpretation of Dreams*, *The Psychopathology of Everyday Life*, *Three Essays on the Theory of Sexuality*.) It is also clear that their circles intersected from at least as early as 1907.[8]

Weber seems never to have felt the need to deal with Freud in the manner that he dealt with Spengler, *Geist an Geist*, as Marianne Weber writes.[9] He does give a short analysis of Freud and his followers in a letter rejecting a submission to the *Archiv für Sozialwissenschaft und Sozialpolitik*; it is worth considering his reasons at some length. The rejected paper had been submitted by Dr Otto Gross, a probably then drug-addicted psychoanalyst, who was at that time in analysis with Jung. (The cross-cutting relations boggle the mind. Freud had refused to analyse Gross, who was a proponent of sexual liberation and was at the time married to a friend of the wife of Weber's co-editor, Edgar Jaffé. Gross was later to become the lover of Jaffé's wife, Else, as well as of her sister Frieda, who in turn was later to marry D. H. Lawrence; Weber was, perhaps not incidentally, later apparently himself to become the lover of Else. Gross died of starvation in 1920.)[10] Weber took special umbrage at the claim apparently advanced in Gross's paper that any repression of affect would lead to inhibition and thus to 'inner falsity'. Weber's reasons were not simply his opposition to any form of ethical *laissez-aller*. Making clear his interest in Freud's project, he argues that psychoanalysis is in fact still in its infancy ('its nappies') and requires for maturation a great deal more *specialized* work.[11] He is especially upset by the tendency in Gross to try and make something practical out of Freud's scientific discoveries — in this case, a means to reduce anxiety. Gross, in effect, turns the value of science into a cost-benefit analysis. Weber calls this a 'hygienic' rather than an 'ethical' orientation. It is the adoption of a 'world-view' rather than a submission to the requirements of science.[12]

Why does Weber respond so strongly to his sense that Gross is refusing the integrity that science demands of him? Indeed, insistences are not unusual in Weber's writing. Both Weber and Freud spent a lot of their more 'methodological' discussions on the topic of 'honesty' and 'integrity'. These virtues are almost a necessary presupposition to the possibility of doing science at all; more threateningly, it is as if the lack of integrity were the greatest danger and the difficulty in detection of such a failing a real threat to knowing itself. Gone from each writer is the satisfied nineteenth-century view that honesty will be enforced by the object of investigation, that, in other words, 'reality' will eventually expose the scientist whose theory, whether out of weakness, error or malice, does not 'fit'. In the earlier understanding, 'honesty' was important but not central, since eventually one would be found out. The source of this anxiety derives, I think, from the imperatives that were derived from the epistemological separation of the natural and historical sciences. Since the *Geisteswissenschaften* dealt with 'realities' that were modified by human intentions and action, 'subjectivity' and 'meaning' was the object of investigation. This meant, however, that the subject matter could no longer be relied on to correct flaws in the analysis. Hence, the door was open to forms of persuasion that had nothing to do with the object of inquiry — if one has to deal with 'meaning', then ideology is immediately a problem.[13]

The source of these concerns may be sought in what the historian Carlo Ginzburg has called a 'semiotic paradigm'.[14] He means by this the development towards the end of the nineteenth-century of an outlook that sought meaning in construction from clues or signs. It is striking that such a shift in the epistemology of investigation appears to have occurred across European culture. In art criticism, for instance, the small, apparently insignificant details, such as the turn of a hand, became the central clues in the identification of a particular painting as an El Greco; content is secondary. Likewise, criminology was transformed by Bertillon with the claim that fingerprints were the soundest way to establish the differences between persons. Indeed, as Steven Marcus has noted, in fiction Sherlock Holmes was making his reputation with an approach epistemologically similar to Freud.[15] A 'sign' in this view does not carry information by itself, but becomes meaningful only when put together with other pieces. The architectonics of the constructing act — what Freud was to call in his dreams book the 'work' — becomes the central focus. We seek to understand precisely how the elements of our world are given meaning and appearance, how, in Thoreau's question, 'these elements precisely make a world'. It is the particular human activity that is now seen as central.

The approach from semiotics raises obvious problems, most specifically of knowing what counts as being 'right'. It seems to open the door to a kind of nihilistic relativism of interpretation, where anything anyone wants to make of the world is all right. It is well known that these accusations have been made about Freud; I want to note here additionally that they have also been made about Weber, both from the left by Lukács and Horkheimer, and from the right by Leo Strauss and other less sympathetic characters.[16]

Central here is the recognition in both Weber and Freud that the subject of their investigations is the meaningful world, and that the world is meaningful because of the activity of human beings. Both Weber and Freud are concerned, therefore, with the production of meaning and thus with the possibilities that human beings will refuse to understand their productions as their own. Responsibility is thus a central value in the epistemology of each thinker. It is probably not too much to assert that responsibility towards self is for each man a prerequisite for making any claims as to 'truth' or accuracy.

The semiotic paradigm poses then the necessity of asking the question of what capacities a person must have before he or she is allowed or, rather, can be understood to make successful claims about our condition. The temptation away from integrity is always present. However, when operating within the semiotic paradigm, external reality does not enforce rectitude upon the investigator by criteria which have a reality independent of the investigator. In Newtonian science, if one got it wrong, reality would let the theory know. From the point of view of the semiotic paradigm, however, reality is not so activist; hence we must pay especial attention to those qualities of the person that preserve that integrity.

With these reflections in mind, let me look more closely at Max Weber. In the 'Objectivity' essay he argues that the 'transcendental presupposition' of the historical sciences is the existence of *historische Individuen*.[17] The term 'transcendental presupposition' is derived directly from Kantian critical philosophy and refers to those criteria one is required to posit to understand how any particular form of knowledge or judgement is possible. Thus, for Weber, the acceptance of the fact that we are 'historical beings' is a prerequisite to making the historical sciences possible. Such an acknowledgement is an acceptance that no act of the understanding is ever transcendent of the object of its understanding. The premiss of the object of such a science – that is, of human culture – is that it is meaningful and that its meaning has been conferred and continued to be conferred by human beings.

In 'Science as a vocation', therefore, Weber speaks of the relentless honesty that the man of science must have towards himself. I have argued elsewhere that there is a close relation between this demand for honesty and the successful elaboration of Weber's central scientific tool, the ideal type.[18] The central recognition here is that, for Weber, the ideal type establishes the *right* to make claims about the world. Weber refers to the ideal type as a 'utopia', designed with the purpose of providing 'an unambiguous means of expression to a description' of the world. There need not have been, indeed there *cannot* even have been in history a set of circumstances that 'looks' just like the 'spirit of capitalism'; the justification of the ideal type comes from the fact that it is a construction of all those traits 'which in their singularity draw upon and respond to their truth from the meaningful traits of our culture'.[19] Keeping in mind that the source of the ideal type are the 'meaningful traits of our culture', three things follow for Weber. First, the more we are aware of the inchoate complexities that make up 'reality' (and thus of the fact that meaning is something that we have constructed), the more the ideal types that we use will be honest as a response to our condition. Hence, the more honest our self-understanding and acknowledgement of who we are (as *historische Individuen*) the closer we will be to doing good social science. This is the significance of the famous story reported by Marianne Weber: when asked what all his learning meant to him and why he did it, Weber answered: 'I want to see how much I can bear.'[20] Secondly, the ideal type is thus also an enforcement on the individual of the meaning of precisely where he stands in history. The ideal type is the scientific equivalent of the Lutheran '*Hier stehe ich*', which Weber gives as the watchword of the man of vocation at the beginning of the conclusion of 'Politics as a vocation'. Thirdly and lastly, the criterion for a 'better' ideal type must be the *power* that the ideal type has over the material it controls and the person seeking understanding of that material. 'There is', Weber wrote, 'only one standard: that of *success* in the recognition of concrete cultural phenomena in their interdependence, in their causal determinedness and their *significance*.'[21]

We might say that the ideal type is something like what Stanley Cavell has called a 'categorical declarative', meaning by that a statement that teaches or reminds us that 'the "pragmatic implications" are ... meant ... [and] something we are responsible for'.[22] The ideal type functions both to make a world available to us and to let us know what can be done in and with that world. It is thus historical in the sense that it has a human origin, but functions in what I might call a 'quasi-transcendental' fashion. I mean by this that knowledge based on ideal types is for Weber objective in the sense that it orders the world so that we can see ourselves as we are – as the source of our meaning. It further reminds us, therefore, that it is our necessary human burden and gift to make sense, and perhaps also tells us that the more sense we know ourselves to make, the more human we can acknowledge ourselves to be.

The ideal type thus has a parentage in Kant's critical thought. Weber, however, differs from Kant in that the 'quasi-transcendental' afforded by the ideal type is a historical product and can only be grasped through historical sociology – that is, through the activities of specialists. Objective knowledge is not available simply because one is a human being. Near the end of the 'Objectivity' essay Weber wrote: 'The *objective* validity of all knowledge of experience rests on and only on the ordering of given reality according to categories which are subjective in a specific sense, namely as the *presuppositions* of our knowledge and are tied to the presupposition of the value of that which the knowledge of experience alone is able to give us.'[23] Therefore, for Weber, objectivity is only available to those who are certain kinds of 'historical individuals'. And he goes on immediately to assert that for whomsoever 'this truth is not valued – and the belief in the value of scientific truth [*Wissenschaftliche Wahreit*] is the product of a given culture and not given in nature – to him we have nothing to offer of the means of our science'.[24] To have accepted truth as a criterion for one's own life means to be a person of *Wissenschaft*; however, as Weber informs us in 'Science as a vocation', that means to have accepted what historical sociology enforces upon us. Specifically, it means to have accepted as part of who we are such characteristics as: the permanence of the division of labour; the necessity of specialization; the 'demagification' of the world through the products of one's scientific labours; the end of amateurishness and childishness. Bluntly, it means to have accepted oneself as a bourgeois. Therefore, the acknowledgement of onself as a bourgeois is a precondition for being able responsibly to make a claim to (scientific) truth. Only such persons are able to bear what Weber calls the 'fate of the times' in the manner he enjoins us: 'like a man'.[25]

But, we might ask, what is it that we are bearing? It is precisely not the image of the dispassionate social scientist, as commentators of an early generation tried to enjoin us. It is rather a demand that we take upon ourselves the various and now irreconcilable fragments into which the modern world has been shattered. Our world is now beyond natural coherence: 'We live as did the olden world, not yet disenchanted of its gods and demons, but in another sense: just as the Hellene at times sacrificed to Aphrodite and then to Apollo and before all to the gods of his city, so do we still, but disenchanted and disrobed of the mythic but inwardly true plasticity of that stance. The destiny of our culture is however that we will become again more clearly conscious of these struggles, after our eyes have been for a millenium blinded by the allegedly or presumably exclusive orientation towards the great fervour [*Pathos*] of the Christian ethic.'[26] For Weber, and contrary to a whole millenium of Christianity, we must *refuse* to make sense of the whole world and take that meaninglessness on us as far as we can. The world, for Weber, can ultimately not cohere; the danger that confronts us is that we will constantly be tempted to want to make it cohere. The self-knowledge to which we are enjoined as a prerequisite for responsibility does not, for Weber, take us out of this world. Instead, it throws us back into it and places our feet on the ground of this world. Contrary to Marx, who had hoped to escape from the everyday minutiae of the division of labour, and contrary to Durkheim, who had suggested that happiness was to be found in the divisions of labour, Weber seeks neither escape nor happiness. But he does find in this world, as it is given to us by our history, the only possibility for humanness.[27] Part of the source of his anger against Gross was that Gross sought to escape the here-and-now for the non-existent and, in doing so, did not face up to the givenness of his own humanity.

There is thus a kind of community in Weber, but only a community given by history and to those who share the same history. This is in part the basis of his central emphasis on the nation-state, but here it is also the basis of the community of those who would seek 'objective' knowledge of the world. It is important to realize that Weber is not saying that we are at liberty to make anything we wish of the world. As incarnations of the history and the sociology he has spent his life investigating, we are condemned, as it were, to seek truth: that is what an honest acknowledgement to ourselves requires of us. To adopt a Freudian vocabulary, one might say that Weber resists any totemic foundation to his community.[28]

It is worth noting here that similar considerations are at the basis of Nietzsche's insistence that we are doomed by our genealogy to pursue truth. Nietzsche finds this fate will lead to nihilism. Weber is trying[29] to counter the nihilistic conclusions that Nietzsche found necessary. Freud, however, is, as we shall see, ambivalent. With him, the hopes for a reconciliation to the self and the world seem to be a constant theme from early on. On the other hand, at the end of his life, he often seems to despair of human capacities for understanding themselves and appears to hold out only the hope for a temporary alleviation of our neuroses.[30] In this world, unhappiness is the necessary and ultimately unsupportable human fate.

As it applies to Weber, one may object, and not without reason, to this portrait of man without salvation and a world without redemption. Weber, it must be said, not only shows us how to 'set to work to meet the demands of the day' as he puts it towards the end of 'Politics as a vocation', but also gives a portrait of a heroic leader who, as a responsible Caesar, may make all things new.[31] It is clear that there is something very correct in this portrait. Consider the ending of the 'Politics' essay: 'Certainly all historical experience confirms the truth — that man would not have attained the possible unless time and again he had reached out for the impossible. *But to do that a man must be a leader, and not only a leader but a hero as well, in a very sober sense of the word.*'[32] As befits someone operating from the 'semiotic paradigm', Weber tends to think of the question of 'What is to be done?' in terms of 'Who is entitled to do it?'. Thus the central consideration of the 'Politics' essay is 'What kind of person must one be, if one is to be allowed to set one's hand on the spokes of the wheel of history?'[33] and Weber does appear to hold out the real possibility of, even the hope for, such a hero.[34]

But he does not expect this hero and we must remember the Augustinian concern he shows in the possible identification of heroes. When Augustine confronted the reality of having to use force in the name of love in order to force Christianity upon non-believers against their will, he also spent much thought on the criteria by which a prince who would be entitled to do this could be identified, both by himself and by others.[35] To those who think they have found such a leader and most especially to those who might even think themselves possessed of the 'inner charisma' of such a leader, Weber counsels ten years of patience in a 'polar night of icy darkness'. Weber is rather constantly concerned to *distance* his audience from their desires, much in the manner of a man who truly has a vocation for politics must also have a distance from himself. It is, I think, the intention of the whole lecture on 'Politics as a vocation' both to hold up the image of the transfiguring hero and to make it impossible that his audience recognizes any individual as that hero.

With this, we arrive at the deeper intent, or at least *a* deeper intent of Weber's work. It is therapeutic: he finds his audience(s) possessed with the need and desire for an answer to the question of what is to be done and for a certain answer as to what can be known. To make people come to terms with the actuality of their position in history – with who they are – he cannot simply tell them that they are wrong, he must *enttäuschen* them. He opens the essay with this verb: it has an intended double meaning. On the one hand, he must 'disappoint' their hopes, but they will only recognize the necessity of this if he also 'takes away their illusions' about themselves and their world.[36]

With the theme of *enttäuschen*, we find Weber on a terrain where Freud also often ventured. The unmasking of illusions is a *Leitmotiv* in Freud, where it is coupled, as it is in Weber, with the imperative to 'grow up', to become mature and stop being a child.[37] Weber seems to have what I might call a Protestant hope that such a matured self-honesty is available to all individuals: Freud, as we shall see, is both more pessimistic and more optimistic. Freud brings his thoughts on illusion, maturity and humanity together in the opening chapter of *Civilization and its Discontents*. In this book Freud addresses the problem of civilization as a whole. He chooses to approach it through a comment on religion, which, he had argued some years earlier in *The Future of an Illusion*, is, as a form of group behaviour, a regression resting on illusions about the world. All such behaviours, be they in religion or politics, are manifestations of the (necessarily) insufficiently developed 'I' ('ego') in most humans. For Freud, the person whose vocation is psychoanalysis has risen above all such forms of childhood.[38]

Freud opens his essay by noting that he is unable to resist the conclusion that most men generally use false or impossible standards for themselves, such as power, success or riches. None of these activities has any conceivable point of satiation. There is, he allows, a small group, whose 'attributes and achievements ... are completely foreign to the aims and ideals of the multitude', who seem to be different.[39] But then he warns the reader that it is not as simple as that. He gives next an example of one of the small group: Romain Rolland, who 'calls himself...my friend'. The locution is perplexing, for Freud resists the possibility of saying that Rolland *is* his friend. Freud then proceeds to pick a quiet quarrel with Rolland over religion. Rolland had claimed that Freud had misunderstood the nature of religion and not realized that religion is but a manifestation of a general human feeling, which he (Rolland) calls the 'oceanic feeling'. Freud claims to be upset on the grounds that he can feel nothing like this in himself. In fact, he inscribed the gift copy of *Civilization and its Discontents* that he sent to Rolland with 'To the great oceanic animal from his terrestial beast'.[40] As Freud proceeds with a new discussion of religion, it turns out that those who believe in religion are childish, in that their self is not sufficiently detached from the world. They are still children.

Having disposed of Rolland, Freud goes on to remark in the next chapter that 'The whole thing [religion] is so patently infantile, so foreign to reality, that to anyone with a friendly attitude to humanity it is painful to think that the great majority of mortals will never be able to rise above this view of life'.[41] Again, the locution is strange and indicative: Freud speaks of humanity as something almost external to himself, from which he finds himself slightly repulsed. Those who replace religion with an impersonal abstract concept are so distressing that, says Freud, it is almost enough to drive one to (religious) belief in order to criticize these pretenders. Freud in fact has established a three-level hierarchy: there are those who don't know that religion is an illusion; those who don't know that they don't know that religion is an illusion; lastly, those who see clearly. The people in this last group, for which Freud is an obvious candidate, have found a way to reconcile themselves to a life without illusion and are not infected by the childishness that infects the rest of humanity.

What does it mean to be such a person? The rest of *Civilization and its Discontents* is by and large given over to an investigation of the discontents that the repression necessary for civilization engenders. Freud's answer to this question (which it is interesting to see is like Weber's) comes elsewhere in his discussion of the notions of distance, maturity, of the construction of meaning, of self-acknowledgement, and of vocation. These concepts had all come together in the essay on the 'Moses of Michelangelo', which Freud published anonymously in 1914.[42] At the beginning of this essay, the anonymous Freud worries about his ability to understand Michelangelo's statue of Moses; indeed, his whole sense of himself is called into question and he wonders if he is not part of 'the mob which can hold fast no conviction, which has neither faith nor patience and which rejoices when it has regained its illusory idols'.[43] He then proceeds to dispose of other possible interpretations, mostly by pointing out small details that they have not noticed and which contradict their conclusions.

At this point Freud brings in what he explicitly calls the 'rubbish heap' of our observations. He slowly builds a story that accounts for all the observable details, most centrally the position of one finger on top of the beard while the rest of the hand lies underneath. Central to the approach is the claim that *nothing* can be there by accident. Were that to be the case – that some detail were an 'accident' – then we would have to think *less* of Michelangelo. 'I cannot say', Freud admits, 'whether it is reasonable to credit Michelangelo – an artist in whose works there is so much thought striving for expression – with such an elementary want of precision.'[44] As a work of art the statue is finished, in the way that a human being never can be. Therefore, in the analysis of the work, we reach a point where there is simply nothing more to say. It is important, however, at this point, to note that the facts do not yield up a single, satisfying answer. The conclusion that Freud comes to is, therefore, an imputation of heroism (we sense, to a kindred soul) and a claim about the nature of a person who gives meaning to that which he makes. The choice is either to make powerful and actual sense in the world or simply to produce what Weber was calling 'the sterile excitation ... of a romantic windbag'.

What does it mean to make such a claim? Two things seem at stake and worth bringing out starkly. First, the validity of an interpretive construction depends, as it had in Weber, on its power, i.e. on its ability to control all possible facts.[45] Secondly, Freud notes in general about an interpretation that it must produce 'an *assured conviction* of the truth of the construction which achieves the same therapeutic result as a recaptured memory'.[46] I take 'assured conviction' to mean something like this: the truth of a constructed interpretation means that there are no details which do not 'fit' — no 'inconvenient facts', Weber would have said — and that when this is achieved there is produced a 'conviction' which takes hold and remains. This means for Freud that the threat of chaos of that which is not the self (the it or 'id') has been eliminated by the extension of the self (the 'ego') over that threat. This process is the analytic significance of the watchword of the *New Introductory Lectures* and of *The Ego and the Id*, 'Where It was, there shall I be'. This is a hard doctrine and it is no surprise that, at the end of his life, Freud came increasingly to wonder about the possibility of true termination of analysis for living subjects (as opposed to statues), even by the kind of choice required above.[47]

A way of approaching what such a successful constructive interpretation would look like can be gleaned by returning to an analysis of the Moses figure. We know that Freud admired Moses greatly and identified with him as another stranger who brought the tablets of a new law to an unreceiving people. If we turn to *Moses and Monotheism*, Freud's last book, we find that what Freud thinks most significant about Moses is that he '*stamped* the Jewish people with this trait [of self-confidence and assuredness], one which became so significant to them for all time'.[48] The Hebrews are thus the clay Moses moulded, the coin he made metal; they had no name before he made them.

Here, we have obvious resemblances to and the beginning of an important difference from Weber. The origins of community and collective identity, are not for Freud, as they had been for Weber, given by historical accident and process; rather, they are the result of an artistic–legislative act that stamped out a collective self. If, with this in mind, we return to the Moses statue, we find the source of this ability in precisely the same area as Weber had located it, but without the Augustinian anxiety that Weber had associated with it. Freud writes:

> What we see before us is not the inception of a violent action but the remains of a movement that has already taken place. In his first transport of fury, Moses desired to act, to spring up and take vengeance and forget the Tablets; but he has *overcome* the temptation and he will now remain seated and still, in his frozen wrath and in his pain mingled with contempt. Nor will he throw away the Tablets so that they will break on the stones, for it is on their *especial account* that he has controlled his anger; it was to preserve them that he kept his passion in check. In giving way to his rage and indignation he had to neglect the Tablets, and the hand which upheld them was withdrawn. They began to slide down and were in danger of being broken. This *brought him to himself*. He *remembered his mission* and for its sake renounced an indulgence of his feelings. His hand returned and saved the unsupported Tablets before they had actually fallen to the ground. In this attitude he remained immobilized...[49]

To the objection that this is not after all the Moses of the Bible, who *did* throw the Tablets down, Freud indicates that this new Moses rises to new heights.

> But *Michelangelo has placed a different Moses on the tomb of the Pope, one superior to the historical or traditional Moses.* He has modified the theme of the broken Tables; he does *not let* Moses break them in his wrath, but makes him be influenced by the danger that they will be broken and makes him calm that wrath, or at any rate prevent it from becoming an act. In this way he has added something new and *more than human* to the figure of Moses; so that the giant frame with its tremendous physical power becomes only a concrete expression of *the highest mental achievement that is possible in a man, that of struggling successfully against an inward passion for the sake of a cause to which he has devoted himself.*[50]

Strong stuff this. For Freud, the statue embodies a being who is 'more than human', whose definition of himself in his mission (which *is* who he is, his 'I') has so overpowered his affectual life that he has become something other than the rest of us. It is this capacity that allows Moses to 'stamp' out a people upon the unnamed chaos of the wandering Hebrews; it is presumably this vocational assurance that gives Freud the ability to make sense out of the welter of facts that each individual patient presents to him and to present them with an 'assured conviction' of their own self.[51] When, with his Augustinian anxiety, Weber had described the man who had the right to place his hand on the wheel of history, he had suggested that when such a truly mature (*reif*) man can with all inward honesty say 'Here I stand, I can do no other' then discussion ceased and we could only admire such a being (assuming that we were not 'spiritually dead'). At this point – with which Weber sought to avoid actual confrontation – aesthetics would have replaced moral discourse. Likewise, in Freud, the legislator (analyst?) figure is also placed into a position that transcends the dictates of morality.

Those who need analysts (indeed, by an extension which Freud undertakes very early in his writing, most of humanity) will only have a self to the degree that they are able to perform something like the analytical act – a construction of the self. Most people, however, have neither the will nor even the desire to do this. They are unhappy, not because they do not know what would make them happy or cannot get what would make them happy; they are unhappy because they have to be. Being moral means having operative criteria for both good and evil, but this means in the end to have a self that stands in contradiction to itself.

It is a self that is insufficiently 'I'. The legislator-analyst is the person who knows that the self has no basis in 'reality'. Because the analyst makes this conviction available, he stands in a trans-moral position, both unable to enter and destructive of a community of (moral) discourse with other human beings. By his vocation, he is distanced from the community he creates.

If, with this in mind, we turn to the person Freud himself, who saw himself as the Copernicus of the mind,[52] we see some of the reasons for which he may have insisted on his own separateness. In 'On the history of the psycho-analytic movement', written the same year as the Moses essay, he remarked about himself that he sacrificed at its inception his growing popularity as a doctor and noted that silence followed his talks, that a 'void' formed itself around him. [53] He found, however, that his conviction of 'the general accuracy of [his] observations and conclusions grew even stronger' (no reason is given), and he 'made up his mind that it had been [his] fortune to discover some particularly important facts and connections, and [he] was prepared to accept the fate which sometimes accompanies such discoveries.' [54] Even more tellingly: 'Whatever personal sensitiveness I possessed became blunted during those years, to my advantage.' This enhances him in his conviction, for 'psychoanalytic theory enabled [him] to understand this attitude [of repudiation] in [his] contemporaries and see it as the necessary consequence of fundamental analytic premises'. [55]

The image presented by Freud about himself is obviously close to that of the men of vocation so important to the heart of Weber's writing. There, too, both the man of politics and the man of knowledge confront a world that is ultimately chaos, into which the only meaning has been put by the actions of men, be those of the mind or the body. These activities have no significance beyond themselves: they are convincing only if they convince. Yet, says Weber, the answer to the question of entitlement – 'who is entitled to put his hand on the wheel of history?' – is in the end he whose inner conviction and responsibility to that conviction run so deep that there is nothing that might be said to shake them. Weber finds this true as much for the hero whose vocation is truly for politics as for the man of knowledge. The justification for the categories of understanding that the scientist imposes are, in the end, that they are *powerful* enough to shape and control all those inconvenient facts, especially those of which Weber wants to remind his liberal, socialist and conservative friends.

The resemblances are tantalizing and important. They derive from the fact that both Weber and Freud sought the source for understanding human society in the fact that human beings made sense (though not just as they wished) of their world. They found that the understanding of that fact led them to require of humans special characteristics of honesty: it was as if something extra were required for honesty towards self and others. I would suggest that the source of this, in both Weber and Freud, derives from the common experience of the collapse of available structures of meaning, which overtook Europe in the latter part of the nineteenth century, and the concomitant recognition that human beings will require that there be meaning. [56] This posed a new moral and political problem: epistemology had become politics, as well as the reverse. Such, after all, was the significance of Nietzsche's proclamation that 'God is dead'. He meant that no human action would henceforth be understood satisfactorily to put us into contact with a world that transcended our activity and that every act we undertook to free ourselves from our prison would reinforce our shackles.

But the resemblances are also only partial. For Weber, for those who are not heroes, the self-acknowledgement that in vocation makes responsible action and knowledge possible does not entail an escape from one's past. It consists rather in that one acknowledges that one's historical past is oneself. The possible escape from the past which might be consequent to the achievement of a heroic trans-historical actor has, Weber admits, its attractions. But Weber makes sure that no one will ever be able to recognize any human being as such a figure. There is a good deal of the sober John Winthrop in Weber's puritanism, even when he is most attracted by the 'I want the real thing or nothing at all' of Roger Williams and Anne Hutcheson. If Weber forces us into a world with the sense that it is not a place of happiness, he also makes sure that we understand that there is no good human reason (no reason available to human beings) for escaping it. In fact, as his comments on Otto Gross show, there is good reason for not trying to find such reasons. Freud too, thinks the world to be a vale of tears, and that most people do not have the means by which either to understand or escape that fact. For Freud, escape from the past that binds us is also a heroic act; but, for Freud, such an escape is required for a full acknowledgement of humanity, for only by that escape lies the maturity that Freud thinks he, with a few others, possesses. This is not a stoic affirmation of the past, but a transcendence of time past into the eternal present of the ego, the 'I'. Only a heroic few have the constitution for this.

Freud is thus led (as Weber certainly is not) to biological metaphors and understandings: some individuals are just different. He thus removes his thought from politics, at least from politics in the sense of the slow boring into hard boards. We might say against Weber that he removes any collective vision from his politics. After all, what does keep the men who meet the demands of the day in a common world? For Weber, we are bound together in our day-to-day activities only by externalities. But perhaps that is less dangerous than the requirements of leadership that Freud sees as necessary to found a community.

Although in the end the vision of man-in-the-world diverges sharply between Weber and Freud, it is only in the end that it diverges. Neither man thought that the world would permit harmonious reconciliation and resolution of conflicting claims; both were willing to pursue a vision of knowledge despite the recognition that an at least preliminary consequence would be a sharp delineation of the applicability of moral discourse. Rogers Brubaker makes the point that, for both men, their austere vision involved 'not a new type of society but a new type of individual: one who harbors neither nostalgia for a golden past nor hope for a redeeming future...'[57] To that, we can only add that Weber took the past upon himself, preferring, in Nietzsche's metaphor, to be a camel rather than a child and that Freud, too afraid of children in the world, constructed himself as an adult.

Notes: Chapter 31

1   Quoted in E. Baumgarten (ed.), *Max Weber. Werk und Person* (Tübingen, 1964), p. 554.
2   For the appropriate references for Freud, see T. B. Strong, *Friedrich Nietzsche and the Politics of Transfiguration* (Berkeley, Calif., 1975); for Weber, see the discussion in R. Eden, *Political Leadership and Nihilism: A Study of Weber and Nietzsche* (Gainesville, Fla, 1984).
3   See B. Turner, *For Weber: Essays on the Sociology of Fate* (London, 1981), pp. 61–88.
4   C. E. Schorske, *Fin de siècle Vienna* (New York, 1980).
5   P. Ricoeur, *Freud and Philosophy* (New Haven, Conn., 1970), p. 374.
6   See the suggestive remarks in F. Jameson, 'The vanishing mediator: narrative structure in Max Weber', *New German Critique*, vol. 1 (1974), p. 65–6.
7   F. Meinecke, '"Max Weber: Ein Lebensbild"' in R. König and J. Winckelmann (eds), *Max Weber zum Gedächtnis: Materialien und Dokumente zur Bewertung von Werk und Persönlichkeit* (Cologne, 1963). pp. 143–7; A. Mitzman, *The Iron Cage: An Historical Interpretation of Weber* (New York, 1970); Jameson, 'The vanishing mediator'.

8 See Mitzman, *The Iron Cage*, pp. 277 ff. Towards the end of his life, Weber wrote a full-length account of his illness for a psychiatrist; it was apparently destroyed by his wife 'sometime before 1945' (Baumgarten, ed., *Max Weber*, pp. 641–2).

9 *Lebensbild*, p. 687. See also T. B. Strong, 'Oswald Spengler: Ontologie, Kritik und Enttäuschung', in P. C. Ludz (ed.), *Spengler heute* (Munich, 1980), pp. 74–99.

10 For Gross see Chapter 32 by Wolfgang Schwentker in this volume. See also M. Green, *The von Richthofen Sisters: The Triumphant and the Tragic Mode of Love* (New York, 1974), pp. 32 ff., 366; P. Roazen, *Freud and his Followers* (Glencoe, Ill., 1976), pp. 260, 277.

11 Cf. K. Burke, 'Freud and the analysis of poetry', in idem, *The Philosophy of Literary Form* (New York, 1957), p. 225.

12 See *Biography*, p. 380. Compare here Freud's very similar remarks at the end of the last of his *New Introductory Lectures* (New York, 1964), pp. 181–2.

13 Cf. V. N. Voloshinov, *Marxism and the Philosophy of Language* (New York, 1973), p. 6.

14 C. Ginzburg, 'Clues', *Theory and Society*, vol. 7 (1983), pp. 273–88. See also, Burke, 'Freud', pp. 223, 229.

15 Cf. S. Marcus, 'Introduction', to A. Conan Doyle, *The Adventures of Sherlock Holmes* (New York, 1976), pp. x–xi.

16 See G. Lukács, *The Destruction of Reason* (London, 1957); M. Horkheimer, *The Eclipse of Reason* (New York, 1974); L. Strauss, *Natural Right and History* (Chicago, 1953). See also the discussion in R. Bendix and G. Roth (eds), *Scholarship and Partisanship* (Berkeley and Los Angeles, Calif., 1981), pp. 55–69.

17 WL[4], p. 180, translated in MSS, p. 81,.

18 Cf. T. B. Strong, 'Entitlement and legitimacy: Weber and Lenin on the problems of leadership', in F. Eidlin (ed.), *Constitutional Democracy: A Festschift in Honour of Henry W. Ehrmann* (Boulder, Colo, 1983), pp. 153–80. Some of the following material draws on a portion of this essay.

19 MSS, p. 91.

20 The best discussion of this is in Eden, *Political Leadership and Nihilism*.

21 MSS, p. 92.

22 S. Cavell, *Must We Mean What We Say?* (New York, 1969), p. 32.

23 MSS, p. 110.

24 ibid., pp. 110–11; WL[4], p. 213. See 'Science as a vocation': FMW, p. 154, and compare with F. Nietzsche, *Beyond Good and Evil*, preface.

25 FMW, p. 155.

26 FMW, pp. 148–9; WL[4], pp. 604–5. This passage is mistranslated in FMW.

27 Cf. S. Lukes, 'Alienation and anomie', in P. Laslett and W. D. Runciman (eds), *Philosophy, Politics and Society*, 3rd series (Oxford, 1967), pp. 89–116.

28 Cf. Burke, 'Freud', pp. 234–5.

29 Quite consciously, as Eden (*Political Leadership and Nihilism*) has shown.

30 See S. Diaenos, *Sigmund Freud and the End of Metaphysics* (New Haven, Conn., 1982), pp. 13–15, 42 ff.; T. B. Strong, 'Psychoanalysis as a vocation: Freud, politics and the heroic', *Political Theory*, vol. 12 (1984), pp. 51–79.

31 This picture plays an important part in W. J. Mommsen, *Max Weber and German Politics, 1890–1920* (Chicago, 1984), and in E. Nolte, 'Max Weber vor dem Faschismus', *Der Staat*, vol. 2 (1963), pp. 1–24.

32 FMW, p. 128. My italics.

33 FMW, p. 115.

34 As Spengler remarked in the 1930s about Hitler: 'Wir brauchen einen Helden, nicht einen Heldentenor.' See Strong, 'Oswald Spengler', p. 98.

35 See P. Brown, *Augustine of Hippo* (Berkeley and Los Angeles, 1975), pp. 233–43. For a suggestion of a parallel in Freud, see Burke, 'Freud', p. 225.

36 See W. Schluchter, 'Value-neutrality and the ethic of responsibility', in G. Roth and W. Schluchter, *Max Weber's Vision of History: Ethics and Methods* (Berkeley and Los Angeles, Calif., 1979), pp. 65–116.

37 See Burke, 'Freud'.

38 For an elaboration of this argument, see Strong, 'Psychoanalysis'.

39 S. Freud. 'Civilization and its discontents', in *The Standard Edition of the Complete Psychological Works of Sigmund Freud*, vol. 21 (London, 1961), p. 64.

40 Cf. D. J. Fischer, 'Sigmund Freud and Romain Rolland: the Terrestrial Animal and the Great Oceanic Beast', *American Imago*, vol. 33 (1976), p. 22.

41   Freud, *Standard Edition*, Vol. 21, p. 74.

42   Freud, 'The Moses of Michelangelo', in *Standard Edition*, Vol. 13 (London, 1955), pp. 211–36. Freud published several papers dealing with his self and they are almost all ones in which he separates himself from himself by some device or analytic category. For example, 'Screen memories' (ibid., Vol. 3, London 1962, pp. 301–22), or 'A disturbance of memory on the Acropolis' (ibid., Vol. 22, London 1964, pp. 239–48).

43   Freud, *Standard Edition*, Vol. 13. p. 213.

44   ibid., p. 236.

45   See the discussion in W. Loch, 'Some comments on the subject of psychoanalysis and truth', in J. Smith (ed.), *Thought, Consciousness and Reality* (New Haven, Conn., 1977), pp. 242 ff.

46   S. Freud, *Collected Papers*, Vol. 5 (London, 1953), p. 368.

47   See ibid., pp. 313–15, 316–57.

48   S. Freud, *Moses and Monotheism* (New York, 1957), p. 135. My italics.

49   Freud, *Standard Edition*, Vol. 13, pp. 229–30.

50   ibid., p. 233. My italics.

51   It is important here to remember the fact of Freud's *self*-analysis. It was not undertaken in order to *cure* him from some particular neurosis, but to permit him to have the courage to carry out his 'mission'. Freud specifically attributes to himself no important neuroses. The analysis was required because it permitted him to face up to the fact that his heroic self has in the end no basis in nature or history. Although the moral stance towards life in which most of us live is in no ways grounded in 'nature', most humans have neither the ability nor the courage to go beyond it. But Freud also knows that the revelation that the moral realm has no justification except the necessities of human neuroses is likely to be more dangerous than liberating. Whatever self there is in most people may be threatened by this revelation. Hence his concern with the Moses figure is a concern that exemplifies the sort of personality which was able to face the awe-ful reality of human selfhood and at the same time imprint upon a world, or at least on a person, a new and viable self: a birth of the self out of the spirit of analysis.

52   Although not without some problems attached to it: when Freud was arriving by boat in New York in 1909 to deliver the Clark Lectures, he turned to Jung and remarked, 'They do not know that we bring them the plague'. Cited in J. Lacan, *Ecrits* (Paris, 1973), p. 401.

53   Freud, 'On the history of the psycho-analytic movement', in *Standard Edition*, Vol. 14 (1957), pp. 7–66; here p. 21.

54   ibid., p. 22.

55   ibid., p. 23.

56   See Schorske, *Fin de siècle Vienna*, introduction.

57   R. Brubaker, *The Limits of Rationality: An Essay on the Social and Moral Thought of Max Weber* (London, 1984), p. 112.

32 Passion as a Mode of Life: Max Weber, the Otto Gross Circle and Eroticism

WOLFGANG SCHWENTKER

In the last few years the life and works of the Austrian doctor, psychoanalyst and anarchist Otto Gross have been the object of renewed interest. His central theme, the liberation of the individual from the social and political norms of bourgeois society at the turn of the century, today occupies those who are concerned with establishing how individuals can assert themselves in a world that is increasingly endangered by technocratic penetration and led by increasingly complex administrative and political decision-making processes. In fact, precisely those groups within the so-called alternative movements which seek to evade the external control of the individual by the bureaucratic apparatus and to escape from the optimism of our modern industrial societies by turning to communal forms of living and economic activity have rediscovered Otto Gross as one of their spiritual fathers, praising him as a 'prophet of alternative modes of life'.[1]

Even his contemporaries − comrades from the circle of the literary and artistic avant-garde, political friends and professional colleagues − were likewise fascinated by the works and the man. Intellectual radicalism and personal charisma, as well as the consistency with which Otto Gross placed his own life at the service of his vision of a society free of authority and control, secured him many supporters, particularly from the circle of Munich bohemians and the anarchist community settlement on Monte Verità in Ascona.[2] He inspired many writers, who knew him, to draw literary portraits of him.[3] For Erich Mühsam, the anarchist poet and close friend, who in 1905 took Gross to Ascona for the first time, he was 'Sigmund Freud's most important pupil'.[4] Freud himself considered Gross one of the few original thinkers among his pupils, but did not predict a great career for him because of his dependence on drugs.[5] He reminded Freud's biographer, Ernest Jones, who was personally introduced by Gross to psychoanalytical praxis before the First World War, of the romantic conception of genius.[6] And Max Weber, who made his acquaintance in 1906−7 in the house of Edgar and Else Jaffé, attributed an almost charismatic power to the young psychoanalyst.[7]

I shall attempt below to reconstruct Max Weber's relations with Otto Gross in three stages. First, I shall examine the theoretical works by Gross in so far as they are relevant to Weber's arguments with him; then I shall turn to Weber's attitude to these theories and his part in the lives of their adherents; finally, I shall investigate Weber's interpretations of the relations between eroticism and the modern world.

Otto Gross's origins and education seemed at first to point to a traditional bourgeois career as a doctor. Born in 1877, the son of a well-known professor of criminology in Graz, he studied medicine in Graz, Munich and Strasburg after a privileged schooling. After graduating in a psychiatric subject, Gross obtained a position as assistant doctor in an Austrian clinic. In 1901–2 he published his first scientific works in the *Archiv für Kriminalanthropologie und Kriminalistik*, a journal edited by his father.[8] Even in these early works the question which concerned him was whether basic ethical positions could be defined with the aid of empirical, scientific methods. 'Everywhere people are now beginning to realize', he wrote in one of these essays, 'that the reform and salvation of the human sciences is expected from the natural sciences and the revolution in methodology and knowledge brought about by them.'[9]

Gross shared the typical turn-of-the-century enthusiasm for scientific and technical procedures; he adopted the expectation cherished by the monists that new scientific methods of acquiring knowledge would not merely enrich the separate disciplines, but would also point to new paths in basic philosophical, moral and even religious questions. His own tools in this process were the methods of psychoanalysis made famous by the publications of Freud. The starting point for his theoretical works was the question of what factors constitute the synthesis of the psyche and what causes are responsible for mental disturbances in man. The answers that Gross found to these questions indicated important lines of development for psychoanalysis in years to come. Gross was one of the first to point to the connection between psychopathological conflicts and social problems. Gross did not dispute the idea of the sexual basis of neuroses, which had been very much to the fore in Freudian theory since the early work on *Sexuality in the Aetiology of Neuroses* (1898) and attracted attention beyond the disciplinary boundaries, above all with the *Three Essays on the Theory of Sexuality*, published in 1905.[10] But he stressed, in opposition to Freud, the social and cultural components in the causal framework of mental disturbances, making this an important theme at the Salzburg Congress of Psychoanalysts. The consequences for Gross of this point of view, not only for his scientific activity but also for his personal mode of life, made him the leading figure in an anarchism motivated by sexual politics, and one of the most important protagonists of the 'erotic movement' before the First World War.

In 1913 Gross set out the quintessence of his reflections and experiences in two articles for the left-wing Expressionist journal *Die Aktion*, which like all his works are marked by an over-use of sexual clichés.[11] The point of departure for his theory about the liberation of the prevailing sexual morality of the day was the work of Friedrich Nietzsche, which he greeted with enthusiasm. Gross adopted Nietzsche's view that the existing political and social conditions offered strong personalities equipped with extraordinary talents no possibilities of self-fulfilment. The normative constraints imposed by capitalist society engendered pathogenic personality structures precisely in these exceptional individuals, because no scope could be granted to their striving for inordinate forms of self-realization. It was Gross's firm conviction that the conflict between individual and society resulting from this contradiction was bound to lead to socio-structural and psychic dysfunctions. Nietzsche himself, he claimed, had adequately described the socially pathogenic phenomena and thus founded the 'discipline of biological sociology'. Nietzsche, he asserted, had been able to show that the discrepancy between individual wishes and social demands must necessarily lead 'to the elimination of precisely the healthiest and strongest individuals – those gifted with the greatest tendencies towards expansion – by reprisals on the part of the general public, to a negative selection and hence to a decline of the race, to a progressive growth of hereditary degeneration'.[12] On the other hand, the psychic-pathogenic phenomena, which the repressive grip of social institutions triggered off internally in these personalities only became perceptible with the aid of Freud's researches. They could be described as traumatic experiences, phobias or repressions.

The conflict between individual and society, which 'under the pressure of social cohabitation' necessarily turns into 'a conflict in the individual himself', was for Otto Gross the expression of a fundamental cultural crisis. Patriarchal, authoritarian family structures and a code of morals institutionalized in marriage had, in his view, perpetuated this conflict over the centuries. A first step towards establishing 'the freedom of individuality' – in the sense of an individualist, anarchist Utopia such as had been favoured by Stirner and Kropotkin – must entail the liberation of the individual from the prevailing ethical norms in the sexual sphere. For sexuality was seen as the 'universal motive for an endless succession of inner conflicts, not in itself but as the object of a sexual morality which remains in insoluble conflict with everything that represents value, will and reality'.[13]

In Heidelberg, those who professed this erotic orientation of values and life after coming under the influence of Gross were close friends and acquaintances of Max and Marianne Weber. Marianne Weber painted a vivid picture of the entry of this 'erotic movement' into Heidelberg's academic world:

> Around that time the professorial core of Heidelberg intellectual life received a variety of fresh stimulation from young people without an official position and at all stages of development, who either wished to enter the inner academic circle at some time in the future or who desired to live in an intrinsically intellectual atmosphere. Modern currents flowed from the outside to the hospitable shores of this small town. Young people placed a different life-style, one that was beyond convention, alongside the firmly established structures of the older generation. New types of persons, related to the Romantics in their intellectual impulses, once again called in question bourgeois systems of thinking and living. They questioned the validity of universally binding norms of action and either sought an 'individual law' or denied any 'law' so as to let only *feeling* influence the flow of life.[14]

What explanation is there for the evidently considerable influence of this 'movement', which bears the clear imprint of Gross, on the academic milieu?

With his theories Otto Gross had become a representative of the decadence cult and the often mystically obscured atmosphere of restlessness and upheaval of his day – at first only in the coffeehouses of Schwabing, but then also in the intellectual circles of the south-western university towns.[15] His critique of the respectable bourgeois sexual morality of the nineteenth century, which differed from the aristocratic culture and the peasant life of earlier centuries in its increasing tendency to privatize the sexual sphere, was characteristic of the sub-cultural milieu of the bohemians in general. But this critique was only able to achieve a broader effect, reaching into the liberal educated bourgeoisie, against the background of the development of a new self-awareness among women. This was not simply the result of a desire for social and political participation; it was also a reaction against the stigmatization of the female typical of the turn of the century, as it was to be found in the works of, say, Nietzsche or Otto Weininger.[16] (Weininger's *Geschlecht und Charakter* [Sex and Character], which appeared in 1903 as a philosophical dissertation, became a bestseller and went into its tenth edition in 1912!) There were biological and medical grounds, too. Since the turn of the century, women had to a great extent begun to discard their role as physically disadvantaged.[17] Advances in medicine made it possible for the first time to carry out relatively safe abortions and largely eliminated the risks of childbirth. Women began to rethink their traditional role in marriage and the family, in the state and in society. The demand for political, social, economic and cultural equality, which was now raised most emphatically by the women's organizations, also took in the 'sexual question'. The theme of sexuality and eroticism once again emerged from the private and intimate sphere, and in doing so, it differentiated itself in two aspects. First, it served to nurture an extravagant culture of emotion of an eroticist character. Suffice it to recall the literary manifestation of the erotic in Arthur Schnitzler and D. H. Lawrence, its decorative ornamentation in the visual arts, as in Gustav Klimt or Max Klinger, or its philosophical apotheosis by Lou Andreas-Salomé.[18] Also significant was the emphasis on political emancipation through sexual autonomy in the radical ranks of the bourgeois women's movement.[19] At the same time, however, we can observe how the process of the rationalization of sexuality, which began in the last third of the nineteenth century, received a scientific boost in the years between 1900 and 1920, giving rise to a wave of 'sexological' publications, and eventually leading to the establishment of research institutions. The publication of Iwan Bloch's famous book *Das Sexualleben unserer Zeit in seinen Beziehungen zur modernen Kultur* [The Sexual Life of Our Time in its Relations to Modern Culture] in 1907 is one example; the foundation of the Berlin 'Institute for Sexual Science' by Magnus Hirschfeld in 1918, another. Thus, the rational comprehension of sexuality not only in the natural sciences but also in the cultural sciences overlapped with efforts to achieve its moral liberation.[20]

Max Weber was first confronted with this development, as far as I can see, in the 'Bund für Mutterschutz' (Association for the Protection of Mothers), whose formation he promoted in 1905 in company with Werner Sombart, Friedrich Naumann, Iwan Bloch and others.[21] The activities of the Association, which was closely allied to the left wing of the bourgeois women's movement, were initially supposed to be limited to sociopolitical questions, principally promoting the welfare of unmarried mothers and their children. But when the radical wing of the Association, under the leadership of Helene Stöcker, gained the upper hand from 1906 onwards, problems of sexual politics and matrimonial law became noticeably more important. Within the bourgeois women's movement, this shift of interest triggered off violent disagreements about the relation between sexual and economic emancipation. The Association attacked the conventional ossification of bourgeois marriage and propagated as an alternative a 'new ethic', whereby women could claim the right to engage in sexual relations regardless of material and legal considerations. The right to 'free love' and to the illegitimate child, which fervent adherents of the movement claimed for themselves, was at first rejected utterly by Weber, prompting him to leave the Association as early as 1906. In a letter to Robert Michels, who in late 1906 had sent him an essay devoted to the theme of eroticism, published in the journal of the Association, Weber expressed the brusque verdict: 'This specific *Mutterschutz* [protection of mothers] gang is an utterly confused bunch ... Crass hedonism and an ethics that would benefit only men as the goal of women ... that is simply nonsense.'[22]

The first evidence of the confrontation between the Webers and the representatives of the 'erotic movement' was Marianne Weber's book *Ehefrau und Mutter in der Rechtsentwicklung* [Wife and Mother in the Development of Law], which Max Weber had read in manuscript in the summer of 1906.[23] In the final chapter of this book ('Critique of marriage, interpretation of marriage and extramarital sexual relations') Marianne Weber had strongly criticized Gross's theory of libertinage for its bizarre medicinal pretensions and its alluring moral-philosophical language. She had done so from the standpoint of the wing of the bourgeois women's movement that was principally concerned with the legal equality of women and less with their economic and moral emancipation. At this time she avoided a radical confrontation, lest she should become ensnared 'in a struggle involving questions of *Weltanschauung*'.[24] She considered untenable the connection between scientific knowledge and pragmatic moral recipes. She thus opened a line of argument that Max Weber was to take up again in a similar form a year later in an assessment of an essay by Otto Gross.

The themes of the 'erotic movement' also occupied Max and Marianne Weber the following year, 1907. At the request of Adolf von Harnack, Marianne Weber gave a lecture at the Evangelical-Social Congress in Strasbourg on 'Sexual-ethical questions of principle', which seems to have been heavily influenced by Max Weber.[25] It is interesting to note that in this talk she defends the ethical and legal norms of modern marriage by drawing on the theory of rationalization, introducing evolutionary motifs, which Max Weber takes up again a few years later, in part word for word, in passages dealing with sexuality in the 'sociology of religion' section of *Economy and Society* and in the 'Intermediate reflections' in the 'Economic Ethics of the World Religions'.[26] Marriage as a lasting, exclusive life-companionship between man and woman, with mutual obligations, was in her eyes the 'product of a cultural development'. It had arisen with the purpose of attenuating by contract the 'originally brutal power of the male'. From this viewpoint she interpreted the theories of the 'sexual-ethical sceptics' as a 'reaction against the degradation of sexuality by the ideals of asceticism'. She reproached the adherents of these doctrines with 'ethical complacency, adjustment of ethical demands to the given "facts", to the *actual* state of sexual morality'.[27]

This public discussion was accompanied by innumerable private arguments with supporters of the 'erotic movement' in the same year. Gross's wife Frieda had been associated with the Webers since the Freiburg years, and Else Jaffé, an old friend of Marianne, a pupil of Max Weber and wife of Edgar Jaffé (who edited the *Archiv für Sozialwissenschaft und Sozialpolitik* with Weber and Sombart was a close friend of Otto Gross at this time. Weber heavily criticized the moral position of these two women and encouraged Marianne Weber in numerous letters to defend her point of view resolutely, even at the risk of a personal breach.[28] From 1907 onwards, Weber began to deal systematically with psychoanalysis and with the relationship between sexuality and moral philosophy. In this year he read the major works of Freud and, through Else Jaffé, became acquainted at first hand with a scientific work by Gross. In the summer of that year, Gross had submitted an essay to the editors of the *Archiv für Sozialwissenschaft*. Weber rejected the article. He set out the reasons for this decision in a lengthy letter addressed to Else Jaffé,[29] which was quite evidently designed to convince her of the scientific untenability of Gross's theories. From a systematic point of view, this letter is of interest in three respects: it leads Weber to a more subtle assessment of the doctrines of Freud and Gross; based on the antinomy of 'heroic ethics' and 'average ethics', it sketches out an almost idealistic value ethic; it points yet again to the problems of scholarship guided by value-judgements.

Weber acknowledged the works of Sigmund Freud to be a scientific achievement of the highest order. He himself ascribed major importance to psychoanalysis for research into cultural history; but he criticized Freud's early works for a still insufficiently developed casuistry and for semantic inconsistencies in psychoanalytical terminology. In contrast, his critique of Gross's essay had quite a different thrust. He reproached Gross with wanting to derive instructions for practical living from his psychoanalytical findings and, more importantly, with seeking to raise such instructions to the level of an ethical-normative theory. Gross thereby departed – in Weber's eyes – from the 'position of strict science', to move increasingly into the field of 'metaphysical speculation'.

Gross's efforts to adapt ethical norms to the realities of everyday life led Max Weber to a generalization of ethical precepts in general. According to Weber, all ethical codes may be divided into two groups: a kind of 'heroic ethic', which imposes demands of principle on the individual 'to which he is generally not able to do justice, except in the great high points of his existence', and a form of 'average ethic', which is simply designed to meet the demands of everyday life.[30] Weber himself saw at this time an acceptable frame of reference for the life-orientation of the individual in the obligation to the first category only, to an ethical idealism, examples of which were the ethic of early Christianity and that of Kant. One must be ready in one's own conduct to make sacrifices and accept responsibility for the consequences which it might have for the lives of others, even at the risk of not being able to fulfil self-imposed demands.

And, finally, he laid before Gross the charge that his theoretical structure was interspersed with value-judgements, which made it impossible to accept his contribution for a scholarly journal. Science was 'technique, teaches technical methods', and was not called upon to provide sweeping interpretations of meaning. Weber thus set out a critique which was to come very close to Freud's. After Gross had spoken on the 'cultural perspectives of science' at the International Congress of Psychoanalysts in 1908, Freud is said to have replied to him: 'We are doctors, and wish to remain doctors'[31] – an objection that Gross quite simply could not accept. Weber and Freud both objected to Gross's attempt to instrumentalize scientific medical knowledge with a view to changing society.

After this letter, Weber's 'contact' with Gross was broken off for the time being. But the continued arguments of the Webers with those of Gross's supporters who lived in Heidelberg led in the years that followed to an extension of the original set of problems. It was not merely questions of erotic emancipation that came up for discussion, but also increasingly questions pertaining to the cultural role of women in modern professional life, in so far as women entered the world of impersonal systems and value-spheres, performing cultural work in a specifically female life-context. [32] In the circle of Gross's disciples, the discussion centred fundamentally on the question of whether ethical ideals alone, or emotions too, should be the guiding principle for the conduct of the individual; when ethical norms must claim unconditional validity; and (in a confused revival of Nietzschean ideas with the postulates of the 'erotic movement') 'whether the gods were not permitted what was forbidden to the average human being'. [33] In the course of these controversies, Max Weber's thinking came to be increasingly occupied with issues relating to the manner in which the individual's chances of leading his life were dependent on ethical-cognitive or ethical-aesthetic value-spheres. As Marianne Weber notes in her biography, 'Weber was greatly interested in the effects of a norm-free eroticism upon the total personality, for the latter now seemed to him what was important in the final analysis.' [34]

It was against this background that Weber wrote in 1908 a comprehensive review of the book by the Prague philosopher Christian von Ehrenfels, entitled *Sexualethik* [Sexual Ethics], which was above all of considerable importance for the further development of psychoanalytical sexual theory. [35] In this study, Ehrenfels developed a moral justification of polygamy as being in the interest of preserving the 'tribe' and its 'upwards procreation', which according to Weber came close to that of the Anabaptists, at least in its theoretical underpinning. (The Anabaptists placed the polygamy of the men of the chosen people, and thus the cream of 'virile potency', at the service of a divine mission, according to the commandment in Genesis.) Ehrenfels offered a sexual doctrine characterized by biological reductionism. At its beginning is the differentiation of 'natural' and 'cultural' sexual morality. The characteristic of *natural sexual morality* is that under its rule a 'human tribe' is able to maintain itself constantly in a state of health and vitality by way of continuous selection. Its constitutive foundation is the 'virile factor', defined as the excess of male reproductive potency over female fertility and readiness for intercourse. The resultant male rivalry achieves its best result in the sense of preserving and maintaining the race by 'allowing the qualitative optimum of the rivals to achieve the quantitative maximum of reproduction, referring the defeated remainder of men to hetaeric satisfaction'. [36] In contrast to this, *cultural sexual morality* owes its origins to the circumstance that reproduction and birth are linked with the same organs as the excretion of body waste and therefore these organs need aesthetic concealment. One consequence of this was, according to Ehrenfels, the triumph of the 'feminine sexual virtues' of chastity and modesty. These virtues were culturally stimulating in that they channelled the generatively unexpended excess of masculine sexuality in the direction of religious, artistic-creative or cognitive-systematizing productivity, thus favouring a process which ever since Freud we have termed the 'sublimation' of sexual needs. Theoretically, sexual morality in the Occident lies somewhere between the Romance, Catholic monastic ideal and the Germanic, Protestant pastoral ideal of monogamy as the self-surrendering union of souls. In secularized everyday life it produced two variants of sexual morality: for the woman, the single or monogamous; for the man, a double sexual morality which is monogamous in its official appearance but is unofficially polygamous. This double morality is heavily criticized by von Ehrenfels, and thereby reinterpreted in an anti-feminist manner. In the cultural sphere, he says, it favours the 'rule of hypocrisy' and in the physiological sphere it damages 'popular health' by legally sanctioning Christian monogamy and hence excluding the 'fittest', who have dedicated themselves to a 'generative and reproductive idealism of ruthless and unconditional tenacity of purpose', from the biological process of evolution.

Doubtless the idea behind this argument was the notion of a presumed progressive pathogenesis of Western culture. Thus, at the conclusion of his study, Ehrenfels pointed out that the West could only avoid its destruction in the face of the 'expansionist Mongol sway' if sexual morality became once more biologically oriented and the culturally stifled sensuality of the male was once again enlisted into the service of rational racial ends.[37] According to Weber, Ehrenfels was *in principle* harking back to a moralism to which early Puritanism, rationalistic Pietism and the Enlightenment had been committed.[38] They had permitted sexual intercourse exclusively for the divine purpose of procreation. The fundamental difference, as compared with Ehrenfels's 'sexual ethics', consisted, certainly, in the *means*. The sexual moral code of Puritanism had prescribed monogamy and had nevertheless been successful from the point of view of population. Ehrenfels's legitimation of polygamy was supported, he said, by the allegedly greater success of China in this respect.

This evolutionary model of development had little in common with the sexual political anarchism of Otto Gross, apart from its recourse to a mode of life that was 'true to nature' and had to lend itself to the selection of exceptional individuals. Ehrenfels was a strict moralist. The moral foundations of sexual reform must not on any account be libertinistic. Rather, a morally liberal sexual reform was intended to serve the man who acted with a strong moral purpose, and only him. Its mission was definitely not to create a moral free zone for an erotic-emotional culture of experience; rather, it had to commit its actors — as Weber formulated it — 'to the rationalization of the sexual drive into the reproductive urge'.

If we return to the biographical level and trace the relevant passages of Marianne Weber's *Lebensbild* for the following years, it is noticeable that there is a shift in Weber's assessment of the 'erotic movement' in the course of the numerous personal confrontations which he had with its protagonists. It is no longer the moral obligation as such, the individual's striving for the ethically highest goals, that is morally favoured, but the individual's possibilities of attaining the maximum degree of self-realization. The idealistic 'heroic ethic' is supplanted by a 'new insight': 'There is a gradation of the ethical. If the ethically highest step is unattainable in a concrete case, one must try to achieve the second or third best. What that is cannot be derived from a theory, only from the concrete situation.'[39] From this position, Weber gave up his strict moral rejection of the adherents of an erotic-emotional life-style, even defending them from personal attack. He replied quite sharply to a reproach by Rickert that a sexually promiscuous life has a debilitating effect on the character of women (like Frieda Gross) in particular.[40] But despite his readiness to show understanding, Weber held firm to moral demands in interpersonal relations. In this vein he wrote to Georg Lukács, shortly before his first visit to the communes in Ascona in spring 1913: 'What is formed is, of course, not *only* what can be *valued*, which rises above what can be experienced; *formed* is also the *erotic*, diving into the depths and delving into the furthermost crannies of the dungeon. It shares the fate of the guilt-laden with all formed life, and is even close to the aesthetic attitude in the quality of its opposition to everything that belongs to the realm of the form-alien God.'[41]

Weber did not fail to give personal assistance to the followers of Gross's doctrines. In spring 1913 and 1914, he spent several weeks each year in Ascona in order to provide Frieda Gross with legal assistance in a trial involving issues of maintenance and guardianship. Frieda had accompanied Otto Gross to Ascona in 1910 to support him in his efforts to establish a free college on Monte Verità, from which to attack Western civilization with scientific means.[42] Gross was unable to carry out this plan. This was probably due to the opposition to him that existed in the various settlements. For, in the immediate prewar years, Monte Verità no longer housed a homogeneous community. Established in 1899 by the Antwerp industrialist's son Henri Ödenkoven as a natural sanatorium, a few years after the foundation of the first vegetarian commune, Ascona had already developed into a cult centre and a tourist attraction for all those who – as Erich Mühsam, first an enthusiastic supporter of Monte Verità, and then in the 1920s an equally fierce critic, put it – 'had fled from capitalism, civilization, European bustle and social hypocrisy in order to provide a social example in voluntary association and in individual community, in accordance with their own moral and social principles'.[43] For this reason, anthroposophists and sun-worshippers, natural healing reformers and anarchists, artists, writers and scientists came together in several communal settlements on Monte Verità. When Otto Gross settled there in 1910, his theories were at first received with a lack of understanding by many residents. There were enough inhabitants who had subjected their daily life to a strict self-discipline and preferred meditative forms of self-realization. They did not adopt the doctrines and life praxis of Otto Gross. Others emphatically welcomed the 'sexual revolution' proclaimed by Gross. They even submitted to his claims for recognition to the extent of permitting him to allocate life-partners. In the ranks of his 'disciples' this led to a number of personal crises. For more than a few of those affected, suicide was the only way out of a dead-end in their personal development. These events finally brought the authorities to the scene and resulted in Gross's prosecution. In the meantime, he isolated himself increasingly from the inhabitants of Monte Verità.[44]

For these reasons, among others, his influence was short-lived, and in the history of the commune it remained no more than an episode. In 1913, Gross turned his back on it in disappointment and, leaving his wife, children and some supporters behind, he joined the left-wing circles in Berlin. Having meanwhile become heavily addicted to drugs and mentally ill, he was arrested in the same year for alleged anarchist activities, committed to an Austrian lunatic asylum and declared incapable of managing his own affairs. A press campaign, initiated by political friends in Maximilian Harden's *Zukunft* and elsewhere, at first obtained some improvements in his personal situation. In the meantime, his father was taking legal steps to deprive Frieda Gross of guardianship of her son, in order to ensure that he, at least, grew up in 'civilized circumstances'. Her plea for help caused Weber to go to Ascona in 1913 and to champion her rights in what proved to be a long-drawn-out trial. Otto Gross and his fate hardly played any part in the matter now. Weber only approached him once more, and this was about a legal question.[45] Gross was released in July 1914. After the outbreak of war, he went to Hungary as an epidemiologist and fought in the years that followed for the guardianship imposed on him to be lifted. During the 1918–19 revolution he became politically active once again in socialist groups and produced several publications.[46] In the spring of 1920 he died, gravely ill and utterly alone, in Berlin.

In contemporary Weber scholarship, it would appear to be beyond dispute that the elucidation of the rationalization problem, with its importance for all areas of life, runs as a central theme through all Max Weber's sociological works. At first glance it may, then, seem surprising that Weber's personal interest – notwithstanding all the intellectual and political differences – was often engaged by the mode of life of people who had sought their place far away from our rationalized and disenchanted world. Otto Gross and his circle, who attempted to restore the 'magic of love' to its rightful place, belonged to them, as did the type of the literary prophet (Stefan George) and the group of young intellectuals who wanted to set up a communist community in Siberia after the German revolution and to whom Max Weber offered his services as an economic adviser (in 1920!).[47] Nevertheless, he was always sceptical about the striving for a mode of living that sought to escape from the world, and warned of false prophets. In the numerous conversations that he had at Monte Verità with Gross's supporters, he never conceded any chance of success to their desire to 'achieve the consummation of kindness and brotherly love through the acosmism of eroticism',[48] in a world to which brotherliness was alien.

The topic broached in these arguments was developed by Weber in the context of a systematic inquiry into the history and sociology of religion, above all in the section dealing with sexuality and eroticism in the chapter 'Religious Ethics and the World' in *Economy and Society*, and in the thematically related part of the 'Intermediate reflections' in 'Economic Ethics of the World Religions', which sprang from it.[49] Here, he is largely detached from real historical references and personal life-experiences, and free of psychologizing reflections (such as Otto Gross still had in mind), rather concentrating on an 'ideal-typical' process model. In these passages, Weber presented eroticism as one of those orders of life that exist in the tension between a religious-minded ethical, more strictly world-renouncing orientation and the objective demands of the modern world. He describes the original relation between sexuality and the ethics of salvation as initially extremely close.

Examples are the forms of magical orgiastic practices, in which passion heightened to the point of ecstasy is consummated as a cultic act. It was only the regulation of sexuality in favour of marriage that initiated a process which led to a steady dissolution of the originally close relation and, in a second phase of differentiation, as it were, favoured the sublimation of sexuality into 'eroticism' in the sense of a 'consciously cultivated sphere that is hence beyond the routine of living'. Weber thus ties in the denaturizing of sexuality with the 'universal patterns of rationalization', but this, in his view, by no means dispels the thoroughly ambivalent nature of eroticism. On the contrary, precisely because it is experienced as something consciously enjoyed and at the same time assumes an increasingly strong emotive, sensational nature, it clears the way 'to the most irrational and thus most real core of life as opposed to the mechanisms of rationalization'.[50]

According to Weber, we are here dealing with a process that is completed in stages, which we can localize historically with relative accuracy. Accordingly, the capacity for erotic experience in men of the pre-Christian, mythological era had its limits. The passion of the female bacchantes was experienced by the men in classical Euripedean tragedy only as a power conflict. It was denied to them, and was diverted on to the 'youth' as the central object of desire, culminating in the platonically cultivated form of eroticism. Christianity was first to intrude problems of guilt into the erotic sphere, which increasingly strengthened the 'value accent of the purely erotic sensation as such', making an essential contribution to its cultural manifestation in a feudal code of honour. Weber cites the courtly love poetry of the Middle Ages as an example. The development of erotic convention then takes a more permissive and playful course from the Renaissance to the aristocratic 'salon culture' of the eighteenth century, for which mutual conversation about 'sexual experience' has, on the one hand, the moral effect of dispelling taboos, and, on the other, appeared to be welcome as a kind of amatory stimulation.[51] Then, according to Weber, eroticism underwent a final 'value enhancement' as a form of 'internal salvation from the rational' with the asceticism of modern 'occupational humanity'. It permitted sensual enjoyment only in the context of a rational orientation to a system of discrete individual ends; procreation was its command. But with this the irrational sphere of the erotic is in a state of double tension: in the first place to the modern, rationally constructed everyday world, which permits only that sex life which is 'beyond the everyday routine of living, hence especially outside marriage, as the sole bond . . . linking the human being who has now completely stepped out of the cycle of the simple old peasant existence with the natural source of all life'.[52] On the other hand, the erotic sphere comes into conflict with all religiously inspired ethics of brotherliness as soon as it itself assumes the character of an excessive love of one's neighbour and seeks to convert. It is then transformed into its opposite, producing a most unbrotherly egoism, which can only be fulfilled in sensations that are no longer communicable to others.[53] Consistent religious ethics of brotherliness adopt an attitude which is, for several reasons, radically opposed. Eroticism strives for inner-wordly salvation and thus hampers the orientation towards a transcendent god. In addition, certain psychological affinities between other-worldly religious devotion and inner-wordly sexual surrender exacerbate this conflict; both demand of the person concerned a consistency that has to reckon with the loss of personal autonomy. And finally, according to Weber, the very passionate nature of the erotic relationship must, owing to its loss of self-control, appear suspect to all religious ethics of brotherliness, which are based on the 'rational good sense of divinely willed systems'.

In conclusion, let us return to the questions we posed at the outset. In Otto Gross we encounter a contemporary of Weber, whom Weber treated with rejection and dismissal. Weber subjected Gross's teachings to massive criticism; he scarcely took any interest in him as a person. Yet not only did he show sympathy concerning the destiny of many of Gross's supporters, but he frequently had links of friendship with them also, giving them his support when they came into conflict with the 'world'. Close personal ties with other women may have played a part in this connection. For the development of the theme of eroticism, these relationships are hard to evaluate; for the status of this theme in his work, they are largely irrelevant.[54] The theme of sexuality and eroticism never occurs in its own right, but always remains closely tied up with the material analyses of the sociology and history of world religions, changing only slightly in the course of various reworkings.[55] The interpretation of individual passages from the works from a contemporary angle has its limitations; it contributes little to an understanding of the work as a whole.[56] On the other hand, Weber's account of the history of eroticism enables us to understand Otto Gross and his circle as more than simply interesting peripheral figures in the history of culture.[57] Obviously, Gross's theories – and this may explain the current interest in them – shed some light on the dark side of our industrial and supposedly impersonal mass society. Gross was one of those who have tried, from a naturalist need for harmony, to adapt their mode of life to erotic and aesthetic forms of 'world acquisition', described as irrational by Weber, and who have attempted to reconcile love as an expression of life that fundamentally transcends everyday routine with the accompanying demands and needs of the modern everyday world. Gross lived out this desire in a personal and radical form and proclaimed it as a doctrine of salvation in a world of assumed lovelessness. For Weber, however, the retreat to the state of innocence was an impassable path. It is true that in his view, sexuality and eroticism in the final analysis evaded all rationalization strategies, were irreconcilably opposed to any form of a religious-minded orientation towards an ethic of conviction, and, as almost mystical experiences, 'escaped the cold skeletal hands of rational systems just as much as the dullness of everyday routine'.[58] But for him the irreconcilability of erotic-aesthetic forms of conduct with the realities of our modern world constituted an insuperable state of tension, which it was necessary to acknowledge as a fundamental fact of human existence.

Notes: Chapter 32

This chapter was translated by Barrie Selman.

1   See, for example, the latest anthology of the major works by Gross with the spectacular title *Von geschlechtlicher Not zur sozialen Katastrophe* [From Sexual Privation to Social Catastrophe], ed. K. Krieler (Frankfurt, 1980). The title, by the way, is not taken from Gross but was used by his friend Franz Jung as the rubric for an outline history of his life and

works. On the question of Gross's current relevance, the editor writes in the appendix, p. 149, 'The modern revolt is that of creative common interests versus the bureaucratic organization of life and work, that of personal integrity versus the standardization of aspiration and (erotic) fantasy.' Gross's importance for the history of psychoanalysis is described in the latest biography by E. Hurwitz, *Otto Gross. Paradies-Sucher zwischen Freud und Jung* (Zürich, 1979), especially pp. 90 ff. For the relationship with the New Left, cf. J. Dvorak, 'Kokain und Mutterrecht. Die Wiederentdeckung von Otto Gross', *Neues Forum*, nos 295/296 (1978), pp. 52–61. From the point of view of literary history, I find the contribution of Thomas Anz interesting: 'Zwischen Freud und Schwabing. Otto Gross, ein vergessener Kulturrevolutionär im Wilhelminischen Deutschland', *Süddeutsche Zeitung*, no. 35, 11/12 February 1978. Gross's life and work against the background of cultural history and political development are best portrayed by A. Mitzman, 'Anarchism, Expressionism and Psychoanalysis', *New German Critique*, vol. 10 (1977), pp. 77–104.

2   The master–disciple relationship and his adherents' tendencies towards adoration are described by H. Kreuzer, *Die Boheme. Beiträge zu ihrer Beschreibung* (Stuttgart, 1968), p. 181. For Gross's activities in Ascona, see E. Hurwitz, 'Otto Gross. Von der Psychoanalyse zum Paradies', in H. Szeemann *et al.* (eds), *Monte Verità. Lokale Anthropologie als Beitrag zur Wiederentdeckung einer neuzeitlichen sakralen Topographie*, exhibition catalogue (Milan, 1980), pp. 107–16. See also, J. Dvorak, 'Die Paradiessucher. Otto Gross und die "Degenerierten"', in K. Sotiffer (ed.), *Das grössere Österreich. Geistiges und soziales Leben von 1880 bis zur Gegenwart* (Vienna, 1982), pp. 157–61.

3   I refer the reader to novels by L. Frank, *Links wo das Herz ist* (Munich, 1953) and F. Werfel, *Barbara oder die Frömmigkeit* (Berlin, 1933). See also the autobiographical novel by B. Lask, *Stille und Sturm* (Munich, 1975), pp. 154 ff., in which Max Weber, under the pseudonym Max Wortmann, likewise plays an important part.

4   E. Mühsam, *Namen und Menschen – Unpolitische Erinnerungen* (Berlin, 1958), p. 150.

5   Cf. E. Jones, *Sigmund Freud: Life and Work*, Vol. 2 (London, 1958), p. 37.

6   Cf. M. Green, *The von Richthofen Sisters: The Triumphant and the Tragic Modes of Love* (New York, 1974), p. 43. Green's book presents an informative cultural–historical group portrait and constitutes the hitherto most extensive work on Weber and Gross, without, however, entering into a systematic, comparative discussion of the theme of eroticism on the level of the works.

7   See Max Weber's letter to Else Jaffé of 13 September 1907, partially reprinted in E. Baumgarten (ed.), *Max Weber. Werk und Person* (Tübingen, 1964), pp. 644–8. Gross's close friend Franz Jung reports in a biographical sketch that in order to prepare a postdoctoral thesis Gross had gone to Heidelberg, 'where he came into close contact with some German scholars such as the brothers Alfred and Max Weber and the future Munich finance scholar Edgar Jaffé, who of all his academic friends was probably the only one who was always ready to lend him a helping hand in later years'. Cf. Gross, *Von geschlechtlicher Not*, p. 133.

8   O. Gross, 'Zur Frage der sozialen Hemmungsvorstellungen', *Archiv für Kriminalanthropologie und Kriminalistik*, vol. 7 (1901), pp. 123–31; idem, 'Zur Phyllogenese der Ethik', ibid., vol. 9 (1902), pp. 100–3.

9   ibid., p. 100.

10   S. Freud, 'Die Sexualität in der Ätiologie der Neurosen', in idem, *Gesammelte Werke*, Vol. 1 (London, 1952), pp. 491 ff., idem, 'Drei Abhandlungen zur Sexualtheorie', ibid., Vol. 5 (London, 1949), pp. 27 ff.

11   O. Gross, 'Zur Überwindung der kulturellen Krise', *Die Aktion*, vol. 3 (1913), pp. 384–7, and idem, 'Die Einwirkung der Allgemeinheit auf das Individuum', ibid., pp. 1091–5.

12   idem, 'Die Einwirkung der Allgemeinheit auf das Individuum', reprinted in idem, *Von geschlechtlicher Not*, p. 17.

13   Gross, 'Zur Überwindung der kulturellen Krise', reprinted in ibid., p. 14.

14   *Biography*, p. 370.

15   In a letter written at this time to Frieda Weekly, Else Jaffé's sister, Gross wrote: 'You know my belief that a new life-harmony can only arise through decadence – and that the marvellous age in which we live is destined, as the age of decadence, to become the womb of the great future.' Quoted from Green, *Richthofen Sisters*, p. 111.

16   On this point, see the brilliant study by N. Wagner, *Geist und Geschlecht. Karl Kraus und die Erotik der Wiener Moderne* (Frankfurt, 1982), pp. 7 ff. The wing of the bourgeois women's movement that could be aligned with the 'erotic movement' had, by contrast, a thoroughly positive image of Nietzsche. See, for example, H. Stöcker, 'Nietzsches

Frauenfeindschaft', in idem, *Die Liebe und die Frauen* (Munich, 1905), pp. 65 ff. and p. vii, where it says: 'It was *one* artist in particular – one of the greatest of the past century – who gave us a religion of joy which spiritualizes, enhances and idolizes everything earthly. Friedrich Nietzsche taught us how to "overcome" the passions. For centuries the Church has known only one means to deal with them: castration. Nietzsche understood that with such a radical cure we destroy life itself, that we attack life itself at the roots. Thus he teaches the spiritualization of sensuality, "love" as the greatest triumph over sterile asceticism.'

17   This thesis is propounded by E. Shorter, *History of Women's Bodies* (London, 1983).

18   On Schnitzler and Klimt, see the beautiful book by C. E. Schorske, *Fin-de-siècle Vienna. Politics and Culture* (New York, 1980), pp. 10 ff. and pp. 208 ff. Cf. also L. Andreas-Salomé, *Die Erotik* (Frankfurt, 1910).

19   On this point, see B. Greven-Aschoff, *Die bürgerliche Frauenbewegung in Deutschland 1894–1933* (Göttingen, 1981), pp. 66 ff.

20   For the problem of the scientific approach to the theme of sexuality and its cultural and personal preconditions, see the contribution by A. Bejin and M. Pollak, 'La rationalisation de la sexualité', *Cahiers internationaux de sociologie*, vol. 67 (1977), pp. 105 ff.; A. Bejin, 'Niedergang der Psychoanalytiker, Aufstieg der Sexologen', in P. Ariès *et al.* (eds), *Die Masken des Begehrens und die Metamorphosen der Sinnlichkeit. Zur Geschichte der Sexualität im Abendland* (Frankfurt, 1982), p. 226, finds the origins of sexology in the second half of the nineteenth century. For the period after the turn of the century, however, it seems to be characteristic that the theme of sexuality and eroticism tended more and more to emerge from the sphere of scientific interest and become a more acceptable subject of discussion socially.

21   See the foundation appeal, signed by Weber and others, of the 'Bund für Mutterschutz', Bundesarchiv Koblenz, Adele Schreiber papers, no. 29. For the history of the association, see R. J. Evans, *The Feminist Movement in Germany 1894–1933* (London, 1976), pp. 115 ff.

22   Max Weber to Robert Michels, 11 January 1907, quoted in *Biography*, p. 373. Weber was referring to the article by Robert Michels, 'Erotische Streifzüge: Deutsche und italienische Liebesformen – Aus dem Pariser Liebesleben', *Mutterschutz*, vol. 1 (1906), pp. 362 ff. Michels's theme in this essay was the public manifestations of intimate erotic situations and the relation between love and morality in the milieu of prostitution in France.

23   *Biography*, p. 366.

24   Marianne Weber, *Ehefrau und Mutter in der Rechtsentwicklung* (Tübingen, 1907), p. 515.

25   *Biography*, p. 373. The statement, 'Max Weber assisted her', must refer to the preparation of the lecture, as he was not present at the congress itself. At any rate, the list of participants does not include his name. Cf. *Verhandlungen des 18. Evangelisch-Sozialen Kongresses in Strassburg* (Göttingen, 1907). The exact title of Marianne Weber's lecture was 'Die Bekämpfung der Unsittlichkeit mit besonderer Beziehung auf den Schutz der Jugend', ibid., pp. 114–25.

26   Thematic overlapping is most evident in the part of the paper that deals with the history of religion and culture, particularly in the account of the Lutheran conception of marriage; cf. Marianne Weber's remarks in *Verhandlungen*, pp. 117–18: 'True, the Reformation rejected the outbidding of inner emotional morality by monastic celibacy as the "work of man". Only Luther's view of marriage remained basically the same. For him, as for monasticism, it was in principle a "spital of the sick", only distinguishable from whoredom in that *God* had expressly instituted it, that it was his "institution and foundation". Therefore God, as he says, "turns a blind eye" to "sin" in marriage.' There are other correspondences. See WuG[5], pp. 364–5 and RS, Vol. 1, p. 563.

27   *Verhandlungen*, p. 118.

28   *Biography*, p. 381.

29   See Max Weber's letter to Else Jaffé of 13 September 1907, reprinted in Baumgarten (ed.), *Max Weber*, pp. 644–8. A handwritten copy of the letter in Else Jaffé's hand mentions the title of the essay by Gross, 'Über psychologische Herrschaftsordnung. I. Der Psychologismus seit Nietzsche und Freud', Zentrales Staatsarchiv Merseburg, Rep. 92, Max Weber papers, no. 30. The essay itself is not extant. The slim volume by Gross, *Über psychopathische Minderwertigkeiten* (Vienna and Leipzig, 1909) may possibly be an elaborated version of the essay. The title and parts of the text mentioned by Else Jaffé seem to fit. For Mitzman, 'Anarchism', p. 91, this article represents 'the first detailed formulation of Gross's ideas'. In it, Gross combines the findings of Freudian psychopathology with Nietzsche's racial ideology and proceeds to criticize the culturally conditioned reduction of natural selection.

30 Letter from Max Weber to Else Jaffé, 13 September 1907, Baumgarten (ed.), *Max Weber*, p. 646.
31 Gross, *Von geschlechtlicher Not*, p. 154.
32 Of great influence in this context was the book by Marie Luise Enckendorff (that is, Gertrud Simmel), *Realität und Gesetzlichkeit im Geschlechtsleben* (Leipzig, 1910), which gave rise to an impassioned argument between Gertrud Simmel and Stefan George in the winter 1911–12. Stefan George's copy of the book bears the characteristic note: 'To see things of the house religiously is more important than any "female occupation". The modern woman can only transcend the "house" in an entirely urbanized, mechanized rootless world.' Cf. S. George and F. Gundolf, *Briefwechsel*, ed. R. by Boehringer and G. Landmann (Munich, 1962), pp. 229–30. Evidence of the development of a new female self-awareness is also found in Marianne Weber's essay, 'Die Frau und die objektive Kultur' (1913), in idem, *Frauenfragen und Frauengedanken. Gesammelte Aufsätze* (Tübingen, 1919), pp. 95–133; the essay represents a penetrating analysis of Georg Simmel, 'Weibliche Kultur', in AfSSP, Vol. 33 (1911), pp. 1 ff.
33 A nice, if bombastic, example of the manner in which the schematism of sensuality and reason was broken in the course of the academic conversation about eroticism as a way of life may be found in Marie Luise Enckendorff (that is, Gertrud Simmel), *Vom Sein und Haben der Seele. Aus einem Tagebuch* (Leipzig, 1906), pp. 22–3: 'It is in the extremely rare and chosen ones that the most sublime quality of mankind is realized: a deep, broad and wide life, brought together by one strong hand. In humble everyday life, however, whose teachings must be reckoned with, it transpires that the rich and emotionally vital and agile natures – precisely those which harbour the finest possibilities of seizing the life-enhancing force firmly, resolutely and joyfully – are greatly exposed to the danger of being torn apart and breaking up. This is the reason why "affect", emotion, has rather fallen into disrepute with all moralism, which always takes the bourgeois safe course; and the word "passion", which designates a form of inner emotional movement, is employed as though it meant that this movement had another base, ignoble content.'
34 *Biography*, p. 387.
35 C. v. Ehrenfels, *Sexualethik* (Wiesbaden, 1907). Max Weber's review in AfSSP, Vol. 27 (1908), pp. 613–17. Ehrenfels's book prompted Sigmund Freud to write in 1908 the famous article 'Die "kulturelle" Sexualmoral und die moderne Nervosität' ('"Civilized" Sexual Morality and Modern Nervous Illness'), which represented, thematically, the sociological extension of the essays on sexuality, which had appeared three years before and adopted a wholly psychoanalytical perspective. Cf. S. Freud, *Gesammelte Werke*, Vol. 7 (London, 1947), pp. 143 ff.
36 Weber, 'Ehrenfels', p. 614.
37 Ehrenfels, *Sexualethik*, p. 90.
38 Weber, 'Ehrenfels', p. 615.
39 *Biography*, p. 388. Translation altered (see *Lebensbild*, p. 392).
40 Cf. Max Weber's letter to Heinrich Rickert of 18 April 1908, Zentrales Staatsarchiv Merseburg, Max Weber papers, no. 25.
41 Cf. Max Weber's letter to Georg Lukács of 10 March 1913, in G. Lukács, *Briefwechsel 1902–1917*, ed. E. by Karádi and E. Fekete (Stuttgart, 1982), pp. 320–1.
42 Cf. Hurwitz, *Otto Gross*, p. 119.
43 See Erich Mühsam's reviews of R. Landmann, *Monte Verità – Ascona. Die Geschichte eines Berges* (Berlin, 1930), in the *Berliner Tageblatt*, 31 July 1930, reprinted in Szeemann et al. (eds), *Monte Verità*, p. 37.
44 Cf. R. Landmann, *Ascona – Monte Verità. Auf der Suche nach dem Paradies*, 2nd edn (Frankfurt, 1979), pp. 106–7.
45 Max Weber's letter to Frieda Gross of 14 May 1914, Zentrales Staatsarchiv Merseburg, Max Weber papers, no. 13. The letter to Otto Gross mentioned there is presumably no longer extant.
46 Gross's activities in the final years of his life are well described in Green, *Richthofen Sisters*, pp. 71–2.
47 *Biography*, pp. 674–5.
48 Letter from Max Weber to Marianne Weber, ibid., p. 490. Translation altered (see *Lebensbild*, p. 497).
49 Cf. WuG⁵, pp. 362–5, and RS, Vol. 1, pp. 556–64.
50 ibid., p. 558.

51   The many and various ways in which this process has left its mark on the semantics of love in European literature may now be studied in N. Luhmann, *Liebe als Passion. Zur Kodierung von Intimität*, 4th edn (Frankfurt, 1984), which also contains an interpretation (pp. 81–2) of the *Lettres portugaises* mentioned by Weber, which raised female love correspondence to the level of literature for the first time.

52   RS, Vol. 1, p. 560.

53   This point of view is also stressed by Wolfgang Schluchter in his interpretation of the 'Zwischenbetrachtung'; W. Schluchter, 'Weltflüchtiges Erlösungsstreben und organische Sozialethik. Überlegungen zu Max Webers Analysen der indischen Kulturreligionen', in idem (ed.), *Max Webers Studie über Hinduismus und Buddhismus* (Frankfurt, 1984), p. 24.

54   Eduard Baumgarten represented the opposite view in *Max Weber*, pp. 472 ff. He is concerned with demonstrating that the section on sexuality and eroticism in the eleventh chapter, 'Religious Ethics and the World', in the part of *Economy and Society* that deals with the sociology of religion, and in the two versions of the 'Zwischenbetrachtung' of 1915 and 1920, changed against the background of his personal experiences. Other writers have followed him and have attributed Weber's manner of treating this topic to his personal circumstances. A historical, biographical interpretation of Max Weber's relations with Otto Gross and with women, including the treatment of the theme of eroticism in Weber's work, is offered by A. Mitzman, *The Iron Cage: An Historical Interpretation of Max Weber* (New York, 1970), pp. 278 ff. For an example of biographical psychologizing, see Nicolaus Sombart's review of Martin Green's book: 'Gruppenbild mit zwei Damen. Zum Verhältnis von Wissenschaft, Politik und Eros im Wilhelminischen Zeitalter', *Merkur*, vol. 30 (1976), pp. 972–90.

55   Cf. W. Schluchter, 'Die Paradoxie der Rationalisierung. Zum Verhältnis von "Ethik" und "Welt" bei Max Weber', in idem, *Rationalismus der Weltbeherrschung, Studien zu Max Weber* (Frankfurt, 1980), pp. 212 ff., and recently a more detailed account by the same scholar in 'Weltflüchtiges Erlösungsstreben', pp. 59–61. In the various revised versions it is primarily a question of amplifications, as Baumgarten has already demonstrated. The third version of the 'Zwischenbetrachtung' of 1920 ends with a completely new passage on Quaker ethics. The revisions between 1915 and 1920 chiefly consist in a 'standardization of concepts'. 'Refinement' becomes 'sublimation', *bestialisch* becomes *animalisch*, *virtuosenhaft* in a few cases becomes *heldenhaft*, and in some places *Virtuose* becomes *Held*. In addition to this, Baumgarten (*Max Weber*, pp. 473–4) has drawn attention to the fact that, compared with the first version of the chapter in the part of *Economy and Society* dealing with the sociology of religion, the mood of the exposition in all later versions is different: 'As before the style of the account is marked by detachment and composure. But not until now has the section had an inner affinity with the following section on art. Now, both appear as provinces of *one* power – *beauty* – which, indivisible, has its place of realization in both domains.'

56   In a judiciously argued paper on 'Max Webers Darstellung der "Sexualorgastik" in der hinduistischen Sektenreligiosität' Hermann Kulke has pointed out that Weber's arguments with Otto Gross and the erotic movement constituted *one* reason for the over-emphasis of the erotic aspect of Hindu religion. Cf. H. Kulke, 'Orthodoxe Restauration und hinduistische Sektenreligiosität im Werk Max Webers', in Schluchter (ed.), *Max Webers Studie über Hinduismus und Buddhismus*, pp. 302 ff.

57   According to Kulke (ibid., p. 309) the 'distancing preterite' employed in the 'Zwischenbetrachtung' cannot disguise the fact that in his account of the relations between eroticism, religion and the modern world Weber 'was speaking of the (or rather, his own) present'.

58   RS, Vol. 1, p. 561.

33 Ernst Bloch and Georg Lukács in Max Weber's Heidelberg

ÉVA KARÁDI

Ernst Bloch and Georg Lukács are influential members of an anti-capitalist intellectual tradition in twentieth-century history of ideas. Several generations of left-wing intellectuals have regarded their works as obligatory theoretical points of reference. Bloch expressed this in one of his late letters to Lukács, when he wrote: 'Circumstances have placed us in a better and truer relationship with each other than we ourselves ... have managed to do. We have almost exactly the same friends, pupils, "followers". Together we are regarded as the representatives of the intelligentsia who have made apparent in the most unmistakable way the high standards and perspectives that make up the wealth of knowledge and humanity of Marxism.'[1]

The relationship between Max Weber and this anti-liberal school of thought in the younger generation would have required investigation, even if there had been no direct contact between them. But a personal relationship did exist: Lukács and Bloch turned up in Heidelberg in 1912, took part in the Webers' Sunday gatherings and, with absences of varying duration, remained in Max Weber's immediate vicinity in Heidelberg until 1915, in Bloch's case, and until the end of 1917, in Lukács's.[2] Honigsheim was the first to point out that these two curious figures, 'Ernst Bloch, Jewish Apocalyptist, along with his acolyte Lukács', belonged to Max Weber's Heidelberg circle as much as did Friedrich Gundolf of the Stefan George circle.[3] They feature in the most diverse memoirs as young Eastern philosophers, apocalyptic metaphysicians, gnostics who aired their theosophical fantasies among friends, and were regarded by some as saints.[4] A joke by Lask makes fun of their portentous behaviour: 'Who are the four Evangelists? Matthew, Mark, Lukács and Bloch.'[5] They are also mentioned among potential *Habilitanden* (post-doctoral students) who, seeking enlightenment, flocked from all over the world to Heidelberg, the unofficial intellectual capital of Germany.[6] Above all, they added new splashes of colour to the intellectual life of the town, which was receptive to anything new and modern. 'At that time Heidelberg was like Noah's Ark: it possessed one example of every new variation of intellect', wrote Radbruch.[7] In similar vein, Lask comments in a letter on Lukács's appearance in Heidelberg: 'so that, in addition to the Stefan George circle with Gundolf at its head, we shall see the most varied circles and schools of thought gathered here.'[8]

Some saw them as representative of certain fashionable trends, a decisive anti-liberalism and a new religious mentality: 'a rejection of the bourgeois life-style, big city life, instrumental rationality, quantification, academic specialization and whatever else was abominated at the time.'[9] 'It was the time when religion began to become fashionable – in salons and cafés – when one naturally read the mystics and "Catholicized", and when despising the eighteenth century ... was the done thing.'[10] In the name of a liberalism that had been put on the defensive, Honigsheim noted disapprovingly: 'like almost every movement of those days, this one made ripples in the house in the Ziegelhäuser Landstraße.'[11]

Many have seen in Weber's receptiveness to this movement another symptom of a tendency to favour the extraordinary and the extreme, revealed also by his attitude to modernism, Bohemianism and anarchism, and by his statement that he would admit only Russians, Poles and Jews to his seminar.[12] In my opinion, Weber was interested in the influential intellectual movements of the day, in ideas and their effects, regardless of whether or not he identified with them. This was true of his relationship with the George circle, and must also have been true in the case of Bloch and Lukács.[13]

Weber himself classified Bloch and Lukács as 'figures from the opposite pole'[14] – opposite to that represented by Stefan George. Weber wrote in a letter to Lukács: 'quite by chance I mentioned your name as a representative of German eschatologism and the opposite pole to Stefan George.'[15] Marianne Weber interprets this contrast as follows: 'These young philosophers were moved by eschatological hopes of a new emissary of the transcendent God ... The ultimate goal is salvation *from* the world and not, as for George and his circle, *in* it.'[16]

Where did these young 'Eastern' philosophers come from, and in what sense is Lukács to be regarded as an acolyte of the metaphysical Apocalyptist, Bloch? They had come from the Simmel circle in Berlin, where they had been admitted to Simmel's *Privatissimum* [exclusive tutorial]. They had been among his favourite students, 'members of the younger generation of thinkers with a real gift for philosophy, who wanted to be more than intelligent or diligent scholars in a narrow field'.[17] Lukács always emphasized that his meeting with Bloch had been of great importance to him. Many years later he wrote: 'A philosophy in the classical style (and not in the pale imitative style of today's universities) has been revealed to me by Bloch's personality, and has thus also opened up for me as a path through life.'[18] Immediately after their first meeting he noted: 'Just now somebody of the greatest value to me was here – Dr Bloch.'[19]

Some of the people close to Lukács, members of his circle of friends in Budapest, were of a different opinion in this respect. 'An intellectual Condottiero', wrote Béla Balázs of Bloch in his diary, 'who is only likeable because he is also a Don Quixote – and a child. He has a strongly hypnotic effect on Gyuri, which makes me uneasy. He is bad for Gyuri – he is not to be relied upon.'[20] Balázs, who found the new religion that accompanied each cigar rather disreputable, concentrated more on the amusing aspects of the whole affair. Admitting that Bloch inspired an extraordinary productivity in Lukács, he described Messianism as 'Gyuri's new philosophy' and a homogeneous world as the ultimate goal of redemption. But he thought that Lukács behaved unconvincingly when with Bloch: 'The role of a prophet, a visionary, does not suit Gyuri's basically thorough and sober way of thinking, because he does not believe in it enough, because he hesitates a little and is anxious, as if he were in a strange house.'[21]

Lukács and Bloch had a common aim: to overcome Simmel's philosophical impressionism, which strongly influenced their own way of thinking. They were not satisfied by his pluralism, his 'perhaps-philosophy', and regarded him as a collector of many points of view circling around the truth, who did not want to, or could not, possess it. Bloch wrote that 'calling him a relativist on principle is treating him with too much terminological stringency'.[22] Lukács and Bloch were looking for an unequivocal, fixed world-view, a definite answer to the ultimate question. I see this as the basis of their various philosophical attempts, sometimes extreme, to find a solution.

The first period during which they worked creatively together was dominated by systematic plans conceived on a large scale. They systematized strictly in the style of the ancient, classical philosophers, allocating all things their metaphysical space and regarding topology as halfway to cognition. This was a reaction against the disorder, superficiality, subjectivism and relativism of impressionist philosophy. 'So – the pathos of order against the pathos of freedom, against Bohemianism, against feuilletonism.'[23] Bloch called this period of his 'seigneurial scholarly bachelor life' with Lukács in Heidelberg[24] the time of their intellectual symbiosis, a time of 'symphilosophizing', when they communicated so closely that they had to define a 'protected area of differences' so that they would not always say the same things at social gatherings. They inspired each other and were uplifted by the exceptional circumstances of their meeting, by the deeply rooted irrationality of their spiritual and metaphysical brotherhood, and by the fact that they 'continually met in regions where no one else could breathe, while nobody else had an inkling of this'.[25]

If they were really fully in accord and inseparable, why did Weber react so differently to them? The main reason, apparently, was Bloch's upbringing: his lack of respect and his unwillingness to reciprocate the large degree of tolerance Weber showed towards him. Social conventions were *adiaphora* to Bloch. On one occasion at the Webers, Bloch bombarded Friedrich Naumann, a friend of the family, with questions derived from the heights of his apocalyptic speculations, embarrasing everyone present. The Webers realized that the atmosphere of their Sunday gathering was being endangered by Bloch's scandalous behaviour – he had become *persona non grata* in polite society.[26] Honigsheim may have been right in saying that ultimately it was not Bloch's thought that irritated Weber so much as his behaviour. Weber had no 'ear' for Bloch's prophetic qualities. Bloch expressed the task of a true philosopher as follows: 'The philosopher ... must ... rise above all creatures like a sun, so that he may aid them towards a manifestation of God. And philosophy's power to designate, reveal, create, inform, and, finally, identify, is so great, that even a totally denuded Now, the complete realization of our experience of Nowness, that even this possible task of the Messiah and the all-transforming apocalypse is, as a task of identification, a philosophical task.'[27]

Bloch apparently once claimed that a true philosopher could not have a thought that did not somehow contain within itself his whole system. Like the Arab conquerors, therefore, he could say: burn the libraries – you will find it all in my head.[28] Bloch himself subsequently confirmed this hostility towards culture: 'I used to say that I knew only Karl May and Hegel; everything else is an unhomogeneous mixture of the two – why should I read it?[29] In this respect, Lukács was immeasurably his superior – not for nothing did Bloch call him a local patriot of culture. Bloch wrote to Lukács about the effect he expected his work to have: 'Georg, I assure you, everyone, both in Russia and here in the West, will feel as if they have been taken by the hand, they will be moved to tears and they will be shaken and find redemption in the great binding idea ... I am the Paraclete, and those to whom I have been sent will experience and understand the returning god within themselves.'[30] It is obvious that Weber must have seen this as a case of false prophecy, as outrageous presumption, an attitude that permitted no doubts or counter arguments and demanded unconditional faith.

Honigsheim once attempted to put in a good word for Bloch with Weber, referring to Weber's principle of recognizing the autonomy of different opinions. He pointed out that what Bloch was proclaiming was, after all, new and independent, and therefore deserved to be respected. But Weber thought Bloch was not worth taking seriously as a scholar. According to Weber, Bloch lacked intellectual integrity and a willingness to justify what he said, to underpin it epistemologically and to expose it to discussion. 'This man is full of his god, and I happen to be a scholar', said Weber.[31] Hans Staudinger is the only person to report any acknowledgement of Bloch by Weber. In his memoirs,[32] Staudinger writes that Bloch inundated Weber with his philosophical, mystical and prophetic observations, and that Weber admired his vast knowledge, his ability to put things together and his powers of expression. According to Staudinger, Weber saw Lukács as a scholar (*Wissenschaftler*), and Bloch as a presentient metaphysicist. Other people's memories are closer to Plessner's. He remembers Bloch making temperamental pronouncements on eschatology in a strong Mannheim dialect at the Webers' gatherings, causing Weber to wrinkle his forehead threateningly and to pull at his beard, which Paul Honigsheim insists was a true value-judgement.[33]

Weber reveals his true opinion of Bloch's early work, *Geist der Utopie*, in a letter to Bloch's friend and reviewer, Margarete Susman. Weber writes that at the time he had helped – not without certain misgivings – to find a publisher for this book. His opinion was that, in addition to containing the most abysmal belletristic rubbish, the book had something valuable to say. Weber emphasizes that he had good reason to be generally tolerant of Bloch's singularity, 'but the formlessness and arrogance – and the immaturity! – of large sections' of the book which he had tried to read were so abhorrent to him that he had put it aside and not read any further.[34] Weber's report on *Philosophie der Musik*, which he must have sent to the publisher Duncker & Humblot with a few lines of recommendation, helped to get the book published. We do not have the text of this review, apart from the paragraph that appeared in the first edition of Bloch's *Durch die Wüste*, in the section 'Einige Kritiker': 'His very comprehensive control of material is most praiseworthy. The assessment of Beethoven and of chamber music is absolutely correct, and the book in general contains a wealth of important and accurate observations on the subject; I am genuinely indebted to the author for a large number of points.'[35]

Although Bloch liked to quote Weber when defending himself against Paul Bekker's criticisms, he was not at all satisfied with Weber's views. Bloch responded to them, in a letter to Lukács, by saying that Weber's facility in finding fault with or praising inessential aspects, and in rejecting or not even seeing the rest, was so remarkable that had his own name not been expressly mentioned he would not have known that it was a review of his *Musik*.[36] 'On the basis of this review, which is not metaphysically indifferent, that is, merely specialist, but metaphysically negative ... you will allow me to continue to differ with you in my opinion of W[eber].'[37] In this connection, he put to Lukács the question that we have also asked: Why was Weber's relationship with these two closely related thinkers so different? 'How can a man like him, who has so little idea of my abilities, of my whole *Spezificum* ... how can this man be intellectually so close to you?' asks Bloch. 'How can he understand anything of yours, after his devastating misrepresentation of my sublimity?'[38]

How did this intellectual intimacy between Weber and Lukács come about? Lukács came to Heidelberg with the intention of pursuing post-doctoral studies and wanted to approach Windelband or Rickert. He brought with him only a volume of essays, *Die Seele und die Formen* (1911) and his new, ambitious plans for a system. It was his friends in Heidelberg, the Lederers, who made him aware of Weber's importance and advised him to enlist Weber's support for his project.[39] This shows too that during Weber's lifetime his personality had a greater impact than his writings. Before meeting Weber, Lukács had almost no knowledge of his works.

Lukács wanted to take up contact with Windelband, the famous representative of the Southwest German School of philosophy, and asked Weber, among others, for help. Weber did his best. And although Lukács did not succeed in arousing Windelband's interest, Weber was more helpful and understanding than Lukács had dared to hope. 'With some', he wrote in retrospect, 'I found more understanding than ever before in my life. Naturally I soon saw that Max Weber and Lask were extraordinary phenomena in the intellectual life of Germany of that time.'[40]

As Lask points out in a letter, Weber was the only non-reactionary German professor.[41] Weber's relationship with Lukács, too, shows that Weber considered it his moral duty, even if the situation was hopeless, to help talented young people 'with something to say', who were discriminated against for religious, ethnic or political reasons. Their relationship allows us to examine in a specific case the principles Weber put forward in his famous lectures.

In 1912, when the idea that Lukács should prepare a *Habilitation* [post-doctoral thesis] first came up, Weber wrote to his brother: 'I must urgently ask you to say absolutely nothing about the possibility of Dr v. Lukács writing a *Habilitation* – perhaps! I do not think that Windelband will co-operate. He has a sort of "hydrophobia" when it comes to anything "modern".'[42] The Webers saw the essayist Lukács as representing modern writing, as a pupil of Simmel who was prepared to overcome his essayistic tendencies in favour of a more systematic approach. Marianne Weber reported to her husband along these lines: 'Yesterday Lukács, who wants to speak to you soon – he is an amazing intellect! I really believe that he will create a philosophical system – aesthetic things represent for him only a preliminary stage, he said.'[43] Emil Lask recommended Lukács's essay to his sister, adding: 'He is no longer an essayist – he has changed completely into a systematic philosopher, and great things are expected of him.'[44] For Lask to recommend Lukács to Rickert on the basis of his essays was as hopeless as for Weber to recommend him to

Windelband. Rickert's opinion was: 'While he does not seem to me to be a particularly profound "scientific" philosopher, he certainly seems to be a very brilliant man.'[45]

The Webers established a close friendship with Lukács. They entertained him regularly, apart from the Sunday gatherings. They tried to separate him from Bloch, showed an interest in his personal life and counted him among their best people. The mode of address in their letters soon changes from the formal *Verehrter Herr Doktor* to the more informal *Lieber Freund*, and his name occurs frequently in the Webers' personal correspondence, as do references to his visits, his manuscripts, his nicotine poisoning, his 'Russian girlfriend',[46] his temporary inability to work, etc. In the autumn of 1913, they went to Rome together;[47] in the summer of 1916, Weber visited Lukács in Budapest and wrote to his wife: 'I am very much looking forward to being with him.'[48] Weber's memoirs make it obvious that he valued Lukács above all as a stimulating partner in conversation. He used to say: 'A conversation with Lukács gives me things to think about for days.'[49] Weber preferred Lukács to Bloch because of his intellectual level, his refinement (he was a sensitive connoisseur of poetry),[50] because of the originality of his intellect and his intellectual integrity. Lukács was willing and able to justify his philosophical statements in strictly epistemological terms; this made discussions with him possible and rewarding. Weber's approval is first expressed in his letters: 'Rickert should be made aware of your intellect.' 'He [Lask] wanted to get the benefit of your intellect for the university.'[51] This is also an indication that Weber did not want to be surrounded by hangers-on and yesmen, but by independent, original and inspiring people of a high intellectual calibre.

The 'magnificent building blocks' of Lukács's philosophy of art, however, fundamentally changed his relationship with Weber. When Weber had become familiar with it, he no longer saw Lukács merely as representing one of the types of German eschatology and another kind of independent thinker, but as a potential companion, and as an ally in his field. Weber thought that the way in which Lukács posed the question that his philosophy of art addressed was not only original but also definitively correct: 'Works of art exist – how are they possible?'[52] The question is expressed in Kantian terms, but attempts to eliminate the subjective, psychologistic elements of Kant's philosophy. Lukács does not start from an aesthetic judgement, as Kant does, but from the actual existence of the individual work of art. Weber was relieved to see that after aesthetics had been written from the point of view of the receiver, and then from that of the creator, the work was finally being allowed to speak for itself.[53] Important elements of Lukács's philosophy of art pointed towards the *Logos* movement, the cultural philosophy that came closest to Weber's position: the conviction that individual intellectual spheres were autonomous and followed their own immanent dynamic, and that they could not be reduced to or derived from positivistic naturalism or Hegelian logicism. Lukács argued that values existed independently of empirical recognition or acknowledgement, and advocated a resolute anti-psychologism in the field of aesthetics. This is why Weber and Lask expected so much of him.

Immediately after Lask met Lukács for the first time, he reported to his master Rickert: 'A knowledgable Hungarian, a prospective lecturer, wants to disseminate our ideas in his home country and establish "scientific" philosophy there.'[54] 'The most recent star to rise in Heidelberg is still Georg von Lukács, who intends to settle here', wrote Lask in another letter.[55] He wanted to send Lukács's manuscript to Rickert in Freiburg, with the request at least to glance at it in order to get some idea of the man.[56] 'My impression was very strong', wrote Weber to Lukács,[57] and the strength of this impression is confirmed by his letters and by his works. Lukács's ideas are recognizable in Weber's work, not only where his name is cited, as in 'Science as a vocation', for example,[58] but also in other works such as 'Economic Ethic of World Religions', and almost everywhere that Weber deals with art, contrasting and comparing the relationship between art and science and art and religion. In addition to a neo-Kantian tendency, however, elements of *Lebensphilosophie* can be detected in Lukács's philosophy of art. What really interested him was not a theoretical system of aesthetics, but the significance of works of art in the context of life. The question: 'How are they possible?' implies also: 'How are they possible in this world where art is regarded as something alien?'[59] This way of seeing the question was not far removed from Weber's tragic awareness, from his conception of pluralism and the inevitable collision of fundamental values. But, in his view, it had to be separated from 'scientific' reasoning.

Lukács's receptiveness to 'scientific' philosophy allowed his relationship with Weber to turn into an 'asymmetrical partnership' similar to that which W. J. Mommsen has described between Michels and Weber.[60] Weber was prepared to further Lukács's academic career, but he also made exacting demands on him. He did not want to make matters too easy by pointing out short cuts,[61] and advised Lukács to take the difficult path dictated by his nature and real interests, and follow it to the end. He demanded that Lukács systematically complete the work he had started, and revise it where consistency required. If he could not do this, if he lacked the asceticism required by 'science', then he should give up the idea of writing a *Habilitation* and find another profession.[62] This shows how much Lukács may have contributed to forming and underpinning the point of view Weber presented in 'Science as a vocation'. Weber did not want Lukács to be lost to philosophy, and therefore constantly had to combat Lukács's tendency to take the opposite direction. The difference between Lukács's two aesthetic fragments from the Heidelberg period, *Kunstphilosophie* and *Ästhetik*,[63] can be explained only by reference to Weber's and Lask's influence respectively. To Weber, grounding a philosophy of art in a *Lebensphilosophie* and in the concept of experiential reality was problematical; Lask thought the first chapter should be revised, probably advising Lukács to adopt a consistently transcendental philosophical position. Lukács, in fact, did this in his *Ästhetik*, where he separated the everyday from the aesthetic subject.[64] In his smaller works, published in the *Archiv für Sozialwissenschaft und Sozialpolitik* – such as the Croce review and his debate with Alfred Weber about the functions and methods of a sociology of culture[65] – Lukács apparently also attempted to fulfil Weber's expectations; he shows himself here to be an orthodox and militant advocate of the brand of neo-Kantianism represented by Windelband and Rickert.

But, at the same time, Lukács was exposed to Bloch's influence, which tended to push him in the opposite direction. A letter written in the summer of 1914 reports: 'At the moment Lukács is not in Heidelberg, but I hear a great deal about him from Lask and others; he has a good position in society, and is doing a lot of work, but everything I hear suggests that, under Bloch's influence, he is ridiculing "scientific" philosophy and building a system of grotesquely complicated and peculiar schemas (eschatology, the twelve steps of receptive behaviour, etc.). His plans to write a *Habilitation* failed because of Windelband. So did Bloch's, and "old Goethe" is very angry with him.'[66] The failure of Lukács's plans to write a *Habilitation* can ultimately be explained[67] by his vacillation between 'professional' philosophy and his 'essayistic' tendency, or between an academic career and a literary life – as Weber expresses it in his letters on the subject. Lukács himself in retrospect summed up: 'Throughout my youth a deep and irreconcilable conflict existed within me between a striving towards philosophical generalization in the manner of the great old philosophers, and a tendency towards pure "scientific" philosophy.'[68]

Weber did not give up in the struggle for Lukács. He was prepared to tolerate even his most extreme metaphysical theories, so long as they were kept separate from his 'scientific' theories. A good example is found in 'Science as a vocation', where Weber cites Lukács's aesthetic position, claiming that this way of expressing the problem was characteristic of modern aesthetics. He suggests that it can co-exist with a metaphysical conception of art, but only if they are kept strictly separate. And here he unmistakably refers to Lukács's theory of the Luciferian nature of art, quoting it almost verbatim: 'Take a discipline such as aesthetics. The fact that works of art exist is accepted as given in aesthetics. It attempts to explore the conditions under which this is so. But it does not raise the question of whether the realm of art is not, perhaps, a realm of diabolical splendour.'[69] This rather curious Lukácsian idea, which is often mentioned in his memoirs,[70] does not appear in the revised version of *Ästhetik*; here, he evidently tried to follow Weber's directive to keep his immanent, 'scientific' aesthetic theory separate from his transcendent, metaphysical one. Lukács's ambivalence can also be interpreted as a struggle between Weber and Bloch for his soul; and Lukács's two great unfinished works of the Heidelberg period – *Ästhetik* and *Theory of the Novel* – can be seen as reflecting these two tendencies. This is illustrated by Weber's and Bloch's positive reactions to those works which fulfilled their respective expectations, and their passionate rejection of those works displaying the opposed tendency. Bloch remarked that, from the very beginning, he felt estranged by large parts of Lukács's *Ästhetik*.[71] And Weber said he hated *Theory of the Novel*, because Lukács's sudden switch from the unfinished *Ästhetik* to Dostoevsky seemed to give credence to those who said that he was a born essayist and would not stick to systematic work.[72]

What finally decided the battle? In general terms, it was the outbreak of war, the advent of the Apocalypse proclaimed by Bloch and the impotence and bankruptcy of 'scientific' philosophy when faced with brutal reality. The refusal of the neo-Kantians to come to grips with ultimate questions seemed less and less justifiable. Weber presumably felt this too. It could be one factor in explaining the change he underwent at the end of his life, when he was prepared to discuss these ultimate questions not only in private but also in public.

Lukács and Bloch were brought together again by their anti-militarism. Lukács was disappointed in the enthusiastic reaction to war displayed by German intellectuals, including Weber and Lask.[73] He again felt isolated, and tried, on the basis of Dostoevsky's novels, to work out his own ethics, his theory of the substantiality of the soul and its priority over structures (*Gebilde*), institutions and the 'Jehovian' world, and to justify the reality of the world of the soul in theoretical terms.[74] This project made Lukács a moral genius in Bloch's eyes, and the planned book on Dostoevsky a clearly conceived major work, an *Ethics* to rival Spinoza's in range and intellectual rigour, but with an even greater right than his to be given a title spanning all disciplines. 'Lukács will follow the theoretical path marked out by Tolstoy and Dostoevsky right to the end.'[75] With the outbreak of war, then, the Blochian tendency in Lukács gained the upper hand. Bloch freed him of his neo-Kantian inhibitions and opened up the path towards an all-encompassing metaphysics and historicism in the Hegelian sense – as the two completed parts of Lukács's work on Dostoevsky, in his *Theory of the Novel* (1916), show. Although Weber 'hated' this book – primarily, no doubt, because of Lukács's reversion to the Blochian line, and the mixture of value-judgements and aesthetic analysis that it contained – he was prepared, despite his reservations, to assist in finding a publisher for it (as in the case of Bloch's *Geist der Utopie*). Lukács's ethical reflections did not leave Weber totally unmarked.

Lukács's first ethical work, a dialogue entitled 'Von der Armut am Geiste' ['On spiritual poverty'] (1912), 'in which the creative love that brings about salvation is conceded the right to break through the ethical norm',[76] had already evoked a response from Weber. He mentions it in a letter, together with Dostoevsky's *Brothers Karamazov*.[77] Lukács's work traces the shortcomings and limits of Kant's system of ethics. He shows that a respect for the dignity of the other (his or her incognito, in Kierkegaard's terminology), in fact sanctions loneliness and isolation when seen from the other side, and displays indifference and a lack of compassion towards the other. Lukács attempts to overcome Kant's ethics by taking the direction indicated by Dostoevsky. This approach is taken further in his fragmentary work, *Theory of the Novel*. The key idea in these fragments is the contrast between what Lukács calls a 'first' and a 'second' morality: the normative ethic of the isolated European individual, on the one hand, and the Russian ethic of goodness, love and solidarity, which breaches this isolation, on the other.[78] A knowledge of this theory may also play a crucial part in our understanding of Weber's ethics, as in the 'Intermediate reflections', for example, where a priori rigorism and the ethic of religious fraternity are subsumed under the same category of the ethics of ultimate ends.[79]

Weber wrote to Lukács that the first parts of *Theory of the Novel* were 'almost incomprehensible for anyone who *does not know you*'.[80] But Weber knew Lukács well; for many years they had weekly if not more frequent discussions. Staudinger attributed Weber's interest in Dostoevsky to Lukács's influence. Honigsheim emphasized that for some time Lukács figured prominently in Weber's thinking, and he could not remember a Sunday afternoon conversation in which Dostoevsky's name had not been mentioned at some stage.[81] These conversations left traces in the cultural references frequently drawn upon by both Weber and Lukács. The examples that appear most frequently in Lukács's ethics can also be found in Weber's writings on the same subject: the Sermon on the Mount, Saint Francis of Assisi, an Indian monk, a member of the Russian Narodniki, Tolstoy, the Grand Inquisitor scene in Dostoevsky, etc. Lukács's ideas to a large extent influenced the way in which Weber expressed his own ideas on these moral problems. He could respect these forms of the ethic of ultimate ends if they were carried through consistently and shaped one's personal life-conduct, but he saw that they were incompatible with other life-principles, and he did not believe in the possibility of an ethical homogenization of the world.

After 1915, the ethical problem of terrorism was an important component of Lukács's ethics. Lukács interprets the morality of the Russian revolutionaries as a logical extension of Dostoevsky's teachings, as an ethic of taking sin on oneself and sacrificing one's own moral purity for the sake of others. He sees this as a new form of the old conflict between a 'first' and a 'second' morality, of duty towards structures and the imperatives of the soul. 'Order of precedence always undergoes peculiar dialectical complications when the soul is not concerned with itself, but with humanity as a whole, as is the case with political people, with revolutionaries. In order to save the soul — the soul has to be sacrificed.'[82] Lukács's notes for the Dostoevsky book he planned to write use the Italian term *sacrifizio dell' anima* to describe this phenomenon. The origin of this category is revealed in Weber's lecture, 'Politics as a vocation', where he refers to Machiavelli's *History of Florence* in dealing with the same problem. The analysis of these questions, therefore, obviously derives from discussions they had together, but their answers diverge to a greater and greater extent. After the separation of 1918–19, this dialogue of many years' standing continued in letters and other writings. This does not imply, of course, that Weber's lectures were addressed only to Lukács; what it does mean is that the intellectual exchange he maintained with Lukács for years gave Weber the opportunity to articulate his position on these issues for himself. Lukács was a typical example — one whom Weber happened to know well — of the *Gesinnungsethiker* and political crusaders with whom he argued so passionately, but to so little purpose, at the end of his life.

How did Weber react to Lukács's political volte-face, which led to his assumption of a leading role in the Hungarian revolution of 1919? Weber cannot have been totally unprepared for this development. Lukács's antimilitarism and his sympathy for the Russian social revolutionaries meant that he had been seen as a revolutionary socialist in Heidelberg. Thus, Edgar Salin, for example, mentions his name: 'with the rising generation of revolutionary socialists ... with Ernst Bloch — their prophet, Georg v. Lukács — their philosopher, and Emil Lederer — their economist.'[83] Honigsheim and Staudinger recall a discussion that took place between Weber and Lukács about historical materialism.[84] Perhaps we could go so far as to suggest that, at that time, Weber was closer than Lukács to Marxism. Later, it was the Messianic element in Marxism[85] to which Lukács could relate as a consequence of his political decision to join the Communist Party.

Albert Salomon's memoirs give us some idea of how guests at the Webers' Sunday afternoon gatherings saw Lukács's interpretation of the connection between socialism and Marxism. Salomon writes that Lukács initially saw Marxism as a necessary element in an eschatological dialectic. He saw

Marxism as the best remedy for the calamities produced by capitalist society, and for the organic deficiencies and uncertainties of industrial society. According to Lukács, until total socialism had come about, and external structures had liberated the individual and the community from the oppressive burden of uncertainty, a liberated humanity would not be capable of experiencing and understanding true suffering, genuine passion and pain beyond social structures. For only genuine lack of hope and humility could bring about a religious and eschatological renaissance.[86] This was the tenor of Lukács's views shortly before his association with the Communist movement began. Characteristically, he – like Michels – referred to Weber and his decisionism in the theoretical justification of his decision made in 'Taktik und Ethik' (1919).[87] Weber apparently said that Lukács's political reversal, unlike Ernst Toller's, must have been the result of a fundamental change in his convictions and ideas. In Toller's case, it revealed no more than emotional confusion.[88] Although Lukács, in retrospect, insisted that his personal relationship with Weber did not survive his change of political allegiance,[89] existing documents suggest that the reality was not so straightforward. Lukács told his students that he had written to Marianne Weber, saying that any further contact between himself and Weber could only be like that between Gyges and Candaules: former friends who, despite their mutual liking for each other, were condemned to destroy each other.[90] Weber responded to Lukács's political convictions with paternal understanding: 'Dearest friend, *of course* political opinions divide us.'[91] He believed that these experiments would, indeed could, only result in socialism being discredited; he saw revolutions as bloody carnivals and warned against dilettantism in the economy and in politics. He had not yet given up the struggle for Lukács, and wanted to tempt him back to scholarship. 'What seems to me to be most important', he wrote to Lukács's father, 'is that your son gets back to his *work*.'[92] He emphasized that Lukács 'must give up his totally sterile involvement in *politics*. His talents are wasted, not to mention the fact that he has got on to completely the wrong track.'[93] The relationship between Weber and Lukács reveals Weber facing a dilemma that was typical for him. He and Lukács had totally different opinions on whether politics or scholarship was Lukács's true vocation – but, by his own principles, he had to respect the other's decision, even though he thought it was wrong. 'But in this case, understandably enough, you reserve the right to decide alone.'[94]

Lukács, like Michels, felt that, in any relationship with Weber, political differences could not be allowed to have the last word.[95] Both were convinced that, given the opportunity to have a personal conversation 'about the human element in what we are living through (quite apart from whether what we are doing is right or not)', the old understanding could be re-established: 'Everything that divides us ... could be torn down, destroyed by a few words between human beings.'[96] Weber's sudden death, which affected Lukács deeply, meant that these words could never be spoken. Their dialogue became a monologue in the decades that followed.[97]

The characteristic difference between these two thinkers, derived from their final positions, lies in their relationship with the modern world, Western civilization and culture. For Lukács, culture was the ultimate value;[98] commodity society's hostility towards culture meant that, from the start, he was anti-capitalist and anti-liberal. Weber explained this by saying that Lukács drew from the history of art the lesson that culture can exist only when it is embedded [in life].[99] This conflict of values was, for Weber, an integral part of seeing reality without illusion; he was passionately against seeing civilization and culture as opposed to each other. Individual autonomy and the disenchanting power of science were more important for Weber than for Lukács, who was prepared to sacrifice his individual morality and his intellect, to make the *sacrifizio dell' anima* and the *sacrifizio dell' intelletto*. Weber looked for the possibility of a rational conduct of life within an irrational whole; Lukács wanted to make the whole meaningful and homogenize it with the help of ethics or politics. Weber's arguments against this attitude and its consequences are more relevant than ever today. It is instructive to reconsider them in the light of his relationship with the anti-liberal movements, Marxism and socialism, and with their philosophers, Lukács and Bloch.

Notes: Chapter 33

This chapter was translated by Angela Davies.

1   Ernst Bloch to Georg Lukács, 11 June 1955, in M. Mesterházi and G. Mezei (eds), *Ernst Bloch und Georg Lukács. Dokumente. Zum 100. Geburtstag* (Budapest, 1984), pp. 141–2.
2   Bloch divided his time between Garmisch and Heidelberg; Lukács had to go to Budapest for a year in the autumn of 1915 to do his military service.
3   P. Honigsheim, 'Der Max Weber–Kreis in Heidelberg', *Kölner Vierteljahreshefte für Soziologie*, vol. 5 (1926), p. 283.
4   ibid., p. 286, *Biography*, p. 466; K. Jaspers, 'Heidelberger Erinnerungen', *Heidelberger Jahrbücher*, vol. 5 (1961), p. 5.
5   ibid., p. 5.
6   ibid., p. 4.
7   G. Radbruch, *Der innere Weg. Aufriss meines Lebens* (Stuttgart, 1951), pp. 87–8.
8   Emil Lask to Berta Lask, 16 November 1912, Heidelberg University Library, Lask papers.
9   Paul Honigsheim, 'Max Weber in Heidelberg', in R. König and J. Winckelmann (eds), *Max Weber zum Gedächtnis. Materialien zur Bewertung von Werk und Persönlichkeit* (Cologne and Opladen, 1963), p. 238.
10   Honigsheim, 'Max Weber–Kreis', p. 284.
11   ibid.
12   ibid.
13   For this, see Hans Staudinger's recollections of Max Weber's explanation of his real research interest: 'Cultural history, he said, not sociology, was his real research interest: the relationships, dependent on time, between values and ideas, that is, subjective motivations and the driving forces behind human actions, social forms and institutions. Cultural relationships, which change according to time and space, were the subject of his interest ... What he wanted to do was to see subjective values, faith and superstition, as well as linguistic and other traditions of any given period in various delimited parts of the world objectively as the driving forces behind human decisions, actions, social arrangements, institutions and forms of artistic expression.' H. Staudinger, *Wirtschaftspolitik im Weimarer Staat. Lebenserinnerungen eines politischen Beamten im Reich und in Preußen 1884–1934* (Bonn, 1982), pp. 7–8.
14   *Biography*, p. 465.
15   Max Weber to Georg Lukács, 6 March 1913 (Zentrales Staatsarchiv Merseburg, Rep. 92. Max Weber papers, no. 22); French translation in Georges Lukács, *Correspondence de jeunesse 1908–1917*, ed. É. Fekete and É. Karádi (Paris, 1981), p. 234. In this letter, Weber recommends Gaston Riou, a French journalist from *Figaro*, to Lukács. Riou was interested in the religious and quasi-religious movements prevalent in Germany at the time, and wanted to put together a book of interviews about them. He had already interviewed Troeltsch, Windel-

band, Weber and others, and now wanted to interview German writers. Although this book was never published, it would be worth finding these interviews, if they still exist.

16 *Biography*, p. 466.
17 G. Lukács, 'Georg Simmel (1858–1918)', *Pester Lloyd*, 2 October 1918. See also K. Gassen and M. Landmann (eds), *Buch des Dankes an Georg Simmel* (Berlin, 1958), p. 171.
18 G. Lukács, *Gelebtes Denken. Eine Autobiographie im Dialog*, ed. I. Eörsi (Frankfurt, 1981), p. 251.
19 Georg Lukács to Leo Popper, 11 February 1911, in G. Lukács, *Briefwechsel 1902–1917*, ed. É. Karádi and É. Fekete (Stuttgart, 1982), p. 202.
20 B. Balázs, *Tagebuch* (Hungarian) (Budapest, 1982), p. 596. On Lukács's group of friends in Budapest, which was known as the *Sonntagskreis* and included Karl Mannheim, Arnold Hauser, Frederick Antal, Charles de Tolnay, Béla Fogarasi, Ervin Sinko, Lajos Fülep and Anna Lesznai, see the volume of their writings: É. Karádi and É. Vezér (eds), *Lukács, Mannheim und der Sonntagskreis* (Frankfurt, 1985).
21 Balázs, *Tagebuch*, p. 597.
22 E. Bloch, *Geist der Utopie* (Berlin, 1918), pp. 246–7.
23 idem., 'Erbschaft aus Dekadenz? Ein Gespräch mit Iring Fetscher und Georg Lukács', in R. Traub und H. Wieser (eds), *Gespräche mit Ernst Bloch* (Frankfurt, 1975), p. 32. Constantly changing plans for a voluminous system do not fill only Bloch's letters at this time; a draft of a similar system can also be found in Lukács's papers, in his handwriting: 'Three books on the division of the world. *Book I*: Theory of Abstract Forms (1) Logic; (2) Reality of experience. *Book II*: Theory of Methodological Forms (1) Natural science; (2) Philosophy of history; (3) Political science and ethics; (4) Aesthetics; (5) Philosophy of religion; (6) Philosophy. *Book III*: Theory of Metaphysical Forms (1) Ontology; (2) Rational psychology; (3) Cosmogony.' (Lukács Archive, Budapest).
24 E. Bloch, *Tendenz–Latenz–Utopie* (Frankfurt, 1978), p. 20; idem, 'Erbschaft', pp. 32–3.
25 Bloch to Lukács, summer of 1915 and 16 August 1916, in Mesterházi and Mezei (eds), *Ernst Bloch und Georg Lukács*, pp. 98 and 105.
26 Honigsheim, 'Max Weber', p. 167.
27 E. Bloch, 'Über motorisch-mystische Intention in der Erkenntnis', *Die Argonauten*, vol. 4 (1921), p. 186.
28 E. Ritook, *Die Abenteurer des Geistes. Roman* (Hungarian), 2 Vols. (Budapest, 1922), Vol. 1, p. 145.
29 Bloch, 'Erbschaft', p. 33.
30 Ernst Bloch to Georg Lukács, 18 October 1911, in Mesterházi and Mezei (eds), *Ernst Bloch und Georg Lukács*, p. 29.
31 Honigsheim, 'Max Weber', p. 187.
32 Staudinger, *Wirtschaftspolitik*, p. 13.
33 H. Plessner, 'In Heidelberg 1913', in König and Winckelmann (eds), *Max Weber zum Gedächtnis*, p. 31.
34 Max Weber to Margarete Susman, 19 October 1919 (Max Weber Archive, Munich).
35 E. Bloch, *Durch die Wüste* (Berlin, 1923), p. 58.
36 Ernst Bloch to Georg Lukács, 16 August 1916, in Lukács, *Briefwechsel 1902–1917*, p. 375.
37 Ernst Bloch to Georg Lukács, 24 August 1916, in Mesterházi and Mezei (eds), *Ernst Bloch und Georg Lukács*, p. 107.
38 Ernst Bloch to Georg Lukács, 16 August 1916 (as in n. 36 above).
39 Emil Lederer, editor of the *AfSSP*, was married to a Hungarian, Emmy Lederer-Seidler, the sister of Irma Seidler, to whose memory Lukács dedicated his volume of essays, *Die Seele und die Formen* (1911). Emmy Lederer reported from Heidelberg to Lukács in Budapest that his essay, 'Die Metaphysik der Tragödie' (1911), which had been published in *Logos*, had been accepted. See Lukács, *Briefwechsel 1902–1917*, pp. 14–15.
40 See É. Fekete and É. Karádi (eds), *Georg Lukács. Sein Leben in Bildern, Selbstzeugnissen und Dokumenten* (Stuttgart, 1981), p. 364.
41 Emil Lask to Otto Baensch, 19 February 1906, Heidelberg University Library, Lask papers (as in n. 8 above).
42 Max Weber to Alfred Weber, 9 November 1912, privately owned.
43 Marianne Weber to Max Weber, 27 October 1912, privately owned.
44 E. Lask to Berta Lask, 16 November 1912, Heidelberg University Library, Lask papers (as in n. 8 above).
45 Heinrich Rickert to Emil Lask, 20 June 1912, ibid.

46   At the end of 1913 Lukács became engaged to Jelena Grabenko, a Russian painter and revolutionary. He married her in the spring of 1914. The marriage was not happy and lasted only a few years. Weber seems to have disapproved of this change in Lukács's personal circumstances: although he was prepared to help Jelena Grabenko to get a passport after the war, he felt it necessary to point out, when there was talk of finding a job for Lukács, that it would be easier without his Russian wife: 'Anything from Russia *at present* faces particular difficulties, in this atmosphere' (Max Weber to Joseph von Lukács, 9 January 1920, Zentrales Staatsarchiv Merseburg).

47   Several letters from Marianne Weber to Lukács (Lukács Archive, Budapest) concern preparations for this trip, renting a flat for the three of them, and her husband's eagerness to be able to talk to Lukács at last.

48   Max Weber to Marianne Weber, 28 May 1916, privately owned.

49   Honigsheim, 'Max Weber', p. 187. See also *Biography*, p. 468: 'Only few guests, like Gundolf or Lukács, were able to express their ideas well enough to become independent points of interest.' Or, another memory: 'Karl Jaspers, Georg von Lukács and Friedrich Gundolf were Max Weber's real partners in conversation – he listened to them and could enjoy a genuine intellectual exchange with them. In the ritual which developed at these Sunday afternoon gatherings these three in particular played the role of Weber's antagonists,' K. Loewenstein, 'Persönliche Erinnerungen an Max Weber', in K. Engisch *et al.* (eds), *Max Weber. Gedächtnisschrift der Ludwig-Maximilians-Universität München zur 100. Wiederkehr seines Geburtstages 1964* (Berlin, 1966), p. 30.

50   Jaspers, 'Heidelberger Erinnerungen', p. 5.

51   Max Weber to Georg Lukács, 14 August 1916 and 23 August 1916, in Lukács, *Briefwechsel 1902–1917*, pp. 371 and 376.

52   ibid., p. 322. See Lukács, *Heidelberger Philosophie der Kunst (1912–1914)*, aus dem Nachlaß herausgegeben von G. Markus and F. Benseler (Darmstadt and Neuwied, 1974).

53   ibid., p. 321.

54   Emil Lask to Heinrich Rickert, 18 June 1912, Heidelberg University Library, Lask papers (as in n. 8 above).

55   Emil Lask to Berta Lask, 16 November 1912, ibid.

56   Emil Lask to Heinrich Rickert, 7 May 1913, ibid.

57   Max Weber to Georg Lukács, 22 March 1913, in Lukács, *Briefwechsel 1902–1917*, p. 322.

58   WL⁴, p. 610.

59   See F. Fehér, 'Am Scheideweg des romantischen Antikapitalismus', in A. Heller *et al.*, *Die Seele und das Leben. Studien zum frühen Lukács* (Frankfurt, 1977), p. 266.

60   See Chapter 8 by Wolfgang J. Mommsen in this volume.

61   Lukács could have written his *Habilitation* with Alfred Weber, on the basis of his sociology of drama (see *AfSSP*, vol. 38, 1914, pp. 303–45 and 622–706). Weber's reaction to this possibility reveals his conception of the relationship between philosophy and sociology: 'You were undecided as to whether to write your *Habilitation* as a professor of the "meaning" of the spiritual, or of its (empirical) "being" (in this latter case, as a sociologist), but if it were possible, you would prefer the former', Lukács, *Briefwechsel 1902–1917*, p. 371). See also ibid., p. 290: 'The presentation of something *complete* in itself, not just a chapter but a "finished" work, provides *by far* the best chance of a positive solution.'

62   Max Weber to Georg Lukács, 14 August 1916 and 23 August 1916, ibid., pp. 372 and 376.

63   See G. Markus, 'Lukács' "erste" Ästhetik: Zur Entwicklungsgeschichte des jungen Lukacs', in Heller *et al.*, *Die Seele und das Leben*, pp. 192–240.

64   Max Weber to Lukács, 22 March 1913, in Lukács, *Briefwechsel 1902–1917*, p. 321: 'You will probably not be able to clear up the problematical aspects of the category "reality of experience" – that would take you too far. But *that* is the source of the incompleteness which one is aware of.' And ibid., p. 376: '. . . whether he will ever decide *really* to revise the *first* one?' As a result of this revision, Lukács's work forfeited much of its originality. Bloch later mentioned, with a great deal of satisfaction, that Lukács had been bored while doing this work. See Mesterházi and Mezei (eds), *Ernst Bloch und Georg Lukács*, p. 307.

65   G. Lukács, 'Benedetto Croce, Zur Theorie und Geschichte der Historiographie', *AfSSP*, vol. 39 (1915), pp. 878–85; idem, 'Zum Wesen und Methode der Kultursoziologie', *AfSSP*, vol. 39 (1915), pp. 216–22.

66   Béla Fogarasi to Emma Ritoók, in Emma Ritoók, 'Erinnerungen' (Hungarian), privately owned.

67   That is, disregarding external causes (his origins, the fact that the *Habilitation* thesis was in-

complete, the absence of both Max and Alfred Weber, etc.). Weber thought, in retrospect, that the main errors had been ones of form. See his letter of 9 January 1920 to Lukács's father (Zentrales Staatsarchiv Merseburg). Documents relating to the *Habilitation* are in the Heidelberg University Archive, III, Fakultätsakten 1918/19, Vol. I. Dekanat Domaszewski, 5a 186.

68 Max Weber to Georg Lukács, 14 August 1916 and 23 August 1916, in Lukács, *Briefwechsel 1902–1917*, pp. 372, 376. Georg Lukács to Frank Benseler, at the end of 1961, quoted in J. Kammler, *Politische Theorie von Georg Lukács* (Darmstadt and Neuwied, 1974), p. 245.

69 WL[4], p. 600.

70 Marianne Weber describes this idea as follows: 'For Lukács the splendour of inner-worldly culture, particularly its aesthetic side, meant the Anti-Christ, the "Luciferian" competition against God's effectiveness' (*Biography*, p. 466). Bloch also explained the origin of this category: '"Luciferian" was one of his favourite categories, taken from our great teacher Marcion, 200 AD, of course ... So he said art is "Luciferian", that is, it is in upheaval – and it has been from the start – against myth.' Mesterházi and Mezei (eds), *Ernst Bloch and Georg Lukács*, p. 302.

71 Ernst Bloch to Georg Lukács, 24 August 1916, ibid., p. 107.

72 Max Weber to Georg Lukács, 14 August 1916, in Lukács, *Briefwechsel 1902–1917*, p. 372.

73 See G. Lukács, 'Die deutschen Intellektuellen und der Krieg (1915)', *Text und Kritik*, no. 39/40 (1973), pp. 65–9. Georg Simmel to Marianne Weber, 14 August 1914, in Gassen and Landmann (eds), *Buch des Dankes*, p. 133: 'But surely our times are unique in that at last, at last, the demands of the day coincide with those of the idea. Of course this can only be grasped "intuitively", or rather, by practical experience, and if Lukács lacks this experience, it cannot be demonstrated to him. In that case, it is quite consistent for him to see "militarism" everywhere.' In an interview in 1974 in New York, Hans Staudinger told Erzsébet Vezér (Lukács Archive, Budapest), that Lukács was very bitter about Weber's patriotism during the war. In Lukács's and Bloch's eyes, Weber made a fool of himself by donning uniform and trying to be useful in the administration of military hospitals.

74 'The power of structures seems to be increasing more steadily than that of things which really exist. But – this is the experience of war for me – we must not admit it. We have to go on emphasizing that we are the only essential things, our soul, and even its eternally a priori objectivizations are (to use Ernst Bloch's nice metaphor) only paper money, whose value depends on the gold it stands for. The real power of structures cannot, of course, be denied ... Yes, the state is a power – but does it therefore have to be recognized as possessing real existence, in a philosophical utopian sense, in the essentially active sense of true ethics? I think not. And I intend to protest vigorously in the non-aesthetic parts of my Dostoevsky book' – Georg Lukács to Paul Ernst, 14 April 1915, in Lukács, *Briefwechsel 1902–1917*, p. 349.

75 E. Bloch, 'Zur Rettung von Georg Lukács', *Die weißen Blätter*, vol. 6 (1919), p. 529.

76 *Biography*, p. 466.

77 Max Weber to Marianne Weber, 5 April 1914, privately owned.

78 G. Lukács, *Dostojewski. Notizen und Entwürfe*, aus dem Nachlaß herausgegeben von K. Nyiri (Budapest, 1985); extracts also in Karádi and Vezér (eds), *Lukács, Mannheim und der Sonntagskreis*. The best analysis of these fragments is by Fehér in Heller et al., *Die Seele und des Leben*, pp. 290–327.

79 RS, Vol. I, p. 554. See W. Schluchter, *Rationalität der Weltbeherrschung* (Frankfurt-on-Main, 1980), p. 248.

80 Max Weber to Georg Lukács, 23 December 1915, in Lukács, *Briefwechsel 1902–1917*, p. 363.

81 Staudinger, interview; Honigsheim, 'Max Weber', pp. 184 and 241.

82 Georg Lukács to Paul Ernst, 14 May 1915, in Lukács, *Briefwechsel 1902–1917*, p. 352.

83 E. Salin, 'Max Weber und seine Freunde', *Die Zeit*, 24 April 1964.

84 Honigsheim, 'Max Weber', p. 187. Staudinger, interview: 'Weber said, "I accept historical materialism as a heuristic principle, but as a dogma – no".'

85 *Biography*, p. 466.

86 A. Salomon, 'Karl Mannheim', *Social Research*, vol. 15 (1947), pp. 350–64. See also E. Bloch, 'Wie ist Sozialismus möglich?', *Die weißen Blätter*, vol. 5 (1918), pp. 193–201.

87 To investigate Weber's impact on Lukács would go far beyond the scope of this study. The relationship between Weber and Lukács has already been dealt with to some extent in the literature. See especially, J. Habermas, *Theorie des kommunikativen Handelns*, 2 Vols (Frankfurt, 1981) especially Vol. 1, pp. 474 ff.; M. Weyembergh, 'M. Weber et G. Lukács',

Revue internationale de philosophie, vol. 27 (1973), pp. 474–500; I. Fetscher, 'Zum Begriff der "objektiven Möglichkeit" bei Max Weber und Georg Lukács', ibid., pp. 501–25.

88　'Lukács on his life and work', *New Left Review*, no. 68 (1971), p. 54.

89　ibid.: 'But I had no relations with him from that time on.'

90　Heller *et al.*, *Die Seele und das Leben*, pp. 320–1.

91　Max Weber to Georg Lukács, spring 1920, privately owned.

92　Max Weber to Joseph von Lukács, 9 January 1920 (Zentrales Staatsarchiv Merseburg).

93　ibid.

94　Max Weber to Georg Lukács, spring 1920, privately owned.

95　Michels, in his work on Max Weber, expresses a feeling similar to Lukács's. Michels writes about the break in the old friendly relationship: 'a break which, as far as can humanly and psychologically be anticipated, would have healed if we had been able to meet and have it out after the war.' R. Michels, *Bedeutende Männer* (Leipzig, 1927), p. 114.

96　Georg Lukács to Marianne Weber, n.d. [1920], privately owned.

97　See Georg Lukács, 'Marx und das Problem des ideologischen Verfalls', *Einheit*, vol. 1 (1946), pp. 108–23; idem, 'Die deutsche Soziologie vor dem Ersten Weltkrieg', *Aufbau*, vol. 1 (1946), pp. 476–89; idem, 'Die deutsche Soziologie zwischen dem Ersten und Zweiten Weltkrieg', *Aufbau*, vol. 1 (1946), pp. 585–600; idem, *Die Zerstörung der Vernunft* (Berlin, 1955).

98　See G. Markus, 'Die Seele und das Leben. Der junge Lukács und das Problem der "Kultur"', in Heller *et al.*, *Die Seele und das Leben*, pp. 99–130.

99　Honigsheim, 'Max Weber', p. 187.

34 Max Weber, Oswald Spengler, and a Biographical Surmise

DOUGLAS WEBSTER

The surmise that I place before you emerged from a different concern – a comparison between two contemporaries, Max Weber and Oswald Spengler. Since 1918, the works of Spengler have enjoyed something of a *réclame*. In February 1920 certain meetings took place between Weber and Spengler known from the accounts by Marianne Weber[1] and Eduard Baumgarten,[2] and a 1925 paper on their political philosophies exists, written by Otto Koellreutter, then professor of public law at Jena.[3] In terms of influence, I would hold that in fact neither savant exerted the slightest influence on the ideas or behaviour of the other. However, one contrast between them, stressed by Koellreutter, leads to my surmise about the intellectual biography of Max Weber.

Which policy is right in the interests of the state, which policy must be wrong? Koellreutter points out that Max Weber's whole analysis is *economic*, by which he means based on the competing manoeuvres and policies of *individuals*.

> In contrast to Max Weber, whose concern with politics is centred in an economic approach, Spengler considers politics purely from the point of view of the state. ... It is precisely the natural cast of the mind of the private enterpriser, the pursuit of his private interest, that Spengler rejects for the political guidance of the state.[4]

This leads Weber (says Koellreutter) to be untrue to his own ideal of cultural history; it leads him to entertain the notion of transplanting to German culture features that work well enough in an alien culture: notably British or Anglo-Saxon parliamentary ideas, a constitution based on political parties, and the choice of leaders – ministers of departments, presidents – in the cut-and-thrust of party politics; leaders who avowedly and unashamedly are in politics to further the interests that they personally judge most important. In this, Weber allies himself with the 'abstracting' tendencies of the eighteenth-century Enlightenment, but both Spengler and Koellreutter say that such cultural grafting is doomed to failure. Only what is utterly consonant with the whole, the totality (*Gesamtheit*) can be 'the true political leader of the state':

> The ethos ... of the personality who takes the whole as the object for his responsibility ... The official, not working for his own interests but imbued with the moral ethos of officialdom as service to the state.[5]

This broad contrast between 'the whole' (as in Spengler) and 'the natural cast of mind of the private enterpriser' (Weber) is the one that I shall use here.

A Biographical Surmise

It can hardly be doubted that Max Weber – at least in what Schumpeter calls the epoch of his ripest thought – was an individualist and strove always to think and reason in terms of individuals. Unity is an illusion. Not a government which hands down a solution to any social problem, but a constitution which leaves it free for groups and individuals to fight for their interests. Social sciences – and a history – which state their problems and seek their answers in terms of individuals acting with a mind to the actions and reactions of other social actors (known or typical), and the direct and indirect results of that action. People today speak of Weber's 'methodological individualism'. (I shall argue below that this term is misleading.) This picture of the mature Weber is well-nigh universally agreed,[6] and Part One of *Economy and Society* is taken as unequivocal evidence.[7] But two facts complicate the issue. First, did not Weber's greatest work enable us to make sense precisely of the large scale? Is it not *about* the large scale, *about* structures of social formations? Is *that* not where its fascination and explanatory force lie? And, secondly, the individualistic approach is by no means as clearly seen in Weber's earlier work as it was in 1920. Further questions follow: Was Weber's earlier work perhaps conceived wholly in terms of social formations, and not individualistic at all? And when did the individualistic emphasis first come in?

These questions were suggested, but not considered in detail, in the paper published in 1952 by John Watkins: 'Ideal types and historical explanation'.[8] Watkins was concerned not with Max Weber but with the logic of historical explanation; he argued – rightly – that ideal types of any kind do not in themselves constitute an explanation, and he argued in favour of methodological individualism. Watkins pointed out a curious fact: in his 1904 'Objectivity' essay, Weber mentions, as examples of ideal types, mostly concepts that Watkins describes as 'essential traits of a situation considered as a whole' and Weber described as 'synthetic constructions' or 'a unitary internally consistent *thought* picture' (such as the 'city economy' of the Middle Ages; 'feudalism'; 'individualism');[9] in 1920, his examples of pure types are much more concepts based on the form of individual actors' dispositions, the state of their information, and their relationships (such as the four pure forms of social action or the three pure types of legitimate domination).[10] The first of these Watkins labelled *holistic*, the second *individualistic*. The contrast is not really as clear-cut as Watkins made out, for Weber does give other examples as well. But that is a quibble. There is an important truth in what Watkins says.[11]

Watkins's paper in 1952 had two unintended results. First, it started a controversy (of course welcome to Watkins) on methodological individualism and holism, which raged for years in the learned journals in the 1950s and 1960s. No-one who lived through it could wish to revive that debate, and I do not try your patience by citing details. The participants finally sank back exhausted in stalemate. The general feeling of frustration, that the issue was wrongly formulated and perhaps a bogus issue, has remained ever since. Badly formulated the issue may be. But bogus? To Max Weber it was a real issue, a central issue, like the issue of *Sein* and *Sollen*, *is* and *ought*, which met with the same frustration and incomprehension. In each case it seemed impossible that

Weber could really mean what he said. But Weber really did mean what he said. And he had an uncanny knack of putting his finger on the issue, however baffling, that really matters. So we must be chary of ruling this one out of court.

The second unintended result was this. Watkins remarked *en passant* that, in Weber, the individualistic examples of ideal types tend to come later and that 'the later Weber' 'tacitly abandoned' the holistic 'in favour of' the individualistic. [12] His remark was *obiter dictum*; it was not central to his thesis (which applied alike to all ideal types) and it was assumed, not established in any strict scholarly way. Yet, *prima facie*, it looked obviously true. It involved conflating (for Weber) three things, which I shall consider separately: individualism, methodological individualism, and individualistic ideal types. It involved an implicit story: Max Weber grew up in an atmosphere and tradition overwhelmingly 'holistic' – holistic politically, philosophically and academically; somewhere in the early years of this century, he started changing his tune; probably there was some cause that we have not discerned yet (perhaps to do with his breakdown, perhaps connected with his other battles, perhaps an indirect result of the *Methodenstreit*). [13] Highly plausible. I suspect that most scholars taking part in or watching the quarrel over methodological individualism accepted this implicit story as true and, having had more than enough of the main battle, forgot about that side issue.

So Watkins suggests the question: *When (and perhaps why) did Max Weber first become imbued with the individualistic approach?* It was not Watkins's business to give an answer. I now pose the question afresh and suggest the answer.

The Child is Father of the Man

My thesis is twofold. First, in its origins Max Weber's individualism was religious in nature, and throughout his life it retained a very strong religious character, from which its other aspects separated out: ethical, political, economic, social, methodological. Second, the crucial time of its birth was the period around Max Weber's confirmation, roughly the first half of 1879, shortly before and shortly after his fifteenth birthday.

I present a benign picture of Max Weber, which today may seem old-fashioned and naive. There are two reasons: one hermeneutic (any figure of the past is puzzling and contradictory – seek first a 'soft' and sympathetic picture and leave judgement till later) and one factual (on balance the benign picture of Weber is much closer to the truth than the malign). I speak with great reserve. There must exist many early documents that I have not been able to consult.

My interpretation [14] depicts a boy in his early teens, unusually active intellectually, possessed of formidable knowledge, argumentative, just beginning to be consciously aware of his relations with other individuals and the connections binding any person to the groups of which he is a member; typically working these out explicitly by using words, discussion, argument; being spurred to explicit awareness of his position, his theory, by the requirements of his religious confirmation and the classes and discussions leading to the ceremony. No doubt the process was a gradual one, which worked itself out over a long period. The most important persons contributing to the process were Weber's mother, to a lesser degree his father, and other relatives, especially his grandmother Emilie Fallenstein, Hermann and Ida Baumgarten, Adolf Hausrath and, in the role of passive confidant, Fritz Baumgarten. Other important influences, such as Otto and Emmy Baumgarten, arrived after the deed was done and consolidated it; Friedrich Naumann, later still. But, to an overwhelming degree, the main impulse came from within Max Weber himself, and all other forces were secondary: fuel to a fire that fed on itself.

I draw attention to these five ranges of facts: the young Weber's hobbies and interests; earliest historical essays, up to about Christmas 1878; early reading and the use made of it; confirmation and the Christian community; independent opinion and the power structure. They cannot be detailed without some quotation of known material. For this I crave indulgence.

The young Weber's hobbies and interests we know from at least three sources: his early letters, Marianne Weber's biography, and Heinrich Rickert. Apart from his reading, writing letters, and arguing on an impressive scale (on which, see below), two interests are worth mentioning: constructing historical maps and genealogical tables, and collecting antique coins. Thus, when only twelve years old, in September 1876, he offers to construct, as a present, 'a few definitive genealogical tables, for instance of the Merovingians or the Carolingians or the Hohenstaufen or the Hohenzollern or the Hapsburgs'[15] – a fairly ambitious offer. And two years later, in September 1878, again writing to his grandmother, he tells how he has been

busy with a historical map of Germany in 1360. This map is costing me a lot of effort, because first I have to gather together the material for it from all sorts of genealogical tables, local histories, and encyclopaedias. Often – who knows how often – I have to look up the general reference book and other places for information about the most insignificant village ... I think that once I have mastered the history through the map, I shall get a lot of enjoyment out of it.[16]

Rickert knew Weber when they were boys at Gymnasium and reports:

As a boy Weber possessed a collection of coins, and when he showed it to me, he displayed a wealth of historical knowledge that well nigh intimidated me. In this field he seemed to me to be of such overwhelming superiority that I could not help being terrified I could give him nothing in exchange.[17]

Trivial? No. Certainly these passages contain nothing conclusive on my thesis. Yet so far as they go, they are wholly consistent with the picture my thesis paints: of a boy of unusual erudition and great industry in the service of scholarship (we can see him soon, slaving over these 'hundreds of Italian and Spanish collections of statutes'),[18] who essentially must come to understand artefacts and large-scale historical phenomena in terms of actual individuals, families of persons engaged in different trades, dynasts, inhabitants of the 'most insignificant village'. Naturally, we must beware of reading too much into scanty evidence.

The second range of evidence in part presents an opposite picture. It consists of three youthful essays apparently written in the same period, when Weber was twelve to fourteen years old, for which the only source is Marianne Weber.[19] Their titles: 'About the course of Germany history, with special reference to the positions of the Emperor and the Pope', 'About the period of Imperial Rome from Constantine to the migration of nations' (decorated with a family tree and with portraits apparently copied from antique coins), and (about Christmas 1878, when he was fourteen) 'Observations on the ethnic character, development and history of the Indo-Germanic nations'. Marianne Weber says of the third essay, which must have been in her hands: 'It aims at an understanding of the entire history of civilized nations and seeks to clarify the "laws governing their development".' It uses concepts of *Volksgemüt* (national emotions) and *Volksgeist* (national spirit) and, on the 'laws governing their development', Marianne Weber gives a quotation from the essay: 'Nations cannot abandon the course on which they have set out any more than can celestial bodies − provided that there are no external disturbances (by which the paths of the stars are also modified).' Thus, in the third essay, the young Weber expressed a thoroughgoing version of historicism, of what Hayek has called 'scientism',[20] and of the approach referred to above as 'holism'. It need not surprise us if an intellectually active young man of fourteen, growing up near Berlin in the 1870s, listening daily to discussions on national politics, should exhibit that form of analysis − all features of which the mature Weber went out of his way to condemn.

The third range of evidence refers to young Weber's reading. He read on a daunting scale. No short résumé can give a fair picture. I select two points only. First, at the age of fifteen − perhaps no great age − Weber was still quite capable of falling under the sway of romanticism. He says of Ossian: 'I am almost inclined to place him above Homer, but surely he is his equal, although he is infinitely far removed from him.'[21] 'Above Homer': hardly the judgement a more sober mind would make, although Weber argues his case soberly and points out that his is a minority view. Secondly, the fourteen-year-old Weber made a detailed analysis of Cicero's series of speeches directed against the attempted rebellion of Catilina in 64 BC, with suggestions on how Cicero should more honourably and effectively have behaved.[22] It is a truly remarkable piece of sustained analysis: analysis, note, in terms of the motives and decisions of persons acting in a complex changing situation, having in mind the actions of numerous other persons. The form of analysis is totally 'individualistic' (in complete contrast to the 'Observations on the ethnic character ...' mentioned above, which followed after this letter) and is fully reminiscent of numerous analyses of political and economic situations in the years that follow: to mention only one, since it is a late one and there are several accounts of it, Weber's analysis of policies in the Arco affair.[23]

So, by the end of 1878, with Weber at the age of fourteen, we find both clear evidence and possible predisposing factors of an individualistic approach and personality, and equally clear indications of an anti-individualistic stance in longer written work. The next event was Max Weber's confirmation − my fourth range of evidence.

The precise nature of confirmation varies from one Christian church to another, and its theological significance is a matter of some dispute. However, it is widely regarded as the occasion on which a child or youngster is admitted to communion, to full membership of the Christian community, and hence often 'provides a regular opportunity for giving adolescents systematic instruction in the Christian faith'.[24] In Max Weber's family, we follow discussions about the events and meaning of confirmation for three of the boys, Max (in 1879, just before his 15th birthday), Alfred (1884), and Karl (1886), both in Marianne Weber's biography and in letters that flowed back and forth between members of the Weber, Baumgarten, and Hausrath families and Grandmother Fallenstein. From these, five points emerge.

It is apparent that the young Max Weber was not 'naturally' inclined to the religious life and had to argue himself intellectually into it.[25] He did this slowly but with some success, and remained very knowledgeable about and sensitive and sympathetic towards spiritual matters for the rest of his life.[26] This may explain the stilted tone of his early letters on the meaning of confirmation, which lack the spontaneity and vigour of his usual expression. It is seen equally in his letter to Fritz Baumgarten of January 1879, in that to Alfred Weber in March 1884, and in his letter to his mother in March 1886 about Karl's confirmation: dutiful elder brother helping the younger ones, and reassuring everyone earnestly that it is a difficult time whose significance is hard to grasp.[27]

The second point concerns rights and duties. Before Alfred Weber's confirmation Max wrote him on 25 March 1884:

It will become all the time clearer to you, just as it did to me ... that you have laid yourself under the obligation of certain rights and duties. As a member of the Christian community you take upon yourself the right and the obligations of labouring, for your own part, towards the development of the great Christian culture and thus of mankind as a whole.[28]

This stress remained Max Weber's stress: the individual entering a world which is composed of earlier individuals, taking on rights and obligations, and thus coming – this is the third point – to constitute and to create that world, a world of rights and obligations, 'in the adjustments and arrangements of the whole of human society, in its modes of thought and behaviour'.[29] This picture is stressed again in his letter about Karl's confirmation in March 1886, as is the aspect (the fourth point to note) that both the theoretical teachings and the ceremony come first, the actual practice and practical understanding only later (which may explain why, all his life, Weber remained a preacher):

But – on the one hand – at this age one is not yet completely called upon to take an active part in this practical side of things (for the time being one's obligations do not change either in extent or in kind). And on the other hand, the understanding of the practical meaning of Christianity in everyday life is something that in general *can* only come to one on another occasion.[30]

Dutiful, stilted, even 'forced', these reflections by Max Weber may be, because he was setting himself consciously to perform a duty to himself and his family. Nevertheless the interpretation that he worked out was precisely (a somewhat secular version of) that which the best Christian thinkers would give for the purpose of confirmation: an initiation rite, the official entrance of a youngster, as a matured individual, into a great moral and spiritual community. The community that Weber speaks of in this connection, in his late teens, is always Christendom, the community of the Christian church, which is represented as embracing the world. We can easily see analogues in other religions, the Jewish barmitzvah, for instance, and of course Max Weber sees them. His interpretation (fifth point) later comes to be applied to the manifold world which embraces Christendom and much else too; that is, it is generalized; but it remains the same interpretation.

There remains one range of evidence in Weber's youth to mention. We have the individual faced with a great community, into which he is absorbed (with some difficulty) so that we can see that this community consists of individuals. Which is more important, to which should we grant more consideration, the individual or the community?

This question also was faced by Max Weber, but, it seems to me, less explicitly and rather later. Gradually it comes to be distasteful to him to contemplate an individual having to bow his judgement too much to the dictates of the structure, the regimes, the organizations. Each person has several, perhaps many, allegiances. Each has grown to have rights within and obligations towards several different groupings. It is for the individual, not for others, to decide and insist which is most important for him. Heteronomy becomes distasteful, autonomy claimed more clearly. Thus, when Fritz Baumgarten suggested that Weber's acute comments on classical writers had perhaps been copied from the books of others, the fourteen-year-old replied with moderation and dignity, but also with some indignation: yes, we do take almost all our thoughts from others, but no, in his matter 'I have not been able to admit thus far that I have let myself be overly swayed by any book or any words from the mouth of our teacher'.[31] Again, though without giving an exact date, his biographer tells us that, stimulated by lectures, Max Weber 'learned Hebrew in order to study the Old Testament in the original language'[32] – as later, for the same reason (not to depend on commentators), he taught himself Russian. From his youth, Weber preferred independence of thought in a preacher (and teacher) and independence from tightly prescribed ritual. At university, he found what he wanted. You must take the rough with the smooth, but 'the text of the sermon is not obligatory but the free choice of the preacher, and the sermon itself was not delivered with the tedious pathos of most of our preachers'.[33]

I suspect – so far only another surmise – that Weber became able to state explicitly a thesis of individual autonomy only during his final school year and his studies at the University of Heidelberg. I conjecture that the crucial factor was his reading of Immanuel Kant, begun when he was seventeen[34] and carried on for several years. Kant's ethical writings of the 1780s – particularly *Foundations of the Metaphysics of Morals* (1785), *Critique of Practical Reason* (1787), and *Critique of Judgement* (1790) – work out and express exactly the concept of a rational being that Weber was groping towards: a *person* or human individual who is 'free' in being endowed with the capacity of choice, and hence of responsibility, of human dignity, who must be used 'at all times as an end as well, and never as a means only'. Individuals must form their own personal set of values, must remain free to choose and decide, must choose after hard thought, and must live with the consequences. This theme or Leitmotiv is repeatedly voiced by the mature Weber. Perhaps, since I suggest its origin in Weber was religious, it can be summed up in two biblical texts. The first, quoted by him in November 1882: 'As thou hast believed, so be it done unto thee.' (Matt. 8:13)[35] The second, the text taken for Max Weber's confirmation in March 1879: 'Now the Lord is the spirit: and where the spirit of the Lord is, there is freedom.' (2 Cor. 3:17) As his biographer comments: 'Hardly any other biblical text could have better expressed the law that governed this child's life.'[36]

This law, by which the mature Weber was possessed, is well symbolized by his individualism. That individualism was attained in the late 1870s by intellectual effort expended to answer religious demands and problems in a context where family tensions were beginning to come to the surface; the religious was intertwined with the ethical; its central concern was the ethical relations between the individual and other structures of human beings; it later spread and took on a form that was political, economic, social, methodological. That is my case.

Max Weber's Version of Individualism

Thus far my evidence, the biographical core of my interpretation. There is no attempt to test it critically here. Now a final section to explore its meaning by looking at five connected questions: For Max Weber, what was the relation between individuals and structures, between *Einzelnen* and *Gebilden*? Can we throw light on standard objections to his position? Why did Weber speak so very emphatically on this topic? Where did Weber himself stand between two 'laws'? And can we throw new light – even today – on Weber's 'nationalism' and his attitude to the state?

To clarify Weber's version, we do not need to inquire into the many different senses of individualism[37] or seek to 'define' the word. If we speak of 'the actions of one or a smaller or larger number of separate individuals', what then is the nature, the ontological status of social structures or constructs, what is the relation between individuals and structures? Consider the strong statement in *Economy and Society*, in the section on 'social relationships'.[38] Weber expresses himself very emphatically, that so-called social structures or social institutions (*soziale Gebilde*) – a state, church, association, marriage, and such constructs – must only be thought of in terms of the probability (*Chance*) that given forms of action by individuals will occur. 'It is vital to be continually clear about this in order to avoid the "reification" of those concepts.' This strong statement forms part of Weber's general battle against all approaches that explain (or explain away) individual behaviour and responsibility as arising from, emanating from, controlled by, accounted for by, or reduced to any general external concept of any kind.[39] And it explains his detestation of the Hegelian tradition.

Weber's repeated onslaughts led critics to a standard answer, which in fact amounts to an (ontological) misinterpretation, express or implied, and may be paraphrased thus: 'What! You say that only individuals exist, and social structures — institutions, bureaucracies, armies, prisons — do not exist. Ridiculous! — as anyone knows who has tried to get the better of them.' True. In the sense of colliding with something like a stone wall, a social construct or structure (a prison, a Kafkaesque bureaucracy) certainly does exist.[40] Individuals can achieve their separate aims more effectively if they combine. We can hardly suppose that Max Weber, obsessed with 'the types of domination' and 'the economy and the arena of normative and de facto powers' and the 'coercive apparatus' of communities and organizations, in any way held that structures are like fairies or leprechauns, that in our calculations in life we can simply disregard them. No nominalistic argument denies that they are there. The difference lies elsewhere. A social structure exists solely because of the judgements, intentions, decisions and actions of individuals; individuals cause it to exist; it represents the probability that individuals have acted or do act or will act in a given way. The structure cannot itself judge (judge, say, that actions are unjust), or decide (say, to right the wrong), or form intentions or plans, or act, or be held responsible for decisions; only individuals can do that. And any structure can be changed, because we individuals can change it, though it is a great mistake to think that it can be changed easily or quickly or in the way we want. The fact remains: what man has built up, man can cast down. So, in approach and method, we can understand and explain social constructs and structures only in terms of individuals. More: we can make sense of the life of man, and the pathos of Fate, only if we insist that men, not constructs, have plans, make decisions, act, and are to be held responsible for the decisions and actions. Yet more: responsible, even though everyone knows that things will almost certainly go wrong for two cardinal reasons: partly (the structural argument of, say, Wolfgang Schluchter or Bryan Turner) because of the massy immovable reality of structures and material interests, which can only be changed slowly and painfully; but more because of the perverseness of the outcome of our deliberate acts (other individuals, with other aims, react to them) — which in principle can never be changed at all. (Hence an 'impossible' demand for responsibility, reminiscent of strict liability in law, and adopted for the same reason — as being the only way to secure decent standards in a dangerous, tightly packed, industrial world.)

I have said that the standard answer to a position like Weber's (the answer: social structures *exist*) amounts to an ontological misinterpretation. We may ask: Is it a question of ontology, of what exists, of *Sein*; or of ethics, of 'ought', of *Sollen*? In Kantian language, of *quid facti* or *quid juri*? For any system of ethics of the Kant–Weber type, the issue lies at the meeting place of three problems: of the individual, the person, of 'ought', and of freedom. For a Kant–Weber system, it seems at first sight to be a *fact* that an individual person is that entity which is endowed with choice. But, more accurately, this is the main original premiss or presupposition; develop this premiss and we get the whole ethical system; and thence the postulate that for analysis and explanation (both ethical and empirical) we must always seek out the individual. Which comes first, the chicken or the egg? In Weber's biography, the ethic comes first, and the 'method' follows. From first to last, it is not a question of ontology at all.[41]

Thus, we see, it is a mistake to phrase the question solely in terms of 'methodological' individualism. In the case of Weber (and of other thinkers of a like disposition), it is only when we widen the discussion to his individualism as a whole that we understand aright what he is saying. And it is this moral origin of Weber's individualist approach, and his intuitive distaste for all reductionist, determinist alternatives, which account for the great *wertrational* and emotional emphasis in his arguments.

Consider two final corollaries of Max Weber's brand of individualism.

First: It was Weber's habit to contrast two ethics or forms of commitment. The details vary, but commonly he spoke of some contrast between an ethic of conviction (*Gesinnungsethik*) or sometimes 'the ethic of the Sermon on the Mount' and an ethic of responsibility (*Verantwortungsethik*).[42] In fact, however, there was a contrast between three courses of action. The first – the *Gesinnungsethik* – Weber identified early in the teachings of Channing and of the young Friedrich Naumann; later, in the extreme pacifists or political radicals (say, Ernst Toller), whom he defended but strongly disagreed with; ideally, in Tolstoy. (He might have added Kant, but though he loves pulling Kant's leg he does not – I think – mention Kant in quite this way.) Where it was sincere, this was a course that Weber admired and respected (and it is 'responsible' in that its proponents are willing themselves to accept the consequences of their choice); Weber himself always hankered after it and in practice often adopted it; it was the course idealized by his mother and his aunt, Ida Baumgarten; but since it takes too little account or no account of the structures and massy interests of the real world, he could not recommend it. The second course is the opposite of this: in the extreme, the course of the time-server, the person who accepts too completely the behest of the real world, the power of the organized structure, the powers that be. In his father's circle of politicians and men of the world, and in ruthless industrialists, there were ample models. This course Weber (while always applauding realism) condemned as well, and more harshly. Thus, the supposed power of the state to be 'the ultimate value' is 'a wholly inadmissible change of interpretation from facts in the sphere of *is* into norms in the sphere of *ought*'.[43] This second course is the antithesis of Weberian responsibility. What matters supremely is autonomy, not heteronomy; choice, not determinism (psychological, ethical, political, social, or economic). The *Verantwortungsethik* was not a straight alternative to *Gesinnungsethik*. It was a third and more difficult course, which recognized and respected but differed from both of the first two. Men are Homeric heroes pulled and wrenched by daemonic forces and gods – including Tolstoyian ideals, scientific and logical truth, monomanias, obsessions, phobias, allegiances to disparate groups and interests[44] – but we must come to see that in principle these cannot all be reconciled, and we must acknowledge both the ideals and the brute facts of the world.[45] There is no one true policy that the nature of the world forces on all men. Policies must always fight it out. Thus Weber's own account is verbally misleading. We must picture Weber, and Weber in fact pictures mankind, as facing a choice between three laws.

Return now to his open letter of February 1916, 'Zwischen zwei Gesetzen' or 'Between two laws', with its strong emphasis on the destiny and obligations of any state that joins the power struggle. Here, Weber discusses Jacob

Burckhardt's argument for the civilizing value of the small state and against the greed for power of large nation-states. Does Weber's individualism conflict with his patriotism, his 'nationalism', the fascination that the power-state held for him (an aspect of his doctrines much discussed in recent years)?[46] Weber's remarks were certainly heated, even fevered, yet I suggest that he did give a clear answer to this question. He viewed any human being as born into and sustained in numerous persisting human groups or allegiances (the nation or state being one of them, or the Christian community, or a social class, or a kin group, or a 'calling' as scholar or politician), and in each case slipping into considerable specific benefits, loyalties and obligations. The benefits and obligations are not of our invention. They result from countless other people. We take them on whether we like them or not, and they are very onerous. We cannot exist naked without them. They add up to our *Beruf*: the reason why we are here in the world. It is not utterly impossible to slough off certain of these rights and duties (to change our nationality, say, from being German to being Swiss, to become a complete pacifist, to found a self-sufficient commune); but it is very difficult, and in each case the allegiances and demands are different and very strong. Burckhardt was a citizen of Switzerland, and Weber and Spengler of imperial Germany. Therein lies each man's fate.

So: Goodbye to Oswald Spengler. I find no trace of influence between him and Max Weber, and I do not play the academic game of relentless comparison. But one contrast between them – in terms of individualism – reveals something of much greater interest in the Weber biography.

Notes: Chapter 34

Wherever possible, reference is made to the known English-language editions. Occasionally I have supplied my own translation of a term or phrase; in that case, I cite both English and German sources.

1 *Biography*, pp. 674–5.
2 E. Baumgarten (ed.), *Max Weber. Werk und Person* (Tübingen, 1964), pp. 554 5.
3 O. Koellreutter, 'Die staatspolitischen Anschauungen Max Webers und Oswald Spenglers', *Zeitschrift für Politik*, vol. 14 (1925), pp. 481–500. Cf. also idem, *Die Staatslehre Oswald Spenglers. Eine Darstellung und eine kritische Würdigung* (Jena, 1924).
4 Koellreutter, 'Die staatspolitischen Anschauungen ...', pp. 499, 500.
5 Ibid., p. 500.
6 Not universally. A few disagree. Thus, Bryan Turner holds that Weber does not practise what he preaches, namely that Weber misunderstands his own reasoning. B. S. Turner, *For Weber: Essays on the Sociology of Fate* (London, 1981).
7 Or the earlier version: Weber, 'Some categories of interpretive sociology' [1913], *Sociological Quarterly*, vol. 22 (1981), pp. 145–80, especially p. 158; WL[4], pp. 427–74, especially p. 439. Or Weber's letter to Robert Liefmann of 9 March 1920: 'Supposing I am now a sociologist (according to my letter of accreditation), then the essential reason is to put an end to the trafficking in collective concepts that still haunts us. In other words, sociology itself can only be carried on by proceeding from the actions of one or few or many separate individuals, it must be strictly "individualistic" in its method.' Quoted in H. H. Bruun, *Science, Values and Politics in Max Weber's Methodology* (Copenhagen, 1972), pp. 38–9, n. 3. Weber cast around for some years, trying out one name after another to label the philosophy that he urged on us. He chose 'sociology', perhaps 'because he knows it teases'. In fact most persons then and since who adopt the label 'sociologist' have espoused the opposite of Weber's individualism.

8   J. W. N. Watkins, 'Ideal types and historical explanation', *British Journal for the Philosophy of Science*, vol. 3 (1952–3), pp. 22–43, especially pp. 23–4. Also idem, 'The principle of methodological individualism', ibid., pp. 186–9.

9   '"Objectivity" in social science and social policy', in MSS, pp. 49–112; see pp. 89–93; WL⁴, pp. 190–3.

10   ES, Vol.1, pp. 24–5; 215–6. Also WG, 'Introduction on concepts', pp. 1–17 (not translated in GEH).

11   Watkins reports that the idea behind his distinctions was derived from W. Eucken, *The Foundations of Economics*, transl. by T. W. Hutchison from the 6th German edn (London, 1950). The analogous terms in Eucken are: 'real type' and 'ideal type'. The contrast already appears in the first edition: Eucken, *Die Grundlagen der Nationalökonomie* (Jena, 1939). The contrasted words 'holistic' and 'individualistic' were first used, so far as I know, by Karl Popper.

12   Watkins, 'Ideal types', pp. 23, 27, 29.

13   The narrative would need a whole biography. In particular, Weber's relations to the Austrian economists have never had the attention they deserve. His attitude to Carl Menger was equivocal; yet he was on friendly terms with several others of the Austrians, among them Wieser (who took part in the famous 1909 Vienna meeting of the Verein für Sozialpolitik and wrote the early volume on economic theory for the *Grundriss*), Felix Somary the banker, Schumpeter, and von Mises (later surely the clearest exponent of individualism). A first step in discussion is: L. M. Lachmann, *The Legacy of Max Weber* (London, 1970).

14   One of the few discussions of this question, and almost certainly the best, is P. Honigsheim, 'Max Weber: his religious and ethical background and development', *Church History*, vol. 19 (1950), pp. 219–39. My thesis (coming from guesswork) coincides almost exactly with that of Honigsheim (based on some twelve years' personal experience and on intimate knowledge of Weber's work). If our thesis is right, the credit is his.

15   *Jugendbriefe*, pp. 3–4; shortened version in *Biography*, p. 46.

16   *Jugendbrief*, p. 16; *Biography*, p. 46.

17   H. Rickert, 'Max Weber und seine Stellung zur Wissenschaft', *Logos*, vol. 15 (1926), pp. 222–37; quotation on pp. 225–6. This paper is an extended version of a review of the *Lebensbild* in *Frankfurter Zeitung*, 16 June 1926, reprinted in R. König and J. Winckelmann (eds), *Max Weber zum Gedächtnis* (Cologne and Opladen, 1963), pp. 109–15. The *Logos* paper is slightly fuller at this point.

18   *Biography*, p. 113.

19   ibid., pp. 46–7. If the *Max Weber-Gesamtausgabe* would reveal such documents to the public, it would do a signal service.

20   F. A. Hayek, *The Counter-Revolution of Science: Studies on the Abuse of Reason* (New York, 1955). (The relevant papers first appeared in the journal *Economica* in 1941–44.) Cf. idem, *Studies in Philosophy, Politics and Economics* (London, 1967), Preface, p. viii.

21   *Biography*, p. 55 (letter of 19 December 1879).

22   ibid., pp. 52–5 (letter of 9 September 1878).

23   For example, W. J. Mommsen, *Max Weber und die deutsche Politik, 1890–1920* (Tübingen, 2nd edn 1974), Anhang VII, p. 536 (Weber's written notes, omitted from the English edition of Mommsen) and p. 346, note 152 (Weber's report to Mina Tobler, pp. 321–2 in the English edition); *Biography*, pp. 672–3; Baumgarten (ed.), *Max Weber*, pp. 555–6; F. J. Berber, 'Aufzeichnungen (1919/1920)', in König and Winckelmann (eds), *Max Weber zum Gedächtnis*, pp. 21–4; M. Rehm, 'Erinnerungen an Max Weber', in ibid., pp. 24–8.

24   F. L. Cross (ed.), *Oxford Dictionary of the Christian Church* (Oxford, 1957), p. 328 (art. s. v. 'Confirmation').

25   cf. *Jugendbriefe*, p. 121, on reading Channing in mid-1884: 'For several years over which I can think back, it is the first time that anything religious has achieved for me a more than purely objective interest.'

26   Weber included himself among those he called 'unmusical' in religious matters. We must not misunderstand the phrase: this was a category which he contrasted with 'heroic' or 'virtuoso' religiosity as expressed by religious ascetics, monks, active members of sects (see FMW, p. 287). He himself was extremely sensitive to all the nuances of religious feeling and action; cf. his own many writings on religious topics; P. Honigsheim, 'Max Weber' (see n. 14); Th. Heuss, 'Max Weber in seiner Gegenwart', Geleitwort in GPS², p. xiii.

27   *Jugendbriefe*, pp. 20–1, 105–8, 211–2. In marked contrast (since it is not on doctrinal questions and no doubt shows great relief that the ordeal is over) is Weber's happy letter to his

grandmother of 2 April 1879 after his own confirmation: 'The day of the confirmation was a lovely day. Throughout the week rain and cold had been the order of the day, but on Sunday morning the sun broke through the clouds and warmed up body and soul. I don't think I shall soon forget again that beautiful day; the confirmation was extremely beautiful and solemn, it made a big impression on all of us.' (ibid., p. 24.)

28 ibid., p. 107; Baumgarten (ed.), *Max Weber*, p. 25.

29 ibid.

30 *Jugendbriefe*, p. 212.

31 *Biography*, p. 54 (letter of 25 October 1878).

32 ibid., p. 57.

33 *Jugendbriefe*, p. 45 (9 May 1882, to his father).

34 *Biography*, pp. 45, 87–8, 156–7; cf. *Jugendbriefe*, pp. 251–62 (letter to Emmy Baumgarten, 5 July 1887).

35 *Jugendbriefe*, p. 61; *Biography*, p. 69.

36 *Jugendbriefe*, p. 24; *Biography*, p. 59.

37 Cf. PESC, p. 222, n. 22 to ch. IV: 'The expression "individualism" includes the most heterogeneous things imaginable . . . A thorough analysis of these concepts in historical terms would at the present time be highly valuable to science.'

38 ES, Vol. 1, p. 27.

39 The main onslaught was launched in the essays of 1903–6 now translated as *Roscher and Knies: The Logical Problems of Historical Economics* (New York, 1975); cf. WL[4], pp. 1–145. The attack was not on social constructs as such, but on *any concept or entity external to or other than an individual human mind or spirit*, on the *misuse of such concepts in argument*, especially political argument. The concepts and uses were very various, and Weber constantly found another one to shoot at.

40 A vigorous statement of this fact is given by the arch-individualist L. v. Mises, *Human Action: A Treatise on Economics* (London, 1949), pp. 42, 43: 'If we scrutinize the meaning of the various actions performed by individuals we must necessarily learn everything about the actions of collective wholes. For a social collective has no existence and reality outside of the individual members' actions. The life of a collective is lived in the actions of the individuals constituting its body. There is no social collective conceivable which is not operative in the actions of some individuals . . . A collective whole is a particular aspect of the actions of various individuals and as such a real thing determining the course of events.' This book is a rewritten version of v. Mises, *Nationalökonomie. Theorie des Handelns und Wirtschaftens* (Geneva, 1940). See there especially pp. 31–4.

41 The battle over 'methodological individualism' raged inconclusively through the 1950s and 1960s and subsided into sulky disagreement. So far as I am aware, it was only late in that battle – after the screams and groans had died away – that this ethical point was made explicitly by J. Agassi, 'Institutional individualism', *British Journal of Sociology*, vol. 26 (1975), pp. 144–55. (Agassi, like Watkins, would not claim to be a Weber scholar. He assigns the joint invention of methodological individualism to Max Weber and Ludwig von Mises.)

42 See, for example, Weber, 'The meaning of "ethical neutrality" . . .', in MSS, p. 16; 'Politics as a vocation', in FMW, pp. 118 ff.; 'Zwischen zwei Gesetzen', in GPS[3], pp. 142–5, and in MWG, Vol. I/15, pp. 93–8. The last denotes Weber's formulation: between two laws (or precepts, or ethics).

43 'The meaning of "ethical neutrality" . . .', in MSS, p. 46; WL[4], p. 539.

44 ES, Vol. 1, pp. 575–6; cf. R. Eden, *Political Leadership and Nihilism: A Study of Weber and Nietzsche* (Gainsville, Fla, 1984), p. 90 and passim.

45 In 'Politics as a vocation', Weber puts it: 'An ethic based solely on convictions and an ethic of responsibility are not absolute contrasts; rather they complement each other, and only the two together can make up the true man – the man who *can* have the "calling for politics".' (Compare the alternative translations by E. Matthews in Weber, *Selections in Translation*, ed. by W. G. Runciman (Cambridge, 1978), p. 224; and by Gerth and Mills in FMW, p. 127.)

46 Thus Ernst Troeltsch, who knew Weber well: 'The European . . . could revere only *one* value-god, draw out one value-god from the irreparable discords of values: for Weber it was national strength and greatness.' *Der Historismus und seine Probleme* (Tübingen, 1922), p. 161. Recent discussion of this contentious issue has stemmed from Mommsen's book first published in 1959 and now happily available in English: W. J. Mommsen, *Max Weber and German Politics, 1890–1920* (Chicago, 1984).

35 Karl Jaspers: Thinking with Max Weber in Mind

DIETER HENRICH

I

At a commemorative ceremony in the Great Hall of the University of Heidelberg, a month after the death of Max Weber, on 17 July 1920, Karl Jaspers delivered the eulogy to the assembled body of students. It is well attested that the eulogy had a deep, even overwhelming effect. Jaspers accorded Max Weber exemplary importance in the realm of modern life and thought. For forty years, he kept to the basic elements of his interpretation of Weber, as can be seen from the long series of assessments and explanations of Weber's work and way of thinking which followed the commemorative address, and from his invocation of Weber to establish the truth of his own philosophy. In his written work and published statements, Jaspers would constantly cite Weber, and these invocations, whether in the form of quotations or allusions, permeate his entire *oeuvre*.

One thing that impressed itself immediately both on those who heard the eulogy and on Jasper's contemporaries, but which needs to be re-emphasized today, is that in his commemorative address Karl Jaspers was speaking for the first time as a philosopher about philosophy. The address begins and reaches a climax in the proposition that Max Weber was really a philosopher. In part Jaspers, as a young associate professor who had only just moved from psychology to philosophy and who was deeply shaken by the death of a man he had loved and admired, was trying to define the source of Weber's fragmentary work and the reason for its vital appeal. At the same time, he was constructing a model and erecting the signposts to a way of thinking that were to direct philosophy itself along its path, temporarily abandoned, but the only one essential to it and therefore unavoidable. 'He gave the philosophical life present-day importance. In him we could see what it was to be a philosopher in our time, if we doubted whether there were still any philosophers left.' By speaking of Weber in this way, Jaspers was committing himself to follow the same path in his own life, and at the same time he was embarking inevitably on a confrontation with the philosophical theory of his age and with the leading figure in the department of philosophy in his own faculty, Heinrich Rickert.

Jaspers himself was to indicate subsequently that it was Max Weber's early death that first caused him to see clearly his own task as a philosopher and to devote himself to it: 'Only after his death, and then increasingly, it became apparent to me what he signified and how important he was.' Jaspers felt that 'what always needs to be done was not being done, namely, to call to mind what it really means to be a philosopher. In 1920 Max Weber died. The man whose presence had made me aware of the true refuge of the mind was no longer there. I felt as if I had entered into a void. If others will not act, I may be permitted to do so.' Max Weber's last words to him took on the meaning both of a confirmation and of a challenge. Weber had thanked Jaspers for his recently published *Psychologie der Weltanschauungen* [Psychology of World Views] (1919) and had added: 'This has been very worth while, I hope you will continue to be productive.'[1] Jaspers would refuse to accept praise for the power of his commemorative address, saying that Max Weber had spoken out of him and that he could take no credit.

In a very literal sense, the philosophy of Jaspers originated in the life and death of Weber: it provided him with an aim in life and with a programme that organized his entire work. It is only against this background that it becomes apparent that Jaspers's whole philosophy developed with Max Weber in mind. That this really was the case Jaspers continued to attest throughout his academic career, in words that hardly varied: 'We have no great man left who could bring us to ourselves in this way. For that reason our lives are still determined by the thought of him today', he wrote in his Weber essay in 1932, intending to remind a confused Germany of real greatness while there was still time. The autobiography of 1957 says, this time with reference to Jaspers's own life as a philosopher: 'It is as if we only began to do philosophy with an eye on somebody else ... Max Weber was to provide me again and again with an irreplaceable reassurance.' And the notes for Jaspers's last public lecture on 'The Great Philosophers' contain the observation: 'I can only hint at the continuity of this attentive gaze in myself for fifty years, to the fact that in all those years none of my philosophy was done without thinking of Max Weber.'

Having Max Weber always in mind, Jaspers's philosophy differs from those kinds of theory that can be elaborated without regard to the roots from which they grow and without regard to their capacity to generate a true consciousness of the self. The commentator who helps the reader to enter into this perspective is most likely to make Jaspers's own thought accessible. He will be able to distil that distinctive manner of philosophizing from the imposing tomes in which Jaspers presented himself, and which offer themselves to the young with what looks like a frozen inaccessibility. The attempt to come to terms with Jaspers in this way is facilitated by the fact that we look back over a century to the beginning of Jaspers's life. It was, among other things, the life of a tireless commentator, devoted to interpreting the thought of the great philosophers in the light of the living impulse that rules their thinking and through which alone they can exert an influence on the open history of philosophy. This method should appeal even to those who think it proper to try to reach a fresh understanding of the intellectual climate at the place where both Max Weber and Karl Jaspers prepared and wrote their works. Max Weber's work, and the way in which Jaspers's thought developed with constant reference to Weber, have long been regarded as essential to any description of the distinctive features of the intellectual climate of Heidelberg in the first half of the century. Traditions are not established and continued commemorations. The power by which they survive is not generated solely by memory or by appropriation through memory. When, in 1920, Jaspers publicly associated himself with Max Weber by means of his wholly original interpretation of him, he introduced into what had previously looked like a proud and established domain with continuing influence a surprising modification, which was immediately felt to be a provocation as well. This should mean that subsequent generations, too, ought to reach an understanding of Jaspers's association with Weber and of its effect on his thought not by quotations alone but by exerting themselves to arrive at an independent interpretation of it. But the fact of the matter is that, as we try to come to terms with this relationship, the documentary evidence obliges us to take account of a troublesome complication. Although Jaspers continued to emphasize right to the end of his academic career the extent to which he was guided by Weber, in his old age he was to frustrate all attempts to view this relationship as an unproblematical basis for the interpretation of his work. Jaspers's last words on the subject of Max Weber did not call his greatness into question, but they did cast doubt on the unity which had seemed to bind together the figure of Weber and the essential impulse of Jaspers's thought.

In Jaspers's last autobiographical sketch, the references to Weber have an altogether new tone: 'I believe that I see in his life a complete and incurable fragmentation (*Zerrissenheit*); a man who cannot be reduced to a single common denominator, and with whom I feel very ill at ease.' But had not Jaspers reduced Weber to a single common denominator when he said that he 'had given the philosophical life its present-day character', not least through the 'plain fact of his life'? True, the refuge for the mind that Jaspers found in Weber had never been located outside the antinomies of human existence – indeed, Weber more than anybody else had made people aware of those antinomies. But it was a refuge precisely because it could find a place among them and make it possible to lead a life without any loss of truthfulness. The doubts about the accuracy of his interpretation of Weber, an interpretation which grew out of the consciousness of being sheltered and at home in Weber's spirit, colour Jaspers's last words about Weber in a way that cannot be ignored.

The editor of Jaspers's works has recently communicated to me the fact that Jaspers left notes that convey a new picture of Weber, and provide the beginning for a new interpretation of Weber's work in terms of this picture. When Jaspers died, the dossier containing these notes was found on his desk. No attempt to enter into the perspective of Jaspers's thought can afford to ignore the existence of this dossier. It obliges us to revise our interpretation of Jaspers's ideas about the continuity of his own perspective on Max Weber with its fifty-year history.

It is evident that Jaspers himself thought that he could do no more than hint at this final new development. Nowhere in his publications does he explicitly revoke any of his previous statements about Weber as a figure, nor does any of the documents that have been published explain what caused him to offer a new interpretation. But the necessity of undertaking a revision was perfectly apparent to him. On one page of the dossier he writes, 'Something inside me resists saying anything about this Max Weber. But I cannot escape it. It seems as if I am obeying his own demand.'

Jaspers's dossier was entrusted to me. Knowing it as I do, and with all the caution and the reservations appropriate to a new beginning, I shall embark on the attempt to give an account of Jaspers's thinking in relation to Max Weber in the various stages of its development, and I shall do so in such a way as to make it possible to understand both the manner in which Jaspers understood his connection with Max Weber and the final shift in his relationship with him.[2]

II

Weber's influence on Jaspers's work had begun long before Jaspers's commemorative address. The two books that Jaspers published before he decided to devote himself to philosophy can only be understood if it is realized that Max Weber was their intended reader. Weber is to be thought of not as a student or user of the books, but as the one reader who would find in them that his whole view of things had been attended to, confirmed and extended to include new insights about the field of investigation opened up in these works. This early influence was based largely on what was visible in Weber's scholarly work. It is proper, therefore, to begin to recall those aspects of Weber's work that were relevant for Jaspers.

In a series of studies on the methodology of the social sciences, Weber had analysed the methods used and reached three main conclusions: (1) The knowledge made available by the social sciences is reliable even when it is only partial. (2) The use of the two methods available to the social sciences, causal analysis and the interpretation of subjective intentions and meanings, neither one of which can be reduced to the other, is dependent on interests of the inquiring mind, whether explicitly formulated or merely implied. These themselves are determined by historical circumstances and can never be transformed into a complete knowledge of reality. (3) Theories are instruments, indispensable for acquiring knowledge, but they can never offer a comprehensive knowledge of the world.

During Weber's time in Heidelberg, the defence of this methodology went hand in hand with the development of his investigations into the sociology of religion. The aim of these investigations was to give an account of the particular features of the form of rationality that became predominant in Western science, economy and society, and to demonstrate that it had its origins in modes of living that were themselves governed by religious interpretations of the world. With this intention, Weber also analysed the world-images and ethical systems of the great religions of all other cultures, in order to illustrate the ways of life in which they originate and which they generate, with the aim of shedding light on the particular features of the history and present-day life of the West.

It is obvious that Weber's theses concerning methodology and the philosophy of religion are interdependent. But, in both fields of study, there is another implicit focus of interest to which Jaspers's later philosophy devoted scant attention: in relation to attitudes both to science and to life, reason functions under conditions which it can itself neither control nor completely comprehend, but which first set reason free and enable it to serve its own purposes. The result is that rationality, once achieved, does not in the last resort distance itself from the conditions of its emergence. Even in those cases where life develops in harmony with reflection and a rational view of the world, it remains linked to those conditions that have opened up the space and a sense of direction for this activity of reflection. This awareness of a ground of material fact, which does not simply limit the exercise of reason but actually makes it possible, is evidently linked in the case of Weber with something more than a narrowly scientific standpoint. It is an integral part of the lived experience of his life and the precondition of that diagnostic concreteness and penetration which so impressed Jaspers. Because of it, even the most famous of Weber's texts take on the restrained form of a pathos, in which talk of fate and the postulate of a rational order governing both knowledge and life are grasped in a simple thought which, however, is not worked out and made explicit.

It can now be shown how in Jaspers's first books of 1913 and 1919, which adopt and develop an independent position, the programme of research set out in those works of Weber published during the years immediately preceding is taken up and applied. Jaspers's *General Psychopathology* (1913) explicitly proclaims its relation to Weber's methodological writings, and the *Psychologie der Weltanschauungen*, taking Weber's methodology as its premiss, refers to Weber's work on the sociology of religion. Both books are systematically constructed in that they are concerned with organized wholes of possible knowledge, but without aiming at cognitive totality. They do not attempt to cover whole theoretical areas or even parts of them. That any kind of systematic approach can be achieved under such conditions, and that it can allow for an approach that permits an inner dynamism in the development of its ideas – we are far removed from Linnaeus's system of classification or from the logic of Leibniz – is the result of the particular way in which the works are set out. This early outline of a system which rejects totality should be seen as an original achievement on the part of Jaspers – one that he could not have adopted from Weber directly, but which may well have been conceived because he began from Weber's work and kept it continually in view.

General Psychopathology begins by distinguishing two irreducible and contrasting methods: explanation from established causes and explanation from intelligible motives. First, it separates and distinguishes those events which, whether as subjective states of consciousness or as simply objective disorders, can be concretely established. Then it derives inferences from the causal or intelligible circumstances connected with those events. Finally, on the basis of these second-order elements and their combination, an attempt is made to establish a general model of types of illness. It is perfectly plain that Weber's theory of ideal types provides the methodological framework for this undertaking. It must be said that this kind of typology, as it relates both to complex cases and to the survey of pathological elements, is designed to encompass the whole field of psychic illness. Yet this survey is intended only as a typology, not as an explanatory theory to be proved by procedures adopted in advance of any evidence of their usefulness in diagnosis. There is no intention to offer any prospect of arriving at some final truth concerning an illness or the personality of a patient. In this way, it becomes clear how, with the application of Weber's theories in Jaspers's first book, a theme achieves prominence that can be traced back to Kant's theory of ideas: a whole can never be grasped *in concreto*, yet it remains the unattainable target of every effort of understanding. This applies especially to the conscious subject's understanding of itself: even the person, in so far as it is a totality, is an idea

– it cannot be reduced to any objective scientific status, but is left to itself in the search for unity.

Already, at the time when he was writing the *General Psychopathology*, Jaspers was affected by Weber's vivid presence. But this personal influence initially makes itself felt only in the emphatic rigour of the obligation for value-free analysis which he imposes on himself and in his attempt to apply Weber's programme for founding a doctrine of categories for sociology within the domain of psychiatry, for which Jaspers wanted to achieve just this. *Psychologie der Weltanschauungen* extends this programme to include a comprehensive general psychology and concentrates accordingly on the psychology of cultural forms of life. In this way, Jaspers directly follows Weber's sociology of religion, which is the only contemporary source he cites. He sees its special merit as the achievement 'of concrete analysis with systematic thought', a combination which had previously seemed impossible. Just what that means will be explained presently. But, first, we need to keep in mind that, in its own way, this work also follows the outline of a taxonomy developed in the book on psychopathology. It, too, begins with an irreducible antithesis, the difference being that this time that antithesis is located within the domain of meanings that can be grasped through empathy or *Verstehen*. Subjective attitudes are distinguished from general images of the world as elements that are to be placed in relation to each other. But this relationship between attitudes and images of the world is constituted in individuals and in ways of thinking that are themselves the product of what Jaspers calls 'forces' or 'ideas'. As forms of 'mind', they are prior to any distinction between the world and an attitude towards it. Just like the kinds of illnesses in psychopathology, they provide the actual means for the analysis of world views. But their particular formation is governed by a further condition: a variegated doctrine of antinomies between the various orientations of the life-process. This doctrine of antinomies was to assume a fundamental importance for Jaspers's philosophy. It already appears in *Psychologie der Weltanschauungen* as a doctrine of antinomies of 'limit' situations (*Grenz-situationen*). It is no longer merely, as in Kant, the idea of the totality of a world that is harnessed to antithesis, but the dynamic of the mind itself in its elaboration of conceptions of the world as a whole. Examples would be irreconcilable conflicts of values, such as the conflict between the longing for immortality and the desire to achieve practical ends, between chance and reason. This dynamic unfolds and intensifies in the vital task of gaining a foothold in *Grenzsituationen* and of reaching a clear awareness of the fact that the mind is actually caught in such situations. The possible ways of doing this have in turn to be formulated in antinomies. So it is that Jaspers comes to develop a set of concepts and a language by means of which he is able to penetrate deeply into the development of what had in preliminary fashion to be referred to as a 'world view'. The result is something completely different from an undirected method of description, which adapts smoothly and easily to phenomena through interpretive empathy; it has nothing to do either, with simply registering events in such a way that they are merely opaque for the observer, in the end. Soon Jaspers was to call the interpretation of what in his second major work were defined as 'types of mind' 'the illumination of existence' (*Existenzerhellung*).

Max Weber sent Jaspers offprints of his series of essays on the sociology of religion, which were published in 1916 and 1917 in the volumes of the *Archiv für Sozialwissenschaft und Sozialpolitik*. Jaspers had them bound. There can hardly be any doubt that he studied them attentively and in their entirety. It must then be assumed that the 'Intermediate reflections' at the end of the first series of essays is the text that explains Jaspers's remark about systematic thought in relation to research at its most concrete. In this essay, Weber underpinned his comparative studies of the roots of types of rationality with a typology of forms of rejection of the world from which forms of practical life can develop. This typology is constructed in the form of antinomies. It shows, by means of stages in the development of its set of antinomies, which are generated by the impact of ways of rejecting the world on various dimensions of life, that almost imperceptible differences in external behaviour can correspond to radically distinct forms of consciousness. This kind of systematic comparison could not fail to confirm and strengthen Jaspers's intentions. In the meantime, he had studied Kierkegaard's dialectic of existence. He had also – again by resorting to the formal means of the Kantian theory of antinomies – established a correspondence between Nietzsche's work and Kierkegaard. But Weber's notion of antinomies was even more universal in scope and, rather like Hegel's phenomenology, it had been constructed with regard to the history of mankind. Moreover, Weber had kept his typology free of theories with claims to universal validity and had presented it only as a methodological aid to empathic analysis or *Verstehen*. For his part, Jaspers wished to have his typology of world views taken only as a means of scientific investigation and not as any kind of practical guide to life. The way in which, during the course of his argument, he referred to Weber's postulate of value-free analysis, makes plain the extent to which Weber functioned as the intended reader of his work. After Weber's death, when he turned to philosophy, Jaspers was to see his own work, and consequently also the typology of Weber's 'Intermediate reflections', in a different light. Even in the late Weber dossier, and in the context of his reassessment, the antithesis between self-interpretation and the conditions under which this great text came into being is emphasized: 'He presents the ideas as a useful tool to aid the understanding, but his argument rests on experiences which cost him his life's blood.'

Purely on the grounds of their similar design and the fact that this design is of the same sort in both despite the disparateness of their subject matter, it has to be acknowledged that Jaspers's two early major works are an important achievement. They projected and established a completely autonomous account of a systematizing principle for the human sciences. And they did this in areas of analysis for which no such concept had previously been worked out. Furthermore, they succeeded in opening up a well-structured perspective within which practical analyses could be undertaken, and within which the facts and inner workings of conscious experience (*bewußtes Leben*) could be laid bare without curtailment or deformation. It is easy to understand that this achievement could give Jaspers reason for self-confidence and that he could firmly believe, after his late decision to develop a philosophy that would not abandon its essential subject matter to the requirements of academic form, that he could find his way along the path that he had chosen for himself, and that he could rely on his ability to generate conceptual frameworks.

It is relevant to point out that Jaspers's philosophical works, especially the *Philosophy* of 1932, keep to the basic design of the first two books, although they do transform it into a new method of exposition. Jaspers's particular talent lay in his ability to combine clarity of method, the distinctive feature of his early work on psychiatry, with a facility for exposing implicit intentions and conflicts. This facility derived from a well-developed and universal sense of the hidden propensities that underlie all conscious life and govern all abstract thoughts and all explicitly formulated convictions. As far as he was concerned, the effort to construct theories was a hindrance to the possibility of arriving at this sort of insight, although such insights nevertheless retain both their methodological transparency and their own kind of responsibility in the face of the various forms of scientific knowledge and of academic philosophy. It was not only theory that was alien to him but also the type of analysis that is concerned that the ideas used to understand phenomena and preconceived views about the admissibility of a given approach to phenomena may, in their turn, generate unclarified and inappropriate assumptions. It was for this reason that even Jaspers's *Philosophy* seemed to some of its critics to be nothing more than a psychological study that had gone wrong and to others a kind of thinking, altered only in style, whose means had been adopted almost without question from tradition. But Jaspers placed his reliance on the methodological clarity, the explanatory power and the systematic design of his procedures. He admitted suppressing questions about antecedents when outlining his premisses, and, in the matter of the sequences of abstract arguments, which are of prime importance as well in the formulation of interpretations of the world on the part of the living subject, he considered reliable the basic configurations that have remained constant in the philosophical tradition.

III

In his early books, Jaspers knew himself to be closely allied to Max Weber in delineating and systematically organizing whole new areas of knowledge. The fact that Weber had worked out his methodology not as a philosopher but as a sociologist, he took to be a special testimony to its soundness. He saw the accuracy and strength of Weber's political judgements as being related to the concreteness of his thought, which drew on the widest possible expertise in his subject. Jaspers reports that Weber's Sunday summaries of Germany's political situation and prospects during the First World War first brought him to politics and to lasting political clarity. They were the words of a man for whom no political priority was greater than national interests, but who saw politics in terms of cultural tasks and detested all forms of chauvinism. He placed every decision within the broadest context, outlining its consequences, offering a whole string of reliable prognoses, making it clear that political power requires a refusal of its shortsighted uses and that any political system needs to be measured, above all, against the degree of freedom of responsible action that it permits. All of this was set out with a precision and firmness of thought and expression that brought others besides Jaspers to the view that Max Weber was political rationality personified and destined to become a political leader in a democratized Germany. In Hitler, he was subsequently to see the perversion of Max Weber's charismatic qualities of leadership – a description in which he made use of notions coined by Max Weber. Jaspers's own political writings cannot be understood without the model provided by Weber and without an awareness on the part of Jaspers that he was in a way Weber's successor. The conviction that Weber's political diagnoses were of an incomparable profundity was to survive even the doubts later expressed in the dossier. The very image of the man who provided Jaspers with a refuge for thought derives to a large extent from Jaspers's exposure to Weber's political reason, intensified as it was by a passion for clarity.

But this image of Weber, outlined for the first time in the commemorative address, is by no means independent of a theme that helped shape the structure of Jaspers's early books and provided the form of their systematic construction. It is of vital importance for an understanding of the way Jaspers thought with Max Weber in mind to make this connection clear. The structure of the early works is dependent on attitudes that stand in insuperable antithesis to one another and yet are indissolubly linked. The whole progression of these works is to be seen as the working-out of this conflict. But, in this working-out, more occurs than the deepening and intensifying of this conflict to its most extreme. The movement of thought aims, rather, at a synthesis. This synthesis, indeed, was to be of a kind that would in no way lessen or deny the conflict itself. But the principle of Jaspers's system-construction is inseparable from the idea that the resolution of the conflict generates conceptual categories and leads to modes of realization in the realm of analysis that are closer to the origins of the conflict than the point at which the conflict begins, or at which the conflict's innate tendency to assume a definite form is held off or even repressed. Jaspers's analysis achieves systematic form precisely by virtue of the fact that the line of development of the conflict converges with another line in which, within the conflict itself, a unity is realized that stands above the conflict. This convergence is of methodological importance in that it is only with the results of the process that we are given the instruments for diagnosing it. It is important for the dynamics governing the reality of the conflict under consideration that the final stages of the working-out of the conflict are the very stages at which life in its search for understanding can find a foothold and achieve peace and quiet.

Again, it was Kant's theory of ideas that provided a theoretical justification for the assumptions inherent in the systematic form of Jaspers's work. It was only necessary for Jaspers first to link the theory of ideas with Kant's theory of antinomies, for then the never-ending approach to infinity coincided with the development of irreconcilable antinomies, determining the life of the person who was himself infinite. But it was not only this in the end very simple Kantianizing combination of ideas that gave such a way of proceeding an unquestioned power of conviction for Jaspers. There was another, quite different reason. Truthfulness in the observation of the fundamental facts of human life depends on a life led in the endurance and the living-out of conflicts. But this very truthfulness allows us to recognize that life only attains inner freedom and fullness when it, at the same time, transcends those conflicts and achieves more than could be explained by reference to the position it adopted within the struggle. Thus, the form of the early works comes together with fundamental convictions that have their origins in Jaspers's picture of himself and in his early experience of life.

In Jaspers's later philosophy, the theory of the absoluteness and inner infinity of communication has a central position and one that is characteristic of his convictions. It is dependent on the perception and the personal certainty that, even where there is insuperable division, the undivided can be and is present. In Jaspers's *Philosophische Logik* (1947), communication has become the *definiens* of reason itself, which sets out towards ideas and so reaches beyond all division. What makes man more than just the sum of those things to which he binds his life, and what authenticates and liberates that act of binding is the fact that it is sustained and proved in communication and thereby in its solidarity with other lives, which as such need not be in harmonious accord with it.

Jaspers's thought in its orientation towards Max Weber cannot, however, be understood only as a form of conversation with Weber. Jaspers regarded Weber too much as a model for that, and confessed that he was always shy in Weber's presence. When, at this time, Jaspers attempts to come to terms with the possibilities of greatness, he does so in a further portrait of Max Weber, but without mentioning his name. There, he concedes in respect of the great man that, for his own protection, he needs to adopt an attitude that maintains a certain distance. But, at the same time, he praises Weber's openness, his willingness to associate with everybody on equal terms, his delight in being contradicted, his gratitude, his limitless readiness to offer help and his reliability in providing that help. Jaspers takes it entirely for granted that Weber's most personal being was also lived within the medium of such reliable community and communication.

But what is inherent, without any denial of separateness, in the form of personal encounter that Jaspers named 'communication', that essence which he described in the time-honoured words which oppose the ultimacy of division as 'Being' or 'the One', seemed to him to be decisively present in Weber's life and character. In a finite world, Jaspers argued, the truth of the Whole can be established only if any direct attempt to make it the subject of discussion or the object of reflection is excluded. But Jaspers was as convinced that Weber's decisiveness contained the Whole within itself, as he was that there can be no authentic life that does not stand in this relation to 'the One' or 'the Origin'. The manner in which Weber is described in the commemorative address often culminates in statements that project on to Weber's vehemence in finite affairs and on to the fragmentary character of his work a reflection of the Absolute: 'He might appear to be an uncompromising relativist, and yet he was the man with the strongest belief of any in our time. For it is only such belief that is able to bear the relativizing of everything that we perceive as an object and therefore as something individual and separate.' Writing of Weber in 1932, Jaspers observes: 'He lived in the only way in which an immortal man could live in such a time, by breaking through all appearances to reveal the very springs of humanity.'

In the commemorative address, Jaspers's philosophy made its first entry into the public world, and it is fair to say that the address contains practically every distinctive feature of that philosophy. Needless to say, its detailed elaboration involved a long and wearisome journey through broad territories of problems and forms of life that had to be probed and interpreted. This philosophy as a whole does not wish to argue and does not wish to prove. Its intention is to capture these currents of life in the universal context in which they develop, to explain mental contents by locating them at the point at which they can be grasped in lived experiences. But its final aim is, in the end, only to help this life to attain to itself, which means summoning it to realize its possibilities. For Jaspers, bringing alive the figure of Max Weber and striving for the completion of his own work have a single common origin and intention. In keeping with this, the *Philosophy* of 1932 closes with a statement that quite plainly invokes Max Weber as a witness to the essential truth of the work as a whole, by including an indirect quotation from Weber's essay 'Science as a vocation': 'It is not by reveling in perfection but by suffering, by seeing the grim features of mundane existence, by unconditionally being itself in communication that my possible *Existenz* can achieve what I cannot plan, what becomes an absurdity when I wish it: in foundering to experience being.'[3]

By training and in his initial influence Jaspers was a psychiatrist. As a psychiatrist, in keeping with the method of his psychopathology, he saw illness as a deformed but conscious mode of life that physical factors do no more than influence. For this reason, he could acknowledge the possibility of transforming illness into productivity and could recognize the extraordinary power of insight that can be released in those who are threatened by psychic illness. His study of Strindberg and Van Gogh develops a typology for this kind of understanding, which is diametrically opposed to monocausal explanations of the relationship between genius and illness. The fact that the *Psychologie der Weltanschauungen* could revert to both Nietzsche and Kierkegaard and bring the two for the first time into the relationship that has since become commonplace owes much to Jaspers's particular psychiatrically based approach. In an age caught up in illusions, professing allegiance to an insipid rationality and so concealing from itself its unavoidable conflicts, Jaspers saw Kierkegaard and Nietzsche as founding a new possibility for reason. They could not themselves take full advantage of it. They only delineated the boundaries through which, as Jaspers puts it in his book on Nietzsche, reason has to break 'in order in the end to re-encounter and regain itself through its actions'. In life, Kierkegaard and Nietzsche remain outsiders and finally succumb to illness, the illness that had previously ensured that their analytical talents maintained a critical detachment from the world and from which they had to wrest the formal control that characterized their thinking. They are not so much victims of illness as victims of their age, which imposes a lonely passing on clarity of vision.

Max Weber, too, was burdened with a whole complex of maladies. They obliged him to become a patient at the psychiatric clinic where Jaspers worked. Even early on, Jaspers knew more about Weber's illness than the simple fact that he had had to resign his professorship. Later, Jaspers was to become completely familiar with the symptoms thanks to a pathographic self-portrait by Weber, the uncompromising truthfulness of which made the greatest impression on Jaspers. He considered it to be a document of historic importance, but he encouraged Weber's widow Marianne in her inclination to destroy it when there was a danger that it might fall into the hands of Nazi cultural bureaucrats. His familiarity with the pressure of suffering that weighed inescapably on Weber's existence only heightened his admiration for the man who was the model and supplied the outline of his thought. When he began to discuss Weber's illness in his later lectures, he rejected any comparison with Nietzsche or Kierkegaard: 'His illness did not touch his personality.'

IV

However, the Weber dossier on Jaspers's desk attests even more clearly than Jaspers's last self-portrait (in *Schicksal und Wille* [Fate and Will] in 1967) that this was not his last word on the matter. If the shift in attitude is to be understood, the circumstances that led up to it cannot go unmentioned. In the closing years of his life, some letters of Weber's were brought to Jaspers's attention. Their recipient (Else Jaffé, née von Richthofen) had made them over to Weber's designated biographer (Eduard Baumgarten, a relative of Weber), but she had bound him to quote only passages dealing with objective matters and which demonstrated the richness of Weber's mode of experience – for example, of works of art. He was then to guard the letters, and thereby their personal aspects, against inspection by any third party by destroying them. But a disagreement with Jaspers over the character of Weber induced Baumgarten to use the letters in discussion with and against Jaspers as documentary evidence of decisive importance. Jaspers found himself confronted with love letters, which were not only full of boyish passion but with yet other peculiarities not in keeping with his picture of the man who had hitherto supplied him with a home and refuge for the mind, peculiarities which inevitably reminded him of elements in Weber's pathographic self-portrait. The only fact to which Jaspers attributed decisive importance, however, was that Max Weber had gone to great lengths to conceal from his wife Marianne the true nature of the relationship on which he had embarked, and had resorted to all kinds of tricks and ruses to sustain the pretence.

It may well be thought that Jaspers should have disregarded information of this kind. After all, it amounted to no more than what even the most trivial sociological knowledge would lead one to suspect about small provincial universities. It would even be possible to give Max Weber credit for being large-spirited enough not to raise himself above such things. But such platitudes are too obvious for them to do justice to Jaspers's reactions, especially if they are used to bring about a cheap evaluative criticism of Jaspers's attachment to Max Weber. The fact is that, for Jaspers, the trait that most clearly and directly expressed the essence of Weber's personality was his truthfulness. He saw Weber's research, his political reason, his whole life as being rooted in that truthfulness, and from the very beginning his fundamental perception was opposed to any division between work, intellectual motive and real life. He had believed, he had had to believe, that anybody who looked the world truthfully in the face derived the strength to do so from an undivided and essentially human base, which is further testified to by what Jaspers termed 'communication'. For that reason, a man who wove a web of deceit into the very centre of his personal life could not be a measure for all greatness possible for us. And so, Jaspers found himself, in old age, having to revise his view of Weber, but without being able to forget his experience of the living man, who had once directed and encouraged him into the path of philosophy.

We must concern ourselves now with the nature of the revision Jaspers undertook and at the same time with the change in his understanding of his own work, which necessarily followed from it. In the process, questions will arise that are related to the very possibilities of thinking in our own time, so that our reflections will have to consider the dimension in which Jaspers's work, today and in the future, will take its place and have to assert itself.

Since, in attempting to explain Jaspers's shift of attitude in regard to Weber, there is the inevitable danger of becoming all too personal, let us enter as a caveat against any over-hasty associations the following remark alone: Jaspers unfortunately had only a very incomplete knowledge of the circumstances in which Weber's life moved to its close. As soon as a biography of Max Weber that is free of childish curiosity or embarrassment details those circumstances in full, then it will become apparent that on the part of all those who were directly involved, and not least on the part of Marianne Weber, who was not completely ignorant of what was going on, there was a far greater degree of delicacy and magnanimity than Jaspers can ever have appreciated. But the facts that Jaspers derived from the letters and that were the immediate cause of his change of attitude still remain.

The fresh evidence with which Jaspers was confronted drew him into a protracted revaluation of Weber as a figure. It will be readily understood that Jaspers sometimes felt angry that the witness of his life's work should once have presented himself in a way that kept vital features of his own life hidden. In such moments, he could write: 'Max Weber was guilty of treachery towards Marianne, towards himself, towards all of us who saw his image'. But at once he enters objections against this assertion, and his anger did not get in the way of his attempts to arrive at a proper understanding. When it came to the interpretation of the impulses underlying modes of thought, Jaspers displayed a special talent and a determination to get things straight, which have never been matched since. With these assets, he turned again to Max Weber, the only great man with whom he was on friendly terms for more than a decade. He read Weber's works again, especially the 'Intermediate reflections', and soon the outlines of a new interpretation emerged. He came to see how Weber's personal suffering had left its mark on his work. He detected this in the way in which Weber thought in opposites, in his factual objectivity, which suppressed the philosophical implications of his questions, in his agitated style, in the fragmentary composition of the texts of a man who could never be satisfied, in his proud gestures of defiance and, in particular, in his talk of an inevitable fate. 'We must see in the work what moves and speaks through it, otherwise we can have only a superficial understanding of it.'

He came to discern in Weber's life a detachment from everything he did, a detachment which was not simply designed to protect what was most important, but which was rather an expression of the impossibility of being completely given over to anything. It was the product of an unconquerable loneliness, which in turn originated in the fact that Weber regarded as obscure his own being, from which came all the threatening symptoms, and that he found himself uncanny. In the last resort, Weber lived in a silence that had a counterpart only in the dumbness of that ground of his being to which he could not penetrate. That loneliness could erupt in an unrelenting attitude in quite petty matters, which even Jaspers terms immoderate, but which in its very lack of moderation generated renewed self-control. Yet Weber was always ready to help, he was kind and extravagantly grateful for the smallest tokens of friendship. Jaspers, who now sees this attention to the little things in life as deriving from a completely different motive, speaks in a new and emotional way of Weber's 'heartfelt sympathy for everything that human beings are and can be'. But when Weber talks about his gratitude to Fate for being a German, the stress is not on gratitude; when he speaks of God, it is as if he is talking about an opponent who is pursuing him, about Shylock wishing to have his pound of flesh.

This does nothing to diminish, but rather offers a fresh explanation of the form taken by Weber's rationality. It remains 'that very reason, which knows its own limitations', the 'truthfulness of the perception of limits'. So, too, it does nothing to diminish but rather explains the depth of his perception, which of course always presupposed his intellectual gifts and the strength of his vision.

Jaspers had once traced the origins of his *Psychologie der Weltanschauungen* back to Kierkegaard and Nietzsche as well as to Weber. Now he observes: 'How close he comes to Kierkegaard and Nietzsche', and 'that he stood with [them] on the same foundation made bottomless by the fact of being an outsider'. Yet, even in this completely revised scheme, the special importance of Max Weber is emphasized, with Jaspers no longer simply calling him 'the great' but even more strongly, almost the 'only' man. He had great vitality, which gave a manly air to his figure, his bearing and his way of thinking, even in the darkness of his life. In him the 'poser of truth' was so great that even when it seemed to him that silence and 'treachery' were unavoidable, he found it impossible to remain stubbornly in a condition of untruthfulness by trying to justify himself. Even in his thinking he endured inner fragmentation, whereas Kierkegaard and Nietzsche had prepared avenues of escape for themselves.[4] And far from him lay all vanity of being an outsider. Not only that, but Jaspers detects in Weber's life and even in what he considered he had to accept as his treachery an 'immense striving for normality', which attested to this truthfulness in a different and completely new way.

Weber's place in history also seems to Jaspers to deserve comparison with that occupied by Kierkegaard and Nietzsche. The categories that he had developed in his studies of them he now applies to Weber. Is he 'the sacrifice which was made by an obscure Fate in order that there should emerge in the light the knowledge which could speak to our age'?

In no sense could Jaspers simply push himself away from this other, new Max Weber. For he was soon to imbue him with doubts concerning essential aspects of his own work. Weber's whole attitude seems determined by an awareness of the hopelessness of communication in those areas in which the currents of life arise. At all events, his loneliness was not that kind of loneliness which – according to Jaspers's theory – has to precede any effort to enter into that form of communication in which a man may find a foothold and at the same time be 'at home'. Jaspers himself posed the question: 'Does that abyss of loneliness somehow exclude communication?'

Jaspers might possibly have been able to answer this question in the affirmative, even in respect of an authentic existence not broken by illness, without having to abandon his philosophical position. But, in Weber, he sees in addition the development of a form of rationality that comes to resist the tendency not to question the universalist premiss of his own thought, a tendency that was active from the outset and determined the shaping of his work. This tendency had also been uncritically incorporated in the interpretation of Weber in terms in which he had philosophized throughout his life. The premiss was precisely that, in every essential conflict, the One in which it has its origins becomes apparent. As Jaspers comes to detach his thought from Weber's thought, he is obliged to propound the thesis underlying it on its own grounds and in its own right. In an important note we read: 'Weber's personal rationality reveals its complete openness to experience, its inner turmoil, its struggles, but not the essential oneness ... I have long assumed that such a unity could be taken as self-evidently operative in Max Weber. This assumption is clearly not correct. There remains the insoluble question as to how far it would have been possible in the case of Max Weber ... to communicate with him about something which cannot be delimited and defined merely as a standpoint – where rational discussion moves beyond the interpretation of values into ... questions of the communication of Being. I had no inkling of any of this during Max Weber's lifetime, and subsequently did not make it an object of my reflection for decades – for my part living on the basis of something which Max Weber would perhaps not affirm but which he would interpret for himself as a "standpoint" and tolerate.'

So, for Jaspers, Max Weber, for almost his whole life the chief witness to the truth of his thought, is transformed into the very opposite in the one question that is absolutely decisive. And, for that very reason, what is at first merely the unhappy fact that Jaspers in old age was confronted with letters that were not meant to be seen by anyone takes on a positive significance. From this point on, Jaspers's work, although still done out of an orientation to Max Weber, although a new one, will speak only in the name of its author. In this way, Jaspers himself makes it our task to decide whether his way and the premiss that led him along it, bearing in mind the importance of Max Weber's life and work for comparison, should be seen as grounded in truth or, in the last resort, in a too great and therefore illusory confidence.

And this question, in turn, leads us finally to an open view of fundamental problems of human thought. Is the sense of unity towards which reason gropes only one of its methods of operation, or should it be seen as capable of yielding truth? In what way can unity in conscious experience (*bewußtes Leben*) be realized and at the same time be preserved and grasped in a mode of thought that proves itself by its appropriation of such an experience? Is that which Jaspers proclaims as unity and origin real in a quite different way than is present in general attempts of comprehension or in the infinite *focus imaginarius* of the antinomies of life and thought? Could a different 'One' perhaps not be realized in Weber's fragmentation from which Jaspers in the end saw all unity vanish? What is really important in the philosophy of our time can be related to questions such as these, which are far from being adequately formulated.

A philosophy that evades these questions is confined to the country cottage in which Jaspers found the professorial colleagues of his day comfortably ensconced – at the very moment when, deeply shaken by Weber's death, he set out on his own road as a philosopher. Today, the summer house has become a kind of laboratory, but it is as confined as ever and affords perhaps a still more fatal contentment. A form of thought that leaves it behind, just as Jaspers once did in his commemorative address, will, like his, only approach the truth again if it can survive in the light of Max Weber's strenuous insights.

As neighbours, and yet in quite different ways, Max Weber and Karl Jaspers revealed deep dimensions of the movement of conscious experience. Jaspers knew and proclaimed that such insights are by their very nature philosophical. But there is another important point to be understood about the nature of philosophy, which emerges from Jaspers's early association with Weber and from his later, no less profound portrait of him: namely, that all genuine insights come from the movement of life to which they are directed. In his earlier and later years, Karl Jaspers devoted all his energies to sketching pictures of Max Weber. In them, he put at stake his whole path and the whole movement of his thought. His pictures make plain, for all the differences between them, the extent to which Weber's work proceeded from the heavy-laden struggle of his whole life towards reason. What we cannot make present to ourselves without being touched by it, must become a teaching for us. We must never forget that thinking only arises irresistibly and only combines profundity with truth when, in the words of Hölderlin ('Der Archipelagus'),

> die reißende Zeit mir
> Zu gewaltig das Haupt ergreift und die Not und das Irrsal
> Unter Sterblichen mir mein sterblich Leben erschüttert.

> [Time, as it rushes on ruthless
> Seizes my head too firmly, and need, and this walking bewildered,
> Lost, among mortals at last should shatter my mortal existence.] [5]

Notes: Chapter 35

This chapter was translated by Adrian Stevens.

1 Jaspers recorded Weber's comment in his personal copy of the first edition of his *Psychologie der Weltanschauungen*. Cf. *Hannah Arendt-Karl Jaspers: Briefwechsel*, ed. by L. Köhler and H. Saner (Munich, 1985), p. 828.
2 I am grateful to Hans Saner for his trust in making available the dossier, and also for many suggestions. This text, which is based on an only slightly revised version of the lecture I gave in the Great Hall of the University of Heidelberg on the occasion of Jaspers's own hundredth birthday in 1983, is the result of my study of the dossier, which has not yet been transcribed, and of an investigation of its factual and biographical basis in the life and work of Max Weber, which goes back much further. The sheer bulk of the material, and still more the occasion of the lecture, made annotations seem inapposite. I have also made no attempt to provide references to quotations from published works. All the quotations serve the common purpose of interpreting the development of Jaspers's work in the light of its references to Max Weber, and also of elucidating the way in which Jaspers, in old age, by revising his view of Max Weber, reached the point of allowing his own work to speak in his name and his name alone. The quotations from the dossier are based on my own preliminary transcriptions.

3   K. Jaspers, *Philosophy*, Vol. 3, transl. by E. B. Ashton (Chicago and London, 1971), p. 208.

4   In a letter dated 29 April 1966 (which was published after my lecture), Jaspers explained to Hannah Arendt that his new understanding of Max Weber had led him to see Kierkegaard and Nietzsche 'with somewhat different eyes'. Only Max Weber 'has really practised boundless truthfulness'. The sentence from the dossier that Max Weber is 'the only man' can be understood only in opposition to the weakness displayed even by Kierkegaard and Nietzsche, who in the end had to fall back on evasions. Jaspers now recognizes Weber's manliness also in the composure of the dying man: his last words – *Das Wahre ist die Wahrheit* – he now interprets as the refusal to regret. Cf. *Hannah Arendt-Karl Jaspers: Briefwechsel*, p. 671 ff.

5   F. Hölderlin, *Poems and Fragments*, transl. by M. Hamburger (Cambridge, 1980), p. 231.

Part V

*Max Weber –
the Enduring Contemporary*

36 Max Weber and the World since 1920

EDWARD SHILS

Sociology is said by some of its present practitioners to be a science aiming to discover comprehensively general laws about human actions and institutions; these general laws are expected to be applicable to all human actions and institutions in whatever epoch and place. Other sociologists are less insistent on this view of their subject, claiming that their first task is to obtain precise knowledge of their contemporary society. In fact, most sociologists conduct their investigations into their own contemporaneous societies; this is partly a necessity of their preferred techniques of direct observation and interview and is partly a result of their paramount interests in their own societies. (It is also, in more recent decades, a result of the fact that an increasingly large proportion of sociological research is supported by governments that are interested in obtaining reliable information about contemporary conditions in their own society.) There are exceptions to this generalization; there are sociologists who study societies of the past and who go outside their own national boundaries; they have been increasing in number, but they are still a very small minority. Most sociologists study contemporary Western societies.

The most eminent figures in the history of sociology have had a much broader perspective than the practising sociologists of the present day who conduct studies of particular contemporary factories or towns or of living families. Some of these eminent figures were concerned about the stages in the history of mankind and the 'laws' that described or determined the movement from stage to stage; others, like some contemporary sociological theorists, attempted to transcend history by the formulation of categories and hypotheses that were alleged to be valid for all societies in all times. (Of course, none of them was successful.) None the less, all of these founding and contemporary sociological theorists regardless of whether they thought of general laws ostensibly of universal applicability, like the laws of physics or chemistry which had no regard for epochs or territories, or whether they thought of laws of historical evolution, were, in fact, primarily interested in modern Western societies in their relative distinctiveness compared with societies in other times and in other parts of the world; they wanted to explain how the unique phenomenon of the typical modern Western liberal, democratic, capitalistic, national society came about and how it worked.

I

Max Weber, the corpus of whose work is, in my opinion, the most fundamental and most learned achievement of sociology, went further than any other sociologist in the pursuit of these combined aims of understanding human societies in a universal setting and modern Western society in its uniqueness. He produced the most differentiated set of categories for the analysis of all societies regardless of epoch and territory, he analysed a number of particular civilizations and cultures – China, India and ancient Judaism – in order to contrast them with modern Western societies, and to discover what there was in them which disposed them to move along paths other than that taken by Western civilization in arriving at its modern pattern. Max Weber's general categories, which he intended to be applicable to all societies, were also intended to permit the discernment of the distinctiveness of modern societies. Although he did not believe in 'laws of historical development' or in a 'philosophy of history' that purported to describe a meaningful pattern in the temporal sequence of societies or civilization, he did regard 'rationalization', which was present in some degrees and forms in all large-scale societies and in all civilizations and which he thought reached its most pervasive and most penetrating ascendancy in modern Western society, as both a universally applicable category and as a means of delineating the unique features of particular societies.

Efforts to be systematic, to eliminate contradictions, to establish consistency among observations and between observations and theories, and to make theories internally consistent are acts of cognitive rationalization. Not only the growth of the natural sciences but the numerous efforts to advance the social sciences are such acts of rationalization. Efforts to bring scientific knowledge into the chains of practical action in political, economic and social life are as much acts of rationalization as are the efforts to bureaucratize administration in every sphere and to order our knowledge of the world. 'Scientific management' is a rationalization. Bureaucratization is a rationalization of the actions of corporate bodies: governmental, ecclesiastical, military, academic, industrial and commercial. Secularization is a form of rationalization; it is a movement towards a unitary view of the world and away from seeing the world as made up of unconnected fragments and sectors. Secularization is the elimination of belief in the powers of transcendent spirits and the ostensible replacement of such belief by the mode of analysis and action that seeks to understand and influence the world in accordance with empirical observations made consistently with rationally defined criteria of validity and rational, logical principles constructed on the basis of such observations and criteria.

Societies could be compared with respect to the degree to which and the form in which their institutions were rationalized; patterns of thought – religious, scientific and juridical – could be compared with respect to the degree of their rationalization; institutions could also be compared with respect to their degree of rationalization.

Max Weber characterized modern Western society, ideal-typically, as follows: (1) rationalized, privately owned, economic enterprises oriented towards market conditions and seeking to maximize the profitability of their investments, calculated in monetary terms; (2) these enterprises availed themselves of a rational scientific technology; (3) a formally free market for labour, allowing mobility and hence rationality in the allocation of labour; (4) citizenship with rights and obligations within the national state; (5) bureaucracy, i.e. rationalized administration in government, economic enterprises and other institutions; (6) a legal order and a corresponding judicial system permitting stability of legal norms and hence a far-reaching predictability of consequences; (7) representative political institutions associated with competitive political parties seeking the support of an electorate constituted by approximately universal suffrage; (8) a pervasive secularization (*Entzauberung*) of the view of the world and society: this comprised the extinction of magic, the refusal to admit the operation of 'spiritual' forces, and the ascendancy of a rationalized, naturalistic, scientific outlook; (9) the rule that rewards should be rationally commensurate with achievement. This last feature was not explicitly listed by Max Weber in his enumeration of the features of modern society. Yet it was pervasively implicit in his characterization of the modern society that he studied. In contrast with the traditional society that placed such great emphasis on lineage or descent as a qualification for the possession of property, income, status and office, the modern outlook − contained in the Protestant ethic and in the spirit of capitalism that grew out of it − required that exertion and skill be the legitimate basis for reward. It should be added that Max Weber attributed much importance to the nation as a social and cultural formation. This is, however, more taken for granted than elaborately, systematically treated in his sociological writings; in his political writings it is given considerable prominence, but it is not analysed with the careful attention that he gave to most other features of modern societies.

These were the attributes of modern Western societies, not fully or equally realized in all Western societies but still, to a far-reaching extent, sufficiently developed to make these societies unique in world history. This was Max Weber's view of Western societies as they functioned in his lifetime.

II

Max Weber died in 1920. Approximately two-thirds of a century have now passed since then. Western societies have changed drastically in many respects during the last sixty-five years. Industry has become much more productive; scientific knowledge has been drawn upon for the development of industrial technology far more than was the case at the time of Max Weber's death. All these societies are consequently much wealthier now than they were sixty-five years ago; the mass of the population lives at a much higher standard of material well-being than it did. Extensive provisions for welfare have practically eliminated poverty, as it was then conceived, from these societies. The sphere of the free market, in which enterprises seek to maximize their profits in competition with each other, still exists, but its sphere has been much reduced by an extension of governmentally owned enterprises and by a more penetrating and restrictive regulation by government. The market for labour, which economic theory assumes to be free, has been much eroded by legislation and by the strength of trade unions, which restrict entry into certain occupations, which restrain dismissal and which affect the rates of remuneration that would otherwise be fixed by competition in the market for labour; they restrict output and resist technological innovation by formal and informal agreements, thus limiting the rationalization of business enterprises. Citizenship, with its obligations to the payment of taxes and the performance of military service and its rights to preference over non-citizens in the enjoyment of certain guarantees and political activities, has undergone an uneven development. The obligation to the payment of taxes has been extended throughout the population, the refusal of military service has become more frequent and more tolerated; the differences between the rights of citizens and those of non-citizens have been much diminished at a time when the rights of all residents within the national boundaries have been much increased. There has been a great increase in the demands of individuals throughout modern Western societies for higher incomes, more governmentally provided amenities, and protection and greater freedom in private and public spheres. Previously subordinated and submissive groups, ethnic, regional and social, have become more assertive and demanding. The press, printed and electronic, has become more free, more inquisitive and more critical towards existing institutions and the authorities who rule them. Patriotism, which was once an attribute of citizenship, has been attenuated.

The technology of communications and transportation has greatly increased both the ease and the amount of travel; more of the citizenry can now be reached more speedily and more often by the new methods of electronic communication. Societies have become more integrated through the greater concentration of resources and authority in the hands of central government; they have also become more integrated in the sense of possessing a common body of knowledge of current events through a common focus of attention on central government and through the substance transmitted by a relatively few nationally pervasive organs of communication. The attention of the mass of the population has become more focused on the central government; there has been an increase in demands for the protection of what people assert to be their rights and, in each society, the mass of the population directs these demands towards its central government. Bureaucratization has grown enormously throughout the length and breadth of society.

Despite several setbacks in Italy between 1923 and 1945, and in Germany between 1933 and 1945, and in Spain from the late 1930s until the late 1970s, and in Portugal for a longer period, political democracy now prevails in all these countries as well as in those in which it was never eclipsed. Politicians have become more ready to attempt to gratify the demands of the electorate and to regard themselves as its instruments, while the electorate, for its part, has become more fickle in its loyalty and more sceptical about the merits of its political representatives. The relationship between the electorate and their elected representatives has become more labile, partly in consequence of a diminution of deference towards persons in positions of authority and of the establishment of the sample surveys of public opinion, which bring before politicians (both incumbents and candidates for elective office), the desires and evaluation of 'the public'. 'Party machines' have been weakened by this greater assertiveness and demandingness of the electorate, and particularly by the agitation of intellectuals and social and political reformers who have gained in influence over the functionaries of party machines. Various forms of populism, most of them actually the agitation of organized intellectual and sometimes radical political groups claiming to speak on behalf of 'the people', have placed professional politicians at a disadvantage in their relations with the mass of the population.

The higher educational level of the population – larger proportions of the relevant age-cohorts attend secondary schools and universities – has contributed to greater assertiveness and demandingness and to a more critical attitude towards politicians. Public demonstrations and agitation by particular interest groups have proliferated. Strikes were at one time a monopoly of the industrial working class. This is no longer the case. Employees in civil services and nationalized industries have become as ready to strike as employees in private industry. White-collar workers and professionals also strike on behalf of their demands for higher salaries, shorter working weeks and other benefits. Farmers and peasants have become more insistent in their demands on central governments.

The much greater 'consumption' of mass communication, especially of television broadcasts, by the mass of the population has increased the sensitivity of politicians to the views of the public. Politicians are now more alert to how their 'image' is represented in newspapers and periodicals and on television. Because the electorate is more concerned with issues of domestic policy, politicians have also become much more occupied with domestic issues than with the issues of foreign policy, although they cannot disregard these as much as many of them would like.

The demandingness of the populace is a demandingness addressed to government for services, payments and protection from whatever misfortunes can befall human beings. One major consequence of this has been the growth of the 'welfare-state' and a very great enlargement of the civil service. In most European countries, the size of the public services has been further increased by the nationalization of various branches of industry and of particular firms. Socialists, communists and collectivist liberals press for more nationalization and for a more and more comprehensive regulation and direction of private business enterprises.

The power of bureaucracy has accordingly expanded immensely. The legislature enacts more laws than ever before, but the individual legislators are less powerful. In some systems, legislators are under the control of the cabinet and the party leadership; in the United States, they are increasingly under the influence of their own staffs, originally appointed to help them cope with the executive branch, including the civil service, on the one side, and their demanding constituents, on the other. In the United States, also, the federal judiciary has increasingly claimed jurisdiction over subjects that were unknown to it before.

The intellectuals in their many different intellectual and intellectual–practical activities have become more visible and more influential. University teachers have become much more active as advisers to governments and as incumbents of high political offices. Economic ideas generated in academic situations and in the course of academic debates have been assimilated into governmental policies, although not always with satisfactory practical results. Governments employ more social scientists, not only as staff members in the executive civil service but also for the promulgation and evaluation of policies. The ideas of academic social scientists have been incorporated into public opinion to an unprecedented extent. Politicians are more responsive to the opinions of such academics. The ideas of academics enter into public opinion through the media of mass communication. The academic community on its own side has become more politicized, and universities in many countries have become the platform for radical political ideas to an extent practically unknown in Max Weber's lifetime.

The amount of scientific research in physics, chemistry, astronomy, biology, medicine, agriculture and technology has increased greatly in volume, the number of scientists has grown vastly and the cost of research has increased disproportionately. The promotion and execution (as well as the control) of scientific research in the natural sciences have been taken into the agenda of governments; the chief support of such research comes from central governments, and governments thereupon take it on themselves to attempt to guide the direction of research into paths that they regard as being of practical economic, political and military value. In the course of this, natural scientists have come to occupy important roles in the institutions designated by governments to guide the direction of scientific research; natural scientists have acquired more influential roles as advisers to governments on problems and decisions that require scientific knowledge. Governments have created divisions of research within many of their departments or ministries and maintain many research institutions. The substance of the natural sciences is immune from politicization because of the nature of scientific knowledge, the strength of the traditions of the scientific community and the obstacles that are inherent in the efforts of laymen to control activities which are so complicated as to be intelligible only to those who have studied them for a long time; however, there has never been a time in the history of science when governments have attempted to intrude so much into the sphere of scientific work.

Literary authors also have become more politicized, frequently on behalf of radical causes. The same has been true of the recently much expanded sociological profession, whose members have tended to judge their respective societies from the standpoint of a Utopian egalitarian ideal. The ideal of most intellectuals who have become more or less active in politics has been an ideal of rationalization. Such people have generally been in favour of more control and planning by central governments in most spheres; most of those who are not so active or so favourable acquiesce in such programmes of rationalization.

The progress of rationalization and, even more, of the ideal of the rationalization of society and of the scientific view of the world reaches deeply into the sphere of religion. A striking development of the past sixty-five years is the reduced position of the Christian churches in most Western societies, the decline in the prestige of their leaders and the faded state of Christian belief within the population at large. Regular attendance at services of worship has decreased; Christian belief and imagery come less frequently and less prominently into the idiom of the public speech of politicians. Whereas, at the beginning of the period under consideration, these societies were considered by their members to be 'Christian' – without going further into what that meant – this is no longer the case. This has happened to some extent even in Latin countries of Southern Europe, where the Roman Catholic Church and Roman Catholic belief have, in the past, made fewer concessions to modern secularism. The pressure to conciliate secular desires and to accept secular beliefs has become strong in Roman Catholicism; it is, and has been, even stronger in the major Protestant churches and sects.

Priests and pastors and ministers of religion have become more assertive politically than at any time since the Restoration following the Napoleonic Wars, but now they do not act in defence or for the promotion of their churches and their theological beliefs. They do not act so much 'in the religious interest' as they do on behalf of secular ideals of equality and popular sovereignty outside the churches. The clergy of the Roman Catholic Church, in which more has been required in the way of beliefs and observance, has also lost some of its confidence in the truth of the traditional theological teachings in which its predecessors had believed. The decline in the numbers of vocations and the increase in the number of priests who have requested release from their vows indicate this. In some respects, the crisis of authority in the Roman Catholic Church is more severe than it is in the Protestant churches, in which authority has always been somewhat more limited in its demands on the faith of the clergy and their flocks; the special position of the Papacy adds to the obligations of faith of Roman Catholics, as do the traditional demands of the Church for specific acts and abstentions by the faithful, and both are now more in question than they were in Weber's lifetime.

Ritual and ceremonial have been forced into more and more confined occasions; their elaborateness has been simplified where it has not been obliterated. Ritual and ceremonial have always been associated with the affirmation of authority, with the invocation of higher powers to legitimate earthly powers through the attribution of a sacred significance to earthly things. It may be said that the reduction and confinement of ritual and ceremonial is a manifestation of a secular, rationalizing outlook that denies the existence of the higher powers to which ritual and ceremonial appeal. It should also be said that there is a coincidence of secularist attitudes with attitudes that are hostile towards superordination and towards the exercise of authority and towards any superiority of status. Ritual and ceremony entail superior authority, earthly as well as transcendent, and when authority itself is so critically assessed, ritual and ceremony are bound to be distrusted.

The situation of Christian authority in the past sixty five, and particularly in the past thirty-five years, is only one instance of the situation of authority more generally. There is more questioning of the authority of teachers and officials in universities and in schools, of the authority of officers in armies, of the authority of employers in factories and offices, of the powers of the police in dealing with suspected criminals, of governments vis-à-vis the press in the disclosure of confidential information and the protection of the press's sources of confidential information; these are all parts of the far-flung mosaic of the diminution of deference towards authority.

There is a passion for equality – the argument for it remains very vague – but the burden of proof has passed to those who are reluctant to accept the demand for equality; the argument for equality has become an argument resting on self-evidence. The passion for equality and the efforts to restrict the powers traditionally allowed to offices of authority are probably closely akin to each other; the common element is the postulate of the dignity of the individual human being. This passion and these efforts have gone hand in hand with the readiness to accord greater powers and a greater share of the national income to central government.

The emphasis on the irreducible dignity of every human being is linked to a belief that human beings also have unequal abilities, although those who support the first thesis sometimes deny that they believe the second. They obviously do believe that the equal dignity of human beings is not paralleled by their equal abilities, because it is characteristic of the arguments for equality that they also demand that governments occupy themselves with enforcing equality by a great number and a wide variety of costly and un-precedentedly intrusive measures. The equality of human beings, although alleged to be 'natural', must be assured by measures that have behind them the coercive power of government. Although there is still a belief, more common in Max Weber's lifetime, that rewards should be commensurate with achievement – this was a common belief of the liberalism in which Max Weber shared – it is now qualified by the contradictory belief that inequality of rewards must be reduced in accordance with the postulate of the fundamental equal dignity of all human beings.

The belief in equality permeates the collectivistic liberal and social-democratic outlooks that have been dominant throughout most of the period since the death of Max Weber. It combines distrust towards authority, egalitarianism and secularism, and the belief that only governmental activity is capable of realizing the great ideals of the abolition of authority and the entrenchment of equality.

These have been the salient features of modern Western societies for the last sixty-five years, but they have not been the only features. In some of these societies – specifically in Italy and in Germany – regimes of quite different features have appeared, suppressing individual and civil freedoms, abolishing the institutions of representative government, the rule of law, the freedom of the press, the rights of expression, association and assembly, the competition of two or more political parties; in varying degrees, they have abolished the mechanism of the market, and persecuted ethnic and religious groups to the point of extinction. They have preached vehemently the pre-eminence of the national community to the exclusion of all other social formations save the state, and to the state they have assigned the responsibility of driving to an extreme the paramountcy of nationality within its own society and abroad.

In the other Continental European countries, and to only a very small extent in the United States and Great Britain, there have been organizations that mimicked the German and Italian groups inimical to the liberal democratic social order, but they have remained very small and inconsequential minorities.

There have also been other political movements that wished to displace the liberal-democratic social order and to replace it by a totalitarian order of a sort somewhat different from that contended for by the Nazis and Fascists. These communist movements were intended to instal regimes like that prevailing or thought optimistically to prevail in the Soviet Union, centralized and planned by a dictatorial centre of a single party, without any freedoms, private or corporate. The economy was to be wholly controlled by the central political authority; private economic enterprise was to be wholly abolished except for very marginal activities. The communist ideal was territorially expansive: the communist parties of the Western countries sought to extend the power and pattern of the Soviet Union to their own countries. The communist movement has failed to attain its basic objective in any Western country either before the

Second World War or after it. It attained great size in Germany before 1933 and in France and Italy after the Second World War. In other countries, including the Federal Republic of Germany, it has not been able to gain large numbers of adherents nor has it been able to exercise much influence except by infiltration into trade unions and by its often camouflaged appeals to intellectuals.

Nevertheless, all the Western countries where liberal democracy was established have been obdurate in opposing the efforts of the Communists, just as all but Germany and Italy and Spain were resistant to the Nazi and Fascist efforts to gain control.

The failures of the major movements of subversion – the Communists and the Fascists – have left behind them residues of small, unstable groups of individuals who refuse to reconcile themselves to the liberal democratic societies in which they live. They refuse to live at peace with their societies; they engage in assassinations and the explosion of bombs in crowded places of symbolic importance. Germany, Italy and Ireland, the three countries of the West in which political violence was most pronounced after the First World War, have in recent times been scenes of such terrorist activities.

The institutions for the protection and enforcement of public order have had only partial success in the prevention of these violent disruptions of public order. Limited by legal restraints on the use of force and frustrated by the ingenuity and the numbers of the perpetrators of acts of terror and the help which they receive from ideological sympathizers, the police and security services have not been very effective. (Nor for that matter have they been able to cope with the greatly increased number of ordinary crimes such as armed robbery, burglary, rape and murder or with the great increase in the frequency of 'economic crimes' such as embezzlement.)

Despite severe criticisms from within and attempts at subversion, most of the liberal-democratic countries have persisted and developed. Even Germany and Italy, the two countries that could not resist the totalitarian movements within them, were able, once their tyrants were destroyed in the Second World War, to turn to the liberal-democratic path; they have, moreover, stayed there – the West Germans very successfully, the Italians less successfully but sufficiently so to remain clearly liberal-democratic. In all Western countries, collectivist liberalism and social democracy have gained the ascendancy during the two-thirds of a century under consideration here.

In the last decade and a half, several developments in the direction of a reversal of these tendencies have occurred. In Western Germany, Great Britain and the United States, a more conservative body of political philosophers and publicists has emerged and more conservative parties have acceded to power. They wish to restore greater opportunities to private business and to make it possible for the initiatives of private enterprise to be successful; they wish their societies to rely to a larger extent on the market. They would reduce the share of the gross national product taken by government through taxation and leave more of it to private individuals and enterprises. They are less egalitarian in their fundamental ideals, less emancipationist in their attitude towards the expression of emotional impulses. They have more sympathy with traditional religious beliefs, and are more inclined to affirm the virtues of traditional family life, and of the responsibility of parents for the care of their children.

In general, they are more willing to give the benefit of the doubt to established legitimate authorities in state, school and church, when these are in conflict with the desires of individuals. At the same time, they wish individuals to take more responsibility for providing for themselves and their families. They believe that rewards should be commensurate with effort.

Although they espouse the values of individualistic liberalism, i.e. the values of individual effort in work and the opportunities to gain the rewards of that effort, they would also restore to the family and church their previously esteemed positions. They would give more responsibilities to local and regional governments and would reduce the powers of central government. Yet they would maintain and strengthen the nation, that amorphous and inclusive society-wide collectivity, the most comprehensive consensus-bearing frame of all other individual and collective activities. They would therefore nurture patriotism, or at least not deride it.

This restoration of individualistic liberalism, in combination with the more traditional communal values of patriotism and authority of family and church, has been successful in electing governments that are in principle committed to such values. Nevertheless, it has not succeeded in restoring the patterns of society that were dominant in Western societies in Max Weber's lifetime.

III

Several other very great changes have occurred since Max Weber's lifetime. One is the establishment of so many new sovereign states in Asia and Africa, in what were former colonies of the Western societies that were the central focus of Max Weber's interests. The formation of the new states of Asia and Africa in the formerly colonial territories is one of the most prominent features of the world since Max Weber's lifetime. They are the creation of the influence of nationalism in the colonial territories and represent a changed attitude towards the paraphernalia of the powerful national state in the Western liberal-democratic societies.

The growth of colonial nationalism is very much a product of the experience and the culture of Western societies. Both the idea of a national society and the demand for its congruence with a sovereign state, although foreshadowed in Antiquity and the Middle Ages, came to prominence in Asia in the 1930s and in Africa in the 1940s and 1950s. By 1985, the 'process of decolonization' was practically complete. The aspirants to sovereignty and the rulers who executed it were not willing to reinstate their pre-colonial condition. They wished to become 'modern' almost in the style of the societies analysed by Max Weber as specifically Western. They wanted a rational bureaucratic state, rational scientific industrial technology, modern institutions such as armies, universities, hospitals. Since they arrived late on the historical scene, they absorbed social democratic and quasi-communist aspirations. Hence, they desired economic planning rather than the market. Although they usually began with the desire for political democracy, parliamentary government, the rule of law, competitive elections with a plurality of political parties, freedom of expression and the rest of the panoply of political democracy, these concepts were the first victims of the hard life of self-government. In very many of these countries, civilian governments moved towards the one-party state: first civilian, then military. In some of the new states, the changes in regimes are rapid. Coups d'état in Black Africa have become as characteristic of the regimes there as they became in Latin America after those societies gained sovereignty about a century earlier. These changes in regimes were frequently justified by the newly ensconced rulers as necessitated by the urgent, all-overriding aim of economic development through the mobilization of all resources. The aim has not been realized except in those few states that have abstained from the temptations and pretences of a centrally planned economy. Although most of these states have increased their industrial and agricultural production, and have received considerable financial assistance from their former rulers and other Western societies and international organizations, their populations have grown more rapidly than their economies; their governments have expanded their bureaucracies and spent more than their resources. In consequence, inflation, corruption and resentment are rife on the part of those sections of the population who think that others are being disproportionately favoured by governmental policies. All disorder and misgovernment notwithstanding, in most of the new sovereign territories the standard of living has risen for the new middle class and a larger percentage of the population has become literate. Urbanization has not destroyed the traditional culture: it has, in some respects, intensified attachment to it; ethnic conflicts have become aggravated and sectionalism has grown more rapidly than civic orientation.

The other great change in the world since Max Weber died is the industrialization of East Asia and particularly of Japan. Japan was already acquiring some of the features of Western societies when Weber was still alive: rationalized legal codes, newspapers, universities, rationalized military and economic organizations. But after 1920, and particularly after the Second World War, Japan adopted and developed much more of the pattern of modern Western societies, except in the traditionalism of its religious beliefs and practices — although here, too, secularization has made much progress — and in the greater reverence for authority.

The third major change since Max Weber's time is the establishment of dictatorial and totalitarian communist regimes in territories of the Russian and Chinese empires. Although both the Soviet Union and the People's Republic of China are very inimical towards Western liberal-democratic societies, and are particularly hostile towards the capitalist economies of the West, they both seek to promote the rational scientific technology of the West by reproducing it or purchasing it. They emulate the Western objects of their aggressive attitudes, claiming to have overcome illiteracy by universal education; they are emphatically secularized; they would extirpate the traditional culture; they are, at least in declaration, wholly scientific in their view of the world. Like the impoverished, disorganized and disorderly new states of Asia and Africa, the ideals which their elites allege to pursue are drawn from what they regard as the major features of modern Western societies. Although, in their political arrangements, they depart most widely from the pattern of those societies, they claim none the less to be democratic! Non-Western societies have, by and large, changed very much since Max Weber's lifetime; their changes have been engendered mainly through their ambition to become like Western societies.

Much of the modern Western society, of which Max Weber was the great analyst, has continued to exist: the belief in the necessity of economy and efficiency, the belief in the value of scientific knowledge and scientific technology, the belief that rewards should be commensurate with achievements, the belief that citizenship confers prerogatives which are not to be granted to non-residents living within the same national territory. These beliefs, somewhat eroded, and with some ebbing and rising, have many adherents, and even those who reject them do not do so wholeheartedly. Patriotism still persists, as do nationality and nationalism. Private enterprise oriented towards profit in a competitive market also still exists, quite vigorously. Religious belief still exists, as do believing priests and ministers, and believing laymen. The Western world is far from wholly secularized. Deference towards authority still exists, as does obedience to the commands of authority. The attitudes and institutions that have taken shape in the sixty-five years since the death of Max Weber, and particularly in the forty years since the end of the Second World War, have not by any means completely replaced the institutions and attitudes that prevailed earlier. Nevertheless, despite similarities and continuities, real changes in those societies have occurred. They are for the most part extensions and unfoldings of traditions already present in Max Weber's lifetime. Nothing has sprung into life by a disjunctive mutation. None the less, the unfolding from a state of potentiality in a tradition is different from that same tradition when what was potential had still not become unfolded. (The formation in Asia and Africa and Eastern Europe of societies possessing some of the features of modern Western societies, or at least striving to do so, has not occurred in consequence of the unfolding of indigenous traditions.) The question that I wish to put is: are Max Weber's ideas, as we can construct them from his writings, adequate or helpful to understand the world of Western – and non-Western – societies, as it has taken shape since his time?

V

In one respect, Max Weber's account of the society of his time remains more pertinent to the societies of our time than it was in that earlier phase of modern societies. This is his idea of the preponderance, the central importance, of bureaucracy. Max Weber was not the first to see this in its most general outlines. Alexis de Tocqueville, in the second volume of *De la Démocratie en Amerique*, published in 1840, had pointed out the unceasing progress of the regulatory power of central government. Max Weber gave a more refined analysis of the character of bureaucratic administration than Tocqueville or any other writer before or since. Our depiction and understanding of the present could not begin without Max Weber's account of bureaucracy as the characteristic mode of administration of a government legitimated, in his terminology, on rational-legal grounds.

Max Weber thought that bureaucracy would triumph over all other alternative types of administration because it was the most efficient. He thought that a bureaucracy could consolidate itself in power because it possessed expert knowledge and, because it could withhold that knowledge, it could gain the upper hand over the legislature. He thought that once a bureaucracy became dominant in a government it could not be dislodged from its position except by charismatic leadership on the part of the elected politicians. He did not, however, say just how this process of overpowering the stronghold of a bureaucracy by charismatic politicians would be effected. His account of why bureaucratic authority would be difficult to dislodge is still valid; his argument that a charismatic political leader can reverse the directions in which bureaucracy presses remains plausible. But the evidence for it is scanty, indeed for the very reason that bureaucrats have such tenacious resistive power, and not many politicians can overcome it. The experience of the Reagan administration in the United States and the Thatcher administration in Great Britain are instances of the difficulties experienced by powerful elected politicians in resisting and setting aside the power of the bureaucracy.

In his admiration for the efficacy of bureaucracies, Max Weber did not consider the possibility that a bureaucracy, expanded to such an extent in size and in the complexity and numbers of its tasks as bureaucracies have been in these past six and a half decades, might not be able to act successfully. The complexity of the tasks delegated to it and arrogated by it and the multiplicity of the interconnections of those tasks, as well as an illusionary faith in its capacity to carry out every task and any sets of tasks, have in fact resulted in many failures of bureaucracies to cope effectively with the tasks that they have undertaken. It is true that they do more than has ever been done before, but they often fall far short of their own objectives, which sometimes are not only not fulfilled but are in fact turned into results very different and frequently contrary to what has been sought.

What Max Weber had to say about bureaucracy obviously does not present an adequate account of the growth, vicissitudes, triumphs and failures of bureaucracy since his death. Nevertheless, he, more than any other writer of his own age and probably since, compelled observers to perceive the bureaucratic component of modern societies. His picture of the structure and the consequences — failures and repercussions — and the problems of controlling its growth and action are in need of revision, but only revision and not rejection.

According to Max Weber, the continuous expansion of rationalization was a major feature of modern society; bureaucratization is only one manifestation of this process. Rationalization is a process that takes many forms. It is operative in the organization of civil government and of armies; it is operative in economic life. It is no less present in the effort to understand the world by empirical scientific research and by systematic speculation; it is present in the organization of education and scientific research. It is certainly present in the organization of the media of mass communication as well as in the publication of literary and scientific works.

It is no less present in the substance of intellectual activities, above all in the study of nature, man and society. Here also Max Weber's analysis presents a fruitful approach to the understanding of modern societies, both Western and non-Western. One of Max Weber's most persisting observations about modern Western societies was his view that they had become *entzaubert*. Taken literally, *Entzauberung* is the denial of the validity of propositions asserting the existence of the powers that are dealt with by magical techniques; in that sense, it does not include spiritual forces that are not manipulated by magical techniques. In fact, however, Max Weber regarded the *Entzauberung der Welt* as the elimination of both magical and spiritual forces from the picture of the world; he regarded the refusal to acknowledge these powers as a culmination of one current of the process of rationalization. Other writers, less melodramatically and with less insight into its constitution and its affinity with other movements of belief and practice, have called this process 'secularization'. The process of *Entzauberung* was not complete in Max Weber's time but, discerning its steady expansion in the development of Western theological thought and, in modern times, in the various spheres of social life, Weber seems to have thought that, in the course of time, the eradication of belief in magical and spiritual forces would be complete.

Max Weber was not the first to anticipate such a development. It had been both a factual prediction and a desideratum for Condorcet; Comte took for granted that it would occur in the course of the nineteenth century or shortly thereafter, once the 'positive' method found universal acceptance. Since most of the important sociologists of the nineteenth and twentieth centuries were not believers in the existence of magical and spiritual forces, and since they believed that the prospectively dominant and already visible trend of opinion in the most 'progressive' societies was the increasingly unencumbered expansion of the dominion of reason and sense-experience, they anticipated a totally secular society, a society without religious beliefs. The expectation of a wholly secular future was, thus, not a discovery of Max Weber. His originality consisted in placing the secularization of belief in the wider setting of the rationalization of practically all spheres of life. He was not really consistent when he left open the possibility of a recursion to less secularized beliefs. His profundity consisted, however, in his assertion that the secularization of the world must inevitably leave unanswered the question concerning the meaning of cosmic and earthly existence. The ultimate meaninglessness of the world for those who believe that scientific knowledge is the only valid kind of knowledge was stressed in 'Science as a vocation'; he had already intimated that at the end of the *Protestant Ethic*, but he said nothing about the lasting and universal predominance of a view of the world that left that question unanswered.

Weber gave much attention to theodicy in the world religions: that is, to their efforts to provide a rational justification for the anomaly of the prosperity of the wicked on earth and the sufferings of the good. He is strikingly silent on the position of theodicy in the secularized rationalization of beliefs in his own time; he suggested that its place had been taken, in the outlook of the modern working man, by a naturalistic view of the world, which interpreted the anomalous injustices of the world as the products of a historically changing, economically determined social system. A belief in the rightfulness of a regime of equality in this world could be interpreted as a secular rectification of the anomalous injustice, which a transcendental theodicy placed in the next world.

Whether Max Weber thought of modern egalitarianism in this way cannot be asserted with confidence because he dealt very little with sacred beliefs, and such surrogates as they might have, in the modern society pervaded by *Entzauberung*.

Weber either thought that rather contradictory tendencies would be at work or else he had contradictory views. On the one side, there were religious dispositions, needs for redemption, purification, needs for explaining the meaning of the world, needs for rectifying the injustice that was generated by the evil of this world. On the other side, there was a naturalistic outlook, partly a product of the scientific rationalization of the world, partly a product of religious insensitivity and of the experience of coping effectively with the biological and ecological necessities of individual and collective survival in this world. Max Weber did not deal explicitly with the balance of these two tendencies in the modern world and, hence, it cannot be said that the period which followed his lifetime has confirmed or invalidated his view, since his own beliefs in this matter are obscure.

The fact remains, however, that the rationalization of the world has not by any means taken complete possession of the whole of any Western society. There are still many Christians in Protestant countries; there is an even larger proportion of observant Christians in the Southern European Latin countries and in North America. Among those who call themselves non-believers, many adhere to fragments of traditional Christian belief; many ostensible non-believers have recourse to traditional Christian ceremonials for christening, marriage and burial. Furthermore, charismatic religious enthusiasm thrives in most Western societies, not only among the less educated but among the more highly educated as well. It is perhaps even more common now than it was sixty years ago, although it was not rare then, especially in Protestant countries. The churches as institutions now have fewer prerogatives in the non-ecclesiastical sphere, but the activities of churchmen in that sphere are numerous and not wholly without influence among the many competitors for the attention of the public. There are probably no countries in the West today where secularized politicians think that they may disregard the views of the leading churchmen. The *Entzauberung der Welt* is far from complete in the sphere of religious beliefs. Despite Weber's apparent conviction about the drive towards *Entzauberung*, much of his discussion of the grounds of religious belief throws light on the recalcitrance of religious belief in the face of this movement of *Entzauberung*.

In non-Western countries, where the process of secularization never advanced as far as it has in the West, there has been a traditionalistic resurgence of religious beliefs. This has been especially true of the Islamic societies. This is a subject with which Max Weber did not deal. It goes without saying that he did not write about the syncretistic religious movements in Black Africa. Yet in both cases an approximation to understanding is afforded by his discussions of the Israelitic prophecy and his observations about salvational religions.

Science is a body of knowledge that corresponds most closely to the ideal type of rationalization. That is the way in which Max Weber saw it. Nevertheless, the entire body of scientific knowledge has never been wholly rationalized into a single unitary system. Such a unitary system of knowledge is, however, a postulate of scientific explanation; the growth of scientific knowledge is in part a subsumption of particular observations under more general, more abstract propositions. The now very numerous profession of science has for a long time been inclined to think that, in the course of time, a wholly rationalized account of the universe and of human existence will be produced; many non-scientists believe the same. They also believe that this rationalized body of scientific knowledge will also provide valid criteria of ethical judgement as well. These views are shared by many laymen.

Max Weber did no more than touch on the social and cultural consequences of the belief in the rationalizability of the world. He criticized the scientific position when he assessed the power of social-scientific knowledge to arrive at evaluative judgements, both political and moral; he criticized scientism more profoundly when he pointed out the incapacity of scientific knowledge to disclose the ultimate meaning of life and the ultimate criteria of choice in practical action. A realistic account of the world as we know it would require that the consequences of scientism for modern society and culture be reckoned with. It would have been consistent with Max Weber's views about modern Western society and culture to have observed this spread of scientism and to have discussed the relationship between bureaucratization and scientism. He did not do so, but what he did do, in fact, opened the possibility of our identification and understanding of the belief in scientific solutions to moral and political problems.

It should also be pointed out that belief in the ultimate scientific rationalization of the world has not been universally shared in modern Western societies, even by scientists whose thought was taken by Max Weber to be the prototypical rationalization of symbolic configurations. There have always been scientists who have not shared the scientistic view and, in recent years, many scientists have lost their confidence in the rationalizability of the universe by scientific discovery. Some assert the complementarity of religious faith – most often, Christian religious faith – and scientific knowledge. Others speak more vaguely of the 'two spheres', the conflict-less and separate existences of faith and science. 'Values' are repeatedly emphasized in the non-scientific discourse of scientists addressing laymen. The scientific rationalization of the world has many supporters, but there are also many who do not regard it as having been achieved in the present or likely to be achieved in the future.

Thus, the belief in the ultimate scientific rationalization of the world view might have lost some of its adherents in recent decades. At the same time, the belief in the desirability of the rationalization of the management and strategy of enterprises in industry and agriculture, and particularly of governments, has continued to gain adherents in the period under consideration. (Max Weber himself, with some qualifications, could be counted among these adherents.)

The promotion of the study of the social sciences and the support of social research (although it is partly prompted out of the social scientists' desire for rational understanding, i.e. the cognitive rationalization, of the real world) is supported by its patrons mainly because they think that it will help to 'solve social problems'. Earlier in the present century, it was thought that the 'solution' would lie in making the problematic sectors of society subject to 'rational self-control'; now it is thought to lie in the rational rearrangement of institutions and governmental practices. A large part of the history of modern social science is to be understood as one element in the hope of rationalizing society, both cognitively and practically. This is largely a matter of aspiration; the realization inevitably lags considerably behind.

Max Weber's effort to understand the world sociologically was part and parcel of that process of intellectual rationalization. He also went to some pains, in his essay on *Wertfreiheit*, to show what social science could contribute to the rationalization of decisions about practical social matters; he thought that, at least in principle, it could throw light on the costs of carrying out practical decisions; it could clarify, i.e. make more rational, the analysis of objectives, the means of achieving them and the consequence of using those means. His own attempts to understand the intellectual and practical potentialities of social science, despite vast changes in the scale and technical sophistication of social research, continues to provide the best point of departure for the analysis of the relationship between social science and social policy.

Weber's belief in the possibility and necessity of the scientific rationalization of society and the effort to apply it in practice is a ramification of his conception of bureaucratization. Rationalized bureaucratic practices and the application of scientific knowledge now affect larger proportions of the population than they did in Max Weber's time, and they affect them in more departments of their existence. This, too, is in accord with Max Weber's analysis; indeed he did in fact predict this expansion. They were not predicted in a particular form by Max Weber, but they are intelligible only in the setting of his analysis. Likewise, the developments in econometrics, systems-analysis, social psychology and 'management-science' were unforeseen in their particulars by Max Weber, but their application can best be understood in accordance with his view about the continuing rationalization, i.e. bureaucratization, of modern societies. None the less, the scope and penetration of bureaucratization are far greater now than they were in Max Weber's lifetime. Moreover, the aspiration to increase the rationalization of society is, if not more intense, then at least unabated. Our understanding of these changes, at least descriptively, has been rendered possible by the prior absorption of Max Weber's ideas. The fact that we raise these questions about the degree of rationalization means that we are putting questions and proffering answers to them that have been made possible by Max Weber's own questions, although he did not describe the situations that we now see.

The cognitive and moral disenchantment of the world has, it is true, not gone as far as the rationalization of the organization and management of corporate bodies and the state itself. That too is incomplete. Even though Max Weber's anticipation of the 'disenchantment of the world' has not been realized, our assessment of the limitations of his view could not be rendered without our acceptance of the categories within which he interpreted the world, and within his setting of the problem. In fact, our grasp of the limitations of the process of disenchantment draws on Weber's own elaboration of the conception of charisma and his subsequent analysis of the range of variation of charismatic qualities, between attenuated and intense and between the dispersed and the concentrated distributions of charismatic qualities.

The concept of charisma is a necessary logical presupposition of the analysis of situations in which it is extremely attenuated; Max Weber's idea of routinized charisma was a step towards this further analysis.

Many years ago, I undertook, in the course of an examination of the economic policies of the poor, in recently colonial countries, to try to understand why the political leaders and the higher civil servants in these countries believed that they alone could provide the initiative for the economic improvement of their countries. My knowledge of this matter was not a direct result of applying Max Weber's ideas about charisma; that idea came to me only while I was delivering an address to an academic society about economic policy and public opinion in underdeveloped countries. The idea came to me as I was reading my paper, which contained no reference to charismatic authority. Suddenly, in the course of delivery, the pattern of my thought about the making of economic policy changed; I formulated a distinction between 'concentrated' and 'dispersed' charismatic qualities. (Later, I added the distinction between 'intense' and 'attenuated' charismatic qualities.) It turned out to be illuminating to extend the idea of charismatic authority to the beliefs that educated higher civil servants and leading politicians held and to the contrast that they saw between their own capacities and those of the rest of the members of their own societies. It could be said that the distinctions which I then formulated were already implicitly contained in Max Weber's work; that might be true, but only in the sense that Weber himself employed the distinctions in reference to particular situations, without making them explicit. Once made, the potentiality of extension – the extensibility of the idea – was realized.

The idea of attenuated charisma was implicit in the concept of charismatic authority as it was formulated by Max Weber, although he himself did not formulate such an idea. The idea of attenuated charisma permits a richer analysis of Weber's ideas about charisma and the *Entzauberung der Welt*, while at the same time enabling us to recognize the limitations of his original formulation of the idea of *Entzauberung*.

The concept of rationalization is similarly extensible. It is valuable for the assessment of the extent to which rationalization has in fact occurred, but it is also valuable for the analysis of situations in which the prospect of ceaselessly advancing rationalization has fallen short and seems bound to fall short of the extreme possibility implied by Max Weber. It puts problems to us regarding an inherent tendency towards self-annulment in the process of rationalization. The further it advances, the more likely its frustration. Max Weber did not discuss such questions directly, except in some passages regarding the limits of the formal rationalization of the legal system, arising from demands for substantive rationality. But he turned our attention to the extension of rationalization, and this itself raised questions about possible causes of its breakdown.

Max Weber was a liberal in the sense that he viewed with abhorrence the growing power of the state at the cost of the freedom of the individual. He was also an unsentimental supporter of the rudimentary welfare state as it existed in Germany in his time, although his grounds for giving support had more to do with its contribution to national solidarity and national strength than they had to do with humanitarian principles or sentiments. Weber was also a democrat, but again with a difference: he was not a democrat because he believed in the rights of man or in popular sovereignty – in fact he derided such ideas – but because he thought that representative institutions are the best of possible arrangements for training and selecting the political leadership which any national society needs to keep its position in the larger competitive world of national societies and to protect the freedom of creative individuals from the constriction of conformity imposed by a powerful bureaucracy. He was far from a 'grass-roots democrat'. Not only did he have no sympathy with the idea of popular sovereignty, he regarded its realization as plainly impossible. Max Weber believed in the possibility, under modern conditions, of mass democracy – a system of political parties competing for the support of an electorate defined by universal suffrage and then forming a government on the basis of the support given to one of the parties by a majority of the electorate.

Weber did not say why democracy was necessary 'under modern conditions'. Tocqueville explicitly acknowledged and described the irresistible, onward flow of greater 'equality of condition'. Weber did not speak in those terms. He did not sympathize with theories of the 'rights of man'; he was far from a sentimental exponent of the virtues of the laborious poor; he expressed his contempt for policies concerned to eradicate the misery of the poor, which he disparaged as *Miseribilismus*. His acceptance of democracy probably was inspired by his belief in the value of the national state and of national culture; his democracy probably derived from his nationalism. He thought that the national state could be effective in the world if it were based on a coherent national society and that such a society depended on the attachment of all classes to it. The national society had to incorporate the lower classes, who otherwise would be alienated from it and hostile to it. Because of the large populations of modern societies, democracy had to be 'mass democracy'. The power of the mass of the electorate was confined, in this view, to a retroactive assessment of what the politicians in office had done and to voting for their retention in or dismissal from office. The only power of the electorate is the power exercised through voting; it has no substantive demands that a politician in office or contending for office must heed, satisfy or distract. 'Mass democracy', Weber thought, could work only under the control of 'party-machines' and of charismatic leaders. The electorate could initiate nothing, it could only respond to leaders selected by 'party-bosses' or by the competition of outstanding individual politicians formed through and brought forward in the electoral and parliamentary struggle. The notion of an electorate that was an effective power with substantive demands of its own and which did more than merely ratify or approve the actions of the political elite was not conceived by him to be possible; certainly it was most unlikely. The idea of politicians quailing before reports of public opinion polls or trimming their sails to gain a few additional percentage points in such a poll, and of calculating their actions to satisfy the specific demands of particular blocs within the electorate had little place in his analysis of political democracy in modern Western societies. To think that political democracy could work in that way would have appeared to him to be the fantasy of sentimental populists and of unrealistically idealistic democrats. His studies of Russian and American politics made him very aware of populism, but he thought that populistic politicians were either sentimental, self-deceiving idealists or demagogues who flattered their audiences.

This was an important gap in Max Weber's views about political systems. A demanding electorate and politicians attentive to its demands were omitted from Max Weber's ideas about modern society. They are features of modern Western society that Max Weber's ideas did not really comprehend. The mass of the electorate is probably not as rational in the perception and pursuit of its own advantage as some theorists of democracy have believed it is, although the possibility should not be wholly dismissed. Nor is the electorate as concerned for the common good as some theorists have thought, although this possibility too should not be completely dismissed. However these things may be, the mass of the electorate, in modern Western societies, especially since the Second World War, is certainly demanding of benefits from its governments and its political leaders. Once the mass of the population became aware of the substantial benefits which it could receive from governments, its demands on government increased. The possibility that this could happen was never articulated by Max Weber.

Is there anything in the body of Max Weber's thought that could help us to fill this gap? I think that Max Weber's own ideas, if extended, contain in a fruitful potentiality the ideas needed to correct his own too limited view of the working of present-day political democracy. It seems to me that the extension of Weber's ideas about charismatic authority does offer such help in the task of attempting to explain the increase in self-assertiveness and demands of the mass of the population in Western societies in the present century. The ordinary man in these societies has increasingly come to believe himself to possess those attributes or qualities that entitle him to the deference of others and to the goods and services related to the enhancement of status that he demands. This does not, of course, explain why the dispersion of beliefs about one's possession of charismatic qualities has occurred so pronouncedly in the last three decades, and why it was so slow to emerge in Germany in Weber's time that he failed to observe it in its embryonic manifestations. (In concrete observation, Max Weber did see this phenomenon as early as 1895 in his inaugural lecture at Freiburg on 'The national state and economic policy'.[1])

Although Weber did not examine the belief in 'human rights' and in the dignity of all human beings as a force in conduct, he was well aware that the German working man had a sense of his own dignity that he wished to be acknowledged in German society. The trade unions and the Social Democratic Party were the beneficiaries of that aspiration to dignity. In his discussion of social classes and status groups (no more than a few notes) Weber does not assert any connection between the granting of deference and the acknowledgement of charismatic qualities. Nor does he treat it in his often very sharp observation of citizenship in modern societies. Yet, to make explicit and to emphasize that implied link not only makes Weber's analysis more coherent but it also deepens the discussion of modern political democracy in a way that Weber failed to do himself.

There is another important deficiency in Max Weber's writings, namely, his rather narrow treatment of the grounds for the increase in the power of governmental bureaucracy. Weber thought that bureaucracy became established mainly because rulers saw that it was more efficient and more economical in the use of scarce resources than other types of administration, and that it freed them as rulers from dependence on personal clients and vassals or great landowners, who were their rivals in the struggle for power in their realm. These explanations are sound historically, but they do not contribute much to the explanation of the bureaucratization of governmental administration in the nineteenth and twentieth centuries. It certainly does not explain the great expansion in the size and powers of governmental bureaucracies in the period since Weber's death.

Max Weber also spoke of bureaucratization as one manifestation of a deeper drive towards rationalization, which was integral to Western civilization. More important was his statement that bureaucratization became imperative as the tasks assumed by governments became more elaborate, required more expert knowledge and skill, more probity and more efficiency. This is true, but why did the bureaucracy and the politicians accept such elaborate and far-reaching tasks and so many of them that the size and the powers of the civil services had to be so greatly increased?

It is at this point that Max Weber's failure to foresee the demands of electorates also carried with it a failure to explain the growth of the bureaucratic authority of government over society as a whole.

It is also at this point that we can see the ways in which certain fundamental ideas, which are implicitly contained in Weber's writings, can serve to correct the deficiencies of what is explicitly stated in them. Weber did not see that some of the impulsion for this drive towards the expansion of the power of central government comes from the electorate working through the legislative branch. Bureaucrats usually do not simply seize power against the will of other parts of the government and against the will of the electorate. It is true that they hold firmly to and try to expand any authority that is conferred on them, but it should not be overlooked that the authority that they have exercised increasingly over society has been conferred on them by actions of the legislature. These actions are impelled partly by the legislature's acceptance of current beliefs about the moral responsibilities and capacities of governments and partly by their desire to conform to the wishes of the more pressing sectors of the electorate, which share these current beliefs. The motive force is the electorate's demands for goods and services to which it thinks itself entitled and the politicians' competition for the suffrage of the electorate. Here, as elsewhere, the correction that I would add is not intended as a refutation of Weber's views but rather as an extension of his fundamental, enduringly valid insight into the characteristics of modern societies. As in so many other sides of an assessment of the relevance of Max Weber's ideas to the understanding of modern societies, his shortcomings can often be corrected by the extension of some of his more basic ideas.

In this review of the fittingness of some of Max Weber's ideas for the understanding of important developments in the Western world that have arisen in the sixty-five years since his death, I should also say something about the hedonism and 'emancipationism', i.e. emancipation of impulse from the restraints of reason, convention, institutional rules and tradition, which seem to have displaced in some measure the Protestant ethic. The drive toward the rationalization of economic activity was derived by Max Weber from 'the Protestant ethic', that body of normative beliefs arising from the urgent yearning for certainty of eternal salvation, which was the tradition received by various Puritan sects from Calvinism. It was from this source that, according to Max Weber, much of the motivating force for capitalistic enterprise had sprung; it was to be found in the Puritanical attitude towards work as well as in entrepreneurial initiatives.

The sense of obligation in the individual to work steadily and efficiently at a calling and the rationalized discipline of all his activity in the service of an end higher and more remote than immediate sensual gratification represented for Max Weber the most characteristic and unique feature of modern Western societies. Max Weber thought that this Protestant ethic was already in an advanced state of attenuation in his own lifetime; it was with reference to this attenuation that he spoke of the uninspired continuation of the process of rationalization that threatened to lead the world into a rationalized subjugation to bureaucracy – another facet of the comprehension of *Entzauberung* that would penetrate into every sphere of life.

Weber did not anticipate the stagnation or the disruption of the movement towards rationalization, even though it had lost its most powerful motive-force. The process of rationalization, with all the discipline which it entailed, would, he thought, continue; but it would have no meaning without the theological foundation which the progress of *Entzauberung* was undermining. It is certainly true that rationalization continues in institutions and in the quest for scientific knowledge. There are still many individuals to whom rationalization is a good in itself, or who expect substantial improvement from it in economic organization and in the pursuit of truth through scientific research.

In the conduct of individuals outside organizational and scientific activities, however, the self-discipline and the acceptance of external discipline that were manifested respectively in the 'Protestant ethic' and in the 'spirit of capitalism' have lost much although not all of their force. Emancipation from external and even from internal discipline is the condition that many persons nowadays regard as the right one. The elevation of the immediate gratification of impulse to the highest value certainly existed in Max Weber's time and he was well aware of it. He understood very well the new forms of romantic belief and sensibility at the turn of the century; he was well aware of the antinomic tendencies in modern literature and he was well acquainted with the culture of bohemianism to which he did not refer except in passing in his writings. (He referred contemptuously to *Literaten* but when he did so he did so with reference to the Utopian, doctrinaire or hypernationalistic political ideals of political publicists and literary men; he did not have in mind the 'liberation' of impulse, particularly erotic impulse, which was being so highly praised by certain Bohemian intellectuals whom he knew.) He apparently did not think that the Bohemian culture of the free expression of impulse would ever find a large following; he did not quite perceive the significance of what he disparaged as the desire to be a 'personality'.

Nevertheless, this has happened, and what was once the culture of a very small circle within a generally self-disciplined society – or one which at least justified the principle of self-discipline in pursuit of careers and in familial and sexual relations – has now become much more widespread in most Western societies than it was in his time. In part, this could be deduced – after the fact – from Max Weber's views about the decay of the Protestant ethic, but it is also in certain respects antithetical to his ideas about the unceasingness of the process of rationalization.

Max Weber's writings on religion are full of penetrating remarks about orgiastic and mystical religiosity which breaks through or circumvents institutional religious practice and traditionally set religious beliefs. He also defined a basic category of individual action which he called 'affectual'. Yet, in the rest of his writings, he did not anticipate these phenomena consequent on the evaporation of the Puritanical motive underlying the movement of rationalization. Throughout his writings, sensual gratification and impulse-dominated conduct are regarded as overwhelmed by conduct directed by individual or group 'interest' (meaning the desire for pecuniary benefits and advantages of power and deference) and by beliefs, mainly traditional, in the validity of certain norms or rules.

Weber was well aware that actions to gratify affective impulse and to enjoy sensual pleasures existed and could never be expunged from human life, but he seems to have thought that they were not likely to be very widely practised in any society. He was probably more right than wrong in this view. Human beings can never become exclusively biological organisms, orienting their actions primarily towards biological gratifications. Nevertheless, such an idea has nowadays considerably more adherence in principle and in practice than it had in Max Weber's time; more individuals think that the gratification of impulse and the experience of emotions are of the highest importance. This is in one respect a by-product of the *Entzauberung der Welt*, but it is also a consequence of the relocation of the site of charisma. Max Weber's failure to attribute more importance in his writings to this element indeed presents a shortcoming in any literal application of his ideas to the world since 1920. Its correction entails, however, only an extension of some of his ideas and an elaboration of their potentialities. In a perverse way, contemporary emancipationism is a manifestation of the dispersion of charisma; it is a manifestation of the phenomenon to which Weber himself alluded in his understanding of those sects of extreme Protestantism that insisted that all individuals have within themselves a spark of divinity.

Max Weber, sympathetic though he was towards the industrial working classes, often although not always thought of the lower classes — the working and clerical classes — as rather amorphous, uninspired aggregations, except in times of crises when their charismatic receptiveness and their attractability by charismatic initiative were heightened. He thought that Puritanism had stirred, maintained and disciplined this sensitivity. None the less, apart from this moment of creativity, the lower classes seemed to him to be singularly unproductive. Intellectuals, priests, prophets, charismatic persons were required, if they were to be animated; otherwise, they were only capable of responding, they could not initiate. There is undoubtedly some truth in this view, but it is like some of Weber's other ideas, which require correction if we are to understand this most recent age.

It certainly would be too much to say that the lower classes have become creative in the sixty-five years since Max Weber's death, but they have certainly become less inert and less confined to reacting to external situations. They make more 'demands on life' now than they did formerly and this involves more demands on persons in positions of authority. The demands might be said to be largely for the enhancement of their material advantages — 'interests' as the current idiom has it — but they are also demands with moral or ideal content. Even what they regard as the objects of their 'interests' are things that they think they are morally entitled to have. They feel more justification for making these demands; suffrage is for them not merely a way of selecting leaders but of communicating, in however blurred and inchoate a manner, an indication to those leaders of what they want from them and of what they are 'entitled' to, by virtue of their dignity as citizens and human beings. Modern democracy, for better or worse, is a phenomenon of the dispersion of charisma. Weber intimated as much in his occasional remarks, but he did not do so in his main sociological writings. The failure to state this explicitly, and to incorporate it into his analysis of social stratification, is one of the shortcomings of Max Weber's work. The correction of this failure is made possible, here as elsewhere, by the opening up of the potentialities of some of his own ideas.

VI

Finally, I wish to refer to the applicability of Max Weber's ideas to the new states of Asia and Africa. Max Weber's beliefs did not foresee the end of the European empires in Asia and Africa. Weber did not interest himself in colonial societies; there are practically no references to modern Indian society in *Hinduismus und Buddhismus*. He was certainly acutely aware of 'imperialism' and his brief discussion of the subject is full of shrewd and illuminating observations. But on the societies subjugated by imperialism he is practically silent.

Max Weber regarded it as in the nature of things for 'great powers' to be expansive as a condition for 'holding their own' in the universal struggle for existence. Expansion entailed – at least in most cases – colonies. He accepted the existence of colonies, although he thought imperial Germany had come too late upon the scene to acquire colonies. Colonies were not as central to Max Weber's sociological ideas as rationality, and it is not surprising, therefore, that he did not give much attention to social developments in colonial societies.

Nevertheless, it is not unreasonable to raise the question of whether we can find in his writing ideas that are fruitfully applicable to the understanding of the course of events in the new states of Asia and Africa. There are a few instances where the conception of charismatic authority is directly applicable: for example, in the cases of some of the great figures of the movements for independence such as Gandhi, Soekarno, Nkrumah, Ho Chi Minh. The tension between the charismatic leader and the bureaucratic party-machine needed for the organization of the movement and then for the ruling of the new state may also be interpreted directly in his terms. Apart from these instances, his writings are silent. Nevertheless, as in the analysis of the developments in Western societies after 1920, many clues to understanding can be derived from his fundamental ideas.

The most important of these clues come only from a considerable extension of Weber's explicitly stated ideas. Let us take as one example the ideals of the founders and the first leaders of the new states, particularly the idea of a unitary 'modern' society, bureaucratically administered, with popular elections to a representative legislative body, a planned or rationalized industrial economy with bureaucratic governmental control over agriculture, a bureaucratically organized army, the employment of scientific technology in industry and agriculture. Such ideas were not indigenous; they were acquired from models perceived, correctly or incorrectly, as practised in advanced societies such as the United States, Great Britain, France, Holland and the Soviet Union, which were the centres for the peripheral societies of Asia and Africa.

Now, the ideas of centre and periphery are not to be found in Max Weber's writings, neither in his analyses of the working of modern societies nor in his much scantier analyses of the relations between societies. Yet, the ideas of centre and periphery, as I have developed them in my own studies and as others have done since then, owe a great deal to the elaboration and extension of the idea of charisma. The instabilities of the new states, the weakness of their internal 'modern' centre, the strength of the primordial attachments of the lineages, tribes, ethnic and linguistic groups in these newly constituted states, which in many respects scarcely form national societies, become more intelligible to contemporary students of the subject through an amplification, which Max Weber did not envisage, of ideas contained in his writings.

VII

In these observations, which are intended to show that Max Weber's ideas still have value for the understanding of relative developments in Western liberal–democratic societies and in other societies outside the circle of modern Western societies, I have had no intention of vindicating Max Weber's standing as a sociological interpreter of the modern age. It is far from my desire to assert that all that Max Weber said is true or that all that needs to be done is to go on studying his texts and interpreting them. I do not intend to imply that there is a 'fundamental Weber' whose fundamental ideas have been misunderstood and distorted by those who have hitherto studied his writings. There are many features of Western and especially non-Western societies as they have developed since 1920 for which Max Weber's ideas do not provide any illumination. I think here, for example, of the Holocaust of European Jewry by the National Socialist regime, but there are others. There are also other features of these societies about which Weber's ideas were simply not correct; I think here of the limits on the capacities of bureaucracies to carry out any policies which are assigned to them or which they arrogate to themselves.

Nevertheless, it has seemed clear to me that there is more in Max Weber's ideas than what he formulated explicitly, and that what is below the surface of his texts contains possibilities for understanding the world as it is which are richer than what is on the surface in the text. This does not mean that any effort to study modern societies must begin with an exegesis on Weber's writings. On the contrary, all that I am recommending is that classics of the sort in which Weber's works are comprised should be read freely and not just exegetically. There is a place for exegesis in intellectual history, but not in sociological analysis. What I have tried to show in this paper, on the basis of my own experience with Max Weber's writings and my own studies, is that classics have a continuing intellectual value for understanding the world. They have a life beyond themselves.

Max Weber touched on the deepest elements of the existence of human societies. The elements he touched are of permanent importance. But these elements appear in human history in different forms and combinations. The elements themselves are difficult to define precisely; there are almost inevitable ambiguities. These ambiguities are sometimes obstacles to understanding and sometimes fruitful. Max Weber's ambiguities were more often fruitful than obstructive. They contained within themselves potentialities for extension to situations with respect to which they were not originally propounded. They are susceptible to reinterpretation, extension and above all correction; they have the great merit, because of their pregnancy, of permitting and even compelling these reinterpretations, extensions and corrections. That is why so many of Max Weber's ideas are still of living value for understanding a world that is, in so many ways, very different from the one in which he lived.

The very rough, very general portrayal of some of the chief features of the Western societies of the past sixty-five years, and the even sketchier references to non-Western societies which have been essayed here, and the no less un-refined assessment of the utility of Max Weber's ideas for the understanding of that society which he did not live to know, throw some light on the after-life − the *Nachleben* − of great works of social and political analysis. Their greatness, their standing as classics, consist not just in their simple and straightforward applicability to the historical situations that their authors themselves did not know, but in an application through interpretation which draws out ideas that were not originally and knowingly formulated in them.

It is in the nature of the subject-matter of political and social theory that it changes through time. It does not change in every respect. Societies remain societies bound by the compelling necessities that are inherent in the nature of human beings and the societies that are formed from them. No two situations are identical and no society remains the same through time. The quality that constitutes a classic of social and political analysis is its pertinence to the understanding of the unforeseen societies that have grown out of antecedent societies.

The analytical process or the logical structure of the drawing out of the potentialities of an idea is very obscure. This drawing out is done, even though it is very difficult to say how it is done. The value of an idea − not its only value − lies in its possession of such potentialities. Such potentialities cannot be foreseen by their authors. They can only be seen by those who, at a time, later than the time of their authorship, modified and adapted those ideas. Works that are constituted by such ideas are the classics in their fields. The classics are not merely historical monuments, fixed and settled forever. They must also be capable of a vital after-life through reinterpretation. Treated in this way, they are capable of directing thought on to unforeseen objects and to new tasks.

There are undoubtedly sociological questions of importance that Max Weber's ideas, whether in their literal form or in their potentiality − their unintended variant − cannot answer. That should be recognized. It should also be recognized that the labour of maintaining Max Weber's reputation is not a worthy activity. Max Weber's reputation does not need that vindication. There is no need for those who study Max Weber's works to adopt that protec-tive attitude, which devotees of Marx and Engels have often taken when they sought to vindicate the theory of surplus-value or the theory of increasing poverty or of relations between 'substructure' and 'superstructure'.

An intellectual tradition should not be regarded as sacrosanct. For those who live within it, as sociologists cannot avoid living within the tradition in which Max Weber is the greatest figure, the task must be to use it as well as it can be used. Its shortcomings must not be disregarded, but the fertility that it contains and the intellectual benefits that it offers to deeper understanding of the world — and not just of the text — should not be eschewed. Respect for a tradition should rest not just on the praise that it acquired in the past, but on its present merit as a point of departure for better understanding and deeper, more realistic knowledge.

Note: Chapter 36

1 In attempting to explain why German agricultural labourers were not willing to work as day-workers or seasonal workers on the large East Prussian estates, Weber referred to the conditions of work in the large estates in which there were only masters and drudges, who saw no prospect even for their remote descendants to do anything other than menial labour on some one else's land. 'This dim, largely unconscious glimpse into the future contains an element of primitive idealism. One who does not grasp this, does not know the magic of freedom.' Later, he says that it is 'one of the most primordial dispositions of the human heart' (GPS[4], p. 7)

37 Max Weber and Modern Social Science

RALF DAHRENDORF

At first sight, there is a look of *embarras de richesse* about the subject, Max Weber and modern social science. Is there any modern social science without Max Weber? He has been called an 'authority', a 'founder', even a 'law-giver'. The list of those who see themselves in the succession of Max Weber is long and distinguished, the list of those who acknowledge some debt to the Weber tradition reads like a *Who's Who?* of social science.

This is worth noting, if only because the Weberians of the late twentieth century are in one respect very different from, say, the Hegelians of the mid-nineteenth century. The Hegelians, while more or less grudgingly admitting their debt to the great master, felt oppressed by his shadow, unable to step out into the light of new thought, and were thus mere epigones and, worse, the last epigones of philosophy because they believed that, after Hegel, there was little if anything to say. Not so our modern Weberians, who seem, on the contrary, to be happy epigones, eager to acknowledge their debt to the master, unworried by his shadow. In many ways, Weber is not seen as a source of shadows at all, but as a pervasive light that inspires social science.

The reason for the difference is simple. Hegel's was a closed system. Whoever entered it, had no way out. Even turning it upside down or, conversely, from the head, on which it was standing, on to its feet, betrayed the commitment. The end of history was nigh; if it had not arrived already, it only required another revolution of the wheel of time. Max Weber certainly does not proffer a closed system. Whoever enters the world of his thought remains free to choose a variety of subjects and approaches. Weber's methodology is far from one-dimensional. It is not simply neo-Kantian, let alone Popperian. But it is above all non-Hegelian. The commitment to Max Weber is never total. Weber's happy epigones are all eclectics, which is another way of saying that they are social scientists.

Using the term, social science, in this way clearly begs more questions than it answers. So be it. But one or two of these questions are useful keys to our subject. Why is it, for example, that the most dynamic and influential modern social science, economics, would not recognize a debt to Max Weber? After all, Weber began as an economist, and always remained a political economist. The German term, *Nationalökonomie*, describes even better one major source of Weber's work, unless we want to revive the strangely old-fashioned yet important notion used to describe the series in which that great quarry of ideas, *Economy and Society*, first appeared: socioeconomics, *Sozialökonomik*.

But modern economics has moved in quite different directions. Even welfare economists regard Max Weber as a sociologist, which is not intended to be a compliment. Modern economics has chosen several paths forward, none of which can sensibly be traced back to Max Weber. Economic theory has constructed a non-Euclidean world of assumptions, which are open for the Cartesian mechanics of Pareto but not for Weber's Germanic historical economics. What we now call, econometrics, is a complicated descriptive technique, of which Weber would have approved though he did not invent it. Applied economics, as the notion is understood today, owes more to Kenneth Arrow, and through him to the technicians of economic science, than to Weber's type of analysis.

Even the remnants of political economy, sparse and academically unrecognized as they often are, can hardly be called Weberian. Milton Friedman and Kenneth Galbraith have all kinds of godfathers, but Max Weber is not among them. The same could be said of Friedrich von Hayek and Gunnar Myrdal, whose joint Nobel Prize was in any case a bow, by the Committee, to a nearly extinct branch of economic thought. If there is any one man who has inspired the modern theory of economic policy, it is John Maynard Keynes, who is still rediscovered, re-interpreted, or rejected by the relatively few who make serious claims to the scholarly analysis of real economic problems.

One strand of work in which the institutional tradition of social and political economics has recently come to blossom again, would have been objectionable to Weber on methodological grounds. This is policy research, the attempt to apply the accumulated knowledge of socioeconomic processes to the issues and the time-scales that decision-makers encounter: what are the conditions of sustained growth here and now after two oil shocks and the interest rate explosion? How can we reduce the budget deficit quickly without unintended transfer effects for already disadvantaged groups? Here, the boundary between description and prescription, facts and values is systematically blurred. Small wonder, then, that the Brookings Institution and the American Enterprise Institute are not populated by Weberians.

More seriously still, the only major recent attempt to re-integrate economic analysis into a general social science, that by Talcott Parsons, has in this respect been a total failure. Economists have ignored Parsons's system, and other social scientists have largely ignored the economic aspects of his ambitious cartography of society. It could be argued that both have paid a price, not so much for ignoring Parsons as for discontinuing an intellectual tradition by which Weber was moulded, with so many of his contemporaries who are the subjects of this book. There is something dismal about economic science, much as other social scientists may admire the growth of an effective scientific community and the technical sophistication of journal articles and conference papers. It has become possible to apply general equilibrium theory to money without ever mentioning banks, or chancellors of the exchequer. There is correspondingly something lacking in a social science for which economic analysis has become residual if not expendable.

Indeed, what is left of social science, once socioeconomic macroanalysis is deducted, has characteristically been strongly influenced by another intellectual tradition alien to Max Weber. To call it psychological is perhaps a terrible simplification: it is concerned with the perceptions, motives and attitudes of individuals as individuals rather than as social actors or players of roles. When Parsons advanced his theory of social action, he could base his language on the 'basic concepts' in the early paragraphs of *Economy and Society*, but in fact he owed more to Freud and to that other strand of social thought which Jürgen Habermas has recently revived in his interpretation of George Herbert Mead. Adam Smith is dead, and it is clear who killed him and how. If one wants to identify a single perpetrator, it is Jean-Jacques Rousseau. The Rousseauan bent of modern social science is its single greatest weakness. At times, it appears that what we call social science is but the study of the sub-institutional realities of social life, with political economy forgotten or banned along with institutional social analysis.

What then is left of Max Weber, the authority, the founder, the law-giver? Economics has gone its own separate way, the psychological tradition was never Weberian; thus, we are talking after all about sociology in all its multifariousness and ambiguities. This includes, to be sure, segments and aspects of political science, of history and philosophy, and of numerous specialisms that go by the name of social science in contemporary universities. It is these more tenuous disciplines – undisciplined disciplines in many ways – which like to and perhaps need to invoke the hero, Max Weber. There are probably two main reasons why they find it tempting to do so.

The first is that not just *Economy and Society* but the whole of Weber's work can be described as a quarry. It is not only not Hegelian, but it is not a system in any sense of the term. To describe Weber's work as a mere assemblage of bits and pieces would clearly be unfair, but it is certainly possible for almost any author to pull out bits and pieces and use them to give authority to his own endeavours. The theory of action, the study of bureaucracy, the analysis of class and party, the sociology of religion, the empirical investigation of agricultural labour, the understanding of the role of universities are but some of dozens and dozens of examples. There will be no end of articles devoted to this or that aspect of Weber's work, or to this or that facet of the real world in the light of Weber's analysis. The range of Weber's interests and the conceptual bent of his mind have combined to provide a language for large areas of social science, one moreover that has the ring of legitimacy without involving a theoretical commitment to the primacy of the forces of production, or the unconscious, let alone a practical commitment to the proletarian revolution or psychoanalysis.

Such statements apply most clearly to *Economy and Society*, of course. Even the editorial history of that disorganized, disjointed work betrays its character. It will be interesting to see how the editors of the first critical edition of Weber's works deal with the strong views held by successive authorities – Marianne Weber, Eduard Baumgarten, Johannes Winckelmann – about the organization of this *opus magnum*, though one suspects that it will still be a quarry when it appears, one in which some will mine gold, whereas others cart away rubble, a book which will be quoted more than read, which will provide elements of a language rather than a framework of theory.

The other reason for the great temptation to invoke Max Weber has to do with the extraordinary ambiguities, not to say the explosive contradictions of his work. Take the analysis of the origins of capitalism in the *Protestant Ethic*. In one sense it is, and has been taken to be, a conclusive refutation of Marx. It is not the new productive forces of technology and social organization that have eroded the old relations of production and removed from power a class with a vested interest in their retention, but a new 'spirit', which has spread and turned people's actions in unheard-of directions. However, in another sense, this is not Weber's argument at all. It is, rather, that economic, social and religious developments have formed a whole that defies all attempts to disentangle them. Weber is careful not to establish causalities. Marxist authors, such as Georg Lukács and Lucien Goldmann, or the critical critics of the Holy Family of Frankfurt, did thus not find it difficult to incorporate Weber's ideas in their 'holistic' claims. A similarity, after all, with the conflicting schools of Hegelians before and after 1848?

The two most serious ambiguities in the work of Weber concern what many would regard as the two centrepieces of his social science. There is, first, the curious and fateful dialectics of rationality. Few Weberian notions have gained wider currency in social analysis than that, rationality. Purposive rationality is at the very heart of the values of modern societies. Rational, or legal authority has replaced traditional ways of legitimizing power. The concept itself is complicated. It seems to say little about ends and much about means. Rational action achieves given objectives in a fairly well-defined manner; but it is doubtful whether, at least in Weber's use of the term, there can be rational objectives. Weber alludes to the enlightened concept of reason, but uses for the most part the narrower one of Latin authors such as Pareto, *raison* rather than *Vernunft*. Weber is not an emphatic, philosophical rationalist, despite the crucial importance of the notion in his analysis of modern society.

Perhaps this is the reason behind the ambiguity of his position. When Weber talks about the *Entzauberung* of the modern world, his very choice of words betrays the split in his feelings. *Entzauberung* is not just an objective process of demystification, or even the subjective experience of disenchantment, but it means that the magic has gone out of life, all charm and emotional appeal. This appeal is also very much a part of Weber's (and his self-appointed successors') fascination with charisma, with the unusual, the unexpected, the unique, which alone can force open the rigidities of the rational world. For Weber not only calls our world rational: he also invokes that cage of bondage in which modern man is likely to find himself if he relies exclusively on the rationality of all his means. Thus there remain important unanswered questions: what are the objectives that Max Weber has in mind, be they the intrinsic values of modern society, or the desirable purposes of political action? Is it really an accident that Weber could be interpreted both as a defender of democracy and as an advocate of more personalized leadership? Do we actually know what Weber wanted, or do we merely know what he could not support?

All the time, we are edging towards the most explosive ambiguity in Weber's thought, his methodology. The position that he took in the historical debates of the Verein für Sozialpolitik is clear. Statements of fact are one thing, statements of value another, and any confusion of the two is impermissible. Some would say that the thrust of his two famous lectures, 'Science as a vocation' and 'Politics as a vocation', is equally clear, as is the distinction between an ethics of conviction and an ethics of responsibility. One has to make up one's mind whether one wants to be guided by the duty of the academic to abstain from stating value-preferences, or whether one chooses to let the reins of measured judgement fall and passion have its way. One has to recognize that following absolute moral imperatives is not easily compatible with accepting the exigencies of real quandaries.

But if this is so clear, why do Weber's methodological distinctions have that curiously emotional effect that has accompanied them from the *Werturteils-streit* of 1912, through the ideological critique of sociology in the 1920s and the debate on positivism in the 1960s, all the way to the very practical contro-versy about the deployment of theatre nuclear weapons in the 1980s? More to the point, why did Weber himself find it all but unbearable to live with his distinctions? Could it be that the distinctions are, at the same time, intellec-tually compelling and impossible to sustain in practice? Are they a prescription for breakdown?

There is still a shroud of surmise and guesswork about Max Weber's illness. But we do know that the great man presented and represented many of the forces of his time and his place, even if he could not easily contain them. The traditional scholar did not always succeed in tempering the political animal; the emotional German suffered from his country even as he loved it; in his restless mind, the broad sweep of history entered into an uneasy alliance with concern for the immediate, unrestricted submarine warfare, or entry rules to the civil service. As one thinks about the man whom Marianne Weber has tried to camouflage, and Karl Jaspers to idealize (both, incidentally, by glorifica-tion), the man whose rare photographs puzzle as much as they inform (who is this austere bourgeois apparently lecturing Ernst Toller and Erich Mühsam at Burg Lauenstein in 1917?), one is struck above all by the precarious unity of contradictions. For the personal answer is, in the end, the only one which might overcome the ambiguities of fact and value, science and responsibility: one has to live with these conflicts. This works sometimes, and sometimes it does not. The social scientist has to be more than a mere practitioner of social science. The politician has to be more than a mere practitioner of politics. The social scientist cannot escape the value-laden decisions of the world of action; the politician cannot evade the burden of uncommitted analysis. Or rather, they both can, but if they do, and remain as persons in the cage of abstract distinctions, they cease to be adequate in what they are doing, *sophós* in the Greek sense: that is, simply, good social scientists, good politicians.

Weber's ambiguities are resolved in his method, his range, his personality. All three have clear contours. Not for Weber the systematic imprecision of what Hegelians call dialectic. Not for him the wobbliness and woolliness of sub-institutional sociology, either. *Verstehen* may be an untranslatable word, and as such a little suspicious, but the combination of hard facts and empathy which it entails does not lack incisiveness. It may be difficult to teach, but it is easy to recognize. Marx's *Eighteenth Brumaire*, Durkheim's *Suicide*, some of Simmel's cameo pieces such as the 'Excursus on the stranger', later Michels's *Political Parties*, Geiger's *Social Stratification of the German People*, Merton's 'Social structure and anomie', Baechler's 'Dying at Jonestown', and, of course, also the *Protestant Ethic and the Spirit of Capitalism* are examples of the best in social analysis, of *Verstehen* in Max Weber's sense. They all show how too literal an application of the logic of scientific discovery to things social can become arid. One must not be discouraged by the legitimate demand to make statements that are capable of falsification, from acknowledging dimensions of understanding that defy the hypothetico-deductive method. On the other hand, one must not be misled by the complexity of things social into believing that anything goes. It is always useful to wonder whether the statements we make could also be wrong, or whether they are so full of *ceteris paribus* clauses and other qualifications that the question of falsehood cannot arise. The approach called *Verstehen* is thus not an excuse for arbitrariness, indistinctness and imprecision; it is, on the contrary, an intricate web of historical depth, systematic evidence, and an acute sense of the complexity of human situations, all governed by strict criteria of truth and falsehood.

Weber's range needs few additional comments. What his sociopolitical and socioeconomic understanding of processes means has been alluded to already. We have also seen that much of the great tradition for which Weber stands has since been lost. There are reasons for this — Weberian reasons, one is tempted to say. For, once again, it must be noted that such a range is all but impossible to teach. If young scholars do not start with a detailed study of the position of agricultural labourers in East Elbea, but try to come to grips, in their very first work of scholarship, with some vast endeavour of theory, the result is likely to be pathetic, and soon forgotten. On the other hand, if the non-controversial nature of their early work leads them to keep even their inaugural lecture clear of outrageous generalizations and value-judgements, they merely join the army of research assistants who populate the bureaucratized establishments of higher education. It is, after all, not easy to be an epigone, as Max Weber himself has told us in his remarks on the routinization of charisma. To keep avenues of progress open, we might do well to remember that as often as not scholarship, like history, advances by moving sideways, to different subjects and approaches. The important and difficult task for a social science that does not want to lose its roots is to proceed in this manner — like the knight in the chess game, onward and sideways in one move — without ever forgetting where it came from and that its heroes are more than statues in its museum.

Some of the comments made earlier about *Economy and Society* and, to an extent, about Max Weber's work more generally being a quarry for later generations to mine, must not be misunderstood. Rome's Colosseum lives on in many other structures, whereas the Venus de Milo remains an object of admiration and imitation. The analogy is dangerous. In the arts, unlike the sciences, the perfection of the unique may well be preferable to the utility of the complex; in any case, there is a difference in the significance of building blocks, on the one hand, and patterns of design, on the other. The point about Weber and modern social science is that the manifold uses to which his work is put prove the vitality of this work. Comte and Spencer have become museum pieces of social science. Marx is invoked by those who need a label to add importance to their products. Pareto and, to some extent, Durkheim are remembered for particular theorems. Weber's ubiquity, at least in the 'soft' social sciences, makes him unique and justifies the description of him as a founder and an authority.

Yet all this has to do with what we have called the temptation of Max Weber. His method, *Verstehen*, and his range of institutional analysis, both conceptual and applied, take us to the harder core of Weber's achievement, but they still fail to reach their unique source. Max Weber the quarry is useful, Max Weber's ambiguities are intriguing and a reason for his wide appeal, yet underlying them there is a nucleus of power that holds it all together, gives it strength and meaning. It is, I believe, Max Weber the person. This is not a very original thing to say, nor is it only true for Max Weber. But contrary to what the author of *The Great Philosophers*, Karl Jaspers, believed, there are few who make it as important to try and make sense of their lives and their entire intellectual personalities as Max Weber does. It is in the achievement and aspirations, battles and frustrations of his life that the strands of his writings come together.

Fortunately, much has been added to the early emphatic biographies of Max Weber. Today, we understand better Max Weber's involvement in German politics, his obsession with religion, the psycho-sociology of the cage of bondage which he sensed. Yet one would hope that one day someone will come along and write a truly great Life of Weber, one that fills the gaps of knowledge which still remain, but above all one that welds his life, his works and his times into a whole in the best tradition of *Verstehen*. Clearly, Weber has become an authority in important areas of social analysis, such as the study of power. It is probably right to call him a founder so far as the respectability of social science, albeit in a somewhat narrow sense, is concerned. He can be described as a law-giver rather like the constitution-makers of countries, in that he has provided methodological and thematic guidelines of rare comprehensiveness, which remain relevant even with the occasional need to amend them. But it is above all the explosive unity of his ambiguities that modern social science should remember. All the many things that have fallen apart since Max Weber, and at times by using his name in vain, once belonged together, not in a system, but in a human being. Whoever manages to write such a Life might even give some of the magic back to what has become the barren landscape of modern social science.

Contributors

Rita Aldenhoff is a research assistant at the Arbeitsstelle und Archiv der Max Weber-Gesamtausgabe of the Bavarian Academy of Sciences (Munich). She is a specialist on German liberalism in the nineteenth century. Her book, *Schulze-Delitzsch: Ein Beitrag zur Geschichte des Liberalismus zwischen Revolution und Reichsgründung*, was published in 1984.

David Beetham is Professor of Politics at the University of Leeds. He is the author of *Max Weber and the Theory of Modern Politics* (2nd edition, 1985) and *Marxists in the Face of Fascism*. His book, *Bureaucracy*, will be published in 1987.

John Breuilly is Senior Lecturer in History at the University of Manchester. He is the author of *Nationalism and the State* (1982) and, with Wieland Sachse, of *Joachim Friedrich Martens (1806–1877) und die deutsche Arbeiterbewegung* (1984). He has published a number of articles on comparative labour history in nineteenth century Europe.

Roger Chickering is Professor of History at the University of Oregon. His major books are *Imperial Germany and a World without War: The Peace Movement and German Society, 1892–1914* (1975) and *We Men Who Feel Most German: A Cultural Study of the Pan-German League, 1886–1914* (1984). He is presently working on a study of Karl Lamprecht.

Dittmar Dahlmann is a research assistant at the Arbeitsstelle der Max Weber-Gesamtausgabe at the University of Düsseldorf where he is especially concerned with Max Weber's writings on Russia. His major publication is *Land und Freiheit. Machnovščina und Zapatismo als Beispiele agrarrevolutionärer Bewegungen* (1986).

Ralf Dahrendorf is Professor in the Faculty of Social Sciences at the University of Konstanz. His numerous works include *Class and Class Conflict in Industrial Society* (1959), *Society and Democracy in Germany* (1965–66), *The New Liberty: Survival and Justice in a Changing World* (1975), *Life Chances: Approaches to Social and Political Theory* (1979) and *Law and Order* (1985).

Eberhard Demm teaches history at the University of Paris X (Nanterre). He is the author of *Reformmönchtum und Slawenmission im 12. Jahrhundert* (1970) and the editor of *Alfred Weber als Politiker und Gelehrter* (1986). He is currently working on a political biography of Alfred Weber.

Robert Eden is Professor of Political Science at Dalhousie University, Halifax, Nova Scotia. His book, *Political Leadership and Nihilism: A Study of Weber and Nietzsche*, was published in 1984.

David P. Frisby is Reader in Sociology at Glasgow University. His publications include *Sociological Impressionism* (1981), *The Alienated Mind* (1983), *Georg Simmel* (1984), *Fragments of Modernity* (1986) and, with Derek Sayer, *Society* (1986). He has translated, with Tom Bottomore, Georg Simmel's *The Philosophy of Money* (1978).

Dick Geary is Senior Lecturer and Head of German Studies at the University of Lancaster. He is the author of *European Labour Protest, 1848–1939* (1981), *Arbeiterbewegung und Arbeiterprotest* (1983) and *Karl Kautsky* (1986). With Richard J. Evans he has edited *The German Unemployed* (1986). His book, *Revolution and the German Working Class, 1848–1933*, will be published shortly.

Anthony Giddens is Professor of Sociology in the University of Cambridge. Among his most recent books are *Central Problems in Social Theory* (1979), *The Constitution of Society* (1984) and *The Nation-State and Violence* (1985).

Friedrich Wilhelm Graf is Privatdozent of Systematic Theology at the University of Munich. He is the editor of *Profile des neuzeitlichen Protestantismus* (1986) and, with Horst Renz, of *Troeltsch-Studien* (1982 ff.). His other books include *Die Politisierung des religiösen Bewußtseins* (1978), *Theonomie* (1986) and a study of David Friedrich Strauss: *Kritik und Pseudo-Spekulation* (1982).

Wilhelm Hennis is Professor of Political Science at the University of Freiburg im Breisgau. His books include *Politik und praktische Philosophie* (1963), *Politik als praktische Wissenschaft* (1968), *Organisierter Sozialismus* (1977) and *Politik und praktische Philosophie: Schriften zur politischen Theorie* (1977). His book, *Max Weber: Essays in Reconstruction*, will be published in 1987.

Dieter Henrich is Professor of Philosophy at the University of Munich. He is the author of numerous books, among them *Die Einheit der Wissenschaftslehre Max Webers* (1952), *Der Ontologische Gottesbeweis* (1960), *Hegel im Kontext* (1971), *Identität und Objektivität* (1976), *Selbstverhältnisse* (1982) and *Fluchtlinien* (1982). His most recent book is a study of Hölderlin: *Der Gang des Andenkens* (1986).

Gangolf Hübinger is Lecturer in Political Science at the University of Freiburg im Breisgau. He is the collaborative editor of volume 15 of the *Max Weber-Gesamtausgabe* (1984). Besides *Georg Gottfried Gervinus* (1984) he has published articles on Max Weber, the history of historiography and on culture in Wilhelmine Germany.

Eva Karádi is Assistant Professor of Philosophy at the University of Budapest. She is the editor or co-editor of *Georg Lukács: His Life in Pictures and Documents* (1981), *Georg Lukács: Briefwechsel 1902–1917* (1982) and *Georg Lukács, Karl Mannheim und der Sonntagskreis*. She has published several articles in German on the Hungarian contribution to modern German intellectual history.

Jürgen Kocka is Professor of History at the University of Bielefeld. His main fields of interest are German and American social history and the history and methodology of historiography. His numerous books include *Unternehmensverwaltung und Angestelltenschaft am Beispiel Siemens 1847–1914* (1969), *White-Collar Workers in America, 1890–1940* (1981), *Lohnarbeit und Klassenbildung* (1983) and *Facing Total War: German Society 1914–18* (1984). He is the editor *of Max Weber, der Historiker* (1986).

Dieter Krüger is the author of *Nationalökonomen im wilhelminischen Deutschland* (1983) and of articles on the history of social science in Imperial Germany and on Allied financial policy after 1945. He now works as an archivist.

Carl Levy is a research fellow at Eliot College, University of Kent at Canterbury. He has edited *Socialism and the Educated Middle Classes, 1870–1914* (1986). His articles deal with Italian anarchism, British labour history and Antonio Gramsci.

J. G. Merquior is Minister at the Brazilian Embassy in London and former visiting professor at King's College, London. His books include *Rousseau and Weber* (1980), *Foucault* (1985), *Western Marxism* (1986) and *From Prague to Paris: A Critique of Structuralist and Post-Structuralist Thought* (1986).

Arthur Mitzman is Professor of History at the University of Amsterdam. He is the author of *Sociology and Estrangement: Three Sociologists of Imperial Germany*. His book, *The Iron Cage: An Historical Interpretation of Max Weber*, was re-issued in 1985.

Wolfgang J. Mommsen is Professor of History at the University of Düsseldorf. From 1977 to 1985 he was Director of the German Historical Institute London. He is a co-editor of the *Max Weber-Gesamtausgabe* and the author of *Max Weber and German Politics, 1890–1920* (1984) and *The Age of Bureaucracy: Perspectives on the Political Sociology of Max Weber* (1974). He has published numerous books and articles on modern German and European history, on the history and theory of imperialism and on the theory of historiography.

Guy Oakes is Professor of Philosophy at Monmouth College, New Jersey, and Senior Lecturer in Sociology at the Graduate Faculty of the New School for Social Research. He has published articles on Max Weber, Georg Simmel and on the philosophy of the social sciences. He is a translator of works by Max Weber, Georg Simmel, Heinrich Rickert and Carl Schmitt.

Jürgen Osterhammel is Akademischer Rat in Political Science at the University of Freiburg im Breisgau. From 1982 to 1986 he was a research fellow at the German Historical Institute London. He is the author of *Britischer Imperialismus im Fernen Osten* (1983) and of articles on modern Chinese history, British imperialism and the history of higher education in Germany.

Pietro Rossi is Professor of the Philosophy of History at the University of Turin. He is a leading translator of Max Weber's works into Italian. His books include *Lo storicismo tedesco contemporaneo* (1956), *Storia e storicismo nella filosofia contemporanea* (1960), *Max Weber: razionalità e razionalizzazione* (1982) and *Cultura e antropologia* (1983). His Heidelberg Max Weber Lectures, given in 1985, will be published in 1987 (*Vom Historismus zur Historischen Sozialwissenschaft*).

Alan Ryan is Fellow and Tutor in Politics at New College, Oxford. Among his books are *J. S. Mill* (1974), *The Philosophy of John Stuart Mill* (1970), *The Philosophy of the Social Sciences* (1970) and *Property and Political Theory* (1984). He has edited *The Idea of Freedom* (1979).

Manfred Schön is a research assistant at the Arbeitsstelle der Max Weber-Gesamtausgabe at the University of Düsseldorf. He is preparing a major study of Gustav Schmoller.

Ernst Schulin is Professor of History at the University of Freiburg im Breisgau. He is the author of *Die weltgeschichtliche Erfassung des Orients bei Hegel und Ranke* (1958), *Handelsstaat England* (1969), *Walther Rathenau* (1979) and *Traditionskritik und Rekonstruktionsversuch: Studien zur Entwicklung von Geschichtswissenschaft und historischem Denken* (1979). He is the editor of *Universalgeschichte* (1974) and a co-editor of the *Walther Rathenau-Gesamtausgabe* (1977 ff.).

Wolfgang Schwentker is Lecturer In Modern History at the University of Düsseldorf. He is a collaborative editor of Volume 16 of the *Max Weber-Gesamtausgabe* (1986) containing Max Weber's political writings and speeches from 1918 to 1920. His book, *Die konservative Vereinsbewegung in der deutschen Revolution 1848–49*, will be published in 1987.

Edward Shils is Professor of Sociology at the University of Chicago and Fellow of Peterhouse, Cambridge. He has contributed to many different fields within the social sciences. Some of his most recent books are *The Intellectuals and the Powers* (1972), *Center and Periphery* (1975), *Tradition* (1981), *The Constitution of Society* (1982) and *The American Ethic* (1984).

Tracy B. Strong is Professor of Political Science at the University of California, San Diego. He is the author of *Friedrich Nietzsche and the Politics of Transfiguration* (1975) and, with Helene Keyssar, of *Right in Her Soul: The Life of Anna Louise Strong* (1985). He has published articles on political, literary and aesthetic theory, on the philosophy of social science and on human rights.

Friedrich H. Tenbruck is Professor of Sociology at the University of Tübingen. Among his books are *Jugend und Gesellschaft* (1962), *Kritik der planenden Vernunft* (1971), *Die unbewältigten Sozialwissenschaften oder die Abschaffung des Menschen* (1984), *Geschichte und Gesellschaft* (1986). He has published numerous articles on the sociology of culture and on the history and theory of the social sciences, especially on Max Weber, Georg Simmel, Emile Durkheim and George Herbert Mead.

Peter Theiner is Head of Section at the Carl Duisberg Centre, Cologne. His book, *Sozialer Liberalismus und deutsche Weltpolitik: Friedrich Naumann im Wilhelminischen Deutschland (1860–1919)*, was published in 1983.

W. R. Ward is Professor of Modern History at the University of Durham. His books include *Georgian Oxford* (1958), *Victorian Oxford* (1965), *Religion and Society in England 1790–1850* (1972), *Theology, Sociology and Politics: The German Protestant Social Conscience 1890–1933* (1979) and, as editor, *Early Victorian Methodism:*

The Correspondence of Jabez Bunting 1830–1858 (1976). He is preparing a new edition of John Wesley's *Journal*.

Douglas Webster is now Visiting Fellow in the department of sociology and anthropology at the University of Salford. His research has been mainly in social pathology and criminology, and includes *The Social Consequences of Conviction* (1971).

Sam Whimster is Senior Lecturer in Sociology at the City of London Polytechnic. He is the editor, with Scott Lash, of *Max Weber: Rationality and Modernity* (1987). He has published articles on history as an academic discipline and its relation to Max Weber's historical sociology and on power and rationality in decision making.

Index

Abbé, Ernst 93
Abramowski, Günter 339
Abū Bekr 254
Agnelli, Giovanni 386
Althoff, Friedrich 27
Amos 254
Andreas-Salomé, Lou 486
Ansaldo, Giovanni 387
Antal, Frederick 511
Antoni, Carlo 2, 386, 452–3
Arco zu Valley, Anton Graf von 519
Arendt, Hannah 544
Aristotle 30, 32, 38, 161
Aron, Raymond 2, 4, 165
Arrow, Kenneth 575
Augustine, Saint 474
Avenarius, Richard 458

Badaloni, Nicola 400
Baechler, Jean 578
Balázs, Béla 500
Ballin, Albert 332
Barth, Karl 204
Barth, Paul 423
Barth, Theodor 305
Bassermann, Ernst 211, 308, 324, 326
Baudelaire, Charles 430–1
Bauer, Otto 108
Baumgarten, Eduard 215, 498, 515, 539, 576
Baumgarten, Emmy 518
Baumgarten, Fritz 518, 520–1
Baumgarten, Hermann 27, 163, 518, 520
Baumgarten, Ida 518, 520, 524
Baumgarten, Otto 9, 195–8, 204, 216, 229, 230, 518, 520
Baur, Ferdinand Christian 204
Bebel, August 124, 136, 211, 308, 326, 356, 360, 362–3, 364
Becker, Carl Heinrich 230, 260
Beetham, David 4, 121, 161, 394, 399
Bekker, Immanuel 40
Bekker, Paul 502
Bell, Daniel 4
Below, Georg von 146, 237, 240–1, 257–61, 263, 265, 273–4, 277–80, 281, 282
Bendix, Reinhard 3
Bentham, Jeremy 171–2
Bergson, Henri 16, 166
Berlin, Sir Isaiah 166
Berman, Marshall 428
Bernays, Marie 92–4
Bernhard, Georg 317
Bernhard, Ludwig 72

Bernstein, Eduard 13, 159, 163–4, 305, 345–54, 355–6, 358–60, 362, 455–6
Berti, Giuseppe 389
Bertillon, Alphonse 471
Bertoni, Luigi 367
Bethmann Hollweg, Theobald von 308–9, 315, 321, 328–9
Bismarck, Otto Fürst von 36, 55, 72, 187, 276, 305, 315, 324, 384, 420
Björnson, Björn 374
Bloch, Ernst 18, 422, 499–514
Bloch, Iwan 486
Bloch, Joseph 351
Böhm-Bawerk, Eugen von 56, 60, 89, 106, 108
Borchardt (Saxon pastor) 201
Bornemann, Wilhelm 208
Bouglé, Celestin 423
Bourricaud, François 167
Bousset, Wilhelm 209, 229
Boutroux, Emile 184
Brandes, Georg 105
Braun, Heinrich 31
Brendicke, Dr 27
Brentano, Lujo 29, 61–4, 67, 72–8, 80–1, 84, 88–91, 110, 263, 306, 308, 350, 364, 372
Brinkmann, Carl 262
Brubaker, Rogers 480
Bruun, Hans Henrik 162
Bryce, James (Viscount Bryce of Dechmont) 126
Buci-Glucksmann, C. 395
Bücher, Karl 72–4, 76, 82, 91–2, 237, 243, 324
Budde, Ernst 327
Bueck, Henry Axel 328
Bukharin, Nikolay Ivanovich 318, 388, 390
Bülow, Bernhard Fürst von 76–7, 79, 81, 307, 308, 313
Bultmann, Rudolf 469
Burckhardt, Jacob 166, 273, 283, 524–5
Burresi, Piero 452
Burschell, Friedrich 372
Burzio, Filippo 387

Cantimori, Delio 453
Caprivi, Leo Graf von 36, 77
Carlyle, Thomas 171–2, 174, 213
Cavell, Stanley 472
Cerroni, Umberto 400
Chadwick, Sir Edwin 175
Channing, William 524, 526
Charles X, King of France 104

Chickering, Roger 353
Cicero, Marcus Tullius 519
Clairvaux, Bernard of 206
Clare, Saint 371
Cohen, Hermann 127
Cohn, Gustav 67
Coleridge, Samuel Taylor 171–2
Coli, Daniela 464
Comte, Auguste 25–6, 41, 63, 142, 159,
    172–3, 176–7, 182, 184, 283, 560, 579
Condorcet, Marie Jean Antoine, Marquis de
    560
Conrad, Johannes 64, 78
Cooley, Charles Horton 390
Cournot, Antoine Augustin 159
Cremer, August Hermann 197
Croce, Benedetto 3, 16, 159, 382, 384–7,
    391–2, 396, 399, 447–67, 505

Dahrendorf, Ralf 4, 19
Darwin, Charles Robert 91, 274, 356
David, Eduard 361–2
Deininger, Jürgen 10
Deissmann, Adolf 218
Delbrück, Hans 65, 194, 219, 273, 314
Dernburg, Bernhard 219
Deutsch, Felix 320
Diederichs, Eugen 316, 368
Dietzel, Heinrich 53, 77
Dilthey, Wilhelm 171, 257, 448, 458–9, 469
Disraeli, Benjamin 114
Domela-Nieuwenhuis, F. 123, 367
Dorso, Guido 387–8
Dostoevsky, Fyodor Mikhailovich 506–8, 513
Drews, Paul 208
Dreyfus, Alfred 185
Droysen, Johann Gustav 121
Durkheim, Emile 1, 3, 8–9, 25–6, 160, 164,
    182–9, 260, 271–3, 390, 394, 423, 430,
    473, 578–9

Ebbinghaus, Hermann 272
Ehrenberg, Hans 54
Ehrenberg, Richard 72, 84, 89, 312, 327–8,
    332
Ehrenfels, Christian von 489, 490, 497
Eichhorn, Albert 204, 209, 216
Einaudi, Luigi 385, 387, 453
Eisner, Kurt 369–70, 372–3, 376, 379, 380
Elijah 254
Elster, Ludwig 67
Enckendorff, Marie Luise, *see* Simmel,
    Gertrud
Engels, Friedrich 151, 356, 455, 572
Eucken, Walter 526
Eulenburg, Franz 82, 283

Fallenstein, Emily 518, 520
Fanfani, Amintore 453
Federn, Karl 447

Feige, Hermann Albert Otto Max (also
    known as Ret Marut and later as B.
    Traven) 372
Feiler, Arthur 318
Femia, Joseph 391, 394
Ferrero, Guilhelmo 131
Ferri, Enrico 364
Feuerbach, Ludwig 204
Fichte, Johann Gottlieb 438, 440, 446
Finke, Heinrich 273, 277
Finley, Sir Moses I. 4
Fischbeck, Otto 332
Fischer, Kuno 40, 446
Flaubert, Gustave 102
Fleischmann, Eugène 14
Foerster, Friedrich Wilhelm 57, 369, 370, 378
Fogarasi, Béla 511
Ford, Henry 387
Forster, E. M. 103
Francis of Assisi, Saint 371, 375, 508
Frank, Leonhard 495
Freud, Sigmund 3, 7, 17, 102, 468–82,
    483–5, 488–90, 497, 576
Frick, Ernst 367–8
Friedeberg, Raphael 367–8
Friedman, Milton 575
Friedrich II, King of Prussia (Frederick the
    Great) 419
Friedrich Wilhelm IV, King of Prussia 276
Fuchs, Carl J. 72, 78–9
Fülep, Lajos 511

Galbraith, John Kenneth 575
Galli, Giorgio 392
Galli della Loggia, E. 399
Gallino, L. 395
Gandhi, Mohandas Karamchand (Mahatma)
    570
Geary, Dick 350
Geiger, Theodor 578
Gellner, Ernest 167
Gentile, Giovanni 384–5, 391, 451, 456
George, Stefan 17–18, 100, 103, 166, 422,
    492, 497, 499–500
Gerhardt, Uta 427
Gerlach, Ludwig von 276
Gerth, Hans C. 2
Gierke, Otto von 270, 282
Ginzburg, Carlo 471
Giretti 385
Gobetti, Piero 387–9, 453
Goebel, Max 206, 210
Goethe, Johann Wolfgang von 66, 166, 171
Göhre, Paul 9, 93, 195, 197–9, 204, 208,
    219, 301
Goldmann, Lucien 577
Goldscheid, Rudolf 81–2, 317
Goldstein, Professor 370, 375
Gomperz, Theodor 171
Goriely, Georges 163

Gossen, Hermann Heinrich 62
Gothein, Eberhard 64, 77–8, 280, 281, 426
Gottl-Ottlilienfeld, Friedrich von 42, 448
Gouldner, Alwin W. 184
Grabenko, Jelena 512
Graf, Oskar Maria 372
Grafe, Eduard 216
Gramsci, Antonio 14, 382–402
Graziadei, Antonio 390
Gross, Frieda 367, 487, 491–2
Gross, Otto 17, 367, 377, 470, 474, 480,
    483–98
Grosse, Ernst 423
Grossmann, Henryk 390
Gumplowicz, Ludwig 25
Gundolf, Friedrich 18, 499, 512
Gunkel, Hermann 203, 209

Haase, Hugo 374
Habermas, Jürgen 410, 428–9, 576
Haeckel, Ernst 274
Halbe, Max 374
Hänisch, Konrad 74
Harden, Maximilian 313, 320, 492
Harms, Bernhard 67, 84
Harnack, Adolf von 9, 65, 194–7, 203–5,
    208–9, 212–13, 214, 314, 317, 487
Hartmann, Ludo Moritz 330
Hasenclever, Walter 378
Haupt, Hans 217–18, 230
Hauptmann, Carl 101, 374, 378
Hauser, Arnold 511
Hausrath, Adolf 518, 520
Haußmann, Conrad 12, 330
Hayek, Friedrich A. von 118, 519, 575
Hegel, Georg Wilhelm Friedrich 10, 57,
    159 60, 176, 276 7, 356, 405, 408, 412,
    438–9, 451, 456, 501, 534, 574
Heilmann, Ernst 317
Heine, Wolfgang 371, 379
Hellpach, Willy 279
Helphand, Aleksander 357
Henckell, Karl 378
Hengstenberg, Ernst Wilhelm 204
Hennis, Wilhelm 89, 215, 241
Henrich, Dieter 18, 50
Hensel, Paul 217
Heppe, Heinrich 207
Herder, Johann Gottfried von 26, 160, 273
Herkner, Heinrich 72–5, 78–9, 82, 89, 91–2
Herrmann, Wilhelm 204
Hertling, Georg Graf von 332
Hesse, Albert 82
Heuss, Theodor 326
Heussi, Karl 452
Hildebrand, Bruno 30, 33, 48
Hilferding, Rudolf 364
Hinneberg, Paul 221, 232
Hintze, Otto 1, 11, 241, 247, 279 80,
    284–95

Hirschfeld, Magnus 486
Hitler, Adolf 481, 536
Ho Chi Minh 570
Hobson, John Atkinson 165
Hofmannsthal, Hugo von 105
Hölderlin, Friedrich 543
Holl, Karl 249–50
Holtzendorff, Arndt von 332
Homer 519
Honigsheim, Paul 2, 215, 230, 242, 256,
    499–502, 507–8, 526
Hont, Istvan 55
Horkheimer, Max 471
Hughes, H. Stuart 3, 168
Husserl, Edmund 16, 448
Hutcheson, Anne 480

Iggers, Georg G. 277
Ihering, Rudolf von 53
Isaiah 254

Jäckh, Ernst 328
Jaffé, Edgar 31, 74, 99, 123, 317, 372, 470,
    483, 487, 495
Jaffé, Else (*née* von Richthofen) 470, 483,
    487–8, 496, 539
Jameson, F. 469
Jaspers, Karl 7, 18, 260, 512, 528–44, 578,
    580
Jatho, Carl 230
Jaurès, Jean 384
Jellinek, Camilla 231
Jellinek, Georg 7, 25, 56, 217, 223, 231, 455
Jevons, William Stanley 108, 455
Joan of Arc 254
Jones, Ernest 483
Jung, Carl Gustav 470, 482
Jung, Franz 494, 495

Kaftan, Julius 209–10
Kahler, Erich von 166
Kaiser, Georg 372
Kalberg, Stephen 163, 428
Kant, Immanuel 62, 75, 183, 205, 273, 418,
    436–8, 440, 446, 473, 488, 504, 507, 521,
    523–4, 532–3, 536
Kapp, Wolfgang 324, 330
Kautsky, Karl 14, 353, 355–63, 364, 393,
    455–6
Kelly, Alfred 274
Kessler, Harry Graf 333
Keynes, John Maynard (Baron Keynes of
    Tiltson) 390, 575
Kierkegaard, Søren 507, 534, 538–9, 541,
    544
Klimt, Gustav 486
Klinger, Max 486
Knapp, Georg Friedrich 63, 78, 314, 423

Knies, Karl 7, 15, 30, 32–5, 38, 40–1, 42–8, 49–50, 52, 54, 55, 56, 57, 58, 89, 239, 425, 447–8, 450, 459
Kocka, Jürgen 94
Koellreutter, Otto 515
Kolakowski, Leszek 166
Koselleck, Reinhart 55
Kräpelin, Emil 91, 93–4
Kraus, Karl 109
Kropotkin, Pyotr Alekseyevich, Prince 485

Labriola, Antonio 121, 159, 395, 453–6
Lamprecht, Karl 10–11, 159, 268–83
Landauer, Gustav 367–72, 374, 379
Lang, Otto 101
Lange, Friedrich Albert 455
Lask, Berta 495, 503
Lask, Emil 15–16, 25, 230, 368, 434, 435–6, 438–40, 446, 499, 503–7
Lassalle, Ferdinand 393
Lawrence, D. H. 470, 486
Lawrence, Frieda (*née* von Richthofen) 470
Lazarus, Moritz 431
Le Bon, Gustave 151, 423
Le Poittevin, Alfred 102
Lederer, Emil 503, 508, 511
Lederer-Seidler, Emmy 503, 511
Leibniz, Gottfried Wilhelm von 532
Legien, Karl 124
Lenin, Vladimir Ilyich 14, 19, 164, 318, 357–8, 388, 392–4
Lensch, Paul 74, 317
Lenz, Max 273
Lessing, Gotthold Ephraim 110
Lesznai, Anna 511
Levenstein, Adolf 91, 93, 353
Levien, Max 371, 374
Levine, Donald N. 425, 428
Leviné, Eugen 374–5, 379
Lévy-Bruhl, Lucien 390
Lexis, Wilhelm 67
Liebknecht, Karl 127, 363
Liefmann, Robert 54, 78, 525
Linnaeus, Carolus 532
Lipps, Theodor 272, 448–50
List, Friedrich 30–2, 54, 237
Lloyd George, David 318, 394
Löwenstein, Karl 2
Löwenstein, Fürst Karl zu 380
Löwith, Karl 383
Loofs, Friedrich 204, 208
Loria, Achille 121, 123, 453, 456
Lotz, Walther 72, 76, 78
Lotze, Rudolf Hermann 446
Louis Philippe, King of France 104
Ludendorff, Erich 315, 328
Lukács, Georg 4, 18, 106, 167, 229, 391, 422, 469, 471, 491, 499–514, 577
Lukács, Joseph von 509, 513
Luther, Martin 205–6, 222, 336, 443, 496

Luxemburg, Rosa 127, 160, 355–8, 360, 362, 364, 390
Luzzatto, Gino 453

McClelland, Charles 335
MacDonald, Ramsay 352
Mach, Ernst 275, 458
Machiavelli, Niccolò 27, 30, 392, 419, 508
Malthus, Thomas Robert 180
Mann, Heinrich 372, 378
Mann, Thomas 374, 380
Mannheim, Karl 96, 390, 511
Marcion 513
Marcks, Erich 69
Marcus, Steven 471
Marcuse, Herbert 4, 166
Marshall, Alfred 30–1, 108, 455
Martersteig, Max 374
Marut, Ret, *see* Feige, H. A. O. M.
Marx, Karl 5, 41, 56, 95, 100, 107–8, 112, 117, 151, 159–60, 162, 164, 166, 172, 182, 204, 210–11, 260, 343, 355–9, 383, 400, 405, 453–7, 466, 468, 473, 572, 576, 578–9
Masaryk, Thomas 388–9
Maurenbrecher, Max 316, 369
Mauss, Marcel 390
May, Karl 501
Mayer, Adolf 321
Mayer, Jakob Peter 4
Mead, George Herbert 576
Mehring, Franz 281
Meinecke, Friedrich 2, 66, 262, 273–8, 282, 314, 469
Meitzen, August 58, 123
Melanchthon, Philipp 222
Menger, Carl 38, 50, 56, 60–2, 69, 73, 89, 108, 110–12, 147, 526
Merton, Robert K. 578
Meyer, Eduard 10, 57, 160, 234–67, 273, 279
Michelangelo, Buonarroti 476, 478
Michelet, Jules 103, 105
Michels, Robert (Roberto) 7–8, 121–38, 139, 159, 345, 358, 363, 367, 385, 388–90, 392–3, 453, 487, 496, 505, 509, 514, 578
Mill, James 171–2
Mill, John Stuart 6, 8, 35, 53, 107, 155–6, 170–81, 418
Mills, C. Wright 2
Miquel, Johannes von 304
Mises, Ludwig von 111, 118, 526, 527
Mitzman, Arthur 8, 161, 469
Moellendorff, Wichard von 74, 317–18
Mohammed 254–5
Mohl, Robert von 31
Molo, Walter von 378
Momigliano, Arnaldo 4
Mommsen, Theodor 10, 131, 209
Mommsen, Wolfgang J. 5, 31, 76, 101–2, 165, 264, 333, 340, 350, 368, 379, 396, 417, 505, 527

Montaigne, Michel Eyquem, Seigneur de 411–12, 420
Montesquieu, Charles Louis de Secondat, Baron de 30
Mosca, Gaetano 8, 11, 121, 128, 131, 139–58, 384, 388–9, 399
Moses 476–8, 482
Mühsam, Erich 368, 371, 373, 377, 378, 483, 491, 497, 578
Müller, Adam 30, 32
Müller-Meiningen, Ernst 12
Münsterberg, Hugo 25, 272, 448
Mussolini, Benito 134–5, 155, 388
Myrdal, Gunnar 575

Nairn, Tom 382
Napoleon III 173
Nathusius, Martin von 204
Naumann, Friedrich 9, 12, 63–5, 77–8, 80–1, 90, 94–5, 196–7, 199, 204, 208, 210–11, 214, 218, 229, 299–310, 311, 321, 325–6, 328, 330, 331, 332, 355, 452, 486, 501, 518, 524
Nedelmann, Birgitta 431
Nettlau, Max 367
Neumann, Carl 217
Neumann, Friedrich Julius von 64
Neurath, Otto 82, 372
Niekisch, Ernst 371–3
Nietzsche, Friedrich 5, 6, 14–16, 38, 48, 50–2, 54, 55, 67, 100, 114, 163, 178, 384, 405–21, 426, 468, 474, 479–80, 484, 486, 495–6, 534, 538–9, 541, 544
Nieuwenhuis, F., *see* Domela-Nieuwenhuis
Nkrumah, Kwame 570

Oakes, Guy 347
Ödenkoven, Henri 491
Oldenberg, Karl 76, 82, 194, 313
Omar 254
Oncken, Hermann 273
Oppenheimer, Franz 312, 317
Orzechowski, Marian 19
Ossian (James Macpherson) 519
Ostrogorski, Maurice 126, 130
Ostwald, Wilhelm 263, 274–5, 279
Otto the Great, Emperor of the Holy Roman Empire 336

Paggi, Leonardo 388
Pannekoek, Anton 358
Pantaleoni, Maffeo 455
Pareto, Vilfredo 1, 3, 8, 11, 108, 121, 128, 131, 135, 139–58, 384, 388, 399, 453, 455, 575, 577, 579
Parkin, Frank 165
Parsons, Talcott 2, 25, 163, 260, 262, 575
Parvus, *see* Helphand, Aleksander
Perroux, François 107
Peters, Carl 80

Pfister, Bernhard 262
Philippovich, Eugen von 79
Pitts, Jesse 103
Plato 38, 161, 412
Plehanov, Georgy Valentinovich 159, 356
Plenge, Johann 72–4, 82–3, 316–17
Plessner, Helmuth 502
Pohle, Ludwig 67, 72, 76–8, 82, 84–5
Poincaré, Henri 111
Popper, Sir Karl Raimund 3, 111, 178, 411, 526
Preuss, Hugo 314, 330
Proudhon, Pierre-Joseph 163, 166

Quesnay, François 32

Rachfahl, Felix 215, 225, 232, 273, 277
Radbruch, Gustav 331, 378, 499
Rade, Dora 208
Rade, Martin 194–7, 204, 208–10, 212, 216
Ranke, Leopold von 160, 209, 276–7, 291
Rathenau, Walther 12, 311–22, 371, 387, 452
Reagan, Ronald 559
Renan, Ernest 160, 162, 395
Renner, Karl 109, 317
Rex, John 4
Ricardo, David 33, 39, 107, 455
Richter, Eugen 305–6
Rickert, Heinrich 15, 25, 60, 63, 246, 248, 422, 426, 434–6, 438–45, 446, 448, 450, 458–9, 465, 491, 503–5, 518, 528
Ricoeur, Paul 469
Riehl, Alois 446
Rigdon, Sidney 254
Ringer, Fritz K. 275
Riou, Gaston 510
Ritschl, Albrecht 194, 196, 203–10, 216, 222
Ritschl, Otto 204
Rizzi, Bruno 397
Rodbertus, Johann Karl 237
Röhrich, Wilfried 122, 136
Rolland, Romain 475–6
Roscher, Wilhelm 15, 30, 33, 38–40, 49–51, 68, 237, 239, 270, 279, 282, 425, 447–8, 450, 459–60
Rossi, Mario Manilio 387, 453
Roth, Guenther 167, 405, 408–11
Rothfels, Hans 379
Rousseau, Jean-Jacques 26, 32, 38, 95, 105, 115, 127, 576
Ruggiero, Guido de 401
Ruhland, Gustav 76
Runciman, W. D. 4, 418
Ruta, Enrico 452
Ryan, Alan 418

Saint-Simon, Comte de 185
Salin, Edgar 508
Salomon, Albert 508
Salvemini, Gaetano 384–5

Samuelsson, Kurt 5
Sapori, Armando 453
Sassoon, A. Showstack 394
Saul 254
Savigny, Friedrich Carl von 176
Say, Jean-Baptiste 39
Schäfer, Dietrich 13, 277, 282, 334–44
Schäffle, Albert 25, 39, 183
Scheidemann, Philipp 317
Scheler, Max 16, 230
Schelting, Alexander von 50
Schleiermacher, Friedrich Daniel Ernst 204, 227
Schluchter, Wolfgang 5, 10, 162–3, 232, 405, 408–11, 420, 523
Schmidt, Julian 26
Schmitt, Carl 2, 35, 55, 134
Schmoller, Gustav von 7–8, 38–9, 48, 50, 59–70, 72–4, 77–80, 82–4, 88–92, 95, 108, 257–8, 260, 294, 313–14, 321, 423
Schnabel, Peter-Ernst 425
Schnitzler, Arthur 486
Schönberg, Gustav von 89, 230, 251
Schopenhauer, Arthur 105, 163, 166
Schorske, Carl 469
Schubert, Hans von 216
Schütz, Alfred 16
Schult, Tatiana 383
Schulze-Gävernitz, Gerhart von 72–7, 79–81, 88, 312, 314, 317
Schumann, Wolfgang 312
Schumpeter, Joseph A. 8, 29, 35, 42, 72, 82–3, 106–20, 131, 139, 156, 161, 390, 516, 526
Scoccimarro, Mauro 389
Seeberg, Reinhold 220
Seidler, Irma 511
Sering, Max 63–4, 76–8
Sestan, Ernesto 453
Sheehan, James J. 384
Shils, Edward 410
Siebeck, Paul 53, 219, 226, 230
Sieveking, Heinrich 77
Simmel, Georg 15–16, 25, 145, 163, 183, 217, 247, 334, 389, 422–33, 448, 453, 458, 497, 500–1, 503, 578
Simmel, Gertrud (Marie Luise Enckendorff) 497
Simons, Eduard 216
Sinko, Ervin 511
Sinzheimer, Ludwig 94
Small, Albion 424
Smith, Adam 30–2, 38–41, 54, 455, 576
Smith, Joseph 254–5
Snowden, Philip 352
Socrates 176, 411–12
Soden, Hermann von 195–7, 204
Soekarno, Achmed 570
Sohm, Rudolf 9, 211, 249–50, 253, 255, 302
Somary, Felix 526

Sombart, Werner 8, 25, 31, 54, 65, 67, 72–4, 76–9, 81, 84–5, 88, 99–105, 112, 123, 147, 223, 306, 311–12, 316–17, 321, 387, 389, 425, 453, 455, 486, 488
Sorel, Georges 8, 121, 159–69, 387, 391, 395, 455, 469
Spann, Othmar 82–3, 426–7, 431
Spaventa, Bertrando 399
Spencer, Herbert 25–6, 41, 142, 159, 270, 390, 579
Spener, Philipp Jacob 207
Spengler, Oswald 159, 166, 470, 481, 515, 525
Spiethoff, Arthur 72–3, 82
Spinoza, Baruch 507
Sraffa, Piero 383, 390
Srbik, Heinrich Ritter von 274
Stalin, Joseph 393–4
Stammler, Rudolf 159, 263, 423, 444, 456–8, 462
Stanley, John 163–4
Staudinger, Hans 502, 507–8, 510, 513
Steding, Christoph 2
Steenson, Gary 356
Stein, Lorenz von 31
Steinberg, Hans-Josef 356
Steinthal, Ch. Heymann 431
Stepun, Fedor 374
Sternberger, Dolf 6
Stewart, Dugald 30
Stieda, Wilhelm 194
Stinnes, Hugo 318
Stirner, Max 485
Stoecker, Adolf 193–7, 201, 203–4, 208–9, 300–1
Stöcker, Helene 486
Stoltenberg, Hans Lorenz 260
Strauss, David Friedrich 46, 204
Strauss, Leo 410, 418, 471
Strauss, Richard 105
Stresemann, Gustav 12–13, 323–33
Strindberg, August 538
Struve, Walter 165
Stumm-Halberg, Karl Freiherr von 326
Susman, Margarete 502

Taine, Hippolyte 172
Tarde, Gabriel 160, 168, 423
Tawney, R. H. 2
Tenbruck, Friedrich H. 5, 25–6, 50, 57, 162–3, 215, 424
Thatcher, Margaret 559
Thoreau, Henry David 471
Thyssen, August 318
Tirpitz, Alfred von 337
Tocqueville, Alexis de 32, 171, 173–5, 406, 558, 565
Todt, Rudolf 203
Tönnies, Ferdinand 15, 25, 72–7, 81, 88,

99–101, 145, 183, 247, 260, 312, 314, 390,
  423, 425, 430
Togliatti, Palmiro 383
Toller, Ernst 367–81, 509, 524, 578
Tolnay, Charles de 511
Tolstoy, Lev 129, 367, 507, 524
Traven, B., *see* Feige, H. A. O. M.
Treitschke, Heinrich von 26, 39, 53, 275,
  278, 334–5, 337–8
Troeltsch, Ernst 9, 25, 52, 160, 203–4,
  206–7, 209–13, 214, 215–33, 307, 311,
  314, 317, 387, 452, 510, 527
Troeltsch, Martha 217
Trotsky, Leon 388, 397
Turner, Bryan 523

Ullman, Hans-Peter 326

Vacca, G. 400
Vaihinger, Hans 469
Valéry, Paul 413
Van Gogh, Vincent 538
Veblen, Thorstein 166, 390
Vernon, Richard 162–3
Vezér, Erzsébet 513
Vico, Giambattista 160–1
Voegelin, Eric 410
Vogelstein, Theodor 78
Voigt, Andreas 72, 78, 84
Vossler, Karl 447, 450 3, 465

Wagner, Adolph 53, 64, 72–4, 76, 79–80,
  88, 194–5
Waitz, Georg 336
Walras, Léon 30, 41, 108, 113
Washington, George 176
Watkins, John 516
Webb, Beatrice 394
Webb, Sidney James (Lord Passfield) 394
Weber, Adolf 67
Weber, Alfred 8, 64–5, 77–82, 85, 88–98,
  312–17, 321, 329, 333, 389, 495, 503, 505,
  512, 513, 520

Weber, Carl David 91
Weber, Helene (*née* Fallenstein) 518, 520,
  524
Weber, Karl 520
Weber, Marianne 18, 28, 50, 55, 57, 215,
  217–19, 229, 230, 248–9, 251, 265, 284,
  340, 367, 375, 383, 434, 446, 469, 472,
  485, 487–90, 496, 497, 500, 503–4, 509,
  512, 513, 515, 518–22, 538–40, 576, 578
Weber, Max (sen.) 518, 524
Weininger, Otto 486
Weiß, Johannes (sociologist) 199
Weiss, Johannes (theologian) 209
Werfel, Franz 495
White, Hayden 336
Wichern, Johann Hinrich 299–300
Wiemer, Otto 332
Wiese, Leopold von 72, 81, 83–5, 317
Wieser, Friedrich von 60, 108, 110–11, 526
Wilberforce, William 175
Wilbrandt, Robert 55, 72, 74, 81–3, 88
Wilde, Oscar 103
Wilhelm I, German Emperor and King of
  Prussia 203
Wilhelm II, German Emperor and King of
  Prussia 304
Williams, Roger 480
Winckelmann, Johannes 4, 53, 576
Windelband, Wilhelm 234, 434–40, 446, 447,
  458, 503–6, 510–11
Winthrop, John 479
Wittgenstein, Ludwig 469
Wolf, Julius 72, 84, 89
Wolff, Theodor 321, 329, 332–3
Wordsworth, William 171
Wrede, Wilhelm 208–9
Wundt, Wilhelm 60, 91, 183, 272, 275, 279,
  448

Zinovjev, Grigory Ycvscycvich 388
Znaniecki, Florian Witold 390
Zoroaster 255
Zwiedineck-Südenhorst, Otto von 82, 84, 91